Frank A. Beach
(1911–1988)

Grant money comes from taxes; taxes come from a lot of folks who don't have much money. Spend that money wisely.

To what degree should my choice of research work be governed by human needs, by social imperatives, and how am I going to justify spending all of my energies on any research that does not bear directly on pressing human problems? . . . The solution, or rationalization, that I have finally come up with is that it is a perfectly worthwhile way of spending one's life to do your level best to increase human knowledge, and it is not necessary nor is it always even desirable to be constrained by possible applicability of what you find to immediate problems. This may sound very peculiar to some young people, but it is a value judgment which I myself have made and which I can live with.

Jerre Levy

I was one of those children who drive their parents to distraction with persistent "whys" in response to every answer received. I have changed little since childhood, the major difference being that I now drive myself to distraction with my questions. . . . I believe that real meaning and satisfaction from living must come from a conscious attempt to continue in our individual lives the evolution that made us human. I chose the field that I did not only because of curiosity regarding man's origins, but also because of concern for his destiny, and though I am not so arrogant as to believe that what I do can make any real difference, my values compel me, nevertheless, to make the attempt.

David Hubel

Brain science is difficult and tricky, for some reason; consequently one should not believe a result (one's own or anyone else's) until it is proven backwards and forwards or fits into a framework so highly evolved and systematic that it couldn't be wrong.

Candace Pert

People are too easily influenced by negative data. It is often hard to make things work right. If you can never prove your idea, maybe the idea was wrong, but maybe you never did the experiment right.

Curt P. Richter
(1894–1988)

I enjoy research more than eating.

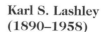

Karl S. Lashley
(1890–1958)

Psychology is today a more fundamental science than neurophysiology. By this I mean that the latter offers few principles from which we may predict or define the normal organization of behavior, whereas the study of psychological processes furnishes a mass of factual material to which the laws of nervous action in behavior must conform.

Biological Psychology

About the Author

James W. Kalat (rhymes with *ballot*) is Professor of Psychology at North Carolina State University. Born in 1946, he received an A.B. degree *summa cum laude* from Duke University in 1968 and a Ph.D. in psychology in 1971 from the University of Pennsylvania. He is also the author of *Introduction to Psychology,* the third edition of which was published by Brooks/Cole in 1993.

FIFTH EDITION

Biological Psychology

JAMES W. KALAT
North Carolina State University

Brooks/Cole Publishing Company

I(T)P™ An International Thomson Publishing Company

Pacific Grove • Albany • Bonn • Boston • Cincinnati • Detroit • London • Madrid • Melbourne
Mexico City • New York • Paris • San Francisco • Singapore • Tokyo • Toronto • Washington

Project Development Editors: *Pat Gadban and Richard Flyer*
Sponsoring Editor: *Jim Brace-Thompson*
Editorial Associates: *Cathleen S. Collins and Patsy Vienneau*
Production Coordinator: *Kirk Bomont*
Project Management and Composition: *GTS Graphics, Inc.*
Marketing Team: *Carolyn Crockett and Jean Vevers Thompson*

Interior Design: *Jamie Sue Brooks*
Technical Illustrations: *James Dowdalls, Darwen and Valley
Hennings, Joel Ito, Carlyn Iverson, Precision Graphics,
Nadine Sokol, John and Judy Waller*
Cover Design: *Roy R. Neuhaus*
Cover Illustration: *Jeena Keller*
Cover Printing: *Phoenix Color Corporation, Inc.*
Printing and Binding: *Quebecor Printing Hawkins*

For more information, contact:

BROOKS/COLE PUBLISHING COMPANY
511 Forest Lodge Road
Pacific Grove, CA 93950
USA

International Thomson Publishing Europe
Berkshire House 168-173
High Holborn
London, WC1V 7AA
England

Thomas Nelson Australia
102 Dodds Street
South Melbourne, 3205
Victoria, Australia

Nelson Canada
1120 Birchmount Road
Scarborough, Ontario
Canada M1K 5G4

International Thomson Editores
Campos Eliseos 385, Piso 7
Col. Polanco
11560 México D.F. México

International Thomson Publishing GmbH
Königswinterer Strasse 418
53227 Bonn
Germany

International Thomson Publishing Asia
221 Henderson Road
#05-10 Henderson Building
Singapore 0315

International Thomson Publishing Japan
Hirakawacho Kyowa Building, 3F
2-2-1 Hirakawacho
Chiyoda-ku, Tokyo 102
Japan

Printed in the United States of America

10   9   8   7   6   5   4   3   2

Library of Congress Cataloging-in-Publication Data

Kalat, James W.
   Biological psychology / James W. Kalat. — 5th ed.
      p.   cm.
   Includes bibliographical references and index.
   ISBN 0–534–21108–9
   1. Neuropsychology.   2. Psychobiology.   I. Title.
QP360.K33   1995
612.8—dc20
                                        94 - 27415
                                           CIP
                                           AC

To Ann

Brief Contents

Contents

Preface

*B*iological psychology is the most interesting topic in the world. I am sure every professor or textbook author feels that way about his or her own topic. But the others are wrong; this really *is* the most interesting topic. By this statement, I do not mean that memorizing the names of brain parts is more interesting than memorizing geographical terms or dates in history. I mean that biological psychology's ultimate questions are so profound that they should interest virtually everyone.

Actually, I shall back off enough to acknowledge that cosmology is in the running with biological psychology for having the profoundest questions. Cosmology, the study of the origin of the universe, asks how the universe came to be and why it exists at all. Biological psychology asks why, in a universe composed of matter and energy, conscious experience exists.

My primary goal in writing this text has been to engage readers' interest. I have tried to focus on the biological mechanisms that are most relevant to key issues in psychology—topics such as the mind-body problem, the development of language and learning, sexual behavior, alcoholism, psychosomatic illnesses, anxiety, aggressive behavior, recovery from brain damage, depression, and schizophrenia. I hope that by the end of the book readers will no longer be asking, "What does all this brain stuff have to do with real psychology?" I hope they will understand that this brain stuff *is* psychology.

Every chapter in this text has been revised since the previous edition. The organizational changes are as follows:

- The chapter on development has been moved from Chapter 8 to Chapter 5. It now includes a new module on the evolution of the brain. The module on development of vision has been moved to the vision chapter, and the module on abnormalities of development has been deleted, with parts of it moved to other sections of the text.
- The order of the chapters on vision and nonvisual senses has been reversed, so that vision now comes first.
- The chapter on lateralization and language has been moved from Chapter 5 to Chapter 14. It has moved around quite a bit from one edition to the next. Instructors who like to discuss it early in the course will find that they can still do so; it does not presuppose a great deal of background. In fact, I know of at least one professor who assigns this chapter first, as a way of grabbing students' interest at the start of the semester.

All chapters except Chapter 1 are divided into modules, each beginning with its own introduction and finishing with its own summary and questions. This organization makes it easier for instructors to assign part of a chapter per day instead of assigning a whole chapter per week. An instructor can also omit a given module or ask students to read the modules in an order different from the one I have used.

Instructors adopting this text for classroom use may obtain from the publisher a copy of the Instructor's Manual, written by Thomas Stonebraker of Greenville College. Contained in the manual are approximately two thousand multiple-choice test items, which are also available on diskette for IBM and Macintosh computers. Also available is a set of overhead transparencies. A Study Guide, written by Elaine Hull of SUNY-Buffalo, is available for student purchase. I am grateful for the excellent work of Stonebraker and Hull.

Packaged free with every new copy of the text is a brief *Dictionary of Biological Psychology*. Useful as a reference for students who are writing papers or studying for exams, this dictionary is also available at a nominal price for students purchasing used copies of the text.

Also available for your biological psychology course is Timothy Teyler's software program *The Graphic Brain: Neurophysiology.* This courseware includes three hours of computer-animated presentations of physiological functions that are difficult to convey via print alone. It is sold on a single-user basis for professors who wish to use it for in-class demonstrations and on a site-license basis for student review in a computer lab. Selected modules from the full program are also available for sale in *The Graphic Brain: Student Edition,* which includes specific references to appropriate pages in *Biological Psychology,* Fifth Edition. In this text, you will notice computer icons in the margins; these indicate the relevant modules of *The Graphic Brain: Student Edition.* To purchase a copy of *The Graphic Brain,* contact the Brooks/Cole fulfillment center at 1–800–354–9706. For information or site-license purchases, call Brooks/Cole marketing at 1–800–354–0092.

Let me tell you something about researchers in this field: As a rule, they are amazingly cooperative with textbook authors. A number of my colleagues have sent me comments, ideas, and published materials; others supplied me with photos for use in this text. I thank especially Israel Abramov, Brooklyn College; Jeffrey Alberts, Indiana University; Suzanne Corkin, Massachusetts Institute of Technology; Terence Deacon, MacLean Hospital; Gary H. Duncan, University of Montreal; Bart Hoebel, Princeton University; Dennis M. D. Landis, Case Western Reserve University; John Liebeskind, UCLA; Jacqueline Ludel, Guilford College; Merriel Mandell, United States International University; Morris Moscovitch, Erindale College of the University of Toronto; Jim Murphy, Indiana University-Purdue University at Indianapolis; Roberto Refinetti, College of William and Mary; Duane Rumbaugh and Sue Savage-Rumbaugh, Georgia State University; Carla Shatz, Stanford University; Thomas Scott, University of Delaware; and Byron Ward, Villanova University.

I appreciate the helpful comments provided by the following reviewers: Linda Bartoshuk, Yale University; Stephen R. Coleman, Cleveland State University; Carl Erickson, Duke University; Bart Hoebel, Princeton University; Elaine Hull, SUNY-Buffalo; Neil Rowland, University of Florida; Kurt Schlesinger, University of Colorado at Boulder; Ronald Skelton, University of Victoria; and Robert Zacharko, Carleton University.

After preparing the first four editions with Wadsworth Publishing Company, this is the first edition I have written with Wadsworth's sibling company, Brooks/Cole. I have been most fortunate to work with Jim Brace-Thompson, who has been a very helpful and supportive editor. Kirk Bomont of Brooks/Cole and Margaret Pinette and Richard Lange of GTS Graphics have done an excellent job of overseeing the production of this edition; I am grateful to have had an opportunity to work with them. I thank Kyrrha Sevco, Pat Gadban, and Richard Flyer for coordinating and planning the illustration program; Sheila Pulver for her excellent copyediting, Jamie Sue Brooks for the design of the book, and Roy Neuhaus for the cover. Thanks and congratulations to James Dowdalls, the artist who had to take my very rough sketches and descriptions and turn them into the excellent new illustrations in this edition. I thank Faith Stoddard, Dorothy Bell, and Tessa McGlasson for supervising production of the supplements. To all these people, my thanks and applause.

Thanks to my wife, Ann, and my daughter, Robin, who listened every time I wanted to talk about the latest thing I had read. And thanks to my department head, David Martin, for his support and encouragement.

I welcome correspondence from both students and faculty. Write: James W. Kalat, Department of Psychology, Box 7801, North Carolina State University, Raleigh, NC 27695-7801. Fax: (919) 783-7468. E-mail: kalat@poe.coe.ncsu.edu.

James W. Kalat

THE GLOBAL ISSUES OF BIOLOGICAL PSYCHOLOGY

A biological psychologist tries to explain any behavior, such as the behavior of this mother gorilla toward her baby, not in terms of subjective experiences like "love" but in terms of its physiology, its development, its evolution, and its function. (Photo courtesy of the Cincinnati Zoo.)

CHAPTER ONE

1. Biological psychologists seek to explain behavior in terms of its physiology, its development, its evolution, and its function.

2. Mind and brain are closely related, but we do not know the exact nature of their relationship or what mind really is. Both philosophers and scientists would like to know whether minds could exist independently of brains, whether brains could function equally well if they did not give rise to minds, and what aspects of brain activity are responsible for conscious experience.

3. Direct electrical stimulation of the brain can induce behavioral changes and subjective experiences. Studies of electrical stimulation of the brain provide strong evidence that the brain is responsible for mental activity.

4. Many experiments in biological psychology use animal subjects. Some of those experiments inflict pain or distress. The ethics of such experiments has become controversial.

It is often said that Man is unique among animals. It is worth looking at this term "unique" before we discuss our subject proper. The word may in this context have two slightly different meanings. It may mean: Man is strikingly different—he is not identical with any animal. This is of course true. It is true also of all other animals: Each species, even each individual is unique in this sense. But the term is also often used in a more absolute sense: Man is so different, so "essentially" different (whatever that means) that the gap between him and animals cannot possibly be bridged— he is something altogether new. Used in this absolute sense the term is scientifically meaningless. Its use also reveals and may reinforce conceit, and it leads to complacency and defeatism because it assumes that it will be futile even to search for animal roots. It is prejudging the issue.

Niko Tinbergen (1973)

*H*uman beings are part of nature. Although much sets us apart from other animal species, we have much in common with other species, too. To understand who we are, we need to understand our relationship to the rest of the animal kingdom.

To understand the nature of our experiences—our "minds," if you wish— we need to understand the physical structure that is responsible for them. Our experience, our behavior, our sense of personal identity—all are products of the brain. **Biological psychology** is an attempt to understand how the brain and the rest of the nervous system generate those products.

Biological psychology encompasses a number of specializations and fields, ranging from teaching and research to various branches of medicine; Table 1.1 describes some of them. If you do not enter one of these fields, but enter a related field, such as clinical psychology or school psychology, you may frequently find yourself using information about the relationship between brain disorders and behavior. And even if you choose a career in an unrelated field, biological psychology offers much that is worth knowing and thinking about.

Biological psychologists deal with many important practical questions: Can biological measurements determine which people are most likely to develop alcoholism, depression, schizophrenia, or impulsive violent behavior? How can disorders such as insomnia, hyperactivity, and anxiety attacks be prevented? How do tranquilizers, antidepressant drugs, and other medical treatments for psychological disorders work? Is it possible to promote behavioral recovery following brain damage?

In addition to the practical questions, biological psychologists wrestle with broad philosophical issues: What is the relationship between the mind and the brain? Could a mind exist independently of a brain? If not, then what is it about the physical structure and functioning of the brain that gives rise to the mind?

How does heredity influence behavior? Our capacity for behavior is a product of our evolutionary history. But did that evolutionary history leave us with genes that *force* us to think and act in certain ways? Did it leave us with genes that make it easier for us to develop certain behaviors instead of others? Or did it leave us with genes that are completely adaptable to the influences of the environment, so that our thinking and behavior are entirely a product of the way we were brought up?

And what about our sense of personal identity? Each of us has a feeling that "I am a single individual," with one mind and one personality. Yet we know that the brain is composed of billions of cells communicating with one another by paths that are sometimes long and indirect. Under certain circumstances, one

Table 1.1 Some of the Major Specializations in Biological Psychology

Specialization	Description
Physiological psychologist (also known as psychobiologist, biopsychologist, or behavioral neuroscientist)	Graduate degree: Ph.D., probably in psychology or related field. May hold position in a research institution, but more likely in a college or university. Conducts research on how behavior relates to the physiology of the brain and other organs of the body.
Comparative psychologist	Graduate degree: Ph.D. in psychology. Conducts research on animal behavior. Similar to an ethologist, a zoologist who studies animal behavior. (Called a "comparative" psychologist because he or she compares different animal species with one another.)
Neuroscientist	Graduate degree: Ph.D. or M.D. Conducts research on the nervous system, including any area from brain anatomy to behavior. Depending on specialty, the person may be a neuroanatomist, neurophysiologist, neurochemist, psychopharmacologist, psychophysiologist, etc.
Neurologist	Graduate degree: M.D. with specialization in treatment of brain damage. Usually holds position in hospital or clinic.
Neuropsychologist	Graduate degree: Ph.D. in psychology, probably with some courses in medical school. Tests the abilities and disabilities of brain-damaged or otherwise impaired people.

part of the brain may fail to communicate with another part of the brain. How, then, does our sense of an undivided personal identity arise? And is it an illusion?

Biological psychologists do not have firm answers to any of these questions, but most of them are motivated by curiosity about such questions. Although our scientific investigations may not directly answer the great philosophical questions, they may improve the quality of our speculations.

In this chapter, we focus on the global issues of biological psychology. First, we consider examples of biological explanations of behavior—the kinds of explanations that we shall consider throughout this text—and the philosophical issues related to such explanations. Then we turn to the ethics of experimentation on animals. In later chapters, we shall examine numerous biological explanations in more detail.

Biological Explanations of Behavior

Psychologists try to explain behavior. Biological psychologists try to explain behavior in biological terms. For example, consider how various kinds of psychologists try to explain human language: Cognitive psychologists study the relationship between what is said and the meaning behind it. Developmental psychologists study how children's language capacities increase as the children grow older. Social psychologists explore the relationship between language and culture and how social pressures influence speech. Learning researchers examine the ways in which reinforcements and punishments influence the frequency and content of speech. Biological psychologists try to determine what goes on in the brain that makes speech possible.

The explanations that biological psychologists seek are not necessarily restricted to brain activity, however. Tinbergen (1951) distinguished four types of biological explanations: physiological, ontogenetic, evolutionary, and functional.

A **physiological explanation** relates an activity to how the brain and other organs function, even at the cellular and chemical levels. The body is a machine and, like any other machine, it converts one kind of energy into another kind of energy. Among other things, the body converts chemical energy into various kinds of brain activity and into the movement of various parts of the body. We can try to understand the "why" of behavior by a detailed study of the brain's machinery. Ultimately, researchers want not only to break the brain's machinery down into its component parts but also to put it back together again, to see how the parts combine forces to produce a coherent whole (Teitelbaum & Pellis, 1992).

The term *ontogenetic* comes from Greek roots meaning "to be" and "origin" (or genesis). Thus, an **ontogenetic explanation** describes how a structure or a behavior develops. When possible, it begins with the genes and traces how those genes combine with the influence of the environment to produce the final outcome.

An **evolutionary explanation** relates a structure or a behavior to the evolutionary history of a species. For example, humans have tiny hair follicles on most of our skin. Most of these hairs are too short to be of any real use; they are a remnant of the longer hairs that our remote apelike ancestors had. Similarly, our capacities for behavior are evolutionarily modified from the capacities that other mammals exhibit. (Appendix A describes the principles of evolution.)

A **functional explanation** describes *why* a structure or behavior evolved as it did. Suppose individuals with gene G are slightly more successful at finding mates and reproducing than are individuals with gene g. In the next generation, the percentage of individuals having gene G will increase and the percentage of individuals having gene g will decrease. (A change in gene frequencies within the population is what evolution is all about.) We can reverse this reasoning: If gene G has become widespread in the population, then individuals having this gene must have been more successful than other individuals were in reproducing. A functional explanation demonstrates how a particular gene increased reproductive success.

An Example: Birdsong

Let us consider how these four types of biological explanation apply to a specific example of behavior. That example is birdsong. You may or may not find birdsong a fascinating topic in its own right. (If not, perhaps you will learn to appreciate it.) But apart from its interest as a behavior, birdsong offers an excellent illustration of how physiological, ontogenetic, evolutionary, and functional explanations apply to a single behavior.

The question is, Why do birds sing? But we can make the question more specific. Not all birds sing. Even among songbirds, adult males generally do most of the singing. Depending on the species, females and immature males may sing less or not at all. The adult males sing vigorously in spring and early summer (the mating season); in most species, they become silent or sing only an occasional fragment of a song during the fall and winter. So the question becomes, Why do particular kinds of birds sing at the particular times they do?

First, let us note what is *not* an explanation: We cannot explain birdsong by saying that it is an instinct. The term *instinct* is at best a label for a category of behaviors that depend more on species membership than on individual experience. But labeling a behavior "instinctive" does not tell us *how* the behavior developed or *why* the species evolved the set of genes promoting this behavior. It is too easy to say that birds sing because they have an instinct to sing, that mother squirrels take care of their babies because they have a maternal instinct, or that cats attack mice because they have a hunting instinct. In each of these cases, people may believe that they have explained the behavior, but they have only named it. For this reason, many investigators of animal behavior avoid the term *instinct* altogether.

A Physiological Explanation of Birdsong

Birdsong depends on two areas of the brain (known as the caudal nucleus of the hyperstriatum ventrale and the robust nucleus of the archistriatum). These areas are well developed in songbirds, such as sparrows and finches; they are small or absent in birds with only simple vocalizations, such as chickens and pigeons. In the songbirds, the relevant brain areas are larger in males than they are in females (Arnold, 1980). (See Figure 1.1.)

The size of these brain areas depends on testosterone, a hormone generally occurring in higher levels in males than in females. At the start of the breeding season, testosterone levels rise in males, causing the brain areas responsible for birdsong to increase in size. When those areas grow large enough, the bird begins to sing. If the testes are surgically removed from a male songbird, his testosterone level drops, the brain areas responsible for song decrease in size, and he stops singing. Similarly, if an investigator damages the relevant brain areas, the bird stops singing.

What do you suppose happens if an experimenter injects large amounts of testosterone into a female? The revelant areas of her brain grow, and she begins to sing—even in species in which females seldom if ever sing! This evidence indicates that both the size of the brain areas and the ability to sing depend on testosterone, not on being a genetic male (Nottebohm, 1980a). (It also indicates that at least a few brain areas can change their size in adult vertebrates.)

Further, what do you suppose happens if an investigator damages the song-control brain areas in a female bird? The damage cannot decrease her singing, because she did not sing even with an intact brain. The effect on her behavior is that she no longer recognizes the song of her species. For example, a female canary adopts a sexually receptive position only if she hears a male singing a normal canary song. After damage to her song-control areas, she adopts that

Figure 1.1
In songbirds, certain areas of the brain are larger in males (left) than in females (right). Generally, only the males sing. (Photos courtesy of Arthur P. Arnold.)

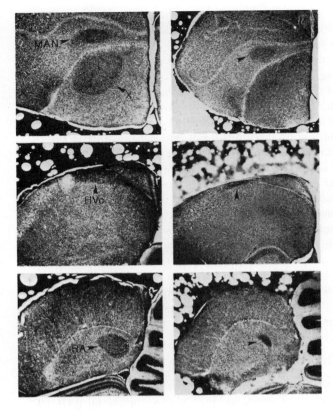

A song sparrow learns its song by imitating others of its species. (Ed Reschke.)

Chapter 1
The Global Issues of Biological Psychology

6

receptive position even after hearing other kinds of bird songs, such as sparrow songs (Brenowitz, 1991).

In short, the physiological explanation states that testosterone causes the growth of certain brain areas necessary for the production and recognition of birdsong. Note that this explanation is somewhat incomplete: It does not specify how the brain areas control the muscles to produce song. The answer to that question is known to some extent (Arnold, 1982), though not completely. As is usually the case in science, answering one question leads to other, more detailed questions.

An Ontogenetic Explanation of Birdsong

As mentioned, certain areas of the brain make it possible for a bird to sing. But how does it know *what* to sing? The answer is more complicated for some species than it is for others (Nottebohm, 1980b).

Pigeons, doves, chickens, and turkeys make only simple coos and cackles, which ornithologists (bird biologists) do not classify as songs. These species do not need to learn their calls. In fact, even if they are deafened early in life, they develop normal calls. (Note that these observations do not explain how pigeons and the others acquire their calls. They merely indicate that we should look for the answers in the embryology of the nervous system, not in the individual's experience.)

In other species, however, each bird has to learn its song by listening to others of its species. For example, in several sparrow species, a male reared in isolation from the sounds of his own species will develop a distinctly abnormal song. To develop a normal song, a male must hear the song of his own species, either from adult males or from tape recordings (Marler & Peters, 1977). He can learn the song from a tape recording only during a **sensitive period** early in life. The sensitive period varies from species to species; in song sparrows, it lasts from about age 20 days to about age 60 days. Exposure to that recording before age 20 days or after age 60 days has little effect (Marler & Peters, 1987, 1988). However, a bird that listens to a live tutor can learn its song during a much longer sensitive period, lasting until at least age 100 days (Baptista, 1985; Baptista & Petrinovich, 1984).

This is a most unusual type of learning. A male sparrow that learns his song during the first two months or so of life cannot begin to practice the song until he reaches sexual maturity the following spring—more than half a year later! As spring approaches, the young sparrow begins to sing. At first, his song is like the babbling of a human infant, a disorganized mixture of many sounds. As time passes, the sparrow eliminates some of his sounds and rearranges the others into an order that comes closer and closer to matching what he heard the previous summer. For example, male song sparrows at first produce songs of six or more notes at a time before eventually settling on the three-note call that is typical of their species (Marler & Peters, 1981, 1982).

What about the female? In nature, females do not sing, but they do learn their song. A female that is injected with enough testosterone will sing her species' song if she was exposed to it during the sensitive period (Marler, 1970). Like a male, she sings an abnormal song if she never heard her species' song.

In short, sparrows (and numerous other songbirds) ordinarily hear their song early in life. During that time, they form a **template** (or model) of what their song should sound like. Later, if and when their testosterone levels are high enough to enable them to sing, they engage in an apparent trial-and-error process to match their own song to the template.

An Evolutionary Explanation of Birdsong

Through natural selection, each species evolves adaptations that distinguish it from other species. But because such changes are mostly slow and gradual, we can see in each species certain remnant characteristics of its ancestors. In some cases, we can roughly reconstruct how a particular feature may have evolved.

For example, two species of birds that appear to be closely related (based on their anatomy) generally produce similar vocalizations. To the trained ear, the song of each species of sparrow is recognizable and the song of each species of warbler is recognizable. Yet it is also possible to hear an unfamiliar species and say, "That's probably some kind of sparrow," or "That sounds like a warbler of some sort." Even though each species has evolved a unique song, it also retains general features characteristic of its ancestors.

In certain cases, biologists can use birdcalls and birdsongs to infer something about the evolutionary relationship among various species. For example, the many species of sandpipers emit similar calls, presumably because they share a common ancestor. Two species—dunlins and Baird's sandpipers—give their calls in distinct pulses. (Other sandpipers do not.) This resemblance

The similarity of the dunlin's song (top) to that of a Baird's sandpiper (below) suggests that the two species are closely related. (Top; Russell Fieber/FPG International Corp. Bottom; Rod Planck.)

implies that these two species are more closely related than the others, that they share a recent evolutionary link (Kroodsma & Miller, 1982).

A Functional Explanation of Birdsong

If a bird species has genes that enable it to learn its song and to sing it at the appropriate time (spring), then natural selection must have favored those genes for certain reasons. What might those reasons be? The song of a male bird serves two functions. First, it attracts females of the species and primes them to engage in reproductive behaviors. For example, a female canary that hears a large number and variety of canary songs is quick to respond to a male sexually, quick to lay eggs, and likely to lay a large number of eggs (Kroodsma, 1976). Second, a male's song alerts other males to his presence and announces that he is defending that territory. In this way, he may deter competition for his nesting site and the female with which he mates.

Given these principles, we can understand why males sing frequently during the breeding season and rarely during fall and winter. They sing only when they are defending a territory and seeking a mate. (Can you imagine any *disadvantages* to a bird that sings out of season?)

We can also see why each species sings its own song: A male song sparrow, for example, gains an advantage by attracting female song sparrows and driving away other male song sparrows. He would gain no advantage if his song were easily confused with those of other species (Miller, 1982).

Finally, a functional explanation can apply to some of the physical characteristics of birdsongs. A singing bird gains an advantage by being heard throughout the territory he can defend. A song heard more widely offers no advantage; it might even be harmful if it attracts cats and other predators. For this reason, most birds produce songs with notes ranging from 1 kHz (kilohertz) upward—frequencies that do not carry well over long distances in a forest (Konishi, 1969).

In summary, when biological psychologists ask why an animal shows a certain behavior, they look for several kinds of answers:

- Physiological (How does the brain generate the behavior?)
- Ontogenetic (How did the capacity for this behavior develop?)
- Evolutionary (How did this capacity evolve from the capacities of related species?)
- Functional (Why did this capacity evolve? What good does it do for the animal?)

Note the relationship between evolution and physiology. The bird has the physiology that it does because evolution has favored that physiology. Note also that we do not have to assume that the bird *knows* why it sings at all, much less why it sings at a particular time and place. Evolution has equipped it with the tendency to sing in certain ways and at certain times, but we need not assume that the bird knows its evolutionary history or the purposes its song may serve. (Similarly, we humans do not have to be consciously aware of the ultimate functions of all our own behaviors. When people are asked why they play, laugh, have sexual relations, or take care of babies, they sometimes reply that they simply "like to" or "want to" do these things. Evolution presumably constructed us to "like" certain activities because those activities increase our chance of passing on our genes.)

Biological Explanations of Human Behavior

Most of us raise no objection to a biological explanation of birdsong. We may feel differently about a similar explanation of human behavior, however. For example, later in this text you will encounter evidence that chemical changes inside your brain increase or decrease the chance that you will act aggressively. Anatomical differences among people's brains may (and I emphasize *may*) predispose certain people to have a better memory than others or may influence whether people develop a homosexual or heterosexual orientation. Some people object that "I am angry when I *choose* to be angry, and I can control my mood or change any of my other behaviors." A biological psychologist will agree but point out that the "I" that chooses and controls behaviors is a biological organism that follows the principles of biology, chemistry, and physics.

The psychologist will go on to distinguish between two types of biological explanation: biological factors that *force* a behavior to occur and biological factors that *enable* a behavior to occur.

Sometimes, the properties of the brain or the rest of the body force certain behaviors to occur. I shall list some human examples. People sweat when they become too hot. The pupil of the eye constricts in the presence of bright light. The leg jerks upward when the knee is tapped in a certain place (the knee-jerk reflex). The flow of saliva increases when a person drinks unsweetened lemon juice. Such behaviors call for a relatively simple biological explanation.

In other cases, a biological influence may make a behavior possible but not absolutely necessary. For example, although a pattern of activity in certain areas of your brain may increase the likelihood of your engaging in aggressive behavior, you may or may not attack someone, depending on the activity in certain other brain areas—the areas that assess the probable consequences of your behavior. An increase in the levels of sex hormones in your blood may increase your sexual motivation, but your actual behavior will depend on your past experiences, the current social setting, and your other current motivations.

The full explanation of such behaviors is complicated, but nevertheless biological. Your past experiences exert their effects by means of your brain. Your perception of the current situation is a brain activity. So are your competing motivations. The point is that behavior, especially human behavior, is the product of many forces. For the sake of simplicity, I shall not always point this out, but you should always bear it in mind when you listen to any biological explanation of behavior.

The Mind-Brain Relationship

A moment ago, I suggested that many of us feel uncomfortable with the idea that our thoughts and actions are the result of physical processes in the brain. Why? Because we have been taught since early childhood that each of us has a "mind" that is separate from the body but capable of interacting with it in some way. For example, it seems to me that I make a conscious decision to do something and then I do it.

Table 1.2	Philosophical Positions on the Mind-Brain Problem
Position	**Explanation**
DUALISM	Holds that mind and brain are fundamentally different and that each can exist independently of the other.
Interactionism	Mind and brain, which exist separately, interact with each other and influence each other. (*How* they might do so has always been unclear.)
Parallelism	Mind and brain exist separately but do not affect each other. Activities of mind and brain nevertheless agree, much as two accurate clocks may always give the same time, even though neither one influences the other.
MONISM	Holds that the universe consists of only one kind of substance, variously viewed as either physical, mental, or some combination of the two.
Materialism	Only the material world exists; minds either do not exist at all or at least do not exist independently.
Mentalism (or immaterialism)	The physical world exists only in one's mind or only in the mind of God. That is, the material world could not exist independently of a conscious subject to perceive it.
Identity position	Mind and brain are two ways of talking about the same thing. Only one kind of substance exists; that substance is neither mind nor material, but mind-material.
Emergent property position	Mind is not a property of matter itself, but emerges as a new property when the matter is organized in a particular way. For analogy, the properties of water emerge when hydrogen and oxygen are combined, even though neither hydrogen nor oxygen by itself has those properties.

How can that be, if my action is governed by a series of chemical processes in the brain? Somehow, there must be a close relationship between mind and brain, but what is the nature of that relationship? This is the **mind-body problem,** or **mind-brain problem.**

The Difficulty of the Problem

Let us consider four interpretations of the relationship between the mind and the brain, along with the strengths and weaknesses of each. Table 1.2 outlines these four, plus several others.

According to the **dualist position,** the mind exists independently of the brain; the two are different kinds of substance. According to the most widespread version of dualism, called **interactionism,** the two kinds of substances somehow interact; that is, the brain sends messages to the mind, which in turn sends messages to control the brain. How could such an interaction occur? The French philosopher René Descartes imagined that the mind received messages through the tiny pineal gland and later pushed or pulled the pineal gland in order to alter brain activity (Figure 1.2). *Strength:* The dualist view fits with

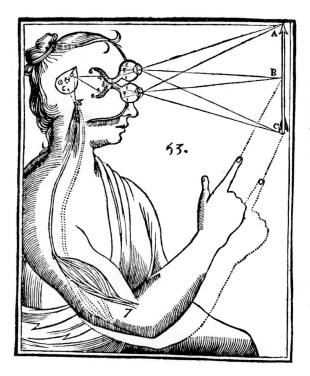

Figure 1.2
René Descartes's concept of mind-brain interaction
He imagined that the mind, separate from the brain, exchanged messages with the brain at the pineal gland, a small unpaired organ at the base of the brain.

our commonsense notion of what the mind is and does. *Weaknesses:* The brain and the rest of the body consist of matter and energy. According to one of the most central tenets of physics, any change in the movement of matter and energy reflects the influences of other matter and energy. If mind is not a type of matter or energy, how could it possibly alter the electrical and chemical activities of the pineal gland or any other part of the brain?

The dualist position is no doubt the most popular position with the general public, but nearly all philosophers and neuroscientists reject it. Indeed, if minds could exist independently of a physical substance (the brain), a biological approach to psychology would fail. Certain scientists, such as the distinguished brain researcher Roger Sperry (1993), maintain that mental processes can control behavior, but even so, Sperry regards those mental processes as inseparable from, and virtually synonymous with, brain activity.

In short, I recommend your being very cautious about using the term *mind*, if you use it at all. If your use of the term implies that you think of the mind as a thing, separate from brain activity, you should be prepared to explain how a nonphysical thing, having no matter or energy of its own, can affect the matter and energy of the brain.

The alternative to dualism is monism, or the **monist position**—the view that the universe consists of only one kind of substance, not two. Various forms of monism differ with regard to whether they hold that this one kind of substance is physical, mental, or some combination of the two.

According to one version of monism, the **materialist position,** the brain is a machine and consciousness is irrelevant to its functioning. *Strengths:* The brain is indeed a machine, and, so far as we can tell, it follows the same physical and chemical principles as any other machine. Investigators find no evidence for any mysterious force that acts on the brain from the outside. *Weaknesses:* As Descartes pointed out, it is impossible to doubt the existence of one's own mind. (As he put it, "I think, therefore I am.") If the brain is a

The Mind-Brain Relationship

machine, it is at least a conscious machine and one that is capable of talking about its own consciousness.

According to another version of monism, the **identity position,** the mind is the same thing as brain activity, just described in different terms. For example, we could describe Michelangelo's statue *David* as a piece of marble with such-and-such dimensions. This physical description would sound very different from a description of the same object as a work of art. The identity position implies that a conscious mind cannot exist without brain functioning, but it also implies that the brain cannot function independently of a conscious mind. *Strengths:* This view accepts the idea that the mind exists and yet describes it as part of the physical universe. Many scientists find this an appealing theory. *Weaknesses:* This view is so vague. Why and how does the brain give rise to conscious experience? And why are we conscious of some activities that take place in the nervous system (such as vision) but not of others (such as spinal reflexes)?

The emergent property position is a modified version of the identity position. According to the **emergent property position,** consciousness is not a property of all brain activity; it emerges when the brain is organized in certain ways. For analogy, when hydrogen and oxygen combine, the properties of water "emerge" even though they were not apparent in either hydrogen or oxygen alone. Similarly, consciousness may emerge from certain interactions among neurons. *Strengths:* This view acknowledges that some kinds of brain activity are conscious while others (such as spinal reflexes) are not. It also allows the possibility that the brains of different animal species, being organized in somewhat different ways, could produce different kinds of mental experience. *Weaknesses:* Again, the problem is vagueness. What kind of brain organization produces consciousness, and why and how? For example, chemists can explain how the properties of water emerge from the hydrogen-oxygen-hydrogen angle of the water molecule. Ideally, we should have some analogous explanation of how brain organization produces mental experience.

The mind-brain relationship is exceedingly difficult to investigate scientifically. The main reason for this difficulty is that, although each of us is directly aware of his or her own conscious mind, we cannot observe anyone else's mind. (Indeed, none of us can be certain that any other person is conscious at all. If you insisted that you are the only conscious being in the universe, what could anyone else say or do to convince you otherwise?)

Although it is hard to imagine scientific evidence that would solve the mind-body problem, it is nevertheless possible to collect scientific evidence that bears on some related questions: Does losing part of the brain mean losing part of the mind? (As we shall see throughout this book, the answer is yes.) And does stimulation of part of the brain elicit behaviors and experiences? If stimulating brain areas can elicit a wide variety of experiences, then brain activity must be responsible for mental events. Let us deal with that issue now.

Control of Behavior by Electrical Stimulation of the Brain

In 1870, Gustav Fritsch and Eduard Hitzig reported that mild, nondestructive electrical stimulation of portions of a dog's cerebral cortex could cause muscle movements. At low intensities, the electrical current stimulated discrete, limited movements—always on the side of the body opposite the stimulation. Depending on the exact point stimulated, the dog would move its neck, back, abdomen, tail, leg, or some other part of its body. Repeated stimulation of the same point consistently elicited the same response. Later experiments yielded similar results for many species.

Electrical activity occurs naturally in the brain at all times. Ordinarily, nerves carrying messages from the sense organs cause this electrical activity. Their impulses combine with the electrical activity already present in certain areas of the brain to produce activity in other areas, which then activate still other areas. Eventually, the areas of the brain that control movement generate activity. Fritsch and Hitzig had directly stimulated the movement-controlling areas, bypassing all the preliminary stages.

Electrical Stimulation of Complex Behaviors   Electrical stimulation of the brain can evoke not only simple muscle movements but also more complex sequences of behavior, particularly if the animal is awake during the stimulation and free to move about. Working with chickens, Erich von Holst and Ursula von St. Paul (1960) implanted electrodes permanently into lower parts of the brain and cemented the electrodes on the skull to hold them in place. Later, they attached wires to the exposed electrodes and passed a weak electrical current to the chicken's brain while it was awake and moving about.

Stimulation of various areas elicited such behaviors as feeding, drinking, cackling, grooming, turning the body to one side, sitting down, sleeping, escape flight, and aggressive attack (Figure 1.3). Similarly, W. R. Hess (1944) found that electrical stimulation of certain brain areas could induce an animal to fall asleep suddenly. The behavior elicited depends on the exact location of the electrode and the intensity of the stimulation. (Stronger current can stimulate more distant cells.)

The elicited behavior also varied depending on environmental stimuli. For instance, in experiments with rats, stimulation at a specific point caused eating if only food was present and drinking if only water was present (Coons, Levak, & Miller, 1965; Valenstein, Cox, & Kakolewski, 1970).

Electrical Stimulation of the Human Brain   We cannot, of course, experiment on human brains just for research purposes. However, a variety of medical purposes allow us to investigate the electrical stimulation of human brains.

Electrical stimulation has most often been used with humans in attempts to identify the part of a person's brain responsible for **epilepsy,** a syndrome caused by abnormal repetitive activity of nerve cells in the brain. This abnormal activity originates in a damaged or malfunctioning area of the brain called the **focus** of the epilepsy. The focus is located in different places for different individuals. The abnormal repetitive activity spreads outward from the focus until a large portion of the cerebral cortex is involved, causing uncontrollable convulsions in some people. Epilepsy is usually treated with drugs; however, some people have frequent major seizures that do not respond to drug therapy. In such cases, surgeons sometimes remove the focus area.

The first step is to find the focus. Because the brain has no pain receptors, surgeons can explore it by anesthetizing only the scalp, leaving the brain itself awake and alert during the surgery. The surgeon exposes part of the brain and then applies an electrode to stimulate small areas of the cortex, one after another. Eventually, as the surgeon stimulates some point, the patient says, "That makes me feel the way I feel when I'm about to have a seizure." This

Figure 1.3
Before stimulation (a), the rooster ignores the stuffed polecat. With low-level stimulation (b) of some points in the brain (not identified), the rooster orients toward the model but does not attack. With stronger stimulation (c, d), he attacks the model. At the end of the attack, after the stimulation is turned off (e), he makes a triumphant call (f). (From von Holst & von St. Paul, 1960.)

point is identified as the focus of the epilepsy and can be surgically removed. Ordinarily, the surgery greatly reduces or eliminates the epileptic seizures, and the effects of losing a small piece of brain are usually not serious (Penfield & Roberts, 1959).

While trying to find the focus, the surgeon can note the effects of stimulating other parts of the patient's brain. As in nonhuman brains, stimulation of some points produces motor responses. For instance, in one person, stimulation caused a series of hand movements; if the man was holding a newspaper at the time, he would fold it and rotate it or feel around its edge, as long as the stimulation continued (Bickford, Dodge, & Uihlein, 1960).

Some years ago, a few people were given electrical stimulation of the so-called pleasure areas of the brain in an attempt to provide them with relief from severe pain or depression. R. G. Heath (1964) described a patient whose septal area was stimulated (without his knowledge) by remote control during a psychiatric interview. Before the stimulation, he was on the verge of tears as he described his father's illness and his own imagined responsibility for it. Within 15 seconds after the stimulation, he suddenly grinned and started discussing a plan to seduce his girlfriend.

Because electrical stimulation of the brain can elicit not only sensations and movements but also emotional changes, it appears that brain activity is responsible for what we call "mind." This is, to be sure, not a new conclusion, but the results of brain stimulation provide particularly strong evidence for it.

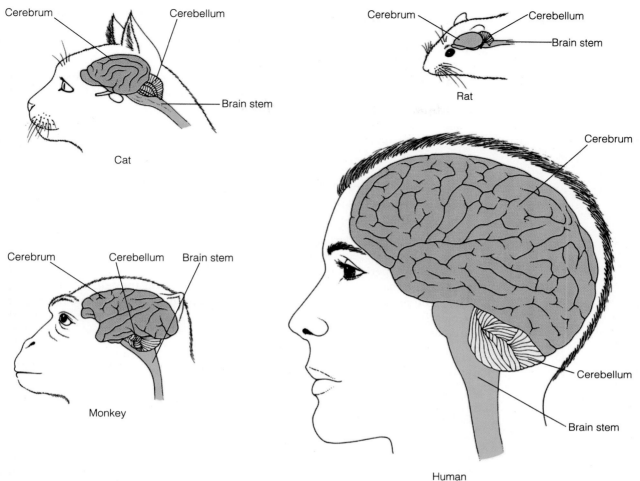

Figure 1.4
Brains of several species
The general plan and organization of the brain are similar for all mammals, even though the size varies from species to species.

Why Investigators Study Animals, and the Ethics of Animal Research

Although studies of animals account for only 7 or 8 percent of all published research in psychology as a whole (Gallup & Suarez, 1980), they account for a much higher percentage of the studies in biological psychology. The brains and behavior of nonhuman animals are not identical to those of humans, but chemically, anatomically, and functionally, their nervous systems are organized in a similar manner (see Figure 1.4). About 95 percent of the animals used in psychology are rats, mice, or birds. Psychological research on dogs, cats, and rabbits used to be fairly common, but has been declining since the 1960s (Viney, King, & Berndt, 1990). Cats are frequently used for certain kinds of vision research.

Given that most biological psychologists want to understand the human brain and human behavior, why do they study nonhuman animals? Here are five reasons:

1. *The underlying mechanisms of behavior are similar across species and sometimes are easier to study in a nonhuman species.* If you wanted to understand how a complex machine works, you might begin by examining a smaller, simpler machine that operates on the same principle. The same is true for studying brain-behavior relationships. For example, much of the early research on nerve cells was conducted on squid nerves, which are similar to human nerves but thicker and therefore easier to study. Or if we wanted to study how certain behaviors change from infancy to old age, we might use mice or rats, which have a life expectancy of two to three years, instead of humans, who live eighty years or more.

2. *Sometimes a certain process is highlighted or exaggerated in animals and therefore is easier to notice than it is in humans.* Consider, for example, the sensitive period for birdsong learning. The evidence shows that certain experiences have a stronger effect at an early age than they do at a later age. The same principle may or may not be true of humans, but once we have seen it clearly in nonhumans, we at least have a good idea of what to look for in humans.

3. *We are interested in animals for their own sake.* Humans are by nature curious. We would like to understand why birds sing, why the Druids built Stonehenge, where the moon came from, and how the rings of Saturn formed, regardless of whether or not such information turns out to be useful for any practical purpose.

4. *What we learn about animals sheds light on human evolution.* What is the place of humans in nature? How did we come to be the kinds of beings that we are? One way to approach such questions is to examine other species. Can we find some trace of language capacity in chimpanzees and other nonhuman species? How much intelligence do monkeys, rats, and other species show? Humans did not evolve from chimpanzees, monkeys, or rats, but we do share common ancestors with these modern animals, and comparing the structure and function of various animal nervous systems with our own provides important clues to our evolution.

5. *Certain experiments are impossible with humans because of legal or ethical restrictions.* For example, investigators sometimes insert electrodes into the brain cells of rats or other animals to determine the relationship between brain activity and behavior. Such experiments answer questions that investigators cannot address in any other way.

Let us focus on the fourth and fifth reasons in more detail: the relationship of animal studies to an understanding of human evolution and the ethics of experimenting with animals.

Evolutionary Relationships among Species

The basic concept of evolution is well established in biology, partly because the fossil evidence shows that species change, but also partly because what we know of genetics makes evolution a logical necessity (see Appendix A). Still, it remains difficult to specify several important details about evolutionary history. For example, biologists are confident that humans and chimpanzees evolved from a common ancestor, but they are less certain about exactly when the two species separated and are still less certain about how our common ancestor may have looked or acted.

The basic line of inference goes like this: Humans are more similar to chimpanzees than they are to any other species, in a wide variety of details including the specific chemical structure of our proteins and our chromosomes. Those similarities point to the probability of a common ancestor from which both humans and chimpanzees inherited most of their genes. As we trace back the fossils of humans and chimpanzees, the more and more ancient fossils become more and more alike, until eventually we cannot distinguish one from the other. Both humans and chimpanzees are more like monkeys than they are like rats and other rodents, more like rats than they are like opossums, and more like opossums than they are like platypuses. Therefore, the common ancestors of the primates (humans, apes, and monkeys) probably separated from the common ancestors of the rodents somewhat more recently than they separated from the ancestors of the opossums. Using similar reasoning, evolutionary biologists have constructed an "evolutionary tree" that shows the relationships among various species (see Figure 1.5).

Evolutionary relationships guide investigators' choice of experimental animals to some extent. A researcher interested in the mechanisms of human memory and intelligence generally chooses a species closely related to humans, one that presumably has highly similar brain mechanisms. However, an investigator who is studying the structure and chemistry of nerve cells could select any convenient multicellular animal because the most basic principles vary little from one species to another. Someone interested in the chemical pathways within cells could study even single-celled animals, or even yeast, because the main chemical reactions have been very conservative indeed over evolutionary time.

⬛➡ *Current Controversies:*
Ethical Issues in Animal Research

In this book, you will read about experiments in which animals were subjected to electrical shocks, brain damage, surgery, brain stimulation, injections of drugs or hormones, and other treatments that could not be given to human beings. Some people regard such animal experimentation as cruelty to animals and have reacted either with peaceful (though vociferous) demonstrations (Figure 1.6) or with more extreme tactics, such as breaking into research labs, stealing lab animals, vandalizing lab property, and threatening researchers.

If certain kinds of research are unethical with humans, can they ever be ethical with nonhuman animals? This is indeed a difficult question. On the one hand, it is undeniable that laboratory animals sometimes undergo painful or debilitating procedures that are *not* intended for their own benefit. Anyone with a conscience (including scientists) is bothered by this fact. On the other hand, experimentation with animals is essential for learning more about both human and animal physiology (American Medical Association, 1988). Animal experimentation was an essential step in the medical research that led to our ability to prevent or treat polio, diabetes, measles, smallpox, massive burns, heart disease, and other conditions. The majority of Nobel prizes in physiology or medicine have been

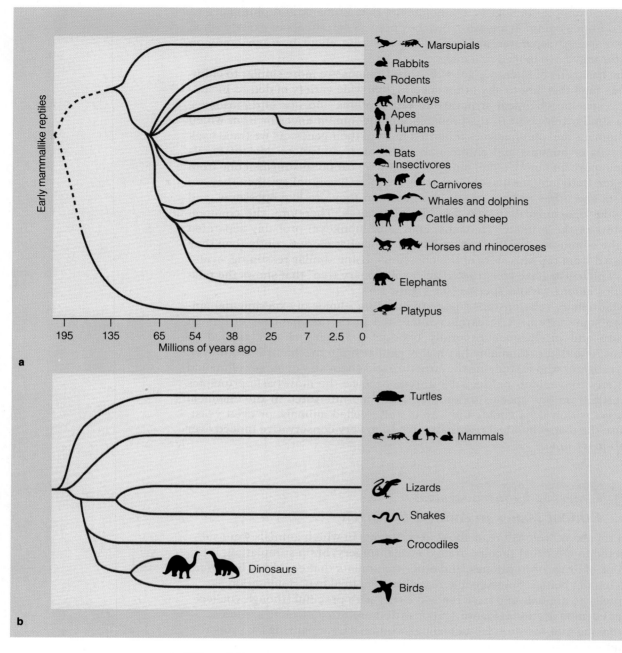

Figure 1.5
(**a**) Evolutionary relationships among various species of mammals.
(**b**) Evolutionary relationships among mammals, birds, and several kinds of reptiles. The relationships that are more remote in time (toward the left side of the figure) are less well established.

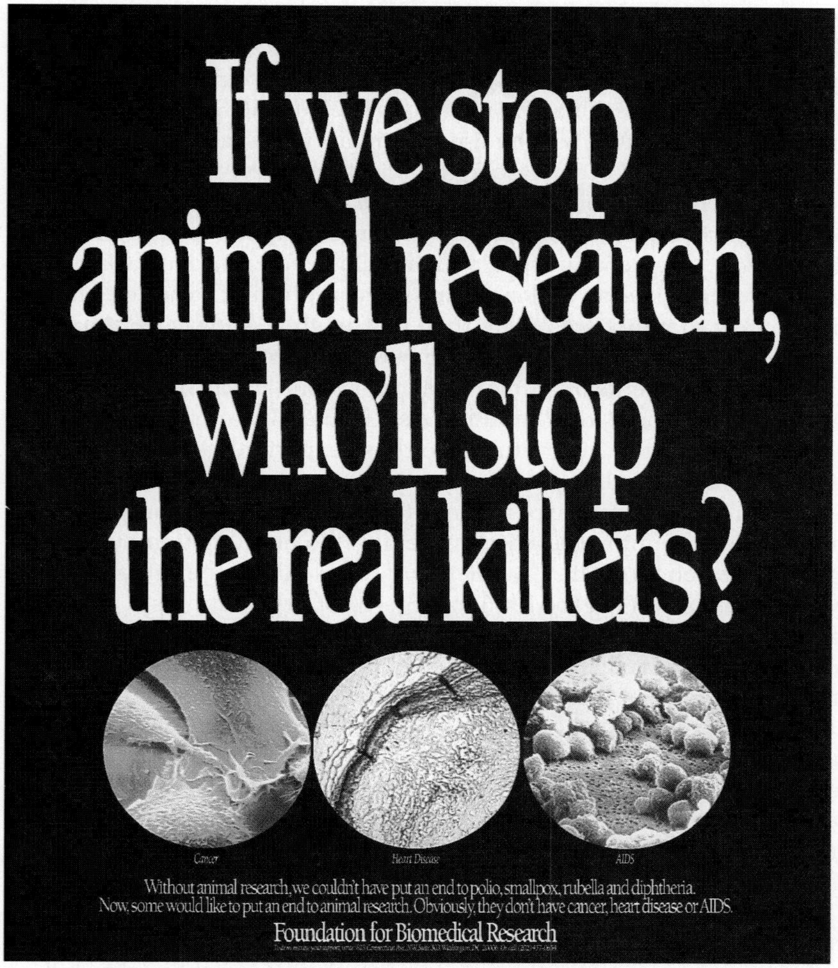

Figure 1.6
For many years, opponents of animal research have been protesting against experimentation with animals. This ad represents a reply by supporters of such research. (Courtesy of the Foundation for Biomedical Research.)

awarded for research conducted on nonhuman animals. The hope of finding methods to treat or prevent AIDS and various brain diseases (such as Alzheimer's disease) rests largely with animal research. In biological psychology, when we deal with certain questions about brain functioning, our only choice is between conducting research on animals or not answering the questions at all.

The ethical issue has much in common with other ethical dilemmas. For example, should a woman have the option of aborting an unwanted pregnancy? Should we permit land developers to destroy wetlands and forests to make room for more houses? In each case, intelligent and well-meaning people on each side of the issue can put forward a legitimate "moral" argument and fail to understand how any other intelligent, well-meaning person could disagree. In each case, compromises are possible, though sometimes difficult when people on both sides have taken heated or extreme stands.

In this debate, people often fail to notice the substantial government regulation of animal research. In the United States, for example, laws require all animal laboratories to meet certain standards of cleanliness and animal care. Professional organizations such as the Society for Neuroscience publish guidelines for the use of animals in research (see Appendix C). All colleges and other research institutions receiving federal funds are required to have Laboratory Animal Care Committees that evaluate proposed experiments and ensure that they are designed to minimize pain and discomfort. Such committees, which include veterinarians and community representatives as well as scientists, can prohibit experiments that are more likely to inflict great pain than to gain great knowledge. Analogous regulations and committees govern research on human subjects.

Still, some opponents of animal research remain unsatisfied and uncompromising. Some, the "minimalists," would like to reduce animal research to a minimum, restricting it to those experiments that are clearly worthwhile and that inflict little if any pain. Others, the "abolitionists," wish to prohibit all animal experimentation without exception. According to one opponent of animal research, "We have no moral option but to bring this research to a halt. Completely. . . . We will not be satisfied until every cage is empty" (Regan, 1986, pp. 39–40). For abolitionists, animal research is always wrong, whether or not the animals are treated well and regardless of how valuable the results may be. Such people maintain that all life is equally valuable and that any animal has the same rights as any human. Keeping an animal (presumably even a pet) in a cage is slavery. Killing an animal to eat it, to use its fur, or to gain scientific knowledge is murder. Most biological scientists support animal *welfare* and work toward improving conditions for laboratory animals, but they deny that animals have the same *rights* as humans (Johnson, 1990).

If society takes the equal-rights-for-animals position, it has a price to pay. For example, the best current treatment for people with a defective heart valve is to transplant a valve from a pig's heart. If we decide that a pig's life has the same value as a human's life, then it is unethical to kill a pig to save a human, and people with defective heart valves will have to settle for some treatment with a lower chance of success. Similarly, if the value of a rat's life or a monkey's life is the same as that of a human's life, then we will have to tell people suffering from AIDS, spinal cord damage, and other incurable diseases and handicaps, "Sorry, we must greatly slow down the progress toward a treatment for your condition." Many victims of incurable diseases have organized to oppose animal-rights groups and to support animal research (Feeney, 1987).

Biological psychologists believe that many of the claims made by abolitionists are exaggerated, unfair, and in some cases simply untrue. A few examples:

Claim: Laboratory animals are given intense, repeated, inescapable shocks until they can no longer even scream in pain. They are left to die of hunger and thirst. Extreme pain and stress are inflicted upon them in attempts to drive them insane.

Reply: Caroline Coile and Neal Miller (1984) examined the psychological studies published over five years and could not find a single example to support any of these charges. Even over the whole history of psychology, experiments that inflicted severe pain on animals have been rare.

Claim: Research on animals leads to no useful discoveries.

Reply: Nearly all of our progress in medicine and in biological psychology is traceable in part to pioneering studies conducted on animals. While it is undeniable that much research on animals leads to little of immediate practical value—and the same is true of research in any field—animal research has led to the development of antianxiety drugs, new methods of treating pain and depression, an awareness of how certain drugs can impair fetal development, an understanding of the effects of old age on memory, methods to help people overcome neuromuscular disorders, and numerous other advances (N. E. Miller, 1985). Unfortunately, it is difficult to predict which research projects will lead to valuable advances and which ones will lead to dead ends.

Claim: Psychologists have been remiss in failing to consider alternative research methods that do not require animals, such as studying embryos, plants, tissue cultures, and computer simulations.

Reply: That criticism is simply puzzling (Gallup & Suarez, 1985). Embryos, plants, and tissue cultures do not behave in ways that would make them suitable subjects for psychological experiments. It is possible to program a computer to simulate a behavior *after* one understands the behavior, but not *before*. Although computer simulations may be suitable as classroom demonstrations, they are no substitute for using real animals in research.

However, even if we disregard the exaggerated or doubtful claims made by the opponents of animal research, a legitimate moral question remains: Under what circumstances, if any, is it justifiable to conduct research on animals (which, after all, did not volunteer for the studies) and sometimes to inflict varying degrees of distress upon them? Even ardent defenders of animal research agree to the need for limits and guidelines.

Most investigators wish to conduct research on animals only if the expected value of the results is greater than whatever suffering the animals might experience. However, applying that principle in practice can be difficult. Many apparently promising experiments produce inconclusive results, and a less promising experiment sometimes leads to unexpected and important results (Gallistel, 1981). Further, we have no standard measurement of animal suffering. Even if we did, we have no reasonable formula to compare the value of results to the expected suffering. In general, investigators are less disturbed about performing potentially painful procedures on insects than on rats and less disturbed about using rats than about using monkeys. But even that kind of distinction rests on loose, vague judgments. In short, investigators try to balance the value of the expected results against the cost to the animals, but in specific cases there is much room for disagreement. ◆◆◆

Summary

1. Biological psychology encompasses the work of many kinds of specialists, including psychologists, biologists, and medical doctors. (p. 2)

2. Biological psychologists try to answer four types of questions about any given behavior: How does it relate to the physiology of the brain and other organs? How does it develop within the individual? How did the capacity for the behavior evolve? And why did the capacity for this behavior evolve? (That is, what function does it serve?) (p. 4)

3. For example: Birds sing because of activity in certain brain areas that enlarge under the influence of the hormone testosterone. Many birds learn to sing their song by

hearing it early in life, even though they cannot practice it until the following year. Many species have songs that roughly resemble those of related species, presumably because both species evolved from a common ancestor. In most species, males sing more than females do, and they sing mostly during the breeding season; available evidence indicates that the song's function is to attract and stimulate a mate and to deter rival males. (p. 4)

4. Biological psychologists' attempts to explain human behavior and experience in biological terms seem to conflict with our impression that a conscious mind controls behavior. (p. 9)

5. Both philosophers and scientists try to understand the relationship between mind and brain. Various people have proposed that the brain is a machine, that the mind is independent of the brain, or that the mind and brain are identical. Although the results of brain research are more compatible with some proposals than with others, no theory seems fully satisfactory at present. (p. 9)

6. Studies of electrical stimulation of the brain indicate that specific kinds of brain activity can alter behavior and experience in complex ways. Such studies support the hypothesis of an inseparable relationship between brain activity and mental activity. (p. 12).

7. The ethics of using animals in research is controversial. Some research does inflict stress or pain on animals; however, many research questions can be investigated only through animal research. (p. 15)

Review Questions

1. What is the difference between an evolutionary explanation and a functional explanation? (p. 4)

2. Give a physiological explanation of why male birds sing more than females do. Give a functional explanation also. (pp. 5, 8)

3. What is meant by the "sensitive period" for learning birdsong? In what way do certain birds learn a song from a live tutor differently from the way that they learn it from a tape recording? (p. 7)

4. What is the "mind-brain problem"? Describe the pros and cons of some major positions on this question. (p. 10)

5. Describe one type of evidence that seems relevant to the mind-brain problem. (p. 12)

6. Describe at least one reason why biological psychologists sometimes conduct their research on nonhuman animals. (p. 16)

Thought Questions

1. Marler (1970) found that white-crowned sparrows have "dialects"—that is, their song varies noticeably from one part of the country to another. How might such dialects develop? Would pigeons and chickens be more likely or less likely than sparrows to have dialects?

2. Suppose a philosopher asks you what findings about the brain and its control of behavior philosophers should

know about. That is, what scientific information is relevant to the mind-body problem? What would you answer? (Keep this question in mind as you read this book; see what relevant information you can find.)

Suggestions for Further Reading

Dennett, D. C. (1991). *Consciousness explained*. Boston: Little, Brown, and Co. The title notwithstanding, I am not convinced that Dennett has "explained" consciousness, but he has certainly offered some outstanding insights. This book is highly recommended for anyone seriously interested in the mind-brain relationship.

Logan, C. A. (1992). Developmental analysis in behavioral systems: The case of bird song. *Annals of the New York Academy of Sciences, 662,* 102–117. An insightful review of research on birdsong and its general implications for the study of behavior.

Valenstein, E. (1973). *Brain control*. New York: Wiley-Interscience. A critical treatment of electrical brain stimulation and psychosurgery.

Terms

biological psychology study of the biological principles underlying behavior (p. 2)

physiological explanation concept that relates an activity to how the brain and other organs of the body function (p. 4)

ontogenetic explanation description of how a structure or a behavior develops (p. 4)

evolutionary explanation hypothesis that relates a structure or a behavior to the evolutionary history of a species (p. 4)

functional explanation description of why a structure or behavior evolved as it did (p. 4)

sensitive period a time (generally early in life) when a particular type of experience has an especially strong and long-lasting effect on the development of behavior (p. 7)

template a model that an individual attempts to match or to copy (p. 7)

parallelism theory that mind and brain exist separately but do not affect each other (p. 10)

mentalism theory that the physical world exists only if a conscious mind perceives it (p. 10)

mind-body problem or **mind-brain problem** question of how the mind is related to the brain (p. 10)

dualist position belief that the mind exists independent of the brain and exerts some control over it (p. 10)

interactionism theory that the mind and the brain are separate but interact with each other and influence each other (p. 10)

monism theory that only one kind of substance exists in the universe (not separate physical and mental substances) (p. 11)

materialist position belief that the brain is a machine and that consciousness is irrelevant to its functioning (p. 11)

identity position belief that the mind is the same thing as brain activity, described in different terms (p. 12)

emergent property position theory that the mind emerges as a new property when matter is organized in a particular way (p. 12)

epilepsy a syndrome caused by abnormal repetitive activity of the nerve cells in the brain (p. 14)

focus a damaged or malfunctioning area of the brain from which an epileptic seizure originates (p. 14)

NERVE CELLS AND NERVE IMPULSES

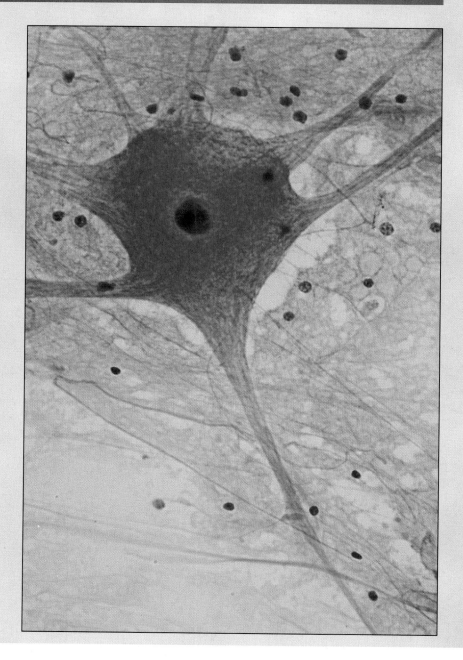

(Ed Reschke)

CHAPTER TWO

MAIN IDEAS

1. Two kinds of cells compose the nervous system: neurons and glia. Only the neurons transmit impulses from one location to another.

2. The structure of a neuron is somewhat plastic throughout life. The fibers of a neuron can increase or decrease their branching pattern as a function of experience, age, and chemical influences.

3. Many molecules in the bloodstream that are free to enter other body organs are unable to enter the brain.

4. The nerve impulse, known as an action potential, is an electrical charge across the membrane of a neuron, caused by the sudden flow of sodium ions into the neuron followed by a flow of potassium ions out of the neuron.

5. Myelin is an insulating sheath that increases the velocity of transmission in certain vertebrate neurons.

6. Many small neurons convey information without action potentials, through graded electrical potentials that vary in intensity.

A society is composed of many people. A chemical compound is composed of two or more atoms. Similarly, a nervous system is composed of many individual cells.

The nervous system is in many regards more like a chemical compound than it is like a society of people. Although we sometimes speak of a society as taking collective action, the individuals who compose that society never entirely lose their capacity for individual action. The nervous system is more like a chemical compound: When oxygen and hydrogen combine, they lose the properties ordinarily associated with oxygen and hydrogen and form water, which has a very different set of properties. Similarly, the combination of many cells in a nervous system has properties that are very different from those of a single cell.

Although we cannot understand what people do and why by studying a single cell, it is the logical place to begin. Just as a chemist must know about atoms to make sense of compounds, a biological psychologist must know about cells of the nervous system to understand how the nervous system works. (Advice: Parts of this chapter and the next deal with chemistry. If you need to refresh your memory of basic chemistry, read Appendix B.)

The Cells of the Nervous System

Until the late 1800s, the best available microscopic views of the nervous system revealed little detail about the organization of the brain. Brain cells are small and generally colorless; before the discovery of staining techniques, they were hard to distinguish from their background. Long, thin fibers were observed between one nerve cell and another. Several of the most respected authorities maintained that these fibers actually merged one cell into another; that is, they denied that any gap separated one cell from the next.

In the late 1800s, Santiago Ramón y Cajal demonstrated that a single nerve cell, or *neuron,* does not merge with its neighbors. Each cell is distinct; a small gap separates it from each neighboring cell.

Philosophically, we can see some appeal in the old concept that one neuron might merge into another. We each experience our conscious awareness as a single thing, not as a combination of many. In a way, it seems right that all the cells in the brain should join together physically as a single unit. Yet we now know that they do not. The adult human brain contains a great many neurons (Figure 2.1)—approximately 100 billion, according to one estimate (Williams & Herrup, 1988). (Because certain areas of the brain contain a large number of very small cells, an accurate count is difficult.) Those billions of cells combine to produce both unified experience and coordinated, organized behavior. Before we can begin to contemplate how they act together, we need to know a little about the properties of the individual cell.

Neurons and Glia

In this chapter, we shall deal with some detailed information about neuron structure and function. At times it may not be obvious why a student of psychology needs to know such things. However, to theorize about how the brain controls behavior, a psychologist needs to know a little about what neurons can and cannot do. Moreover, certain important points about behavior can be related directly to what we know about the individual neuron. For example, a kind of memory loss called Korsakoff's syndrome (see p. 500) is caused by a deficiency in the nutrition of neurons; alcohol exerts some of its long-term effects by changing the structure of neurons; anesthetic drugs prevent the transmission of information by neurons. To understand these and other examples, we need a basic understanding of what neurons are, what they do, and how they do it.

The nervous system consists of two kinds of cells, neurons and glia. **Neurons** are cells that receive information and transmit it to other cells by con-

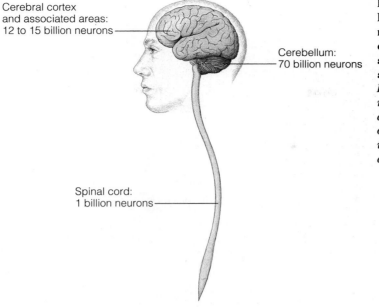

Cerebral cortex
and associated areas:
12 to 15 billion neurons

Cerebellum:
70 billion neurons

Spinal cord:
1 billion neurons

Figure 2.1
Estimated numbers of neurons in the human central nervous system, according to R. W. Williams and K. Herrup (1988)
Because of the small size of many neurons and the variation in cell density from one spot to another, obtaining an accurate count is difficult.

ducting electrochemical impulses; they are the cells that people usually mean when they refer to "nerve cells." The various types of glia and their functions will be described later. Neurons resemble other body cells in certain basic properties, so we shall begin with some information common to all animal cells.

The Structures within an Animal Cell

Figure 2.2 illustrates a neuron from the cerebellum of a mouse, magnified × 23,000. It contains the same basic structures as most other animal cells, even though the cell's size and shape are quite distinctive.

Every cell is surrounded by a **membrane** (often called a *plasma membrane*), a structure composed of two layers of fat molecules, which are free to flow around one another. (Figure 2.12 shows this arrangement in more detail.) The membrane controls the flow of materials between the inside of the cell and the outside environment. A few chemicals, such as water, oxygen, carbon dioxide, and many fat-soluble molecules, move fairly freely across the membrane. A few larger molecules can cross through specialized protein channels. Other large or electrically charged molecules, for which no specialized protein channels exist, cannot cross the membrane at all. The fluid inside the cell membrane is the **cytoplasm.**

All animal cells (except red blood cells) have a **nucleus,** the structure that contains the chromosomes. A **mitochondrion** (plural: mitochondria) is the site where the cell performs metabolic activities, which provide the energy that the cell requires for all its other activities. Mitochondria require fuel and oxygen to function. **Ribosomes** are the sites at which the cell synthesizes new protein molecules. Proteins provide building materials for the cell and facilitate various chemical reactions. Some ribosomes float freely within the cell; others are attached to the **endoplasmic reticulum,** a network of thin tubes transporting newly synthesized proteins to other locations. **Lysosomes** contain enzymes that break down many chemicals into their component parts so they can be

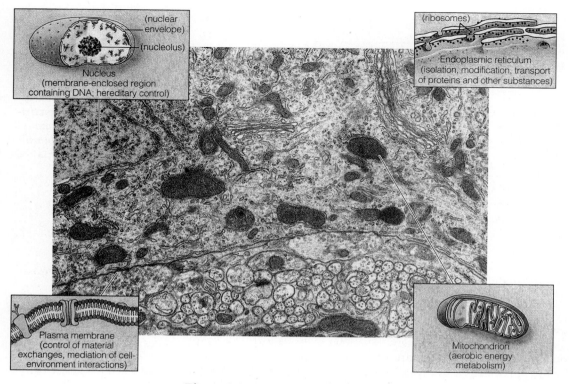

Nucleus
(membrane-enclosed region
containing DNA; hereditary control)

(nuclear
envelope)

(nucleolus)

(ribosomes)

Endoplasmic reticulum
(isolation, modification, transport
of proteins and other substances)

Plasma membrane
(control of material
exchanges, mediation of cell-
environment interactions)

Mitochondrion
(aerobic energy
metabolism)

Figure 2.2
A neuron from the cerebellum of a mouse, magnified × 23,000
The nucleus, membrane, and other structures are characteristic of most animal cells. (Micrograph courtesy of Dennis M. D. Landis.)

recycled for other uses. The **Golgi complex** is a network of vesicles preparing hormones and other products for secretion.

The Structure of a Neuron

A neuron (Figure 2.3) contains a nucleus, a membrane, mitochondria, ribosomes, and the other structures typical of animal cells. What sets a neuron apart from other cells is its shape. From the central body of the neuron, many small, thin fibers may emanate. Some of those fibers extend great distances; some branch widely. The size and shape of neurons vary almost endlessly. The distinctive shape of a given neuron determines its connections with other neurons and thereby determines how it will contribute to the overall functioning of the nervous system. For example, certain neurons send axon branches to wide areas of the brain, transmitting the same message to a great many cells. Other neurons have widely branching dendrites, which enable them to receive and compare input from many sources. Still other neurons with shorter axons and dendrites exchange information with fewer sources.

Figure 2.4 shows one example of a neuron, a motor neuron that has its cell body in the spinal cord and one fiber extending to a muscle. It would be misleading to call this a "typical" neuron; neurons vary so widely in their shape that no one neuron is typical of all others any more than an artichoke is typical of all vegetables. Nevertheless, the motor neuron contains all the parts found in other neurons.

Most neurons have three major components: the cell body, dendrites, and an axon. The **cell body,** or **soma** (Latin for *body*), contains the nucleus, some ribosomes and mitochondria, and other structures found in most cells. Much of the metabolic work of the neuron occurs here. Cell bodies of neurons range in diameter from 0.005 mm to 0.1 mm in mammals and up to a full millimeter in certain invertebrates, such as the squid.

The **dendrites** are thin, widely branching fibers that get narrower as they get farther from the cell body. (The term *dendrite* comes from a Greek root word meaning *tree;* a dendrite's shape resembles that of a tree.) The dendrite's surface is lined with specialized junctions, called *synapses,* at which the dendrite receives information from other neurons. (Chapter 3 discusses synapses in more detail.) The greater the surface area of a dendrite, the more information it can receive. Some dendrites branch widely and therefore have a large surface area. Some also contain **dendritic spines**, short outgrowths as shown in Figure 2.5. The specialized synapses that form on dendritic spines apparently play an important role in the formation of learning and memory (Koch & Zador, 1993).

The **axon** is a single fiber thicker and longer than the dendrites. (The term *axon* comes from a Greek word meaning *axis;* in some ways it resembles a long axis extending from one pole of the neuron.) Mature neurons have either one axon or none. In contrast, a neuron may have any number of dendrites. However, an axon may have many branches, generally near the tip of the axon, remote from the cell body.

In large neurons, the point where the axon begins is marked by a swelling of the soma known as the **axon hillock.** The hillock is the point at which impulses, or *action potentials,* begin. The axon maintains a constant diameter along its entire length. Generally, an axon carries an impulse from the cell body toward other cells. Some axons are a meter or more in length—for example, the axons going from your spinal cord to your feet. A neuron without an axon can convey information only to other neurons immediately adjacent to it.

The axon of a motor neuron is covered with an insulating material called a **myelin sheath.** Myelin covers some, but not all, vertebrate axons. Invertebrate axons do not have myelin sheaths.

Each branch of an axon swells at its tip, forming a **presynaptic terminal,** or *end bulb.* This is the point from which the axon releases chemicals that cross through the synapse (the junction between one neuron and the next) and influence the next cell. The synthesis, release, and reuptake of these chemicals requires considerable energy; consequently, the presynaptic terminals have many mitochondria.

Table 2.1 lists the anatomical distinctions between dendrites and axons. Occasionally, however, we encounter a structure that strains the definitions. For example, each neuron carrying information from touch receptors toward the spinal cord has its cell body located on a stalk (see Figure 2.8c). One long fiber conveys impulses from the sensory receptor toward the cell body. Because it conveys information toward the cell body, it functions as a dendrite, yet its structure is that of an axon.

You will note in Table 2.1 the frequent use of the word *usually.* The structure of neurons varies enormously, and there are exceptions to practically any rule about dendrites and axons. Many neurons, especially the smaller ones, violate the rule that dendrites receive information and axons conduct it to other cells. In some cases, dendrites and cell bodies transmit information directly to the dendrites and cell bodies of other neurons, without the intervention of an axon.

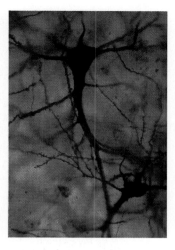

**Figure 2.3
Neurons, stained to appear dark**
The distinctive characteristic of each neuron is its shape. Because neurons differ greatly in their branching patterns, some pool information from many sources and some send their output over great distances. Other neurons have a much more restricted region of input and output. (McCoy/Scheibel/Rainbow.)

Figure 2.4
The components of a motor neuron
The cell body of a motor neuron is located in the spinal cord. The various parts are not drawn to scale; in particular, a real axon is much longer in proportion to the size of the soma.

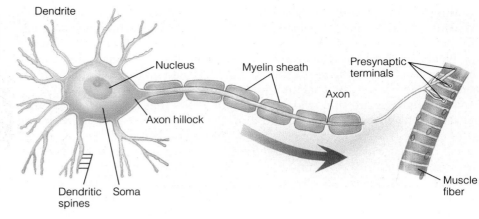

Dendrite

Nucleus

Myelin sheath

Presynaptic terminals

Axon hillock

Axon

Dendritic spines

Soma

Muscle fiber

Figure 2.5
Dendritic spines
The dendrites of certain neurons are lined with spines, short outgrowths that receive specialized incoming information. That information apparently plays a key role in long-term changes in the neuron that mediate learning and memory. (From Harris & Stevens, 1989.)

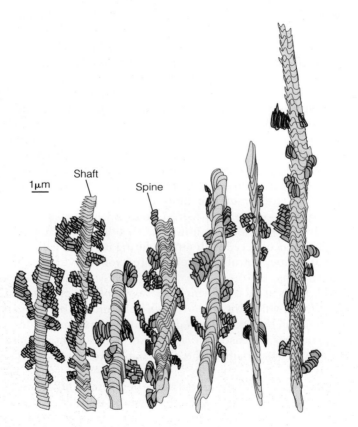

1μm

Shaft

Spine

Variations among Neurons

For some purposes it is useful to distinguish among three types of neurons: receptor neurons, motor neurons, and interneurons. A **receptor** or **sensory neuron** (Figure 2.6) is specialized to be highly sensitive to a particular type of stimulation, such as light, sound waves, touch, or certain chemicals. As a rule, each receptor is highly sensitive to one kind of stimulus and relatively insensitive to most others. For example, a few molecules of an airborne chemical can excite the olfactory receptors in the nose but not the receptors in the eye. A single photon of light can affect receptors in the eye but not the olfactory

Table 2.1 Anatomical Distinctions between Dendrites and Axons	
Dendrites	*Axons*
A neuron may have many dendrites, each with many branches.	A neuron may have one axon or none. An axon may have many branches.
Usually shorter than the axon. Some neurons have a long "apical" dendrite with branches (see Figure 2.8d).	May be any length, in some cases up to 1 meter or longer.
Diameter usually tapers toward the periphery of the dendrite.	Diameter usually constant over the length of the axon until the presynaptic terminal.
No hillock.	Relatively large axons join the cell body at a distinct swelling called the axon hillock.
Usually branch at acute angles.	Usually branch perpendicular to the main trunk of the axon.
Seldom covered with myelin (an insulating sheath).	Often covered with myelin (among vertebrates only).
Usually have ribosomes.	Usually have few ribosomes or none.

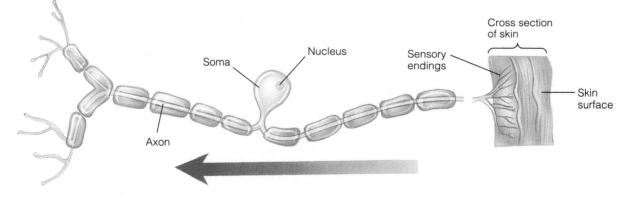

Figure 2.6
A sensory neuron

receptors. However, this selectivity is not absolute; all receptors can be stimulated by electricity and other intense stimuli.

A **motor neuron** (Figure 2.4) receives excitation from other neurons and conducts impulses from its soma in the spinal cord to muscle or gland cells. **Interneurons** (Figure 2.8b) receive information from other neurons (either receptor neurons or interneurons) and send it to either motor neurons or interneurons. Many interneurons connect only to other interneurons, not to receptor or motor neurons. Most of the neurons in the human nervous system are interneurons.

Some other terms that you may encounter are *efferent, afferent,* and *intrinsic.* An **efferent axon** carries information away from a structure; an **afferent axon** brings information into a structure. Every axon that is efferent *from* one

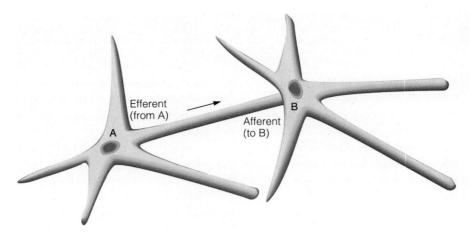

Figure 2.7
Cell structures and axons
It all depends on the point of view. An axon from A to B is an efferent axon from A; it is an afferent axon to B, just as a train from Washington to New York is exiting Washington and approaching New York.

Efferent (from A)

Afferent (to B)

A

B

structure is afferent *to* some other structure, as Figure 2.7 shows. An **intrinsic neuron** is one whose axons and dendrites are all confined within a given structure. For example, an intrinsic neuron of the cerebral cortex has no dendrites or axons that extend beyond the borders of the cortex.

The shape of neurons varies greatly, as Figure 2.8 illustrates. The function of a neuron is closely related to its shape (Palay & Chan-Palay, 1977). For example, the dendrites of the Purkinje cell of the cerebellum (the neuron in Figure 2.8a) branch extremely widely within a single plane; this cell is capable of integrating an enormous amount of incoming information. The neurons in Figure 2.8d and f also have widely branching dendrites that receive and integrate information from many sources. The neuron in Figure 2.8b, an interneuron, has an axon and dendrites that branch diffusely but only within a small radius. It is well suited to engage in extensive feedback, influencing some of the same cells that influence it.

The neurons in Figure 2.8c are the sensory neurons of the spinal cord. They receive information from touch receptors at the periphery of the body and convey it over a long axon that does not branch until it reaches the spinal cord. The neuron in Figure 2.8e, a bipolar cell of the retina in the eye, conveys information about excitation of the visual receptors. Note that the dendrites of the bipolar cell branch over a limited area and that its axon is short, with only a few branches. If either its dendrites or its axon branched widely, vision would be blurry because information from different parts of the retina would not remain distinct.

Glia

Besides neurons, the other major components of the nervous system are **glia** (or *neuroglia*). The term *glia* is derived from a Greek word meaning *glue*. Originally, investigators believed that glia were like glue or putty that held the neurons together (Somjen, 1988). Although that concept is obsolete, the term remains.

On the average, a glial cell is about one-tenth the size of a neuron. Glia are about ten times more numerous than neurons in the human brain, somewhat less in the brains of most other species. Thus, in the human brain, glia occupy about the same total space as the neurons (see Figure 2.9).

Because neurons are larger than glia, investigators can measure the electrical and other activities of neurons much more easily than they can with glia. Consequently, our knowledge of glia is less complete. In contrast to neurons,

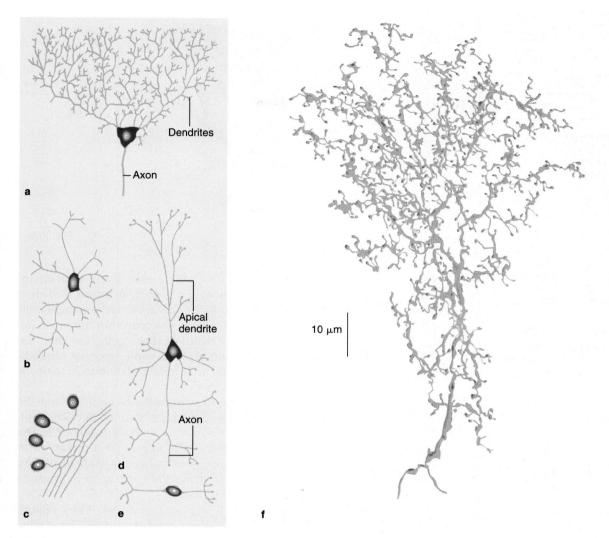

Figure 2.8
The diverse shapes of neurons
(*a*) *Purkinje cell, a cell type found only in the cerebellum;* (*b*) *interneuron of the spinal cord;* (*c*) *sensory neurons from skin to spinal cord;* (*d*) *pyramidal cell of the motor area of the cerebral cortex;* (*e*) *bipolar cell of retina of the eye;* (*f*) *Kenyon cell, from a honeybee. (Part (f) courtesy of R. G. Goss.)*

glia do not transmit information from one cell to another. They perform a variety of other functions, however (Kimelberg & Norenberg, 1989; Varon & Somjen, 1979):

1. Two kinds of glia build the myelin sheaths that surround and insulate certain vertebrate axons: **oligodendrocytes** (OL-i-go-DEN-druh-sites) in the brain and spinal cord and **Schwann cells** in the periphery of the body. Even the unmyelinated axons of the central nervous system are in contact with oligodendrocytes. For unmyelinated axons, the main function of the oligodendrocytes is to separate one axon from another.
2. The very small **microglia** and the larger, star-shaped **astrocytes,** also known as astroglia, remove waste material, particularly that created when neurons die. After brain damage, such as that caused by a stroke,

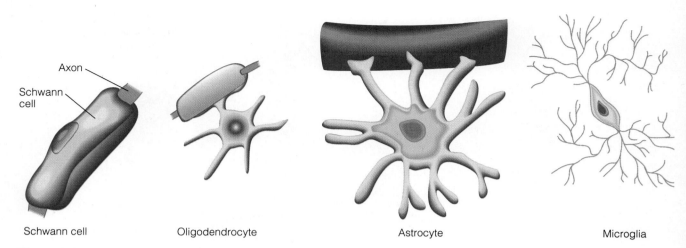

Axon
Schwann cell

Schwann cell   Oligodendrocyte   Astrocyte   Microglia

Figure 2.9
Shapes of some glia cells
Glia perform a number of important roles in the nervous system. Among other functions, they guide the growth and migration of neurons, produce the myelin sheaths that insulate certain vertebrate axons, and remove waste products from the brain.

both kinds of glia enter the damaged area and release a variety of chemicals. Some of those chemicals promote the growth of axons and dendrites by healthy neurons that remain in the area. Other chemicals, such as nitric oxide, kill those cells that were weakened but not yet dead. In effect, the nitric oxide hastens the death of those cells. For this reason, people who suffer a stroke frequently lose some neurons immediately after the damage and then lose an additional population of neurons 1 to 3 days later (Lees, 1993).

3. **Radial glia,** a type of astrocyte, guide the migration of neurons and the growth of their axons and dendrites during embryonic development. Schwann cells perform a related function after damage to axons in the periphery, guiding a regenerating axon to the appropriate target. After the brain is mature, biologists believe that radial glia transform into other forms of astrocytes that provide structural support to help axons and dendrites hold their shape and position.

4. Astrocytes exchange chemicals with adjacent neurons. They absorb potassium and larger chemicals when a neuron releases them; later, they either return them to the neuron or pass them to the blood.

Glia probably perform other functions besides those just listed, including guiding the plasticity of neurons' structures and synapses, removing old structures, and guiding the formation of new structures (Raisman, 1991). Future research may identify additional functions.

Changes in the Structure of Neurons and Glia

Skin cells and cells in many other parts of the body can divide at any time during life to replace cells that have died. However, most areas of the adult vertebrate brain cannot replace lost neurons. As neurons develop their complex shape and function, they lose their ability to divide and reproduce.

Neuroscientists have identified a very few exceptions to this rule. One is in the olfactory system. Olfactory receptors, being exposed to the outside world and its toxic chemicals, have a short life expectancy; if we could not replace them, we would lose our sense of smell at an early age. Fortunately for our

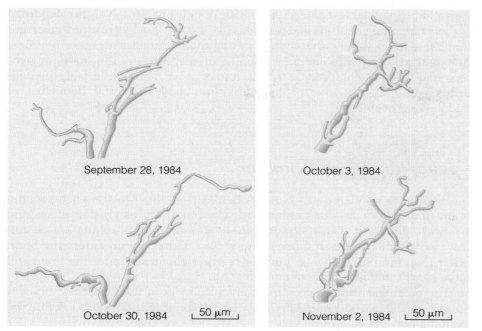

September 28, 1984

October 3, 1984

October 30, 1984   50 μm

November 2, 1984   50 μm

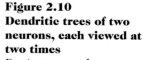

Figure 2.10
Dendritic trees of two neurons, each viewed at two times
During a month, some branches elongated and others retracted. The shape of the neuron is in flux even during adulthood. (From Purves & Hadley, 1985.)

sense of smell, a small population of neurons in the nose remains immature throughout life. When one of the mature olfactory receptors dies, an immature neuron divides, forming one neuron that will become mature and one that will remain immature, waiting for the next time it needs to divide (Graziadei & deHan, 1973; Graziadei & Monti Graziadei, 1985).

A few populations of immature neurons also remain in isolated parts of the rat brain; in those areas, even the adult brain can form new neurons—always small ones with short axons (Bayer, 1985; Kaplan, 1985). However, adult monkey brains are apparently incapable of developing even these small new neurons (Rakic, 1985).

Cancer is an abnormal proliferation (reproduction) of cells. Because most neurons cannot proliferate, brain cancers are generally—maybe always—limited to glial cells, which can and do divide throughout life.

Although most of the adult vertebrate brain does not develop new neurons, the neurons that it already has can change their structure and their connections—rapidly and frequently at a subcellular, molecular level, and more slowly at a visible level. Dale Purves and R. D. Hadley (1985) developed a method of injecting dye into a neuron that enabled them to examine the structure of a living neuron at two times, days to weeks apart. They found that dendritic patterns gradually change. Some branches grow and extend, while others retract. Some new dendrites grow, and old ones disappear altogether (see Figure 2.10). Evidently, the anatomy of the brain is in constant plasticity at the microscopic level as neurons change their connections with other neurons.

Alcohol can impair the dendritic branching of neurons. Pregnant rats that are forced to drink large amounts of alcohol give birth to offspring with abnormal patterns of dendritic branching (West, Hodges, & Black, 1981). The dendritic branches of mice retract after the mice are exposed to alcohol, even in adulthood (Riley & Walker, 1978).

People over age 70 may have either wider or narrower dendritic branches than middle-aged people do. When S. J. Buell and P. D. Coleman (1981) examined the brains of people who had died at various ages, they found that normal, alert old people had lost a certain number of neurons. However, the dendrites of their remaining neurons had compensated for the loss by growing longer and branching more widely, thereby increasing their contact with other neurons. Among the elderly who had grown senile, the dendrites of the surviving neurons had failed to compensate for the loss of other neurons. In fact, the dendrites were slightly shorter and less branched than the dendrites of middle-aged people.

The Blood-Brain Barrier

Have you ever wondered why certain chemicals produce greater effects on the brain than others do—for example, why heroin produces greater effects and stronger addictions than morphine does? (Heroin and morphine are chemically very similar to each other.) One reason is that heroin enters the brain faster than morphine does. A number of other chemicals enter the brain still more slowly, and most cannot enter it at all.

The mechanism that keeps most chemicals out of the vertebrate brain is known as the **blood-brain barrier** (Cserr & Bundgaard, 1986). Before we examine how the blood-brain barrier works, let us consider why we need it.

Why We Need a Blood-Brain Barrier

From time to time, a number of harmful substances enter the body—viruses, for example. When viruses enter one of the body's cells, mechanisms within the cell extrude one of the virus particles through the cell's own membrane, so that *natural killer cells* (part of the immune system) can find the virus. When they do, they not only attack the virus, but they also kill the cell that contains it. In effect, the cell that exposes the virus through its membrane is committing suicide; it says, "Look, immune system, I'm infected with this virus. Kill me and save the others."

That plan works fine if the virus-infected cell is, say, a skin cell or a red blood cell. After the body loses such a cell, it can simply make a replacement. But a mature vertebrate brain cannot make any replacement neurons. Any cell that the brain loses is gone forever. To prevent any loss of neurons, the body literally builds a wall along the sides of the brain's blood vessels, a wall that keeps most viruses, bacteria, and other dangerous intruders out.

"If that works so well for the brain," you might ask, "why don't we have a similar wall around the rest of the body's organs?" The answer is that we pay a price for having a blood-brain barrier: The barrier that keeps the viruses out also keeps out most forms of nutrition.

"What happens if a virus does enter the brain?" you might also ask. After all, certain viruses do find a way to break through the blood-brain barrier. Neurons, unlike other body cells, do not commit suicide by exposing a virus through the membrane (Joly, Mucke, & Oldstone, 1991). Because natural killer cells of the immune system do not attack virus-infected neurons, the infected neurons survive, but so do the viruses. Certain viruses, including the herpes virus, enter the nervous system and then survive for the rest of the person's life.

The body does defend itself against certain viruses in neurons, but through a different mechanism: Antibodies can enter the neurons and prevent certain viruses from reproducing (Levine et al., 1991).

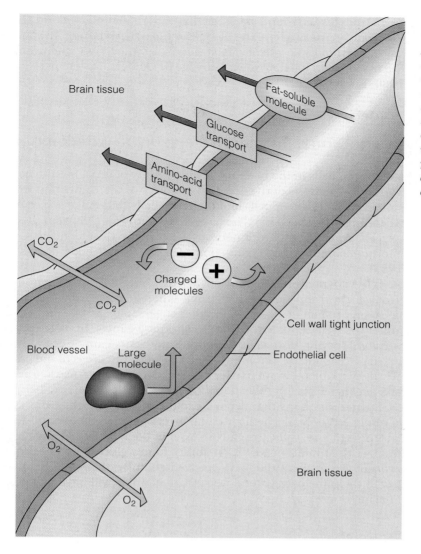

Figure 2.11
The blood-brain barrier
Most large molecules and electrically charged molecules cannot cross from the blood to the brain. A few small, uncharged molecules such as O_2 and CO_2 can cross; so can certain fat-soluble molecules. Active transport systems pump glucose and certain amino acids across the membrane.

How the Blood-Brain Barrier Works

The blood-brain barrier depends on the arrangement of endothelial cells that form the walls of the capillaries (Bundgaard, 1986; Rapoport & Robinson, 1986). In most parts of the body, such cells are separated by gaps large enough to allow the passage of large molecules. In the brain, the endothelial cells are tightly joined to one another. Many molecules simply cannot pass through those joints.

Some kinds of molecules do cross the blood-brain barrier. Oxygen, carbon dioxide, and a few other small, uncharged molecules pass freely back and forth. Because heroin, nicotine, and cannabinol (the active substance in marijuana) are soluble in fats, they can dissolve in the fats of the capillary walls and cross. Heroin crosses more freely and therefore produces stronger effects on the brain than morphine does.

A mechanism called an *active transport system* pumps into the brain certain important chemicals that would not be able to pass through the barrier otherwise. For example, one transport system pumps glucose into the brain; another pumps in certain large amino acids. Figure 2.11 illustrates the blood-brain barrier.

The Cells of the Nervous System

Astrocytes surround most of the endothelial cells along the capillaries, especially in areas where the blood-brain barrier is strong. In ways that are not yet understood, the astrocytes strengthen the barrier; when they are absent, the blood-brain barrier is generally weak (Anders, Dorovini-Zis, & Brightman, 1980; Bradbury, 1979).

The Nourishment of Vertebrate Neurons

Most of the cells in the body use a wide variety of fuels, but the neurons do not. Vertebrate neurons derive the vast majority of their nutrition from **glucose**, a simple sugar. (Cancer cells and the testis cells that make sperm also rely overwhelmingly on glucose.) The metabolic pathway that uses glucose requires oxygen; consequently, the neurons—especially their dendrites—consume an enormous amount of oxygen compared with other body organs (Wong-Riley, 1989).

Why do neurons depend so heavily on glucose? Apparently, it is not because they are incapable of using other fuels. Neurons have the enzymes necessary to metabolize certain other sugars, plus lactate and ketone fats. The infant brain does, in fact, use these alternative fuels. In most parts of the adult vertebrate brain, however, these other nutrients cannot cross the blood-brain barrier in significant amounts (Gjedde, 1984). But areas of the brain with a relatively weak blood-brain barrier can and do sometimes use ketone fats and certain sugars for part of their nutrition (Hawkins & Biebuyck, 1979).

Even for neurons that depend exclusively on glucose, a shortage of glucose is rarely a problem. The liver can convert many carbohydrates, proteins, and fats into glucose; thus, the glucose level in the blood is almost always sufficient to meet the brain's needs. An inability to *use* glucose can be a problem, however. To use glucose, the body needs vitamin B_1, **thiamine.** If a person's diet is low in thiamine over several weeks, the neurons will have increasing difficulty in using glucose.

Summary

1. Santiago Ramón y Cajal used newly discovered staining techniques in the late 1800s to establish that the nervous system is composed of separate cells, now known as neurons. (p. 26)

2. Neurons receive information from, and transmit information to, other cells. The nervous system also contains *glia,* cells that do not exchange information with other cells. (pp. 26, 32)

3. Neurons include four major parts: dendrites, a cell body, an axon, and presynaptic terminals. Neuron shape varies greatly, depending on the function of the neuron and the connections that it makes with other cells. (p. 28)

4. As a rule, the mature vertebrate nervous system cannot form new neurons to replace damaged ones. The olfactory receptors are exceptions to this rule; so are neurons in a few areas of the rat brain. (p. 34)

5. Neurons can alter their shape as a result of experience or as a result of exposure to alcohol or other drugs. Healthy, alert old people have an increased proliferation of dendritic branches, whereas senile people have slightly shrunken dendrites. (p. 35)

6. Because of a set of mechanisms known as the blood-brain barrier, many molecules, especially large molecules, cannot enter the brain. The blood-brain barrier prevents fuels other than glucose from entering most areas of the brain. For this reason, neurons rely heavily on glucose for their nutrition. (pp. 36, 38)

Review Questions

1. Identify nucleus, mitochondrion, ribosomes. (p. 27)

2. Suppose you were looking at a small fiber in the brain; how could you tell whether it was a dendrite or an axon? (p. 28)

3. Distinguish among receptor neurons, motor neurons, and interneurons. Distinguish between afferent and efferent. (p. 30–31)

4. Describe an example of how a neuron's shape relates to its function. (p. 32)

5. What are the functions of the glia? (p. 33)

6. What is the current belief about whether new neurons can form in an adult vertebrate brain? (p. 34)

7. What mechanisms cause the blood-brain barrier? Under what circumstances is the barrier weakened? (p. 37)

8. What is the primary fuel of neurons in the adult vertebrate brain? Why do most brain neurons use very little of other fuels? (p. 38)

9. Which vitamin is necessary for neurons to use their primary fuel? (p. 38)

Thought Question

1. Fetal alcohol syndrome is a condition in which the babies of alcoholic mothers are born with a variety of physical deformities and behavioral abnormalities. What abnormalities would you expect to find in the brain structure of such children?

Suggestions for Further Reading

Kimelberg, H. K., & Norenberg, M. D. (1989, April). Astrocytes. *Scientific American, 260* (4), 66–76. An overview of the functions of glia.

Science, November 4, 1988. A special issue devoted to neurons and the nervous system.

Terms

neuron cell that receives information and transmits it to other cells by conducting electrochemical impulses (p. 26)

membrane structure that surrounds a cell (p. 27)

cytoplasm fluid inside the cell membrane (p. 27)

nucleus structure within a cell that contains the chromosomes (p. 27)

mitochondrion (plural: **mitochondria**) the structure where the cell performs the metabolic activities that provide energy (p. 27)

ribosome the site at which the cell synthesizes new protein molecules (p. 27)

endoplasmic reticulum a network of thin tubes within a cell that transports newly synthesized proteins to other locations (p. 27)

lysosome structure within a cell that contains enzymes that break down many chemicals into their component parts (p. 27)

Golgi complex a network of vesicles within a cell that prepares hormones and other products for secretion (p. 28)

cell body or **soma** structure of a cell that contains the nucleus (p. 29)

dendrite thin, widely branching fiber that emanates from a neuron (p. 29)

dendritic spine short outgrowth along the dendrites (p. 29)

axon a single fiber that extends from a neuron (p. 29)

axon hillock a swelling of the soma, the point where the axon begins (p. 29)

myelin sheath an insulating material that covers many vertebrate axons (p. 29)

presynaptic terminal the tip of an axon, the point from which the axon releases chemicals (p. 29)

receptor or **sensory neuron** a neuron specialized to be highly sensitive to a specific type of stimulation (p. 30)

motor neuron a neuron that receives excitation from other neurons and conducts impulses from its soma in the spinal cord to muscle or gland cells (p. 31)

interneuron a neuron that receives information from other neurons and sends it to either motor neurons or interneurons (p. 31)

efferent axon a neuron that carries information away from a structure (p. 31)

afferent axon a neuron that brings information into a structure (p. 31)

intrinsic neuron a neuron whose axons and dendrites are all confined within a given structure (p. 32)

glia a type of cell in the nervous system that, in contrast to neurons, does not conduct impulses to other cells (p. 32)

oligodendrocyte glia cell that surrounds and insulates certain axons in the vertebrate brain and spinal cord (p. 33)

Schwann cell glia cell that surrounds and insulates certain axons in the periphery of the vertebrate body (p. 33)

microglia a very small type of glia cell that removes waste material in the brain (p. 33)

astrocyte (astroglia) a relatively large, star-shaped glia cell (p. 33)

radial glia a type of glia cell that guides the migration of neurons and the growth of their axons and dendrites during embryological development (p. 34)

blood-brain barrier the mechanism that keeps many chemicals out of the brain (p. 36)

glucose a simple sugar, the main fuel of vertebrate neurons (p. 38)

thiamine (vitamin B_1) a chemical necessary for the metabolism of glucose (p. 38)

The Nerve Impulse

Touch your desk with your finger, paying close attention to exactly when you feel the touch. Do you feel the sensation as soon as your finger contacts the desk? Or is there a delay while you wait for the sensation to travel from your finger to your brain?

It probably seems to you that you feel the sensation instantly. (For that reason, people once believed that the sensation actually took place in the finger itself.) We now know that there is a delay between the time that your finger contacts the surface and the time that you become aware of it. The delay is short—less than a tenth of a second—and it will probably never inconvenience you. It nevertheless exists, and its existence indicates that your perception of touch takes place in your brain, not in your finger. (See Digression 2.1.) It also indicates that axons transmit information at a finite, measurable velocity.

Given that axons must convey information to the brain before the information is perceived, here is something else to think about: What if sensory information faded as it was transported over a distance? That is, suppose the longer it took for information to reach your brain, the weaker the signal became. In that case, you might feel a pinch on your upper arm more clearly than you felt a similar pinch on your finger. A pinch on the tip of your toes would feel even weaker. Short people would feel a pinch on their toes more clearly than tall people would.

Fortunately, your axons are specialized to transmit sensory information over a distance without any loss of intensity or clarity. It takes you a bit longer to feel a pinch on your toes than to feel a pinch on your shoulder, but you do not feel it any less clearly or distinctly. The rest of this chapter explains how axons manage to transmit information over a distance.

The Resting Potential of the Neuron

The membrane of a neuron is specialized to control the exchange of chemicals between the inside and outside of the cell; it also maintains an electrical gradient necessary for neural signaling. All parts of a neuron are covered by a membrane about 8 nanometers (nm) thick (just less than 0.00001 mm), composed of two layers of fat molecules with protein molecules embedded in the fats (see Figure 2.12). Each of the fat molecules has a water-soluble end and a water-insoluble end. The water-soluble ends point outward (toward the exterior of the cell on one side and the interior on the other), while the water-insoluble

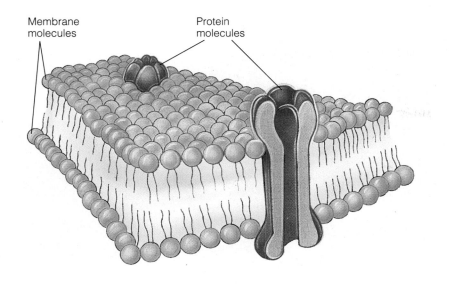

Membrane molecules

Protein molecules

Figure 2.12
The membrane of a neuron
Embedded in it are protein channels that permit certain ions to cross through the membrane at a controlled rate. The membrane is composed mostly of two layers of fat molecules called phospholipids. Each phospholipid molecule has a water-attracting "head" and two fatty water-repelling "tails."

Digression 2.1 — How to Determine the Delay between Finger Contact and the Perception of Touch

You were asked to touch your desk with your finger and to pay attention to exactly when you perceived the touch. Although there actually is a short delay between finger contact and the sensation of it, you are not aware of it. Why not?

The delay is simply too short. Try tapping yourself on the shoulder. Because your shoulder is closer to your brain than your finger is, theoretically you should feel the touch on your shoulder before you feel it on your finger. However, the two sensations arrive at your brain only a couple hundredths of a second apart, and you are not aware of any delay between them. (Vision and hearing are sensitive to very short time delays; touch is not.)

Although you do not notice a delay yourself, an experimenter can measure the delay. Suppose an experimenter taps you sometimes on the shoulder and sometimes on the finger—or better yet, sometimes on the shoulder and sometimes on the ankle. You respond, perhaps by pressing a button, as soon as you feel the touch. Your response time will be longer for a touch on the finger or on the ankle than for a touch on the shoulder, because your shoulder is closer to your brain. The extra delay indicates how long it takes for the touch information to travel the extra distance.

Still, for this experiment to produce meaningful results, the experimenter must be able to measure your response time to the hundredth of a second. Here is a way to make an approximate measurement without fancy equipment: First, arrange a group of about 20 people in a row, with each person holding the ankle of the next person. Pinch the first person's ankle and start timing. As soon as each person feels a pinch, he or she pinches the next person. When the last person feels the pinch, he or she says "Now," and you measure how much time has passed since the first pinch. (Repeat this procedure a few times until you get consistent results.) Then repeat the procedure, but this time have everyone grab the next person's shoulder. You will find that the pinch travels down the line faster when people are pinching shoulders than when they are pinching ankles (Rozin & Jonides, 1977).

The Nerve Impulse

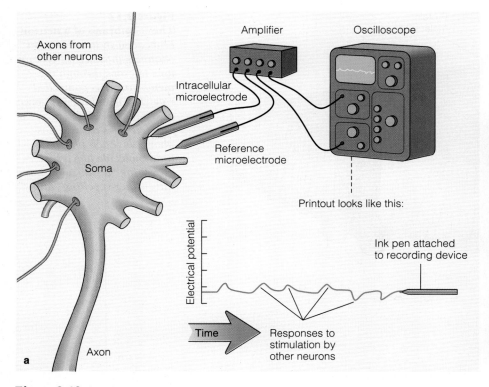

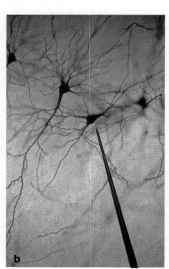

a

Amplifier

Oscilloscope

Axons from
other neurons

Intracellular
microelectrode

Soma

Reference
microelectrode

Printout looks like this:

Electrical potential

Ink pen attached
to recording device

Time

Responses to
stimulation by
other neurons

Axon

b

Figure 2.13
(a) Diagram of the apparatus for recording a neuron's response to stimulation. (b) A microelectrode and neurons, magnified hundreds of times by a light microscope.
Brain tissue has been sliced and stained to make the neurons easy to see. In a living organism, microelectrodes like this one can record the electrical activity of a neuron. (Fritz Goro.)

ends point toward one another. This structure provides the membrane with a good combination of flexibility and firmness and retards the flow of chemicals across the membrane.

In the absence of any outside disturbance, the membrane undergoes electrical **polarization**; that is, the neuron inside the membrane has a slightly negative electrical potential with respect to the outside. In a resting neuron, this electrical potential, or difference in voltage, is called the **resting potential.** It is produced by the unequal distribution of ions between the inside and outside of the neuron.

When the neuron is at its resting potential, a number of common ions are distributed unequally across the membrane. The difference in distribution is called a **concentration gradient.** Sodium is more than ten times more concentrated outside the membrane than it is inside; potassium is more than twenty times more concentrated inside than outside (Guyton, 1974).

Researchers can measure the resting potential by inserting a very thin **microelectrode** into the cell body, as Figure 2.13 shows. The diameter of the electrode must be as small as possible so that it can enter the cell without causing damage. By far the most common electrode is a fine glass tube filled with a concentrated salt solution, such as 2 to 3 molar (mol) potassium chloride, and tapering to a tip diameter of 0.0005 mm or less. This electrode, inserted into the neuron, is connected to recording equipment. A reference electrode placed somewhere outside the cell completes the circuit. Connecting the electrodes to a voltmeter, we find that the neuron's interior has a potential somewhere in the range of −30 to −90 millivolts (mV) relative to its exterior.

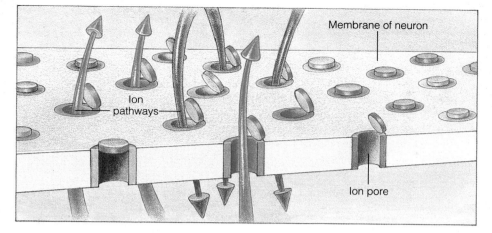

Membrane of neuron

Ion pathways

Ion pore

Figure 2.14
Ion gates in the membrane of a neuron
When a gate opens, it permits one kind of ion to cross the membrane. When it closes, it prevents passage of that ion.

The Forces behind the Resting Potential

One mechanism that maintains the resting potential is the selective permeability of the neuron membrane to the passage of chemicals. **Selective permeability** means that some molecules pass much more freely through the membrane than others do. Oxygen, carbon dioxide, urea, and water cross directly through the membrane in either direction at all times. Most larger or electrically charged ions and molecules cannot cross the membrane at all. However, a few biologically important ions, such as potassium, chloride, and sodium, cross the membrane through gates (or channels) in specialized proteins embedded in the membrane. Each of these ions travels through a different kind of gate, and the gates control the rate at which their ions pass. When the membrane is at rest, the potassium and chloride gates permit potassium and chloride ions to pass at a moderate rate, but the sodium gates are closed, restricting sodium flow to a very low rate. Figure 2.14 illustrates these gates. As we shall see later, certain kinds of stimulation can open the sodium gates.

Membrane

How did sodium ions become so much more concentrated outside the neuron than inside it? The ultimate driving force is a protein complex called the **sodium-potassium pump.** This pump transports sodium ions out of the cell while simultaneously drawing potassium ions into the cell. To be precise, the pump ejects three sodium ions for every two potassium ions that it brings in. Since both sodium and potassium ions carry a +1 electrical charge, the result is a net movement of positive ions out of the cell. The sodium-potassium pump is an **active transport** (one that requires energy) as opposed to the passive flow of ions through open gates in the membrane.

By itself, the sodium-potassium pump would establish only a small difference in charge across the membrane. The selective permeability of the membrane greatly increases the size of the effect. The action of the sodium-potassium pump establishes the concentration gradients for sodium and potassium, with sodium being more highly concentrated outside the neuron and potassium more concentrated inside. Because potassium can cross the membrane at a moderate rate, many of the potassium ions pumped into the cell diffuse back out, carrying a positive charge with them. The sodium ions do not balance this flow by entering the cell, because they cross the membrane at a much slower rate. Figure 2.15 illustrates this process.

The concentration of potassium is the result of an equilibrium of competing forces. The sodium-potassium pump actively moves potassium into the

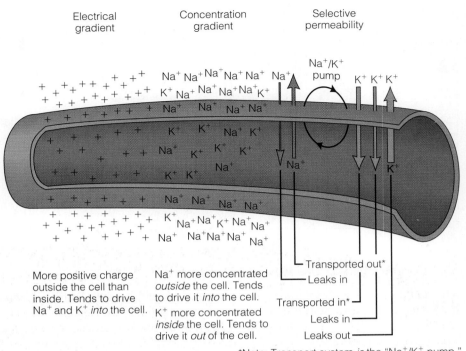

Electrical gradient | Concentration gradient | Selective permeability

Na⁺/K⁺ pump

More positive charge outside the cell than inside. Tends to drive Na⁺ and K⁺ *into* the cell.

Na⁺ more concentrated *outside* the cell. Tends to drive it *into* the cell.

K⁺ more concentrated *inside* the cell. Tends to drive it *out* of the cell.

Transported out*
Leaks in
Transported in*
Leaks in
Leaks out

*Note: Transport system *is* the "Na⁺/K⁺ pump."

Figure 2.15
Factors controlling sodium and potassium gradients for a membrane at rest
The sodium-potassium pump brings two potassium (K^+) ions into the cell for every three sodium (Na^+) ions it pumps out. A few of the potassium ions leak out; almost none of the sodium ions leak in. As a result, sodium ions are much more concentrated outside the cell; the potassium ions are more concentrated inside the cell. Because ions tend to move from an area of greater concentration to an area of lesser concentration, the concentration gradient tends to push Na^+ ions into the cell and K^+ ions out. Because the total positive charge is greater outside the cell than inside, the electrical gradient tends to push both Na^+ and K^+ ions into the cell. For K^+ ions the two gradients virtually cancel each other out. For Na^+ ions both gradients push in the same direction; sodium stays outside the cell only because the sodium gates are closed.

neuron; that is, it expends energy. The potassium ions then flow passively from their area of greater concentration to the area of lesser concentration. The **electrical gradient** also plays a part: Because the inside of the cell is negatively charged with respect to the outside, potassium ions are attracted into the neuron and thus remain more abundant there than they would be if the concentration gradient were the only influence.

Similarly, the concentration gradient of sodium ions is the result of the sodium-potassium pump, which actively moves sodium out of the cell, and the very slow passive diffusion of sodium into the cell, driven by both a concentration gradient and an electrical gradient.

Why a Resting Potential?

Presumably, evolution could have equipped us with neurons that were electrically neutral at rest. The sodium-potassium pump uses energy; presumably, it must provide some benefit to justify this expense.

Resting

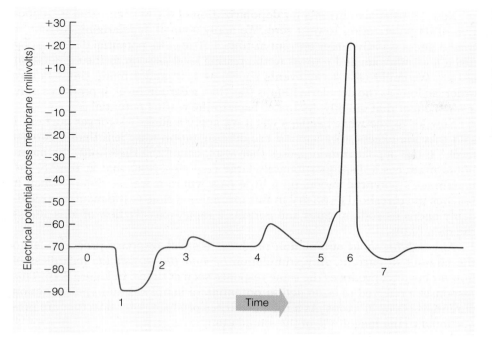

Figure 2.16
**Electrical potentials across
a neuron membrane during
artificial stimulation**
*Time 1 is a hyperpolariza-
tion; 3, 4, and 5 are three
degrees of depolarization.
See text for a further
explanation.*

The advantage is that the resting potential prepares the neuron to respond rapidly to a stimulus. As we shall see in the next section, an excitation of the neuron opens the sodium gates, enabling sodium to enter the cell explosively. Because the membrane did its work in advance by maintaining the concentration gradient for sodium, the cell is prepared to respond strongly and rapidly to a stimulus.

The resting potential of a neuron can be compared to a poised bow and arrow: An archer who pulls the bow in advance and then waits is ready to fire as soon as the appropriate moment comes. Evolution has applied the same strategy to the neuron.

The Action Potential

The resting potential can remain stable as long as the animal remains healthy and the neuron is not stimulated. In nature, stimulation of the neuron takes place at the synapse. We shall consider the synapse in Chapter 3.

Figure 2.16 shows the measured electrical potential inside an axon as a function of time. We can measure the potential using the apparatus shown in Figure 2.13b, with the addition of an extra electrode to stimulate the axon. The extra electrode is placed on the membrane surface close to the intracellular electrode.

Time 0 shows the resting potential, before any stimulus is applied to the neuron. At time 1, we stimulate the neuron by applying a negative charge through the additional electrode, which further increases the negative charge inside the neuron. The change is called **hyperpolarization,** meaning increased polarization. As soon as the artificial stimulation ceases, the cell's charge returns to its original resting level (time 2).

Now, let us apply currents for **depolarization** of the neuron—that is, reduction of its polarization toward zero. We apply a small depolarizing current at time 3 and a slightly larger current at time 4. The cell's potential decreases by just a few millivolts and returns to the resting level as soon as the stimulation ceases. We could repeat the events shown at 1, 3, and 4 many times in any order; so long as the depolarization is less than a certain level, it produces only a small effect that quickly dissipates back to the resting potential.

Now let us see what happens when we apply a slightly stronger current: I said that the effects were small if the depolarization was "less than a certain level." If the depolarization passes that level, called the **threshold,** the membrane produces a disproportionately large response. Note that at time 5, the membrane's potential shoots up a little past where it was at time 4; when it reaches the threshold (-55 mV in this example) at time 6, the membrane suddenly opens its sodium gates and permits a rapid, massive flow of ions across the membrane.

Any *subthreshold* stimulation produces a small response proportional to the amount of current. Any stimulation *beyond the threshold,* regardless of how far beyond, produces the same response seen at time 6 in Figure 2.16. This response is referred to as an **action potential,** or simply as an impulse. Action potentials occur in axons. As a rule, dendrites produce potentials that are proportional to the magnitude of the stimulation.

Within a given cell, all action potentials are approximately equal in size and shape (amplitude) under normal circumstances. This is the **all-or-none law:** *The size and shape of the action potential are independent of the intensity of the stimulus that initiated it.*

As a consequence of this law, a neuron's messages are analogous to those of a telegraph. A neuron cannot send larger action potentials any more than a telegraph operator could send louder dots and dashes. In both cases, the message is conveyed by the time sequence of impulses and pauses. For instance, a neuron might signal "dim light" by a low frequency of action potentials and "brighter light" by a higher frequency. It is also possible that impulses in clusters, such as

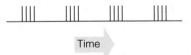

Time

might signal something different from the same number of impulses more evenly distributed:

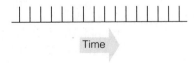

Time

Molecular Basis of the Action Potential

The action potential can be related to the distribution of ions across the membrane of an axon. Remember that the sodium concentration is much higher outside the neuron than inside. In addition to this concentration gradient, sodium ions are attracted to the inside of the neuron by an electrical gradient because of the negative charge inside the neuron. If sodium ions were free to flow across the membrane, they would diffuse rapidly into the cell. Ordinarily, the membrane is almost impermeable to sodium, but during the action potential, its permeability increases sharply.

The membrane proteins that form the sodium gates are **voltage-activated gates;** that is, their permeability to sodium depends on the voltage difference across the membrane. As the membrane of the neuron becomes even slightly depolarized, the sodium gates begin to open and sodium flows more freely. If the depolarization is less than the threshold, the increased entry of sodium ions is balanced by an increased exit of potassium ions. (Potassium ions ordinarily cross the membrane at a restricted rate through potassium channels that are independent of voltage. Some additional voltage-activated potassium channels open when the membrane is depolarized. When the membrane is depolarized, the electrical gradient no longer holds the potassium ions inside the cell.)

Impulse

When the potential across the membrane reaches threshold, the sodium gates open wide enough that sodium enters the cell faster than potassium can exit. The entering sodium ions depolarize the cell still further, opening the sodium gates even wider. Sodium ions rush into the neuron until the electrical potential across the membrane passes beyond zero to a reversed polarity (point 6 on Figure 2.16).

Compared to the total number of sodium and potassium ions in and around the axon, only a small percentage cross the membrane during an action potential. Even at the peak of the action potential, sodium ions continue to be far more concentrated outside the neuron than inside. An action potential increases the sodium concentration inside a neuron by less than 1 percent in most cases. Because of the persisting concentration gradient, sodium ions should still tend to diffuse into the cell. However, they are no longer attracted into the cell by an electrical gradient; in fact, the interior of the neuron has become temporarily positive with respect to the outside. This reversed electrical gradient blocks the further entry of sodium.

After the peak of the action potential, what brings the membrane back to its original state of polarization? The answer is *not* the sodium-potassium pump. (The pump is simply too slow for this purpose.) At about the peak of the action potential, the sodium gates close, but the potassium gates open wider than usual. Potassium ions (positively charged) rapidly leave because they are much more concentrated inside and are no longer attracted by a negative charge. The exit of potassium ions returns the membrane to its original state of polarization. In fact, because of the opening of the potassium gates, enough potassium ions leave to drive the potential a bit beyond the normal resting level to a temporary hyperpolarization (time 7 in Figure 2.16). Figure 2.17 summarizes the movements of ions during an action potential.

At the end of this process, the membrane has returned to its resting potential, and everything is back to normal except that the inside of the neuron has slightly more sodium ions and slightly fewer potassium ions than it used to have. Eventually, the sodium-potassium pump restores the original distribution of ions, but that process takes time. In fact, if a series of action potentials occurs at a sufficiently rapid rate, the pump cannot keep up with the action, and sodium may accumulate somewhat within the axon. (Under natural conditions, it will not accumulate enough to interfere with neuronal functioning.)

For the neuron to function properly, sodium and potassium must flow across the membrane at just the right pace. At the peak of the action potential,

Figure 2.17
The movement of sodium and potassium ions during an action potential
Note that sodium ions cross during the peak of the action potential and that potassium ions cross later in the opposite direction, returning the membrane to its original polarization.

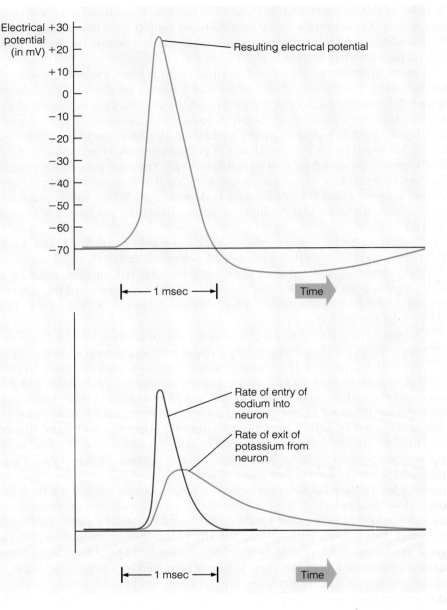

sodium ions must stop entering the cell and potassium ions must exit to return the membrane to its resting potential. Scorpion venom attacks the nervous system by keeping sodium channels open and closing potassium channels (Pappone & Cahalan, 1987; Strichartz, Rando, & Wang, 1987). As a result, the membrane goes into a prolonged depolarization that makes it useless for conveying information.

Local anesthetic drugs such as Novocain and Xylocaine attach to the sodium gates of the membrane, preventing sodium ions from entering (K. W. Miller, 1985). In doing so, such drugs block action potentials in the affected area. If anesthetics are applied to sensory nerves, such as nerves carrying pain messages, they block the messages in those nerves from reaching the brain.

General anesthetics, such as ether and chloroform, decrease brain activity in a different way. They open the potassium gates, promoting the flow of potassium ions out of the neuron. Therefore, they hyperpolarize the neuron and decrease the probability of an action potential (Nicoll & Madison, 1982). Because the neurons fire few action potentials, the nervous system becomes unresponsive to most stimuli.

The Refractory Period

While the electrical potential across the membrane is returning from its peak toward the resting point, it is still above the threshold. Why does the cell not produce another action potential during this period? Evidently, there is a brief period when the cell is resistant to reexcitation. During a period of 1 or more milliseconds (ms) after an action potential, the cell is in such a **refractory period.** During the first part of this period, called the **absolute refractory period,** the membrane cannot produce an action potential in response to stimulation of any intensity. During the second part, the **relative refractory period,** a stimulus must exceed the usual threshold to produce an action potential. Throughout the total refractory period, permeability to sodium ions is low and permeability to potassium ions is higher than normal.

The refractory period sets a maximum on the firing frequency of a neuron. If the absolute refractory period were 1 ms, for example, no stimulus could produce more than 1,000 action potentials per second. Stimuli that were weaker than the maximum would produce lower frequencies, depending on the relative refractory period.

Propagation of the Action Potential

Up to this point, we have dealt with the action potential as it occurs at one location along the axon. It is now time to consider how it moves down the axon toward some other cell. Remember, because axons have to convey messages over great distances, it is important for axons to convey impulses without any loss of strength over distance.

An action potential begins on the axon hillock. It cannot be conducted any great distance down the axon in the manner that electricity is conducted in a wire, because the axon is a poor conductor of electricity. Rather, each point along the membrane regenerates the action potential in much the same way that it was generated initially.

At the time of the action potential, sodium ions enter one point along the axon, bearing positive charges. That location temporarily is positively charged with respect to neighboring areas along the axon. The positive charge flows both down the axon and across the membrane, as Figure 2.18 shows. If the resistance to electrical flow is great across the membrane and relatively low inside the axon, the charge will flow relatively far along the axon. If, on the other hand, the resistance is slight across the membrane and greater inside the axon—as it is in the thinnest axons—the charge will flow only a short distance along the axon before crossing the membrane.

As the charge passes down the axon, it slightly depolarizes the adjacent areas of the membrane. The areas closest to the action potential are depolarized enough to reach their threshold and to generate an action potential of their own. In this manner, the action potential is regenerated. The action potential passes as a wave along the axon. If we could record the electrical

Figure 2.18
Current that enters an axon at the point of the action potential flows down the axon, thereby depolarizing adjacent areas of the membrane. The current flows more easily through relatively thick axons. Behind the area of sodium entry, potassium ions exit.

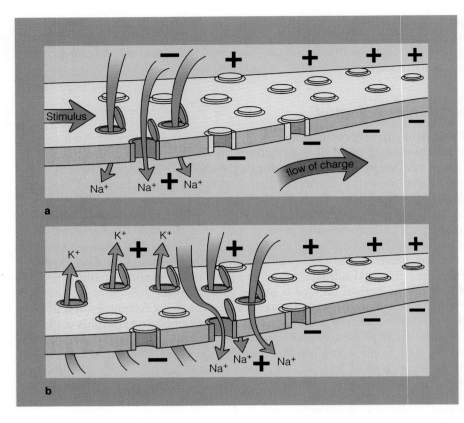

Figure 2.19
Two action potentials as waves traveling along the axon
Note that they are depicted here as a function of location on the axon rather than as a function of time.

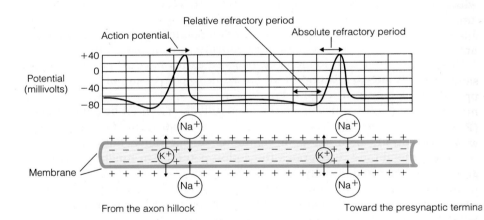

potentials from all points along the axon simultaneously, the result would resemble Figure 2.19.

The **propagation of the action potential** refers to the transmission of an action potential down an axon. The propagation of an animal species is the production of babies; in a sense, the action potential gives birth to a new action potential at each point along the axon. In this manner, the action potential can be just as strong at the end of the axon as it was at the beginning. The action potential is much slower than electrical conduction because it requires the diffusion of sodium ions at successive points along the axon. The thinnest axons are the slowest; their action potentials travel at a velocity of less than 1 meter per second (m/s). In the thickest unmyelinated axons, action potentials reach a velocity of about 10 m/s. In axons surrounded by myelin, which we shall discuss in the next section, the velocity may reach or exceed 100 m/s. In comparison, electricity travels at 300 million m/s.

Let us reexamine Figure 2.18 for a moment. What is to prevent the electrical charge from flowing in the other direction, opposite to the direction that the action potential is traveling? Nothing. In fact, the electrical charge does flow in both directions. In that case, what prevents an action potential near the center of an axon from reinvading the areas that it has just passed? The answer is that the areas just passed are still in their refractory period.

The Myelin Sheath and Saltatory Conduction

As just noted, the maximum velocity of action potentials in the thickest unmyelinated axons of vertebrates is about 10 m/s. At that speed, an impulse from a giraffe's foot would take about a second to reach the brain. Even in smaller animals, a speed of 10 m/s is too slow for the coordination of rapid responses. Myelin sheaths increase speed to make such coordination possible.

Before we discuss how myelin sheaths accelerate action potentials, consider the following analogy. Suppose it were my job to carry written messages over a distance of 3 kilometers (km), without using any mechanical device. One solution would be for me to run with the message over the 3 km. That would be analogous to the propagation of the action potential along an unmyelinated axon; it would get the job done but not very rapidly. An alternative would be for me to tie the message to a baseball and throw it. The problem with that approach is that I cannot throw a ball even close to a distance of 3 km. The ideal compromise would be to station people at moderate distances along the 3 km and to throw the message-bearing ball from person to person until it reaches its destination.

The principle behind **myelinated axons** (axons covered with myelin) is the same. Many vertebrate axons are covered with a myelin sheath, a coating made up largely of fats. The myelin sheath is interrupted at intervals of approximately 1 mm by short unmyelinated sections of axon called **nodes of Ranvier** (RAHN-vee-ay) (see Figure 2.20). Each node is only about one micrometer wide.

Suppose that an action potential is initiated at the axon hillock. It is propagated along the axon until it reaches the first myelin segment. The action potential cannot regenerate along the membrane between one node and the next for two reasons: First, the myelin sheath increases the resistance to electrical transmission at every point between the nodes. Second, sodium gates are located in abundance at the nodes but are virtually absent in the myelinated areas between nodes (Catterall, 1984). Thus, sodium ions cannot cross the membrane between one node and the next. After an action potential occurs at a node, positively charged ions in the interior of the axon carry enough electrical charge to depolarize the membrane at the next node and regenerate the action potential (see Figure 2.21). This flow of ions is considerably faster than the regeneration of an action potential at each point along the axon; consequently, the transmission of impulses is faster in myelinated axons than in axons without myelin—in some cases as fast as 120 m/s. The jumping of action potentials from node to node is referred to as **saltatory conduction,** from the Latin word *saltare,* meaning *to jump.* In addition to providing very rapid con-

Figure 2.20
An axon surrounded by a myelin sheath and interrupted by nodes of Ranvier
The lower part shows a cross section through both the axon and the myelin sheath. Magnification approximately × 30,000.

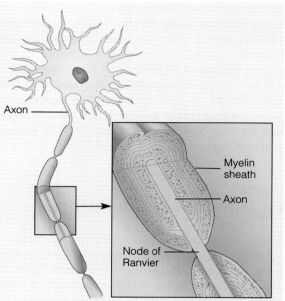

Axon

Myelin sheath

Axon

Node of Ranvier

Cutaway view of axon wrapped in myelin

Figure 2.21
Saltatory conduction in a myelinated axon
An action potential at the node triggers flow of current to the next node, where the membrane regenerates the action potential.

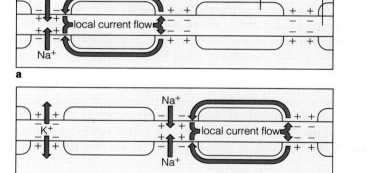

duction of impulses, saltatory conduction has the added benefit of conserving energy: Instead of admitting sodium ions at every point along the axon, and then having to pump them out via the sodium-potassium pump, a myelinated axon admits sodium only at its nodes.

Some diseases, such as multiple sclerosis, destroy myelin sheaths. The result is at least to slow down action potentials and in most cases to stop them altogether. An axon that has lost its myelin is not the same as one that has never had any myelin. A myelinated axon develops sodium gates almost exclusively at the nodes (Waxman & Ritchie, 1985). After the axon loses its myelin, it still lacks sodium gates in the areas previously covered with myelin. Therefore, when the membrane is depolarized in those areas, an action potential cannot arise.

The nervous system contains enormous numbers of very small "local" neurons that play special roles in processing information. But many years ago, long before neuroscientists had any way to investigate the functions of these local neurons, all they knew about them was that they were small. Given that nearly all knowledge about the nervous system reflected the activities of large neurons, the small neurons seemed an anomaly, a mistake. Many scientists assumed that the small neurons were "baby" neurons. As one textbook author put it, "Many of these [neurons] are small and apparently undeveloped, as if they constituted a reserve stock not yet utilized in the individual's cerebral activity" (Woodworth, 1934, p. 194).

In other words, the small cells were noncontribu-tors that could start to contribute to behavior only if they could grow. Perhaps this misconception about the function of local neurons led to the origin of that widespread, nonsensical belief that "they say we use only 10 percent of our brain." (It is difficult to imagine any other origin of that belief. Surely no one maintained that a person could lose 90 percent of the brain and still behave as before. And surely no one maintained that only 10 percent of neurons are active at any given moment.) Whatever the origin of that belief, it became popular, presumably because people wanted to believe it. Eventually, they were simply quoting one another long after everyone forgot what evidence they had (or didn't have) for it in the first place.

Signaling without Action Potentials

What we have just discussed concerning action potentials pertains only to axons. Dendrites and somas do not produce action potentials; they produce small depolarizations and hyperpolarizations, depending on the stimulation affecting them. These depolarizations and hyperpolarizations decay as they travel; they do not follow the all-or-none law. The action potential, with its all-or-none law, starts at the beginning of the axon.

Very small neurons also do not produce action potentials. Such neurons, known as **local neurons,** have either a very short axon or no axon at all, at least not in the usual sense. A local neuron receives information from other neurons in its immediate vicinity and produces **graded potentials,** membrane potentials that vary in magnitude; that is, graded potentials do not follow the all-or-none law. When a local neuron is stimulated, it depolarizes or hyperpolarizes in proportion to the intensity of the stimulus. The change in membrane potential is conducted to adjacent areas of the cell, gradually decaying as it travels. At various points along the cell, it may transmit information to other cells, also in its immediate vicinity. (Remember, a local neuron has either a short axon or none at all, so it cannot transmit information to more distant cells.)

Local neurons are somewhat difficult to study, just because they are small. An investigator who tries to insert an electrode into a cell is most likely to enter a large neuron, simply because it is difficult to insert an electrode into a small cell without damaging it. A disproportionate amount of our knowledge, therefore, has come from large neurons. (See Digression 2.2.) A large neuron with a long axon is specialized to transmit messages over long distances, such as from the spinal cord to the muscles, or from one part of the brain to another. Its dendrites receive information on one end of the cell, and its axon transmits information to its target at the other end. Local neurons do not have such a polarity between one end and the other; they can receive information at various points along their membrane and transmit the information in either direction. In the discussion of the retina (Chapter 6), we shall discuss in some detail a particular example of a local neuron, the *horizontal cell.*

This chapter has concentrated on what happens within a neuron, as if each neuron acted independently. That is a bit like studying the telephone system by examining what happens in a single telephone: Although that is a reasonable place to start, a telephone would be useless if it were not connected to a network of other telephones. Similarly, a neuron contributes to behavior only because of its connections within a vast network. In Chapter 3, we examine what happens at those connections.

Summary

1. At rest, the inside of a neuron has a negative charge with respect to the outside. Sodium ions are actively pumped out of the neuron, while potassium ions are pumped in. Potassium ions are moderately free to flow across the membrane of the neuron, while the flow of sodium ions is greatly restricted. (p. 40)

2. The magnitude of the action potential is independent of the size of the stimulus that initiated it; this statement is the all-or-none law. (p. 46)

3. When the charge across the membrane is reduced, sodium ions can flow more freely across the membrane. If the change in membrane potential is sufficient to reach the threshold of the neuron, then sodium ions enter explosively and the charge across the membrane is suddenly reduced and reversed. This event is known as the action potential. (p. 46)

4. Immediately after an action potential, the membrane enters a refractory period, during which it is resistant to starting another action potential. (p. 49)

5. The action potential is regenerated at successive points along the axon by a combination of electrical flow through the axon and the diffusion of sodium ions across the membrane. The action potential maintains a constant magnitude as it passes along the axon. (p. 49)

6. In axons that are covered with myelin, action potentials form only in the nodes between myelinated segments. Between the nodes, ions flow faster than the action potential propagates in axons without myelin. (p. 51)

7. Many small local neurons transmit messages over relatively short distances by graded potentials that decay over time and space, instead of by action potentials. (p. 53)

Review Questions

1. What is the difference between a hyperpolarization and a depolarization? What is an action potential? (p. 45)

2. State the all-or-none law of the action potential. (p. 46)

3. Explain the ion movements responsible for the action potential and the return to the resting potential. (p. 47)

4. Distinguish between the absolute refractory period and the relative refractory period. (p. 49)

5. How does the refractory period limit the maximum frequency of action potentials in an axon? (p. 49)

6. How does an action potential propagate along an axon? (p. 49)

7. How does myelin increase the velocity of the action potential? Why does loss of myelin severely impair the ability of an axon to conduct action potentials? (p. 51)

8. What is a graded potential? How does a local neuron differ from a neuron with a long axon? (p. 53)

Thought Questions

1. Suppose that the threshold for some neuron were the same as that neuron's resting potential. What would happen? At what frequency would the cell produce action potentials?

2. In the laboratory, researchers can apply an electrical stimulus at any point along the axon and thereby set up action potentials traveling in both directions from the point of stimulation. An action potential traveling in the usual direction, away from the axon hillock, is said to be traveling in the *orthodromic* direction. An action potential traveling toward the axon hillock is traveling in the *antidromic* direction. If we started an orthodromic action potential at the axon hillock and an antidromic action potential at the opposite end of the axon, what would happen when they met at the center? Why? Can you imagine any research that might make use of antidromic impulses?

Suggestions for Further Reading

Shepherd, G. M. (1983). *Neurobiology.* New York: Oxford University Press. The first seven chapters provide additional details about neurons, the membrane, and the action potential.

Terms

polarization an electrical gradient across a membrane (p. 42)

resting potential electrical potential across a membrane when a neuron is not being stimulated (p. 42)

concentration gradient difference in concentration of a solute across some distance (p. 42)

microelectrode a very thin electrode, generally made of glass and filled with an electrolyte solution (p. 42)

selective permeability tendency to permit certain chemicals but not others to cross a membrane (p. 43)

sodium-potassium pump mechanism that actively transports sodium ions out of the cell while simultaneously drawing potassium ions in (p. 43)

active transport transfer of chemicals across a membrane by expenditure of energy, as opposed to passive diffusion (p. 43)

electrical gradient difference in electrical potential across some distance (p. 44)

hyperpolarization increased polarization across a membrane (p. 45)

depolarization reduction in the level of polarization across a membrane (p. 46)

threshold level of depolarization at which a brief stimulation triggers a rapid, massive electrical change by the membrane (p. 46)

action potential depolarization of an axon produced by a stimulation beyond the threshold (p. 46)

all-or-none law principle stating that the size and shape of the action potential are independent of the intensity of the stimulus that initiated it (p. 46)

voltage-activated gate gate in the neuronal membrane that opens as the membrane becomes depolarized (p. 47)

local anesthetic drug that blocks action potentials in the nerves in a particular area where the drug is applied (p. 48)

general anesthetic chemical that depresses brain activity as a whole (p. 48)

refractory period brief period following an action potential, when the cell resists reexcitation (p. 49)

absolute refractory period time immediately after an action potential, when the membrane cannot produce an action potential in response to stimulation of any intensity (p. 49)

relative refractory period time after an action potential, when a stimulus must exceed the usual threshold to produce an action potential (p. 49)

propagation of the action potential transmission of an action potential down an axon (p. 50)

myelinated axon axon covered with myelin (p. 51)

node of Ranvier short unmyelinated section of axon between segments of myelin (p. 51)

saltatory conduction alternation between action potentials at nodes and a more rapid conduction by the flow of ions between nodes (p. 51)

local neuron a small neuron with no more than a short axon (p. 53)

graded potential membrane potential that varies in magnitude (p. 53)

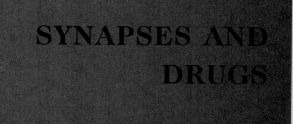

SYNAPSES AND DRUGS

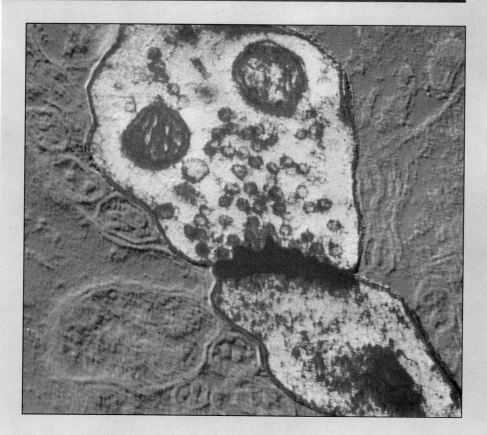

False-color TEM synapse between neurons (© Custom Medical Stock Photo)

CHAPTER THREE

MAIN IDEAS

1. At a synapse, a neuron releases a chemical known as a neurotransmitter that excites or inhibits another cell.

2. A single release of neurotransmitter produces only a subthreshold response in the receiving cell. This response summates with other subthreshold responses to determine whether or not the cell will produce an action potential.

3. Because different neurotransmitters contribute in different ways to the control of behavior, many behavioral abnormalities can be traced to the excess or deficit of transmission at a particular type of synapse.

4. Many of the drugs that affect behavior and experience do so by altering activity at synapses.

If you had to communicate with someone and you were not allowed to use speech or any other auditory information, what would you do? Chances are, your first choice would be some sort of visual code, such as sign language or written words. If that failed, you might try some sort of touch code or you might try communicating with electrical impulses like computers.

You might not even think of communicating by passing chemicals back and forth. Chemical communication is, however, the primary method of communication for the neurons in your nervous system. Considering how well the human nervous system works, chemical communication is evidently a more versatile system than we might have guessed. Neurons communicate by transmitting chemicals at specialized junctions called *synapses*. The synapses are central to all comparison and integration of information in the brain.

The Concept of the Synapse

In the late 1800s, Ramón y Cajal's observations demonstrated that neurons do not physically merge into one another; a narrow gap separates one neuron from the next. No one knew what takes place at that gap. As far as anyone knew, information might be transmitted across the gap in the same way that it was transmitted along an axon.

Then, in 1906, Charles Scott Sherrington inferred that a specialized type of communication occurs at this gap between neurons. He labeled the point of communication between neurons the **synapse** and predicted most of the major properties of the synapse. What makes Sherrington's accomplishment particularly impressive is that he based his conclusions almost entirely on behavioral data. Decades later, when techniques became available to measure and record the processes that Sherrington had inferred, most of his predictions turned out to be correct.

The Properties of Synapses

Sherrington conducted most of his experiments on **reflexes,** automatic responses to stimuli. In a simple reflex, receptors excite interneurons, which excite effector neurons, which excite muscles, as Figure 3.1 shows. This circuit is called a **reflex arc.** Because a reflex depends on communication from one neuron to another—not just on the transmission of action potentials along an axon—Sherrington reasoned that the properties of a reflex might reveal some of the special properties of synapses.

In a typical experiment, a dog was strapped into a harness suspended above the ground. Sherrington pinched one of the dog's feet; after a short delay, the dog *flexed* (raised) the pinched leg and *extended* the others. Both the flexion and the extension were reflexive movements—automatic reactions to the stimulus. Furthermore, Sherrington found the same movements after he made a cut that disconnected the spinal cord from the brain; evidently, the flexion and extension were controlled by the spinal cord itself. In an intact animal, the brain could modify the reflexive movements but was not necessary for their occurrence.

Sherrington observed several properties of reflexes suggesting that some special process must occur at the junctions between neurons: (1) Reflexes are slower than conduction along an axon; consequently, there must be some delay at the synapses. (2) Several weak stimuli presented at slightly different times

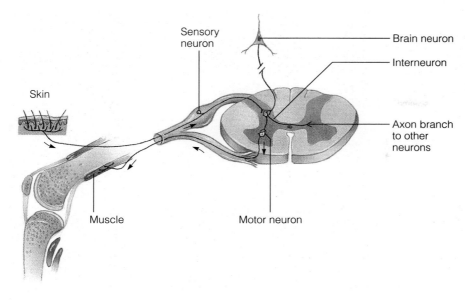

Sensory neuron

Brain neuron

Interneuron

Skin

Axon branch to other neurons

Muscle

Motor neuron

Figure 3.1
A reflex arc through the spinal cord, simplified to show the relationship among sensory neuron, interneuron, and motor neuron

or slightly different locations produce a stronger reflex than a single stimulus does. Therefore, the synapse must be able to *summate* different stimuli. (3) When one set of muscles becomes excited, a different set becomes relaxed. Evidently, synapses are connected so that the excitation of one leads to a decreased excitation, or even an inhibition, of others. We shall consider each of these points in some detail.

Speed of a Reflex and Delay of Transmission at the Synapse

When Sherrington pinched a dog's foot, the dog flexed that leg after a short delay. During the delay, an impulse had to travel up an axon from a skin receptor to the spinal cord, then an impulse had to travel from the spinal cord back down the leg to a muscle. Sherrington measured the total distance that the impulse traveled from skin receptor to spinal cord to muscle and calculated the speed at which the impulse must have traveled to produce a muscle response after the measured delay. He found that the overall speed of conduction through the reflex arc was significantly slower than the known speed of conduction along an axon. Therefore, he deduced, transmission between one neuron and another at the synapse must be slower than transmission along an axon (see Figure 3.2).

Temporal Summation

Sherrington's work with reflex arcs suggested that repeated stimuli occurring within a brief time can have a cumulative effect. He referred to this phenomenon as **temporal summation.** When Sherrington pinched a dog's foot very lightly, the leg did not move. After the same light pinch was repeated several times in rapid succession, however, the leg flexed slightly. The more rapid the series of pinches, the greater the response. Sherrington surmised that a single pinch produced a weak synaptic transmission but not enough to produce an

The Concept of the Synapse

Figure 3.2
Sherrington's evidence for synaptic delay
An impulse traveling through a synapse in the spinal cord is slower than one traveling through a similar distance along an uninterrupted axon.

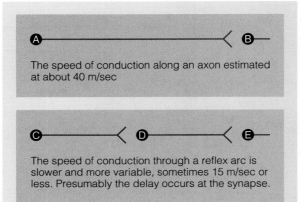

The speed of conduction along an axon estimated at about 40 m/sec

The speed of conduction through a reflex arc is slower and more variable, sometimes 15 m/sec or less. Presumably the delay occurs at the synapse.

action potential in the next cell. That is, the excitation would be less than the threshold of the second cell, the **postsynaptic neuron.** (The neuron that delivers the synaptic transmission is the **presynaptic neuron.**) Sherrington suggested that this subthreshold excitation begins to decay within a fraction of a second but is capable of combining with a second small excitation that quickly follows it. A rapid succession of pinches produces a series of weak activations at the synapse, each of them adding its effect to what was left of the previous excitations. If the excitations occur rapidly enough, they can combine to exceed the threshold and therefore produce an action potential in the postsynaptic neuron.

Decades after Sherrington's work, it became possible to measure some of the single-cell properties he had inferred. To record the activity evoked in a neuron by synaptic input, researchers insert a microelectrode into the neuron and measure changes in the electrical potential across the membrane. Using this method, John Eccles (1964) was able to demonstrate temporal summation in single cells. He attached stimulating electrodes to some of the axons that formed synapses onto a neuron. He then recorded from the neuron while stimulating one or more of those axons. For example, after he had briefly stimulated an axon, Eccles recorded a slight depolarization of the membrane of the postsynaptic cell (point 1 in Figure 3.3).

Note that this partial depolarization is a graded potential. Unlike action potentials, which are always depolarizations, graded potentials may be either depolarizations (excitatory) or hyperpolarizations (inhibitory). A graded depolarization is known as an **excitatory postsynaptic potential,** abbreviated **EPSP.** Like an action potential, an EPSP results from the entry of sodium ions into the cell (see Chapter 2). The synaptic activation opens some number of sodium gates and increases the entry of sodium ions across the membrane. However, transmission at a single synapse does not open enough sodium gates to provoke an action potential. Unlike an action potential, an EPSP is a subthreshold event that decays over time and space; that is, its magnitude decreases as it travels along the membrane.

When Eccles stimulated the axon twice in close succession, two consecutive EPSPs were recorded in the postsynaptic cell. If the delay between EPSPs was short enough, temporal summation occurred; that is, the second EPSP added to what was left of the first one (point 2 in Figure 3.3). The summation of two EPSPs might or might not be enough to exceed the threshold of the post-

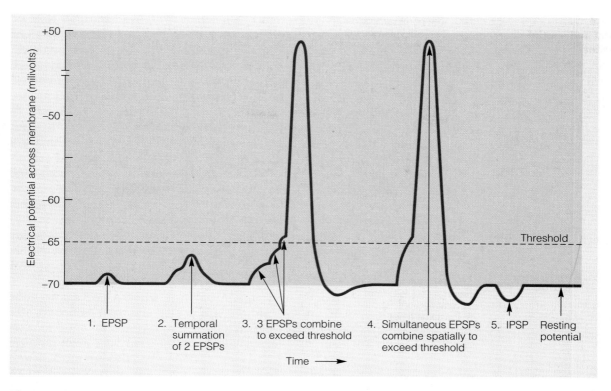

Figure 3.3
Recording from a postsynaptic neuron during synaptic activation, showing (1) an EPSP, (2) subthreshold temporal summation of EPSPs, (3) summation of EPSPs leading to an action potential, (4) spatial summation of simultaneous EPSPs leading to an action potential, and (5) an IPSP

synaptic cell, depending on the size of the EPSP, the time between the two, and the threshold of the postsynaptic cell. In Figure 3.3 at point 3, three consecutive EPSPs combine to exceed the threshold and produce an action potential.

Spatial Summation

Sherrington's work with reflex arcs also suggested that synapses have the property of **spatial summation:** Several synaptic inputs originating from separate locations can exert a cumulative effect on a neuron. To study this phenomenon, Sherrington again began with a pinch that was too weak to elicit a response. But this time, instead of repeating the pinch, he gave the dog simultaneous pinches at two points on the foot. Although neither pinch alone would elicit a movement, the two together did elicit a response. Sherrington's interpretation was that pinching two points on the foot activated two sensory neurons, each of which sent an axon to the same interneuron. Excitation from either axon alone would excite a synapse on the interneuron, but one excitation would be insufficient for an action potential. When both excitations were present at the same time, however, their combined effect exceeded the threshold for producing an action potential (see Figure 3.4).

Again, Eccles was able to confirm Sherrington's inference by recording from single cells. He demonstrated the spatial summation of EPSPs: If two axons

Figure 3.4
Temporal and spatial summation

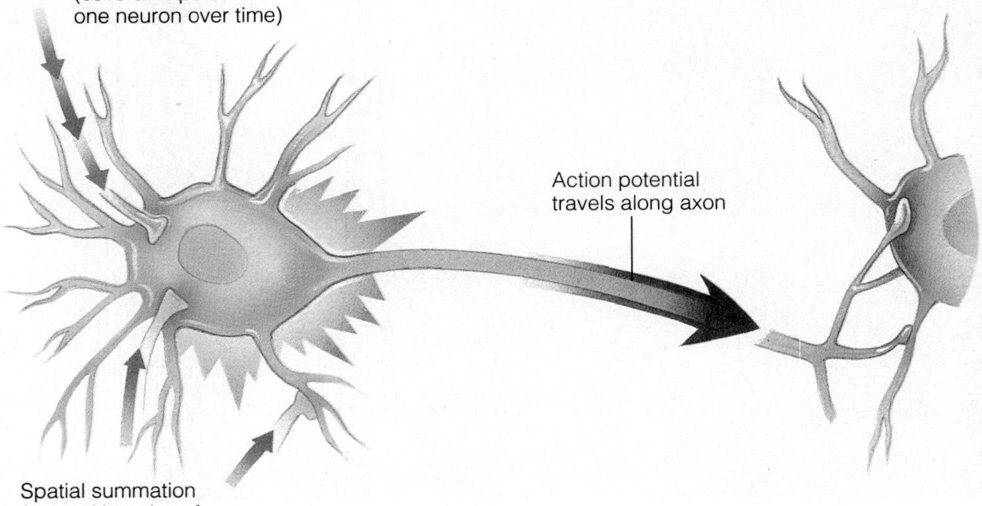

Temporal summation (several impulses from one neuron over time)

Action potential travels along axon

Spatial summation (several impulses from several neurons at the same time)

have excitatory synapses onto a neuron and either one can produce an EPSP, then activating both simultaneously produces a larger EPSP. If the combination exceeds the threshold of the cell, an action potential will begin (point 4 in Figure 3.3). Note that temporal summation and spatial summation produce the same result: Either one generates an action potential in the postsynaptic cell.

Inhibitory Synapses

When Sherrington vigorously pinched a dog's foot, the dog contracted the flexor muscles of that leg and the extensor muscles of the other three legs (see Figure 3.5). At the same time, the dog relaxed the extensor muscles of the stimulated leg and the flexor muscles of the other legs. Sherrington's explanation for this series of coordinated and adaptive movements depended, again, on the synapses and in particular on the connections among neurons in the spinal cord: A pinch on the foot sends a message along a sensory neuron to an interneuron in the spinal cord, which in turn excites the motor neurons connected to the flexor muscles of that leg. Sherrington surmised that the interneuron also sends a message that decreases excitation of motor neurons connected to the extensor muscles in the same leg. He did not know whether the interneuron actually formed an inhibitory synapse onto the motor neuron to the extensor muscles or whether it simply decreased the amount of excitation. In either case, the result was to prevent the flexor and extensor muscles of the leg from contracting at the same time.

Eccles and other later researchers demonstrated that the interneuron actually has an inhibitory synapse onto the motor neuron of the extensor muscle. At these synapses, input from the axon hyperpolarizes the postsynaptic cell, increasing the cell's negative charge and decreasing the probability of an action potential by moving the potential further from the threshold (point 5 in Figure 3.3). This temporary hyperpolarization—called an **inhibitory postsynaptic**

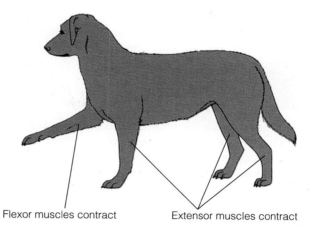

Figure 3.5
Flexor muscles (which draw an extremity toward the trunk of the body) and extensor muscles (which move an extremity away from the body)
Flexor muscles are antagonists of extensor muscles.

Flexor muscles contract   Extensor muscles contract

potential, or **IPSP**—resembles an EPSP except that it changes in the opposite direction. An IPSP occurs when synaptic input selectively opens the gates for potassium ions to leave the cell (carrying a positive charge with them) or for chloride ions to enter the cell (carrying a negative charge).

Inhibition is more than just the absence of excitation; it is an active "brake" that can suppress irrelevant or competing responses. If the inhibition is strong enough, it can cancel the simultaneous excitation at other synapses of the same postsynaptic cell.

Relationship among EPSP, IPSP, and Action Potential

Under normal circumstances, it would be rare for any neuron to be exposed to a single EPSP or IPSP at a time. A neuron may have thousands of synapses along its surface, some that excite the neuron and others that inhibit it. Any number and combination of synapses may be active at any time, giving rise to a continuing combination of temporal and spatial summation. The momentary balance between EPSPs and IPSPs determines whether the neuron reaches its threshold and produces an action potential. The greater the number of EPSPs, the greater the probability of an action potential; the greater the number of IPSPs, the lower the probability of an action potential.

Moreover, some synapses have more influence than others do because of their locations. EPSPs and IPSPs are graded potentials; they decrease in strength as they flow from their point of origin toward other parts of the neuron. For that reason, a synapse located close to the axon hillock, where action potentials originate, has a greater influence than a synapse near the far end of a dendrite.

In many neurons, the EPSPs and IPSPs merely modify the frequency of action potentials that the neuron would fire spontaneously. That is, many neurons have a **spontaneous firing rate,** producing many action potentials per second even without synaptic input. EPSPs increase the frequency of action potentials in these neurons, while IPSPs decrease it. For example, if the neuron's spontaneous firing rate were 10 per second, a steady stream of EPSPs

The Concept of the Synapse

might increase the rate to 15 or 20 or more, whereas a steady stream of IPSPs might decrease the rate to 5 or fewer action potentials per second.

The Neuronal Decision Process

The neuron can be compared to a thermostat, a smoke detector, or any other device that detects something and triggers a response: The area of the neuron that receives synaptic input is analogous to the sensor. When input reaches a certain level, the neuron triggers an action potential, just as the thermostat turns on the furnace or the smoke detector triggers a fire alarm.

That is, the synapses enable the postsynaptic neuron to integrate information. They provide for the convergence and comparison of messages from different cells at different times. For instance, a given neuron may be stimulated simultaneously at both synapses that produce EPSPs and synapses that produce IPSPs. The EPSPs compete against IPSPs, and the net result is a complicated, not exactly algebraic summation of the two effects. We could regard the summation of EPSPs and IPSPs as a "decision"; that is, the postsynaptic cell "decides" to fire or not based on the combination of "information" (EPSPs and IPSPs) that it receives.

Although we may think of a neuron as "deciding" whether to fire action potentials, we should not imagine that any neuron decides between eggs and toast for breakfast. A great many neurons are involved in any behavior, and behavior depends on a whole network, not a single neuron. The translation between activity of a neuron and activity of the whole animal is complex. We cannot even assume, for instance, that an inhibitory synapse tends to inhibit behavior. In many cases, one cell has an inhibitory synapse onto a second cell, which in turn inhibits a third cell. The first synapse, by inhibiting an inhibitor, has the net effect of increasing the excitation of the third cell. This principle of double negatives, or inhibition of inhibition (called *disinhibition*), is common in the nervous system.

Summary

1. The synapse is the point of communication between two neurons. Charles S. Sherrington first inferred the properties of synapses, based on his observations of reflexes. (p. 58)

2. Because transmission through a reflex arc is slower than transmission through an equivalent length of axon, Sherrington inferred that there is a delay of transmission at the synapse. (p. 59)

3. Graded potentials (EPSPs and IPSPs) summate their effects. The summation of graded potentials from stimuli at different times is temporal summation. The summation of graded potentials from different locations is spatial summation. (p. 59)

4. A single stimulation at a synapse produces a brief graded potential in the postsynaptic cell. An excitatory graded potential (depolarizing) is an EPSP. An inhibitory graded potential (hyperpolarizing) is an IPSP. (pp. 60, 62)

5. An EPSP occurs when sodium gates open in the membrane; an IPSP occurs when potassium or chloride gates open. (pp. 60, 62)

6. At any time, the EPSPs on a neuron compete with the IPSPs; the balance between the two determines the rate of firing of the neuron. (p. 63)

Review Questions

1. What evidence did Sherrington use to support his conclusion that transmission at a synapse is different from transmission along an axon? (p. 59)

2. What is the difference between temporal summation and spatial summation? What evidence did Sherrington have for their existence? (p. 59)

3. What evidence did Sherrington have for inhibition in the nervous system? (p. 62)

4. What ion gates in the membrane open during EPSPs? What gates open during IPSPs? (pp. 60, 62)

5. What does the phrase *spontaneous firing rate* mean in a neuron? (p. 63)

Thought Questions

1. When Sherrington measured the reaction time of a reflex (that is, the delay between stimulus and response), he found that the response occurred faster after a strong stimulus than after a weak one. How could you explain this finding? Remember that all action potentials—whether produced by strong or weak stimuli—travel at the same speed along a given axon.

2. A pinch on an animal's right hind foot leads to excitation of an interneuron that excites the motor neurons connected to the flexor muscles of that leg; the interneuron also inhibits the motor neurons connected to the extensor muscles of the leg. In addition, this interneuron sends impulses that reach the motor neuron connected to the extensor muscles of the left hind leg. Would you expect the interneuron to excite or inhibit that motor neuron? (*Hint:* The connections are adaptive. When an animal lifts one leg, it must put additional weight on the other legs to maintain balance.)

3. Neuron X has a synapse onto neuron Y, and Y has a synapse onto Z. Presume here that no other neurons or synapses are present. An experimenter finds that excitation of neuron X causes an action potential in neuron Z after a short delay. However, she determines that the synapse of X onto Y is inhibitory. Explain how the stimulation of X might produce excitation of Z.

Terms

synapse point of communication between two neurons or between a neuron and a muscle (p. 58)

reflex automatic response to a stimulus (p. 58)

reflex arc circuit of neurons and their connections that is responsible for producing a reflex (p. 58)

temporal summation combination of effects of more than one synaptic input at different times (p. 59)

postsynaptic neuron neuron on the receiving end of a synapse (p. 60)

presynaptic neuron neuron on the releasing end of a synapse (p. 60)

excitatory postsynaptic potential (EPSP) graded depolarization of a neuron (p. 60)

spatial summation combination of effects of activity from two or more synapses onto a single neuron (p. 61)

inhibitory postsynaptic potential (IPSP) temporary hyperpolarization of a membrane (p. 62)

spontaneous firing rate speed of action potentials that a neuron produces in the absence of synaptic input (p. 63)

Chemical Events at the Synapse

Although Charles Sherrington accurately inferred many properties of the synapse, he reached one major incorrect conclusion: He thought that synaptic transmission relied on an electrical impulse, believing that it occurred too quickly to be a chemical reaction. Later research found that, in the vast majority of cases, synaptic transmission relies on chemical processes that are much faster than Sherrington thought possible and far more versatile than anyone would have guessed.

The Discovery that Most Synaptic Transmission Is Chemical

In 1905, a young British scientist, T. R. Elliott, demonstrated that the hormone *adrenaline* closely mimics the effects of the sympathetic nervous system, a set of nerves that control the internal organs (see Chapter 4). For example, stimulation of the sympathetic nerves accelerates the heartbeat, relaxes the stomach muscles, and dilates the pupils of the eyes. Applying adrenaline directly to the surface of the heart, the stomach, and the pupils produces those same effects. Elliott therefore suggested that the sympathetic nerves stimulate muscles by releasing adrenaline or something similar. This suggestion implied that synapses in general may operate by releasing chemicals. Elliott's evidence was not decisive, however; perhaps adrenaline merely mimicked certain effects that are ordinarily produced by electrical stimulation. Sherrington's prestige was so great that most scientists ignored Elliott's results and continued to assume that synapses transmitted information by electrical impulses.

Otto Loewi, a German physiologist, was also attracted to the idea that synapses operate by releasing chemicals, although he did not see how he could test the theory decisively. So for almost twenty years, he set it aside. Then in 1920, he aroused from sleep with a sudden idea. He wrote himself a note and then went back to sleep. Unfortunately, the next morning he could not read his own note. The following night at 3 A.M., when he awoke with the same idea, he rushed to the laboratory and performed the experiment at once.

He repeatedly stimulated the vagus nerve to a frog's heart, causing the heart rate to decrease. He then collected fluid from that heart, transferred it to a second frog's heart, and found that the second heart also decreased its rate of beating. (This experiment is diagrammed in Figure 3.6.) In a later experiment, he stimulated the accelerator nerve to the first frog's heart, causing the heart rate to increase. When he collected fluid from that heart and transferred it to the second heart, this fluid caused the heart rate to increase. That is, stimulating

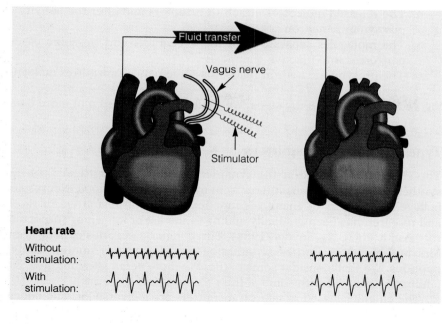

Figure 3.6
Loewi's experiment demonstrating that nerves send messages by releasing chemicals

He stimulated the vagus nerve to one heart, decreasing the heartbeat. Then he transferred fluid surrounding that heart to another heart, decreasing its heartbeat too.

one nerve to the heart released something that inhibited heart rate, and stimulating a different nerve released something else that increased heart rate. Those "somethings" had to be chemicals. (The fluids that Loewi transferred could not have held loose electricity!) Therefore, Loewi concluded that nerves send messages by releasing chemicals.

Loewi later remarked that if he had thought of this experiment in the light of day, he probably never would have tried it (Loewi, 1960). Even if synapses did release chemicals, his daytime reasoning went, there was little chance that they would release enough of the chemicals to make collecting them easy. Fortunately, by the time he realized that the experiment was unlikely to work, he had already completed the research, for which he later won the Nobel Prize.

Although we now know that most synapses operate by transmitting chemicals, a few electrical synapses do exist. They occur mostly in situations where it is important for two neurons to synchronize their activities exactly, such as synapses controlling rapid escape movements in certain fish and invertebrates.

The Sequence of Chemical Events at a Synapse

A great many medical conditions and drugs that affect behavior do so by altering neurotransmission. Consequently, an understanding of the chemical events occurring at a synapse is fundamental to much of current research in biological psychology. The events at a synapse, in summary form, are as follows:

1. The neuron synthesizes chemicals that serve as neurotransmitters or neuromodulators. (In a while, we shall address the distinction between neurotransmitters and neuromodulators.)
2. The neuron transports these chemicals to the terminals of its axons.
3. An action potential causes the release of the neurotransmitters or neuromodulators from the terminals.

4. The released molecules attach to receptors and alter the activity of the postsynaptic neuron.
5. The molecules separate from their receptors and (in some cases) are converted into inactive chemicals.
6. The presynaptic neuron reabsorbs some neurotransmitter molecules.

Figure 3.7 summarizes the steps. We shall discuss each step in more detail.

Types of Neurotransmitters

The chemicals released at the synapse are **neurotransmitters.** Each neuron synthesizes its neurotransmitters from materials in the blood. Neuroscientists believe that dozens of chemicals function as neurotransmitters in the brain, and research has been gradually adding to the list of known or suspected neurotransmitters (S. H. Snyder, 1984). Three major categories of neurotransmitters are **biogenic amines** (containing an NH_2 group), **amino acids,** and **peptides.** We shall consider some of these in more detail later; for now, you can familiarize yourself with some of their names (see Figure 3.8).

The chemicals used as neurotransmitters are a diverse lot. The oddest and most surprising of the apparent or probable neurotransmitters is **nitric oxide** (chemical formula NO). Nitric oxide, unlike other transmitters discovered so far, is ordinarily a gas. (Within the body, it is, of course, dissolved in water.) Moreover, it is a poisonous gas, at least in large quantities. To add even further to the mystery, nitric oxide is difficult to synthesize chemically. Chemists find it difficult to make in a laboratory, except by use of large quantities of energy, comparable to a bolt of lightning. Yet certain neurons have an enzyme that enables them to make this poisonous gas. Exactly what the brain does with this gas is unknown; researchers are investigating a wide variety of possibilities (Snyder, 1992). Nitric oxide occurs mostly in small local neurons, not in neurons with long axons. (Do not confuse nitric oxide, NO, with nitrous oxide, N_2O, sometimes known as "laughing gas.")

Synthesis of Transmitters

Every cell in the body builds some of the materials that it needs by chemical reactions, converting substances provided by the diet into other chemicals necessary for normal functioning. The neuron is no exception. Each neuron synthesizes its neurotransmitters from precursor molecules that reach the cell by way of the blood, derived originally from foods that the individual ate. Many neurotransmitters can be synthesized both in the cell body and in the terminal, close to their point of release. The peptide neurotransmitters, however, are synthesized only in the cell body. Under normal circumstances, the brain maintains fairly constant levels of each neurotransmitter, even during periods of fasting. Nevertheless, if the diet has a high or low concentration of the precursors necessary for making a particular neurotransmitter, the brain may produce a slightly higher or lower than usual amount of that neurotransmitter (R. J. Wurtman, 1982, 1983; Wurtman, Hefti, & Melamed, 1981).

Figure 3.9 illustrates the chemical steps in the synthesis of acetylcholine, serotonin, dopamine, epinephrine, and norepinephrine. Note the relationship among epinephrine, norepinephrine, and dopamine—three closely related compounds known as **catecholamines.** Some neurons synthesize dopamine;

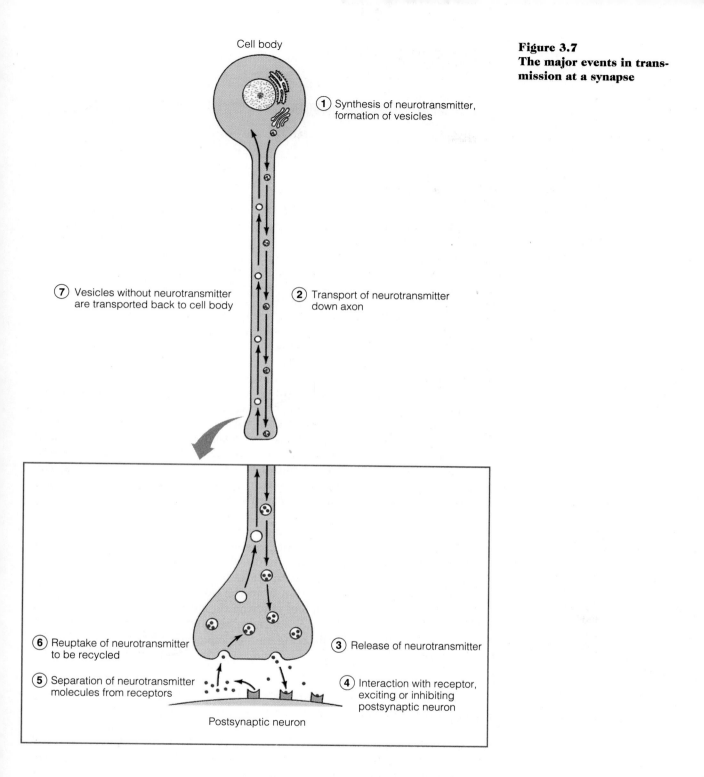

Cell body

1 Synthesis of neurotransmitter, formation of vesicles

7 Vesicles without neurotransmitter are transported back to cell body

2 Transport of neurotransmitter down axon

6 Reuptake of neurotransmitter to be recycled

3 Release of neurotransmitter

5 Separation of neurotransmitter molecules from receptors

4 Interaction with receptor, exciting or inhibiting postsynaptic neuron

Postsynaptic neuron

**Figure 3.7
The major events in transmission at a synapse**

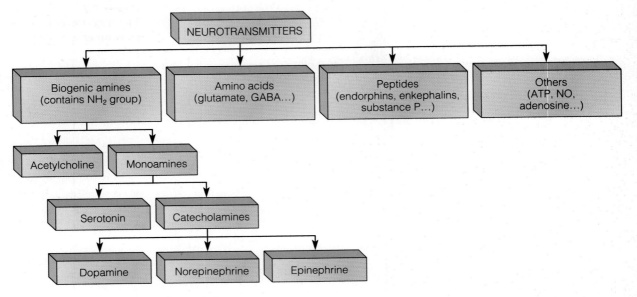

Figure 3.8
Some neurotransmitters

others have an additional enzyme that converts dopamine to norepinephrine; still others can convert norepinephrine to epinephrine.

Each pathway in Figure 3.9 begins with substances found in the diet. Acetylcholine, for example, is synthesized from choline, which is abundant in cauliflower and milk. The body can also make choline from lecithin, a component of egg yolks, liver, soybeans, butter, peanuts, and several other foods. The amino acids phenylalanine and tyrosine, constituents of most proteins, are precursors of dopamine, norepinephrine, and epinephrine.

The amino acid **tryptophan** is the precursor to serotonin, and a special "transport system" enables tryptophan to cross the blood-brain barrier. However, tryptophan shares its transport system with several other amino acids (including phenylalanine) that are almost always more prevalent in the diet. Thus, after a meal rich in protein, the level of tryptophan reaching the brain may be low because of competition from the other amino acids. One way to increase the amount of tryptophan entering the brain is to eat carbohydrates with the protein. Carbohydrates increase release of the hormone **insulin,** which takes a number of competing amino acids out of the bloodstream and into cells throughout the body, thus decreasing the competition against tryptophan for entry into the brain (J. J. Wurtman, 1985).

Transport of Transmitters

The synthesis of peptide neurotransmitter molecules takes place in the cell body. From there, the peptide is transported down the axon to the terminal, where it can be released. The speed of transport varies from only 1 millimeter per day to more than 100 mm per day, depending on the diameter of the axon.

Even at the highest speeds, transport from cell body to terminal may take hours, sometimes days in the longest axons. Consequently, neurons take a long time to replenish their supply of peptides after releasing them. Neurons synthesize the nonpeptide transmitters mainly in the terminals, close to their point of release. They also reabsorb and recycle many of the nonpeptide trans-

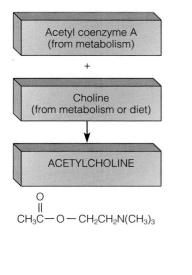

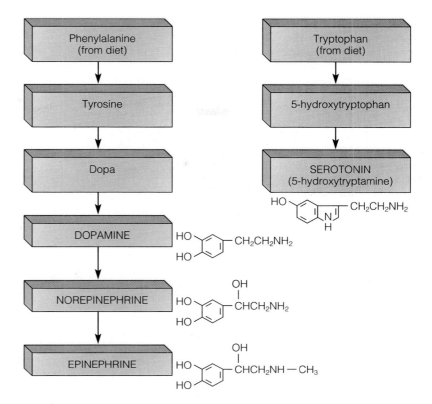

Figure 3.9
Steps in the synthesis of acetylcholine, serotonin, dopamine, norepinephrine, and epinephrine
Arrows represent chemical reactions.

mitters. For these reasons, a neuron can release acetylcholine, for example, much more frequently than it can a peptide.

Release and Diffusion of Transmitters

The presynaptic terminal stores high concentrations of neurotransmitter molecules in **vesicles,** tiny near-spherical packets (Figure 3.10). (Nitric oxide, the gaseous neurotransmitter mentioned earlier, is an exception to this rule. Neurons do not store nitric oxide for future use; they synthesize it immediately before they release it.) In addition to the neurotransmitter stored in vesicles, the presynaptic terminal also maintains substantial amounts outside the vesicles.

When an action potential reaches the end of an axon, the depolarization changes the voltage across the membrane and opens voltage-dependent calcium gates in the presynaptic terminal. This calcium inflow must be carefully regulated. Certain spider venoms either increase or decrease the flow of calcium through these channels; in either case, the result can be fatal (Kawai, 1991). Under normal circumstances, as calcium flows through specialized channels into the presynaptic terminal, it causes the neuron to release a certain amount of its neurotransmitter during the next 1 or 2 milliseconds (Augustine, Charlton, & Smith, 1987). The neuron may do so either by emptying some of its vesicles into the synaptic cleft or by releasing neurotransmitter molecules that were not bound in vesicles. The percentage of neurotransmitter release that comes from the vesicles is still in dispute (Tauc & Poulain, 1991).

Synapse

*Chemical Events
at the Synapse*

Figure 3.10
(a) *Diagram of a synapse. The end of the presynaptic axon swells to form the terminal, which releases the neurotransmitter.* (b) *An electron micrograph, showing a synapse from the cerebellum of a mouse, magnified × 93,000. The small round structures are vesicles. (From Landis, 1987.)* (c) *Electron micrograph showing axon terminals onto the soma of a neuron. Magnified × 11,000. (From Lewis et al., 1969.)*

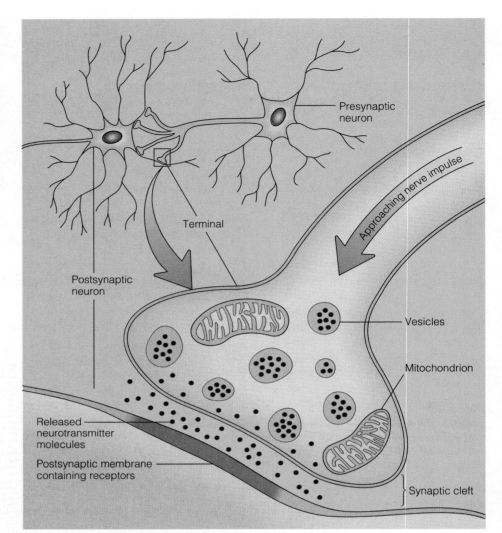

Presynaptic neuron

Approaching nerve impulse

Terminal

Postsynaptic neuron

Vesicles

Mitochondrion

Released neurotransmitter molecules

Postsynaptic membrane containing receptors

Synaptic cleft

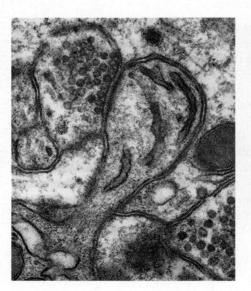

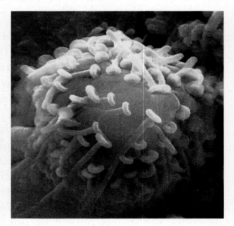

The presynaptic terminal releases neurotransmitter in outbursts of a fixed quantity called a **quantum.** The quantum is the minimum amount of transmitter that a neuron terminal can release at one time. When it releases larger amounts, the larger amounts are always integral multiples of the quantum. For example, an EPSP could be 30 times the quantum or 31, but never 30.5.

After the presynaptic cell releases the neurotransmitter, the chemical diffuses across the synaptic cleft to the postsynaptic membrane, where it attaches to a receptor. The cleft is only 0.02 to 0.05 microns wide, and the neurotransmitter takes no more than 10 microseconds to diffuse across the cleft. The total delay in transmission across the synapse, including the time that it takes for the presynaptic cell to release the neurotransmitter, is 0.5 to 2 milliseconds (Martin, 1977; Takeuchi, 1977).

The brain as a whole uses dozens of neurotransmitters, but no single neuron releases them all. For many years, investigators believed that each neuron released just one neurotransmitter. This generalization is known as *Dale's law* or *Dale's principle.* According to later studies, it appears that many, perhaps most, neurons release two, three, or even more transmitters (Hökfelt, Johansson, & Goldstein, 1984). However, consistent with the general idea behind Dale's law, each neuron probably releases the *same combination* of transmitters from all branches of its axon. For example, if one branch of the axon releases norepinephrine and enkephalin, then all its branches release norepinephrine and enkephalin—though perhaps in different ratios at different branches or at different times (Eccles, 1986).

Why does a neuron release a combination of transmitters instead of just one transmitter? Investigators are not certain, but a combination of transmitters probably enables the neuron to send a more complex message. One transmitter might excite or inhibit the postsynaptic neuron, while another prolongs or limits the effects of the first (Hökfelt et al., 1986).

Although a neuron releases only a limited number of neurotransmitters (generally at its terminal), it may receive and respond to a number of different neurotransmitters at various synapses (generally on its dendrites and soma). For example, it might respond to acetylcholine released at one synapse, serotonin at another synapse, GABA at still another, and so on. Although the neuron produces only a few types of neurotransmitters, it can apparently produce enough types of receptors to respond to a great variety of incoming neurotransmitters.

Activation of Receptors of the Postsynaptic Cell

In English, the term *fern* refers to a small plant. In German, *fern* means far away. In French, it means nothing at all. The meaning of any word depends on who hears it or reads it. The same is true of neurotransmitters: The meaning of a neurotransmitter depends on the receptor that receives it. For example, the neurotransmitter acetylcholine may have a rapid but brief effect on one neuron, a slow but prolonged effect on another neuron, and no effect at all on still another, depending on the receptors of the postsynaptic neurons.

Neurotransmitters can affect other neurons in many ways. For convenience, we distinguish three major types of effects: ionotropic, metabotropic, and modulatory.

Ionotropic Effects   Some neurotransmitters exert **ionotropic effects** on the postsynaptic neuron. This means that the neurotransmitter attaches to a receptor on the membrane and thereby almost immediately opens the gates for

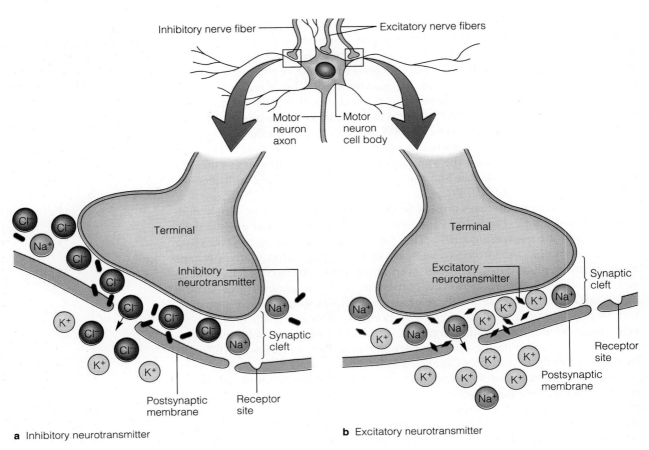

a Inhibitory neurotransmitter

b Excitatory neurotransmitter

Figure 3.11
Ionotropic synapses
At an ionotropic synapse, a neurotransmitter may open (a) chloride or potassium gates, hyperpolarizing the membrane, or (b) sodium gates, depolarizing the membrane.

Channels

some type of ion (see Figure 3.11). For example, when the neurotransmitter *glutamate* attaches to certain receptors, it opens sodium gates, thereby enabling sodium ions to enter the postsynaptic cell. The sodium ions, bringing with them a positive charge, partially depolarize the membrane. Consequently, glutamate is generally an *excitatory* neurotransmitter. The flow of ions is controlled by a molecular complex called an *ionophore,* which includes both the receptor and the ionic gate.

GABA is another neurotransmitter that exerts ionotropic effects, but its effects are generally *inhibitory.* When GABA attaches to its receptors on the membrane, it opens chloride gates, enabling chloride ions, with their negative charge, to cross the membrane into the cell more rapidly than usual.

Acetylcholine exerts ionotropic effects at some synapses but not at others. The synapses at which it produces ionotropic effects are known as *nicotinic* synapses because they can be stimulated by the drug *nicotine.* When acetylcholine attaches to one of its nicotinic receptors, the membrane-bound proteins shown in Figure 3.12, it opens the gates for sodium ions to cross the membrane for about 1 to 3 ms (Changeux, Devillers-Thiéry, & Chemouilli, 1984; Giraudat & Changeux, 1981). Ionic effects at synapses are rapid but

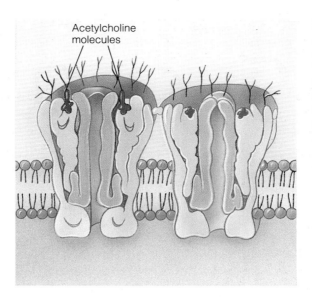

Acetylcholine
molecules

Figure 3.12
**Acetylcholine receptors
embedded in a membrane**
*The receptors on the left
have acetylcholine molecules
attached to them; conse-
quently, their ion pores are
open. (From Lindstrom,
1979.)*

short-lived. Typically, the neurotransmitter opens the ion channels within 10
ms after its release and keeps them open for about 10 to 20 ms (North, 1989;
Westbrook & Jahr, 1989). Ionotropic synapses are therefore useful for conveying information about visual and auditory stimulation, muscle movements, and
other events that change rapidly.

Metabotropic Effects and "Second Messenger" Systems   At certain other
synapses, neurotransmitters exert **metabotropic effects.** These effects take
place through a sequence of metabolic reactions; they are slower, longer lasting, and more complicated than the ionic effects. The effects emerge about 30
ms after the release of the transmitter (North, 1989); they may last seconds or
longer—in some cases, much longer.

Figure 3.13 shows a receptor molecule for epinephrine, a neurotransmitter
that exerts metabotropic effects. The receptor is a protein (a long chain of
amino acids) that winds back and forth across the membrane. When an epinephrine molecule attaches to its receptor, it alters the configuration of the
rest of the protein, although the exact mechanisms are not yet understood. The
altered protein enables a portion of the protein inside the neuron to react with
other molecules, as described in Figure 3.13 (Levitzki, 1988; O'Dowd,
Lefkowitz, & Caron, 1989).

Here are the main points of Figure 3.13: The receptor molecule, which
loops back and forth across the membrane, has a portion outside the membrane that binds to a neurotransmitter. It also has a portion inside the membrane that binds to a *G-protein.* A **G-protein** is a protein coupled to guanosine
triphosphate (GTP), an energy-storing molecule. When the neurotransmitter
binds to its site outside the membrane, the receptor molecule activates the G-
protein, which in turn increases the concentration of a **second messenger,**
such as cyclic adenosine monophosphate (cyclic AMP), inside the cell. Just as
the "first messenger" (the neurotransmitter) carries a message to the postsynaptic cell, the second messenger carries a message to several areas within
the postsynaptic cell. That message may vary from cell to cell; the second messenger may open or close an ion channel in the membrane or alter the production of proteins or the structure of the postsynaptic cell. Metabotropic

*Chemical Events
at the Synapse*

Figure 3.13
Sequence of events at a metabolic synapse, using a second messenger within the postsynaptic neuron

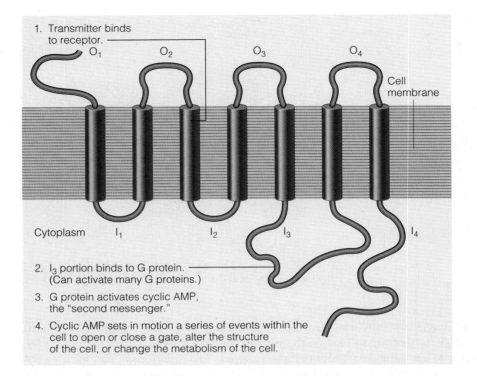

1. Transmitter binds to receptor.
   O_1 O_2 O_3 O_4

Cell membrane

Cytoplasm I_1 I_2 I_3 I_4

2. I_3 portion binds to G protein. (Can activate many G proteins.)

3. G protein activates cyclic AMP, the "second messenger."

4. Cyclic AMP sets in motion a series of events within the cell to open or close a gate, alter the structure of the cell, or change the metabolism of the cell.

changes are relatively slow and long lasting compared with the effects of ionotropic synapses.

Neuromodulators, Including Peptides   A neurotransmitter is like a telephone line; it conveys a message directly and exclusively from the sender to the receiver. Hormones (discussed in later chapters) are more like a radio station; they convey a message to any receiver that happens to be tuned in to the right station. A **neuromodulator** is intermediate between a neurotransmitter and a hormone—perhaps like a CB radio. Like a hormone (or a radio station), it conveys a message to any receiver that happens to be tuned in, but the signal does not travel very far.

Neurons release neuromodulators generally but not necessarily at their terminals. They diffuse to other neurons in their region, perhaps even to the neuron that released them. They affect all those nearby cells that have receptors for them—that is, all the cells "tuned to the right station" (Vizi, 1984). Just as the strength of a CB radio signal fades rapidly over a mile or two, the effect of a neuromodulator is greatest for nearby cells. As the modulator diffuses to greater distances, its concentration decreases.

The distinction between a neurotransmitter and a neuromodulator is not a sharp one. After all, once released, any chemical can diffuse away from its point of release and affect nearby cells. In most cases, the neuromodulators exert their effects by second messengers, like the metabotropic neurotransmitters.

Many neuromodulators are **peptides**—chains of two or more amino acids. The total number of peptides that act as neuromodulators is probably more than 40 (Bloom, 1987). Each of these peptides has other functions in the body as well; in fact, most of them originated in the stomach, intestines, or other visceral organs. (The body uses the same chemicals for different functions instead of synthesizing a new chemical for each function.)

Table 3.1   Differences Between Neurotransmitters and Peptide Neuromodulators

	Neurotransmitters	Peptide Neuromodulators
Location of synthesis	Partly in cell body but mostly in the terminal, near point of release.	Entirely in cell body.
Potential for repeated release	Many molecules recycled; others synthesized near point of release. Can be released at high frequency.	Generally not recycled; newly synthesized molecules may take hours to reach the terminal. Can be released only at a low frequency.
Location of effects	Generally limited to the postsynaptic neuron.	In some cases may diffuse to nearby cells.
Type of effects	Ionotropic: open gates in membrane for some type of ion.	Prolong or limit the effects of a neurotransmitter. Effects are slow but long lasting.
	Metabotropic: more slowly open ion gates or alter the metabolism for structure of the neuron.	
Onset of effects	Ionotropic: less than 10 ms.	Slower than neurotransmitters.
	Metabotropic: 30 ms.	
Duration of effects	Ionotropic: 10–20 ms.	Seconds, maybe minutes, maybe hours?
	Metabotropic: less than a second to a few seconds, maybe longer.	

Based on Bloom, 1987; Carlsson, 1987: Millborn et al., 1989; Shepherd, 1988; Vizi, 1984.

As a rule, the neuromodulators, especially the peptide neuromodulators, by themselves produce little effect on a neuron. This is why they are called "modulators"; they modulate (alter) the effect of neurotransmitters (Millhorn et al., 1989). For example, certain neuromodulators prolong or limit the effect of a neurotransmitter. Such neuromodulators are said to have a "conditional" effect; they produce an effect only when the neurotransmitter is present. Other neuromodulators have other effects, such as limiting the release of neurotransmitter from the presynaptic neuron. Table 3.1 highlights some differences between neurotransmitters and peptide neuromodulators.

Recall that most neurons release two or more chemicals from their terminals. In many cases, one of them is a neurotransmitter such as acetylcholine, and the other is a peptide neuromodulator. Such a combination can have highly adaptive effects. For example, stimulation at one set of synapses leads to salivation. Acetylcholine starts the salivation; a peptide neuromodulator released with it causes the salivation to continue. The effect of acetylcholine by itself would be too brief, and the effect of the peptide by itself would be too

Figure 3.14
Two types of presynaptic receptors
(*a*) *A norepinephrine synapse with an inhibitory receptor, probably sensitive to some other neurotransmitter.* (*b*) *A norepinephrine synapse with an autoreceptor, sensitive to norepinephrine. Autoreceptors may contribute to negative feedback, although the evidence for this function is not yet solid.*

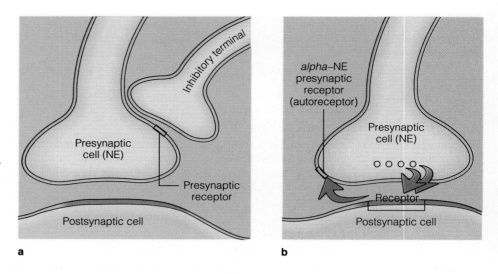

weak and too slow. In other cases, a peptide may reduce or halt the effect of acetylcholine (Crawley, 1990).

Presynaptic Receptors

In one special kind of synapse, the receptor is located on the terminal at the tip of an axon. Such a receptor is known as a **presynaptic receptor.** At most sites, activation of a presynaptic receptor inhibits the later release of neurotransmitter from the terminal; in some cases, however, it facilitates release.

In many cases, a receptor on the presynaptic neuron is sensitive to some neurotransmitter other than the one that the neuron itself releases (Starke, 1981). In many other cases, the presynaptic neuron has receptors sensitive to the same neurotransmitter that the neuron releases (Dubocovich, 1984; Roth, 1984). A presynaptic receptor that responds to the neuron's own neurotransmitter is known as an **autoreceptor.** Many investigators believe that autoreceptors provide negative feedback. That is, after the terminal releases the neurotransmitter, some transmitter molecules return to the presynaptic neuron where they activate autoreceptors, which in turn inhibit further release of the neurotransmitter (see Figure 3.14). However, the evidence to support this view is only indirect and not entirely conclusive (Kalsner, 1990). Therefore, some investigators consider that the role of the autoreceptors is still uncertain.

Inactivation and Reuptake of Neurotransmitters

A neurotransmitter does not normally linger at the postsynaptic membrane for long. If it did, it might continue exciting or inhibiting the postsynaptic neuron indefinitely. Various neurotransmitters are inactivated in different ways.

After acetylcholine activates a receptor, it is broken down by the enzyme **acetylcholinesterase** (a-SEE-til-ko-lih-NES-teh-raze) into two fragments, acetate and choline. Acetate by itself cannot stimulate the receptor, and choline does so only weakly (Krnjević & Reinhardt, 1979). The choline diffuses back to the presynaptic neuron, which takes it up and reconnects it with acetate already in the cell to form acetylcholine again. That is, the brain recycles its choline. The process is highly efficient but not perfect; after a rapid series of transmissions at a synapse, the number of quanta released per transmission declines—presumably because the cell has used up its acetylcholine faster than it can reassemble it.

If the enzyme acetylcholinesterase is not present in adequate amounts, acetylcholine may remain at the synapse for an abnormally long time and continue to excite it. This leads to a strategy in some drug therapies: Certain disorders, such as myasthenia gravis, are associated with a deficit of transmission at acetylcholine synapses. One way to elevate someone's acetylcholine transmission is to give drugs that inhibit acetylcholinesterase.

Serotonin and the catecholamines (dopamine, norepinephrine, and epinephrine) are not broken down into inactive fragments at the postsynaptic membrane. They simply detach from the receptor. The presynaptic neuron takes up most of these neurotransmitter molecules intact and reuses them. This process is called **reuptake.**

Some of the serotonin and catecholamine molecules, either before or after being reabsorbed, are converted into inactive chemicals that cannot stimulate the receptor. The enzymes that convert catecholamine transmitters into inactive chemicals are **COMT** (catechol-o-methyltransferase) and **MAO** (monoamine oxidase, which affects serotonin as well as catecholamines). We shall encounter MAO again later; certain antidepressant drugs act by inhibiting MAO.

Neurotransmitters and Behavior

The brain uses a great many chemicals as neurotransmitters and neuromodulators. Adding to the complexity, each of the widely investigated neurotransmitters has more than one type of receptor. For example, acetylcholine has at least four types of nicotinic receptors and five types of muscarinic receptors (McCormick, 1989). Norepinephrine has several types of alpha and beta receptors (Surprenant, 1989); dopamine has at least five types of receptors (Schwartz, Giros, Martres, & Sokoloff, 1992); serotonin has at least ten types of receptors (Humphrey, Hartig, & Hoyer, 1993). GABA has some receptors that respond to benzodiazepine tranquilizers such as Valium and Xanax, and other receptors that do not (Stephenson & Dolphin, 1989).

Why are there so many neurotransmitters and so many types of receptors? It is probably for the same reason that our alphabet has more than just three or four letters. The nervous system needs a large number of elements that can be combined in different ways to produce complex behavior. To be more specific: Different neurotransmitters control different aspects of behavior. Stimulation of serotonin type 2C receptors may promote certain types of behavior or experience, while stimulation of type 1F receptors facilitates others.

Now, imagine that certain individuals have a bit more of one kind of receptor or a bit less of another. The probable consequence is that, if both people take a given drug, they may experience quite different side effects. Even without taking drugs, the fact that people have different amounts of different receptors may give them different spontaneous behaviors. In other words, the chemistry of synapses and receptors may be responsible even for what we call "personality" and for certain psychological abnormalities. At this point, the relationship between receptor chemistry and spontaneous behavior is based partly on research and partly on speculation. How far this principle will carry us is a matter for future research to determine.

Summary

1. Most synapses operate by the transmission of a neurotransmitter from the presynaptic cell to the postsynaptic cell. (p. 66)

2. It is possible to increase or decrease the production of a given neurotransmitter, at least briefly, by consuming food with a high or low concentration of the precursors to that neurotransmitter. (p. 70)

3. Many chemicals are used as neurotransmitters. As far as we know, each neuron releases the same combination of neurotransmitters from all branches of its axon. (p. 73)

4. At certain synapses, a neurotransmitter exerts its effects by attaching to a receptor that opens the gates to allow a particular ion, such as sodium, to cross the membrane more readily. At other synapses, a neurotransmitter may lead to slower but longer-lasting changes inside the postsynaptic cell. (p. 73)

5. Presynaptic receptors are on the terminal of an axon. Activation of such receptors may inhibit or facilitate the release of a neurotransmitter from that axon. (p. 78)

6. After a neurotransmitter has activated its receptor, some of the transmitter molecules are reabsorbed by the presynaptic cell. Other molecules are metabolized into inactive chemicals and eventually excreted. (p. 78)

7. Different neurotransmitters contribute to behavior in different ways. Certain behavioral abnormalities can be traced to an excess or deficit of chemical activity at particular types of synapses. (p. 79)

Review Questions

1. What evidence did Loewi offer to show that transmission at a synapse depends on the release of chemicals? (p. 66)

2. How can changes in diet modify the levels of certain neurotransmitters in the brain? (p. 68)

3. What is a "quantum" of neurotransmitter? (p. 73)

4. Distinguish between ionotropic and metabotropic effects at synapses. (p. 73)

5. What does a "second messenger" do? (p. 75)

6. List differences between neurotransmitters and neuromodulators. (p. 77)

7. What is an autoreceptor and how does it contribute to negative feedback? (p. 78)

8. After acetylcholine excites its receptor and then detaches from it, what prevents it from attaching and exciting the receptor again? (p. 78)

Thought Question

1. Suppose that axon A enters a ganglion (a cluster of neurons) and axon B leaves on the other side. An experimenter who stimulates A can shortly thereafter record an impulse traveling down B. We would like to know whether B is just an extension of axon A, or whether A formed an excitatory synapse on some neuron in the ganglion, whose axon is axon B. How could an experimenter determine the answer? You should be able to think of more than one good method. Presume that the anatomy within the ganglion is so complex that you cannot simply trace the course of an axon through it.

Suggestions for Further Reading

Allman, W. F. (1989). *Apprentices of wonder.* New York: Bantam Books. Certain neuroscientists have developed mathematical models of how enormous populations of neurons and synapses mediate complex behavior. This book describes those attempts in nontechnical language.

Levitan, I. B., & Kaczmarek, L. K. (1991). *The neuron.* New York: Oxford University Press. A thorough treatment of the mechanisms of synaptic communication.

Terms

neurotransmitter chemical released at a synapse (p. 68)

biogenic amine neurotransmitter containing an amine group (NH_2) (p. 68)

amino acid an acid containing an amine group (NH_2); one of the components of peptides (p. 68)

peptide a chain of amino acids; some peptides are neurotransmitters (p. 68)

catecholamine compound such as dopamine, norepinephrine, and epinephrine that contains both catechol and an amine (NH_2) (p. 68)

acetylcholine, glutamate, GABA, endorphins, enkephalins, substance P, ATP, NO, adenosine, serotonin, dopamine, norepinephrine, and **epinephrine** chemicals believed to act as neurotransmitters at various places in the nervous system (p. 70)

tryptophan amino acid that serves as the precursor to serotonin (p. 70)

insulin hormone that increases the conversion of glucose into stored fat and facilitates the transfer of glucose across the cell membrane (p. 70)

vesicle tiny, nearly spherical packet near the axon terminals filled with the neurotransmitter (p. 71)

quantum the minimum size of an EPSP or IPSP in a postsynaptic neuron (p. 73)

ionotropic effect synaptic effect that depends on the rapid opening of some kind of gate in the membrane (p. 73)

metabotropic effect effect at a synapse that produces a relatively slow but long-lasting effect through metabolic reactions (p. 75)

G-protein a protein coupled to GTP (guanosine triphosphate, an energy-storing molecule); an important part of the receptor molecule found in many synapses (p. 75)

second messenger chemical activated by a neurotransmitter, which in turn initiates processes that carry messages to several areas within the neuron (p. 75)

neuromodulator chemical that has properties intermediate between those of a neurotransmitter and those of a hormone (p. 76)

presynaptic receptor receptor located on the terminal at the tip of an axon (p. 78)

autoreceptor presynaptic receptor that responds to its own neurotransmitter (p. 78)

acetylcholinesterase enzyme that breaks acetylcholine into acetate and choline (p. 78)

reuptake reabsorption of a neurotransmitter by the presynaptic terminal (p. 79)

COMT catechol-o-methyltransferase, an enzyme that metabolizes catecholamines (p. 79)

MAO monoamine oxidase, enzyme that converts catecholamines and serotonin into synaptically inactive forms (p. 79)

Synapses, Drugs, and Behavior

Drugs affecting the brain can be either helpful or harmful. Physicians prescribe antidepressant drugs, tranquilizers, and so forth to help people deal with psychological troubles; meanwhile, society tries to combat the use of drugs for recreational purposes. Many drugs—such as morphine, amphetamine, even cocaine—have legitimate medical uses as well as dangerous or addictive uses. The difference between a "good" drug and a "bad" drug is partly a matter of the drug itself and partly a matter of how much of the drug a person is taking, and when and why.

Nearly all the drugs with strong effects on the brain exert their behavioral effects mainly by influencing the synapses. We shall consider here a few of the basic mechanisms by which drugs affect the nervous system and behavior, focusing on drugs known more for their abuse than for their medical use. In later chapters, we shall discuss drugs known mostly for their psychiatric value.

How Drugs Can Affect Synapses

A drug can mimic or increase the effects of a given neurotransmitter, or it can block those effects. A drug that blocks the effects is called an **antagonist,** meaning *enemy.* A drug that mimics or increases the effects is called an **agonist.** (*Antagonist* is sometimes used in everyday speech, while *agonist* is seldom used except in discussions of drug effects. The term *agonist* is derived from a Greek word meaning *contestant;* an antagonist is an "anti-agonist," or member of the opposing team.)

Drugs can exert their effects in a wide variety of ways, such as facilitating or inhibiting the synthesis of a neurotransmitter, increasing or decreasing the release of a neurotransmitter, or altering what happens to the transmitter after it attaches to its receptors. Figure 3.15 illustrates the sequence of events at a norepinephrine synapse and some of the ways that drugs can alter the events. Ordinarily, tyrosine from the diet is converted into dopa, which in turn gives rise to dopamine and then to norepinephrine. Action potentials in this axon release norepinephrine, which diffuses to the postsynaptic cell and binds with receptors there. After detaching from the receptors, some of the norepinephrine is reabsorbed by the presynaptic cell, and the rest is broken down into inactive chemicals by the enzymes MAO and COMT.

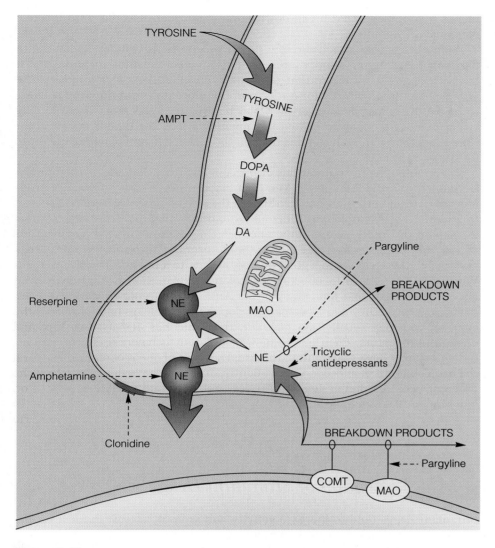

Figure 3.15
Events at a norepinephrine synapse and the drugs that can inhibit each step
AMPT blocks the conversion of tyrosine to dopa. Reserpine causes leakage from the vesicles that store norepinephrine. Amphetamine increases the release. Clonidine stimulates the presynaptic receptors that inhibit release of norepinephrine. Tricyclic antidepressants block reuptake. Pargyline blocks MAO (monoamine oxidase), an enzyme that breaks down norepinephrine and similar transmitters.

Drugs can facilitate or interfere at any step along the way (see Figure 3.15). For example, alpha-methyl-para-tyrosine (*AMPT*) blocks the enzyme that converts tyrosine into dopa; the result is a decreased production of dopa and ultimately a decreased production of norepinephrine. *Reserpine* causes leakage from the vesicles that store norepinephrine. *Amphetamine* increases the release of norepinephrine and also decreases its reabsorption after its release. *Tricyclic antidepressant* drugs specifically inhibit the reabsorption. *Pargyline* blocks the enzymes that break down norepinephrine molecules into inactive chemicals.

Some drugs also attach directly to the receptors. Investigators say that a particular drug has an **affinity** for a particular type of receptor, meaning that it has a tendency to attach to that receptor, somewhat like a lock and key. The stronger the drug's affinity for a receptor, the more powerful the drug is likely to be as an agonist or antagonist. Upon binding to a receptor, the drug may either excite the receptor (like a key opening a lock) or inhibit the receptor (like a key that *almost* fits, failing to open the lock itself, and blocking the route for the correct key).

If you or anyone you know has ever taken any drug that affects the brain— tranquilizers, antidepressants, even high-blood-pressure drugs—you are probably aware that both the effectiveness and the side effects vary from one person to another. For example, antischizophrenic drugs sometimes produce serious movement disorders, sexual impotence, dizziness, drowsiness, excessive salivation, and other undesirable effects. Some users of antischizophrenic drugs experience these effects to a great degree; others, to a mild degree or not at all. Why such differences in effects? Part of the explanation is that each drug affects more than one kind of synapse. Antischizophrenic drugs exert their benefits because they can block certain dopamine pathways in the brain. However, as you may recall from page 79, the brain has at least five kinds of dopamine receptors. Each has somewhat different behavioral effects, and an individual may have greater than the usual amount of one receptor or less than the usual amount of another. Consequently, drugs can have different effects on different people. A major goal of drug research is to find drugs that affect just one kind of receptor and not others.

Modes of Action of Stimulant Drugs

Stimulant drugs tend to increase activity and arousal, at least in most people under most circumstances. (Statements about drugs generally need qualifications such as "for most people" and "in most circumstances." For example, although stimulant drugs arouse most people, they seem to calm hyperactive children.) Different classes of stimulant drugs act on the nervous system in different ways.

Amphetamine and Cocaine

Amphetamine and **cocaine** are strong stimulant drugs with medical uses as well as a powerful potential for abuse. Amphetamine and related drugs are often prescribed for hyperactive children, occasionally for certain types of epilepsy, and sometimes (not very successfully) as an appetite suppressant (see Chapter 10). Cocaine, in addition to its overall effects as a stimulant, has anesthetizing properties similar to those of Novocain (a very similar compound). Cocaine is sometimes used as an anesthetic drug, especially during eye surgery.

Amphetamine and cocaine are widely abused because of their ability to intensify pleasures and provide a sense of well-being. They produce these

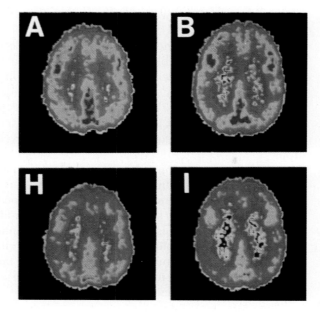

Figure 3.16
Sometimes "your brain on drugs" is not like throwing something into a frying pan, a popular analogy; it is more like throwing it into the refrigerator. As these positron emission tomography (PET) scans show, the brain has lower metabolism and lower overall activity under the influence of cocaine than it has ordinarily. Red indicates highest activity, followed by yellow, green, and blue. A and B represent brain activity under normal conditions; H and I show activity after a cocaine injection. (From London et al., 1990.)

stimulant effects by increasing the activity at dopamine synapses. They have additional effects by increasing activity at norepinephrine and certain other synapses. Drugs that activate dopamine synapses tend to be habit-forming or addictive; conversely, most habit-forming drugs produce some activation of dopamine synapses (Harris, Brodie, & Dunwiddie, 1992; Wise & Bozarth, 1987). In fact, certain kinds of dopamine synapses, using what are known as D_2 and D_3 dopamine receptors, are particularly important for addiction (Caine & Koob, 1993; Uhl, Blum, Noble, & Smith, 1993). The transmitter acetylcholine apparently has opposing effects. In certain brain areas, addicting drugs such as morphine increase the release of dopamine and decrease the release of acetylcholine. In contrast, when a morphine user goes into withdrawal, the result is a decrease in dopamine release and an increase in acetylcholine (Pothos, Rada, Mark, & Hoebel, 1991; Rada, Pothos, Mark, & Hoebel, 1991).

Amphetamine stimulates dopamine synapses in two ways: First, it increases the release of dopamine. Second, it blocks the reuptake of released dopamine by the presynaptic cell; thus, the released dopamine remains in the synaptic cleft longer than usual, capable of stimulating and restimulating the postsynaptic receptors for longer than usual.

Cocaine also blocks the reuptake of norepinephrine and dopamine, thus prolonging their effects. At low doses, cocaine stimulates mostly dopamine's D_2 receptors, leading to an excitation of postsynaptic neurons. At higher doses, it stimulates mostly D_1 receptors, which inhibit the postsynaptic neurons (Nantwi & Schoener, 1993). Ordinarily, the net effect of cocaine is to decrease the total amount of activity in many parts of the brain (London et al., 1990). (See Figure 3.16.)

How, you might wonder, could a drug that decreases overall brain activity lead to increased arousal and activity? The answer is that total brain activity is far removed from total muscle activity. For example, suppose that neuron A inhibits neuron B. Inhibition of A would remove inhibition from B, making B

*Synapses, Drugs,
and Behavior*

more active. (Indeed, we sometimes describe the behavior of drug users as "uninhibited.")

The effects of cocaine and amphetamine on dopamine synapses are necessarily brief. When they block the reuptake of dopamine, dopamine builds up to higher-than-usual concentrations. The excess dopamine in the synaptic cleft stimulates D_2 receptors on the presynaptic terminal, exerting a negative feedback effect (North, 1992). That is, when the concentration of dopamine in the synaptic cleft is high, it inhibits the presynaptic terminal from releasing additional dopamine. Consequently, the dopamine levels in the cleft soon begin to drop.

As time passes, dopamine stimulation drops still further because the dopamine in the cleft, unable to reenter the presynaptic neuron, diffuses away. Ordinarily (in the absence of amphetamine or cocaine), the presynaptic neuron reabsorbs much of the released dopamine and recycles it for future use. When drugs prevent this recycling, the presynaptic neuron needs additional time to rebuild its supplies. As a result, amphetamine and cocaine users often report that, within a couple of hours after they take the drugs, they "crash" into a depressed state, much the opposite of the pleasant, aroused state that the drug initially produced.

One more point about cocaine, which illustrates a general principle about drugs: For many years, cocaine abuse was a relatively minor problem, compared with other drugs. But then, after "crack" cocaine became available in the mid-1980s, cocaine abuse became much more common and much more severe, surpassing all other addictions in its prevalence and severity (Gawin, 1991). Crack cocaine is cocaine that has been converted to the *free base* form (by removing a hydrochloride group); it can be smoked, producing a rush of cocaine to the brain within a few seconds. Other things being equal, the faster any drug gets to the brain, the more powerful the experience and the more likely the drug is to become addictive.

Caffeine

Caffeine, a drug found in coffee, tea, and many soft drinks, acts as a stimulant in at least two ways. First, it dilates the blood vessels, increasing heart rate and blood flow to the brain as well as to other organs. Second, it interferes with the effects of the neurotransmitter *adenosine*. Recall that many neurons have presynaptic receptors—receptors on the presynaptic terminal that facilitate or inhibit the release of transmitter. Adenosine acts at certain presynaptic receptors to inhibit the release of the excitatory transmitter glutamate. Because caffeine blocks the effects of adenosine, which inhibits the release of glutamate, the net effect of caffeine is to increase the release of glutamate (Silinsky, 1989).

Nicotine

Nicotine, a compound present in tobacco products, produces complicated effects (Schelling, 1992). Although it has strong stimulant effects on heart rate and blood pressure, many (though not all) cigarette smokers say that smoking relaxes them. Researchers have not yet resolved that contradiction, but part of the answer may lie in nicotine's effects on breathing rate: Nicotine increases breathing rate in some smokers and decreases it in others (Jones, 1987). Because breathing rate is such a noticeable response, a smoker with a decreased breathing rate is likely to report "relaxation" even if the nicotine has simultaneously acted as a stimulant for heart rate. (How nicotine decreases the breathing rate in some smokers is, however, still mysterious.)

Nicotine directly stimulates one type of acetylcholine receptor, conveniently known as the *nicotinic receptor,* which is found both in the central nervous system and at the nerve-muscle junction of skeletal muscles. Whereas nicotine can substitute for acetylcholine in stimulating the nerve-muscle junction (sometimes causing twitching), drugs that block the nicotinic receptor can cause paralysis. One such drug is *curare* (kyoo-RA-ree). Since long ago, South American Indians put curare on the tips of their arrows, because they had discovered that they could paralyze their prey with this substance.

Nicotine also indirectly stimulates dopamine receptors. It probably has a number of additional synaptic effects, paralleling its multiple behavioral effects (Stolerman, 1991).

Some Other Commonly Abused Drugs

Opiates

Opiate drugs are drugs derived from, or similar to those derived from, the opium poppy. Familiar opiates include morphine, heroin, and methadone. Opiates give rise to a generally pleasant state, an overall withdrawal from reality, and decreased sensitivity to pain. Morphine is often used medically as a painkiller. Opiate drugs when taken for medical reasons are very seldom habit-forming; when taken recreationally, they are strongly addictive.

People smoked or injected morphine and other opiates for centuries before anyone knew how they affected the brain. Then, Candace Pert and Solomon Snyder found that morphine and other opiate drugs attach to specific receptors in the brain (Pert & Snyder, 1973). It was a safe guess that mammals had not evolved such receptors just to enable us to become addicted to derivatives of the opium poppy; the brain must produce some chemical of its own that attaches to these receptors. And, indeed, investigators soon found that the brain has a previously unknown class of neurotransmitters, now known as the *endorphins*—a contraction of *endo*genous *m*orphines. We shall discuss the endorphins in more detail in the section on pain (Chapter 7); at this point, let us simply note that the endorphins serve as a brake on pain and probably contribute to pleasant experience. Opiate drugs are an artificial way of tapping into that brain system.

Note I said earlier (p. 85) that most of the widely abused drugs stimulate dopamine synapses. Indirectly, opiates fit that pattern. Endorphin synapses inhibit neurons that release GABA, a transmitter that inhibits dopamine release (North, 1992). Because of this inhibition of inhibition, the net effect is increased dopamine release.

The opium poppy, from which opiate drugs can be derived. (Scott Camazine/ Photo Researchers Inc.)

Marijuana

The leaves of the marijuana plant contain the chemical Δ^9-*tetrahydrocannabinol* (Δ^9-THC) and other **cannabinoids** (chemicals related to Δ^9-THC), which people inhale when they smoke the leaves. The result is an intensification of

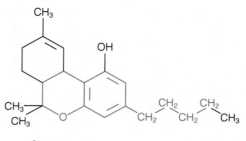

Δ⁹THC

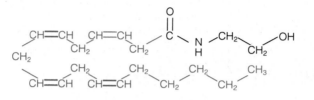

Anandamide

Figure 3.17
Anandamide and Δ⁹-tetrahydrocannabinol
Note the similarity between one part of the naturally occurring brain chemical and one part of the marijuana derivative.

sensory experience and an illusion that time is passing very slowly. Marijuana users frequently experience a lack of energy and ambition; they sometimes also experience impairments of attention, learning, and memory, especially the first few times that they use the substance. Marijuana is sometimes used medically to relieve pain or nausea or to combat glaucoma (an eye disorder).

Marijuana can be habit-forming, although few users experience the same intense cravings that cocaine or opiate users do. Cannabinoids dissolve in the body's fats and leave the body very slowly. One consequence is that users do not experience a sudden "crash" a couple of hours after taking the drug, as cocaine and opiate users do. Another consequence is that a marijuana user can "test positive" for cannabinoids in the urine days or weeks after quitting all use.

Marijuana users face certain health risks: Driving while under the influence of marijuana produces risks analogous to those of driving under the influence of alcohol. And long-term smoking of marijuana cigarettes increases the risk of lung cancer, similar to the effects of smoking tobacco cigarettes. However, marijuana users do not typically "overdose" the way that cocaine and opiate users do; that is, even an unusually large dose of marijuana is unlikely to interfere with breathing or heartbeat.

For years, investigators could not explain the effects of marijuana on the brain. It was known to have some general effects on neuronal membranes, but nothing very spectacular. Then, investigators localized specific receptors for cannabinoids (Devane, Dysarz, Johnson, Melvin, & Howlett, 1988). Those receptors are widespread in the hippocampus, the basal ganglia, and the cerebellum; overall, they are among the most numerous receptors in the brain

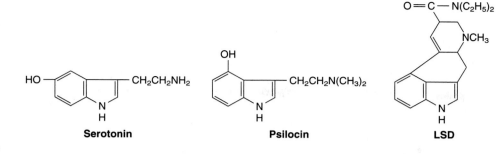

Figure 3.18
Resemblance of the neurotransmitter serotonin to two chemicals with hallucinogenic effects

(Herkenham, 1992; Herkenham, Lynn, deCosta, & Richfield, 1991). However, they are virtually absent from the medulla and the rest of the brain stem. That absence is significant, because the medulla and brain stem include the centers that control breathing and heartbeat; we begin to understand why even large doses of marijuana do not threaten breathing or heartbeat.

Just as the discovery of opiate receptors in the brain led to a successful search for the brain's endogenous opiates, the discovery of cannabinoid receptors prompted investigators to search for some brain chemical that binds to those receptors. One such chemical has been found, referred to as **anandamide** (from the Sanskrit word *ananda,* meaning *bliss*). (See Figure 3.17.) Anandamide binds strongly to the cannabinoid receptor; injections of anandamide to laboratory animals produce some of the same effects as cannabinoids (Devane et al., 1992). Now the question is, why does the brain produce marijuanalike chemicals? What is the function of those chemicals in normal behavior? We must await future research for the answers.

Hallucinogenic Drugs

Drugs that grossly distort perception are called **hallucinogenic drugs.** Examples are lysergic acid diethylamide (LSD), phencyclidine (PCP), and mescaline. Their effects vary from person to person and from one use to another; most often, the effect is described as a dreamlike state.

Just as opiates and cannabinoids closely resemble neurotransmitters, so do LSD and other hallucinogenic drugs. The difference is that hallucinogens resemble a transmitter that has been well known for a long time—serotonin (see Figure 3.18). Because of this resemblance, LSD can attach to a serotonin receptor and act as an agonist. Contrast this mode of action to that of amphetamine: Amphetamine acts by releasing norepinephrine and dopamine from the presynaptic neurons; if the neurons have a low supply of these neurotransmitters, amphetamine is ineffective. In contrast, even after the complete removal of the presynaptic neurons that release serotonin, LSD still exerts its full effect. It may even produce a greater-than-normal effect: After the removal of the serotonin-containing neurons, the postsynaptic neuron may develop an increased number of serotonin receptors as a kind of "compensation." The increased number of receptors makes LSD more effective (Jacobs, 1987).

Serotonin (5-HT) has several types of receptors, each with slightly different properties and no doubt different roles in behavior. LSD, it turns out, has a strong affinity for only one of these types, the 5-HT$_2$ receptor (Jacobs, 1987). Receptors of that type are abundant in much of the brain. By binding to this receptor, LSD stimulates it at abnormal times and blocks serotonin from stimulating it in the normal way.

Does this account of LSD explain its effects on behavior? Only in part. We know what LSD does chemically but not how it produces hallucinations and other changes in experience. Presumably the 5-HT$_2$ receptors contribute in some way to perception, and an abnormal pattern of stimulation of those receptors leads to abnormal perceptions. But in contrast to our knowledge of the chemistry, our understanding of how synaptic activity relates to experience is sketchy.

Alcohol

The most widely abused drug is alcohol. Alcohol by itself does not make people feel happy; however, it increases people's susceptibility to social influences. That is, although you are unlikely to elevate your mood much by drinking alone, drinking at a party may reduce your inhibitions and help you enjoy the party more. Alcohol also helps people to forget their tension, anxiety, and other problems (Cowan, 1983).

Many people eventually cross the line from "social drinker" to "problem drinker," and alcohol abuse is certainly the most common form of substance abuse in the United States and most other countries. Many problem drinkers suffer serious health hazards and a variety of cognitive deficits, including impairments of reasoning and retrieval of memories (see, for example, Nelson, McSpadden, Fromme, & Marlatt, 1986). Problem drinkers who abstain from alcohol will gradually improve in performance of cognitive tasks, especially if they quit drinking before age 40 (Goldman, 1983). The later someone quits, the slower and less certain the recovery.

Alcohol exerts its effects on behavior through many routes. It inhibits the flow of sodium across the membrane, expands the surface of all membranes, and generally interferes with nervous system activity. In addition to these nonspecific effects on neurons throughout the brain, alcohol alters one type of GABA receptor, the GABA$_A$ receptor, making it more responsive. As a result, the neurotransmitter GABA has greater effects than usual. Because GABA transmission leads to relaxation and decreased anxiety, alcohol promotes calmness.

No doubt you have noticed that different people react differently to alcohol: Some drink only occasionally or not at all and feel no desire to drink more. Others develop severe and disruptive drinking habits. Why do some people like alcohol so much more than others do?

Many factors contribute, some of them biological and some of them social. One of the biological factors is a genetic predisposition, or perhaps one should say several genetic predispositions. A person who is closely related to one or more alcoholics has an increased probability of becoming an alcoholic too, even if raised in an adoptive family without alcohol abusers (Cloninger, Bohman, & Sigvardsson, 1981; Gabrielli & Plomin, 1985; Vaillant & Milofsky, 1982). However, this trend depends on several genes with quite different effects, not just one gene.

One such gene, associated with a visible marker on one of the human chromosomes, has been found in 69% of alcoholics, as compared to 20% of nonalcoholics; it is also more common in other kinds of drug abusers than it is in non-drug-abusers (S.S. Smith et al., 1992). Thus, that gene seems to predispose people to an increased chance of just about any kind of drug abuse, not specifically to alcoholism. (*How* it does so is a different, quite fascinating, and unanswered question.) The existence of such a general, all-purpose addiction gene is not surprising; some people switch back and forth between alcohol abuse, abuse of other substances, and even compulsive gambling, which does not require any drug at all.

Other genes are apparently more specific to alcohol use. For example, certain genes affect the rate of metabolism of alcohol. After a person drinks **ethyl alcohol,** enzymes in the liver metabolize it to **acetaldehyde,** a poisonous substance. The enzyme *acetaldehyde dehydrogenase* then converts acetaldehyde to **acetic acid,** which the body can use as a source of energy:

$$\text{Ethyl alcohol} \longrightarrow \text{Acetaldehyde} \xrightarrow{\text{Acetaldehyde dehydrogenase}} \text{Acetic acid}$$

Over a long time, acetaldehyde can cause cirrhosis of the liver and damage to other organs. Even in the short term, it can cause illness if its concentration in an organ is high enough.

Most humans have ample amounts of acetaldehyde dehydrogenase, but about half of all Asians have low amounts (Harada et al., 1982; Reed, 1985). For this reason, many people of Asian ancestry feel ill, or at least experience intense flushing in the face, after drinking alcohol (Helzer et al., 1990). The gene that impairs acetaldehyde metabolism is probably a major reason why alcohol abuse is less common among Chinese and Japanese people than it is among people of European or African ancestry.

"Why is alcohol abuse especially common in certain groups of Native Americans?" you might ask. The answer is not known, but it probably has nothing to do with acetaldehyde dehydrogenase. Native Americans have no excess of that enzyme; they do, however, tend to metabolize alcohol to acetaldehyde more rapidly than other groups do (Reed, 1985). The possible relevance of that fact to alcohol abuse remains uncertain.

The drug *disulfiram,* which goes by the trade name **Antabuse,** decreases a person's levels of acetaldehyde dehydrogenase. Antabuse inactivates all copper-containing enzymes, including acetaldehyde dehydrogenase. For at least a couple of days after taking an Antabuse pill, preferably longer, people must avoid all contact with alcohol, at the risk of grave illness. Antabuse is sometimes used to help people stop abusing alcohol (Peachey & Naranjo, 1983). The idea is that such a person will learn an aversion to the taste of alcohol because of the illness that follows. In fact, however, the drug may be effective mostly because of its threat value. Many of the people who take Antabuse abstain from drinking completely, never experiencing the illness that alcohol would cause them (Fuller & Roth, 1979). Those who drink in spite of taking the pill do get ill, but they are as likely to stop taking the pill as to stop drinking alcohol. Evidently, Antabuse functions mostly as a way for an alcoholic to make a daily reaffirmation of the decision to abstain from alcohol.

Summary

1. Drugs can act as agonists (facilitators) or antagonists (inhibitors) of a neurotransmitter by altering any step in the total sequence of transmission, from synthesis of the transmitter to its reuptake or breakdown following transmission. (p. 82)

2. Drugs that enhance dopamine transmission tend to be habit-forming or addictive. Amphetamine and cocaine enhance dopamine transmission by blocking the reuptake of dopamine after its release from the presynaptic terminal, thus prolonging its presence in the synaptic cleft. Amphetamine also enhances release. (p. 85)

3. Caffeine dilates blood vessels, thus increasing blood flow to the brain and other organs, and prevents adenosine from inhibiting glutamate release. (p. 86)

4. Nicotine exerts a variety of effects, some of them by stimulating certain kinds of acetylcholine receptors. (p. 86)

5. Opiate drugs and cannabinoids attach to brain receptors sensitive to specific neurotransmitters. In the case of cannabinoids, we still know little about the natural function of the corresponding neurotransmitter, anandamide. (p. 87)

6. Hallucinogenic drugs, such as LSD, attach to a particular type of serotonin receptor, stimulating it at inappropriate times and therefore altering perception. (p. 89)

7. Alcohol exerts many effects on the nervous system, including a facilitation of transmission at GABA synapses. (p. 90)

8. Several genes increase a person's predisposition to alcoholism. At least one gene increases the tendency to both alcohol and other drugs. Another gene alters the metabolism of alcohol, causing a buildup of acetaldehyde and thus making the experience of drinking alcohol unpleasant. (p. 90)

Review Questions

1. Why do drugs have stronger effects for some people than for others, and different side effects from one person to another? (p. 84)

2. Name some medical uses of amphetamine, cocaine, morphine, and marijuana. (pp. 84–88)

3. Does cocaine increase or decrease overall brain activity? Explain. (p. 85)

4. Why is "crack" cocaine more addictive than other forms of cocaine? What does this observation tell us in general about drug addiction? (p. 86)

5. Why did South American Indians put curare on their arrow tips? (p. 87)

6. What are the steps in metabolic breakdown of ethyl alcohol by the liver? (p. 91)

7. What is a biological explanation for why many people of Asian ancestry are unlikely to become alcohol abusers? (p. 91)

8. How does Antabuse help people break a habit of alcohol abuse? (p. 91)

Thought Questions

1. Ordinarily, amphetamine and cocaine produce strong stimulant effects on behavior through effects on dopamine synapses. Suppose that someone takes a massive dose of AMPT, which blocks the synthesis of dopamine and norepinephrine, before taking amphetamine or cocaine. Will amphetamine or cocaine have the same behavioral effects as usual, or less, or more? Why?

2. Ordinarily, LSD produces effects by stimulating serotonin synapses. Suppose that someone takes a massive dose of a drug that blocks the synthesis of serotonin, before taking LSD. Will LSD have the same behavioral effects as usual, or less, or more? Why?

3. Suppose that haloperidol, which blocks dopamine synapses, is found to suppress the symptoms of the newly discovered disease X. One possible explanation of its effectiveness is that disease X is caused by supersensitive dopamine receptors. What other explanations are possible?

Suggestions for Further Reading

Hamilton, L. W., & Timmons, C. R. (1990). *Principles of behavioral pharmacology.* Englewood Cliffs, NJ: Prentice-Hall. An excellent description of the ways in which drugs can affect behavior.

Snyder, S. H. (1986). *Drugs and the brain.* New York: Freeman. A description of the effects of tranquilizers, antidepressants, antischizophrenic drugs, and illegal drugs.

Vaillant, G. E. (1983). *The natural history of alcoholism.* Cambridge, MA: Harvard University Press. Report of a long-term study of alcoholic men.

Terms

antagonist drug that blocks the effects of a neurotransmitter (p. 82)

agonist drug that mimics or increases the effects of a neurotransmitter (p. 82)

affinity tendency of a drug to bind to a particular type of receptor (p. 84)

stimulant drugs drugs that tend to increase activity and arousal, at least in most people under most circumstances (p. 84)

amphetamine and **cocaine** strong stimulant drugs that prolong the stimulation of dopamine synapses by blocking the reuptake of dopamine by the presynaptic neuron (p. 84)

caffeine a drug that dilates blood vessels and prevents adenosine from inhibiting glutamate release (p. 86)

nicotine a drug that, among other effects, stimulates certain acetylcholine receptors (p. 86)

opiate class of drugs that stimulate endorphin receptors in the nervous system (p. 87)

cannabinoids chemicals related to Δ^9-THC, the component of marijuana that alters experience (p. 87)

anandamide a naturally occurring brain chemical that stimulates the same receptors as cannabinoids (p. 89)

hallucinogenic drugs drugs that grossly distort perception, such as LSD (p. 89)

ethyl alcohol (or ethanol) the type of alcohol that people drink (in contrast to methyl alcohol, isopropyl alcohol, and others) (p. 91)

acetaldehyde toxic substance produced in the metabolism of alcohol (p. 91)

acetic acid chemical that is used as a source of energy (p. 91)

Antabuse trade name for disulfiram, a drug that helps people break an alcohol habit by changing the way that they metabolize alcohol. (p. 91)

ANATOMY OF THE NERVOUS SYSTEM AND METHODS OF INVESTIGATION

(FPG International)

CHAPTER FOUR

MAIN IDEAS

1. Each part of the nervous system has specialized functions, although the parts must work together to produce behavior. Damage in different areas leads to different types of behavioral deficits.

2. The cerebral cortex, the largest structure in the mammalian brain, performs elaborate processing of sensory information and provides for fine control of movement.

3. A variety of investigative techniques can determine how the functioning of various brain areas relates to behavior.

Trying to learn neuroanatomy (the anatomy of the nervous system) from a book is much like trying to learn geography from a road map. A map can tell you that Mystic, Georgia, is about 40 km north of Enigma, Georgia, and that the two cities are connected by a combination of roads including U.S. Route 129. Similarly, a book can tell you that the habenula is about 4.6 mm from the interpeduncular nucleus in a rat's brain (slightly farther in a human brain) and that the two structures are connected by a set of axons known as the habenulopeduncular tract, also sometimes known as the fasciculus retroflexus. But these two little gems of information are likely to seem both mysterious and enigmatic unless you have some interest in that part of Georgia or in that area of the brain.

This chapter does not try to provide a detailed road map of the brain. It is more like a world globe, describing the large, basic structures (analogous to the continents) and a few distinctive features of each. The chapter also describes the most important methods used to study the role of various brain structures in the control of behavior. Later chapters fill in some additional detail on specific parts of the brain as they become relevant in the discussion of particular behaviors.

Basic Subdivisions of the Vertebrate Nervous System

A little animal called a eugnot lives in the jaws of a great monster. The teeth of that monster are sharp and its jaw muscles are ferocious. The monster chews up all sorts of other animals that are nearly the same size, shape, and flavor as the eugnot. But it hardly ever bites the eugnot; even when it does, the bites are almost always gentle. The eugnot seems fearless; it ventures right up to the teeth and sometimes right between the upper and lower teeth. But before the jaws bite down hard, it manages to get out of the way. What do you suppose accounts for the charmed life of this little animal?

That little "animal" is your tongue. (Eugnot is tongue spelled backward.) It lives in your jaws, an extremely vulnerable place, and yet your teeth do not bite it. Not often, anyway. The reason is the central nervous system, a mechanism that coordinates the actions of each part of the body with the actions of the others, enabling the neurons that control your jaw muscles to stay in close contact with the neurons that control your tongue muscles. The neurons that control your left hand communicate with those that control your right hand, enabling you to play a piano, thread a needle, and perform other tasks that require close coordination of the hands. Still, no single "monarch" area of the nervous system governs all the others. The coordinated behavior of the nervous system as a whole emerges from the communication among various areas, not from a single dominant area.

Invertebrate neurons (those of animals without a backbone) operate by the same basic principles as vertebrate neurons, and we can learn much from them about nerve conduction, synaptic transmission, and even the possible single-cell mechanisms of learning. However, their organization into a structural whole differs substantially from that of vertebrates, and in this book we deal mainly with vertebrates.

The vertebrate nervous system consists of two major divisions: the central nervous system and the peripheral nervous system (see Figure 4.1). The **central nervous system (CNS)** contains the spinal cord and the brain (forebrain, midbrain, and hindbrain). The **peripheral nervous system (PNS)** has two divisions: the autonomic nervous system and the somatic nervous system. The **somatic nervous system** consists of the nerves that convey messages from the sense organs to the CNS and from the CNS to the muscles and glands. The **autonomic nervous system** is a set of neurons that controls the heart, the intestines, and other organs.

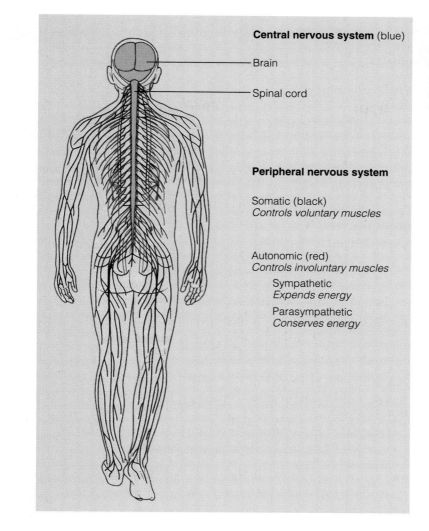

Central nervous system (blue)

— Brain

— Spinal cord

Peripheral nervous system

Somatic (black)
Controls voluntary muscles

Autonomic (red)
Controls involuntary muscles
    Sympathetic
    Expends energy
    Parasympathetic
    Conserves energy

Figure 4.1
The human nervous system consists of the central nervous system and the peripheral nervous system. Each of these divisions has the major subdivisions shown.

Some Terminology

If you were trying to learn the road map of a state or country, you would have to memorize many names of places. The same is true in learning about the brain: You will have to memorize a great many terms. Furthermore, the directional terms for a state are simple: north, south, east, west. Because the brain is a three-dimensional structure, however, we need a greater variety of directional terms. Table 4.1 and Figure 4.2 present some of the basic terms that people use to describe the anatomy of the brain.

In Figure 4.2, note that the terms *dorsal* and *ventral* mean toward the back and toward the stomach. In a four-legged animal, the top of the brain (with respect to gravity) is dorsal (on the same side as the animal's back) and the bottom of the brain is ventral (on the stomach side). Because humans assume an upright posture, the dorsal side of the human brain is at right angles to the dorsal side of the spinal cord, and the ventral side of the brain is at right angles to

Table 4.1 Anatomical Terms Referring to Directions

Term	Definition
Dorsal	Toward the back, away from the ventral (stomach) side. The top of the brain is considered dorsal because that is its position in four-legged animals.
Ventral	Toward the stomach, away from the dorsal (back) side. (*Venter* is the Latin word for belly. It also shows up in the word *ventriloquist,* literally meaning *stomach-talker.*)
Anterior	Toward the front end.
Posterior	Toward the rear end. In humans, the ventral spinal cord is sometimes called *anterior,* and the dorsal cord is called *posterior.*
Rostral	Toward the head, or toward the front of the head, near the nostrils.
Caudal	Toward the rear, away from the head.
Superior	Above another part.
Inferior	Below another part.
Lateral	Toward the side, away from the midline.
Medial	Toward the midline, away from the side.
Proximal	Located close (approximate) to the point of origin or attachment.
Distal	Located more distant from the point of origin or attachment.
Ipsilateral	On the same side of the body (left or right).
Contralateral	On the opposite side of the body (left or right).
Coronal plane (or frontal plane)	A plane that shows brain structures as they would be seen from the front.
Sagittal plane	A plane that shows brain structures as they would be seen from the side.
Horizontal plane (or transverse plane)	A plane that shows brain structures as they would be seen from above.

the ventral side of the spinal cord. We maintain this terminology because it is convenient: The terms *dorsal* and *ventral* always have the same meaning in the brain, regardless of the species of animal under consideration.

Table 4.2 introduces some additional terminology that relates to clusters of neurons and anatomical structures of the brain. Such technical terms, or jargon, enable investigators to communicate with one another with precision and a minimum of ambiguity.

The Spinal Cord and Its Communication with the Periphery

The **spinal cord** is the part of the CNS that communicates with the sense organs and muscles below the level of the head. It is a segmented structure, with each segment having both a sensory nerve and a motor nerve on its left and right sides, as Figures 4.3 and 4.4 show. The sensory nerves enter the spinal cord on the dorsal (back) side; the axons of the motor nerves leave on the ventral (stomach) side. The **Bell-Magendie law** refers to the observation that the dorsal roots of the spinal cord carry sensory information and the ventral roots carry motor information to

Table 4.2   Terms Referring to Parts of the Nervous System

Term	Definition
Lamina	A row or layer of cell bodies separated from other cell bodies by a layer of axons and dendrites.
Column	A set of cells perpendicular to the surface of the cortex, having similar properties.
Tract	A set of axons within the CNS, also known as a *projection*. If axons extend from cell bodies in structure A to synapses onto B, we say that the fibers "project" from A onto B.
Nerve	A set of axons in the periphery, either from the CNS to a muscle or gland, or from a sensory organ to the CNS.
Nucleus	A cluster of neuron cell bodies within the CNS.
Ganglion	A cluster of neuron cell bodies, usually outside the CNS (as in the sympathetic nervous system), or any cluster of neurons in an invertebrate species.
Gyrus (plural: gyri)	A protuberance on the surface of the brain.
Sulcus (plural: sulci)	A fold or groove that separates one gyrus from another.
Fissure	A long, deep sulcus.

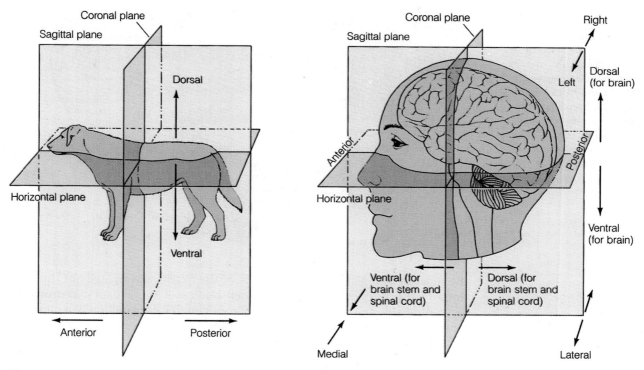

Figure 4.2
Terms describing anatomical directions in the nervous system
In four-legged animals, dorsal and ventral point in the same direction for the head as they do for the rest of the body. However, humans' upright posture has tilted the head relative to the spinal cord, so the dorsal and ventral directions of the head are not parallel to the dorsal and ventral directions of the spinal cord.

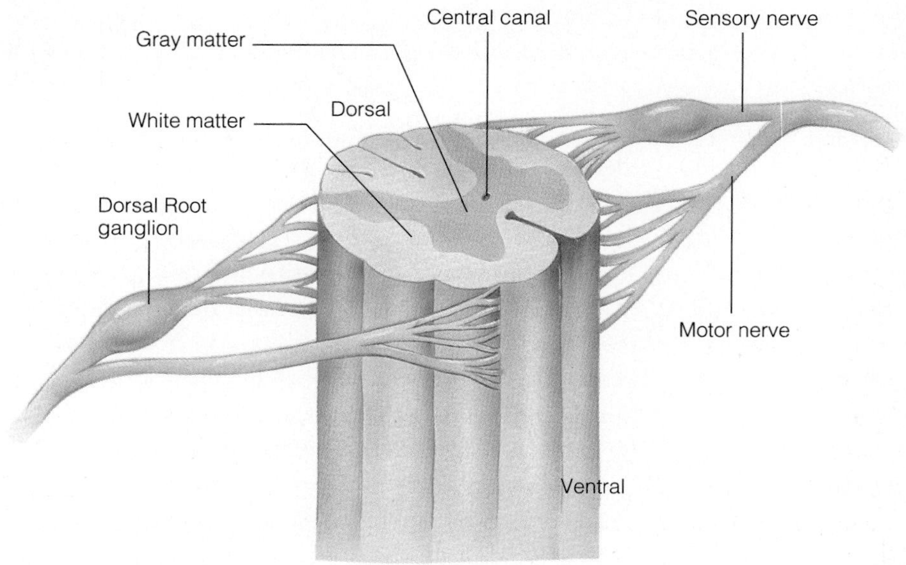

Figure 4.3
Diagram of a cross section through the spinal cord
The dorsal root on each side conveys sensory information to the spinal cord; the ventral root conveys motor commands to the muscles.

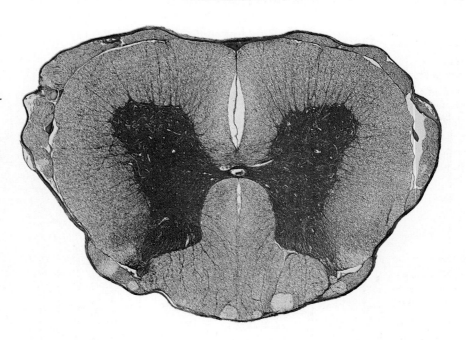

Gray matter

White matter

Central canal

Dorsal

Dorsal Root ganglion

Sensory nerve

Motor nerve

Ventral

Figure 4.4
Photo of a cross section through the spinal cord
The H-shaped structures in the center are gray matter, composed largely of cell bodies. The surrounding white matter is composed of axons. The axons are organized in tracts; some carry information from the brain and higher levels of the spinal cord downward, while others carry information from lower levels upward. (Manfred Kage/Peter Arnold, Inc.)

the muscles and glands. (This was one of the first discoveries about the functions of the nervous system.) The cell bodies of the sensory neurons are located outside the cord in the **dorsal root ganglia.** (A ganglion is a cluster of neurons outside the CNS.) Cell bodies of the motor neurons are located within the spinal cord.

Spinal Pathways

The sensory nerves that enter a segment of the spinal cord make synapses with interneurons within the spinal cord. These in turn make synapses with other interneurons and with motor neurons. In the cross section through the spinal cord shown in Figure 4.5, the H-shaped **gray matter** in the center of the cord is

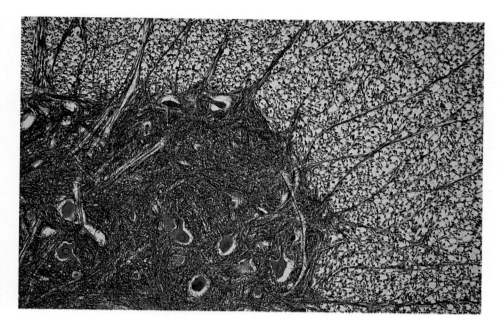

Figure 4.5
A section of gray matter of the spinal cord (lower left) and white matter surrounding it
Note that axons enter the gray matter from the white matter and extend from the gray matter into the white matter. (Manfred Kage/Peter Arnold, Inc.)

densely packed with cell bodies and dendrites, with few myelinated axons. Many of the interneurons' axons form branches that leave the gray matter and travel toward the brain in the white matter. The **white matter** is composed mostly of myelinated axons, which are white.

Each segment of the spinal cord contains neurons that communicate with a particular region of the body; it also contains spinal paths conveying messages between the segments above it and below it. If the spinal cord is cut, the brain loses sensation from and control over all parts of the body served by the spinal cord below the cut.

The Autonomic Nervous System

The autonomic nervous system is a set of neurons that receives information from and sends commands to the heart, intestines, and other organs. It is composed of two parts: the sympathetic and parasympathetic nervous systems (see Figure 4.6). The **sympathetic nervous system** consists of two paired chains of **ganglia** (collections of neuron cell bodies) lying just to the left and right of the spinal cord in its central regions (the thoracic and lumbar areas) and connected by axons to those spinal cord regions. *Postganglionic* axons extend from the sympathetic ganglia to the body's organs. The sympathetic nervous system prepares the body for "fight or flight" activities: It increases the heart rate and breathing rate and it decreases digestive activity. Because all the sympathetic ganglia are closely linked, they tend to act as a single system, "in sympathy" with one another.

The term *para* means *beside* or *related to;* the **parasympathetic nervous system** has functions that are related to, and generally opposite to, those of the sympathetic nervous system. Although the sympathetic and parasympathetic systems act in opposition to one another, they are usually both active at the same time, to varying degrees. At times, parts of one system may be highly active along with parts of the other system.

Basic Subdivisions of the Vertebrate Nervous System

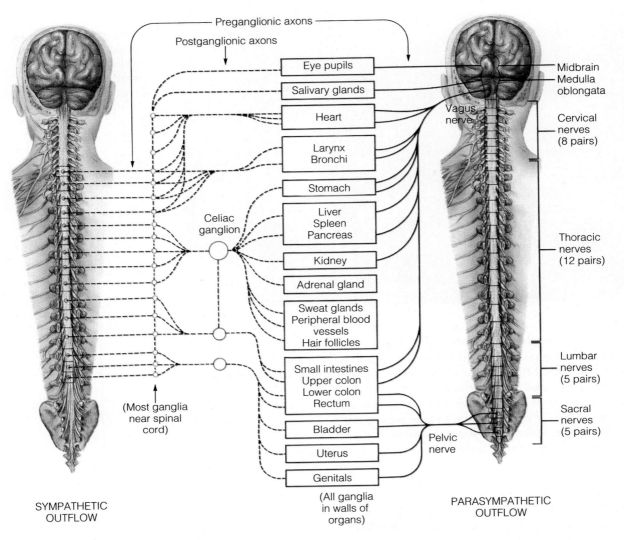

Figure 4.6
The sympathetic nervous system (dashed lines) and parasympathetic nervous system (solid lines)
(From Starr & Taggart, 1989.)

The parasympathetic nervous system is sometimes also known as the craniosacral system because its nerves originate from the cranial nerves and the sacral spinal cord (Figure 4.6). Unlike the ganglia in the sympathetic system, the parasympathetic ganglia are not arranged in a chain near the spinal cord. Rather, long *preganglionic* axons extend from the spinal cord to parasympathetic ganglia close to each internal organ; shorter *postganglionic* fibers then extend from the parasympathetic ganglia into the organs themselves. Because the parasympathetic ganglia are not linked to one another, they sometimes act more independently than the sympathetic ganglia do. Activity of the parasympathetic system decreases heart rate, increases digestive rate, and in general promotes energy-conserving, nonemergency functions.

The sweat glands, the adrenal glands, the muscles that constrict blood vessels, and the muscles that erect the hairs of the skin have sympathetic input

Chapter 4
Anatomy of the Nervous
System and Methods of
Investigation

102

Erection of the hairs, known as "gooseflesh" or "goose bumps," is controlled by the sympathetic nervous system. What does this response have to do with the "fight or flight" functions that are usually associated with the sympathetic nervous system?

Human body hairs are so short that erecting them accomplishes nothing of importance; the response is an evolutionary relic from ancient ancestors with furrier bodies. Erecting the hairs helps nonhuman mammals to conserve their body warmth in a cold environment by increasing their insulation. It also serves several species as a defense against enemies in fight or flight situations. Consider, for example, the

Halloween cat, or any other frightened, cornered animal; by erecting its hairs, it looks larger and may thereby deter its opponent.

The porcupine's quills, which are an effective defense against potential predators, are actually modified body hairs. In a fight or flight situation, sympathetic nervous system activity leads to erection of the quills, just as it leads to erection of the hairs in other mammals (Richter & Langworthy, 1933). The behavior that makes the quills so useful, their erection in response to fear, evidently evolved before the quills themselves did.

only. (See Digression 4.1.) Other organs are controlled by both the sympathetic and parasympathetic systems, generally in opposite directions. For example, the sympathetic nervous system increases heart rate; the parasympathetic nervous system decreases it. The parasympathetic nervous system increases digestive activity; the sympathetic nervous system decreases it.

The parasympathetic nervous system's postganglionic axons release the neurotransmitter acetylcholine. Most of the postganglionic synapses of the sympathetic nervous system use norepinephrine, although a few, such as the ones that control the sweat glands, use acetylcholine. Because the two systems use different transmitters, certain drugs may excite or inhibit one system or the other. For example, over-the-counter cold remedies exert their effects largely by blocking parasympathetic activity or by increasing sympathetic activity (which in turn competes with parasympathetic activity). This action is useful because the flow of sinus fluids is a parasympathetic response; thus, drugs that block the parasympathetic system inhibit sinus flow. The common side effects of cold remedies also stem from their tendency to decrease parasympathetic activities: The drugs inhibit salivation and digestion and increase heart rate.

The Hindbrain

The brain itself (as distinct from the spinal cord) consists of three major divisions: the hindbrain, the midbrain, and the forebrain. (See Figure 4.7 and Table 4.3.) Brain investigators—unfortunately—use a variety of terms synonymously. For example, instead of the English terms *hindbrain, midbrain,* and *forebrain,* some people prefer words with Greek roots: *rhombencephalon, mesencephalon,* and *prosencephalon.* In this text, we shall use the words with English roots, but you may encounter the Greek terms in other reading.

The **hindbrain** (the most posterior part of the brain) consists of the medulla, the pons, and the cerebellum. The medulla and pons, plus the midbrain and certain central structures of the forebrain, constitute the **brain stem** (see Figure 4.8).

Basic Subdivisions of the Vertebrate Nervous System

Figure 4.7
Three major divisions of the vertebrate brain.
The forebrain, midbrain, and hindbrain are clearly visible as separate bulges in the brain of a fish. In adult mammals, the forebrain grows so large that it surrounds the entire midbrain and part of the hindbrain.

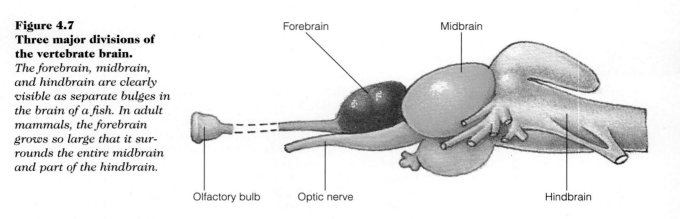

Forebrain Midbrain

Olfactory bulb Optic nerve Hindbrain

Table 4.3	Major Divisions of the Vertebrate Brain	
Area	*Also Known As*	*Structures*
Hindbrain	Rhombencephalon (literally, parallelogram-brain)	Medulla, pons, cerebellum
Midbrain	Mesencephalon (literally, middle-brain)	Tectum, tegmentum, superior colliculus, inferior colliculus, substantia nigra
Forebrain	Prosencephalon (literally, forward-brain)	
	Diencephalon (literally, between-brain)	Thalamus, hypothalamus
	Telencephalon (literally, end-brain)	Cerebral cortex, hippocampus, basal ganglia, other subcortical structures

The **medulla,** or medulla oblongata, is a structure just above the spinal cord; in many ways, it might be regarded as an enlarged, elaborated extension of the spinal cord, although it is located in the skull rather than in the spine. The medulla controls a number of vital reflexes—such as breathing, heart rate, vomiting, salivation, coughing, and sneezing—through the **cranial nerves.** Damage to the medulla is frequently fatal. Because of the vital importance of the medulla, large doses of drugs that affect the medulla—such as opiates or cocaine—can easily be fatal. In contrast, drugs that have little effect on the medulla—such as marijuana—seldom produce life-threatening effects, even though they produce major effects on other parts of the brain (Herkenham et al., 1990).

As the lower parts of the body are connected to the spinal cord via sensory and motor nerves, the skin and muscles of the head and internal organs are connected to the brain by twelve pairs (one right, one left) of cranial nerves.

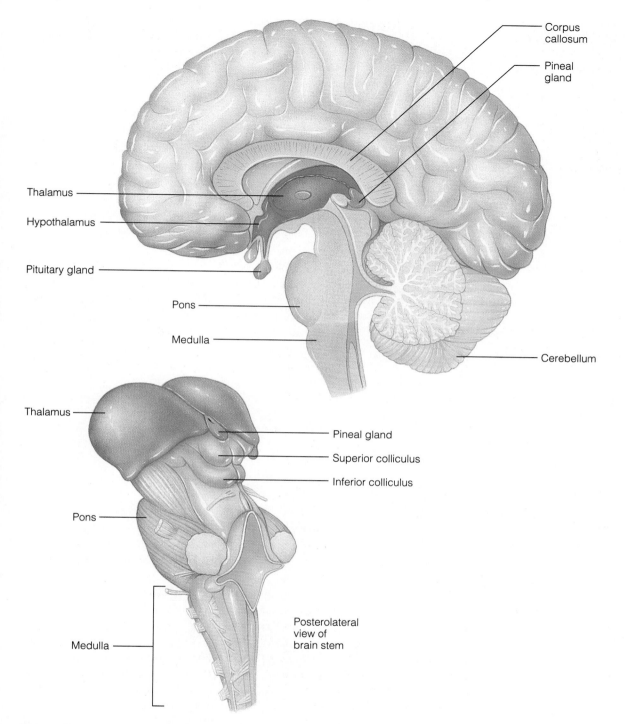

Figure 4.8
Midline structures of the human brain, with a separate drawing of the brain stem

Table 4.4   The Cranial Nerves

Number and Name	Function of Sensory Component	Function of Motor Component
I. Olfactory	Smell	(no motor nerve)
II. Optic	Vision	(no motor nerve)
III. Oculomotor	Sensations from eye muscles	Eye movements, pupil constriction
IV. Trochlear	Sensations from eye muscles	Eye movements
V. Trigeminal	Sensations from skin of face, nose, and mouth	Chewing, swallowing
VI. Abducens	Sensations from eye muscles	Eye movements
VII. Facial	Taste from the anterior two-thirds of the tongue, visceral sensations from the head	Facial expressions, crying, salivation, and dilation of blood vessels in the head
VIII. Statoacoustic	Hearing, equilibrium	(no motor nerve)
IX. Glossopharyngeal	Taste and other sensations from throat and posterior third of tongue	Swallowing, salivation, dilation of blood vessels
X. Vagus	Taste and sensations from neck, thorax, and abdomen	Swallowing, control of larynx, parasympathetic nerves to heart and viscera
XI. Accessory	(no sensory nerve)	Movements of shoulders and head; parasympathetic to viscera
XII. Hypoglossal	Sensation from tongue muscles	Movement of tongue

Figure 4.9
Cranial nerves II through XII
(Based on Braus, 1960.)

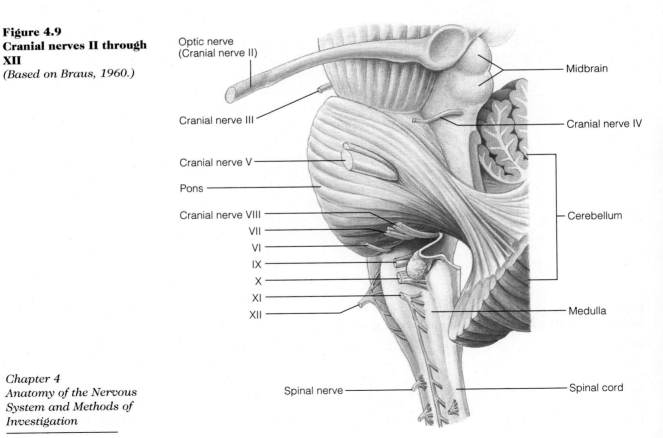

Optic nerve (Cranial nerve II)
Cranial nerve III
Cranial nerve V
Pons
Cranial nerve VIII
VII
VI
IX
X
XI
XII
Spinal nerve
Midbrain
Cranial nerve IV
Cerebellum
Medulla
Spinal cord

Most cranial nerves include both sensory and motor components, although some include just one or the other (see Table 4.4). Each cranial nerve originates in a **nucleus** (a cluster of neurons within the CNS) that integrates the sensory information and regulates the motor output. The cranial nerve nuclei for nerves V through XII are located in the medulla and pons of the hindbrain. Those for cranial nerves I through IV are located in the midbrain and forebrain (see Figure 4.9).

The **pons** lies anterior to the medulla; like the medulla, it contains the nuclei for several cranial nerves. The term *pons* is Latin for *bridge;* the name reflects the fact that many axons in the pons cross from the left side of the brain to the right, or from the right to the left.

The medulla and pons also contain the **reticular formation** and the **raphe system.** These systems send axons diffusely throughout the forebrain, controlling the overall state of nervous system arousal, as we shall see in Chapter 9.

The **cerebellum** is a large hindbrain structure with a great many deep folds. It is best known for its contributions to the control of movement, which will be discussed in Chapter 8. In addition, the lateral parts of the cerebellum contribute to the speed and skill of acquiring language and cognition (Leiner, Leiner, & Dow, 1989). That is, individuals with cerebellar damage sometimes have problems with their memory or finding the right word.

The Midbrain

The **midbrain** starts as the middle of the brain, although in mammals it is eventually dwarfed and surrounded by the forebrain. In birds, reptiles, amphibians, and fish, the midbrain is proportionately much larger than it is in mammals. The roof of the midbrain is called the **tectum.** (*Tectum* is the Latin word for *roof;* the same root shows up in the geological term *plate tectonics.*) The two swellings on each side of the tectum are the **superior colliculus** and the **inferior colliculus** (see Figures 4.8 and 4.12), both part of important routes for sensory information.

Under the tectum is the **tegmentum,** the dorsal part of the midbrain. (In Latin, *tegmentum* means a covering, such as a rug on the floor.) The tegmentum includes the nuclei for the third and fourth cranial nerves, parts of the reticular formation, and extensions of the pathways between the forebrain and the spinal cord or hindbrain. Another midbrain structure is the **substantia nigra,** an area whose cells and axons deteriorate in Parkinson's disease (see Chapter 8).

The Forebrain

The **forebrain** is the most anterior and prominent portion of the mammalian brain. The outer portion is the cerebral cortex. (*Cerebrum* means *brain; cortex* means *covering.*) Under the cerebral cortex lie other forebrain structures, including the thalamus, which provides the main source of input to the cerebral cortex. A set of structures known as the basal ganglia plays a major role in certain aspects of movement. A number of other structures, known as the **limbic system,** form a border (or limbus) around the brain stem. These structures,

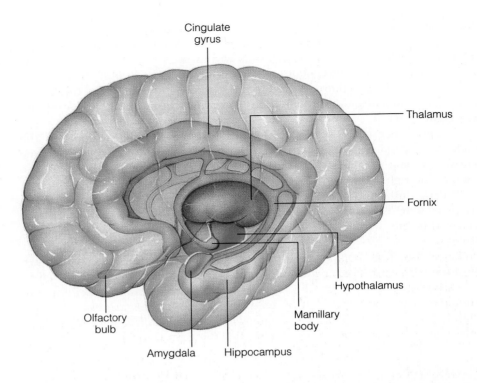

Cingulate gyrus

Thalamus

Fornix

Hypothalamus

Mamillary body

Hippocampus

Amygdala

Olfactory bulb

heavily linked with one another, are particularly important for motivated and emotional behaviors, such as eating, drinking, sexual behavior, anxiety, and aggressive behavior. The larger structures of the limbic system are the olfactory bulb, hypothalamus, hippocampus, amygdala, and cingulate gyrus of the cerebral cortex. Figure 4.10 shows the positions of these structures in a three-dimensional perspective. Figures 4.11 and 4.12 show coronal and sagittal sections through the human brain. Figure 4.11 also includes a view of the ventral surface of the brain.

In describing the forebrain, we shall begin with the subcortical areas and then examine the cerebral cortex in greater detail. Later chapters return to each of these areas.

Hypothalamus

The **hypothalamus** is a small area located near the base of the brain just ventral to the thalamus (see Figures 4.8 and 4.12). It has widespread connections with the rest of the forebrain and the midbrain. The hypothalamus contains a number of distinct nuclei. Damage to one of the hypothalamic nuclei leads to abnormalities in one or more motivated behaviors, such as feeding, drinking, temperature regulation, sexual behavior, fighting, or activity level.

The hypothalamus also regulates the secretion of hormones through its effects on the pituitary gland. The hypothalamus conveys messages to the pituitary gland, partly through nerves and partly through hypothalamic hormones, to alter the release of hormones by the pituitary.

Pituitary Gland

The **pituitary gland** is an **endocrine** (hormone-producing) **gland** attached to the base of the hypothalamus by a stalk that contains neurons, blood vessels,

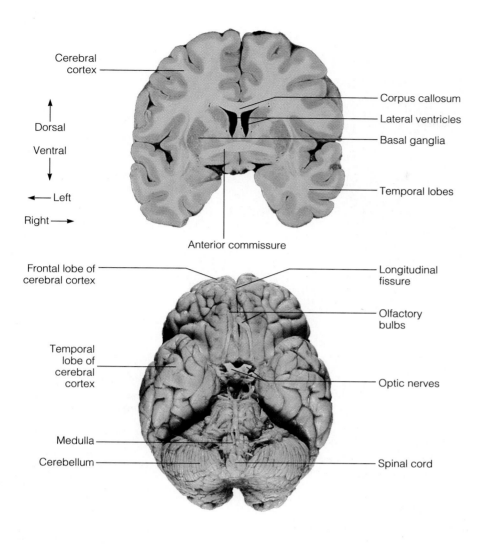

Figure 4.11
Views of the human brain.
Top: Coronal section.
Bottom: Ventral surface.
The optic nerves are the nerves from the eyes to the brain. (Photos courtesy of Dr. Dana Copeland.)

Cerebral cortex

Dorsal

Ventral

Left

Right

Corpus callosum

Lateral ventricles

Basal ganglia

Temporal lobes

Anterior commissure

Frontal lobe of cerebral cortex

Temporal lobe of cerebral cortex

Medulla

Cerebellum

Longitudinal fissure

Olfactory bulbs

Optic nerves

Spinal cord

and connective tissue (see Figure 4.8). In response to messages from the hypothalamus, the pituitary synthesizes and releases hormones into the bloodstream, which carries them to other organs. The pituitary is sometimes called the "master gland" of the body because its secretions control the timing and amount of hormone secretion by the other endocrine organs, such as the thyroid, the adrenal glands, and the ovaries or testes.

Basal Ganglia

The **basal ganglia,** a group of subcortical structures left and right of the thalamus, include three major structures: the caudate nucleus, the putamen, and the globus pallidus (see Figure 4.13). Some authorities include several other structures as well.

The basal ganglia are damaged in Parkinson's disease, Huntington's disease, and other conditions that impair the control of movement. The basal ganglia do not control movement directly, however; they send no axons directly to the medulla or spinal cord. Rather, they send messages to the thalamus and the

Basic Subdivisions of the Vertebrate Nervous System

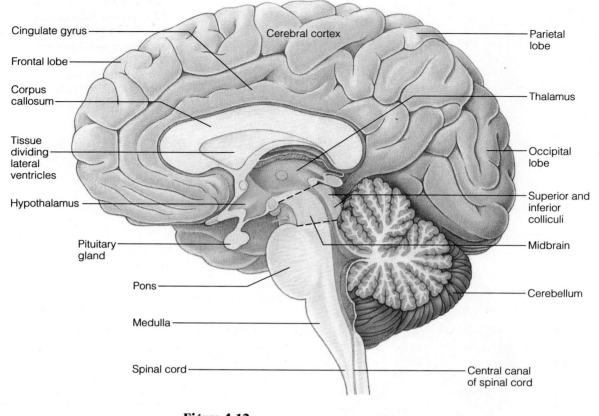

Cingulate gyrus

Frontal lobe

Corpus callosum

Tissue dividing lateral ventricles

Hypothalamus

Pituitary gland

Pons

Medulla

Spinal cord

Cerebral cortex

Parietal lobe

Thalamus

Occipital lobe

Superior and inferior colliculi

Midbrain

Cerebellum

Central canal of spinal cord

Figure 4.12
A sagittal section through the human brain
(After Nieuwenhuys et al., 1988.)

midbrain, which relay information to the cerebral cortex, which in turn sends messages to the medulla or spinal cord. The basal ganglia also contribute to speech and other complex behaviors (Damasio, 1983).

Hippocampus

The **hippocampus** (from a Latin word meaning *sea horse*) is a large structure between the thalamus and the cerebral cortex, mostly toward the posterior of the forebrain, as shown in Figure 4.10. Two major axon tracts, the **fornix** and the **fimbria**, link the hippocampus with the hypothalamus and several other structures. (The fornix was named after an ancient Roman arch that was a famous gathering place for prostitutes. That arch also gave us the word *fornication*.) We consider the role of the hippocampus in memory in Chapter 13.

Thalamus

The **thalamus** resembles two footballs joined side by side. The term *thalamus* was derived from a Greek word meaning *anteroom, inner chamber,* or *bridal bed* (Jones, 1985). One nucleus of the thalamus is called the *pulvinar,* meaning *pillow;* it is shaped a little like a pillow on the bridal bed. (The neu-

Chapter 4
Anatomy of the Nervous
System and Methods of
Investigation

110

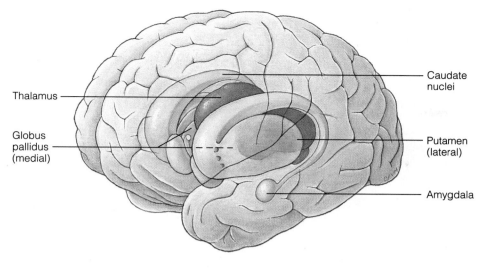

Figure 4.13
The basal ganglia
(After Nieuwenhuys et al., 1988.)

Thalamus

Globus
pallidus
(medial)

Caudate
nuclei

Putamen
(lateral)

Amygdala

roanatomists from long ago who came up with these names thought they were talking dirty.)

The thalamus is the main source of input to the cerebral cortex and almost the only source of sensory information. A few other subcortical areas send axons to the cortex, but most of their information controls arousal and attention rather than sensation (Foote & Morrison, 1987).

Some investigators have described the thalamus as a way station for information going to the cerebral cortex. It is much more than just a passive relay, however. The sensory information has been processed through other synapses before it reaches the thalamus, and it is processed again in the thalamus before being sent to the cortex.

Each nucleus of the thalamus sends its axons to, and receives axons from, a particular part of the cerebral cortex. Figure 4.14 diagrams the routes of axons from five of the many thalamic nuclei. We shall consider the cerebral cortex in more detail because of its great size and importance in the human brain.

The Ventricles

The cerebral **ventricles** are fluid-filled cavities within the brain. The nervous system begins its development as a tube surrounding a fluid canal. The canal persists into adulthood as the **central canal** of the spinal cord and, with much expansion, as the ventricles of the brain. Two large lateral ventricles are located within the two hemispheres of the forebrain (see Figure 4.15). Toward the posterior, they connect to the third ventricle, which connects to the fourth ventricle in the medulla.

The ventricles and the central canal of the spinal cord contain **cerebrospinal fluid (CSF)**, a clear fluid similar to blood plasma. CSF is formed by a group of cells called the *choroid plexus,* located inside the four ventricles. CSF flows from the lateral ventricles to the third and then to the fourth ventricle. From the fourth ventricle, part flows into the central canal of the spinal cord, but the larger part goes through an opening into the thin **subarachnoid space,**

Basic Subdivisions of the Vertebrate Nervous System

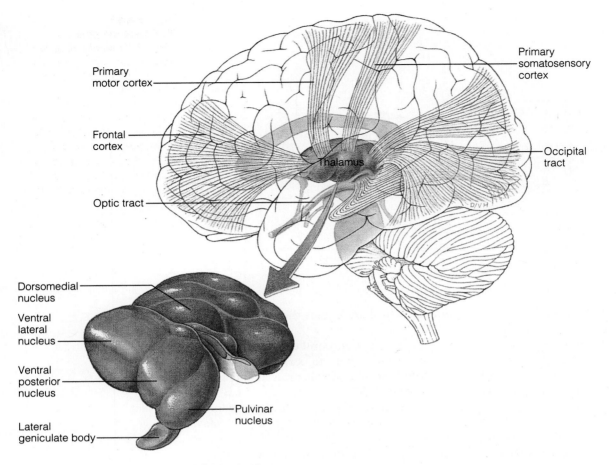

Primary motor cortex

Frontal cortex

Optic tract

Thalamus

Primary somatosensory cortex

Occipital tract

Dorsomedial nucleus

Ventral lateral nucleus

Ventral posterior nucleus

Lateral geniculate body

Pulvinar nucleus

Figure 4.14
Routes of information from some specific nuclei of the thalamus to limited areas of the cerebral cortex
(After Nieuwenhuys et al., 1988.)

between the brain and one of the thin membranes that surround it. From the subarachnoid space, CSF is gradually reabsorbed into the blood vessels of the brain.

Cerebrospinal fluid cushions the brain against mechanical shock when the head moves. It also provides buoyancy; just as a person weighs less in water than on land, the cerebrospinal fluid helps to support the weight of the brain. The CSF also provides a reservoir of hormones and nutrition for the brain and spinal cord.

Sometimes the flow of CSF is obstructed and it accumulates within the ventricles or in the subarachnoid space, thus increasing the pressure on the brain. When this occurs in infants, the skull bones may spread, causing an overgrown head. This condition, known as **hydrocephalus** (HI-dro-SEFF-ah-luss), is usually associated with mental retardation.

Chapter 4
Anatomy of the Nervous
System and Methods of
Investigation

112

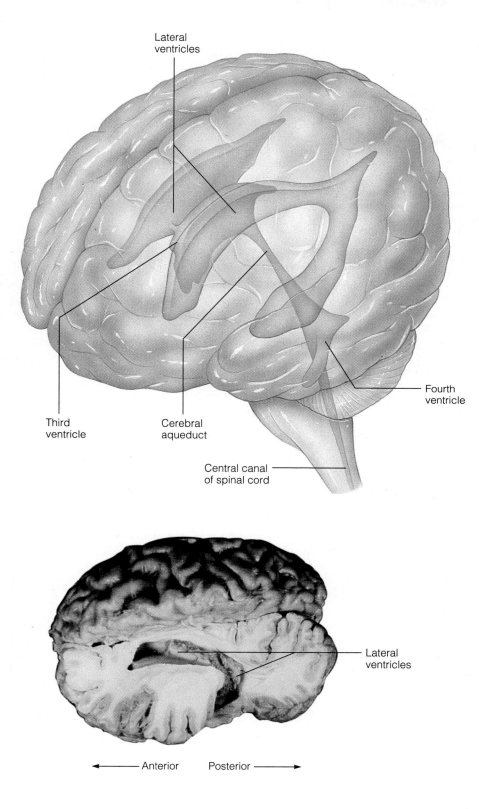

Lateral
ventricles

Third
ventricle

Cerebral
aqueduct

Central canal
of spinal cord

Fourth
ventricle

Lateral
ventricles

◄——— Anterior   Posterior ———►

Figure 4.15
The cerebral ventricles
Top: Diagram showing positions of the four ventricles. Bottom: Photo of a human brain, viewed from above, with a horizontal cut through one hemisphere to show the position of the lateral ventricle. Note that the two parts of this figure are seen from different angles. (Photo courtesy of Dr. Dana Copeland.)

Summary

1. The main divisions of the vertebrate nervous system are the central nervous system and the peripheral nervous system. The central nervous system consists of the spinal cord, the hindbrain, the midbrain, and the forebrain. (p. 96)

2. Each segment of the spinal cord has a sensory nerve on each side and a motor nerve on each side. Several spinal pathways convey information to the brain. (p. 98)

3. The sympathetic nervous system (one of the two divisions of the autonomic nervous system) activates the body's internal organs for vigorous activities. The parasympathetic system promotes digestion and other nonemergency processes. (p. 101)

4. The hindbrain consists of the medulla, pons, and cerebellum. The medulla and pons control breathing, heart rate, and other vital functions through the cranial nerves. The cerebellum contributes to movement. (p. 103)

5. The subcortical areas of the forebrain include the hypothalamus, pituitary gland, basal ganglia, hippocampus, and thalamus. (p. 107)

6. Each area of the cerebral cortex receives input from a nucleus of the thalamus. The thalamus processes that information before sending it to the cortex. (p. 111)

Review Questions

1. What are the functions of the sympathetic and parasympathetic nervous systems? Where are their ganglia located? (p. 101)

2. Why do certain drugs excite either the sympathetic or the parasympathetic nervous system but not the other? (p. 103)

3. Name the principal structures of the hindbrain and the midbrain. (p. 103)

4. What do the cranial nerves do? (p. 104)

5. Cover the labels in Figures 4.10 through 4.14 and identify the structures shown. (p. 108)

6. Which subcortical area is the main source of input to the cerebral cortex? (p. 110)

7. What do the ventricles contain? (p. 111)

Thought Question

1. The drug phenylephrine is sometimes prescribed for people suffering from a sudden loss of blood pressure and for other medical disorders. It acts by stimulating norepinephrine synapses, including those that constrict blood vessels. One common side effect of this drug is gooseflesh. Explain why. What other side effects might the person expect to experience?

Suggestions for Further Reading

Blakemore, C. (1977). *Mechanics of the mind.* New York: Cambridge University Press. An interesting, highly readable introduction to brain functioning.

Goldberg, S. (1979). *Clinical neuroanatomy made ridiculously simple.* Miami: Medmaster. A short paperback reviewing features of the human CNS that are most important in medicine.

Terms

neuroanatomy the anatomy of the nervous system (p. 95)

invertebrate animal lacking a backbone (p. 96)

central nervous system (CNS) the brain and the spinal cord (p. 96)

peripheral nervous system (PNS) nerves outside the brain and spinal cord (p. 96)

somatic nervous system nerves that convey messages from the sense organs to the CNS and from the CNS to muscles and glands (p. 96)

autonomic nervous system set of neurons that regulates functioning of the internal organs (p. 96)

dorsal toward the back, away from the ventral (stomach) side (p. 98)

ventral toward the stomach, away from the dorsal (back) side (p. 98)

anterior toward the front end (p. 98)

posterior toward the rear end (p. 98)

rostral toward the head, or toward the front of the head (where the nostrils are) (p. 98)

caudal toward the rear, away from the head (p. 98)

superior above another part (p. 98)

inferior below another part (p. 98)

lateral toward the side, away from the midline (p. 98)

medial toward the midline, away from the side (p. 98)

proximal located close (approximate) to the point of origin or attachment (p. 98)

distal located more distant from the point of origin or attachment (p. 98)

ipsilateral on the same side of the body (left or right) (p. 98)

contralateral on the opposite side of the body (left or right) (p. 98)

coronal plane a plane that shows brain structures as they would be seen from the front (p. 98)

sagittal plane a plane that shows brain structures as they would be seen from the side (p. 98)

horizontal plane a plane that shows brain structures as they would be seen from above (p. 98)

spinal cord portion of the central nervous system found within the spinal column (p. 98)

Bell-Magendie law observation that the dorsal roots of the spinal cord carry sensory information and that the ventral roots carry motor information toward the muscles and glands (p. 98)

lamina a row or layer of cell bodies separated from other cell bodies by a layer of axons and dendrites (p. 99)

column a set of cells perpendicular to the surface of the cortex (p. 99)

tract a set of axons within the CNS (p. 99)

nerve a set of axons in the periphery, either from the CNS to a muscle or gland, or from a sensory organ to the CNS (p. 99)

nucleus a cluster of neuron cell bodies within the CNS (p. 99)

ganglion a cluster of neuron cell bodies, usually outside the CNS (as in the sympathetic nervous system), or any cluster of neurons in an invertebrate species (p. 99)

gyrus (plural: **gyri**) a protuberance on the surface of the brain (p. 99)

sulcus (plural: **sulci**) a fold or groove that separates one gyrus from another (p. 99)

fissure a long, deep sulcus (p. 99)

dorsal root ganglion set of sensory neuron somas on the dorsal side of the spinal cord (p. 100)

gray matter areas of the nervous system with a high density of cell bodies and dendrites, with few myelinated axons (p. 100)

white matter area of the nervous system consisting mostly of myelinated axons (p. 101)

sympathetic nervous system network of nerves innervating the internal organs that prepare the body for vigorous activity (p. 101)

ganglion (plural: **ganglia**) a cluster of neuron cell bodies (p. 101)

parasympathetic nervous system system of nerves innervating the internal organs, tending to conserve energy (p. 101)

hindbrain most posterior part of the brain, including the medulla, pons, and cerebellum (p. 103)

brain stem the hindbrain, midbrain, and posterior central structures of the forebrain (p. 103)

medulla hindbrain structure located just above the spinal cord (p. 104)

cranial nerve part of a set of nerves controlling sensory and motor information of the head, connecting to nuclei in the medulla, pons, midbrain, or forebrain (p. 104)

nucleus a cluster of neurons within the central nervous system (p. 107)

pons hindbrain structure, anterior or ventral to the medulla (p. 107)

reticular formation network of neurons in the medulla and higher brain areas, important for behavioral arousal (p. 107)

raphe system group of neurons in the pons and medulla whose axons extend throughout much of the forebrain (p. 107)

cerebellum a large, highly convoluted structure in the hindbrain (p. 107)

midbrain middle part of the brain, including superior colliculus, inferior colliculus, tectum, and tegmentum (p. 107)

tectum roof of the midbrain (p. 107)

superior colliculus midbrain structure active in vision, visuomotor coordination, and other processes (p. 107)

inferior colliculus part of the auditory system located in the midbrain (p. 107)

tegmentum dorsal part of the midbrain (p. 107)

substantia nigra midbrain area that gives rise to a dopamine-containing pathway (p. 107)

forebrain the most anterior part of the brain, including the cerebral cortex and other structures (p. 107)

limbic system interconnected set of subcortical structures in the forebrain, including the hypothalamus, hippocampus, amygdala, olfactory bulb, septum, other small structures, and parts of the thalamus and cerebral cortex (p. 107)

hypothalamus forebrain structure located just ventral to the thalamus (p. 108)

pituitary gland endocrine gland whose secretions regulate the activity of many other hormonal glands (p. 108)

endocrine gland gland that releases hormones (p. 108)

basal ganglia set of subcortical forebrain structures including the caudate nucleus, putamen, and globus pallidus (p. 109)

hippocampus large forebrain structure between the thalamus and cortex (p. 110)

fornix tract of axons connecting the hippocampus with the hypothalamus and other areas (p. 110)

fimbria band of axons along the medial surface of the hippocampus (p. 110)

thalamus structure in the center of the forebrain (p. 110)

ventricle any of the four fluid-filled cavities in the brain (p. 111)

central canal fluid-filled channel in the center of the spinal cord (p. 111)

cerebrospinal fluid (CSF) liquid similar to blood serum, found in the ventricles of the brain and in the central canal of the spinal cord (p. 111)

subarachnoid space area beneath the arachnoid membrane that surrounds the nervous system (p. 111)

hydrocephalus accumulation of excessive fluid in the head (p. 112)

The Cerebral Cortex

The surface of the forebrain consists of two cerebral hemispheres, one on the left side and one on the right, covering all the other forebrain structures (Figure 4.16). Each hemisphere is organized to receive sensory information mostly from the contralateral (opposite) side of the body and to control muscles mostly on the contralateral side through axons to the spinal cord and the cranial nerve nuclei.

The cellular layers on the outer surface of the cerebral hemispheres form gray matter known as the **cerebral cortex** (from the Latin word *cortex,* meaning *bark*). Large numbers of axons extend inward from the cortex, forming the white matter of the cerebral hemispheres (Figure 4.11). Neurons in each hemisphere communicate with neurons in the corresponding part of the other hemisphere by two bundles of axons, the **corpus callosum** (Figures 4.11, 4.12, and 4.16) and the smaller **anterior commissure** (Figure 4.11). (Several other commissures link subcortical structures.)

Organization of the Cerebral Cortex

The microscopic structure of the cells of the cerebral cortex varies substantially from one cortical area to another. These differences in appearance relate to differences in function. Much of the research on the cerebral cortex has been directed toward understanding the relationship between structure and function.

Laminae and Columns of the Cerebral Cortex

The cerebral cortex of humans and most other mammals contains up to six distinct **laminae,** layers of cell bodies parallel to the surface of the cortex and separated from each other by fiber layers (see Figure 4.17). The laminae vary in thickness and prominence from one area of the cortex to another, and a given lamina may be absent from certain parts of the cortex. Lamina V, which sends long axons to the spinal cord and other distant areas, is thickest in the motor cortex, the area with the greatest control of the muscles. Lamina IV, which receives axons from the various sensory nuclei of the thalamus, is prominent in all the primary sensory areas (visual, auditory, and somatosensory), but absent from the motor cortex. Anecdotal reports have found lamina IV to be

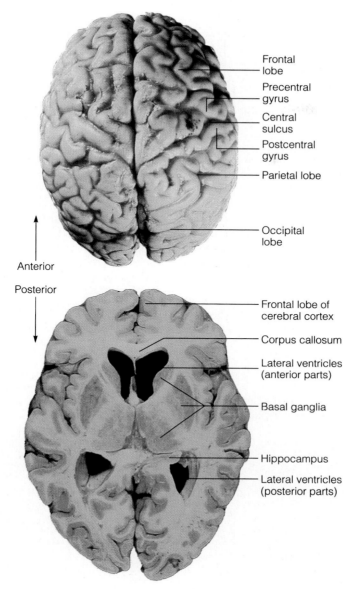

Figure 4.16
Dorsal view of the brain surface and a horizontal section through the brain
(Photos courtesy of Dr. Dana Copeland.)

Frontal lobe

Precentral gyrus

Central sulcus

Postcentral gyrus

Parietal lobe

Occipital lobe

Anterior

Posterior

Frontal lobe of cerebral cortex

Corpus callosum

Lateral ventricles (anterior parts)

Basal ganglia

Hippocampus

Lateral ventricles (posterior parts)

even thicker than normal in the visual cortex of a person with "photographic memory" and in the auditory cortex of a musician with "perfect pitch" (Scheibel, 1984).

The cells of the cortex are also organized into **columns** of cells perpendicular to the laminae (Mountcastle, 1957). (See Figure 4.18.) The cells within a given column have similar or related properties. For example, if one cell in a given column responds to touch on the palm of the left hand, then the other cells in that column also respond to touch on the palm of the left hand. If one cell responds to a particular pattern of light at a particular location in the retina, then the other cells in that column respond to the same pattern of light in the same location.

The Cerebral Cortex

Figure 4.17
**The six laminae of the
human cerebral cortex**
*(Adapted from Ranson &
Clark, 1959.)*

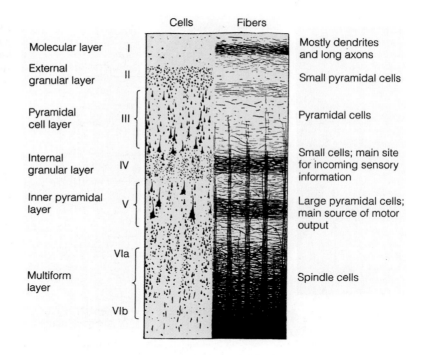

Cells   Fibers

Molecular layer	I	Mostly dendrites and long axons
External granular layer	II	Small pyramidal cells
Pyramidal cell layer	III	Pyramidal cells
Internal granular layer	IV	Small cells; main site for incoming sensory information
Inner pyramidal layer	V	Large pyramidal cells; main source of motor output
Multiform layer	VIa / VIb	Spindle cells

**Figure 4.18
Columns in the cerebral
cortex**
*Each column extends
through several laminae.
Neurons within a given column have similar proper-
ties. For example, in the
somatosensory cortex, all the
neurons within a given column respond to stimulation
of the same area of skin.*

Surface of cortex

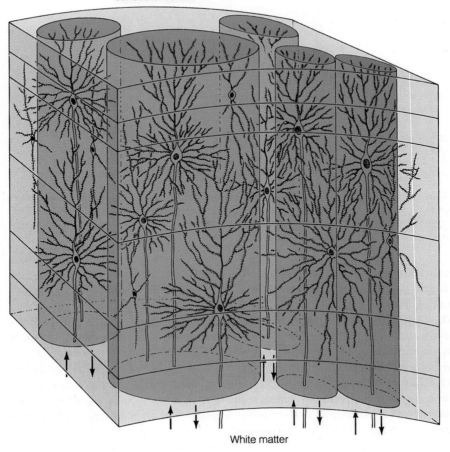

White matter

*Chapter 4
Anatomy of the Nervous
System and Methods of
Investigation*

118

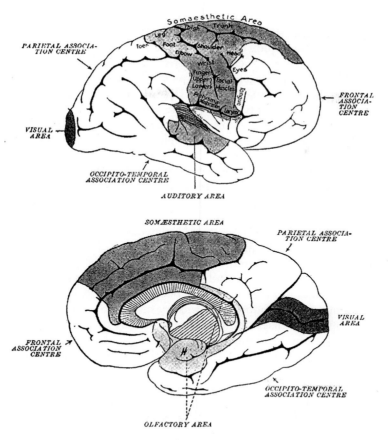

Figure 4.19
An illustration from an old introductory psychology textbook (Hunter, 1923)
Note the designation of certain areas as "association areas." Neuroscientists used to believe that information went first to the cortex's sensory areas, which relayed it to association areas, which then sent commands to the motor areas. Today's researchers are more likely to label those so-called association areas as "additional sensory areas," because they get most of their input from thalamic sensory areas.

Sensory, Motor, and Association Areas of Cortex

Many authorities divide the cerebral cortex into three types of areas: sensory areas, motor areas, and association areas (Figure 4.19). This division reflects some assumptions and interpretations about the brain that were popular long ago. Although this idea is not exactly right, it is not exactly wrong, either. It is, however, misleading.

The original reasoning behind the sensory-motor-association distinction went as follows: The brain has distinct sensory and motor areas. For example, visual information from the thalamus goes directly to the primary visual cortex. Damage to the primary visual cortex in the human brain results in blindness. The primary auditory cortex and primary somatosensory cortex play analogously central roles for hearing and the skin senses. We can also distinguish certain motor areas in the cortex; damage to those areas impairs movement in various ways. After accounting for the primary sensory and motor areas, we have certain other areas "left over." Damage to those areas does not lead to complete loss of any sense, nor does it produce paralysis. So what do those areas do? Perhaps, the reasoning went, those areas "associate." They link vision with hearing, or hearing with touch, or touch with taste, or whatnot; or they link current sensory impressions with memories of previous experiences. This description fit with a commonsense view of what the mind does:

The Cerebral Cortex

First it gets sensory information, then it "thinks" about it, then it acts. The idea of an association cortex quickly became popular because it matched the popular view of the mind (Zeki, 1993).

But does the association cortex really associate? Well, not exactly. The association areas engage in more elaborate processing of information than the primary sensory areas do (Van Hoesen, 1993). However, the association cortexes do not associate, or link, one kind of sensory information with another, as the original idea specified. For example, the association cortex next to the primary visual cortex consists of cells that are responsive to visual information; few if any of its cells respond selectively to anything other than visual information. Similarly, the association cortex next to the primary auditory cortex consists of cells that are responsive to auditory information.

Furthermore, the input to the "association" areas does not come exclusively from other areas of the cerebral cortex, as neuroanatomists of an earlier era once supposed. These areas receive some input from other cortical areas, to be sure, but they also receive much input directly from sensory areas of the thalamus (I. T. Diamond, 1979, 1983).

You will continue to find a number of books and articles today that use the term *association cortex*. In this book, however, I shall generally refer to those cortical areas as "additional sensory areas" to avoid the implication that they link different senses or contribute especially to thinking and reasoning.

"But, then," you might ask, "what about the idea that the sensory areas get the sensation, the association areas think about it, and the motor cortex acts? If the association cortex doesn't think about the information, what area does?" We find ourselves back discussing the mind-brain question, as we did in Chapter 1. The answer is that, so far as we can determine, thinking does not depend on any single spot in the cortex and maybe not entirely on the cortex. The brain has no single site at which all information funnels into a hidden observer—a "little person in the brain"—who unifies all the information. Thinking, or "information processing," depends on separate, simultanous processes throughout the brain.

We now turn to some of the specialized functions of different parts of the cortex. We can distinguish fifty or more areas of the cerebral cortex, based on differences in the thickness of the six laminae and on the appearance of cells and fibers within each lamina. For convenience of discussion, however, we shall group these areas into four *lobes* named for the skull bones that lie over them: occipital, parietal, temporal, and frontal.

Occipital Lobe

The **occipital lobe**, located at the posterior (caudal) end of the cortex (Figure 4.20), is the main target for axons from the thalamic nuclei that receive input from the visual pathways. The very posterior pole of the occipital lobe is known as the *primary visual cortex* or as the *striate cortex* because of its striped appearance in cross section. Destruction of any part of the striate cortex causes loss of vision in part of the visual field. The location of the damage determines which part of the visual field will become blind. For example, extensive damage to the striate cortex of the right hemisphere causes blindness in the left visual field (the left side of the world from the viewer's perspective). Blindness from occipital lobe damage is called *cortical blindness*. A person with

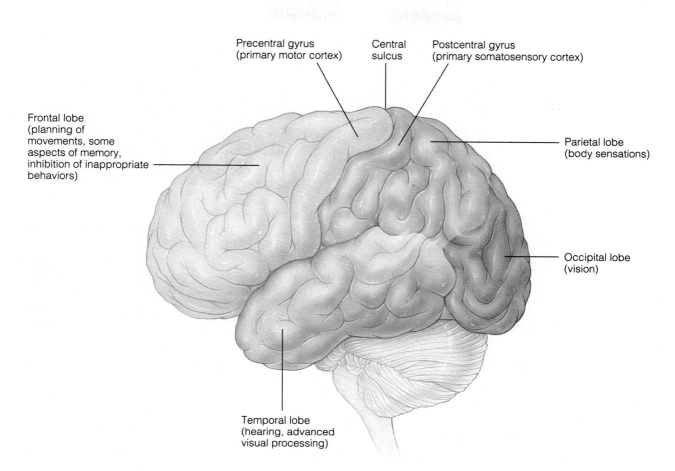

Precentral gyrus (primary motor cortex)

Central sulcus

Postcentral gyrus (primary somatosensory cortex)

Frontal lobe (planning of movements, some aspects of memory, inhibition of inappropriate behaviors)

Parietal lobe (body sensations)

Occipital lobe (vision)

Temporal lobe (hearing, advanced visual processing)

Figure 4.20
Some major subdivisions of the human cerebral cortex, with indications of a few of their primary functions

cortical blindness has normal eyes, normal pupillary reflexes, and some eye movements, but no pattern perception and no awareness of visual information.

Parietal Lobe

The **parietal lobe** lies between the occipital lobe and the **central sulcus,** one of the deepest grooves in the surface of the cortex (see Figure 4.20). The parietal lobe is specialized primarily for dealing with body information, including touch, muscle-stretch receptors, and joint receptors.

The area just posterior to the central sulcus, called the **postcentral gyrus** or the *primary somatosensory cortex,* is the primary target for touch sensations and other skin and muscle information. Direct electrical stimulation of the postcentral gyrus evokes sensations on the opposite side of the body, often described as tingling or unnatural sensations.

The postcentral gyrus includes four bands of cells running parallel to the central sulcus. Along each band are separate areas that receive information from different parts of the body, as Figure 4.21a shows. Two of the bands receive mostly light-touch information, one receives deep-pressure informa-

The Cerebral Cortex

Figure 4.21
**Organization of (a) sensory
areas of the postcentral
gyrus and (b) motor areas
of the precentral gyrus**
*Each location along either
gyrus is primarily involved
in sensations or motor control for one area in the opposite half of the body. (After
Penfield & Rasmussen,
1950.)*

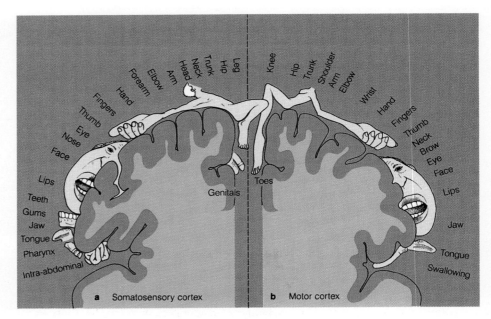

tion, and one receives a combination of both (Kaas, Nelson, Sur, Lin, & Merzenich, 1979). That is, the postcentral gyrus contains four separate representations of the body.

The representation of the body in the postcentral gyrus varies from one species to another and even from one individual to another (Cusick, Wall, & Kaas, 1986). The representation of the paws is unusually large in raccoons; the representation of the snout is unusually large in rats. The pattern for bats, which use their feet to hang upside down and their forelimbs as wings instead of legs, is quite distorted compared with the one shown in Figure 4.21 (Calford, Graydon, Huerta, Kaas, & Pettigrew, 1985).

Following damage to the parietal lobe, people do not completely lose the sense of touch, or the muscle and joint senses, at least not permanently. Rather, they suffer a variety of symptoms that suggest difficulty in interpreting such information and in using it to control movement (J. C. Lynch, 1980). Some common symptoms include:

1. Impairment of ability to identify objects by touch. For example, a blind person who suffers damage to the parietal lobe loses the ability to read Braille (Gloning, Gloning, Weingarten, & Berner, 1954).
2. Clumsiness on the side of the body opposite the damage.
3. Neglect of the opposite side of the body, especially neglect of the left side after right-hemisphere parietal lobe damage (Bisiach & Luzzatti, 1978; Levine, Warach, Benowitz, & Calvanio, 1986). People with such damage may fail to dress the left side of the body, read only the right side of a page, and describe from memory only the right side of a familiar scene. When asked to draw an object, they generally draw only its right side. When asked to draw a mark to divide a line in half, they draw the mark well to the right side of the line (ignoring or distorting the left side), unless the line is very short (Marshall & Halligan, 1990). (See Figure 4.22.)

*Chapter 4
Anatomy of the Nervous
System and Methods of
Investigation*

122

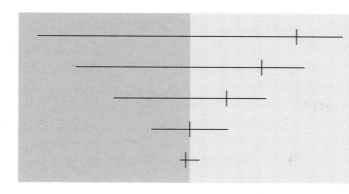

4. Distortion of body image. One young man suffered damage to his parietal lobe in an automobile accident. After recovering from the immediate effects of the injury, he began to complain about sensations from his left eye. In fact, both eyes were normal and both had 20/20 vision. He nevertheless demanded surgical removal of the eye, threatened suicide when surgeons refused to remove it, and eventually tried (unsuccessfully) to remove the eye himself with a pellet gun (Dalby, Arboleda-Florez, & Seland, 1989).
5. Inability to draw and follow maps, describe how to get somewhere, or say what something might look like when viewed from a different angle.

The parietal cortex is also important for relating visual information to spatial information. Certain parietal cells may be responsible for your knowing that something you have looked at is still the same object after you have tilted your head and looked at it from a different angle (Andersen, Essick, & Siegel, 1985). After parietal lobe damage, a person may find it necessary to focus directly on an object with the center of the retina to identify it (J. C. Lynch, 1980). To recognize a group of objects, such a person must look at the objects one at a time.

Temporal Lobe

The **temporal lobe** is located laterally in each hemisphere, near the temples (see Figure 4.20). It is the primary cortical target for auditory information. In humans, the temporal lobe—especially the left temporal lobe in most cases—is essential for understanding spoken language.

The temporal lobe also contributes to some of the more complex aspects of vision, including perception of complex patterns such as faces. A tumor in the temporal lobe may give rise to elaborate visual hallucinations, whereas a tumor in the occipital lobe ordinarily evokes only simple sensations, such as flashes of light. In humans, the left temporal lobe is also important for the comprehension of language.

The temporal lobes also play a part in emotional and motivational behaviors. Temporal lobe damage can lead to a set of behaviors known as the **Klüver-Bucy syndrome** (named for the investigators who first described it). Monkeys with damaged temporal lobes fail to display normal fears and anxieties (Klüver & Bucy, 1939). Previously wild and aggressive monkeys can be handled easily

Squirrel monkey

Cat

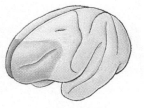

Rhesus monkey

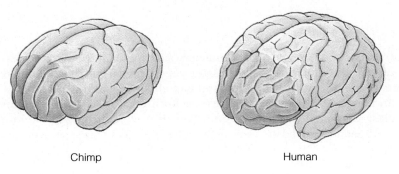

Dog

Chimp

Human

Figure 4.23
The prefrontal cortex (shaded area) in the brains of six species
Note that the prefrontal cortex constitutes a larger proportion of the human brain than of the brains of these other species. The human midbrain is not visible from the outside because the forebrain covers it. (After Fuster, 1989.)

after such surgery. They put almost anything they find into their mouths. They attempt to pick up snakes and lighted matches (which intact monkeys consistently avoid). It is hard to determine how much of this behavior results from an emotional change and how much from a visual deficit. For example, a monkey might handle a snake because it is no longer afraid of snakes or because it does not recognize what the snake is.

Frontal Lobe

The **frontal lobe** (which contains the motor cortex and the prefrontal cortex) extends from the central sulcus to the anterior limit of the brain (see Figure 4.20). The posterior portion of the frontal lobe is the **precentral gyrus,** which is specialized for the control of fine movements, such as moving one finger at a time. It has separate areas responsible for different parts of the body (Figure 4.21), mostly on the contralateral side of the body, but with slight control of the ipsilateral side, too.

The most anterior portion of the frontal lobe, the **prefrontal cortex,** is a fairly large structure, especially in species with a large brain overall, such as humans (Figure 4.23). It is not the primary target for any single sensory system, but it receives information from all the sensory systems, including sensations from the interior of the body. The prefrontal cortex is the only cortical area known to receive input from all sensory modalities (Stuss & Benson, 1984).

The prefrontal cortex was the target of **prefrontal lobotomies,** an infamous type of brain surgery conducted in attempts to control certain types of psychological disorder (see Digression 4.2). As a consequence of the surgery, people generally lost their initiative and failed to inhibit socially unacceptable impulses. They also showed impairments in certain aspects of memory and in their facial expressions of emotion.

In the late 1940s and early 1950s, about 40,000 **prefrontal lobotomies** were performed in the United States (Shutts, 1982). The operation consists of damaging the prefrontal cortex or cutting the connections between the prefrontal cortex and the rest of the cortex. The impetus to performing this operation was a report that damage to the prefrontal cortex of primates in the laboratory had made them tamer without impairing their sensory or motor capacities in any striking way. It was reasoned that the same operation might help people suffering from severe and otherwise untreatable psychiatric disorders.

The largest number of lobotomies in the United States was performed by Walter Freeman, a medical doctor who had never been trained in surgery. His techniques were amazingly crude, even by the standards of the 1940s. He performed many of the operations in his office or in other sites outside the hospital. (Freeman carried his equipment, such as it was, around with him in his car, which he called his "lobotomobile.")

Freeman and others became increasingly casual about deciding who should get a lobotomy. At first, the technique was used only in cases of severe, untreatable schizophrenia. Lobotomy did calm some schizophrenic people, but the effects were often disappointing, even to Freeman and others who performed the operations. (We now know that the frontal lobes of many severe schizophrenics are partly shrunken and less active than normal; lobotomy was therefore damaging a structure that had already been impaired.) As time went on, Freeman tried lobotomy for people with an assortment of other major and minor disorders. Some would, in fact, be considered normal by today's standards.

After antischizophrenic and antidepressive drugs became available in the mid-1950s, the use of lobotomy declined sharply. Freeman, who had been praised by some of his colleagues and barely tolerated by others, lost his privilege to practice at most hospitals and faded into the same obscurity as lobotomy itself. Lobotomy

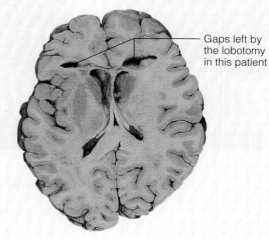

Gaps left by the lobotomy in this patient

A horizontal section of the brain of a person who had a prefrontal lobotomy many years previously. The two holes in the frontal cortex are the visible results of the operation. (Photo courtesy of Dr. Dana Copeland.)

has been an exceedingly rare operation since the mid-1950s (Lesse, 1984; Tippin & Henn, 1982).

Among the common consequences of prefrontal lobotomy were apathy, a loss of planning and initiative, memory disorders (Chapter 13), distractibility, generally blunted emotions, and a loss of facial expression (Stuss & Benson, 1984). People with such damage lose their social inhibitions; they behave in a tactless, callous manner and ignore the rules of polite, civilized conduct. If the damage is extensive, these people have trouble suppressing one behavior and substituting another (Damasio, 1979). For example, after they have learned to sort a set of cards by color, it is difficult for them to shift to sorting them by the numbers or patterns on the cards.

However, the results of prefrontal lobotomies provided only a superficial understanding of what the prefrontal lobes do and how they do it. The work of Patricia Goldman-Rakic and others has led to a more advanced understanding. According to Goldman-Rakic (1988), the prefrontal cortex is particularly important for behaviors guided by an "internal representation" of the world. For example, a monkey without its prefrontal cortex is fully capable of learning always to go toward the green light to find food and never to go toward a blue light. That task does not require an internal representation of the world; it

The Cerebral Cortex

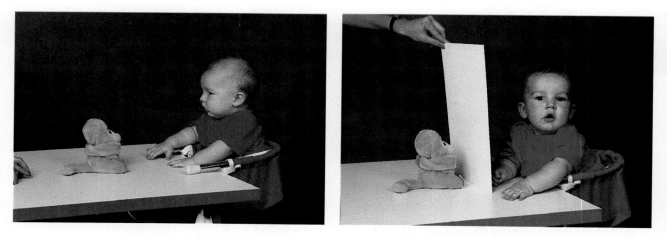

Figure 4.24
Piaget's object permanence task
An infant sees a toy; then an investigator places a barrier in front of the toy. Infants younger than about 9 months old fail to reach for the hidden toy. This task is similar to the delayed-response task, which infant monkeys cannot master until their prefrontal cortex matures. (Doug Goodman/Monkmeyer Press.)

requires only a response to stimuli present at the time. The same monkey is greatly impaired on **delayed-response tasks,** in which it must remember, for example, where it saw a green light last and go toward it 30 seconds after it was turned off. There are many versions of the delayed-response task, but the basic procedure is always to provide a signal indicating the correct response, turn off the signal, impose a delay, and then test whether the animal can still make the correct response. A correct response to a delayed-response task requires an internal representation of past stimuli. Goldman-Rakic's research indicates that the prefrontal cortex includes a great many separate circuits representing past stimuli of different types—visual, auditory, and so forth.

Research on the prefrontal cortex has led to a biological explanation of a well-known observation in child development. In a developmental psychology course, you may have learned about Jean Piaget's concept of object permanence. In the object permanence task, an observer shows a toy to an infant, places the toy behind a barrier, and then watches whether or not the child reaches for it. Generally, a child less than 9 months old does not reach for it (Figure 4.24). Goldman-Rakic (1987) noted the similarity between this task and the delayed-response task: In both cases, the individual must respond to a signal that was once present but is now gone.

Monkeys, it turns out, fail the delayed-response task until they are about 2 to 4 months old. Most of the synapses in the monkey's prefrontal cortex develop between ages 2 and 4 months. Presumably, the monkeys become capable of responding correctly on the delayed-response task at 2 to 4 months because the synapses of the prefrontal cortex develop at that time.

The prefrontal cortex develops more slowly in humans than it does in monkeys. Massive numbers of synapses develop in the human brain between ages 7½ and 12 months. Perhaps infants fail the object permanence task before about age 9 months because this task requires activity in the prefrontal cortex, and the necessary synapses are not present until about that age (Goldman-Rakic, 1987).

Summary

1. The cerebral cortex is composed of six laminae (layers) of neurons. A given lamina may be absent from certain parts of the cortex. The cortex is organized into columns of cells arranged perpendicular to the laminae. (p. 116)

2. Almost every cortical area has sensory, associational, and motor functions, although the degree of each varies. (p. 119)

3. The occipital lobe of the cortex is primarily responsible for vision. Damage to part of the occipital lobe leads to blindness in part of the visual field. (p. 120)

4. The parietal lobe deals with body sensations. The post-central gyrus contains four separate representations of the body. (p. 121)

5. The temporal lobe contributes to hearing and to complex aspects of vision. (p. 123)

6. The frontal lobe includes the precentral gyrus, which controls fine movements. It also includes the prefrontal cortex, which is essential for behaviors guided by an internal representation of the world. The prefrontal cortex receives information from each of the sensory systems. (p. 124)

Review Questions

1. In what way do the neurons within a given column resemble one another? (p. 117)

2. Why is it an overstatement to divide the cerebral cortex into distinct sensory, associational, and motor areas? (p. 120)

3. How does cortical blindness differ from blindness caused by damage to the eyes? (p. 120)

4. What kind of brain damage leads to sensory neglect of the left half of the body? (p. 122)

5. What is the Klüver-Bucy syndrome? What kind of brain damage is associated with it? (p. 123)

6. Give a biological explanation of why 9-month-old children fail Piaget's object permanence task. (p. 126)

Thought Question

1. When monkeys with Klüver-Bucy syndrome pick up lighted matches and snakes, it is not obvious whether they are displaying a deficit in emotional response or a difficulty identifying what the object is. What kind of research might help to answer this question?

Suggestions for Further Reading

Klawans, H. L. (1988). *Toscanini's fumble and other tales of clinical neurology*. Chicago: Contemporary Books. Fascinating description of cases of human brain damage and other neurological conditions.

Sacks, O. (1986). *The man who mistook his wife for a hat: And other clinical tales*. New York: HarperCollins. Tantalizing reports of people with various kinds of brain damage; unfortunately, often short on explanations.

Valenstein, E. S. (1986). *Great and desperate cures*. New York: Basic Books. Account of the rise and fall of prefrontal lobotomies.

Terms

cerebral cortex layer of cells on the outer surface of the cerebral hemispheres of the forebrain (p. 116)

corpus callosum large set of axons that connects the two hemispheres of the cerebral cortex (p. 116)

anterior commissure set of axons connecting the two cerebral hemispheres; smaller than the corpus callosum (p. 116)

lamina (plural: **laminae**) a layer of cells (p. 116)

column collection of cells having similar properties, arranged perpendicular to the laminae (p. 117)

occipital lobe one of the four lobes of the cerebral cortex (p. 120)

parietal lobe one of the lobes of the cerebral cortex (p. 121)

central sulcus a large groove in the surface of the primate cerebral cortex, separating frontal from parietal cortex (p. 121)

postcentral gyrus gyrus of the cerebral cortex just posterior to the central gyrus; a primary projection site for touch and other body sensations (p. 121)

temporal lobe one of the lobes of the cerebral cortex (p. 123)

Klüver-Bucy syndrome condition in which monkeys with damaged temporal lobes fail to display normal fears and anxieties (p. 123)

frontal lobe one of the lobes of the cerebral cortex (p. 124)

precentral gyrus gyrus of the cerebral cortex just anterior to the central sulcus; a primary point of origin for axons of the pyramidal system of motor control (p. 124)

prefrontal cortex the most anterior portion of the frontal lobe of the cerebral cortex (p. 124)

prefrontal lobotomy surgical disconnection of the prefrontal cortex from the rest of the brain (p. 124)

delayed-response task assignment in which an animal must respond on the basis of a signal that it remembers but that is no longer present (p. 126)

Methods of Investigating How the Brain Controls Behavior

In the nineteenth century, Franz Joseph Gall observed (or so he thought) that people with an excellent verbal memory had bulging, protruding eyes. He drew the inference that verbal memory depended on a part of the brain immediately behind the eyes and that overdevelopment of this part of the brain pushed the eyes forward. If this were so, Gall reasoned, bulges and depressions elsewhere on the skull might also reflect overdevelopment or underdevelopment of the underlying brain areas. Thus, by comparing skull features among people and relating them to those people's behavior, it should be possible to identify the activities conducted by each part of the brain. And after identifying the functions of all brain areas in this manner, one should be able to determine the personality of an unknown person by feeling bumps and depressions on his or her head. These were the basic premises of **phrenology**. Figure 4.25 shows a typical phrenologist's map of the human skull.

The phrenologists' methods were a classic example of pseudoscience. In many cases, phrenologists identified an area on their map of the brain by observing only one or two people. Moreover, they ignored discrepancies when someone's behavior did not fit the theory.

Nevertheless, researchers today maintain one of the phrenologists' basic assumptions: Different parts of the brain do control different aspects of behavior. If brain area A controls behavior X, then individuals with a deficiency of behavior X should have some deficiency in brain area A. Individuals with a greater-than-normal amount of behavior X should have an excess of activity in area A; area A may even be larger than normal in such individuals (Scheibel, 1984).

Current research differs from phrenology in several major respects, however. Psychologists no longer attempt to localize such personality traits as self-esteem, reverence, or "marvellousness." Rather, we attempt to understand how the brain produces such biological functions as vision, control of finger movements, and temperature regulation. We consider not only localized brain areas but also diffuse systems of neurons that may not be confined to one region. And we examine the electrical and chemical activity of brain areas and systems, not just their size. That is, a behavior may be deficient because some brain area is inactive, not just because that brain area is small or damaged. Still, a major goal of current research is to determine what functions differentiate one area of the brain from other areas. A number of techniques have been developed in pursuit of this goal; a few of the most common are described here.

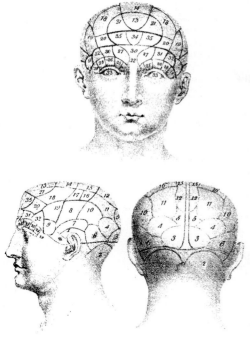

AFFECTIVE.

I.—PROPENSITIES.

† Desire to live.
* Alimentiveness.
No. 1. Destructiveness.
   2. Amativeness.
   3. Philoprogenitiveness.
   4. Adhesiveness.
   5. Inhabitiveness.
   6. Combativeness.
   7. Secretiveness.
   8. Acquisitiveness.
   9. Constructiveness.

II.—SENTIMENTS.

10. Cautiousness.
11. Approbativeness.
12. Self-esteem.
13. Benevolence.
14. Reverence.
15. Firmness.
16. Conscientiousness.
17. Hope.

18. Marvellousness.
19. Ideality.
20. Mirthfulness.
21. Imitation.

INTELLECTUAL.

I.—PERCEPTIVE.

No. 22. Individuality.
   23. Configuration.
   24. Size.
   25. Weight and Resistance.
   26. Coloring.
   27. Locality.
   28. Order.
   29. Calculation.
   30. Eventuality.
   31. Time.
   32. Tune.
   33. Language.

II.—REFLECTIVE.

34. Comparison.
35. Causality.

Figure 4.25
A phrenologist's map of brain areas
(From Spurzheim, 1908.)

The Stereotaxic Instrument

Investigators sometimes wish to study the effects of stimulating or damaging a small area buried deep in an animal's brain, or they wish to record the activity of such an area. To do so, they use a **stereotaxic instrument.** Figure 4.26 shows a stereotaxic instrument for a rat, by far the most commonly used animal in research of this type. The rat is anesthetized and then positioned in the stereotaxic instrument. Ear bars and a clamp around the nose and mouth hold the head in place. Any part of the brain can be located fairly accurately from the position of two landmarks on the head: the ear bars and **bregma** (the point where the frontal and parietal skull bones join, as shown in Figure 4.27).

To calculate the position, the researcher refers to a **stereotaxic atlas** (or map) of the animal's brain areas in relation to the external landmarks. Such atlases have been published for the brains of many species. Figure 4.28, from Pellegrino and Cushman's (1967) atlas, illustrates one slice through the brain of an adult rat. The scale at the bottom indicates distances in millimeters left or right from the center of the skull. The scales at the left and right indicate distances dorsal and ventral from the top surface of the brain and from the ear bars, respectively. The notations in the upper corners indicate that this slice is 6.0 mm anterior to the ear bars and 0.2 mm anterior to bregma. Other pages of the atlas present slices at 0.2-mm intervals.

An experimenter who wants to insert an electrode into, say, the ventromedial hypothalamus (VMH in Figure 4.28) places an anesthetized animal in the stereotaxic instrument, drills holes at the appropriate spot on the skull, inserts

Methods of Investigating
How the Brain Controls
Behavior

Figure 4.26
A stereotaxic instrument for locating brain areas in small animals

Figure 4.27
Skull bones of a rat and the position of bregma

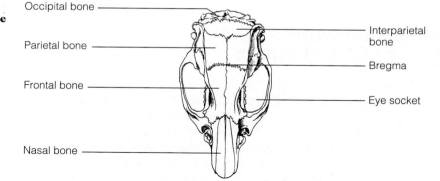

Occipital bone

Parietal bone

Frontal bone

Nasal bone

Interparietal bone

Bregma

Eye socket

the electrode, and lowers it to the target area. The investigator can then use the electrode to record from cells in that area, stimulate those cells, or overstimulate and thereby destroy cells.

Lesions and Ablations

A **lesion** is destruction or functional disruption of an area of the brain. An **ablation** is removal of part of the brain. Lesions and ablations can be produced intentionally by experimenters with laboratory animals, or they can occur naturally, as when a person has a stroke or a head wound. When a lesion or

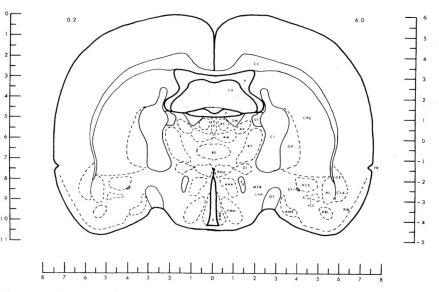

Figure 4.28
A typical page from a stereotaxic atlas of the rat brain showing a coronal section 6.0 mm anterior to the ear bars
The surrounding unlabeled area is the cerebral cortex. Abbreviations refer to various areas of the brain; for example, CC = corpus callosum. (From Pellegrino et al., 1979.)

ablation leads to a deficit in some behavior, we assume that the damaged area had some role in the control of that behavior, although its exact role may be difficult to determine. The lesion technique has been widely used throughout the history of biological psychology.

Methods of Producing Lesions and Ablations

Lesions and ablations can be produced in experimental animals in several ways. To remove a large area on the external surface of the brain, an experimenter can cut back a flap of skull and then remove the desired brain tissue with a knife or with vacuum suction. To make smaller lesions, especially lesions beneath the surface of the brain, the investigator inserts an electrode using the stereotaxic device and then applies a current.

The electrode inevitably kills a few cells on the way to the target. To find out the effects of such accidental damage and to separate them from the effects of the lesion itself, an experimenter produces a **sham lesion** in a control group. That is, the experimenter goes through all the same procedures but does not apply the electrical current. Any behavioral difference between the lesioned group and the sham-lesion group must result from the lesion itself and not from damage caused by inserting the electrode.

Histological Techniques

Suppose that an investigator has made a lesion in a rat's brain and then has tested the behavioral effects of the lesion. When the experiment is over, the

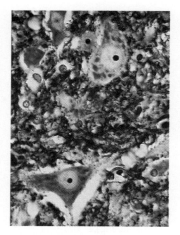

A slice of rat brain treated with Nissl stain. (Ed Reschke, Peter Arnold, Inc.)

investigator usually examines the rat's brain to determine the size and the exact location of the lesion.

The rat is deeply anesthetized, then perfused with chemicals that preserve the tissues. Then the brain is removed and stained. Without some special treatment, brain tissue looks fairly uniform; it is difficult to identify even the major nuclei and tracts. Therefore, investigators use various histological procedures to highlight the kinds of brain tissue that they wish to examine. (*Histology* is the branch of biology that deals with the structure of tissues.)

First, investigators harden the brain tissue either by freezing it or by forcing a chemical into it that hardens it. (Using such a chemical is called "embedding" the tissue.) Then the brain is divided into slices just a few microns thick by means of a device called a microtome. Finally, the tissue is stained with chemicals that selectively attach to certain structures. For example, Nissl stain attaches selectively to cell bodies; Weigert stain attaches to axons.

Difficulties of Interpreting the Results of Lesion Experiments

The results of lesion experiments are sometimes hard to interpret. As an analogy, suppose that no one understood how a television works. To find out, an investigator explodes a small firecracker inside the set, damaging nearby structures, and then examines the results. Suppose that exploding a firecracker in one given location destroys the sound without affecting the picture. That result implies that something in the area of the explosion contributes to the sound in some way. We have taken an important first step, but only a first step. We need to determine exactly which structure in the damaged area was important and exactly how it contributed to sound production.

Investigating a brain by making lesions poses some analogous difficulties. Suppose, for example, that a lesion in some brain area disrupts maze learning. That result by itself means very little; researchers need to determine whether the lesion has its effect by impairing vision, or body location sense, or hunger motivation, or some aspect of memory, or any of a number of other behavioral features relevant to maze performance.

One important strategy for evaluating lesion effects is to look for a **double dissociation of function**: a demonstration that lesion 1 impairs behavior A more than behavior B, while lesion 2 impairs behavior B more than behavior A. For example, if one lesion impairs maze learning for food reward but not for temperature reward, and some other lesion impairs learning for temperature reward but not for food reward, then we may conclude that these brain areas contribute to hunger and to temperature regulation and that they do not control vision, body sensations, learning, or memory.

Stimulation of and Recording from the Brain

The lesion methods determine what behaviors occur when certain areas of the brain are damaged. Alternative ways to study brain functioning are to insert electrodes into the brain and briefly stimulate certain areas (to see how increased activity of those areas affects behavior) and to use the electrodes to record spontaneous brain activity (to determine what behaviors accompany that activity).

Researchers feel more confidence in a conclusion if they can support it through different types of experiments. For example, lesion experiments have shown that damage to the lateral hypothalamus causes an animal to stop eating, while experiments with implanted electrodes have demonstrated that stimulating the same area increases eating. Recording of neurons in this area has revealed that spontaneous activity is high around the time of a meal. All these lines of evidence indicate that the lateral hypothalamus has something to do with eating. Although the results do not tell us how the lateral hypothalamus contributes to eating, at least they tell us where in the brain to look for further information.

Labeling Brain Activity

Several methods adopt the strategy of labeling certain chemicals in the brain so that investigators can observe their distribution. Two such methods are autoradiography and immunohistochemistry.

Autoradiography

An autograph is a person's signature. An autoradiograph is a signal produced radioactively by a chemical. **Autoradiography** is a method of determining where a chemical is located in the brain.

To conduct autoradiography, an investigator begins by injecting a radioactively labeled chemical, such as radioactively labeled glucose, amino acids, or drugs, into a laboratory rat. After the injection, the investigator waits a few minutes for the chemicals to reach the brain and then kills the rat and slices its brain into thin sections. The investigator then places each section against a piece of x-ray film, which records all the radioactivity that the labeled chemicals emit. In that manner, it creates a map of the relative amounts of radioactivity in different parts of the rat's brain.

For example, an investigator might inject radioactively labeled glucose or 2-deoxy-D-glucose, which neurons take up when they absorb glucose. (The advantage of 2-deoxy-D-glucose is that it is metabolized much more slowly than glucose and so remains in the cell longer.) The most active neurons take up more glucose than less active neurons do; consequently, the autoradiography provides a map of relative activity levels in the brain (Hibbard, McGlone, Davis, & Hawkins, 1987). By the same logic, researchers can inject radioactive amino acids and later look for the brain areas that incorporated them into proteins or inject radioactively labeled drugs to find the receptors to which they attach.

Immunohistochemistry

The term *immunohistochemistry* is a combination of *immuno,* referring to the immune system, *histo,* meaning tissues, and *chemistry.* **Immunohistochemistry,** therefore, is a method of using the immune system to label particular types of tissues.

First, investigators purify a protein or peptide in which they are interested—say, the acetylcholine receptor of rhesus monkeys. Then they inject that protein into some other species, such as rabbits, whose immune system will form antibodies to it. (The acetylcholine receptors are very similar across species but not identical; thus, the rabbit's immune system attacks the monkey's acetylcholine receptors as intruders.) Investigators collect the antibodies from the rabbit's blood, chemically attach them to dyes, and expose those antibodies to a slice of a monkey's brain. The rabbit's antibodies, carrying the dye with them, attach to acetylcholine receptors. The investigators then observe where the dye attaches and use this distribution to map the location of acetylcholine receptors.

Studies that Use the Natural Development of the Brain

Sometimes an investigator wishes to study a set of cells that is intermingled thoroughly with other cells, making it impossible to stimulate or damage one set of cells without equally affecting the others. Investigators cannot make the surgical manipulations themselves, but they may be able to let nature do the work for them. For example, certain individuals may lack one type of cell or another for genetic reasons. And because different parts of the brain mature at different rates, an individual may lack certain types of cells at one age but have those cells at a later age.

Genetic Lesions and Arrested Development

Sometimes a genetic mutation can remove a structure that a surgeon could not. For example, one mutation prevents granule cells from developing in the cerebellum of mice. Such mice have great difficulty maintaining their balance. Their legs tremble constantly, and they can hardly take a step without falling over. Such evidence is at least a start toward understanding the role of the granule cells (Sidman, Green, & Appel, 1965).

Another way to remove a particular type of cell is to interfere with brain maturation at a particular stage. Different cell types mature at different times. If experimenters expose the brain to x-rays or to the neurotoxin methylazoxymethanol acetate (MAM), they can destroy the cells that are dividing and developing at that time, while sparing mature cells (Anderson & Altman, 1972; Sanberg, Pevsner, Autuono, & Coyle, 1985). When the researchers repeat the experiment at different ages, they can examine the contributions of different populations of cells.

Correlation of Developing Brain with Developing Behavior

Suppose that a certain structure or system in the brain and a certain behavior both reach maturity fairly suddenly at the same time. With caution, we can use this as evidence that the structure is responsible for the behavior.

For example, the retina of a frog contains four anatomical types of cells known as constricted tree, E-tree, H-tree, and broad tree, according to their shape. Physiological recordings from cells in the retina reveal that different cells respond best to four different stimuli: edges, convex edges, moving contrast, and dimness. Each of the four anatomical types of cells probably responds best to a different stimulus. But which is which? The question is not

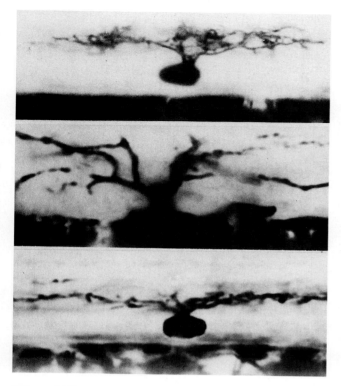

Figure 4.29
Three cell types in the tadpole retina
From top to bottom, E-tree, H-tree, and broad tree. (From Pomeranz & Chung, 1970.)

easy to answer because the physiological responses of cells can be recorded only when they are alive, and their anatomy can be determined only by staining them after they are dead.

Pomeranz and Chung (1970) were able to relate two of the anatomical types to visual responses by studying the retinas of tadpoles (baby frogs) (see Figure 4.29). They noted that tadpoles lack the constricted tree cells and have no cells that respond best to edges. They therefore inferred that constricted tree cells respond to edges. Moreover, E-tree cells could be found only in the center of the tadpole's retina, and cells responsive to convex edges could be recorded only in the center of the retina. Thus, E-trees are apparently responsive to convex edges. The researchers were unable to pair up the other two types of cell, however.

Studies of the Structure of Living Human Brains

Suppose that we want to investigate whether a given person has any kind of brain abnormality. Experimenters could hardly insert electrodes into that person's brain. To study the brains of living people, investigators turn to other

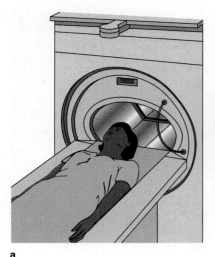
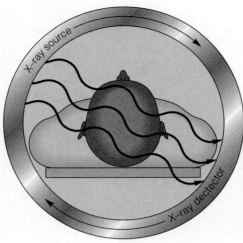
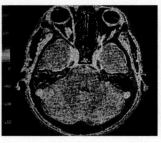

a

b

Figure 4.30
CT scanner
A person's head is placed into the device (a), and then a rapidly rotating source sends x-rays through the head while detectors on the opposite side make photographs. A computer then constructs an image of the brain. (b) A view of a normal human brain generated by computerized axial tomography (CT scanning). (Dan McCoy/Rainbow.)

methods, sometimes called "noninvasive" or "less invasive" methods because they do not require surgical invasion of the brain. We begin with methods of examining the structure of living brains.

Computerized Axial Tomography

Is Alzheimer's disease associated with any loss of brain tissue? Is schizophrenia? One way to find out is to use **computerized axial tomography,** better known as a **CT scan** or **CAT scan** (Andreasen, 1988). A CT scan makes use of x-rays, but x-rays generally reveal very little contrast between one part of the brain and another. To increase the contrast, a physician begins by injecting a dye into the blood. The physician then places the person's head into a CT scanner like the one shown in Figure 4.30a. X-rays are passed through the head and recorded by detectors on the opposite side. The CT scanner is rotated 1 degree at a time and the procedure is repeated until a measurement has been taken at each angle over 180 degrees. From the 180 measurements, a computer can reconstruct images of the brain. Figure 4.30b shows a CT scan of a normal brain; CT scans also show that the cortex is atrophied (shrunken) in patients with Alzheimer's disease and that the cerebral ventricles are enlarged in certain people with schizophrenia.

Magnetic Resonance Imaging

A second method of examining brain anatomy in a living person is **magnetic resonance imaging (MRI),** also known as nuclear magnetic resonance (NMR). Magnetic resonance imaging can produce images with a high degree of resolution without exposing the brain to any radiation at all (Moonen, van Zijl, Frank,

LeBihan, & Becker, 1990). This method uses the fact that any atom with an odd atomic weight—such as hydrogen—has an inherent rotation. Ordinarily, each atom's axis of rotation points in a random direction, but an outside magnetic field can align the axes of rotation. A radio frequency field can then make all these atoms move like tiny gyros. When the radio frequency field is turned off, the atomic nuclei release electromagnetic energy as they relax. By measuring that energy, MRI devices form an image of the brain, such as the one in Figure 4.31. Like CT scans, an MRI image can reveal structural defects such as an enlarged ventricle or an atrophied cortex.

The most serious limitation of MRI has been that the process is slow, taking about 15 minutes to complete. The resultant image can therefore reveal only stationary structures, not movement. An improved apparatus, known as *echoplanar MRI,* can now form clear images of the brain in less than a tenth of a second, fast enough to observe the blood flowing through the brain (Alper, 1993). As this device becomes more widely available, investigators will be able to record rapid changes in brain activity and to answer previously unanswerable questions.

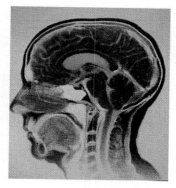

Figure 4.31
A view of a living brain generated by magnetic resonance imaging
Any atom with an odd atomic weight (such as hydrogen) has an inherent rotation. An outside magnetic field can align the axes of rotation. A radio frequency field can then make all these atoms move like tiny gyros. When the radio frequency field is turned off, the atomic nuclei release electromagnetic energy as they relax. By measuring that energy, we can obtain an image of a structure such as the brain without damaging it. (Dan McCoy/Rainbow.)

Measurement of Human Brain Activity

At any moment, certain areas of the brain are more active than others. For example, the visual cortex becomes more active during visual stimulation, and the olfactory bulb becomes more active during olfactory stimulation. Investigators have developed several noninvasive ways to measure changes in brain activity.

The Electroencephalograph

A device called the **electroencephalograph (EEG)** records electrical activity of the brain via electrodes attached to the scalp. It enables investigators to make gross determinations of brain activity in humans and other animals without actually cutting into the skull. Electrodes, generally eight or fewer, are attached with glue or other adhesive to various locations on the surface of the scalp. The output of those electrodes is then amplified and recorded. From an examination of EEG records, an investigator can determine whether the person is asleep, dreaming, awake, or excited. Abnormalities in the EEG record may also suggest the presence of epilepsy, a tumor, or other medical problems located in a brain region under a particular electrode.

With the **evoked potential** method, experimenters use the EEG apparatus to record the brain's activity in response to sensory stimuli. Any sensory stimulus evokes electrical activity with a very short latency (delay) over a limited area of the cerebral cortex. If the individual reacts to the stimulus as meaningful and attention getting, another electrical response appears with a latency of about 0.3 second. Digression 4.3 describes a fascinating attempt to develop this method to communicate with totally paralyzed people (see also Figure 4.32).

PET Scans

Positron-emission tomography (PET) provides a high-resolution image of brain activity. PET scans rely on the fact that the radioactive decay of certain

Suppose you became completely paralyzed. You cannot move your lips to talk; you cannot move your hands or feet to write. But you can still hear, see, and feel; you would like to be able to communicate with others. (If nothing else, you want to tell your physician where you hurt.) Would there be any way for you to communicate?

Maybe. If you can see, your brain will exhibit evoked responses to visual stimuli. When people see anything that is especially meaningful to them, they produce a special kind of evoked response called a *P300 wave*. It is called "P300" because it is positive (P) and occurs about 300 milliseconds following a stimulus. The P300 wave is generally considered to be an indication of attention or interest.

L. A. Farwell & E. Donchin (1988) set up a device that uses the P300 response. Suppose that you are thinking of the word *neck* (because you want to tell someone that your neck hurts). The investigator shows you a display like the one in Figure 4.32 and asks you to pay special attention to the first letter of your word (*n*) and silently to count all the times that it

is highlighted. Various rows and columns are highlighted in a random order. If all goes according to plan, you show a clear P300 wave whenever the third column or the second row is lit, because they include the letter *n*. The information from your brain waves feeds to a computer which eventually determines that you are thinking of the letter *n*. You then go on to the letter *e*, and so forth. If your P300 waves are not entirely reliable, the computer may make a mistake—for example, it may say that you were thinking of *d* when you were really thinking of *e*. You would then think of *"bksp"* (backspace) for your next letter, erasing the *d*.

This technology is a bit awkward, at least in its current stage of development. At best, it enables people to spell out two or three letters per minute. So it might take you 10 or 15 minutes to say "Give me more pain medicine." Still, the method enables people who cannot move any muscles at all to communicate.

Could this method be used to "read someone's mind"? No. Fortunately or unfortunately, depending on your point of view, it cannot read the mind of someone who does not want to cooperate.

---

elements emits a positron. A positron is an antimatter particle with the same mass as an electron but an opposite charge.

First, the person receives an injection of glucose or some other chemical with a radioactive label of ^{11}C, ^{18}F, or ^{15}O. (These chemicals have half-lives ranging from 110 minutes for ^{18}F to 2 minutes for ^{15}O. Because their half-lives are so short, the investigators must make them in a cyclotron near the PET scanner. Cyclotrons are very large and expensive. Consequently, PET scans are available only at the largest research hospitals.) The chemical chosen for injection depends on the nature of the research question. For example, glucose goes to the most active areas of the brain and is suitable for finding which areas of the brain are most active at a given moment. When a radioactive label decays, releasing a positron, the positron immediately collides with a nearby electron. When a positron and an electron collide, they emit two gamma rays in exactly opposite directions. The person's head is surrounded by a set of gamma ray detectors. When the detectors record two gamma rays at the same time, they identify a spot halfway between those two detectors as the point of origin of the gamma rays. Using this information, a computer can determine how many gamma rays are coming from each spot in the brain—and, therefore, how much of the radioactively labeled chemical is located in each area (Phelps & Mazziotta, 1985). Figure 4.33 includes several examples of PET scans of the human brain.

PET scans enable physicians to localize tumors, certain types of epilepsy, and other disorders that alter the metabolic rate of a given brain area. They also enable researchers to answer some questions that could not be answered any other way. For example, Harry Chugani and Michael Phelps (1986) performed PET scans on infant brains to determine when various brain structures

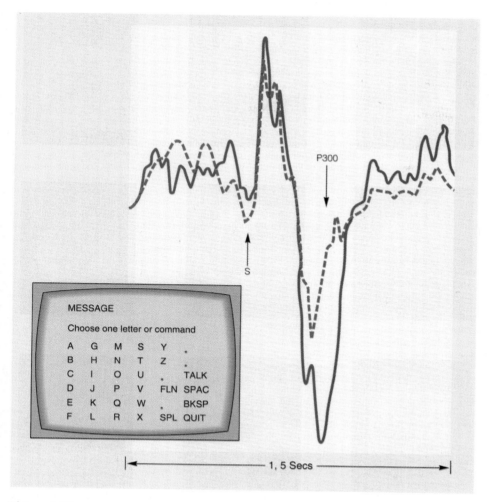

Figure 4.32

A computer display that enables people to communicate through brain waves
One row or column at a time is highlighted at random. The viewer who is trying to communicate one letter counts the number of times that letter is highlighted. Doing so makes that letter especially meaningful and causes a P300 wave. The computer determines which letter most reliably causes a P300 wave and thereby determines which letter the person is thinking about. The extra symbols: SPAC = space, BKSP = backspace (delete previous letter), FLN = file name (used to store a message on a disk or call up a message already stored on a disk), SPL = special (a preprogrammed special message). The asterisks (*) are placeholders where additional options or messages can be added later. (From Farwell and Donchin, 1988.)

become active. They found that the thalamus and brain stem showed fairly high rates of activity by age 5 weeks. Most of the cerebral cortex and the outer part of the cerebellum were immature at 5 weeks but much more advanced by 3 months. The frontal lobes of the cerebral cortex showed little sign of activity until the age of 7½ months.

Regional Cerebral Blood Flow

When an area of the brain becomes more active, its blood supply, its use of glucose, and its synthesis of proteins increase. Researchers can capitalize on this fact by administering small amounts of certain radioactive chemicals and then

Figure 4.33
PET scans of normal people, showing differences during various tasks
Red indicates the greatest level of brain activity; blue indicates the least. Left column: Brain activity with no special stimulation and during passive exposure to visual and auditory stimuli. Center column: Activity while listening to music, language, or both. Right column: Activity during performance of a cognitive task, an auditory memory task, and a task of moving fingers of the right hand in a fixed sequence. Arrows indicate regions of greatest activity. (Courtesy of Michael E. Phelps and John C. Mazziotta, University of California, Los Angeles, School of Medicine.)

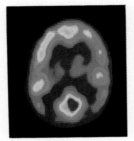 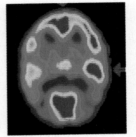 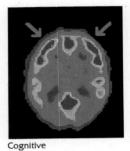

Resting state

Music

Cognitive

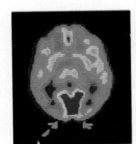 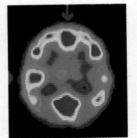 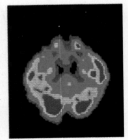

Visual

Language

Memory

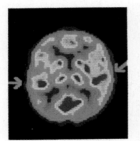 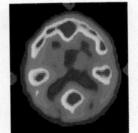 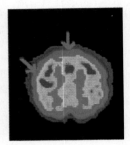

Auditory

Language and music

Motor

Figure 4.34
No, it's not a state-of-the-art hairdo; it's a type of PET scanner. A person engages in a cognitive task while attached to this apparatus that records regional cerebral blood flow in the brain to determine which areas become more active, and by how much. (Burt Glinn/Magnum.)

Chapter 4
Anatomy of the Nervous System and Methods of Investigation

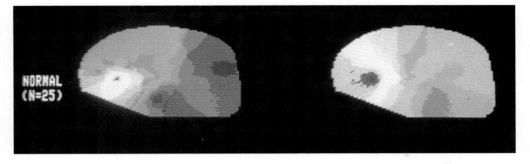

Figure 4.35
An rCBF image of a normal human brain
Red indicates the greatest amount of blood flow and therefore of brain activity.
Yellow shows the next greatest amount, followed by green and blue. (Karen Berman
and Daniel Weinberger, National Institute of Mental Health.)

monitoring these chemicals to measure the relative activity of various areas of
the brain. We already encountered this strategy in autoradiography. With a few
changes in procedure, it can be applied to a living human brain.

In the **regional cerebral blood flow** method **(rCBF),** an investigator uses a
chemical that dissolves in the blood. One such substance is xenon (^{133}Xe), a
radioactive gas. After a person inhales xenon, it enters the bloodstream.
Because it does not react chemically with anything in the body, the xenon goes
wherever the blood goes. Thus, the radioactivity recorded from a particular
part of the brain will be proportional to the amount of blood flow to it. The
investigator places the person's head in a PET scanner or similar device (see
Figure 4.34). A computer then uses that information to construct an image of
the brain in full color, like those in Figure 4.35. Areas with a great deal of
radioactivity appear red. Areas of decreasing activity appear orange, yellow,
green, blue, and violet. The areas that appear red are the most active; blue or
violet areas are the least active.

I have told you that blood flow increases to the brain areas with the greatest activity. You might ask, how does the blood "know" which brain areas are
most active? The answer is that certain neurons, when active, release chemicals that dilate the nearby blood vessels. First, just as a natural result of a series
of action potentials, potassium ions leave the neuron and accumulate in the
glia cells, which pump them to the walls of nearby arteries. Potassium dilates
(expands) the artery walls and thereby increases the flow of blood to that part
of the brain (Paulson & Newman, 1987). A second, evidently more important,
mechanism is that certain neurons, when active, release nitric oxide (NO),
which strongly but briefly dilates nearby blood vessels (Iadecola, 1993). The
result of the released potassium, NO, and probably other chemicals as well is to
increase blood flow to the most active areas of the brain, as the rCBF method
reveals.

A typical way of using the rCBF method is to ask a person to engage in a
series of tasks, such as listening to music, solving a problem, and moving the
fingers in a certain way. The investigator then uses the rCBF results to compare
the type of brain activity that occurs during the various tasks (Andreasen,

Methods of Investigating
How the Brain Controls
Behavior

1988). This method can be used to detect possible brain abnormalities in people with psychological disorders. For example, when most people sort cards according to a complex set of rules, activity in the prefrontal cortex increases. When people with schizophrenia perform the same task, many of them fail to show that increase (Berman, Zec, & Weinberger, 1986). Those who fail to show increased blood flow to the prefrontal cortex generally perform poorly on the task.

The brain is a complex structure. You have encountered a great deal of terminology and many facts in this chapter. Do not become discouraged if you cannot remember everything. It will help to refer back to this chapter to review the anatomy of certain structures as you encounter their functions again in later chapters. Gradually, the material will become more familiar.

Summary

1. A stereotaxic device can enable an investigator to implant electrodes deep in the brain to make lesions or to stimulate neurons or record from them. (p. 129)

2. One of the most common methods of studying brain functioning is by examining the effects of lesions (brain damage). (p. 130)

3. Lesion studies help to locate the brain areas most critical to a particular behavioral function, but they do not indicate how that area controls behavior. (p. 132)

4. Autoradiography is a way of measuring the activity of various brain areas at a given time. Histochemistry is a method of identifying the distribution of a particular chemical in various parts of the brain. (p. 133)

5. To study the role of a particular type of cell, investigators examine individuals whose brain developed abnormally or they compare the behaviors of individuals at various stages of development. (p. 134)

6. CT scans and MRI images can reveal the structure of the brain in a living person. (p. 136)

7. Electroencephalographs, PET scans, and rCBF images can indicate the activity taking place in various parts of a human brain at a given time. (p. 137)

Review Questions

1. Describe the method for inserting an electrode into an area of an animal's brain that cannot be seen from the surface. (p. 129)

2. What are some of the difficulties in interpreting the results of a lesion experiment? (p. 132)

3. Describe methods used to study the structure of a living human brain. (p. 135)

4. Describe methods used to study the functioning of a living human brain. (p. 137)

Thought Questions

1. One of the many kinds of cells in the cerebral cortex is the stellate cell, which is an unusually small neuron. Stellate cells are more numerous in adults than in children and more numerous in humans than in other species. How might one determine what special role, if any, stellate cells have in the control of behavior? Describe at least three possibilities. (For one attempt to answer this question, see Scheibel & Scheibel, 1963.)

2. Multiple sclerosis destroys the myelin sheaths of axons. Why should we expect that evoked potentials would have longer-than-normal latencies in people with this disease?

Suggestion for Further Reading

Morihisa, J. M. (1984). *Brain imaging in psychiatry.* Washington, DC: American Psychiatric Press. Provides more information on PET scans and similar methods.

Terms

phrenology nineteenth-century theory that personality types are related to bumps on the skull (p. 128)

stereotaxic instrument device for the precise placement of electrodes in the head (p. 129)

bregma a point on the skull where the frontal and parietal bones join (p. 129)

stereotaxic atlas an atlas of the location of brain areas relative to external landmarks (p. 129)

lesion damage to a structure (p. 130)

ablation removal of a structure (p. 130)

sham lesion control procedure for an experiment, in which an investigator inserts an electrode into a brain but does not pass a current (p. 131)

double dissociation of function demonstration that one lesion impairs behavior A more than it impairs behavior B, while a second lesion impairs behavior B more than it impairs behavior A (p. 132)

autoradiography method of injecting a radioactively labeled chemical and then mapping the distribution of radiation in the brain (p. 133)

immunohistochemistry method of using the immune system to label particular types of tissues (p. 133)

computerized axial tomography (CT scan, CAT scan) method of visualizing a living brain by injecting a dye into the blood and then passing x-rays through the head and recording them by detectors on the other side (p. 136)

magnetic resonance imaging (MRI) method of imaging a living brain by using a magnetic field and a radio frequency field to make atoms with odd atomic weights all rotate in the same direction and then removing those fields and measuring the energy that the atoms release (p. 136)

electroencephalograph (EEG) device that records the electrical activity of the brain through electrodes on the scalp (p. 137)

evoked potential electrical activity recorded from the brain, usually via electrodes on the scalp, in response to sensory stimuli (p. 137)

positron-emission tomography (PET) a method of mapping activity in a living brain by recording the emission of radioactivity from injected chemicals (p. 137)

regional cerebral blood flow (rCBF) method of estimating activity of different areas of the brain by dissolving radioactive xenon in the blood and measuring radioactivity from different brain areas (p. 141)

DEVELOPMENT AND EVOLUTION OF THE BRAIN

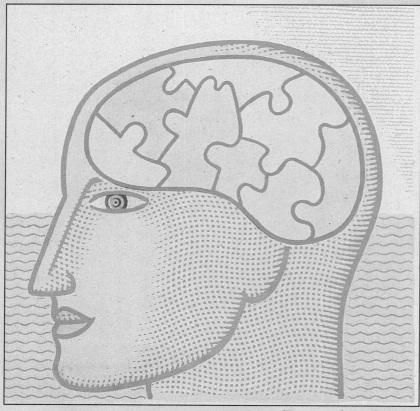

(Tim Grajek/Stockworks)

1. Axons find their way to their targets in a relatively specific way, not at random. To some extent, they identify appropriate target cells by chemical markers on those cells. The postsynaptic cells select among the axons that attach to them. They accept synapses from some axons and reject others.

2. The human brain is the product of many evolutionary modifications of the overall vertebrate brain organization. We generally assume that larger brains have greater behavioral abilities than smaller brains do, but the exact role of brain size is still uncertain and elusive.

"Some assembly required." Have you ever bought a device with those ominous words on the package? Sometimes all you have to do is to attach two or three parts, maybe tighten a few bolts. But in other cases, "some assembly required" means facing page after page of incomprehensible instructions. I remember once putting together my daughter's bicycle and wondering how something that looked so simple could be so complicated. The human nervous system comes with an enormous amount of assembly required. The structure and potential of the nervous system have changed enormously over the course of evolution; they also change enormously as we progress from the embryonic stage to adulthood.

The instructions for assembling the nervous system are different from those for assembling, say, a bicycle. Instead of just saying, "Put this piece here and that piece there," the instructions for the brain say, "Put these axons here and those dendrites there, and then wait to see what happens. Keep the connections that seem to be working well, move some of the others around, throw away the rest, and then make some new ones similar to the ones that you kept." Moreover, the brain continues moving connections around as long as it is alive and healthy. The assembly of the brain is never complete; it literally takes a lifetime to put your brain together.

Development of the Brain

As a college student, you can probably perform a number of feats today that you could not possibly have performed several years ago: solve calculus problems perhaps, or read a foreign language, or convincingly pretend that you understand James Joyce. Have you developed these new skills because your brain has grown? No. Your brain has no doubt moved a number of synapses around, but its overall size and structure are about the same as before.

Now think of all the things that 2-year-old children can do that they could not do the day they were born: walk, talk, pick up small objects, draw simple pictures, and control their bowel and bladder functions. Have they developed these new skills because of brain growth? To a large extent, yes. The brain of a newborn cannot learn to walk and talk until it has grown and matured in many ways. But much of behavioral development in children depends also on experience and on moving synapses around in much the same way that an adult brain does.

Often it seems reasonable to distinguish between learning (which can occur at any age) and maturation (which is most prominent early in life). But, as we shall see, many processes of brain development depend on experience in complex ways that sometimes blur the distinction between learning and maturation.

Growth and Differentiation of the Vertebrate Brain

The human central nervous system begins to form when the embryo is about two weeks old. First, the dorsal surface of the embryo thickens and then long thin lips rise and curl, merging to form a neural tube surrounding a fluid-filled cavity (see Figure 5.1). The tube sinks under the surface of the skin and continues to develop. The forward end enlarges and differentiates into the hindbrain, midbrain, and forebrain (see Figure 5.2); the rest becomes the spinal cord. The fluid-filled cavity within the neural tube becomes the central canal of the spinal cord and the four ventricles of the brain. The fluid inside the canal and ventricles is the cerebrospinal fluid (CSF). This same basic process occurs in all other vertebrates as well, varying mostly in speed. For example, the nervous system matures rapidly in mice, slowly in elephants.

At birth, the human brain weighs about 350 grams (g). Certain areas of the forebrain are immature for the first few weeks, as indicated by their low levels of glucose use. Development is rapid, however, and areas of the brain that are almost silent at birth approach adult patterns of activity within 7 to 8 months (Chugani & Phelps, 1986). At the end of the first year, the brain weighs 1,000 g, not much less than the adult weight of 1,200 to 1,400 g.

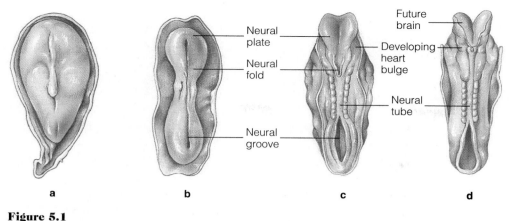

Figure 5.1
Early development of the human central nervous system
The brain and spinal cord begin as folding lips surrounding a fluid-filled canal. Stages shown occur at approximately ages 2 to 3 weeks.

The Growth and Development of Neurons

As the brain grows, what happens at the microscopic level? Does the brain simply produce more neurons that do exactly what infant neurons were doing? Or do the new cells lead to some kind of reorganization of the brain's structure? The cerebral cortex is composed of columns and similar repeating units. The adult cortex has more columns than the infant cortex has, but the average size of columns is not proportionately larger than it was in the infant.

Anthony-Samuel LaMantia and Dale Purves (1989) created a way to stain and photograph the living brain of an infant mouse and then to photograph the same area of brain later in development. They found that brain anatomy is stable over short periods of time. However, from age 4 to 6 days until two weeks later, the brain adds new units. The glomeruli of the olfactory bulb are good examples of such units. As Figure 5.3b shows, the glomeruli present in the first week of life are still present two weeks later, but some new glomeruli have also appeared. Evidently, the brain develops partly by the expansion of old units and partly by the addition of new units. A similar principle holds across species: Primate brains, which are larger than the brains of most other mammalian species, also have more columns and specialized subdivisions of the cortex (Kaas, 1989; Killackey, 1990).

Development of the nervous system naturally entails production and alteration of neurons. Neuroscientists distinguish four major stages in the development of neurons: proliferation, migration, differentiation, and myelination.

Proliferation is the production of new cells. Early in development, cells lining the ventricles of the brain divide to make new cells. Some of these new cells remain where they are, continuing to divide and redivide. Others become primitive neurons and glia that **migrate** (move) toward their eventual destinations in the brain. The cerebral cortex develops from the inside out; that is, each arriving wave of new cells migrates beyond the previous cells.

At first, primitive neurons look much like any other cell of the body. Gradually, a neuron **differentiates**, forming the axon and dendrites that provide its distinctive shape. Generally, the axon grows before the dendrites; in fact, the axon may grow while the neuron is migrating. (Some neurons leave an axon growing behind them, somewhat like a long tail.) After the neuron reaches its

Development of the Brain

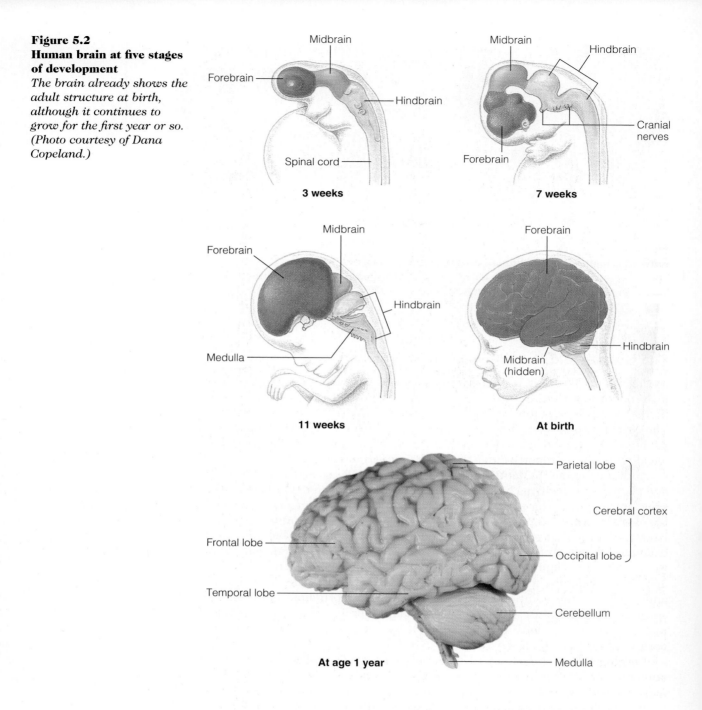

Figure 5.2
Human brain at five stages of development
The brain already shows the adult structure at birth, although it continues to grow for the first year or so. (Photo courtesy of Dana Copeland.)

3 weeks
Midbrain
Forebrain
Hindbrain
Spinal cord

7 weeks
Midbrain
Hindbrain
Cranial nerves
Forebrain

11 weeks
Forebrain
Midbrain
Hindbrain
Medulla

At birth
Forebrain
Hindbrain
Midbrain (hidden)

At age 1 year
Parietal lobe
Cerebral cortex
Frontal lobe
Occipital lobe
Temporal lobe
Cerebellum
Medulla

final location, dendrites begin to form, very slowly at first. Most dendritic growth occurs later, at the time when incoming axons are due to arrive.

Not only does a neuron differentiate to look different from other kinds of body cells, but neurons in different parts of the brain differentiate to look different from one another. Neurons in various parts of the cerebral cortex differ greatly in the size and shape of their dendritic trees. When and how does a neuron "decide" which kind of neuron it is going to be? Evidently, its destiny is not determined until fairly late in development. Experimenters can transfer immature, proliferating neurons from one part of the developing cortex to another;

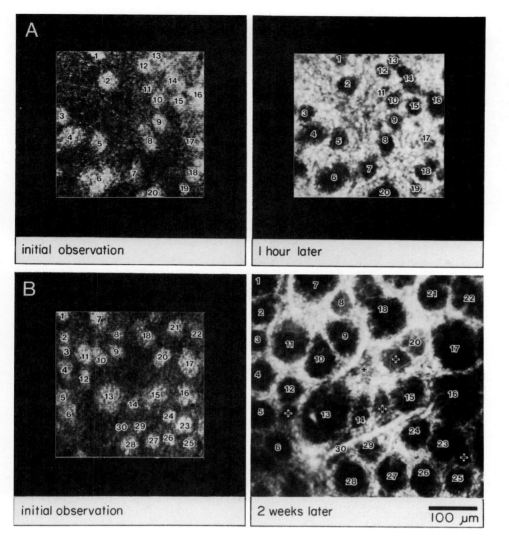

Figure 5.3
Photos of sections of the olfactory bulbs of mice
*The initial observations (**left**) were taken in mice 4 to 6 days old. The later observations (**right**) were taken an hour later or two weeks later, using a different staining procedure. In (**a**), note the consistency of appearance over one hour; each glomerulus is easily recognized and is in the same position. In (**b**), the 30 original glomeruli are still present two weeks later, but five new glomeruli have appeared. The brain develops partly by growth of old units and partly by addition of new units. (From LaMantia & Purves, 1989.)*

the transplanted neurons develop the shape and properties appropriate to their new location. The final shape and function of a neuron is determined by chemical interactions with all the neurons around it (McConnell, 1992).

Finally, some axons myelinate, as glial cells produce the insulating sheaths that make rapid transmission possible. Neurons can be functional before they develop myelin, although the myelin certainly improves their function. In humans, myelin forms first in the spinal cord and then in the hindbrain, midbrain, and forebrain.

Development of the Brain

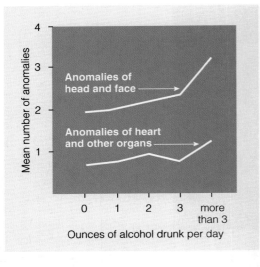

Figure 5.4
(*a*) *Mean number of anomalies in children born to mothers who drank different amounts of alcohol during pregnancy. Examples of anomalies are small head, folds around the eyes, malformed ears, and heart murmurs. (Based on data of Ernhart et al., 1987.)* (*b*) *Child with fetal alcohol syndrome. (George Steinmetz)*

Vulnerability of the Developing Brain

The developing brain is more vulnerable to the effects of toxic chemicals and infections than is the mature brain. For example, if a pregnant woman suffers from syphilis or rubella (German measles) during pregnancy, her baby's developing brain may be seriously damaged (Berg, 1986). Exposure to the same infections in adulthood does not cause immediate brain damage. (Long-term, untreated syphilis does produce brain damage, even in adults.)

A deficiency of iodine in the diet is also more dangerous to the developing fetus or infant than it is to an adult. An iodine deficiency leads to inadequate production of thyroid hormones, and inadequate thyroid hormones early in life lead to **cretinism,** a type of mental retardation characterized by fairly normal appearance at birth but slow mental and physical development (Pollitt, 1988). Thyroid deficiency in adulthood produces other disorders but not mental retardation. Iodine deficiency was more common long ago than it is today. Table salt today is nearly always fortified with iodine, so it would be difficult to consume a diet deficient in iodine.

Exposure to alcohol also impairs the developing brain much more than it does the mature brain. The children of mothers who drink heavily during pregnancy may be born with **fetal alcohol syndrome,** a condition marked by decreased alertness, hyperactivity, varying degrees of mental retardation, motor problems, heart defects, and facial abnormalities (Streissguth, Barr, & Martin, 1983). Dendrites tend to be short, with less branching than in most other people. The more alcohol the mother drinks, the greater the risk (Figure 5.4), but researchers are not sure whether there is a threshold for the effect of alcohol on the brain. That is, no one knows whether a small amount of alcohol is safe or whether even small amounts may be dangerous at certain times of brain development. Studies with nonhuman animals suggest that small amounts can have detectable effects on the brain (Jones, 1988). To play it safe, pregnant women should avoid alcohol (and other drugs) as much as possible during pregnancy.

Modification by Experience

Your genes contain the instructions that specify approximately how to assemble your nervous system—but *only* approximately. In certain invertebrate species, such as slugs or houseflies, the genes specify the assembly of the nervous system with much greater precision. In those species, development does not have to wait for experience to guide it, because the experience is highly predictable. Every slug has pretty much the same way of life as any other slug alive today, or any slug that ever lived. Its genes can set up a nervous system to deal with all the likely situations that the animal will face.

Because vertebrate life is much less predictable, we have evolved the ability to redesign our brains (within limits) based on our experience (Shatz, 1992). Our genes set up an enormous number of neurons, connections, and potential connections, and then experience determines how many and which ones will survive.

Let's start with a relatively simple example of this principle: If you live in a complex and challenging environment, you will need an elaborate and complex nervous system. Ordinarily, a laboratory rat lives in about the simplest, least challenging environment that one could imagine: a small, bare gray cage with food and water. Now imagine some other rats that spend their lives in a more stimulating environment: a larger cage, among ten or so other rats, with a few little pieces of junk to explore or play with. Researchers sometimes call this an "enriched" environment, but it is "enriched" only by contrast to the very impoverished environment of the usual rat cage.

Rats in the more stimulating environment develop more glial cells and a wider pattern of dendritic branches than do rats kept in individual cages (Greenough, 1975; Uphouse, 1980). The anatomical changes are known to last at least a month, and probably much longer, after the animals have been removed from the enriched environment (Camel, Withers, & Greenough, 1986). Similar results have been reported for jewel fish (Coss & Globus, 1979) and honeybees (Coss, Brandon, & Globus, 1980). (See Figure 5.5.)

Let's consider another example: Remember the discussion of birdsong learning in Chapter 1? Baby birds of certain species learn their song by selecting some elements out of a set of "possible song components" and discarding other possible elements (Marler & Nelson, 1992). They apparently do so by magnifying some dendritic branches and shrinking others. One portion of the brain of mynah birds is known to be essential to its ability to sing. (Mynah birds, like parrots and mockingbirds, excel at learning to imitate other birds' songs.) In that brain area, one kind of neuron has a great many *dendritic spines* (little outgrowths) early in the first year of life. At this time, the mynah bird is rapidly learning a variety of new songs. By the end of the first year, each of those neurons has far fewer dendritic spines than it had at the start of the year, but the surviving spines are much larger than they used to be (Figure 5.6). Evidently, the multitude of tiny dendritic spines at the start of the year made it possible for the bird to learn an unpredictable variety of new songs. By the end of the year, the mynah bird had learned many songs and strengthened

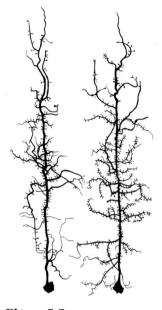

Figure 5.5
Comparison of structures of neurons from the brains of jewel fish reared in isolation (left) and reared with others of their own species (right)
Note the richer branching pattern in the neuron on the right. (Photo courtesy of Richard Coss.)

Development of the Brain

Figure 5.6
Dendritic spines in the song-control area of a mynah bird's brain
(*a*) *Early in its first year of life, the bird has an enormous number of tiny spines, each of them evidently corresponding to the enormous variety of potential song elements that the bird might learn.* (*b*) *About a year later, the bird has far fewer spines, but the surviving spines have grown much larger. These presumably correspond to song elements that the bird has actually learned to produce. (From Rausch & Scheich, 1982.)*

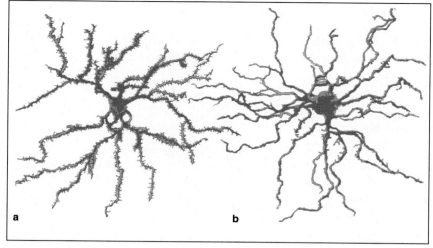

the spines needed for those songs, but by losing other spines it virtually lost the ability to learn additional songs.

Pathfinding by Axons

For the nervous system to operate properly, axons must reach their proper targets, forming synapses with the correct neurons. How do they find their way?

Basic Strategies for Directing an Axon to Its Target

Suppose you operate a federal government office in Washington, D.C. You need to convey some secret messages—so secret that you cannot use telephones or the mail. You decide to install private telegraph cables to the places where you expect to send messages. You tell one of your employees, "Here, Carlos, take this cable and run it across the street to the Office of Bureaucratic Mismanagement." Because it is so near, you hardly give a thought as to how he is going to find the way. Then you tell another employee, "Here, Carla, take this very long cable and stretch it to the mayor's office in Truth or Consequences, New Mexico." (Carla got the tough job.) Now you definitely have to worry: Will Carla find a reasonably direct route from here to there? Will she find her way at all? You would have to make sure that she has a map and a compass and that she knows how to read street signs. Or, if some other employee had made the same trip last week and had carefully left a trail, you could just tell Carla to follow the purple arrows along the side of the road.

The developing nervous system faces a similar problem. It sends some of its axons over enormous distances. For example, the cerebral cortex sends certain axons all the way to the spinal cord, and the spinal cord sends motor axons to muscles in the arms, legs, and elsewhere. How do these axons find their way to the correct locations? And does the nervous system ever know that its axons have reached their targets?

Chemical Pathfinding by Axons

A famous biologist, Paul Weiss (1924), once conducted an experiment in which he grafted an extra leg to a salamander and then waited for axons to grow into it. (Such an experiment could never work with a mammal. Salamanders and other amphibians can regenerate many parts of their bodies, including limbs, that mammals cannot. They also generate new axon branches to an extra, grafted-on limb.) After the axons reached the muscles, Weiss observed the animal's behavior. The extra leg, positioned right next to one of the hind legs, moved in perfect synchrony with the normal adjacent leg.

One possible interpretation of these results is that each axon to the normal limb had developed a branch that found its way to exactly the same muscle in the extra limb. Weiss dismissed that interpretation as unbelievable. He suggested instead that the nerves attached to muscles at random and then sent a variety of messages, each one "tuned" to a different muscle. In other words, it did not matter which axon was attached to which muscle. The muscles were like a series of radios, each tuned to a different station. They all received the same signals through the air, but each one responded only to the station to which it was tuned.

Weiss's theory has not stood the test of time. Later evidence supported the interpretation Weiss had dismissed as unbelievable: that the salamander's extra leg moved in synchrony with its neighbor because each axon had sent a branch to each leg and each branch had attached to exactly the same muscle. That is, a growing axon finds its way to the correct target.

Since the time of Weiss's work, most of the research on axon growth has dealt with how sensory axons find their way to the correct targets in the brain. (The issues and difficulties are the same as those for axons finding their way to muscles in the periphery.) Roger Sperry, who was a student of Weiss, conducted much of the decisive research in this area. In one study, he cut the optic nerve of some newts. In amphibians, unlike mammals, a damaged optic nerve grows back and contacts the **tectum,** the main visual area of fish, amphibians, reptiles, and birds (see Figure 5.7). Sperry found that when the new synapses formed, the newt regained normal vision.

To discover how the axons find their targets, Sperry (1943) repeated the experiment, but this time, after he cut each optic nerve, he rotated the eye by 180 degrees. When the axons grew back to the tectum, would the axons rotated to the dorsal side of the eye go where axons from the dorsal side ordinarily go, and would the axons now on the ventral side go where axons on the ventral side ordinarily go? Or would each axon ignore the fact that it was in a new position and find its way back to its *original* target, indicating that it "knew" where to go? Sperry found that the axons from what had originally been the dorsal side of the retina (which was now on the ventral side) grew back to their original target area of the tectum—the area responsible for vision in the dorsal side of the retina. Likewise, axons from what had once been the ventral side of the retina (now on the dorsal side) grew back to the tectal area responsible for vision on the ventral side of the retina. The newt now saw the world upside down and backward. It responded to stimuli in the sky as if they were on the ground, and to stimuli on the left as if they were on the right (see Figure 5.8). Evidently, each axon regenerated to the area of the tectum where it had originally been—the area where it "knew" it belonged.

In another experiment, Domenica Attardi and Roger Sperry (1963) damaged parts of the retina in a group of goldfish and cut their optic nerves. The optic nerve from the intact part of each retina grew back to the tectal area that

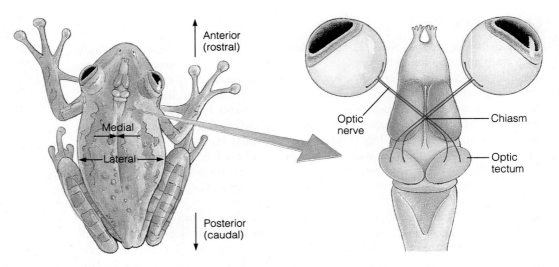

Figure 5.7
The optic tectum is a large structure in fish, amphibians, reptiles, and birds. In location, it corresponds to the midbrain of mammals, but its function is more elaborate, analogous to what the cerebral cortex does in mammals. (After Romer, 1962.)

Figure 5.8
Summary of Sperry's experiment on nerve connections in newts
After he cut the optic nerve and inverted the eye, the optic nerve axons grew back to their original targets, not the targets corresponding to the eye's current position.

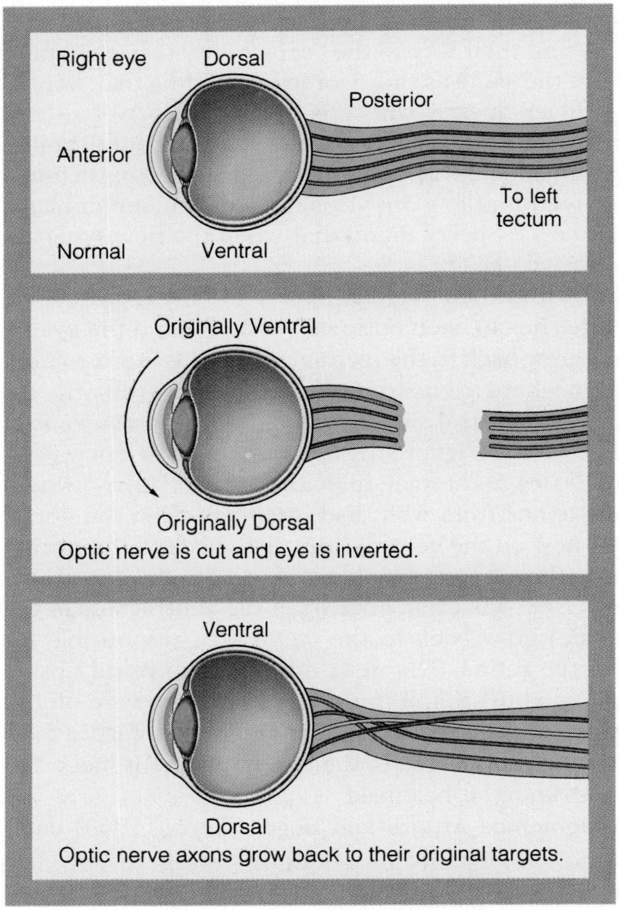

Right eye   Dorsal

Posterior

Anterior

To left
tectum

Normal   Ventral

Originally Ventral

Originally Dorsal
Optic nerve is cut and eye is inverted.

Ventral

Dorsal
Optic nerve axons grow back to their original targets.

Chapter 5
Development and Evolution
of the Brain

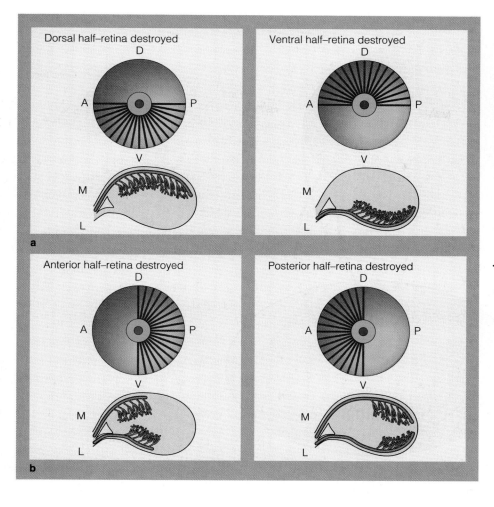

Figure 5.9

After half of the goldfish retina is destroyed and the optic nerve from the other half is cut, the optic nerve grows back to just half of the optic tectum, the part that it ordinarily innervates. (a) After the destruction of the dorsal or ventral half-retina, axons from the remaining half-retina regenerate to the medial-dorsal or lateral-ventral half of the tectum, respectively. (b) After the destruction of the anterior or posterior half-retina, axons from the remaining half of the retina regenerate to the appropriate half of the tectum. (Based on Attardi & Sperry, 1963.)

it ordinarily innervated, as Figure 5.9 shows. Again, each axon found its appropriate target. The tectal areas originally innervated by the damaged parts of the retina now had vacant synapses, with no incoming axons. As with the previous experiment, these results suggested that each axon might be following a chemical trail to its destination, like a bloodhound sniffing its way through the forest. We now know that some cells emit chemicals that attract a given axon, while other cells emit chemicals that repel the axon (Pini, 1993).

The next question was how specific a target the axon might have. Did an axon from an amphibian's or goldfish's retina have to find the tectal cell with exactly the right chemical marker on its surface, like a key finding the right lock? Such a mechanism would be barely plausible. Just think of the billions of axons that the nervous system has. Does the body have to synthesize a separate chemical marker for each one of them?

No. Neurons in the retina are marked with a gradient of chemicals, and so are the neurons in the tectum. One such chemical is a protein known as TOP_{DV} (TOP for *top*ography; DV for *d*orso-*v*entral). This protein is 30 times more concentrated in the neurons of the dorsal retina than it is in the neurons of the ventral retina, and it is 10 times more concentrated in the ventral tectum than in the dorsal tectum. As axons from the retina grow toward the tectum, the

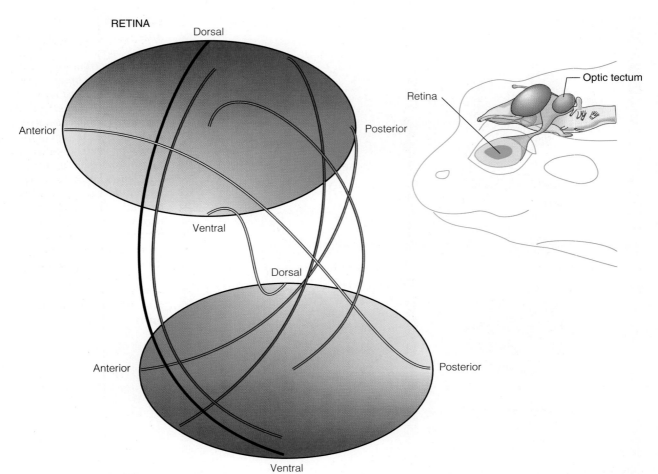

RETINA

Dorsal

Anterior

Posterior

Ventral

Dorsal

Anterior

Posterior

Ventral

OPTIC TECTUM

Retina

Optic tectum

Figure 5.10
Retinal axons match up with neurons in the tectum by following two gradients
The protein TOP$_{DV}$ is concentrated mostly in the dorsal retina and the ventral tectum. Axons rich in TOP$_{DV}$ attach to tectal neurons that are also rich in that chemical. Similarly, a second protein directs axons from the posterior retina to the anterior portion of the tectum. To illustrate the gradient, the drawing at left is diagrammatic; it is not anatomically realistic.

retinal axons with the greatest concentration of TOP$_{DV}$ connect to the tectal cells with the highest concentration of that chemical; the axons with the lowest concentration connect to the tectal cells with the lowest concentration. A similar gradient of another protein aligns the axons along the anterior-posterior axis (Sanes, 1993). (See Figure 5.10.)

Retinal axons can find their way to the correct target even if they do not start off in the normal location. For example, in one series of studies, experimenters took retinal tissue of fetal rats and transplanted it into the interior of the brain, far from the normal location of the eyes. The retinal axons grew from that odd location to the same locations where vertebrate retinal axons normally go (Craner, Hoffman, Lund, Humphrey, & Lund, 1992). (As a consequence, these rats would have been constantly watching the inside of their own heads, if there had been any light there.) Evidently, axons have a powerful ability to follow chemical paths to their appointed destinations.

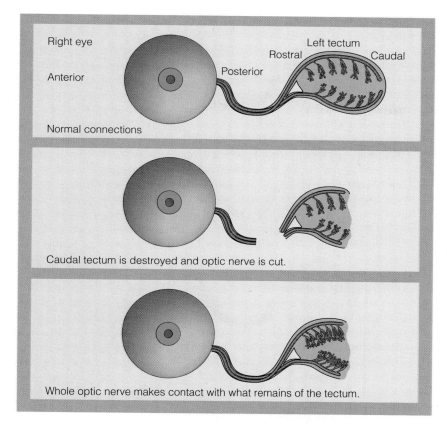

Figure 5.11
Results of experiments on regeneration of the goldfish optic nerve after damage to the optic tectum
Experimenters cut the optic nerve and destroyed the caudal part of the tectum. Then the axons that ordinarily innervate the caudal tectum grew back to the most caudal part of the remaining tectum. Other axons arranged themselves in the correct order as before, though not on the same target cells as before. (Based on results of Gaze & Sharma, 1970; Yoon, 1971.)

Once an axon reaches the correct brain location, it does not have to search for its one and only possible target. Suppose that an axon reaches its approximately correct destination, only to discover that its target cells have been destroyed. For example, axons from the anterior ventral part of an amphibian retina might reach the tectum, only to find that something has destroyed the tectal neurons to which these axons ordinarily should connect. The axon does not necessarily die; it may make contact with the nearest approximation that it can find to its normal target. In two similar experiments, investigators removed the caudal half of the tectum of goldfish and cut the optic nerve. Ordinarily, axons from the anterior side of the retina make contact with the caudal tectum. When those axons reached the tectum, they formed synapses with the most caudal portion of what was left of the tectum (Figure 5.11). That is, the whole optic nerve made a compressed projection onto the now-small tectum (Gaze & Sharma, 1970; Yoon, 1971).

In a related experiment, investigators destroyed the anterior half of the retina of goldfish and then cut the optic nerve, letting the axon from the posterior half-retina regenerate. Initially, it connected only to its normal area, the rostral part of the tectum. Months later, however, some of the axons began creeping from the edge of the rostral tectum into the adjacent areas of the caudal tectum (Figure 5.12). This process continued until the axons had spread themselves evenly over the entire tectum (Schmidt, Cicerone, & Easter, 1977).

These experiments suggest an alternative interpretation of how axons attach to targets: Imagine the growing axons as males and the target cells as females. Generally, the northernmost males mate with the northernmost females, and the southernmost males mate with the southernmost females.

Figure 5.12
Results of an experiment on regrowth of a goldfish's optic nerve after damage to half of the retina

Experimenters destroyed the anterior retina and cut the optic nerve. At first, axons from the posterior retina grew back to their original target cells in the caudal tectum (as they did in the earlier experiment by Attardi and Sperry). However, as months passed, connections moved into the vacant rostral portion of the tectum and eventually spread out over the whole tectum. (Based on results of Schmidt, Cicerone, & Easter, 1977.)

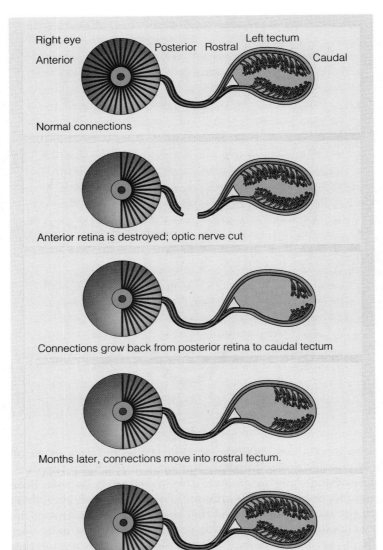

Normal connections

Anterior retina is destroyed; optic nerve cut

Connections grow back from posterior retina to caudal tectum

Months later, connections move into rostral tectum.

Eventually, connections spread out over whole tectum.

Similarly, the axons and cells have a gradient of preferences. The axons from the most anterior regions of the retina pair with the most caudal cells available, the axons from the most posterior retina pair with the most rostral cells, and the intermediate axons space themselves out as evenly as they can.

Competition among Axons

Let us continue with this analogy of axons as males pairing with target cells as females. In human dating, males are selective about which females they pursue, but females are just as selective, or more so, about which males they will accept as potential suitors. Axons show selectivity in that they grow toward certain targets and not toward others. Are those target cells also selective?

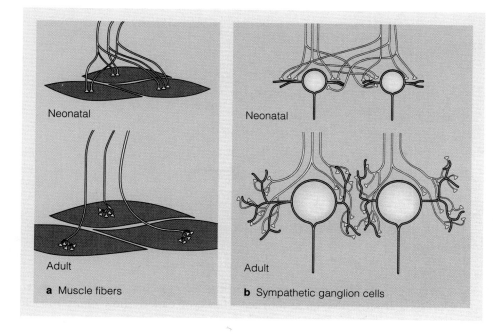

a Muscle fibers   **b** Sympathetic ganglion cells

Figure 5.13
Development by elimination of synapses
(*a*) *Early in development, each muscle fiber receives synapses from branches of several motor axons. The muscle fiber gradually strengthens its synapse with one axon and rejects the others. (However, an axon can form synapses with many muscle fibers.)* (*b*) *Early in development, neurons in the ganglia of the sympathetic nervous system receive synapses from many axons. Later, each cell rejects the incoming axons from some neurons and accepts the axons from others. Although the cell as a whole may accept axons from numerous different neurons, typically, each dendrite forms lasting synapses with only one axon. That axon may, however, form a great many branches and therefore a great many synapses onto that dendrite. (After Purves & Lichtman, 1980.)*

That is, do they accept synapses from any and all axons, or do they accept some and reject others?

The answer: They do accept some and reject others; their selectivity plays an important part in the construction of the nervous system (Easter, Purves, Rakic, & Spitzer, 1985; Purves & Lichtman, 1980). In the early stages of embryonic development, the nervous system overproduces neurons and axons. Many parts of the CNS develop two or three times as many neurons as will actually survive into adulthood. Their axons then grow out toward their targets and establish more-or-less correct connections. At this point, each axon forms synapses onto a number of target cells, and each target cell receives synapses from a large number of axons. And then gradually certain synapses are eliminated. The postsynaptic cell develops a strong connection with some of those axons, but not all. In many cases, one cell accepts an axon that another cell rejects. Figure 5.13 summarizes the results: At first, axons and postsynaptic cells have many tentative connections with one another; later they develop fewer but stronger attachments.

As the postsynaptic cells favor some axons and reject others, each axon grows additional branches onto each postsynaptic cell that accepts it, while it withdraws from others. Neurons whose axons fail to form synapses degenerate and die. Each part of the brain has a period of massive cell death when it is littered with dead and dying cells (Figure 5.14). This does not indicate that something is wrong; it is a natural part of development (Finlay & Pallas, 1989).

Why does the CNS produce more neurons than it needs? There are at least two explanations:

1. The extra neurons enable the postsynaptic cells to be selective. In a sense, overproduction of neurons followed by cell death provides an opportunity for "survival of the fittest." Perhaps each postsynaptic cell has a greater opportunity to find an acceptable axon if it can choose among many.
2. The extra neurons enable the CNS to compensate for unpredictable variations in body size. For example, when the motor neuron axons begin

Development of the Brain

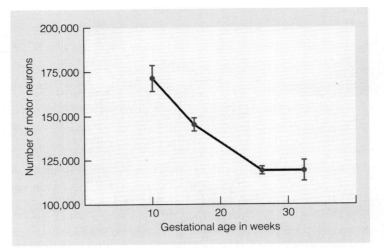

Figure 5.14
Mean number of motor neurons in the ventral spinal cord of human fetuses at ages 11 weeks to 32 weeks
Note that the number of motor neurons is highest at 11 weeks and drops steadily until about 25 weeks. This is when motor neuron axons make synapses with muscles. Those that fail to make synapses die. (From Forger & Breedlove, 1987.)

growing from the spinal cord toward the leg muscles, there is no way to predict exactly how large that leg will be or exactly how many muscle fibers it will have. The spinal cord sends out a great many axons; the larger the leg is, the more axons survive. In short, the death of excess axons enables the body to end up with just the necessary number.

How does a postsynaptic neuron "decide" which axon or axons to accept and which to reject? We can imagine several possible mechanisms; here are two: First, just as axons approach some targets and not others because of their chemical markers, the postsynaptic cells may recognize chemical markers on the axons that identify them as more acceptable or less acceptable. Second, in many cases, the postsynaptic cell is more likely to form synapses with combinations of axons that are simultaneously active, instead of combinations that send uncorrelated messages.

Let's consider one example of that second mechanism: One part of the thalamus, the *lateral geniculate* (Figure 4.14), receives its input from the retinas of the eyes. At first, each cell in the lateral geniculate receives input from a rather erratically chosen group of axons. Gradually, it cleans up its mistakes and selects a smaller group of axons, which originated from spots near one another in the retina. Now, how did that lateral geniculate cell "know" which axons started off in the same part of the retina? The answer is that, during prenatal development, long before the eyes are open and before they would be exposed to any light, the retinal receptors are spontaneously active. Repeated waves of activity sweep over the retina from one side to the other. Consequently, axons from adjacent areas of the retina become active almost simultaneously. Each lateral geniculate cell selects a group of axons that are simultaneously active at this time; the result is a group of axons from adjacent areas of the retina (Meister, Wong, Baylor, & Shatz, 1991).

Chemical Mechanisms of Neuron Death and Neuron Survival

Exactly *how* does a postsynaptic cell accept some axons and reject others? Or to put it another way, how does a neuron know whether its axon has been accepted or rejected?

Investigators have long known that the spinal cord sends out many motor neuron axons to a body area with many muscles and fewer to an area with fewer muscles. At one time, neuroscientists believed that the muscles sent some sort of message to tell the spinal cord how many axons to generate. (The more muscles, the more of that message and therefore the more neurons.)

Thanks to the research of Nobel Prize winner Rita Levi-Montalcini, we now know that each area of the spinal cord generates its normal number of axons regardless of how many muscles are present in the corresponding body area. The muscles do not determine how many axons grow; they only determine how many axons *survive*.

For example, when a neuron of the sympathetic nervous system forms a synapse onto an organ muscle, that muscle delivers a protein called **nerve growth factor (NGF)** that promotes the survival and growth of the axon (Levi-Montalcini, 1987). An axon that does not receive enough nerve growth factor degenerates, and its cell body dies. In other words, various axons in the sympathetic nervous system compete with one another for NGF, which they need for survival. NGF is like a magic potion that tells an axon, "Yes, you can survive."

Nerve growth factor is a **trophic factor**, a chemical that promotes survival and activity. (The word *trophic* is derived from ancient Greek for *nourishment*.) NGF is just one of the body's trophic factors and is effective only for certain kinds of axons. Other trophic factors influence other types of neurons. For example, one trophic factor specifically promotes the survival of neurons that release dopamine as their transmitter (Lin, Doherty, Lile, Bektesh, & Collins, 1993). That factor may prove to be a useful treatment for Parkinson's disease, which is caused by a gradual loss of dopamine-containing neurons.

Certain trophic factors enable axons in the brain to find their correct destinations. Consider the following: The thalamus sends axons to the cerebral cortex, specifically to lamina IV (Figure 4.17), the main sensory lamina of the cortex. Somehow, those axons have to find lamina IV; they have to grow far enough, but not too far. The cortex produces trophic factors that guide the growth of those axons. At an early stage of development, the thalamus matures faster than the cerebral cortex. When axons from the thalamus reach the outskirts of the cortex, they wait there—for several days in primates—until the cells of the cortex reach maturity. At that point, the cortical neurons begin to produce trophic factors that promote the growth of thalamic axons. The thalamic axons grow through laminae VI and V, which produce substantial amounts of the trophic factor. However, the neurons in lamina IV do not produce the trophic factor. Thus, when the axons get to lamina IV, they stop growing. In short, the trophic factors from the cortex keep the thalamic axons growing just until they reach the point at which they are supposed to make synapses (Götz, Novak, Bastmeyer, & Bolz, 1992). Figure 5.15 summarizes this result.

Competition among Axons as a General Principle of Neural Functioning

To some theorists, the principles we have considered so far in this chapter suggest a possible general principle of brain functioning, a principle that Gerald Edelman (1987) calls **neural Darwinism**. The basic principle of Darwinian evolution is that, during reproduction, gene mutations and gene reassortment produce individuals with variations in structure and function (see Appendix A). Natural selection favors some variations while weeding out the rest.

Figure 5.15
How trophic factors route thalamic axons to the correct layer of the cerebral cortex

In primates, thalamic neurons and their axons develop days before the cerebral cortex does. The thalamic axons wait at the outskirts of the cortex until cortical cells are ready. At that point, cells in layers VI and V secrete trophic factors that promote the growth of the thalamic axons. Those axons grow through layers VI and V, but stop in layer IV because cells in that layer fail to produce the trophic factor.

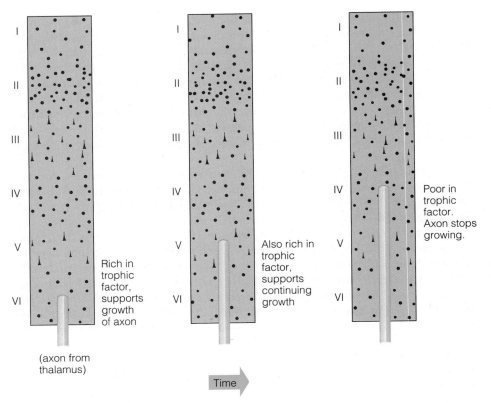

Rich in trophic factor, supports growth of axon

(axon from thalamus)

Also rich in trophic factor, supports continuing growth

Time

Poor in trophic factor. Axon stops growing.

Similarly, in the development of the nervous system, we start with more neurons and synapses than we shall keep. Synapses form somewhat randomly at first, and then a selection process keeps some and rejects others. A muscle fiber selects only one incoming axon, based mostly on chemical factors. Neurons are more complicated. A neuron selects the most active incoming axon, or combinations of two or more incoming axons, especially if those axons generally send synchronized signals. In this manner, the most successful axons or axon combinations survive; the less active or less informative ones fail to sustain active synapses.

The principle of competition among axons is an important one, although we should handle the analogy with Darwinian evolution cautiously. So far as we know, mutations in the genes occur completely at random. The growth of axonal branches and new synapses is partly random but partly controlled by chemical guidance and trophic factors. Still, in both cases, we can talk about the most successful types proliferating at the expense of the less successful. And in both cases, a change in the environment can cause a different type of individual to thrive.

Pioneer Neurons

The development of connections to and from the cerebral cortex poses some special problems. The human cerebral cortex forms extensive connections with the thalamus and other subcortical structures that are fairly well developed and ready for synaptic contacts by the 35th day of embryonic development. But the cerebral cortex itself is slow to mature. The first cortical neurons appear during the seventh week of fetal development, and the others develop gradually until at least the 16th week (Rakic, 1978). So the subcortical areas are ready to form synapses with cortical cells before most of the cortical cells themselves are ready. And by the time the cortical cells are ready, the cortex has grown so large that these cells are far from the subcortical areas with which they must exchange connections. If the axons are to find their way from cortex to thalamus, or from thalamus to cortex, they will have to travel a substantial distance, past an enormous number of other cells and axons. How do they do so?

Earlier in this chapter, I suggested that one way people could find their way from Washington, D.C., to New Mexico would be to follow a path left by a previous traveler. The CNS uses that principle in connecting the cortex to subcortical structures. Early in embryonic development, when neurons in the cerebral cortex are all immature, the brain develops neurons called **subplate cells** just below where the cerebral cortex is developing. Axons from the thalamus and other subcortical areas synapse with these subplate cells; the subplate cells extend their axons back to the subcortical areas, to other subplate cells, and across the corpus callosum to the opposite hemisphere. The subplate cells maintain much neural activity, but they do so only temporarily. When the neurons of the cerebral cortex mature, they extend their axons down through the cortex to the subplate cells and then follow the axons of the subplate cells to their various targets, including the subcortical areas of the brain. Then the thalamic axons that had made contact with the subplate neurons extend their axons farther, making synapses in the cerebral cortex. After these new synapses are formed, the subplate neurons die. In this manner, the subplate neurons act as "pioneer neurons"; they survive only briefly themselves, but they establish paths to be used by later-developing, permanent neurons (McConnell, Ghosh, & Shatz, 1989).

Summary

1. In vertebrate embryos, the central nervous system begins as a tube surrounding a fluid-filled cavity. The human CNS grows to about one-fourth of adult size by birth and to almost adult size by age 1 year. (p. 146)

2. During development of the nervous system, growing axons manage to find their way to approximately the right locations. Over the years, investigators have discovered some of the mechanisms by which axons find their way. (p. 152)

3. In many nonmammalian species, a damaged optic nerve can regenerate. When it does so, the axons grow back to more or less their original targets, apparently identifying their target cells chemically. (p. 153)

4. Axons identify their targets relatively, not absolutely. For example, an axon that ordinarily connects to the extreme caudal part of the tectum will, if deprived of its normal target, connect to the most caudal area available. (p. 157)

5. Initially, many axons attach to each postsynaptic cell. The postsynaptic cell selects one or more of these axons and delivers to them a trophic factor, a chemical that promotes survival and growth. Nerve growth factor is one trophic factor. (p. 161)

6. An axon that does not receive the trophic factor withdraws from that cell. Axons that do not establish a lasting synapse with any target cell degenerate, and their cell bodies die. (p. 161)

7. Development of the cerebral cortex poses special problems because its cells reach maturity far later than the neurons of the thalamus, with which they must make contact. To solve this problem, the thalamic cells form synapses with temporary "pioneer" neurons just below the developing cortex. When the cortical neurons become mature, their axons follow the paths of the pioneer cells' axons. (p. 162)

Review Questions

1. How did Roger Sperry establish that each axon finds its way to a relatively specific target, instead of connecting at random? (p. 153)

2. Suppose that the optic nerve of a fish or amphibian is cut and permitted to regenerate, but part of the tectum has

been destroyed. What will happen to the axons that ordinarily make contact with the now-damaged area? (p. 157)

3. In what sense do axons compete with one another? (p. 158)

4. At what age does the nervous system have the largest number of neurons: during early embryonic development, infancy, or adulthood? (p. 159)

5. What is nerve growth factor and how does it contribute to the development of the nervous system? (p. 161)

6. What does the term *neural Darwinism* mean? (p. 161)

7. Why does the brain need a population of temporary "pioneer" neurons, the subplate neurons? (p. 163)

Thought Questions

1. Biologists can develop antibodies against nerve growth factor (that is, molecules that inactivate nerve growth factor). What would happen if someone injected such antibodies into a developing nervous system?

2. Ordinarily, cells in one part of the thalamus, the lateral geniculate, send their axons to the primary visual area of the cerebral cortex, in the occipital lobe. Suppose that the primary visual cortex is destroyed in newborn kittens. What is likely to happen to the lateral geniculate cells?

Suggestions for Further Reading

Edelman, G. (1987). *Neural Darwinism.* New York: Basic Books. Detailed theoretical treatment of how neurons and synapses are selected through competition with one another.

Levi-Montalcini, R. (1988). *In praise of imperfection.* New York: Basic Books. Autobiography by the discoverer of nerve growth factor.

Purves, D. (1988). *Body and brain.* Cambridge, MA: Harvard University Press. An excellent account of research on the growth of axons and the development of the vertebrate nervous system.

Shatz, C. J. (1992, September). The developing brain. *Scientific American, 267 (3),* 60–67. Excellent review of current research and theory of brain development, by one of the leading researchers.

Terms

proliferation the production of new cells (p. 147)

migration movement of neurons toward their eventual destinations in the brain (p. 147)

differentiation formation of the axon and dendrites that gives a neuron its distinctive shape (p. 147)

cretinism a type of mental retardation characterized by fairly normal appearance at birth but slow mental and physical development, caused by an iodine deficiency that leads to inadequate production of thyroid hormones early in life (p. 150)

fetal alcohol syndrome condition resulting from prenatal exposure to alcohol and marked by decreased alertness, hyperactivity, varying degrees of mental retardation, motor problems, heart defects, and facial abnormalities (p. 150)

tectum the main visual area of fish, amphibians, reptiles, and birds (p. 153)

nerve growth factor (NGF) protein that promotes the survival and growth of axons in the sympathetic nervous system and certain axons in the brain (p. 161)

trophic factor chemical that promotes survival and activity (p. 161)

neural Darwinism principle that, in the development of the nervous system, synapses form somewhat randomly at first, and then a selection process keeps some and rejects others (p. 161)

subplate cell temporary neuron that forms just below the area where the cerebral cortex is developing (p. 163)

Evolution of the Brain and Its Capacities

We humans like to think of ourselves as the dominant animal species on earth. By "dominant," we do not mean that we are the most numerous, but that we largely control the environment. We tear down forests, replant forests, extract gas and oil from the ground, bury our garbage underground, tunnel through mountains, build bridges over rivers, and in countless other ways rebuild the world to fit our desires. We capture and domesticate animals useful to us, like horses. We kill animals that threaten us, like grizzly bears, until their numbers dwindle to near-extinction, and then we protect them. In one way or another, we make decisions that affect life and death for all or nearly all other species.

What gives us this great power? Our brains do, of course. But what aspect of our brains is important? Is it the total size, or some detail of brain structure or organization?

Furthermore, how and why did humans evolve the kinds of brains we have? And if our kind of brain is so useful, why didn't raccoons or kangaroos or some other species evolve this kind of brain too?

One more issue: If a certain kind of brain size or structure is what enables humans to do so much more than other animals can, does brain structure also account for some of the differences among humans? That is, if humans can do more than other species can because of our large brains, is it also true that some humans are more intelligent than others because they have larger brains?

I shall warn you at the start that these are difficult, slippery issues and that this chapter will not reach firm conclusions on any of the main questions. But the topic is worth exploring nevertheless, if only to outline what we *don't* know, and why. By the end of this section, you may not know all the answers, but at least you should better understand the questions.

Difficulties of Inferring Evolution of Brain or Behavior

Shortly we shall be examining some differences among animal brains, as shown in Figure 5.16. No doubt you have seen similar illustrations in other texts, and you will probably see them again in the future. If I do not explain carefully, you may assume that you are looking at some sort of evolutionary sequence—for example, the codfish brain evolved into the frog brain, which evolved into the alligator brain, and so forth until it reached the human brain. In reality, nothing of the sort is true (Campbell & Hodos, 1991). The ancient ancestors that gave rise to today's species were not the same as any of today's fish, amphibians, reptiles, and so forth; each species has changed over evolutionary time.

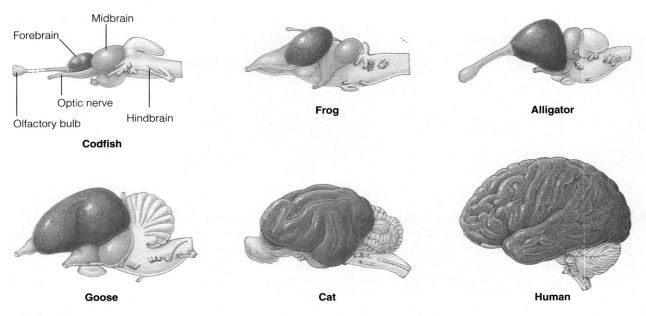

Forebrain
Midbrain
Optic nerve
Olfactory bulb
Hindbrain

Codfish

Frog

Alligator

Goose

Cat

Human

Figure 5.16
The brains of six verte-brates (not drawn to the same scale)
The human forebrain covers the dorsal surface of the midbrain and part of the hindbrain. (After Romer, 1962.)

What *did* the brains of our ancient ancestors look like, and how did they behave? We cannot answer with certainty. Behavior, with very few exceptions, does not fossilize. ("Exceptions?" you might ask. "How could any behavior ever leave fossils?") Occasionally, investigators find fossil footprints, from which they can reconstruct the animal's gait. But that's about the limit of fossilized behavior.) Investigators also find no fossil brains. The closest they can come is to find fossil skulls. In contemporary animals, the brain more or less fills the skull; assuming that the same was true for animals of the past, we can infer the size and shape of the brain for animals of the remote past.

Can we go beyond that very limited inference, to reconstruct also the organization of the brain? To a limited extent, and with certain reservations, we can use current species to make inferences about ancient species. For example, we find that in all mammals the main route of visual information goes to a particular section of the occipital cortex, the *primary visual cortex*. Because all of today's mammals have their primary visual cortex in the same location, we infer that the original, ancestral mammals had a similar organization, and that all of today's mammals inherited the relevant genes from a common ancestor. Still, we must be ever cautious when discussing the "primitive" mammalian brain; the line separating reasonable inferences from mere guesswork is often a blurry one indeed (Deacon, 1990b).

Structures that differ strikingly among today's mammals probably represent evolutionary additions in one line or another. For example, although all mammals have a primary visual cortex, some species have additional, supplementary visual areas, while others do not. These additional visual areas were, we infer, added at various times in various mammalian lines, including the line that eventually led to primates. The language areas of the human cortex are much elaborated even in comparison with other primates; neuroscientists therefore infer that those areas of the cortex represent relatively recent evolutionary changes.

In short, we can with caution draw a few inferences about how various brains evolved and what kinds of brains ancestral species had. But we do not assume that something like today's codfish evolved into reptiles, or reptiles into mammals, or that one of today's monkeys evolved into humans.

Chapter 5
Development and Evolution of the Brain

166

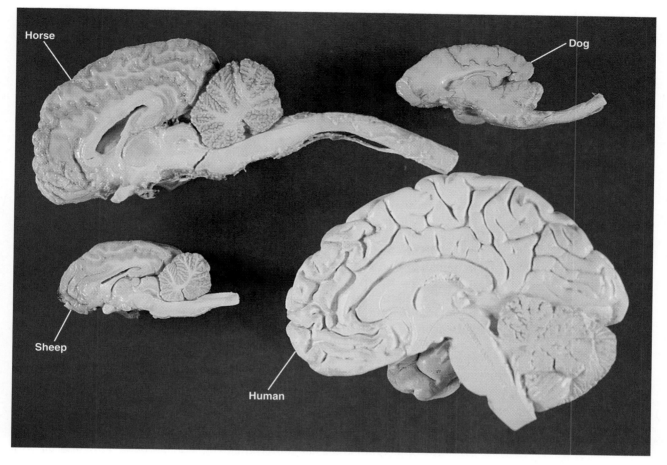

Labels on image: Horse, Dog, Sheep, Human

Figure 5.17
Similarities and differences in mammalian brains
The general structure and organization of the brain is the same across species, but each species has adaptations to its own way of life. For example, primates have large visual areas and small olfactory bulbs. Species that rely heavily on hearing have elaborations in the auditory area. (Photo by David Hinds.)

Human Brains and Other Brains

Throughout this text, you will find numerous studies of rat brains and other nonhuman brains, conducted by investigators who are ultimately concerned to understand human brains. Their justification for studying nonhuman brains is that the fundamental principles of nervous functioning—how axons and synapses work, for example—are largely the same throughout the animal kingdom, and that the general structure of the nervous system is about the same throughout the vertebrates. Even the neurotransmitters are the same; in fact, most of our neurotransmitters are found throughout the entire animal kingdom, not just in fellow vertebrates (Erbas, Meinertzhagen, & Shaw, 1991). That is, evolution alters a number of the details of the nervous system, but it keeps the basic principles intact.

Figure 5.16 illustrates the structures of six vertebrate brains. In all six species, we can distinguish three major areas: the *forebrain,* the *midbrain,* and the *hindbrain.* Note that the forebrain forms a larger proportion of the brain in mammals, such as rats and humans, than in fish, amphibians, and reptiles.

If we compare the human brain to the brain of cat, monkey, or any other mammal, we find striking similarities (Figure 5.17). In each case, the forebrain

*Evolution of the Brain and
Its Capacities*

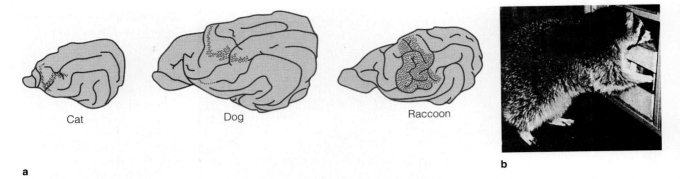

Cat   Dog   Raccoon

a   b

Figure 5.18
Relationship between brain specialization and behavioral capacities
(*a*) *Representations of the cerebral cortex of cat, dog, and raccoon. The stippled area indicates the section of the somatosensory cortex devoted to sensations from the paws. In the case of the raccoon, it seems more appropriate to call them "hands" than "paws" because of their great sensitivity.* (*b*) *A raccoon reaches through a barrier to feel two objects. To get a food reinforcement, it must pull the ball and not the square. Raccoons learn to make fine touch discriminations about as accurately as college students do.* (*From Rensch & Dücker, 1963.*)

is the largest structure, covering the dorsal midbrain and part of the hindbrain. However, within the constraints of this overall plan, different brain areas are emphasized in different species. You may note in Figure 5.16 that the olfactory bulbs form a smaller percentage of the human brain than they do of most other mammalian brains. This trend corresponds to the fact that most other mammals rely on olfaction more heavily than humans do. Humans, on the other hand, have large and highly elaborate visual areas in the cerebral cortex. The brain areas essential for localizing sounds are unusually large in dolphins and bats, which find their way about by echolocation (Harrison & Irving, 1966). Raccoons, whose sense of touch is very precise, have an unusually large area of the cerebral cortex devoted to touch (Rensch & Dücker, 1963; see Figure 5.18).

Conversely, in species that make little use of a particular sense, the cortical area devoted to that sense tends to be small. For example, certain fish have evolved to live in completely dark caves. Over evolutionary time, their eyes have become blind, and the area of their brain devoted to vision has become much smaller than in other fish (Voneida & Fish, 1984). In short, the relative size of various brain areas has something to do with the behavioral abilities and deficits of an animal.

Recall from Chapter 4 that the cell bodies of the cerebral cortex line its outer surface; the interior of the cerebral cortex consists almost entirely of axons. Because the information-processing ability of the cortex depends on the number of cell bodies, dendrites, and synapses, an evolutionary increase in processing capacity requires an evolutionary increase in the surface area of the cortex. However, the head has only so much room available; beyond a certain point, the best way to expand the surface of the cortex is to fold it back and forth. **Primates** (monkeys, apes, and humans) have extensive folding in their cerebral cortex, resulting in the gyri and sulci evident on the surface of our brains. Nonprimate mammals with large heads and large brains—bears, antelopes, and so forth—also have a fair amount of folding in the surface of their cerebral cortex, but primates have an even greater degree of folding than one would predict from the overall volume of their brains (Zilles, Armstrong, Moser, Schleicher, & Stephan, 1989). In short, the evolution of primates has been characterized by greater development of the cerebral cortex than in other mammals. (*Why* this is true is a matter of speculation.)

The evolution of the primate brain apparently has proceeded mainly by adding new areas, instead of just expanding the old areas (Killackey, 1990; Rakic, 1988). For example, the primary visual cortex does not vary much from one mammalian species to another. Naturally, it is larger in humans than it is in hedgehogs, for example, but it has not proportionately increased in size compared with the total volume of the human cortex. Similarly, the primary auditory cortex and the primary somatosensory cortex have not expanded proportionately as the human brain as a whole expanded. Instead, new sensory

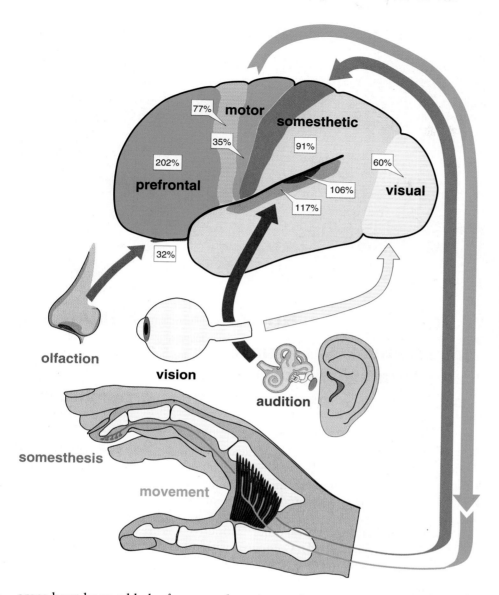

**Figure 5.19
Size of various areas of
human cortex, in
comparison with size of the
same areas in other
primates**
*T.W. Deacon calculated how
large each cortical area
would be in an "average"
nonhuman primate if its
overall brain size were as
large as that of humans. He
then determined how large
each human area is in comparison with that of the nonhuman primates. Note that
the motor and visual areas
are proportionately smaller
in humans than they are in
other primates, while the
prefrontal area is substantially larger. (From Deacon,
1990a.)*

areas have been added—for example, primates have second, third, and fourth
visual areas that process the same visual information in different ways,
enabling us to identify multiple relationships among visual stimuli.

One remarkable characteristic of the human brain in comparison with
other primate brains is the great expansion of our prefrontal cortex. Figure
5.19 diagrams some major areas of the human cortex. If we took the average of
a number of nonhuman primate brains and expanded the resulting brain to
match the human brain in size, some parts of the human brain would be larger
and some would be smaller. The percentages shown on Figure 5.19 show how
large each area of the human brain is in comparison with the corresponding
area of the "average" primate brain. Note that our motor cortex is relatively
small; that is, it has not kept pace with the proportional growth of the rest of
the brain. The primary visual cortex is also proportionately smaller in humans
than it is in other primates; so is the olfactory bulb. However, the prefrontal
cortex is about twice as large in humans as it is in other primates. (The prefrontal cortex is not the primary receiving site for any of the senses; however,
it receives all kinds of sensory information that other brain areas have already

*Evolution of the Brain and
Its Capacities*

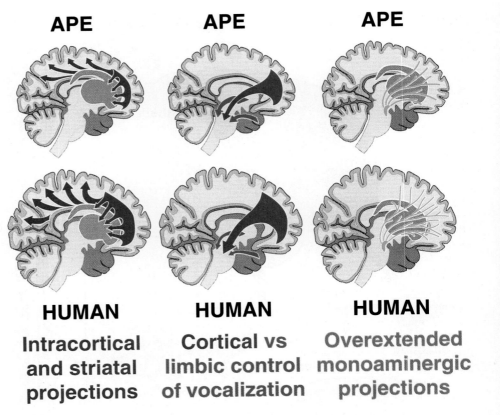

Figure 5.20
A representation of a generalized ape brain and a human brain, drawn as if they were the same size (*a*) *The human brain has more axons from one cortical area to another and from the cortex to the basal ganglia.* (*b*) *While apes and humans have similar areas in the limbic system that control vocalizations, humans have proportionately greater control by the cortex.* (*c*) *Axons releasing monoamines, such as dopamine and norepinephrine, are proportionately more widespread in humans than they are in apes. (From Deacon, 1992; Deacon, in press.)*

APE APE APE

HUMAN HUMAN HUMAN

Intracortical and striatal projections **Cortical vs limbic control of vocalization** **Overextended monoaminergic projections**

processed.) Based on the results shown in Figure 5.19, Terrence Deacon (1990a) has argued that the important point about the evolution of the human brain is not simply its increase in overall size, but rather its reorganization, which highlighted or exaggerated certain features at the relative expense of others.

Figure 5.20 illustrates several other distinctive features of the human brain (Deacon, 1992; Deacon, 1994). Compared with other primates, humans have a larger number of axons from one cortical area to another and from the basal ganglia to the cortex, thus providing somewhat different kinds of communication than occur in other primates. The control of vocalizations in apes depends mostly on the limbic system, which produces emotional grunts and squeals. Humans have that system too, but we also have a more extensive set of connections from the cortex, responsible for our more precise control of vocalizations. Note also that humans have more widespread monoamine axons (dopamine, norepinephrine, and related transmitters) than other primates have.

Brain Size and Intelligence

The size of a sensory area of the brain (such as the visual cortex) roughly corresponds to how much or how well a species uses that sense. What, then, can we say about the size of the brain as a whole? Does total brain size correspond to total behavioral capacity — "intelligence"?

Brain Size, Body Size, and Intelligence across Species

Consider the size of the human brain (Figure 5.21): Considering all the functions that it controls—vision, language, hunger and thirst, sense of humor, and so on—the human brain seems tiny. However, compared with the brains of most other mammals, the human brain is large. (In fact, our large brain size causes us a problem: An infant's head grows so large that it barely fits through the birth canal.)

However, the human brain is not the largest mammalian brain. Several other species—including whales, dolphins, and elephants—have substantially larger brains. Now, maybe that fact implies that humans are not really the most intelligent species. After all, we made up the rules on what constitutes intelligence; if dolphins or elephants were defining intelligence, humans might not score so highly. Still, even if we let our species-centric definition of intelligence stand unchallenged, is there any way to reconcile our belief in our own great intelligence with the fact that we do not have the largest brains?

Perhaps, if we assume that the critical measurement of the brain is not brain *size* itself, but brain size *in proportion to body size*. As a general rule, the size of an animal's brain is roughly proportional to the size of its body. That is, an elephant has a large brain and a large body; a mouse has a small brain and a small body. Humans have an unusually large brain in proportion to body size.

As Figure 5.22 illustrates, the logarithm of body mass is generally an accurate predictor of the logarithm of brain mass (Jerison, 1985). That is, if we know how large an animal's body is, we can predict with fair accuracy the size of its brain.

Note on Figure 5.22 that the whole polygon representing mammals shows a higher brain-to-body proportion than does the polygon representing reptiles. This tendency corresponds to our notion that, in general, mammals have greater behavioral flexibility—that is, greater intelligence—than reptiles have. Moreover, humans and other primates have a higher brain-to-body ratio than other mammals have. Thus, brain-to-body ratio fits pretty well with our informal estimates of animal intelligence.

Problems of Measuring Animal Intelligence   Note that I said "informal estimates." Unfortunately, those estimates are indeed informal, and problems arise when we try to measure animal intelligence more rigorously (Thomas, 1980). When we are talking about humans, we have trouble enough defining what we mean by "intelligence." When we are talking about differences among species, the difficulties of defining intelligence become much more severe. Most of us will have little trouble agreeing that monkeys are more intelligent than rats are, and still more intelligent than frogs are, but if someone asks exactly what we mean by that statement, we find ourselves admitting that we are not quite sure.

We could, no doubt, list a great many tasks that monkeys can learn to perform that rats and frogs cannot. But how much of the monkeys' advantage is really a matter of intelligence, as opposed to reflections of the monkeys' greater vision, hearing, motor skills, and so forth? (For analogy, a skilled human athlete can perform many tasks that an old or injured person could not perform. But we do not attribute those differences to intelligence.)

The study of animal learning is littered with examples in which investigators at first alleged that some species could not learn something, only to discover later that the species could indeed learn, under somewhat different training conditions. For example, suppose that we offer an animal three objects

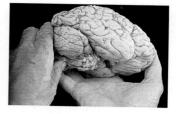

Figure 5.21
The size of the human brain relative to that of a hand
Although it weighs only 1,200 to 1,400 grams—about the same weight as this book—the brain can produce a wealth of complex and sophisticated behaviors. (Dan McCoy/Rainbow.)

Figure 5.22
Relationship between brain mass and body mass across species
Each species is one point within one of the polygonal areas. Note that primates in general and humans in particular have a high ratio of brain mass to body mass. (Based on Jerison, 1985.)

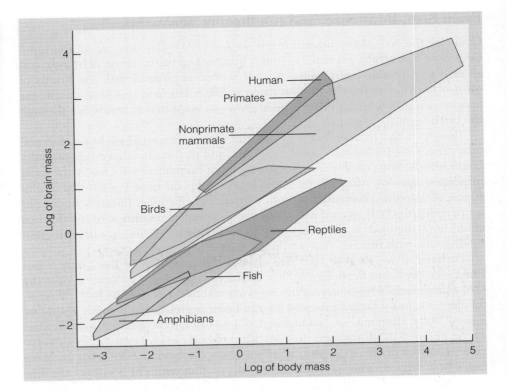

(two look the same, one looks different); the animal can find food by looking under the different one. (This task may be familiar to you from *Sesame Street:* "One of these things is not like the others. . . .") Monkeys master this principle quickly; rats do not. For years, psychologists maintained that rats "could not grasp the idea of oddity." And then another investigator demonstrated that rats readily learned to pick the object that *smelled* different from the others (Langworthy & Jennings, 1972). Evidently, rats do not lack the concept of oddity; they simply fail to recognize or apply it to visual discriminations. (How quickly would humans learn to pick the object that smells different from the others? Might a rat experimenter studying humans conclude that we lack the concept of oddity?)

Euan Macphail (1985), after a review of the literature on animal learning, found no evidence for any intellectual skill that was demonstrable in so-called "higher" animals, such as monkeys, and clearly not present in *adequately tested* lower animals, such as rats or frogs.

A more worrisome problem arises if we ask which is more intelligent, a monkey or a dolphin. (Remember, a monkey has a slightly higher brain-to-body ratio, but a dolphin has a larger absolute brain size.) How can we measure the comparative intelligence of monkeys and dolphins? They have such different ways of life that we simply cannot ask either of them to perform the same tasks as the other one.

In summary, let us look again at Figure 5.22. We can *ask* whether animal intelligence corresponds better to absolute brain size or to brain-body ratio. But we cannot responsibly *answer* the question until we find some better way to measure animal intelligence.

Doubts About the Value of Brain-to-Body Ratio   Although we cannot reasonably compare the intelligence of monkeys with that of dolphins, because we cannot ask them both to perform the same task, we can make somewhat more reasonable comparisons if we limit ourselves to closely related species. For example, Bernhard Rensch compared several types of mice with one another, several species of chickens with one another, and several species of freshwater fish with one another. In each case, the species being compared were similar in their sensory and motor capacities; thus, several types of mice could be given the same task in the same apparatus and the task should be about equally fair (or unfair) to all of them.

For a group of closely related species, such as various mice, the brain-to-body ratio is about the same for all species (Pagel & Harvey, 1989). However, the larger species have a larger brain in absolute terms. Rensch found that in each comparison—mice with mice, chickens with chickens, and fish with fish—the largest members of each group, having the largest brains, learned fastest, retained longest, suffered the least interference when they learned several tasks, and generalized most readily from a trained stimulus to similar stimuli (Rensch, 1964, 1971, 1973). In other words, within a group of closely related species—where we can most sensibly make comparisons of learning performance—bigger brains can do more than smaller brains can, even though brain-to-body ratio remains constant.

Now, does that mean that absolute brain size is the primary anatomical determinant of intelligence and that brain-to-body ratio is unimportant? No, we cannot draw that conclusion, either. An elephant with a mouse-sized brain would hardly be the equal of a mouse in intelligence.

However, Rensch's results do tell us that intelligence must depend on something more complicated than a simple brain-to-body ratio. Indeed, it never made good sense to take that ratio too seriously. Presumably, the underlying point was that intelligence depends on how many neurons and synapses an animal has "left over" after it attends to all the necessary functions of operating its body. But the number needed to attend to those necessary functions probably depends on something such as muscle mass or metabolic rate, not simply on total body mass (Harvey & Krebs, 1990). For example, much of a whale's mass is composed of blubber; a whale probably does not need many neurons to take care of its blubber, and we should not count the blubber against it when we are estimating its intelligence.

Variations in Brain Size and Intelligence among Humans

Among nonhuman animals, the research indicates that some species do at least learn faster and remember longer than other species do, even if we are not sure that we can find any qualitative differences. Furthermore, the data are consistent with the idea that learning ability has vaguely something to do with brain size, even though we are not sure whether to measure brain size by absolute mass, brain-to-body ratio, or some other formula.

Now we come to humans. Humans differ in intelligence as measured by intelligence quotient (IQ) tests, school performance, and similar tasks. Granted, IQ tests are far from perfect; after decades of research, psychologists are still not agreed on how well these tests measure intelligence, as opposed to motivation, exposure to a certain culture, and so forth. I presume that we would all welcome a new and improved intelligence test, but in the meantime, the standard IQ tests do provide us with something to work with. As with nonhuman animals, the question here is: Do differences in IQ scores correspond to any differences in brain size or structure?

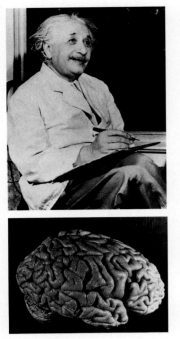

Figure 5.23
After the death of the great scientist Albert Einstein, biological researchers dissected his brain to look for any clue as to what made him such a genius. They were not sure what they were looking for, and whatever it was, they never found it. So far as researchers could tell, Einstein's brain looked pretty much the same as other people's. The relationship between intelligence and brain structure remains unresolved. (Top photo; Historical Pictures Services, Chicago/ FPG: Bottom Photo; Dr. Thomas Harvey)

Biological Factors Influencing Brain Size   Just as the largest animal species generally have the largest brains, larger humans tend to have larger brains than smaller individuals do. The proportionality is only approximate, however. Most of the variation in human brain size is determined by age 1 year. Up to that age, the brain grows in about the same proportion as the rest of the body. Certain genes promote growth; so do good nutrition and good health. But beyond about age 1 year, the rate of brain growth decreases. Neurons continue to increase in size, though not in number, until about adolescence; at that point, the brain has reached its full size. (It produces new dendrites and synapses throughout life, but those changes do not noticeably affect total brain size.) The rest of the body, however, continues to grow for many years, including a big "growth spurt" during adolescence. In short, the variation in human brain size has to do with what happened before birth or during childhood, while much of the variation in body size has to do with what happened after age 10 years. Consequently, adult brain size has only an approximate relationship to adult body size (Riska & Atchley, 1985). As a rule, taller or otherwise larger people tend to have somewhat larger brains in absolute terms, but somewhat smaller brain-to-body ratios.

Correlations between Brain Size and Intelligence   Do any of these size variations have anything to do with intelligence? For many years the answer appeared to be, for all practical purposes, *no*. (See Figure 5.23). One typical study found a correlation of only 0.1 between IQ score and estimated brain size—too low a correlation to have any practical value or even much theoretical interest (Passingham, 1979).

However, those results were based on rather inaccurate estimates of brain size. Investigators either weighed the brains of recently deceased people—whose brains tend to dry out and gradually shrink—or they estimated brain size from the size of the skull. Either method introduced a fair degree of error.

Investigators today can use the more modern MRI technique (p. 136) to visualize and measure accurately the brains of living people. In one such study, investigators measured the brains of 20 male and 20 female college students, selected on the basis of their IQ scores. Half of the students (10 male and 10 female) had IQ scores of 130 or above; half had IQ scores of 103 or below. The investigators found that the higher-IQ students had significantly larger brains than did the lower-IQ students (Willerman, Schultz, Rutledge, & Bigler, 1991). They further found that IQ scores correlated 0.51 with brain-to-body ratio and slightly less with absolute brain volume. That correlation is somewhat inflated because the sample consisted of two groups differing by at least 27 IQ points; the authors estimated that the correlation for a representative population would be about 0.35.

Do these results mean that human IQ is strongly related to brain size? Maybe; we shall need to see more data, drawn from larger and more representative samples. However, these results do suggest that we should no longer disregard the possibility of a relationship between IQ and brain size.

⇒ *Current Controversies:*
Possible Relationship to Race or Ethnic Differences

Finally, with fear and trepidation, let us examine the most controversial and potentially most explosive issue related to this topic: Do brain differences correspond to the measured differences in IQ scores among racial or ethnic groups?

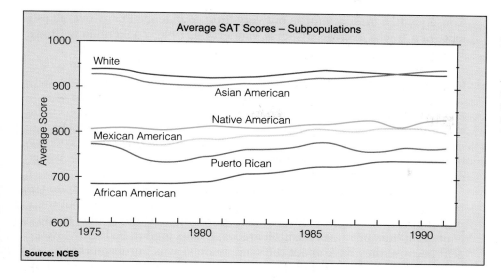

Figure 5.24
Mean SAT scores for six U.S. subpopulations, 1975–1991
Note a gradual increase in mean scores by several minority groups. (From Carson, Huelskamp, & Woodall, 1993.)

Like it or not, the fact is that, within the United States, people of Asian ancestry get, on average, higher IQ scores than do people of European ancestry, who in turn get higher scores on average than do people of African ancestry. Figure 5.24 presents Scholastic Aptitude Test (SAT) scores, which are related to IQ scores, though not interchangeable with them. On the SAT, the Asian-American mean has surpassed the mean for European-Americans, even though some Asian-Americans learned English as a second language (Carson, Huelskamp, & Woodall, 1993).

Repeat: These are differences on the average; they do not tell us what to expect from any given individual.

Do Asian-Americans also have larger brains, followed by European-Americans? First, note that this question is independent of the relationship between IQ and heredity. Environmental differences clearly contribute substantially to differences in brain size, as they do to differences in IQ scores. For example, the average size of heads and brains in the United States is significantly larger at the end of the 20th century than it was at the start of the 20th century—for people of Asian, European, and African ancestry alike. That increase happened too fast to be a result of heredity; it reflects advances in health and nutrition. Any contemporary difference among the races in brain size could likewise reflect differences in health, nutrition, prenatal care, and the like.

At any rate, how do the races compare in brain size? According to one review of the literature (Rushton, 1988), people of Asian ancestry have larger brains than people of European ancestry do (by about 1–3 percent), while people of European ancestry have slightly larger brains than people of African ancestry do. However, that conclusion was based on a miscellaneous and dubious assortment of measurements. For example, the mean for "Africans" reflects results from several populations within Africa, including some impoverished and disease-ridden populations, plus several studies of African-Americans, many of them conducted with inaccurate measurement techniques prior to World War II. (Since then, few researchers have chosen to study biological differences among the races.) The mean brain sizes vary quite strikingly from one African population to another, as well as from one European or Asian population to another.

Evolution of the Brain and Its Capacities

Consequently, most scientists put very little confidence in any overall estimate of a "racial average" (Cain & Vanderwolf, 1990; Zuckerman & Brody, 1988).

Philippe Rushton, however, has argued that, even if the measured differences are not very accurate, the trends are worth taking seriously. For example, he has maintained that even if the difference between Asians and Europeans in brain size sounds small (1–3 percent)—in fact, even if the difference in absolute brain size were *zero*—the results would be meaningful anyway because of the resulting brain-to-body ratios. That is, because most Asians are shorter and lighter than most Europeans, Asians on the average have a higher ratio of brain size to body size.

On the average, Asians do appear to have the highest ratio of brain size to body size. However, recall some of the doubts raised earlier about the meaning of brain-to-body ratio. We can raise some further doubts in the context of humans: If, as Rushton argues, Asians tend to be highly intelligent because they have about the same brain size as Europeans but smaller bodies, then we should observe a similar advantage in small, short Europeans. Short people of European ancestry have a high brain-to-body ratio, comparable to that of Asians. They do not, however, have consistently high IQ scores comparable to those of Asians (Willerman, 1991). In short, if we want to explain why Asians do so well on IQ tests and the like, we probably need to look to something other than differences in brain size.

In Closing

Where does all this leave us? Unfortunately, we are stuck with a lot of maybes and probablys. Intelligence is difficult to measure (or even to define) for humans; it is an even more problematic concept when we are comparing species. If we had a better measurement of it, we could ask in more detail how it relates to absolute brain size, brain-to-body ratio, or some other, better formula. As it is, we can say vaguely that it is probably better to have a large brain than to have a small brain, but we cannot say anything for sure about the relationship between overall brain size and human intelligence. The next time that you hear someone talking nonsense about either animal intelligence or biological bases for race differences, you might point out some of the difficulties inherent in those issues.

Ultimately, if we are ever going to understand the relationship between brain structures and intelligence—and no doubt some such relationship does exist—our understanding will have to come from studies at a more microscopic level. That is, we can never get very far by studying the relationship between whole-brain size and intelligence as a whole. We need to know how the functioning of neurons and synapses in various specific brain areas contributes to specific behavioral abilities — specific sensory and motor skills, specific types of memory, and so forth. In subsequent chapters, we move to consider investigations of these more detailed processes. ◆◆◆

Summary

1. The fossil record leaves us only limited information about how the brain evolved or about how ancient animals behaved. We can make certain inferences based on current animals. For example, we infer that brain structures common to all current mammals must have derived from a common remote ancestor. (p. 166)

2. The overall structure and organization of the brain, including the cerebral cortex, are fairly similar from one mammalian species to another. Individual areas, such as cortical areas representing a sensory system, are larger or smaller in given species, depending on that species' way of life. (p. 167)

3. Primate brains have an unusually large amount of folding of the cerebral cortex, providing for a larger surface and therefore a larger number of neurons. (p. 168)

4. In general, brain size is roughly proportional to body size across species. Among the individuals within a species, such as humans, we find a less precise relationship between brain size and body size, because of the adolescent growth spurt that produces variations in adult body size. (pp. 171, 174)

5. In general, mammals have a greater brain-to-body ratio than do reptiles, and primates have a higher ratio than most other mammals. Loosely speaking, brain-to-body ratio corresponds to our informal estimates of animal intelligence. However, it is very difficult (and possibly meaningless) to compare intelligence across animal species. (p. 171)

6. Among closely related species, which differ in absolute brain size but not in brain-to-body ratio, the species with larger absolute brain size tend to learn faster and remember better than do species with smaller brains. (p. 173)

7. Among humans, measurements of brain size correlate positively, if not always highly, with IQ scores. (p. 174)

8. Human races differ, on the average, in their IQ scores. The relationship between those differences and possible differences in brain size is controversial and at this point highly uncertain. (p. 175)

Review Questions

1. Why do neuroscientists believe that the language cortex of the human brain evolved relatively recently, while the visual cortex is ancient? (p. 166)

2. Did brain evolution proceed mostly by expanding old brain areas or by adding new brain areas? (p. 168)

3. Which major sections of the cerebral cortex are proportionately larger in humans than they are in other primates? Which areas are proportionately smaller in humans? (p. 169)

4. What are the arguments for and against using brain-to-body ratio as a gauge of overall intelligence? (p. 171)

5. Why is it difficult and possibly meaningless to try to compare intelligence across animal species? (p. 171)

6. Why did old studies find such a low correlation between human IQ and brain size? What advance in research methods led to a higher estimate? (p. 174)

7. Why should we *not* assume that individual differences or race differences in brain size are under genetic control? (p. 175)

Thought Question

1. How can we study the evolution of behavior? Behavior leaves no fossils, with the exception of occasional footprints. (*Hint:* How might you study the evolution of the heart, kidney, or other internal organs, which also leave few fossils?)

Term

primate member of the mammalian order including humans, monkeys, apes, and their relatives (p. 168)

VISION

CHAPTER SIX

1. Vertebrate vision depends on two kinds of receptors: cones, which contribute to color vision, and rods, which do not.

2. Three types of cones enable us to distinguish among colors. For genetic reasons, some people do not perceive colors in the same way that most people do. Color blindness has several types.

3. Within the retina, a process called lateral inhibition enhances the contrast between a brightly lit area and a neighboring dimmer area.

4. After visual information reaches the brain, different pathways analyze different aspects of the information, such as shape, color, and movement.

5. The properties of the neurons in the visual cortex are to a large degree molded by experience. Neurons become more responsive to common stimuli and less responsive to uncommon stimuli.

Some years ago, a graduate student was taking his final oral exam for a Ph.D. degree in psychology. He had answered without difficulty many questions, most of them about animal behavior, his specialty. Then one member of his committee asked, "How far can an ant see?" The student suddenly turned pale. He did not know the answer, and evidently he was supposed to know it. (Do you know the answer? Think about it for a minute before you read on.)

Quickly, the poor graduate student mentally reviewed everything he had read about the compound eyes of insects. He remembered reading about how insects can detect light and about their color vision and their ability to detect movement . . . but nothing about how far they can see. Finally, he gave up and admitted he did not know.

With an impish grin, the professor told him, "Presumably, an ant can see 93 million miles—the distance to the sun." Yes, this was a trick question—a beaut, as trick questions go. But it illustrates an important point: How far an ant can see, or how far you or I can see, depends on how far the light travels. Good eyes cannot see farther than bad eyes. We fall into a trap because we perceive the objects we see as being "out there," when in fact the stimulation is on the retinas of our eyes. The light out there stimulates a pattern of activity on the retinas, which in turn stimulates a pattern of activity in the brain, enabling us to perceive objects as being "out there." How does all this happen?

Visual Coding and the Retinal Receptors

Imagine that you are a piece of iron. I admit that's not easy to do. A piece of iron doesn't have a brain, and even if it did it would not have much experience. But try to imagine it anyway.

So there you are, sitting around doing nothing, as usual, when along comes a drop of water. What will be your perception, your experience, of the water?

You will have the experience of rust. From your point of view, water is above all else *rustish*. Now return to your perspective as a human. You know that the property rustish is not really a property of water itself; it is a property of the way water interacts with iron.

The same is true of human perception. In vision, for example, when you look at the leaves of a tree, you perceive them as *green*. But green is no more a property of the leaves themselves than rustish is a property of water. The greenness is what happens when the light bouncing off the leaves interacts with the neurons in the back of your eye, and eventually with the neurons in your brain. That is, the greenness is really in us—just as the rust is really in the piece of iron.

Reception, Transduction, and Coding

When light reaches our eyes, or when any stimulus reaches any receptor, it starts a series of three steps that take us from stimulus to perception: reception, transduction, and coding (see Figure 6.1). **Reception** is simply the absorption of physical energy by the receptors. **Transduction** is the conversion of that physical energy to an electrochemical pattern in the neurons. **Coding** is the one-to-one correspondence between some aspect of the physical stimulus and some aspect of the nervous system activity. For example, molecules from a squeezed lemon strike receptors in the nose (reception); they lead to a chemical reaction that changes the polarization across the membrane of the receptor cell (transduction); and the resulting activity in that neuron and other neurons sends a distinctive message to the brain (coding).

Each receptor is specialized to absorb one kind of energy and transduce it into an electrochemical pattern that the brain can read. For example, visual receptors can absorb and respond to as little as a single photon of light and transduce it into a **generator potential,** a local depolarization or hyperpolarization of a neuron membrane. The generator potential determines what message the neuron passes along to the next neuron on the way to the brain.

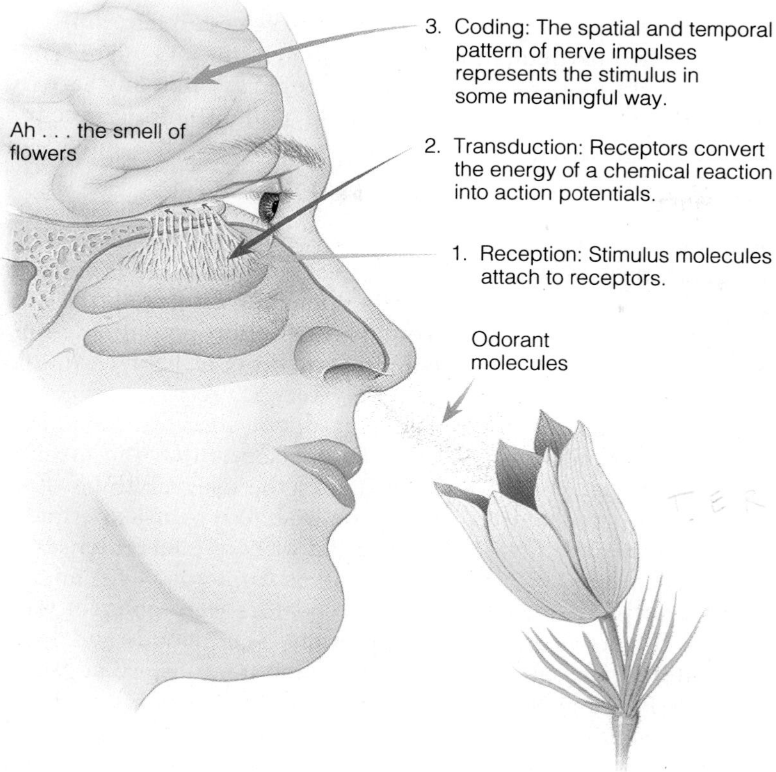

3. Coding: The spatial and temporal pattern of nerve impulses represents the stimulus in some meaningful way.

2. Transduction: Receptors convert the energy of a chemical reaction into action potentials.

1. Reception: Stimulus molecules attach to receptors.

Ah . . . the smell of flowers

Odorant molecules

Figure 6.1
Three steps in the sensation and perception of a stimulus

From Neuronal Activity to Perception

After the information gets to the brain, how does the brain make sense of it? The rest of this chapter and the next will attempt to find an answer, but first let us consider what is *not* an answer. Centuries ago, scientists and philosophers, such as René Descartes, believed that the brain's representation of a physical stimulus would have to resemble the stimulus itself. That is, when you look at a table, the nerves from the eye would project a pattern of impulses onto your visual cortex to produce a pattern of excitation shaped like a table—a pattern representing the top of the table would be near the top of the visual cortex, a pattern shaped like legs would stretch toward the bottom of the visual cortex, and so forth. Neuroscientists have long since discarded that conception (Dennett & Kinsbourne, 1992). You do not have a "little person in the head" to view a pattern on a screen, and therefore the pattern of impulses in your cortex could be right-side-up, upside-down, inside-out, or completely unrelated to the shape of a table. In other words, the coding of visual information in your brain *does not duplicate* the shape of the object that you see.

(Consider a computer analogy: When a computer stores instructions for what to write on the top and bottom of the page, its instructions for what to write at the top of the page do not have to be stored near the top part of the computer. The same principle applies to the way that your brain stores visual information.)

General Principles of Sensory Coding

One important aspect of all sensory coding is *which* neurons are active. A given frequency of impulses may mean one thing when it occurs in one neuron and something quite different in another. In 1838, Johannes Müller described

*Visual Coding and the
Retinal Receptors*

181

this basic insight as the **law of specific nerve energies.** Müller held that whatever excited a particular nerve established a special kind of "energy" unique to that nerve. In more modern terms, we could say that any activity by a particular nerve always conveys the same kind of information to the brain. The brain "sees" the activity of the optic nerve and "hears" the activity of the auditory nerve.

Another way of stating the law of specific nerve energies: No nerve has the option of sending the message "high C note" at one time, "bright yellow" at another time, and "lemony smell" at yet another. It sends only one kind of message—action potentials. The brain somehow interprets the action potentials from the auditory nerve as sounds, the action potentials from the olfactory nerve as smells, and those from the optic nerve as light. (Admittedly, that word *somehow* glosses over a profound mystery.)

If you poke your eye or rub it hard, you may see spots or flashes of light even if the room is totally dark. The reason is that the mechanical pressure excites some receptors in the retina of the eye; anything that excites those receptors is perceived as light. (If you wish to try this experiment, press gently on your eyeball with your eye shut and without contact lenses on the eye.)

If it were possible to take the nerves from your eyes and ears and cross-transplant them so that the visual receptors were connected to the auditory nerve and vice versa, you would literally "see" sounds and "hear" lights. This implies that perceptions depend on which neurons are active and how active each one is at a given time.

Although the law of specific nerve energies is still considered fundamentally correct a century and a half after it was first stated, we must add some important qualifications. First, certain cells with a spontaneous rate of firing may signal one kind of stimulus by an increase in firing and a different kind by a decrease in firing. For instance, certain cells in the visual system increase their firing rate in response to red light and decrease below the spontaneous rate in response to green light. The same cell, therefore, may contribute to the perception of both red and green.

Second, it is possible that the "rhythm" of impulses may code certain kinds of information (DiLorenzo & Hecht, 1993). For example, the following three records of impulses over time may convey different information, even though they represent the same mean frequency in the same cell:

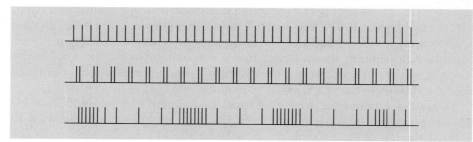

Third, the exact meaning of an impulse in a single neuron may depend on what other neurons are active. Just as the meaning of the letter *h* depends on what letters surround it, the activity of a given neuron might contribute to the sensation of green, yellow, or white, depending on the activity of other neurons.

To understand how we perceive light and color, we begin with the reception and transduction by the receptors in the eyes.

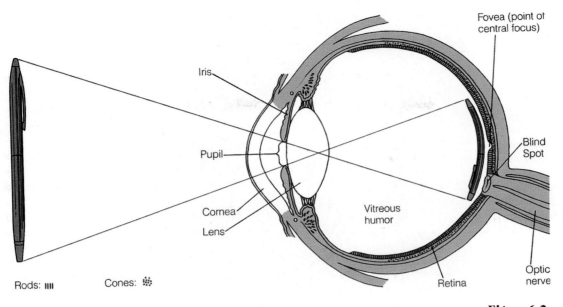

Fovea (point of central focus)

Iris

Pupil

Cornea

Lens

Vitreous humor

Blind Spot

Optic nerve

Retina

Rods: ⅠⅠⅠⅠ   Cones: ※

**Figure 6.2
Diagrammatic cross section
of the vertebrate eye,
showing the projection of
an image onto the retina**

The Eye and Its Connections to the Brain

Eventually, visual information has to reach the brain, but we can explain certain phenomena of perception simply in terms of the structure of the eye. Figure 6.2 illustrates the basic structures of the eye. Light enters through an opening in the eyeball called the **pupil** and is focused by the cornea and lens onto the **retina** (Figure 6.2), which is the rear surface of the eye, lined with visual receptors—rods and cones. As in a camera, the light rays are focused so that the image is reversed: Light from the left side of the world strikes the right half of the retina and vice versa. Light from above strikes the bottom half of the retina; light from below strikes the top half of the retina.

The Fovea

An area called the **fovea** (meaning *pit*) in the center of the human retina is specialized for acute, detailed vision. Because blood vessels and ganglion cell axons are almost absent near the fovea, the fovea has the most unimpeded vision available in the eye. The tight packing of receptors further aids perception of detail.

Different species have their area of greatest visual sensitivity in different parts of the retina, not always in the center (Land & Fernald, 1992). For example, both rabbits and cheetahs have a highly sensitive *visual streak* stretching horizontally through the center of the retina, suited to scanning the horizon.

You have heard the expression "eyes like a hawk." In many bird species, the eyes occupy more than half the volume of the head, as compared to only 5 percent of the head in humans. Furthermore, many bird species have two foveas per eye. Each eye has one fovea pointing ahead and one pointing to the side (Wallman & Pettigrew, 1985). The two foveas enable such birds to perceive detail in their peripheral vision.

Hawks and other birds of prey have a greater density of visual receptors on the top half of their retinas (looking down) than they have on the bottom half

*Visual Coding and the
Retinal Receptors*

183

Figure 6.3

One owlet has turned its head almost upside down to see above itself. Birds of prey have a great density of receptors on the upper half of the retina, enabling them to see down in great detail during flight. But they see objects above themselves very poorly, unless they turn their heads. Take another look at the prairie falcon at the start of this chapter. It is not a one-eyed bird; it is a bird that has tilted its head. Do you now understand why? (Chase Swift.)

of their retinas (looking up). That arrangement is highly adaptive, because predatory birds spend most of their day soaring high in the air, looking down. However, it does pose a problem when the bird lands and needs to look up. To see above itself, the bird must turn its head, as Figure 6.3 shows, so that it can focus the light from above on the part of its retina that has the greatest density of receptors (Waldvogel, 1990).

Conversely, certain of the animals that hawks prey on, such as rats, have their greater density of receptors on the bottom half of the retina (Lund, Lund, & Wise, 1974). As a result, they can see objects above them in more detail than they can objects below them.

The Route of Visual Information within the Retina

In a sense, the retina is built inside-out. If you or I were designing an eye, we would probably let the light strike the receptors and then have the receptors send their messages directly back to the brain. In the vertebrate retina, however, the receptors, located on the back of the eye, send their messages not toward the brain but toward other neurons, called *bipolar neurons,* located closer to the center of the eye. The bipolar neurons send their messages to *ganglion cells,* located still closer to the center of the eye. Only at that point do the axons from the ganglion cells join one another, loop around, and exit the eye en route toward the brain. (See Figure 6.4.)

One consequence of this anatomy is that light has to pass through those ganglion cells and bipolar cells before it reaches the receptors. However, because the ganglion cells and bipolar cells are highly transparent, they distort vision only minimally.

A more serious consequence of the eye's anatomy is the *blind spot* of the eye. The ganglion cell axons band together to form the **optic nerve** (or optic tract), which loops around to exit through the back of the eye. The point at which it leaves is called the **blind spot** because it has no receptors. (See Figure 6.2 and Digression 6.1). Blood vessels also enter the eye through the blind spot.

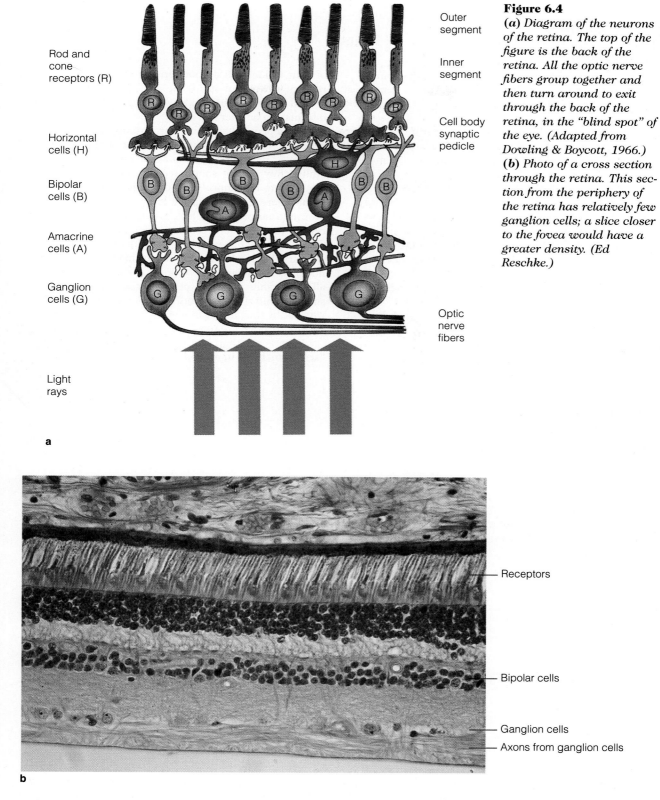

Figure 6.4
(*a*) *Diagram of the neurons of the retina. The top of the figure is the back of the retina. All the optic nerve fibers group together and then turn around to exit through the back of the retina, in the "blind spot" of the eye. (Adapted from Dowling & Boycott, 1966.)* (*b*) *Photo of a cross section through the retina. This section from the periphery of the retina has relatively few ganglion cells; a slice closer to the fovea would have a greater density. (Ed Reschke.)*

Outer segment

Inner segment

Cell body synaptic pedicle

Optic nerve fibers

Rod and cone receptors (R)

Horizontal cells (H)

Bipolar cells (B)

Amacrine cells (A)

Ganglion cells (G)

Light rays

a

Receptors

Bipolar cells

Ganglion cells

Axons from ganglion cells

b

Visual Coding and the Retinal Receptors

185

Every person is blind in part of each eye—the point at which the optic nerve exits the eye. You can demonstrate your own blind spot using Figure 6.5. Close your left eye and focus your right eye on the o in the top part. Then move the page back and forth, noticing what happens to the x. When the page is about 25 cm (10 inches) away, the x disappears because its image strikes the blind spot of your retina.

Now repeat the procedure with the lower part of the figure. When the page is again about 25 cm away from your eyes, what do you see? The *gap* disappears! But although you no longer see the gap, do you see something *inside* the gap? You might say that you see an x in the middle of the gap, suggesting that your brain had filled in the gap. Many observers argue, however, that you do not exactly *see* an x; rather, you make an inference (Dennett, 1991). When you don't see an x but you don't see a gap either, your brain "knows" that there must be an x there. In the same way, you can look at this page and know the sizes, shapes, and colors of the objects out in the periphery

of your vision. You do not actually see all that detail right now. You saw it a while ago when you actually looked at those objects; now you simply know the information or infer it.

Some people have much larger blind spots in their retinas, because glaucoma or other diseases have destroyed receptors or parts of the optic nerve. Generally, they do not spontaneously notice their large blind spots any more than other people notice the point where the optic nerve leaves the retina. Some are quite surprised, in fact, when an optician's test reveals that they have lost virtually half of their visual field. Why don't they notice their loss of vision? Two answers: First, what they "see" in their blind areas is not blackness, but simply *nothing*—no sensation at all, the same as other people experience in their smaller blind spots. Second, their brains know or infer what is in that blind area, just as you did with the lower part of Figure 6.5.

Here is another way that people can reportedly "see" something in a blind part of the retina: Suppose

Figure 6.5
Two demonstrations of the blind spot of the retina
Close your left eye and focus your right eye on the o in the top part. Move the page toward you and away, noticing what happens to the x. At a distance of about 25 cm (10 inches), the x disappears. Now repeat this procedure with the bottom part. At that same distance, what do you see?

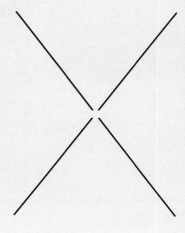

that your retina and optic nerve were intact, but your visual cortex were damaged. Now, depending on which part of your visual cortex were damaged, and how much of it, you would become blind in some part of your visual field. If someone showed you something on the corresponding part of your retina and asked what it was, you would insist that you saw nothing.

However, if instead of asking you to *say* what the object was, the investigator asked you to point to it or to turn your eyes toward it, your accuracy would be surprisingly good—surprising even to yourself, since you would continue to insist that you saw nothing (Bridgeman & Staggs, 1982; Weiskrantz, Warrington, Sanders, & Marshall, 1974). This ability to localize visual objects within an apparently blind field of vision is called **blindsight.**

The explanation for blindsight remains controversial. In some cases, the person who is reportedly blind in a large portion of the visual field has tiny islands of healthy tissue surviving within an otherwise damaged portion of the visual cortex. Those tiny islands are not large enough to provide any shape perception or conscious perception of vision at all, but they nevertheless provide enough information for blindsight (Fendrich, Wessinger, & Gazzaniga, 1992).

Surviving islands in the visual cortex may not be the whole explanation in all cases, however. In addition to the information sent to your visual cortex, you have other branches of your optic tract that go to the superior colliculus (Figure 6.6) and to other noncortical structures. The superior colliculus, known to be important for the control of eye movements and other visually guided movements, may provide nonconscious responses to visual stimuli after damage to parts of the visual cortex (Rafal et al., 1990).

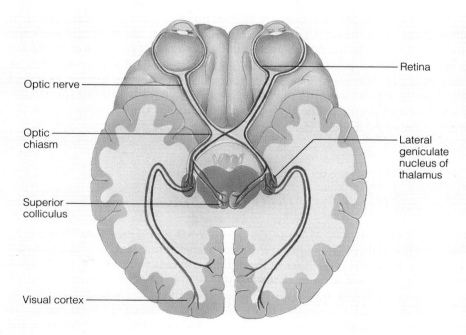

Optic nerve

Optic chiasm

Superior colliculus

Visual cortex

Retina

Lateral geniculate nucleus of thalamus

Figure 6.6
Major connections in the visual system of the brain
Part of the visual input goes to the thalamus and from there to the visual cortex. Another part of the visual input goes to the superior colliculus.

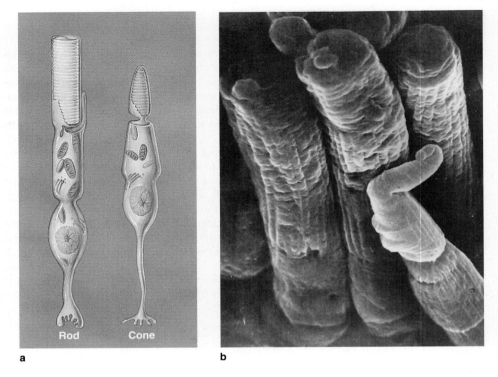

a   b

Note that some ganglion cells are located much closer to the blind spot than other ganglion cells are. All other things being equal, the messages from the closer ganglion cells would reach the brain sooner, and the person would see events in different parts of the retina just slightly out of synchrony. But all other things are not equal: The axons from ganglion cells farther from the blind spot conduct their action potentials slightly faster (Stanford, 1987). Consequently, stimuli striking different parts of the retina at the same time reach the brain at the same time.

Visual Receptors: Rods and Cones

Retina

The retina contains two types of receptors: **rods** and **cones** (see Figure 6.7). The cones, which are specialized for color vision, are more sensitive to detail and are located near the center of the retina, whereas the rods are more sensitive to dim light and are found toward the periphery of the retina. Table 6.1 summarizes the functional distinctions between the two. These differences are reflected in several aspects of our experience. For detailed vision, we try to focus an object on the fovea, where cones are concentrated and acuity is the greatest. To perceive the dimmest lights, such as faint stars in the night sky, we often find it better to look slightly to the side so that the light rays from the target fall outside the fovea.

We can see dim lights better in the periphery of the retina for two reasons. One is simply that rods are more sensitive to light than cones are. The second is that, near the fovea, only a small number of receptors convey input to a given postsynaptic cell, but in the periphery, great numbers of rods funnel their input

Table 6.1 Functional Distinctions between Rods and Cones

Characteristic	Rods	Cones
Location	Absent from fovea; increasingly common toward periphery	More common toward center of the retina
Sensitivity to detail (acuity)	Low because many rods funnel onto a single postsynaptic neuron	Greater because fewer cones funnel onto a single postsynaptic neuron
Sensitivity to dim light	Greater	Lesser
Contribute to color vision?	No	Yes
Species more abundant in	Rodents, other nocturnal animals	Birds, primates

into each postsynaptic cell. That is, in the periphery, the summation of many inputs increases detection of dim light, at the expense of perceiving details.

Chemical Basis for Receptor Excitation

Both rods and cones contain **photopigments,** chemicals that release energy when struck by light. Photopigments consist of 11-*cis*-retinal (a derivative of vitamin A) bound to proteins called *opsins.* The 11-*cis*-retinal is stable in the dark, but even a single photon of light can convert it to another form, all-*trans*-retinal. (The light is absorbed in this process; it does not continue to bounce around in the eye.) When the light converts 11-*cis*-retinal to all-*trans*-retinal, it triggers changes in the opsin, converting hundreds of second-messenger molecules to their active state, ultimately closing a number of ion channels in the cell membrane (Lamb & Pugh, 1990; Nathans, Thomas, & Hogness, 1986). This is similar to what happens at many inhibitory synapses in the brain; in fact, rhodopsin (the kind of opsin found in rods) is chemically related to many neurotransmitter receptors.

(Do not be confused by the fact that light inhibits the activity of the receptor cell. It is possible to convey just as much information by a decrease in a signal as by an increase.)

Although 11-*cis*-retinal is so sensitive that a single photon can activate it, it seldom discharges a false alarm in the dark. The average molecule of this chemical has about a 50 percent chance of a spontaneous activation within a thousand years. Because each rod has an estimated 200 billion of these molecules, however, the average rod cell has about one spontaneously active molecule per minute (Yau, Matthews, & Baylor, 1979).

The conversion of 11-*cis*-retinal to all-*trans*-retinal releases energy that decreases the permeability of the receptor's membrane to sodium. (This is the *transduction* process.) The result is a graded hyperpolarization of the receptor—not a depolarization: the greater the light, the greater the hyperpolarization. Ordinarily, even in the dark, the receptor is in a steady state of partial depolarization and is constantly sending inhibitory synaptic transmission to the bipolar cells, which are the next cells in the pathway of the visual system.

Visual Coding and the Retinal Receptors

Figure 6.8
A beam of light separated into its wavelengths
Although the wavelengths vary over a continuum, we perceive them as several distinct colors.

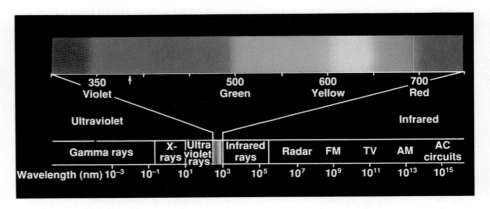

When light hyperpolarizes the receptor, it slows the rate of inhibitory transmission to the bipolars and thereby leads to a net excitation of the bipolar cells.

Color Vision

Color vision apparently evolved more than once in the animal kingdom, and the extent of color vision varies widely even among vertebrates. Of all the vertebrates that researchers have tested, only one—the skate—has no cones at all (Dowling, 1987). However, having a few cones does not necessarily provide color vision; to have color vision, an individual must have different kinds of cones, selectively responsive to different wavelengths of light. For example, rats have just one kind of cone (Neitz & Jacobs, 1986). Although their cones probably enable rats to see better during the day than they would with only rods, rats cannot discriminate between colors. Mice have only one kind of cone in the ventral half of their retina, but two kinds in the dorsal half (Szél et al., 1992). Presumably, they have a limited amount of color vision in part of their visual field but not in other parts.

In the human visual system, the shortest visible wavelengths, about 400 nm (1 nm = nanometer, or 10^{-9} m), are perceived as violet; progressively longer wavelengths are perceived as blue, green, yellow, orange, and red, near 700 nm (Figure 6.8). Discrimination among colors poses some special coding problems for the nervous system. A cell in the visual system, like any other neuron, can vary only its frequency of action potentials or, in a cell with graded potentials, its membrane polarization. If the cell's response indicates the brightness of the light, then it cannot simultaneously be a code for color. Conversely, if each response indicates a different color, the cell has no way to signal brightness. The inevitable conclusion is that no single neuron can simultaneously indicate brightness and color; our perceptions must depend on patterns of responses by a number of different neurons.

Color vision depends on different processes in different parts of the nervous system. Two major processes were described in the 1800s, in terms known as the trichromatic theory and the opponent-process theory.

The Trichromatic (Young-Helmholtz) Theory

The **trichromatic theory** of color vision, also known as the **Young-Helmholtz theory,** was first proposed by Thomas Young and later modified by Hermann

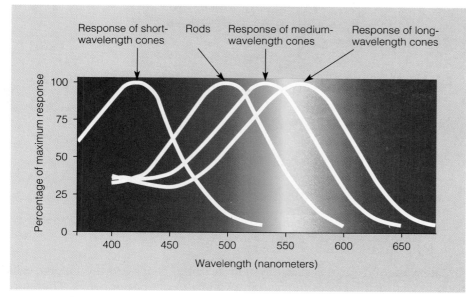

Figure 6.9
Response of rods and three kinds of cones to various wavelengths of light
Note that each kind responds somewhat to a wide range of wavelengths but best to wavelengths in a particular range. (Based on data of Bowmaker & Dartnall, 1980.)

von Helmholtz. According to this theory, we perceive color through the relative rates of response by three kinds of cones, with each kind maximally sensitive to a different set of wavelengths (*trichromatic* means *three colors*). Figure 6.9 shows wavelength-sensitivity functions for the three cone types, which we shall call *short-wavelength, medium-wavelength,* and *long-wavelength* cones. Note that each cone is sensitive to a broad range of wavelengths, not just to a narrow band, but is more responsive to some wavelengths than to others.

According to the trichromatic theory, we discriminate among wavelengths by the ratio of activity across the three types of cones. That is, light at 500 nm excites the medium-wavelength cone to about 65 percent of its maximum, the long-wavelength receptor to 40 percent of its maximum, and the short-wavelength receptor to 30 percent of its maximum. This ratio of responses among the three cones defines the color perception, in this case blue-green. More intense light would increase the activity of all three cones but would not greatly alter the ratio of responses. When all three types of cones are equally active, we see white (or gray).

Note that, in the trichromatic theory, a given response rate by a given cone is ambiguous. For example, a low response rate by a middle-wavelength cone might indicate low-intensity 540-nm light, or brighter 500-nm light, or still brighter 460-nm light. Even a high response rate is ambiguous; it could equally well indicate bright light specifically at 540 nm or bright white light, which includes 540 nm. The nervous system can determine the color and brightness of the light only by comparing the responses of the three types of cones.

Originally, the Young-Helmholtz theory was based strictly on **psychophysical observations,** reports by human observers concerning their perceptions of various stimuli. For example, observers find that they can match any possible color by mixing appropriate amounts of just three wavelengths. So we conclude that three types of cones are sufficient to account for human color vision. Modern methods have clearly established physical differences among the three kinds of cones. Although all cones contain 11-*cis*-retinal, different opsins are bound to it in the three kinds of cones. The opsins modify the sensitivity of the photopigment to light to produce the three different peaks of wavelength absorption (Wald, 1968).

Visual Coding and the Retinal Receptors

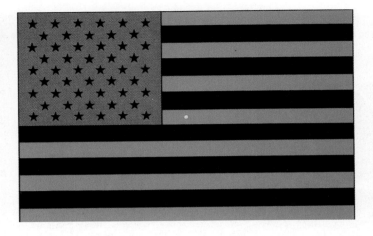

Figure 6.10
Stimulus for demonstrating negative color afterimages
Stare at the dot in the center of the flag under bright light for about a minute and then look at a white field. You should see a red, white, and blue flag.

The Opponent-Process Theory

The next neurons in the visual system after the cones are the bipolar cells. Each bipolar cell receives input from two or three types of cones. Therefore, the trichromatic theory does not apply at this level or beyond. We can identify a long-wavelength cone, but not a long-wavelength bipolar cell.

For example, one type of bipolar cell receives excitatory synapses from medium-wavelength cones and inhibitory synapses from long-wavelength cones. Green light shining on the cones connected to it will depolarize this bipolar cell; red light hyperpolarizes it. Yellow, blue, white, or gray light has little effect.

Note that the response of such a bipolar cell is *less* ambiguous about color than the response of any cone is. From the response of a given medium-wavelength cone, we cannot determine whether the cell is stimulated by green light, by white light, or even by bright red or blue light. But imagine a bipolar cell that depolarizes in the presence of green light, hyperpolarizes in the presence of red light, and remains unchanged in the presence of white light. When that cell depolarizes, the brain knows that it is looking at something approximately green. It might be a yellowish green or a bluish green, but it cannot be red or white. In effect, the bipolar cell has subtracted the amount of red light from the amount of green light.

The **opponent-process theory** of Ewald Hering, a nineteenth-century rival of Helmholtz, describes this manner of coding color information. According to the opponent-process theory, we perceive color in terms of paired opposites: white versus black, red versus green, and blue versus yellow (Hurvich & Jameson, 1957). In modern terms, we have neurons that are excited by green and inhibited by red, or excited by red and inhibited by green, and so forth. Hering supported his view with psychophysical observations, such as the phenomenon of color afterimages: If you stare at something yellow for about a minute and then look at a white background, you see blue. Similarly, if you stare at blue, red, or green, you see a yellow, green, or red afterimage, respectively (Figure 6.10). These **negative afterimages** represent the results of fatiguing one or another kind of response by bipolar cells. For example, in the prolonged presence of green light, a particular bipolar cell may have undergone prolonged excitation. When the green light is removed, the cell becomes hyperpolarized, and its output is perceived as red.

Beyond the level of the cones, color coding in many neurons of the visual system resembles Hering's opponent processes (DeValois & Jacobs, 1968).

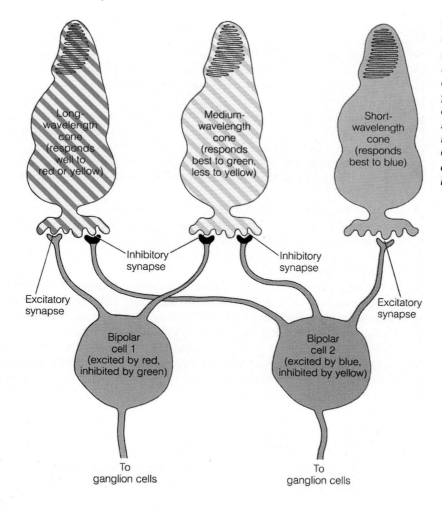

Figure 6.11
Connections between three types of cones and the bipolar cells enable the bipolar cells to show opponent-process properties. For example, when red light strikes this group of receptors, it excites bipolar cell 1. Green light inhibits bipolar cell 1. Red, green, or yellow light inhibits bipolar cell 2.

Many bipolar cells, ganglion cells, and cortical cells are excited by green light on the retina and inhibited by red light or are excited by red light and inhibited by green. Other cells are excited by yellow or blue and inhibited by the other. White-black cells are most strongly stimulated by a combination of all wavelengths (white). There is no such thing as black light. White-black cells are most effectively inhibited when the light shining on their cones is much fainter than the light shining on other cones surrounding them.

Although we do not know exactly how the three kinds of cone connect to the bipolar cells, Figure 6.11 illustrates one possibility. Note that the activity of bipolar cell 1 depends on the ratio of activity between the medium-wavelength and long-wavelength cones. For example, red light, which excites the long-wavelength cone, excites bipolar cell 1. Green light excites the medium-wavelength cone and thus inhibits bipolar cell 1. Yellow light excites both the long-wavelength cone and the medium-wavelength cone and therefore produces little net effect on bipolar cell 1.

Color Blindness

A colleague once sent a survey to me and a number of other psychologists asking what "discoveries" psychologists had made. That is, the encyclopedias are full of examples of discoveries in astronomy, biology, chemistry, and other sciences, but they seldom designate anything as a "discovery in psychology." Have psychologists made any discoveries, and if so what were they?

You might give that question some thought. To be a "psychological discovery," a finding should be clearly part of psychology, formerly unknown, but now well established. I shall leave it to you to devise your own list, but let me tell you what I believe was the first real discovery in psychology: the phenomenon of color blindness. Before color blindness was discovered in the 1600s (Fletcher & Voke, 1985), people took it for granted that vision copies the objects we see. That is, if an object is round, we see the roundness; if it is yellow, we see the yellowness; if it is moving, we see the movement. Investigators *discovered* that it is possible to have otherwise satisfactory vision without seeing color.

We now recognize several types of color blindness. For genetic reasons, some people lack long-wavelength, medium-wavelength, or short-wavelength cones. Some lack two kinds of cones, having only one intact (Nathans et al., 1989). Other people have all three types of cones, but have low numbers or defective forms of one type.

In the most common form of color blindness, red-green color blindness, people have trouble distinguishing red from green. The reason is an alteration of the genes coding for the opsins in the long- and medium-wavelength cones (Nathans, Piantanida, Eddy, Shows, & Hogness, 1986). Those genes are recessive genes located on the X chromosome. That is, they are sex-linked genes (see Appendix A). About 8 percent of males are red-green color blind, as compared with about 1 percent of females.

Summary

1. Each type of receptor transduces a particular kind of energy into a generator potential. (p. 180)

2. Sensory information is coded so that the brain can process it. The coded information bears no physical similarity to the stimuli being coded. (p. 181)

3. According to the law of specific nerve energies, the brain interprets any activity of a given sensory neuron as representing the kind of sensory information that neuron is tuned to. (p. 182)

4. Light passes through the pupil of a vertebrate eye and stimulates the receptors lining the retina at the back of the eye. (p. 183)

5. Visual receptors are most densely packed in the fovea, the central area of the retina. (p. 183)

6. The receptors in the retina pass their information to bipolar cells, which in turn stimulate ganglion cells, all within the eyeball itself. The axons from the ganglion cells join to form the optic tract, which exits from the eye at a point called the blind spot. (p. 184)

7. The retina has two kinds of receptors: rods and cones. Rods are more sensitive to dim light. Cones, which are located mostly near the center of the retina, are more sensitive to detail. Cones contribute to color vision; rods do not. (p. 188)

8. Light stimulates the receptors by triggering a change in molecules of 11-*cis*-retinal, which release energy, thereby activating second messengers within the cell. (p. 189)

9. According to the trichromatic (or Young-Helmholtz) theory of color vision, color perception begins with the stimulation of three types of cones in the retina. Each wavelength of light stimulates a distinctive ratio of responses by the three types of cones. (p. 190)

10. According to the opponent-process theory of color vision, visual system neurons beyond the receptors themselves respond with an increase in activity to indicate one color of light and a decrease to indicate the opposite color. The three pairs of opposites are red-green, yellow-blue, and white-black. (p. 192)

11. For genetic reasons, certain people are unable to distinguish one color from another in the same way that most people do. The most common type of color blindness is an inability to distinguish between red and green. (p. 194)

Review Questions

1. What is the difference between transduction and coding? (p. 180)

2. When light from the environment strikes the retina, it is

reversed left-right and up-down. Does the nervous system turn the image right side up? If so, where and how? If not, does the reversal of the image cause any difficulties? (p. 181)

3. What is the law of specific nerve energies, and how must it be modified in light of modern knowledge of the nervous system? (p. 182)

4. Why is perception of detail better in the fovea than it is toward the periphery of the retina? Why is perception of dim light better in the periphery? (pp. 183, 188)

5. What makes the blind spot of the retina blind? (p. 184)

6. What are the differences between rods and cones? (p. 188)

7. How does 11-*cis*-retinal contribute to the detection of light? (p. 189)

8. Describe the Young-Helmholtz theory and the opponent-process theory. (p. 190)

9. Why is color blindness more common in men than in women? (p. 194)

Thought Question

1. How could you test for the presence of color vision in a bee? Examining the retina will not help; invertebrate receptors resemble neither rods nor cones. It is possible to train bees to approach one visual stimulus and not another. The difficulty is that if you trained some bees to approach, say, a yellow card and not a green card, you would not know whether they solved the problem by color or by brightness. Because brightness is different from physical intensity, you cannot equalize brightness by any physical measurement, nor can you assume that two colors that are equally bright to humans are also equally bright to bees. How might you get around the problem of brightness to study the possibility of color vision in bees?

Suggestion for Further Reading

Dowling, J. E. (1987). *The retina.* Cambridge, MA: Harvard University Press. Detailed, well-illustrated review of research on retinal receptors and their connections to other neurons within the eye.

Terms

reception the absorption of physical energy by the receptors (p. 180)

transduction the conversion of that physical energy to an electrochemical pattern in the neurons (p. 180)

coding the one-to-one correspondence between some aspect of the physical stimulus and some aspect of the nervous system activity (p. 180)

generator potential a local depolarization or hyperpolarization of a neuron membrane (p. 180)

law of specific nerve energies statement that each nerve always conveys the same kind of information to the brain (p. 182)

pupil opening in the eyeball through which light enters (p. 183)

retina the rear surface of the eye, lined with rods and cones (p. 183)

fovea area in the center of the human retina specialized for acute, detailed vision (p. 183)

optic nerve (or optic tract) bundle of axons from the ganglion cells of the retina to the brain (p. 184)

blind spot point in the retina that lacks receptors because the optic nerve exits at this point (p. 184)

blindsight ability to point toward objects or turn the eyes toward objects in a damaged area of the visual field (p. 187)

rod one type of retinal receptor, not contributing to color perception (p. 188)

cone one type of retinal receptor, contributing to color perception (p. 188)

photopigment chemical that releases energy when struck by light (p. 189)

trichromatic theory or **Young-Helmholtz theory** theory that we perceive color through the relative rates of response by three kinds of cones, with each kind maximally sensitive to a different set of wavelengths (p. 190)

psychophysical observations reports by human observers concerning their perceptions of various stimuli (p. 191)

opponent-process theory theory that we perceive color in terms of paired opposites: white versus black, red versus green, and blue versus yellow (p. 192)

negative afterimages perceptions resulting from the fatigue of one kind of neuron, such as the perception of green that people experience after prolonged viewing of something red (p. 192)

Neural Basis of Visual Perception

Recall I said that color blindness was a discovery (p. 194). Some people with otherwise satisfactory vision cannot distinguish reds from greens, for example. Before the discovery of color blindness, almost everyone assumed that anyone who saw an object at all would see everything about the object — its shape, its color, its movement.

Because you have grown up since early childhood knowing about color blindness, you may find it hard to understand how its discovery would have been so surprising. And yet you yourself may be surprised—as psychologists of the late 20th century were—by the analogous phenomenon of *motion blindness:* Some people with otherwise satisfactory vision often fail to detect that some object is moving. Or, if they do detect that it is moving, they have more than the usual trouble determining in which direction it is moving or how fast it is moving. "How could anyone see something without seeing that it is moving?" you might ask. If so, your question is not much different from the question raised in the 1600s, "How could anyone see something without seeing what color it is?"

The fundamental fact about the visual cortex is one that takes a little getting used to: You have no little person in the head, no hidden observer who sees each object as if projected on a screen. Different parts of your cortex "see" different aspects of the object. One part analyzes the shapes, while another part analyzes colors, and still another part analyzes movement. So far as we can tell, no "central processor" neurons see all aspects at once.

An Overview of the Mammalian Visual System

Let us begin with a general outline of the anatomy of the mammalian visual system. Then we shall examine in more detail the processes occurring at certain stages along the route.

We have already discussed the receptors (rods and cones). They make synaptic contact with **horizontal cells** and **bipolar cells** (Figure 6.12). The bipolars make synapses onto **amacrine cells** and **ganglion cells.** All these cells are located within the eyeball.

The axons of the ganglion cells form the optic nerve, which leaves the retina, traveling along the lower surface of the brain. The optic nerve from the left eye and the optic nerve from the right eye meet at the optic chiasm (Figure 6.6), where, in humans, half of the axons from each eye cross to the opposite side of the brain. The percentage of crossover varies from one species to another, depending on the location of the eyes. In species that have their eyes

Figure 6.12
A bipolar cell from the retina of a carp, stained with Procion yellow
Bipolar cells get their name from the fact that a fibrous process is attached to each end (or pole) of the neuron. (From Dowling, 1987.)

25 μm

far toward the sides of the head, as do rabbits and guinea pigs, nearly all the axons cross to the opposite side of the head.

Most of the axons in the optic nerve go to the **lateral geniculate nucleus** of the thalamus. (The term *geniculate* comes from the Latin root *genu,* meaning *knee.* To *genuflect* is to bend the knee. In some species, the lateral geniculate nucleus is shaped like a knee . . . if you use some imagination!) Some axons go to the superior colliculus, and a smaller number go to several other areas. A very few axons go to a section of the hypothalamus that keeps waking-sleeping schedules synchronized with the day-night cycles of the world. (See Chapter 9.)

At any rate, most of the optic nerve axons, and thus most of the visual information, goes to the lateral geniculate. The lateral geniculate, in turn, sends its axons to the visual areas of the cerebral cortex.

The cerebral cortex has a number of distinguishable visual areas, each with its own functions, each analyzing visual information in its own way. However, the division of labor begins much earlier. Way back at the level of the ganglion cells, we can distinguish several types of cells, with different sizes of cell bodies, different conduction speeds, and different roles to play in perception. Those different kinds of cells give rise to different pathways that remain largely separate in the lateral geniculate and then again in the cerebral cortex. The story of what these different pathways do is both complex and fascinating. To understand it, we need to begin with some general principles.

Mechanisms of Processing in the Visual System

The human retina contains roughly 120 million rods and 6 million cones. If we were aware of the activity in every receptor, we would be flooded with information. We do not need or want information about 126 million points of light. We merely need to know what objects are out there, where their borders are,

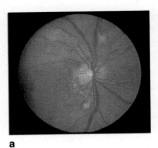

a

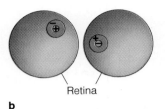

Retina

b

Figure 6.13
(a) View of the retina through an ophthalmoscope. (Don Wong/Science Source/PR.) (b) Diagrams of two typical receptive fields of bipolar cells (greatly magnified).

and how they are moving. To provide this information, the cells of our visual system have to compare what is happening in one part of the retina with what is happening in other parts, especially adjacent parts.

Receptive Fields

In tracing what happens to visual information as it passes from the retina to various points in the brain, we rely on a concept known as the **receptive field.** In the visual system, the receptive field of a neuron is the portion of the retina in which light will affect the activity of that neuron. For example, we can speak of the receptive field of a cell in the visual cortex. The receptive field of that cell is a part of the retina where the receptors stimulate bipolar cells, which in turn stimulate ganglion cells, and so forth until eventually the message reaches the cortical cell in question. If light in some retinal area leads to excitation of the cortical cell, we say that area is part of the cell's excitatory receptive field. If light somewhere inhibits the cortical cell, that area is part of the cell's inhibitory receptive field. And, of course, if light neither excites nor inhibits, then it is not part of that cell's receptive field at all. (It is presumably part of the receptive fields of other cortical cells.)

We can describe the receptive field of a visual cell in two ways. The first is to describe it as an area of the retina, as in Figure 6.13. The second is to describe it as an area of the visual field. Due to the fact that every spot on the retina receives its input from one point in the visual field, the two ways are equivalent.

To map the receptive fields of neurons in the visual system, an investigator can shine light on specific receptors in the retina while recording from a cell in the brain. If light on a particular receptor either increases or decreases the firing rate of a brain cell, then that receptor is part of the cell's receptive field. If the light has no effect, the receptor is outside the receptive field.

Customarily, neuroscientists often say that a particular neuron in the visual system responds to a particular pattern of light: For example, "this cell in the cerebral cortex responds best to a green horizontal line." The investigator does not mean that light shining on the neuron excites it. Rather, the neuron is excited when that pattern of light shines on the neuron's receptive field in the retina.

Lateral Inhibition

Neurons in the cerebral cortex have some very complicated receptive fields. Instead of simply being excited or inhibited by light, a cortical cell may respond only when its receptive field sees, say, a horizontal green line moving upward, or some other, even more complicated pattern. These advanced and complicated receptive fields arise through interactions among various cells in the visual system. One of the most basic examples of such an interaction is lateral inhibition.

Lateral inhibition is the reduction of activity in one neuron by activity in a neighboring neuron (Hartline, 1949). Lateral inhibition ordinarily serves to heighten the contrast at borders; it can also produce some other curious effects. For example, examine Figure 6.14. Do you see dark diamonds at the crossroads among the black squares? By the end of this section, you should be able to explain how lateral inhibition produces the illusion of dark diamonds in this figure.

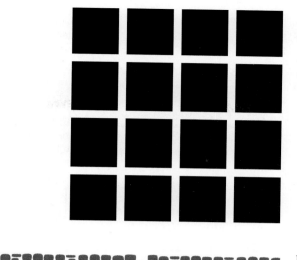

Figure 6.14
An illustration of lateral inhibition
Do you see dark diamonds at the "crossroads"?

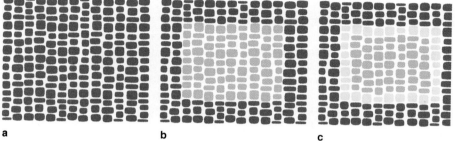

a   b   c

Figure 6.15
(*a*) *Diagram representing receptive fields in part of the retina.* (*b*) *Diagram showing the same fields while light is falling on one part of the retina (the part highlighted). Because each excited receptive field inhibits those next to it (via lateral inhibition), the cells on the outer rim of the stimulated region will receive the greatest net excitation, as shown in* (*c*). *The fields along the rim get the same amount of stimulation as those on the interior, but they get less inhibition.*

A general outline of lateral inhibition follows. Suppose that Figure 6.15a represents the receptive fields in some portion of the retina. (Don't think of these as individual receptors, but as receptive fields of bipolar or ganglion cells.) Figure 6.15b shows light falling on a rectangular-shaped area of the retina. Now, suppose that each receptive field is excited in proportion to the amount of light falling on it. In addition, in proportion to this excitation, each receptive field *inhibits* each of its immediate neighbors. What will be the result?

Each of the fields near the center of the rectangle will get a certain amount of excitation from the light, plus a certain amount of inhibition from each of the fields surrounding it. The net result is excitation, but to a limited degree. Now consider the fields around the rim of the rectangle. They too get excitation from the light, the same amount as do the receptive fields near the center of the rectangle. But the ones along the rim get less inhibition. Their neighbors on one side are inhibiting them, but their neighbors on the other side are silent. As a result, the receptive fields along the rim of the rectangle will be more excited than any of the receptive fields on the interior. In this manner, lateral inhibition increases the apparent contrast at the edges of an illuminated area of the retina. It thereby helps to define the borders of an object.

To further clarify the principle, consider an analogy: If I place a wooden block on a surface of gelatin, the block depresses the gelatin beneath it while raising the surrounding surface (Figure 6.16a). The depression is analogous to the excitation of a neuron; the rise in the surrounding gelatin is analogous to lateral inhibition of surrounding neurons. Then I place a second block next to the first. As the second block sinks into the gelatin, it slightly raises the first (Figure 6.16b). Finally, I try placing a row of blocks on the gelatin. The blocks at the beginning and end of the row sink deeper than the others (Figure 6.16c).

Neural Basis of Visual Perception

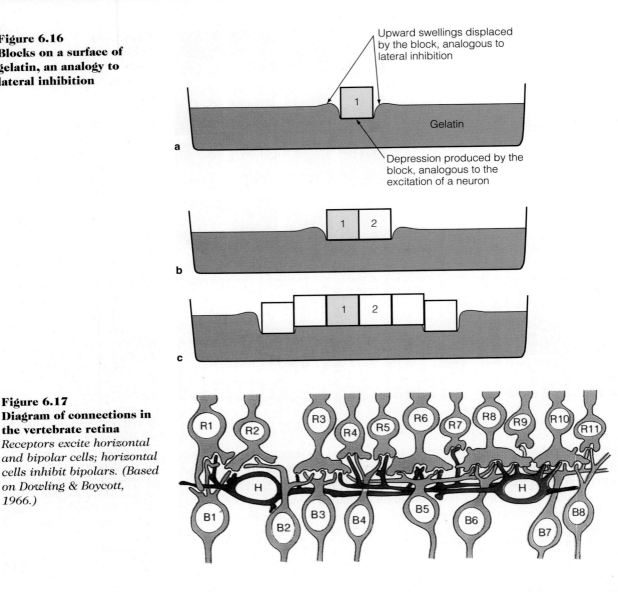

Figure 6.16
Blocks on a surface of gelatin, an analogy to lateral inhibition

Upward swellings displaced by the block, analogous to lateral inhibition

Gelatin

Depression produced by the block, analogous to the excitation of a neuron

Figure 6.17
Diagram of connections in the vertebrate retina
Receptors excite horizontal and bipolar cells; horizontal cells inhibit bipolars. (Based on Dowling & Boycott, 1966.)

Why? Because each block in the interior of the row is subject to an upward pressure from both sides, while the blocks at the beginning and end of the row are subject to that pressure from one side only.

Here is how the connections in the vertebrate retina accomplish lateral inhibition: Each receptor cell excites one or more bipolar cells, as Figure 6.17 shows. It also excites a large, widely branching horizontal cell (H), which *inhibits* that bipolar cell somewhat, although the combined effect from the receptor and the horizontal cell leaves a net excitation in the bipolar cell. The horizontal cell also inhibits other, nearby bipolar cells; in other words, it produces lateral inhibition. (See Figure 6.18.)

How Receptive Fields Are Built

Lateral inhibition is one element that goes into building the receptive field of a neuron in the visual system. Examine cell B3 in Figure 6.17. Cell B3 can be excited when light strikes receptor R3. It is also connected to a horizontal cell

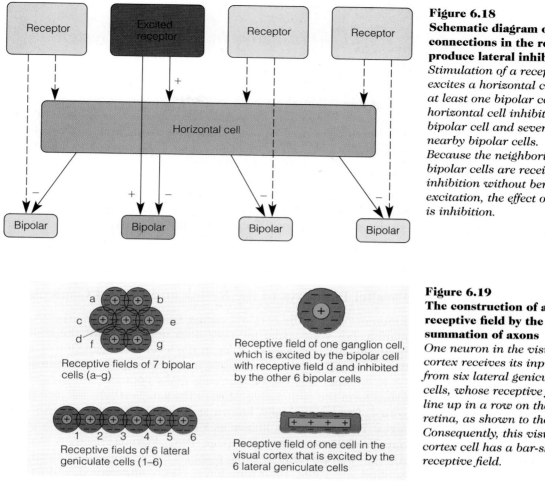

Figure 6.18
Schematic diagram of how connections in the retina produce lateral inhibition
Stimulation of a receptor excites a horizontal cell and at least one bipolar cell. The horizontal cell inhibits that bipolar cell and several nearby bipolar cells. Because the neighboring bipolar cells are receiving inhibition without benefit of excitation, the effect on them is inhibition.

Receptive fields of 7 bipolar cells (a–g)

Receptive field of one ganglion cell, which is excited by the bipolar cell with receptive field d and inhibited by the other 6 bipolar cells

Receptive fields of 6 lateral geniculate cells (1–6)

Receptive field of one cell in the visual cortex that is excited by the 6 lateral geniculate cells

Figure 6.19
The construction of a receptive field by the summation of axons
One neuron in the visual cortex receives its input from six lateral geniculate cells, whose receptive fields line up in a row on the retina, as shown to the left. Consequently, this visual cortex cell has a bar-shaped receptive field.

that receives input from receptors R1 through R8, thus receiving lateral inhibition from any of those cells. We say that receptors R1 through R8 constitute the receptive field of cell B3. That is, stimulation anywhere in that area affects the cell by either exciting or inhibiting it. Figure 6.17 shows cells along only one dimension. If we present the entire retina in two dimensions, the receptive field of a cell such as B3 looks like the drawing in Figure 6.13b. Some bipolar cells have the reverse receptive field, with an inhibitory region in the center and an excitatory field in the surround.

A group of bipolar cells sends its output to ganglion cells; in turn, a group of ganglion cells sends its output to cells in the lateral geniculate, and so on. The neurons at each level have receptive fields made by combining the receptive fields of all incoming fibers. Therefore, cells at successively later stages of the visual system tend to have larger and larger receptive fields.

When a set of neurons sends its axons to some other cell at the next level of the visual system, the sum of their receptive fields constitutes the receptive field of the next cell. For example, suppose that six neurons in the lateral geniculate each have a circular receptive field on the retina, as shown in Figure 6.19. All six cells have excitatory synapses onto a cell in the visual cortex. The receptive field of that cortical cell is the sum of the receptive fields of the six lateral geniculate cells—a bar shape, as shown on the right in Figure 6.19b.

Parallel Pathways in the Visual System

Look out your window. Perhaps you see someone walking by. A perception so simple that you take it for granted is actually a combination of many kinds of visual information: shape, size, color, brightness, distance, movement. . . . How does your visual system keep track of such different kinds of information?

Although your perception of that person walking by seems to you a single, integrated whole, different parts of your brain are analyzing different aspects. One set of neurons identifies the person's shape, another set concentrates on the colors of skin and clothing, and another sees which direction the person is walking and how fast (Livingstone, 1988; Livingstone & Hubel, 1988; Zeki & Shipp, 1988). The various pathways necessarily communicate with one another to some extent (Kaas, 1989); still, each carries on its functions with far greater independence than we might have imagined.

Parallel Pathways in the Retina and Lateral Geniculate

Different parts of the cerebral cortex analyze different aspects of visual information, but your visual pathway does not wait until the cerebral cortex to begin this division of labor. Even at the level of the ganglion cells in the retina, different cells are already reacting in different ways to the same input.

Remember that the bipolar cells make contact onto ganglion cells, whose axons form the optic nerve. Most of the ganglion cells fall into two major categories. The smaller cells, known as **X cells,** are located mostly in or near the fovea. The larger cells, known as **Y cells,** are distributed fairly evenly throughout the retina (Sherman & Spear, 1982; Fukuda, Hsiao, & Watanabe, 1985). Another category, the **W cells,** respond rather sluggishly (Raczkowski, Hamos, & Sherman, 1988); their function is poorly understood, and we shall not consider them further in this text.

Not only are the X cells physically small themselves; they have small receptive fields. Thus, they are well suited to respond to small details. They are also highly sensitive to color. That is, each neuron is excited by light of one color (such as red) in its receptive field and inhibited by another color (such as green). This high sensitivity to detail and to color makes sense when you recall that X cells are located mostly in and around the fovea, the part of the retina where we have our best perception of detail and color.

The Y cells, in contrast, have larger receptive fields and are color blind; that is, they do not signal a difference between one color and another. Furthermore, the Y cells respond best to a moving stimulus, giving only a brief response to a stationary stimulus. Again, this pattern makes sense: The Y cells become increasingly dominant toward the periphery of the retina. In the periphery of your visual field, you do not see details or color as you do toward the fovea, but you are quite sensitive to movement.

(You might try this demonstration: Take a stack of colored photographs, or baseball cards, or anything similar you have handy. Shuffle them face down, then pick one, hold it in the extreme periphery of your vision, and turn it face toward you. At that location, you cannot identify what is in the picture and you will see little if any color, but if you shake the picture, you will have no trouble detecting the movement.)

Table 6.2   Distinctions between Parvocellular and Magnocellular Neurons in the Lateral Geniculate

Characteristic	Parvocellular Neurons	Magnocellular Neurons
Input	97% from X cells (with small cell bodies), 3% from Y cells (with large cell bodies)	60% from X cells, 40% from Y cells
Cell bodies	Smaller	Larger
Receptive fields	Smaller	Larger
Color sensitive?	Yes	No
Response	Sustained response; adapted for detailed analysis of stationary objects	Fast, transient responses; adapted to detect movement and broad outlines of shape

(References: Livingstone, 1988; Livingstone & Hubel, 1988; Marrocco, 1986.)

Most Y cells and apparently all X cells send their axons to the lateral geniculate nucleus of the thalamus. The X cells, the smaller of the two kinds of ganglion cells, are mostly responsible for the input to some relatively small lateral geniculate cells, known as **parvocellular neurons.** Parvocellular means *small celled,* from the Latin root *parv,* meaning *small.* Both X and Y cells send their axons to certain larger lateral geniculate cells, known as **magnocellular neurons.** Magnocellular means *large celled,* from the Latin root *magn,* meaning *large.* (The same root appears in *magnify* and *magnificent.*)

Table 6.2 summarizes the differences between parvocellular and magnocellular neurons. The parvocellular system is generally more sensitive to color and to fine detail; the magnocellular system is generally more sensitive to larger shape patterns, depth, and movement.

The distinction between parvocellular and magnocellular pathways has certain implications for human vision (Livingstone, 1988; Livingstone & Hubel, 1988). For example, consider the painting in Figure 6.20. The artist has indicated shadows by distinct colors. The result is a painting that does not look entirely realistic, and yet the shadows enable us to perceive the illusion of depth about as well in the color version as in the black-and-white version. The reason is that the magnocellular pathway, which is more important for depth perception, is highly sensitive to brightness and not to color.

For another example, consider Figure 6.21, which has yellow-to-gray borders. Because the yellow and gray are about equally bright, the photo has very little brightness contrast. The parvocellular pathway, which is color sensitive, can detect the stimulus. However, the magnocellular pathway, which is highly sensitive to brightness contrast but not to color, detects this stimulus only weakly. The parvocellular pathway is more important for analysis of the details of form; if you focus on one point at a time, you can see each detail of the photo. However, the magnocellular pathway is more important for perceiving the overall pattern or outline of the object. Because the magnocellular system is poorly stimulated, we are slow to see the bicycle in the photo.

VIS-PATH

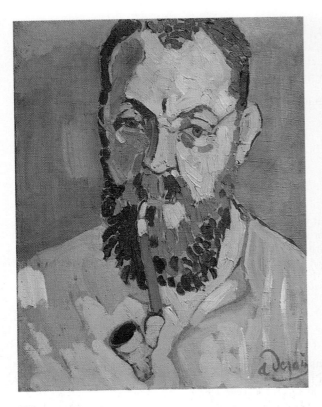 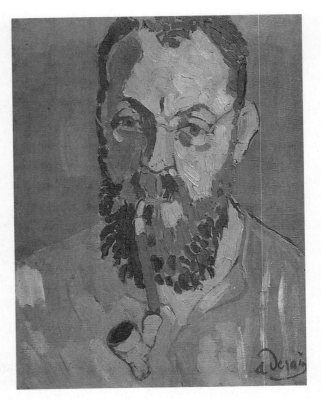

Figure 6.20
The artist André Derain (1880–1954) has shown depth with colored shadows in this portrait of painter Henri Matisse (1905). Although the painting does not look realistic, we perceive the depth easily because the magnocellular pathway (responsible for depth perception) is color blind. Note that we perceive depth about equally well in the color painting and in the black-and-white version. (Tate Gallery, London/Art Resource, NY.)

Figure 6.21
The left image can be seen only by color, because the yellows and grays are about equally bright. Therefore, seeing it depends on the parvocellular system, which is specialized for perceiving details but not overall form. Notice that you can perceive detail in this photo by looking at one spot at a time but that you have trouble seeing the bicycle as a whole. The image on the right excites your magnocellular system as well; note how easily you see the overall pattern of this bicycle. (From Livingstone & Hubel, 1988.)

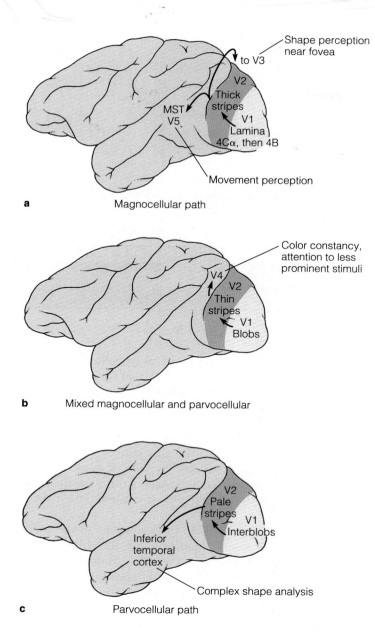

a Magnocellular path

Shape perception near fovea

to V3

V2
Thick stripes

MST
V5

V1
Lamina 4Cα, then 4B

Movement perception

b Mixed magnocellular and parvocellular

Color constancy, attention to less prominent stimuli

V4
V2
Thin stripes

V1
Blobs

c Parallel path

V2
Pale stripes

V1
Interblobs

Inferior temporal cortex

Complex shape analysis

Figure 6.22
Three visual pathways in the cerebral cortex, each beginning with neurons in area V1
(a) Neurons in lamina 4B of area V1 send information to the thick stripes of V2, which send information to both V3 and V5. (b) Neurons in the blobs of V1 send information to the thin stripes of V2, which send information to area V4. (c) Neurons in the interblobs of V1 send information to the pale stripes of V2, which send information to the inferior temporal cortex. Although these three pathways are partly independent of one another, they also communicate back and forth.

Parallel Pathways in the Cerebral Cortex

The bulk of the visual information from the lateral geniculate area of the thalamus goes first to the **primary visual cortex,** also known as area **V1,** also known as the *striate cortex* because of its striped appearance. Much of the information from the primary visual cortex goes to the **secondary visual cortex** (area **V2**), which also gets some input directly from the thalamus. From the secondary visual cortex, information branches out to areas V3, V4, and V5. (See Figure 6.22.); some also goes back to area V1 (Mignard & Malpeli, 1991). Each of those areas has subdivisions, and each sends information to additional brain areas. In total, neuroscientists distinguish twenty or more brain areas receiving visual input, occupying more than half of the primate cerebral cortex (Kaas & Krubitzer, 1991; Knierim & Van Essen, 1992).

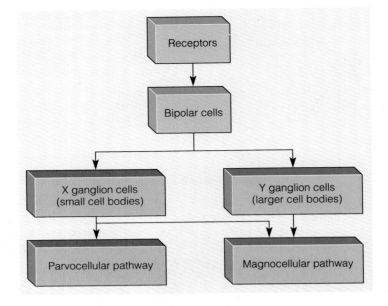

Within the cerebral cortex, the parvocellular and magnocellular pathways split from two pathways into three. Part of the parvocellular pathway continues as a system that is sensitive primarily to details of shape. The main part of the magnocellular pathway continues as a system that is highly sensitive to movement. A third system gets some of its input from the parvocellular pathway and some from the magnocellular pathway. This third system is sensitive to brightness and color. Actually, within this system, although the parvocellular cells and magnocellular cells lie side by side, they do not mingle their responses much. The parvocellular components of this system are sensitive to color (Ts'o & Gilbert, 1988); the magnocellular components are sensitive to black-and-white brightness.

Figure 6.22 diagrams these three systems in the cortex. You will note certain terms on that figure, such as blobs, interblobs, pale stripes, thin stripes, and thick stripes. Those terms refer to anatomical structures within certain parts of the visual cortex. You would certainly need to become familiar with these anatomical terms if you became a visual cortex researcher; at this point, however, do not worry too much about these details. Figure 6.23 summarizes the relationship of the X and Y cells to the parvocellular and magnocellular pathways.

Cerebral Cortex: The Shape Pathway

In the 1950s, David Hubel and Torsten Wiesel began a research project in which they shone various light patterns on the retina while using microelectrodes to record from cells in the animal's brain. They found that each cell was highly responsive to a particular "preferred" stimulus, and unresponsive or only slightly responsive to other stimuli in the same part of the retina. This research, for which Hubel and Wiesel shared a Nobel Prize, has often been called "the research that launched a thousand microelectrodes" because of the

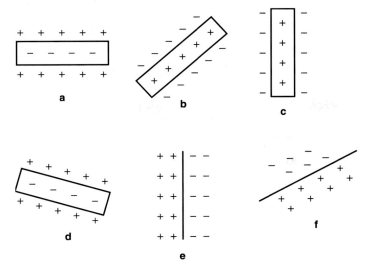

Figure 6.24
Typical receptive fields for simple visual cortex cells of cats and monkeys
Areas marked with a plus (+) are the excitatory receptive fields; areas marked with a minus (−) are the inhibitory receptive fields. (Based on Hubel & Wiesel, 1959.)

way it inspired further research. By now, their research has probably launched a million microelectrodes.

Hubel and Wiesel found that most neurons in the primary visual cortex of cats and monkeys have binocular receptive fields. That is, they respond to portions of both eyes. Moreover, most visual cortex cells have receptive fields shaped like a bar or an edge (Hubel & Wiesel, 1959). The cells may therefore serve as **feature detectors**—neurons whose responses indicate the presence of a particular feature. They distinguished three categories of neurons in the visual cortex: simple, complex, and hypercomplex cells.

Simple Cells

The receptive fields shown in Figure 6.24 are typical of **simple cells,** which are found exclusively in the primary visual cortex. Each simple cell can be excited by a point of light anywhere in the excitatory part of its receptive field and inhibited by light anywhere in the inhibitory part. The more light that falls in the cell's excitatory field, the more the cell responds. The more light that falls in the inhibitory field, the less the cell responds. For example, a cell with a receptive field like that depicted in Figure 6.24c is maximally responsive to a vertical bar of light in its receptive field. The response of the cell decreases sharply if the bar of light is moved slightly to the left or right or if it is tilted even slightly from the vertical, because light then strikes the inhibitory regions as well. (See Figure 6.25.) The receptive fields for different cortical cells have different orientations, which include vertical, horizontal, and intermediate angles.

Complex Cells

Complex cells, located in either area V1 or V2, have a larger receptive field than simple cells do. Unlike the receptive fields that we have encountered up to this point, the receptive fields of complex cells cannot be mapped into fixed excitatory and inhibitory zones.

Figure 6.25
Responses of a cat's cortical cell to a bar of light presented at varying angles
The short horizontal lines indicate the time when light is on. (From Hubel & Wiesel, 1959.)

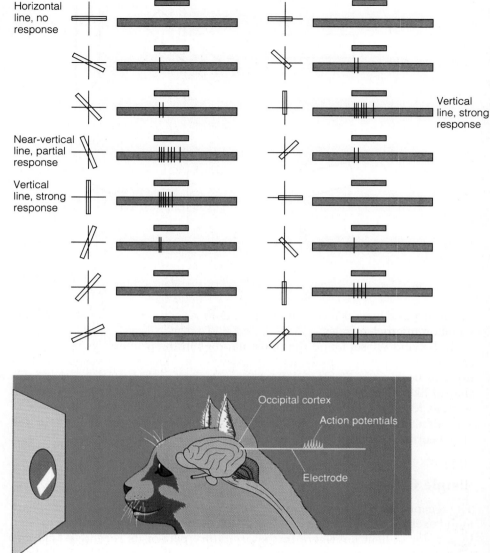

Horizontal line, no response

Near-vertical line, partial response

Vertical line, strong response

Vertical line, strong response

Occipital cortex

Action potentials

Electrode

A complex cell is practically unaffected by a small point of light in the retina. Instead, it responds to a pattern of light in a particular orientation (for instance, a vertical bar), preferably moving perpendicular to its axis. (For example, a vertical bar produces its greatest response if it is moving horizontally.) Any stimulus with the right orientation and movement within the large receptive field excites the cell, regardless of the exact location of the stimulus within that receptive field (see Figure 6.26).

We have two ways of determining whether a given cell in the visual cortex is a simple cell or a complex cell: (1) Find a bar of light to which the cell vigorously responds, and then move the light slightly to one side or the other. If the cell responds to light only in one location, it is a simple cell. (2) Shine small spots of light instead of a bar. If any spot produces significant excitation or inhibition, the cell is a simple cell.

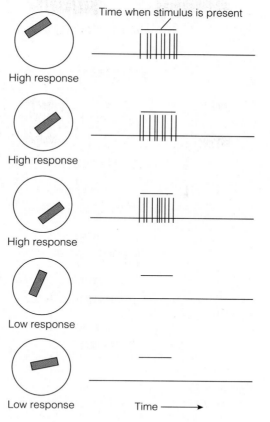

Time when stimulus is present

High response

High response

High response

Low response

Low response

Time ⟶

Figure 6.26
The receptive field of a complex cell in the visual cortex
It is like a simple cell in that its response depends on a bar of light's angle of orientation. It is unlike a simple cell in that the complex cell's response is the same for a bar in any position within the receptive field.

Hypercomplex Cells

Hypercomplex cells resemble complex cells with one additional feature: A hypercomplex cell has a strong inhibitory area at one end of its bar-shaped receptive field. The cell responds to a bar-shaped pattern of light anywhere in its broad receptive field, provided that the bar does not extend beyond a certain point (see Figure 6.27). Table 6.3 summarizes the properties of simple, complex, and hypercomplex cells.

Columnar Organization of the Visual Cortex

Various cells in the visual cortex respond best to horizontal lines, vertical lines, and various diagonals. The cells having these properties are not arranged haphazardly throughout the cortex; cells with similar properties are grouped together in columns perpendicular to the surface of the cortex (Hubel & Wiesel, 1977). (See Figure 4.18.)

VIS-CRTX

For example, Figure 6.28 shows the results when an investigator lowers an electrode into the visual cortex and records from each cell that the electrode encounters. Each red line represents a neuron and shows the angle of orientation of its receptive field. In electrode path B, the first 12 cells show orientations parallel to one another. Electrode path A is not exactly perpendicular to the surface of the cortex, and it encounters receptive fields that change gradually from one cell to the next.

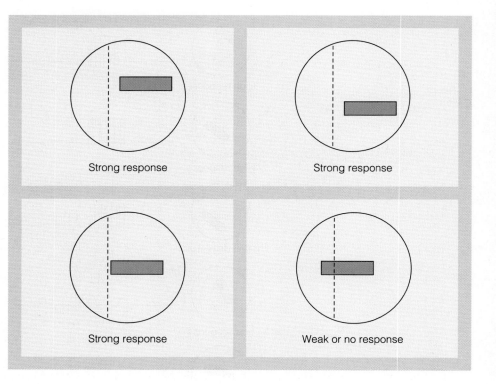

Figure 6.27
The receptive field of a hypercomplex cell responds to a bar in a particular orientation (in this case, horizontal) anywhere in its receptive field, provided that the bar does not extend into a strongly inhibitory area.

Table 6.3 Summary of Cells in the Primary Visual Cortex

Characteristic	Simple Cells	Complex Cells	Hypercomplex Cells
Location	V1	V1 and V2	V1 and V2
Binocular input?	Yes	Yes	Yes
Size of receptive field	Smallest	Medium	Largest
Response to single point of light	Excited or inhibited, depending on location	No response	No response
Best stimulus	Bar of light in particular location	Bar of light anywhere in receptive field	Same as complex cells but with strong inhibitory field at one end
Sensitive to orientation of stimulus?	Yes	Yes	Yes

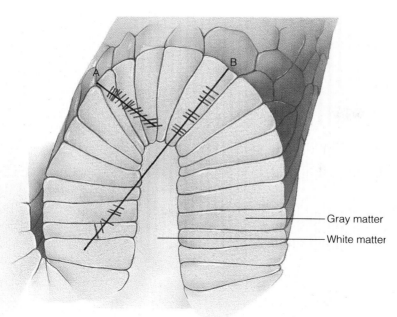

Figure 6.28
Columns of neurons in the visual cortex
When an electrode passes perpendicular to the surface of the cortex, it encounters a sequence of neurons with parallel receptive fields. (The colored lines show the angle of orientation of the receptive field for each cell.) When an electrode passes at some other angle, it encounters neurons with a variety of receptive fields. (From Hubel, 1963.)

Gray matter

White matter

Furthermore, if one cell in a column is equally responsive to both eyes, the others are also. In another column, all the cells might be responsive mostly to the left eye or the right eye. As a rule, if the cells in a given column are sensitive to color, they are all maximally excited by the same color. In short, the cells within each column all deal with more or less the same information, although they may process it in somewhat different ways.

Feature Detectors and Human Vision

Each cell in the visual cortex responds vigorously to a bar of light with a particular orientation, in a particular location. But what does such a cell have to do with perception?

Figure 6.29 (from Blakemore & Sutton, 1969) offers one demonstration: Cover the two stripe patterns on the right and stare at the little rectangle in the middle of the left half for a minute or so. As you do so, you fatigue a set of cortical neurons responding to wide stripes in the upper part of your visual field and another set responding to narrower stripes in the lower part of your visual field. Then look at the small square in the center of the right half of the figure. Note that the stripes in the upper set look narrower than those in the lower set. The reason is that you have fatigued two sets of neurons (feature detectors), which are now contributing less than usual to your perception. Your perception is now dominated by neurons sensitive to narrow stripes in the upper part of your visual field and wide stripes in the lower part.

Similar phenomena demonstrate other feature detectors in human vision. For example, if you stare at a waterfall for a minute or more and then look away, the rocks and trees next to the waterfall appear to be flowing upward. This effect, termed the *waterfall illusion,* is caused by the fatigue of feature-detector neurons responsive to downward motion.

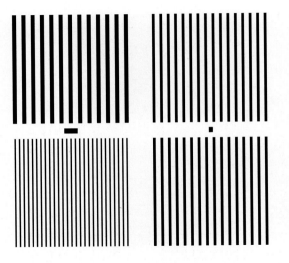

Figure 6.29
Stimulus for demonstrating width aftereffects
First stare at the little rectangle in the left half of the figure for a minute or so. Then look at the small square in the right half of the figure. Does one set of stripes look narrower than the other?

Shape Analysis beyond the Primary and Secondary Visual Cortices

As visual information goes from the simple cells of the primary visual cortex to the complex cells of the primary and secondary visual cortex, receptive fields become larger and more complex. As visual information proceeds to areas specialized for further shape analysis, the receptive fields become still larger and still more complex.

One important area for shape analysis is area **V3,** part of the magnocellular system (Figure 6.22). Area V3 is probably most important for identification of the overall shape or outline of an object. Another important area is the **inferior temporal cortex.** Cells in this area have a median width of 26 degrees of the visual field, always including the fovea (Desimone & Gross, 1979). Some cells in this area respond preferentially to stimuli with a highly complex shape, such as the shape of a hand or a face (Desimone, 1991; Desimone, Albright, Gross, & Bruce, 1984).

As a rule, the cells in the inferior temporal cortex respond vigorously to their preferred shape regardless of its exact size or position on the retina. Cells responsive to, say, a square also respond about equally to a black square on a white background, a white square on a black background, or a square-shaped pattern of dots moving across a stationary pattern of dots (Sáry, Vogels, & Orban, 1993). Face-sensitive cells in macaque monkeys respond to a face in left profile or to the same face in right profile. The ability of such cells to ignore changes in size and direction probably contributes to our capacity for **shape constancy**—the ability to recognize an object's shape even as it approaches or retreats or rotates.

Disorders of Object Recognition

Given that the visual cortex has a specialized pathway devoted to pattern recognition, we can predict that damage to this pathway should lead to specialized deficits in people's ability to recognize objects. Can we find people with such specialized deficits? Yes. In fact, neurologists have been reporting such cases for decades, although the reports frequently met with skepticism. Now that we understand *how* such specialized defects might arise, we find it easier to believe that they actually occur.

An inability to recognize visual objects is called **visual agnosia** (literally meaning *lack of knowledge*). A person with agnosia is not blind. He or she can point to visual objects and describe many of their features (though, in some cases, very slowly). Yet the person has trouble determining what the object is, despite years of experience with the object prior to brain damage.

For example, one patient, when shown a key, said, "I don't know what that is; perhaps a file or a tool of some sort." When shown a stethoscope, he said that it was "a long cord with a round thing at the end." An examiner showed him a pipe. When he could not identify it, the examiner said that it was a pipe. He then replied, "Yes, I can see it now," and pointed out the stem and bowl of the pipe. Then the examiner asked, "Suppose I told you that the last object was not really a pipe?" The patient replied, "I would take your word for it. Perhaps it's not really a pipe" (Rubens & Benson, 1971). In short, the patient was unable to identify what he saw with any confidence.

Some people experience visual agnosia limited to one or a few kinds of stimuli. For example, some brain-damaged people lose the ability to recognize once-familiar faces. This specialized deficit is known as **prosopagnosia.** Imagine that you conduct the following experiment on yourself (or you could actually conduct it if you feel that ambitious): Borrow the high-school yearbook from someone who lived in a different town from you. Study the names of all the people on facing pages until you can recite them all once. Then wait about six months, go back to those pages, and see how many you remember. Chances are, you will remember none of them. People with prosopagnosia have this problem even with the faces of their friends and relatives (Wallace & Farah, 1992).

Some people lose the ability to recognize faces without much loss of other abilities. That is, they may be able to read and write and to recognize many objects other than faces, and they can recognize their friends and relatives from the sounds of their voices, so the problem is not an overall loss of memory. When they look at a face, they can describe whether the person is old or young, male or female, and so forth. However, they cannot identify who the person is, and they may even be unsure whether this is a familiar face or an unfamiliar face (Etcoff, Freeman, & Cave, 1991).

Some people who suffer prosopagnosia also have trouble recognizing different kinds of animals, plants, or cars (Farah, 1990). So the deficit is, at least in some cases, a general difficulty with complex visual discriminations and not exclusively a problem with faces. Typically, however, the people who complain of trouble recognizing faces have no trouble recognizing letters or words. Conversely, brain-damaged patients who lose the ability to read seldom complain of trouble in recognizing faces. Evidently, the human brain has two kinds of shape recognition systems: one that identifies faces and similar patterns and one that identifies letters, words, and similar symbols (Farah, 1992).

How does the human brain recognize a face? We know that the inferior temporal cortex has some very complex feature detectors, including some that respond selectively to faces (Gross & Sergent, 1992; Ojemann, Ojemann, & Lettich, 1992). That is, such a cell will respond vigorously to certain faces, less vigorously to other faces, and hardly at all to stimuli other than faces.

What does one of these cells record? We could imagine that each cell detects and identifies a particular face—one cell for your grandmother, another for your psychology professor, another for the girl who sat beside you in 12th-grade math. That mechanism, while conceivable, would be extremely vulnerable. For example, if you happened to suffer damage to your "grandmother neuron," you would suddenly become unable to recognize your grandmother, even though you could still recognize everyone else. That kind of loss simply does not occur. Brain-damaged people who have trouble recognizing faces have trouble with all faces, not just certain ones.

Research on monkeys has found that, although each cell responds more to some faces than it does to others, each cell will respond fairly strongly to a large number of faces (Gross & Sergent, 1992; Young & Yamane, 1992). Therefore, no one cell acts as a detector for your grandmother or for any other individual. In order to perceive a face, you have to rely on a distinctive pattern across a population of face-selective neurons.

Cerebral Cortex: The Color Pathway

Although many parts of the visual cortex are sensitive to color and presumably contribute to color perception, one area, area **V4** of the cortex, seems especially important. Each cell in area V4 responds selectively to a particular color in its rather large receptive field (Zeki, 1980). V4 receptive fields always include areas in or near the fovea.

Area V4 may be critical for **color constancy**—the ability to recognize the color of an object despite changes in the lighting (Land, Hubel, Livingstone, Perry, & Burns, 1983; Land & McCann, 1971). If you were to put on green-tinted glasses, or if you replaced your light bulb with a green-tinted bulb, you would still be able to identify all the objects in the room. You would of course notice the greenish tint, but you would still identify the bananas as yellow, the paper as white, the walls as brown (or whatever), and so forth. You do so by comparing the color of one object with the color of another, in effect subtracting a fixed amount of green from each. Color constancy depends on this comparison; if you focused the green light on just one kind of object, with nothing else around for comparison, that object would look green, not its original color.

After extensive damage in and around area V4, some patients become color blind. Some retain a limited amount of color vision, especially for reds (Zeki, 1990). After less extensive damage in this area, a person may retain color vision but lose color constancy (Zeki, 1980, 1983). If you sustained damage there, you would still be able to see colors, but you would not be able to compensate for green-tinted glasses or green-tinted lighting; you would indeed see everything as green. Monkeys with damage to area V4 can learn to pick up a yellow object to get food, but if the overhead lighting is changed from white to blue, the monkey can no longer find the yellow object (Wild, Butler, Carden, & Kulikowski, 1985).

If you refer to Figure 6.23, you will notice that area V4 receives input from both the magnocellular and parvocellular pathways. You may find that confusing, since the magnocellular pathway does not contribute to color vision. The explanation is that area V4 has some additional functions unrelated to color vision, particularly some functions relating to visual attention. Monkeys with damage in V4 have trouble learning to focus their eyes on the smaller, slower, or duller of two visual stimuli (Schiller & Lee, 1991).

Cerebral Cortex: The Motion and Depth Pathways

Many of the cells of the magnocellular pathway are specialized for **stereoscopic depth perception**—the ability to detect depth by differences in what the two eyes see. To illustrate, hold a finger in front of your eyes and look at it, first with just the left eye and then with just the right eye. Try this again, holding your finger at different distances. Note that the two eyes see your finger differently and that the closer your finger is to your face, the greater the difference between the two views. Certain cells in the magnocellular pathway are highly sensitive to the amount of discrepancy between the two views, presumably mediating stereoscopic depth perception. (When you look at something with just one eye, those cells are almost unresponsive.)

Structures Important for Motion Perception

Another branch of the magnocellular pathway, specialized for motion perception, goes to an area in the middle of the temporal lobe, area **V5** (also known as area MT, for middle-temporal cortex) and to an adjacent region, area **MST** (medial superior temporal cortex). (See Figure 6.22.) The cells in those areas respond selectively based on the speed and direction of movement. For example, a particular cell might respond most vigorously in the presence of an object moving to the left at 15 degrees of visual arc per second; another cell might respond best to something moving upward at 10 degrees per second. Such cells are almost indifferent to *what* is moving; that is, they respond about equally to a large or small, bright or dark object, provided that it is moving in the correct direction at the correct speed (Albright, 1992; Lague, Raiguel, & Orban, 1993).

Various neurons in this area have somewhat different kinds of preferred stimulus. Some cells, especially in area V5, respond best to any kind of light-dark border moving within a fairly small receptive field of the retina. That is, they would respond well to either a moving small object or the moving edge of a larger object. Other cells, located in the dorsal part of area MST, respond best to an expansion, contraction, or rotation of a large visual scene, as illustrated in Figure 6.30. That is the kind of experience that occurs when the observer moves forward or backward or tilts the head. Presumably, these cells help to record the movement of the head with respect to the world.

Finally, these two kinds of cells—the ones that record movement of single objects and the ones that record movement of the entire background—funnel their messages into neurons in the ventral part of area MST, where cells respond whenever an object moves in a certain direction *relative to its background*. That is, such a cell might respond either when a small object moves to the right against a stationary background, or when the object remains in one place on the retina while the background moves to the left (Tanaka, Sugita, Moriya, & Saito, 1993). (See Figure 6.31.) An object would stay in one place on the retina while the background moved left if, say, the observer's head were moving to the right while the object itself was also moving to the right.

A cell with such properties could be enormously useful in determining the motion of objects. When you move your head from left to right, all the objects in your visual field move across your retina as if the world itself had moved right to left. (Go ahead; try it.) Yet you do not perceive anything as moving; the world looks stationary. Indeed, all the objects are stationary—with respect to

**Figure 6.30
Stimuli that excite certain cells in the dorsal part of area MST**
Cells in this area have large receptive fields; they respond not to the movement of a single object or border, but rather to an expansion, contraction, or rotation of a large scene, as would happen if the observer moved forward or backward or tilted his or her head.

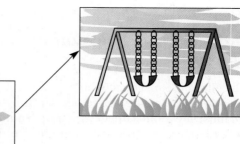

expansion

rotation

**Figure 6.31
Stimuli that excite certain cells in the ventral part of area MST**
Cells in this area respond best when a small object moves relative to its background. That could occur if the object's image either moved on the retina or remained in one place while the background moved.

one another. But if, while you are moving your head left to right, some object in your visual field really is moving, you do see the movement. The mechanism, evidently, is that cells in the ventral part of area MST in your brain detect the motion of objects relative to their background. Such cells enable you to perceive moving objects independently of whether your head itself is moving.

Motion Blindness

After damage in and around area V5, a person becomes **motion blind.** That is, he or she can see objects, but has trouble determining whether an object is moving or stationary. One such patient reported that she felt uncomfortable in a room with people walking around, because "people were suddenly here or there but I have not seen them moving." She could not cross a street without someone to help her: "When I'm looking at the car first, it seems far away. But then, when I want to cross the road, suddenly the car is very near." Even such a routine task as pouring coffee became very difficult; the flowing liquid appeared to be frozen and unmoving, and she would not stop pouring until she had overfilled the cup (Zihl, von Cramon, & Mai, 1983).

Is Motion Perception Color Blind?

Many neuroscientists characterize areas V5 and MST as "color blind." That characterization, though true in a sense, may be misleading.

It is certainly true in the sense that the neurons in areas V5 and MST do not give different responses depending on the color of an object. However much a neuron responds to, say, a white moving object, it responds the same way to a green or yellow or red moving object. Thus, these cells do not contribute to identifying the color of an object.

Furthermore, examine Figure 6.32. Because the red and green lines differ in color, but only slightly in brightness, this display should only slightly stimulate the magnocellular system. If a computer display shows lines like this moving steadily in one direction or the other, people sometimes have trouble seeing the movement, or if they do see it, they underestimate its speed (Logothetis, 1991). Observations of this sort imply that the motion-detection system of the human brain does not see color, or at least that it sees color poorly.

However, if we carry this description to its extreme, we might conclude that one part of the brain sees only shape, another sees only color, and still another sees only motion. Now, we can imagine seeing a colorless, motionless shape or a shapeless, motionless blob of color, but can you imagine a shapeless, colorless "something" in motion? Ordinarily, the perception of motion is the perception of an *object* in motion. Various parts of our visual system combine forces to define something we see as "an object." We can perceive an object because it stands out from its background in brightness, texture, depth, monocular disparity, or color (Stoner & Albright, 1993). Once we have detected an object by its color, we can perceive this colored object as moving. In other words, even though the cortical systems that detect movement do not help us detect color, the systems that help us detect color do contribute (at least a little) toward helping us perceive movement.

Figure 6.32
A pattern of lines that stimulates the parvocellular pathway much more than the magnocellular pathway
Movement of such lines is difficult to detect because the magnocellular pathway is responsible for movement detection.

Cerebral Cortex: Communication among the Pathways

The main points of this section of the chapter have been as follows:

- Each cell in the visual system has a receptive field—a portion of the retina to which it is responsive.
- Each cell in the visual system responds to specific features of a stimulus in its receptive field—features such as shape, color, or movement.
- Separate pathways in the visual system attend to different aspects of the visual system.
- Certain kinds of brain damage can impair specific aspects of visual perception.

Figure 6.22 summarizes the three major visual pathways in the cerebral cortex—one responsible mostly for perception of color, one responsible mostly for perception of fine detail, and one responsible mostly for perception of movement and depth. Each of these areas is in fact subdivided, and each passes information on to additional areas not shown.

Why do we have so many visual areas? What can we do with a large number of visual areas that other animals with fewer visual areas, such as hedgehogs, cannot do? Surely it is nothing simple; hedgehogs respond to the shape, color, and movement of visual stimuli. Somehow the extra visual areas may facilitate subtle capacities such as color constancy, or they may simply increase the precision of the same capacities that hedgehogs have (Kaas, 1989).

How do we put together the information from different pathways? For example, when you look at a rabbit, you do not see a rabbit-shaped thing, a brown thing, and a hopping thing; you see one thing—a rabbit. What part of the brain "puts the rabbit together"?

The apparent answer, perhaps surprisingly, is that *no* part of the brain puts it together. Even in the prefrontal cortex, known as an "association area," certain neurons store memories of shapes and other neurons store memories of locations (Wilson, Ó Scalaidhe, & Goldman-Rakic, 1993). Apparently, the brain has no central "self" cell where all the information comes together.

"But, then," you might ask, "if different parts of my brain see color, shape, location, motion, and so forth, how do I perceive all of those as aspects of a single object?" In asking this, you are reformulating the mind-brain question: "What is the relationship between conscious experience and the activity of countless cells in the brain?" The answer is not obvious. One possibility stems from the discovery that neurons stimulated by the same object often produce 40 cycle-per-second oscillations ("brain waves") in synchrony with one another (Engel, König, Kreiter, & Singer, 1991). Perhaps those oscillations are a way of connecting the responses from different parts of the brain. Perhaps, perhaps not. What is most remarkable is that this question of how we perceive a unified stimulus has begun to look like a scientific question, and not just a philosophical one.

Summary

1. The optic tracts of the two eyes join at the optic chiasm, where half of the axons from each eye cross to the opposite side of the brain. Most of the axons then travel to the lateral geniculate nucleus of the thalamus, which communicates with the visual cortex. (p. 196)

2. Each neuron in the visual system has a receptive field—an area of the retina to which it is connected. Light on the receptive field can excite or inhibit the neuron, depending on the light's location, color, movement, and so forth. (p. 198)

3. Lateral inhibition is a mechanism by which stimulation in any area of the retina suppresses the responses in neighboring areas. It enhances the contrast at light-dark borders. (p. 198)

4. Receptive fields of higher-level neurons are built up by excitatory and inhibitory connections from lower-level neurons. In the simplest case, the receptive field of a higher-level neuron is the sum of the receptive fields of all the lower-level neurons connected to it. (p. 200)

5. The mammalian vertebrate visual system has much division of labor. X ganglion cells (smaller) and Y ganglion cells (larger) give rise to the parvocellular (smaller) system and magnocellular system (larger) in the thalamus and cerebral cortex. In general, the parvocellular system is specialized for perception of color and fine details; the magnocellular system is specialized for perception of depth, movement, and overall patterns. (p. 202)

6. One system in the cerebral cortex is responsible for shape perception. Within the primary visual cortex, neuroscientists distinguish simple cells, which have a fixed excitatory and inhibitory field, from complex cells, which respond to a light pattern of a particular shape regardless of its exact location. Hypercomplex cells are similar to complex cells, except that they have a strong inhibitory field at one end. (p. 207)

7. Within the cortex, cells with similar properties cluster together in columns perpendicular to the surface of the cortex. (p. 209)

8. Neurons sensitive to shapes or other visual aspects serve as feature detectors. Prolonged staring at a particular

pattern can fatigue certain feature detectors and lead to aftereffects such as the waterfall illusion. (p. 211)

9. One of the advanced pathways for shape perception is the inferior temporal cortex, which is apparently critical for shape constancy. (p. 212)

10. Damage to certain cortical areas can impair recognition of specific objects, such as faces. (p. 213)

11. Another pathway through the visual cortex, largely dependent on area V4, is important for color constancy. (p. 214)

12. Motion perception depends on cells in area V5 and the medial superior temporal cortex. People with damage in those areas have severe troubles identifying the direction and speed of moving objects. (p. 215)

Review Questions

1. Where in the brain do axons of the optic nerve go? (p. 196)

2. What is and where is the receptive field of a cell in the visual cortex? (p. 198)

3. Suppose light shines equally on all the receptors in a square area of the retina. In which part of the retina will the bipolar cells show the greatest activity? Why? (p. 199)

4. How does a horizontal cell produce lateral inhibition in the vertebrate eye? (p. 200)

5. Visual cortex cells have bar-shaped receptive fields. How are those built up from the input from lateral geniculate cells that have circular receptive fields? (p. 201)

6. What are the differences between parvocellular neurons and magnocellular neurons? (p. 203)

7. How could an investigator determine whether a given cell in the visual cortex is simple or complex? (p. 208)

8. Describe the role of feature detectors in the waterfall illusion. (p. 211)

9. What is shape constancy, and what part of the brain is especially important for this function? (p. 212)

10. What does the study of agnosias tell us about the possible existence of separate shape representation systems in the visual cortex? (p. 213)

11. What is color constancy, and what part of the brain is especially important for this function? (p. 214)

12. How does the visual system distinguish between a moving object and an image moving across the retina because of the observer's own movement? (p. 215)

13. If a repeating pattern of red and green lines (about equally bright) moves across a computer screen, why do people have trouble perceiving the movement? (p. 217)

Thought Questions

1. Explain the dark diamonds you see in Figure 6.14 in terms of lateral inhibition.

2. After a receptor cell is stimulated, the bipolar cell receiving input from it shows an immediate burst of response.

A fraction of a second later, the bipolar's response rate decreases, even though the stimulation from the receptor cell remains constant. How can you account for that decrease? (*Hint:* What does the horizontal cell do?)

3. Cortical cells have receptive fields with preferred orientations of horizontal, vertical, and intermediate angles. Why would it be unsatisfactory for an animal to have only two kinds of cells, horizontal and vertical, without the intermediates? Note that such an animal would not necessarily be blind to intermediate angles. Even a 45-degree line could give rise to a slight response by both cells. (*Hint:* How could the animal tell the difference between a line at a 5-degree angle and one at a 10-degree angle or between a 45-degree angle and a 135-degree angle?)

Suggestions for Further Reading

Livingstone, M. S. (1988, January). Art, illusion and the visual system. *Scientific American, 258* (1), 78–85. Interesting discussion of the three pathways in the visual system of the cerebral cortex.

Masland, R. H. (1986, December). The functional architecture of the retina. *Scientific American, 255* (6), 102–111. Description of how bipolar cells, horizontal cells, and amacrine cells combine to produce the receptive fields of ganglion cells.

Van Essen, D. C., Anderson, C. H., & Felleman, D. J. (1992). Information processing in the primate visual system: An integrated systems perspective. *Science, 255,* 419–423. A summary of research on parallel visual pathways through the cerebral cortex.

Terms

horizontal cell a cell type in the vertebrate eye, responsible for lateral inhibition (p. 196)

bipolar cell one of the cell types in the eye (p. 196)

amacrine cell local neuron within the eye having no axon (p. 196)

ganglion cell type of neuron within the eye (p. 196)

lateral geniculate a thalamic nucleus that receives incoming visual information (p. 197)

receptive field region of the receptive surface (such as retina or skin) that can excite or inhibit a given neuron (p. 198)

lateral inhibition restraint of activity in one neuron by activity in a neighboring neuron (p. 198)

X cell small ganglion cell, located mostly in or near the fovea (p. 202)

Y cell relatively large ganglion cell, distributed fairly evenly throughout the retina (p. 202)

W cell type of ganglion cell that is only weakly responsive to visual stimuli (p. 202)

parvocellular neuron small-celled neuron of the visual system that is sensitive to color differences and visual details (p. 203)

magnocellular neuron large-celled neuron of the visual system that is sensitive to changing or moving stimuli (p. 203)

primary visual cortex or area **V1** area of the cortex responsible for the first stage of visual processing (p. 205)

secondary visual cortex or area **V2** area of the visual cortex responsible for second stage of visual processing (p. 205)

feature detector neuron whose responses indicate the presence of a particular feature (p. 207)

simple cell type of visual cortex cell that can be excited by a point of light anywhere in the excitatory part of its receptive field and inhibited by light anywhere in the inhibitory part (p. 207)

complex cell cell type of the visual cortex that responds best to a light stimulus of a particular shape anywhere in its receptive field; its receptive field cannot be mapped into fixed excitatory and inhibitory zones (p. 207)

hypercomplex cell cell of the visual cortex that responds best to stimuli of a precisely limited type, anywhere in a large receptive field, with a strong inhibitory field at one end of its field (p. 209)

V3 area of the visual cortex responsible for detailed spatial perception, especially in and near the fovea (p. 212)

inferior temporal cortex portion of the cortex where neurons are highly sensitive to complex aspects of the shape of visual stimuli within very large receptive fields (p. 212)

shape constancy ability to perceive the shape of an object despite the movement or rotation of the object (p. 212)

visual agnosia impaired ability to identify visual objects, despite otherwise satisfactory vision (p. 213)

prosopagnosia impaired ability to recognize or identify faces (p. 213)

V4 area of the visual cortex responsible for processing color information (p. 214)

color constancy ability to recognize the color of an object despite changes in lighting (p. 214)

stereoscopic depth perception ability to detect depth by differences in what the two eyes see (p. 215)

V5 a portion of the middle temporal cortex, where neurons are highly sensitive to the speed and direction of movement of visual stimuli (p. 215)

MST medial superior temporal cortex, an area in which neurons are sensitive to expansion, contraction, or rotation of the visual field or to the movement of an object relative to its background (p. 215)

motion blindness impaired ability to perceive the direction or speed of movement, despite otherwise satisfactory vision (p. 216)

Development of the Visual System

Suppose that you had lived all your life in the dark. And then today, for the first time, you came out into the light for the first time and looked around. Would you be able to make any sense of what you saw?

Chances are, you did have this experience once—on the day you were born. We cannot know how much sense babies make of what they see; presumably, the world looks fairly mysterious to them. Yet, within a few months to a year or so, they can recognize familiar faces, they can crawl toward a toy they see at the other side of a room, and they may even show signs of recognizing themselves in a mirror. How do they develop these impressive skills?

As we shall see, much of visual development depends on the formation and selection of synapses: Once axons get to approximately their correct targets, they form a large number of synapses, only some of which will survive. The selection of synapses depends partly on experience.

Infant Vision

When cartoonists want us to see a character as an infant, they draw the eyes large in proportion to the head. Infant eyes look large because they approach full size sooner than the rest of the head does. There is a good reason for this tendency: Infant eyes form an enormous number of complex attachments to the brain. If the eyes grew substantially after making those attachments and then sent new axons to the brain, the brain would have to reorganize its connections continually to use the additional information. One way to minimize this problem is to have the eyes reach full size early, as they do in mammals. Evolution found a different solution for fish, as Digression 6.2 describes.

Although human infants at first have very little control of movement, they have surprisingly well-developed sensory capacities. Within the first day or two after birth, human infants spend more time looking at faces, circles, or stripes than they spend looking at a patternless display (see Figure 6.35). However, the receptors in and around the fovea are immature at birth (Abramov et al., 1982). Therefore, infants, unlike older children and adults, see better in the periphery than they do in the center of vision.

Another special feature of infant vision is that infants have trouble shifting their attention. For example, infants less than 4 months old may stare at some highly attractive display, such as twirling dots on a computer screen, and be unable to shift their gaze onto some other object (Johnson, Posner, & Rothbart,

Haplochromis burtoni, an African fish, grows enormously over the course of its life. As its body grows, its eyes grow as well. Its eyes may triple in size during the first two months; eventually, each eye may be larger than the whole fish was when it hatched (see Figure 6.33b). Its neural connections were set up back when the eye was tiny. What readjustments does the fish have to make as the eye grows larger?

As Figure 6.34 shows, a large eye sees the same amount of the world as a smaller eye does. As the retina expands, the original receptors grow only a little, and they become separated over a wider area. So a receptor that originally occupied a certain arc of the radius of the infant eye occupies a much smaller arc of the adult eye—and consequently sees a smaller arc of the visual field (Figure 6.34b). If no new receptors formed, the fish's retina would have large gaps with no receptors and therefore large blind spots in its visual field.

In fact, new receptors do fill in the gaps. But most of these receptors are rods, not cones. Why does the proportion of receptors change?

Vision in bright light depends almost entirely on cones, and the acuity (precision) of vision depends on the number of cones per degree of visual angle. If the fish added many new cones, its visual acuity might

a

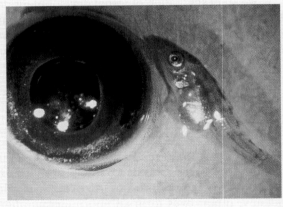

b

Figure 6.33
The African fish *Haplochromis burtoni*
(*a*) *A pair of adult fish.* (*b*) *Size comparison between adult and infant. Note that the eye of the adult is larger than the entire body of the infant fish. (Photo courtesy of Russell D. Fernald.)*

1991). Occasionally, infants stare at one object until they begin crying in distress! Slightly older infants can shift their gaze away from the most attractive display in the room, but only briefly; they almost immediately shift their gaze back to it (Clohessy, Posner, Rothbart, & Veccra, 1991). Not until about age 6 months can an infant explore one object and then shift attention to something else.

To describe visual development in more detail, investigators turn to studies of animals. The research in this area has greatly expanded our understanding of brain development and has offered implications for alleviating certain human abnormalities.

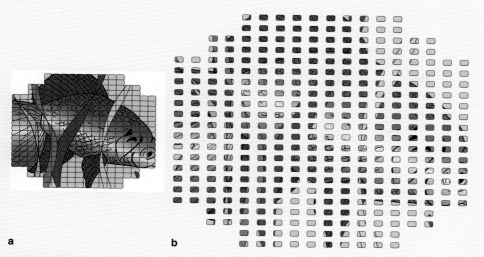

Figure 6.34
Vision through a growing eye
*As the retina expands, the cones spread out over a larger area. Each cone becomes
sensitive to a smaller degree of visual arc, and the fish has larger gaps among its
cones. This figure represents an artist's reconstruction of what the world might look
like to an infant fish (**a**) and to the same fish a year later (**b**).*

improve, but only if all the synapses in its tectum were reorganized to take advantage of the new information. That reorganization could conceivably happen, but the evidence says that it does not (Fernald, 1989). As the retina expands, the number of cones grows only slightly, and acuity stays about the same as it was. The cones do widen, so each one takes in more light than before.

Rods contribute little to the perception of detailed patterns. Their main function is to detect dim light. Many rods funnel their input into each ganglion cell; the more rods attached to a given ganglion cell, the greater the capacity of that cell to detect dim light. As the retina expands, newly formed rods fill the gaps in the retina. These new rods funnel their input into the same ganglion cells as the old rods (Fernald, 1989).

In summary, as the retina grows, the fish maintains the same acuity as before (because of the nearly constant number of cones), but its ability to see in dim light improves (because of the increased number of rods funneling into each ganglion cell). In the retina of a newly hatched fish, about 50 percent of the receptors are rods; in a full-grown adult, the percentage rises to almost 95 percent.

Development of Binocular Interaction

Most neurons in the visual cortex of an adult cat or primate respond to stimuli in both eyes, producing **binocular vision**. Furthermore, they respond to approximately corresponding areas in the two retinas. For example, if a neuron responds to a stimulus 10 degrees above the center of vision in the left eye, it also responds to a stimulus in about the same position in the right eye (Figure 6.36).

The cortical neurons of kittens have properties surprisingly similar to those of adult cats. Ordinarily, kittens open their eyes for the first time at about age

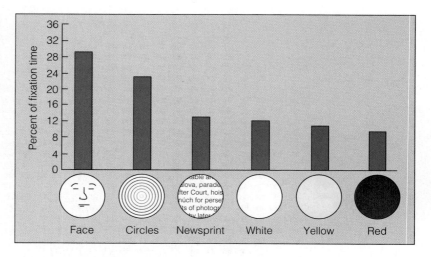

**Figure 6.35
Amount of time infants
spend looking at various
patterns**

*Even in the first two days
after birth, they look more at
faces and other complex patterns than at a plain color
or at incomprehensible
newsprint. (Based on Fantz,
1963.)*

9 days. At that time, these visually inexperienced kittens have cortical neurons
that respond to stimuli in both eyes. However, abnormal experience after age 9
days can disrupt the normal organization of the cortex.

Effects of Early Lack of Stimulation of One Eye

Although the cortical neurons are responsive to both eyes from the time that
the kitten's eyes open, visual experience is necessary, not only to fine-tune the
neurons' properties but even to maintain them. Suppose that an experimenter
sutures shut one eyelid of a kitten for the first 4 to 6 weeks of life, so that the
kitten sees with the other eye only (see Figure 6.37a). Within a week, thalamic
axons representing the deprived eye have begun to degenerate (Antonini &
Stryker, 1993). By the end of 4 to 6 weeks, those axons have lost most of their
synapses onto cortical cells (Hockfield & Kalb, 1993). The kitten is now nearly
blind in the deprived eye (Wiesel, 1982; Wiesel & Hubel, 1963).

This effect occurs only if the kitten is deprived of normal experience in one
eye during the first few weeks of life. A similar abnormal experience in adulthood does not impair the cortex. Evidently, the first three months of a kitten's
life constitute a **sensitive period** or **critical period** for the development of the
cat's visual cortex, because experiences at this time produce major, lasting
effects.

Effects of Early Lack of Stimulation of Both Eyes

If one of a kitten's eyes remains shut throughout its entire sensitive period,
the cortical neurons become unresponsive to stimulation in that eye. What do
you suppose happens if *both* eyes remain shut throughout the sensitive
period?

Surprisingly, the cortex remains somewhat responsive to both eyes,
although cells do respond rather sluggishly (Figure 6.37b). Evidently, when one
eye remains shut during the sensitive period, the cells of the visual cortex
become insensitive to axons from that eye mainly because axons from the
other eye are *more* active. The more active synapses displace the less active
synapses. If neither eye is active, no axon displaces any other.

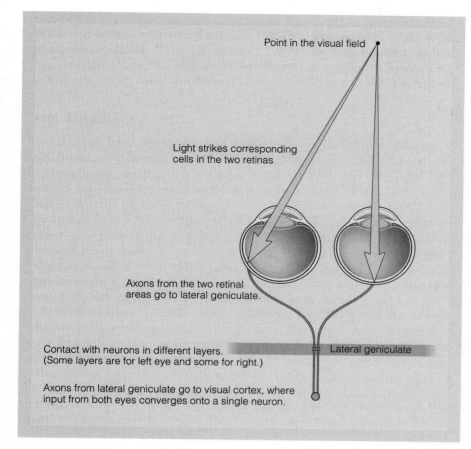

Point in the visual field

Light strikes corresponding
cells in the two retinas

Axons from the two retinal
areas go to lateral geniculate.

Contact with neurons in different layers.
(Some layers are for left eye and some for right.)

Lateral geniculate

Axons from lateral geniculate go to visual cortex, where
input from both eyes converges onto a single neuron.

Figure 6.36
The anatomical basis for binocular vision in cats and primates
Light from a point in the visual field strikes one point in the left retina and another point in the right retina. Then those two retinal areas send their axons to separate layers of the lateral geniculate. In turn, neurons in the lateral geniculate send axons to the visual cortex, where the inputs from the two eyes finally converge onto a single cell. That cell is connected (via the lateral geniculate) with corresponding areas of the two retinas.

Restoration of Response after Early Deprivation of Vision

After the cortical neurons have become insensitive to the inactive eye, can experience restore their sensitivity? Yes and no. No, *normal* experience cannot restore sensitivity to stimuli in the formerly deprived eye. If the cat simply lives its normal life with both eyes open, the deprived eye remains functionally blind. However, if the previously active eye is covered for a few months, the cortical cells do regain some responsiveness to the previously deprived eye (Smith, 1981).

This animal research has clear relevance to a human condition. Some children suffer from **lazy eye**, also known by the fancier term **amblyopia ex anopsia**, a condition in which the child ignores one eye, sometimes not even focusing it in the correct direction. Based on the animal research, we can predict that the best way to facilitate normal vision in the ignored eye would

Figure 6.37

Reduced activity in either or both eyes affects the responsiveness of neurons in the visual cortex. Visual cortex neurons lose responsiveness to an inactive input only if there is competition from a more active input.

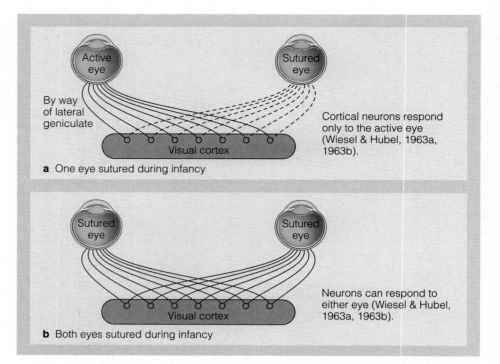

be to prevent use of the active eye. To correct the condition, a physician puts a patch over the active eye, forcing the child to use the other eye. The child gradually increases his or her attention to vision in the previously ignored eye. Eventually, the child is permitted to use both eyes together. Wearing an eye patch is likely to be most effective if it begins in early childhood. We do not know, however, exactly how long the sensitive period lasts in humans.

Deprivation of the Simultaneous Use of Both Eyes

In animals with binocular vision, cortical neurons that respond to both eyes generally respond to approximately corresponding portions of the two eyes. This arrangement enables the development of **stereoscopic depth perception,** the perception of depth by comparing the slightly different inputs from the two eyes.

Stereoscopic depth perception requires the brain to detect **retinal disparity,** the discrepancy between what the left eye sees and what the right eye sees. But how do we fine-tune cortical neurons so they will be sensitive to just the right amount of retinal disparity? The genetic instructions by themselves could not be sufficient; different individuals have slightly different head sizes, and the genes cannot know exactly how far apart the two eyes will be. The fine-tuning of binocular vision must depend on experience.

And indeed it does. Suppose that an experimenter sets up a procedure in which a kitten can see with the left eye one day, the right eye the next day, and so forth. The kitten therefore receives the same amount of stimulation in both eyes, but it never sees with both eyes at the same time. After several weeks, almost every neuron in the visual cortex responds to one eye or the other, but almost none respond to both. The cat, therefore, has no stereoscopic depth perception.

Similarly, suppose that a kitten has defective or damaged eye muscles, so that its two eyes cannot focus in the same direction at the same time. In this case, both eyes are active simultaneously, but no neuron in the visual cortex gets the same message from both eyes at the same time. Again, the result is that each neuron in the visual cortex chooses one eye or the other and becomes fully responsive to it (Blake & Hirsch, 1975; Hubel & Wiesel, 1965).

Again, a similar phenomenon occurs in humans. Certain children are born cross-eyed or wall-eyed; that is, their eyes never look in the same direction at the same time. This condition is known as **strabismus.** Such children do not develop stereoscopic depth perception; they perceive depth no better with two eyes than they do with one. A surgical operation in adulthood to correct the strabismus does not improve their depth perception (Banks, Aslin, & Letson, 1975; D. E. Mitchell, 1980). Presumably, the sensitive period for cortical development is over long before then; a much earlier operation might improve binocular vision.

The mechanism behind all these results is probably that a postsynaptic cell identifies groups of axons with synchronized activity and somehow increases its responsiveness to those axons (Singer, 1986). For example, if a portion of the left retina frequently focuses on the same object as some portion of the right eye, then axons from those two retinal areas frequently carry synchronous messages. A cortical cell would be likely to establish strong synapses with both of them. However, if the eye muscles are damaged, or if one eye at a time is always covered, the cortical cell does not receive simultaneous inputs from the two eyes. Consequently, it establishes strong synapses with axons from one eye and weakens those with axons from the other eye.

Recall from Chapter 5 that postsynaptic cells promote the survival of certain axons by delivering nerve growth factor (NGF) to them; axons that fail to get enough NGF become inactive or die. The same process apparently applies in the visual cortex. In one experiment, investigators produced strabismus in one group of infant rats. In these rats, most cortical cells became responsive to one eye only, instead of responding to both eyes. In another group, however, the investigators again produced strabismus, but in this case injected large amounts of NGF into the brain. The result was that most cells showed a strong response to both eyes, just as if the rats had grown up with normal visual experiences (Domenici, Parisi, & Maffei, 1992). The likely explanation is that, because of the massive amounts of NGF floating around in the brain, almost all axons got enough NGF to survive. They did not need to compete with one another for the NGF provided by the postsynaptic cells, and the axons that would have been rejected managed to survive.

Development of Pattern Perception

How does a cell in the visual cortex develop its property of responding only to, say, a vertical line? Although such properties are present in rough form at birth, visual experience helps to sharpen them.

Figure 6.38
Procedure for restricting a kitten's visual experience during early development
For a few hours a day, the kitten wears goggles that show just one stimulus, such as horizontal stripes or diagonal stripes. For the rest of the day, the kitten stays with its mother in a dark room without any mask. (Photo courtesy of Helmut V. Hirsch.)

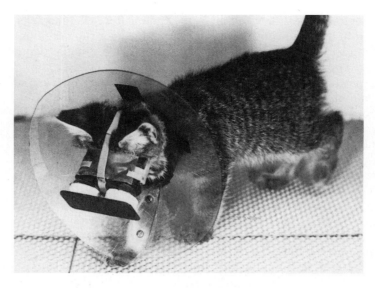

Effects of Early Total Visual Deprivation

Kittens normally open their eyes for the first time at age 9 days. Hubel and Wiesel (1963) opened the eyes of an 8-day-old kitten and recorded the response of cortical cells to light stimulation of the retina. They found simple and complex cells with receptive fields similar to those of a normal adult cat. However, many of the kitten's cells responded sluggishly or lacked the clearly defined bar-shaped receptive fields found in adults' simple and complex cells. If a kitten is reared in a dark environment, cells remain in this immature condition (Buisseret & Imbert, 1976).

Occasionally, human infants are born blind for some reason that can be corrected surgically at a later age; that is, they have no visual experience in early infancy but they begin to see later. Such children do respond to visual stimuli after the operation; for example, they can identify the brightness of light and the direction from which it is coming. However, they find it difficult to identify objects just by looking at them, or even to describe the shapes of the objects they see. They also have trouble using vision to find their way around (Valvo, 1971). In some cases, they may even choose to close their eyes and rely on touch and sound cues to maneuver through a hallway or down the stairs.

Effects of Early Exposure to a Limited Array of Patterns

If animals receive only abnormal visual experience during the early sensitive period, their cortical cells develop abnormally. For example, if a kitten spends its early sensitive period wearing goggles, so that it can see only the horizontal lines painted on the goggles (Figure 6.38), then nearly all its simple and complex cortical cells become responsive primarily to horizontal lines (Stryker & Sherk, 1975; Stryker, Sherk, Leventhal, & Hirsch, 1978). A few months later, when the cat is exposed to vertical lines and objects, it virtually ignores them and continues to show impaired vision even after years of living in a normal environment (D. E. Mitchell, 1980).

What would happen if infants, like the kittens in the experiments, were exposed mainly to vertical lines or to horizontal lines, and not to both equally? You might wonder under what circumstances such a bizarre thing could happen to any child. No parents would let an experimenter subject their child to such a procedure, and it would never happen accidentally in nature. Right?

Wrong. In fact, there is a greater than 50-50 chance that it happened to you! About 70 percent of all infants have **astigmatism,** a blurring of vision for lines in one direction (such as horizontal, vertical, or one of the diagonals). Astigmatism is caused by an asymmetric curvature of the eyes (Howland & Sayles, 1984). The prevalence of astigmatism declines to about 10 percent in 4-year-old children, as a result of normal growth.

You can informally test yourself for astigmatism with Figure 6.39. Do the lines in one direction look darker or sharper, while those in another direction look fainter or blurrier? If so, rotate the page. You will notice that the faintness or blurriness of certain lines depends on how you hold the page. If you wear corrective lenses, try this demonstration with and without your lenses. If you see a difference in the lines only when looking without your lenses, then your lenses have corrected your astigmatism.

If your eyes had strong astigmatism during your early childhood (that is, during the sensitive period for development of your visual cortex), you saw lines in one direction more clearly than you saw lines in another direction. If your astigmatism was not corrected during the first 5 to 7 years of your life, then the cells of your visual cortex probably became more responsive to the kind of lines you saw more clearly (D. E. Mitchell, 1980). In that case, you will continue to see lines in one direction or another as slightly faint or blurry, even if your eyes later became completely spherical (Freedman & Thibos, 1975).

Figure 6.39
An informal test for astigmatism
Do the lines in one direction look darker or sharper than the other lines do? If so, notice what happens when you rotate the page or rotate your head. The lines really are identical; certain lines appear darker or sharper because of the shape of your eye. If you wear corrective lenses, try this demonstration both with and without your lenses.

Development of Other Aspects of Vision

Experience molds the visual cortex in other respects as well. For example, consider what would happen if kittens grew up without seeing anything move. You can imagine the difficulty of arranging such a world; even if nothing else in the world moved, the kitten's head would be sure to move. Max Cynader and Garry Chernenko (1976) found an ingenious way to prevent an animal from seeing anything in motion: They raised kittens in an environment illuminated only by a strobe light, which flashed eight times a second for 10 microseconds each. In effect, the kittens' visual world was a series of still photographs. After 4 to 6 months in this odd environment, each kitten's visual cortex had neurons that responded normally to shapes but few neurons that responded strongly to moving stimuli. In short, the kittens had become motion blind.

Still, early experience does not modify all aspects of vision. One monkey was kept for its first three months in an environment with only a narrow bandwidth of red light. Humans in that environment found themselves unable to distinguish the colors of objects. At the end of this period, the monkey was given normal visual experience and was tested for color vision. It learned color discriminations about as well as a monkey did that had normal color experience from the start (Brenner, Cornelissen, & Nuboer, 1990).

In Conclusion

This has been one of the most detailed and complex chapters in the book, even though I have omitted enormous amounts of information. Neuroscientists have a more thorough understanding of the visual system than they do of any of the other sensory systems, and certainly more than they do of motivation, emotion, and other topics that we shall discuss in later chapters.

One reason for our progress in understanding vision is that the research is relatively easy to conduct. Vision researchers may be stunned to have me call their research "easy," so let me explain: It is easier to do additional research in an already well-understood area than it is to do ground-breaking work in a new area. (In other words, good research leads to more good research.) Because of advances long ago in physics and engineering, today's researchers can readily control light stimuli, varying their intensity, wavelength, timing, and so forth. Controlling olfactory stimuli is more difficult; controlling motivational or emotional stimuli is still more difficult. Furthermore, we already have good ways of measuring visual responses; in many other areas of behavior, we are still debating the proper methods of measurement.

However, the ease of making progress is hardly the only, or main, reason why neuroscientists have concentrated so much effort on vision. Vision is fundamentally important; our eyes are to a major extent our "windows on the world." Understanding our vision helps us to understand much about the brain and about the mind-brain relationship; when research does not answer all the questions, it at least clarifies what the questions mean.

Summary

1. Human infants have nearly normal peripheral vision at birth, although their foveal vision matures later. In mammals, the eyes approach their full size earlier than the rest of the head does. (p. 221)

2. The cells in the visual cortex of infant kittens have nearly normal properties. However, visual experience is necessary to maintain and fine-tune those properties. For example, if a kitten has visual experience in one eye and not in the other during an early sensitive period, its cortical neurons become responsive only to the open eye. (p. 224)

3. Cortical neurons become unresponsive to axons from the inactive eye mainly because of competition from axons from the active eye. If both eyes are closed, cortical cells remain responsive to axons from them both. (p. 224)

4. If cortical cells have become unresponsive to an eye because it was inactive during the early sensitive period, normal visual experience later does not restore normal responsiveness. However, prolonged closure of the previously active eye can increase the response to the previously inactive eye. (p. 225)

5. Ordinarily, most cortical neurons of cats and primates respond to portions of both retinas. However, if the two eyes are seldom open at the same time during the sensitive period, or if they consistently focus in different directions, then each cortical neuron becomes responsive to the axons from just one eye and not the other. (p. 226)

6. If a kitten sees only horizontal or only vertical lines during its sensitive period, most of the neurons in its visual cortex become responsive to the kind of lines it saw. For the same reason, children who have a strong astigmatism early in life may develop a permanently decreased responsiveness to one or another kind of lines. (p. 228)

7. Other aspects of vision, such as motion perception, also depend on early experience for their proper development. (p. 229)

Review Questions

1. In what way is the visual attention of human infants different from that of adults? (p. 221)

2. The retina of the fish *Haplochromis burtoni* grows enormously from hatching to adulthood. How does the fish deal with the additional receptors without establishing a huge number of new synapses in the brain? (p. 222)

3. What happens to neurons in a kitten's visual cortex if

one of its eyes is closed throughout its early development? What if both eyes are closed? (p. 224)

4. How could an investigator determine the duration of the sensitive period for development of the visual cortex? (p. 224)

5. What is "lazy eye"? How can it be treated? (p. 225)

6. What experience is necessary in early life to maintain binocular input to the neurons of the visual cortex? (p. 226)

7. What is strabismus, and how does it affect the development of the visual cortex? (p. 227)

8. Does an injection of NGF increase or decrease the effects of abnormal visual experience? Why? (p. 227)

9. What is astigmatism, and how does early childhood astigmatism sometimes affect the development of the nervous system? (p. 229)

10. What evidence indicates that perception of movement depends on having early experience in watching movement? (p. 229)

Thought Questions

1. A rabbit has eyes on the sides of its head instead of in front. Would you expect rabbits to have many cells with binocular receptive fields—that is, cells that respond to both eyes? Why or why not?

2. Would you expect the cortical cells of a rabbit to be just as sensitive to the effects of experience as are the cells of cats and primates? Why or why not?

Suggestions for Further Reading

Greenough, W. T., & Jusaska, J. M. (Eds.) (1986). *Developmental neuropsychobiology.* Orlando, FL: Academic Press. A collection of 16 articles on the development of brain and behavior. Four of them deal with the development of vision.

Hubel, D. H. (1988). *Eye, brain, and vision.* New York: Scientific American Library. Excellent source by co-winner of the Nobel Prize. See especially Chapter 9.

Terms

binocular vision sight based on simultaneous stimulation of two eyes (p. 223)

sensitive period or **critical period** time of development when experiences produce major, lasting effects (p. 224)

lazy eye or **amblyopia ex anopsia** reduced vision resulting from disuse of one eye, usually associated with failure of the two eyes to point in the same direction (p. 225)

stereoscopic depth perception sensation of depth by comparing the slightly different inputs from the two eyes (p. 226)

retinal disparity difference in locations of the two retinas stimulated by a single item (p. 226)

strabismus condition of the two eyes pointing in different directions (p. 227)

astigmatism blurring of vision for lines in one direction because of the nonspherical shape of the eye (p. 229)

THE NONVISUAL SENSORY SYSTEMS

CHAPTER SEVEN

1. Our senses have evolved not to give us complete information about all the stimuli in the world but to give us the information most useful to us.

2. Different sensory systems code information in different ways, ranging from a one-axon, one-message system to a system in which the message depends on a pattern across many axons.

According to a Native American saying, "A pine needle fell. The eagle saw it. The deer heard it. The bear smelled it" (Herrero, 1985). Different species are sensitive to different information. Bees and many other insects can see short-wavelength (ultraviolet) light that is invisible to humans; conversely, humans see long-wavelength (red) light that these insects cannot see. Bats produce sonar waves at 20,000 to 100,000 hertz (cycles per second) and then localize insect prey by listening to the echoes. Most adult humans cannot hear any sounds in that range, although children may hear the lower part of the range (Griffin, Webster, & Michael, 1960).

Many animal species are sensitive to only a small range of stimuli that are most useful to their way of life. For example, a frog's eyes include cells that respond selectively to small, dark moving objects such as insects (Lettvin, Maturana, McCulloch, & Pitts, 1959). The ears of the cricket frog, *Acris crepitans,* are highly sensitive to sounds around the frequencies 550 and 3,550 Hz—the frequencies found in the adult male's croak. The frog's ear is poorly sensitive to other sounds. In frog species in which the male produces other sounds, the ears are "tuned" to respond to the particular sounds that those males make (Capranica & Frishkopf, 1966; Capranica, Frishkopf, & Nevo, 1973). Similarly, 17-year locusts are highly sensitive to the songs produced by their own species and are virtually deaf to other sounds (Simmons, Wever, & Pylka, 1971).

We generally assume that human sensory systems simply reflect the physical world. Granted, human visual and auditory abilities are broader and less specialized than those of frogs and locusts, perhaps because a wider range of stimuli is biologically relevant to us than to them. However, humans have some important sensory specializations. For example, we can detect the sweet taste of certain nutritious substances and the bitter taste of poisons at low concentrations (Richter, 1950; Schiffman & Erickson, 1971). Conversely, we fail to taste many substances that are irrelevant to our nutrition (for instance, sand and cellulose). Our olfactory systems are sensitive to a wide variety of gases but completely insensitive to others, including some that it would be useless for us to detect (nitrogen, for example). Thus, this chapter concerns not how our sensory systems enable us to perceive actual reality, but how they enable us to get biologically useful information.

Audition

If a tree falls in an uninhabited forest where no one is present to hear it, does it make a sound? The answer depends on what we mean by "sound." If we mean sound waves, then of course a tree falling in an uninhabited forest makes a sound. Sound waves, a physical phenomenon, are sure to occur when a falling tree hits the ground. But the term *sound* usually refers not to the sound waves themselves but to a perception, an experience. By that definition, nothing can make a sound unless someone is present to hear it.

The human auditory system enables us to hear not only falling trees but also the birds singing in the trees and the wind blowing through the leaves. Some blind people learn to walk down a hallway clicking their heels against the floor and listening to the echoes to localize the walls and other obstructions. Our auditory systems are amazingly well adapted for detecting and interpreting an enormous variety of information.

Sound

Sound waves are periodic compressions of air, water, or other media. When a tree hits the ground, both the tree and the ground vibrate, setting up sound waves in the air that strike someone's ears. If a similar object hit the ground on the moon, where there is no air, people would not hear it—unless, perhaps, they put an ear to the ground.

Sound waves vary in two ways, amplitude and frequency. The **amplitude** of a sound wave is its intensity. A very intense compression of air, such as that produced by a bolt of lightning, produces sound waves of great amplitude, which a listener hears as great loudness. **Loudness** is the *perception* of intensity; it is not the same thing as amplitude. If the amplitude of a sound doubles, its perceived loudness increases but it does not double.

The **frequency** of a sound is the number of compressions per second, measured in hertz (Hz, cycles per second). **Pitch** is a perception closely related to frequency. As a rule, the higher the frequency of a sound, the higher its pitch.

Figure 7.1 illustrates the amplitude and frequency of sounds. In each part of the figure, the height of the waves corresponds to amplitude, and the number of waves per second corresponds to frequency.

The average adult human can hear air vibrations ranging from about 15 or 20 Hz to somewhat less than 20,000 Hz. Perception of high frequencies decreases with age; preschool children are better than adults at hearing frequencies of 20,000 Hz and above (B. A. Schneider, Trehub, Morrongiello, & Thorpe, 1986). For middle-aged adults, the upper limit for hearing decreases

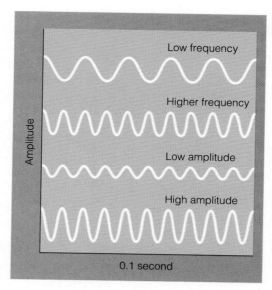

Figure 7.1
Four sound waves
The period (time) between the peaks determines the frequency of the sound, which we experience as pitch. Here, the top line represents 5 sound waves in 0.1 second, or 50 Hz—a very low-frequency sound that we would experience as a very low pitch. The other three lines represent 100 Hz. The vertical extent of each line represents its amplitude or intensity, which we experience as loudness.

by about 80 Hz every six months (von Békésy, 1957). The upper limit drops even faster for those exposed to loud noises.

Structures of the Ear

You may have heard of a "Rube Goldberg" device. Rube Goldberg (1883–1970) was a cartoonist who drew enormously complicated inventions to perform simple tasks. For example, a person's tread on the front doorstep would pull a string that raised a cat's tail, awakening the cat, which would then chase a bird that had been resting on a balance, which would swing up to strike a doorbell. The functioning of the ear may remind you a little of a Rube Goldberg device, since sound waves are transduced into action potentials through a many-step, roundabout process. Unlike Rube Goldberg's inventions, however, the ear actually works.

The first step in hearing is the entry of sound waves into the auditory canal, as Figure 7.2 shows. At the end of the auditory canal, vibrations strike the **tympanic membrane,** or eardrum, which vibrates at the same frequency as the sound waves that strike it. The tympanic membrane is attached to three bones in the middle ear that transmit the vibrations to the *oval window* of the inner ear. These bones are sometimes known by their English names (hammer, anvil, and stirrup) and sometimes by their Latin names (malleus, incus, and stapes.) The tympanic membrane has an area about 20 times larger than the footplate of the stirrup, connected to the oval window. As in a hydraulic pump, the vibrations of the tympanic membrane are transformed into more forceful vibrations when they reach the smaller stirrup. The net effect of the system is to convert the sound waves into waves of greater pressure on the small oval window. This is important because more force is required to move the viscous fluid inside the oval window than to move the eardrum, which has air on both sides of it.

The auditory receptors are located in the inner ear in a snail-shaped structure called the **cochlea** (KOCK-lee-uh, Latin for *snail*). A cross section through

hammer, anvil, stirrup
malleus, incus, stapes

Figure 7.2
Structures of the ear
When sound waves strike the tympanic membrane in (a), they cause it to vibrate three tiny bones—the hammer, anvil, and stirrup—that convert the sound waves into stronger vibrations in the fluid-filled cochlea (b). Those vibrations displace the hair cells along the basilar membrane in the cochlea. (c) A cross section through the cochlea. (d) A close-up of the hair cells.

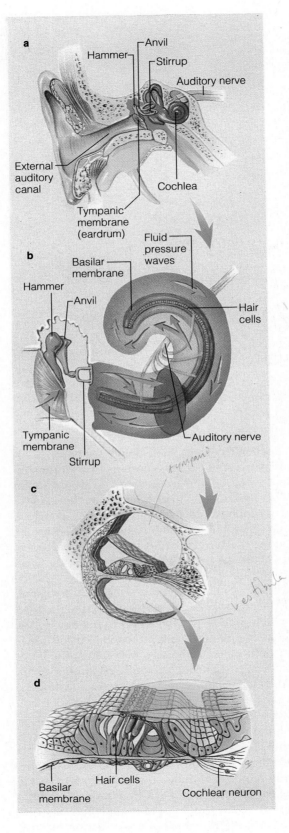

a
Hammer
Anvil
Stirrup
Auditory nerve
External auditory canal
Cochlea
Tympanic membrane (eardrum)

b
Basilar membrane
Fluid pressure waves
Hammer
Anvil
Hair cells
Tympanic membrane
Stirrup
Auditory nerve

c
tympani
vestibule

d
Basilar membrane
Hair cells
Cochlear neuron

Figure 7.3
Hair cells from the auditory systems of three species
(*a, b*) *Hair cells from a frog sacculus, an organ that detects ground-borne vibrations.* (*c*) *Hair cells from the cochlea of a cat.* (*d*) *Hair cells from the cochlea of a fence lizard. Kc = kinocilium, one of the components of a hair bundle. (From Hudspeth, 1985.)*

the cochlea, as in Figure 7.2c, shows that it contains three long fluid-filled tunnels: the scala vestibuli, scala media, and scala tympani. The stirrup contacts the oval window at the entrance to the scala vestibuli; from there, vibrations are transmitted to the rest of the cochlea. When the vibrations reach the **basilar membrane,** which forms the floor of the scala media, they displace the **hair cells** that lie along the basilar membrane (Figure 7.2d). As the scala media is pushed up and down by the pressure waves, the hair cells are bent between the tectorial and basilar membranes. The hair cells respond within microseconds to a displacement as small as 10^{-10} meter (0.1 nanometer, about the diameter of one atom), thereby opening ion channels in the membrane of the neuron (Fettiplace, 1990; Hudspeth, 1985). Figure 7.3 shows electron micrographs of the hair cells of three species. The hair cells stimulate the cells forming the auditory nerve, which carries information to the brain.

Hearing

Pitch Perception

Our ability to understand speech or to enjoy music depends on our ability to differentiate among sounds of different frequencies, even when the sounds are presented for brief periods in rapid succession. How do we do so?

According to one early theory, the **frequency theory,** the basilar membrane vibrates in synchrony with a sound and causes auditory nerve axons to produce action potentials at the same frequency. For example, a sound at 500 Hz would cause 500 action potentials per second in the auditory nerve. The downfall of this theory in its simplest form is that adults can distinguish frequencies up to 20,000 Hz and children can hear even higher frequencies. The refractory period of neurons prevents them from maintaining such high rates of action potentials.

According to the **place theory,** an alternative proposed by Hermann von Helmholtz, the basilar membrane resembles the strings of a piano in that each area along the membrane is tuned to a specific frequency and vibrates whenever that frequency is present. Thus, according to this theory, a sound at any frequency activates the hair cells at only one place along the basilar membrane. The nervous system distinguishes among frequencies on the basis of which neurons are activated. The downfall of this theory in its original form is that no portion of the basilar membrane has physical properties like those that cause a piano string to resonate to a tone. Moreover, the various parts of the basilar membrane are bound together, so no one part could resonate without carrying neighboring parts with it.

According to the currently prevalent theory (Corso, 1973; Gulick, 1971), the mechanism differs for low and high frequencies. For low-frequency sounds (up to about 100 Hz), the frequency theory seems to apply. The basilar membrane vibrates in synchrony with the sound waves, and auditory nerve axons generate one action potential per wave. Weak sounds activate only a small number of neurons, while stronger sounds activate greater numbers. Thus, at low frequencies, the frequency of impulses identifies the pitch, and the number of cells firing identifies the loudness.

Beyond about 100 Hz, a given neuron cannot keep up with the frequency of the sound waves. A neuron may nevertheless produce action potentials phase-locked to the peaks of the sound waves (that is, always occurring at the same phase in the sound wave), as illustrated here:

Sound wave
(about 100 Hz)

Action potentials
from one auditory
neuron

Additional auditory neurons also produce action potentials phase-locked with peaks of the sound wave but not necessarily in phase with the action potentials of the first neuron:

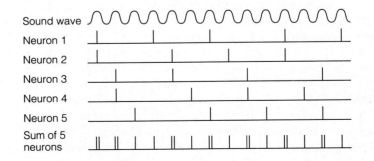

Sound wave
Neuron 1
Neuron 2
Neuron 3
Neuron 4
Neuron 5
Sum of 5
neurons

If we consider the auditory nerve as a whole, including a large number of individual fibers, we find that each sound wave of moderately high frequency produces a volley of impulses by various fibers; that is, at least a few neurons fire

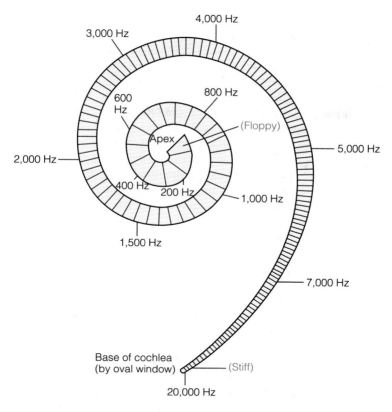

Figure 7.4
The basilar membrane of the human cochlea
High-frequency sounds produce their maximum displacement near the base. Low-frequency sounds produce their maximum displacement near the apex.

Labels in figure: 4,000 Hz; 3,000 Hz; 800 Hz; 600 Hz; (Floppy); Apex; 2,000 Hz; 5,000 Hz; 400 Hz; 200 Hz; 1,000 Hz; 1,500 Hz; 7,000 Hz; Base of cochlea (by oval window); (Stiff); 20,000 Hz

synchronously with each wave in, say, a 600-Hz tone. Although no individual fiber can produce impulses at a rate of 600 per second, the auditory nerve as a whole can have volleys of impulses at 600 per second. This is the **volley principle** of pitch discrimination (Rose, Brugge, Anderson, & Hind, 1967).

Do such volleys really contribute to pitch perception? Investigators have demonstrated that volleys of impulses do occur in the auditory nerve, and biological psychologists generally assume that the brain can use any information produced by neurons. In this case, however, we do not know how the brain uses the volleys, if it does.

At some tone near 5,000 Hz, the volley principle becomes inadequate; even staggered volleys of impulses cannot keep pace with the sound waves. Before this point is reached, however, another mechanism comes into play, similar to the mechanism postulated by the place theory.

At its **base,** where the stirrup meets the cochlea, the basilar membrane is thin (about 0.15 mm) and stiff. It is wider (0.5 mm) and only one-hundredth as stiff at the other end of the cochlea, the **apex** (von Békésy, 1956; Yost & Nielsen, 1977). (See Figure 7.4.) You may be surprised that the basilar membrane is thinnest at the base, where the cochlea itself is widest. The difference is made up of a bony shelf that attaches to the basilar membrane. When a vibration strikes the basilar membrane, it sets up a **traveling wave.** As the wave travels along the membrane, it produces some displacement at all points, but the amount of displacement varies because of differences in the thickness and stiffness of the membrane.

Vibrations at different frequencies set up traveling waves that peak at different points along the basilar membrane, as Figures 7.4 and 7.5 illustrate. The

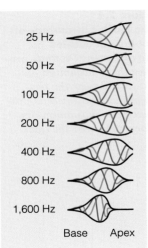

25 Hz

50 Hz

100 Hz

200 Hz

400 Hz

800 Hz

1,600 Hz

Base Apex

Figure 7.5
Traveling waves in the basilar membrane set up by different frequencies of sound
Note that the peak displacement is closer to the base of the cochlea for high frequencies and is toward the apex for lower frequencies. In reality, the peak of each wave is much narrower than shown here.

Many people without hearing utilize American Sign Language as an alternative communication. (Photo courtesy of Gallaudet Univ.)

traveling wave for a low-frequency vibration peaks at or near the apex, where the membrane is large and floppy. For progressively higher frequencies, the point of maximum displacement gets closer to the base. In fact, the highest frequencies produce practically no displacement of the membrane near the apex. The waveforms in Figure 7.5 are drawn fairly broadly to be easily visible. In healthy tissues, however, the waves are sharply defined, falling rapidly on both sides of the maximum displacement (Zwislocki, 1981).

To summarize, we identify the lowest-frequency sounds by the frequency of impulses. We discriminate among high frequencies in terms of the place along the basilar membrane at which the receptors show their greatest activity; the higher the frequency, the closer the maximum displacement to the base of the cochlea. We discriminate intermediate frequencies (about 60 to 5,000 Hz) through a combination of frequency (perhaps aided by the volley principle) and place.

Deafness

Complete deafness is rare. About 99 percent of deaf people can hear at least certain frequencies if they are loud enough. We distinguish two categories of hearing impairment: nerve deafness and conductive deafness.

Nerve deafness, or **inner-ear deafness,** results from damage to the cochlea, the hair cells, or the auditory nerve. The damage can occur in any degree. It may be confined to one part of the cochlea or to neurons in one part of the cochlea. The result is an impairment in hearing pitches in one range of frequencies—most often the high frequencies. Although nerve deafness is permanent, hearing aids can compensate for the loss.

Nerve deafness can be inherited. It can also develop from a variety of prenatal problems or disorders of early childhood (Cremers & van Rijn, 1991; Robillard & Gersdorff, 1986), including:

- Exposure of one's mother to rubella (German measles), syphilis, or other contagious diseases during pregnancy
- Exposure of one's mother to various toxins during pregnancy
- Inadequate oxygen to the brain during the birth process
- Inadequate activity of the thyroid gland
- Certain diseases, including multiple sclerosis and meningitis
- Childhood reactions to certain drugs, including aspirin

Prolonged exposure to loud noises is one of the most common causes of hearing loss in adults. Some degree of nerve deafness is also common in old age (Corso, 1985).

Conductive deafness, or **middle-ear deafness,** occurs if the bones of the middle ear fail to transmit sound waves properly to the cochlea. Such deafness can be caused by certain diseases and infections or by a tumorous growth of bones in and around the middle ear. Conductive deafness is sometimes temporary. If it persists, it can sometimes be corrected by surgery. Because people with conductive deafness have a normal cochlea and auditory nerve, they can hear sounds that bypass the middle ear. For example, they can hear their own voices, which can be conducted through the bones of the skull directly to the cochlea.

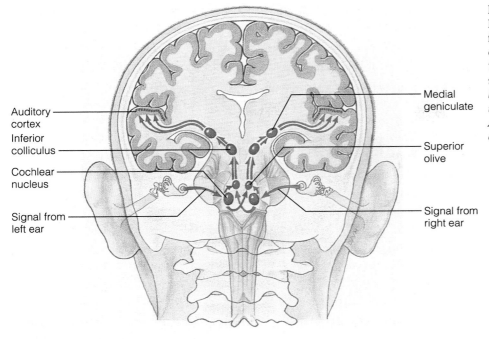

Figure 7.6
Route of auditory impulses from the receptors in the ear to the auditory cortex
The cochlear nucleus receives input from the ipsilateral ear only (the one on the same side of the head). All later stages have input originating from both ears.

Labels in figure:
- Auditory cortex
- Inferior colliculus
- Cochlear nucleus
- Signal from left ear
- Medial geniculate
- Superior olive
- Signal from right ear

Localization of Sounds

Determining the direction and distance of a sound is complicated. Unlike touch, for which receptors are spread over the whole body, or even vision, in which each eye has receptors focused on separate points in space, audition requires a comparison between the two ears—which are in effect just two points in space—to locate the sources of stimuli. And yet this system can be accurate enough for owls to hunt mice on dark nights solely by their sounds, identifying not only the left-right direction of a sound source but its elevation as well (Knudsen & Konishi, 1978).

Information from the two ears progresses through several subcortical structures on its way to the auditory cortex, as Figure 7.6 illustrates. Virtually all aspects of the auditory system, from the external ear to the auditory cortex, show adaptations that facilitate the localization of sounds.

Two methods are used for the localization of sound direction (Yost & Nielsen, 1977). The first is the difference in loudness between the two ears. The head impedes the passage of sound waves, especially if the wavelength is shorter than the width of the head; that is, for short-wavelength (high-frequency) sounds, the head creates a *sound shadow* (Figure 7.7). Consequently, the sound is louder for the closer ear. In adults, this mechanism produces accurate sound localization for frequencies above 3,000 Hz and progressively less accurate localization for lower frequencies.

The second method of localization is the difference in *time of arrival* at the two ears. A sound coming from a source directly in front of a person reaches both ears at the same time. A sound coming directly from the left will reach the left ear about 600 microseconds (6×10^{-6} seconds) before it reaches the right

Figure 7.7
Differential loudness as a cue for sound localization

The sound shadow shown does not include the effects of diffraction, or "bending" of sound waves around the head. (After Lindsay & Norman, 1972.)

Figure 7.8
What it means for sound waves to be in phase and out of phase

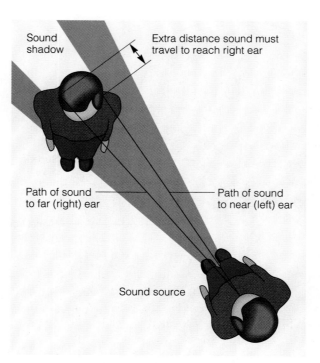

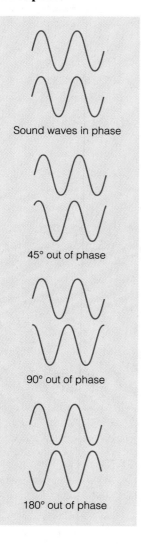

Sound waves in phase

45° out of phase

90° out of phase

180° out of phase

ear. Sounds coming from intermediate locations will reach the two ears at times 0 to 600 microseconds apart.

The time of a sound's onset is useful for localizing sounds with a distinct, sudden onset, such as the sound of an object hitting the floor. It is less useful for localizing sounds with a gradual onset. When threatened by a predator, many birds give alarm calls that increase gradually in loudness; such calls are difficult for the predator to localize.

However, for low-frequency sound waves, even gradual-onset sounds can be localized. Any sound wave has phases, with two consecutive peaks 360 degrees apart. Figure 7.8 shows sound waves that are in phase and sound waves that are 45, 90, and 180 degrees out of phase. If a sound comes from one side of the head, the sound wave striking one ear will be slightly out of phase with the same sound wave striking the other ear. In Figure 7.9a, note that the sound waves in the left ear are out of phase with those in the right ear. For each wave, the receptors in the ear closer to the sound source will fire slightly sooner than those in the farther ear will. A large difference in phase between the two ears indicates that the sound source is almost directly to the side; a small difference indicates that the sound source is approximately straight ahead or straight behind. However, phase differences are useless for localizing high-frequency sounds. As Figure 7.9b shows, with high-frequency sounds, it would be easy to confuse the phase of one wave with the phase of another wave. Phase differences provide information that is useful for localizing sounds with frequencies up to about 1,500 Hz.

In short, humans localize low frequencies (up to 1,500 Hz) by differences in phase and time of onset. We localize high frequencies (above 3,000 Hz) by loudness differences. We are less accurate at localizing the intermediate frequencies.

The usefulness of both methods of localization depends on the size of the head. For a small species such as the mouse, the ears are so close together that

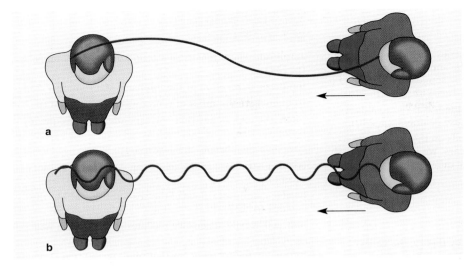

Figure 7.9
**Phase differences between
the ears as a cue for sound
localization**
*Note that a low-frequency
tone (a) arrives at the ears
slightly out of phase. The ear
for which the receptors fire
first (here, the person's left
ear) is interpreted as being
closer to the sound. If the
difference in phase between
the ears is small, then the
sound source is close to the
center of the body. However,
with a high-frequency sound
(b), the phase differences
become ambiguous. The person cannot tell which sound
wave in the left ear corresponds to which sound
wave in the right ear.*

the animal cannot detect phase differences between sounds even at low frequencies. Small animals therefore have trouble localizing low-frequency tones.
They also have some trouble localizing sounds of 3,000 Hz or so, which
humans easily localize by differences in loudness. High-frequency tones are
louder to one ear than to the other because the head creates a sound shadow.
But the head creates a shadow only when the wavelength of the sound is less
than the width of the head. A tone at 3,000 Hz has a short wavelength relative
to the width of the human head, but not relative to a mouse's head. The smaller
the animal, the higher the frequency must be before the animal can use loudness as a cue to direction. Thus, small-headed species such as mice cannot use
phase differences for localization at all, and they can use loudness differences
only for higher frequencies than humans can.

During the course of evolution, each species seems to have evolved a sensitivity to those frequencies that it can easily localize. Rodents and other small
animals are less sensitive to low-pitched sounds than humans are, but they are
more sensitive to higher frequencies, up to 40,000, 60,000, or even 100,000
Hz. Vervets, a species of monkeys with relatively small heads, are more sensitive to high frequencies than other monkeys are but less sensitive to low frequencies (Owren, Hopp, Sinnott, & Petersen, 1988). The hearing range of
larger mammals is shifted toward lower frequencies. The upper limit for elephants is just 10,000 Hz (Heffner & Heffner, 1982). These findings underscore
a point made at the beginning of this chapter: Each species is most sensitive to
the information that is most useful to it.

The two methods of sound localization depend on different brain structures. Localization based on loudness depends on the lateral part of the superior olive (in the medulla); localization based on phase differences depends on
the medial part. Small-headed species, such as the mouse, which cannot use
phase differences to localize sound, have no medial superior olive at all; they
have just the lateral superior olive (Masterton, 1974).

*Large-headed animals, such
as elephants, can readily
localize low-frequency tones
by phase and onset differences between the two ears.
(Telegraph Colour
Library/FPG)*

Summary

1. We detect the pitch of low-frequency sounds by the frequency of action potentials in the auditory system. We detect the pitch of high-frequency sounds by the area of greatest response along the basilar membrane. (p. 238)

2. Damage to the nerve cells or to the bones that conduct sounds to the nerve cells can cause deafness. (p. 240)

3. We localize high-frequency sounds on the basis of differences in loudness between the ears. We localize low-frequency sounds on the basis of differences in phase. (p. 241)

Review Questions

1. Differentiate among the frequency theory, the volley principle, and the place theory of pitch perception. (p. 238)

2. How do our mechanisms of pitch perception vary among low-, medium-, and high-pitched tones? (p. 238)

3. What are the two major categories of deafness, and what causes each? (p. 240)

4. What mechanisms enable an animal to localize sounds? How does the effectiveness of each method depend on the size of the animal's head? (p. 241)

Thought Questions

1. Why do you suppose that the human auditory system evolved sensitivity to sounds in the range of 20 to 20,000 Hz instead of some other range of frequencies?

2. The text explains how we might distinguish loudness for low-pitched sounds on the basis of the frequency theory. How might we distinguish loudness for high-pitched sounds?

Suggestions for Further Reading

Goldstein, E. B. (1989). *Sensation and perception* (3rd ed.). Belmont, CA: Wadsworth. A general textbook on the sensory systems, emphasizing vision and hearing.

Zwislocki, J. J. (1981). Sound analysis in the ear: A history of discoveries. *American Scientist, 69,* 184–192. An excellent review of transduction and coding of auditory information.

Terms

amplitude the intensity of a sound or other stimulus (p. 234)

loudness perception of the intensity of a sound (p. 234)

frequency the number of sound waves per second (p. 234)

pitch the experience that corresponds to the frequency of a sound (p. 234)

tympanic membrane the eardrum (p. 235)

cochlea structure in the inner ear, containing auditory receptors (p. 235)

basilar membrane floor of the scala media, within the cochlea (p. 237)

hair cell a type of sensory receptor shaped like a hair (p. 237)

frequency theory concept that pitch perception depends on differences in frequency of action potentials by auditory neurons (p. 237)

place theory concept that pitch perception depends on which part of the inner ear has cells with the greatest activity level (p. 238)

volley principle tenet that a sound wave of a moderately high pitch may produce a volley of impulses by various fibers even if no individual fiber can produce impulses in synchrony with the sound waves (p. 239)

base (of tympanic membrane) point at which the stirrup meets the cochlea (p. 239)

apex one end of the cochlea, farthest from the point where the stirrup meets the cochlea (p. 239)

traveling wave wave that travels along a surface, producing some displacement at all points, though possibly more at some than at others (p. 239)

nerve deafness or **inner-ear deafness** hearing loss that results from damage to the cochlea, the hair cells, or the auditory nerve (p. 240)

conductive deafness or **middle-ear deafness** hearing loss that occurs if the bones of the middle ear fail to transmit sound waves properly to the cochlea (p. 240)

The Mechanical Senses

The next time you turn on your radio or stereo set, place your hand on its surface and feel the vibrations. The vibrations you feel in your hand are the same vibrations you hear.

If you were to practice enough, could you learn to "hear" the vibrations with your fingers? No. You might improve your ability to recognize a particular pattern of vibrations, but they would still feel like vibrations, and the detectors in your skin would never become sensitive to the airborne vibrations that you experience as sounds.

If a species with no ears had enough time, might its vibration detectors evolve into sound detectors? Yes! In fact, that is probably how our remote ancestors did evolve the ability to hear. Fish have no ears as such; they have a lateral line system consisting of a long row of touch receptors on each side of the body. Those touch receptors produce sensations that provide the equivalent of hearing for fish. (Snakes also lack ears and apparently do not detect airborne vibrations. Instead, they are able to detect vibrations in the ground.) Primitive vertebrates probably had a variety of touch receptors, perhaps somewhat like today's fish. From those touch receptors, we ultimately evolved our organs of hearing. But we also evolved receptors that are responsive to mechanical stimulation; these receptors generally receive little attention in psychology, but their importance becomes clear as soon as we contemplate what it would be like to live without them.

We categorize several senses as *mechanical senses* because they respond to pressure, bending, or other distortions of a receptor. These senses include touch, pain, and other body sensations, as well as vestibular sensation, a system specialized to detect the position and movement of the head. Audition could be regarded as a mechanical sense as well, because the hair cells are modified touch receptors. However, it is convenient to keep audition separate because it provides information about objects at a distance, while the other mechanical senses provide information about what is happening to one's own body.

Vestibular Sensation

Try this demonstration: Attempt to read this text while you jiggle your head up and down, back and forth. It is a little inconvenient, you will find, but not too bad. Now hold your head steady and jiggle the book up and down, back and forth. Suddenly, reading becomes much more difficult. Why?

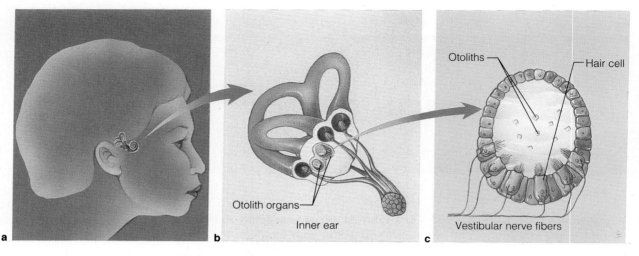

Figure 7.10
(*a*) *Location of the vestibular organs.* (*b*) *Structures of the vestibular organs.*
(*c*) *Cross section through an otolith organ. Calcium carbonate particles, called otoliths, press against different hair cells, depending on the direction of tilt and rate of acceleration of the head.*

When you move your head, the **vestibular organ** adjacent to the cochlea monitors each movement and directs compensatory movements of your eyes. When your head moves left, your eyes move right; when your head moves right, your eyes move left. Almost effortlessly, you keep your eyes focused on what you want to see. When you move the page, however, the vestibular organ cannot help you keep your eyes on target. Vestibular sensations (sensations from the vestibular organ) detect the direction of tilt and the amount of acceleration of the head. These sensations seldom enter our conscious awareness; nevertheless, they contribute to the guidance of both eye movements and balance.

Figure 7.10 shows the anatomy of the vestibular organ. It consists of two otolith organs and three semicircular canals. Like the hearing receptors, the vestibular receptors are modified touch receptors. One **otolith organ** has a horizontal patch of hairs; the other has a vertical patch. Calcium carbonate particles called *otoliths* lie next to the hair cells in the otolith organs. When the head tilts in different directions, the otoliths push against different sets of hair cells and excite them (Gresty, Bronstein, Brandt, & Dieterich, 1992).

The three **semicircular canals,** oriented in three different planes, are filled with a jellylike substance and lined with hair cells. An acceleration of the head in any plane causes the jellylike substance in one of these canals to push against the hair cells. Action potentials initiated by the cells of the vestibular system travel via part of the eighth cranial nerve to the brain stem and cerebellum.

Chemsen

Somatosensation

The **somatosensory system,** the sensation of the body and its movements, is not one sense but many. We can distinguish discriminative touch (by which we

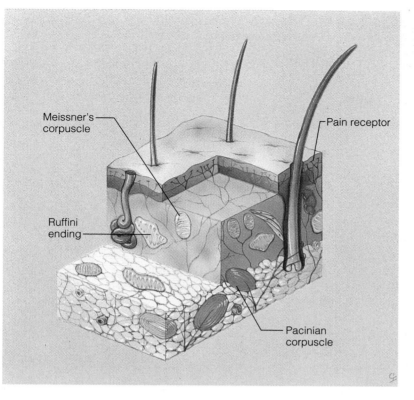

Figure 7.11
Some sensory receptors
found in the skin, the
human body's largest organ

Meissner's corpuscle

Pain receptor

Ruffini ending

Pacinian corpuscle

identify the shape of an object), deep pressure, cold, warmth, pain, and the sense of position and movement of joints.

Somatosensory Receptors

The skin is packed with a variety of somatosensory receptors. Figure 7.11 shows some of the major receptor types found in mammalian skin, and Table 7.1 lists some of their probable or primary functions (Iggo & Andres, 1982). Many of these receptors in fact respond somewhat to several kinds of stimuli, such as touch and temperature. Other receptors, which the list does not include, respond to deep stimulation, movement of joints, and movement of muscles.

A touch receptor may consist of a simple bare ending (such as pain receptors), an elaborated neuron ending (Ruffini endings and Meissner's corpuscles), or a bare ending surrounded by nonneural cells that modify its function (Pacinian corpuscles). Some of the more sensitive areas of skin, such as the fingertips, have as many as 700 touch cells in 2 square millimeters of surface.

One example of a receptor is the **Pacinian corpuscle** (Figure 7.12), which detects a sudden displacement of the skin or high-frequency vibration on the skin. Inside the onionlike surround is a neuron membrane. When mechanical pressure bends the membrane, its resistance to sodium flow decreases, and sodium ions enter, depolarizing the membrane (Loewenstein, 1960). The onionlike outer structure provides a mechanical support such that a gradual or constant pressure on the skin does not bend the neuron's membrane; only a sudden or vibrating stimulus can bend it.

Mechsen

The Mechanical Senses

Table 7.1 Somatosensory Receptors and Their Probable Functions

Receptor	Location	Responds to	Rate of Adaptation to a Prolonged Stimulus
Free nerve ending (unmyelinated or thinly myelinated fibers)	Around base of hairs and elsewhere in skin	Pain, warmth, cold	Uncertain
Hair-follicle receptors	Hair-covered skin	Movement of hairs	Rapid
Meissner's corpuscles	Hairless areas	Sudden displacement of skin; low-frequency vibration (flutter)	Rapid(?)
Pacinian corpuscles	Both hairy and hairless skin	Sudden displacement of skin; high-frequency vibration	Very rapid
Merkel's disks	Both hairy and hairless skin	Indentation of skin	Slow
Ruffini endings	Both hairy and hairless skin	Stretch of skin	Slow
Krause end bulbs	Hairless areas, perhaps including genitals; maybe some hairy areas	Uncertain	Uncertain

Figure 7.12
A Pacinian corpuscle, a type of receptor that responds best to sudden displacement of the skin or to high-frequency vibrations
Pacinian corpuscles respond only briefly to steady pressure on the skin. The onion-like outer structure provides a mechanical support to the neuron inside it so that a sudden stimulus can bend it but a sustained stimulus cannot. (Ed Reschke.)

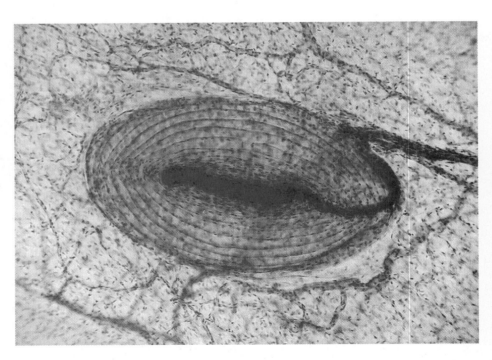

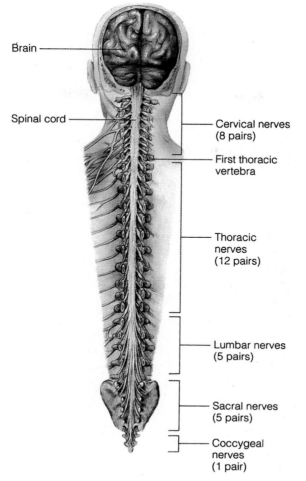

Figure 7.13
The human central nervous system (CNS)
Spinal nerves from each segment of the spinal cord exit through the correspondingly numbered opening between vertebrae. (From Starr & Taggart, 1989.)

Brain

Spinal cord

Cervical nerves
(8 pairs)

First thoracic
vertebra

Thoracic
nerves
(12 pairs)

Lumbar nerves
(5 pairs)

Sacral nerves
(5 pairs)

Coccygeal
nerves
(1 pair)

Many of the body senses are still not well understood—itching, for example. An itching sensation depends on the same spinal nerves that carry pain sensations, and most people who are insensitive to pain also fail to report itching. However, morphine, a powerful painkiller, has no effect on itching. Furthermore, no one knows which receptor or combination of receptors is responsible for itching (McMahon & Koltzenburg, 1992).

Input to the Spinal Cord and the Brain

Information from the various touch receptors enters the spinal cord and passes toward the brain. The spinal cord has 31 segments and therefore 31 sets of sensory and motor nerves, the **spinal nerves** (see Figure 7.13). Beginning at the top, we distinguish eight cervical nerves, twelve thoracic nerves, five lumbar nerves, five sacral nerves, and one coccygeal nerve.

Each spinal nerve innervates a limited area of the body. The skin area innervated by a sensory spinal nerve is called a **dermatome**. Figure 7.14 shows the locations of the dermatomes. For example, the third thoracic nerve (T3) innervates a strip of skin just above the nipples on the chest plus the underarm

Figure 7.14

Dermatomes innervated by the 31 sensory spinal nerves

Areas I, II, and III of the face are not innervated by the spinal nerves, but instead by three branches of the fifth cranial nerve. Although this figure shows distinct borders between dermatomes, the dermatomes actually overlap one another up to about one-half of their width.

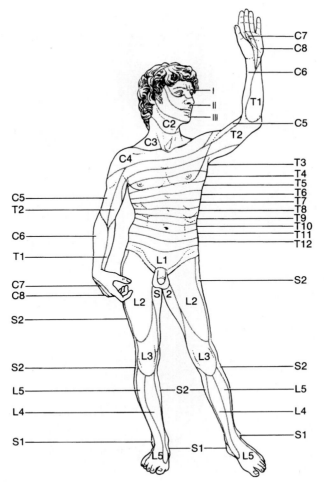

area. But the borders between dermatomes are not so distinct as Figure 7.14 implies; there is actually one-third to one-half overlap between adjacent pairs.

The sensory information that enters the spinal cord travels in well-defined pathways up the spinal cord toward the brain. Figure 7.15 depicts two of the major somatosensory paths of the spinal cord. The point of this figure is certainly not to provide details for you to try to memorize, but merely to demonstrate that different types of sensory information have different routes to the brain and that they project to different brain areas.

Information that travels up different routes in the spinal cord also reaches different parts of the thalamus and cerebral cortex. For example, one area of the ventral-posterior thalamus responds to activity of the Pacinian corpuscles. Within that area, different parts respond to different parts of the body. At least three other nearby areas of the thalamus respond to different receptors or combinations of receptors (Dykes, Sur, Merzenich, Kaas, & Nelson, 1981).

The various areas of the somatosensory thalamus send their impulses to different areas of the somatosensory cortex, located in the parietal lobe. The somatosensory cortex includes four parallel strips, each of which has its own representation of the entire body (see Chapter 4). Two of the strips respond mostly to touch on the skin; the other two respond mostly to deep pressure and

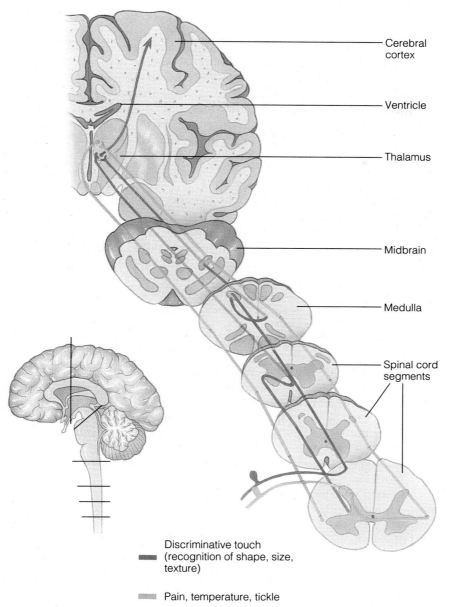

Figure 7.15
Two major pathways ascending the spinal cord
Note that the sensory input enters through the dorsal roots of the spinal cord and that different kinds of sensory information travel through different pathways.

Cerebral cortex

Ventricle

Thalamus

Midbrain

Medulla

Spinal cord segments

▬▬▬ Discriminative touch (recognition of shape, size, texture)

▨▨▨ Pain, temperature, tickle

movement of the joints and muscles (Kaas, 1983). In short, various aspects of somatosensation remain at least partly separate from one another at all levels, from the receptors to the somatosensory area of the cerebral cortex.

Because touch perception itself depends on activity in the cerebral cortex, people sometimes experience touch sensations that do not correspond to what is happening on the skin. An extreme example is **phantom limb,** the sensation of a body part even after that part has been amputated. After the loss of an arm, leg, or other body part, most people feel some sensation "in" that body part, such as a tingling or a sense of movement. Some continue to feel the pains that they used to feel in that body part, such as the pain from a too-tight ring on the finger (Melzack, 1990). In most cases, the phantom sensations decline gradually, although they last for years in some people.

The Mechanical Senses

After damage to parts of the somatosensory cortex, people sometimes experience a loss of sensation in parts of their bodies. One patient with Alzheimer's disease, who had damage in the somatosensory cortex as well as elsewhere, had much trouble getting her clothes on correctly. Also she could not point correctly in response to such directions as "show me your elbow" or "point to my knee," although she pointed correctly to various nonbody objects in the room. When told to touch her elbow, her most frequent response was to feel her wrist and arm and suggest that the elbow was probably around there, somewhere. She acted as if she had only a blurry map of where the body parts were located (Sirigu, Grafman, Bressler, & Sunderland, 1991).

Pain

Pain is a sensation evoked by a harmful stimulus, including cuts, diseases, chemical irritation, and intense heat or cold. Pain is a message to get away from the source of harm. Some people are born with an almost complete insensitivity to pain. Others are born with indifference to pain; although they can detect that something is sharp or hot or cold, they do not find those experiences distressing.

People with insensitivity to pain sustain a seemingly endless series of injuries. They frequently bite their tongues; some even bite off the tip. They have frequent severe burns, scratches, and cuts, because they do not receive the early warning signal of impending harm. They may injure their mouths by drinking very hot coffee or injure their feet by exposing them too long to the cold. Many such people also injure their bones and tendons by sitting in a single position for too long at a time. Ordinarily, most of us shift positions every few minutes without even thinking about it, not from pain but just from mild discomfort. People lacking a sense of pain generally do not even feel that discomfort.

A woman with pain insensitivity once took a casserole out of the oven and carried it with her bare hands. Her husband screamed to be careful because the casserole was burning hot, but she calmly set it on their cardboard table. Not until the cardboard table burst into flames did she realize that she had made a mistake (Comings & Amromin, 1974).

However, while lack of pain is dangerous, prolonged pain is not only unpleasant but also unnecessary. A variety of physiological mechanisms inhibit pain after it starts; because of these mechanisms, the intensity of pain varies from one person to another and also from one situation to another for a given individual (Liebeskind & Paul, 1977). For example, some soldiers and athletes report little pain from serious injuries; occasionally, they do not even notice an injury until the action is over.

To account for such variations in pain responsiveness, Ronald Melzack and P. D. Wall (1965) proposed a highly influential theory of pain known as the **gate theory.** According to this theory, certain areas of the spinal cord receive messages not only from pain receptors but also from other receptors in the skin and from axons descending from the brain. If these other inputs to the spinal cord are sufficiently active, they close the "gates" for the pain messages. In other words, the brain can increase or decrease its own exposure to pain information.

Although Melzack and Wall's gate theory included certain details that turned out to be wrong, the general principle is valid: Various kinds of nonpain

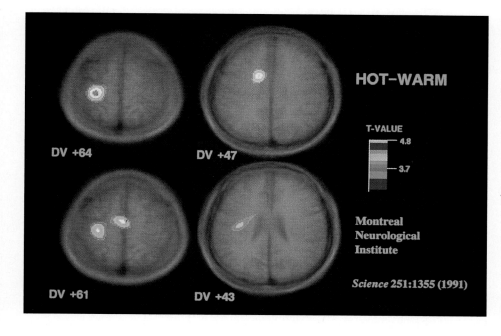

HOT-WARM

DV +64   DV +47

T-VALUE
4.8
3.7

DV +61   DV +43

Montreal
Neurological
Institute

Science 251:1355 (1991)

Figure 7.16
Representation of pain in the human brain
Investigators used PET scans and MRI data to record the activity of various brain areas during exposure to painful heat and to non-painful warmth, both on the right arm. Then the investigators subtracted the activity during warm stimulation from the activity during painful heat to find the activity attributable to pain itself. The areas marked in white showed the greatest response to pain, followed by the red, yellow, blue, and violet areas. Response was greatest in a portion of the somatosensory cortex contralateral to the stimulated arm. (From Talbot et al., 1991.)

stimuli can modify the sensation of pain. We begin with the neurons and neurotransmitters that convey pain information; then we shall turn to the mechanisms that inhibit pain.

Pain Neurons and Their Neurotransmitters

Unmyelinated axons and some thinly myelinated axons carry pain information to the spinal cord, releasing a neurotransmitter known as **substance P** to the neurons that they contact in the spinal cord (Levine, Fields, & Basbaum, 1993). The spinal cord neurons in turn send their information to the ventrobasal nucleus of the thalamus, which relays it to certain parts of the cingulate cortex and the somatosensory cortex (Talbot et al., 1991). (See Figure 7.16.) The projection to the cingulate cortex is interesting, as that part of the brain has been linked to emotional responses.

What effect would you expect if an investigator injected substance P, an important pain transmitter, into an animal's brain or spinal cord? The animal would scratch, bite, and show other indications of pain—not pain in the spinal cord itself, but pain felt in the part of the body that ordinarily sends information to that section of the spinal cord.

An animal also shows signs of pain and distress after a spinal injection of **capsaicin,** a chemical that causes neurons containing substance P to release it suddenly. An injection of capsaicin causes an animal to react about the same way as it would after an injection of substance P itself. After a few minutes, however, because the neurons released substance P far faster than they could resynthesize it, they have less ability than usual to release it. Consequently, the animal becomes relatively insensitive to pain for a long time, sometimes months (Gamse, Leeman, Holzer, & Lembeck, 1981; Jancsó, Kiraly, & Jancsó-Gábor, 1977; Yarsh, Farb, Leeman, & Jessell, 1979).

Capsaicin occurs in nature in jalapeño peppers and other hot peppers. When you eat a hot pepper, the capsaicin in the pepper causes certain neurons in your tongue to release substance P, giving you a sensation of pain or heat.

The Mechanical Senses

After the heat sensation wears off, you may experience a pleasant state of relief, probably accompanied by a decreased sensitivity to pain on your tongue.

Capsaicin is therefore sometimes used for pain relief. Capsaicin rubbed onto a sore shoulder, an arthritic joint, or other painful area produces a temporary, mild sting followed by a longer period of decreased pain. Do not, however, try *eating* hot peppers to help reduce pain. Because very little ingested capsaicin enters the blood, the capsaicin you eat will not relieve pain—unless you happen to have pain on the tongue (Karrer & Bartoshuk, 1991).

Opiates and Endorphins

For centuries, people have been using morphine and other opiate drugs to relieve pain, induce sleep, and stimulate pleasure, although no one knew how the drugs worked. A classic example of a nonexplanation came from a physician in one of Molière's plays who said that opium induces sleep "because of its dormitive properties." (*Dormitive* is just a fancy word for sleep inducing.) We can do better than that today, although we still cannot offer a complete explanation of how opiates affect behavior.

Beginning in the 1950s, investigators discovered that most drugs with behavioral effects interact with one or another of the synaptic receptors. It was natural, therefore, to look for some sort of receptor with which opiate drugs might interact. For years, those presumed receptors remained elusive. Then Candace Pert and Solomon Snyder (1973) identified brain receptors that bind specifically to morphine and related drugs. They also demonstrated that the opiate receptors are concentrated in certain areas of the brain—the same areas where substance P is concentrated (McLean, Skirboll, & Pert, 1985). Apparently, opiate receptors play an important role in inhibiting or limiting the pain-producing effects of substance P (Figure 7.17).

But presumably evolution did not equip us with receptors just to deal with drugs derived from the opium poppy. The discovery of opiate receptors implied that the brain must have its own natural substances with opiatelike effects. Before long, those substances were discovered. The brain produces two opiate-like peptide neurotransmitters, composed of five amino acids each: **met-enkephalin** and **leu-enkephalin** (Hughes et al., 1975). (The term *enkephalin* refers to the fact that these chemicals were first found in the brain, or encephalon. The two enkephalins are the same except at one end, where met-enkephalin has methionine and leu-enkephalin has leucine.) Although the enkephalins have chemical structures very unlike morphine, they interact with the same receptors as morphine. In addition, the pituitary gland produces two hormones with opiate-type effects: *beta-endorphin* and *dynorphin.* These two chemicals also serve as neurotransmitters. Collectively, met-enkephalin, leu-enkephalin, beta-endorphin, and dynorphin are known as **endorphins,** a contraction of *endogenous morphines.* They are the brain's own morphines. Brain investigators use the term *endorphins* to refer to any or all of these chemicals; they use the term *enkephalins* to refer specifically to the two short peptides.

What is the role of endorphins in behavior? Like other neurotransmitters, they contribute to a variety of behaviors. They produce **analgesia** (relief from pain); they also promote positive reinforcement. The enkephalin synapses are concentrated mostly in the **periaqueductal gray area** of the brain stem and surrounding areas (Figure 7.18). Activity at these synapses probably blocks the release of substance P from pathways responsible for pain, both in the brain and in the spinal cord (Reichling, Kwiat, & Basbaum, 1988; Terman, Shavitt, Lewis, Cannon, & Liebeskind, 1984). (You may recognize this as the basic idea

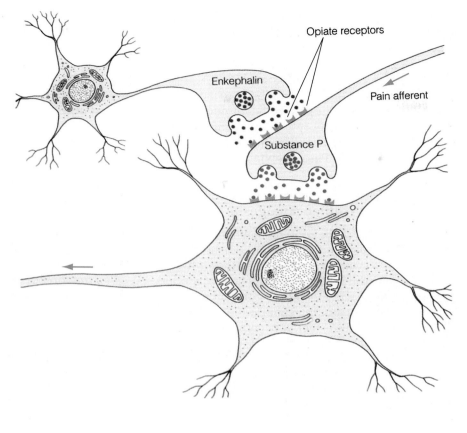

Figure 7.17
Synapses responsible for pain and its inhibition
The pain afferent neuron releases substance P as its neurotransmitter. Another neuron releases enkephalin at presynaptic synapses; the enkephalin inhibits the release of substance P and therefore alleviates pain.

Opiate receptors

Enkephalin

Pain afferent

Substance P

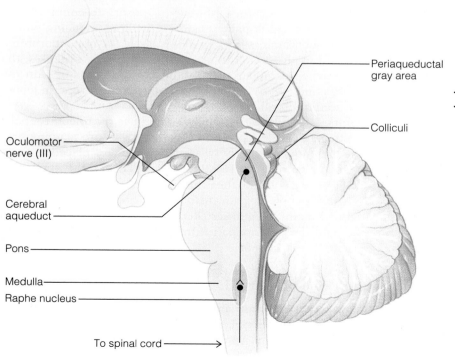

Figure 7.18
The periaqueductal gray area, where electrical stimulation relieves pain
Periaqueductal means "around the aqueduct," a passageway of cerebrospinal fluid between the third and fourth ventricles.

Periaqueductal gray area

Colliculi

Oculomotor nerve (III)

Cerebral aqueduct

Pons

Medulla

Raphe nucleus

To spinal cord

The Mechanical Senses

of Melzack and Wall's gate theory of pain.) For people suffering from severe pain, physicians have sometimes implanted electrodes and provided stimulation to the periaqueductal gray area. Up to 60 percent of people suffering from severe pain experience noticeable analgesia, which may last for hours after the stimulation ends (Barbaro, 1988).

Either enkephalins or electrical stimulation of the periaqueductal gray area can yield analgesia, but neither one produces the nausea that people typically report after receiving morphine injections. Why not? Morphine injections produce effects not only in the brain but also in the digestive system (Bechara & van der Kooy, 1985). The enkephalins act only in the brain; hence, they do not produce nausea.

Stimuli that Produce Analgesia

The endorphins relieve pain, presumably at times when pain is more disruptive than informative. Under what circumstances would neurons release endorphins? That is, what stimuli or situations initiate the release of endorphins?

One such stimulus is pain itself. After pain has served its function of alerting and warning the individual, continuous, intense pain is unnecessary, and we have mechanisms for suppressing it. For example, after an animal has received a shock to its feet, it becomes somewhat less responsive than usual to the next painful stimulus.

Stressful situations can also reduce pain. The mere presence of a cat temporarily decreases rats' response to pain (Lester & Fanselow, 1985). Other stressors, such as loud noises or being forced to swim for a few minutes, also reduce pain.

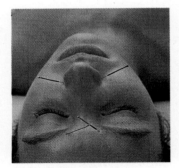

Patient undergoing acupuncture treatment. Acupuncture relieves pain under certain circumstances. (Tim Malyon/Paul Biddle/Science Photo Library/PR)

Pain-induced and stress-induced analgesia depend on the release of endorphins in some situations but not in others. For example, exposure to intermittent or low-intensity continuous shock induces the release of endorphins. We know that endorphins are necessary because the effect is blocked by **naloxone,** a drug that blocks opiate receptors. However, exposure to continuous, high-intensity shock also decreases pain sensitivity without inducing endorphin release (Terman & Liebeskind, 1986). In many cases, the nonendorphin analgesia can be blocked by drugs that interfere with glutamate synapses; that is, certain glutamate synapses apparently inhibit certain kinds of pain (Mogil, Sternberg, & Liebeskind, 1993). In short, mammals have several independent mechanisms for inhibiting pain.

Medical doctors and physical therapists sometimes try to control patients' pain by stimuli that release endorphins. Two examples are acupuncture, an ancient Chinese technique of gently twisting thin needles placed in the skin, and **transcutaneous electrical nerve stimulation (TENS),** the application of prolonged, mild electrical shock to the arms, legs, or back. TENS provides relief for more than half of people in pain, with almost none of the side effects or risks associated with painkilling drugs (Pomeranz, 1989). Note that, because TENS decreases pain through nonpain stimulation, it constitutes an example supporting the gate theory of pain.

The Pros and Cons of Morphine Analgesia

Suppose that a patient is suffering serious pain after a surgical operation or as a result of cancer. Should a physician prescribe enough morphine to suppress the pain? Or should the patient just suffer through the pain?

Some physicians hesitate to prescribe morphine, partly because of the fear of addiction. Actually, morphine taken under hospital conditions almost never becomes addictive.

A more serious concern is that opiates, by themselves, temporarily weaken the immune system and leave the body vulnerable to certain diseases and even to the spread of certain kinds of cancer. That danger, however, lasts only a couple of days before the immune system returns to full force. Prolonged pain or stress, however, weakens the immune system for much longer (Mogil, Sternberg, & Liebeskind, 1993). Morphine, by alleviating pain, in the long run actually strengthens the immune system and enhances the defenses against the spread of certain cancers (Page, Ben-Eliyahu, Yirmiya, & Liebeskind, 1993). Consequently, vigorous efforts to relieve pain are beneficial not just because they comfort the patient, but also because they promote long-term recovery.

Summary

1. The vestibular system is a sensory system that detects the position and acceleration of the head and adjusts body posture and eye movements based on that information. (p. 245)

2. The somatosensory system depends on a variety of receptor types sensitive to different kinds of stimulation of the skin and internal tissues. The brain maintains several parallel somatosensory representations of the body. (p. 246)

3. Because body sensation lies in the brain, not in the body itself, people sometimes experience sensations from amputated parts of the body. (p. 251)

4. A certain harmful stimulus may give rise to a greater or lesser degree of pain, depending on other current and recent stimuli. According to the gate theory of pain, other stimuli can close certain gates and block the transmission of pain. (p. 252)

5. Pain messages are transmitted by axons that predominantly release substance P as a neurotransmitter. (p. 253)

6. Opiate drugs attach to a particular type of receptor in the brain. The brain produces its own opiate-type chemicals, including the neurotransmitters leu-enkephalin and met-enkephalin and the hormones beta-endorphin and dynorphin. The enkephalins decrease pain sensations, probably by blocking the release of substance P. (p. 254)

7. Pain and stress can release endorphins and thereby decrease sensitivity to pain. (p. 256)

8. Although morphine by itself temporarily impairs the immune system, pain impairs the immune system more. Morphine, by relieving pain, actually produces a net enhancement of the immune system. (p. 257)

Review Questions

1. If a person suffers damage to the vestibular system, he or she has trouble reading street signs while walking. Why? (p. 246)

2. In what way is touch several senses instead of just one sense? (p. 246)

3. Why is lifelong insensitivity to pain dangerous? (p. 252)

4. Which neurotransmitter do pain-receptor neurons release? (p. 253)

5. Why do jalapeño peppers produce a hot sensation? (p. 253)

6. What evidence do we have that mild foot shock produces analgesia by releasing endorphins while prolonged, intense shocks to the feet produce analgesia in some other manner? (p. 256)

Thought Question

1. Why is the vestibular sense generally useless under conditions of weightlessness?

Suggestion for Further Reading

Snyder, S. (1989). *Brainstorming: The science and politics of opiate research.* Cambridge, MA: Harvard University Press. Fascinating "insider's" history of the discovery of endorphins.

Terms

vestibular organ component in the inner ear that detects tilt of the head (p. 246)

otolith organ an organ responsible for vestibular sensation (p. 246)

semicircular canal canal lined with hair cells and oriented in three planes, sensitive to the direction of tilt of the head (p. 246)

somatosensory system sensory network that monitors the surface of the body and its movements (p. 246)

Pacinian corpuscle a receptor that responds to a sudden displacement of the skin or high-frequency vibration on the skin (p. 247)

spinal nerve nerve that conveys information between the spinal cord and either sensory receptors or muscles in the periphery (p. 249)

dermatome area of skin connected to a particular spinal nerve (p. 249)

phantom limb a sensation that feels like a body part even after that part has been amputated (p. 251)

gate theory assumption that stimulation of certain nonpain axons in the skin or in the brain can inhibit transmission of pain messages in the spinal cord (p. 252)

substance P a neurotransmitter released by nerves that are sensitive to pain (p. 253)

capsaicin a chemical that causes neurons containing substance P to release it suddenly (p. 253)

leu-enkephalin and **met-enkephalin** each, a chain of five amino acids believed to function as a neurotransmitter that inhibits pain (p. 254)

endorphin category of chemicals the body produces that stimulate the same receptors as do opiates (p. 254)

analgesia relief from pain (p. 254)

periaqueductal gray area area of the brain stem that is rich in enkephalin synapses (p. 254)

naloxone drug that blocks opiate receptors (p. 256)

transcutaneous electrical nerve stimulation (TENS) method of relieving pain by applying prolonged, mild electrical shock to the arms, legs, or back (p. 256)

The Chemical Senses

Suppose you had the godlike power to design a new species of animal, but you could equip it with only one sensory system. Which sense would you give it?

Your first impulse might be to choose either vision or hearing. After all, those senses are extremely versatile and valuable to humans. But an animal with only one sensory system is not going to be much like humans, is it? To have any chance of survival, it will probably have to be small and rather slow, perhaps even a one-celled animal. What sense will be most useful to such an animal?

Most theorists believe that the first sensory system of the earliest animals was probably a chemical sensitivity (G. H. Parker, 1922). A chemical sense enables a small animal to cope with the basics of survival: finding food, distinguishing food from nonfood, identifying certain kinds of danger, and even locating mates.

Now, imagine that you as a human have to choose one of your senses to *lose*. Which one will it be? Most of us would not choose to lose vision, hearing, or touch. Losing sensitivity to pain can be dangerous. You might choose to sacrifice your olfaction or taste.

Curious, isn't it? If an animal is going to survive with only one sense, that sense almost has to be a chemical sense, and yet if an animal such as ourselves has many other well-developed senses, the chemical senses seem dispensable. Perhaps we underestimate the importance of these senses.

General Issues about Chemical Coding

Suppose you run a bakery and you need to send frequent messages to your supplier two blocks away. Suppose further that you can communicate only by ringing three large bells on the roof of your bakery. You would have to work out some sort of code.

One possibility would be to label the three bells: The high-pitched bell means "I need flour." The medium-pitched bell means "I need sugar." And the low-pitched bell means "I need eggs." Then you simply ring the right bell at the right moment. The more you need something, the faster you ring the bell. We shall call this the "labeled-line code" because each bell has a single, unchanging label.

Another possibility would be to set up a code that depends on a relationship among the three bells: Ringing the high and medium bells equally means that you need flour. The medium and low bells together call for sugar; the high and low bells together call for eggs. Ringing all three together means you need vanilla extract. Ringing mostly the high bell while ringing the other two bells slightly means you need hazelnuts. And so forth. We call this the "across-fiber pattern code" because the meaning depends on the pattern across bells.

The across-fiber pattern code has the advantage of being more versatile; with just three bells, you can call for all sorts of necessary ingredients. Its disadvantage is that it is complicated. If your supplier forgets the code or cannot hear your bells clearly, you may get a truckload of iodized salt when you asked for a bottle of maple syrup.

A sensory system could use either type of coding. In a system relying on **labeled lines**, each receptor responds to a limited range of stimuli, and each receptor has a direct line to the brain. In a system relying on an **across-fiber pattern**, each receptor responds to a wider range of stimuli and contributes to the perception of each of them. In other words, a given level of response by a given sensory axon means little unless the brain knows what a number of other axons are doing at the same time.

We have already encountered a clear example of each kind of code. Pitch perception in audition uses labeled lines; the firing of a particular axon in the auditory nerve unambiguously indicates "F-sharp below middle C" or whatever other pitch that axon is tuned to detect. Color perception, however, uses an across-fiber pattern; each color-sensitive cell responds best to certain stimuli, but, because it also responds to other stimuli, its message out of context is ambiguous. For example, a given cone that responds best to green light might produce the same response to a moderate green light or to a brighter yellow, blue, or red light. To decode this cell's response, the nervous system must compare it with the simultaneous responses of other cells.

Which kind of code does the nervous system use for taste and smell? As you will see, neuroscientists are still not certain. On this and many other basic questions about the chemical senses, our understanding lags decades or even centuries behind our understanding of vision and hearing.

Taste

When we talk about the "taste" of food, we generally mean a combination of taste and smell. The term *flavor* would be better for that purpose; *taste* should refer to the stimulation of the taste buds. When people complain of losing their sense of taste, they generally mean that they have an impaired sense of smell. A true loss of taste is very rare.

Taste Receptors

The receptors for taste are not true neurons but modified skin cells. Like neurons, taste receptors have excitable membranes and release neurotransmitters to excite neighboring neurons, which in turn transmit information to the brain. Like skin cells, however, taste receptors are gradually sloughed off and replaced, each one lasting about 10 to 14 days (Kinnamon, 1987).

Mammalian taste receptors are located in **taste buds,** located in **papillae,** structures on the surface of the tongue (Figure 7.19). A given papilla may contain any number of taste buds from none to ten or more (Arvidson & Friberg, 1980), and each taste bud contains about 50 receptor cells. Each of the neurons carrying impulses from the taste bud receives synaptic contacts from a number of receptors (Altner, 1978).

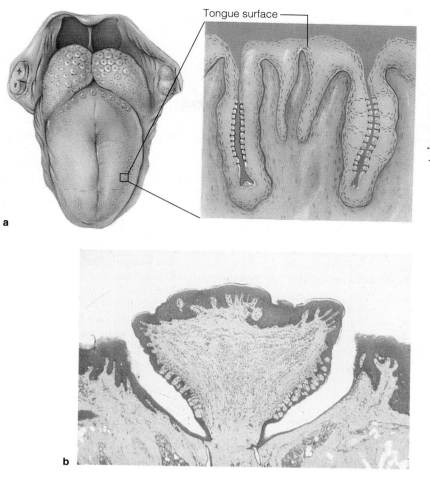

Figure 7.19
The organs of taste
(*a*) *The tip, back, and sides of the tongue are covered with taste buds. Taste buds are located in papillae.*
(*b*) *Photo showing cross section of a taste bud. Each taste bud contains about fifty receptor cells. (SIU/Peter Arnold, Inc.)*

In adult humans, taste buds are located almost exclusively along the outside edge of the tongue, with very few in the center. You can demonstrate this to yourself as follows: Soak one end of a cotton swab in sugar water, salt water, or vinegar. You might try one of each. Then touch it lightly on various portions of your tongue. You should experience a clear taste when you touch the edges of your tongue, but very little sensation in the center.

Now change the procedure a bit: Wash your mouth out with water and prepare a cotton swab as before. Touch the soaked portion to one edge of your tongue and then slowly stroke it to the center of your tongue. Now it will seem as if you are moving the taste to the center of your tongue. In fact, you are getting only a touch sensation from the center of your tongue; you refer the taste you had on the side of your tongue to every other spot you stroke (Bartoshuk, 1991).

How Many Kinds of Taste Receptors?

We can describe most if not all tastes with the four terms *sweet, sour, salty,* and *bitter,* though a few tastes defy such categorization (Schiffman & Erickson, 1980; Schiffman, McElroy, & Erickson, 1980). Do we have separate receptors for sweet, sour, salty, and bitter tastes? And do we have any additional taste receptors?

The Chemical Senses

Although the miracle berry, a plant native to West Africa, is practically tasteless, it temporarily changes the taste of other substances. Miracle berries contain a protein, *miraculin,* that modifies sweet receptors in such a way that they can be stimulated by acids (Bartoshuk, Gentile, Moskowitz, & Meiselman, 1974). If you ever get a chance to chew a miracle berry (and I do recommend it), for about the next half hour all acids (which are normally sour) will taste sweet. They will continue to taste sour as well.

Miraculin was, for a time, commercially available in the United States as a diet aid. The idea was that dieters could coat their tongue with a miraculin pill and then eat and drink unsweetened, slightly acidic substances. Such substances would taste sweet without providing many calories.

A colleague and I once spent an evening experimenting with miracle berries. We drank straight lemon juice, sauerkraut juice, even vinegar. All tasted extremely sweet. Somehow we forgot how acidic these substances are. We awoke the next day to find our mouths full of ulcers.

Other taste-modifying substances include an extract from the plant *Gymnema sylvestre,* which makes people temporarily insensitive to a great variety of sweet tastes (Frank, Mize, Kennedy, de los Santos, & Green, 1992), and the chemical *theophylline,* which reduces the bitterness of many substances (Kodama, Fukushima, & Sakata, 1978). After eating artichokes, some people report a sweet taste from water (Bartoshuk, Lee, & Scarpellino, 1972).

Have you ever tasted orange juice just after brushing your teeth? And did you wonder why something that usually tastes so good suddenly tasted so bad? Most toothpastes contain sodium lauryl sulfate, a chemical that intensifies bitter tastes while weakening sweet tastes (DeSimone, Heck, & Bartoshuk, 1980; Schiffman, 1983). Evidently, it disrupts the membrane surfaces, preventing molecules from binding to sweetness receptors. Fortunately, the effect wears off in a few minutes.

Chemsen

One way to answer these questions is to find procedures that affect one taste without affecting others. For example, certain chemicals can alter the response of sweetness receptors without affecting other taste receptors (see Digression 7.1). Therefore, we conclude that there must be a sweetness receptor, independent of receptors for other tastes.

Further evidence for at least four receptors comes from studies of the following type: Suppose that you soak your tongue for 15 seconds in some sour solution, such as unsweetened lemon juice. Then try tasting some other sour solution, such as dilute vinegar. You will find that it tastes less sour than usual. Depending on the concentrations of the lemon juice and the vinegar, the second solution may not taste sour at all. We call this phenomenon **adaptation;** it presumably reflects the fatigue of receptors sensitive to sour tastes. Now try tasting something salty, sweet, or bitter. Those substances taste about the same as usual. In short, you experience little or no **cross-adaptation** (reduced response to one stimulus because of exposure to some other stimulus). Additional tests will show that exposure to a sweet, sour, salty, or bitter taste generally produces little cross-adaptation to the other three kinds of taste (McBurney & Bartoshuk, 1973). Therefore, the four tastes probably rely on different receptors.

But might we have more than four receptors? Research suggests a possible separate receptor for "umami," the taste of MSG (monosodium glutamate). MSG tastes fairly similar to salt, but certain chemicals that interfere with salty tastes have no effect on the taste of MSG (Scott & Plata-Salaman, 1991).

Another possibility is that we may have more than one kind of bitter or sweet receptor. The enormous variety of substances that taste bitter have little in common with one another, except that nearly all of them are in some way

*Chapter 7
The Nonvisual
Sensory Systems*

harmful to the body. The strongest evidence for multiple bitter receptors comes from studies of the taste of PTC (phenylthiocarbamide) and similar substances containing an H-N-C=S chemical group. To most people, these substances taste bitter; to others, they are tasteless. Those who cannot taste them also tend to be less sensitive than other people are to the taste of caffeine and saccharin (Gent & Bartoshuk, 1983; Hall, Bartoshuk, Cain, & Stevens, 1975), but they have a nearly normal sensitivity to quinine. One interpretation of these results is that people may have several kinds of bitter receptors, which can be lost independently of one another.

Sweetness may also depend on more than one receptor. To humans, aspartame (Nutrasweet®) tastes sweet. When given a choice between aspartame and water, apes and Old World monkeys strongly prefer aspartame, while New World monkeys and prosimians (a primitive kind of primate) show no preference one way or the other (Glaser, van der Wel, Brouwer, Dubois, & Hellekant, 1992). The conclusion: The evolutionary line leading to humans, after diverging from the line that led to New World monkeys, developed either an altered sweetness receptor or a second kind of sweetness receptor.

Mechanisms of Taste Receptors

Neuroscientists know the properties of some, but not all, taste receptors. (After all, even the total number of taste receptors is still in doubt.) The best-understood taste receptor is the salty detector (or, at least, one type of salty detector). Recall that a neuron produces an action potential when sodium ions cross its membrane. A saltiness receptor cell, which detects the presence of sodium, does not need a specialized membrane site sensitive to sodium. It simply permits sodium ions on the tongue to cross its membrane. The higher the concentration of sodium on the tongue, the greater the response of this receptor. Chemicals such as amiloride, which prevents sodium from crossing the membrane, reduce the intensity of salty tastes (Desimone, Heck, Mierson, & Desimone, 1984; Schiffman, Lockhead, & Maes, 1983). The chemical *bretylium tosylate,* which facilitates the passage of sodium across the membrane, intensifies salty tastes (Schiffman, Simon, Gill, & Beeker, 1986).

Sour receptors operate on a different principle. When an acid binds to the receptor, it closes potassium channels, preventing potassium from leaving the cell. The result is an increased accumulation of positive charges within the neuron and therefore a depolarization of the membrane (Shirley & Persaud, 1990).

Sweetness and bitterness receptors apparently operate like a metabotropic synapse (p. 75). After a molecule binds to one of these receptors, it activates a G protein that releases a second messenger within the cell (Margolskee, 1993).

The Coding of Taste Information

How do we perceive tastes? According to the simplest explanation, the labeled-line theory, each kind of receptor—sweet, sour, salty, bitter, possibly one or more others—has its own direct route to the brain. That is, each axon carries information about just one taste.

Although you may consider it self-evident that four kinds of receptors imply four routes to the brain, researchers are not sure that this hypothesis is entirely correct. According to the alternative theory, the across-fiber pattern theory, several types of receptors pool their information into each axon toward the brain, and the brain must examine the pattern of firing across several axons to distinguish one taste from another.

Figure 7.20
Major routes of impulses related to the sense of taste in the human brain
The thalamus and cerebral cortex receive impulses from both the left and the right sides of the tongue.

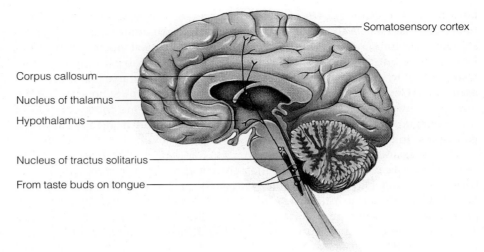

The truth may lie somewhere between these two theories (Hettinger & Frank, 1992). Each axon responds best to a particular taste—such as sweet or salty—but it responds somewhat to other stimuli also (Pfaffmann, Frank, & Norgren, 1979; Scott & Perrotto, 1980; Yaxley, Rolls, & Sienkiewicz, 1990). The neurons that respond best to sweet substances are essential for sweet tastes; in their absence, the remaining cells would not be able to distinguish sweet tastes from other substances (Smith, VanBuskirk, Travers, & Bieber, 1983b).

However, if we examine *only* the responses of the cells that respond best to sweet tastes, we find somewhat ambiguous information (Scott, 1987). For example, a moderate level of response could indicate a dilute sugar solution, or it could indicate a fairly concentrated salt solution. Only by comparing these cells' responses with those of the neurons that respond best to salt can the brain determine what the tongue is tasting.

In other words, evidently each taste axon contributes to all tastes, but it contributes more to the experience of one taste than it does to others (Scott & Chang, 1984). If all this sounds a bit confusing, it is because it really is confusing. The full story about taste coding is not yet understood.

Taste Coding in the Brain

Information from the receptors in the anterior two-thirds of the tongue is carried to the brain along the chorda tympani, a branch of the seventh cranial nerve (the facial nerve). Taste information from the posterior tongue and the throat is carried along branches of the ninth and tenth cranial nerves. Those three nerves project to different parts of the **nucleus solitarius** in the medulla (Travers, Pfaffmann, & Norgren, 1986). From the nucleus solitarius, information branches out, reaching (among other areas) the pons, the lateral hypothalamus, the amygdala, the ventral-posterior thalamus, and two areas of the cerebral cortex, one of which is responsible for taste and one of which is responsible for the sense of touch on the tongue (Pritchard, Hamilton, Morse, & Norgren, 1986; Yamamoto, 1984). Figure 7.20 diagrams a few of these major connections.

With any sensory system, the brain must determine not only what the stimulus is, but also what it means. The latter decision is particularly critical in taste, which tells the brain whether to swallow something or to spit it out. In rats, even cells in the nucleus solitarius (the first stop in the brain) code the meaning of the taste and not just its physical identity. For example, rats deficient in sodium show an increased preference for salty tastes. Recordings from the nucleus solitarius show that after rats become sodium deficient, salty substances begin to excite cells that ordinarily respond mostly to sweets! Researchers cannot yet say whether the salty substance actually tastes "sweet" to the rat or whether it just tastes "good." In either case, it is impressive that neurons at the level of the medulla have already classified the acceptability of a taste.

Conversely, if a rat has become nauseated after drinking sugar water, it decreases its preference for sugar, and the nucleus solitarius now responds to sugar in almost the same way that it responds to quinine, a bitter substance. In short, if experience has shown a substance to be good for the rat, the substance actually starts to taste good; if experience has shown a substance to be dangerous, it starts to taste bad (Scott, 1992). Monkeys show similar results, but only after taste information reaches the cerebral cortex, not the nucleus solitarius.

Olfaction

Olfaction, the sense of smell, is the detection and recognition of chemicals in contact with the membranes inside the nose. In an ordinary day, most of us pay little attention to what we smell, and an entire industry—the deodorant industry—is dedicated to removing one type of smell from our experience. But olfaction is important for appreciating food, discriminating good wine from poor wine, recognizing that old meat is rotting. Natural gas companies put a strong odor into their gas so that people can smell a leak in the gas line. Most mammals, including humans to some extent, alter their social responses to one another because of odors (see Digression 7.2). Olfaction is more important than we sometimes realize. But we have few words to describe what we smell.

Suppose you have two bottles of clear liquid, differing only in their smell. You have labeled one of them A and the other B. You are on the telephone trying to explain to someone who has the same two bottles of liquid which one to label A and which to label B. Could you describe the smells well enough for the other person to understand you?

Depending on the contents of the bottles, you might soon find yourself frustrated, clearly able to distinguish between the two, yet unable to describe that difference to someone else. With practice, you would improve, however. In one study, adults tried to identify common objects—such as bananas, popcorn, cigarette butts, mothballs, and tuna—just from their smell. At first, most could identify only a few. After several hours of practice, they learned to identify 64 objects with greater than 90 percent accuracy (Desor & Beauchamp, 1974). Evidently, human olfaction can identify a great many odors.

Olfaction can be impaired at least briefly by a number of medical conditions, including vitamin B_{12} deficiency. A loss of olfaction is a common side effect of many medical drugs, although physicians seldom ask their patients about this possible trouble (Schiffman, 1983).

Olfactory Receptors

The neurons responsible for smell are the **olfactory cells,** which line the olfactory epithelium in the rear of the nasal air passages (see Figure 7.21). In mammals, each olfactory cell has cilia (threadlike structures) that extend from the cell body into the mucous surface of the nasal passage. The fundamental structure of an olfactory receptor is about the same in all species, with variations

A **pheromone** is an odorous chemical released by one animal that affects the behavior of other members of the same species. Most mammalian species use pheromones in sexual attraction; they can determine from another animal's smell whether it is a male, a female in estrus, or a female not in estrus. Pheromones can also produce longer-lasting effects (Bronson, 1974): The odor of a group of female mice can stop another female mouse's estrous cycle, and the odor of a male can restore the estrous cycle.

Humans also secrete and respond to a variety of odorous chemicals. If you were given two T-shirts, identical except that one had been slept in by your brother or sister and the other had been slept in by someone you do not know, could you identify which shirt was which, just by the smell? In one study, 27 of 40 adults chose the correct shirt (Porter, Balogh, Cernoch, & Franchi, 1986).

In the same study, people were given two shirts, one that had been worn by a baby in their own family and one that had been worn by an unrelated baby. Nearly all the mothers as well as most of the fathers, grandmothers, and aunts were able to identify which was which, just by sniffing the two shirts. Some said, "This smells like our baby." Others said that it smelled like the mother or the father and therefore probably belonged to a family member (Porter et al., 1986).

Do people's odors affect other people's sex-related behaviors, as pheromones do in other species? The clearest evidence relates to the timing of women's menstrual cycles. Many of the women who live together in a college dormitory gradually synchronize their menstrual cycles, unless they are taking birth control pills (McClintock, 1971). (Presumably, our ancestors evolved this tendency to synchronize cycles, but why they did so is hardly obvious.) To test whether pheromones are responsible for the synchronization, researchers in two studies exposed young volunteer women to the underarm secretions of a donor woman. In both studies, most of the women exposed to these odors became synchronized to the donor woman's menstrual cycle (Preti, Cutler, Garcia, Huggins, & Lawley, 1986; Russell, Switz, & Thompson, 1980).

Another study dealt with the phenomenon that women who have an intimate relationship with a man tend to have more regular menstrual periods than other women do. One hypothesis is that the man's odors somehow promote this regularity. In one study, young women who had no heterosexual activity were exposed daily to a man's underarm secretions. Gradually, over 14 weeks, most of these women's menstrual periods became more regular than before, with a mean of about 29–30 days each (Cutler et al., 1986). In short, human body odors apparently do have some effects on hormones and behavior, although these effects are more subtle than they are in nonhuman mammals.

reflecting each species' nose shape and way of life (Menco, 1992). Olfactory receptors, almost alone among mature mammalian neurons, are replaceable. When such neurons die, new receptors form to replace them.

The olfactory receptor sites are probably located on the cilia. Because odorant molecules must pass through a mucous fluid before they reach the receptors, we experience a delay—perhaps as much as 300 ms—between inhaling a substance and smelling it (Getchell & Getchell, 1987). After a molecule excites receptors, those receptors produce a response that gradually fades (Breer & Boekhoff, 1992). So, unlike vision, olfaction does not respond rapidly enough to record sudden changes or movements, nor does it provide a lasting response, like what you see when you stare at an unmoving object.

After an olfactory cell is stimulated, its axon carries an impulse directly to the olfactory bulb, from which connections extend to the cerebral cortex, hippocampus, amygdala, and hypothalamus (Scalia & Winans, 1976).

Behavioral Methods to Identify Olfactory Receptors

How many kinds of olfactory receptors do we have? Certainly we must have more than one kind; a single receptor could not signal the differences in both the type of smell and the intensity. On the other extreme, we could hardly

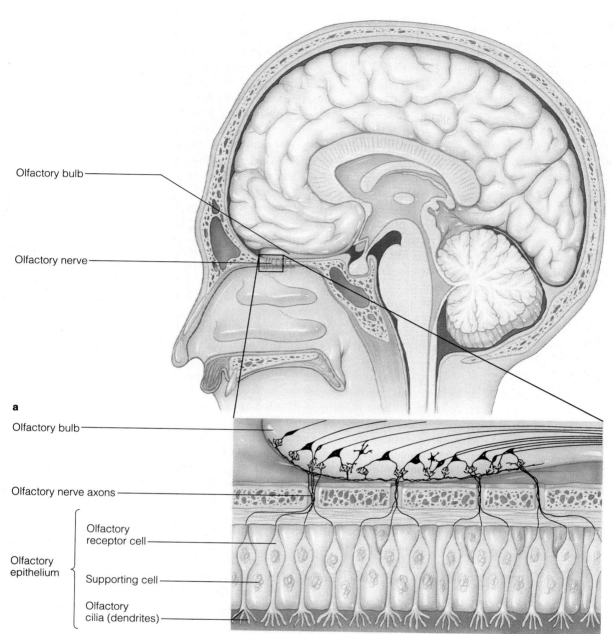

Olfactory bulb

Olfactory nerve

a

Olfactory bulb

Olfactory nerve axons

Olfactory epithelium

Olfactory receptor cell

Supporting cell

Olfactory cilia (dendrites)

b

Figure 7.21
Olfactory receptors
(*a*) *Location of receptors in nasal cavity.* (*b*) *Close-up of olfactory cells.*

imagine a separate receptor for every smell that humans can distinguish. Surely, for example, evolution did not equip us with receptors waiting for every perfume that some company might invent.

But do we have two or three kinds of olfactory receptors, or seven, or twenty, or what? Researchers answered the analogous question for color vision more than a century ago, using only behavioral observations. They found that,

The Chemical Senses

by mixing various amounts of three colors of light—say, red, green, and blue—they could match any other color that people can see. Researchers therefore concluded that we must have three, and probably only three, kinds of color receptors (which we now call cones).

We could imagine doing the same experiment for olfaction: Take some small number of odors—say, almond, lilac, and skunk—and test whether people can mix various proportions of those odors to match all other odors. If three odors are not enough, then add another, and another, and another, until eventually we find that we can mix them to match every other possible odor.

So far as I am aware, no one has ever tried that experiment, or anyone who did try must have given up before completing it. Certainly, this would be an extremely difficult experiment, considering the enormous number of possible odors and the expense of obtaining a bottle of each.

Another possible way to estimate the number of olfactory receptor types is to study people who have trouble smelling one type of odor. A general lack of olfaction is known as **anosmia;** an inability to smell a single chemical is a **specific anosmia.** For example, about 2 to 3 percent of all people are insensitive to the smell of isobutyric acid, the smelly component of sweat (Amoore, 1967). (They seldom complain about this "disability.") Because people can lose the ability to smell just this one chemical, we may assume that there is a receptor specific to isobutyric acid. We might then search for additional specific anosmias on the theory that each specific anosmia represents the loss of a different type of receptor.

One investigator identified at least five other specific anosmias—musky, fishy, urinous, spermous, and malty—with less convincing evidence suggesting twenty-six other possible specific anosmias (Amoore, 1977). Additional research indicates that specific anosmias are partly inherited but also partly dependent on experience: After prolonged exposure to some chemical, an individual with a specific anosmia to that chemical starts to smell it, presumably by developing new olfactory receptors (Wang, Wysocki, & Gold, 1993).

Research on specific anosmias suggests that people probably have a fairly large number of olfactory receptors. However, the larger the number of olfactory receptors, the more discouraging the prospects for identifying them all through specific anosmias. That is, if researchers found, for example, just five specific anosmias, with a large number of cases of each, we would begin to believe that people have just five kinds of receptors. But if researchers find 31 kinds of specific anosmias, some of them very rare, then we wonder how many other rare specific anosmias might exist that we have not yet discovered.

Biochemical Identification of Receptor Types

Ultimately, the best way to determine the number of olfactory receptor types is to isolate the receptor molecules themselves. In 1991, researchers apparently accomplished that task. Linda Buck and Richard Axel (1991) identified in olfactory receptors a family of proteins as shown in Figure 7.22. Each of these proteins traverses the cell membrane seven times, just like a neurotransmitter receptor. Also like a neurotransmitter receptor, the olfactory receptors respond to a chemical outside the cell (here, an odorant molecule instead of a neurotransmitter) by triggering changes in a G-protein inside the cell; the G-protein then provokes chemical activities that lead to an action potential.

These olfactory receptor proteins occur only in the olfactory receptors, not in other parts of the brain or other organs of the body. Moreover, different receptor cells have different receptor proteins. Buck and Axel identified 18 dif-

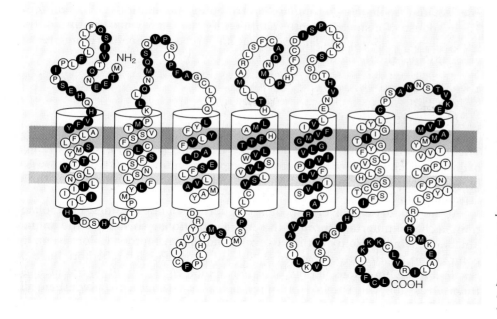

Figure 7.22
One of the olfactory receptor proteins
If you compare this protein with the synaptic receptor protein shown in Figure 3.13, you will notice great similarity. Each is a protein that traverses the membrane seven times; each responds to a chemical outside the cell and triggers activity of a G-protein inside the cell. The protein shown is one of a family; different olfactory receptors contain different proteins, each with a slightly different structure. Each of the little circles in this diagram represents one amino acid of the protein. The white circles represent amino acids that are the same in most of the olfactory receptor proteins; the black circles represent amino acids that vary from one protein to another. (From Buck & Axel, 1991.)

ferent receptor proteins, varying in their amino acid composition at certain sites (Figure 7.22). Other researchers since then have identified additional receptor proteins (Raming et al., 1993). Investigators estimate the total number of olfactory receptor proteins at 100 or more.

Implications for Coding

Most neuroscientists were surprised by the large number of olfactory receptors. After all, we have only three kinds of cones, one kind of auditory receptor, and either four or slightly more than four kinds of taste receptors. By analogy, most people imagined that we would have only a few kinds of olfactory receptors. Having so many kinds makes possible a great specialization of olfactory receptors.

To illustrate: In color vision, because we have only three kinds of cones with which to see a great variety of colors, each cone must contribute to almost every color perception. In olfaction, we can afford to have some "specialists," receptors that contribute strongly to perception of certain odors and not at all to others.

In fact, each olfactory receptor has a "preferred" odor to which it responds most strongly, but it also responds somewhat to at least a few other similar chemicals and perhaps to some other, more distantly related chemicals. That is, olfaction is not a pure labeled-line system. It is closer to being a labeled-line system than color vision is, however. The response of one olfactory receptor might mean "I smell a fatty acid with a straight chain of about 3–5 carbon atoms." The response of another receptor might mean "I smell either a fatty acid or an aldehyde, with a straight chain of about 4–6 carbon atoms." The response of either cell alone would be slightly ambiguous, but the responses of just a few cells might be enough to remove the ambiguity. The responses of other cells could identify alcohols, alkanes, and other types of odorous molecules (Imamura, Mataga, & Mori, 1992; Mori, Mataga, & Imamura, 1992). In short, each odorous molecule stimulates a limited population of receptors,

The Chemical Senses

and related molecules stimulate overlapping populations of receptors. The response of a single receptor can identify the approximate nature of the molecule; the response of a larger population of receptors enables more precise recognition of the molecule.

In Conclusion

The question may have occurred to you, "Why did evolution go to the bother of designing a hundred or so different olfactory receptor types? Couldn't we get by with some smaller number? After all, color vision gets by with just three types of cones."

At the risk of being overly speculative, here are a few musings: First, olfaction has been important through the entire evolutionary history of the animal kingdom, giving us plenty of time to evolve multiple receptors. Color vision, by comparison, is a relative newcomer. Second, our olfactory receptors have to respond to an enormous variety of airborne molecules, which do not arrange themselves along any single continuum such as wavelength. To detect them all, we may need some variety of receptors.

Third, the variety of receptors is not as great as it may seem. We have perhaps a hundred or so types of olfactory receptors, but all of them are variations on a single pattern. Just as you could rearrange a small pile of blocks into a seemingly endless variety of shapes and patterns, your cellular biochemistry rearranges a few chains of amino acids to produce a great variety of olfactory receptors.

Summary

1. Sensory information can be coded either in terms of a labeled-line system or in terms of an across-fiber pattern system. (p. 259)

2. Taste receptors are modified skin cells located in taste buds in papillae on the tongue. (p. 260)

3. The tongue has at least four kinds of receptors, one each for sweet, sour, salty, and bitter. It may have additional receptors, including more than one kind of sweet or bitter receptor. (p. 261)

4. Salty receptors respond simply to sodium ions crossing the membrane. At sweet receptors, sucrose or other substances activate a second messenger within the neuron. (p. 263)

5. Each taste axon responds best to one kind of substance but also responds somewhat to other kinds. (p. 263)

6. Brain neurons change their response to a taste to reflect its meaning. Sodium deficiency makes salt taste more pleasant; associating a taste with nausea makes it taste less pleasant. These changes in response occur even in the nucleus solitarius of rats, but not until the cortex in primates. (p. 264)

7. People are generally poor at describing odors, although they can improve greatly with practice. (p. 265)

8. Olfactory receptors are proteins, each showing its strongest response to one chemical, weaker responses to similar chemicals, and little or no response to unrelated chemicals. Vertebrates have a large number of olfactory receptor types, probably a hundred or more. (p. 268)

Review Questions

1. What is the difference between the labeled-line theory and the across-fiber pattern theory? (p. 259)

2. How long does a taste receptor last before it is replaced? (p. 260)

3. What are the effects of miraculin and *Gymnema sylvestre* extract on sweetness receptors? (p. 262)

4. What evidence indicates that we have more than one kind of bitter receptor? (p. 262)

5. How does amiloride block salty tastes? (p. 263)

6. Why is the response of any single taste neuron in the brain somewhat ambiguous? How does comparing it with other neurons remove the ambiguity? (p. 264)

7. What is a pheromone? (p. 266)

8. What is a specific anosmia? (p. 268)

9. How do olfactory receptors resemble synaptic receptors? (p. 268)

Thought Question

1. Suppose a chemist synthesizes a new chemical, which turns out to have a smell. Presumably we do not have a specialized receptor for detecting that chemical. Explain how our receptors presumably detect this chemical.

Suggestions for Further Reading

Bolles, R. C. (Ed.). (1991). *The hedonics of taste.* Hillsdale, NJ: Lawrence Erlbaum. See especially Linda Bartoshuk's excellent chapter on taste and smell.

Finger, T. E., & Silver, W. L. (Eds.). (1987). *Neurobiology of taste and smell.* New York: Wiley. A scholarly review of research on taste and smell.

Terms

labeled-line principle concept that each receptor responds to a limited range of stimuli and has a direct line to the brain (p. 260)

across-fiber pattern principle notion that each receptor responds to a wide range of stimuli and contributes to the perception of every stimulus in its system (p. 260)

taste bud structure on the tongue that contains taste receptors (p. 260)

papilla structure on the surface of the tongue, containing taste buds (p. 260)

adaptation decreased response to a stimulus as a result of recent exposure to it (p. 262)

cross-adaptation reduced response to one stimulus because of recent exposure to some other stimulus (p. 262)

nucleus solitarius area in the medulla that receives input from taste receptors (p. 264)

olfaction sense of smell (p. 265)

olfactory cell neuron responsible for smell, located on the olfactory epithelium in the rear of the nasal air passages (p. 265)

pheromone odorous chemical released by one animal that affects the behavior of other members of the same species (p. 266)

anosmia general lack of olfaction (p. 268)

specific anosmia inability to smell one type of chemical (p. 268)

MOVEMENT

©Al Tielemans/Duomo

1. An individual can recruit different muscles at different times for a similar task, depending on how difficult the task is at a given moment.

2. Movements vary in their sensitivity to feedback, their skill, and their variability in the face of obstacles.

3. Different parts of the brain control different aspects of movement, such as fast movements versus slow movements and fine movements versus cruder movements.

4. Neurological disorders impair people's control of movement.

Imagine that you are a limpet, a small shellfish that lives on a rock at the edge of the ocean. When the tide is out, you cling tightly to the rock. When the tide is in, you loosen your grip enough to capture and eat algae and other tiny plants that float in on the waves. Your main enemies are shorebirds such as oystercatchers. Whenever you loosen your grip on the rock, a shorebird can rip you right out of your shell and swallow you whole. You are almost defenseless against this attack; the birds can see exactly where you are, while your vision can barely distinguish light from dark. Even if you could see them, you would be unable to defend yourself; the shorebirds are bigger, stronger, faster, and smarter than you are. Under the circumstances, what hope do you have?

You do have one chance: You might happen to be in a rock crevice or some other location where the shorebirds cannot reach you. They gobble up every limpet they can easily reach and then move on. You have no way of knowing whether you are in a safe location, but the longer you have been in one place without getting eaten, the better your chances. If you start moving around, sooner or later you are going to wander into a dangerous spot, and then the birds will probably get you. So your best bet is to stay right where you are. Most limpets do exactly that (Frank, 1981). The moral of the story: If your enemies are bigger and stronger and faster and smarter than you are, you might as well stay in one place and hope they don't find you.

In other words, if you have little in the way of brains, you should not move much. The reverse is also true: If you are not going to move much, you do not need an elaborate nervous system. To take the extreme case, most plants do not move at all, and they have no nervous system. Animals need a nervous system to coordinate movements with one another and with sensory stimuli.

Although the ultimate function of the nervous system is to control movement, most psychologists pay little attention to movement. Compared with the study of visual perception, learning, social interactions, motivation, or emotion, the study of muscle contractions seems somehow less impressive, less "psychological."

And yet, consider: Although it takes a typist at least one-fourth of a second to type a single letter in response to a stimulus, many skilled typists type an average of eight or more characters per second (Salthouse, 1984). (Evidently they start each character well before finishing the previous one.) Sometimes a professional baseball player hits a ball thrown at 90 miles per hour, even though his eyes cannot move fast enough to maintain focus on the ball for the last 5 or 6 feet of its travel (Bahill & LaRitz, 1984). Highly skilled movements have to be planned ahead and executed as a coordinated unit, with little margin for error. To understand how such movements occur is a significant challenge for psychology as well as biology.

The Control of Movement

Suppose you decide to walk down to the store and buy a newspaper. If you are in good health, the weather is good, and the street is not too hilly, you probably think of your task in global terms: "I'm going to the store." You never even think about your individual muscle movements.

Now imagine a slightly more complex task: You have to change your car's flat tire. You have done so once or twice before, but you are still a little unsure of yourself. Now you think of the task not in global terms ("changing a tire") but in terms of subtasks: "First I take off the hubcap and loosen the bolts a little. Then I get out the jack and put it here. Then . . . "

Finally, imagine a still more difficult task: You are standing on your head with your feet balanced against the wall. While upside down you are going to try to pick up an awkwardly shaped mug, pour some water into your mouth, and swallow it. (I don't know why you would be doing this, but let's just say you are.) For such a difficult task, you must concentrate on each individual movement, breaking it down into its component parts (Vallacher & Wegner, 1987).

Regardless of whether or not we are aware of it, every task consists of many component parts. It is a tribute to the motor control systems of our brains that we ordinarily put together complex sequences of movement without even thinking about them.

Muscles and Their Movements

All animal movement depends on the contraction of muscles. Vertebrate muscles fall into three categories (see Figure 8.1): **smooth muscles,** which control movements of internal organs; **skeletal,** or **striated, muscles,** which control movement of the body with respect to the environment; and **cardiac muscles** (the heart muscles), which have properties intermediate between those of smooth and skeletal muscles.

Each muscle is composed of many individual muscle fibers, as Figure 8.2 illustrates. A given axon may innervate more than one muscle fiber, in some cases a great many fibers. For example, the eye muscles have a ratio of about one axon per three muscle fibers, while the biceps muscles of the arm have a ratio of one axon for more than a hundred fibers (Evarts, 1979). Generally, when an axon innervates relatively few muscle fibers, as in the eye muscles, movements can be more precise than when a single axon innervates many fibers.

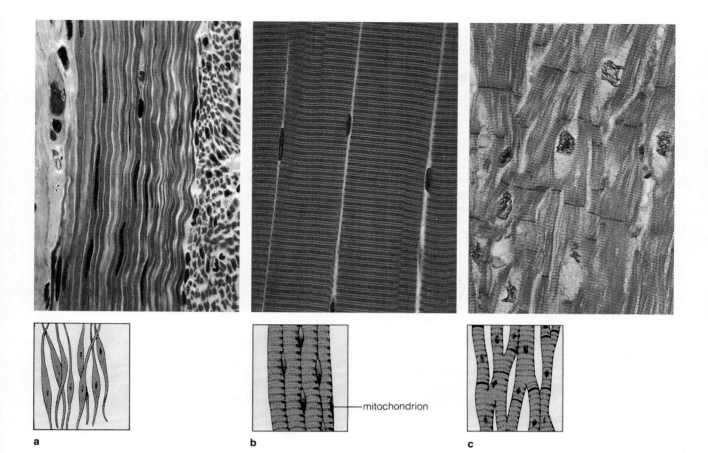

a   b   c

Figure 8.1

The three main types of vertebrate muscles

(a) *Smooth muscle, found in the intestines and other organs, consists of long, thin cells.* (b) *Skeletal muscle consists of long, cylindrical fibers with stripes.* (c) *Cardiac muscle, found in the heart, consists of fibers that fuse together at various points. Because of those fusions, cardiac muscles contract together, not independently. (After Starr & Taggart, 1989. Photos from Ed Reschke.)*

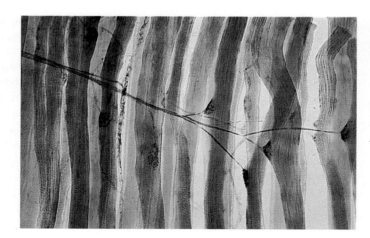

Figure 8.2
Photograph showing how an axon can branch to innervate separate muscle fibers within a muscle
Movements can be much more precise where each axon innervates only a few fibers, as with the eye muscle, than where it innervates many fibers, as with the biceps muscle. (Photo from Ed Reschke.)

The Control of Movement

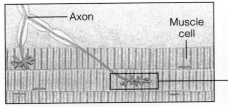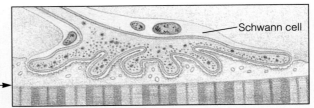

Neuromuscular junction (boxed)

Motor end plate (troughs in muscle cell membrane)

Figure 8.3
A neuromuscular junction, the synapse between a motor neuron and a muscle
The terminal of the axon forms many branches, each of which enters a trough in the membrane of the muscle cell. (After Starr & Taggart, 1989.)

Figure 8.4
A pair of antagonistic muscles
The biceps of the arm is a flexor; the triceps is an extensor. (After Starr & Taggart, 1989.)

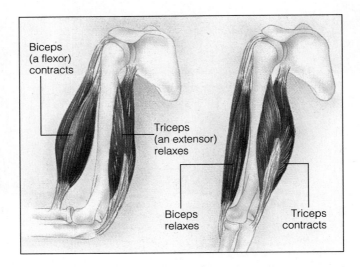

A **neuromuscular junction** is a synapse where a motor neuron's axon meets a muscle fiber (Figure 8.3). In skeletal muscles, every axon releases acetylcholine at the neuromuscular junction, and the acetylcholine always has an excitatory effect; that is, the transmitter always causes the muscle to contract.

Each muscle has just one movement—contraction—and so just one direction of movement. In the absence of excitation, it relaxes, but it never moves actively in the opposite direction. Moving a leg or arm in two directions requires opposing sets of muscles, called **antagonistic muscles.** An arm, for example, has a **flexor** muscle that flexes or raises it and an **extensor** muscle that extends or straightens it (Figure 8.4). Walking, clapping hands, or any other coordinated sequence of movements requires a regular alternation between contraction of one set of muscles and contraction of another.

The motor nerves of mammals originate from neurons in the spinal cord or the medulla. All sensory neurons enter the dorsal side of the spinal cord, and all motor neurons leave through the ventral side (see Figure 4.3). The axon of a motor neuron extends all the way from the spinal cord or medulla to the muscle that it innervates. Diseases of the spinal cord can impair the control of movement in various ways. (See Table 8.1.)

Table 8.1   Some Disorders of the Spinal Cord

Disorder	Description	Cause
Paralysis	Lack of voluntary movement in part of the body.	Damage to motor neurons in the spinal cord or their axons in the periphery.
Flaccid paralysis	Inability to move one part of the body voluntarily, accompanied by low muscle tone and weak reflexive movements.	Damage to motor neurons in the spinal cord. Can be temporary result of damage to axons from brain to spinal cord.
Spastic paralysis	Inability to move one part of the body voluntarily, although reflexive movements and tremors remain. Muscles are stiff and muscle tone is higher than normal. Reflexes are strong and jerky.	Damage to axons from the brain to the spinal cord. (Such damage initially causes flaccid paralysis, which eventually gives way to spastic paralysis.)
Paraplegia	Loss of sensation and voluntary muscle control in both legs. Reflexes remain in legs. Although no messages pass between the brain and the genitals, the genitals still respond reflexively to touch. Paraplegics feel nothing in their own genitals, but they can function sexually, satisfy their partners, and still experience orgasm (Money, 1967).	Cut through the spinal cord above the segments attached to the legs.
Quadriplegia	Loss of sensation and muscle control in all four extremities.	Cut through the spinal cord above the level controlling the arms.
Hemiplegia	Loss of sensation and muscle control in the arm and leg on one side.	Cut halfway through the spinal cord or (more commonly) damage to one of the hemispheres of the cerebral cortex.
Tabes dorsalis	Impaired sensation in the legs and pelvic region, impaired leg reflexes and walking, loss of bladder and bowel control.	Late stage of syphilis. Dorsal roots of the spinal cord deteriorate gradually.
Poliomyelitis	Paralysis.	Virus that damages cell bodies of motor neurons.
Amyotrophic lateral sclerosis (Lou Gehrig's disease)	Gradual weakness and paralysis, starting with the arms and later spreading to the legs. Both motor neurons and axons from the brain to the motor neurons are destroyed.	Unknown.

Fast and Slow Muscles

At the start of this chapter, I asked you to imagine that you were a limpet. Now imagine that you are a small fish. You are in constant danger of attack by larger fish, turtles, and birds; your only defense is your ability to get away (Figure 8.5). Are you in any special danger when the water is cold? Remember, as a fish, you cannot maintain a constant body temperature. If the water temperature drops from 20°C to 5°, your body temperature drops from 20° to 5°.

Any muscle fiber contracts more vigorously at high temperatures than it does at low temperatures. Therefore, you should be able to swim faster at high temperatures; at low temperatures, your sluggish movements should leave you

Figure 8.5
Fish are "cold blooded," but many of their predators (such as this pelican) are not. At cold temperatures, a fish must maintain its normal swimming speed, even though every muscle in its body contracts more slowly than usual. To do so, a fish calls upon white muscles that it would otherwise use only for brief bursts of speed. (Bill Curtsinger)

extremely vulnerable to attack, especially by warm-blooded animals such as birds. Right?

Strangely, that is not so. A fish swims just as fast at low temperatures as it does at high temperatures, even though every muscle fiber contracts more vigorously at higher temperatures than it does at lower temperatures. The fish maintains its swimming speed by recruiting more muscles at low temperatures than it does at high temperatures (Rome, Loughna, & Goldspink, 1984).

A fish has three kinds of muscles: red, pink, and white. Red muscles produce rather slow movements, but they can continue to respond almost indefinitely without fatigue—like the muscles you use for sitting or standing. White muscles produce the fastest movements, but they can act only for brief periods before becoming fatigued. Pink muscles are intermediate in both speed and fatigue. At high temperatures, a fish relies mostly on its red muscles and a few pink muscles, using its white muscles only when it needs a brief burst of speed. At colder temperatures, the red and pink muscles produce only slow and weak contractions, and the fish relies more and more on its white muscles. By recruiting enough white muscles, the fish can maintain its usual swimming speed in all water temperatures. However, the fish fatigues faster at low temperatures because of its increased dependence on white muscles.

All right, you can stop imagining that you are a fish. What is the message here for humans? Mammals have **fast-twitch fibers** that produce fast contractions but fatigue rapidly (corresponding to the fish's white muscles) and **slow-twitch fibers** that produce less vigorous contractions without fatiguing (corresponding to the fish's red muscles). We also have a variety of intermediate fibers. Unlike fish, our fast-twitch, intermediate, and slow-twitch fibers are all mixed together (Hennig & Lømo, 1985). The fish's muscles are distinctly separated. (Take a look the next time you go to the supermarket.) Although we mammals do not need to concern ourselves much with varying temperatures, we call mostly on fast-twitch fibers for some situations and mostly on slow-twitch fibers for others. For standing, walking, and nonstrenuous aerobic exercise, we rely on our slow-twitch and intermediate fibers. For running up a flight of stairs at full speed, we use our fast-twitch fibers.

People vary substantially in their relative amounts of fast-twitch and slow-twitch fibers, and apparently certain kinds of exercise can increase the percentage of one kind or the other. For example, competitive sprinters have about 70% intermediate- and fast-twitch fibers in certain leg muscles, suitable for brief bursts of great speed. Marathon runners, however, have about 60% slow-twitch fibers, with increased capillary blood flow to those muscles (Crenshaw, Fridén, Thornell, & Hargens, 1991; Sjöström, Johansson, & Lorentzon, 1988). The Swedish ultramarathon runner Bertil Järlaker built up so many slow-twitch fibers in his legs that he once ran 3,520 km (2,188 miles) from Finland to Sweden in 50 days (an average of 1.7 marathons per day), with only minimal signs of pain or fatigue (Sjöström, Friden, & Ekblom, 1987). However, he had developed these slow-twitch fibers at the expense of his fast-twitch fibers. Consequently, his speed for short-distance races fell to a mediocre 6 minutes per kilometer (more than 9 minutes per mile).

Another application of the distinction between different kinds of muscle fibers: As you may recall from Chapter 1, male birds generally sing more than females do because of anatomical differences in their brains. In frogs, males croak more than females do because males have about eight times as many muscles in their throats, including mostly intermediate- to fast-twitch fibers, capable of the rapid contractions that produce frog sounds. Females have fewer

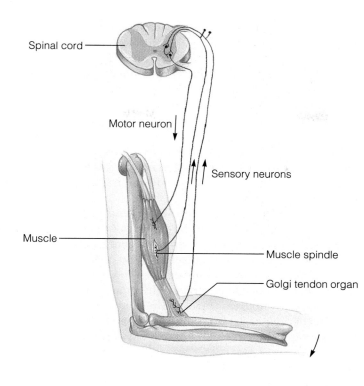

Figure 8.6
**Two kinds of
proprioceptors regulate the
contraction of a muscle**
*When a muscle is stretched,
the nerves from the muscle
spindles transmit an
increased frequency of
impulses, resulting in a contraction of the surrounding
muscle. Contraction of the
muscle stimulates the Golgi
tendon organs, which act as
a brake or shock absorber to
prevent a contraction that is
too quick or extreme.*

throat muscles overall and a higher percentage of slow-twitch fibers (Sassoon, Gray, & Kelley, 1987).

Muscle Control by Proprioceptors

You are walking along on a slightly bumpy road. What happens if the messages that your spinal cord sends to your leg muscles are not exactly correct? You might set your foot down a little too hard or not quite hard enough, depending on whether you step onto a bump or into a little dent in the road, and on whether you have recently gained weight or lost weight, and on whether the wind is with you or against you. Nevertheless, you adjust your posture almost immediately and maintain your balance without even thinking about it. How do you do that?

A baby is lying on its back. You playfully tug on one of its feet and then let go. At once the leg bounces back to its original position. How did that happen?

In both cases, the mechanism is under the control of proprioceptors (see Figure 8.6). A **proprioceptor** is a receptor sensitive to the position and move-ment of a part of the body—in these cases, a muscle. Proprioceptors detect the stretch and tension of a muscle and send messages that enable the spinal cord to adjust its signals. When a muscle is stretched, the spinal cord sends a reflex-ive signal to contract the muscle. This **stretch reflex** is *caused* by a stretch; it does not *result* in a stretch.

One kind of proprioceptor is the **muscle spindle**, a stretch receptor parallel to the muscle (Merton, 1972; Miles & Evarts, 1979). Whenever the muscle spindle is stretched, its sensory nerve sends a message to a motor neuron in the spinal cord, which in turn sends a message back to the muscles surround-ing the spindle, causing muscle contractions. Note that this reflex provides for

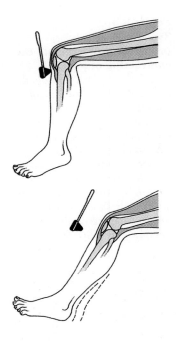

Figure 8.7
Knee-jerk reflex

negative feedback: When the muscle and its spindle are stretched, the spindle sends a message that results in a muscle contraction.

For example, you set your foot down on a slight bump on the road. Your knee bends a bit, stretching the extensor muscles of that leg. The sensory nerves of the spindles send action potentials to the motor neuron in the spinal cord, and the motor neuron sends action potentials to the extensor muscle. Contraction of the extensor muscle straightens the leg, adjusting for the bump on the road.

A physician who asks you to cross your legs and then taps you just below the knee (Figure 8.7) is testing your stretch reflexes. The tap below the knee stretches the extensor muscles and their spindles, resulting in a message that jerks the lower leg upward.

Another proprioceptor, the **Golgi tendon organ,** responds to increases in muscle tension. Located in the tendons at both ends of a muscle, it acts as a brake against an excessively vigorous contraction. Some muscles are so strong that they could damage themselves if too high a percentage of fibers contracted at once. Golgi tendon organs detect the contraction of the muscle. The more vigorously the muscle contracts, the greater the response of the Golgi tendon organs. Their impulses travel to the spinal cord, where they inhibit the motor neurons via messages from interneurons. In short, a vigorous muscle contraction activates the Golgi tendon organs, inhibiting further contraction.

Units of Movement

The stretch reflex is one example of movement. Others include speaking, walking, threading a needle, and throwing a basketball through a hoop while off balance and trying to evade two defenders. In many ways, these movements are different from one another, and they depend on different kinds of control by the nervous system.

Voluntary and Involuntary Movements

Reflexes are consistent, automatic responses to stimuli. The stretch reflex is one example; another is the constriction of your pupil in response to bright light; still another is the knee-jerk reflex in response to a tap on the knee. We generally think of reflexes as *involuntary* because they are sensitive to external stimuli but insensitive to reinforcements, punishments, and motivations.

Many behaviors are a complex mixture of voluntary and involuntary influences. Take swallowing, for example. You swallow periodically during the day without thinking about it, involuntarily. You also swallow when eating, more because of the food in your mouth than because of any deliberate decision. You can voluntarily decide to swallow or to inhibit swallowing, but only within certain limits. Try to swallow ten times in a row, voluntarily. The first swallow is easy; the second almost as easy; but before long, you will find additional swallows difficult, unpleasant, eventually almost impossible. Now try to inhibit swallowing for, say, 20 minutes. Chances are, you will give in long before you reach that goal. (No fair spitting during the 20 minutes.)

Can you think of an example of a purely voluntary movement—that is, one that is independent of external stimuli, one that has no unintentional components? That probably sounds like an easy question, and you start to generate examples: walking, talking, scratching your head . . . However, on close inspection, most examples turn out to include some involuntary components. Consider walking: When you walk, you automatically compensate for the bumps and irregularities in the road. You probably also swing your arms a bit as you walk. You could voluntarily increase or decrease the amount of swing, but ordinarily it occurs as an automatic, involuntary consequence of walking.

Certain visual stimuli greatly facilitate walking, at least in certain people. A patient with Parkinson's disease has much trouble walking under ordinary circumstances but can walk surprisingly well when following a parade. Also, if someone marks lines across the floor at approximately one-step intervals, a Parkinson's patient can step across each line much more easily than he or she can walk down an unmarked hall (Teitelbaum, Pellis, & Pellis, 1991). So is the walking voluntary or involuntary? Evidently, it is a mixture of both; the person chooses to walk, but the stimuli of following a parade or crossing lines greatly facilitate the behavior. In short, the distinction between voluntary and involuntary is often a blurry one.

Movements with High or Low Sensitivity to Feedback

The military uses two kinds of missiles: ballistic missiles and guided missiles. A ballistic missile is simply launched toward the target, much as someone throws a ball. Once launched, there is no way to correct the missile's aim. A guided missile, however, detects the target's location and shifts its trajectory one way or the other to correct for any error in the original aim.

Similarly, some movements are ballistic and others are corrected by feedback. A **ballistic movement** is executed as a whole; once someone has initiated a ballistic movement, he or she cannot alter it or correct its aim. Reflexes (simple, automatic responses to a stimulus), such as the stretch reflex or the contraction of the pupils in response to light, are ballistic movements. We can observe certain reflexes in infants that are absent in adults. (See Digression 8.1.)

Oscillators, repetitive alternations of movements, are another type of more or less ballistic movements (Gallistel, 1980). Examples include wing flapping in birds and insects, fin movements in fish, and the repetitive shaking movements that a wet animal makes to dry itself off. We may regard an oscillator as a kind of reflex because a stimulus consistently elicits the same response. Although a stimulus starts an oscillator, it does not control the frequency of repetition of the alternating movements. For example, consider the **scratch reflex.** C. S. Sherrington found that when he lightly irritated a dog's skin, the dog would raise a limb and scratch the irritated area repetitively. The scratching movement, a well-timed alternation of extensor and flexor muscles, occurred at a constant rate of four to five scratches per second. If the amount of irritation increased, the length and strength of each scratching movement increased, but the rhythm stayed the same. Even if the experimenter tickled the skin rapidly or slowly, the muscles still produced four or five scratches per second. Therefore, Sherrington reasoned, the scratching rhythm is generated by some set of cells in the spinal cord, not by the sensory input.

Many other movements depend to a greater extent on moment-by-moment feedback. For example, when you thread a needle, you make a slight movement and then observe the new positions of the thread and the needle. If your aim was slightly off in one direction or another, you try to correct that error with your next movement. For another example, when a soprano holds a single note for a prolonged time, the pitch of her voice will inevitably waver slightly from the intended note. When she hears a slight change of pitch, she

The vigorous body shaking of a wet mammal is one example of an oscillator. The frequency of shakes is nearly constant for a given species. (©Johnny Johnson/Natural Selection)

The Control of Movement

Certain reflexes are present in infants but not in older children or adults. For example, if you place an object firmly in an infant's hand, the infant will reflexively grasp it tightly (the **grasp reflex**). If you stroke the sole of the foot, the infant will reflexively extend the big toe and fan the others (the **Babinski reflex**). If you touch the cheek of an awake infant, the head will turn toward the stimulated cheek and the infant will begin to suck (the **rooting reflex**). The rooting reflex is not a pure example of a reflex; its intensity depends on the infant's alertness, hunger, and so forth. Still, this reflex, like the others, is characteristic of infants and seldom present in healthy adults.

Although such reflexes fade away over age, the reflexive connections behind them remain intact. They are not lost but rather suppressed by axons from the maturing brain. If the cerebral cortex is damaged, the infant reflexes are released from inhibition. In fact, neurologists and other physicians frequently test for infant reflexes. If a physician has ever stroked the sole of your foot during a physical exam, he or she was probably looking for evidence of brain damage. This is hardly the most dependable test, but it is among the easiest. If stroking the sole of your foot makes you fan your toes as a baby does, you may be suffering from some impairment of your cerebral cortex.

The infant reflexes sometimes also return temporarily if activity of the cerebral cortex is depressed by alcohol, carbon dioxide, or other chemicals. (You might try testing for infant reflexes in a friend who has consumed a little too much alcohol.)

Infants and children also have a stronger tendency than adults do to display certain *allied reflexes*. If a cloud of dust blows in your face, you will reflexively close your eyes, close your mouth, and probably sneeze. These reflexes are *allied* in the sense that each of them tends to elicit the others. If you suddenly see a bright light—as when you emerge from a dark the-

ater on a sunny afternoon—you will reflexively close your eyes and you may also close your mouth and perhaps sneeze. Some adults do so; a higher percentage of young children do (Whitman & Packer, 1993).

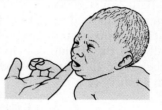

Rooting reflex

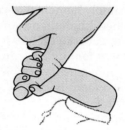

Grasp reflex

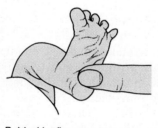

Babinski reflex

compensates and quickly brings her voice back to the original note. The importance of the feedback becomes apparent if we distort it. If a device records the soprano's singing and plays it back to her through earphones after a delay of a few seconds, her voice may drift off the intended note for several seconds before she hears her error. She then begins to correct the error, but by the time she hears her correction, several seconds later, she has already overcorrected. Her voice swings back and forth widely around the intended note. This procedure, called *delayed auditory feedback,* disturbs anyone's speech patterns, although one can learn to minimize the effect.

Skilled and Unskilled Movements

In general, an unskilled sequence of movements is slow and requires moment-by-moment feedback. If you ever learned to play a musical instrument, you began by learning to play one note. You had to make sure you got that note right before you tried another one. After more practice, you could play a long sequence of notes as a familiar "chunk." Similarly, an expert gymnast plans and performs a complex series of movements as a unit, although he or she will pause momentarily between large units to make corrections in aim and balance. In other words, the development of movement skills is mainly a matter of stringing together many individual movements into larger, more or less ballistic units.

A large coordinated chunk of movements depends on a nervous-system mechanism called a **motor program.** A motor program can be either learned or built into the nervous system, but, once established, it may be fairly inflexible. A species-specific motor program that develops almost automatically in any normal environment is called a **fixed action pattern.** One example is the grooming behavior of mice (Fentress, 1973). Periodically during the day, a mouse sits up, licks its paws, wipes its paws over its face, closes its eyes as the paws pass over them, licks the paws again, and so forth. The mouse begins with a series of rapid rubs on the nose and then follows with longer, slower strokes. Even mice that lack forelimbs assume the typical posture for grooming and then wiggle their stumps back and forth. Periodically, they extend their tongues and close their eyes in synchrony with the movements of the limb stumps, just as if intact paws were passing back and forth over the face. Moreover, they begin with rapid stump movements and then shift to slower movements, like normal mice. In short, once the motor program (or fixed action pattern) for this sequence of movements is triggered, it runs to completion.

By comparing species, we can gain some insight into how a motor program can be gained or lost through evolution. For example, if you hold almost any bird several feet above the ground and then drop it, the bird will stretch its wings and flap them. Provine (1979, 1981) found that chickens with featherless wings or amputated wings made the same movements, even though they failed to break their fall. On the other hand, penguins, emus, and rheas, which have not used their wings for flight in countless generations, do not extend or flap their wings when they are dropped (Provine, 1984). Although their ancient ancestors presumably had this motor program, it has been lost over the course of evolution.

Do humans have any built-in motor programs? Yawning is one example (Provine, 1986). A yawn is composed of the opening of the mouth, a prolonged inhalation, often accompanied by stretching, and a shorter exhalation. Yawns are very consistent in duration, with a mean of just less than 6 seconds.

The repetitive grooming behavior of a mouse is one example of a fixed action pattern. (©L. West/The National Audubon Society/PR)

Summary

1. An overall movement may depend on a great many muscle contractions. We attend to the individual contractions only when a task is particularly difficult. (p. 274)

2. Vertebrates have skeletal, cardiac, and smooth muscles. (p. 274)

3. The neuromuscular junction is a specialized type of synapse. (p. 276)

4. Skeletal muscles range from slow muscles that do not fatigue to fast muscles that fatigue quickly. We rely on the slow muscles most of the time, but we recruit the fast muscles for brief periods of strenuous activity. (p. 277)

5. Proprioceptors are receptors sensitive to the position and movement of a body part. Two kinds of proprioceptors—

muscle spindles and Golgi tendon organs—help to regulate muscle movements. (p. 279)

6. Some movements, especially reflexes, proceed as a unit, with little if any guidance from sensory feedback. Other movements, such as threading a needle, are constantly guided and redirected by sensory feedback. (p. 281)

7. Someone who develops skill at a movement comes to execute large chunks of the movement as a whole, with little dependence on moment-by-moment feedback. (p. 283)

Review Questions

1. Why can the eye muscles be moved with greater precision than the biceps muscles? (p. 274)

2. What transmitter is released at the neuromuscular junction of skeletal muscles? (p. 276)

3. How does a fish manage to swim at the same speed in water of different temperatures, even though temperature affects the vigor of contraction of each muscle fiber? (p. 278)

4. Someone who runs extraordinary distances builds up muscles that enable long-distance running without fatigue. What disadvantage is likely? Why? (p. 278)

5. While you are holding your arm straight out, someone pulls it down slightly. Immediately it bounces back to its original position. What proprioceptor is responsible? (p. 279)

6. What is the function of Golgi tendon organs? (p. 280)

7. Give an example of a movement that is highly sensitive to feedback and one that is relatively insensitive. (p. 281)

8. What is the evidence that the rhythm of the scratch reflex is generated within the animal's own nervous system? (p. 281)

9. Give an example of a motor program or a fixed action pattern. (p. 283)

Thought Question

1. Would you expect jaguars, cheetahs, and other great cats to have mostly slow-twitch, nonfatiguing muscles in their legs or mostly fast-twitch, quickly fatiguing muscles? What kinds of animals might have mostly the opposite kind of muscles?

Suggestions for Further Reading

Brooks, V. B. (1986). *The neural basis of motor control.* Oxford, England: Oxford University Press. Detailed description of research on how the nervous system controls the muscles; not easy reading but highly informative.

Gallistel, C. R. (1980). *The organization of action: A new synthesis.* Hillsdale, NJ: Erlbaum. Provocative analysis of the units of movement, featuring reprints of some classic articles.

Terms

smooth muscle muscle that controls movements of internal organs (p. 274)

skeletal muscle or **striated muscle** muscle that controls movement of the body with respect to the environment (such as arm and leg muscles) (p. 274)

cardiac muscle muscle of the heart (p. 274)

neuromuscular junction synapse where a motor neuron's axon meets a muscle fiber (p. 276)

antagonistic muscle muscle that moves a limb in opposite directions (for example, extensor and flexor) (p. 276)

flexor muscle that flexes a limb (p. 276)

extensor muscle that extends a limb (p. 276)

fast-twitch muscle muscle that produces fast contractions but fatigues rapidly (p. 278)

slow-twitch muscle muscle that produces less vigorous contractions without fatiguing (p. 278)

proprioceptor receptor that is sensitive to the position and movement of a part of the body (p. 279)

stretch reflex reflexive contraction of a muscle in response to a stretch of that muscle (p. 279)

muscle spindle receptor that responds to the stretch of a muscle (p. 279)

Golgi tendon organ receptor that responds to the contraction of a muscle (p. 280)

reflex a consistent, automatic response to a stimulus (p. 280)

ballistic movement motion that proceeds as a single organized unit that cannot be redirected once it begins (p. 281)

oscillator repetitive alternation between two movements (p. 281)

scratch reflex reflexive alternation of extension and flexion of a limb in response to irritation of the skin (p. 281)

grasp reflex reflexive grasp of an object placed firmly in the hand (p. 282)

Babinski reflex reflexive flexion of the big toe when the sole of the foot is stimulated (p. 282)

rooting reflex reflexive head turning and sucking after a touch on the cheek (p. 282)

motor program fixed sequence of movements that occur as a single unit (p. 283)

fixed action pattern motor program that develops almost automatically in any normal environment (p. 283)

Brain Mechanisms of Movement

Suppose you go through a sequence of actions: You stand up, walk across the room, sit at the piano, place your hands in position, and start to play. So far as you are consciously aware, you merely decide to perform these actions and then they happen. However, much of your nervous system devotes its time to making them happen. Furthermore, different parts of your brain are responsible for different kinds of movement. Figure 8.8 outlines the major motor areas of the mammalian central nervous system. Don't get too bogged down in their details at this point; we shall attend to each of these areas in due course.

The Role of the Spinal Cord

Have you ever heard the expression "running around like a chicken with its head cut off"? A rather gruesome image, but a chicken with its head cut off *can* run around . . . for a little while. Naturally, it does not run toward anything or away from anything; it just runs. Nevertheless, it maintains its balance even while running on bumpy ground or up or down a slope. In short, the spinal cord can control walking and running.

In fact, the spinal cord largely controls walking and running even when the brain is intact, even in humans. That is, the motor program for walking is located in the spinal cord. The spinal cord and medulla also have motor programs for chewing, swallowing, breathing, scratching, and a number of other common behaviors (Shik & Orlovsky, 1976). The cerebral cortex does not direct the individual muscle contractions necessary for such movements; it merely turns on the appropriate motor programs.

The spinal cord's motor program for the scratch reflex has received considerable research attention. In cats, the reflex has a rhythm of three or four scratches per second. Cells in the third through fifth lumbar segments of the spinal cord generate that rhythm (Deliagina, Orlovsky, & Pavlova, 1983). A stroking of the skin stimulates certain neurons in that area of the spinal cord to produce impulses at a rate of three or four per second. The rate of scratching remains the same even if those neurons are isolated from all cerebral input, so it appears that the rhythm originates in the spinal cord. Furthermore, those cells generate the rhythm even if the muscles themselves are paralyzed, so the rhythm does not require feedback from muscle movements.

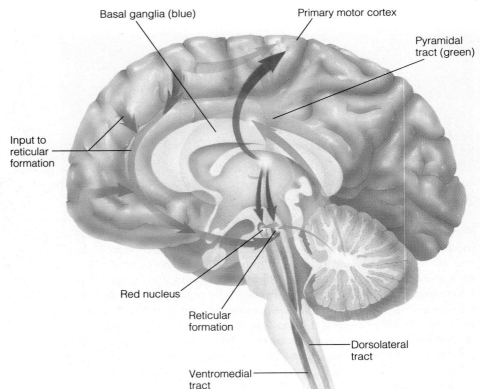

Figure 8.8
Outline of the major motor areas of the mammalian central nervous system
The cerebral cortex, especially the primary motor cortex, sends axons directly to the medulla and spinal cord; it also sends axons to the red nucleus, reticular formation, and other brain-stem areas, which in turn send axons to the medulla and spinal cord. The medulla and spinal cord control all muscle movements. The basal ganglia and cerebellum influence movement indirectly through their communication back and forth with the cerebral cortex and brain stem.

Basal ganglia (blue)

Primary motor cortex

Pyramidal tract (green)

Input to reticular formation

Red nucleus

Reticular formation

Ventromedial tract

Dorsolateral tract

The Role of the Cerebellum

The cerebellum is important for motor control, including learned motor responses. The term *cerebellum* is Latin for *little brain*. Although it is smaller than the rest of the brain, the cerebellum contains so many neurons and so many connections that its potential for information processing is comparable with that of the cerebral cortex.

Physiologists long believed that the role of the cerebellum was merely to improve the coordination of muscles and to maintain equilibrium. The cerebellum does make those contributions, but it has other functions as well. In particular, we now know that cerebellar neurons are active before movements begin, not just during and after them. That is, the cerebellum contributes to generating and planning movements. It is also important for various kinds of motor learning, including classically conditioned responses (see p. 450).

Effects of Damage to the Cerebellum

People with cerebellar damage have trouble with any sequence of rapid movements that requires accurate aiming and timing. For example, they have trouble tapping a rhythm, pointing at a moving object, and adapting to prisms that distort vision (Daum et al., 1993). They also have trouble with speaking, writing, typing, playing a musical instrument, and athletic skills. Even simple alter-

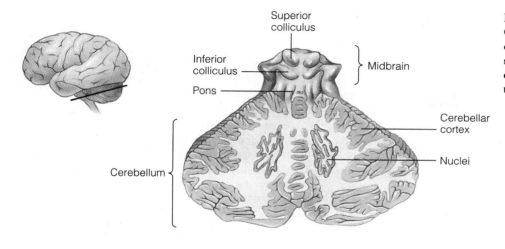

nating movements such as clapping hands or dribbling a basketball become difficult; the person has to pause after each movement to plan the next one.

Ordinarily, certain movements accompany one another. For example, when pulling the right arm back in preparing to throw a ball, a normal person will put more weight on the right leg, raise the left leg and the left arm, and shift the pelvis and the neck. After cerebellar damage, a person may throw with the right arm without making the usual movements with the rest of the body.

The cerebellum is generally large in species that make many rapid, well-aimed movements, such as birds. The sloth, on the other extreme, is a mammal proverbial for its slowness. When M. G. Murphy and J. L. O'Leary (1973) made cerebellar lesions in sloths, they could detect no change in the animals' movement patterns.

Tests of Cerebellar Functioning

Here is one quick way to test how well someone's cerebellum is functioning: Ask the person to focus on one spot, then to move the eyes quickly to focus on some other object. **Saccades** (sa-KAHDS), ballistic eye movements from one fixation point to another, depend on impulses from the cerebellum and the frontal cortex to the cranial nerves. A normal, healthy person moves his or her eyes from one fixation point to another by a single movement or by one large movement plus a small correction at the end. Someone with cerebellar damage, however, has difficulty programming the angle and distance of eye movements (Dichgans, 1984). The eyes make many short movements until, by trial and error, they eventually focus on the intended spot.

Another test of cerebellar damage is the *finger-to-nose test*. The person is instructed to hold one arm straight out and then, at command, to touch his or her nose as quickly as possible. A normal person does so in three steps: First, the finger moves ballistically to a point just in front of the nose. This *move* function depends on the cerebellar cortex (the surface of the cerebellum), which sends messages to the nuclei (clusters of cell bodies in the interior of the cerebellum; see Figure 8.9). Second, the finger remains steady at that spot for a fraction of a second. This *hold* function depends on the nuclei alone (Kornhuber, 1974). Finally, the finger moves to the nose by a slower movement that does not depend on the cerebellum.

After damage to the cerebellar cortex, a person has trouble with the initial, rapid movement. Either the finger does not go far enough or it goes too far, striking the person in the face. If certain nuclei of the cerebellum have been damaged, the person may have difficulty with the hold segment; after the finger reaches a point just in front of the nose, it wavers wildly.

The symptoms of cerebellar damage markedly resemble those of alcohol intoxication. Drunken individuals as a rule are clumsy, their speech is slurred, and their eye movements are inaccurate. A police officer testing someone for possible drunkenness may use the finger-to-nose test or other tests that are also used for diagnosing damage to the cerebellum because it is one of the first areas of the brain to show the effects of alcohol intoxication.

Cellular Organization of the Cerebellum

The cerebellum receives input from the spinal cord, from each of the sensory systems by way of the cranial nerve nuclei, and from the cerebral cortex. That information eventually reaches the **cerebellar cortex,** the surface of the cerebellum (see Figure 8.9).

The cerebellar cortex has an extremely regular arrangement of neurons, as Figure 8.10 shows. The **Purkinje cells** are very flat cells arranged in a plane. The **parallel fibers** running perpendicular to that plane supply much of the input to the Purkinje cells.

The Purkinje cells provide the output, transmitting an inhibitory message to cells in the interior **nuclei of the cerebellum** and to cells in the vestibular nuclei in the brain stem. The cells from the nuclei of the cerebellum in turn send output fibers to the thalamus and to the **red nucleus,** a structure in the midbrain. The thalamus sends information to motor areas of the cerebral cortex; the red nucleus sends information directly to the spinal cord.

Note how a single parallel fiber can activate a long string of Purkinje cells, one after the other. If all those Purkinje cells send their output to the same target cell, then one after another of them inhibits that cell, producing a prolonged effect. The greater the number of Purkinje cells responding, the longer they will collectively inhibit their target cell. The target cell receives much excitation from other sources; the inhibition from the Purkinje cells selects which cells will not respond and, therefore, which other cells will. By controlling the target cell for varying periods, the Purkinje cells control the duration (and therefore distance) of ballistic motor responses (Kornhuber, 1974; Llinás, 1975).

The Role of the Basal Ganglia

The term *basal ganglia* applies collectively to a group of large subcortical structures in the forebrain (see Figure 8.11): the **caudate nucleus,** the **putamen,** the **globus pallidus,** the **substantia nigra,** and the **subthalamic nucleus** (DeLong et al., 1984). Each of these areas exchanges information with the others. The main receptive areas are the caudate nucleus and the putamen, which receive sensory input from much of the thalamus and the cerebral cortex. The main output area is the globus pallidus, which sends information to the primary motor cortex and several surrounding areas (Hoover & Strick, 1993).

The basal ganglia contribute to both movement and cognitive functions. In the control of movement, they are apparently not responsible for selecting which muscles will be active at a given time. Rather, they control the direction

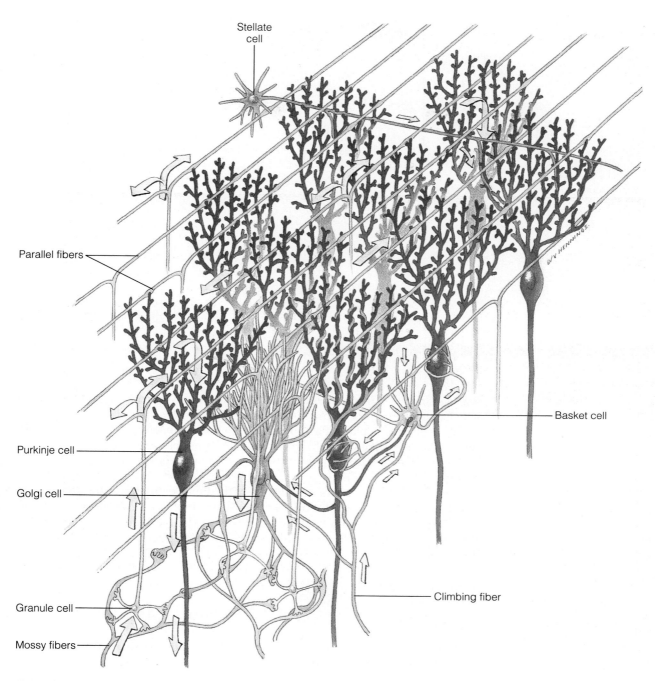

Stellate cell

Parallel fibers

Purkinje cell

Golgi cell

Granule cell

Mossy fibers

Basket cell

Climbing fiber

Figure 8.10
Cellular organization of the cerebellum
Parallel fibers activate one Purkinje cell after another. Purkinje cells inhibit a target cell in one of the nuclei of the cerebellum. The more Purkinje cells that respond, the longer the target cell is inhibited. In this way, the cerebellum controls the duration of a movement.

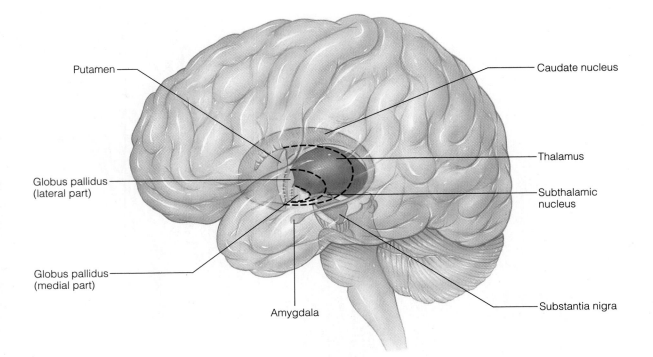

Putamen

Globus pallidus
(lateral part)

Globus pallidus
(medial part)

Amygdala

Caudate nucleus

Thalamus

Subthalamic
nucleus

Substantia nigra

**Figure 8.11
Location of the basal
ganglia**

and distance of movements, especially postural movements. Cells in the basal
ganglia become active before movements begin; for that reason, we believe that
they participate in planning and organizing the movements, not just in coordinating them. Unlike cells of the cerebellum, most basal ganglia cells are more
active prior to gradual movements than they are before fast, ballistic movements (DeLong, 1974).

Two medical disorders associated with damage to the basal ganglia are
Parkinson's disease and Huntington's disease, which we shall consider later in
this chapter. People who have impairments in the basal ganglia can move all
their muscles, but weakly and without coordination (DeLong et al., 1984; Marsden, 1984).

The Role of the Cerebral Cortex

Since the pioneering work of Gustav Fritsch and Eduard Hitzig (1870), neuroscientists have known that direct electrical stimulation of the motor cortex can
elicit movements. However, the motor cortex has no direct connections to the
muscles; it sends axons to the medulla and spinal cord, which in turn send
axons to the muscles. Electrical stimulation of the motor cortex generally produces a coordinated movement of several muscles, not an isolated movement
of a single muscle (Asanuma, 1981). In other words, the cortex (unlike the
spinal cord) is in charge of overall plans of movement, not individual muscle
contractions. The cerebral cortex is particularly important for the control of
complex actions. It contributes little to the control of coughing, sneezing, gag-
ging, laughing, or crying (Rinn, 1984). (Perhaps this lack of control by the cerebral cortex has something to do with why it is hard to perform those actions
voluntarily.)

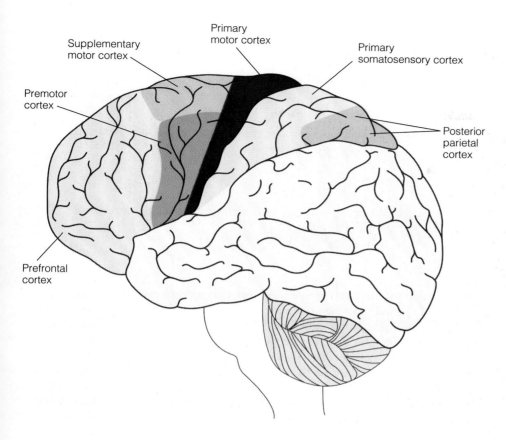

Primary
motor cortex

Supplementary
motor cortex

Primary
somatosensory cortex

Premotor
cortex

Posterior
parietal
cortex

Prefrontal
cortex

Figure 8.12
Principal areas of the motor cortex in the human brain
Cells in the premotor cortex and supplementary motor cortex are active during the planning of movements, even if the movements are never actually executed.

The Primary Motor Cortex and Neighboring Areas

The **primary motor cortex,** the greatest source of output to the spinal cord, is surrounded by other areas contributing to motor control, as shown in Figure 8.12. Those surrounding areas also send axons to the spinal cord, but in addition they help to guide the activity of the primary motor cortex.

The somatosensory cortex is the primary receiving area for touch and other body information. The somatosensory cortex sends a substantial number of axons to the spinal cord itself, as well as communicating with the primary motor cortex. The **prefrontal cortex** responds mostly to the sensory signals that lead to a movement (Goldman-Rakic, Bates, & Chafee, 1992). The **premotor cortex** is mostly active during the preparations before a movement and less active during the movement itself. The **supplementary motor cortex** is most active during the preparation before a rapid series of movements, such as if you were getting ready to touch your thumb to each of your four fingers in a particular order, as fast as possible (Roland, Larsen, Lassen, & Skinhøj, 1980). Cells in the premotor cortex and the supplementary motor cortex are active during the planning of a movement, even if the movement itself is never carried out.

Here is an experiment that illustrates the contributions of the prefrontal cortex and the premotor cortex: Monkeys were presented with a red or green light, which signaled whether they would later have to touch the red or green pad to get food. After a 1.25 second delay, the monkeys saw a second light, which meant that it was almost time to respond. The monkeys then had to wait at least another 1.25 seconds, but not more than 3.5 seconds, before touching

Brain Mechanisms of Movement

Figure 8.13
Movement vectors in the primary motor cortex
The direction of the line indicates that neurons tuned to that direction of movement are more active than other neurons are. The longer the line, the greater the dominance by the neurons tuned to that direction.

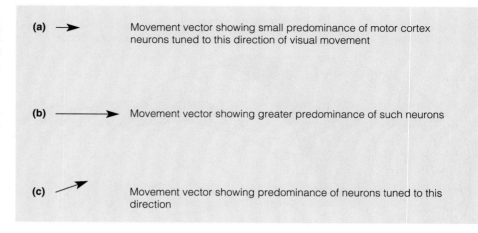

(a) → Movement vector showing small predominance of motor cortex neurons tuned to this direction of visual movement

(b) ⟶ Movement vector showing greater predominance of such neurons

(c) ↗ Movement vector showing predominance of neurons tuned to this direction

the correct pad, in order to receive some juice as a reinforcement (that is, the monkeys had to time their response correctly). The initial stimulus (the red or green light) provoked activity mostly in the prefrontal cortex. The second stimulus (indicating that the monkey needed to wait another 1.25 seconds before responding) also provoked activity mostly in the prefrontal cortex. Toward the end of that delay, just before the movement, cells in the premotor cortex became active (DiPelligrino & Wise, 1991). Thus, preparation for a movement seems to consist of waves of activity, first in the prefrontal cortex, then in the premotor cortex, then mostly in the primary motor cortex, and ultimately in the spinal cord and the muscles.

The Coding of Movement in the Primary Motor Cortex

Within the primary motor cortex, each area controls a different part of the body, as shown in Figure 4.21. This figure is, however, somewhat simplified; cells in a given location are most active during movement of a particular part (such as a finger), but also active to some extent during movement of adjacent parts (Schieber & Hibbard, 1993).

For the area responsible for control of the arm, most neurons are tuned to an approximate direction of movement. For example, one neuron might be most responsive in preparation for arm movements directly away from oneself, and slightly less active for movements a bit to the left or right of that target. Other neurons have other preferred directions, representing all possible angles.

At any point in time, an investigator can determine a *movement vector* to represent the activity of neurons in the motor cortex. For example, if the neurons tuned to a left-to-right movement are slightly more active than other neurons, we could represent this trend with a short line to the right, as in Figure 8.13a. A longer line to the right, as in Figure 8.13b, indicates that neurons tuned to a left-to-right movement are a great deal more active than are other neurons. A line at a different angle, as in Figure 8.13c, shows a predominant activity by neurons preferring some other angle of movement.

Now let us apply this system to the results of one experiment: Monkeys were trained to hold a lever in the center of a circle and then, under certain conditions, to pull that lever toward a light that flashed at some point along the radius of the circle. Under these conditions, the signal quickly elicited a move-

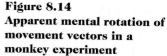

Figure 8.14
Apparent mental rotation of movement vectors in a monkey experiment
The monkey saw a light appear at the 0° direction; it had to move the lever to a position 90° counterclockwise from that direction. Just after the presentation of the light, the movement vector pointed weakly in the direction of the light. Over the next 0.3 seconds, the movement vector moved toward the correct direction. In effect, these results enable us to watch the monkey's brain activity as it mentally rotates the stimulus. (From Lurito, Georgakopoulos, & Georgopoulos, 1991.)

ment vector pointed toward the light, the same as the direction of the movement. So far, no surprise.

Then, under other conditions, the monkey had to move the lever to a spot 90° counterclockwise from the direction of the light. Here, the results looked like those in Figure 8.14: At first, the movement vector was short and pointed almost in the direction of the light. Over the next 0.3 seconds, the movement vector gradually changed, growing longer and moving in the direction of the eventual movement (Lurito, Georgakopoulos, & Georgopoulos, 1991). The gradual change in neural activity suggests that the monkey is doing a "mental rotation" from the direction of the original stimulus to the direction of the actual movement.

Connections from the Brain to the Spinal Cord

Axons from the brain to the spinal cord form systems that can be divided in several ways. One way is the distinction between the pyramidal system and the extrapyramidal system. The **pyramidal system** consists mainly of the axons from the primary motor cortex and adjacent areas. The axons of this system descend until they reach the medulla, at which point, most of them cross between the left and right sides of the nervous system in distinctive swellings called **pyramids,** as Figure 8.15a shows. The axons then continue to interneurons or motor neurons in the medulla and spinal cord. For that reason, the pyramidal system is also called the corticospinal tract.

The **extrapyramidal system** consists of all the movement-controlling areas other than the pyramidal system. As Figure 8.15b illustrates, axons from the basal ganglia and diffuse areas of the cerebral cortex converge onto the red nucleus, the reticular formation, the **vestibular nucleus,** and some adjacent areas. Each of those areas then sends axons to the medulla and spinal cord. You will sometimes hear the expression **extrapyramidal symptoms;** for example, certain drugs produce extrapyramidal symptoms as side effects. That expression refers to clumsy, ill-coordinated movements similar to those associated with damage to the basal ganglia and other extrapyramidal structures.

Another distinction is the one between the dorsolateral tract and the ventromedial tract. The pyramidal system largely overlaps the dorsolateral tract and the extrapyramidal system largely overlaps the ventromedial tract. But the pairs of terms are not synonymous; there are some important distinctions.

Figure 8.15
The dorsolateral tract and the ventromedial tract

(a) *The dorsolateral tract, which controls the most precise and most discrete movements, especially in peripheral muscles such as those of a hand or finger.*

Facing page: (b) *The ventromedial tract, which controls trunk movements and bilateral movements, including standing, walking, and adjusting posture.*

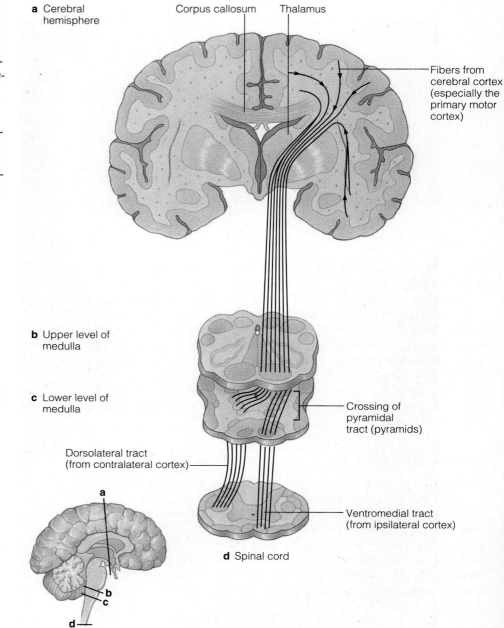

a Cerebral hemisphere

Corpus callosum   Thalamus

Fibers from cerebral cortex (especially the primary motor cortex)

b Upper level of medulla

c Lower level of medulla

Crossing of pyramidal tract (pyramids)

Dorsolateral tract (from contralateral cortex)

Ventromedial tract (from ipsilateral cortex)

d Spinal cord

The **dorsolateral tract** of the spinal cord includes the cortical fibers that cross from one side to the other at the pyramids, plus the fibers from the red nucleus (which also cross). (See Figure 8.15a.) The **ventromedial tract** is composed of the remaining fibers from the cortex—the fibers that did not cross—plus all the fibers from the reticular formation and the vestibular nucleus (which do not cross). (See Figure 8.15b.) Once the ventromedial tract reaches the spinal cord, its axons contact cells that branch to both sides of the cord; thus, the impact of the ventromedial tract is bilateral, not just ipsilateral.

Figure 8.15 continued

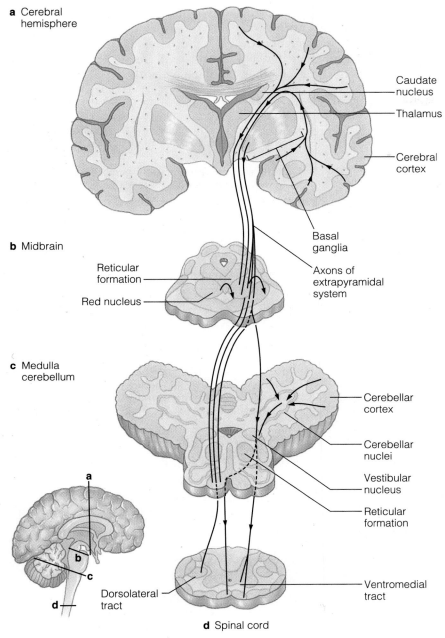

a Cerebral hemisphere

Caudate nucleus

Thalamus

Cerebral cortex

b Midbrain

Reticular formation

Red nucleus

Basal ganglia

Axons of extrapyramidal system

c Medulla cerebellum

Cerebellar cortex

Cerebellar nuclei

Vestibular nucleus

Reticular formation

Dorsolateral tract

Ventromedial tract

d Spinal cord

b

The dorsolateral tract controls movements in the periphery of the body, such as the hands, fingers, and toes. The dorsolateral tract from one side of the brain controls the opposite side of the body. After damage to this system, people suffer at least a temporary paralysis of those movements.

The ventromedial tract controls movements near the midline of the body, such as bending and turning of the trunk, back, or neck (Kuypers, 1989). Note that these movements are necessarily bilateral; you can move your fingers on one side and not the other, but you cannot move your neck on one side and not

Brain Mechanisms of Movement

the other. Damage to the ventromedial tract impairs walking, turning, bending, standing up, and sitting down.

Ordinarily, most movements rely on both pyramidal and extrapyramidal influences and both dorsomedial and ventrolateral tracts. The motor systems work in cooperation with each other, not independently.

Summary

1. The spinal cord contains the mechanisms for many motor programs such as walking, running, and scratching. It can generate rhythmic movements on its own. (p. 285)

2. The cerebellum helps to generate ballistic movements and to link individual movements into rapid, coordinated sequences. (p. 286)

3. After damage to the cerebellum, people have trouble with rapid alternating movements, saccadic eye movements, and rapid movements requiring accurate aim. (p. 286)

4. The cells of the cerebellum are arranged in a very regular pattern that enables them to produce outputs of well-controlled duration. (p. 288)

5. The basal ganglia are a group of large subcortical structures that control the direction and amplitude of movements, especially postural movements. (p. 288)

6. The pyramidal system is a set of neurons, located mostly in the primary motor cortex and adjacent areas, whose axons extend directly to the medulla and spinal cord. The pyramidal system controls fine movements, especially of the extremities. (p. 293)

7. The extrapyramidal system includes cortical and other neurons that send information to the red nucleus, the reticular formation, and other structures in the midbrain. Those structures in turn send their output to the medulla and spinal cord, controlling less precise movements than the pyramidal system does. The extrapyramidal system is especially important for postural movements. (p. 293)

8. Most of the pyramidal system fibers and some of the extrapyramidal system fibers cross to the opposite side of the spinal cord, forming the dorsolateral tract. The dorsolateral tract controls movements in the periphery of the body. (p. 294)

9. The fibers that do not cross sides in the spinal cord constitute the ventromedial tract. The ventromedial tract controls bilateral movements near the midline of the body. (p. 294)

Review Questions

1. What evidence supports the conclusion that the spinal cord directly controls certain motor programs? (p. 285)

2. Do cells in the cerebellum and basal ganglia become active before a movement or only during and after the movement? (pp. 286, 290)

3. What kind of brain damage produces motor effects that resemble those of alcoholic intoxication and why? (p. 288)

4. From what structures does the cerebellum receive input? To which structures does it send output? (p. 288)

5. Name the structures that compose the basal ganglia. (p. 288)

6. List the main differences between the pyramidal system and the extrapyramidal system. (p. 293)

7. What is the difference in function between the dorsolateral and ventromedial tracts of the spinal cord? (p. 294)

Thought Question

1. Human infants are at first limited to gross movements of the trunk, arms, and legs. The ability to move one finger at a time matures gradually over more than the first year. What hypothesis would you suggest about which brain areas controlling movement mature early and which ones mature later?

Suggestion for Further Reading

Georgopoulos, A. P. (1991). Higher order motor control. *Annual Review of Neuroscience, 14,* 361–377. Review of the contributions of various brain areas to the control of movement.

Terms

saccade rapid movement of the eyes from one fixation point to another (p. 287)

cerebellar cortex outer covering of the cerebellum (p. 288)

Purkinje cell a neuron type in the cerebellum; the type of neuron responsible for all the output from the cerebellar cortex to the cerebellar nuclei (p. 288)

parallel fiber axon that runs perpendicular to the planes of the Purkinje cells in the cerebellum (p. 288)

nuclei of the cerebellum clusters of neurons in the interior of the cerebellum that send axons to motor-controlling areas outside the cerebellum (p. 288)

red nucleus nucleus midbrain structure whose axons join the dorsolateral tract of the spinal cord, controlling distal muscles of the body such as those in the hands and feet (p. 288)

caudate nucleus, putamen, globus pallidus, substantia nigra, subthalamic nucleus structures of the basal ganglia (p. 288)

primary motor cortex area of the frontal cortex just anterior to the central sulcus; a primary point of origin for axons of the pyramidal system of motor control (p. 291)

prefrontal cortex the anterior portion of the frontal lobe of the cortex (p. 291)

premotor cortex area of the frontal cortex, just anterior to the primary motor cortex, active during the planning of a movement (p. 291)

supplementary motor cortex area of the frontal cortex active during the planning of a movement (p. 291)

pyramidal system structure originating mostly in the precentral and postcentral gyri whose axons cross in the pyramids of the medulla and extend to neurons in the medulla or spinal cord; important for control of discrete movements (p. 293)

pyramid swelling in the medulla where pyramidal system axons cross from one side of the brain to the opposite side of the spinal cord (p. 293)

extrapyramidal system movement-controlling areas other than the pyramidal system, especially the basal ganglia, red nucleus, reticular formation, vestibular nucleus, and adjacent areas (p. 293)

vestibular nucleus cluster of neurons in the brain stem, primarily responsible for motor responses to vestibular sensation (p. 293)

extrapyramidal symptoms disruption of movement resulting from damage to part of the extrapyramidal system (p. 293)

dorsolateral tract a path of axons in the spinal cord from the ipsilateral hemisphere of the brain, controlling movements of peripheral muscles (p. 294)

ventromedial tract a path of axons in the spinal cord providing bilateral control of the trunk muscles (p. 294)

Disorders of Movement

Even if your nervous system and muscles are completely healthy, you may sometimes find it difficult to move in the way you would like. For example, if you have just finished a bout of unusually strenuous exercise, your muscles may be so fatigued that you can hardly move them voluntarily, even though they constantly twitch. Or if your legs "fall asleep" while you are sitting in an awkward position, you may stumble and fall when you try to walk.

Certain neurological disorders produce exaggerated and lasting movement limitations. Some people suffer permanent fatigue and constant twitching. Others lose the ability to perform even simple, everyday movements, although their muscles are intact. We shall consider a few examples of such disorders.

Myasthenia Gravis

Myasthenia gravis (MY-us-THEE-nee-uh GRAHV-iss) is an autoimmune disease—that is, a disease in which the immune system forms antibodies against part of itself. In myasthenia gravis, the immune system attacks the acetylcholine receptors at neuromuscular junctions (Shah & Lisak, 1993). A rare condition, myasthenia gravis is responsible each year for the deaths of about two or three people per 100,000 over the age of 75; it affects younger people less often (Chandra, Bharucha, & Schoenberg, 1984).

The symptoms of myasthenia gravis are progressive weakness and rapid fatigue of the striated muscles. As a result, any repeated movement rapidly gets weaker unless the person pauses to rest. Because the muscles have fewer than the normal number of acetylcholine receptors, the remaining receptors need the maximum amount of transmitter to move the muscles normally. After any motor neuron has fired a few times in quick succession, later action potentials release fewer quanta of acetylcholine. A slight decline in acetylcholine is no problem for healthy people, because they have an abundance of acetylcholine receptors. In people with myasthenia gravis, transmission at the neuromuscular junction is precarious at best, and even a slight decline in acetylcholine availability has powerful effects (Drachman, 1978).

Myasthenia gravis can be treated with drugs that suppress the immune system (Shah & Lisak, 1993). That approach has its limitations, of course, because suppression of the immune system leaves the patient vulnerable to other illnesses. Many physicians also prescribe drugs that inhibit the enzyme

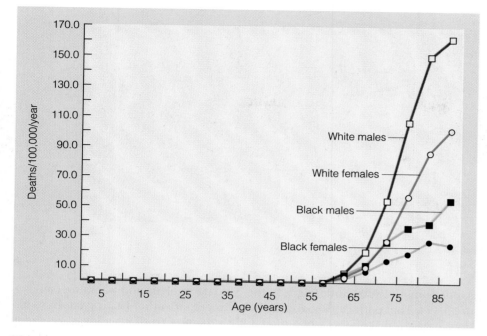

Figure 8.16
The number of people who die from causes related to Parkinson's disease
Note that the number increases rapidly after age 65 and that the disorder affects more white than nonwhite people. (Based on Chandra et al., 1984.)

acetylcholinesterase, which breaks down acetylcholine. By inhibiting the breakdown of acetylcholine, such drugs prolong the action of acetylcholine at the neuromuscular junction. A physician must monitor the dose carefully, however, as an excess can impair the muscles just as badly as myasthenia gravis does.

Parkinson's Disease

Parkinson's disease and Huntington's disease are called extrapyramidal disorders because they result from a disorder somewhere in the extrapyramidal system. Both are characterized by abnormal movements, not by paralysis. **Parkinson's disease** is an affliction that occurs mostly in the elderly. The main symptoms are slow movements, difficulty initiating movements, rigidity of the muscles, tremors, and sometimes intellectual impairment and depressed mood (Miller & DeLong, 1988). The symptoms vary substantially from one person to another, making diagnosis difficult (Koller, 1992). Among people over age 75, Parkinson's disease is responsible for the death of about one person per 1,000, with a higher rate among whites than blacks in the United States (Chandra, Bharucha, & Schoenberg, 1984). (See Figure 8.16.)

The immediate cause of Parkinson's disease is the gradual, progressive degeneration of various parts of the brain, especially the dopamine-containing

Figure 8.17
**The pathway from the
substantia nigra to the
caudate nucleus and
putamen**
*This is the location of the
most severe brain damage in
Parkinson's disease.*

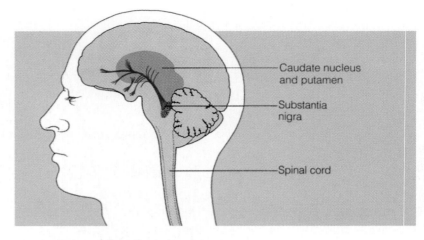

axons from the substantia nigra to the caudate nucleus and putamen (see Figure 8.17). That pathway apparently helps to prepare other brain systems to initiate organized sequences of actions. With damage to that pathway, a person has trouble getting started on either a movement or a cognitive task such as problem solving (Marsden, 1992; Robbins & Everitt, 1992).

Possible Causes of Parkinson's Disease

Parkinson's disease, in contrast to most other serious neurological or psychological disorders, does not appear to have a strong hereditary basis. In most cases, even having an identical twin with Parkinson's disease does not greatly increase one's risk of contracting the disease (Duvoisin, Eldridge, Williams, Nutt, & Calne, 1981). However, when one identical twin has Parkinson's and the other does not, the non-Parkinson's twin generally has somewhat below-normal levels of dopamine synapses, intermediate between the normal level and the typical Parkinsonian level (Burn et al., 1992). A likely interpretation is that certain genes may increase or decrease a person's vulnerability to Parkinson's, as indicated by the dopamine synapses, although something in the environment determines whether the predisposition progresses to the stage of being a noticeable disorder.

Possible environmental factors include an interruption of blood flow to certain parts of the brain, prolonged exposure to certain drugs, a history of encephalitis or other viral infections, and exposure to toxic substances (Jenner, 1990). The possibility of a toxic cause for Parkinson's disease was discovered by accident (Ballard, Tetrud, & Langston, 1985). In 1982, several young adults (ages 22 to 42) in northern California developed symptoms of Parkinson's disease after using a heroin substitute, which all of them had bought from the same dealer. (See Digression 8.2.) At first, physicians resisted diagnosing their condition as Parkinson's disease, because the patients were so young. Eventually, however, it became clear that the symptoms matched those of Parkinson's disease. Before the investigators had a chance to alert the community to the danger of the heroin substitute, a number of other people had used it. Some of them developed severe, eventually fatal Parkinson's disease. Others

The United States enforces laws against the manufacture, sale, or use of many drugs that are regarded as harmful. Heroin is one such drug. One way to evade the law is to sell a drug that produces similar effects but is chemically different, even if the difference is as minor as, say, substituting a methyl group for a single hydrogen ion. The laws apply to heroin and other drugs that the federal government has chemically identified and listed. They do not apply to new drugs that have never been sold before.

Because of this enormous loophole in the legal system, certain drug dealers manufacture "designer drugs"—drugs that may produce effects similar to heroin (or whatever) and that remain technically legal until the government obtains enough of them to determine what they are and passes a law against them. Although the risk to the drug dealer is low, the risk to the user is unknown and may in certain cases be severe.

developed milder symptoms (Tetrud, Langston, Garbe, & Ruttenber, 1989). Still others have developed no symptoms so far, although their substantia nigras have suffered some damage (Calne et al., 1985). These people are probably at serious risk for developing Parkinson's disease later in life.

The heroin substitute that these people used was a mixture of two chemicals: MPPP and MPTP. The body converts **MPTP** to a related chemical, **MPP$^+$**, which accumulates in, and then destroys, neurons that release dopamine as their neurotransmitter (Nicklas, Saporito, Basma, Geller, & Heikkila, 1992). Postsynaptic neurons compensate for the loss of their usual dopamine input by increasing their number of dopamine receptors (Chiueh, 1988; see Figure 8.18). The symptoms of Parkinson's disease result partly from the decrease in dopamine input and partly from the jumpy overresponsiveness of the extra receptors (Miller & DeLong, 1988).

No one supposes that illegal drug use causes very many cases of Parkinson's disease. A more likely hypothesis is that people sometimes expose themselves to MPTP or similar chemicals present in air or water pollution. A number of herbicides and pesticides, including *paraquat,* have a chemical structure similar to that of MPTP and MPP$^+$ (see Figure 8.19). One study of Parkinson's patients with early onset of symptoms (at 50 years or less) found that a higher-than-normal proportion of them had been exposed to large amounts of insecticides and herbicides (Butterfield, Valanis, Spencer, Lindeman, & Nutt, 1993).

The toxin-exposure hypothesis has some problems, however (Jenner, Schapira, & Marsden, 1992; Spencer, Ludolph, & Kisby, 1992). One is the time course: If a toxic substance causes Parkinson's disease, why does the condition generally start in old age and grow gradually, steadily worse over time? A possible but speculative answer is that the effects of exposure to a toxin early in life combine with the effects of a natural loss of neurons through the aging process (Morgan & Finch, 1988). The brain can withstand a moderate loss of neurons in the substantia nigra; symptoms of Parkinson's disease emerge only after the number of surviving neurons dips below about one-fifth of the original total (Zigmond et al., 1990).

A second problem is the geographical distribution: Presuming that toxins occur in some places and not others, we might expect near-epidemics in some regions and few cases elsewhere. The actual distribution is more scattered. For

Figure 8.18
The results of injecting MPP⁺ into one hemisphere of a rat brain, as revealed by autoradiography
The upper part shows D_2 dopamine receptors; the lower part shows axon terminals that contain dopamine. Red indicates the highest level of activity, followed by yellow, green, and blue. Note that the MPP⁺ greatly depleted the number of dopamine axons and that the number of D_2 receptors increased in response to this lack of input. However, the net result is a great decrease in dopamine activity. (From Chiueh, 1988.)

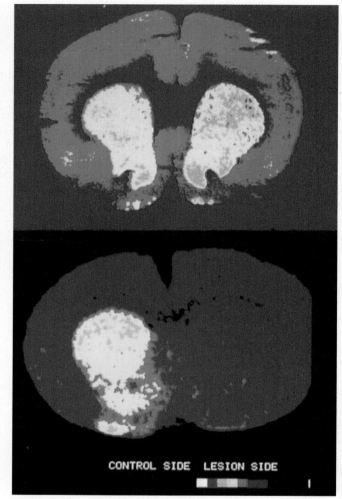

CONTROL SIDE   LESION SIDE

Figure 8.19
The chemical structures of MPPP, MPTP, MPP⁺, and paraquat

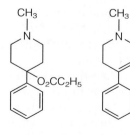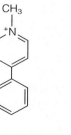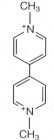

MPPP   **MPTP**   **MPP⁺**   **Paraquat**

this problem, a possible reply is to suggest an interaction between toxic substances and genetic differences in vulnerability, perhaps based on genes that control the body's defenses against certain harmful chemicals (C. Smith et al., 1992).

L-dopa Treatment for Parkinson's Disease

The traditional goal of therapy has been to replace the missing dopamine. A patient cannot simply take dopamine pills or injections because dopamine does not cross the blood-brain barrier. **L-dopa**, a precursor to dopamine (see Figure 3.9), does cross the barrier, however. Most people with Parkinson's disease take L-dopa pills daily, often in conjunction with other drugs. After L-dopa reaches the brain, neurons convert it to dopamine, which largely relieves the symptoms of Parkinson's disease. It does not cure the underlying problem, however, and the gradual destruction of dopamine-containing axons continues.

Moreover, L-dopa produces harmful side effects, including nausea, restlessness, sleep problems, low blood pressure, stereotyped movements, and occasionally hallucinations and delusions. Drugs that stimulate dopamine receptors produce similar repetitive movements in rats, including walking forward, circling, pivoting tightly, and moving the forequarters from side to side. If the rat walks into a corner or to the end of a tube, it may get trapped there, unable to turn around or back up (Szechtman, Ornstein, Teitelbaum, & Golani, 1985). Evidently, while L-dopa relieves the symptoms of dopamine deficiency, it occasionally overstimulates certain dopamine synapses.

The side effects of L-dopa can be relieved somewhat by additional drugs that prevent L-dopa from being converted to dopamine before it enters the brain (Dakof & Mendelsohn, 1986). They can also be minimized by delivering L-dopa through various slow-release devices. The usual forms of delivery—pills or injections—subject the brain to sudden pulses of large quantities of L-dopa, which lead to changes in the dopamine receptors and ultimately to periods of overstimulation (T. N. Chase et al., 1989; Obeso et al., 1989). Slow release minimizes those changes.

The side effects of L-dopa generally grow worse after someone has taken the medication for a long time. Some physicians delay giving the medication as long as possible in hopes of minimizing the side effects. The research does not support the effectiveness of those delays, however (Markham & Diamond, 1981); the side effects probably grow worse over time simply because the underlying disease grows worse over time, not because of the cumulative effects of taking L-dopa.

New Therapies for Parkinson's Disease

The research on MPTP has led to a new treatment for Parkinson's disease. MPTP itself is harmless; it becomes dangerous after an enzyme called *monoamine oxidase B* converts it to MPP$^+$. Consequently, any drug that blocks monoamine oxidase B prevents the damage caused by MPTP.

Even if MPTP itself is not ordinarily the cause of Parkinson's disease, other similar chemicals might be. With that in mind, investigators tested the effect of **deprenyl** (an inhibitor of monoamine oxidase B) on Parkinson's disease. Two groups of human patients with mild Parkinson's disease were randomly assigned to receive either deprenyl or a placebo. Those receiving the placebo deteriorated more rapidly (Tetrud & Langston, 1989). In other words, deprenyl actually slowed the progress of the disease. In contrast, L-dopa merely decreases the symptoms, while the underlying disease continues at its own pace.

Another possible strategy is to transplant fetal cells into the damaged portion of the brain, producing a "brain graft" that provides the missing dopamine (Björklund, 1992). We shall consider that possibility more fully in Chapter 15; at this point, let me simply say that the results have been inconsistent, and the possibility remains uncertain and controversial.

Still another approach: It is possible to grow cells in tissue culture, genetically alter them so that they produce large quantities of L-dopa, and then transplant them into the brain. The drawback to this approach is that such altered cells often cause tumors. Various neuroscientists are trying to find a way to produce cells with the desired properties without the tumorous tendencies (Jiao, Gurevich, & Wolff, 1993).

Huntington's Disease

Huntington's disease, also known as *Huntington's chorea,* is a severe neurological disorder related to damage in the caudate nucleus and putamen. The motor symptoms usually begin with a facial twitch; later, tremors spread to other parts of the body. Walking, speech, and other voluntary movements become slow and clumsy at first; eventually, they become impossible (McHugh, 1989).

In addition, people with Huntington's disease suffer psychological disorders, which may be noticed before the motor symptoms. Among the psychological symptoms are depression, memory impairment, anxiety, hallucinations and delusions, poor judgment, alcohol and drug abuse, and anything from a total lack of sexual responsiveness to indiscriminate sexual promiscuity (Shoulson, 1990).

The most common age of onset is 30 to 50, although cases are known with onset in childhood or in old age. Once the symptoms emerge, both the psychological and the motor symptoms grow progressively worse over a period of about 15 years, culminating in death (Chase, Wexler, & Barbeau, 1979). About 50 people per million in the United States eventually develop Huntington's disease.

Nature of the Brain Damage in Huntington's Disease

Huntington's disease is characterized by a progressive loss of neurons, especially in the caudate nucleus, putamen, and globus pallidus, with some loss in the cerebral cortex. The overall brain weight may decline by 15 to 20 percent before death (Sanberg & Coyle, 1984). Unlike patients with Parkinson's disease, who suffer damage mostly in just the substantia nigra, patients with Huntington's disease suffer more widespread damage. They especially lose cells with glutamate receptors in the basal ganglia (Young et al., 1988).

An injection of **kainic acid** or **quinolinic acid** into the caudate nucleus and putamen of rats produces both movement disorders and a pattern of brain damage that mimic Huntington's disease (Meldrum, 1990). Both kainic acid and quinolinic acid resemble the neurotransmitter *glutamate;* they damage neurons by overstimulating them. Thus, one hypothesis is that people with Huntington's disease produce chemicals that overstimulate and kill neurons.

Heredity and Presymptomatic Testing for Huntington's Disease

Huntington's disease is controlled by an autosomal dominant gene. That is, a person who has the gene will eventually develop the disease and will transmit the gene to about half of his or her children, on the average.

Imagine that, at the age of 20, you learn that one of your parents has Huntington's disease. You now know that you have a 50 percent chance of developing it yourself, probably in about 20 years. In addition to your grief about your parent's agony, your life will change in two ways. First, whenever you do something clumsy or experience a slight tremor anywhere in your body, you will fear that it is the start of Huntington's disease. Second, you may have trouble deciding whether to have children. You may decide that you would not want to have children if you have the gene for Huntington's disease. But how can you find out whether you have the gene, while you are still young enough to start a family?

Investigators worked for many years to discover an accurate **presymptomatic test**—a test of whether someone who seems healthy now is likely to develop the disease later. In the 1980s, they developed a partially accurate method based on direct examination of the chromosomes. At that time, they established that the gene for Huntington's disease was located on human chromosome number 4, although they did not yet know the gene's exact location. To determine whether or not a person was at high risk for Huntington's disease, one would examine certain markers on that person's chromosome 4 and then compare those with chromosomal markers for various relatives. If the person's markers matched those of relatives with Huntington's disease, then that person had a high risk of getting Huntington's disease as well (Folstein et al., 1985; Gusella et al., 1983). This test had its limitations: It required the cooperation of a number of relatives, even under the best circumstances it was only about 95% accurate, and it was sometimes completely indecisive. (For example, if the parent with Huntington's disease had the same markers as the other parent, then the results for the children could be ambiguous.)

Then, in 1993, researchers identified the Huntington's gene itself (Huntington's Disease Collaborative Research Group, 1993). Now it is possible to predict whether or not someone will get Huntington's disease, with nearly 100% accuracy, by examining that person's chromosomes. (No tests of relatives are necessary.) If you had a parent with Huntington's disease, would you want to have your chromosomes examined? Many do; others decide they would rather live with uncertainty than run the risk of getting bad news. When people who take the test do get bad news, they generally accept it with no apparent increase in distress or depression (Wiggins et al., 1992). Nevertheless, anyone taking the test should have access to counseling to deal with the results.

Now that researchers have identified the gene causing Huntington's disease, that information may lead to a greater understanding of the disease itself. The affected gene, in its normal form, includes at one point a sequence of bases "C-A-G" (cytosine, adenine, guanine), repeated 11 to 24 times, and occasionally as many as 34 times in some individuals. In people with Huntington's disease, that sequence is repeated at least 42 times, sometimes 66 or more times (Huntington's Disease Collaborative Research Group, 1993). Those extra repetitions are apparently the source of the disease. At this point, no one knows what the resulting protein actually does. We know that it occurs fairly widely in the brain, but we do not know what it is doing there. After neuroscientists learn more about this protein, perhaps they will find ways to prevent or alleviate the symptoms of this dreadful disease.

A few comments in conclusion: The control of movement is an important topic for psychology as well as for biology. The inability to make certain movements may mean that the muscles are paralyzed, but it can also mean that the brain has difficulty planning the movements or conveying the plan from one part of the brain to another. Disorders such as Parkinson's disease and Huntington's disease are known mostly for their effect on movement, but they are also linked to abnormalities of thought and mood. In short, the brain mechanisms that control movement are not tacked on at the end of all the "psychological" processes; they are an integral part of everything that the brain does.

Summary

1. In myasthenia gravis, the body's immune system attacks the neuromuscular junctions. The disease is treated by suppressing the immune system and by prolonging the actions of acetylcholine at the neuromuscular junction. (p. 298)

2. Parkinson's disease is characterized by slow movements, tremor, rigidity, and, in most cases, depression. It is associated with degeneration of dopamine-containing axons from the substantia nigra to the caudate nucleus and putamen. Generally, it is treated with L-dopa, which the brain can convert into dopamine, or with deprenyl, which inhibits the enzyme monoamine oxidase B. (p. 299)

3. The chemical MPTP selectively damages neurons in the substantia nigra and leads to the symptoms of Parkinson's disease. Certain herbicides and pesticides are chemically similar to MPTP. Drugs that prevent the breakdown of MPTP into MPP^+ appear to be useful in slowing the progress of Parkinson's disease. (p. 300)

4. Huntington's disease is a hereditary condition marked by deterioration of motor control, plus depression, memory impairment, and other cognitive disorders. It generally has its onset at age 30 to 50. (p. 304)

5. In Huntington's disease, numerous brain cells, especially in the basal ganglia, die. It is possible to mimic the disease in animals by injections of kainic acid or quinolinic acid. (p. 305)

6. By examining a portion of chromosome 4, physicians can determine whether or not a person is likely to develop Huntington's disease later in life. (p. 305)

Review Questions

1. What causes myasthenia gravis? How can the condition be treated? (p. 298)

2. Which two drugs are used in the treatment of Parkinson's disease? How does each of them work? (p. 303)

3. What are the symptoms of Huntington's disease? What is the usual age of onset? (p. 304)

4. What chemicals can produce brain damage that mimics the damage found in Huntington's disease? How do they do so? (p. 305)

5. What procedure enables physicians to determine which people are most likely to get Huntington's disease? (p. 305)

Thought Question

1. What effect would haloperidol probably have for someone suffering from Parkinson's disease?

Suggestion for Further Reading

Geschwind, N. (1975). The apraxias. *American Scientist, 63,* 188–195. Discusses movement disorders in relationship to localized human brain damage.

Terms

myasthenia gravis autoimmune disease in which the body forms antibodies against the acetylcholine receptors at neuromuscular junctions (p. 298)

Parkinson's disease malady caused by damage to a dopamine pathway, resulting in slow movements, difficulty initiating movements, rigidity of the muscles, and tremors (p. 299)

MPTP, MPP$^+$ chemicals known to be toxic to the dopamine-containing cells in the substantia nigra, capable of producing the symptoms of Parkinson's disease (p. 301)

L-dopa chemical precursor of dopamine and other catecholamines (p. 303)

deprenyl drug that inhibits the enzyme monoamine oxidase B; found to slow the progress of Parkinson's disease (p. 303)

Huntington's disease an inherited disorder characterized by tremor, movement disorder, and psychological symptoms, including depression, memory impairment, hallucinations, and delusions (p. 304)

kainic acid chemical similar to glutamate that destroys cell bodies in contact with it but does not destroy passing axons (p. 305)

quinolinic acid chemical resembling glutamate that kills certain neurons by overstimulating them (p. 305)

presymptomatic test exam to predict the onset of a disease, conducted before any symptoms appear (p. 305)

RHYTHMS OF WAKEFULNESS AND SLEEP

NASA

CHAPTER NINE

1. Wakefulness and sleep, as well as temperature and other body activities, vary on a cycle of approximately 24 hours. The body itself generates this cycle.

2. People can suffer insomnia if their biological rhythm is out of phase with the prescribed time for sleeping.

3. Sleep progresses through four stages, which differ in brain activity, heart rate, and other signs of arousal.

4. A special type of stage 1 sleep, known as paradoxical sleep or REM sleep, is light sleep in some ways and deep sleep in others. It is associated with dreaming, especially with vivid dreaming.

5. The reticular formation is important for arousal of the brain. Certain areas of the brain are believed to be important for the control of sleep, although the exact nature of their contribution is not yet clear.

6. For a variety of reasons, many people do not sleep well enough to feel rested the following day.

Suppose you are an astronaut who has just made the flight to Daynite, a planet in another solar system. Daynite rotates on its axis only once a year; that is, it always keeps the same side facing its sun, and no part of the planet alternates between day and night. Nearly all animals and plants live in a "twilight zone" around the border between light and dark. The animals, having had a very different evolutionary history from any species on Earth, exhibit numerous peculiarities. One is that none of them ever sleeps.

Although you may be surprised to find animals that never sleep, your reaction hardly compares with the reaction of the Daynitian astronauts who simultaneously make their first visit to Earth. They marvel that about once every 365th of a year each animal lies down and stops moving. After these strange Earthlings appear to have been dead for a few hours, they spontaneously come back to life again! The Daynitians wonder, "What on Earth is going on?"

For the purposes of this chapter, let us adopt the perspective of the Daynitians and ask why animals as active as we are spend one-third of our lives doing so little.

The Alternation of Waking and Sleeping

When you learn that your body spontaneously generates its own rhythm of wakefulness and sleep, you are, I suspect, not particularly surprised. Psychologists of an earlier era, however, considered that idea revolutionary. The research of Curt Richter (1922) and others strongly suggested that the body generates its own cycles of activity and inactivity, but psychologists were ill-prepared to accept this news. According to psychological theories prevalent from the 1920s through the 1950s, nearly all behavior is a reaction to a stimulus. Therefore, cycles of wakefulness and sleep must depend on some cycle in the outside world—cycles of sunrise and sunset, or temperature fluctuations, or something else.

Gradually, the evidence became stronger, and eventually undeniable, that animals generate approximately 24-hour cycles of wakefulness and sleep even in an environment with unchanging light, temperature, noise, and every other variable that one can imagine. Thus, at least part of the impetus for behavior comes from within the body. This conception of wakefulness and sleep was an important discovery for psychology and an important step toward a view of the organism as an active producer of behaviors, not just a responder to stimuli.

Endogenous Cycles as a Preparation for External Changes

An animal that produced its behavior entirely as a response to current stimuli would be at a serious disadvantage; in many cases, an animal has to prepare for changes in sunlight and temperature before they occur. For example, most migratory birds start on their way toward their winter home while the weather in their summer home is still fairly warm. A bird that waited for the first frost would be in serious trouble. Similarly, squirrels begin storing nuts and putting on extra layers of fat in preparation for winter long before food becomes scarce. Animals that mate during only one season of the year go through extensive changes in both their anatomy and their behavior as the reproductive season approaches.

How do animals know what time of day or what time of year it is? For example, what tells migratory birds when to start flying? To some extent, they respond to changes in sunlight. When the ratio of daylight hours to dark hours declines to a certain point, it is time for the bird to head south. (Temperature is a much less reliable cue.) But after a bird has wintered in the tropics, how does it know when to return north? The ratio of daylight to dark is not a helpful cue because, in the tropics, it does not vary much from one season to

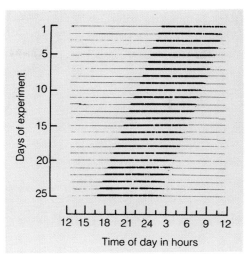

**Figure 9.1
Activity record of a flying squirrel kept in constant darkness**
The thickened segments indicate periods of activity as measured by a running wheel. Note that the free-running rhythm of activity and rest in this animal under conditions of constant darkness lasts slightly less than 24 hours. (From DeCoursey, 1960.)

another. For the same reason, temperature is uninformative. Migratory birds need an internal mechanism to judge when it is spring—in effect, an internal calendar. In one experiment, willow warblers (a European species) were captured from the wild and kept in cages with 12 hours of light alternating with 12 hours of darkness each day (Gwinner, 1986). For the next three years, the birds showed a characteristic *migratory restlessness* every fall and every spring.

Evidently, a mechanism somewhere in the bird's body generates a rhythm that prepares the bird for seasonal changes. We refer to that rhythm as an **endogenous circannual rhythm.** (*Endogenous* means *generated from within. Circannual* comes from the Latin words *circum,* for *about,* and *annum,* for *year.* An endogenous circannual rhythm is thus a self-generated rhythm that lasts about a year.) Similar mechanisms underlie a mammal's seasonal changes in reproduction, body fat, and hibernation. In nature, the daily onset of light and darkness fine-tunes such mechanisms to prevent them from running too fast or too slow.

Similarly, animals produce **endogenous circadian rhythms**—rhythms that last about a day. (*Circadian* comes from *circum,* for *about,* and *dies,* for *day.*) Our most familiar endogenous circadian rhythm is the one that controls wakefulness and sleepiness. If you go without sleep all night—as most college students do, sooner or later—you feel sleepier and sleepier as the night goes on, until early morning. But as morning arrives, you actually begin to feel less sleepy. Evidently, your urge to sleep depends on the time of day, not just on how recently you have slept.

Figure 9.1 represents the activity of an animal (in this case, a flying squirrel) kept in total darkness for 25 days. Each horizontal line represents one 24-hour day. A thickening in the line represents a period of activity by the animal. Even in this unchanging environment, animals generate a regular rhythm of activity and sleep. The self-generated cycle may be slightly shorter than 24 hours, as in Figure 9.1, or slightly longer, depending on whether the environment is constantly light or constantly dark and on whether the species is normally active in the light or in the dark (Carpenter & Grossberg, 1984). The cycle may also vary from one individual to another, even in the same environment. Nevertheless, the rhythm is highly consistent for a given individual in a given environment.

The Alternation of Waking and Sleeping

Figure 9.2
**Mean rectal temperatures
for nine adults**
*Body temperature reaches
its low for the day about 2
hours after sleep onset; it
reaches its peak about 6
hours before sleep onset.
(Based on data of Morris,
Lack, & Dawson, 1990.)*

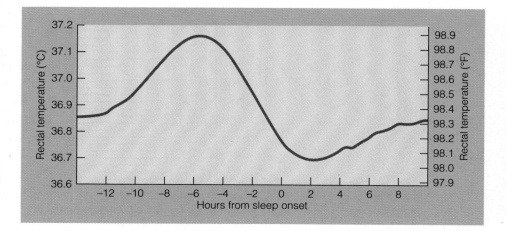

Mammals, including humans, have circadian rhythms in their waking and
sleeping, frequency of eating and drinking, body temperature, secretion of certain hormones, volume of urination, sensitivity to certain drugs (Moore-Ede,
Czeisler, & Richardson, 1983b), frequency of yawning (Anías, Holmgren, Urbá
Holmgren, & Eguíbar, 1984), and many other variables. For example, although
we ordinarily think of human body temperature as 37°C (98.6°F), normal temperature fluctuates over the course of a day from a low of about 36.7°C during
sleep to about 37.2°C in late afternoon or early evening (see Figure 9.2.) Ordinarily, all these cycles stay in synchrony with one another, suggesting that they
depend on a single master clock.

Setting and Resetting the Cycle

Although an animal's circadian rhythm can persist in the absence of light, light
is critical for periodically resetting the **biological clock** that underlies the
rhythm. A biological clock is the internal mechanism for controlling a behavior—such as sleep or migration—that recurs on a regular schedule. As an analogy, consider a wristwatch. I used to have a windup wristwatch that lost about
2 minutes per day. If I continued to wind the watch but never reset it, it would
be an hour slow after a month. We could say that it had a **free-running rhythm**
of 24 hours and 2 minutes. The biological clock is similar to my wristwatch.
Because its free-running rhythm is not exactly 24 hours, it has to be reset daily.
The stimulus that resets it is often referred to by the German term **zeitgeber**
(TSITE-gay-ber), meaning *time giver.* Light is the dominant zeitgeber for land
animals (Rusak & Zucker, 1979). (The tides are a more important zeitgeber for
certain marine animals.)

If a light cycle is not available as a reliable zeitgeber—for people living in a
cave, for example, or for blind people or astronauts in space—noises, meals,
social interactions, and temperature fluctuations can also act as zeitgebers.
However, the effectiveness of these nonvisual zeitgebers varies from one person to another. Most blind people manage to maintain a nearly normal circadian rhythm, but some do not. One blind man had a circadian rhythm of about
24¼ hours despite keeping a very regular activity schedule. Whenever his circadian rhythm happened to be in phase with his schedule, he slept well. When
it drifted out of phase, he slept poorly (Klein et al., 1993).

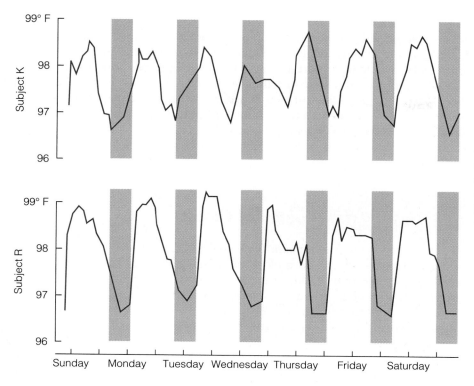

Figure 9.3
Curves of weekly body temperature of two men under an artificial routine of 19 hours of wakefulness and 9 hours of sleep
Shaded areas represent time in bed. Subject K's weekly record has seven 24-hour curves, but subject R adapted fairly well to the 28-hour schedule; the shaded areas show his temperature minima. (From Kleitman, 1963.)

Attempts to Alter the Biological Clock

Is it possible to change a person's biological clock so that it will produce a different endogenous rhythm? If humans moved to a planet with, say, 20-hour days or 30-hour days, would they adjust easily, or would they have to undergo countless generations of evolutionary change before they felt really at home? In an effort to answer such questions, two volunteers spent a month deep in an isolated part of Mammoth Cave in Kentucky (Kleitman, 1963). The temperature (12°C) and relative humidity (100 percent) were constant at all times, and the only light they saw was the artificial light controlled by a fixed schedule.

Throughout the month in the cave, the set schedule was a 28-hour day, with 19 hours of activity alternating with 9 hours of sleep. One subject (R in Figure 9.3) adjusted reasonably well to the new schedule; his body temperature cycle matched his activity cycle, with low body temperature occurring while he slept. However, he was always sleepy well before the scheduled bedtime, and he had trouble awakening at the scheduled times. The other subject (K in Figure 9.3) was much less successful. He continued to feel sleepy only at his usual bedtime, once every 24 hours, and his body temperature continued to fluctuate on a 24-hour cycle. He had great trouble getting to sleep when the artificial cycle was out of phase with his original cycle. Even by the end of the month, he showed no sign of adjusting to the 28-hour schedule.

Other experimenters have also attempted to train people or laboratory animals to follow a cycle other than 24 hours. As a rule, the adjustment is more successful if the imposed cycle is close to 24 hours. In one experiment, a group of 12 young people lived in a cavelike environment, isolated from natural light and other time cues, for 3 weeks. They agreed to go to bed when the clock said

The Alternation of Waking and Sleeping

11:45 P.M. and to awaken when it said 7:45 A.M. Although they did not know it, the clock initially ran normally and then gradually ran faster, until it was completing a day in only 22 hours. When the clock was completing a day in 23 hours, the people were alert during their wakeful periods and reported no trouble awakening on schedule or falling asleep on schedule. On a 22-hour schedule, however, only one subject kept pace with the clock. For the others, alertness rose and fell on a free-running 24-hour cycle that quickly drifted out of phase with the waking-sleeping schedule (Folkard, Hume, Minors, Waterhouse, & Watson, 1985). Evidently, humans find it difficult to adjust to a waking-sleeping cycle much different from 24 hours per day.

Resetting the Biological Clock

When evolution built in humans' biological clock, it missed. Instead of giving us a 24-hour clock, it gave us a clock of about 24½ or 24¾ hours. We have to readjust our internal workings every day to stay in phase with the outside world. On weekends, when most of us are freer to follow the dictates of our nature, we tend to stay awake later than usual and awaken later than usual. By Monday morning, when the electric clock says the time is 7 A.M., the biological clock says it is about 5 A.M. (Moore-Ede, Czeisler, & Richardson, 1983a). People who travel across time zones or who work odd schedules face special problems in resetting their biological clocks.

Jet Lag

Because the human biological clock tends to run slower than 24 hours, most of us find it easier to adjust to crossing time zones going west than going east. Going west, we stay awake later at night and awaken later in the morning than we would have at home. Going east, we go to sleep earlier and awaken earlier. In one study, a group of healthy young men reported psychological discomfort and unsatisfactory sleep after crossing seven time zones going east; they took 11 days to return to normal. A trip west over seven time zones produced no serious complaints (Désir et al., 1981). A disruption of biological rhythms due to crossing time zones is known as **jet lag** (Figure 9.4). (Before the rise of air travel, this phenomenon was known as "boat lag," experienced by transatlantic boat travelers.)

Shift Work and Night Shifts

People who have to sleep irregularly—such as pilots and truck drivers, medical interns, and shift workers in certain factories—find that their duration of sleep depends on their time of going to sleep. When they go to sleep in the morning or early afternoon, after working all night, they sleep only briefly (Frese & Harwich, 1984). They sleep the longest when they go to sleep in the early or middle part of the night. If they do not get to sleep until very late at night or early in the morning, they do not sleep for long (Winfree, 1983).

Some people work in factories or other jobs on a night shift, such as midnight to 8 A.M., and then sleep during the day. Even after working months or years on such a schedule, many workers fail to adjust fully. They continue to feel a little groggy while on the job, they do not sleep soundly during the day, and their body temperature continues to peak during the day, like that of most people, instead of peaking at night while they are working. In general, night-

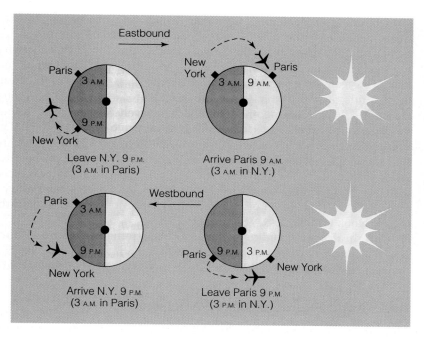

Figure 9.4
Jet lag
When people travel east, their new time is later than their home time. People who travel six time zones east must wake up when their biological clocks say it is the middle of the night; they must go to bed when their biological clocks say it is just late afternoon. Most people adjust more easily when they travel west; they stay up later at night and sleep later in the morning.

shift workers perform less well and have more accidents than day workers. In short, working at night does not reliably shift the circadian rhythm.

However, exposure to bright lights does. In one study, two groups of young men were active all night and slept during the day. One group was exposed to very bright lights (7,000 to 12,000 lux) during their night activity periods; the other was not. That level of lighting is extremely bright, comparable to the noonday sun. (A normally lit room at night has about 150 lux.) Within 6 days, the men who were exposed to the bright lights had readjusted. They were alert at night, they slept well during the day, and their body temperature reached its peak at night. The other group showed no signs of adjusting to the new schedule (Czeisler et al., 1990). The moral of the story: Night-shift workers should be exposed to bright lights during their work period.

Location and Nature of the Biological Clock

Given that our biological cycles are generated within the body, we must have a clock somewhere—a physical mechanism that produces 24-hour rhythms. The biological clock might depend on any number of possible mechanisms. We might imagine a device that counts heartbeats or breaths, for example, as an indication of the passage of time. Such a mechanism would be inaccurate, however; its speed would depend on the activity of the individual. Ideally, it should be like your wristwatch in its ability to keep time accurately no matter where you are or what you are doing.

Interference with the Biological Clock

Curt Richter found that the biological clock is insensitive to most forms of interference. An animal's circadian rhythm of activity and sleep remains intact

The Alternation of Waking and Sleeping

after blinding or deafening, although it may drift out of phase with the real world because of the loss of zeitgebers. The circadian rhythm is hardly disturbed at all by procedures that greatly modify the total level of activity, including food or water deprivation, x-rays, tranquilizers, LSD, alcohol, anesthesia, lack of oxygen, long periods of forced activity, long periods of forced inactivity, most kinds of brain damage, or the removal of any of the hormonal organs (Richter, 1967). Electroconvulsive shock severely depresses an animal's activity for about a week, but it does not disrupt the biological clock. The animal eventually resumes its activity periods at the normal time of day, indicating that the biological clock has been keeping track of the time during the animal's week of just sitting. In hamsters and certain other small animals, it is possible to lower body temperature for several hours, inducing a temporary hibernation. Even an hour or so of induced hibernation often fails to disturb the biological clock (Gibbs, 1983; Richter, 1975).

Certain drugs, including caffeine, other stimulants, and barbiturates, can act as zeitgebers to reset the clock (Ehret, Potter, & Dobra, 1975; Mayer & Scherer, 1975), although they do not change the length of the period.

Role of the Suprachiasmatic Nucleus

The surest way to disrupt the biological clock is to damage one key area of the hypothalamus—the **suprachiasmatic** (soo-pruh-kie-as-MAT-ik) **nucleus,** abbreviated **SCN.** It gets its name from the fact that it is located just above the optic chiasm (see Figure 9.5). The optic nerve sends some axons directly from the retina to the SCN. (Researchers are not sure whether those axons can be traced back to input from rods and cones, or whether they rely on input from some other, as yet undiscovered, kind of receptor.) If the SCN is damaged, or if it loses its input from the optic nerve, light can no longer reset the biological clock (Rusak, 1977). However, mice with a certain genetic condition that destroys almost all their rods and cones become virtually blind, even though light continues to reset the biological clock (Foster, 1993). In short, the visual pathway to the SCN is separate from the pathways responsible for pattern vision.

The SCN generates rhythms itself. If neurons of the SCN are removed from an animal's brain, or if they are left in place but are disconnected by cuts from the rest of the brain, the SCN neurons nevertheless produce a pattern of impulses that follows a circadian rhythm (Green & Gillette, 1982; Inouye & Kawamura, 1979). The mechanism by which SCN neurons generate circadian rhythms is still unknown.

The SCN alone is responsible for an animal's circadian rhythm of waking and sleeping. One group of experimenters discovered some hamsters bearing a mutant gene that caused them to produce not a 24-hour rhythm, but a 20-hour rhythm (Ralph & Menaker, 1988). They surgically removed the SCN from adult hamsters and then transplanted SCN tissue from hamster fetuses into the adults. When the experimenters transplanted SCNs from fetuses with a 20-hour rhythm, the recipients produced a 20-hour rhythm. When the experimenters transplanted SCNs from fetuses with a 24-hour rhythm, the recipients produced a 24-hour rhythm. The recipients' rhythm no longer matched their own genes, but the genes of the SCN donors (Ralph, Foster, Davis, & Menaker, 1990).

For an intact animal, the SCN is apparently the dominant force in all the body's circadian rhythms—for activity versus sleep, temperature, and so forth (Refinetti & Menaker, 1992). After damage to the SCN, animals' activity pattern becomes inconsistent and no longer responds to environmental patterns

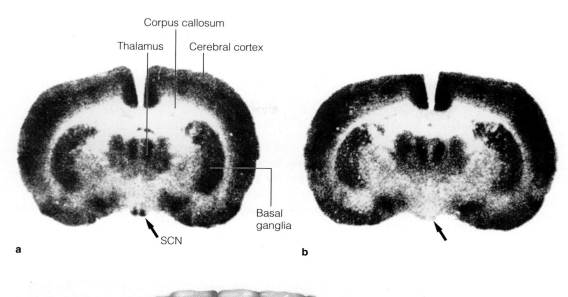

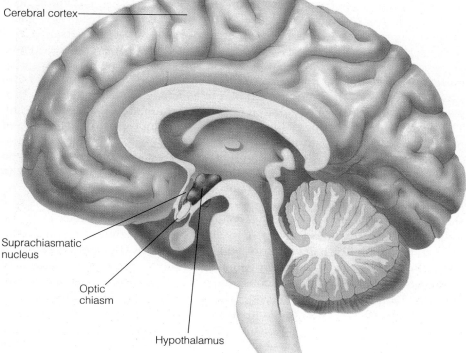

Figure 9.5
The suprachiasmatic nucleus (SCN) of rats, studied by autoradiography
*The SCN is located at the base of the brain, just above the optic chiasm, which has torn off in these coronal sections through the plane of the anterior hypothalamus. Each rat was injected with radioactive 2-deoxyglucose, which is absorbed by the most active neurons. A high level of absorption of this chemical produces a dark appearance on the slide. Note that the level of activity in SCN neurons is much higher in section (**a**), in which the rat was injected during the day, than it is in section (**b**), in which the rat received the injection at night. (From Schwartz & Gainer, 1977.) (**c**) A sagittal section through a human brain, showing location of the SCN.*

of light and dark. Their activity level rises and falls with other stimuli, however, such as the feeding schedule, or social stimuli, or the time when an experimenter cleans their cages (Mistlberger, 1992; Stephan, 1992).

The Functions of Sleep

The suprachiasmatic nucleus and other mechanisms of the biological clock control the timing of sleep, but they are not responsible for sleep itself, any more than they are responsible for eating, drinking, urinating, or any other activity that follows a circadian rhythm.

Presumably, animals would not have evolved mechanisms that provide alternating periods of activity and sleep unless sleep serves some important function. But exactly what is that function?

The Repair and Restoration Theory of Sleep

According to the **repair and restoration theory of sleep,** the function of sleep is to enable the body to repair itself after the exertions of the day. Many restorative processes—such as digestion, removal of waste products, and protein synthesis—occur during sleep (Adam, 1980). However, these same processes also occur during the waking state, and some of them actually occur more during the waking state than they do during sleep. James Horne's (1988) extensive review of the literature led him to conclude that sleep does not provide any special repair or restoration functions in humans, except in the brain. That is, the organs outside the brain get just as much repair during a relaxed wakeful state as they do during sleep.

The brain, however, is another story. You can rest your muscles while you are awake, but not your brain. A certain amount of sleep may be necessary to restore the brain to full functioning (Horne, 1988).

One way to examine how sleep restores the brain is to observe the effects of sleep deprivation. People who have gone without sleep for a week or more, either as an experiment or as a publicity stunt, report dizziness, impaired concentration, irritability, hand tremors, and hallucinations (Dement, 1972; Johnson, 1969). Prolonged sleep deprivation in animals (mostly rats) generally produces much more severe consequences, even death (Rechtschaffen, Gilliland, Bergmann, & Winter, 1983). There are good reasons for this apparent difference in species: First, the humans who went without sleep did so voluntarily, knowing they could quit if they found the strain unbearable. The rats had no way to predict or control their situation. (Stressors take a greater toll when they are unpredictable and uncontrollable.) Second, because the rats were not participating voluntarily, the experimenters constantly had to prod them and stimulate them in various ways to keep them awake. The rats' health deteriorated not only from sleep deprivation but also from continuous stimulation (Horne, 1988).

Still, the behavioral impairments that humans experience after sleep deprivation confirm that sleep does serve restorative functions. Sleep is not analogous to stopping to catch your breath after running a race, however. If sleep were restorative in that simple sense, we should expect people to sleep significantly more after a day of great physical or mental exertion than after an uneventful day. Great physical or mental exertion does increase sleep dura-

Some Facts about Hibernation

1. Hibernation occurs in certain small mammals such as ground squirrels and bats. It is a matter of definition whether we can say that bears hibernate. Bears sleep most of the winter, but they do not lower their body temperatures the way small hibernating animals do. *Microcebus*, a primate that lives in Madagascar, sleeps 4 to 6 hours more per day in the winter than it does in the summer (Barre & Petter-Rousseaux, 1988).

2. Hamsters sometimes hibernate. If you keep your pet hamster in a cold, poorly lit place during the winter, and it appears to die, make sure that it is not just hibernating before you bury it!

3. Hibernation retards the aging process. Hamsters that spend longer times hibernating have proportionately longer life expectancies than other hamsters do (Lyman, O'Brien, Greene, & Papafrangos, 1981).

4. Hibernating animals produce a chemical that suppresses metabolism and temperature regulation. H. Swan and C. Schätte (1977) injected extracts from the brains of hibernating ground squirrels into the brains of rats, a nonhibernating species. The rats decreased their metabolism and body temperature. Similar brain extracts from nonhibernating ground squirrels had no apparent effect on the rats.

5. Hibernating animals awaken in the spring around the time when food becomes available. Male ground squirrels awaken a few days earlier than the females. Their early awakening is presumably an evolutionary adaptation to the fact that the males compete with one another for mates and that mating occurs as soon as the females awaken. (Males who awaken early are sure to be ready as soon as the females are. Males who awaken at about the same time as the females might miss a chance at any female who awakened a bit early.) Because the males awaken before the females, who awaken at about the time that food becomes available, the males must survive several days without food. They have to gain an enormous amount of weight in the fall to get through both the winter and a few days of full activity in the spring before they can find any food (French, 1988).

tion, but only slightly (Horne & Minard, 1985; Shapiro, Bortz, Mitchell, Bartel, & Jooste, 1981). Apparently, the amount of sleep that we need does not depend much on our activity level during the day.

Moreover, a few people manage to satisfy their restorative needs in far less than the customary 7 to 8 hours. Two men have been reported to average only 3 hours of sleep per night and to awaken feeling refreshed (Jones & Oswald, 1968). A 70-year-old woman was reported to average only 1 hour of sleep per night; many nights, she felt no need to sleep at all (Meddis, Pearson, & Langford, 1973).

The Evolutionary Theory of the Need for Sleep

Given that the duration of sleep bears little relationship to the activity of the previous day, several theorists have offered an alternative explanation of why we sleep. According to the **evolutionary theory of sleep** (Kleitman, 1963; Webb, 1974), the function of sleep is similar to that of **hibernation,** a special adaptation of certain mammalian species to a season when food is scarce (see Digression 9.1). Hibernating animals' heart rate, breathing, brain activity, and metabolism decrease greatly; they generate only enough body heat to prevent themselves from freezing.

Hibernation is a true need; a ground squirrel that is prevented from hibernating can get as disturbed as a person who is prevented from sleeping. However, the function of hibernation is not to recover from a busy summer; it is simply to conserve energy when the environment is hostile. Similarly, according to the evolutionary theory of sleep, the primary function of sleep is to force

The Alternation of Waking and Sleeping

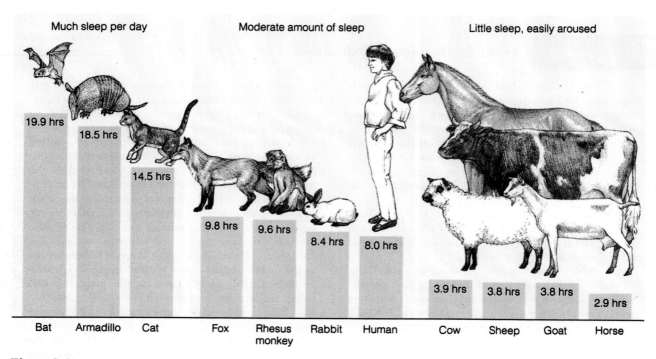

Much sleep per day   Moderate amount of sleep   Little sleep, easily aroused

19.9 hrs
18.5 hrs
14.5 hrs
9.8 hrs
9.6 hrs
8.4 hrs
8.0 hrs
3.9 hrs
3.8 hrs
3.8 hrs
2.9 hrs

Bat   Armadillo   Cat   Fox   Rhesus monkey   Rabbit   Human   Cow   Sheep   Goat   Horse

Figure 9.6
Hours of sleep per day for various animal species
*Generally, predators and others that are safe when they sleep tend to sleep a great
deal; animals in danger of being attacked while they sleep spend less time asleep.*

us to conserve energy when we would be relatively inefficient. The evolutionary theory does not deny that we need to sleep; it merely asserts that evolution
built that need into us for a special reason.

The evolutionary theory predicts that animal species should vary in their
sleep habits depending on how much time each day they must devote to the
search for food, how safe they are from predators when they sleep, and other
aspects of their way of life. In general, the data support these predictions (Allison & Cicchetti, 1976; Campbell & Tobler, 1984).

Horses, cows, and other animals that graze most of the day sleep relatively
few hours. Cats and other predators that usually eat just one meal per day sleep
much longer. Species that are frequently attacked by predators and whose only
defense is their ability to run away (for example, rabbits, sheep, and goats)
sleep relatively little and awaken easily. Cats, dogs, and other species that are
seldom attacked spend more hours sleeping. So do bats, which live in caves
that offer excellent protection against predators. (See Figure 9.6.)

Although the evolutionary theory of sleep has considerable appeal, it also
has its critics (for example, Hauri, 1979). In particular, they argue, the theory
seems to predict that sheep, goats, and similar species should not sleep at all,
since they are vulnerable to attack when they sleep. The fact that they do sleep
suggests that every animal needs some sleep to survive.

The evolutionary theory makes one prediction that has not been tested: A
species that has evolved in an environment that does not change during the
day should not sleep at any consistent time of day, if indeed it sleeps at all. For

*Chapter 9
Rhythms of Wakefulness
and Sleep*

example, deep-sea fish and cave-dwelling fish live in an environment with no light and almost no changes in temperature. Little is known about the sleep habits of such species. In fact, little is known about the sleep of fish in general (Karmanova, 1982).

Which theory of sleep is right? Actually, adherents of each theory concede that the other is partly right. Suppose you believe that the main function of sleep is to repair and restore the brain. Surely you will grant that each species confines its sleep to those hours when it is least efficient at doing anything else and, furthermore, that species that can afford long periods of inactivity (predators) will evolve a tendency to sleep longer than species that must remain constantly vigilant (prey). Now suppose you believe that the main function of sleep is to conserve energy. Surely you will agree that, while an animal is lying around doing nothing else anyway, sleep might be a good time for some repair and restoration functions. In short, the two theories do not directly conflict with each other.

Summary

1. Animals, including humans, have internally generated rhythms of activity and other functions, approximating both a 24-hour cycle and a one-year cycle. (p. 310)

2. Although the biological clock can continue to operate in constant light or constant darkness, the onset of light at a particular time can reset the clock. (p. 312)

3. The biological clock can reset daily to match an external rhythm of light and darkness slightly different from 24 hours, but if the discrepancy exceeds 1 to 2 hours, the biological clock generates its own rhythm instead of resetting. (p. 313)

4. It is easier for people to follow a cycle longer than 24 hours than to follow a cycle shorter than 24 hours. (p. 314)

5. Many factors that temporarily block overall body activity have little effect on the biological clock. (p. 315)

6. The suprachiasmatic nucleus, a part of the hypothalamus, generates the body's circadian rhythm. (p. 316)

7. Sleep probably serves at least two functions: (1) repair and restoration and (2) conservation of energy during a period of relative inefficiency. (p. 318)

Review Questions

1. Why is it advantageous for a migratory bird to have an internal mechanism that predicts the changing seasons, instead of relying entirely on changes in the light/dark patterns in the environment? (p. 310)

2. What stimulus is the most effective zeitgeber for resetting the biological clock? (p. 312)

3. What evidence indicates that the human body has an internal biological clock, instead of timing its activities entirely on the basis of light and other external cues? (p. 313)

4. For people who are scheduled to work consistently at night, what procedure is most effective for resetting their circadian rhythms to favor night activity? (p. 314)

5. What are some factors that do and do not interfere with the biological clock? (p. 315)

6. What is the evidence that the suprachiasmatic nucleus generates circadian rhythms of activity? (p. 316)

7. State the strengths and weaknesses of the repair and restoration theory and the evolutionary theory of the need for sleep. (p. 318)

Thought Questions

1. Hummingbirds, smaller than any other bird or mammal, need to consume almost their weight in nectar each day to maintain their body temperature and activity. During periods of food shortage, they go into a state resembling hibernation at night, greatly lowering their activity and body temperature. What does this observation imply about the functions of sleep?

2. Is it possible for a blind person to reset his or her circadian rhythms based on the onset of light and dark each day? Would the answer depend on the cause of blindness? Explain.

Suggestion for Further Reading

Horne, J. (1988). *Why we sleep.* Oxford, England: Oxford University Press. Thorough study of the functions of sleep, including the results of sleep deprivation.

Terms

endogenous circannual rhythm self-generated rhythm that lasts about a year (p. 311)

endogenous circadian rhythm self-generated rhythm that lasts about a day (p. 311)

biological clock internal mechanism for controlling rhythmic variations in a behavior (p. 312)

free-running rhythm circadian or circannual rhythm that is not being periodically reset by light or other cues (p. 312)

zeitgeber stimulus that resets a biological clock (p. 312)

jet lag disruption of biological rhythms caused by travel across time zones (p. 314)

suprachiasmatic nucleus (SCN) area of the hypothalamus where damage disrupts the biological clock (p. 316)

repair and restoration theory of sleep concept that the function of sleep is to enable the body to repair itself after the exertions of the day (p. 318)

evolutionary theory of sleep concept that the function of sleep is to conserve energy at times of relative inefficiency (p. 319)

hibernation condition in which heart rate, breathing, brain activity, and metabolism greatly decrease as an adaptation to conserve energy during winter (p. 319)

Sleeping and Dreaming

Advances in scientific research usually result from improvements in our ability to measure something. Sleep research is no exception. The electroencephalograph (EEG), mentioned in Chapter 4, records a gross average of the electrical potentials of the cells and fibers in a particular part of the brain by means of an electrode attached to the scalp (see Figure 9.7). It displays a net average of all the neurons' potentials. That is, if half the cells increase their electrical potentials while the other half decrease, the EEG recording is a flat line. The EEG record rises or falls only when a number of cells fire in synchrony—doing the same thing at the same time. You might compare it to a record of the noise in a crowded football stadium: It shows only slight fluctuations from time to time until some event gets everyone yelling at once.

The EEG provides an objective way for brain researchers to determine whether people are awake or asleep without relying on the people's self-reports. The EEG also enables researchers to compare brain activity at one time of night with activity at a different time of night. Such research has led to the identification of several distinct stages of sleep.

The Stages of Sleep

Figure 9.8 shows the EEG and eye movement records from a male college student during the various stages of sleep. Figure 9.8a begins with a period of relaxed wakefulness for comparison. Note the steady series of waves at a frequency of about 10 per second, known as **alpha waves.** Alpha waves are characteristic of the relaxed state, not of all wakefulness.

In Figure 9.8b, the young man has just fallen asleep. During this period, called stage 1 sleep, brain activity is said to be desynchronized; the neurons are not all doing the same thing at the same time. The EEG in stage 1 is dominated by **theta waves,** which are irregular, jagged, and low in voltage.

As Figure 9.8c shows, the most prominent characteristics of stage 2 are sleep spindles and K-complexes. A **sleep spindle** is a burst of 12- to 14-Hz waves lasting at least half a second. A **K-complex** is a sharp high-amplitude negative wave followed by a smaller, slower positive wave. Sudden stimuli can evoke K-complexes during other stages of sleep (Bastien & Campbell, 1992), but they are most common in stage 2.

In each succeeding stage of sleep, heart rate, breathing rate, and brain activity are slower than in the previous stage, and the percentage of slow, large-amplitude waves increases (see Figure 9.8d and e). By stage 4, more than half

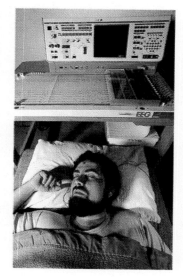

Figure 9.7
Sleeping person with electrodes in place on the scalp for recording brain activity
The printout above his head shows the readings from each electrode. (Photo from Richard Nowitz.)

323

Figure 9.8
**Polysomnograph records
from a male college student**
*A polysomnograph includes
records of EEG, eye move-
ments, and sometimes other
data, such as muscle tension
or head movements. For
each of these records, the top
line is the EEG from one
electrode on the scalp; the
middle line is a record of eye
movements; and the bottom
line is a time marker, indicating 1-second units. Note
the abundance of slow
waves in stages 3 and 4.
(Records provided by T. E.
LeVere.)*

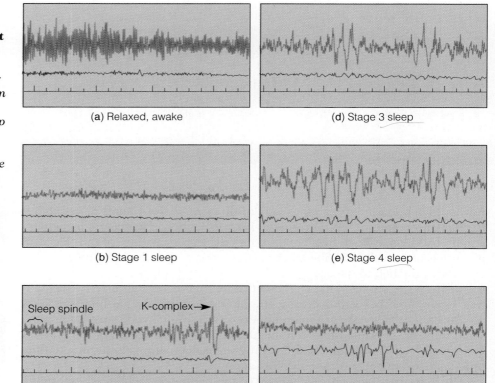

(a) Relaxed, awake

(d) Stage 3 sleep

(b) Stage 1 sleep

(e) Stage 4 sleep

(c) Stage 2 sleep

(f) REM, or "paradoxical" sleep

the record includes large waves of at least a half-second duration. Stages 3 and 4 are known together as **slow-wave sleep (SWS).**

Slow waves indicate that neuronal activity is highly synchronized. In stage 1 or in wakefulness, the cortex receives much input, so various cells are rapidly excited and inhibited out of phase with one another. By stage 4, however, sensory input to the cerebral cortex has been greatly reduced, and the few remaining sources of input can synchronize many cells. As an analogy, imagine the barrage of stimuli arriving at the brain of an alert person as being like dropping hundreds of rocks into a pond over the course of a minute; the resulting waves will largely cancel one another out. Although the surface of the pond will be choppy, it will have few large waves. Contrast that with the effect of dropping just one rock: The surface will have larger waves, like those seen in stage 4 sleep.

Paradoxical, or REM, Sleep

A person who has just fallen asleep enters stage 1 sleep. Later in the night, people may or may not return to stage 1; more commonly, they enter a related but very special stage, which two sets of researchers discovered accidentally at almost the same time.

In France, Michel Jouvet was trying to test the learning abilities of cats after complete removal of their cerebral cortex. To cope with the fact that decorticate cats hardly move at all, Jouvet electrically recorded slight movements of the cats' muscles while he also recorded EEGs from the hindbrain. He found that, during periods of apparent sleep, the cats had almost complete relaxation of their neck muscles but high levels of brain activity. Jouvet named this phenomenon **paradoxical sleep** because it is in some ways the deepest sleep and in other ways the lightest. (The term *paradoxical* means *apparently self-contradictory.*)

Meanwhile, in the United States, Nathaniel Kleitman and Eugene Aserinsky were observing eye movements of sleeping people as a means of measuring depth of sleep, based on the simple assumption that eye movements would decrease as a person fell asleep. At first, they recorded only a few minutes of eye movements per hour, partly because the recording paper was expensive and partly because they did not expect to see anything interesting in the middle of the night anyway. When they sometimes recorded periods of eye movements in people who had been asleep for hours, the investigators assumed at first that something was wrong with their machines. Only after repeated, careful measurements did they conclude that people have periods of rapid eye movements during their sleep (Dement, 1990). They called these periods **rapid eye movement (REM) sleep** (Aserinsky & Kleitman, 1955; Dement & Kleitman, 1957a). They soon concluded that rapid eye movement sleep was synonymous with what Jouvet was calling *paradoxical sleep*. Researchers more commonly use the term *REM sleep* when referring to humans; they prefer the term *paradoxical sleep* when dealing with certain animals, especially those without eye movements.

During paradoxical or REM sleep, the EEG shows irregular, low-voltage fast waves, which suggest a considerable amount of brain activity. Heart rate and breathing rate are higher and more variable than in stages 2 through 4. In those regards, REM sleep is light. However, during REM sleep, the postural muscles of the body, such as those that support the head, are more relaxed than in any other stage. In this regard, REM sleep is deep. This stage of sleep is also associated with erections in males and vaginal moistening in females. It is not obvious whether we should consider erections and vaginal secretions as indications of deep or light sleep. In short, REM sleep combines deep sleep, light sleep, and ambiguous features. Consequently, it is best to avoid using the terms *deep* and *light* sleep.

In addition to these steady characteristics, REM sleep has certain intermittent characteristics, including facial and finger twitches and the characteristic back-and-forth movements of the eyes (Figure 9.9). Figure 9.8f provides the **polysomnograph** (a combination of EEG and eye-movement records) for a period of REM sleep. The EEG record is similar to that for stage 1 sleep, but notice how different the eye-movement records are. The stages other than REM are sometimes known as **non-REM sleep,** abbreviated **NREM.**

Sleep Cycles

A person who falls asleep enters stage 1 and slowly progresses through stages 2, 3, and 4 in order. External stimuli can halt this progression, however. For example, noises during stage 3 can prolong this stage or cause a reversion to stage 2, stage 1, or even wakefulness.

About 60 to 90 minutes after going to sleep, the person begins gradually to cycle from stage 4 back through stage 3, stage 2, and then REM sleep. After a period of REM sleep, the sequence repeats, with each complete cycle lasting about 90 to 100 minutes. Early in the night, stages 3 and 4 predominate.

**Figure 9.9
A double-exposure photograph representing rapid
eye movements**
*(Photo from Dr. J. Allan
Hobson/PR Inc.)*

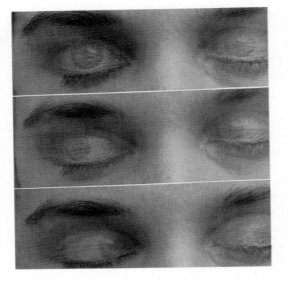

Toward morning, the duration of stage 4 grows shorter and the duration of REM sleep grows longer. Figure 9.10 shows typical sequences.

REM Sleep and Dreaming

REM sleep is associated with dreaming, although the relationship is not perfect. Researchers can determine a person's sleep stage by monitoring EEG records and eye movements. William Dement and Nathaniel Kleitman (1957b) awakened adult volunteers during various stages of sleep. They found that people awakened during REM sleep reported dreams about 80 to 90 percent of the time. Those dreams often included elaborate visual imagery and complicated plots. People awakened during slow-wave sleep reported dreams less frequently. The percentage of reported dreams in non-REM sleep varies from one investigation to another, from less than 10 percent to more than 70 percent. Much of this discrepancy depends on whether investigators include vague, thoughtlike experiences as dreams or whether they limit dreams to complex experiences with well-defined visual imagery (Foulkes, 1967).

By awakening people during REM sleep, investigators have been able to answer questions that were previously a matter for speculation. For example, as far as we can determine, all normal humans dream. Everyone studied in the laboratory has had periods of REM sleep. When people who claim they never dream are awakened during an REM period, they generally report dreams. Most of their dreams are less vivid than those of other people, however. Apparently, they believe that they do not dream only because they forget their dreams.

Furthermore, we now know that dreams last about as long as they seem to last, contrary to a once-popular belief that a dream lasts only a second or two. Dement and E. A. Wolpert (1958) awakened people after they had been in REM sleep for varying periods of time. The length of the dreams they reported corresponded closely to the length of the REM period prior to awakening, up to a limit of about 15 minutes. Beyond 15 minutes, the volunteers did not report still longer dreams, perhaps because they had already forgotten the beginning of the dream by the time they got to the end of it.

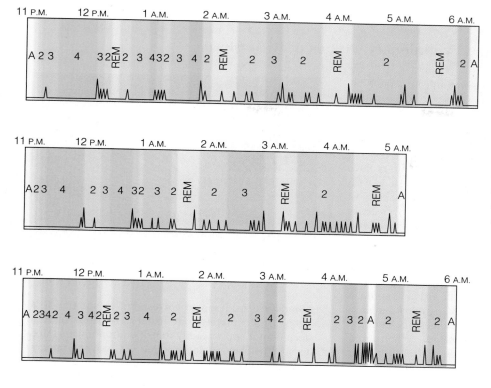

Figure 9.10
Sequence of sleep stages on three representative nights
Columns indicate awake (A) and sleep stages 2, 3, 4, and REM. Deflections in the line at the bottom of each chart indicate shifts in body position. Note that stage 4 sleep occurs mostly in the early part of the night's sleep, while REM sleep becomes more prevalent toward the end. (Based on Dement & Kleitman, 1957a.)

The Functions of REM Sleep

An evolutionary point of view teaches us to look for functional explanations of behavior (see p. 4). An average person spends about one-third of his or her life asleep and about one-fifth of the sleep time in REM sleep. Overall, REM sleep occupies about 600 hours per year. If people and a wide variety of other animal species are going to devote that much time to REM sleep, presumably it serves some biological function. But what function? To approach this question, we can examine what kinds of people or animals get more REM sleep than others do, and we can examine the effects of being deprived of REM sleep.

Individual and Species Differences in REM Sleep

Nearly all mammals and birds show at least a small amount of REM sleep, indicating that the capacity for REM sleep is part of our ancient evolutionary heritage. (See Digression 9.2.) Some species, however, get a great deal more than others. The pattern that stands out is that the species that get the most total sleep also get the highest percentage of REM sleep. Cats, which spend up to 16 hours a day sleeping, spend much or most of it in REM sleep. Rabbits, guinea pigs, and sheep, which sleep much less, spend very little time in REM sleep.

Within a species, infants have a higher percentage of REM sleep than adults do. Figure 9.11 demonstrates this relationship for humans. The general trend is the same for most other mammalian species. REM sleep occupies an even greater percentage of total sleep time in premature infants (Astic, Sastre, & Brandon, 1973; Dreyfus-Brisac, 1970). It is difficult to distinguish between an

Nearly all mammals and birds show at least some REM sleep, and so do a few reptiles such as the desert tortoise *Gopherus flavomarginatus* (Ayala-Guerrero, Caldéron, & Pérez, 1988). Apparently, the capacity for REM sleep evolved long ago in ancient reptiles.

One species of mammal does not have REM sleep: the spiny anteater, or echidna. Spiny anteaters have long periods of slow-wave sleep but no periods with eye movements or aroused EEG or total relaxation of the postural muscles (Allison & Goff, 1968). Because spiny anteaters are among the most primitive of surviving mammals, we naturally wonder whether the original mammals (the ancestors of all of today's mammals) also lacked REM sleep. Maybe, but maybe not. Opossums, which are also very primitive mammals, have REM periods like those of other mammals (VanTwyver & Allison, 1970). Perhaps spiny anteaters have lost a trait that their ancient ancestors had.

Fish and amphibians have periods of behavioral inactivity (sleep), although stimuli can arouse them fairly easily during these periods (Karmanova, 1982). They do not have two separate sleep states, corresponding to REM and NREM, but only one sleep state,

(Tom McHugh/PR Inc.)

generally considered to correspond to our non-REM sleep. Unfortunately, our usual definitions of REM sleep do not apply readily to fish or amphibians (Meddis, 1979). They do not produce EEG waves comparable with those of mammals, and they have few eye movements even while awake. And we can hardly ask them about their dreams.

Figure 9.11
The percentage of time spent by people of different ages in waking, REM sleep, and NREM sleep
REM sleep occupies about 8 hours a day in newborns but only 2 hours per day (or less) in most adults. The sleep of infants is not quite like that of adults, however, and the criteria for identifying REM sleep are not the same.

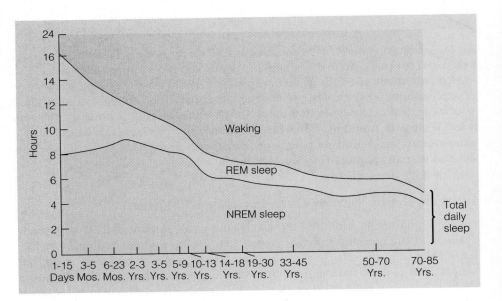

infant in REM sleep and an infant who is awake but has his or her eyes closed (Lynch & Aserinsky, 1986). For that reason, the data on infants may not be entirely accurate.

The adult humans who get the most sleep per night (9 or more hours) have the highest percentage of REM sleep. Those who get the least total sleep (5 hours or less) spend the lowest percentage of their sleep on REM. From all these data, a pattern emerges: Across species, across ages, and across individuals, the greater the total amount of sleep, the greater the percentage of REM sleep.

In short, the amount of non-REM sleep varies relatively little from one species to another or from one age to another; an individual that gets extra sleep fills most of the extra time with REM sleep. Horne (1988) has therefore suggested that much of our REM sleep, perhaps as much as half of it, is "optional"; we could easily survive without it. Thus, the study of individual variations in REM sleep time tells us disappointingly little about why we need REM sleep at all.

The Effects of REM Sleep Deprivation in Humans

To say that much of our REM sleep is optional is not to say that all of it is unnecessary, however. What would happen if someone had almost no opportunity for REM sleep? William Dement (1960) observed the behavior of eight men who agreed to be deprived of REM sleep for four to seven consecutive days. During that period, they slept only in a laboratory. Whenever the EEG and eye movements indicated that a given subject was entering REM sleep, an experimenter promptly awakened him and kept him awake for several minutes. The subject was then permitted to go back to sleep until he started REM sleep again.

Over the course of the four to seven nights, the experimenters found that they had to awaken the subjects more and more frequently. On the first night, an average subject had to be awakened 12 times. By the final night, this figure had increased to 26 times. That is, the subjects had increased their "attempts" at REM sleep.

During the deprivation period, the subjects reported mild, temporary personality changes. Most reported irritability, increased anxiety, and impaired concentration. Five of the eight experienced increased appetite and weight gain. Control studies found that a similar number of awakenings not linked to REM sleep did not produce similar effects. The disturbances were therefore due to REM deprivation, not just to the total number of awakenings.

After the deprivation period, seven subjects continued to sleep in the laboratory. During their first uninterrupted night, five of the seven spent more time than usual in REM sleep; 29 percent of the night was devoted to REM sleep, as compared with 19 percent before the deprivation. One of the seven showed no increase. (The investigators discarded the results from the seventh subject, who came to the laboratory drunk that night. Alcohol suppresses REM sleep, so results from this subject would be unreliable.)

The Effects of Paradoxical Sleep Deprivation in Nonhumans

Similar experiments have been done with laboratory animals, for which it is possible to impose much longer periods of paradoxical-sleep deprivation. Cats have been deprived of paradoxical sleep for up to 70 consecutive days (see Dement, Ferguson, Cohen, & Barchas, 1969). Do not imagine shifts of experimenters monitoring cats 24 hours a day and prodding them whenever they enter paradoxical sleep. Rather, they kept each cat on a tiny island surrounded by water. As soon as the cat entered paradoxical sleep its postural muscles relaxed, it lost its balance, and it fell into the water. It could have no more than a few seconds of paradoxical sleep at a time before awakening. Over the course of days, the cats placed in this situation made progressively more attempts to enter paradoxical sleep.

These and similar studies indicate that animals deprived of paradoxical sleep become generally disturbed in a number of ways. However, they leave unanswered the question of what function paradoxical sleep, or REM sleep, actually serves. Psychologists and others have speculatively linked it to brain growth, the need for periodic arousal of the brain during the night, the dampening of excessively strong motivations, and so forth.

A number of animal studies have linked paradoxical sleep to the process of strengthening memories. Animals that are given new learning experiences generally show an increase in paradoxical sleep time, and animals that are deprived of the opportunity for paradoxical sleep show impairments of learning (Hobson, 1992). Also, when a group of rats learns a new, challenging task, the fastest learners show the greatest increase in paradoxical sleep during the 24 hours after learning (Smith & Wong, 1991). In short, new learning tends to increase paradoxical sleep, and paradoxical sleep facilitates new learning. Exactly how it does so, we do not know.

A Biological Perspective on Dreaming

Dreams are real while they last. Can we say more of life?
—Havelock Ellis

For decades, psychologists have been heavily influenced by Sigmund Freud's theory of dreams, which was based on the assumption that hidden and often unconscious wishes cause dreams. Although Freud was certainly correct in asserting that dreams reflect the dreamer's personality and recent experiences, his theory of the mechanism of dreams depended on a now-obsolete view of the nervous system (McCarley & Hobson, 1977). He believed, for example, that brain cells were inactive except when nerves from the periphery brought them energy. Freud was also hampered by relying on dream reports that his patients gave him hours or days after the dream occurred.

In a search for a more modern view of dreams, contemporary investigators have offered several new theories. According to one influential idea, called the **activation-synthesis hypothesis,** during sleep various parts of the brain are activated—either by random spontaneous activity or by stimuli in the room—and the brain synthesizes some sort of story to make sense of all the activity (Hobson & McCarley, 1977; McCarley & Hoffman, 1981). According to a slightly different version of this hypothesis, the brain is aroused and ready to process information during REM sleep, but the environment provides few stimuli. Therefore, the individual begins processing information stored in memory, treating the stream of thought and imagery as if it were the real world (Antrobus, 1986).

While we sleep, we do not completely lose contact with external stimuli. (For example, except in early childhood, we seldom roll out of the bed.) We incorporate many of the external stimuli into our dreams, at least in some modified form. If water is dripping on someone's foot, he or she may dream about swimming or about walking in the rain. In addition to the external stimuli, bursts of activity occur spontaneously in certain parts of the cerebral cortex, including the visual, auditory, and motor cortexes, plus various subcortical areas that contribute to motivation and emotion.

Occasional bursts of vestibular sensation are also common during REM sleep, perhaps because a sleeping person is generally lying prone instead of maintaining the usual upright position. According to the activation-synthesis hypothesis, the brain incorporates those vestibular sensations into the common dreams of falling, flying, or spinning.

Have you ever dreamt that you were trying to move, but couldn't? It is tempting to relate such dreams to the fact that the major postural muscles are virtually paralyzed during REM sleep. That is, when you are dreaming, you really *can't* move. However, that explanation becomes less convincing when we realize how often people dream that they *are* moving. (The muscles are relaxed during both kinds of dreams.)

The activation-synthesis hypothesis and various modifications of it remain controversial. Some dream researchers consider this approach fruitful; others find it too vague. Certainly, the activation-synthesis hypothesis does not account for all the phenomena of dreams. For example, it does not explain why many people have repetitive dreams or other dreams full of personal meaning (Winson, 1993). Haphazard sounds and other stimuli may be more important for scene shifts and miscellaneous details of a dream than they are for the dream's overall plot.

Summary

1. Sleep is composed of distinct stages that EEG records can identify. Stage 1 is a transition from wakefulness to sleep; stage 4 has the least brain activity. (p. 323)

2. One special stage of sleep is rapid eye movement (REM) sleep. During REM sleep an individual has much brain activity, very relaxed postural muscles, and many eye movements. (p. 324)

3. During a night's sleep, people cycle from stage 1 or REM sleep down to stage 4 and then back to REM or stage 1 again. A complete cycle lasts about 90 to 100 minutes. (p. 325)

4. People are more likely to report dreams, especially their more vivid dreams, when they are awakened from REM sleep than when they are awakened from other stages of sleep. (p. 326)

5. REM sleep is most common in those individuals and species that spend the most total hours asleep. (p. 327)

6. People who are deprived of REM sleep become irritable and report trouble in concentrating. After the end of a period of REM deprivation, people compensate for the loss by spending more time than usual in REM sleep. (p. 329)

7. According to the activation-synthesis hypothesis, dreams are the brain's attempts to make sense of limited, shifting, and somewhat random stimuli when the brain is aroused and ready to process information. (p. 330)

Review Questions

1. What is the EEG pattern when neuronal activity is synchronized? What is the pattern when activity is desynchronized? (p. 324)

2. How can an investigator determine whether a person is in sleep stage 1, 2, 3, 4, or REM? (p. 324)

3. Why do many sleep researchers avoid the terms *light sleep* and *deep sleep*? (p. 325)

4. Which sleep stages are most common early in the night? Which ones predominate later in the night? (p. 325)

5. What kinds of dreams (if any) occur during non-REM sleep? (p. 326)

6. Do all people dream? If so, why do some people believe that they do not? (p. 326)

7. Which animal species have the largest amount of REM sleep? (p. 327)

8. What are the effects of REM sleep deprivation? (p. 329)

9. What is the apparent relationship between REM sleep and memory? (p. 330)

10. According to the activation-synthesis hypothesis of dreams, what determines the content of our dreams? (p. 330)

Suggestions for Further Reading

Dement, W. C. (1992). *The sleepwatchers.* Stanford, CA: Stanford Alumni Association. Fascinating, entertaining account of sleep research by one of its leading pioneers.

Moorcroft, W. H. (1993). *Sleep, dreaming, & sleep disorders: An introduction.* (2nd ed.) Lanham, MD: University Press of America. Excellent and thorough review of research on sleep and dreams.

Winson, J. (1990, November). The meaning of dreams. *Scientific American, 263* (5), 86–96. Discusses theories of the function of REM sleep and the meaning of dreams.

Terms

alpha wave rhythm of 8 to 12 brain waves per second, generally associated with relaxation (p. 323)

theta wave irregular, jagged, low-voltage brain wave at a rhythm of 4 to 7 cycles per second (p. 323)

sleep spindle burst of 12- to 14-Hz brain waves lasting at least half a second (p. 323)

K-complex sharp, high-amplitude, negative wave followed by a smaller, slower, positive wave (p. 323)

slow-wave sleep (SWS) stages 3 and 4 of sleep, which are occupied largely by slow, large-amplitude brain waves (p. 324)

paradoxical sleep stage of sleep characterized by complete relaxation of the large muscles but high activity in the brain (p. 325)

rapid eye movement (REM) sleep sleep stage with rapid eye movements, high brain activity, and relaxation of the large muscles (p. 325)

polysomnograph a combination of EEG and eye-movement records, and sometimes other data, for a sleeping person (p. 325)

non-REM sleep sleep stages other than REM sleep (p. 325)

activation-synthesis hypothesis hypothesis that the brain synthesizes dreams from spontaneous brain activity occurring during sleep (p. 330)

Brain Mechanisms in Sleep and Its Disorders

Suppose I buy a new radio. After I play it for 4 hours, it suddenly stops. To explain why it stopped, I would try to discover whether the batteries were dead or whether the radio needed repair. Suppose I discover that the radio will operate again a few hours later even without repairs or a battery change. I also discover that the radio always stops whenever I play it for 4 hours. I begin to suspect that the manufacturer designed it this way on purpose, perhaps to prevent me from wearing it out too fast or to prevent me from listening to the radio all day. I might then try to find the device in the radio that turns it off whenever I play it for 4 hours. Notice that I am now asking a new question. When I thought that the radio stopped because it needed repairs or new batteries, I would not have thought to ask which device turned the radio off. I ask that question only when I think of the stoppage as something other than an accidental, passive process.

The same is true for sleep. If we think of sleep only as a passive cessation of activity, similar to catching one's breath after running a race, we do not ask which part of the brain is responsible for sleep. But if we think of sleep as a specialized state evolved to serve particular functions, we may look for the devices that control it.

Wakefulness and the Reticular Activating System

Making a cut through the midbrain, separating the forebrain and part of the midbrain from the rest of the midbrain, pons, medulla, and spinal cord (line A in Figure 9.12) produces the **cerveau isolé** (SEHR-voh EE-so-lay) preparation (French for *isolated forebrain*). The cerveau isolé animal goes into a prolonged state of sleep. The brain shows no signs of wakefulness in the EEG for the next week or so, and only brief periods of wakefulness later.

Most sensory information enters the nervous system at levels below the cut; thus, the cut isolates the brain from most sources of sensory stimulation. It may seem obvious, therefore, that the cut produces prolonged sleep by isolating the brain from the sensory stimuli that normally activate it. However, the effect of this cut is very different from the effect of cutting off each sensory source individually. Because each sensory tract enters the brain through a well-defined path, it is possible to cut the individual tracts while sparing the rest of the spinal cord and brain stem. As more and more sensory tracts are cut, the animal becomes responsive to fewer and fewer sensory stimuli. Nevertheless, it continues to have normal periods of sleep and wakefulness.

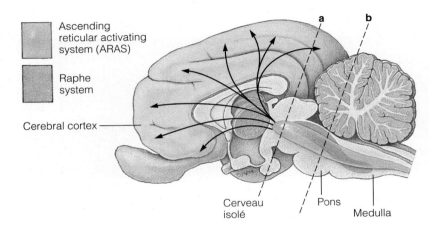

Figure 9.12
Location of systems in the cat brain that play critical parts in wakefulness and sleep
A cut at line A leads to prolonged sleep; a cut at line B leads to prolonged wakefulness. This evidence pointed to a brain system, now known as the ARAS, which arouses the brain, and to other brain systems, largely in the pons and midbrain, which promote sleep.

Legend: Ascending reticular activating system (ARAS); Raphe system; Cerebral cortex; Cerveau isolé; Pons; Medulla; a; b

Apparently, the cerveau isolé cut decreases wakefulness by some means other than just reducing sensory input.

In 1949, Giuseppe Moruzzi and H. W. Magoun found that wakefulness depends not on the sensory tracts themselves but on a system of heavily interconnected neurons extending from the medulla into the forebrain, called the **ascending reticular activating system (ARAS),** which is part of the reticular formation. It is called the *ascending* reticular formation to distinguish it from the axons of the reticular formation that descend toward the spinal cord, controlling motor output. Although the ARAS depends on the sensory tracts for much of its input, it also can generate activity on its own. High-frequency stimulation of the ARAS awakens a sleeping individual or increases alertness in one already awake. It also desynchronizes the EEG. Damage to the ARAS or a cut that separates it from the anterior parts of the brain leads to prolonged sleep or inactivity. Clearly, it is critical for wakefulness and alertness.

Figure 9.12 shows the position of the ARAS in a cat brain. The borders shown are only approximate. The term *reticular* (based on the Latin word *rete*, meaning *net*) describes the widespread, diffuse reach of the ARAS. It extends forward at least into parts of the thalamus and hypothalamus; some authorities maintain that it extends all the way into the cerebral cortex.

The individual neurons of the ARAS are heavily interconnected, as in parts of a net. Its neurons are characterized by long, widely branching dendrites. The connections among neurons do not form straight chains but include multisynaptic paths and looping axon branches.

The input and output of the ARAS are somewhat nonspecific in comparison with any of the sensory pathways. The cranial nerves send input to the ascending reticular formation, in addition to their primary targets. Thus, the ARAS can be activated by practically any stimulus. The ARAS also generates spontaneous activity of its own. Cells in the ARAS, in turn, send impulses widely throughout the cerebral cortex.

The ARAS differs in an important way from the sensory systems. The lateral geniculate nucleus of the thalamus, for example, receives input mostly from the retina and sends its output mostly to the occipital cortex. Similarly, structures in other sensory systems receive limited kinds of input and project their axons to limited targets. The widespread projections of the ARAS to other parts of the brain make it well adapted for serving an energizing function, for controlling arousal and wakefulness. Any strong stimulation—sound, touch, pain— activates the ARAS, thereby activating wide regions of the cerebral cortex.

Physiological Mechanisms of Sleep and REM Sleep

We discussed the effects of a cut through the midbrain of a cat at line A in Figure 9.12. If, however, we make the cut at line B, we still isolate the brain from most sensory input, but, instead of increasing sleep, this cut increases wakefulness! A cat with such a cut stays awake 70 to 90 percent of the time, about twice as long as a normal cat (Batini, Magni, Palestini, Rossi, & Zanchetti, 1959; Batini, Moruzzi, Palestini, Rossi, & Zanchetti, 1958, 1959; Batini, Palestini, Rossi, & Zanchetti, 1959). Evidently, the cut at B spares enough of the ARAS to permit wakefulness but damages a system that promotes sleep; that is, a sleep-promoting area must exist near or below the cut.

Sleep-Inducing Areas

Matters might seem simple if we could point to one sleep-inducing area between lines A and B. Early research did implicate a single area, the *raphe system*. *Raphe* is a Greek word meaning *seam* or *stitching*. The seam referred to here is the line joining the halves of the hindbrain; the raphe system is located near the midline of the brain stem. After damage to certain parts of the raphe system, a cat or rat remains awake for a day or more (Jouvet & Renault, 1966; Żernicki, Gandolfo, Glin, & Gottesmann, 1984), suggesting that the raphe system might be responsible for inducing sleep.

However, the animal begins sleeping within a few days after damage to the raphe system or after depletion of its neurotransmitter, serotonin. Furthermore, most neurons in the raphe system are more active during wakefulness than they are during sleep. They are particularly inactive during REM sleep, and researchers now believe the raphe system inhibits REM sleep. It no longer appears to be critical for the onset of sleep, however.

The brain apparently does have sleep-inducing areas, but the evidence suggests control by several areas, not just one master area. Sleep can be triggered or facilitated by neuronal activity in various parts of the hypothalamus, thalamus, and the brain stem. Stimulation of any of these areas can increase the probability of sleep; damage can decrease sleep (Culebras, 1992; Steriade, 1992).

The Biochemistry of Sleep

Several chemicals circulating in the blood can influence waking and sleeping. For example, prostaglandin D_2 binds mostly to forebrain neurons and induces sleep (Hayaishi, 1988). It also lowers body temperature, a factor that can greatly influence sleepiness (Satinoff, 1988). The link between sleep and prostaglandins is interesting because both of them are also linked to the immune system. Infections and illnesses generally lead to both an increase in prostaglandin production and an increase in sleep.

A small glycopeptide, designated **Factor S,** which can be isolated from the nervous system or bloodstream of sleeping animals, can induce sleep, mostly slow-wave sleep, when it is injected into other animals (Inoué, Uchizono, & Nagasaki, 1982; Krueger, Pappenheimer, & Karnovsky, 1982). Evidently, various neuronal mechanisms are responsible for initiating sleep, but hormonal factors may be important for maintaining it.

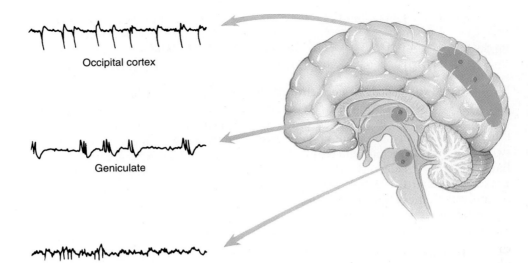

Figure 9.13
PGO waves start in the pons (P), then show up in the lateral geniculate (G) and the occipital cortex (O). Each PGO wave is synchronized with an eye movement in REM sleep.

REM-Inducing Areas

Michel Jouvet (1960) was the first to suggest that a particular area of the brain, probably in the brain stem, might trigger the events that produce REM sleep. REM sleep begins with a distinctive pattern of high-amplitude electrical potentials that can be detected first in the pons, then in the lateral geniculate of the thalamus, and finally in the occipital cortex (Brooks & Bizzi, 1963; Laurent, Cespuglio, & Jouvet, 1974). Those potentials are known as **PGO waves** for pons-geniculate-occipital (see Figure 9.13). The PGO waves begin at or just before the start of REM sleep; they continue during REM sleep. Each PGO wave is synchronized with an eye movement (Cespuglio, Laurent, & Jouvet, 1975).

Animals compensate for lost PGO waves more precisely than they compensate for lost REM time (Dement, Ferguson, Cohen, & Barchas, 1969). During a prolonged period of REM deprivation, PGO waves begin to emerge during stages 2 to 4 sleep—when they do not normally occur—and even during wakefulness, often in association with strange behaviors, as if the animal were hallucinating. At the end of the deprivation period, when animals are permitted to sleep without interruption, their REM periods have an unusually high density of PGO waves.

The Biochemistry of REM Sleep

The cells apparently responsible for starting REM sleep are pons cells that release acetylcholine as their neurotransmitter (Hobson, 1992; Winson, 1993). Those neurons activate parts of the thalamus, which in turn activate the cerebral cortex, producing the desynchronized EEG, the PGO waves, and the rapid eye movements characteristic of REM sleep. Injection into the pons of the drug *carbachol* (which stimulates ACh synapses) quickly produces an REM state (Baghdoyan, Spotts, & Snyder, 1993).

At about the same time that these acetylcholine-containing neurons send messages to arouse the forebrain, other cells in the pons use the neurotransmitter glutamate to send messages to certain neurons in the *descending* portion of the reticular formation, which in turn send messages to inhibit motor neurons in the spinal cord (Lai & Siegel, 1991). Those messages are responsible for the inactivity of the muscles during REM sleep.

Abnormalities of Sleep

Have you ever stayed awake extremely late at night to finish some project and then found yourself making one mistake after another the next morning? If so, you are not alone. An estimated 8 to 15 percent of adults in the United States have chronic sleep complaints (Weitzman, 1981), and a great many more than that have at least occasional or mild complaints. People who work long or irregular hours are especially likely to have sleep problems; so are people with psychiatric problems such as depression, schizophrenia, and substance abuse (Benca, Obermeyer, Thisted, & Gillin, 1992). Unsatisfactory sleep is a major cause of accidents on the job, comparable with the effects of drugs and alcohol.

Insomnia

How much sleep is enough? How much is too little? Some people get along fine with six hours of sleep per night. For others, eight hours may not be enough, especially for people who awaken repeatedly during the night. The best gauge of **insomnia** is whether the person feels well rested the following day. Anyone who consistently feels sleepy during the day is not sleeping well enough at night.

Insomnia can result from many causes, including excessive noise, worries and stress, drugs and medications, uncomfortable temperatures, sleeping in an unfamiliar place, or trying to fall asleep at the wrong time in one's circadian rhythm (Kales & Kales, 1984). A friend of mine suffered insomnia for months until he realized that he dreaded going to sleep at night because he dreaded waking up in the morning and doing his daily jogging. After he switched his jogging time to late afternoon, he no longer had any trouble sleeping. Before trying sleeping pills or any other method of combating insomnia, a person should carefully identify the reasons for his or her sleep troubles.

It is convenient to distinguish three categories of insomnia: onset insomnia, maintenance insomnia, and termination insomnia. People with **onset insomnia** have trouble falling asleep. Those with **maintenance insomnia** awaken frequently during the night. And those with **termination insomnia** wake up too early and cannot get back to sleep. It is possible to have more than one of the three types.

Certain cases of insomnia are related to abnormalities of biological rhythms (MacFarlane, Cleghorn, & Brown, 1985a, 1985b). Ordinarily, people fall asleep while their temperature is declining and awaken while it is rising, as in Figure 9.14a. Some people's body temperature rhythm is *phase delayed,* as in Figure 9.14b. If they try to fall asleep at the normal time, their body temperature is higher than normal for going to sleep. Such people are likely to experience onset insomnia (Morris, Lack, & Dawson, 1990). Other people's body temperature rhythm is *phase advanced,* as in Figure 9.14c. They are likely to suffer termination insomnia. Those who suffer from maintenance insomnia may have major irregularities of their circadian rhythms.

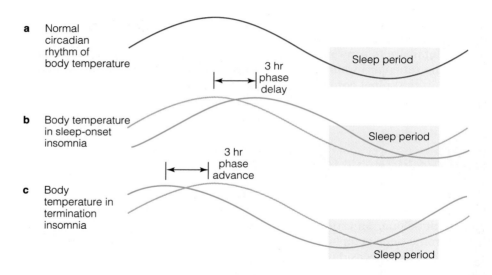

Figure 9.14
How a delay or advance in the circadian rhythm of body temperature can relate to insomnia

a   Normal circadian rhythm of body temperature

3 hr phase delay

Sleep period

b   Body temperature in sleep-onset insomnia

Sleep period

3 hr phase advance

c   Body temperature in termination insomnia

Sleep period

REM sleep occurs mostly during the rising phase of the temperature cycle. For most people, this is the second half of the night's sleep, as Figure 9.14a shows. For people with termination insomnia, or anyone else who falls asleep after the temperature cycle has already hit bottom, REM sleep may start shortly after the person falls asleep (Czeisler, Weitzman, Moore-Ede, Zimmerman, & Knauer, 1980). Because depression is often associated with termination insomnia, many depressed people enter REM sleep earlier in the night than nondepressed people do.

Sleep Apnea

One special cause of insomnia is **sleep apnea,** an inability to breathe while sleeping (Weitzman, 1981). Many people breathe irregularly during REM sleep, and about 10 to 15 percent of all adults have occasional periods of at least 10 seconds without breathing. Sleep apnea to that degree is considered normal and unrelated to insomnia (Kales & Kales, 1984). A few people, however, may go a minute or more without breathing and then awaken, gasping for breath (Weitzman, 1981). Such people may stay in bed more than 8 hours per night but sleep only about half that time. In many cases, the person does not remember awakening repeatedly during the night; he or she is aware only of feeling poorly rested the next morning.

Obesity is one of several possible causes of sleep apnea. Some obese people, especially men, have trouble finding a sleeping position that enables them to breathe easily. More frequently, especially in older people, the origin of sleep apnea lies in brain mechanisms for respiration that cease functioning while a person is asleep.

Overuse of Sleeping Pills

Another cause of insomnia is, paradoxically, sleeping pills. Most sleeping pills are also tranquilizers; they operate at least in part by decreasing synaptic stimulation by norepinephrine, dopamine, or histamine—three neurotransmitters that tend to increase arousal.

Although tranquilizers may help a person to fall asleep, taking such drugs a few times may cause dependence on them for getting to sleep. Such a person who tries going to sleep without the drug may go into a withdrawal state that prevents sleep (Kales, Scharf, & Kales, 1978). He or she may react to the sleep-lessness by taking the sleeping pills again, setting up a cycle from which it is difficult to escape.

Certain short-acting tranquilizers, such as midazolam and triazolam, have become popular because their effects wear off before morning. Unlike certain other drugs, they do not leave the person sleepy the next day. Unfortunately, because their effects wear off so quickly, they may produce withdrawal effects during the night. As a result, someone who takes such drugs may awaken very early as a side effect of the drug and find it impossible to get back to sleep (Kales, Soldatos, Bixler, & Kales, 1983).

A final point regarding tranquilizers as sleeping pills: Certain tranquilizers may either phase-advance the biological clock or phase-delay it, depending on when a person takes them (Turek & Losee-Olson, 1986). Especially if such pills are taken to combat the sleep disorders of jet lag, they may aggravate the problem instead of relieving it, depending on when the person takes the pills and which direction the person has flown.

Periodic Movements in Sleep

Another factor occasionally linked to insomnia is **periodic movements in sleep,** a repeated involuntary movement of the legs and sometimes arms (Weitzman, 1981). The legs may kick once every 20 to 30 seconds for a period of minutes or even hours, mostly during non-REM sleep. Periodic movements are more common in older people than in younger people and are particularly rare before age 30. If they become extremely frequent or severe, they may awaken the person. They may also cause the person to fall out of bed. Many normal people experience a mild to moderate degree of periodic movements (Kales & Kales, 1984). Such movements may not be a problem unless they annoy the person's sleeping partner.

Narcolepsy

Narcolepsy is a condition characterized by frequent unexpected periods of sleepiness in the middle of the day (Aldrich, 1993). The condition strikes about one person in a thousand, generally running in families.

Four symptoms are generally associated with narcolepsy, although most patients do not report all four:

1. Gradual or sudden attacks of extreme sleepiness during the day.
2. Occasional **cataplexy**—an attack of muscle weakness while the person remains awake. Cataplexy is often triggered by strong emotions, such as anger or great excitement.
3. Sleep paralysis—a complete inability to move just as the person is falling asleep or waking up. Other people may experience sleep paralysis occasionally, but people with narcolepsy experience it more frequently.
4. *Hypnagogic hallucinations*—dreamlike experiences that the person has trouble distinguishing from reality, often occurring at the onset of sleep.

All of these symptoms can be interpreted as intrusions of an REM-like state into wakefulness; REM sleep is associated with muscle weakness (cataplexy), paralysis, and dreams (Mahowald & Schenck, 1992). Certain cells in the medulla become active during REM sleep, sending messages to the spinal cord to suppress muscle responsiveness. Many of those same cells in the medulla become active when a narcoleptic individual experiences cataplexy (Siegel et al., 1991). Various stimulant drugs, such as amphetamine, help to control narcolepsy; those same drugs tend to suppress REM sleep. However, because of amphetamine's other effects and its potential for abuse, many physicians are cautious about prescribing it (Kryger, 1993).

Night Terrors, Sleep Talking, and Sleepwalking

Night terrors are experiences of intense anxiety from which a person generally awakens screaming in terror. A night terror should be distinguished from a *nightmare,* which is simply an unpleasant dream that occurs during REM sleep in people of any age. Night terrors occur during non-REM sleep and are far more common in children than in adults.

Many people talk in their sleep occasionally, often unaware that they do. *Sleep talking* has about the same chance of occurring during REM sleep as during non-REM sleep (Arkin, Toth, Baker, & Hastey, 1970).

Sleepwalking occurs mostly in children, especially ages 2 to 5, and is most common early in the night, during stage 3 or stage 4 sleep. Its causes are not known, other than the fact that it runs in families. Sleepwalking is generally harmless, both to the sleepwalker and to others. No doubt you have heard people say, "You should never waken someone who is sleepwalking." In fact, it is not harmful or dangerous to awaken a sleepwalker, although the person is likely to feel very confused (Moorcroft, 1989).

REM Behavior Disorder

For most people, the major postural muscles are relaxed and inactive during REM sleep. However, a few people move around vigorously during their REM periods, apparently acting out their dreams. This condition is known as **REM behavior disorder.** Many of their dreams are violent, and they may punch, kick, and leap about, often damaging property and injuring themselves or other people. Their dreams correspond to their movements; that is, they dream that they are kicking when they are actually kicking.

A possible explanation for such behavior is damage to the brain areas responsible for inhibiting muscles during REM sleep. For example, after cats have received damage to various areas of the pons and midbrain, their muscles do not relax during REM sleep. Evidently, those areas send inhibitory messages to the motor neurons during REM sleep, probably by releasing the neurotransmitter glycine (M. H. Chase, Soja, & Morales, 1989). After damage to those areas, the cats' motor neurons are released from inhibition. During their REM periods, the cats occasionally walk, chase, attack, and perform other actions as if they were acting out dreams (Henley & Morrison, 1974; Jouvet & Delorme, 1965). Similarly, one study of people with REM sleep disorder found multiple areas of damage in the pons and midbrain (Culebras & Moore, 1989). Although the data do not point to a single critical brain area, they do suggest that REM sleep disorder is associated with impaired inhibition of the motor neurons.

Summary

1. The ascending reticular activating system (ARAS) sends diffuse messages throughout the cerebral cortex, regulating general arousal. A cat whose forebrain is cut off from the ARAS sleeps most of the day. (p. 334)

2. Several other brain areas produce activity that tends to promote sleep, although research has not identified a single master area for inducing sleep. (p. 335)

3. REM sleep begins with PGO waves—waves of brain activity transmitted from the pons to the lateral geniculate to the occipital lobe. (p. 336)

4. Acetylcholine neurons in the pons trigger REM episodes. After sleep has begun, certain circulating chemicals help to maintain it. (p. 336)

5. Insomnia sometimes results from a shift in phase of the circadian rhythm of temperature relative to the circadian rhythm of sleep and wakefulness. It can also result from a difficulty in breathing while asleep, overuse of tranquilizers, and numerous other causes. (p. 337)

6. People with narcolepsy grow very sleepy in the middle of the day. (p. 339)

7. Among other sleep disorders are night terrors, sleep talking, sleepwalking, and REM behavior disorder. (p. 340)

Review Questions

1. A cut through one level of the brain stem leads to constant sleeping; a cut through a more posterior level leads to constant wakefulness. Why? (p. 334)

2. How does the structure of the ARAS make it well suited to control the brain's arousal? (p. 334)

3. What are PGO waves? Where do they originate? (p. 336)

4. What is the apparent role of acetylcholine in sleep? (p. 336)

5. Describe some of the possible causes of insomnia. (p. 337)

6. What are the disadvantages of using sleeping pills to combat insomnia? (p. 338)

7. Describe the characteristics of narcolepsy. (p. 339)

8. Are night terrors more common in REM sleep or non-REM sleep? What about sleep talking? Sleepwalking? (p. 340)

Thought Question

1. When cats are deprived of REM sleep for various periods, the amount of rebound increases for the first 25 to 30 days but does not increase further with a longer deprivation. What prevents the need from accumulating beyond that point? Consider PGO waves in your answer.

Suggestion for Further Reading

Moorcroft, W. H. (1993). *Sleep, dreaming, & sleep disorders: An introduction.* (2nd ed.) Lanham, MD: University Press of America. Discusses the functions of various brain areas in sleep and clearly describes sleep disorders.

Terms

cerveau isolé preparation in which the forebrain and part of the midbrain are separated from the rest of the midbrain, hindbrain, and spinal cord (p. 333)

ascending reticular activating system (ARAS) system of heavily interconnected neurons extending from the medulla into the forebrain (p. 334)

Factor S small glycopeptide found in the nervous system and bloodstream of sleeping animals (p. 335)

PGO wave pattern of high-amplitude electrical potentials that occurs first in the pons, then in the lateral geniculate, and finally in the occipital cortex (p. 336)

insomnia lack of sleep, leaving the person feeling poorly rested the following day (p. 337)

onset insomnia difficulty falling asleep (p. 337)

maintenance insomnia frequent awakening during the night (p. 337)

termination insomnia tendency to awaken early and to be unable to get back to sleep (p. 337)

sleep apnea inability to breathe while sleeping (p. 338)

periodic movement in sleep repeated involuntary movement of the legs and sometimes arms during sleep (p. 339)

narcolepsy condition characterized by unexpected periods of sleep in the middle of the day (p. 339)

cataplexy attack of muscle weakness while a person remains awake (p. 339)

night terror experience of intense anxiety during sleep, from which a person awakens screaming in terror (p. 340)

REM behavior disorder condition in which people move around vigorously during REM sleep (p. 340)

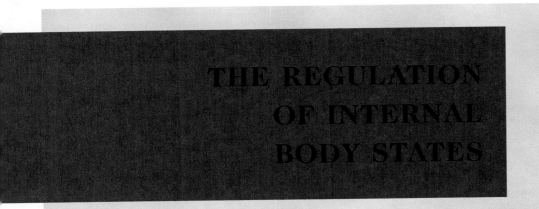

THE REGULATION OF INTERNAL BODY STATES

CHAPTER TEN

1. Many physiological and behavioral processes act to maintain a near-constancy of certain body variables, although they often anticipate a need rather than react to a need.

2. Mammals regulate body temperature by such physiological processes as shivering and by such behavioral processes as selecting an appropriate environment. Brain areas that control body temperature respond both to their own temperature and to the temperature of the skin and spinal cord.

3. Thirst may act to anticipate and prevent water need. Thirst also responds to the osmotic pressure of the blood and the total volume of blood.

4. Hunger and satiety are regulated by several factors, including taste, stomach distention, and glucose availability to the cells.

What is life? Life is many things and can be defined in different ways depending on whether our interest is medical, legal, philosophical, or poetic. At the most basic biological level, we can say that *life is a coordinated set of chemical reactions.* Not every coordinated set of chemical reactions is alive, but life cannot exist without a coordinated set of chemical reactions.

Every chemical reaction in the body takes place in a water medium at a rate that depends on the concentration of molecules in the water, the identity of those molecules, the temperature of the solution, and the presence of any contaminants. To continue the chemical reactions that we call "life," we need to prepare the ingredients according to a most precise recipe. Much of our behavior is organized to keep those ingredients present in the right proportions and at the right temperature.

Temperature Regulation

Many people try to lose weight by exercising. They quickly discover that it takes an amazing amount of exercise to lose a noticeable amount of weight (Després et al., 1991); your body uses almost as much fuel on an inactive day as it does on a day when you exercise. Where does all the rest of that fuel go? Most of it goes to **basal metabolism,** the rate of energy used while the body is at rest. Humans' basal metabolism is as high as it is because of the energy that we require to maintain a constant body temperature. Reptiles and amphibians, which do not maintain a constant body temperature, need a great deal less fuel each day than we do.

In short, temperature regulation is one of your body's top priorities, even if it is not one of your main topics of thought and conversation. By the end of this module, I hope to convince you that it deserves more attention than it usually gets from psychologists.

Homeostasis

Physiologist Walter B. Cannon (1929) introduced the term **homeostasis** (HO-mee-oh-STAY-sis) to refer to temperature regulation and other biological processes that work to keep certain body variables within a fixed range. To understand how a homeostatic process works, we can use the analogy of the thermostat in a house. Someone fixes a set range of temperatures on the thermostat. When the temperature in the house drops below that range, the thermostat triggers the furnace to provide heat until the house temperature returns to the set range. When the temperature rises above the maximum of the range, the thermostat triggers the air conditioner to cool the house.

Similarly, homeostatic processes in animals trigger certain physiological and behavioral activities when some variable passes beyond the limits of its set range. In many cases, the range is so narrow that we refer to it as a **set point.** For example, if calcium is deficient in your diet and its concentration in the blood begins to fall below the set point of 0.16 g/L (grams per liter), storage deposits in your bones will release additional calcium into the blood. If the calcium level in the blood rises above 0.16 g/L, part of the excess is stored in the bones and part is excreted in the urine and feces. Analogous mechanisms maintain constant blood levels of water, oxygen, glucose, sodium chloride, protein, fat, and acidity (Cannon, 1929).

In the mammalian body, temperature regulation, thirst, and hunger are *nearly* homeostatic processes. They are not *exactly* homeostatic because they anticipate future needs as well as reacting to current needs (Appley, 1991). For example, if you are planning to take an 8-hour hike, you might eat a larger-than-usual breakfast before you start. Even our temperature-regulation mechanisms anticipate future needs. In a frightening situation that might call for vigorous activity, you begin to sweat even before you start to move. People describe this experience as a "cold sweat."

Set points for body temperature, body fat, and other variables are not quite fixed; they change depending on time of day, time of year, and other conditions (Mrosovsky, 1990). Set points also differ among species. Most mammals have a body temperature close to that of humans, 37°C, while birds are significantly warmer, generally around 41°C.

Reproductive cells require a somewhat cooler environment. Birds sit on eggs instead of keeping them inside the body because the birds' internal temperature of 41°C is too hot for the embryo to survive, at least in the early stages. Similarly, in most male mammals, the scrotum hangs outside the body because sperm production requires a temperature a bit cooler than the rest of the body. (A man who wears his undershorts too tight begins producing fewer healthy sperm cells than before.) Pregnant women are advised to avoid hot baths or anything else that would expose a developing fetus to excessive heat.

Mechanisms of Controlling Body Temperature

Amphibians, reptiles, and most fish are **poikilothermic**; their body temperature is the same as the temperature of their environment. They can control their body temperature to some extent by selecting an appropriate location in the environment, but they lack physiological mechanisms of temperature regulation such as shivering and sweating. A few kinds of fish maintain a nearly constant temperature in the brain, if not in the rest of the body (Block, Finnerty, Stewart, & Kidd, 1993).

Mammals and birds are **homeothermic**; they use physiological mechanisms to maintain an almost constant body temperature despite large variations in the environmental temperature. Mammals and birds keep their body temperature close to a set point under normal circumstances.

Homeothermy requires an expenditure of effort, and therefore of fuel. An animal generates heat in proportion to its total mass; it radiates heat in proportion to its surface area. A small animal, such as a mouse or a hummingbird, has a high surface-to-volume ratio and therefore radiates heat rapidly. Such animals need a great deal of fuel each day in order to maintain their body temperature. The largest animals are better insulated against heat loss.

Why have we evolved mechanisms to control body temperature? What difference would it make if body temperature fluctuated over a range of 20 degrees or so each day? Why is constancy of body temperature important enough to be worth all the energy that it requires?

Part of the answer has to do with the effect of temperature on chemical reactions. Although the rates of all chemical reactions increase when the temperature rises, the rates of different reactions do not increase equally. For instance, imagine a sequence of chemical reactions of this form:

$$A \xrightarrow{\quad 1 \quad} B \xrightarrow{\quad 2 \quad} C$$

The letters stand for chemicals and the numbers represent reactions. Suppose that a 10° increase in temperature triples the rate of reaction 1 but only doubles the rate of reaction 2. As a result, chemical B may be generated faster than it can be converted to chemical C. The resulting accumulation of B might be harmful. In short, a constant body temperature makes it possible to evolve precise coordinations among the various reactions in the body.

A constant body temperature also makes it easier for the animal to stay active when the environment turns cold. Recall from Chapter 8 that a fish has trouble maintaining a high activity level at a low temperature. To move at a normal speed, it must recruit muscle fibers that fatigue rapidly. By maintaining a constant internal temperature, birds and mammals can be ready for action at any temperature, without needing to recruit different sets of muscles.

Brain Mechanisms of Temperature Regulation

The body defends the temperature at its core—including the brain and the other internal organs—more carefully than it defends the temperature of the skin. When the body cools below the set point, the blood vessels to the skin constrict, preventing the blood from being cooled by the cold air around the skin. Although the skin may grow very cold, the brain, heart, and other internal organs remain warm. To generate more heat, the muscles contract rhythmically (shivering), or the animal runs about. The fur of a mammal becomes erect, increasing insulation from the cold environment.

If the body begins to overheat, more blood than usual flows to the skin, where it can be cooled by contact with the air (which is almost always cooler than the body). An animal may decrease its heat production by decreasing body activity. Depending on the species, animals sweat, pant heavily, or lick themselves; evaporation of the saliva cools the body.

All these physiological changes depend predominantly on certain areas within the hypothalamus, a small structure at the base of the brain (see Figure 10.1). The hypothalamus contains a number of nuclei, each of which apparently serves a different function. The most critical area for temperature control is the **preoptic area**, located adjacent to the anterior hypothalamus. (It is called *preoptic* because it is located next to the optic chiasm, where the optic nerves cross.)

The preoptic area monitors body temperature partly by monitoring its own temperature (Nelson & Prosser, 1981). When an experimenter heats the preoptic area, an animal pants or sweats, even in a cool environment. If the same area is cooled, the animal shivers, even in a warm room. These responses are not simply reflexive. When an experimenter heats or cools the preoptic area, an animal will learn to press a lever or to do other work for cold air or hot air reinforcements (Laudenslager, 1976; Satinoff, 1964).

Besides monitoring their own temperature, the cells of the preoptic area also receive input from temperature-sensitive receptors in the skin and spinal cord. The animal shivers most vigorously when both the preoptic area and the other receptors are cold; it sweats or pants most vigorously when both are hot.

Damage to the preoptic area impairs a mammal's temperature regulation. It can no longer shiver, so its body temperature plummets in a cold environment (Satinoff, Valentino, & Teitelbaum, 1976). Moreover, even in an environment with a steady temperature, the animal's body temperature fluctuates over a range of 10 degrees or more (Satinoff, Liran, & Clapman, 1982).

The preoptic area is the dominant area for temperature control, but temperature-sensitive cells also exist in other parts of the hypothalamus, else-

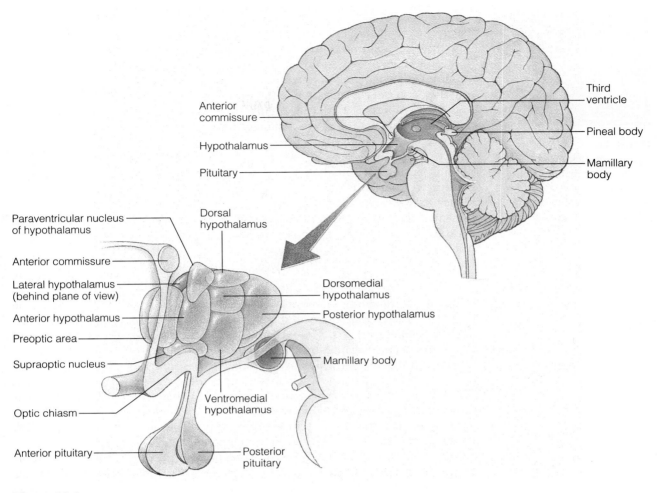

Figure 10.1
Major subdivisions of the hypothalamus and pituitary
(After Nieuwenhuys et al., 1988.)

where in the brain, and in the spinal cord. Fragmentary shivering and sweating can still occur after preoptic area damage.

Behavioral Mechanisms of Temperature Regulation

Although the body temperature of fish, amphibians, and reptiles matches that of their environment, their temperature seldom fluctuates wildly. They regulate their temperature by choosing their environment (Crawshaw, Moffitt, Lemons, & Downey, 1981). A desert lizard burrows into the ground in the middle of the day, when the surface is too hot, and again in the middle of the night, when the surface is too cold. While on the surface, it will choose a spot in the sun or in the shade to keep its body temperature fairly constant.

Mammals, too, use behavioral means to regulate their body temperature. They do not sit on an icy surface shivering when they can build a nest, or sweat and pant in the sun when they can find a shady spot. The more they can regulate their temperature behaviorally, the less they need to rely on physiological changes (Refinetti & Carlisle, 1986a).

Figure 10.2
Infant rats regulate body temperature by burrowing into the pile of other infant rats to keep warm and by passively floating to the top when they are already warm enough. (©Stephen Dalton/ Photo Researchers, Inc.)

During infancy, behavioral mechanisms compensate for inadequate physiological mechanisms. For example, infant rats have no fur for insulation. An infant rat isolated in a cold room cannot generate heat nearly as fast as it loses it. A litter of ten to 12 infant rats, however, can huddle together and collectively maintain a normal body temperature. As the ones on top cool off, they burrow into the center of the mass, while the warm ones near the center passively float to the top (Alberts, 1978). (See Figure 10.2.)

Adult mammals that have a damaged preoptic area can also regulate their temperature by behavioral means. In a cold environment, they will press a lever to keep a heat lamp on long enough to keep their body temperature near normal (Satinoff & Rutstein, 1970; Van Zoeren & Stricker, 1977). Their temperature regulation is not as good as normal, however; their temperature gets higher than normal during the day and colder than normal during the night (Szymusiak, DeMory, Kittrell, & Satinoff, 1985). Behavioral regulation of temperature is partly under the control of the preoptic area, partly under the control of the posterior hypothalamus (Refinetti & Carlisle, 1986b), and partly under the control of other brain areas.

Fever

People with bacterial and viral infections generally have a fever—an increase in body temperature. As a rule, the fever is not part of the illness; it is part of the body's defense against the illness.

When the body is invaded by bacteria, viruses, fungi, or other foreign bodies, it mobilizes, among other things, its *leukocytes* (white blood cells) to attack them. The leukocytes release a protein called *interleukin-1*, which in turn causes the production of **prostaglandin E_1**, which then causes cells in the preoptic area to raise body temperature (Dascombe, 1986; Dinarello & Wolff, 1982). Prostaglandin E_1 elevates body temperature even in animals not suffering any infection; rats injected with the chemical also show an increased preference for the warmer areas in the environment (Marques, Spencer, Burks, & McDougal, 1984). All these effects depend on the preoptic area.

Newborn rabbits, whose hypothalamus is immature, do not get fevers in response to infections. If they are given a choice of environments, however, they will select an unusually warm environment and thereby raise their body temperature (Satinoff, McEwen, & Williams, 1976). That is, they will develop a fever by behavioral rather than physiological means. Fish and reptiles do the same if they can find a warm enough environment (Kluger, 1978).

Does a fever do the animal any good? Certain types of bacteria grow less vigorously at high temperatures than at normal mammalian body temperatures (Kluger & Rothenburg, 1979). Animals that develop moderate fevers, up to about 2.25 degrees above normal temperature, have a better chance of surviving a bacterial infection than do animals that fail to develop a fever (Kluger & Vaughn, 1978). If the fever goes higher than that, the animal's probability of survival declines.

Temperature Regulation and Behavior

When we are watching an animal's behavior and trying to interpret it, we can easily overlook the importance of temperature regulation. Let us consider three examples of how psychologists can reinterpret or better understand their results when they acknowledge the importance of body temperature.

Body Temperature and the Development of Animal Behavior

Over a number of years, psychologists observing the development of behavior in rats concluded that infant rats were incapable of certain behaviors and that the capacity for those behaviors developed at some point in the first three weeks or so of life. (Three weeks is a much longer time in a rat's life than it is in a human's.) The list of such behaviors included odor conditioning, female sexual behavior, certain aspects of eating and drinking, and others. After extensive attempts to study the developmental psychology of such behaviors, researchers discovered that rats could perform all these behaviors in the first week of life, sometimes even in the first day of life, if the researchers tested the rats in a warm enough room. The problem was simply that researchers generally work at "normal room temperature," perhaps 20°–23°C, which is comfortable to you or me, but dangerously cold for an isolated baby rat. (See Figure 10.3.) Testing baby rats under those conditions would be analogous to testing the intelligence of adult humans while they are submerged in ice water. When baby rats are placed in a room at 33°–35°C, their behavioral capacities improve markedly (Satinoff, 1991).

Body Temperature and "Distress Calls"

Here is a second example of the wide-ranging relevance of temperature regulation: Occasionally a baby rat accidentally wanders outside its nest. When it does so, it emits very high-pitched vocalizations, about 40 kHz—much too high for adult humans to hear, but well within the range for adult rats. If the mother rat is nearby, she responds to those vocalizations by retrieving the lost rat pup to the nest. Now, why does the baby rat emit those calls?

At first glance, the answer may seem obvious: "It's a distress call; the infant is calling for help." But the obvious answer may be incorrect, or at least misleading. Consider this analogy: Suppose you get lost on a camping trip. After wandering around for a while, you start a fire to warm yourself up. Unbeknownst to you, a rescue party had been searching for you, and now the campfire enables them to find you. The fire served the function of getting help, but you did not set it for that purpose.

The same is true for the baby rat. A baby rat that wanders out of its nest utters very few vocalizations if the temperature is within the **thermoneutral zone**—the range of environmental temperatures for which the animal needs to expend little energy in order to maintain its normal body temperature. (See Figure 10.4.) But if the air is too cold or too hot, the baby rat has to expend a great deal of energy to maintain its temperature, and, in order to get all the oxygen that it needs, it has to breathe hard and exhale vigorously. The vigorous exhalation produces the high-pitched sounds (Blumberg & Alberts, 1990; Blumberg, Efimova, & Alberts, 1992). That is, in the process of trying to stabilize its temperature, the baby rat's breathing accidentally makes sounds that attract the mother.

When we at first interpreted the baby's vocalizations as distress calls, we were guilty of the error of **anthropomorphism** (literally, "human-shape-ism"), the error of treating animals as if they were humans. When adult humans vocalize, we are almost always trying to communicate. We are therefore quick to assume that animals—or, indeed, baby humans—also intend some communication by their vocalizations. That assumption, though seemingly natural, needs to be challenged.

Figure 10.3
The special difficulties of temperature regulation for a newborn rodent
A newborn rat has no hair, thin skin, and little body fat. If left exposed in a cool room, its body temperature quickly falls. This difficulty in regulating body temperature impairs the young rat's performance in many psychological experiments. (©Cosmos Blank/NAS/Photo Researchers, Inc.)

Figure 10.4
Vocalizations by isolated infant rats at various temperatures
At a room temperature of 32°C or 35°C, rat pups can easily maintain their body temperature of 37°C, and they vocalize very little. At cooler or warmer temperatures, they vocalize more frequently. (Based on data of Blumberg, Efimova, & Alberts, 1992.)

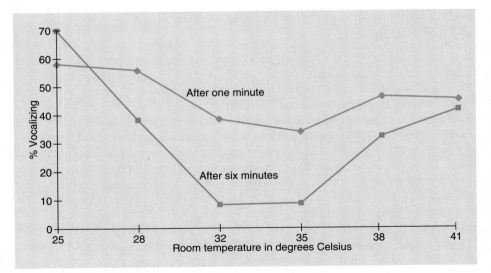

Figure 10.5
When a predator captures a young chick, the chick adopts a posture of "tonic immobility," failing to move for at least a few seconds, sometimes as much as hours. The cessation of this posture depends on changes in body temperature.

Body Temperature and the Tonic Immobility Response

One more example: When a chick or other baby bird is grabbed by a predator, its first response is generally to adopt a position known as **tonic immobility,** in which it becomes limp and motionless except for an occasional muscle twitch (Figure 10.5). Observers say the chick is "feigning death." One does not necessarily imagine that the chick is doing this intentionally; still, the effect of the chick's immobility is to decrease the predator's probability of attacking it. After all, the predator is predisposed to attack its prey until the prey stops moving; once the prey stops moving, the predator stops attacking.

So, the functional advantage of the chick's immobility response is that it stops the predator from attacking. Eventually, the predator might drop it or give the chick some other opportunity to escape. Granted, the chances are not good, but any chance is better than none at all.

The chick may stay in this position for just seconds or for several hours. As a rule, the longer, the better; if it gets up and starts moving again too soon, the predator will react to the movement by attacking before the chick has a chance to escape. But what determines how soon the chick quits "feigning death" and starts moving?

The answer is, simply, body temperature. Ordinarily, chicks maintain a body temperature that is one or more degrees cooler than that of adult chickens, and they control their body temperature largely by behavioral means. When they lie or sit motionless, they increase body temperature; when they stand and move a bit, they decrease body temperature. Ordinarily, a chick alternates between sitting and standing. In the tonic immobility position, the chick remains sitting and its body temperature begins to increase. When body temperature reaches 41.4°C. (the normal body temperature of an adult chicken), the chick gets up and starts moving (Rovee-Collier, Kupersmidt, O'Brien, Collier, & Tepper, 1991). Moving incurs the risk of a possible attack by the predator, but staying still would incur the certain danger of overheating.

The moral of the story: Even when we are studying some more dynamic behavior such as predator-prey relations, we should not forget the contribution that temperature regulation makes to animal behavior.

Summary

1. Homeostasis is a tendency to maintain a body variable near a set point. Temperature, hunger, and thirst are almost homeostatic, but they anticipate future needs as well as reacting to current needs. (p. 344)

2. A constant body temperature enables an animal to evolve chemical reactions that are precisely coordinated. It also enables the animal to be equally active and equally resistant to fatigue at all environmental temperatures. (p. 345)

3. The preoptic area of the hypothalamus is critical for temperature control. It monitors both its own temperature and that of the skin and spinal cord. (p. 346)

4. Even homeothermic animals rely partly on behavioral mechanisms for temperature regulation, especially in infancy and after damage to the preoptic area. (p. 347)

5. Fever is caused by the release of prostaglandin E_1, which stimulates cells in the preoptic area. A moderate fever may help an animal combat an infection. (p. 348)

6. Temperature regulation often influences behaviors that seem unrelated to temperature; psychologists must sometimes reinterpret their results after they consider the relevance of the animal's body temperature. (p. 349)

Review Questions

1. In what ways are certain motivations homeostatic? (p. 344)

2. What evidence do we have that the preoptic area controls body temperature? (p. 346)

3. In what way can an animal continue to regulate body temperature after damage to the preoptic area? (p. 348)

4. What processes in the brain are responsible for fevers? (p. 348)

5. Why should we not assume that an isolated infant rat's vocalizations are attempts to get help? (p. 349)

6. What is anthropomorphism, and why should psychologists try to avoid it? (p. 349)

7. After a predator has captured a chick, why does the chick feign death longer in a cool environment than in a warm environment? (p. 350)

Thought Question

1. Speculate on why human body temperature is 37°C. Is that figure just an accident? Would it have been as easy to evolve temperature regulation around a body temperature of 21° or 47°C? Why do birds have higher body temperatures than mammals have? If you were asked to predict the body temperature of beings on some other planet, what would you want to know about conditions on that planet before making your prediction?

Terms

basal metabolism rate of energy use while the body is at rest, used largely for maintaining a constant body temperature (p. 344)

homeostasis tendency to maintain some variable, such as temperature, within a fixed range (p. 344)

set point level at which homeostatic processes maintain some variable (p. 344)

poikilothermic maintaining the body at the same temperature as the surrounding environment (p. 345)

homeothermic maintaining nearly constant body temperature over a wide range of environmental temperatures (p. 345)

preoptic area brain area adjacent to the anterior hypothalamus, important for temperature control (p. 346)

prostaglandin E_1 chemical produced during an infection that stimulates an increase in body temperature (p. 348)

thermoneutral zone range of environmental temperatures for which an individual can maintain a normal body temperature without expending much effort (e.g., neither shivering nor sweating) (p. 349)

anthropomorphism the unjustified attribution of human characteristics to nonhuman animals (p. 349)

tonic immobility limp and nearly motionless condition of the body's postural muscles (p. 350)

Thirst

Water constitutes an estimated 70 percent of the mammalian body. Because the rate of all chemical reactions in the body depends on the concentration of the chemicals in water, the body's water must be regulated within narrow limits. The body also needs enough fluid in the circulatory system to maintain normal blood pressure.

Mechanisms of Maintaining Water Balance

To maintain a constant amount of water in the body, we have to balance the water we take in with the water we excrete. We take in water by drinking, of course, but also by eating. Certain foods, such as lettuce, contain a great deal of water, and even dry foods yield some water during digestion. We lose water by urinating, defecating, and sweating. We also lose a little in every breath that we exhale and a little by evaporation from the eyes, the mouth, and other moist body surfaces.

Different species have adopted different strategies for balancing water intake and loss. Beavers and other species that live in or near the water drink plenty of water and eat foods with a high water content; they excrete copious amounts of dilute urine and moist feces. However, gerbils and other desert animals may go through their entire lives without ever drinking water; they gain a little by eating, but they cannot afford to lose much. They have evolved ways of excreting very dry feces and very concentrated urine. They do not sweat; to keep cool, they enter deep burrows during the heat of the day. Their highly convoluted nasal passages minimize the amount of water lost when they exhale.

Humans can use either the beavers' strategy or the gerbils' strategy, depending on circumstances. If you have access to ample supplies of highly palatable beverages, you will probably drink much and urinate much, as beavers do. In that case, you do not concern yourself with drinking the "right" amount; you let your kidneys discard the excess. However, if you cannot find anything good to drink, or if you have already lost a fair amount of water by sweating or other means, you will conserve your water, as gerbils do. You conserve fluid mainly by decreasing the amount of water in your urine. When body fluids are low, the posterior pituitary (see Figure 10.1) releases a hormone called **vasopressin** because it raises blood pressure by constricting the blood vessels (the vascular system). Vasopressin is also known as **antidiuretic hormone (ADH)** because it enables the kidneys to reabsorb water and therefore to secrete highly concentrated urine. (*Diuresis* means *urination.*) In short, you can maintain your water balance either by increasing your water intake or by decreasing your loss.

The Multiple Causes of Drinking

We drink for many reasons. At one time, physiologists believed that all drinking was a response to a dry throat (Fitzsimons, 1973). Today, we regard dryness of the throat as only a minor contributor to thirst. Although someone with inactive salivary glands does drink more than usual during a meal just to wash down the food, such a person drinks only a normal amount over the course of a day. If an animal's esophagus is cut and connected to a tube that empties outside the body, the animal continues drinking enormous amounts, even though its throat is constantly moist (Blass & Hall, 1976).

We drink the greatest amount during meals. Drinking with meals is adaptive because food increases the concentration of solutes in the body and thus the need for water. But we do not wait until those solutes enter our cells; we drink long before the food is digested and sometimes at the very start of the meal (Kraly, 1990).

People also sometimes drink just because a beverage tastes good or because they like to socialize with friends over a drink or two. In a way, thirst is almost a backup system, a way of ensuring that we drink enough when taste, socializing, and eating-related drinking do not supply enough water to the system.

Although we speak about "thirst" as if it were a single entity, we experience one kind of thirst after an increase in the solute concentrations in the body and a different kind of thirst after a loss of overall fluid volume. Correspondingly, thirst researchers distinguish between osmotic thirst and hypovolemic thirst.

Osmotic Thirst

The concentration of all solutes combined in the body fluids remains at a nearly constant level of 0.15 M (molar) in mammals. (A concentration of 1.0 M has a number of grams of solute equal to the molecular weight of that solute, dissolved in 1 liter of solution.) This fixed concentration of solutes can be regarded as a set point, similar to the set point for temperature. Any deviation from the set point activates mechanisms that act to restore the concentration of solutes to the set point.

The solutes produce an **osmotic pressure,** defined as the force exerted by the concentration of a solute in a water solution toward other solutions separated from it by a semipermeable membrane (a membrane through which water, but not solutes, can pass). Loosely speaking, osmotic pressure is the force with which a solution holds its water and attracts water from an adjacent solution. The osmotic pressure of a solution is proportional to the total number of molecules in the solution per unit volume. In osmosis, water diffuses across a membrane from the side with low solute concentration to the side with high solute concentration. That is, water flows from the area of high water

Figure 10.6
Two dishes of solution separated by a semipermeable membrane
(*a*) *Two solutions of unequal solute concentration are introduced.* (*b*) *Water flows by osmosis toward the area with a higher concentration of solutes.*

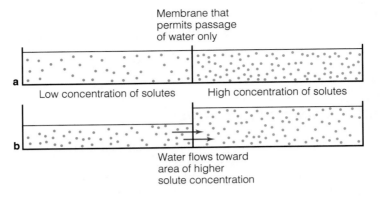

Membrane that permits passage of water only

a Low concentration of solutes | High concentration of solutes

b

Water flows toward area of higher solute concentration

concentration to the area of low water concentration, until the concentration of solutes in water is equal on both sides (see Figure 10.6).

If the concentration of solutes increases in the body, then the osmotic pressure of its fluids increases. This can occur either because the body has lost water or because it has gained solutes. Generally, the body compensates by excreting a concentrated urine, to rid the body of excess solutes, and by drinking, to increase water. The resulting thirst is known as **osmotic thirst.**

Osmotic thirst occurs when a high concentration of solutes outside the cells causes water to flow out of the cells. For example, if concentrated sodium chloride is injected into the blood, the sodium does not readily cross the membranes of cells. Water flows out of the cells and into the blood, shrinking the volume of the cells. The result is increased thirst (Fitzsimons, 1961). An injection of concentrated glucose does not have the same effect because glucose readily crosses the membrane. Therefore, no gradient of osmotic pressure withdraws water from the cell.

How does the body "know" when its osmotic pressure is low? The answer is that it has some neurons specialized for this purpose, located in areas around the third ventricle of the brain (Figure 10.7). The areas surrounding the third ventricle are not protected by a blood-brain barrier; hence, they are in a position to detect chemicals circulating in the blood, including the overall solute concentration of the blood (Ramsay & Thrasher, 1990). The area principally responsible for detecting osmotic pressure is known as the **OVLT** (*organum vasculosum laminae terminalis*).

Neurons in the OVLT relay their information to several parts of the hypothalamus, including the **supraoptic nucleus** and the **paraventricular nucleus,** which control secretion of vasopressin, the hormone that regulates blood pressure and urine concentration. The OVLT neurons also relay information to the nearby **lateral preoptic area.** The lateral preoptic area directs drinking and water-seeking behaviors. A lesion in the lateral preoptic area decreases a rat's drinking response to an injection of sodium chloride into the blood (Blass & Epstein, 1971; Peck & Novin, 1971). We cannot say that the rat fails to respond to the sodium chloride, however. Rather, it deals with the sodium chloride the way that a gerbil does (as previously described): It excretes small quantities of highly concentrated urine, removing as much of the sodium chloride as possible without losing much water (Stricker, 1976; Stricker & Coburn, 1978).

Healthy, intact rats react the same way if they have only bitter-tasting water available (Rowland & Flamm, 1977). In other words, an animal with damage to its lateral preoptic area acts as if it dislikes the taste of water.

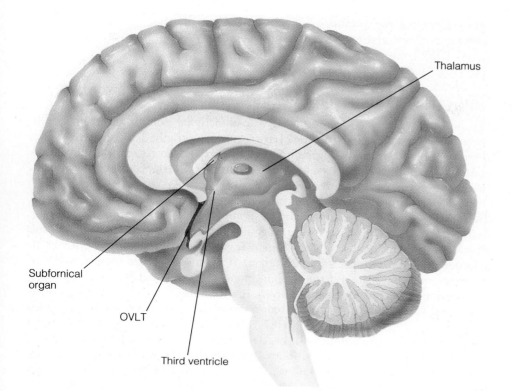

Thalamus

Subfornical
organ

OVLT

Third ventricle

Figure 10.7
Location of the brain's receptors for osmotic pressure and blood volume
*These neurons are located in areas surrounding the third ventricle of the brain,
where no blood-brain barrier prevents blood-borne chemicals from entering the
brain. The primary area for detecting osmotic pressure is the OVLT (organum vacu-
losum laminae terminalis). The primary area for detecting blood volume is the subfornical organ. (Based in part on Weindl, 1973; and DeArmond, Fusco, & Dewey,
1974.)*

Hypovolemic Thirst

The body needs to maintain an adequate blood pressure. If blood volume, and
therefore pressure, is too low, the blood cannot carry enough water and nutrients to the cells. Blood volume may drop sharply after a deep cut or after internal hemorrhaging. The body then needs to replenish not only its water but also
the salts and other solutes that have been lost. The result is **hypovolemic** (HI-
po-vo-LEE-mik) **thirst,** meaning *thirst based on low volume.*

Studying hypovolemic thirst simply by withdrawing blood from an animal
is unsatisfactory because an animal that loses blood rapidly may go into a state
of shock. One way to withdraw blood gradually is by injecting polyethylene gly-
col just under the skin (Stricker & Macarthur, 1974). The solution stays where
it is injected for hours and causes fluid from the blood to accumulate temporarily in that area.

After a reduction in blood volume, an animal increases its drinking, but it
will not drink much pure water. (A large amount of water would dilute its body
fluids.) It will drink much larger amounts of water containing salts (Stricker,

Thirst

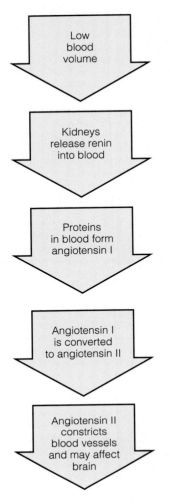

Low
blood
volume

Kidneys
release renin
into blood

Proteins
in blood form
angiotensin I

Angiotensin I
is converted
to angiotensin II

Angiotensin II
constricts
blood vessels
and may affect
brain

**Figure 10.8
Hormonal response to
hypovolemia**

1969). If offered one container of pure water and another of excessively concentrated saltwater, it will alternate between the two to produce a mixture that matches the content of its blood.

Mechanisms of Hypovolemic Thirst

The body has two ways of detecting a loss of blood volume (Epstein, 1990; Ramsay & Thrasher, 1990). First, **baroreceptors** attached to the large veins detect the blood pressure returning to the heart. These receptors relay information to hypothalamic areas, increasing drinking (Rettig, Ganten, & Johnson, 1981; Zimmerman, Blaine, & Stricker, 1981).

The second mechanism depends on hormones. When blood volume drops, the kidneys detect the change and respond by releasing *renin,* a hormone. Renin splits a portion off angiotensinogen, a large protein that circulates in the blood, to form the hormone angiotensin I, which certain enzymes convert to angiotensin II. The hormone **angiotensin II** then causes the blood vessels to constrict, compensating for the drop in blood pressure (see Figure 10.8).

When angiotensin reaches the brain, it stimulates neurons in the **subfornical organ,** which, like the OVLT area, adjoins the third ventricle of the brain (Fitzsimons, 1971). (See Figure 10.7.) Also like the OVLT, the subfornical organ lies outside the blood-brain barrier and is therefore well suited to monitor the blood (Buggy, Fisher, Hoffman, Johnson, & Phillips, 1975; Mangiapane, Thrasher, Keil, Simpson, & Ganong, 1983; Miselis, Shapiro, & Hand, 1979). The subfornical organ relays information to part of the preoptic area in the hypothalamus, which directs drinking. Injections of angiotensin to the subfornical organ and adjacent areas can prompt drinking (Mangiapane & Simpson, 1980). An injection of a drug that blocks angiotensin II receptors strongly inhibits drinking (Fregly & Rowland, 1991). This finding supports the conclusion that angiotensin in the brain promotes certain types of thirst.

Angiotensin and baroreceptors may have a **synergistic effect** (Epstein, 1983; N. Rowland, 1980). If two effects are synergistic, their combined effect is more than twice the effect of either one acting separately. That is, it may take less angiotensin to stimulate thirst if the baroreceptors are also indicating low blood pressure than if they are indicating normal blood pressure.

Table 10.1 summarizes the differences between osmotic thirst and hypovolemic thirst.

Sodium-Specific Cravings

Many people today have to limit their salt intake to control high blood pressure. However, although excessive salt is harmful, a certain amount of sodium chloride and other salts is necessary for life.

Individuals who have lost sodium and other solutes by bleeding or other means often experience a craving for salty tastes along with their hypovolemic thirst. That increased preference develops automatically, apparently without any trial-and-error learning (Richter, 1936). In fact, sodium-deficient animals have an increased preference for many salty-tasting solutions, including those containing lithium salts, which are poisonous (Nachman, 1962). Sodium-specific cravings are the only known specific hunger that emerges as soon as the need exists; specific hungers for other vitamins and minerals have to be learned by trial and error (Rozin & Kalat, 1971). Even after an animal has

Table 10.1 Comparison of Osmotic and Hypovolemic Thirst

Type of Thirst	Stimulus	Best Relieved by Drinking	Receptor Location
Osmotic thirst	High solute concentration outside cells, hence loss of water from cells	Water	OVLT, a brain area adjoining the third ventricle
Hypovolemic thirst	Low blood volume	Saltwater or water containing other solutes	1. Baroreceptors, measuring blood flow returning to the heart 2. Subfornical organ, a brain area adjoining the third ventricle

recovered from sodium deficiency, it continues to show an increased preference for solutions containing sodium (Sakai, Frankmann, Fine, & Epstein, 1989).

Sodium hunger depends largely on hormones (Schulkin, 1991). When the body's sodium reserves are low, the adrenal glands produce the hormone **aldosterone,** which causes the kidneys to conserve sodium when excreting urine. Aldosterone also acts on the OVLT and other areas surrounding the third ventricle to trigger an increased intake of salty tastes. The body also reacts to the decreased sodium reserves by increasing the blood concentrations of angiotensin II. Angiotensin produces different effects in different parts of the brain; in some areas it induces only thirst, but in the medial amygdala it triggers sodium hunger.

The effects of aldosterone and angiotensin are strongly synergistic, perhaps because they act on different parts of the brain. Either one alone produces a small increase in sodium intake; together they produce a much greater effect than either one can alone (Sakai & Epstein, 1990; Stricker, 1983).

Summary

1. Drinking occurs for many reasons, often in anticipation of a need and not just in response to a current need. Most drinking occurs around mealtime, stimulated by food in the stomach. (p. 352)

2. An increase in the osmotic pressure of the blood, which draws water out of cells, causes osmotic thirst. Neurons in the OVLT, an area adjoining the third ventricle, detect changes in osmotic pressure and send information to hypothalamic areas responsible for vasopressin secretion and for drinking. (p. 353)

3. A loss of blood volume causes hypovolemic thirst. Animals with hypovolemic thirst drink more water containing solutes than pure water. The subfornical organ is especially important for detecting changes in blood volume and sending information to trigger hypovolemic thirst. (p. 355)

4. Two stimuli have been identified for hypovolemic thirst: signals from the baroreceptors and the hormone angiotensin II, which increases when blood pressure falls. The two stimuli apparently act synergistically. (p. 356)

5. A loss of sodium salts from the body triggers sodium-specific cravings. The hormones aldosterone and angiotensin II synergistically stimulate such cravings. (p. 356)

Review Questions

1. Why does an injection of sodium chloride produce thirst, while an injection of an equal amount of glucose does not? (p. 354)
2. In what way does an animal with damage to the lateral preoptic area of the hypothalamus resemble an animal that has access only to bad-tasting water? (p. 354)
3. What is the difference between osmotic and hypovolemic thirst? (p. 355)
4. Which hormones synergistically promote a craving for salty tastes? (p. 357)

Thought Question

1. Certain women crave salt during menstruation or pregnancy. Why?

Suggestion for Further Reading

Stricker, E. M. (Ed.) (1985). *Handbook of behavioral neurobiology, Vol. 10: Neurobiology of food and fluid intake.* New York: Plenum Press. A collection of chapters by various specialists; includes articles on hunger as well as thirst.

Terms

vasopressin, also known as **antidiuretic hormone (ADH)** pituitary hormone that raises blood pressure and enables the kidneys to reabsorb water and therefore to secrete highly concentrated urine (p. 352)

osmotic pressure force exerted by the concentration of a solute in water solution toward other solutions separated from it by a semipermeable membrane (p. 353)

osmotic thirst thirst that results from an increase in the concentration of solutes in the body (p. 354)

OVLT *organum vasculosum laminae terminalis,* a brain structure on the border of the third ventricle that is highly sensitive to the osmotic pressure of the blood (p. 354)

supraoptic nucleus and **paraventricular nucleus** two areas of the hypothalamus that control secretion of vasopressin (p. 354)

lateral preoptic area portion of the hypothalamus that is important for control of drinking (p. 354)

hypovolemic thirst thirst provoked by low blood volume (p. 355)

baroreceptor receptor that detects the blood pressure in the largest blood veins (p. 356)

angiotensin II hormone that constricts the blood vessels, monitoring blood volume and contributing to hypovolemic thirst (p. 356)

subfornical organ brain structure adjoining the third ventricle of the brain, where its cells monitor blood volume and relay information to the preoptic area of the hypothalamus (p. 356)

synergistic effect tendency for two influences acting simultaneously to produce more than twice the effect of either influence acting alone (p. 356)

aldosterone adrenal hormone that causes the kidneys to conserve sodium when excreting urine (p. 357)

Hunger

Imagine that your automobile needed a balanced diet, including varying proportions of 20 or more different kinds of fuel, and that the particular balance it needed varied from time to time. Imagine further that you never knew exactly what you were getting at any fuel station. The pumps contain varying combinations of gasoline, kerosene, alcohol, and other ingredients. To say the least, you would have trouble judging how much fuel to add at any time.

Regulating human food intake is even more complicated. Besides needing a balanced diet and never knowing exactly what is in our food, we need different amounts of any one nutrient depending on what other nutrients we are getting. For example, the more carbohydrates we eat, the more thiamine (vitamin B_1) we need. Considering all the complexities, it is amazing that anyone ever gets the right amount and balance of foods.

The Digestive System and Food Selection

Before discussing hunger, let's quickly examine the digestive system, diagrammed in Figure 10.9. Most foods consist of large molecules that cannot be used directly by the cells. The function of the digestive system is to break down the food into smaller, more easily used molecules.

Digestion begins in the mouth, where food is mixed with saliva, which contains enzymes that help break down carbohydrates. When swallowed, the food travels down the esophagus to the stomach. There, it is mixed with hydrochloric acid and several enzymes, which are mostly effective for the digestion of proteins. Between the stomach and the intestines is a round sphincter muscle that closes off the entrance to the intestines. This muscle periodically opens to allow food to enter the intestines, a bit at a time. Thus, the stomach serves as a storage place for food as well as a digestive organ.

Food then passes to the small intestine, which contains enzymes that help to digest proteins, fats, and carbohydrates. It is also the main site for the absorption of digested foodstuffs into the bloodstream; little is absorbed through the walls of the esophagus or stomach. The large intestine absorbs water and minerals and lubricates the remaining materials to pass them as feces.

Digested materials absorbed through the small intestine are carried throughout the body by the blood. If more carbohydrates, proteins, and fats are absorbed than the body can use at one time, the excess is stored as fat. Later, when the body needs additional nutrients, fat reserves are converted into glucose, the body's primary fuel, which is mobilized into the bloodstream.

Figure 10.9
The human digestive system

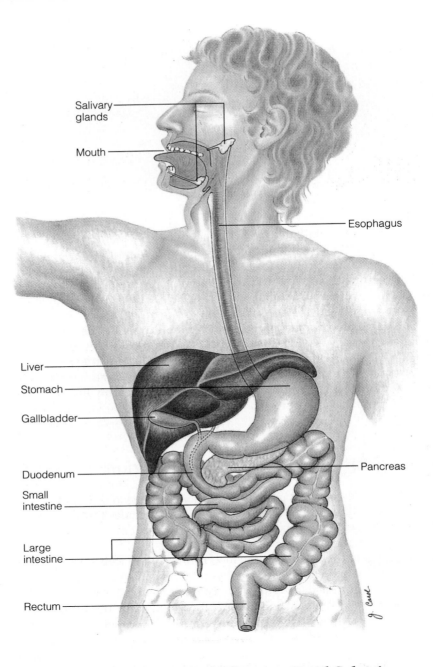

Salivary glands

Mouth

Esophagus

Liver

Stomach

Gallbladder

Pancreas

Duodenum

Small intestine

Large intestine

Rectum

How the Digestive System Influences Food Selection

Newborn mammals survive entirely on a diet of mother's milk. Why do they stop nursing when they grow older? There are several reasons: The milk dries up, the mother pushes the infants away, the infants grow large enough to try other foods. Moreover, after a certain age, most mammals lose their ability to metabolize **lactose,** the sugar in milk, because of declining levels of the intestinal enzyme **lactase,** which is necessary for lactose metabolism. From then on, consumption of milk can cause gas, stomach cramps, or other signs of distress (Rozin & Pelchat, 1988). Adult mammals can drink a little milk, as you may have noticed with a pet dog, but they generally limit the amount. The declining level of lactase may be an evolved mechanism to encourage weaning at the appropriate time.

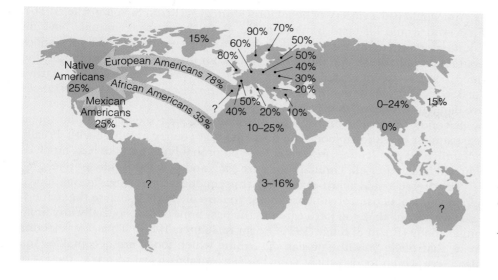

Figure 10.10
The distribution of adult lactose tolerance in different parts of the world
People in areas with high lactose tolerance (such as Scandinavia) are likely to enjoy milk, cheese, and other dairy products throughout their lives. People in areas with low tolerance (such as much of Asia) do not ordinarily consume milk or dairy products as adults. (Based on Flatz, 1988, and Rozin & Pelchat, 1988.)

Humans are the partial exception to this rule. Many adult humans consume milk, cheese, ice cream, and other products derived from cow or goat milk. And their intestinal lactase levels remain at fairly high levels throughout life. Worldwide, however, the majority of adults cannot comfortably tolerate large amounts of milk products. About two-thirds of all adult humans have low levels of lactase because of a recessive gene (Flatz, 1987). Most of these people can tolerate moderate amounts of dairy products but begin to feel uncomfortable if they consume too much. A smaller number of people can hardly consume any dairy products at all. Figure 10.10 shows the worldwide distribution of lactose tolerance. Note that most Europeans and European-Americans tolerate lactose and therefore have no trouble digesting dairy products. Most Africans and Asians have much lower tolerance for lactose. For that reason, Chinese, Japanese, Thai, and other Asian cuisines do not ordinarily use cheese or any other dairy product.

Other Influences on Food Selection

For some animal species, selecting a suitable diet is easy; for others it can be rather difficult. A **carnivore** (meat eater) has a relatively simple task; it eats whatever animal it can catch. However, **herbivores** (plant eaters) and **omnivores** (those that eat both meat and plants) must distinguish between edible and inedible substances.

One way to do so is to learn from the experiences of others. For example, juvenile rats tend to imitate the food selections of their elders, even if the elders had been taught to eat some rather unpalatable foods (Galef, 1992). Human children also learn from their parents and other adults. Children who grow up in the United States or Canada learn that peanut butter is "food," grass is "inappropriate," insects are "disgusting," and meat that has gone unrefrigerated for three days is "dangerous" (Rozin, 1984; Rozin & Fallon, 1987). Children in other parts of the world learn to eat the foods of their own cultures, such as the hot, spicy foods of Mexico (Rozin, 1990).

But remove the effects of culture and then what? If you parachuted onto an island with many unfamiliar plants and no other people to guide your choices, how would you figure out which ones were edible?

Hunger

You would use a variety of behavioral strategies (Rozin & Vollmecke, 1986). First, you would let taste be your guide. People and other animals have an innate preference for sweet tastes; most naturally occurring sweet substances contain carbohydrates, an important part of our diet. If we need more salt, the need triggers an increased preference for salty tastes, as described earlier (p. 356). We also have an innate dislike for bitter tastes; most bitter substances are dangerous to eat (Richter, 1950).

Second, you would probably seek something that seemed familiar, or at least similar to a known food. The first time that you try anything with a really unfamiliar flavor—coffee, for example—you probably do not like it as much as you will later. After all, familiar foods are safe, and new foods may not be.

Third, you could learn about the consequences of eating various foods. When you feel nausea or similar illness, you are likely to associate that experience with foods that you have eaten in the past hour or so, especially any unfamiliar foods (Rozin & Kalat, 1971; Rozin & Zellner, 1985). Thus, by rejecting foods that make you ill, you can determine which foods are acceptable. You also learn which foods satisfy your hunger. Animals learn to prefer flavors of foods that contain sucrose or other high-calorie substances; they show less preference for flavors paired with saccharin, a good-tasting but nutritionally useless substance (Mehiel, 1991). Presumably, you also come to enjoy fruit flavors because they are associated with good nutrition.

Physiological Mechanisms of Hunger and Satiety

Newborn rats, which grow very rapidly, follow a simple rule on the consumption of mother's milk: They nurse as long as milk is available and consume as much as possible (Blass & Teicher, 1980). They stop nursing only if the milk backs up from their stomach into the esophagus so that they cannot breathe!

Bears, even as adults, tend to eat as much as they can (Herrero, 1985). Although bears will eat almost anything, most of them survive largely on nuts and berries, which are in season for only a few days or weeks at a time. When the nuts and berries are available, bears stuff them down nonstop all day long, gaining enough weight to hold them through weeks or months of little food.

In contrast, humans generally eat discrete meals, instead of grazing sporadically like horses, or eating until the food backs up into the esophagus, like infant rats. Something within us tells us when to start eating and when to stop. In fact, we have a number of such mechanisms; if one mechanism fails for any reason, others can do the job.

Those mechanisms work well enough for most of us. However, the enormous market for diet books, diet products, and diet aids attests to the fact that many people fail to adjust their intake to match their need. The diet aids often fail or produce problems of their own. (See Digression 10.1.)

Oral Factors

People eat partly for the sake of taste. In one experiment, college students consumed lunch five days a week without tasting it. Each swallowed one end of a rubber tube and then pushed a button to pump a liquid diet into his or her stomach (Jordan, 1969; Spiegel, 1973). After a few days of practice, each sub-

Amphetamine as an Appetite Suppressant, and Tolerance to It

Some people who wish to lose weight resort to extreme strategies such as surgically removing fat, implanting a balloon in the stomach to occupy space, or wiring their jaws shut. Some also turn to appetite suppressant pills. Amphetamine was used for that purpose for a time, but was abandoned because of its potential for abuse. Other drugs are used today as appetite suppressants, but, regardless of which drug is used, users eventually develop a **drug tolerance** and eat as much as before, in spite of the drug. Why?

In two experiments, rats were given amphetamine or similar drugs 15 to 20 minutes before being offered access to milk for 15 or 30 minutes (Carlton & Wolgin, 1971; Woolverton, Kandel, & Schuster, 1978). The amphetamine suppressed their intake below its normal level, but the rats, being food-deprived, did at least nibble at the food. The following day, they were again injected with amphetamine prior to a meal; this time, they nibbled a bit more. By the end of the week, they were eating as much after the amphetamine injections as they had been eating previously. These rats developed tolerance because they practiced eating while under the drug's influence.

In both experiments, a second group received an amphetamine injection each day *after* the meal. By the end of a week, they had received as many amphetamine injections as the first group, but they had never tried to eat while under the effects of the drug. On the next day, the experimenters injected both groups with amphetamine before a meal. The group that had been receiving amphetamine before meals showed strong tolerance. The group that had been receiving amphetamine after meals showed no tolerance. They just nibbled a little, as the other group had done on the first day.

The conclusion is that drug tolerance is based largely on learning: If animals are repeatedly given an opportunity to practice some behavior (in this case, eating) while under the influence of a drug, the animals eventually develop a tolerance to the drug's effect on that behavior. If animals are injected with a drug the same number of times without practicing the behavior, they develop no tolerance. (See, for example, Campbell & Seiden, 1973; Wenger, Berlin, & Woods, 1980; Wenger, Tiffany, Bombardier, Nicholls, & Woods, 1981.)

These results suggest a way to avoid developing a tolerance to appetite suppressants: Use the pill when you plan to skip a meal altogether, not when you want to eat a very small meal. However, even if this strategy reduced the tolerance, an appetite suppressant probably would not help people lose much weight in the long run, for a different reason: Someone who has skipped a meal (with or without the use of pills) tends to overeat during the next meal (Caul, Jones, & Barrett, 1988).

---

ject established a consistent pattern, pumping in a constant volume of the liquid each day and maintaining a constant body weight. Most subjects found the untasted meals unsatisfying, however. Many reported a desire to taste or chew something. Moreover, when they were allowed to drink the liquid diet in the normal manner while also receiving it through the stomach tube, they drank almost as much as they would have had they received nothing through the tube (Jordan, 1969).

Eating is also sustained by other facial sensations. A rat explores a potential food with its mouth and whiskers before it starts to eat. The tactile sensations are conveyed to the brain via the fifth cranial nerve (the trigeminal nerve). After that nerve is cut, a rat decreases its exploration of foods and its biting of them. It can still eat moist, soft foods, using its jaw as a scoop, but it loses weight. It not only fails to eat properly, but it also will not press a bar as much as normal for food reinforcement. Evidently, a loss of sensation from the mouth leads to a drop in food-related motivation (Zeigler, Jacquin, & Miller, 1985).

Although taste and other mouth sensations contribute to the regulation of eating, they are not sufficient by themselves to determine the amount of food consumed. In **sham-feeding** experiments, an animal is denied nutrition because everything it swallows leaks out a tube connected to the esophagus or

Hunger

stomach. Under such conditions, animals swallow several times as much as normal during each meal (Antin, Gibbs, Holt, Young, & Smith, 1975).

Stomach Stimulation

Ordinarily, we end a meal when we experience a sensation of a full stomach, long before much of the digested food has reached the blood, much less the cells that need fuel. In one experiment, researchers attached an inflatable cuff at the connection between the stomach and the small intestine (Deutsch, Young, & Kalogeris, 1978). When they inflated the cuff, it closed off the passage of food from the stomach to the duodenum. They carefully ensured that the cuff was not traumatic to the animal and did not interfere with feeding, even when inflated. Then they showed that, with the cuff inflated, an animal would eat a normal-sized meal and then stop; that is, it could become satisfied even though the food did not go beyond the stomach. Those results imply that one can get adequate satiety signals from the stomach before the food reaches later parts of the digestive system.

You may have noticed, however, that you feel full fairly rapidly when eating a high-calorie food (such as a chocolate-fudge sundae) but more slowly when eating a low-calorie food (such as vegetable soup). There are at least two reasons for this difference. First, many low-calorie foods pass through the stomach quickly and make room for more, while high-calorie foods delay emptying of the stomach (McHugh & Moran, 1985). Second, the stomach monitors nutrient content as well as total volume. An animal that eats a high-calorie food stops eating long before it fills the stomach; an animal eating a low-calorie food fills much more of the stomach before it stops eating (Deutsch & Gonzalez, 1980).

The stomach conveys satiety messages to the brain via the vagus nerve and the splanchnic nerves. The **vagus nerve** (cranial nerve X) conveys information about the stretching of the stomach walls. Animals with a damaged vagus nerve eat until they overfill the stomach (Gonzalez & Deutsch, 1981). The **splanchnic** (SPLANK-nik) **nerves** (carrying impulses from the thoracic and lumbar parts of the spinal cord to the digestive organs and from the digestive organs to the spinal cord) convey information about the nutrient contents of the stomach (Deutsch & Ahn, 1986).

Could we trigger satiety messages by artificially distending the stomach? In one study, rats were offered a high-fat diet, on which they gained weight. Then the experimenters implanted water-filled balloons to occupy about one-third of each rat's stomach. The rats ate smaller meals than before and lost weight over a period of weeks (Geliebter, Westreich, Hashim, & Gage, 1987). Similar procedures have been attempted with obese people, but the long-term results have not been good, partly because materials implanted into the stomach can make the stomach grow larger.

The Duodenum and the Hormone CCK

The **duodenum** (DYOU-oh-DEE-num or dyuh-ODD-ehn-uhm) is the part of the small intestine adjoining the stomach; it is the first structure of the digestive system to absorb a significant amount of nutrients. When a bulk substance (nutrient or nonnutrient) enters the duodenum, the animal decreases or stops eating (Ehman, Albert, & Jamieson, 1971; Vanderweele, Novin, Rezek, & Sanderson, 1974).

Cholecystokinin (ko-leh-SIS-teh-KI-nehn) **(CCK)**—which the duodenum releases as a hormone and the brain uses as a neurotransmitter—may play an important role in satiety (Gibbs, Young, & Smith, 1973). For example, introducing food into the duodenum causes the duodenum to release CCK. When CCK is injected into a rat before a meal, the rat eats less than normal. The more CCK injected, the smaller the meal consumed (Antin, Gibbs, & Smith, 1978). After a large enough dose, a rat that has not fed will go through a sequence of grooming itself and then resting or sleeping, just as it would after a normal meal (Antin et al., 1975).

These results do not necessarily mean, however, that the CCK released by the duodenum influences the brain as a satiety hormone. Rather, the released CCK helps to close the sphincter muscle between the stomach and the duodenum. That is, food going from the stomach to the duodenum triggers the release of CCK, which inhibits emptying of the stomach and thus promotes stomach distention (McHugh & Moran, 1985).

In support of this interpretation, one study found that an injection of CCK had no effect on human appetite at the start of a meal. It did, however, shorten the meal (Pi-Sunyer, Kissileff, Thornton, & Smith, 1982). In other words, CCK magnifies the satiety-producing effect of food in the stomach.

Blood Glucose

Digested food enters the bloodstream, much of it in the form of glucose. An important source of energy for all parts of the body, glucose is by far the most important fuel of the brain. Jean Mayer (1953) proposed that the supply of glucose to the cells is the primary basis for hunger and satiety. When the cells have too little glucose, the individual gets hungry. When the cells have enough, the individual becomes satiated.

An artificially produced rise in blood glucose decreases feeding (J. D. Davis, Wirtshafter, Asin, & Brief, 1981; Tordoff, Novin, & Russek, 1982), whereas a drug that prevents glucose from entering the cells leads to increased feeding (Thompson & Campbell, 1977). These results support the theory that eating is controlled partly by the availability of glucose to the cells. On the other hand, glucose is certainly not the only factor. Even fructose, a sugar that does not cross the blood-brain barrier and that cannot be converted to glucose, can suppress hunger (Stricker, Rowland, Saller, & Friedman, 1977). So can various other nutrients. Thus, hunger and satiety must be based not on glucose alone but on the availability of all types of nutrients combined (Friedman & Stricker, 1976).

The level of glucose in the blood varies little under normal conditions (LeMagnen, 1981). Even during a period of prolonged fasting, the liver converts stored glycogen, fats, and proteins into glucose to maintain blood glucose levels. However, the availability of glucose to the cells can vary significantly as a function of changes in blood levels of two pancreatic hormones, insulin and glucagon. The hormone **insulin** facilitates the entry of glucose into the cells, which may either use the glucose for current energy needs or store it as fat or glycogen. **Glucagon,** a hormone released by the pancreas, has the reverse effect: It stimulates the liver to convert stored glycogen to glucose, thus raising blood glucose levels. After a meal, insulin levels rise, much glucose enters the cells, and appetite decreases. As time passes, the blood glucose level falls, the pancreas starts releasing more glucagon and less insulin, and hunger returns (Figure 10.11).

Generally, when insulin levels are high, hunger is low (because the blood is supplying the cells with glucose). However, if the insulin level remains high and the glucagon level remains low well after the last meal, the body continues to

Figure 10.11

Insulin and glucagon provide a feedback system to control food intake and use. When glucose levels rise, the pancreas releases the hormone insulin, which causes cells to store the excess glucose as fats and glycogen. The entry of glucose into cells suppresses hunger. Lack of hunger leads to decreased eating, which lowers the glucose level; the pancreas releases glucagon, which stimulates the liver to convert stored glycogen into glucose, which enters the blood. The high ratio of glucagon to insulin also stimulates hunger, and the cycle repeats.

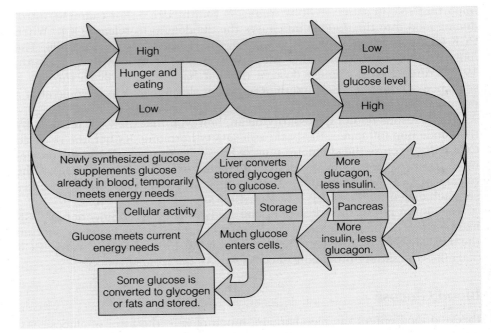

Figure 10.12

Effects of steadily high insulin levels on feeding

Even when the glucose level is low, insulin remains high and much of the blood glucose is stored as fats and glycogen. Consequently, the blood's supply of glucose quickly drops and hunger returns.

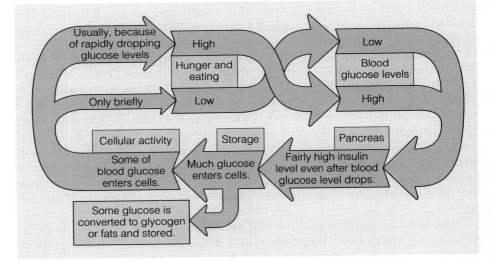

move blood glucose into the cells, and liver cells and fat cells continue to store it as glycogen and fats. Consequently, the blood glucose available for use begins to decline. For example, in late autumn, migratory and hibernating species have high insulin levels and low glucagon levels. They rapidly deposit a large percentage of each meal as fat and glycogen and then grow hungry again (Figure 10.12). Consequently, they gain much weight, which is adaptive as a preparation for a period without food. Similarly, people with chronically high insulin levels tend to eat a lot and gain weight.

When the insulin level is extremely low, as in people with diabetes, blood glucose levels may reach three times the normal level, or even more. However, little of the glucose can enter the cells (Figure 10.13). People and animals suf-

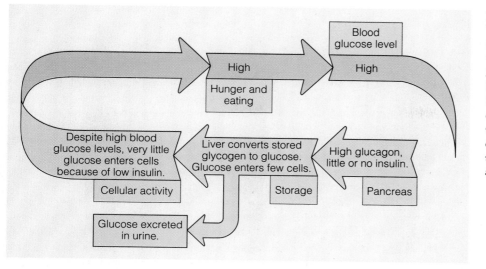

Figure 10.13
Why people with untreated diabetes eat much but lose weight
Because of their low insulin levels, the glucose in their blood cannot enter the cells, either to be stored or to be used. Consequently, they excrete glucose in their urine while their cells are starving.

fering from diabetes eat more food than normal because their cells are starving (Lindberg, Coburn, & Stricker, 1984), but they lose weight because they excrete most of their glucose unused. (Note the paradox that both high and very low levels of insulin can lead to increased eating, although they do so for different reasons. To maintain normal body weight, it is best to have an intermediate level of insulin.)

People produce more insulin when they eat and even when they are getting ready to eat. Up to a point, that is useful, because it prepares the body to let more glucose enter the cells and to store the excess part of the meal as fats. However, obese people produce more insulin than do people of normal weight (Johnson & Wildman, 1983). Their high levels of insulin cause more of their food than normal to be stored as fat, and therefore their appetite returns sooner than normal after a meal (see Figure 10.14).

Metabolic Rate

Weight is the outcome of both the amount of food consumed and the amount of energy used. Most obese people could lose weight by following habits of regular exercise to burn off more calories (Thompson, Jarvie, Lahey, & Cureton, 1982); unfortunately, many of them find it difficult to stick to an exercise program for long.

Most of the calories that people consume are used not for exercise but for basal metabolism, the energy that they use for constant activities such as temperature regulation. People vary somewhat in their basal metabolism, although they do not vary much in body temperature. People with higher metabolic rates produce more heat than others do but radiate it to their environment. People with lower metabolic rates generate less heat but conserve it better.

Because of such differences in metabolic rates, one person will gain weight while eating only a moderate amount, and another person will remain thin while eating much more. Metabolic rates vary depending on many factors, probably including genetics (Bogardus et al., 1986). Similarly, genetic differences strongly influence body weight. According to a Danish study of 540 adopted children who had reached adulthood, their weight correlated strongly with that of their biological relatives, not with that of their adoptive relatives

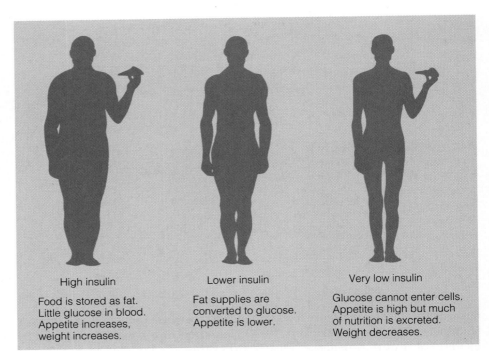

**Figure 10.14
Effects of insulin on glucose, appetite, and weight**
People with high insulin levels eat much and gain weight; people with very low levels also eat a great deal but excrete much of what they eat.

High insulin

Food is stored as fat.
Little glucose in blood.
Appetite increases,
weight increases.

Lower insulin

Fat supplies are
converted to glucose.
Appetite is lower.

Very low insulin

Glucose cannot enter cells.
Appetite is high but much
of nutrition is excreted.
Weight decreases.

(Stunkard et al., 1986). The implication is that genetic differences in metabolic rate are the primary reason behind differences in adult body weight. We cannot draw a firm conclusion until someone conducts a longitudinal study linking early-onset differences in metabolic rate with later-developing differences in body weight. Still, a relationship between the two seems likely.

Unfortunately for those wishing to lose weight, lowering food intake leads to a compensatory decrease in metabolic rate and an increase in the body's efficiency in using its food (Brownell, Greenwood, Stellar, & Shrager, 1986; McMinn, 1984). That is, if you adhere to a low-calorie diet, your metabolic rate will decrease and you will burn fewer calories. People who diet and then regain weight and then diet and regain ("yo-yo dieters") often find that weight loss gradually becomes more and more difficult on each succeeding diet.

Food-Specific Mechanisms of Satiety

Imagine that a food-deprived, water-deprived rat comes upon a tube full of liquid. Given that it does not know what is in the tube, how will it know how much to drink? The answer is simple: Until it tastes the liquid, it does *not* know how much to drink (Mook, 1990).

It tastes the liquid. If the liquid is plain water, the rat drinks a certain amount based on how long it has been deprived of water. If the liquid is sugar water, the rat bases its intake on its need for food, not its need for water. If the liquid contains saccharin, a nonnutritive sweetener, again the rat's intake depends on its need for food. (That is, the rat treats the solution as food, even though it is not.) In short, taste tells the rat whether to use its thirst system or its hunger system to determine satiety. If the rat were salt-deficient as well, a salty-tasting liquid could turn on yet another mechanism.

To some extent, different foods also activate different satiety mechanisms. Suppose you sit down to a meal of baked potatoes. After you eat one or two, your host asks whether you would like another. "No," you reply, "I'm full." You may be too polite to explain, "I'm full of *baked potatoes*. If you had something else, I might be interested in eating again."

The same is true of other animals. A rat that seems fully satiated after eating one substance may begin eating again if it encounters another food (Mook, 1990). (This tendency increases the probability that the rat will eat a varied diet.) Furthermore, taste tells the rat which satiety mechanism to rely on. With most foods, a rat eats more if this is its first meal in 24 hours than if the last meal was just 2 or 3 hours ago. That is, most foods prompt the rat to use satiety mechanisms sensitive to stomach distention, intestinal distention, and blood sugar. However, when the rat finds a concentrated sugar solution, it suddenly relies almost entirely on oral factors to determine satiety. It takes a certain number of licks and then stops, almost independently of the time since the last meal. (For people, certain tasty snacks may be analogous. Would you eat an ice cream cone even when you are not hungry?) Satiety is no simple matter. The conditions for stopping a meal vary depending on the meal.

Brain Mechanisms of Eating and Weight Control

In the 1940s and 1950s, investigators discovered that damage to the lateral hypothalamus decreased eating and that damage to the ventromedial hypothalamus increased eating. Their initial interpretation was that the lateral hypothalamus controlled hunger and that the ventromedial hypothalamus controlled satiety. Later investigators modified and corrected these hypotheses in many ways.

The Lateral Hypothalamus

Several kinds of evidence indicate that the **lateral hypothalamus** (Figure 10.15) is an important area for the control of feeding (Hoebel, 1988). After damage in this area, an animal refuses food and water, grimacing and turning its head away from offered food, as if the food were distasteful. The animal may starve to death in the presence of good food, unless it is force-fed, in which case it gradually recovers much of its ability to eat. (See Figure 10.16.) In an intact animal, electrical stimulation of the lateral hypothalamus stimulates eating. If no food is present, that electrical stimulation increases the rat's bar-pressing, if the rat had previously learned to bar-press for food. In other words, the stimulation increases complex food-seeking behaviors, not just chewing or some other reflex. Furthermore, activity recorded from the lateral hypothalamus shows that neurons in that area become active when a hungry rat is offered food.

Although this evidence is strong, we need to consider one factor that complicates the interpretation: Any investigation that damages or stimulates the lateral hypothalamus is likely to strike not only the neurons with cell bodies in that area, but also a number of dopamine-containing axons that happen to pass through there. To deal with this problem, investigators developed several ways

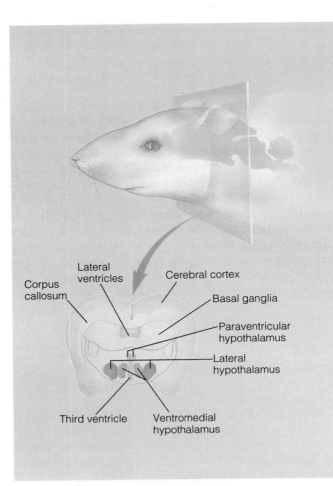

Figure 10.15
Three areas of the rat hypothalamus where stimulation or damage produces marked effects on feeding
The side view of a rat's head above indicates the plane of the coronal section of the brain below. (After Hart, 1976.)

to limit the damage to either the axons or the cells. For example, they may inject 6-hydroxydopamine (6-OHDA), which damages only neurons that manufacture catecholamines, including dopamine. An injection of 6-OHDA to the lateral hypothalamus damages many passing axons that contain dopamine, but spares most of the cell bodies in the hypothalamus. Experiments of this type indicate that the dopamine-containing axons are important for the animal's arousal; damage to those axons leaves an animal chronically inactive and unresponsive to sensory stimuli (Figure 10.17). However, although such animals have trouble finding food (or anything else), they eat normally once they have food in their mouths (Berridge, Venier, & Robinson, 1989).

In other studies, experimenters found ways to damage the cells of the lateral hypothalamus while sparing the passing axons. The result was a major loss of feeding with relatively little loss of arousal or responsiveness to stimuli (Almli, Fisher, & Hill, 1979; S. P. Grossman, Dacey, Halaris, Collier, & Routten-

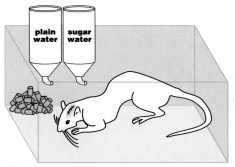

Stage 1. *Aphagia and adipsia.* Rat refuses all food and drink; must be force-fed to keep it alive.

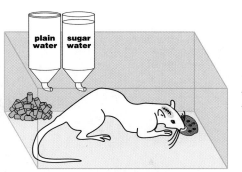

Stage 2. *Anorexia.* Rat eats a small amount of palatable foods and drinks sweetened water. It refuses dry food or plain water. It still does not eat enough to stay alive.

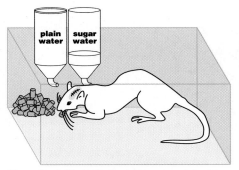

Stage 3. *Adipsia.* The rat eats enough to stay alive, though at a lower-than-normal body weight. It still refuses plain water.

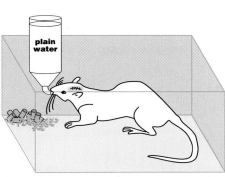

Stage 4. *Near-recovery.* The rat eats enough to stay alive, though at a lower-than-normal body weight. It drinks plain water, but only at mealtimes to wash down its food. Under slightly stressful conditions, such as in a cold room, the rat will return to an earlier stage of refusing food and water.

Figure 10.16
Recovery of feeding after damage to the lateral hypothalamus
At first, the rat refuses all food and drink. If kept alive for several weeks or months by force-feeding, it gradually recovers its ability to eat and drink enough to stay alive. However, even at the final stage of recovery, its behavior is not the same as that of normal rats. (Based on Teitelbaum & Epstein, 1962.)

Figure 10.17
The effect of lateral hypothalamic lesions on arousal and responsiveness to stimulation
(Most such experiments are conducted with rats; in this case, the subject was a cat.) This cat with a lesion in the lateral hypothalamus grasped and picked up a mouse that was placed against its snout; then the cat fell asleep. (From Wolgin, Cytawa, & Teitelbaum, 1976.) The lack of arousal is due mostly to damage to dopamine-containing axons that pass through the lateral hypothalamus.

berg, 1978; Stricker, Swerdloff, & Zigmond, 1978). Evidently, the cell bodies of the lateral hypothalamus contribute mainly to feeding, while the passing fibers contribute to overall arousal.

The question remains: *How* does the lateral hypothalamus contribute to feeding? It contributes in several ways (Hernandez, Murzi, Schwartz, & Hoebel, 1992). First, axons from the lateral hypothalamus extend to the NTS (nucleus of the tractus solitarius) in the pons, part of the pathway responsive to taste (see p. 264). Information from the lateral hypothalamus modifies the activity of some of the NTS cells, either altering the taste sensation or (more likely) increasing the salivation response to the tastes. Second, axons from the lateral hypothalamus extend into several forebrain structures, facilitating ingestion and swallowing. (See Figure 10.18.) Third, activity in the lateral hypothalamus stimulates the release of insulin by the pancreas and digestive juices by the stomach (Morley, Bartness, Gosnell, & Levine, 1985). After damage to the lateral hypothalamus, an animal has low levels of insulin and digestive juices and difficulty digesting its foods. Also, because of the decreased insulin levels, the animal converts much of its fat reserves into blood glucose, and thus has fairly high levels of blood sugar even without eating.

Hunger

Figure 10.18
Pathways from the lateral hypothalamus
Axons from the lateral hypothalamus modify activity in several other brain areas, changing the response to taste, facilitating ingestion and swallowing, and increasing food-seeking behaviors. Also (not shown), the lateral hypothalamus controls stomach secretions and insulin production.

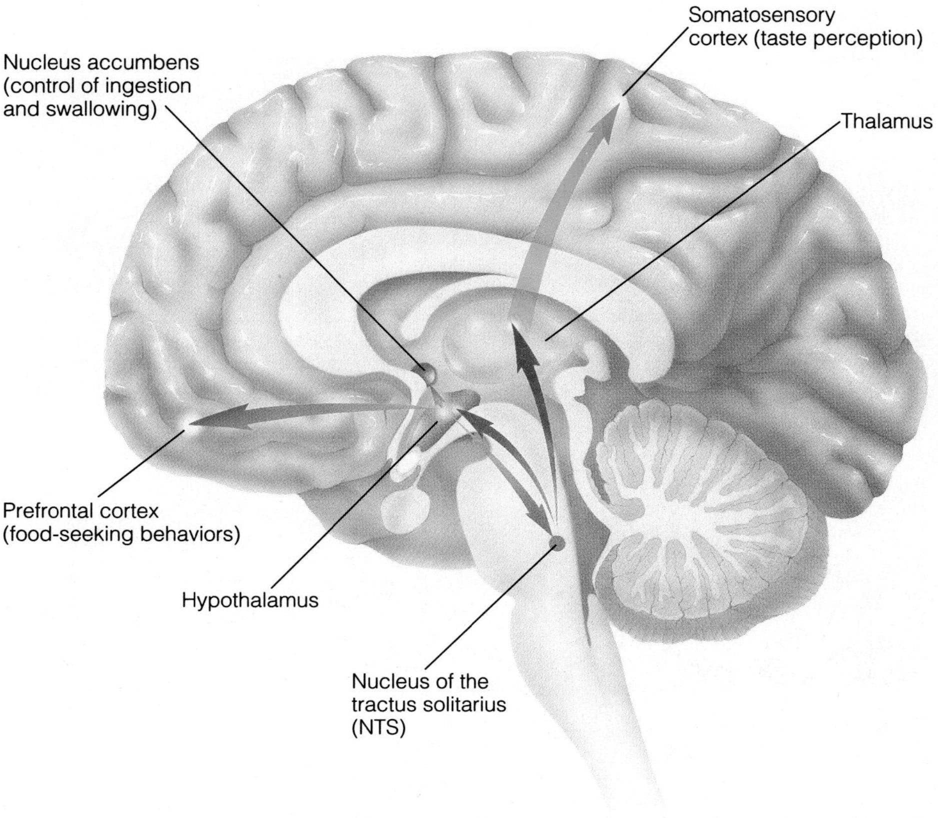

Nucleus accumbens (control of ingestion and swallowing)

Somatosensory cortex (taste perception)

Thalamus

Prefrontal cortex (food-seeking behaviors)

Hypothalamus

Nucleus of the tractus solitarius (NTS)

Medial Areas of the Hypothalamus

Near the lateral hypothalamus is a set of areas with a much different contribution to feeding. Neuroscientists have known since the 1940s that a large lesion centered on the **ventromedial hypothalamus** (Figure 10.15) leads to overeating and weight gain. Some people with a tumor in that area have gained more than 10 kg (22 pounds) per month (Al-Rashid, 1971; Killeffer & Stern, 1970; Reeves & Plum, 1969). Rats with similar damage sometimes double or triple their weight (Figure 10.19). Eventually, however, body weight levels off at a stable, though very high, set point. At that point, total food intake per day is very close to normal levels.

Although these symptoms are generally known as the *ventromedial hypothalamic syndrome,* damage limited to the ventromedial hypothalamus itself does not consistently produce large increases in eating or body weight. To produce a large effect, the lesion must extend outside the ventromedial hypothalamus to invade nearby areas, including the ventral noradrenergic bundle (Figure 10.20), a nearby axon pathway (Ahlskog & Hoebel, 1973; Ahlskog, Randall, & Hoebel, 1975; Gold, 1973).

Rats with damage in and around the ventromedial hypothalamus are finicky eaters. With a normal or sweetened diet, they overeat, sometimes eating day and night instead of sleeping. Yet they eat far less than normal on a bitter or otherwise untasty diet (Ferguson & Keesey, 1975; Teitelbaum, 1955). Consequently, we cannot say that the rats show an overall increase in hunger. We should also not say that they lack satiety. They eat normal-sized meals,

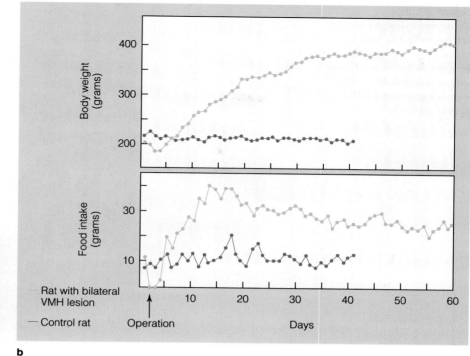

a

b

Rat with bilateral
VMH lesion

— Control rat

Operation

Days

Figure 10.19
The effects of damage to
the ventromedial
hypothalamus
(a) On the right is a normal
rat. On the left is a rat after
damage to the ventromedial
hypothalamus. The brain-
damaged rat may weigh up
to three times as much as a
normal rat. (Yoav Levy/
Phototake.) (b) Changes in
weight and eating in a rat
after damage to the ventro-
medial hypothalamus.
Within a few days after the
operation, the rat begins eat-
ing much more than normal.
As it gains weight, its eating
decreases, although it
remains above normal.
(Adapted from Teitelbaum,
1961.)

demonstrating satiety at the normal time. Their abnormality is that they start their next meal sooner than normal, thus eating more meals per day than a normal rat does (Duggan & Booth, 1986).

Such rats eat more frequently than normal for several reasons (Hoebel & Hernandez, 1993). First, they have increased stomach motility and secretions, and their stomachs empty faster than normal. The faster the stomach empties, the sooner an animal is ready for its next meal. Second, the damage leads to a lasting increase in insulin production (King, Smith, & Frohman, 1984). Because of the increased insulin, a larger-than-normal percentage of each meal is stored as fat. If animals with this kind of damage are prevented from overeating, they gain weight anyway! Mark Friedman and Edward Stricker (1976) have therefore proposed that the animal does not get fat because it overeats; rather, it has to overeat because it stores so much fat and has little fuel left over for its current needs.

Rats with damage in the nearby **paraventricular nucleus (PVN)** of the hypothalamus also overeat, but for a different reason. Instead of eating more frequent meals, they eat larger meals (Leibowitz, Hammer, & Chang, 1981). Thus the PVN appears to be critical for ending meals. In rats, the role of the PVN is especially evident for the rat's first meal after waking up (at the beginning of the night). Ordinarily, rats choose a high-carbohydrate meal, if possible, at that time; later in the night, they eat more fats and proteins. Stimulation of the PVN by either of the neurotransmitters serotonin or CCK (cholecystokinin) greatly decreases intake, particularly of carbohydrates, during the first meal of the night (Cooper, Dourish, & Barber, 1990; Leibowitz, Alexander, Cheung, & Weiss, 1993; Leibowitz, Weiss, & Suh, 1990). (Remember, CCK as an intestinal hormone also decreases food intake through action in the digestive system.) Inhibition of the PVN by the neurotransmitter norepinephrine has the

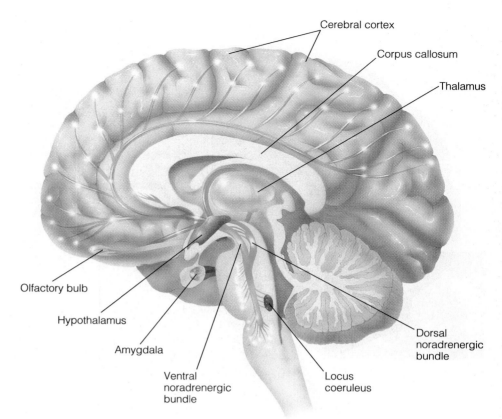

Figure 10.20
Major norepinephrine pathways in the human brain
Damage to the ventral noradrenergic bundle leads to overeating and weight gain. (Based on Valzelli, 1980.)

Cerebral cortex

Corpus callosum

Thalamus

Olfactory bulb

Hypothalamus

Amygdala

Ventral noradrenergic bundle

Locus coeruleus

Dorsal noradrenergic bundle

opposite effect, increasing carbohydrate intake during the first meal of the night (Alexander, Cheung, Dietz, & Leibowitz, 1993; Paez, Stanley, & Leibowitz, 1993). Inhibition by either of the transmitters **neuropeptide Y** or **polypeptide YY** (which are chemically very similar) can enormously increase meal size, as illustrated in Figure 10.21, while also increasing fat storage (Billington & Levine, 1992; Leibowitz & Alexander, 1991; Morley, Levine, Grace, & Kneip, 1985). Neuropeptide Y and polypeptide YY have been speculatively linked with human eating disorders; for example, women with a past history of bulimia (a condition marked by periodic bouts of overeating) have higher-than-normal levels of polypeptide YY in their cerebrospinal fluid (Kaye, Berrettini, Gwirtsman, & George, 1990).

The paraventricular hypothalamus may contribute to diet selection as well as to ending a meal. An injection of norepinephrine to the PVN increases carbohydrate intake; so does an injection of the hormone corticosterone. In contrast, an injection of the hormone aldosterone or the neurotransmitter *galanin* increases fat intake (Tempel, Kim, & Leibowitz, 1993; Tempel, Leibowitz, & Leibowitz, 1988).

Table 10.2 summarizes the effects of lesions in several areas of the hypothalamus.

Eating and Neurotransmitters

A new technology for studying the effects of neurotransmitters on feeding has facilitated a more detailed investigation of events in the hypothalamus. **Microdialysis** is a method for measuring the concentrations of chemicals in a brain

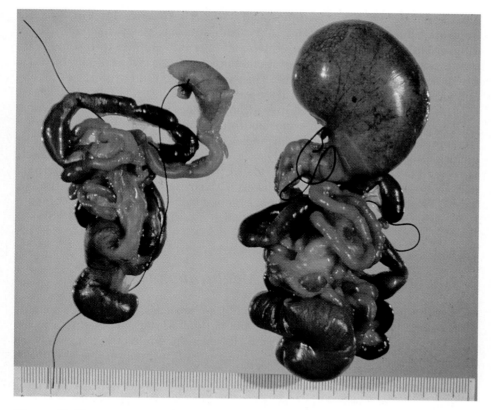

Figure 10.21
The effects of polypeptide YY on eating in rats
On the left is the digestive system of a normal rat. On the right is the digestive system of a rat that had polypeptide YY injected eight times over two days into its paraventricular hypothalamus. It continued eating even though it distended its stomach and intestines practically to the point of bursting. (From Morley, Levine, Grace, & Kneip, 1985.)

Table 10.2	Effects of Lesions in Certain Hypothalamic Areas
Hypothalamic Area	*Effect of Lesion*
Preoptic area	Deficit in physiological mechanisms of temperature regulation
Lateral preoptic area	Deficit in drinking
Lateral hypothalamus	Undereating, weight loss, low insulin level (because of damage to cell bodies); underarousal, underresponsiveness (because of damage to passing axons)
Ventromedial hypothalamus	Increased meal frequency, weight gain, high insulin level
Paraventricular nucleus	Increased meal size, especially increased carbohydrate intake during the first meal of the active period of the day

area. Using stereotaxic procedures, as described in Chapter 4, an investigator implants a fluid-filled tube with a thin membrane, across which chemicals can diffuse. The experimenter brings the membrane into contact with some brain tissue; neurotransmitters or their metabolites can cross from the brain tissue across the membrane into the tube. The experimenter then withdraws the tube and analyzes the chemicals that have entered it.

This procedure has enabled investigators to determine the times at which various brain areas release certain neurotransmitters. For example, research has found that the paraventricular nucleus of the hypothalamus releases tiny quantities of norepinephrine mostly at the start of a meal and serotonin mostly at the end of a meal (Hernandez & Hoebel, 1988; Schwartz, McClane, Hernandez, & Hoebel, 1989; Stanley, Schwartz, Hernandez, Leibowitz, & Hoebel, 1989). The size and frequency of meals may depend on a balance or competition among a number of neurotransmitters and hormones (Hoebel, 1988).

Integration of Multiple Mechanisms

We began this chapter with a discussion of homeostasis. Eating has a roughly homeostatic effect; it tends to maintain a fairly constant supply of fuel to the cells and a fairly constant body weight. However, the brain does not simply try to hold a single variable near a set point. Instead, it monitors blood glucose, stomach distention, duodenal distention, body weight, and probably other physiological variables as well. It anticipates future needs as well as responding to current needs. Integrating such diverse and sometimes contradictory information provides a kind of security: If one system provides faulty information, other systems can override it.

Moreover, people sometimes ignore their physiological signals. They may eat highly attractive foods even when they are satiated and refrain from eating unacceptable foods even when they are hungry. Eating is a complex behavior that depends on an array of cognitive, social, and physiological influences.

Summary

1. The ability to digest a food is one major determinant of preference for eating that food. For example, people who cannot digest lactose generally do not like to eat dairy products. (p. 360)

2. Other major determinants of food selection include innate preferences for certain tastes, a preference for familiar foods, and the ability to learn about the consequences of foods. (p. 361)

3. People and animals eat partly for the sake of taste. However, a sham-feeding animal, which tastes its foods but does not absorb them, eats far more than normal. (p. 362)

4. The primary factor limiting the size of a meal is stomach distention. Nerves from the stomach report information concerning both mechanical distention and nutrient content. (p. 364)

5. When food reaches the duodenum, it stimulates the release of CCK, which decreases food intake by inhibiting the further release of food from the stomach and possibly by other means. (p. 364)

6. Hunger increases when little glucose and other fuels reach the cells; it decreases when a lot of glucose is available to the cells. Such fluctuations ordinarily depend on the hormones insulin and glucagon, which control the storage of food supplies as fat. (p. 365)

7. People differ in their metabolic rates, partly for genetic reasons. It is likely that a low metabolic rate leads to weight gain. (p. 367)

8. The conditions necessary for achieving satiety vary depending on what the meal contains. Different foods trigger the use of different satiety mechanisms. (p. 368)

9. Damage to cells in the lateral hypothalamus leads to decreased eating and loss of weight through effects on other brain areas that control taste and salivation, ingestion and swallowing, and food-seeking behaviors. (p. 369)

10. Damage to the ventromedial hypothalamus increases

meal frequency; damage to the paraventricular nucleus of the hypothalamus increases meal size. Damage to either of these areas can lead to weight gain. (p. 372)

11. Feeding, at least for carbohydrate meals, depends on competition among several neurotransmitters and hormones with competing effects in the paraventricular nucleus of the hypothalamus. (p. 373)

Review Questions

1. Why do Asian cooks seldom, if ever, use cheese and other dairy products? (p. 361)

2. Why are amphetamine pills generally ineffective as a long-term aid to losing weight? (p. 363)

3. What evidence points to stomach distention as a major contributor to satiety? (p. 364)

4. What causes release of the hormone CCK? By what mechanism does CCK probably act in limiting meal size? (p. 364)

5. Why do high levels of insulin and very low levels of insulin *both* lead to increased eating? (p. 365)

6. Describe several biological reasons why certain people may become overweight. (Refer to stomach emptying speed, CCK, insulin levels, and genetic differences in metabolic rate.) (pp. 364–368)

7. What is the role of cell bodies in the lateral hypothalamus, and how does that role contrast with the contribution of dopamine-containing axons passing through the area? (p. 369)

8. How does damage to the lateral hypothalamus affect eating? (p. 371)

9. Through what mechanisms does damage to the ventromedial hypothalamus lead to weight gain? (p. 373)

10. What kind of questions can investigators answer with microdialysis? (p. 374)

Thought Question

1. For most people, insulin levels tend to be higher during the day than during the night. Use this fact to explain why people grow hungry a few hours after a meal during the day, but not so quickly at night.

Suggestions for Further Reading

LeMagnen, J. (1992). *Neurobiology of feeding and nutrition.* San Diego, CA: Academic Press. Thorough description of taste, digestion, and brain mechanisms of feeding.

Logue, A. W. (1991). *The psychology of eating and drinking* (2nd ed.). New York: Freeman. Discussion includes both normal eating and disorders such as anorexia nervosa and bulimia.

Terms

lactose the sugar in milk (p. 360)

lactase enzyme necessary for lactose metabolism (p. 360)

carnivore animal that eats meat (p. 361)

herbivore animal that eats plants (p. 361)

omnivore animal that eats both meat and plants (p. 361)

drug tolerance decreased response to a drug after repeated use of it (p. 363)

sham feeding preparation in which everything that an animal swallows leaks out a tube connected to the esophagus or stomach (p. 363)

vagus nerve tenth cranial nerve, which sends branches to the stomach and several other organs (p. 364)

splanchnic nerves nerves carrying impulses from the thoracic and lumbar parts of the spinal cord to the digestive organs and from the digestive organs to the spinal cord (p. 364)

duodenum part of the small intestine adjoining the stomach (p. 364)

cholecystokinin (CCK) hormone released by the duodenum in response to food distention (p. 364)

insulin hormone that facilitates the entry of glucose into the cells (p. 365)

glucagon pancreatic hormone that stimulates the liver to convert stored glycogen to glucose (p. 365)

lateral hypothalamus area of the hypothalamus in which damage impairs eating and drinking (p. 369)

ventromedial hypothalamus (VMH) one of the nuclei of the hypothalamus, in which damage leads to faster stomach emptying and increased secretion of insulin (p. 372)

paraventricular nucleus area of the hypothalamus that contributes to control of meal size (p. 373)

neuropeptide Y and **polypeptide YY** two peptides found in the brain and digestive system; when injected into the paraventricular nucleus of the hypothalamus, either one increases feeding. (When injected into other locations not described here, they affect body temperature, sexual behavior, grooming, breathing, pain, and other functions.) (p. 374)

microdialysis method for measuring the concentrations of chemicals in a brain area by enabling them to cross a membrane into an implanted, withdrawable tube (p. 374)

HORMONES AND
SEXUAL BEHAVIOR

©Ron Chapple/FPG

CHAPTER ELEVEN

MAIN IDEAS

1. Hormones exert effects on behavior either by attaching to receptors on the membrane of a cell or by attaching to receptors within the cell that alter the expression of the genes.

2. Sex hormones have organizing and activating effects. Organizing effects are permanent effects on anatomy and the brain, exerted during a sensitive period of early development. Activating effects are transient effects exerted at any later time.

3. In mammals, the presence or absence of testosterone determines whether the genitals and hypothalamus will develop in the male or the female manner, although for certain characteristics testosterone must first be converted to estradiol within the cell.

4. Numerous sex hormones, including testosterone and estradiol, can activate specific sexual, aggressive, and parental behaviors, depending on the behavior, species, and sex of the individual.

5. The causes and controls of sexual identity and orientation are complex, but genes, hormones, and brain anatomy evidently contribute, along with various environmental and experiential factors.

Imagine that medical science has developed a new procedure—a drug, let's say—that can totally halt the aging process. If you submit to this procedure, your body will stay as it now is, forever. If you are now 20 years old, you will always look 20 years old. Your hair will not grow gray, your skin will not wrinkle, you will continue to be as athletic and energetic as you are now, and you will not develop any of the deteriorative conditions of old age, such as Parkinson's disease, Alzheimer's disease, or heart problems. The procedure does not guarantee immortality; you could still get hit by a truck or catch some deadly virus. But if you live cautiously, and if humanity manages to avoid wars and does not completely ruin the environment, you might survive for hundreds, maybe even thousands of years, looking and feeling young the whole time.

There is one catch: The government will provide this procedure free for anyone who wants it, but, in order to prevent runaway overpopulation, anyone who submits to this procedure must also agree to irreversible sterilization. That is, if we let people survive for hundreds of years *and* reproduce, the world could become unbearably crowded. So, if you agree to this procedure, you cannot have children. The procedure won't destroy your sex drive, just your ability to have children.

What would you decide?

If you choose to have children, you will someday watch your childless friends continue to swim and play tennis while you hobble with a walker into a nursing home. On the other hand, all the humans of the remote future will descend from people who decided to have children, not from people who decided to stay young.

The opportunity to reproduce is very important to most people; it is essential for the preservation and evolution of the species. The constant reshuffling of genes enables the species to adapt evolutionarily to a changing environment. It also provides enough variability among individuals to prevent any one strain of virus or bacterium from wiping out the population.

Reproduction is not always easy, however. To reproduce, an individual must find a healthy, sexually mature member of the opposite sex of its own species. It must persuade that partner to accept it as a mate and then synchronize its behavior with that of its partner so that both are ready to engage in the sex act at the same time. Then, unless the young are born capable of taking care of themselves, one or both parents must nurture the young until they reach maturity.

Hormones and Behavior

In fall, migratory birds prepare for a long flight. The preparation includes changes in eating and metabolism to store enough fat for the journey, a tendency to join into flocks with others of the species, and a preference for flying in a direction somehow identified as "south." In the spring, the same birds fly back north. At that time, their feathers change to breeding colors, the birds start looking for appropriate mates, and males start singing. The coordination of widespread changes throughout the body, such as those that accompany migration and mating, frequently depends on hormones.

In humans, too, hormones control a wide variety of behaviors; Chapter 10 mentioned the roles of angiotensin, aldosterone, and insulin in drinking and feeding. Hormones are so important to sexual behavior, however, that this is a good context for discussing hormones in general. A **hormone** is a chemical that is secreted by a gland and conveyed by the blood to other organs, whose activity it influences. Figure 11.1 presents the major **endocrine (hormone-producing) glands.** Table 11.1 lists some important hormones and their principal effects.

Mechanisms of Hormone Actions

The effects of hormones on behavior overlap greatly with the effects of neurotransmitters. A number of chemicals—including epinephrine, norepinephrine, angiotensin, and CCK—are classed as both neurotransmitters and hormones. The difference between a neurotransmitter and a hormone is that a neurotransmitter is released directly adjacent to the target cell, while a hormone is carried by the blood to targets throughout the body. But even this distinction can be blurry; neurotransmitters sometimes diffuse over a fairly broad area of the brain.

Types of Hormones

The body produces dozens of known hormones, and new ones are discovered from time to time. Most of these fall into a few major classes. One class is composed of **protein hormones** and **peptide hormones,** composed of a chain of amino acids. (Generally, the longer chains are called proteins, and the shorter chains are called peptides.) Insulin is one example. *Glycoproteins,* a special kind of peptide hormone, consist of a chain of amino acids attached to a carbohydrate. Protein and peptide hormones attach to receptors on the cell membrane, where they activate an enzyme that produces cyclic AMP or some other second messenger. Cyclic AMP then activates a number of enzymes that may

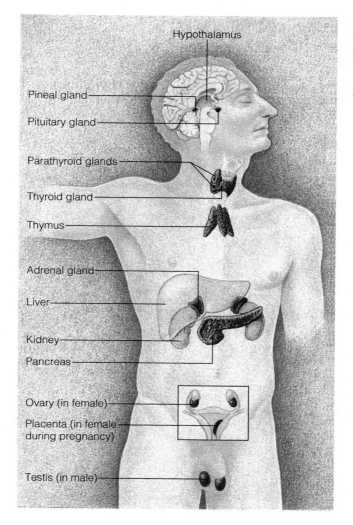

Figure 11.1
Location of some of the major endocrine glands in the human body
(From Starr & Taggart, 1989.)

Hypothalamus

Pineal gland

Pituitary gland

Parathyroid glands

Thyroid gland

Thymus

Adrenal gland

Liver

Kidney

Pancreas

Ovary (in female)

Placenta (in female during pregnancy)

Testis (in male)

alter the metabolism of the cell or the ability of various ions to cross the membrane (Figure 11.2). These changes in the cell may last minutes to hours. Note that peptide hormones affect cells by the same route as peptide neurotransmitters do (Chapter 3).

Another major class of hormones, **steroid hormones,** contain four carbon rings, as Figure 11.3 shows. Steroid hormones exert their effects by entering the cell and attaching to receptors in the cytoplasm, which then move to the nucleus of the cell where they determine which genes will be expressed (see Figure 11.4). Steroids can also exert more rapid effects analogous to those of peptide hormones, altering the transmission of ions across the membrane (Moore & Orchinik, 1991).

Cortisol and corticosterone, steroid hormones released by the adrenal cortex, elevate blood sugar and enhance metabolism. They are particularly important in helping the body adapt to prolonged stress.

Two classes of steroid hormones, the **estrogens** and the **androgens,** turn on the genes that contribute to both the physical and behavioral aspects of sexuality. Circulating levels of estrogens are generally higher in females; androgens, in males. Like other steroid hormones, estrogens and androgens increase the

Hormones and Behavior

Table 11.1 Partial List of Hormone-Releasing Glands

Organ	Hormone	Hormone Functions
Hypothalamus	Various releasing hormones	Promote or inhibit release of various hormones by pituitary
Anterior pituitary	TSH (thyroid-stimulating hormone)	Stimulates thyroid gland
	LH (luteinizing hormone)	Increases production of progesterone (female), testosterone (male); stimulates ovulation
	FSH (follicle-stimulating hormone)	Increases production of estrogen and maturation of ovum (female) and sperm production (male)
	ACTH	Increases secretion of steroid hormones by adrenal gland
	Prolactin	Increases milk production
Posterior pituitary	Oxytocin	Controls uterine contractions, milk release, certain aspects of parental behavior and sexual pleasure
	Vasopressin	Constricts blood vessels, raises blood pressure
Pineal	Melatonin	Inhibits gonadal development; also has roles in puberty onset, sleep-wakefulness cycles
Thyroid	Thyroxine Triiodothyronine	Increase metabolic rate, growth, maturation
Parathyroid	Parathyroid hormone	Increases blood calcium, decreases potassium
Adrenal cortex	Aldosterone	Reduces secretion of salts by the kidneys
	Cortisol, corticosterone	Stimulate liver to elevate blood sugar, increase metabolism of proteins and fats
Adrenal medulla	Epinephrine, norepinephrine	Similar to effects of sympathetic nervous system
Pancreas	Insulin	Increases entry of glucose to cells, increases storage as fats
	Glucagon	Increases conversion of stored glycogen to blood glucose
Ovary	Estrogens	Promote female sexual characteristics
	Progesterone	Maintains pregnancy
Testis	Androgens	Promote sperm production, growth of pubic hair, male sexual characteristics
Liver	Somatomedins	Stimulate growth
Kidney	Renin	Converts a blood protein into angiotensin, which regulates blood pressure and contributes to hypovolemic thirst
Thymus	Thymosin (and others)	Support immune responses

synthesis of certain kinds of RNA and proteins by a factor of 20 to 60 (Shapiro et al., 1989). Some genes that sex hormones activate are called **sex-limited genes** because we see their effects much more strongly in one sex than in the other. For example, estrogen activates the genes responsible for breast development in women, and androgens activate the genes responsible for the growth of facial hair in men. Sex hormones can also increase the expression of certain genes in both sexes. For example, androgens stimulate the growth of pubic hair in both sexes.

Within the brain, estrogen receptors are more abundant in some areas and androgen receptors in others. Thus each hormone affects a different population

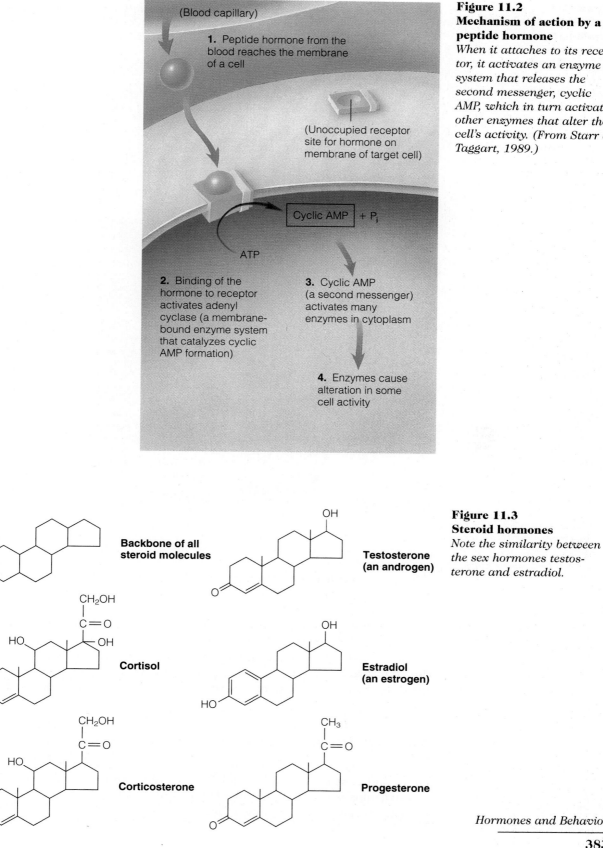

Figure 11.2
Mechanism of action by a peptide hormone
When it attaches to its receptor, it activates an enzyme system that releases the second messenger, cyclic AMP, which in turn activates other enzymes that alter the cell's activity. (From Starr & Taggart, 1989.)

(Blood capillary)

1. Peptide hormone from the blood reaches the membrane of a cell

(Unoccupied receptor site for hormone on membrane of target cell)

Cyclic AMP + P_i

ATP

2. Binding of the hormone to receptor activates adenyl cyclase (a membrane-bound enzyme system that catalyzes cyclic AMP formation)

3. Cyclic AMP (a second messenger) activates many enzymes in cytoplasm

4. Enzymes cause alteration in some cell activity

Backbone of all steroid molecules

Testosterone (an androgen)

Cortisol

Estradiol (an estrogen)

Corticosterone

Progesterone

Figure 11.3
Steroid hormones
Note the similarity between the sex hormones testosterone and estradiol.

Hormones and Behavior

Figure 11.4
Mechanism of action of a steroid hormone
The hormone enters a cell, binds with a receptor in the nucleus, and thereby activates particular genes. As a result, the cell increases its production of specific proteins. (From Starr & Taggart, 1989.)

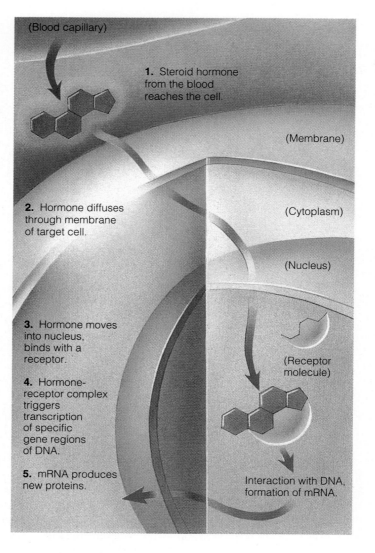

(Blood capillary)

1. Steroid hormone from the blood reaches the cell.

(Membrane)

2. Hormone diffuses through membrane of target cell.

(Cytoplasm)

(Nucleus)

3. Hormone moves into nucleus, binds with a receptor.

(Receptor molecule)

4. Hormone-receptor complex triggers transcription of specific gene regions of DNA.

5. mRNA produces new proteins.

Interaction with DNA, formation of mRNA.

of neurons and therefore different sets of behaviors (McEwen & Pfaff, 1985). Not only do hormones influence behavior; behavior can also influence hormonal patterns. Digression 11.1 describes one example.

In addition to peptide hormones and steroid hormones, other classes of hormones include thyroid hormones (released by the thyroid gland, all of them containing iodine) and monoamines (such as norepinephrine and dopamine). The body also has several miscellaneous hormones that do not fit into any of the described categories, and several "possible" hormones about which researchers are still uncertain.

Control of Hormone Release

Just as circulating hormones modify brain activity, the brain secretes hormones and controls the secretion of many other hormones. Attached to the hypothalamus is the **pituitary gland,** sometimes called the "master gland" of the body because its secretions influence so many other glands. (See Figure

Behavior Can Influence Hormones, Just as Hormones Can Influence Behavior

The mating behavior of the ring-necked dove offers a striking example of how hormones and behavior interact with each other. A newly mated pair of doves goes through a well-synchronized series of behaviors, as outlined in the following table:

	Male	Female
Day 1	Aggressive behavior	Nonaggressive behavior
Days 2–6	Courtship (nest coos) Copulation Nest building (brings twigs)	Courtship (nest coos) Copulation Nest building (arranges twigs)
Day 7		Lays two eggs
Next 2 weeks	Sits on eggs during middle of the day	Sits on eggs from late afternoon to next morning
Next 3 weeks	Tends and feeds chicks	Tends and feeds chicks

The behaviors of the male and female are tightly synchronized. If the female assumes the receptive posture for copulation too early, the male may copulate but then quickly deserts her (Erickson & Zenone, 1976). But properly timed copulation establishes a "pair bond" that keeps the couple together through the mating season and sometimes even into later years.

Both birds normally ignore nesting materials on day 1, begin to build a nest on day 2 or 3, and, if a nest is not completed by day 6 or 7, work frantically on nest building at that time. Neither pays much attention to a nest with eggs before day 7, but they take turns sitting on eggs after that time. Both produce a "crop milk" that they feed to chicks that hatch 14 days after the eggs are laid, but they do not provide milk if chicks hatch much earlier.

Although certain hormone injections would induce any of the observed behaviors, it is also the case that each change in the birds' behavior induces a change in their hormone secretions. The sequence of behaviors depends on a system in which each behavior causes the production of hormones that prepare a bird for the next stage of behavior. On day 1, the male struts around and makes a cooing display. The male's behavior seems to excite the female; her ovaries increase production of estrogen (Erickson & Lehrman, 1964). By day 2, she is ready for courtship and soon after that for copulation. If a researcher simply injects an isolated female with estrogen, she is ready for courtship and copulation almost as soon as a male appears. Thus, the function of the male's behavior on the first day is to stimulate the female's hormonal secretions.

Meanwhile, the male seems to be excited by observing the female on day 1; his androgen production increases. By day 2, he is ready for nest building. Based on studies in other bird species (Adkins & Pniewski, 1978), we can assume that different aspects of the male's courtship and nesting behaviors probably depend on different forms of androgen.

A week of courtship and nest building causes the female to produce first estrogen and then a combination of estrogen and progesterone. If we give estrogen injections to an isolated female for a week, with additional progesterone on the last two days, she becomes ready to incubate eggs even if she has neither seen nor heard a male. Evidently, the courting and nesting experiences produce hormonal changes that make her ready for the next behavioral stage.

Similarly, 14 days of sitting on eggs (or of watching through glass another bird sitting on eggs) causes either the male or the female to produce the hormone prolactin, which stimulates the production of crop milk and disposes the bird to take care of baby doves. If a dove is isolated from other birds and from nests and eggs, a researcher can still get it to care for baby doves by injecting it repeatedly with prolactin.

In short, one behavior causes a hormonal change, which disposes the bird toward a second behavior, which causes a further hormonal change, and so on to the end of the sequence (Lehrman, 1964; Martinez-Vargas & Erickson, 1973).

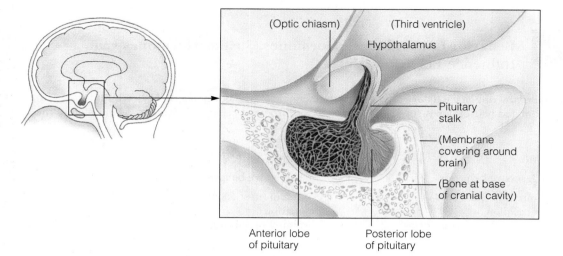

Figure 11.5
Location of the hypothalamus and pituitary gland in the human brain
(From Starr & Taggart, 1989.)

11.5.) The pituitary consists of two distinct glands, the **anterior pituitary** and the **posterior pituitary,** which release different sets of hormones (Table 11.1).

The posterior pituitary, composed of neural tissue, can be considered an extension of the hypothalamus. Neurons in the hypothalamus synthesize the hormones **oxytocin** and **vasopressin** (also known as antidiuretic hormone), plus much smaller amounts of various other peptides (Morris & Pow, 1993). Hypothalamic cells then transport these hormones down their axons to their axon terminals, located in the posterior pituitary, as shown in Figure 11.6. Action potentials release these hormones into the blood.

The anterior pituitary, composed of glandular tissue, synthesizes six hormones itself. However, the hypothalamus controls their release (see Figure 11.7). The hypothalamus secretes **releasing hormones,** which flow through the blood to the anterior pituitary. There they stimulate or inhibit the release of six known hormones, five of which control the secretions of other endocrine organs (see Figure 11.8):

Adrenocorticotropic hormone (ACTH)	Controls secretions of the adrenal cortex
Thyroid-stimulating hormone (TSH)	Controls secretions of the thyroid gland
Follicle-stimulating hormone (FSH) Luteinizing hormone (LH) }	Control secretions of the gonads
Prolactin	Controls secretions of the mammary glands
Somatotropin (also known as growth hormone (GH))	Promotes growth throughout the body

The hypothalamus maintains fairly constant circulating levels of certain hormones. For example, when the level of thyroid hormone is low, the hypothalamus releases one of its hormones, known as *TSH-releasing hormone,* which stimulates the anterior pituitary to release TSH, which in turn causes the thyroid gland to secrete more thyroid hormones. After the level of thyroid hormones has risen, the hypothalamus decreases its release of TSH-releasing hormone (see Figure 11.9).

Chapter 11
Hormones and Sexual
Behavior

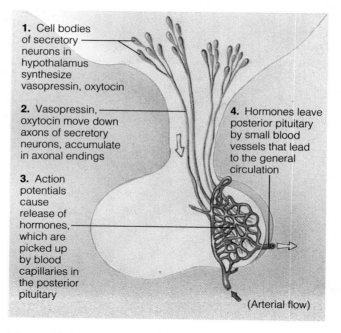

1. Cell bodies of secretory neurons in hypothalamus synthesize vasopressin, oxytocin

2. Vasopressin, oxytocin move down axons of secretory neurons, accumulate in axonal endings

3. Action potentials cause release of hormones, which are picked up by blood capillaries in the posterior pituitary

4. Hormones leave posterior pituitary by small blood vessels that lead to the general circulation

(Arterial flow)

Figure 11.6
Production of oxytocin and vasopressin in the hypothalamus, and their storage and release by the posterior pituitary
(From Starr & Taggart, 1989.)

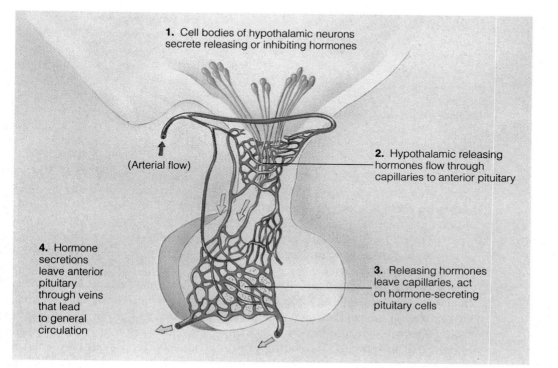

1. Cell bodies of hypothalamic neurons secrete releasing or inhibiting hormones

2. Hypothalamic releasing hormones flow through capillaries to anterior pituitary

(Arterial flow)

4. Hormone secretions leave anterior pituitary through veins that lead to general circulation

3. Releasing hormones leave capillaries, act on hormone-secreting pituitary cells

Figure 11.7
How hypothalamic releasing hormones control the activity of the anterior pituitary
(From Starr & Taggart, 1989.)

387

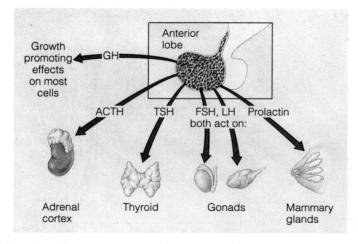

Figure 11.9
Negative feedback in the control of thyroid hormones
The hypothalamus secretes a releasing hormone that stimulates the anterior pituitary to release TSH, which stimulates the thyroid gland to release its hormones. Those hormones in turn act on the hypothalamus to decrease its secretion of the releasing hormone.

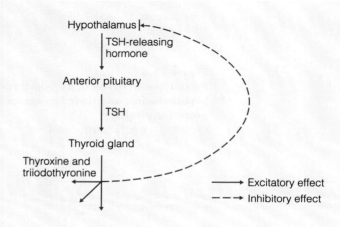

Organizing Effects of Sex Hormones

We generally refer to the androgens, a group of hormones including testosterone and several others, as "male hormones" and to the estrogens, a group of hormones including estradiol and others, as "female hormones." Those designations are overstatements, however. Both males and females produce both types of hormones, and both types have important effects on each sex. However, males secrete more androgens than estrogens, and females secrete more estrogens than androgens.

We distinguish two effects of sex hormones: organizing effects and activating effects. The **organizing effects** of sex hormones, which determine whether the brain and body will develop as a female or as a male, occur mostly at a sensitive stage of development—shortly before and after birth in rats, and well before birth in humans. **Activating effects** occur mostly later in life, when a hormone temporarily activates a particular response; activating effects on an organ last only a little longer than the hormone remains in the organ. Note that I said organizing effects occur "mostly" at an early period and that activating effects occur "mostly" later. In fact, the two kinds of effects are not clearly

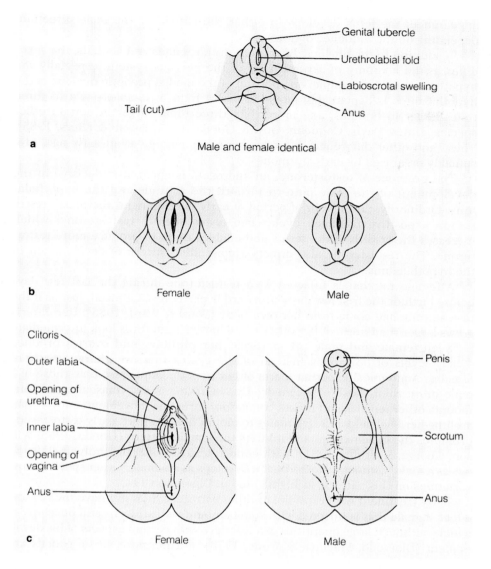

**Figure 11.10
Differentiation of human
genitals from a single set of
precursors**
*(a) At age 6 weeks, male
and female look identical.
(b) In the second trimester,
male and female begin to
differentiate. (c) Appearance
at birth. (Based on Netter,
1983.)*

separated into different eras; hormones early in life can exert activating effects on behavior even while they are organizing body development, and hormones during puberty or later can induce certain long-lasting structural changes (organizing effects) as well as activating effects (Arnold & Breedlove, 1985; Williams, 1986).

Sex Differences in the Gonads and Hypothalamus

During an early stage of prenatal development, the **gonads** (reproductive organs) of every mammalian fetus are the same, and both male and female have a set of Müllerian ducts and a set of Wolffian ducts. The gonads will differentiate into **ovaries** in females and **testes** in males. The **Müllerian ducts** are precursors to female reproductive structures (the oviducts, uterus, and upper vagina); the **Wolffian ducts** are precursors to the male reproductive structures. The fetus also has a set of external structures that differentiate into either female genitals or male genitals (see Figure 11.10). From its initial unisex

Hormones and Behavior

appearance, the fetus develops in either the female or the male direction, depending on the influence of hormones.

In addition to the obvious differences in the gonads and genitals, the sexes differ in the anatomy of several parts of the nervous system, especially the hypothalamus. For example, one portion of the medial preoptic nucleus of the hypothalamus is dependably larger in males than in females—two to three times larger in humans, and more than three times larger in certain other species (Hines, Davis, Coquelin, Goy, & Gorski, 1985; Swaab & Fliers, 1985). These and other differences between the sexes emerge at an early age, presumably organized by early hormones.

The presence of **testosterone**, an androgen, is apparently decisive in the development of the male pattern in both the genitals and the hypothalamus. Ordinarily, during a brief period of early development, the male's testes set up a positive feedback cycle: The testes secrete testosterone, which increases the growth of the testes and enables them to produce more testosterone. The testosterone also directs a masculine pattern of development in the hypothalamus.

A female rat that is injected with testosterone during the last few days before birth or the first few days afterward is partly masculinized, just as if the testosterone had come from her own body (Ward & Ward, 1985). Her clitoris grows larger than normal; her other reproductive structures look intermediate between female and male. At maturity, her pituitary and ovaries produce steady levels of hormones instead of the cycles that are characteristic of females. Anatomically, certain parts of her hypothalamus resemble those of a male more than those of a female. Her behavior is also masculinized: She mounts other females and makes copulatory thrusting movements rather than arching her back and allowing males to mount her. In short, early testosterone promotes the male pattern and inhibits the female pattern (Gorski, 1985; Wilson, George, & Griffin, 1981). With enough testosterone, the individual develops as a male; without testosterone, it develops as a female. Other species show variations on this pattern, as highlighted in Digression 11.2.

Early treatment with estradiol or other estrogens does not have the reverse effect. A male that is injected with small amounts of estrogens still develops as a male, although large quantities can interfere with certain aspects of his development (Diamond, Llacuna, & Wong, 1973). Furthermore, if the gonads are removed from either a male or a female rat just after birth, depriving the animal of its own hormones, the young rat develops to look and behave like a female. (It may need at least a small amount of estrogen to develop a fully normal female pattern, however.)

In short, in the presence of little or no sex hormones, a mammal develops the female pattern of external genitals and hypothalamus. Add estrogens, within normal limits, and the result is still female. Add testosterone and the result is male. Testosterone exerts long-lasting effects only if it is present during an early **sensitive period**—a few days before and after birth for a rat, about the third and fourth months of pregnancy for a human (Money & Ehrhardt, 1972).

According to studies on rodents, testosterone exerts a major part of its effect on the hypothalamus through a surprising route: After it enters a neuron, it is converted to estradiol! Testosterone and estradiol are chemically very similar, as you can see in Figure 11.3. In organic chemistry, a ring of six carbon atoms containing three double bonds is an *aromatic* compound. An enzyme found in the brain can *aromatize* testosterone into estradiol. Other types of androgens that cannot be aromatized into estrogens are less effective in masculinizing the hypothalamus. Moreover, drugs that prevent testosterone from being aromatized to estradiol block the organizing effects of testosterone on

The spotted hyena provides exceptions to most of the generalizations we usually make about males and females (Glickman et al., 1992). (See Figure 11.11.) On the average, female spotted hyenas are larger than the males are, as well as more dominant and more aggressive. The female's clitoris is fully as large as the male's penis and capable of erections like those of a penis. The female urinates through a canal in her clitoris. During puberty, that canal enlarges enough for the male to insert his penis into it in sexual intercourse. Eventually, her first-born baby rips through the wall of the clitoris, often dying in the process. Later-born babies have a higher chance of survival.

We do not have an evolutionary or functional explanation for why female spotted hyenas look and act so much like the males. Perhaps the explanation relates in some way to the overall aggressive nature of this species. (They fight with one another quite vigor-

ously. A pair of brothers or sisters sometimes fight to the death.)

Physiologically and ontogenetically, we are closer to an explanation. During pregnancy, the hyena mother's ovaries produce large amounts of androstenedione, the precursor chemical for both testosterone and estrogen. The placenta has relatively large amounts of the enzyme that converts androstenedione to testosterone, and small amounts of the enzyme that converts it to estrogen (Yalcinkaya et al., 1993). Therefore, at least at certain stages of development, the female fetus is exposed to much higher testosterone levels than are females of most other species. In short, the underlying mechanisms of sexual differentiation for spotted hyenas are much the same as in other mammalian species, even though the final outcome seems rather peculiar.

Figure 11.11
A female spotted hyena pup
Note that her clitoris looks like a penis and that her labia are fused and swollen like a scrotum. Female spotted hyenas are exposed to large amounts of testosterone during prenatal development. Their anatomy and their aggressive behavior become highly masculinized. (Courtesy Kay E. Holekamp)

sexual development. Apparently, androgens must be aromatized to estrogens to exert their organizing effects on the hypothalamus.

Why, then, is the female not masculinized by her own estradiol? During the early sensitive period, immature mammals of many species have in their bloodstream a protein called **alpha-fetoprotein,** which is not present in adults (Gorski, 1980; MacLusky & Naftolin, 1981). Alpha-fetoprotein binds with estrogen and blocks it from leaving the bloodstream and entering the cells that are developing in this early period. Primates have other mechanisms for inactivating estrogen, such as breaking down estrogens into inactive substances. In any event, testosterone is neither bound to alpha-fetoprotein nor metabolized; it is free to enter the cells, where enzymes convert it into estradiol. That is, testosterone is a way of getting estradiol into the cells when estradiol itself cannot leave the blood.

This explanation of testosterone's effects enables us to make sense of an otherwise puzzling fact: Although normal amounts of estradiol have little effect on early development, an injection of a larger amount actually masculinizes a female's development. The reason is that normal amounts are bound to alpha-fetoprotein or metabolized, whereas a larger amount may exceed the body's capacity for inactivation; the excess is thus able to enter the cells and masculinize them.

Testosterone also exerts organizing effects on the nerves and muscles that control the penis. In most mammalian species, a male has certain muscles in or near the penis that are either absent or very small in the area near the female's clitoris. Those muscles receive their neural input from two motor nuclei in the spinal cord; again, those nuclei are present in males and either smaller or absent in females. Early in development, both male and female develop large numbers of neurons in these nuclei. The male's testosterone supports survival of those neurons; in the female, the testosterone levels are lower and most of the neurons die (Goldstein & Sengelaub, 1992). A male also loses most of those neurons if he is treated with testosterone-blocking drugs during an early sensitive period (Grisham, Castro, Kashon, Ward, & Ward, 1992).

Sex Differences in Nonreproductive Characteristics

Males and females obviously differ in their organs of reproduction and in certain aspects of sexual behavior. But they also differ in many characteristics that have only indirect or nonobvious relationships with reproduction: In most mammalian species, males tend to be larger than females and to fight with one another more than females do (Ellis, 1986). Females tend to live longer and to devote more attention to infant care. (Humans are among the few mammalian species in which the male contributes to care for the young.)

Many of these sex differences depend on prenatal hormones. For example, female monkeys exposed to testosterone during their sensitive period engage in more rough-and-tumble play than other females do during youth, are more aggressive, and make more threatening facial gestures (Quadagno, Briscoe, & Quadagno, 1977; Young, Goy, & Phoenix, 1964). Similar effects on play and aggressive behavior have been noted in dogs (Beach, Buehler, & Dunbar, 1982; Reinisch, 1981) and ferrets (Stockman, Callaghan, Gallagher, & Baum, 1986).

In humans, too, males and females differ in their play patterns and aggressive behavior, even at an early age, but the exact role of early hormones is hard to determine. For example, girls who were exposed to elevated testosterone levels during prenatal development tend to spend more time than most other girls do playing with "boys' toys" such as toy cars and fire engines (Berenbaum & Hines, 1992). While that result suggests a possible relationship between early hormones and play preferences, we do not know whether parents and other people may have treated these girls differently from other girls because of their somewhat masculinized appearance.

Activating Effects of Sex Hormones

Long after the early hormones have determined the structure of the genitals and the nervous system, current levels of testosterone or estradiol exert activating effects on sexual behaviors. Activating effects temporarily modify sexual or other activities; they do not permanently alter anatomy, as organizing effects do.

Activating Effects on Sexual Behavior

In general, sexual behavior requires at least a minimum level of sex hormones to activate it. Species such as deer mate only in one season of the year, when their sex hormone levels are high. The activating effects of hormones on sexual behavior vary from one species to another.

Effects on Rats   After removal of the testes from a male rat or the ovaries from a female rat, sexual behavior declines as the sex hormone levels in the blood decline. It may not disappear altogether, partly because the adrenal glands also produce some testosterone and estradiol. An injection of testosterone into a castrated male rat restores sexual behavior, as does an injection of testosterone's two major metabolites, dihydrotestosterone and estradiol (Baum & Vreeburg, 1973). Estrogen followed by at least 2 to 4 hours of progesterone is the most effective combination for stimulating sexual behavior in a female rat (Glaser, Etgen, & Barfield, 1987).

By what mechanism do sex hormones activate sexual behavior? They do so partly by changing sensations. The *pudendal nerve* transmits tactile stimulation from the pubic area to the brain. Estrogens increase the area of skin that excites the pudendal nerve (Komisaruk, Adler, & Hutchison, 1972). Sex hormones also facilitate sexual behavior by binding to receptors in the brain. Estrogens bind especially to receptors in the ventromedial hypothalamus; androgens, to receptors in the preoptic area of the hypothalamus (Davidson, 1966).

Male sexual behavior depends heavily on neurons that release dopamine (Damsma, Pfaus, Wenkstern, Phillips, & Fibiger, 1992; Pfaus & Phillips, 1991). Neurons in the medial preoptic area of the hypothalamus release increased levels of dopamine during male sexual behavior, and not during other activities (Hull, Eaton, Moses, & Lorrain, 1993). Dopamine evidently contributes to different aspects of sexual behavior at different kinds of dopamine receptors. (Recall from page 79 that a given transmitter may stimulate several distinct kinds of receptors.) When the concentration of released dopamine is only moderately high, dopamine stimulates mostly type D_1 receptors, which facilitate erection of the penis. When the concentration of dopamine reaches a higher level, dopamine stimulates mostly type D_2 receptors, which lead to orgasm and ejaculation (Hull et al., 1992). The D_1 receptors tend to inhibit the effects of the D_2 receptors, and the D_2 receptors tend to inhibit the effects of the D_1 receptors. That is, at an early stage of excitation, the male is likely to have an erection but not to ejaculate. At a later, higher stage of excitation, the male is ready to ejaculate but then loses his erection.

Hormones and Behavior

Effects on Dogs and Cats Dogs and cats are less dependent on their levels of sex hormones than rodents are (Beach, 1967, 1970). Male dogs castrated as adults maintain sexual behavior at a somewhat decreased level for several years. Male cats maintain some sexual activity if they have had sexual experience before castration. Female dogs and cats cease sexual activity after removal of their ovaries, however.

For an intact female dog, sexual behavior depends largely on estrogen. Frank Beach taught us to distinguish among three aspects of female sexual behavior: attractivity, receptivity, and proceptivity (Beach, 1976). **Attractivity** is a tendency to attract sexual advances from males. **Receptivity** is a tendency to respond favorably to a male's sexual advances and to accept copulation. **Proceptivity** is a tendency to approach a male and actively to seek sexual contact. Just before the start of a dog's **estrus** period (her "heat" period, the time when she is fertile), her estradiol levels increase and she becomes sexually attractive to males. She begins to show proceptive behaviors (approaching males) but not yet receptive behaviors (accepting copulation). During the estrus period itself, her estradiol levels decline while her progesterone levels increase. Here she shows both proceptive and receptive behaviors, and copulation occurs. At the end of estrus, estrogen and progesterone levels drop sharply, as do proceptivity, receptivity, and attractivity (Beach, Dunbar, & Buehler, 1982).

Effects on Nonhuman Primates Primates (monkeys, apes, and humans) depend even less on current levels of sex hormones than dogs and cats do, although the results differ substantially from one primate species to another. Females of many monkey species are at least moderately receptive to males' sexual advances at all stages of their menstrual cycles (Baum, 1983). Their sex hormones apparently have more influence on their proceptivity than on their receptivity. Estrogen generally increases proceptive behaviors (Dixson, 1987). Female rhesus monkeys approach males and make inviting gestures much more frequently just before or during their fertile period (when estrogen levels are high) than they do after the end of the fertile period (Pomerantz & Goy, 1983; Wallen et al., 1984). For female primates, unlike dogs and rodents, progesterone decreases both sexual behavior and attractivity to males (Baum, 1983).

Male monkeys maintain a moderate amount of sexual activity after castration (Phoenix, Slob, & Goy, 1973), although the frequency does decline. After castration, testosterone injections increase sexual activity; estradiol injections do not (Michael, Zumpe, & Bonsall, 1990). Among intact males, sexual activity correlates positively, but not highly, with testosterone.

Effects on Men Human sexual activity is least dependent on current hormone levels, although an influence is certainly demonstrable. Among males, sexual excitement is generally highest at the age when testosterone levels are highest (about ages 15 to 25). The hormone oxytocin may also contribute to sexual pleasure. The body releases enormous amounts of oxytocin during orgasm, more than tripling the usual concentration in the blood. Several studies support a relationship between oxytocin and sexual pleasure, although the results are not yet conclusive (Murphy, Checkley, Seckl, & Lightman, 1990).

Decreases in testosterone levels generally decrease sexual activity. After castration, for example, most men—though not all—report a decrease in their sexual interest and activity (Carter, 1992). As time passes, they first lose their ability to ejaculate, then their ability to have an erection, and finally their sexual interest. However, low testosterone is not the only basis for **impotence**

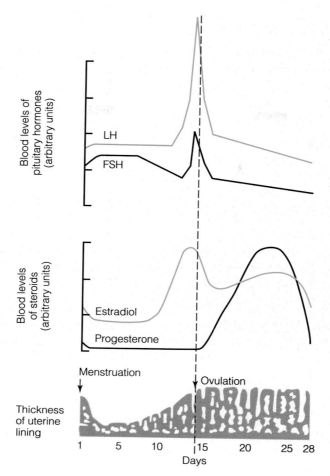

Figure 11.12
Blood levels of four
hormones over the human
menstrual cycle

(inability to have an erection). Some men with normal testosterone levels are impotent, and giving them extra testosterone does not alter their condition (Carani et al., 1990).

Typically, sex offenders (exhibitionists, rapists, child molesters, committers of incest, and so forth) have about average testosterone levels (Lang, Flor-Henry, & Frenzel, 1990). Occasional attempts have been made to control their behavior by administering drugs that lower their testosterone levels. One such drug is *cyproterone*, which blocks the entry of testosterone into cells and the binding of testosterone to receptors within cells. Another drug, *medroxyprogesterone*, blocks testosterone receptor sites in cells and accelerates the breakdown of testosterone into inactive molecules (Bradford, 1988). Most of the treated men cease their offensive behaviors as long as they continue taking the drugs (Bradford, 1988).

Effects on Women   In women and certain other female primates, the hypothalamus and pituitary interact with the ovaries to produce the **menstrual cycle,** a periodic variation in hormones and fertility over the course of approximately one month (see Figure 11.12). After the end of a menstrual period, the pituitary releases **follicle-stimulating hormone (FSH),** which promotes the growth of a follicle in the ovary. The follicle nurtures the *ovum* (egg cell) and produces estrogen. Toward the middle of the menstrual cycle, the follicle builds up more and more receptors to FSH; so, even though the actual concentration of FSH in the blood is decreasing, the effects of FSH on the follicle increase. As a result, the follicle produces increasing amounts of one type of estrogen, **estradiol.** Near the middle of the menstrual cycle, through a mechanism not well understood, the increased release of estradiol causes an increased release of FSH, as well as a sudden surge in the release of **luteinizing hormone (LH)** from the pituitary. (See top graph in Figure 11.12.) FSH and LH cause the follicle to release an ovum. They also cause the remnant of the follicle (now called the *corpus luteum*) to release the hormone **progesterone,** which prepares the uterus for the implantation of a fertilized ovum. Progesterone also inhibits the further release of LH. At the end of the menstrual cycle, the levels of LH, FSH, estradiol, and progesterone all decline (Feder, 1981). If the ovum is fertilized, the levels of estradiol and progesterone increase gradually throughout pregnancy. If the ovum is not fertilized, the lining of the uterus is cast off (menstruation), and the cycle is ready to begin again.

Birth-control pills prevent pregnancy by interfering with the usual feedback cycle between the ovaries and the pituitary. The most widely used and most effective birth-control pill is the *combination pill,* containing both estrogen and progesterone. The pill is so effective because it prevents pregnancy in a variety of ways. High levels of estrogen beginning shortly after the end of the menstrual period suppress the release of FSH, thereby blocking the development of the follicle and preventing the release of an ovum. Progesterone blocks the secretion of luteinizing hormone, thus further guaranteeing that an ovum will not be released.

These hormonal cycles produce only slight effects on women's sexual receptivity. However, at least a minimum level of sex hormones, both estrogen and testosterone, is important. For example, after **menopause** (a time when middle-aged women stop menstruating), women's levels of sex hormones decline. Some postmenopausal women take low levels of testosterone; the effect is generally an increase in sexual desire and sexual enjoyment (Sherwin, 1988). As with nonhuman primates, estrogen appears to be more important for proceptive behaviors than for receptive behaviors. According to two studies, women not taking birth-control pills initiate more sexual activity (either with a partner or by masturbation) about midway between menstrual periods than at other times during the month (Udry & Morris, 1968; Adams, Gold, & Burt, 1978). (See Figure 11.13.) The point midway between the menstrual periods is the time of ovulation and generally the time of the highest estrogen levels.

Activating Effects on Aggressive Behavior

Testosterone tends to activate fighting in the males of many species. In species that mate only in one season of the year, males fight with one another mostly during that season, while their testosterone levels are high (Goldstein, 1974; Moyer, 1974). A castrated male fights little; testosterone injections restore aggressive behavior (Brain, 1979).

Testosterone probably enhances the likelihood of human violence also. Throughout the world, males engage in more violent behavior than females do (Maccoby & Jacklin, 1974; Moyer, 1974). Moreover, the highest incidence of violence, as measured by crime statistics, is in men 15 to 25 years old, who also have the highest levels of testosterone in the blood.

A study of more than four thousand male military veterans found that the men with the higher testosterone levels had a greater frequency of assaults on

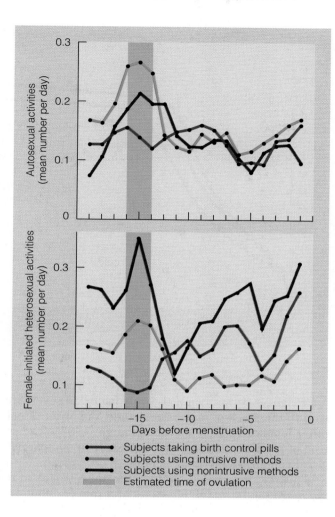

Figure 11.13
Fluctuation of autosexual activities (masturbation and sexual fantasies) and female-initiated heterosexual activities during the monthly cycle
Results are plotted separately for women taking birth-control pills, women using "intrusive" birth-control methods (diaphragm, foam, or condom), and women using "nonintrusive" methods (IUD or vasectomy). Note that women other than pill users increase self-initiated sex activities when their estrogen levels peak. (From Adams, Gold, & Burt, 1978.)

other people, being absent without leave from the military, abusing alcohol and other drugs, and in general getting into trouble (Dabbs & Morris, 1990). However, although these differences were statistically significant, they were fairly small. Testosterone apparently contributes toward violent and impulsive behavior in humans, but it is hardly the only contributor.

Puberty

Puberty, the onset of sexual maturity, usually begins at about age 12 to 13 for girls and a year later for boys in the United States. Because reproduction requires a great deal of energy, the body does not enter puberty until it has enough energy reserves. On the average, a girl experiences **menarche** (muh-NAR-kee; her first menstruation) when she weighs about 47 kg (103 pounds) (see Figure 11.14). Girls who keep their weight very low because of ballet or athletic training or other reasons are slower than others to reach menarche and generally have more irregular menstrual cycles than other girls have. Girls more than 30 percent overweight also have irregular cycles (Frisch, 1983, 1984).

Hormones and Behavior

Figure 11.14
Weight gain and sexual maturation in three samples of girls
Girls start their adolescent growth spurt when their weight reaches about 30 kg (66 pounds). They generally reach menarche (the first menstruation) when they weigh about 47 kg (103 pounds). Girls in 1947 reached menarche at a slightly younger age than girls in earlier studies did, presumably because better nutrition and health enabled them to gain weight faster. (After Frisch, 1972.)

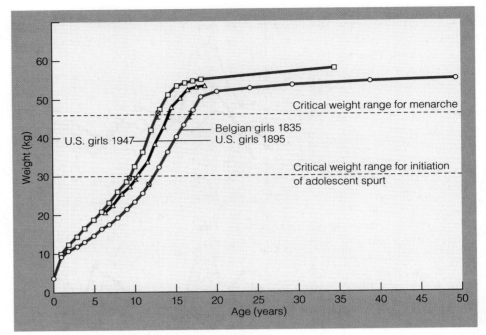

Weight is certainly not the only factor. In several nonhuman species, exposure to the smell of males accelerates the onset of puberty, while the smell of other females retards it (Vandenbergh, 1987). The same may or may not be true of humans; it would be interesting to compare girls in coed schools with girls in all-girl elementary schools.

Puberty starts when the hypothalamus begins to release bursts of *luteinizing hormone releasing hormone* at a rate of about one burst per hour. We do not know what stimulates the hypothalamus to do so, but once it begins, it continues throughout the fertile period. This hormone stimulates the pituitary to secrete LH and FSH, which in turn stimulate the gonads to release estradiol or testosterone (B. D. Goldman, 1981). Estradiol causes breast development and broadening of the hips. Testosterone causes lowering of the voice, beard growth, broadening of the shoulders, and growth of hair on the chest, in the underarms, and in the pubic area. Both boys and girls undergo a growth spurt in response to the increase in hormones.

Parental Behavior

Sexual behavior has a way of leading to babies. During late pregnancy and just after giving birth, mammalian mothers have high levels of estrogen, progesterone, oxytocin, and prolactin. It is natural to expect that those hormonal changes may predispose her to maternal behavior.

This hypothesis is largely correct for a number of nonhuman mammals. However, humans are a special case. Women who have never been pregnant can be devoted parents; so can men. Hormones are apparently not necessary for human parental behavior, except for the ability of the mother to breast-feed the infant.

In rodents, hormones can strongly influence parental behavior. Late in pregnancy, female rats produce a pattern of hormones that is incompatible with parental behavior; if infant rats are presented to a pregnant female 2 to 5 days before she is due to give birth, she is actually *less* responsive to them than a virgin female is (Mayer & Rosenblatt, 1984). However, by the day of delivery, her hormones have changed (with a marked increase in prolactin and oxytocin) and so has her behavior. The hormones of mother rats strongly promote parental behavior. In one study, 30-day-old rats (just a week or so after weaning) were injected with plasma from mother rats, containing all the mothers' hormones. The 30-day-old rats, especially the females, quickly showed typical rat parental behaviors, such as retrieving baby rats and putting them into a nest (Brunelli, Shindledecker, & Hofer, 1987). An injection of estrogen, progesterone, oxytocin, and prolactin into a virgin female rat can induce maternal behavior, although the behavior generally does not appear until a day or two after the injection (Bridges, DiBiase, Loundes, & Doherty, 1985; Lamb, 1975; Moltz, Lubin, Leon, & Numan, 1970; Pedersen, Ascher, Monroe, & Prange, 1982).

Although hormones facilitate maternal behavior, they are not indispensable for it. If a female rat that has never been pregnant is left with some 5- to 10-day-old babies, her interest in them increases over several days. (Because the babies cannot survive without parental care and food, the experimenter must periodically replace them with new, healthy babies.) After about six days, the adoptive mother builds a nest, assembles the babies in the nest, licks them, and does everything else that a normal mother would, except nurse them. Even females whose ovaries were removed respond maternally, although those with intact ovaries show more complete parental behavior (Mayer & Rosenblatt, 1979).

Even male rodents can be induced to parental behavior, although their hormonal patterns never duplicate those of a new mother. A male rat that is caged with infants by himself (with no adult female) may kill them or initially ignore them. Males that ignore the babies gradually come to show parental behavior (R. E. Brown, 1986; Rosenblatt, 1967). In this regard, the males' behavior is somewhat like that of a previously inexperienced female.

In short, exposing adult rats to infants for 5 to 10 days can substitute for the hormonal changes that accompany pregnancy and delivery. Would this effect of exposure ever influence behavior in nature? After all, a baby that needed six days to induce an adult to take care of it would die before the adult got mobilized. Rosenblatt's (1970) answer is that maternal behavior goes through two stages. During the first few days after giving birth, hormones facilitate maternal behavior. After those first few days, the mother's familiarity with the young becomes a sufficient basis to maintain maternal care, with or without hormones. The advantage of this system is that maternal care lasts longer than the hormonal changes that accompany giving birth.

Throughout this section I have been discussing "maternal behavior" as if it were all one unified act. It is not; after different kinds of brain damage, a mother rat can lose a single aspect of maternal behavior, such as her tendency to defend the nest or her tendency to retrieve lost pups (Factor, Mayer, & Rosenblatt, 1993; Hansen, Harthon, Wallin, Löfberg, & Svensson, 1991). I may also have left the misconception that maternal behavior is motivated by the desire to help the young. This is true in humans (generally); in other species, it may or may not be. For example, a mother rat licks her babies all over shortly after their birth and again periodically for the next 2–3 weeks. Licking them provides stimulation that is essential for the babies' survival. However, we have no reason to believe that the mother understands this function. She licks her babies after giving birth because at that time they are covered with her own salty body fluid, and she needs the salt. She continues licking them over the next 2–3 weeks to swallow their urination—again, a source of salt. If an experimenter provides her with ample sources of salt water, she licks the babies much less, and thus the babies get less of her helpful stimulation (Gubernick & Alberts, 1983). In short, a mother rat's motivations are not necessarily synonymous with the ways that her behavior contributes to reproduction. (The same could be said for the motivations of a human having sexual intercourse.)

Summary

1. Three major types of hormones are peptide hormones, thyroid hormones, and steroid hormones. Peptide hormones attach to membrane receptors and exert effects similar to those of neurotransmitters. Thyroid hormones and steroid hormones attach to receptors inside the cell and through those receptors modify the expression of the genes. (p. 380)

2. The hypothalamus controls activity of the pituitary gland by nerve impulses and releasing hormones. The pituitary in turn secretes hormones that alter the activity of other endocrine glands. (p. 384)

3. The organizing effects of a hormone are exerted during an early sensitive period and bring about relatively permanent alterations in anatomy or in the potential for function. (p. 388)

4. In the absence of sex hormones, or with the addition of small amounts of estrogens, the genitals and hypothalamus of an infant mammal will differentiate like those of a female. In the presence of adequate amounts of testosterone, the infant will develop as a male. (p. 390)

5. At least in developing rodents, testosterone is converted within certain cells to estradiol, which actually masculinizes the development of the hypothalamus. Estradiol in the blood does not masculinize development, either because it is bound to proteins in the blood or because it is metabolized. (p. 390)

6. Sex hormones also exert organizing influences on other aspects of behavior. (p. 392)

7. In adulthood, sex hormones can activate sex behaviors, aggressive behaviors, and increased activity levels. The effects of each hormone differ from male to female, from species to species, and from one behavior to another. (p. 393)

8. Puberty begins when the hypothalamus begins to release bursts of luteinizing hormone releasing hormone. The onset of puberty is controlled by many factors, including weight and social stimuli. (p. 397)

9. Hormones released around the time of giving birth facilitate maternal behavior in females of many mammalian species. Nevertheless, mere prolonged exposure to young is also sufficient to induce parental behavior, even in males of certain species. Hormonal facilitation is apparently not essential to human parental behavior. (p. 399)

10. A mother rat's motivations include her own thirst and salt need, not just the welfare of the young. (p. 399)

Review Questions

1. What are the major differences between the anterior pituitary and the posterior pituitary? (p. 386)

2. What is the difference between the organizing and activating effects of a hormone? (p. 388)

3. What are the effects of testosterone in the early sensitive period on the development of the genitals and the hypothalamus? What are the effects of estradiol? Why does the circulating estradiol in a female fetus have little effect on the cells? (p. 390)

4. What is the difference between receptivity and proceptivity? (p. 394)

5. What differences exist among mammalian species in their dependence on current hormone levels for sexual behavior? (p. 394)

6. Describe the evidence that sex hormones activate sexual behavior in men and women. (p. 394)

7. What drugs are sometimes used to suppress sexual interest in sex offenders? How do they work? (p. 395)

8. Describe the hormonal feedback that regulates the menstrual cycle of women. (p. 395)

9. How do combination birth-control pills prevent pregnancy? (p. 396)

10. What are some of the factors that control the onset of puberty? (p. 397)

11. What is responsible for maternal behavior in the first few days after giving birth? What is responsible for parental behavior later? (p. 399)

12. We might assume that a mother rat takes care of her babies because she wants to help them survive. In what way is that assumption an example of *anthropomorphism*, as defined on page 349? (p. 399)

Thought Questions

1. The controversial pill RU-486 produces abortions by blocking the effects of progesterone. Explain how blocking progesterone would abort a pregnancy.

2. The presence or absence of testosterone determines whether a mammal will differentiate as a male or a female; estrogens have no effect. In birds, the story is the opposite: The presence or absence of estrogen is critical (Adkins & Adler, 1972). What problems would determination by estrogen create if that were the mechanism for mammals? Why do those problems not arise in birds? (*Hint:* Think about the difference between live birth and hatching from an egg.)

3. In most mammalian species, females live longer than males do, on the average. Also in most species, females contribute more than males do to infant care. Could these two tendencies be related to one another? (For example, might natural selection have favored a longer life span for females because the infants' well-being depends more on the survival of the mother than on the survival of the father?)

Suggestion for Further Reading

Becker, J. B., Breedlove, S. M., & Crews, D. (1992). *Behavioral endocrinology.* Cambridge, MA: MIT Press. Collection of chapters by various authorities reviewing many aspects of hormones and sexual behavior.

Terms

hormone chemical secreted by a gland and conveyed by the blood to other organs whose activity it influences (p. 380)

endocrine gland organ that produces and releases hormones (p. 380)

protein hormone hormone composed of a longer chain of amino acids (p. 380)

peptide hormone hormone composed of a shorter chain of amino acids (p. 380)

steroid hormone hormone that contains four carbon rings (p. 381)

estrogen a class of steroid hormones that are more abundant in females than in males for most species (p. 381)

androgen a class of steroid hormones that are more abundant in males than in females for most species (p. 381)

sex-limited gene gene that exerts its effects primarily in one sex because of activation by androgens or estrogens (p. 382)

pituitary gland an endocrine gland attached to the hypothalamus (p. 384)

anterior pituitary portion of the pituitary gland (p. 386)

posterior pituitary portion of the pituitary gland (p. 386)

oxytocin hormone released by the posterior pituitary; also used as a neurotransmitter in the brain; important for sexual and parental behaviors (p. 386)

vasopressin (also known as antidiuretic hormone) hormone released by the posterior hypothalamus; raises blood pressure and enables the kidneys to reabsorb water and therefore to secrete highly concentrated urine (p. 386)

releasing hormone hormone released by the hypothalamus that flows through the blood to the anterior pituitary (p. 386)

organizing effect long-lasting effect of a hormone that is present during a sensitive period early in development (p. 388)

activating effect temporary effect of a hormone on behavior or anatomy, occurring only while the hormone is present (p. 388)

gonad reproductive organ (p. 389)

ovary female gonad that produces eggs (p. 389)

testis male gonad that produces testosterone and sperm (p. 389)

Müllerian duct early precursor to female reproductive structures (the oviducts, uterus, and upper vagina) (p. 389)

Wolffian duct early precursor to male reproductive structures (p. 389)

testosterone one type of androgen (p. 390)

sensitive period time early in development during which some event (such as the presence of a hormone) has a long-lasting effect (p. 390)

alpha-fetoprotein protein found in the bloodstream of most immature mammals that binds with estrogen (p. 392)

attractivity tendency to attract sexual advances (p. 394)

receptivity tendency to respond favorably to sexual advances (p. 394)

proceptivity tendency to approach a partner and actively seek sexual contact (p. 394)

estrus period when a female animal is fertile (p. 394)

impotence inability to have an erection (p. 394)

menstrual cycle periodic variation in hormones and fertility over the course of approximately one month in women (p. 395)

follicle-stimulating hormone (FSH) anterior pituitary hormone that promotes the growth of follicles in the ovary (p. 395)

estradiol one type of estrogen (p. 396)

luteinizing hormone (LH) anterior pituitary hormone that stimulates the release of an ovum and prepares the uterus for implantation of a fertilized ovum (p. 396)

progesterone hormone that prepares the uterus for the implantation of a fertilized ovum (p. 396)

menopause time when middle-aged women stop menstruating (p. 396)

puberty onset of sexual maturity (p. 397)

menarche time of a woman's first menstruation (p. 397)

Variations in Sexual Development and Sexual Orientation

One species of fish (*Thalassoma duperry*) ordinarily lives in small schools consisting of one male and a few females. If the male dies, a new male may join the school to take his place. If no new male shows up, one of the females changes into a male (Ross, Losey, & Diamond, 1983). (I don't know how they decide which female will become the male.) The converted female not only looks and acts like a male but also produces sperm and fertilizes the eggs of the other females.

Nothing quite like that happens in mammals, but it should alert us to some of the possible difficulties with the categories of male and female. Certain people develop anatomies that are intermediate between male and female or anatomies that do not match their genetic sex. Some men are sexually aroused by other men, some women by other women. These variations in development are interesting to investigate for their own sake and for what they reveal about sexual development in general.

Sexual development is a very sensitive issue, so let us specify from the start: "Different" does not mean "abnormal" (except in the statistical sense). People differ naturally in their sexual development just as they do in their height, weight, emotions, and memory.

Determinants of Gender Identity

Gender identity—the sex with which one identifies and the sex that one calls oneself—is a uniquely human characteristic. Gender identity is closely related to, but not identical with, the concept of **sex role,** the set of activities and dispositions presumed to be common for one sex or the other in a particular society. While someone who adopts the female gender identity is likely to accept the female sex role, for example, it is also possible to reject all or part of that sex role.

Sex roles are determined to a large extent by one's culture and upbringing. For example, cooking is regarded as women's work by certain societies and as men's work by others. Even within our own society, what we regard as normal behavior for a man or a woman may change sharply from one generation to the next.

Gender identity is undoubtedly also governed to a large degree by one's upbringing. From an early age, a girl is told, "You are a girl, and later if you decide to marry, you will marry a boy." She is dressed in girl's clothing and placed mostly in the company of other girls. Boys receive the inverse treatment. And yet, a few people are clearly dissatisfied with their assigned sex, a

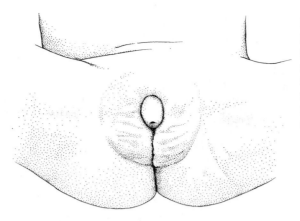

Figure 11.15
External genitals of a
genetic female, age 3
months, masculinized by
excess androgens from the
adrenal gland before birth
(the adrenogenital
syndrome)

small number of them (transsexuals) to such an extreme degree that they insist
on a sex change. Others (homosexuals) have no desire to become a member of
the opposite sex, but they direct their sexual interests toward members of their
own sex. Might some biological factor, such as prenatal hormones, influence
gender identity or sexual orientation? Several kinds of human cases shed some
light on this question, though to date there are no definitive answers.

Intersexes or Pseudohermaphrodites

Recall that testosterone masculinizes the development of the genitals and the
hypothalamus during a sensitive period in early development. If a genetic
female is exposed to more testosterone than the average female but less than
the average male, she may develop an appearance intermediate between male
and female. The same is true of a genetic male who is deprived of some, but not
all, of his own testosterone.

Rarely, human fetuses are exposed to an abnormal hormonal environment
before birth. For example, a female fetus or her mother may have an adrenal
gland that produces an excess of testosterone and other androgens, or the
mother may have taken an antimiscarriage drug that mimics some of the
effects of testosterone. Also, in some women, the placenta lacks the enzyme
that converts testosterone to estrogen (Shozu, Akasofu, Harada, & Kubota,
1991). If for any reason a female fetus is exposed to elevated androgen levels,
the result is partial masculinization of her external anatomy, as Figure 11.15
illustrates. Note in the figure that the genitals appear intermediate between a
clitoris and a penis; swellings near the genitals appear intermediate between
normal labia and a normal scrotum.

Individuals whose genitals do not match the normal development for their
genetic sex are referred to as **hermaphrodites** (from Hermaphroditus, son of
Hermes and Aphrodite, in Greek mythology). There are several types of hermaphrodites. The so-called *true hermaphrodite,* a rarity, has some normal testicular tissue and some normal ovarian tissue—for example, a testis on one
side of the body and an ovary on the other (Simpson, 1976). Individuals whose
development is intermediate between male and female, like the one in Figure
11.15, are variously called **intersexes, pseudohermaphrodites,** or simply
hermaphrodites.

When a baby is born with an intersexual appearance, a decision must be
made: Shall we call the child a boy or a girl? As a rule, intersexes are infertile,

and the chromosomes are a poor guide as to the person's eventual genital appearance, behavior patterns, or social identity. For decades now, the usual policy has been: When in doubt, call the child a girl. Given that plastic surgeons cannot successfully enlarge the penis/clitoris to full penis size, they surgically reduce it to clitoris size and create an artificial vagina or lengthen a short natural vagina. At that point, the child looks like a more-or-less normal female; her parents raise her as a female and her age-mates accept her as such.

And she lives happily ever after, right? Well, not necessarily. Here is a quote from one intersexual adult (Chase, 1993):

> Surgical and hormonal treatment allows parents and physicians to imagine that they have eliminated the child's intersexuality. Unfortunately, the surgery is immensely destructive of sexual sensation as well as one's sense of bodily integrity. Because the cosmetic result may be good, parents and physicians complacently ignore the child's emotional pain in being forced into a socially acceptable gender. This child's body, once violated by the surgery, is again and again subjected to frequent genital examinations. Many "graduates" of medical intersex corrective programs are chronically depressed, wishing vainly for the return of body parts. Suicides are not uncommon. Some former intersexuals become transsexual, rejecting their imposed sex.

So how *should* the child be reared? On that question, psychologists do not agree. What do we learn about the causes of gender identity from a study of intersexes? There too, the answers are inconclusive. Intersexes were subjected to a pattern of prenatal hormones intermediate between the normal male and female patterns. As children, most were reared as girls, some as boys, but we do not know how normal their rearing experiences actually were. As adults, most are more-or-less satisfied with their assigned sex, but some have a rather ambiguous sexual identity, and some reject their assigned sex (Ehrhardt & Money, 1967; Money & Ehrhardt, 1968; Money, 1970). Under these circumstances, we cannot clearly separate the contributions of prenatal hormones from those of postnatal experiences.

Testicular Feminization

Certain individuals with the typical male XY chromosome pattern have the genital appearance of a female. This problem is known as **androgen insensitivity** or **testicular feminization**. Although such individuals produce normal amounts of androgens, their bodies lack the mechanism that enables androgens to bind to genes in a cell's nucleus. Consequently, the cells are insensitive to androgens, and the external genitals develop almost like those of a normal female. Two abnormalities appear at puberty: First, in spite of breast development and broadening of the hips, menstruation does not begin because the body has two internal testes instead of ovaries and a uterus. (The vagina is short and leads to nothing.) Second, pubic hair does not develop, because pubic hair depends on androgens in females as well as males (see Figure 11.16).

A person with androgen insensitivity develops with a fully normal female gender identity. If her condition is medically identified, typically the very short vagina is surgically lengthened and the internal testes removed because internal testes are likely to develop tumors and to cause additional health problems. Her female gender identity should come as no surprise: She looks like a normal

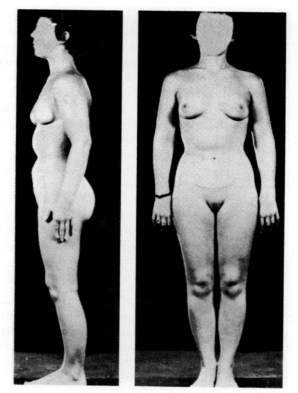

Figure 11.16
A woman with an XY
chromosome pattern but
insensitivity to androgens
Two undescended testes pro-
duce testosterone and other
androgens, to which the
body is insensitive. The
testes and adrenal glands
also produce estrogens that
are responsible for the
pubertal changes. (From
Federman, 1967.)

female, she has been raised unambiguously as a female, and her cells have been exposed only to estrogens since prenatal development. The only discrepancy is that her genetic sex is male (XY).

Discrepancies of Sexual Appearance

Most of the evidence from pseudohermaphrodites does not tell us anything indisputable about the roles of rearing and hormones in determining gender identity. From a scientific viewpoint, the only decisive way to settle the issue would be to raise a completely normal male baby as a female or to raise a normal female baby as a male. If the process succeeded, we would know that upbringing determines gender identity and that hormones do not. Although no one could perform such an experiment intentionally, it is possible to treat accidental events as natural experiments. Here, we shall consider two examples in which children were (presumably) exposed to the hormonal pattern of one sex and then reared (unambiguously, as far as we know) as the opposite sex.

Penis Development Delayed until Puberty Certain genetic males in the Dominican Republic were born with a gene that prevented penis growth early in life. Specifically, they have low levels of the enzyme that converts testosterone to the related hormone DHT (5-alpha-dihydrotestosterone). DHT is more effective than testosterone is for masculinizing the genitals; thus the consequence of the enzyme deficiency is a lack of penis growth during early life. Their testosterone levels were probably normal, however. As infants, they were

Variations in Sexual
Development and Sexual
Orientation

regarded as girls with slightly swollen clitorises and were reared as females. At puberty, their testosterone levels increased enough that, even without DHT, their penises grew. At this point, each was reassigned as a male.

If you had lived your first 12 years or so as a female and then suddenly grew a penis, and your parents said that now you were a boy, how would you react? Perhaps surprisingly, in nearly all cases in which this has happened, the girl-turned-boy developed a clear male gender identity and directed his sexual interest toward females (Imperato-McGinley, Guerrero, Gautier, & Peterson, 1974). One interpretation of these results is that the prenatal testosterone favored a male gender identity, even in children who were reared as females. Another possibility is that gender identity is established by social influences around the time of puberty. In either case, the results make it difficult to argue that early rearing experiences are the sole determinant of gender identity, unless we assume that these children were actually recognized as different from the start and were reared in an abnormal way. (We can only speculate about whether it would be equally easy for someone reared as a male to switch to a female identity.)

Accidental Removal of the Penis　Circumcision is the removal of the foreskin of the penis, a common procedure with newborn boys. One physician, while trying to circumcise a baby boy using an electrical procedure, accidentally used too high a current and burned off the entire penis. The parents elected to rear the child as a female, with the appropriate corrective surgery. What makes this a particularly interesting case is that the subject has a twin brother (whom the parents did not let the physician try to circumcise). If both twins developed satisfactory gender identities, one as a girl and the other as a boy, we would be likely to conclude that rearing was decisive in gender identity and that prenatal hormones were not.

The child reared as a girl was reported to have a normal female gender identity as a prepubertal child, though she also had strong tomboyish tendencies (Money & Schwartz, 1978). However, as a teenager she was reported to be very unhappy, "beset with problems," and unwilling to discuss sexual matters. When asked to "draw a person," she always drew a man (which is not so unusual) and absolutely refused to draw a woman (which is unusual). She looked and walked like a man; fellow students called her a "cavewoman." No one had told her about her operations or sex reassignment, and no one was sure whether she had remembered or suspected. Rearing this child as a girl was far from a complete success and hardly an endorsement for the idea that rearing is the sole determinant of gender identity (Diamond, 1982). More recent reports have not been published, perhaps to protect the family's privacy.

▶ *Current Controversies:*
Possible Biological Bases of Sexual Orientation

Why do some people prefer partners of the opposite sex and other people prefer partners of their own sex? This topic is particularly troublesome to deal with because of the difficulty of separating the scientific issues from the social, political, and moralistic disputes. If we ever do determine the causes of sexual orientation, some people worry about what society might do with the information. Given the emotionally charged atmosphere of this debate, scientific progress is more difficult than it might otherwise

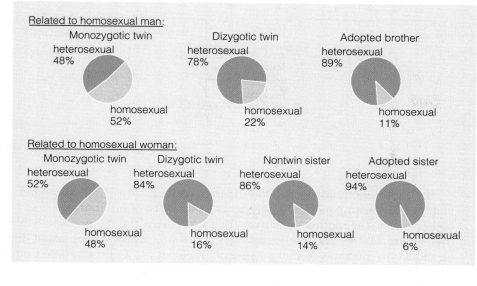

Figure 11.17
Frequency of homosexual and heterosexual orientations in adult family members of a homosexual man or woman
Note that the probability of a homosexual orientation is highest among monozygotic twins of a homosexual individual, lower among dizygotic twins, and still lower among adopted brothers or sisters. These data suggest a genetic contribution toward the development of sexual orientation. (Based on the data of Bailey & Pillard, 1991; Bailey, Pillard, Neale, & Agyei, 1993.)

be. Most of our discussion will focus on male homosexuality, which is more common than female homosexuality and a great deal more heavily investigated.

Most people say that their sexual orientation "just happened," generally at an early age, and that they do not know how or why it developed as it did. Sexual orientation, like left-handedness or right-handedness, is not something that most people voluntarily choose or that they can easily change. Like most other complex human behaviors, it reflects a complex interplay of genetic and nongenetic influences.

Genetics Research suggests that certain genes increase the probability that a person will develop a homosexual orientation. Figure 11.17 shows the frequency of homosexual vs. heterosexual orientations in the adult brothers of homosexual men and the adult sisters of homosexual women. Note that the probability of homosexuality is highest in monozygotic (identical) twins of the originally identified homosexual individual, lower in dizygotic twins, and still lower in adopted brothers or sisters (Bailey & Pillard, 1991; Bailey, Pillard, Neale, & Agyei, 1993). Another study with a smaller sample found similar results (Whitam, Diamond, & Martin, 1993). In short, genetic similarity makes a contribution that goes beyond that of growing up in the same environment. However, homosexual men tend to have more homosexual brothers than homosexual sisters; homosexual women tend to have more homosexual sisters than homosexual brothers (Bailey & Benishay, 1993). Therefore, the genes or other factors promoting male homosexuality are different from those that promote female homosexuality.

Note that the data in Figure 11.17 support a genetic contribution to sexual orientation; note also two limitations on any such conclusion:

- The results are based on limited samples, which may be unrepresentative in some way. As always, it is best to wait for replications on additional samples.
- Even identical twins do not always develop the same sexual orientation. Thus, although genetic factors appear to be important, they are certainly not the only factor.

Variations in Sexual Development and Sexual Orientation

407

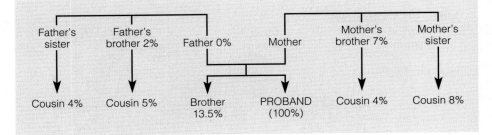

Note that the incidences are higher in the relatives on the mother's side than they are in the relatives on the father's side. Note also that the incidence is higher in sons of the mother's sister than it is in sons of the mother's brother. These results are consistent with a hypothesis that a gene promoting male homosexuality is located on the X chromosome. (From data of Hamer, Hu, Magnuson, Hu, & Pattatucci, 1993.)

If we examine relatives beyond the immediate family of a homosexual male, an interesting pattern emerges: The incidence of homosexuality is higher among the mother's relatives than it is among the father's relatives. (See Figure 11.18.) The likely explanation is that a relevant gene could be on the X chromosome. A man necessarily receives his X chromosome from his mother. If some gene on the X chromosome increases the probability that a man will develop a homosexual orientation, then his mother must have that gene also, even though the gene might have a very different, or even undetectable, effect on her own behavior. The gene would also occur in a fair percentage of the mother's sisters, who could pass it on to some of their sons. The gene would also occur in a fair percentage of the mother's brothers—but not in those brothers' sons. (Remember, the sons get their X chromosomes from their mothers.) The data in Figure 11.18 fit this set of predictions reasonably well. (Hamer, Hu, Magnuson, Hu, & Pattatucci, 1993). In fact, an examination of visible markers on the X chromosomes of homosexual men and their relatives has led to a tentative location for the gene in question, near a region of the chromosome known as Xq28 (Hamer et al., 1993). Eventually, researchers may identify the gene itself.

Until then, we do not know what that gene does. You should not necessarily think of this as a "gene for sexual orientation." Most genes have multiple effects, and the one that we happen to notice may not be a gene's primary effect. For example, psychologists have found evidence for a genetic contribution to television watching (Plomin, Corley, DeFries, & Fulker, 1990). Surely humans did not evolve a gene with that specific effect; the differences in television watching must be a by-product of genetically based differences in activity level or attention span or something else. Similarly, the gene or genes that affect sexual orientation probably affect other behavioral or physiological features as well.

If certain genes promote a homosexual orientation, then why, one might wonder, has evolution not selected strongly against those genes, which clearly decrease the probability of reproduction? One possible explanation is that the genes may produce different effects in different people, sometimes promoting highly beneficial behaviors without altering reproductive behaviors. Another possibility focuses on **kin selection,** selection for a gene that benefits one's kin (relatives). For example, homosexual men and women may perhaps help their brothers or sisters to rear children, and thereby perpetuate genes that the whole family shares (LeVay, 1993). This hypothesis is plausible, although we have no evidence to support it. A third possibility: Recall that the mothers, aunts, and sisters of a homosexual man are likely to have the same gene(s) without manifesting a homosexual orientation. Perhaps the relevant genes provide them with some advantage, increasing their probability of reproducing.

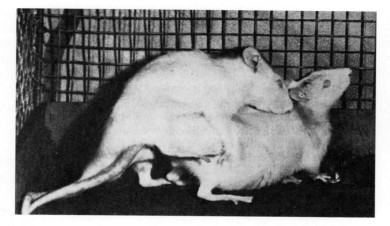

Figure 11.19
A female rat mounting a male
The female was injected with androgens during an early sensitive period; the male was castrated at birth and injected with androgens at adulthood. (From Dörner, 1974.)

Effects of Hormones   Given the importance of hormones for sexual behavior, it seems natural to look for possible effects of hormones on sexual orientation. We can quickly dismiss the hypothesis that sexual orientation depends on adult hormone levels: Most homosexual men have testosterone and estrogen levels well within the same range as heterosexual men.

A more plausible hypothesis is that sexual orientation depends on testosterone levels during some sensitive period of brain development, perhaps from the middle of the second month of pregnancy until the end of the fifth month (Ellis & Ames, 1987). In studies of animals ranging from rats to pigs to zebra finches, males that were exposed to much-decreased levels of testosterone early in life have as adults shown a sexual interest in other males (Adkins-Regan, 1988). Females exposed to extra testosterone during that period show an increased probability of attempting to mount sexual partners in the way that males typically do. (See Figure 11.19.)

However, in many of these animal studies, the hormonal manipulation also led to abnormalities of the genitals. (Homosexual and heterosexual people are anatomically the same.) A more directly relevant animal study is one in which a treatment altered sexual behavior without much effect on anatomy: Ingeborg Ward (1972, 1977) exposed pregnant rats to a stressful experience during the final week of pregnancy by confining them in tight Plexiglas tubes for 135 minutes daily under bright lights. Such stress increases the mother's release of endorphins, some of which cross the placenta and evidently reach the fetuses' developing hypothalamus, where the endorphins produce antitestosterone effects (Ward, Monaghan, & Ward, 1986).

Prenatal stress did not prevent normal development of the males' penis and testes, but it did modify their behavior, presumably because of early effects on the hypothalamus. As adults, the prenatally stressed males responded to injections of either testosterone or estrogen with an increase in female sexual behavior, arching their backs to receive a male partner. Few attempted to copulate with female partners.

Although the sexual behavior of prenatally stressed males is altered, their behavior is typically male in certain other regards, such as level of activity in an open field (Meisel, Dohanich, & Ward, 1979). Evidently, different aspects of sex-differentiated behavior are organized at different times in development or are perhaps sensitive to different types of androgens.

Variations in Sexual Development and Sexual Orientation

Even for sexual behavior, the effects of the prenatal stress varied, depending on social experiences after birth. Prenatally stressed males reared in isolation or with other prenatally stressed males developed a sexual responsivity to males. Those reared with normal males and females became sexually responsive to both males and females (Dunlap, Zadina, & Gougis, 1978; Ward & Reed, 1985).

With regard to human sexual orientation, the rat data are merely suggestive, with serious limitations:

- The hormonal influences associated with sexual behavior differ in several ways between rats and primates and even between one primate species and another.
- The female sexual behaviors shown by the male rats in these studies (such as arching their backs) do not closely mimic human behaviors. In humans, male homosexuals are characterized by their preference for male partners, not necessarily by their preference for female postures or behaviors.

Despite these limitations, the rat studies suggest that investigators should examine any possible relationship between prenatal events and later sexual orientation. One approach is to ask the mothers of homosexual men whether they experienced any unusual stress during pregnancy. One such survey contacted 283 mothers of homosexual and heterosexual men, without letting them know why or how they had been chosen. The survey made no mention of sexual orientation; it merely asked about a variety of illnesses and stressors that the woman might have experienced before, during, or after pregnancy. The mothers of homosexual men reported a significantly greater number of stressful events, especially during the second trimester of pregnancy (Ellis, Ames, Peckham, & Burke, 1988). However, a similar study failed to find any report of increased stress during pregnancies that led to homosexual sons (Bailey, Willerman, & Parks, 1991). Both studies are limited by relying on mothers' memories of pregnancies that occurred more than 20 years previously. A more decisive (though much more difficult) procedure would be to measure stress at the time of pregnancy and follow up later to determine the sexual orientation of the offspring. At this point, the relationship between prenatal stress and human sexual orientation is uncertain.

What about the role of hormones in female homosexuality? In the 1950s and early 1960s, certain pregnant women took the synthetic estrogen **diethylstilbestrol (DES)** to prevent miscarriage or to deal with other problems. DES can exert masculinizing effects similar to those of testosterone. One study found that, of 30 adult women whose mothers had taken DES during pregnancy, 7 reported some degree of homosexual or bisexual responsiveness. By comparison, only 1 of 30 women not prenatally exposed to DES reported any homosexual or bisexual responsiveness (Ehrhardt et al., 1985). Note that, although these results suggest that prenatal hormones play some role, they do not imply a very strong influence.

Brain Anatomy   On the average, men's brains differ from women's in several ways, such as in the relative sizes of parts of the hypothalamus (Breedlove, 1992). Do the brains of homosexual men resemble those of heterosexual men or heterosexual women?

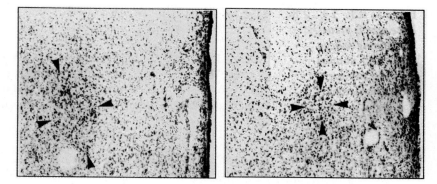

Figure 11.20
Comparison of typical size of interstitial nucleus 3 of the anterior hypothalamus in a heterosexual male (left) and a homosexual male (right)
On the average, the volume of this structure was more than twice as large in a sample of heterosexual men than it was in a sample of homosexual men, for whom it was about the same size as that in women. Animal studies have implicated this structure as particularly important for male sexual activities. (From LeVay, 1991.)

The answer is, in certain ways one, in certain ways the other, and in certain ways perhaps neither. The anterior commissure (see p. 500) is, on the average, larger in women than it is in heterosexual men; in homosexual men, it is at least as large as it is in women, perhaps even slightly larger (Allen & Gorski, 1992). The suprachiasmatic nucleus is also larger in homosexual men than it is in heterosexual men (Swaab & Hofman, 1990). The meaning of those differences is unclear, as neither the anterior commissure nor the suprachiasmatic nucleus has any known relationship to sexual behavior. In contrast, for certain parts of the hypothalamus known to differ between the sexes, homosexual men resemble heterosexual men and not heterosexual women (Swaab & Hofman, 1990).

The most suggestive study of brain differences concerned a particular nucleus of the anterior hypothalamus, known as interstitial nucleus 3, which is generally more than twice as large in heterosexual men as it is in women. Damage to structures in approximately the same location in a male rat's brain can greatly interfere with male sexual behavior.

Simon LeVay (1991) examined interstitial nucleus 3 in 41 people who had died between the ages of 26 and 59. Of these, 16 were heterosexual men, 6 were heterosexual women, and 19 were homosexual men. All of the homosexual men, 6 of the 16 heterosexual men, and one of the 6 women had died of AIDS. He found that the mean volume of interstitial nucleus 3 was 0.12 mm^3 in heterosexual men, 0.056 mm^3 in heterosexual women, and 0.051 mm^3 in homosexual men. Figure 11.20 shows a typical cross section for a heterosexual man and a homosexual man. Figure 11.21 shows the distribution of volumes for the three groups. Note that the difference between heterosexual men and the other two groups is fairly large, and that the cause of death (AIDS vs. other) has no clear relationship to the brain volumes.

These data face certain limitations: Although cause of death does not appear to be a determinant of brain structure for the heterosexual men, it would nevertheless be helpful to examine the brains of homosexual men who died of causes other than AIDS. LeVay (1993) later examined the hypothalamus of one homosexual man who died of lung cancer; that man had a small interstitial nucleus 3, like the homosexual men who died of AIDS. Still, it would be helpful to examine more cases.

A second limitation: We do not know whether the apparent brain differences were present since early childhood or whether they emerged in adulthood—conceivably, a result of sexual activity, instead of a cause. We

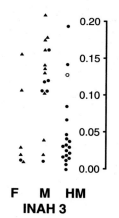

Figure 11.21
Distribution of volumes for interstitial nucleus 3 of the anterior hypothalamus in females (F), heterosexual males (M), and homosexual males (HM)
Each filled circle represents a person who died of AIDS; each triangle represents a person who died from other causes. The one open circle represents a bisexual man who died of AIDS. (From LeVay, 1991.)

could discuss and argue the likelihood that sexual activity might enlarge or reduce the size of some brain structure, but there is no substitute for data on this point.

One final point: In Figure 11.21, note that although the groups differ fairly substantially on average, they also overlap. Consequently, the data do not indicate that brain structure completely determines sexual orientation. At most, brain structure alters the probability of developing one orientation or another. ◆◆◆

Summary

1. It is difficult to determine the role, if any, of prenatal hormones in the development of gender identity. Because the sex defined by rearing usually matches the prenatal hormone pattern, the effects of rearing and hormones are hard to separate. (p. 402)

2. Pseudohermaphrodites are people who were subjected to a hormonal pattern intermediate between male and female during their prenatal sensitive period for sexual development. (p. 403)

3. Although most pseudohermaphrodites accept their assigned sex, a significant number are somewhat or greatly dissatisfied. (p. 404)

4. Certain adolescents develop a sexual appearance that does not match the sex they were reared as. Observations of such individuals suggest that their sexual orientation may have been influenced, directly or indirectly, by prenatal hormones. (p. 405)

5. Certain genes evidently influence the probability of a homosexual or heterosexual orientation; how they exert this influence is unknown. (p. 407)

6. In male rats, procedures that prevent testosterone from masculinizing the brain during a prenatal period lead to an adult pattern of sexual responsiveness toward other male rats. The relationship of this finding to human homosexuality is still speculative. (p. 409)

7. Prenatal exposure to masculinizing hormones may contribute to some instances of female homosexuality, although it does not appear to have a strong influence. (p. 410)

Review Questions

1. What may cause a human to develop as a pseudohermaphrodite, or intersex? (p. 403)

2. Why is each of the observations on gender identity in pseudohermaphrodites scientifically inconclusive? (p. 404)

3. What is testicular feminization, and what are its effects on development? (p. 404)

4. What other kinds of evidence may help to evaluate the possible contribution of prenatal hormones to gender identity? (p. 405)

5. What event in early development can cause a male rat to develop sexual responsiveness to other males and not to females? Through what mechanism does this event probably work? (p. 409)

6. What evidence points to prenatal hormones as a possible contributor to homosexuality in men? What evidence points to prenatal hormones as a possible contributor to homosexuality in women? What are the limitations of such evidence? (p. 410)

Thought Questions

1. On the average, pseudohermaphrodites have IQ scores in the 110 to 125 range, well above the mean for the population (Dalton, 1968; Ehrhardt & Money, 1967; Lewis, Money, & Epstein, 1968). One possible interpretation is that a hormonal pattern intermediate between male and female promotes great intellectual development. Another possibility is that pseudohermaphroditism may be more common in intelligent families than in less intelligent ones or that the more intelligent families are more likely to bring their pseudohermaphroditic children to an investigator's attention. What kind of study would be best for deciding among these hypotheses? (For one answer, see Money & Lewis, 1966.)

2. Recall LeVay's study of brain anatomy in heterosexual and homosexual men (p. 411). Certain critics have suggested that one or more of the men classified as "heterosexual" might actually have been homosexual or bisexual. If so, would that fact strengthen or weaken the overall strength of the conclusions?

Suggestions for Further Reading

Adkins-Regan, E. (1988). Sex hormones and sexual orientation in animals. *Psychobiology, 16,* 335–347. A review of research on the effects of prenatal and early postnatal hormones on the adult sexual behavior of nonhuman animals.

LeVay, S. (1993). *The sexual brain.* Cambridge, MA: MIT Press. Discusses the biological basis of sexual behaviors, including sexual orientation.

Terms

gender identity the sex with which a person identifies (p. 402)

sex role the set of activities and dispositions presumed to be common for one sex in a particular society (p. 402)

hermaphrodite individual whose genitals do not match the normal development for his or her genetic sex (p. 403)

intersex or **pseudohermaphrodite** individual whose sexual development is intermediate between male and female (p. 403)

androgen insensitivity or **testicular feminization** condition in which a person lacks the mechanism that enables androgens to bind to genes in a cell's nucleus (p. 404)

kin selection selection for a gene because it benefits one's kin (p. 408)

diethylstilbestrol (DES) a synthetic estrogen (p. 410)

EMOTIONAL BEHAVIORS AND STRESS

CHAPTER TWELVE

1. Emotional states associated with activation of the autonomic nervous system have been linked to several psychosomatic illnesses.

2. Chronic stress can suppress activity of the immune system and leave an individual highly vulnerable to various illnesses.

3. Pleasure is associated with activity of certain brain pathways in areas that are rich in dopamine synapses, although other transmitters may also contribute.

4. The amygdala appears to be critical for learned fears.

5. Anxiety is linked with high levels of sympathetic nervous system arousal and high levels of norepinephrine activity; GABA synapses can inhibit it.

6. Aggressive behavior is associated with activity of parts of the amygdala and with decreased turnover of serotonin.

If I were tsar, I would make a law that a writer who uses a word whose meaning he can't explain should be deprived of the right to write and receive 100 strokes of the birch.

Leo Tolstoy

If Tolstoy's proposed law ever goes into effect, I shall cease at once to use the word *emotion*. In fact, if you have a pen handy, maybe you could do me a favor and cross out the title of this chapter right now. Seriously, suppose we crossed out the word *emotion* every time that it appears anywhere in psychology. Would psychology be any poorer for the loss of this word?

Of all the terms that psychologists commonly use, *emotion* may be the most difficult to define. To illustrate: Psychologists do not always agree on what memories really are, but they are skilled at detecting and measuring memories in people and animals. Psychologists have even less agreement on what motivation is, but they can generally measure the intensity of a given motivation, such as hunger or thirst. But just try to determine how "happy" a rat is, and you will quickly discover how slippery our concepts of emotions are.

Even though the term *emotion* is poorly defined, however, the behaviors generally associated with it—such as escape and attack—are too important to ignore. And when we observe that people have become "emotional," their behavior is undeniably different from usual. For example, suppose an experimenter locks you in a room with no windows and challenges you to get out. You systematically (and unemotionally) try to pry the door open or to find a secret passageway. If you fail, you may eventually give up and wait for the experimenter to rescue you. Now suppose that a terrorist has locked you in the same room, but this time with a time bomb. Suddenly your behavior becomes "emotional." Frantically you try climbing the walls, breaking down the door, or prying up the floorboards. You keep on trying even after all efforts fail. In short, emotional behaviors tend to be vigorous and persistent (Tomkins, 1980).

Emotion, Autonomic Nervous System Arousal, and Health Problems

When driving a car, you have an accelerator to increase speed and a brake to decrease speed. Emotions are a little like that, although I would not push the analogy too far. Some emotional states speed up your actions to deal with an emergency; others slow you down to be cautious or to conserve energy.

Role of the Autonomic Nervous System in Emotional Behaviors

The two parts of the autonomic nervous system largely govern the vigor of a behavior. The sympathetic nervous system prepares the body for intense, vigorous, emergency activity. The parasympathetic nervous system increases digestion and other processes associated with relaxation. At most times, both systems are active, although at a given moment one may be more active than the other. (To review the structure and function of the sympathetic and parasympathetic nervous systems, see p. 101 and especially Figure 4.6.)

Exactly what is the relationship between autonomic nervous system arousal and emotions? Which comes first: the cognitive appraisal (such as "This is a frightening situation") or the autonomic arousal? Or do they occur simultaneously? Psychologists have debated these issues off and on since William James and Carl Lange first addressed them in the 1880s. Embarrassingly, psychologists have still not resolved them. Nevertheless, although we cannot say much about what an emotion really is, we know a good deal about what happens in the body during emotional states.

Events That Arouse the Sympathetic and Parasympathetic Systems

The sympathetic nervous system is activated, not by stimuli themselves, but by how someone interprets those stimuli. In one study, boys who were given a task and told that it was a test reacted with increased heart rates. Other boys who were given the same task but told that it was a game reacted with decreased heart rates (Darley & Katz, 1973).

In another study, people who received inescapable shocks and knew that the shocks were inescapable had decreased heart rates—a typical parasympathetic response to uncontrollable distress. People who were misled into believing that they might find some way to avoid the shocks had faster heart rates

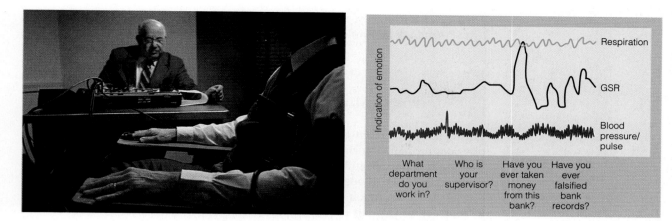

Figure 12.1
The polygraph test, literally a "many measures test"
The examiner asks a series of questions and compares the autonomic responses. One major difficulty is that a heightened response may indicate either nervousness about lying or nervousness about being accused of an offense. (Alon Reiniger/ Contact Press Images/ Woodfin Camp.)

(Malcuit, 1973). In other words, a given task or set of shocks can either increase or decrease sympathetic arousal, depending on what response people think that the situation requires.

One way to increase parasympathetic activity is to remove the stimulus that originally excited sympathetic activity. A sudden decrease in sympathetic activity provokes rebound overactivity of the parasympathetic system. For example, if a serial killer with a chain saw starts chasing you, you will run away, aided by abundant activity of your sympathetic nervous system. When the police grab the attacker and you realize that you are safe, your parasympathetic nervous system takes over, so strongly that you may even faint.

Measurements of Autonomic Arousal

In everyday life, we generally gauge people's emotions from their self-reports. When people say that they are happy, sad, or angry, we believe them. But we need more objective measures for many scientific purposes—certainly when using nonhuman animals and often with humans as well.

For many purposes, investigators measure sympathetic nervous system responses, such as increased heart rate and rapid breathing. Such measurements provide a crude but sometimes satisfactory indicator of "emotionality" in both humans and nonhumans. However, those measurements do not distinguish among fear, anger, intense happiness, or other emotional states that yield similar autonomic responses. We must also be cautious because some people have consistently greater responses than others. (If my heart rate increases twice as much as yours, I may not be twice as frightened or twice as angry.)

The polygraph test—the so-called lie-detector test—is really a measure of sympathetic nervous system arousal (see Figure 12.1): It typically records heart rate, blood pressure, breathing rate, and **galvanic skin response** (determining the electrical conductance of the skin, a measure of the slight sweating caused by sympathetic nerves to the skin). The theory behind the polygraph test is that people become nervous when they lie and that their nervousness elevates the response of their sympathetic nervous system.

Because lying is only loosely related to nervousness, the polygraph is not a highly reliable indicator of truthfulness. Some people can remain calm while lying about their criminal activities; others become nervous even when they are telling the truth. How would you react if someone strapped you into a polygraph device and then asked whether you had stolen a thousand dollars last

Thursday? Ordinarily, about half of all innocent people "fail" the lie-detector test (Forman & McCauley, 1986; Patrick & Iacono, 1989).

Emotions, Autonomic Responses, and Health

Through most of its history, modern medicine has explained diseases in purely physical terms: bacteria, viruses, toxins, or vitamin deficiencies, for example. Researchers have seen little merit in the idea of "will to live" or any other relationship between thoughts and health. Such concepts sounded too mystical, too spiritual, too much like the superstitions that medical doctors were trying to replace. To take an extreme case, when soldiers returned from battle with "shell shock," now called **posttraumatic stress disorder,** many physicians rejected any notion that a soldier's fear might have had something to do with the condition. Instead, they suggested "ionized air caused by cannonballs whistling by" and similar farfetched hypotheses (McMahon, 1975).

Today, there is little doubt that stressful experiences and thoughts of despair can increase the risk of many kinds of disease. Conversely, social support, a sense of humor, and other positive emotions can prolong survival or at least improve the quality of life for people with serious illnesses. Finding a connection between psychological factors and health is neither mystical nor antiscientific, although certain mystics have admittedly made some very nonscientific claims about "mind over matter." What we call "psychological factors" or "mental events" is, according to biological psychologists, merely another term for "brain activity" (see p. 12), which can of course influence body functions.

Appreciating the psychological factors in health is a relatively new idea in Western medicine. It also represents a growing trend in psychology, the focus of **behavioral medicine,** a field that considers the influence of eating and drinking habits, smoking, stress, exercise, and other behaviors on people's health.

Unfortunately, it is easy to slip from the enlightened view that experiences can affect health into an old-fashioned idea that blames the victim for illness. In medieval times, many people believed that illness was a punishment for sin; today's equivalent is the belief that people become ill or fail to recover from illness because they did not control the stress in their lives or because they failed to think sufficiently positive thoughts. Adherents of this view have sometimes inadvertently made patients with cancer and other serious illnesses feel guilty. Psychological factors do have *some* control over health and illness, and it is important to learn more about this control. But they do not have complete control, by any means.

The Autonomic Nervous System and Psychosomatic Illnesses

Most people's autonomic responsiveness is highly consistent over time. Some people show a stronger and quicker sympathetic response to a wide variety of stimuli than other people do. They also tend to show more emotional expression and more overall activity; in addition, they are generally more gregarious, more impulsive, more distractible, and less patient (Shields, 1983). In other words, responsiveness of the sympathetic nervous system is related to much of what we call *personality.*

Figure 12.2
An "executive" monkey (left) and a "passive" monkey (right)
When the executive presses the lever, it temporarily prevents electric shocks for both monkeys. Note the more relaxed bearing of the passive monkey. (From Brady et al., 1958.)

People with a highly responsive sympathetic nervous system also tend to be relatively vulnerable to heart disease and several other medical disorders. In these **psychosomatic illnesses,** the probability of getting the disease or recovering from it depends in part on the person's personality or experiences. A psychosomatic illness is real, not imaginary or pretended. For example, heart disease is psychosomatic in the sense that it is somewhat more common among hostile people than among people who are relaxed and easygoing (Booth-Kewley & Friedman, 1987).

The Role of the Autonomic Nervous System in Ulcer Formation

One illness strongly influenced by autonomic nervous system activity is **ulcers** (open sores on the lining of the stomach or intestines). Ulcers can form in several ways, but people who experience severe work-related stress are believed to be especially vulnerable. Because of the difficulties in studying ulcer formation in humans, experiments have been conducted on animals.

In a pioneering experiment, monkeys were exposed to work-related stress (Brady, Porter, Conrad, & Mason, 1958). Pairs of monkeys were confined to chairs, as Figure 12.2 shows; one foot of each monkey was attached to an electrode that delivered a shock every 20 seconds. One of the monkeys, dubbed the executive monkey of the pair, could forestall the shocks by pressing a lever in front of it. If the executive pressed the lever at least once every 20 seconds, neither monkey received any shocks. But if it waited any longer, both monkeys would receive a shock once every 20 seconds until the executive pressed the lever again. The second, passive monkey had no control over the shocks. The procedure lasted 6 hours at a time, twice a day, every day. Within an hour or two of the first session, each executive monkey had learned the response well and prevented the shocks almost completely from then on.

As the researchers had expected, the executive monkeys got ulcers and the passive monkeys did not. Why? Actually, because the experimental design was imperfect, the results are not easy to interpret. The monkeys were not randomly assigned to the executive and passive roles but rather were assigned on the basis of how well they learned the avoidance response. Conceivably, animals that learn to respond rapidly may also be nervous ones likely to develop ulcers. Regardless of how seriously we worry about that possibility, the experiment does not fully explain why the executives got ulcers and the passives did not. The key factor may have been some combination of emotional strain and physical exertion.

A second experiment sheds important light on the results of the first. E. L. Foltz and F. E. Millett (1964) repeated the executive monkey experiment, except that they used the same passive monkey with three different executives. After one executive monkey had served for a few weeks, it was replaced by a second; this new executive, being inexperienced in the apparatus, took a couple of hours to learn what to do. The passive monkey gyrated vigorously in its chair, screaming and gesturing wildly until the new executive started preventing the shocks consistently. Later, when a third untrained executive replaced the second one, the passive monkey went through the same routine and soon developed a severe case of ulcers.

Evidently, the ulcers came not from "being in charge" but from a state of high arousal, whatever its cause. An executive monkey gets ulcers from struggling to avoid shocks; a passive monkey may get ulcers from receiving many unavoidable shocks.

Similar experiments have been conducted on rats. The executive rats never approached 100 percent shock avoidance, as the monkeys did. The passive rats developed more ulcers than the executives, presumably because they could neither control the shocks nor predict their onset (J. M. Weiss, 1968, 1971a, 1971b). Note that the ulcers did not result from the shocks themselves (since both animals got the same number of shocks) but from the passive rats' lack of an adequate coping response.

Other things being equal, unpredictable shocks cause more ulcers than predictable shocks do (Guile, 1987). When shocks or other stressors are predictable, the individual can be on the alert at the appropriate times. When they are unpredictable, the individual must be alert and tense at all times.

Ulcers do not form during stress periods, while the animals are receiving shocks or pressing levers to avoid them, but during the rest periods afterward (Desiderato, MacKinnon, & Hissom, 1974). The shock period greatly activates the sympathetic nervous system; during the rest period, the parasympathetic system rebounds, releasing an excess of digestive juices that damage the insides of the stomach and intestines, causing ulcers.

Digestive secretions are not the whole explanation, however. During a stress period, and especially during the first two hours after the stress period, the stomach makes many slow but intense contractions. These contractions tend to break up the protective mucus lining of the stomach; they expose parts of the stomach wall to the digestive secretions (Garrick, 1990; Garrick, Minor, Bauck, Weiner, & Guth, 1989).

How could a person at high risk for developing ulcers, unable to prevent a stressful experience, avoid developing ulcers? Eating something just before or after the experience greatly lowers the probability of ulcer formation because food helps to absorb excess digestive secretions. We might well guess that a mild stressor following the major stressor would also help to reduce ulcer formation by enabling the sympathetic system to "calm down" gradually instead of swinging suddenly to a parasympathetic rebound. However, introducing brief, mild stressors during the rest period actually increases the probability of ulcers (Murison & Overmier, 1990; Overmier, Murison, Ursin, & Skoglund, 1987). The reason is uncertain.

Voodoo Death and Related Phenomena

Almost everyone knows of someone with a strong will to live who survived well beyond others' expectations or someone who gave up and died of a relatively minor ailment. An extreme case of the latter is *voodoo death*, in which a healthy person dies apparently just because he or she believes that some curse has destined death.

Such phenomena were generally ignored by scientists until Walter Cannon (1942) published a collection of reasonably well-documented reports of voodoo death. A typical example was a woman who ate a fruit and then was told that it had come from a taboo place. Within hours, she was dead. The common pattern in such cases was that the intended victim knew about the magic spells and believed that he or she was sure to die from them. The person's friends and relatives also believed in the hex and began to treat the victim as a dying person. Overwhelmed with a feeling of hopelessness, the victim refused food and water and died, usually within 24 to 48 hours. In some manner, the terror and hopelessness led to death. (For more examples, see Cannon, 1942; Cappannari, Rau, Abram, & Buchanan, 1975; Wintrob, 1973.) Similar examples occur in our own society—not people who die because they believe they are hexed, but people with minor illnesses or injuries who die because they expect to.

What is the cause of death in such cases? Curt Richter accidentally stumbled on a possible answer while studying the swimming abilities of rats. Ordinarily, rats can swim in turbulent warm water nonstop for 48 hours or more. However, Richter (1957a) found that a rat would die quickly if he cut off its whiskers just before throwing it into the tank. (A rat's whiskers are critical to its ability to find its way around.) The rat would swim frantically for a minute or so and then suddenly sink to the bottom, dead. Richter found that many, but not all, laboratory rats died quickly under these conditions. Wild rats, which are more nervous and "emotional" than domesticated laboratory rats, all died quickly under the same conditions. Autopsies showed that the rats had not drowned; their hearts had simply stopped beating.

Richter's explanation was that dewhiskering the rat and then suddenly throwing it into the water greatly stimulated the rat's sympathetic nervous system and thus its heart rate. After the rat swam frantically for a minute or so and found no escape, its parasympathetic system became highly activated, both as a rebound from the strong sympathetic activation and as the natural response to a terrifying but inescapable situation. Massive parasympathetic response may have stopped the rat's heart altogether.

To confirm the role of apparent escapability or inescapability, Richter performed another experiment. First he placed a rat in the water several times, rescuing it each time. Then he cut the rat's whiskers and put it in the water again. The rescues apparently immunized the rat against extreme terror in this situation; the rat swam successfully for many hours. Richter's results suggest that voodoo death and perhaps certain other cases of sudden death in a frightening situation may be due to excessive parasympathetic activity.

Does that explanation apply to many cases of heart attacks? Probably not. Most heart attacks begin when excessive sympathetic nervous system activity disrupts the normal beating rhythm of the heart (Kamarck & Jennings, 1991). Excessive parasympathetic activity is probably a serious problem only under limited circumstances.

Chronic Stress, the Immune System, and Health

Up to this point, we have considered the effects of fairly brief stressful periods, lasting from a few seconds to a few hours, that call for vigorous action. We sometimes encounter another kind of stress, however—problems that seem to go on forever, problems that we can do little or nothing about. The government builds a toxic waste dump in your neighborhood. A loved one suddenly dies and you have to live without this person you had depended on. Your business is on the verge of failure and you face the constant worry of whether you will be able to pay the bills. The body's response to chronic stressors differs from its response to temporary emergencies. In fact, it has different responses to different chronic stressors; although we often find it convenient to talk about stress as a general concept, we must admit that the term is poorly defined and that most generalizations about stress are subject to many exceptions (Engel, 1985).

Stressors excite both the sympathetic nervous system and an axis composed of the hypothalamus, pituitary gland, and adrenal cortex. With increasingly prolonged stress, the effects of the hypothalamus/pituitary/adrenal axis become more prominent. The hypothalamus induces the anterior pituitary gland to secrete adrenocorticotropic hormone (**ACTH**), which in turn stimulates the adrenal cortex to secrete **cortisol** and several other hormones; cortisol elevates blood sugar and enhances metabolism (see Figure 12.3). The increased fuel supply to the cells enables them to sustain a high level of activity in the face of stress. It is, however, a steady activity instead of the sudden bursts of "fight or flight" activity associated with the sympathetic nervous system. In fact, an individual with elevated cortisol secretion may act withdrawn and inactive much of the time. As cortisol and other hormones shift energy toward increasing blood sugar and metabolism, they shift it away from synthesis of proteins, including the proteins necessary for the immune system. In the short term, that shift may not be a problem; however, stress that continues for weeks or months may weaken the immune system and leave the individual vulnerable to a variety of illnesses. In short, brief or occasional stress poses little threat to health; constant, prolonged stress is a more serious problem.

The Immune System

The **immune system** is a set of structures that protects the body against intruders, such as viruses and bacteria (see Figure 12.4). The immune system is like a police force: If it is too weak, the "criminals" (viruses and bacteria) run wild and create damage. If it becomes too strong or too unselective, it starts attack-

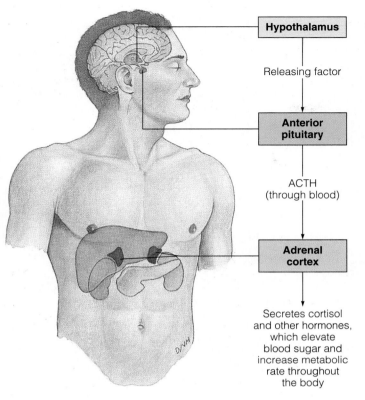

Figure 12.3
The hypothalamus/anterior pituitary/adrenal cortex axis
Prolonged stress leads to the secretion of the adrenal hormone cortisol, which elevates blood sugar and increases metabolism. Those changes help the body to sustain prolonged activity but at the expense of decreased immune system activity.

Hypothalamus

Releasing factor

Anterior pituitary

ACTH (through blood)

Adrenal cortex

Secretes cortisol and other hormones, which elevate blood sugar and increase metabolic rate throughout the body

ing "law-abiding citizens" (the body's own cells). When the immune system attacks normal cells, we call the result an *autoimmune disease*.

The most important elements of the immune system are the **leukocytes,** commonly known as white blood cells (Kiecolt-Glaser & Glaser, 1993; O'Leary, 1990). Leukocytes are produced in the bone marrow; they then migrate to several organs such as the thymus gland, the spleen, and the peripheral lymph nodes. Those organs store the leukocytes and promote their maturation until some foreign body causes their release. The leukocytes patrol the blood and other body fluids, searching for intruders. Each cell has on its surface certain proteins, called **antigens** (antibody-generator molecules). When a leukocyte finds a cell with antigens different from the rest of the body, it responds to that antigen as a signal to attack.

One type of leukocyte, a **B cell** (which matures in the bone marrow) produces specific antibodies to attack an antigen. **Antibodies** are Y-shaped proteins that circulate in the blood, specifically attaching to one kind of antigen, just as a key fits only one lock. The body builds up antibodies against the particular antigens that it has encountered. If you ever had measles, for example, your immune system has developed antibodies against the measles virus and will protect you against a further outbreak of the same disease. The strategy behind a vaccination, such as a measles vaccine or a polio vaccine, is to introduce a weakened form of the virus, so that the body can develop antibodies against the virus without actually getting the disease itself.

Another kind of leukocyte are the **T cells** (so named because they mature in the thymus), which directly attack intruder cells or stimulate added response by other immune-system cells. A T cell may attack a cancer cell, a

Emotion, Autonomic Nervous System Arousal, and Health Problems

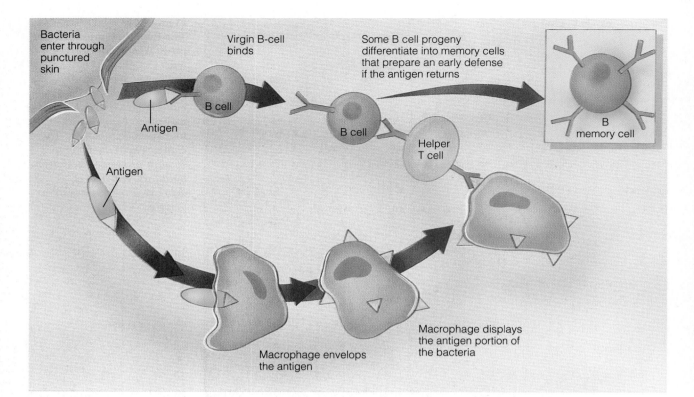

Figure 12.4
Immune system responses to a bacterial infection

A macrophage cell engulfs a bacterial cell and displays one of the bacteria's antigens on its surface. Meanwhile, a B cell also binds to the bacteria and produces antibodies against the bacteria. A helper T cell attaches to both the macrophage and the B cell; it stimulates the B cell to generate copies of itself, called B memory cells, which immunize the body against future invasions by the same kind of bacteria.

Within the figure:

- Bacteria enter through punctured skin
- Antigen
- Virgin B-cell binds
- B cell
- Some B cell progeny differentiate into memory cells that prepare an early defense if the antigen returns
- B cell
- Helper T cell
- B memory cell
- Antigen
- Macrophage envelops the antigen
- Macrophage displays the antigen portion of the bacteria

virus-infected cell, or any other cell that it identifies as foreign. T cells are ordinarily helpful, but after a surgical transplant they become part of the problem: They attack the transplanted tissue, unless physicians can suppress T-cell activity or trick the T cells into accepting the transplanted tissue.

Natural killer cells are blood cells that attach to certain kinds of tumor cells and cells infected with viruses. Natural killer cells are relatively nonspecific in their targets. Unlike an antibody or a T cell, each of which attacks only one kind of intruder, a given natural killer cell can attack several kinds of intruders.

Effects of Stress on the Immune System

Contrary to assumptions long held in biology, we now know that the nervous system has considerable control over the immune system. The study of this control is called *psychoneuroimmunology* (O'Leary, 1990; Vollhardt, 1991). One of the key topics in psychoneuroimmunology is the study of how stress alters the immune response. Unfortunately, the term *stress* applies to a wide variety of events, and different kinds of stress produce different effects on the body.

Certain kinds of prolonged stressful events, such as intermittent foot shocks, can release endorphins, which decrease pain but also suppress blood levels of natural killer cells. Injections of morphine (which stimulate endorphin synapses) can directly decrease the levels of natural killer cells, though not so strongly as foot shocks do (Mogil, Sternberg, & Liebeskind, 1993). After a depression of natural killer cells, animals are highly vulnerable; if they develop a tumor, the tumor grows faster than it does in other animals (Sklar &

Anisman, 1981). Conversely, animals that have strong and stable social relationships tend to have stronger-than-average immune responses (Cohen, Kaplan, Cunnick, Manuck, & Rabin, 1992).

In humans, too, certain stressful experiences release endorphins and suppress immune responses. For example, in 1979, the Three Mile Island nuclear power plant suffered a major accident that was successfully (though barely) contained. The people who continued to live in the vicinity over the next year had lower-than-normal levels of B cells, T cells, and natural killer cells. They also complained of emotional distress and showed impaired performance on a proofreading task (Baum, Gatchel, & Schaeffer, 1983; McKinnon, Weisse, Reynolds, Bowles, & Baum, 1989). Natural killer cells are also fewer than normal in women whose husbands are dying of cancer, women whose husbands died within the last six months, and medical students going through their exam period (Glaser, Rice, Speicher, Stout, & Kiecolt-Glaser, 1986; Irwin, Daniels, Risch, Bloom, & Weiner, 1988).

However, the relationship between stress, immune responses, and health remains uncertain for humans. I mentioned that tumors grow rapidly in rats with suppressed levels of natural killer cells. We cannot assume that the same conclusion holds for humans because most rat tumors are caused by viruses, and the vast majority of human tumors are not. We know that depressed mood correlates strongly with impaired responses of the immune system (Weisse, 1992), but we also know that chronically depressed people have a virtually normal life expectancy, except for their increased probability of suicide and fatal accidents (Stein, Miller, & Trestman, 1991).

A number of studies have shown that stress accelerates the deterioration associated with AIDS (a disease related to impaired immune responses), and that stress-reducing experiences, such as social support, improve the health of cancer patients. Unfortunately, we still know little about what kinds of stress are the most dangerous and what kinds of positive experiences are the most beneficial. Also the research does not tell us how much of these health effects depend on stress-related changes in the immune system and how much of them depend on other factors (Cohen & Williamson, 1991). For example, people who are feeling emotional tension are less likely than other people are to take their medication as prescribed and exercise and eat properly; they are more likely than others are to engage in risky behaviors and to complain about relatively minor ailments. Determining the exact relationship between experiences and illness for humans will be a major, long-term research challenge.

Summary

1. Many emotional stimuli increase the activity of the sympathetic nervous system. Removal of such a stimulus activates the parasympathetic nervous system as a rebound effect. (p. 416)

2. A given event may produce either major sympathetic nervous system arousal, a little, or none at all, depending on how the individual interprets the event. (p. 416)

3. Ulcers can be provoked in part by excessive activity of the parasympathetic nervous system as a rebound after excessive sympathetic activation. (p. 419)

4. Prolonged stressful experiences activate the adrenal cortex and increase the release of endorphins. Those changes tend to suppress the activity of the immune system. The impact of this suppression on human health is still uncertain. (p. 422)

Review Questions

1. What happens to autonomic nervous system arousal just after removal of a stimulus that excited sympathetic nervous system arousal? (p. 417)

2. If periods of stress alternate with periods of rest, when are ulcers most likely to form? Why? (p. 420)

3. Besides excess digestive juices, what other change in the digestive system contributes to ulcer formation? (p. 420)

4. What activity of the autonomic nervous system may be responsible for certain cases of sudden death, as in voodoo death? (p. 421)

5. What are leukocytes and how do they contribute to the immune response? (p. 423)

Thought Question

1. Suppose that someone has just gone through a highly stressful experience and is now at risk for developing ulcers. What kinds of drugs might be helpful in preventing the ulcers: Drugs that increase or decrease activity of the sympathetic system? Drugs that increase or decrease activity of the parasympathetic system?

Suggestions for Further Reading

Brannon, L., & Feist, J. (1992). *Health psychology* (2nd ed.). Belmont, CA: Wadsworth. Discussion of relationships among stress, behavior, and health issues.

Goleman, D., & Gurin, J. (Eds.) (1993). *Mind/body medicine: How to use your mind for better health.* Yonkers, NY: Consumer Reports Books. A collection of articles on stress, emotions, and health.

LeDoux, J. E., & Hirst, W. (1986). *Mind and brain.* Cambridge, England: Cambridge University Press. Chapters 14 through 17 deal with the psychology and biology of emotions.

O'Leary, A. (1990). Stress, emotion, and human immune function. *Psychological Bulletin, 108,* 363–382. Excellent introduction to how psychological factors affect the immune system and thereby health.

Terms

galvanic skin response measure of the electrical conductance of the skin (p. 417)

posttraumatic stress disorder condition characterized by periodic outbursts of anxiety, panic, or depression provoked by reminders of a traumatic experience (p. 418)

behavioral medicine field that considers the influence of eating and drinking habits, smoking, stress, exercise, and other behavioral variables on people's health (p. 418)

psychosomatic illness illness for which personality or experience influences onset or recovery (p. 419)

ulcer open sore on the lining of the stomach or intestines (p. 419)

ACTH adrenocorticotropic hormone, which stimulates the adrenal cortex to release cortisol (p. 422)

cortisol hormone released by the adrenal cortex that elevates blood sugar and enhances metabolism (p. 422)

immune system set of structures that protects the body against viruses and bacteria (p. 422)

leukocyte white blood cell, a component of the immune system (p. 423)

antigen protein on the surface of a microorganism, in response to which the immune system generates antibodies (p. 423)

B cell type of leukocyte that matures in the bone marrow (p. 423)

antibody Y-shaped protein that fits onto an antigen and weakens it or marks it for destruction (p. 423)

T cell immune system cell that directly attacks intruder cells or stimulates added response by other immune system cells (p. 423)

natural killer cell type of leukocyte that destroys certain kinds of tumor cells and cells infected with viruses (p. 424)

Reinforcement, Escape and Attack Behaviors, and the Brain

One of the great accomplishments of chemistry is the periodic table of the elements. The periodic table names all the elements that form every compound that could possibly exist. Moreover, it organizes the elements into a regular, repeating pattern that shows us *why* certain elements are metals, *why* certain others are gases, and *why* no chemist is likely to discover some new naturally occurring element that previous scientists had overlooked.

As a psychologist, I envy the chemists' periodic table. I wish we had a periodic table of emotions or motivations. Some psychologists have tried to list all the emotions or all the motivations, but such lists seem haphazard. For example, Carroll Izard (1977) lists ten emotions: interest, joy, surprise, distress, anger, disgust, contempt, fear, shame, and guilt. But why those particular ten? Is each of those states elemental or are some of them compounds? For instance, is disgust a compound of two parts distress and one part contempt? Could we perhaps reduce the list to, say, eight elementary emotions, or five, or even two—approach and avoidance?

Maybe, maybe not. While we are waiting for someone to develop a periodic table of emotions, in this section we shall examine one set of brain areas—the limbic system—regarded as important for all emotional behaviors. We then turn to three important examples of emotional behaviors: reinforcement (an approach behavior), anxiety (an avoidance behavior), and attack (a special kind of approach behavior).

The Limbic System and Emotions

Emotional behavior depends largely on a group of forebrain structures known as the **limbic system,** including the hypothalamus, hippocampus, amygdala, olfactory bulb, septum, other small structures, and parts of the thalamus and cerebral cortex. Several investigators have contributed to our understanding of the limbic system. In pioneering studies, Philip Bard (1929, 1934) found that, when he removed the entire cerebral cortex of cats, they displayed exaggerated aggressive behaviors and postures in response to various stimuli. Evidently, subcortical areas could generate emotional behaviors; the function of the cerebral cortex was to direct those behaviors toward appropriate targets and, when appropriate, to suppress them.

In 1937, J. W. Papez (rhymes with *grapes*) proposed that the hypothalamus and several other subcortical structures (see Figures 4.10 and 12.5) compose a circuit responsible for emotions. Papez based his theory partly on the fact that cells in parts of the limbic system respond to taste, smell, and pain stimuli, all

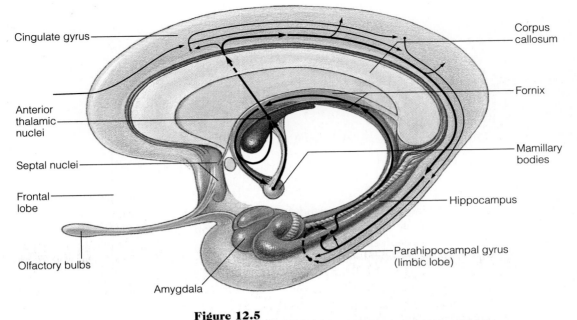

Cingulate gyrus

Corpus callosum

Anterior thalamic nuclei

Fornix

Septal nuclei

Mamillary bodies

Frontal lobe

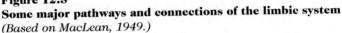

Hippocampus

Olfactory bulbs

Parahippocampal gyrus (limbic lobe)

Amygdala

Figure 12.5
Some major pathways and connections of the limbic system
(Based on MacLean, 1949.)

of which evoke strong emotional reactions. These three sensory modalities also have the properties of slow onset, slow offset, and vagueness about location—properties that characterize emotions as well.

Paul MacLean revived and revised Papez's theory on the basis of later studies of brain damage (MacLean, 1949, 1958, 1970), giving Papez's circuit the name *limbic system* because its structures form a border (*limbus*) around the brain stem and other midline areas. The size of the limbic system is relatively constant across the various mammalian species. By contrast, species vary greatly in the size of their cerebral cortex (see Figure 12.6); MacLean interpreted these species differences to mean that the limbic system controls primitive functions that all mammals share in common.

According to MacLean, the strongest evidence that the limbic system is important for emotion comes from observations of people with temporal lobe epilepsy or other abnormalities in the limbic system. Although most people with temporal lobe epilepsy have no particular emotional experiences with their epileptic seizures, a substantial minority experience aggressive impulses, fear, a dissociation of experience similar to multiple personality (Schenk & Bear, 1981), uncontrollable laughter (Swash, 1972), sexual arousal (Rémillard et al., 1983), or a feeling of extreme bliss, including a sense of oneness with the universe and the Creator (Cirignotta, Todesco, & Lugaresi, 1980). (The latter experience is named *Dostoyevskian epilepsy* after the Russian novelist who had this illness.)

Within the limbic system, MacLean (1970) distinguished three circuits. One circuit, including the amygdala and the hippocampus, affects behaviors related to self-preservation. Damage to various parts of the amygdala can make an animal excessively tame, unaggressive, and emotionally unresponsive (Zagrodzka & Fonberg, 1979; Aggleton & Passingham, 1981). Monkeys and cats with amygdala damage sometimes attempt to eat feces, burning matches, and

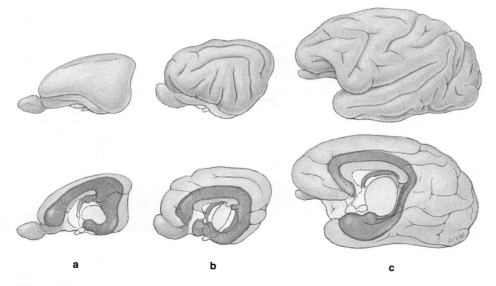

Figure 12.6
Brains of (a) a rabbit, (b) a cat, and (c) a monkey, showing both the lateral surface (top) and the medial surface (bottom)
The limbic system (dark areas) shows less variation in size across mammalian species than does the cerebral cortex. (From MacLean, 1954.)

other objects that they would ordinarily reject. (However, it is hard to be certain whether they have a loss of emotions or whether they no longer recognize the objects.)

A second circuit in the limbic system includes the cingulate gyrus of the cerebral cortex, the septum, and several other structures. (The septum is a fairly large structure in the rat brain but a much less imposing structure in humans.) This circuit seems to relate to sexual enjoyment. Electrical or chemical stimulation of this region in rats often causes penile erection, self-grooming, and related behaviors.

A third circuit, according to MacLean, includes parts of the hypothalamus and anterior thalamus. Believed to be important for cooperative social behavior and certain aspects of sexuality, this circuit is larger in primates than in most other mammals.

Brain Activity and Reinforcement

Pleasure or happiness is an especially difficult state to study scientifically. Unlike pain, pleasure does not correspond to a particular kind of stimulation. And unlike fear and anger, pleasure does not give rise to any consistent, observable response, such as running away or attacking. Happy people sometimes smile, but not always. (If a friend who is not smiling tells you that she is happy, do you disbelieve her?) Dogs wag their tails to display a friendly and presumably happy state, but most other nonhumans have no clear gesture to indicate happiness. So an investigator who wants to determine what goes on in the brain during happiness is handicapped by not having any gauge for happiness.

We can, however, measure reinforcement and can easily determine which brain processes are associated with reinforcement. *Reinforcement* is an event that increases the probability of the preceding response; for example, food is a reinforcement for a food-deprived rat because the rat will increase its frequency of whatever response leads to food. For humans, most events that make us happy serve as reinforcements. However, not all reinforcements make people happy. For example, a paycheck is a reinforcement for a worker, but does not always make the worker *happy*. Some people play video games by the hour; a high score serves as a reinforcement, but is not necessarily a source of happiness. Even with rats, reinforcement is probably not synonymous with pleasure.

Self-Stimulation of the Brain in Nonhuman Animals

The brain mechanisms of reinforcement were discovered by accident. Two young scientists studying the effects of electrical stimulation of the reticular formation, James Olds and Peter Milner (1954), put rats in a situation in which they had to choose between turning left and turning right. Rats typically hesitate, looking one way and then the other, before choosing. Olds and Milner wanted to test whether stimulation of the reticular formation would cause a rat that was looking in one direction to turn in that direction. However, they had implanted the electrode in the rat's septum by mistake. To their surprise, when the rat received the brain stimulation, it would sometimes sit up, look around, and sniff, as rats often react to a favorable stimulus.

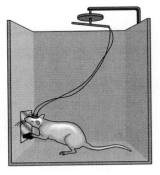

Figure 12.7
A rat pressing a lever for self-stimulation of its brain

Olds and Milner later placed the rat in a Skinner box, where it repeatedly pressed a lever for electrical brain stimulation as a reinforcement (Figure 12.7). That is, it worked for **self-stimulation of the brain.** Olds found that a number of other areas in the limbic system also produce reinforcement; in some cases, rats pressed a lever to stimulate certain brain areas as often as 2,000 times per hour, continuing for hours until collapsing from exhaustion (Olds, 1958b). In similar experiments, monkeys pressed a lever as often as 8,000 times per hour (Olds, 1962).

Follow-up experiments indicated that the electricity was not simply stimulating involuntary movements. Animals will press levers to stimulate areas that extend over about one-third of the brain, certain areas much more vigorously than others. They will also work to turn off stimulation in about 5 percent of the brain.

Why is electrical stimulation of certain brain areas reinforcing? Perhaps the stimulation taps into circuits responsible for eating, sexual behaviors, and other natural reinforcers. But we do not know what the animal is experiencing. In some cases, electrical stimulation produces stronger effects than any natural reinforcer does. In one experiment, rats in a T-maze could choose food by turning in one direction or electrical stimulation of part of the limbic system by turning in the other direction (Spies, 1965). Rats chose the brain stimulation on more than 80 percent of their trials, even though they had been kept on a near-starvation diet for 10 days. In another experiment, rats selected brain stimulation in preference to water and avoidance of shock to the feet (Valenstein & Beer, 1962). Still more impressively, four mother rats abandoned their newborn pups in order to press a lever for brain stimulation (Sonderegger, 1970). Ordinarily, a mother rat will stick with her young at all costs.

In some regards, self-stimulation of the brain may be like an addictive behavior. The animal does not rush to the lever as soon as it is available, but once it starts pressing, it persists for long periods. The stimulation may produce a mixture of pleasant and unpleasant feelings; at times the animal withdraws sharply from the stimulation, only to return a few moments later.

Electrical Stimulation of the Brain and Reinforcement in Humans

Because the brain contains no pain receptors—in fact, no somatosensory receptors of any kind—brain surgery in a conscious patient is possible after anesthetizing only the scalp. In certain cases, it is desirable to do so, so that the surgeon can test several areas until the patient says, "Yes, that made me feel the way I do right before a seizure." During the 1960s, a few surgeons experimented with electrical stimulation of the human brain as a possible therapy for depression or severe pain.

From those medical studies, we have learned something about the subjective experience of reinforcing brain stimulation. One 36-year-old epileptic woman received electrical stimulation in the right temporal lobe of her cortex. She reported a pleasant, tingling sensation on the left side of her body. She giggled, said that she enjoyed the sensation very much, and began flirting with the therapist (Delgado, 1969). Electrical stimulation in the temporal lobe of an 11-year-old boy led him to say, "Hey! You can keep me here longer when you give me these; I like those" (Delgado & Hamlin, 1960; Higgins, Mahl, Delgado, & Hamlin, 1956).

On the other hand, a few patients pressed buttons to stimulate their brains electrically, yet described the experience as not altogether pleasant. One patient described the result of self-stimulation of the brain as "almost orgasm." He continued pressing, hoping to produce the orgasm, but only prolonged the frustration (Heath, 1963). Other patients described a feeling of "having something on the tip of my tongue." They continued pressing in hopes of recovering the memory, but again were frustrated. In other words, self-stimulation of the brain sometimes produces reinforcement without producing pleasure.

Pharmacology of the Reinforcement Systems of the Brain

Although an animal will work to self-stimulate numerous points in the brain, these points are largely concentrated along a few pathways (Gallistel, Gomita, Yadin, & Campbell, 1985). Because these pathways are believed to use only a limited number of neurotransmitters, reinforcement (reward) itself may depend on only a few transmitters.

Most of the areas that mediate reinforcement are rich in catecholamine neurotransmitters, especially dopamine (Wise & Rompre, 1989). A particularly reliable area for eliciting self-stimulation is the **medial forebrain bundle** (Figure 12.8), which contains the main ascending dopamine pathway. Recall from Chapter 3 that most addictive drugs increase the release of dopamine, and recall from Chapter 11 that sexual excitement releases dopamine. Evidently, dopamine has some powerful reinforcing effects.

In addition to dopamine, animals will also work for injections of opiates (Bozarth & Wise, 1984; Wise & Bozarth, 1984; Wise & Rompre, 1989). Opiates stimulate endorphin synapses, which inhibit cells releasing GABA, which in turn inhibit dopamine release. Thus, through inhibition of an inhibitor, the net effect of opiates is to increase the release of dopamine.

Figure 12.8
The major dopamine pathways of the rat brain, shown in a midsagittal section
The medial forebrain bundle is a highly reliable area for eliciting self-stimulation.

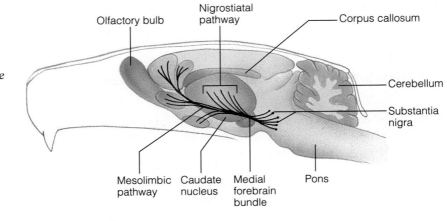

Olfactory bulb

Nigrostiatal pathway

Corpus callosum

Cerebellum

Substantia nigra

Mesolimbic pathway

Caudate nucleus

Medial forebrain bundle

Pons

Fear and Anxiety

We distinguish between fear and anxiety mostly on the basis of when they occur. Fear occurs in a limited, potentially escapable situation, such as being out in a small boat during a storm. Anxiety is a longer-lasting, less escapable state. For example, a person can have anxiety about the future, anxiety about interactions with other people, or general "free-floating" anxiety that is not tied to any identifiable stimulus.

Fear serves a useful function, steering us away from dangers. Mild anxiety may promote cautiousness. But beyond a certain degree, anxiety begins to interfere with normal activity. Much progress has been made toward understanding the physiological basis of fear and anxiety.

The Amygdala and Anxiety

With few exceptions, if any, our fears are either learned or at least modified by experiences. Consider the **startle response** that you make after a sudden, unexpected loud noise. Although you always jump a little after a loud noise, you may make a much stronger response if you were already tense (because someone had yelled at you) or worried (because you were walking through an unfamiliar neighborhood at night). People with posttraumatic stress disorder show an enhanced startle response, compared with other people, at practically all times (Shalev, Orr, Peri, Schreiber, & Pitman, 1992).

Psychologists measure the enhancement of a startle response as a gauge of fear or anxiety. One virtue of this measurement is that it can be used with non-humans as well as humans. Typically, investigators first measure an animal's muscular responses to a loud noise. Then they repeatedly pair some stimulus, say a light, with shock. Finally, they present that light just before the loud noise and determine how much more the animal jumps after the combination of stimuli than it does after the noise alone. (A control group is tested using a light stimulus that has not been paired with shock. We need to be sure that the effect of the light-plus-noise combination is due to what the animal has learned about the light.) Results of such studies consistently show that, after animals have learned an association between some stimulus and shock, that stimulus becomes a "fear signal"; presenting that stimulus just before a loud noise enhances the animal's response to the noise.

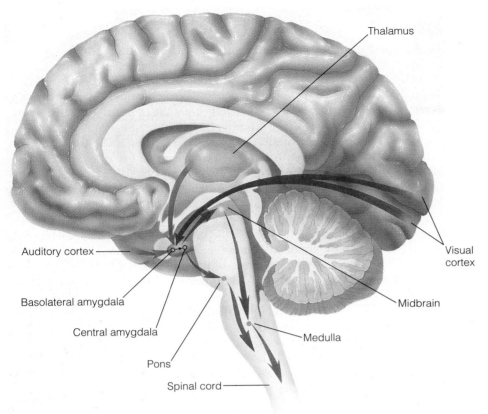

Figure 12.9
The amygdala and its connections relevant to the learning of fears
Cells in the lateral and basolateral parts of the amygdala receive visual and auditory information and then send messages to the central amygdala, which then sends its output to the hindbrain—either to the pons or the medulla or possibly both. The amygdala's output to the hindbrain can enhance fear responses, such as the startle response. Damage at any point along the route from amygdala to hindbrain interferes with learned fears, although it does not block the startle response itself.

Using that basic design, investigators have determined the role of various brain areas in learned fears. The key area is the amygdala. (See Figure 12.9.) A rat with damage to the amygdala, particularly the central nucleus of the amygdala, still shows a normal startle response after a loud noise, but it shows no enhanced startle response to the combination of a "fear signal" plus loud noise (Phillips & LeDoux, 1992). In general, such animals neither learn new fears nor retain learned fears that they may have acquired before the brain damage (Kim & Davis, 1993).

The amygdala sends its output to various parts of the brain; its connections to the hypothalamus control autonomic fear responses (such as increased blood pressure), while its connections to the hindbrain control flinching, freezing, and similar skeletal responses (LeDoux, Iwata, Cicchetti, & Reis, 1988). The exact connections to the hindbrain are still in some dispute. Some of the research suggests a direct connection from the central nucleus of the amygdala to the pons (Rosen, Hitchcock, Sananes, Miserendino, & Davis, 1991); other research suggests a route from the central amygdala to the midbrain, which in turn relays information to the medulla (Yeomans & Pollard, 1993). Figure 12.9 shows both of these proposed routes. In either event, damage at any point along the route from the central amygdala to the hindbrain blocks the effect of experiences on the startle response. A rat with such damage still shows a startle response to loud noises, but it fails to show learned or potentiated fears.

In one study, rats were repeatedly exposed to a light followed by shock, and then tested for their responses to bursts of loud noise, with or without the simultaneous presence of the light. Intact rats showed a moderate startle

Reinforcement, Escape and Attack Behaviors, and the Brain

433

response to the loud noise and an enhanced response to the light plus noise. (That is, the light increased their fear.) In contrast, rats with damage at various points along the path from the central amygdala to the hindbrain showed the same startle response to the loud noise regardless of the presence or absence of the light (Hitchcock & Davis, 1991). Evidently, that path also contributes to some fears that we might have thought of as unlearned, such as a rat's fear of a cat—fears that may or may not be learned, but that certainly require some interpretation of visual or auditory stimuli (Davis, 1992).

Much of the incoming information to the amygdala comes directly from the thalamus. That discovery constituted a serious surprise for researchers, who had imagined that all sensory information would first have to be analyzed by the cerebral cortex. The fact that the amygdala gets information directly from the thalamus implies that the amygdala does not rely on highly detailed or precise information, but that it gets the information fairly rapidly. Some fear conditioning, such as associating a sound with pain, may take place within the thalamus (Cruikshank, Edeline, & Weinberger, 1992). Additional conditioning occurs in the lateral and basolateral parts of the amygdala, where certain cells receive incoming pain information in addition to visual or auditory information (Romanski, Clugnet, & LeDoux, 1993; Sananes & Davis, 1992). The lateral and basolateral amygdala then relay the learned information to the central amygdala, which sends the output to the pons.

In short, we now know much of the circuitry underlying learned fears and anxiety. Presumably, something in this circuit is overactive in people with phobias, posttraumatic stress disorder, and other anxiety disorders, but we do not know exactly what it is. Nor do we yet understand *why* activity in this particular circuit constitutes anxiety. (That question is part of the overall mind-brain question discussed in Chapter 1.)

Anxiety-Reducing Drugs

Decades ago, **barbiturates** (a class of tranquilizers) were the drugs most widely used to combat anxiety. Although barbiturates effectively reduce anxiety, they have two significant drawbacks: They are strongly habit forming, and it is fairly easy to kill oneself with an overdose, either intentionally or accidentally, especially if one combines barbiturates with alcohol.

Another class of antianxiety drugs, **benzodiazepines** (BEN-zo-die-AZ-uh-peens), are currently much more widely used than barbiturates because they are less habit forming than barbiturates are and because an overdose is less likely to be fatal. Besides relieving anxiety, benzodiazepines relax the muscles, induce sleep, and decrease the likelihood of convulsions; they are used not only as tranquilizers but also as sleeping pills and as antiepileptic drugs. Benzodiazepines such as diazepam (trade name Valium), chlordiazepoxide (Librium), and alprazolam (Xanax) have been widely prescribed and used for decades.

Like many other drugs, benzodiazepines were found to be effective long before anyone knew how they worked. Then in the late 1970s and early 1980s, investigators discovered specific benzodiazepine receptors in the CNS to which these drugs bind. The receptors are part of the **GABA$_A$ receptor complex,** shown in Figure 12.10. The complex includes a site that binds the neurotransmitter gamma amino butyric acid (**GABA**) as well as sites that bind other chemicals that modify the sensitivity of the GABA site.

The brain has at least two major categories of GABA receptors: GABA$_A$ and GABA$_B$ receptors. GABA$_A$ sites apparently decrease anxiety, among other

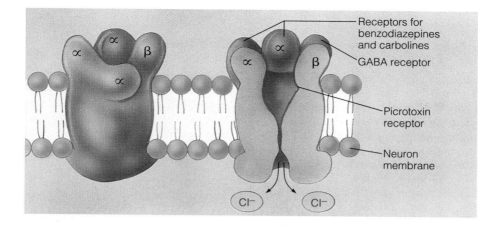

Figure 12.10
The GABA_A receptor complex
Of its four receptor sites sensitive to GABA, the three α sites are also sensitive to benzodiazepines. (Based on Guidotti, Ferrero, Fujimoto, Santi, & Costa, 1986.)

effects. Benzodiazepines facilitate binding of GABA to the GABA_A receptors; in doing so, they help to decrease anxiety.

The heart of the GABA_A receptor complex is a chloride channel. When open, it permits chloride ions (Cl^-) to cross the membrane into the neuron, hyperpolarizing the cell. (That is, the synapse is inhibitory.) Surrounding the chloride channel are four units, each containing one or more sites sensitive to GABA. Three of those four units (labeled α in Figure 12.10) also contain a benzodiazepine receptor. Even though it has no effect by itself on the chloride channel, an attached benzodiazepine molecule facilitates the GABA receptor. Presumably, it alters the shape of the receptor so that the GABA attaches more easily or binds more tightly (Macdonald, Weddle, & Gross, 1986). The net result is an increased flow of chloride ions across the membrane—but only when both the benzodiazepine and the GABA are present.

The GABA_A receptor complex has at least two other binding sites. One of those sites is actually inside the chloride channel itself. Certain drugs such as *picrotoxin* can bind to that site; when they do so, they block the passage of chloride ions, regardless of what the GABA or benzodiazepine molecules are doing. The other binding site (not shown in Figure 12.10) is sensitive to barbiturates and to the metabolites of certain hormones (Majewska, Harrison, Schwartz, Barker, & Paul, 1986). Like the benzodiazepine receptor, the barbiturate receptor facilitates the binding of GABA to its own receptor. Alcohol, a relaxant, also facilitates the binding of GABA and thereby enhances the flow of chloride ions across the membrane (see Digression 12.1).

In using the name "benzodiazepine receptor," we do not mean that benzodiazepines are the only chemicals to bind there. (Would evolution have equipped us with receptors waiting around for drug companies to develop benzodiazepines?) As we might expect, these receptors are also sensitive to some chemicals naturally produced by the brain. Two families of such chemicals are known as the β-**carbolines** and the **endozepines**, a contraction of "endogenous benzodiazepines." The term *endozepine* is unfortunate and confusing, because the endozepines produce effects that are opposite to those of benzodiazepines. The endozepines are actually endogenous antibenzodiazepines. Alas.

The largest and best-studied molecule endozepine is the protein **diazepam-binding inhibitor (DBI)**, which blocks the behavioral effects of diazepam and other benzodiazepines (Guidotti et al., 1983). The two other endozepines are formed by the breakdown of the DBI molecule (Rouet-Smih, Tonon, Pelletier, & Vaudry, 1992).

Ethyl alcohol, the type of alcohol that people drink, has behavioral effects similar to those of benzodiazepine tranquilizers. It decreases anxiety and decreases the effects of punishment. Moreover, a combination of alcohol and tranquilizers depresses body activities and brain functioning more severely than either drug alone would. (A combination of alcohol and tranquilizers can be fatal.) Furthermore, alcohol, benzodiazepines, and barbiturates all exhibit the phenomenon of **cross-tolerance:** An individual who has used one of the drugs enough to develop a tolerance to it will show a partial tolerance to other depressant drugs as well.

We now know the reason behind these relationships: Alcohol promotes the flow of chloride ions through the GABA$_A$ receptor complex, just as tranquilizers do (Suzdak et al., 1986). Exactly how alcohol promotes the chloride flow is not known, but it is unlikely that alcohol attaches directly to any of the receptor sites. A more likely hypothesis is that alcohol alters the membrane structure around the GABA and benzodiazepine binding sites in some manner that makes their binding more effective.

Although this is not the only way that alcohol affects the brain, it is apparently how alcohol exerts both its antianxiety effects and its intoxicating effects. Drugs that block the effects of alcohol on the GABA$_A$ receptor complex also block most of alcohol's behavioral effects. One experimental drug, known as Ro15-4513, is particularly effective in this regard (Suzdak et al., 1986). Besides affecting the GABA$_A$ receptor complex, Ro15-4513 blocks the effects of alcohol on motor coordination, its depressant action on the brain, and its antianxiety effects (Becker, 1988; Hoffman, Tabakoff, Szabo, Suzdak, & Paul, 1987; Ticku & Kulkarni, 1988). (See Figure 12.11.)

Could Ro15-4513 be useful as a "sobering-up" pill or as a treatment to help people who want to quit

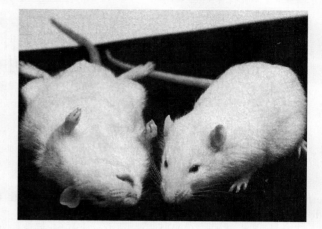

Figure 12.11
Two rats that were given the same amount of alcohol
The one on the right was later given the experimental drug Ro15-4513. Within 2 minutes, its performance on motor tasks improved significantly. (Photo courtesy of Jules Asher.)

drinking alcohol? Hoffman-LaRoche, the company that discovered it, eventually concluded that using the drug would be too risky. People who relied on the pill might try to drive home, thinking they were sober when they were still somewhat impaired. Furthermore, giving such a pill to alcoholics could easily backfire. Alcoholics generally drink to get drunk; a pill that decreased their feeling of intoxication would probably lead them to drink even more. Ro15-4513 reverses the behavioral effects of moderate alcohol doses, but a large dose can still be a health hazard or even fatal (Poling, Schlinger, & Blakely, 1988). For these reasons, Ro15-4513 is used only in laboratories.

The β-carbolines and endozepines attach to the same receptors as benzodiazepines but affect it in the opposite way. Instead of facilitating GABA binding, they inhibit it and thus increase anxiety, motor agitation, and responses to punishment (Corda, Blaker, Mendelson, Guidotti, & Costa, 1983; File, Pellow, & Braestrup, 1985; Lagarde et al., 1990; Martin, Cook, Hagen, & Mendelson, 1989). You might wonder why the body would produce such "feel-bad" chemicals. The functions of these chemicals are as yet far from being well understood, but we can note that different situations call for different degrees of anxiety or fearfulness. The β-carbolines and endozepines may be one way of adjusting the anxiety level.

Obsessions are nagging, intrusive thoughts. *Compulsions* are urges to perform repetitive acts such as hand washing or endless double-checking of every activity (Pollak, 1979). Although **obsessive-compulsive disorder** is considered uncommon in psychiatry, mild or unreported cases are fairly common, affecting 2–3 percent of all people at some point in their lives (Karno, Golding, Sorenson, & Burnam, 1988). For unknown reasons, obsessive-compulsive disorder is especially common among dermatology patients (Rasmussen, 1985). It is also especially common in people with type A blood—again for unknown reasons (Turner, Beidel, & Nathan, 1985).

One clue suggesting a biological basis for obsessive-compulsive disorder is that many patients respond well to **clomipramine** or **fluvoxamine,** two drugs that inhibit the reuptake of serotonin by the presynaptic neuron (Goodman et al., 1990; Leonard et al., 1989; Yaryura-Tobias, 1977). That is, these drugs prolong the effects of serotonin at the synapse. Conversely, drugs that inhibit serotonin synthesis and release tend to aggravate the symptoms of obsessive-compulsive disorder (Hollander et al., 1992).

Clomipramine is also an effective treatment for *trichotillomania,* compulsive hair pulling. People with this condition habitually pull out their eyelashes, eyebrows, scalp hair, even their pubic hair. Some continue until they become bald. Under the influence of clomipramine, such people decrease their hair pulling to about half of what it used to be (Swedo et al., 1989). The drug's effectiveness suggests that the underlying causes of trichotillomania resemble those of obsessive-compulsive disorder.

According to PET scans, obsessive-compulsive people have increased metabolic rates in the caudate nucleus and in parts of the frontal cortex (Baxter et al., 1987). Either drug therapy or behavior therapy lowers the metabolic rates in those areas, but only in patients who respond favorably to the therapy (Baxter et al., 1992). Thus, the symptoms of obsessive-compulsive disorder appear to be closely related to the increased activity in those brain areas.

Panic Disorder

We may be able to learn more about the physiology of anxiety by studying clinical conditions associated with excess anxiety. One such condition is obsessive-compulsive disorder (see Digression 12.2). Another is **panic disorder,** a psychological condition that afflicts about 1 percent of all adults (Robins et al., 1984). People with panic disorder suffer occasional attacks of extreme fear, breathlessness, heart palpitations, fatigue, and dizziness. They generally have an overresponsive sympathetic nervous system, one that swings frequently and rapidly between high and low stimulation of the heart and other organs (Nutt, 1989).

According to one view, many cases of panic disorder arise when people misinterpret respiratory signals in the brain and react as if they were suffocating (Klein, 1993). One of the surest ways to trigger a panic attack is to increase blood levels of lactate and carbon dioxide. Those blood levels increase during suffocation; they also increase after exercise or stress or under various conditions in experiments. People who are subject to panic attacks often respond to moderate increases in blood CO_2 or lactate as if they were suffocating, especially if they believe that they have no control over the situation (Sanderson, Rapee, & Barlow, 1989).

Many people experiencing a panic attack aggravate the problem by **hyperventilating** (breathing more often or more deeply than they need to). A deep breath or two can often be a good way of calming oneself, but what is good in small doses can be harmful in large doses. Prolonged hyperventilation lowers the levels of carbon dioxide and phosphates in the blood, which in turn decreases parasympathetic nervous system activity (George et al., 1989).

Reinforcement, Escape and Attack Behaviors, and the Brain

Thus, a little exercise, a little stress, an injection of lactate, or anything else that elevates blood CO_2 will produce a very large *percentage* increase in CO_2, which in turn stimulates a sharp rise in sympathetic nervous system action (Gorman et al., 1986, 1989; Woods et al., 1986).

People with panic disorder are generally treated with drugs or psychotherapy or both. Tranquilizer drugs help to relieve anxiety directly (Ballenger et al., 1988); also, having tranquilizers available "just in case" also provides reassurance. Psychotherapy can help sufferers to break the cycle of panic attacks leading to hyperventilation that in turn leads to further attacks.

What do we learn about anxiety in general from studying victims of panic disorder? We learn that the chemistry of anxiety is complex, relating to norepinephrine and GABA, operating both in the brain and in the sympathetic nervous system.

Aggressive Behaviors

Fighting among animals generally serves an important purpose—defense of the animal's mating territory or its young. In many species of birds, a male will vigorously attack other males of his own species that approach his nest, his mate, or his young during the mating season. In certain species, the female is also highly aggressive, especially when an intruder threatens her nest or her young. The defending bird usually wins in such encounters (like the home team in human sports), driving the intruder out of the territory, generally without inflicting much injury. The winner thereby removes potential competition for its mate or a threat to its young. The winner also removes a competitor for its food supply, although this benefit is apparently less important. (At the end of the mating season, when fighting would serve only to protect the food supply, fighting generally ceases.)

Humans fight under many of the same circumstances as nonhumans. One of the most common causes of homicide is sexual jealousy—most frequently, two men fighting about a woman (Daly, Wilson, & Weghorst, 1982). But some human violent behavior is rather unemotional. Soldiers and police may be forced into a battle without feeling any anger at all, for example, and people sometimes make "cold-blooded" attacks for financial gain.

Similarly, we have to distinguish between at least two kinds of attack behavior in nonhumans. A cat fighting or threatening another cat shrieks, erects its fur, and shows other signs of emotional arousal. This is known as an **affective attack.** (Do not confuse *affective* with *effective*. *Affective* comes from the noun *affect,* meaning emotion.) The same cat may attack and kill a mouse smoothly, swiftly, and calmly; this is a **quiet biting attack.** As we shall see, these two types of attack depend on different systems in the brain.

Quiet Biting Attack

Electrical stimulation can elicit either a quiet biting (predatory) attack or an affective attack, depending on which brain area is stimulated. Figure 12.12 shows a quiet biting attack in response to stimulation of the perifornical nucleus of the hypothalamus. Similar results follow stimulation of several other areas of the hypothalamus and the midbrain (Siegel & Brutus, 1990; Siegel & Pott, 1988).

Figure 12.12
Quiet biting attack provoked by electrical stimulation of the perifornical nucleus of the hypothalamus in a cat
The cat moved swiftly and with little sign of emotion to bite the rat's neck and kill it. (From Siegel & Brutus, 1990.)

If you have ever watched a cat attack a mouse (or rat), you may have seen it "play" with its prey before killing it. The cat kicks the mouse, bats it with its paws, tosses it in the air, and sometimes picks it up and carries it. Why? Is the cat sadistically tormenting its prey before killing it? That might or might not sound plausible to you, depending on what you think of cats, but it is hardly a scientific explanation. Moreover, considerable evidence indicates that the cat's play is not based on a separate motive; it is a compromise between attack and escape.

When confronted with a prey, some cats swiftly bite it on the neck, killing it in less than 2 minutes. Other cats play with it for 10 minutes or more before either killing it or letting it go. Still others explore it briefly and then withdraw. Those that withdraw tend to be "timid" in a variety of situations; for example, they are slow to explore a new environment. Most cats are highly consistent from one day to the next in how they respond to a potential prey (Adamec, 1975).

Many of the "play" behaviors are defensive movements to avoid the prey's teeth. When the prey faces the cat, the cat is likely to bat, kick, or toss it. When the prey faces away, the cat is more likely to bite at its neck (Pellis et al., 1988). In other words, what appears to be play is actually a combination of attack and defense behaviors.

Various factors can move a cat's behavior one direction or the other along the continuum from withdrawal to attack. When cats become very hungry, those that usually withdraw from the prey start to play with it; those that usually play with it attack more vigorously and kill it. However, if the prey is large or if it fights back vigorously, cats that are usually quick killers start playing with it and those that usually play with it simply withdraw (Adamec, Stark-Adamec, & Livingston, 1980; Biben, 1979). When cats are given benzodiazepine tranquilizers, which presumably lower anxiety and reduce the tendency to withdraw, cats that usually play become quick killers (Pellis et al., 1988). In sum, cats have no separate motive to play; they play when their attack and escape tendencies are about equal. If the balance shifts one way or the other, cats move toward either quicker attack or withdrawal.

Figure 12.13
An affective attack expression, evoked by radio stimulation of the medial hypothalamus of a cat
Because the cat does not direct its attack toward any target, we regard this as just a fragment of a normal attack. (From Delgado, 1981.)

Affective Attack

Facial displays, shrieks, and other signs of autonomic arousal accompany affective attack. In humans, such displays are associated with reports of anger. The physiological basis of affective attacks differs from that of quiet biting attacks.

Nonhuman Animals   Stimulation of several areas in the hypothalamus, amygdala, and brain stem can elicit an affective attack (Siegel & Pott, 1988). As a result of such stimulation, a cat hisses, growls, arches its back, and bares its teeth. Ordinarily, it directs its attack toward any convenient target that is present, but stimulation sometimes elicits just the facial expressions without the rest of the attack sequence (see Figure 12.13).

A full-fledged attack requires sensory cues as well as hypothalamic stimulation. A blindfolded cat shows no signs of attacking in response to brain stimulation. A cat with cortical or thalamic damage hisses and bares its teeth, but generally does not direct its attack toward a target (Flynn, 1973; Flynn, Edwards, & Bandler, 1971). Apparently, the thalamus and cortex use the available sensory information to direct attack toward a suitable target; after damage to those areas, the attack is aimless.

Electrical stimulation of the amygdala (see Figure 12.14) can lead to vigorous affective attacks. Damage to the amygdala most often leads to tameness and placidity. Animals with an epileptic focus in the amygdala often show an increase in aggressive behavior (Pinel, Treit, & Rovner, 1977). **Rabies,** a disease caused by a virus that attacks much of the brain but especially the temporal

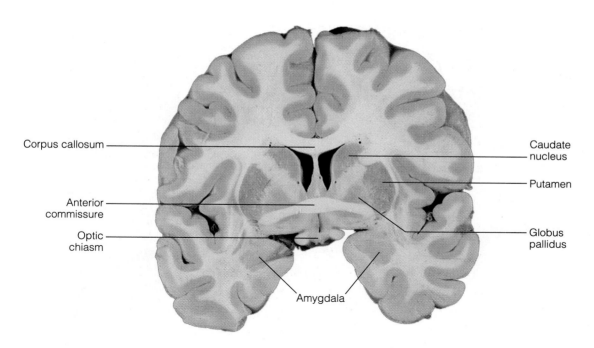

Corpus callosum

Anterior commissure

Optic chiasm

Caudate nucleus

Putamen

Globus pallidus

Amygdala

Figure 12.14
Coronal section through the human brain, showing the location of the amygdala
(Photo courtesy of Dana Copeland.)

lobe (including the amygdala), leads to furious, violent behavior (Lentz, Burrage, Smith, Crick, & Tignor, 1982). (*Rabies* is the Latin term for *rage.*)

Damage to the amygdala does not simply cause or prevent a certain emotion, however. Rather, it changes how animals interpret information. For example, certain monkeys with amygdala lesions have trouble interpreting social stimuli from other monkeys; because of their misinterpretations, they may attack inappropriately or fail to defend themselves when attacked.

H. Enger Rosvold, Allan Mirsky, and Karl Pribram (1954) made an amygdala lesion in the most dominant and aggressive monkey of a group of eight. After the lesion, that monkey quickly sank to the lowest status in the dominance hierarchy. Then they made a lesion in the amygdala of the most dominant remaining monkey, who quickly fell to seventh place. When they made a lesion in the third monkey, however, it did not drop significantly in status or in aggressive behavior. One possible explanation is that the lesions had invaded slightly different parts of the brain in the three monkeys. Another possibility is that the effect of the lesions was modified by the social environment. The first two monkeys returned to an environment with aggressive competitors; the third returned to one without aggressive competitors. It may have been harder for the first two monkeys to maintain aggressive behavior in the face of clear competitors than for the third to do so. Figure 12.15 shows the monkeys' dominance hierarchies before and after the three lesions.

Humans Can irritation of the temporal lobe provoke violent behavior in humans as well as other species? A number of investigators have looked particularly at temporal lobe epilepsy. An epileptic attack occurs when a large group of neurons suddenly produces synchronous action potentials. The symptoms depend on the location of the epileptic focus. When the focus is in the

Reinforcement, Escape and Attack Behaviors, and the Brain

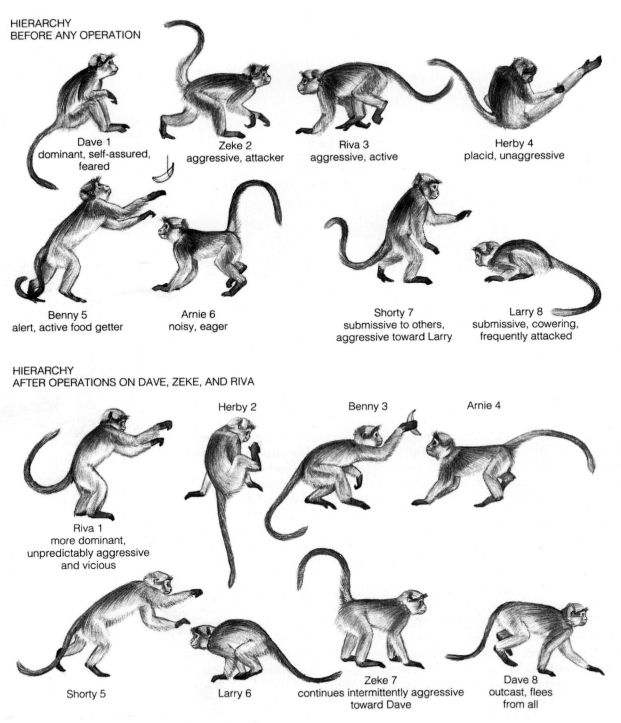

HIERARCHY BEFORE ANY OPERATION

Dave 1
dominant, self-assured, feared

Zeke 2
aggressive, attacker

Riva 3
aggressive, active

Herby 4
placid, unaggressive

Benny 5
alert, active food getter

Arnie 6
noisy, eager

Shorty 7
submissive to others, aggressive toward Larry

Larry 8
submissive, cowering, frequently attacked

HIERARCHY AFTER OPERATIONS ON DAVE, ZEKE, AND RIVA

Riva 1
more dominant, unpredictably aggressive and vicious

Herby 2

Benny 3

Arnie 4

Shorty 5

Larry 6

Zeke 7
continues intermittently aggressive toward Dave

Dave 8
outcast, flees from all

Figure 12.15
The dominance hierarchy for eight male monkeys before brain operations (top) and after amygdala lesions were made (bottom) in Dave, Zeke, and Riva
(From Rosvold, Mirsky, & Pribram, 1954.)

temporal lobe, the symptoms include hallucinations, lip smacking or other repetitive acts, and, in certain cases, emotional behaviors.

Here is an example of a patient with temporal lobe epilepsy who had sudden outbursts of unprovoked violent behavior (Mark & Ervin, 1970):

Thomas was a 34-year-old engineer, who, at the age of 20, had suffered a ruptured peptic ulcer. He was in a coma for 3 days, which caused some brain damage. Although his intelligence and creativity were unimpaired, there were some serious changes in his behavior, including outbursts of violent rage, sometimes against strangers and sometimes against people he knew. Sometimes his episodes began when he was talking to his wife. He would then interpret something she said as an insult, throw her against the wall and attack her brutally for 5 to 6 minutes. After one of these attacks, he would go to sleep for a half hour and wake up feeling refreshed.

Eventually, he was taken to a hospital, where epileptic activity was found in the temporal lobes of his cerebral cortex. For the next 7 months, he was given a combination of tranquilizers, antiepileptic drugs, and other medications. None of these treatments reduced his violent behavior. He had previously been treated by psychiatrists for 7 years without apparent effect. Eventually, he agreed to a surgical operation to destroy a small part of the amygdala on both sides of the brain. Afterwards, he had no more episodes of rage.

According to several reviews, about 10 percent of people with temporal lobe epilepsy have such outbursts of unprovoked violent behavior (Bear & Fedio, 1977; Goldstein, 1974; Pincus, 1980). The accuracy of these estimates has been challenged, however (Volavka, 1990): Temporal lobe epilepsy is difficult to diagnose, violent behavior is not always clearly defined, and, in many cases, the investigator who diagnosed temporal lobe epilepsy also determined the subject's history of violence.

In many instances, antiepileptic drugs have shown promise in controlling episodic violent behavior. When people with a history of unprovoked violence fail to respond to antiepileptic drugs, a few surgeons have surgically destroyed parts of the amygdala or other brain areas (Balasubramaniam & Kanaka, 1976; Mark & Ervin, 1970; Narabayashi, 1972). They reported success in reducing or eliminating the violent outbursts, with only occasional unwelcome side effects, including overeating or diabetes. But it is unclear how carefully their patients have been tested for side effects.

Is brain surgery justifiable when the only goal is to change behavior? Such surgery, known as **psychosurgery**, has a history dating back to lobotomies that hardly inspires confidence. Opponents of psychosurgery object that, because it is conducted to protect society, not to help the patient, it can easily be abused. Defenders of psychosurgery reply that a dangerous person's freedom must be restricted, either by medical intervention or by legal incarceration. At present, psychosurgery is a rare procedure, but the controversy is likely to continue.

Serotonin Synapses and Aggressive Behavior

Although it is unlikely that a single neurotransmitter system controls aggressive behavior, or any other behavior, several lines of evidence indicate that serotonin is especially important in the control of aggressive behavior. In particular, a low serotonin release is associated with a rise in aggressive behavior.

Nonhuman Animals   Part of the evidence for this conclusion comes from the work of Luigi Valzelli, studying aggressive behavior in mice. Valzelli (1973) found that four weeks of social isolation induced a drop in serotonin turnover in the brains of the male mice. **Turnover** is the amount of release and resynthesis of a neurotransmitter by presynaptic neurons. That is, a brain with low serotonin turnover may have a normal amount of serotonin, but the neurons fail to release it and synthesize new serotonin to take its place, making it essentially inactive. Turnover can be inferred from the concentration of 5-hydroxy-indole-acetic acid or **5-HIAA,** a serotonin metabolite, in the blood, cerebrospinal fluid (CSF), or urine. When 5-HIAA levels are low, serotonin turnover is low.

Valzelli further found that, when social isolation lowered a male mouse's serotonin turnover, it also induced increased aggressive behavior toward other males. If he placed two males with low serotonin turnover together, he could count on them to fight. Comparing different genetic strains of mice, he found that the strains with the lowest serotonin turnover fought the most (Valzelli & Bernasconi, 1979). Social isolation does not decrease serotonin turnover in female mice in any genetic strain, and it does not make the females aggressive.

Valzelli also studied interactions between mice and rats. When male rats were socially isolated, some showed increased serotonin turnover, while others showed decreased turnover or no change. When rats that showed a decrease in serotonin turnover were placed with mice, they attacked and killed the mice. Rats that showed no change in serotonin turnover ignored the mice. Those with an increase in serotonin turnover became friendly and nurturing toward the mice (Valzelli & Garattini, 1972).

Humans   Numerous studies have found that people with a history of violent behavior tend to have lower-than-normal serotonin turnover. That trend applies to violence against self as well as violence against others. People who have committed suicide or attempted it by violent means have low levels of 5-HIAA in their CSF or blood, suggesting lower-than-normal release of serotonin (G. Brown et al., 1982; Edman, Åsberg, Levander, & Schalling, 1986; Mann, Arango, & Underwood, 1990). They also have more 5-HT$_2$ (serotonin$_2$) receptors than usual in the cerebral cortex; the increase in receptors is believed to be the brain's compensation for decreased serotonin release (Arango et al., 1990; Mann, Stanley, McBride, & McEwen, 1986). Serotonin turnover is also depressed in people convicted of arson and other violent crimes (Virkkunen, Nuutila, Goodwin, & Linnoila, 1987).

Diet may affect violent behavior in humans as well as animals. According to Mawson and Jacobs (1978), the murder rate is highest in those countries that consume the most corn. Corn contains very little tryptophan, the precursor to serotonin. That is, eating a lot of corn decreases serotonin synthesis (Lytle, Messing, Fisher, & Phebus, 1975). Needless to say, the relationship between corn in the diet and the murder rate could be explained in many other ways, including a relationship to poverty. This point certainly calls for thorough investigation before we draw any conclusions. In the meantime, it may be prudent for people with a history of violent behavior to be cautious about eating lots of corn or other foods low in tryptophan. Similar caution might be advisable about foods high in phenylalanine (such as NutraSweet) because phenylalanine competes with tryptophan for entry into the brain.

Psychologists are far from understanding the connections between serotonin turnover and aggressive behavior. According to one hypothesis, serotonin synapses inhibit behavioral impulses that might lead to punishment or

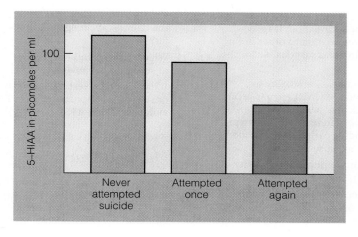

Figure 12.16
Levels of 5-HIAA in the CSF of depressed people who never attempted suicide, those who attempted it once, and those who attempted it again within 5 years after the first attempt
Measurements for the two suicide-attempting groups were taken after the first attempt. Low levels of 5-HIAA indicate low serotonin turnover. (Based on results of Roy, DeJong, & Linnoila, 1989.)

other unfavorable outcomes (Spoont, 1992). Thus, when serotonin turnover is high, the result is restrained behavior. When it is low, the result is impulsive behavior, including outbursts of violence.

Even without a good theoretical understanding, however, psychologists may find serotonin turnover measurements useful in predicting behavior. For example, one study of children and adolescents with a history of aggressive behavior found that the individuals with the lowest serotonin turnover were the ones most likely to get into trouble for additional aggressive behavior in the following two years (Kruesi et al., 1992). According to one follow-up study of people who had survived suicide attempts, those with lower serotonin turnover levels were more likely than others to attempt suicide again, perhaps fatally, within the next five years (Roy, DeJong, & Linnoila, 1989; see Figure 12.16). A follow-up study on people convicted of manslaughter or arson found that, after their release from prison, those with lower serotonin turnover had a greater probability of committing other violent crimes within the next three years. The investigators found that they could have used the serotonin measures to predict violent crime with 84 percent accuracy (Virkkunen, DeJong, Bartko, Goodwin, & Linnoila, 1989).

What uses could we imagine for serotonin turnover measures? We could imagine mental hospitals using blood samples to identify which patients to watch most carefully as possible suicide risks. We could imagine courts or prisons using blood samples as one of several indicators of which convicts are a good risk for probation or parole and which ones are too dangerous for release. Whether or not anyone *should* use serotonin measures in such ways raises difficult ethical, legal, and political issues; after all, predictions based on serotonin turnover are far from perfect.

Summary

1. The brain area most important for emotional behaviors is the limbic system, a circuit that includes the hypothalamus, hippocampus, amygdala, olfactory bulb, septum, other small structures, and parts of the thalamus and cerebral cortex. (p. 427)

2. Animals will work to deliver an electrical stimulation to certain areas of their brains, presumably areas that contribute to natural reinforcements. (p. 430)

3. The reinforcement areas of the brain are generally rich in catecholamines, especially dopamine. Other neurotransmitters such as endorphins may also contribute to reinforcement. (p. 431)

4. The amygdala appears to be a point of convergence for sensory information and pain information; it relays "learned fear" or "anxiety" information to other brain areas, including the hindbrain areas responsible for the startle response. (p. 432)

5. Benzodiazepine tranquilizers decrease anxiety by attaching to a receptor next to the GABA$_A$ synapse on the GABA$_A$ receptor complex. The benzodiazepine receptor is also sensitive to certain naturally occurring chemicals in the brain, including carbolines, that modify the sensitivity of the GABA$_A$ synapse. (p. 434)

6. Alcohol relieves anxiety by increasing the sensitivity of the GABA$_A$ synapse. (p. 435)

7. Panic disorder is a clinical condition marked by intense anxiety attacks; people with panic disorder have overresponsive sympathetic nervous systems. (p. 437)

8. Stimulation of certain areas of the hypothalamus and midbrain can elicit quiet biting attack; stimulation of parts of the amygdala and hypothalamus can elicit affective attack. (p. 438)

9. Cats "play" with their prey when the tendency toward an affective attack is balanced by a tendency toward withdrawal. Various factors can tilt the balance in one direction or the other. (p. 439)

10. Damage to the amygdala of animals can lead to a decrease in aggressive behavior and social rank, partly because the animals misinterpret social stimuli. (p. 441)

11. A small percentage of people with temporal lobe epilepsy have occasional outbursts of violent behavior. Medical treatments to control such violent behavior have shown some promise, but remain controversial. (p. 441)

12. A drop in serotonin release and turnover in the brain is associated with increased aggressive behavior, including violent suicide. (p. 443)

Review Questions

1. What structures compose the limbic system? What function does that system serve? (p. 427)

2. How did researchers discover that specific areas of the brain are responsible for reinforcement? (p. 430)

3. Which neurotransmitters are believed to be critical for reinforcement? (p. 431)

4. How does damage to the amygdala affect the startle response? (p. 432)

5. Describe the GABA$_A$ complex. How do benzodiazepines affect it? (p. 434)

6. What kind of evidence indicates that alcohol relieves anxiety through effects on the GABA$_A$ receptor complex? (p. 436)

7. Physiologically, how do people with panic attacks differ from other people? (p. 437)

8. Why do many people with panic attacks hyperventilate? Does hyperventilation tend to alleviate or aggravate their problem? (p. 437)

9. Why do some cats "play" with a rat or mouse before killing it? What evidence supports this conclusion? (p. 439)

10. How does amygdala damage alter affective attack? Does the damage affect aggressiveness or perception of stimuli? (p. 440)

11. What evidence links aggressive behavior with a decrease in serotonin turnover? (p. 444)

12. What biological test may identify which violent offenders or suicide attempters are most likely to commit other violent acts? (p. 445)

Thought Question

1. According to one interpretation of why electrical stimulation of the brain is rewarding, stimulation of different brain areas produces experiences corresponding to different natural reinforcements. That is, stimulation in one area might produce sexual sensations, and stimulation in another area might produce food or drink sensations. How might one test this hypothesis? (For two tests that came to opposite conclusions, see Frutiger, 1986, and Olds, 1958b.)

Suggestion for Further Reading

Kidman, A. (1989). Neurochemical and cognitive aspects of anxiety disorders. *Progress in Neurobiology, 32,* 391–402. Excellent review of both biological and behavioral aspects of anxiety.

Terms

limbic system set of forebrain areas including the hypothalamus, hippocampus, amygdala, olfactory bulb, septum, other small structures, and parts of the thalamus and cerebral cortex (p. 428)

self-stimulation of the brain response reinforced by direct electrical stimulation of a brain area (p. 430)

medial forebrain bundle main ascending dopamine pathway in the vertebrate brain (p. 431)

startle response the response that one makes after a sudden, unexpected loud noise or similar sudden stimulus (p. 432)

barbiturate class of drugs used as anticonvulsants, sedatives, and tranquilizers (p. 434)

benzodiazepine class of widely used antianxiety drugs (p. 434)

GABA$_A$ receptor complex structure that includes a site that binds GABA, as well as sites that bind other chemicals that modify the sensitivity of the GABA site (p. 434)

GABA gamma amino butyric acid, a neurotransmitter (p. 434)

β-carboline or **endozepine** type of naturally occurring chemical that binds to the same receptors as benzodiazepines (p. 435)

diazepam-binding inhibitor (DBI) brain protein that blocks the behavioral effects of diazepam and other benzodiazepines (p. 435)

cross-tolerance tolerance of a drug because of exposure to a different drug (p. 436)

obsessive-compulsive disorder psychological disorder characterized by intrusive thoughts and urges to perform repetitive acts (p. 437)

clomipramine and **fluvoxamine** drugs that inhibit the reuptake of serotonin by the presynaptic neuron (p. 437)

panic disorder condition characterized by occasional attacks of extreme fear, breathlessness, heart palpitations, fatigue, and dizziness (p. 437)

hyperventilating breathing more often or more deeply than necessary (p. 437)

affective attack attack in which an animal shows signs of emotional arousal (p. 438)

quiet biting attack swift, calm attack with few signs of emotional arousal (p. 438)

rabies disease caused by a virus that attacks much of the brain, especially the temporal lobe, causing violent behavior (p. 440)

psychosurgery brain surgery conducted to change behavior (p. 443)

turnover release and resynthesis of a neurotransmitter (p. 444)

5-HIAA 5-hydroxyindoleacetic acid, a serotonin metabolite (p. 444)

THE BIOLOGY OF
LEARNING AND MEMORY

Dan McCoy/Rainbow

CHAPTER THIRTEEN

MAIN IDEAS

1. Understanding the physiology of learning requires answering two questions: What changes occur in a single cell during learning, and how do changed cells work together to produce adaptive behavior?

2. Psychologists distinguish among several types of memory, each of which can be impaired by a different kind of brain damage.

3. During learning, a variety of brief and more permanent changes occur that either facilitate or decrease the activity at particular synapses.

Suppose I type a short BASIC program into my computer:

```
10 HOME
20 FOR A=1 TO 100
30 PRINT A^(0.5)
40 NEXT A
```

I can now leave the computer, come back later, and type "RUN." Provided that the power has not been interrupted, the computer will print out a list of the square roots of the integers 1 to 100. How does the computer remember what to do?

That question is really two questions that call for two kinds of answers. One is: How does the computer store a representation of the keys that I type? Somehow, my hitting those keys leads to a physical change in some tiny silicon chips inside the computer. To explain how that happens, we would need to understand the physics of the silicon chip.

But understanding a silicon chip does not tell us how the computer as a whole works. To explain how the computer runs my program, we would have to answer a second question: How does the computer put together the information stored in numerous silicon chips to make its response? In other words, we would have to understand the wiring diagram.

Similarly, when we try to explain how a person remembers to stop at a red light or to show up for work at 8 A.M., we are really answering two questions. One is: How does a pattern of sensory information set up a lasting change in the input-output properties of one or more neurons in the nervous system? That question concerns the biophysics of the neuron. The second question is: After the properties of certain neurons have changed, how does the nervous system as a whole produce the appropriate behavior? That question concerns the wiring diagram.

We could begin with either question, but in this chapter we shall begin with the second one: How do the various areas of the nervous system interact to produce learning and memory? Later, we turn to the more detailed physiology of how experience changes the properties of the individual cells and synapses.

Learning, Memory, Amnesia, and Brain Functioning

How would you act if you could not remember from one moment to the next what you had just done? For one thing, you would probably repeat yourself many times without even realizing it.

How would you act if you could not remember from one moment to the next what you had just done? For one thing, you would probably repeat yourself many times without even realizing it.

Some people have exactly this problem. Others can remember what they just did and said, but they have some other specialized memory loss. A study of the effects of accidental brain damage reveals much about the nature of memory.

Localized or Diffuse Representations of Memory

What is the brain's physical representation of learning and memory? One early, influential idea was that it might be a strengthened connection between two brain areas. The Russian physiologist Ivan Pavlov pioneered the investigation of what we now call **classical conditioning** (Figure 13.1a), in which a stimulus comes to elicit a response similar to the response produced by some other stimulus. Ordinarily, the experimenter starts by presenting a **conditioned stimulus (CS),** which initially elicits no response of note, and then presents the **unconditioned stimulus (UCS),** which automatically elicits the **unconditioned response (UCR).** After some pairings of the CS followed by the UCS (perhaps just one or two pairings, perhaps many), the individual begins responding to the CS, producing a **conditioned response (CR).** In his original experiments, Pavlov presented a dog with a sound (CS) followed by meat (UCS), which stimulated the dog to salivate (UCR). After many such pairings, the sound alone (CS) would stimulate the dog to salivate (CR).

By contrast, in **operant conditioning** (Figure 13.1b), an individual's response is followed by a reinforcement or punishment. A **reinforcement** is any event that increases the future probability of the response; a **punishment** is an event that decreases the future probability of the response. For example, when a rat enters one arm of a maze and finds Froot Loops cereal (a potent reinforcement for a rat), the probability of its entering that arm again increases. If it receives a shock instead, the probability decreases.

Some cases of learning are difficult to label as classical or operant. For example, in birdsong learning (Chapter 1), a male songbird hears the song of his own species during his first spring and summer; he imitates it the following year. During the first year, the song that he heard was not paired with any other stimulus, so we cannot call this classical conditioning. He made no overt

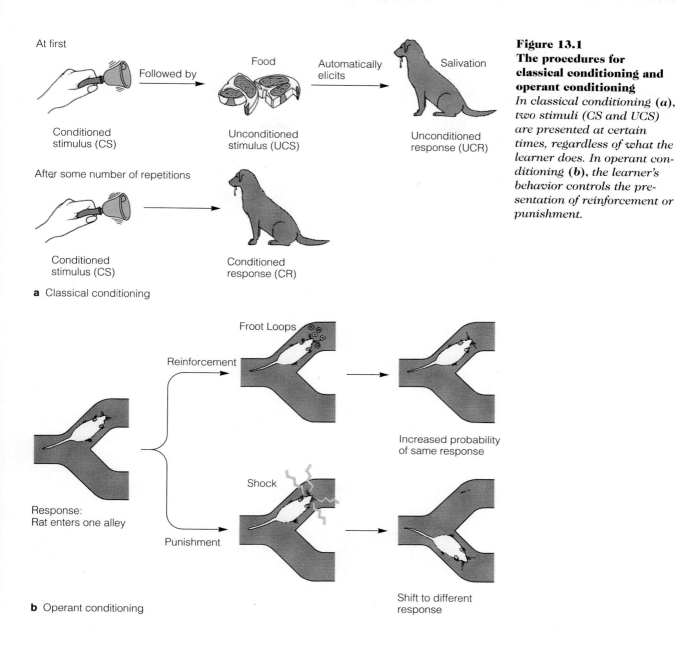

At first

Conditioned
stimulus (CS)

Followed by

Food

Unconditioned
stimulus (UCS)

Automatically
elicits

Salivation

Unconditioned
response (UCR)

After some number of repetitions

Conditioned
stimulus (CS)

Conditioned
response (CR)

a Classical conditioning

Froot Loops

Reinforcement

Increased probability
of same response

Response:
Rat enters one alley

Shock

Punishment

Shift to different
response

b Operant conditioning

Figure 13.1
The procedures for classical conditioning and operant conditioning
In classical conditioning **(a)**, *two stimuli (CS and UCS) are presented at certain times, regardless of what the learner does. In operant conditioning* **(b)**, *the learner's behavior controls the presentation of reinforcement or punishment.*

responses and received no reinforcements or punishments, so we cannot call it operant conditioning. That is, classical and operant conditioning do not exhaust all possible kinds of learning; animals have specialized ways of acquiring new behavior patterns in different situations (Rozin & Kalat, 1971; Rozin & Schull, 1988).

Pavlov believed that classical conditioning reflected a strengthened connection between a brain area that represents CS activity and a brain area that represents UCS activity. Because of that strengthened connection, any excitation of the CS center flows to the UCS center, evoking the unconditioned response (Figure 13.2). Karl Lashley set out to test this highly influential hypothesis. He said that he was searching for the **engram**—the physical representation of learning. (A connection between two brain areas would be one example of an engram but hardly the only possibility.)

Learning, Memory, Amnesia, and Brain Functioning

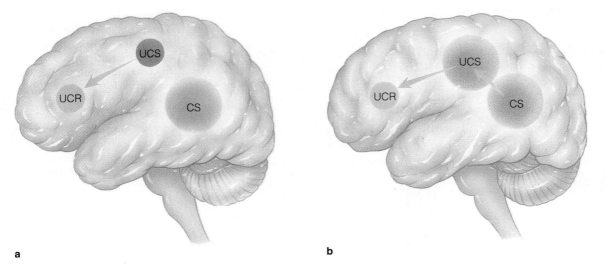

Figure 13.2
Pavlov's view of the physiology of learning
Initially (a), the UCS excites the UCS center, which then excites the UCR center. The CS excites the CS center, which elicits no response of interest. After training (b), excitation in the CS center flows to the UCS center, thus eliciting the same response as the UCS.

a

b

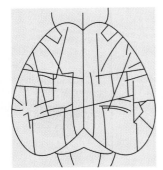

Figure 13.3
Map of cuts that Lashley made in the brains of various rats to see which one(s) would interfere with memory of a maze
None of the cuts interfered with maze memories. (Adapted from Lashley, 1950.)

Lashley reasoned that, if learning depends on new or strengthened connections between two brain areas, then a knife cut somewhere in the brain should interrupt that connection and abolish the learned response. He trained rats on a variety of mazes and a brightness discrimination task and then made one or more deep cuts in varying locations in the rats' cerebral cortexes (Lashley, 1929, 1950; see Figure 13.3). However, none of the knife cuts impaired rats' performance as much as he had expected. Evidently, the types of learning that he studied did not depend on strengthened connections across the cortex.

Lashley also tried to find out whether any portion of the cerebral cortex is more important than others for learning. He trained rats on mazes before or after he removed large portions of their cortex. The lesions impaired the rats' performance, but the amount of retardation depended more on the amount of brain damage than on its location. Learning and memory apparently did not rely on a single cortical area.

Eventually, researchers discovered that Lashley's conclusions reflected two unnecessary assumptions: (1) that the best place to search for an engram is the cerebral cortex, and (2) that all kinds of memory are physiologically the same. As we shall see, investigators who discarded those assumptions have come to some different conclusions.

Various Types of Memory

You will recall from Chapter 6 that different parts of the brain contribute to different aspects of visual perception. The same principle holds for memory, and much of our progress in understanding the physiology of memory has come from progress in distinguishing among different types of memory.

Short-Term Memory versus Long-Term Memory

We could, if we wished, draw an unlimited number of distinctions among different types of memory: memory of recent events versus older events, memory of sounds versus sights, memory of events that happened on Thursday versus those that happened on Friday, and so forth. How could we determine which distinctions (if any) were "natural" ones, reflecting important differences in brain functioning, and which distinctions were not?

Recall the concept of a *double dissociation of function* from Chapter 4: We can feel confident that two functions are physiologically different if some procedure (such as damage to a particular brain area) impairs one of the functions, while some other procedure impairs the other function. By this criterion, we can discard a distinction between "memories of Thursday events and memories of Friday events." No researcher has found any procedure that impairs one of those types of memory without equally impairing the other.

In contrast, several kinds of distinctions do appear to be biologically significant. One is Donald Hebb's (1949) distinction between short-term memory and long-term memory. **Short-term memory** is memory for events that have just occurred. **Long-term memory** is memory for events that do not currently occupy your attention; to recall them, you must retrieve them from storage. Several types of evidence validate this distinction, or at least something similar to it:

- Individuals with damage to the hippocampus can form new short-term memories, but they have great trouble developing new long-term memories.
- People and laboratory animals with certain kinds of sudden head trauma forget the events that happened just before the trauma (events that were in short-term memory) without forgetting earlier events (that were in long-term memory). However, the time after an event when the memory remains vulnerable to destruction varies from one instance to another (Squire & Spanis, 1984). That is, some short-term memories enter long-term memory rapidly, and others enter much more slowly.
- Short-term memory has several properties that differ from those of long-term memory. For illustration, read these letters and then repeat them from memory: CYXGMBF. That was short-term memory. Now try recalling the names of all your high-school teachers. That was long-term memory. Note that your short-term memory stores only a small amount of information at a time, and stores it only briefly unless you constantly rehearse it. (You may have already forgotten CYXGMBF.) Your long-term memory holds vast amounts of material indefinitely, but you may have to spend some effort to recall or reconstruct that information. (If you actually tried naming all your high-school teachers, you know what I mean.)

Consolidation of Long-Term Memories

I would not begin to estimate how much information passes through your short-term memory in a single day. Of all that information, a tiny fraction becomes a readily available long-term memory (e.g., your name, address, and telephone number), a somewhat larger fraction becomes a harder-to-recall long-term memory (e.g., the names of all your high-school teachers), and the largest fraction is forgotten altogether. In other words, we **consolidate,** or strengthen, some short-term memories into long-term memories, but the degree of consolidation varies. How does consolidation occur, and what processes promote or inhibit it?

In Donald Hebb's (1949) original theory, consolidation depended primarily, if not entirely, on time. Any short-term memory would be gradually converted into a long-term memory if it stayed in short-term storage long enough. Hebb guessed that a short-term memory might be represented by a *reverberating circuit* of neuronal activity in the brain, with a self-exciting loop of neurons. If the reverberating circuit remained active long enough, some chemical or structural change would occur that stored the memory permanently.

Although some time is necessary for the formation of long-term memories, most memory researchers no longer believe that simply holding something in short-term memory is sufficient to form a long-term memory. If you want to remember forever that Jakarta is the capital of Indonesia, do not spend the next few minutes repeating "Jakarta is the capital of Indonesia." Rather, think about it from as many angles as possible. Find Jakarta on a map of Indonesia, draw a map and mark Jakarta on it, make up a little story about where the name *Jakarta* came from, and so forth. In short, forming a long-term memory depends on building up lots of meaningful links, not just on waiting for time to pass.

Generally, the more meaningful an event is to you, the faster and more strongly you consolidate a memory of it. For example, suppose that someone you have had your eye on for weeks smiles and says, "I surely would like to go out with you this weekend." Chances are, you won't have to repeat that sentence twenty times to store it in your memory. In contrast, suppose your geography professor tells you the exact latitude and longitude of some city you had never heard of. You may have to study that fact long and hard before you can be sure you have memorized it.

Physiologically speaking, one reason why you remember exciting experiences better than you remember dull experiences is that exciting experiences arouse the sympathetic nervous system, increasing the secretion of epinephrine (adrenaline) into the bloodstream (McGaugh, 1990). For example, if you press a button and get a reward or press a button and get a shock, you are likely to experience a rush of epinephrine into the blood. An injection of epinephrine can also enhance a memory, up to an optimum level of epinephrine. Excessive epinephrine has a less beneficial effect and sometimes even a harmful effect. (People in a panic often have trouble remembering details of the situation later.)

How does epinephrine enhance memory? It does not do so by stimulating brain synapses; little epinephrine from the periphery crosses the blood-brain barrier. Instead, epinephrine converts stored glycogen to glucose and therefore raises the level of glucose in the blood that is available to the brain. Paul Gold and his colleagues have demonstrated that, when a high epinephrine level raises the level of blood glucose, the high glucose level facilitates memory. In fact, injecting glucose (to bypass the epinephrine stage) shortly after an experience enhances future memory of it (Gold, 1987; Hall & Gold, 1990; Lee, Graham, & Gold, 1988). In short, highly arousing events improve memory consolidation simply by increasing the brain's fuel supply.

Explicit Memory versus Implicit Memory

Another useful memory distinction, which psychologists first made in the 1980s, is between *explicit* and *implicit* memory. **Explicit memory** is a memory for facts or specific events; an investigator can test it directly through such questions as "what is your name?", "what did you have for dinner last night?", or "how do you spell *catecholamine*?" **Implicit memory** is memory that does not require any recollection of a specific event; investigators test it indirectly. For example, when you tie your shoelaces or ride a bicycle, you make use of implicit motor-skill memories. If you have been concentrating on your reading while ignoring a television talk show, you may not explicitly remember anything that the people on television said, and yet in your next conversation you may use some of the same words that the television characters used. Psychologists call that phenomenon **priming**, by which they mean that hearing those words "primes" you to use them yourself; priming is another example of implicit memory.

The explicit-implicit distinction is useful because certain kinds of brain damage impair explicit memory without affecting implicit memory. However, the distinction is not very precise, and we are not always sure whether to call a particular memory explicit or implicit. (Indeed, there are probably many borderline cases that are part one and part the other.) With humans, we can sometimes use verbalization as a criterion: If an event influences people's behavior, even though they say they don't remember it, then they have an implicit memory of it. But neuroscientists do much of their research with animals, which cannot verbalize. Researchers then have to infer, "Is this kind of animal memory more like human explicit memories or more like human implicit memories?" In some cases, that is a fairly easy inference; in other cases, the answer is far from obvious (Nadel, 1992).

Instead of the explicit-implicit distinction, many psychologists distinguish between declarative memory and procedural memory. **Declarative memory** is memory that a person can state in words; **procedural memory** consists of motor skills. Declarative memories are mostly explicit, and procedural memories are mostly implicit, but the terms do not overlap exactly.

So far, I have been loosely alluding to observations on brain damage; it is now time to consider those observations in more detail. We shall examine the short-term versus long-term memory distinction, the explicit versus implicit distinction, and others.

Brain Damage and Impairments of Implicit Memory

Let us begin with implicit memory, deferring the longer and more complex discussion of explicit memory. Implicit memory includes conditioned responses, learned motor skills, certain kinds of perceptual learning, and priming effects—quite a variety of phenomena, relying on different types of physiological mechanisms. Those mechanisms are fairly well known in certain instances, less well established in others.

Richard F. Thompson and his colleagues were the first to accomplish Lashley's goal of localizing an engram in the vertebrate brain, to be able to say, "Here is the spot where this particular kind of learning occurs." They localized that engram, not in the cerebral cortex, where Lashley sought it, but in the cerebellum.

Thompson's general procedure has been to study classical conditioning of eyelid responses in rabbits. They present first a tone (CS) and then a puff of air (UCS) to the cornea of the rabbit's eye. At first, a rabbit blinks at the air puff but not at the tone; after repeated pairings, it blinks at the tone by itself. That is, classical conditioning takes place. At various points in this procedure, the investigators record the activity from various brain cells to determine whether or not they change their responses as learning takes place.

Thompson and other investigators have consistently found changes in cells in one nucleus of the cerebellum, the **lateral interpositus nucleus.** That is, at the start of training, those cells show very little response to the training tone, but as learning proceeds, the cells' responses increase (Thompson, 1986). Furthermore, damage to the lateral interpositus nucleus causes a permanent loss of the conditioned response (McCormick & Thompson, 1984; Woodruf-Pak, Lavond, & Thompson, 1985).

Now, the fact that damaging a brain area prevents a learned response does not necessarily mean that the learning took place in that area. (The area could be receiving information from some other area that changed its responses during learning.) To test the role of the cerebellum in learning, two sets of investigators temporarily suppressed activity in the lateral interpositus nucleus at the start of training, either by cooling the area or by injecting a drug into it. Then they presented the CS and UCS as usual and found no learning. Finally, they waited for the effects of the cooling or the drugs to wear off and continued training. At that point, the rabbits began to learn, but they showed no "savings"; that is, they learned at the same speed as animals that had received no previous training. (In effect, these animals *had* received no previous training, since the training took place while the relevant brain area was inactive.)

In contrast, consider what happened when the investigators suppressed activity in the red nucleus, a midbrain motor area that receives input from the cerebellum: When the red nucleus was suppressed during training, the rabbits showed no responses during training. However, as soon as the red nucleus had recovered from the cooling or drugs, the rabbits showed strong learned responses to the tone (Clark & Lavond, 1993; Krupa, Thompson, & Thompson, 1993). In other words, suppressing the red nucleus temporarily prevented the response but did not prevent learning. We conclude, therefore, that this instance of learning takes place in the lateral interpositus nucleus, even though the red nucleus is also necessary for the motor expression of the response. Figure 13.4 summarizes these experiments.

The cerebellum may be central to a variety of conditioned responses, learned motor skills, and even intellectual skills in humans, as well as in rats (Bracke-Tolkmitt et al., 1989; Daum et al., 1993; Glickstein, 1992). However, certain kinds of implicit memory may depend on other brain areas as well. In one series of experiments, investigators presented guinea pigs with a tone (CS) followed by a shock (UCS), while recording activity from cells in the auditory portions of the thalamus and cerebral cortex. Ordinarily, a typical neuron in the auditory system responds most strongly to a sound at one frequency, a little less to some other tones near that frequency, and still less or not at all to tones still further from that frequency. Some neurons are tuned fairly tightly to a particular frequency; others respond more broadly over a wider range. During the course of training, as one tone is paired with shock, an increasing number of neurons become highly responsive to the frequency of that tone, and correspondingly less responsive to other frequencies (Edeline, Pham, & Weinberger, 1993; Edeline & Weinberger, 1992; Lennartz & Weinberger, 1992). In short, cortical cells can change their responsiveness to various stimuli, and such changes may contribute to learning.

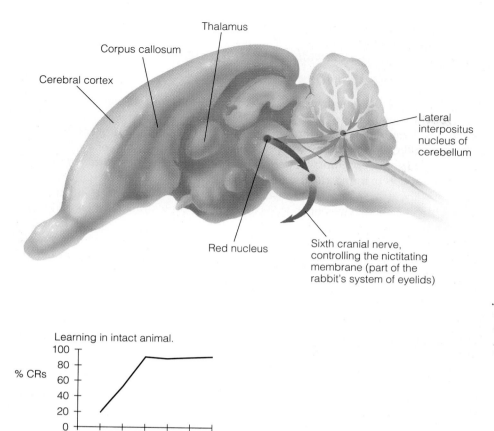

Thalamus

Corpus callosum

Cerebral cortex

Lateral interpositus nucleus of cerebellum

Red nucleus

Sixth cranial nerve, controlling the nictitating membrane (part of the rabbit's system of eyelids)

Figure 13.4
Summary of experiments localizing the engram for a conditioned eyelid response in rabbits
Temporary suppression of activity in the lateral interpositus nucleus of a rabbit blocks all indications of learning, both during the suppression and afterwards. Temporary suppression of activity in the red nucleus blocks the response during the period of suppression, but does not prevent learning itself; the learned response appears as soon as the red nucleus recovers from the suppression. Based on the experiments of Clark & Lavond (1993) and Krupa, Thompson, & Thompson (1993).

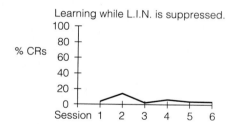

Learning in intact animal.

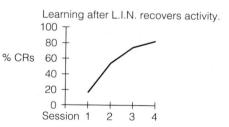

Learning while L.I.N. is suppressed.

Learning after L.I.N. recovers activity.

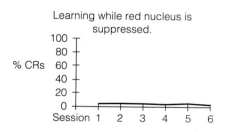

Learning while red nucleus is suppressed.

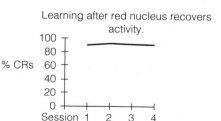

Learning after red nucleus recovers activity.

Brain Damage and Impairments of Explicit Memory

If you someday become a neurologist, you will seldom encounter a patient whose main complaint was, "I no longer show classically conditioned responses." You might encounter occasional patients complaining about a loss of motor skills, although they will probably describe it as a loss of coordination rather than a loss of memory. If people ever lose certain other kinds of implicit memory such as priming effects, they are unlikely to notice the loss, much less complain about it. When people worry or complain about **amnesia** (memory loss), either in themselves or in their loved ones, they almost always refer to a loss of explicit memory.

Much of what psychologists have learned about explicit-memory amnesia comes from studies of brain-damaged people. Those studies have led to experiments on animals, which in turn have led to new studies and new insights about people.

The Story of H. M., a Man with Hippocampal Damage

What gave researchers the idea to focus on the hippocampus? The main impetus was the memory loss of a special individual known to us by his initials H. M., now one of the most famous cases in neurology (Milner, 1959; Penfield & Milner, 1958; Scoville & Milner, 1957).

In 1953, H. M.'s epileptic seizures, which had proved unresponsive to all antiepileptic drugs, became so frequent and incapacitating that he had to quit his job. In desperation, neurosurgeons removed the hippocampus from both sides of his brain (see Figure 13.5), because the seizures seemed to be originating from that structure. They also removed several neighboring structures, including the amygdala. Although the surgeons did not know what to expect from the operation, they took a gamble that this extensive surgery might do H. M. more good than harm. As the results turned out, H. M. probably would have preferred to stick with having epilepsy.

Following the surgery, H. M.'s epileptic seizures did decrease in frequency and severity, and he was able to take less of the antiepileptic medications. His personality and intellect remained the same; in fact, his IQ score increased slightly after the operation, presumably because of the decreased epileptic interference. However, he suffered moderate **retrograde amnesia** (loss of memory for events that occurred shortly prior to brain damage from trauma or disease). That is, he had some trouble recalling events that happened within the last 1 to 3 years before the operation, but no trouble recalling still older events. He also suffered a massive **anterograde amnesia** (loss of memories for events that happened after brain damage). He could store new information briefly, but he had great difficulty in recalling it after any distraction.

For example, after the operation, he could not learn his way to the hospital bathroom. After reading a story, he was unable to describe what had happened in it. He could read a single magazine over and over without any indication of familiarity or any loss of interest. He lived with his parents, and when they moved to a new address, he had great difficulty finding his way home or locating anything within the house. After eight years, he had finally memorized the

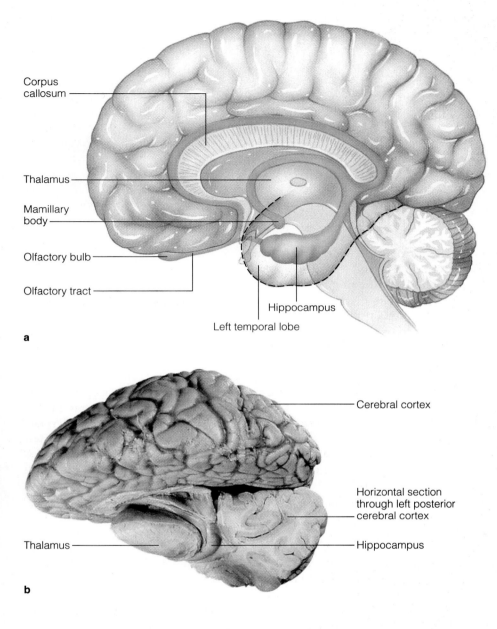

Figure 13.5
(*a*) *Location of the hippocampus in the human brain.* (*b*) *Photo showing part of the hippocampus, which curves into the interior of each hemisphere. In both parts of the figure, note that the hippocampus curves around over the thalamus and under the cerebral cortex. (Photo courtesy of Dana Copeland.)*

Corpus callosum

Thalamus

Mamillary body

Olfactory bulb

Olfactory tract

Hippocampus

Left temporal lobe

a

Cerebral cortex

Horizontal section through left posterior cerebral cortex

Thalamus

Hippocampus

b

floor plan and could find his way from one room to another; however, he still could not find his way home from a distance of more than two blocks (Milner, Corkin, & Teuber, 1968).

In one test of H. M.'s memory, Brenda Milner (1959) asked him to memorize the number 584. After a 15-minute delay without distractions, he was able to recall the number correctly. He explained how he did so. "It's easy. You just remember 8. You see, 5, 8, and 4 add to 17. You remember 8, subtract it from 17, and it leaves 9. Divide 9 in half and you get 5 and 4, and there you are, 584. Easy." A moment later, after H. M.'s attention had been shifted to another subject, he had forgotten both the number and the complicated line of thought he had associated with it.

In 1980, he moved to a nursing home. Four years later, he could not say where he lived or who cared for him. Although he watched the news on television every night, he could recall only a few fragments of events since 1953. For

Learning, Memory, Amnesia, and Brain Functioning

Figure 13.6
The Tower of Hanoi puzzle
The task is to transfer all the disks to another peg, moving just one at a time, without ever placing a larger disk on top of a smaller disk. H. M. has learned to solve this problem, although he says that he does not remember ever seeing it before.

several years after the operation, whenever he was asked his age and the date, he answered "27" and "1953." After a few years, he started guessing wildly, generally underestimating his age by 10 years or more and misestimating the year by as much as 43 years (Corkin, 1984).

H. M. and similar patients are not completely incapable of new memories. They can learn to recall new material if they are given many, many repetitions under conditions designed to minimize interference. Even then, however, they do not remember when or where they learned the material, and even when they answer correctly, they do not answer with much confidence (Freed & Corkin, 1988; Hayman & Macdonald, 1993).

Although H. M. has enormous trouble learning new facts and keeping track of current events in his life, he learns new skills without apparent difficulty. For example, he has learned how to do a simple finger maze, read material written in mirror fashion, and solve the Tower of Hanoi puzzle shown in Figure 13.6 (Cohen, Eichenbaum, Deacedo, & Corkin, 1985). He does not *remember* learning these skills, however. In fact, he says he does not remember seeing the maze or the puzzle before.

Korsakoff's Syndrome and Other Frontal-Lobe Damage

Korsakoff's syndrome, also known as *Wernicke-Korsakoff syndrome,* is a type of brain damage caused by thiamine deficiency. Severe thiamine deficiency occurs almost exclusively in severe alcoholics who go days or weeks at a time eating almost nothing and drinking only alcoholic beverages. In doing so, they become deficient in thiamine (vitamin B_1), which the brain needs in order to metabolize glucose, its primary fuel. Prolonged thiamine deficiency leads to a loss or shrinkage of neurons throughout the brain, especially in the mamillary bodies (part of the hypothalamus) and in the **dorsomedial thalamus,** a nucleus that projects to the prefrontal cortex (Squire, Amaral, & Press, 1990; Victor, Adams, & Collins, 1971). Consequently, their symptoms are similar to those of people with damage to the prefrontal cortex, including apathy, confusion, and memory impairment.

Certain hospitals, especially in large cities, report about one person with Korsakoff's syndrome per 1,000 hospital admissions. Treatment with thiamine can sometimes improve the condition, but the longer a person has remained thiamine-deficient before treatment, the poorer the chances for recovery.

Most Korsakoff's syndrome patients have both retrograde and anterograde amnesia, in varying degrees of severity. Here is an example: A 59-year-old man easily recalls details of his early life and of military experience as a young man, although he can recall almost no recent events. When an interviewer leaves the room after a long conversation and returns a few minutes later, the patient does not recognize the interviewer and does not remember their conversation. He does not recognize any doctors or nurses at the hospital and cannot find his way around. He reads the same newspaper repeatedly, showing surprise at the news items each time. When seated at the dinner table with an empty plate in front of him, he does not remember whether he has just finished eating or has not yet started (Barbizet, 1970).

Patients with Korsakoff's syndrome often show signs of implicit memory, despite their great impairments of explicit memory. For example, after patients in one study read a list of words—such as *defend, helium, convey, modify, sinker, belfry*—they had no explicit memory of the words on the list. When asked to write as many words as they could remember from the list, some replied, "What list?" But then the experimenter gave them a list of word fragments and asked them to fill in complete words:

def_____   he_____   con_____   mod_____   sin_____   bel_____

Each of these fragments can be completed in several ways; for example, *def* can become *defeat, defect, deface, define, defrost,* and so on. However, Korsakoff's syndrome patients generally filled in the blanks to form the words they had seen on the list, even though they insisted that they did not remember the list (Schacter, 1985).

Korsakoff's patients, like other patients with frontal-lobe damage, often have great trouble recalling the temporal order of events. Such patients cannot recall which of a series of world events happened furthest in the past or which one happened most recently; they also cannot recall which events from their own lives happened long ago and which ones happened recently (Shimamura, Janowsky, & Squire, 1990). Answering questions about the timing of events calls for reasoning skills as much as it calls for memory skills (Moscovitch, 1992). Suppose I ask, "Which happened to you most recently: graduation from high school, getting your first driver's license, or reading Chapter 2 of *Biological Psychology*?" You do not simply examine your three memories to decide which one feels "freshest." Instead, you reason it out: "I started driving during my junior year of high school, so that came before high-school graduation. *Biological Psychology* is one of my college texts, so I started reading it after high-school graduation." A person with frontal-lobe damage has trouble with even this simple kind of reasoning; consequently, he or she will make such gross errors as telling you that "I have been married for four months" and then a moment later telling you, "my oldest child is 32 years old" (Moscovitch, 1989).

Alzheimer's Disease

Another cause of severe memory loss is **Alzheimer's disease,** a condition that becomes more and more prevalent with advancing age. Occasionally, people develop the disease before age 50 or even before age 40. By age 65–74, it strikes less than 5 percent of the population, but in people over age 85 it affects almost 50 percent (Evans et al., 1989). The symptoms start with minor forgetfulness, similar to that found in many older people, but the disease progresses to more serious memory loss, confusion, depression, restlessness, hallucinations, delusions, and disturbances of eating, sleeping, and other daily activities (Cummings & Victoroff, 1990).

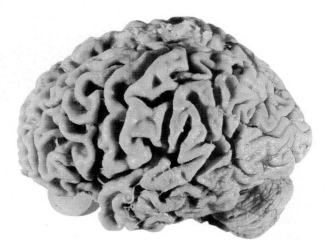 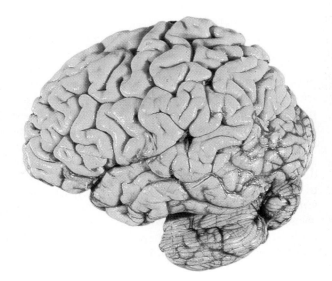

At the start, people with Alzheimer's disease typically have trouble keeping track of what they have just done and what has been going on around them. For example, Daniel Schacter (1983) reported playing golf with an Alzheimer's patient who, although he remembered the rules and jargon of the game correctly, could not remember how many strokes he took on any hole. Five times he teed off, waited for the other player to tee off, and then teed off again, having forgotten his first shot. Even when he did remember not to tee off again, he could not remember where he had hit his ball. He could not say what label was on his ball, although when he picked up a ball he could recognize whether it was his.

As with H. M. and Korsakoff's patients, Alzheimer's patients learn new skills more easily than they learn new facts. In one study, Alzheimer's patients were unable to learn a list of words or recognize new faces. However, they had little trouble learning the skill of maintaining contact between a hand-held pointer and a moving object (Eslinger & Damasio, 1986).

Alzheimer's disease is associated with a widespread atrophy (wasting away) of the cerebral cortex, hippocampus, and other areas, as Figure 13.7 shows (Hyman, Van Hoesen, Damasio, & Barnes, 1984). The most heavily damaged area is the entorhinal cortex, the portion of the cerebral cortex that conducts the greatest amount of communication with the hippocampus (Van Hoesen, Hyman, & Damasio, 1991). A number of neurons degenerate (see Figure 13.8), especially those that release acetylcholine (Mash, Flynn, & Potter, 1985). Large numbers of **plaques** (formed from degenerating axons and dendrites) appear in the damaged areas, as Figure 13.9 illustrates (Rogers & Morrison, 1985). **Tangles** of axons and dendrites are also common.

The plaques contain deposits of a protein known as β-**amyloid**. A lively research controversy concerns whether this chemical is one of the underlying causes of Alzheimer's disease or just another one of the symptoms. Certain studies have found that an injection of β-amyloid into a rat's brain can damage neurons and produce symptoms resembling those of Alzheimer's disease (Kowall, Beal, Busciglio, Duffy, & Yankner, 1991). Such results suggest that excess production of β-amyloid may be one step in the causation of Alzheimer's disease, and many investigators lean toward that conclusion (Rosenberg, 1993). However, a number of investigators who injected β-amyloid

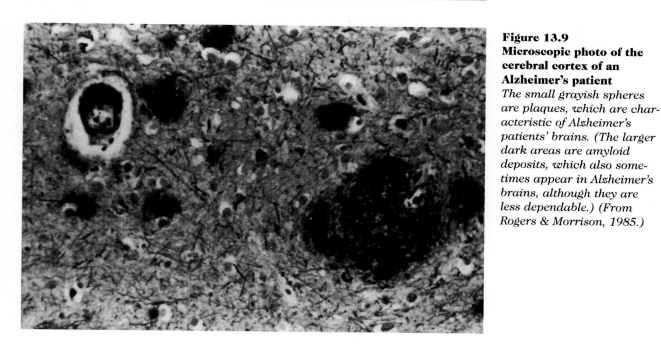

Figure 13.8
Progressive degeneration of
neurons in the prefrontal
cortex during Alzheimer's
disease
(a) *A cell in a normal
human;* (b) *cells from the
same area of cortex in
Alzheimer's disease patients
at three stages of deterioration. Note the shrinkage of
the dendritic tree. (After
Scheibel, 1983.)*

**Figure 13.9
Microscopic photo of the
cerebral cortex of an
Alzheimer's patient**
*The small grayish spheres
are plaques, which are characteristic of Alzheimer's
patients' brains. (The larger
dark areas are amyloid
deposits, which also sometimes appear in Alzheimer's
brains, although they are
less dependable.) (From
Rogers & Morrison, 1985.)*

failed to replicate the evidence of brain damage. The results apparently depend
on a number of details of procedure, and researchers will have to explore those
details before they can reach a consensus on the role of β-amyloid. Ultimately,
to mimic the effects of Alzheimer's disease in a nonhuman animal, researchers
will probably have to induce a gradual accumulation of β-amyloid or other substances in the brain, rather than suddenly injecting large amounts.

Alzheimer's disease runs in certain families, suggesting a genetic basis, but
genetics is certainly not the only factor. The disease sometimes occurs in people unrelated to any other Alzheimer's patients, and it sometimes fails to occur

*Learning, Memory, Amnesia,
and Brain Functioning*

in someone whose identical twin has Alzheimer's disease (Nee et al., 1987). One clue to a possible genetic basis is the fact that people with *Down syndrome* (a type of mental retardation) almost invariably get Alzheimer's disease if they survive into middle age (Lott, 1982). *Down syndrome* is caused by having three copies of chromosome 21 rather than the usual two copies; consequently, researchers have examined chromosome 21 for genes that are possibly related to Alzheimer's disease. The results indicate that Alzheimer's disease, unlike Huntington's disease (p. 304), depends on at least two or three different genes in different families.

For certain families with early-onset Alzheimer's disease, researchers have identified mutations on chromosome 21, in or near the gene that determines the structure of *amyloid precursor protein* (Goate et al., 1991; Murrell, Farlow, Ghetti, & Benson, 1991). (That protein is interesting to theorists because fragments of it can become β-amyloid.) In other families with early-onset Alzheimer's disease, the evidence suggests that the relevant gene is on chromosome 14 (Schellenberg et al., 1992). What that gene does and how it contributes to Alzheimer's disease are simply unknown. In people with late-onset Alzheimer's disease, the genetic basis is less clear. (The dividing line between early-onset and late-onset is not distinct, but is generally set at about age 60 to 65.) Several studies have found a link between late-onset Alzheimer's disease and a gene on chromosome 19 (Corder et al., 1993; Pericak-Vance et al., 1991). However, many cases of late-onset Alzheimer's disease do not show a family basis and may depend largely on nongenetic factors. It is clear, in summary, that Alzheimer's depends on a variety of influences, not just one.

What Amnesic Patients Teach Us: Different Types of Memory

The study of amnesic patients reveals that, when people "lose their memory," they do not lose all aspects of memory equally. H. M. remembers events from long ago, although he has forgotten almost everything that has happened since his operation. He and other patients who have great trouble memorizing facts can learn new skills and retain them indefinitely. Evidently, people have several somewhat independent kinds of memory, depending on different brain areas.

Role of the Hippocampus, Amygdala, and Frontal Cortex

So far, we have seen that damage to the hippocampus and other areas impairs the formation of long-term explicit memories. Can we clarify the role of each brain area in more detail? To gain greater control of the situation, neuroscientists turn to animal studies.

The discovery of how hippocampal damage impaired memory in H. M. and other patients led psychologists to study the effects of hippocampal lesions on rats. In early experiments, they typically made the lesions and then tested the rats' ability to learn a simple discrimination, such as to turn left in a T-maze for food, or to approach a white card instead of a black card or a high-frequency tone instead of a low-frequency tone. To the investigators' surprise, the rats generally did pretty well. Psychologists puzzled over why hippocampal damage

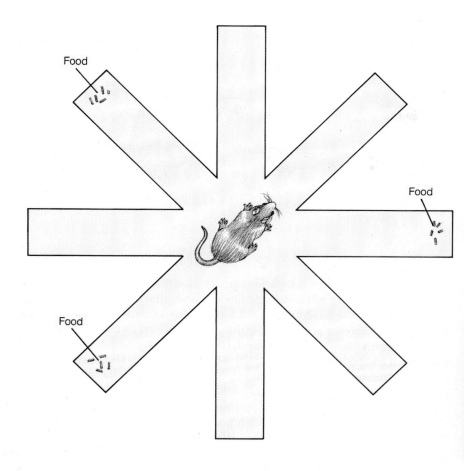

Food

Food

Food

Figure 13.10
An eight-arm radial maze
Food is in some arms, not in others. To perform well, a rat must maintain a working memory of which arms it has already explored. If it reenters one arm before trying other arms, it makes an error of working memory. (Photo Hank Morgan/Rainbow)

seemed to impair human memory so much more than it impaired animal memory (Isaacson, 1972).

But that was before investigators were sensitive to the distinctions between different kinds of memory. Learning to make a particular response to a particular stimulus can be regarded as implicit memory, the kind of memory that is not impaired in H. M. or other brain-damaged amnesic patients. Eventually, investigators discovered that rats with hippocampal lesions performed well on some memory tasks and poorly on others. Let's consider what kinds of performance a hippocampal lesion does and does not impair.

Damage to the Hippocampus in Rats

As with humans, hippocampal damage in rats impairs some kinds of memory and spares other kinds. Figure 13.10 illustrates a **radial maze.** In a typical experiment, a rat is placed in the center of eight or more arms, some of which have a bit of food at the end. For example, the rats might have to learn that the arms with a rough floor never have food or that the arms pointing toward the window never have food. The rat stays in the maze until it has found all the food or until it has gone, say, 2 minutes without finding any more food. After enough training trials, a rat may learn to go down each correct arm once and only once and not to try any of the incorrect arms. A rat can make two types of mistakes: It can go down one of the always-incorrect arms, or it can enter one correct arm repeatedly while failing to enter one of the other correct arms.

Learning, Memory, Amnesia, and Brain Functioning

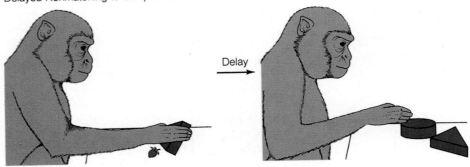

Delayed Nonmatching-to-Sample Test

Delay

Monkey lifts sample object
to get food.

Food is under the new object.

**Figure 13.11
The procedure for delayed
nonmatching-to-sample
with a monkey**

A normal rat makes only a few errors of either kind. Rats with damage to the hippocampus, or with damage to the axons that connect the hippocampus to other structures, seldom enter the never-correct arms. But they frequently reenter some correct arms while failing to try others. Evidently, they lose track of which arms they have already tried (Jarrard, Okaichi, Steward, & Goldschmidt, 1984; Olton & Papas, 1979; Olton, Walker, & Gage, 1978).

The radial maze is one of many tasks on which hippocampal lesions impair performance; on many other tasks, such lesions have little effect. Psychologists have debated how to describe what the hippocampal lesions impair. Some psychologists have emphasized the importance of the hippocampus for spatial tasks (e.g., Kesner, 1990; O'Keefe, 1983), but the lesions also impair performance on many nonspatial tasks (e.g., Eichenbaum, 1992; Rawlins, Lyford, Seferiades, Deacon, & Cassaday, 1993). Another hypothesis is that the hippocampus is necessary for *configural conditioning,* in which the correct response depends on a combination of two or more stimuli rather than any one stimulus. That hypothesis, too, fails to fit all of the data (Davidson, McKernan, & Jarrard, 1993; Whishaw & Tomie, 1991). At this point, the hypothesis that seems most consistent with the data, although it is unfortunately loose and imprecise, is that the hippocampus is critical for declarative, explicit memory (Squire, 1992). I say that this is "loose and imprecise" because the behaviors of rats and other nonverbal species is not directly comparable with the verbal responses of people who are asked about their memories. Choosing the correct arm in a radial maze strikes most investigators as a reasonable rat facsimile of human explicit memory, but we must admit that we have not yet specified adequately the kind of memory to which the hippocampus is relevant.

Damage to the Hippocampus in Primates

Primates are generally tested on some rather complex tasks. In a **delayed matching-to-sample task,** an animal sees an object (the sample) and then, after a delay, gets a choice between two objects, from which it must choose the one that matches the sample. In the **delayed nonmatching-to-sample task** (Figure 13.11), the procedure is the same except that the animal must choose the object that is *different* from the sample. In both cases, there may be a spatial component, but the primary task is to recognize which stimulus is familiar and which is new.

An animal's performance on a task like this varies enormously with apparently minor changes in procedure. For example, on either delayed matching-to-sample or delayed nonmatching-to-sample tests, the subject must remember the sample during the delay, and we might suppose that both tasks would be equally easy or equally difficult. Yet monkeys perform much better on nonmatching than on matching; evidently, they learn to reach for a new item more easily than they learn to reach for a familiar item. Furthermore, the results can vary depending on whether the experimenter uses the same objects repeatedly or uses new objects each time. For example, if a monkey always has to choose between a red triangle and a blue square, damage to the prefrontal cortex impairs performance, but hippocampal damage does not. If a monkey has to choose between different objects every time, damage to either the hippocampus or the prefrontal cortex greatly impairs performance (Aggleton, Blindt, & Rawlins, 1989).

Exactly how does the hippocampus contribute to memory? Clearly, we do not store memories *in* the hippocampus itself. Hippocampal damage makes it difficult to store new memories, but it does not impair old memories. Investigators have offered many interpretations of what the hippocampus does. Here are two: One hypothesis is that the hippocampus acts as a map of where memories are stored in the cerebral cortex—analogous to a library's card catalog (Teyler & DiScenna, 1986). After damage to the hippocampus, an individual has trouble locating the memory that is correct at this moment and distinguishing it from similar memories stored in the past.

A second hypothesis is that hippocampal neurons maintain a temporary store of sensory information through their own continuous activity. In several experiments, rats have been given a visual or auditory stimulus and then required to make some response to it after a delay. Many cells in the hippocampus maintain distinctive response patterns during the delay, varying as a function of the original stimulus or the upcoming response (e.g., Hampson, Heyser, & Deadwyler, 1993; Sakurai, 1990). Their activity may be a way of maintaining memory during the delay.

Contributions of the Prefrontal Cortex

Damage to the prefrontal cortex produces effects similar in some regards to those of hippocampal damage. The hippocampus and amygdala send part of their output to the prefrontal area of the cerebral cortex, so the three areas are closely related.

Damage to the prefrontal cortex impairs performance on a variety of tasks, with the results depending on the location of damage within the prefrontal cortex. After damage to a ventral area of a monkey's prefrontal cortex, the monkey typically shows **perseveration;** that is, once it makes a particular response, such as choosing a blue square, it tends to make the same response repeatedly, even when it should suppress that response and choose something else (Mishkin & Manning, 1978).

Humans with prefrontal damage are severely impaired on the **Wisconsin card-sorting task** (see Figure 13.12). This task requires a person first to sort cards into stacks according to one rule (for example, by shape), then reshuffle them and sort by a different rule (for example, color or number). People with prefrontal damage generally have little trouble sorting according to the first rule, whatever it may be. But they have great trouble shifting to a new rule. For example, after sorting by shape, they have trouble sorting by color (Janowsky, Shimamura, Kritchevsky, & Squire, 1989).

Figure 13.12
The Wisconsin card-sorting task

First, people sort the cards by one rule—in this case, shape. Then they sort them by some other rule, such as color, and then by another rule, such as number. People with prefrontal cortex damage are highly impaired on this task. After they have sorted by one rule, they find it difficult to ignore that rule and follow a different rule.

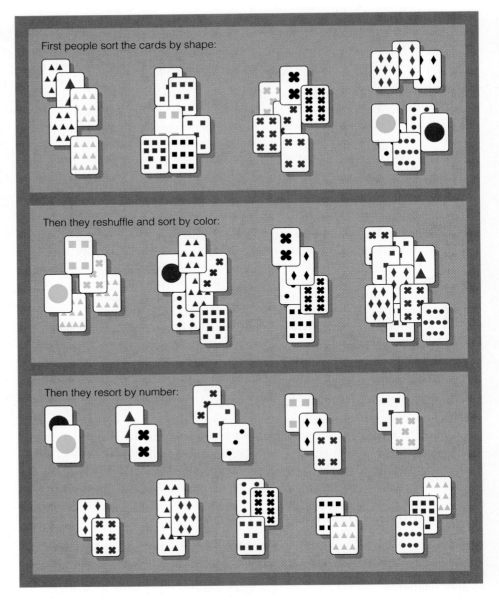

After damage in a dorsal area of the prefrontal cortex, called the *principal sulcus,* monkeys show some specialized deficits with temporary memories, especially on spatial tasks. For example, consider the following tasks: A monkey is trained to stare at a fixation point on a screen. A light appears elsewhere on the screen. At certain times, the monkey is trained to move its eyes at once toward the light. At other times, the light goes off, and the monkey is supposed to continue staring at the fixation point until it disappears a few seconds later. When it disappears, the monkey is to move its eyes toward where the light *used to be.* Note that this second condition, a version of the **delayed-response task,** requires spatial memory, while the first (no delay) condition does not. Monkeys with damage to the principal sulcus of the prefrontal cortex show a severe deficit in the delayed-response task, but no deficit in moving their eyes toward the target without a delay (Goldman-Rakic, 1994). In other words, their problem is specifically with memory, not with vision or muscle control.

Furthermore, if the monkey has damage to just a small part of the principal sulcus, it may lose its memory for just one small part of the visual field. For example, it may be unable to remember to move its eyes to the right, though it is perfectly capable of remembering left, or up, or down. *It can still move* its eyes to the right in the no-delay task; the problem arises only when the monkey has to *remember* a location to the right. The results suggest that the monkey has lost its ability to remember one spot in visual space.

Recall for a moment the discussion at the end of Chapter 5 concerning a possible relationship between overall intelligence and overall brain size. You should now see more clearly why many investigators regard that whole approach as misguided. "Overall intelligence" is just a convenient fiction. In reality, what we call "intelligence" is the sum of a great many separate brain functions, each dependent on very specific modules and pathways. Even "memory" is composed of a great many surprisingly specific abilities.

Brain and Memory in Young and Old

Ideally, investigation of the physiology of learning and memory should lead to insights about why some people have better memories than other people do. For example, why do infants and old people sometimes have memory difficulties?

A possible key to answering this question is that both infants and old people perform well on some memory tasks and poorly on others. For example, psychologists have long puzzled over **infant amnesia,** the phenomenon of remembering very few events from the first 4 or 5 years of our lives. Nevertheless, children less than 4 years old learn many general principles such as "do not touch a hot stove." That is, in our first 4 or 5 years we learn many implicit memories even if we do not form many permanent explicit memories.

In that regard, infant memory resembles that of people with hippocampal damage. Perhaps infants have memory problems because the hippocampus is slow to mature. (Moscovitch, 1985). Both human infants and monkey infants readily learn simple object discriminations (such as "find food under the red triangle"), but conspicuously fail on hippocampus-dependent tasks such as delayed nonmatching-to-sample (Bachevalier & Mishkin, 1984; Overman, Bachevalier, Turner, & Peuster, 1992).

Many old people who have great troubles with recent explicit memories manage to learn new skills (such as walking with a cane) or to adjust old skills. That is, they are impaired mostly on hippocampus-dependent types of memory. Old rats also show deficits similar to those of rats with damage to the hippocampus or prefrontal cortex (Winocur & Moscovitch, 1990). The hippocampus of old rats includes many dead or dying neurons and axons (Greene & Naranjo, 1987); many of the surviving neurons are less active than they are in younger rats (Barnes & McNaughton, 1985).

The prefrontal cortex also deteriorates in old age. Aged monkeys perform poorly on many of the same tasks as do monkeys with prefrontal damage. The deficits of old age may be due in part to a declining number of dopamine and norepinephrine synapses in the prefrontal cortex (Arnsten & Goldman-Rakic, 1985a, 1985b).

Summary

1. Ivan Pavlov suggested that learning depends on the growth of a connection between two brain areas. Karl Lashley showed that learning does *not* depend on new connections across the cerebral cortex. He further demonstrated that damage almost anywhere in the cerebral cortex can impair performance of complex learned behaviors. (p. 450)

2. Psychologists distinguish between short-term memory and long-term memory. Short-term memory holds only a small amount of information and retains it only briefly unless it is constantly rehearsed. Long-term memory retains vast amounts of material indefinitely, but recalling information from long-term memory sometimes requires great effort. (p. 453)

3. Most short-term memories are eventually forgotten; others are consolidated to varying degrees into long-term memories. Epinephrine enhances consolidation by increasing the availability of glucose to the brain. (p. 453)

4. Psychologists also distinguish between explicit and implicit memory. For humans, explicit memories are those that the person identifies as recollections of past events; implicit memories do not require identification of any specific event. The explicit-implicit distinction is more difficult to apply with nonhuman species. (p. 454)

5. Certain classically conditioned responses (a type of implicit memory) depend on localized circuits in the cerebellum. (p. 455)

6. Most of what we regard as amnesia is a loss of explicit memory. People with damage to the hippocampus, such as the patient H. M., have great trouble forming new long-term explicit memories, although they can still recall events from before the damage and form new implicit memories. (p. 458)

7. Patients with Korsakoff's syndrome or other types of frontal-lobe damage have impairments of explicit memory, especially in using their reasoning powers to decide, for example, that "this event must have happened before that other event." (p. 460)

8. Alzheimer's disease is a progressive disease, more common in old age, characterized by a severe impairment of explicit memory. (p. 461)

9. Rats and monkeys with damage to the hippocampus show impaired memory of changeable information, such as which arms of a radial maze a rat has entered recently, or which of two stimuli a monkey saw recently. This deficit can be loosely described as a loss of explicit memory. Animals showing such deficits are less impaired at learning responses to stimuli whose meaning does not change. (p. 465)

10. Damage to the prefrontal cortex produces a variety of memory problems, including perseveration—a tendency to repeat an old learned response instead of substituting a new response that is more appropriate. (p. 467)

Review Questions

1. What does the term *engram* mean? What kind of engram did Karl Lashley expect to find? (p. 451)

2. How does epinephrine enhance consolidation? (p. 454)

3. Describe the type of memory for which an engram has actually been located, and name that location. (p. 456)

4. What kind of learning or memory is least impaired in the patient H. M.? (p. 460)

5. Why is Korsakoff's syndrome more common among alcoholics than among other people? (p. 460)

6. What type of memory process is especially impaired after frontal-lobe damage? (p. 461)

7. What observation first led to the suspicion that chromosome 21 in some people contains a gene that causes Alzheimer's disease? (p. 464)

8. After damage to the hippocampus of a rat, what kinds of memory are most impaired? What kinds are least impaired? What evidence points to the importance of the hippocampus for spatial memories? (p. 465)

9. Why do psychologists conclude that the hippocampus is important for storing certain memories, but that the brain actually stores those memories in some other location? (p. 467)

10. What are the effects of prefrontal cortex damage on a person's performance of the Wisconsin card-sorting task? (p. 467)

11. What kinds of memory are most vulnerable to loss in infancy and in old age? (p. 469)

Thought Questions

1. Lashley sought to find the engram, the physiological representation of learning. In general terms, how would you recognize an engram if you saw one? That is, what would someone have to demonstrate before you could conclude that a particular change in the nervous system was really an engram?

2. Animals that eat immediately after a learning trial tend to learn faster than animals that do not eat (Flood, Smith, & Morley, 1987). Based on material you have read so far in this chapter, offer an explanation.

Suggestions for Further Reading

Cohen, N. J., & Eichenbaum, H. (1993). *Memory, amnesia, and the hippocampal system.* Cambridge, MA: MIT Press. Discussion of memory impairments, especially as they relate to the hippocampus.

Squire, L. R. (1992). Memory and the hippocampus: A synthesis from findings with rats, monkeys, and humans. *Psychological Review, 99,* 195–231. An excellent theoretical review of the literature.

Terms

classical conditioning type of conditioning produced by the pairing of two stimuli, one of which evokes an automatic response (p. 450)

conditioned stimulus (CS) stimulus that comes to evoke a particular response only after the pairing of that stimulus with an unconditioned stimulus (p. 450)

unconditioned stimulus (UCS) stimulus that automatically evokes an unconditioned response (p. 450)

unconditioned response (UCR) response automatically evoked by an unconditioned stimulus (p. 450)

conditioned response (CR) response evoked by a conditioned stimulus as a result of the pairing of that stimulus with an unconditioned stimulus (p. 450)

operant conditioning type of conditioning in which reinforcement or punishment changes the future probabilities of a given behavior (p. 450)

reinforcement event that increases the future probability of the preceding response (p. 450)

punishment event that decreases the future probability of the preceding response (p. 450)

engram the physical representation of learning (p. 451)

short-term memory memory for an event that just happened (p. 453)

long-term memory memory for an event that is not currently in one's attention (p. 453)

consolidation formation and strengthening of long-term memories (p. 453)

explicit memory memory for facts or for specific events, detectable by direct testing such as asking a person to describe a past event (p. 454)

implicit memory memory that does not require any recollection of a specific event, detectable by indirect influences on behavior (p. 455)

priming phenomenon where seeing or hearing a word or words increases the probability that a person will soon use those same words (p. 455)

declarative memory memory that a person can state, identifying it as a memory (p. 455)

procedural memory memory of how to do something (p. 455)

lateral interpositus nucleus a nucleus of the cerebellum that is critical for classical conditioning of the eye-blink response in rabbits (p. 456)

amnesia memory loss (p. 458)

retrograde amnesia loss of memory for events that occurred before brain damage (p. 458)

anterograde amnesia loss of memory for events that happened after brain damage or some other event (p. 458)

Korsakoff's syndrome type of brain damage caused by thiamine deficiency, characterized by apathy, confusion, and memory impairment (p. 460)

dorsomedial thalamus area of the thalamus that sends axons mostly to the frontal cortex; it is damaged in Korsakoff's syndrome (p. 460)

Alzheimer's disease condition characterized by memory loss, confusion, depression, restlessness, hallucinations, delusions, and disturbances of eating, sleeping, and other daily activities (p. 461)

plaque structure formed from degenerating axons and dendrites in the brains of people with Alzheimer's disease (p. 462)

tangle collection of disrupted axons and dendrites found in the brains of people with Alzheimer's disease (p. 462)

β-amyloid a protein found in large quantities in the plaques in brains of people with Alzheimer's disease; a possible cause of Alzheimer's disease (p. 462)

radial maze apparatus with many arms radiating from a central point, generally with food at the end of some or all of the arms (p. 465)

delayed matching-to-sample task task in which an animal sees a sample object and then after a delay must choose an object that matches the sample (p. 466)

delayed nonmatching-to-sample task task in which an animal sees a sample object and then after a delay must choose an object that does not match the sample (p. 466)

perseveration tendency to repeat a previously learned response even though some other response is currently more appropriate (p. 467)

Wisconsin card-sorting task task in which a person first sorts cards according to one rule and then reshuffles them and sorts them according to a different rule (p. 467)

delayed-response task task in which individuals are given some signal to which they must give some learned response after a delay (p. 468)

infant amnesia tendency for people to recall few specific events that occurred before about age 4 or 5 years (p. 469)

Mechanisms of Storing Information in the Nervous System

When you see something, hear something, or do something, your experience probably leaves several traces in your nervous system. But which of these traces are important for memory?

If I walk through a field, are the footprints that I leave "memories"? How about the mud that I pick up on my shoes? In a sense, both are memories. That is, if the police wanted to know who had walked across that field, a forensics expert could compare the footprints with the soles of my shoes and the mud on my shoes to the mud on the field.

Similarly, when a pattern of activity passes through my brain or yours, it leaves a path of physical changes. Any or all of those changes could be memories if something in the brain can use them appropriately, like the forensics expert who knows how to examine footprints. Investigators of the physiology of learning and memory try to determine how an experience lays down lasting traces in the brain and which of those traces the brain uses later. The task is a little like searching for the proverbial needle in the haystack, and researchers have explored many avenues that seemed promising for a while but now seem fruitless (see Digression 13.1).

Learning and the Hebbian Synapse

Ivan Pavlov's concept of classical conditioning lent itself very well to theorizing about the physiological basis of learning. As we have already seen, Pavlov's theories provoked Karl Lashley's unsuccessful search for new connections across the cerebral cortex. Pavlov's theories also stimulated Donald Hebb to propose a mechanism for change at a synapse.

Hebb suggested that, when the axon of neuron A "repeatedly or persistently takes part in firing [cell B], some growth process or metabolic change takes place in one or both cells" that increases the subsequent ability of axon A to excite cell B (Hebb, 1949, p. 62). In other words, an axon that has successfully stimulated cell B in the past becomes even more successful in the future.

Consider how this relates to classical conditioning: Suppose that axon A initially excites cell B only slightly. However, if axon A often fires at the same time as some other axon, say axon C, the combined effect on B may be great, perhaps even producing an action potential. You might think of axon A as the CS and axon C as the UCS. The pairing of activity in axons A and C causes cell B to increase its responsiveness to A. Hebb was noncommittal about where the change occurred; the terminal of axon A might grow, the dendrites of cell B might grow, or a chemical change might occur in one or the other.

A synapse that increases in effectiveness because of simultaneous activity in the presynaptic and postsynaptic neurons is called a **Hebbian synapse.** In

Textbooks, this one included, talk mostly about "successful" research, the studies that led to our current understanding of a field. You may get the impression that science progresses in a smooth fashion, that each study leads to the next and that each investigator simply contributes to an ever-accumulating body of knowledge. However, if you ever look at the old journals or old textbooks in a field, you will find discussions of various "promising" or "exciting" findings that we disregard today. Scientific research does not progress in a straight line from ignorance to enlightenment; it explores one direction after another, a little like a rat in a complex maze, abandoning the arms that lead nowhere and pursuing those that lead further. Many "promising" lines of research turn out to be blind alleys.

The problem with the maze analogy is that an investigator seldom runs into a "wall" that clearly identifies the end of a route. Perhaps a better analogy is a prospector digging in one location after another, never entirely certain whether to abandon an unprofitable spot or whether to keep digging just a little longer. Many once-exciting lines of research in the physiology of learning are now of little more than historical interest. Here are three examples:

1. Wilder Penfield sometimes performed brain surgery for severe epilepsy on conscious patients who had only scalp anesthesia. When he applied a brief, weak electrical stimulus to part of the brain, the patient could describe the experience that the stimulation evoked. Stimulation of the temporal cortex sometimes evoked vivid descriptions such as:

I feel as though I were in the bathroom at school.

I see myself at the corner of Jacob and Washington in South Bend, Indiana.

I remember myself at the railroad station in Vanceburg, Kentucky; it is winter and the wind is blowing outside, and I am waiting for a train.

Penfield (1955; Penfield & Perot, 1963) suggested that each neuron in the temporal cortex stores a particular memory, almost like a videotape of one's life. However, we have several reasons to doubt that the brain stimulation actually evoked old memories. For example, stimulation very rarely evoked a memory of a specific event. More often, patients reported vague sights and sounds or repeated experiences such as "seeing a bed" or "hearing a choir sing 'White Christ-

mas.'" Stimulation almost never elicited memories of doing anything—just seeing and hearing. Also, some patients reported events that they had never actually experienced, such as being chased by a robber or seeing Christ descend from the sky. In short, the stimulation produced something more like a dream than an accurate memory.

2. G. A. Horridge (1962) apparently demonstrated that decapitated cockroaches can learn. First, he cut the connections between a cockroach's head and the rest of its body. Then he suspended the cockroach so that its legs dangled just above a surface of water. An electrical circuit was arranged as Figure 13.13 shows, so that the roach's leg would get a shock whenever it touched the water. Each experimental roach was paired with a control roach that got a leg shock whenever the first roach did; only the experimental roach had any control over the shock, however. (This kind of experiment is known as a "yoked-control" design.)

Over a period of 5 to 10 minutes, roaches in the experimental group "learned" a response of tucking the leg under the body to avoid shocks. Roaches in the control group did not, on the average, change their leg position during the training period. Thus, the changed response apparently qualifies as learning and not as some accidental by-product of the shocks.

These experiments initially seemed like a promising way of studying anatomical and chemical changes after learning has occurred in a very simple nervous system—in this case, a single cockroach ganglion (Eisenstein & Cohen, 1965). This is a case of looking for a needle in a very small haystack. Unfortunately, decapitated cockroaches learn slowly, and the results vary sharply from one individual to another, limiting the usefulness of the results. After a few studies in the 1960s and early 1970s, interest in this line of research faded.

3. In the 1960s and early 1970s, several investigators proposed that each memory is coded as a specific molecule, probably RNA or protein. The boldest test of that hypothesis was an attempt to transfer memories chemically from one individual to another. James McConnell (1962) reported that, when planaria (flatworms) cannibalized other planaria that had been classically conditioned to respond to a light, they apparently "remembered" what the cannibalized planaria had learned. (At least, they learned the response faster than planaria generally do.)

Continued on next page

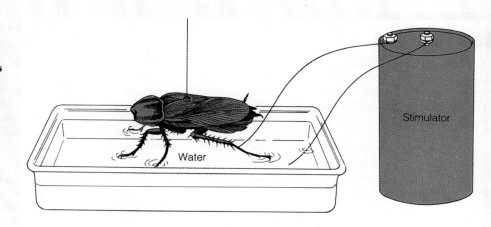

Figure 13.13 Apparatus for shocking a cockroach leg whenever it enters the water
A cockroach in the control group gets a shock whenever this roach does, regardless of the position of the control group roach's leg. (After Horridge, 1962.)

Inspired by that report, other investigators trained rats to approach a clicking sound for food (Babich, Jacobson, Bubash, & Jacobson, 1965). After the rats were well trained, the experimenters ground up the rats' brains, extracted RNA, and injected it into some untrained rats. The recipient rats learned to approach the clicking sound faster than rats in the control group did.

That report led to a sudden flurry of experiments on the transfer of training by brain extracts. In *some* of these experiments, rats that received brain extracts from a trained group showed apparent memory of the task, while those that received extracts from an untrained group did not (Dyal, 1971; Fjerdingstad, 1973).

The results were inconsistent and unreplicable, however, even within a single laboratory (L. T. Smith, 1975). Many laboratories failed to find any hint of a transfer effect. By the mid-1970s, most biological psychologists saw no point in continuing research in this area (Gaito, 1976).

Chapter 5, we encountered many examples of this type of synapse; in the development of the nervous system, postsynaptic neurons increase their responsiveness to combinations of axons that are active at the same time as one another (and therefore as the postsynaptic neuron). Such synapses may also be critical for many kinds of associative learning. Neuroscientists have discovered much about the mechanisms of Hebbian (or almost-Hebbian) synapses.

Single-Cell Mechanisms of Invertebrate Behavior Change

We could imagine many possible physiological mechanisms for learning and memory: changes in dendritic branching, changes in glia, increased or decreased release of some neurotransmitter, or development of new proteins within neurons, for example. If we are going to look for the proverbial needle in a haystack, a good strategy might be to look for a small haystack.

By that reasoning, many researchers have turned to studies of invertebrates. Certainly, the nervous system of an invertebrate is organized differently from that of a vertebrate; for example, many invertebrates have several widely separated ganglia instead of a single structure that we could call a "brain." But

Figure 13.14
***Aplysia*, a marine mollusc sometimes known as the sea hare**
A full-grown animal is a little larger than the human hand. (H. Chaumeton/ Nature.)

the general chemistry of the neuron, the principles of the action potential, and even many of the neurotransmitters are the same. (Many key neurotransmitters can be found in one-celled animals, although we do not know what they are doing there.) If we identify the physical basis of learning and memory in some invertebrate, we cannot assume that vertebrates use the same mechanism, but at least we have a good hypothesis of what *might* work. (Biologists have long used this strategy for studying genetics, embryology, and other biological processes.)

Aplysia as an Experimental Animal

Aplysia, a marine invertebrate related to the common slug, has become a particularly popular animal for studies of the physiology of learning (see Figure 13.14). *Aplysia* has fewer neurons than any vertebrate, and many of its neurons are rather large (up to 1 mm in diameter) and therefore easy to study. Moreover, unlike vertebrates, *Aplysia* has neurons that are recognizable and virtually identical from one individual to another. For example, after an experimenter identifies the properties of the *R2* cell in one specimen, other experimenters can find the same cell in their own animals and can carry the studies further or relate that neuron to other identified neurons. Vertebrates do not show the same kind of similarity from one individual to another.

Much of the research on *Aplysia* deals with changes in behavior as a result of experience. Some of those changes may seem simple, and it is a matter of definition whether we call these changes *learning* or use the broader term *plasticity*. One commonly studied behavior is the withdrawal response: If someone touches the siphon, mantle, or gill of an *Aplysia* (Figure 13.15), the animal vigorously withdraws the irritated structure. Investigators have traced the neural path from the touch receptors through various identifiable interneurons to the motor neurons that direct this withdrawal response. Using this neural pathway, investigators have studied such phenomena as habituation and sensitization.

Habituation in *Aplysia*

Habituation is a decrease in response to a stimulus that is presented repeatedly and accompanied by no change in other stimuli. For example, if your clock chimes hourly, you respond to it less and less after many repetitions.

Figure 13.15
Touch stimulation of an
***Aplysia's* mantle, siphon, or**
gill causes a withdrawal
response
The sensory and motor neu-
rons controlling this reac-
tion have been identified and
studied.

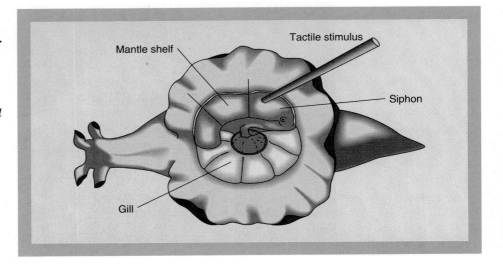

Habituation can be demonstrated in an *Aplysia* by repeatedly stimulating its gills with a brief jet of seawater. At first, it withdraws the gills, but after many repetitions it stops responding.

Several possible mechanisms of habituation can be eliminated. First, we can rule out muscle fatigue because, even after habituation has occurred, direct stimulation of the motor neuron produces a full-sized muscle contraction (Kupfermann, Castellucci, Pinsker, & Kandel, 1970). Second, habituation does not depend on a change in the firing rate of the sensory neuron. After repeated stimulation, the sensory neuron still gives a full, normal response to stimulation; it merely fails to excite the motor neuron as much as before (Kupfermann et al., 1970).

By process of elimination, we are left with the conclusion that habituation in *Aplysia* depends on a change in the synapse between the sensory neuron and the motor neuron (Figure 13.16). To determine the nature of that change, V. Castellucci and Eric Kandel (1974) measured the excitatory postsynaptic potentials (EPSPs) in the motor neuron during habituation. As habituation proceeded, the average size of the EPSP decreased, but each EPSP was still an integral multiple of the quantum of membrane response (as described in Chapter 3), which is presumably based on a quantum of neurotransmitter release. From this evidence, Castellucci and Kandel inferred that habituation reflects a decrease in transmitter release by the presynaptic cell.

Sensitization in *Aplysia*

After a strong electrical shock or any other intense stimulus, a person undergoes **sensitization,** becoming overresponsive to mild stimuli. Similarly, a strong noxious stimulus almost anywhere on *Aplysia's* surface can intensify later withdrawal responses to a touch on the siphon, mantle, or gill. Sensitization may last as briefly as a few seconds or as long as days, depending on the strength and repetition of the sensitizing stimulus.

As with habituation, sensitization in *Aplysia* depends on a change in the number of quanta of neurotransmitter that the presynaptic neuron releases (Dale, Schacher, & Kandel, 1988). The difference is that habituation reflects decreased release, while sensitization reflects increased release. Figure 13.17 diagrams the two relevant synapses: one between the sensory neuron and an interneuron and one between the sensory neuron and the motor neuron.

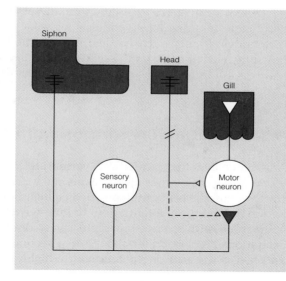

Figure 13.16
Habituation of the gill-withdrawal reflex in *Aplysia* apparently depends on decreased transmission at the synapse between the sensory neuron and the motor neuron
Stimulation at other locations, such as the head, can temporarily reexcite a habituated synapse. (After Castellucci et al., 1970.)

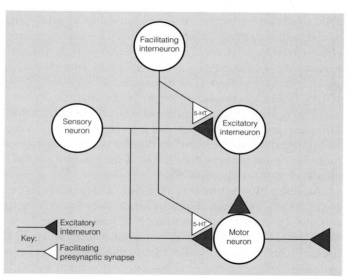

Figure 13.17
Sensitization of the withdrawal response in *Aplysia* depends on the release of serotonin (5-HT) at presynaptic synapses
(After Kandel & Schwartz, 1982.)

Researchers have described the mechanism of that change in some detail (Cleary, Hammer, & Byrne, 1989; Kandel & Schwartz, 1982).

Strong stimulation (of the head, tail, or elsewhere) excites a particular facilitating interneuron, which can be identified in any *Aplysia*. The facilitating interneuron has presynaptic synapses that release serotonin (5-HT) onto the synapses of many sensory neurons. Serotonin interacts with a metabotropic receptor in each sensory neuron, ultimately blocking potassium channels in the membrane. As you will recall from Chapter 2, potassium flows out of the neuron after the peak of the action potential; the exit of potassium restores the neuron to its usual polarization. When the cyclic AMP-dependent enzyme blocks the potassium channels, the net effect is to prolong the action potential and therefore to prolong transmitter release by the presynaptic cell.

If the sensitizing stimulus is repeated, the prolonged elevation of cyclic AMP in the sensory neuron leads to the production of new proteins responsible for long-term sensitization. Unlike the short-term variety, long-term potentiation depends on protein synthesis. Drugs that block protein synthesis can prevent it (Schacher, Castellucci, & Kandel, 1988).

Mechanisms of Storing Information in the Nervous System

The research on *Aplysia* shows us one set of mechanisms for behavior plasticity and therefore one hypothesis for what mechanisms we might find with vertebrates. It shows us that learning can be based on presynaptic changes. Learning need not rely on the same mechanisms in all situations in all species, however. Additional research may discover different mechanisms of learning.

Long-Term Potentiation in the Mammalian Brain

Are the cellular mechanisms of vertebrate learning similar to those of molluscs? If not, what other mechanisms can we find? Within the mammalian nervous system, the best candidate for a cellular basis of learning is a phenomenon known as long-term potentiation. In **long-term potentiation (LTP),** a neuron is bombarded with a brief but rapid series of stimuli—typically, 100 synaptic excitations per second for about 1 to 4 seconds. This burst of intense stimulation leaves the neuron "potentiated" (highly responsive to new input of the same type) for minutes, days, or weeks. LTP can result from repeated stimulation of a single synapse (like sensitization) or from nearly simultaneous stimulation of two or more synapses (more like conditioning). Generally, simultaneous stimulation of different synapses produces a stronger and more lasting effect than stimulation of a single synapse does; this is one reason why LTP is considered promising as a single-cell basis for associative learning.

LTP was first discovered in studies of hippocampal neurons (Bliss & Lømo, 1973). It can also occur in other parts of the nervous system, including the cerebral cortex, the amygdala, and the cerebellum. Many LTP experiments use **hippocampal slices,** sections of the hippocampus removed from the animal and maintained in a culture medium with various nutrients. Such a procedure makes it easier for investigators to stimulate and record from cells and test the effects of various chemicals.

At many hippocampal synapses, LTP depends on the activation of one type of glutamate receptors. The vertebrate nervous system has at least three major types of glutamate receptors, each of which comes in several subtypes (Nakanishi, 1992). One of the major types is known as an **NMDA receptor,** because the artificial chemical NMDA (*N*-methyl-D-aspartate) can stimulate this type of glutamate receptor and not the others (Cotman, Monaghan, & Ganong, 1988). The NMDA receptors are critical for LTP.

Glutamate at its non-NMDA receptors is an excitatory neurotransmitter, opening channels for sodium ions to enter the neuron. At the NMDA receptors, glutamate ordinarily produces no effect at all, being neither excitatory nor inhibitory. In this way, NMDA receptors are different from all the other synaptic receptors that we have encountered so far. The reason for the unresponsiveness of NMDA receptors is that their ion channel is blocked by magnesium ions, which do not pass through the channel but which nevertheless block the channel so that no other ions can pass through. The activation of NMDA receptors requires *both* the neurotransmitter glutamate (or, in the laboratory, a substitute such as NMDA) and the removal of those magnesium ions. (See Figure 13.18a.)

About the only way to activate the NMDA receptors is first to activate the nearby non-NMDA glutamate receptors repeatedly, thereby depolarizing the neuron. The depolarization repels the magnesium ions and enables glutamate to open the NMDA channels, through which both sodium and calcium ions enter (Figure 13.18b). The entry of calcium induces the expression of certain otherwise inactive genes (Bading, Ginty, & Greenberg, 1993); the activity of

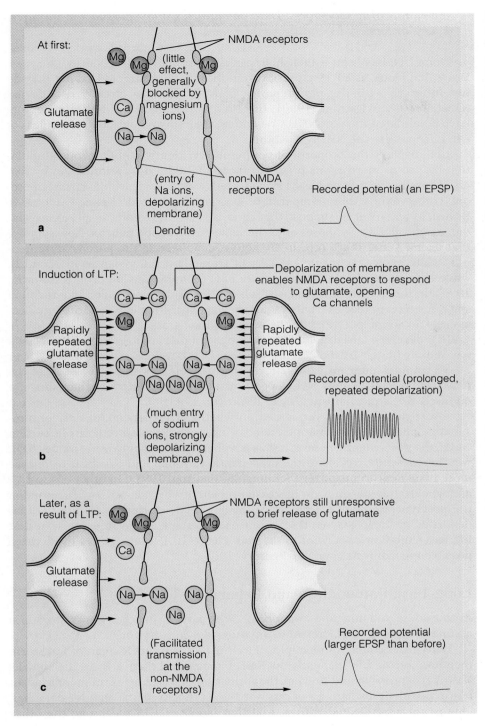

Figure 13.18
One possible arrangement for LTP
(*a*) *At first, glutamate stimulation moderately excites the postsynaptic neuron through the non-NMDA receptors. The nearby NMDA receptor is unresponsive.*
(*b*) *Then LTP is induced by rapidly repeated stimulation; stimulation by two glutamate axons produces more effect than one. This stimulation strongly depolarizes the membrane. Depolarization of the membrane alters the NMDA receptor, enabling glutamate to stimulate it. Thus, the NMDA receptor is effective only when the membrane is strongly depolarized.* (*c*) *After induction of LTP, transmission at non-NMDA receptors is facilitated. The exact mechanism of facilitation is not yet clear, but it probably includes increased release of glutamate, at least in many cases. Although the NMDA receptor was necessary for inducing LTP, it is not necessary for maintaining it. Once LTP is established, drug blockage of the NMDA receptors does not interfere with the facilitated response by the non-NMDA receptors.*

those genes facilitates the future responsiveness of the active non-NMDA receptors in the area (Figure 13.18c).

In short, when glutamate massively stimulates non-NMDA receptors, the resulting depolarization enables glutamate to stimulate nearby NMDA receptors, and stimulation of the NMDA receptors feeds back to potentiate

Mechanisms of Storing Information in the Nervous System

the non-NMDA receptors. That potentiation may persist for minutes, hours, or longer, depending on the synapse.

Once LTP has been established, it no longer depends on NMDA synapses. Drugs that block NMDA synapses prevent the *establishment* of LTP, but they do not interfere with the *maintenance* of LTP that was already established (Gustafsson & Wigström, 1990). In other words, once the NMDA receptors have potentiated the non-NMDA receptors, they stay potentiated, regardless of what happens to the NMDA receptors.

LTP displays the property of **cooperativity:** Nearly simultaneous stimulation by two or more axons produces more LTP than does stimulation by just one. This observation makes LTP an attractive model of learning. Furthermore, only those axons that "cooperated" become facilitated (Kelso, Ganong, & Brown, 1986). That is, suppose that three axons—A, B, and C—all release glutamate and all have synapses onto the same postsynaptic neuron. Now suppose that axons A and B are repeatedly active, depolarizing the postsynaptic neuron, while axon C is inactive. LTP will strengthen the synapses of A and B, while actually weakening the synapses of C (Sejnowski, Chattarji, & Stanton, 1990). In this regard, the synapses subject to LTP are very much like Hebbian synapses, except that LTP only requires a depolarization of a dendrite, not necessarily an action potential by the whole cell.

LTP develops fairly rapidly in the hippocampus but also begins to decay a few minutes later. In the cerebral cortex, LTP develops more gradually over 30–90 minutes after an experience, but then remains stable for at least the next few hours. LTP may well depend on a family of related mechanisms, not on just a single mechanism (Teyler & Grover, 1993).

Investigators are not yet agreed on whether LTP depends mostly on presynaptic changes, postsynaptic changes, or a combination of both. In certain cases, the postsynaptic neuron releases a chemical, probably nitric oxide (NO), which apparently travels to the presynaptic terminal and causes it to release more of its neurotransmitter (Schuman & Madison, 1991). In other cases, LTP almost certainly depends on increased sensitivity by non-NMDA receptors on the postsynaptic neuron (Baudry & Lynch, 1993). A third possibility is that dendrites of the postsynaptic neuron change their shape in some way that increases the flow of current to the cell. Figure 13.19 summarizes these three possible mechanisms (Lynch & Baudry, 1991).

Long-Term Potentiation and Behavior

At this point, you might be wondering, "Who cares?" In other words, how does an understanding of LTP relate to anything else in behavior?

Here are a couple of examples: First, if LTP is a mechanism of long-term memory, and if LTP depends on NMDA receptors, then a drug that blocks NMDA receptors should prevent the formation of new long-term memories. In one experiment, two groups of rats were given shocks in a distinctive chamber. One group was injected with a drug that blocks NMDA receptors; the other group was given a saline injection (NaCl in water). If tested immediately after the shocks, both groups showed a fear response in the test chamber. But if tested more than three minutes later, only the saline group showed any signs of fear. That is, the drug that blocked NMDA receptors had no effect on short-term memory, but it prevented the formation of a new long-term memory of the frightening experience (Kim, Fanselow, DeCola, & Landeira-Fernandez, 1992).

Second example: Recall from Chapter 6 that special kinds of visual experience can alter connections in the visual system only during a critical period of

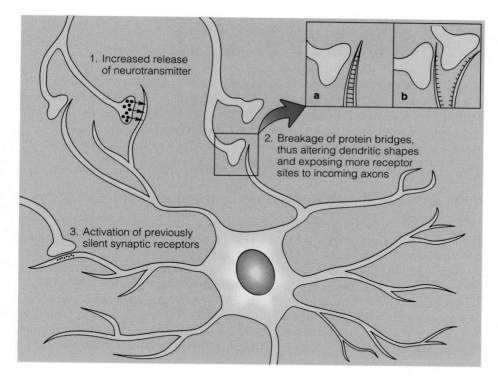

Figure 13.19
**Three possible mechanisms
of long-term potentiation**

1. Increased release
of neurotransmitter

2. Breakage of protein bridges,
thus altering dendritic shapes
and exposing more receptor
sites to incoming axons

3. Activation of previously
silent synaptic receptors

development. What ends that critical period? Apparently, the critical period depends on NMDA receptors, which are easier to excite in the visual areas of the brain during the critical period than they are afterwards (Carmignoto & Vicini, 1992). In one study, injecting a drug that blocks NMDA receptors blocked all effects of visual experience during the critical period (Klein-schmidt, Bear, & Singer, 1987). In another study, prolonged application of NMDA to an amphibian's brain toward the end of the critical period lengthened that period (Udin & Scherer, 1990). These results imply that the modification of synapses during the critical period depends on NMDA synapses; one can shorten the critical period by blocking those synapses or extend it by stimulating those synapses. Presumably, the normal critical period corresponds to a time when NMDA synapses are ordinarily easiest to stimulate.

A third example: Long-term potentiation depends on the entry of calcium ions into postsynaptic neurons. In aged mammals (presumably including humans), calcium channels apparently become somewhat "leaky," resulting in higher-than-normal resting levels of calcium within neurons. For that reason, calcium that enters during a train of stimuli may produce less effect in an older person than it would for a younger individual. In aged mammals, injections of magnesium (which competes with calcium) or of drugs that block calcium channels can enhance learning and memory (Deyo, Straube, & Disterhoft, 1989). Presumably, such treatments lower the resting calcium levels and therefore enhance the effects of calcium entering the cell during stimulation.

LTP is apparently an important contributor for many kinds of vertebrate learning, though probably not all. Drugs that block NMDA receptors prevent some kinds of learning, but have no effect on others (Willner, Gallagher, Graham, & Crooks, 1992). Even when LTP is most clearly necessary, we still have much to learn about how it relates to overall behavior. Certainly, understanding a facilitated synapse is a long way from understanding complex learned behaviors (Fanselow, 1993).

The Biochemistry of Learning and Memory

Studies of the single-cell basis of learning have attributed learning to increases in calcium within neurons, decreases in potassium flow, increased numbers of certain synaptic receptors, and other biochemical changes. Such findings suggest that learning impairments may result from chemical deficiencies in the brain and that certain drugs may impair or improve learning. Research on the biochemistry of learning has followed several routes.

Influence of Protein Synthesis on Learning and Memory

Proteins are an important building block of the body; to produce growth of an axon or dendrite, an increase or decrease in the production of a neurotransmitter, or an alteration of any receptor, protein synthesis is a necessary step. Protein synthesis is known to be critical for *Aplysia* learning and for LTP; both can be prevented by drugs that block protein synthesis.

Drugs that inhibit protein synthesis also impair the long-term storage of memory in rats, although they do not impair short-term retention (Davis & Squire, 1984). The more completely that a drug inhibits protein synthesis, the more completely it retards learning (Bennett, Rosenzweig, & Flood, 1979).

Acetylcholine Synapses and Memory

With the phenomenon of LTP, we have already encountered one neurotransmitter that participates in learning: glutamate. Another neurotransmitter that is important for learning is acetylcholine. For example, the degree of memory loss in old age correlates strongly with the decline in brain acetylcholine levels (Bartus, Dean, Beer, & Lippa, 1982; Davies, 1985).

In several experiments, young adult volunteers received injections of **scopolamine,** a drug that blocks acetylcholine synapses. While under the influence of the drug, they showed clear deficiencies on a variety of memory tasks. Their general pattern of performance resembled that of senile people; that is, they were impaired on the same memory tasks on which senile people have the greatest troubles (Beatty, Butters, & Janowsky, 1986; Drachman & Leavitt, 1974).

Given these results, the question arises, could we improve human memory by using physostigmine or other drugs that prolong the effects of acetylcholine at the synapses? Several studies have found that physostigmine does improve memory, especially in older people and others with poor memories (Davis, Mohs, Tinklenberg, Pfefferbaum, Hollister, & Kopell, 1978; Sitaram, Weingartner, & Gillin, 1978). Unfortunately, the required doses produce prominent, unwelcome side effects such as restlessness, sweating, diarrhea, and excessive salivation (Bartus et al., 1982). So such drug treatments are not clinically useful.

Researchers have also tried to increase acetylcholine production in the brain by providing dietary precursors, such as choline and lecithin. In numerous studies, these substances have been given to senile or brain-damaged people with serious memory failures. Unfortunately, they produced no apparent benefits (Bartus, Dean, Pontecorvo, & Flicker, 1985). Perhaps senility and other memory failures are associated with such a massive depletion of acetylcholine synapses that a slight rise in the availability of the neurotransmitter is ineffective.

Other Synapses and Memory

Besides glutamate and acetylcholine, several other neurotransmitters may be necessary for the expression of learned behaviors. In old age, memory deficits generally accompany a gradual decline in the brain's supply of norepinephrine, serotonin, and dopamine (Wong et al., 1984). Young monkeys suffer similar memory deficits after depletion of norepinephrine and dopamine from their prefrontal cortex. *Clonidine,* a drug that stimulates norepinephrine receptors, reverses these deficits (Arnsten & Goldman-Rakic, 1985a). Drugs that stimulate dopamine receptors have been shown to improve performance on a visual memory task even in healthy, young adult humans (Luciana, Depue, Arbisi, & Leon, 1992).

Chemical Modulators of Attention

Other neurotransmitters and neuromodulators may play a role in attention. The hormones ACTH and vasopressin improve the performance of rats on numerous learning tasks (Edelstein, 1981; Martinez, Jensen, & McGaugh, 1981; Messing & Sparber, 1985). Vasopressin also enhances the memory performance of senile people (Delwaide, Devoitille, & Ylieff, 1980). The brain metabolizes vasopressin to form the chemical AVP_{4-9}, which is more effective than vasopressin itself. AVP_{4-9} focuses the brain's attention on the dominant cues in the environment, as the following experiment illustrates (Bunsey, Kramer, Kesler, & Strupp, 1990):

Rats were confronted with two boxes; on each trial, one box contained some Froot Loops. One group of rats had to learn to choose the box with the correct covering on its sides; the box lid also varied but was irrelevant. Another group of rats had to choose the box with the correct lid; the side covering also varied but was irrelevant. So each rat had to pay attention to the correct stimulus (either sides or lids) and ignore the other stimulus. Figure 13.20 illustrates the situation.

Ordinarily, without drugs or any other treatments, rats learn this task faster when the sides are relevant than when the lids are relevant. That is, they evidently find it easier to pay attention to sides than to lids. In this experiment, an injection of AVP_{4-9} facilitated performance in the group for which the sides were relevant; it impaired performance in the group for which the lids were relevant. That is, AVP_{4-9} evidently focused the rats' attention even more strongly on the stimulus that they would have paid attention to anyway. If that was the relevant stimulus, the rats did well; if it was a distraction, the rats did poorly.

At this point, we can only speculate on the possible implications for humans. Note, however, that ideal performance requires a balance between the ability to focus attention and the ability to shift one's focus from time to time. Some people (such as autistic children) tend to focus their attention on a single stimulus and ignore other stimuli that might be important. Other people (such as those with schizophrenia or attention deficit disorder) are distracted too easily by extraneous ideas and stimuli.

As you have seen in this chapter, an investigator of the physiology of learning must deal with processes ranging from molecular changes to behavior. We cannot say simply that a particular drug or physiological change improves or impairs memory; we must specify the type of memory affected and the way it is affected. In the process, we stand to clarify our understanding, not only of the physiology, but also of memory itself.

*Mechanisms of Storing
Information in the
Nervous System*

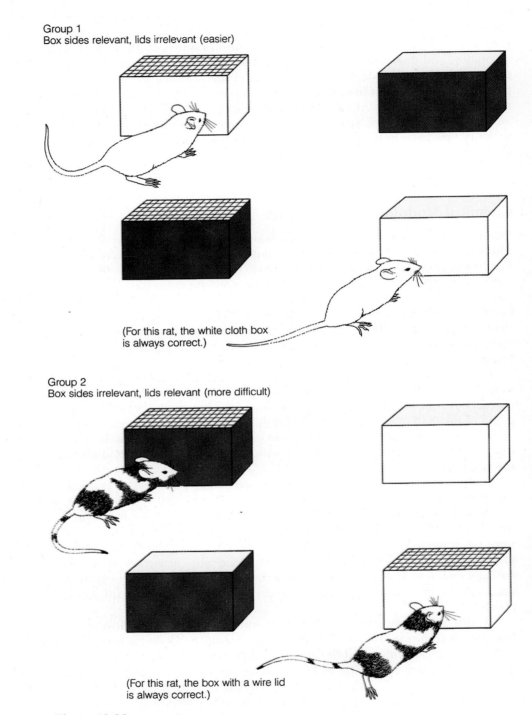

Group 1
Box sides relevant, lids irrelevant (easier)

(For this rat, the white cloth box is always correct.)

Group 2
Box sides irrelevant, lids relevant (more difficult)

(For this rat, the box with a wire lid is always correct.)

Figure 13.20
Procedure for an experiment on attention
For rats in one group, the side of the box is the relevant cue for where to find food, and the type of lid is irrelevant. For rats in the other group, the type of lid is the relevant cue, and the side of the box is irrelevant. The brain chemical AVP$_{4-9}$ enhanced performance when the side was the relevant cue but impaired performance when the lid was relevant. (Bunsey, Kramer, Kesler, & Strupp, 1990.)

Summary

1. A Hebbian or Hebb-type synapse is one that is strengthened if it is active at the same time that the postsynaptic neuron produces an action potential. Much research has sought to identify Hebbian synapses and to discover how they operate. (p. 472)

2. Habituation of the gill-withdrawal reflex in *Aplysia* depends on a mechanism that decreases the release of transmitter from a particular presynaptic neuron. (p. 475)

3. Sensitization of the gill-withdrawal reflex in *Aplysia* depends on the release of an enzyme that blocks potassium channels in a presynaptic neuron and thereby prolongs the release of transmitter from that neuron. (p. 476)

4. Long-term potentiation (LTP) is an enhancement of response at certain synapses because of a brief but intense series of stimuli delivered to a neuron. The effect is greatest when two or more axons stimulate a postsynaptic neuron simultaneously. LTP occurs in many brain areas and is particularly prominent in the hippocampus. (p. 478)

5. LTP in hippocampal neurons occurs as follows: Repeated glutamate excitation of non-NMDA receptors depolarizes the membrane. The depolarization removes magnesium ions that had been blocking NMDA receptors. Glutamate is then able to excite the NMDA receptors, opening a channel for calcium ions to enter the neuron. The calcium activates genes that produce long-term potentiation of the nearby non-NMDA receptors. (p. 478)

6. Drugs or other procedures that block NMDA receptors impair certain kinds of learning. (p. 480)

7. In addition to glutamate, several other transmitters, including acetylcholine, norepinephrine, and dopamine, also contribute to learning. Blockade of transmission at those synapses can impair certain kinds of learning and memory. (p. 482)

8. Certain other chemicals, including one derivative of the hormone vasopressin, alter the distribution of attention between the more-prominent and less-prominent stimuli in the environment. (p. 483)

Review Questions

1. How can a Hebbian synapse account for the basic phenomena of classical conditioning? (p. 472)

2. What are the advantages of research with *Aplysia* and other molluscs as compared with vertebrates? (p. 475)

3. Why do researchers believe that habituation and sensitization in *Aplysia* depend on presynaptic rather than postsynaptic changes? (p. 476)

4. What procedures produce LTP in the mammalian brain? (p. 478)

5. What is an NMDA synapse? Are NMDA synapses responsible for maintaining LTP after it is established? (p. 478)

6. What is "cooperativity" and how does it relate to LTP? (p. 480)

7. What are the possible mechanisms of LTP? (p. 480)

8. How can we explain the ability of magnesium ions to enhance certain kinds of memory in old age? (p. 481)

9. What evidence suggests an important role for acetylcholine in learning and memory? (p. 482)

10. What is the effect of the vasopressin derivative AVP_{4-9} on attention? (p. 483)

Thought Question

1. In one experiment (Castellucci & Kandel, 1974), habituation was attributed to a presynaptic change because the size of the quantum remained the same even though the size of the EPSP decreased. What conclusion, if any, could you draw if the size of the quantum decreased during habituation? Can you think of any other way to decide whether an alteration in EPSP size was due to presynaptic or postsynaptic changes?

Suggestions for Further Reading

Baudry, M., Thompson, R. F., & Davis, J. L. (Eds.) (1993). *Synaptic plasticity.* Cambridge, MA: MIT Press. A collection of articles on LTP and other cellular mechanisms of learning and memory.

Gustafsson, B., & Wigström, H. (1990). Basic features of long-term potentiation in the hippocampus. *Seminars in the Neurosciences, 2,* 321–333. Review of the main findings on LTP.

Terms

Hebbian synapse synapse that increases in effectiveness because of simultaneous activity in the presynaptic and postsynaptic neurons (p. 472)

habituation decrease in response to a stimulus that is presented repeatedly and that is accompanied by no change in other stimuli (p. 475)

sensitization increase in response to mild stimuli as a result of previous exposure to more intense stimuli (p. 476)

long-term potentiation (LTP) increased responsiveness to axonal input as a result of a previous period of rapidly repeated stimulation (p. 478)

hippocampal slice section of hippocampus removed from an animal and maintained in a culture medium (p. 478)

NMDA receptor glutamate receptor that also responds to N-methyl-D-aspartate (p. 478)

cooperativity tendency for nearly simultaneous stimulation by two or more axons to produce more LTP than stimulation by just one (p. 480)

scopolamine drug that blocks acetylcholine synapses (p. 482)

AVP_{4-9} metabolite of vasopressin that has been found to enhance attention toward the dominant cues in the environment (p. 483)

LATERALIZATION
AND LANGUAGE

Telegraph Colour Library/FPG

CHAPTER FOURTEEN

1. The left and right hemispheres of the brain communicate through the corpus callosum. After damage to the corpus callosum, each hemisphere has access to information only from the opposite half of the body and the opposite visual field.

2. In most people, the left hemisphere is specialized for language and "analytical" processing. The right hemisphere is specialized for certain complex visual-spatial tasks and "synthetic" processing.

3. The human brain is specialized for language, although its specializations are not altogether new features, but instead are elaborations of features that are present in other primates.

4. Abnormalities of the left hemisphere can lead to a variety of specific language impairments.

The human brain consists of neurons numbering in at least the tens of billions. Each of those neurons contributes to behavior and experience in its own specialized way. Yet each of us experiences the self as a unity, not a conglomerate of separate voices. Although your brain parts are many, your consciousness is one.

That unity of consciousness comes about through the connections between various brain parts. What happens if major connections are broken? In that case, although different parts of the brain continue their activities, they become unable to communicate with one another. When such disconnections occur in humans, they offer fascinating clues about how the brain operates and raise equally fascinating questions.

Lateralization of Function and the Corpus Callosum

The left hemisphere of the cerebral cortex is connected to skin receptors mainly in the right half of the body, and it has the main control of muscles on the right side of the body. It sees only the right half of the world. The right hemisphere is connected to sensory receptors mainly on the left half of the body and controls muscles on the left side. It sees only the left half of the world.

Each hemisphere has limited sensory input and motor control on its own side of the body. The degree of ipsilateral control (control of the same side of the body) varies from one individual to another. *Why* humans and all other vertebrates evolved so that each hemisphere controls the contralateral side of the body, instead of the ipsilateral side, no one knows.

Ordinarily, the left and right hemispheres exchange information through a set of axons called the **corpus callosum** (Figure 14.1; see also Figures 4.11 and 4.12) and through the smaller anterior commissure and hippocampal commissure. Within 7 to 13 milliseconds, the information that initially entered one hemisphere crosses also to the opposite hemisphere (Saron & Davidson, 1989).

The two hemispheres are not simply mirror images of each other. In most humans, the left hemisphere is specialized for the control of language. The right hemisphere has some functions that are more difficult to summarize, as we shall see later in this chapter. Such division of labor between the two hemispheres is known as **lateralization.** If it were not for the corpus callosum, your left hemisphere could talk only about the information from the right side of your body, and your right hemisphere could perform its functions only on the information from the left side of your body. Because of the corpus callosum, however, each hemisphere deals with the information from both sides of the body. Only after damage to the corpus callosum (or to one hemisphere or the other) do we see the effects of lateralization.

Before we can discuss lateralization in any detail, we must consider some background material concerning the connections from the eyes to the brain. The connections from the left and right eyes to the left and right hemispheres are more complex than you might expect.

Connections of the Eyes to the Brain's Left and Right Hemispheres

Each hemisphere is also connected to the eyes in such a way that it gets input from the opposite half of the visual world; that is, the left hemisphere sees the right side of the world and the right hemisphere sees the left side of the world. For rabbits and other species that have the left eye facing the left side of the world and the right eye facing the right side of the world, the connections from

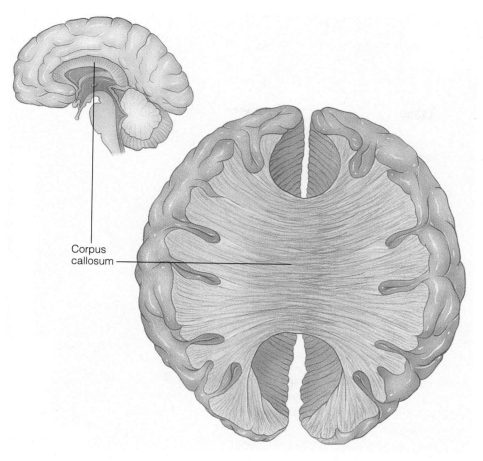

Figure 14.1
Two views of the corpus callosum, a large set of axons conveying information between the two hemispheres
Left: A sagittal section through the human brain. Right: A dissection (viewed from above) in which gray matter has been removed to expose the corpus callosum.

Corpus callosum

eye to brain are easy to describe: The left eye connects to the right hemisphere, and the right eye connects to the left hemisphere. **Your *eyes are not connected to the brain in that way.* Both of your eyes face forward. You can see the left side of the world almost as well with your right eye as you can with your left eye.

Imagine how the eyes would be connected to the brain in a cyclops—the mythical giant with just one eye, located in the middle of its forehead. Presume that, like all other vertebrates, its left hemisphere sees the right half of the world and its right hemisphere sees the left half of the world. In Figure 14.2, note that light from the left half of the world passes through the pupil to strike the right half of the cyclops's eye and that light from the right half of the world strikes the left half of the cyclops's eye. Then the information goes from the left half of the retina to the left half of the brain and from the right half of the retina to the right half of the brain.

Each human eye is located in the front of the head, like the eye of a cyclops. Each of your eyes sends its information to the brain in the same way that the cyclops's eye does. That is, you have two cyclopean eyes.

Figure 14.3 illustrates the connections from the eyes to the human brain. Vision starts with stimulation of the receptors that line the *retina* on the back of each eye. Light from the **visual field**—the part of the world visible to the eyes at a particular moment—enters the eyes; light from the right visual field shines onto the left half of both retinas, and light from the left visual field shines onto the right half of both retinas. The left half of *each* retina connects to the left hemisphere; thus, the left hemisphere sees the right visual field.

Figure 14.2
Connections from the eye to the brain in a mythical being, the cyclops

Notice that the left half of the eye sees the right half of the world and sends its information to the left half of the brain. The right half of the eye sees the left half of the world and sends its information to the right half of the brain. Human eyes are connected to the brain in this same manner, except that we have two such eyes.

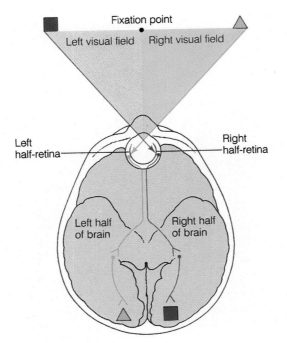

Similarly, the right half of each retina connects to the right hemisphere, which sees the left visual field. (If you have trouble remembering all this, recall that each human eye connects the same way as does the cyclops's eye.) A small vertical strip down the center of each retina, covering about 5 degrees of visual arc, connects to both hemispheres (Innocenti, 1980). In Figure 14.3, note how half of the axons from each eye cross to the opposite side of the brain at the **optic chiasm** (literally, the "optic cross").

Information about each visual field projects to just one side of the cerebral cortex. The auditory system handles information differently. Although each ear receives sound waves from just one side of the head, it sends input to both sides of the brain, though somewhat more strongly to the opposite side. (The reason for this is that people locate sounds in space by comparing the input from the two ears. Any part of the brain that contributes to localizing sounds must receive input from both ears.)

Effects of Cutting the Corpus Callosum

Damage to the corpus callosum blocks the exchange of information between the two hemispheres. A few people have had their corpus callosum cut as a therapy for severe epilepsy. (See Digression 14.1.) Epilepsy can usually be treated with drugs, but some rare individuals fail to respond to any of the antiepileptic drugs. If their seizures are so severe and so frequent as to be incapacitating, they and their attending physicians may be willing to try almost anything to relieve the epilepsy. In certain cases, surgeons have cut the corpus callosum in hopes of preventing epileptic seizures from crossing from one hemisphere to the other, so that, when seizures do occur, they will be less severe because they will affect only half the body. In fact, the operation has generally relieved the epilepsy better than anyone had initially expected. Not

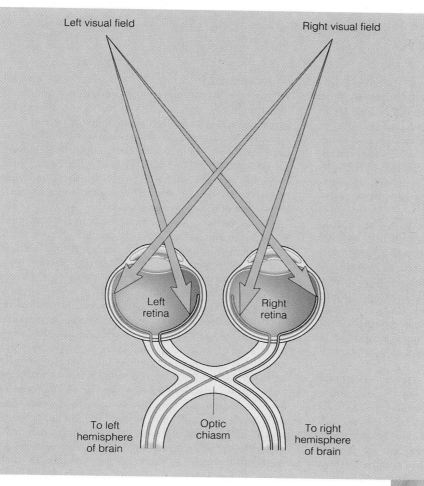

a

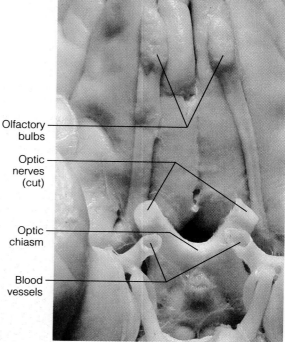

b

Figure 14.3
(*a*) *Route of visual input to the two hemispheres of the brain. Note that the left hemisphere is connected to the left half of each retina and thus gets visual input from the right half of the world, while the opposite occurs with the right hemisphere.* (*b*) *Close-up of olfactory bulbs and the optic chiasm. At the optic chiasm, axons from the right half of the left retina cross to the right hemisphere, and axons from the left half of the right retina cross to the left hemisphere. (Photo courtesy of Dr. Dana Copeland.)*

491

Epilepsy is a condition in which brain neurons have repeated episodes of excessive, synchronized activity and possibly also periods of excessive inhibition (Aird, Masland, & Woodbury, 1984; Pincus & Tucker, 1985). Epilepsy can result from a variety of causes, including genetics, birth injury or other trauma, infection to the brain, exposure to toxic substances, and brain tumors. Epilepsy of genetic origin is likely to begin during childhood or adolescence. Epilepsy of other causes can begin at any age.

Epilepsy can produce a variety of symptoms, depending on which parts of the brain are affected and for how long. Two general categories of epilepsy are *generalized seizures* and *partial seizures*. A **generalized seizure** spreads quickly across neurons over a large portion of both hemispheres of the brain. In the most spectacular form of generalized seizure, a **grand mal seizure,** the person makes sudden, repetitive jerking movements of the head and limbs for a period of seconds or minutes and then collapses in a state of exhaustion and sleep.

In another kind of generalized seizure, a **petit mal seizure** (or *absence seizure*), the person stares, unresponsive to the environment, for a period generally no longer than 15 to 20 seconds. He or she makes no sudden movements, except perhaps for eye blinking or a drooping of the head. Other people who are present may not even be aware of the seizure, and the affected person may not be either. The person may, however, report some confusion and a lack of memory for what just happened.

In contrast to a generalized seizure, a **partial seizure** begins in a **focus** somewhere in the brain and then spreads to nearby areas in just one hemisphere. Depending on the location of the focus, a person with a partial seizure may experience a variety of sensations or involuntary movements, such as a tingling sensation in a hand or a shaking of a leg. Sometimes the effect spreads, such as a twitch starting in a finger and moving up the arm. The person remains conscious but may become confused.

If the focus of a partial seizure is in the temporal lobe, the result is known as a *partial seizure with complex symptomatology* or a *temporal lobe seizure* or a *psychomotor seizure.* Such seizures produce only slight movements, such as lip smacking or chewing, but can lead to complex psychological states, including anxiety, aggression, laughter, repetitive thoughts, dreamlike hallucinations, or a déjà vu experience.

Over the years, medical researchers have accumulated a large array of antiepileptic drugs, which act mostly by blocking sodium flow across the membrane or by enhancing the effects of GABA (an inhibitory transmitter) at its synapses. More than 90 percent of epileptic patients respond well enough to drugs that they can live a reasonably normal life. Some suffer no more problem than the necessity of taking a daily pill. A few, however, continue having frequent seizures in spite of all possible combinations of drugs. In such cases, if the seizure begins at a clearly localizable focus, physicians sometimes remove the focus surgically. Surgery is, however, the method of last resort.

only are the seizures limited to one side of the body, but they also occur less often than before the operation.

How does severing the corpus callosum affect other aspects of behavior? The surgeons who conducted the operations had some idea of what to expect, based on studies with nonhuman animals. Following damage to the corpus callosum, laboratory animals show normal sensation, control of movement, learning and memory, and motivated behaviors. Their responses are abnormal only when sensory stimuli are limited to one side of the body. For example, if they see something in the left visual field, they can reach out to it only with the left forepaw. If they learn to do something with the left forepaw, they cannot do the same thing with the right forepaw, unless they learn the skill all over again with that paw and the left hemisphere (Sperry, 1961).

People who have undergone damage to the corpus callosum show similar tendencies. They can still walk, swim, and carry on other motor activities that use both sides of the body, although their coordination is sometimes slow and

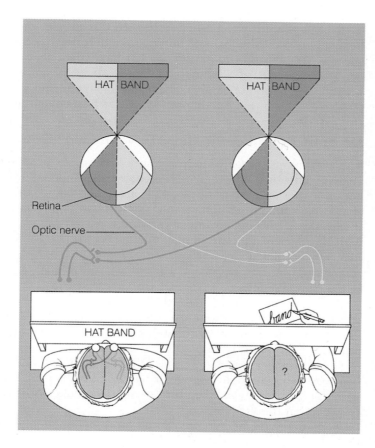

Figure 14.4
Demonstration of the effects of damage to the corpus callosum
When the word hatband *is flashed on a screen, a woman with a split brain can report only what her left hemisphere saw,* band. *However, with her left hand, she can point to a hat, which is what the right hemisphere saw.*

awkward (Zaidel & Sperry, 1977). They suffer little or no impairment of overall intellectual performance, motivation, emotion, or language. However, careful experiments by Roger Sperry and his students (Nebes, 1974) revealed subtle behavioral effects when stimuli were limited to one side of the body or the other.

In one typical experiment, a split-brain patient stared straight ahead as pictures were flashed on the left side of a screen (see Figure 14.4). When the corpus callosum is destroyed, any information that enters one hemisphere cannot pass to the other. Thus, the information went only to the right hemisphere. The picture stayed on the screen long enough for the person to see it clearly in the left visual field but not long enough for the person to move his or her eyes to bring the picture into the other visual field.

The experimenter then told the person (both hemispheres could hear the instructions) to put one hand behind a cloth curtain, to feel the ten or so objects behind the curtain, and to hold up the object that had just been shown on the screen. Split-brain patients consistently performed correctly if permitted to use their left hand (controlled by the right hemisphere, which saw the display on the screen). But if they were told to use their right hand, accuracy fell to the chance level. When the experimenter flashed the display on the right side of the screen, the right hand performed correctly and the left hand failed.

For most people, the ability to speak depends on the left hemisphere of the cerebral cortex. In split-brain people, when a display was flashed in the right visual field, thus going to the left hemisphere, the person could name the object easily. But when it was flashed in the left visual field, thus going to the right hemisphere, the person could not name or describe the object, although he or she was able to point to it with the left hand. The person could even say, "I don't know what it is," while simultaneously pointing to the correct choice with the left hand. (Of course, a split-brain person who watched the left hand pick up an object in the center or right visual field could then name the object.)

Do Split-Brain People Have Two Minds or One?

The two hemispheres of a split-brain person can process information and answer questions independently of each other. Indeed, they seem at times to act as if they are separate people sharing one body. One split-brain person sometimes found himself buttoning his shirt with one hand while unbuttoning it with the other hand. Another split-brain person would pick up a newspaper with the right hand, only to have the left hand (controlled by the less verbal hemisphere) put it down. Repeatedly, the right hand picked it up; an equal number of times, the left hand put it down, until finally the left hand threw it to the floor (Preilowski, 1975).

One split-brain person described his experience—or, rather, his left hemisphere described his experience—as follows (Dimond, 1979): "If I'm reading, I can hold the book in my right hand; it's a lot easier to sit on my left hand, than to hold it with both hands. . . . You tell your hand—I'm going to turn so many pages in a book—turn three pages—then somehow the left hand will pick up two pages and you're at page 5, or whatever. It's better to let it go, pick it up with the right hand, and then turn to the right page. With your right hand, you correct what the left has done."

Such conflicts are reported to be more common soon after surgery than they are later. The corpus callosum does not grow back; however, the brain learns to use certain subcortical connections between the left and right halves of the brain (Myers & Sperry, 1985). Also, the hemispheres gradually find ways to cooperate with each other, sometimes in surprising ways. One split-brain person who was being tested with the standard apparatus shown in Figure 14.4 suddenly seemed able to name what he saw in either visual field. However, the right hemisphere could answer correctly only when the answers were restricted to two possibilities (such as yes/no or true/false) and only when the subject was allowed to correct himself immediately after making a guess. Suppose that something was flashed in the left visual field. The experimenter might ask, "Was it a letter of the alphabet?" The left (speaking) hemisphere would take a guess: "Yes." If that was correct, the person would get credit for a correct answer. But if the left hemisphere guessed incorrectly, the right hemisphere, which saw the display on the screen and heard the left hemisphere's guess, knew that the guess was wrong. The right hemisphere would then make the face frown. (Both hemispheres can control facial muscles on both sides of the face.) The left hemisphere, feeling the frown, would say, "Oh, I'm sorry, I meant no." If such corrections are permitted, split-brain patients can guess the correct answers consistently.

Does the split-brain person have one mind or two? Investigators are not in complete agreement, and the question is complicated by our inability to say exactly what we mean by *mind*. But apparently each hemisphere can answer certain questions on its own, and the two hemispheres sometimes exchange information by facial signals or other means that two separate people might use for communication. Thus, the two hemispheres of a split-brain person seem to be at least partly independent.

Functions of the Right Hemisphere of the Cerebral Cortex

When investigators discovered that the left hemisphere controls speech, many of them thought of the right hemisphere as something like a vice president. That is, it supported the left, "major" hemisphere in various ways but was definitely subordinate to it. Later studies, including some with split-brain patients, have indicated that the right hemisphere is capable of more than researchers had assumed.

First, although it usually cannot control speech or writing, the right hemisphere does understand simple speech and, to a more limited extent, understands some written words (Levy, 1983). A split-brain person who hears a verbal description of an object can feel some objects with the left hand (right hemisphere) and pick up the described object. In a few split-brain patients, the left hand can write or can arrange letter blocks to describe information known only by the right hemisphere (Gazzaniga, LeDoux, & Wilson, 1977; Levy, Nebes, & Sperry, 1971).

In people with an intact, healthy brain, the right hemisphere is less active than the left hemisphere during speech (Papanicolaou, Moore, Deutsch, Levin, & Eisenberg, 1988). However, it contributes to the emotional content of speech. People who have suffered damage to the right hemisphere speak with less than the normal amount of inflection and expression (Shapiro & Danly, 1985). They also have trouble interpreting the emotions that other people express through their tone of voice (Tucker, 1981). And they may fail to appreciate humor and irony in speech.

The right hemisphere may be more specialized for emotional expression in general than the left hemisphere is. After damage to the right hemisphere, people have some trouble both in producing facial expressions of emotion and in understanding other people's facial expressions (Borod, Koff, Lorch, & Nicholas, 1986; Kolb & Taylor, 1981; Rinn, 1984). Moreover, according to the studies of Jerre Levy and her colleagues on normal (brain-intact) people, when the left and right hemispheres perceive different emotions in someone's face, the response of the right hemisphere dominates. For example, examine the faces in Figure 14.5. Each of these was made by combining half of a smiling face with half of a neutral face. Which face looks happier to you: face A or face B? Most people choose face A, the one with the smile on the viewer's left (Heller & Levy, 1981; Hoptman & Levy, 1988). Similarly, a frown on the viewer's left looks sadder than a frown on the viewer's right (Sackeim, Putz, Vingiano, Coleman, & McElhiney, 1988).

The right hemisphere also appears to be more adept than the left hemisphere at recognizing and dealing with complex visual patterns. For example, one young woman, after suffering damage to her posterior right hemisphere as a result of a tumor, had great trouble finding her way through a building or finding her way around town, even in familiar areas. To reach a destination, she had to follow directions that listed specific visual details, such as, "Walk to the corner where you see a building with a statue in front of it. Then turn left and go to the corner that has a flagpole and turn right...." Each of these directions had to include an unmistakable feature; if the instruction said "go to the city government building—that's the one with a tower," she could easily make a mistake and go to some other, very different building that happened to have a tower (Clarke, Assal, & deTribolet, 1993).

Split-brain patients have given us additional information about the specialized functions of the right hemisphere. For example, a split-brain person can

Figure 14.5
Two faces made by combining half of a smiling face with half of a neutral face
Which one looks happier to you? Your answer may suggest which hemisphere of your brain is dominant for interpreting emotional expressions. (From Levy et al., 1983.)

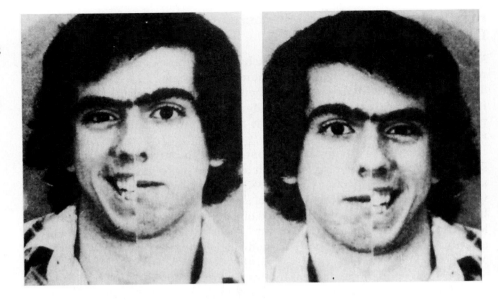

arrange puzzle pieces more accurately with the left hand than with the right. Although the person's right hand can write words much better than the left, the left hand does better at drawing a box, a bicycle, and similar objects.

The right hemisphere is not necessary for *all* visual and spatial tasks, however. In one study, stroke patients who had suffered damage to the right hemisphere performed about as well as normal people did at estimating the positions of nine major cities on an outline map of the United States. They were also as good as normal people were at estimating the distances between points on a sheet of paper. Their impairment became apparent when they had to combine these tasks by imagining the positions of those same nine cities and estimating the distances between them (Morrow, Ratcliff, & Johnston, 1986). Evidently, the right hemisphere is more essential for tasks that require internal representations of visual and spatial information—visual imagination, we might say.

How can we best describe the difference in functions between the left and right hemispheres? It is partly, but not entirely, correct to say that the left hemisphere is specialized for language and the right hemisphere for complex visual functions, spatial functions, and certain aspects of emotions. For example, most people can identify a melody more easily when listening with the left ear (right hemisphere) than when listening with the right ear. Professional musicians, however, can identify melodies better when listening with the right ear, suggesting that they process the music primarily in the left hemisphere (Shanon, 1980). Evidently, what the left hemisphere does best extends to some other tasks besides language. According to John Bradshaw and Norman Nettleton (1981), the left hemisphere is sequential, analytic, and time dependent. That is, regardless of whether it is dealing with speech, music, or visual stimuli, the left hemisphere treats the stimuli as a sequence of units. The right hemisphere, in contrast, is "synthetic" and "holistic," by which Bradshaw and Nettleton mean that it deals with overall patterns instead of breaking them into units. Unfortunately, this description of the left and right hemispheres may be too vague to be useful (Zaidel, 1983). Describing exactly how the left and right hemispheres differ remains difficult.

Evidence for Hemispheric Specializations in Intact People

Although the differences between the two hemispheres are more apparent after damage to the corpus callosum, certain differences can be demonstrated even in a person without brain damage. These differences are, however, generally so small and inconsistent that they emerge only as statistical trends with a large number of people.

Here is a demonstration that you can try yourself: Count how many times a child can tap the index finger of one hand within 1 minute; then repeat with the other hand. Now repeat the measurements while the child taps a finger and talks at the same time. For most right-handers, talking decreases the tapping rate with the right hand more than it does with the left hand (Kinsbourne & McMurray, 1975). Evidently, it is more difficult to do two things at once if both activities depend on the same hemisphere. (Adults may tap too fast for you to count the taps accurately. Have the person tap with a pencil on a piece of paper; later you can count the markings. Or you could ask people to tap a key on a computer and program the computer to count the taps.)

Hemispheric Differences and Cognitive Style

Occasionally, you may hear someone say something like "I don't do well in science courses because those are left-brain courses and I am a right-brain person." That kind of statement is based on two reasonable scientific premises and one doubtful assumption. The scientific premises are that (1) the left hemisphere is specialized for verbal or analytic processing and the right hemisphere is specialized for nonverbal or synthetic processing and (2) certain tasks evoke greater activity in one hemisphere than in the other. The doubtful assumption is that a given individual relies consistently on one hemisphere or the other, regardless of the task or situation.

That assumption is at best a great overstatement. Granted, the left hemisphere may be more active for some tasks and the right hemisphere may be more active for other tasks, but on any task a normal person uses both hemispheres. Furthermore, the relative balance of activity varies from time to time and from task to task. A person will rely mostly on the right hemisphere at one time and mostly on the left hemisphere at another time.

Finally, what evidence do you suppose a person has for a statement like "I do poorly in science courses because I am a right-brain person"? Did the person undergo a CT scan or PET scan to determine that the right hemisphere was larger than the left, or that it had a higher metabolic rate? Not likely. Generally, when people say "I am right-brained," all they mean is that they perform better on creative tasks than on logical tasks. Therefore, the statement really boils down to "I do poorly in science courses because I do poorly in science courses."

Development of Lateralization and its Relationship to Handedness

Because in most people language depends primarily on the left hemisphere, it is natural to ask whether the left hemisphere is anatomically different from the right. If so, is this difference present before speech develops, or is it a result of

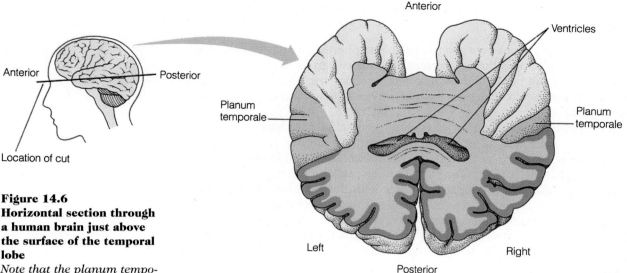

Anterior

Ventricles

Anterior

Posterior

Location of cut

Planum temporale

Planum temporale

Left

Right

Posterior

Figure 14.6
Horizontal section through a human brain just above the surface of the temporal lobe

Note that the planum temporale, an area that is critical for speech comprehension, is substantially larger in the left hemisphere than in the right hemisphere. (From Geschwind & Levitsky, 1968.)

speech? What is the relationship between handedness and hemispheric dominance for speech?

Anatomical Differences between the Hemispheres

For many years, biological psychologists believed that the left and right hemispheres were anatomically the same, in spite of their differences in action. Then Norman Geschwind and Walter Levitsky (1968) reported that one section of the temporal cortex, called the **planum temporale** (PLAY-num tem-poh-RAH-lee), is larger in the left than in the right hemisphere for 65 percent of people (Figure 14.6). The size is about equal for 24 percent and larger in the right hemisphere for 11 percent. The size differences for this area are reasonably large; in fact, they are visible to the naked eye if one knows where to look. The planum temporale includes areas important for language.

The planum temporale is evidently larger in the left than in the right hemisphere even before language develops. Sandra Witelson and Wazir Pallie (1973) examined the brains of 14 infants who had died before the age of 3 months. In 12 of the 14, the planum temporale was larger in the left than in the right hemisphere—on the average, about twice as large. Children who suffer brain damage during their first 4 years of life show more language impairment after left-hemisphere damage than after right-hemisphere damage (Aram & Ekelman, 1986).

One convenient indicator of the size of the planum temporale is the length of the **Sylvian,** or **lateral, fissure** (one of the major fissures, or folds, on the side of the cortex). In humans, the Sylvian fissure is 14 percent larger on the left side than on the right, on the average. Figure 14.12, later in this chapter, shows this fissure (p. 510). In chimpanzees, the fissure is only 5 percent larger on the left side; in monkeys, the two sides are practically equal (Yeni-Komshian & Benson, 1976).

Maturation of the Corpus Callosum

The corpus callosum matures gradually over the first 5 to 10 years of human life, making it one of the last brain structures to reach maturity (Trevarthen,

1974). The developmental process is not so much a matter of growing new axons, however, as it is of selecting certain axons and discarding others.

At an early stage of development, the brain generates far more axons in the corpus callosum than it will have at maturity (Ivy & Killackey, 1981; Killackey & Chalupa, 1986). The reason for this is that any two neurons connected via the corpus callosum need to have corresponding functions. For example, suppose that a given neuron in the occipital cortex of the left hemisphere responds to light in the very center of the retina. It should be connected to a right-hemisphere neuron that responds to light in that same location. During early embryonic development, the genes cannot specify exactly where those two neurons will be. Therefore, a great many connections are made across the corpus callosum, but only those axons that happen to connect very similar cells survive (Innocenti & Caminiti, 1980).

But how does a neuron "know" that it is connected to another neuron with properties similar to its own? Apparently, a neuron recognizes whether the input from the other neuron is synchronized with its own activity. Cats ordinarily have a certain number of connections across the corpus callosum to link the visual areas of the brain. If either or both eyelids are sewn shut for the first 3 months of life, they develop fewer than the normal number of axons across the corpus callosum. The same result occurs if their eye muscles are damaged early in life so they cannot focus both eyes in the same direction at the same time (Innocenti, Frost, & Illes, 1985). In other words, experience sharpens the selection of axons across the corpus callosum, enabling the right axons to survive. Abnormal experiences cause a reduction in the number of axons.

Because the connections across the human corpus callosum take years to develop their mature adult pattern, the behavior of young children resembles that of split-brain adults in some situations. A 9-week-old infant who has one arm restrained will never reach across the midline of the body to pick up a toy on the other side (Provine & Westerman, 1979). Apparently, at that age, each hemisphere has little access to the sensory information or motor control of the opposite hemisphere. By age 17 weeks, however, infants will reach across the midline to pick up a toy more often than not.

In one study, 3- and 5-year-old children were asked to feel two fabrics, either with the same hand or with the opposite hand, and say whether they were the same or different kinds of material. The 5-year-olds did equally well with one hand or with two. The 3-year-olds made 90 percent more errors with the opposite hand than with the same hand (Galin, Johnstone, Nakell, & Herron, 1979). The likely interpretation is that the corpus callosum matures sufficiently between ages 3 and 5 to make the comparison of stimuli across the two hands much easier by age 5.

Development without a Corpus Callosum

Rarely, the corpus callosum fails to form. The problem may be genetic or perhaps a toxin to which the mother was exposed during pregnancy. Whatever the cause, a person born without a corpus callosum develops differently from other people and is in many ways different from a person who once had a corpus callosum and then lost it in split-brain surgery (Chiarello, 1980).

People born without a corpus callosum can perform some tasks that split-brain patients fail. They can verbally describe what they feel with either hand or what they see in either visual field; they can also feel one object with the left hand and another with the right hand and say whether they are the same or different (Bruyer et al., 1985; Sanders, 1989).

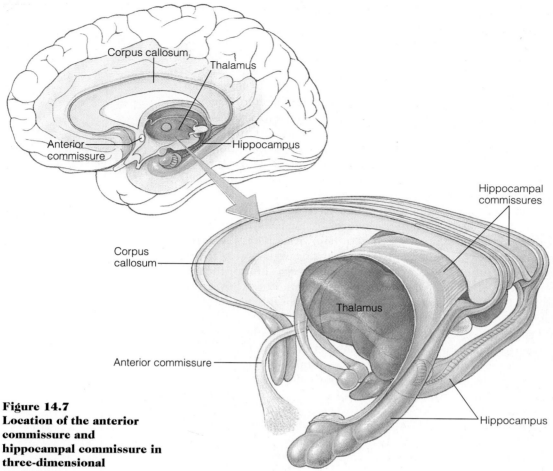

Corpus callosum

Thalamus

Anterior commissure

Hippocampus

Hippocampal commissures

Corpus callosum

Thalamus

Anterior commissure

Hippocampus

Figure 14.7
Location of the anterior commissure and hippocampal commissure in three-dimensional perspective
These commissures exchange information between the two hemispheres, as does the larger corpus callosum. (Based on Nieuwenhuys, 1988, and others.)

How do people born without a corpus callosum manage to perform tasks that usually require a corpus callosum? One possible explanation is that each hemisphere develops speech; thus, the left hemisphere describes what the right hand feels, and the right hemisphere describes what the left hand feels. However, the available evidence argues against any right-hemisphere speech in these people (Lassonde, Bryden, & Demers, 1990). A second possible explanation is that each hemisphere develops pathways connecting it to both sides of the body. Thus, the left (speaking) hemisphere could feel both the left hand and the right hand. A third possibility is that people born without a corpus callosum develop larger-than-normal connections elsewhere in the brain. In addition to the corpus callosum, people have two other major axonal connections in the forebrain: The **anterior commissure** connects the hemispheres in the anterior part of the cerebral cortex, and the **hippocampal commissure** connects the left hippocampus to the right hippocampus (Figure 14.7). In most people, these commissures do not convey enough information to enable the left hemisphere to describe what the right hemisphere sees or feels. But perhaps in people who lack a corpus callosum, the other commissures develop beyond the usual level.

Although people born without a corpus callosum do not show the usual effects of split-brain surgery, they are nevertheless far from normal. For example, although they can coordinate the movements of their two hands to lace and tie their shoes, they do so very slowly (Sauerwein, Lassonde, Cardu, & Geoffroy, 1981). Their language abilities in general are impaired, even on tasks that have nothing to do with the left versus right sides of the body. The exact language impairment varies from one person to another, but may include difficulty thinking of words that rhyme with a particular word (Temple, Jeeves, & Vilarroya, 1989) or understanding passive sentences (Jeeves & Temple, 1987; Sanders, 1989). Evidently the "cost" of reorganizing the brain without a corpus callosum is that the left hemisphere does not develop its full, normal language capacities.

Handedness and Its Relationship to Language Dominance

About 10 percent of all people are left handed or ambidextrous. (Here we shall consider ambidextrous people to be left handed. Indeed, most left-handers are partly ambidextrous.) Of all the surviving prehistoric drawings and paintings that show people using a tool with one hand or the other, more than 90 percent show them using the right hand (Coren & Porac, 1977). Thus, right-handedness appears to be part of our ancient heritage, not a recent development.

The brain of a left-handed person is different from that of a right-handed person, but it is not simply the reverse. For about 99 percent of right-handed people, the left hemisphere is strongly dominant for speech. The left hemisphere is also dominant for speech in about 70 percent of left-handers (Rasmussen & Milner, 1977). Of the remaining 30 percent, most have varying degrees of control by both hemispheres; only a few have complete control by the right hemisphere (Loring et al., 1990). The corpus callosum (especially the anterior corpus callosum) is about 11 percent thicker in left-handers than in right-handers, presumably facilitating cross-hemisphere communication and bilateral representation of functions (Habib et al., 1991; Witelson, 1985).

Why are certain people left handed and others right handed? Genetics is a factor but not the only determinant. The chance of having a left-handed child is higher if both parents are left handed, but the family data on handedness do not suggest any simple Mendelian effects.

Whatever the causes of hand preference, left-handedness is correlated with a wide variety of seemingly disparate biological traits. Norman Geschwind and Albert Galaburda (1985) proposed that these relationships ultimately trace back to the diverse effects of the hormone testosterone. High effects of testosterone at various times in prenatal and postnatal life can impair the growth of the posterior left hemisphere, increase the probability of left-handedness, increase the probability of right-hemisphere language dominance, impair development of the immune system, and produce other effects, as summarized in Figure 14.8. According to this model, testosterone provides an explanation for why left-handers are more likely than right-handers to develop unusual behavioral conditions ranging from dyslexia to mathematical excellence, as well as medical conditions ranging from childhood allergies to immune disorders. The effects of testosterone also help to explain why many of these conditions are more common in males than they are in females.

These observations do *not* mean that left-handedness causes dyslexia or immune disorders, any more than they mean that immune disorders cause left-handedness. They do suggest that the factors leading to left-handedness in some individuals overlap the factors that lead to other biological conditions.

Geschwind and Galburda's hypothesis remains speculative. On the plus side, it brings together a number of phenomena that seemed unrelated, and

Lateralization of Function and the Corpus Callosum

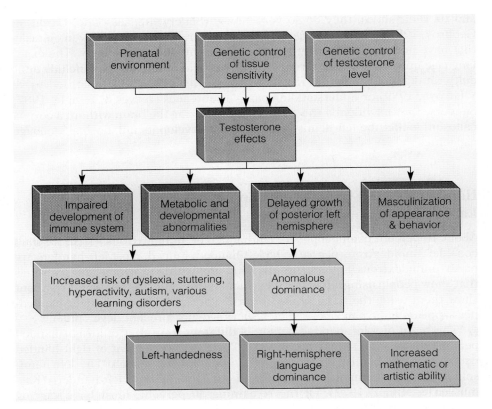

Figure 14.8
Summary of how testosterone may affect handedness, language dominance, and a variety of other biological characteristics
(Based on Geschwind & Galaburda, 1985; McManus & Bryden, 1991.)

Boxes in figure:
Prenatal environment
Genetic control of tissue sensitivity
Genetic control of testosterone level
Testosterone effects
Impaired development of immune system
Metabolic and developmental abnormalities
Delayed growth of posterior left hemisphere
Masculinization of appearance & behavior
Increased risk of dyslexia, stuttering, hyperactivity, autism, various learning disorders
Anomalous dominance
Left-handedness
Right-hemisphere language dominance
Increased mathematic or artistic ability

proposes a mechanism for relating them. On the negative side, the hypothesis is vague on many points and therefore difficult to test decisively (McManus & Bryden, 1991). Furthermore, the theory apparently predicts a large difference between males and females in their hand preference, brain lateralization, and likelihood of developing various disorders. The sexes do differ, but the differences are not enormous. At a minimum, however, Geschwind and Galaburda's hypothesis is provoking new directions in research.

Summary

1. The corpus callosum, a set of axons connecting the two hemispheres, has been surgically cut in a small number of people to relieve severe, otherwise untreatable epilepsy. (p. 490)

2. After the corpus callosum is cut, the left hemisphere can answer questions verbally and can control the right hand. The right hemisphere can control the left hand. Each hemisphere sees the opposite side of the world and feels the opposite side of the body, but neither hemisphere has direct access to the knowledge of the other any longer. (p. 493)

3. Although the two hemispheres of a split-brain person are sometimes in conflict, they find many ways to cooperate and to cue each other. (p. 494)

4. The left hemisphere of most people is specialized for language or for "sequential, analytic" tasks. The right hemisphere is specialized for control of complex visual-spatial functions, especially those that require internal representations of visual and spatial information. It is also specialized for "synthetic, holistic" tasks. (p. 495)

5. The left hemisphere differs anatomically from the right hemisphere even during infancy. Young children have some trouble comparing information from the left and right hands because the corpus callosum is not fully mature. (p. 498)

6. In children born without a corpus callosum, the rest of the brain develops in unusual ways, and the children fail to show the same deficits as adults who sustain damage to the corpus callosum. (p. 499)

7. The brain of a left-handed person is not simply the mirror image of the brain of a right-handed person. Left-handers are more likely to stutter and to have a variety of other medical and psychological anomalies, some of them advantages and others disadvantages. According to one hypothesis, all these effects may be exaggerations of the normal effects of testosterone on development. (p. 501)

Review Questions

1. Why is the left hemisphere of the brain simply connected to the right eye in rabbits, but not in humans? (p. 488)

2. In the human eye, what part of each retina connects to the left hemisphere? To the right hemisphere? What part of the visual field does the left hemisphere see? What part does the right hemisphere see? (p. 489)

3. Can a split-brain person name something after feeling it with the left hand? With the right hand? Why? (p. 493)

4. Describe one way in which the two hemispheres of a split-brain person cooperate. (p. 494)

5. What kinds of tasks can the right hemisphere perform better than the left hemisphere? (p. 495)

6. How does experience affect the development of the corpus callosum? (p. 499)

7. A child born without a corpus callosum can name what he or she feels in the left hand, unlike an adult with a damaged corpus callosum. What is a likely explanation for this difference? (p. 500)

8. According to Geschwind and Galaburda, what may account for the relationship between left-handedness and various disorders, ranging from dyslexia to immune disorders? (p. 501)

Thought Question

1. People born without a corpus callosum show one peculiarity that is not typical of split-brain patients: Whenever they move the fingers of one hand, they involuntarily move the fingers of the other hand, too. What possible explanation can you suggest?

Suggestion for Further Reading

Springer, S. P., & Deutsch, G. (1993). *Left brain, right brain* (4th ed.). New York: W. H. Freeman. Discusses the split-brain phenomenon and the specializations of the two hemispheres evident in normal people.

Terms

corpus callosum large set of axons that connects the two hemispheres of the cerebral cortex (p. 488)

lateralization division of labor or specializations between the two hemispheres of the brain (p. 488)

visual field the part of the world visible to the eyes at a particular moment (p. 489)

optic chiasm point at which parts of the optic nerves cross to the opposite side of the brain (p. 490)

epilepsy a condition in which brain neurons have repeated episodes of excessive, synchronized activity and possibly also periods of excessive inhibition (p. 492)

generalized seizure an epileptic seizure that spreads quickly across neurons over a large portion of both hemispheres of the brain (p. 492)

grand mal seizure type of generalized seizure in which the person makes sudden, repetitive jerking movements of the head and limbs for a period of seconds or minutes and then collapses in a state of exhaustion and sleep (p. 492)

petit mal seizure (or *absence seizure*) type of generalized seizure in which the person stares, unresponsive to the environment, for a period of seconds, making no sudden movements, except perhaps for eye blinking or a drooping of the head (p. 492)

partial seizure epileptic seizure that begins in a focus somewhere in the brain and then spreads to nearby areas in just one hemisphere (p. 492)

focus point in the brain from which a seizure originates (p. 492)

planum temporale area of the temporal cortex that is larger in the left hemisphere than in the right for most people (p. 498)

Sylvian, or **lateral**, **fissure** one of the major fissures, or folds, on the side of the cortex (p. 498)

anterior commissure set of axons that connects the hemispheres in the anterior part of the cerebral cortex (p. 500)

hippocampal commissure set of axons that connects the left hippocampus to the right hippocampus (p. 500)

The Biological Basis of Language

Suppose your physician has just told you that you have a brain tumor. It causes you few problems now, but it will become life threatening in a year or two if it is not surgically removed. After the operation—if you agree to it—you will have a normal life expectancy and you will be entirely healthy, except for one thing: Because of the tumor's location, its removal will damage tissue and leave you virtually incapable of understanding language. In many ways, you will still be able to carry on a normal life. You will understand the meanings of many symbols and signals, including smiles and frowns. But you will make no sense of anything you try to read, and you will understand only a little of what you hear other people say. Under these conditions, will you agree to have the surgery?

Some people say yes and some say no. Even those who say yes are generally hesitant. Losing language comprehension would mean losing an important part of what makes us human.

The Evolution of Language Capacities

The human capacity for language enables us to profit from the experiences of people who live in other parts of the world and of people who lived long ago. Given the great usefulness of language, you may never have paused to wonder *why* our ancestors evolved this capacity. "Obviously," you may reply, "language enabled our ancestors to teach one another skills, to make plans, to communicate between parent and child . . . ."

Okay, but if language is really so useful, why have no other species evolved it?

"Maybe they just couldn't," you might reply. "Maybe a species cannot evolve language unless it first has enough intelligence, and maybe only humans have that much intelligence."

If that is your reply, you have stated one of several current theories of human language evolution—the theory that humans evolved high intelligence and that language came along as a more-or-less accidental by-product of the intelligence. However, this theory is unconvincing. As we saw in Chapter 5, the evolution of the human brain did not consist simply of increasing brain size, but instead of reorganizing the brain. In comparison with other primates, some of our brain areas, especially the prefrontal cortex, are proportionally much larger, while other areas are proportionally smaller. Much of this reorganization probably took place *because* of the growing importance of language. In

Figure 14.9
*One of the Premacks'
chimps, Elizabeth, reacts to
colored plastic chips that
read "Not Elizabeth banana
insert—Elizabeth apple
wash." (Photo courtesy of
Ann Premack.)*

other words, it is not clear that language was a by-product of selection for intelligence. The opposite is at least as likely: Our great intelligence may have been
a by-product of selection for language (Deacon, 1992). So the question of why
humans and only humans evolved language remains a puzzle.

Another puzzle is how the process got started. As a rule, every new feature
evolves from some feature that was already present in some other form, and
not just out of thin air. Bats evolved wings by modifying the forearms of their
predecessors. Porcupines evolved quills by modifying hair cells. Similarly,
humans' capacity for language presumably evolved from behavioral capacities
present in other primates, perhaps serving some other purpose.

Consequently, we might expect that our nearest relatives, the chimpanzees,
would be able to learn at least a simple approximation to language, under
appropriate circumstances. The earliest attempts to teach chimpanzees language focused on spoken language and consistently failed (Premack, 1976).
The next generation of experiments achieved a certain degree of success by
teaching chimpanzees to use American Sign Language or various systems in
which visual stimuli represented concepts (Gardner & Gardner, 1975;
Premack & Premack, 1972). (See Figure 14.9.) In one version, chimps learned
to punch keys bearing symbols to type out messages on a computer (Rumbaugh, 1977). For example, chimps learned to make requests of the computer
(such as "Please machine give me apple" or "Please machine turn on movie").
They also learned to type messages to communicate with other chimps
("Please share your chocolate with me").

Although chimpanzees in these studies learned to produce correct
sequences of symbols, their product was not necessarily "language." For example, we humans might interpret a sequence of four symbols as "please give me
apple," but the chimp might simply have learned, "If I use these four symbols
in just this order, people give me an apple." In these experiments, chimps' use
of symbols differed from human language in several regards (Rumbaugh, 1990;
Terrace, Pettito, Sanders, & Bever, 1979):

- The chimpanzees seldom combined symbols to make new, original "sentences" (as even very young children do).
- The chimpanzees used their symbols almost exclusively to request, almost never to describe.
- If the experimenter varied the word order a little, the chimpanzee seemed not to understand.

Based on such studies, psychologists grew skeptical about chimpanzees' ability to learn language and particularly about their ability to acquire syntax, the rules for combining words to express new meanings. Then some new and surprising results emerged from studies of a rare and endangered species, *Pan paniscus,* which is sometimes known as the pygmy chimpanzee (a misleading name because these animals are almost as large as common chimpanzees) or the bonobo (also a misleading name because it refers to a place in Africa where they do not live).

Pan paniscus has a social order resembling that of humans in several regards. Males and females form strong, sometimes long-term personal attachments. They often copulate in a face-to-face position. The female is sexually responsive throughout the month and not just during her fertile period. Unlike most other primates, these males contribute significantly to infant care. Adults often share food with one another. They stand comfortably on their hind legs. In short, they resemble humans more than any other primates do.

In the mid-1980s, Sue Savage-Rumbaugh, Duane Rumbaugh, and their associates began trying to teach a female *Pan paniscus* named Matata to press symbols that light up when touched; each symbol represents a word (see Figure 14.10). She made very disappointing progress. However, her infant son Kanzi seemed to learn a great deal just by watching her attempts. When given a chance to use the symbol board, he quickly surpassed the performance of his mother and of all common chimps that had been tested, even though Kanzi had never received any formal training. Furthermore, it soon became clear that Kanzi understood a fair amount of spoken language. The experimenters first noticed that whenever anyone said the word "light," he would flip the light switch. By age 5½, he understood about 150 English words and could respond to complex, unfamiliar spoken commands such as "throw your ball in the river," "go to the refrigerator and get out a tomato," and "let's chase to the A-frame" (Savage-Rumbaugh, 1990; Savage-Rumbaugh, Sevcik, Brakke, & Rumbaugh, 1992). Kanzi has demonstrated language comprehension comparable to that of a 2- to 2½-year-old child (Savage-Rumbaugh et al., 1993).

Kanzi and his younger sister Mulika understand far more language than they produce. Both now actually say a few English words, although they continue to communicate mostly by pressing symbols on their symbol boards. Their productions exceed those of other chimpanzees in some important regards: First, they use the symbols to name and describe objects even when they are not requesting them. They also request items that they do not see, such as "bubbles" (I want to play with the bubble-blower) or "car trailer" (drive me in the car to the trailer) (Savage-Rumbaugh, 1991; Savage-Rumbaugh et al., 1993). Second, they occasionally use the symbols to relate events of the past. One time, Kanzi punched the symbols "Matata bite" to explain the cut that he had received on his hand an hour previously. Third, Kanzi and Mulika frequently make original, creative requests. For example, after Kanzi had learned to press the symbols to ask someone to play "chase" with him, he asked one person to chase another person while he watched!

Figure 14.10
Kanzi, a bonobo (*Pan paniscus*), points to answers on a board in response to questions that he hears through earphones
The experimenter with him does not know what the questions are or what answers are expected. (From Georgia State University's Language Research Center, operated with the Yerkes Primate Center of Emory. Photo courtesy of Duane Rumbaugh.)

Why have Kanzi and Mulika been so much more successful than other chimpanzees? One possible explanation is a species difference: Perhaps *Pan paniscus* has greater language capacities than common chimpanzees. A second explanation is that Kanzi and Mulika began language training at an early age, unlike the chimpanzees in most other studies. A third reason may pertain to the method of training: Perhaps learning by observation and imitation promotes better understanding than the formal training methods of previous studies (Savage-Rumbaugh, Sevcik, Brakke, & Rumbaugh, 1992).

Can any nonprimate species learn any aspect of language? Maybe. Dolphins have learned to respond to a system of gestures and sounds, each representing one word. For example, after the command "Right hoop left frisbee fetch," a dolphin takes the frisbee on the left to the hoop on the right (Herman, Pack, & Morrel-Samuels, 1993). A dolphin responds correctly to new combinations of old words, but only if the result is meaningful. For example, the first time that a dolphin is given the command "Person hoop fetch," it takes the hoop to the person. But when told "Person water fetch," it does nothing (because it has no way to take water to the person). But note that this system offers the dolphins neither the opportunity nor the incentive to produce language. The dolphins cannot produce the gestures or sounds to tell a human to take the frisbee to the hoop, and even if they could, it is not clear why they would want to (Savage-Rumbaugh, 1993).

Figure 14.11
*Alex, a gray parrot, has
apparently learned to con-
verse about toy objects in
simple English—for exam-
ple, giving the correct
answer to "What color is the
circle?" He receives no food
rewards. (Photo from David
Carter.)*

Spectacular results have been reported for Alex, an African gray parrot (Figure 14.11). Parrots are, of course, famous for imitating human sounds; Irene Pepperberg was the first to argue that parrots can learn the meaning of the sounds. She kept Alex in a stimulating environment and taught him to say a variety of words in conjunction with specific objects. First, she and the other trainers would say a word many times, then they would offer rewards if Alex approximated the same sound. Here is an excerpt from a "conversation" with Alex early in training (Pepperberg, 1981):

Pepperberg: Pasta! (*Takes pasta.*) Pasta! (*Alex stretches from his perch, appears to reach for pasta.*)
Alex: Pa!
Pepperberg: Better . . . what is it?
Alex: Pah-ah.
Pepperberg: Better!
Alex: Pah-ta.
Pepperberg: Okay, here's the pasta. Good try.

Although this example concerns pasta, Pepperberg generally used toys for rewards. For example, if Alex said "paper," "wood," or "key," she would give him what he asked for. In no case did she reward him for saying "paper" or "wood" by giving him a piece of food.

Alex made gradual progress, learning to give spoken answers to spoken questions! He was shown a tray of 12 small objects and then asked such questions as "What color is the key?" (answer: "green") and "What object is gray?"

(answer: "circle"). In one test, he gave the correct answer to 39 of 48 questions. Even many of his errors were close to being correct. In one case, he was asked the color of the "block" and he responded with the color of the "rock." In another case, the correct answer was "green," and Alex said something that sounded like "gree," but could have been "gray," so the experimenters counted his answer wrong (Pepperberg, 1993).

Is Alex actually learning language? Pepperberg prefers to avoid this question, simply referring to his performance as "language-like." She says that she is using the research to study the bird's concept formation, not its language capacities. Still, Alex has made far more progress than most of us would have thought possible for a nonprimate; these results prompt us to rethink some assumptions about what sort of brain development is necessary for language.

What do we learn about language from studies of nonhuman language abilities? At a practical level, we may gain some insights into how best to teach language to those who do not learn it easily. The methods that we develop for teaching chimpanzees may be useful for brain-damaged people or autistic children (see, for example, Glass, Gazzaniga, & Premack, 1973). At a more theoretical level, we find out something about how special humans are—and are not. Although humans undeniably develop language far more readily than any other species does, our language abilities are an elaboration of abilities that are found to some degree in other species, not an altogether new feature. Finally, these studies call attention to the difficulty of defining language: The main reason that we have such trouble deciding whether chimpanzees or parrots have language is that we have not specified exactly what we mean by the term.

Effects of Brain Damage on Human Language

Biological psychologists have learned much about the brain mechanisms of vision, hearing, and muscle control by studying the brains of other species. With regard to language, their investigations must be based almost entirely on humans. Although chimpanzees and maybe even African gray parrots can learn a certain amount of language, language learning does not come as easily for them as it does for us. The human brain is specialized to facilitate language.

Most of our knowledge about the brain mechanisms of language has come from studies of brain-damaged people. Such information can be useful and sometimes fascinating. However, it is limited to telling us *where* in the brain language comprehension and production take place, not *how* they take place (Caramazza, 1988).

Broca's Aphasia

In 1861, one patient who had been mute for 30 years was taken to the French surgeon Paul Broca because of gangrene. When the patient died 5 days later, Broca did an autopsy on the man's brain and found a lesion restricted to a small part of the frontal lobe of the left cerebral cortex near the motor cortex (Boring, 1950; Schiller, 1979). In later years, Broca examined the brains of other patients whose only problem had been a language impairment of sudden origin; in nearly all cases, he found damage in that same area, which is now known as **Broca's area** (Figure 14.12). The usual cause of the damage was a stroke (an interruption of blood flow to part of the brain).

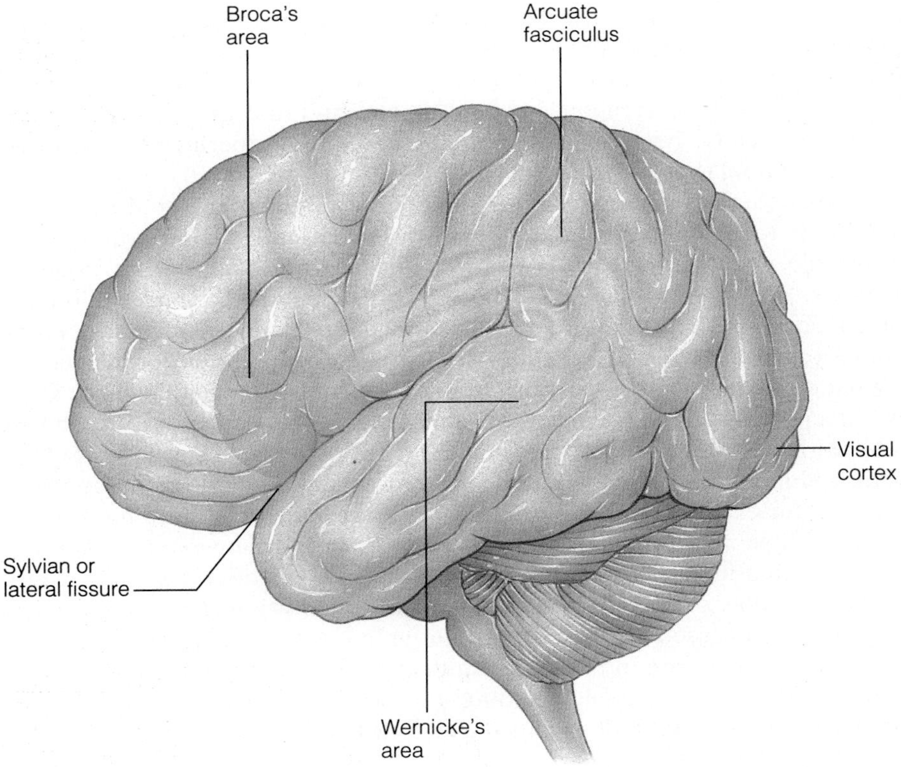

Figure 14.12
Location of the major language areas of the cerebral cortex
In most people, only the left hemisphere is specialized for language.

Broca's area

Arcuate fasciculus

Visual cortex

Sylvian or lateral fissure

Wernicke's area

Later studies confirmed that Broca's area and surrounding areas are damaged in most patients who suffer **aphasia,** a loss of language due to brain damage. The kind of aphasia typically associated with damage to Broca's area is generally known as **Broca's aphasia** or *nonfluent aphasia* because the person cannot speak fluently.

Broca's area is part of a much larger circuit of areas contributing to language. According to modern brain-scanning techniques, when people speak, they have increased activity in much of the frontal, temporal, and parietal cortex in the left hemisphere, plus parts of the left thalamus and basal ganglia (Wallesch, Henriksen, Kornhuber, & Paulson, 1985). (See Figure 14.13.) Investigators have studied the effects of brief electrical brain stimulation on patients undergoing surgery for epilepsy. (Such surgery is often conducted with only the scalp anesthetized, leaving the brain awake.) Stimulation of certain points in or near Broca's area halts all speech, while also impairing recognition of simple speech sounds. Stimulation of various other cortical regions outside Broca's area leaves speech intact, but impairs various aspects of verbal memory (Ojemann & Mateer, 1979; Ojemann & Whitaker, 1978). Evidently, the brain areas controlling speech are not homogeneous; different areas contribute to different aspects. Consequently, the effects of brain damage depend on the exact location of the damage as well as on the exact amount (Alexander, Benson, & Stuss, 1989; Damasio & Geschwind, 1984).

Traditionally, Broca's aphasia has been associated with impaired language production and relatively spared language comprehension (Geschwind, 1970, 1972). That generalization is largely valid, but with some important excep-

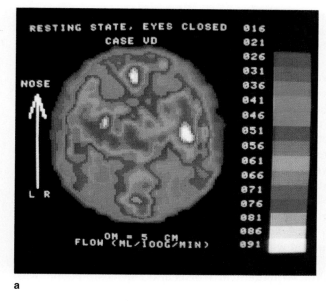

a

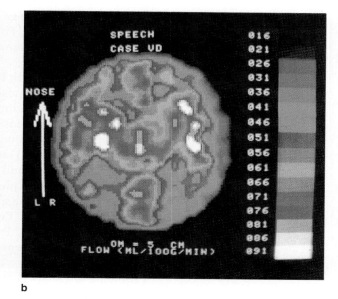

b

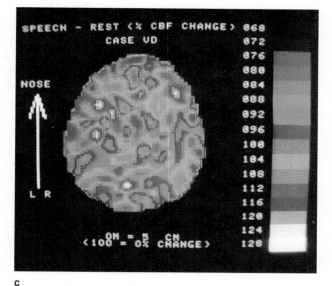

c

Figure 14.13
Records showing rCBF for one normal adult subject
*Red indicates the highest level of activity, followed by yellow, green, and blue. (**a**) Blood flow to the brain at rest. (**b**) Blood flow while subject describes a magazine story. (**c**) Difference between **b** and **a**. The results in **c** indicate which brain areas increased their activity during language production. Note the increased activity in many areas of the brain, especially on the left side. (From Wallesch, Henriksen, Kornhuber, & Paulson, 1985.)*

tions: Both production and comprehension are especially impaired when the meaning of a sentence depends on prepositions, word endings, and other grammatical devices.

Difficulty in Language Production   Some people with Broca's aphasia cannot speak at all, although they may be able to make a variety of sounds and sometimes even hum or sing. Those with less extensive damage can speak, but slowly and inarticulately. However, their problem is not just a lack of control of the throat; such people also have trouble writing and expressing themselves through gestures (Cicone, Wapner, Foldi, Zurif, & Gardner, 1979). In addition, deaf people with damage in and around Broca's area find it difficult to produce sign language (Bellugi, Poizner, & Klima, 1983). They can make only a few brief signs, even though their ability to use their hands may be unimpaired in other ways.

When someone with Broca's aphasia speaks, the speech is meaningful but it omits pronouns, prepositions, conjunctions, helper verbs, quantifiers, and tense and number endings. These omitted words and endings are sometimes known as the *closed class* of grammatical forms because a language rarely adds new prepositions, conjunctions, and the like. In contrast, new nouns and verbs (the *open class* forms) enter the language every year. People with Broca's aphasia can speak nouns and verbs more easily than closed-class words. They find it difficult to repeat a phrase using many prepositions and conjunctions, such as "No ifs, ands, or buts," although they can successfully repeat "The general commands the army." Furthermore, patients who cannot read aloud "To be or not to be" can read "Two bee oar knot two bee" (Gardner & Zurif, 1975). Clearly, the trouble depends on word meanings, not just pronunciation.

Problems in Comprehending Grammatical Words and Devices People with Broca's aphasia understand both spoken and written language better than they can produce it. However, they have trouble understanding the same word categories that they have trouble saying—prepositions, conjunctions, and other relational words—and they have trouble if the meaning depends on an unusual word order. For example, they have difficulty understanding "The girl that the boy is chasing is tall" (Zurif, 1980). They are not sure who is chasing whom and which one is tall. Sometimes the meaning of a sentence is clear enough independent of the relational words and grammatical devices, and sometimes the meaning depends on such words and devices, as Table 14.1 demonstrates. So a person with Broca's aphasia will understand some sentences well and others poorly.

People with Broca's aphasia are not totally lacking in comprehension of grammar. For example, they can generally recognize that something is wrong with the sentence "He written has songs," even if they cannot say how to improve the sentence. However, they are less likely to notice sentences with subtler errors such as "She are baking a cake" (Wulfeck & Bates, 1991).

Wernicke's Aphasia

In 1874, Carl Wernicke (generally pronounced WER-nih-kee in the United States; the German pronunciation is VER-nih-keh), a 26-year-old junior assistant in a German hospital, discovered that damage in part of the left temporal cortex produced language impairment that was very different from what Broca had reported. Patients could produce language, but they had trouble comprehending the verbal and written communications of others. This brain area, now known as **Wernicke's area** (Figure 14.12), is located near the auditory part of the cerebral cortex. Damage in and around Wernicke's area produces **Wernicke's aphasia,** also sometimes known as *fluent aphasia* because the person can still speak smoothly. The typical results are as follows:

1. *Articulate speech.* In contrast to Broca's aphasics, Wernicke's aphasics speak articulately and fluently, except when they pause to try to think of the name of something.

2. *Difficulty finding the right word.* People suffering from Wernicke's aphasia have **anomia** (ay-NOME-ee-uh), a difficulty in recalling the names of

Table 14.1 What Language Might Sound Like to a Person with Broca's Aphasia

In each case, prepositions, conjunctions, relative pronouns, articles, and word endings have been removed from a published text.

Example 1 (*Still mostly understandable*): "Michael Crichton . . . throwback: . . . hard-work . . . pop novel . . . spot . . . trend, . . . research, retool . . . familiar character . . ., work . . . plot, plant . . . clue . . ., tie . . . loose end . . . keep . . . you turn . . . page . . .—. . . clumsy prose." (*Newsweek,* January 17, 1994, p. 52.)

Example 2 (*More difficult*): Pigeon, dove, chicken, . . . turkey make . . . simple coo . . . cackle, . . . ornithologist (bird biologist) do not classify . . . "song." . . . species do not need . . . learn . . . call. . . . fact, . . . they are deaf . . . early . . . life, they develop normal call. (Note . . . observation do not explain . . . pigeon . . . other acquire . . . call. They merely indicate . . . we should look . . . answers . . . embryology . . . nervous system, not . . . individual experience.) (page 6 of this text).

Example 3 (*Almost incomprehensible*): ". . . other public building . . . certain town . . . many reason . . . will be prudent . . . refrain . . . mention . . . I will assign no fictitious name . . . boast . . . one . . . anciently common . . . most town, great . . . small . . . wit . . . workhouse . . . born . . . day . . . date . . . I need not trouble . . . myself . . . repeat . . . it can be . . . no possible consequence . . . reader . . . stage . . . business . . . event . . . item . . . mortality . . . name . . . prefix. . . head . . . chapter." (*Oliver Twist,* by Charles Dickens, opening of Chapter 1).

objects. A typical result follows: "Yes, all the little, little pe-, ah, puh, ah, places the, the ah, big big of-fi-ces then have undergone this here ah, the, ah, the, ah, there and they're there, but they can't hear, hi, hi, can't see them because it's s-so-so big, other big buildings are there" (Martin & Blossom-Stach, 1986). Even when people with Wernicke's aphasia do manage to find some of the right words, they fail to arrange the words properly, saying, for example, "The Astros listened to the radio tonight" (instead of "I listened to the Astros on the radio tonight") (Martin & Blossom-Stach, 1986).

3. *Poor language comprehension.* Wernicke's aphasics have great trouble understanding both spoken and written speech. While many sentences are clear enough without prepositions, word endings, and grammar (which confuse Broca's aphasics), almost no sentences are clear without nouns and verbs (which trouble Wernicke's patients).

The following conversation is between a woman with Wernicke's aphasia and a speech therapist trying to teach her the names of some objects. (The Duke University Department of Speech Pathology and Audiology provided this dialogue.)

Therapist: (*Holding picture of an apron*) Can you name that one?
Woman: Um . . . you see I can't, I can I can barely do; he would give me sort of umm . . . .

Table 14.2 Broca's Aphasia and Wernicke's Aphasia			
Type	*Pronunciation*	*Content of Speech*	*Comprehension*
Broca's aphasia	Very poor	Mostly nouns and verbs; omits prepositions and other grammatical connectives	Impaired if the meaning depends on prepositions, grammar, or unusual word order
Wernicke's aphasia	Unimpaired	Grammatical but sometimes nonsensical; has trouble finding the right word, especially names of objects	Seriously impaired

T: A clue?

W: That's right . . . just a like, just a . . . .

T: You mean, like, "You wear that when you wash dishes or when you cook a meal . . ."?

W: Yeah, something like that.

T: Okay, and what is it? You wear it around your waist, and you cook . . . .

W: Cook. Umm, umm, see I can't remember.

T: It's an apron.

W: Apron, apron, that's it, apron.

T: (*Holding another picture*) That you wear when you're getting ready for bed after a shower.

W: Oh, I think that he put under different, something different. We had something, you know, umm, you know.

T: A different way of doing it?

W: No, umm . . . umm . . . . (*Pause*)

T: It's actually a bathrobe.

W: Bathrobe. Uh, we didn't call it that; we called it something else.

T: Smoking jacket?

W: No, I think we called it, uh . . . .

T: Lounging . . . ?

W: No, no, something, in fact, we called it just . . . . (*Pause*)

T: Robe?

W: Robe. Or something like that.

Unlike hearing people, deaf people who suffer damage to Wernicke's area do not lose their ability to understand sign language. Rather, they lose that ability after damage in the parietal lobe, the area responsible for touch and other body sensations (Bellugi, Poizner, & Klima, 1983).

Table 14.2 contrasts Broca's aphasia and Wernicke's aphasia.

PET Scan Studies of Language Processing

For many years, the study of brain-damaged people was almost the only available method for determining how different parts of the brain contribute to language. The introduction of PET scans has enabled investigators to address some questions that they could not answer with observations on brain-damaged patients.

A typical procedure is this: First, a person looks at some printed words, while the investigators record brain activity with a PET scanner (see p. 137). Then the person stares at a blank card, while the investigators again record brain activity. Finally, a computer subtracts the brain activity on the second task from the activity on the first task; the difference is the activity specifically generated by reading the words.

Figure 14.14 shows the results of one study (Posner, Petersen, Fox, & Raichle, 1988). Note that reading enhanced brain activity in the occipital lobe only. Activity in the occipital lobe was to be expected; after all, the occipital lobe is the brain's primary visual area. The more surprising result was that this task did not activate the temporal lobe. We might have expected that a person would have to convert the written word into sound to read it.

Next, the investigators ask the person to read pairs of words and decide whether they rhyme with each other. Some pairs look similar and rhyme (such as *face* and *pace*), some look similar but do not rhyme (*pint* and *lint*), and some look different but rhyme anyway (*row* and *though*). So to answer the questions, the person must attend to the sounds and not just the appearances of the words. The computer compares the brain areas activated by this task with the brain areas activated by simply looking at words; the result is that this task leads to greater activity in the temporal lobes (Posner et al., 1988). That is, the person must convert the written word into a sound, using the part of the cortex specialized for hearing.

Now the investigators ask the person to read one object-word at a time on a screen and then state a way to use the object. (For example, hammer—pound, or cake—eat). They also ask the person to listen to spoken object-words and state a use for each object. The brain areas activated by these tasks are compared with those activated by simply repeating the word after seeing it or hearing it. Stating uses for words activates much of the frontal cortex, including Broca's area and other nearby areas (Petersen, Fox, Posner, Mintun, & Raichle, 1988; Posner et al., 1988). Furthermore, reading a word and stating a use produces about the same results as listening to a word and stating a use. In short, the frontal cortex processes both spoken and written language in the same way (see Figure 14.15).

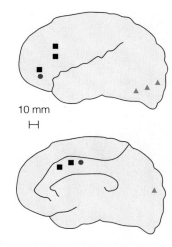

Figure 14.14
Brain areas activated by certain tasks
Passively reading words activates areas in the occipital cortex more than they are activated when the person simply stares ahead (triangles). Reading the name of an object and thinking of a way to use the object activates the areas marked with squares. Listening to words and silently counting dangerous animals activates the areas marked with circles. (From Posner et al., 1988.)

Other Language Deficits

In earlier chapters, we encountered such specific deficits as motion blindness, face blindness, impaired fear learning, and impaired short-term spatial memory. In the realm of language also, people sometimes develop surprisingly specialized deficits and skills.

Word Blindness Despite Ability to Write

A person can suddenly lose the ability to read without losing any other language ability. Even writing ability is spared, although the person cannot read what he or she has just written. This condition is known as word blindness, or **alexia.** Vision is intact in the left visual field but is lost in the right visual field.

The cause? The left visual cortex has been destroyed (by stroke, perhaps), as has the posterior part of the corpus callosum, known as the *splenium,* which contains the fibers from the visual areas of the cortex. The person can see only with the right visual cortex (left visual field), and information in the right visual cortex cannot get to the language areas in the left hemisphere (Greenblatt, 1973; Hécaen & Kremin, 1976; Staller, Buchanan, Singer, Lappin, & Webb, 1978). Spontaneous writing is normal because vision is not necessary for writing; a normal person can, after all, write with his or her eyes closed. Reading is

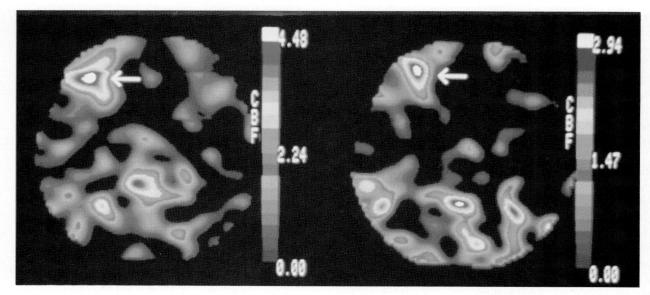

Figure 14.15
PET scans indicating where brain activity increases when people state a use of a word
(such as *cake—eat*) instead of simply repeating the word (such as *cake—cake*)
In the PET scan on the left, people heard the word that they were to respond to; in the
scan on the right, they saw it. In both cases, activity increases markedly in the left
anterior frontal cortex (marked with arrow). (From Petersen et al., 1988.)

impaired, however, because it requires transfer of information from the vision to the language areas of the brain.

Most people suffering from word blindness can name the objects that they see in the left visual field. This may seem surprising, since the fibers that transmit visual information across the corpus callosum have been damaged. Geschwind (1970, 1972) has suggested that the right hemisphere may somehow convert the visual identification of an object into touch or other kinds of sensory representations that can be sent across the intact anterior corpus callosum. Because the right hemisphere cannot convert written words or letters into any nonvisual code, the left hemisphere has no access to them. For the same reason, most people with word blindness cannot name the colors they see.

Certain people have had their posterior corpus callosum cut for medical reasons. When they see something in the left visual field (right hemisphere), they can sometimes transfer enough information across the anterior corpus callosum for the left hemisphere to enable them to describe the object partially, but not necessarily to name it (Sidtis, Volpe, Holtzman, Wilson, & Gazzaniga, 1981). They often describe this phenomenom as a "tip of the tongue" experience; a patient might say, "I saw an article of clothing . . . it's worn by men, mostly in fall. . . . Oh, it's a hunter's cap." It is as if the information is flowing piecemeal across the corpus callosum and the left hemisphere must infer what the object is, instead of seeing it directly.

Inability to Follow Instructions to Move a Limb in Isolation

One brain-damaged man could not follow verbal instructions to use either arm or either leg in isolation or any other single set of muscles by itself (Geschwind, 1975). He could make all the same movements spontaneously, however, and he could follow instructions to stand, walk, bow, kneel, or make other postural movements of the whole body. He could follow instructions to assume a boxer's position but not to punch with one hand.

In this case, the brain damage had disconnected the language areas in this man's left cerebral cortex from his pyramidal system but not from his extrapyramidal system. That is, the damage interrupted fibers from the language areas to the primary motor cortex. Because the primary motor cortex and the entire pyramidal system were intact, his spontaneous movements were normal. However, because the language areas could not send messages to the pyramidal system, he could not move individual limbs in response to verbal instructions. Nevertheless, his language areas could send messages to the more diffuse extrapyramidal system to control gross movements and postures.

Developmental Language Impairment

In one family, 16 of 30 people, ranging over three generations, have shown severe language deficits, despite normal intelligence in other regards. Presumably because of a dominant gene, the 16 affected people all had serious troubles with pronunciation, being almost unintelligible until about age 7, and decidedly inarticulate for years after that (Gopnik & Crago, 1991).

These people also have severe difficulties with simple grammatical rules, even in adulthood. For example, here are the results of some questions about making plurals:

Experimenter's Question	Answers by Person with Developmental Language Impairment
This is a wug; these are . . .	How should I know? [Later] These are wug.
This is a zat; these are . . .	These are zacko.
This is a sas; these are . . .	These are sasss. [Not "sasses"]

In another test, experimenters presented sentences such as the following and asked whether each sentence was correct, or, if not, how one might improve it:

> The boy eats three cookie.
>
> The boy kiss a pretty girl.
>
> Yesterday the girl pet a dog.
>
> The little girl is play with her dog.

The people with developmental language impairment frequently failed to identify errors and also misidentified many correct sentences as "ungrammatical." (Evidently, they were just guessing much of the time.) When they tried to correct a sentence, many of their results were odd. For example,

Original Item	Attempted Correction
The boy eats three cookie.	The boys eat four cookie.

Some of the newspaper reports about this family claimed that the results indicated a "specific gene for grammar." The results support no such conclusion. Affected members of this family have troubles pronouncing, repeating, and understanding speech (Fletcher, 1990; Vargha-Khadem & Passingham, 1990). The important point is that a genetic condition affecting brain development can specifically impair language, without noticeably impairing other functions.

Figure 14.16
A drawing of an elephant and a description of an elephant by an 18-year-old woman with Williams syndrome, IQ 49
The labels on the drawing were provided by the investigator, based on what the woman said she was drawing. (From Bellugi, Wang, & Jernigan, 1994.) Copyright Ursula Bellugi, The Salk Institute for Biological Studies.

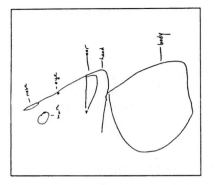

And what an elephant is, it is one of the animals. And what the elephant does, it lives in the jungle. It can also live in the zoo. And what it has, it has long gray ears, fan ears, ears that can blow in the wind. It has a long trunk that can pick up grass, or pick up hay....If they're in a bad mood it can be terrible...If the elephant gets mad it could stomp; It could charge, like a bull can charge. They have long big tusks. They can damage a car...It could be dangerous. When they're in a pinch, when they're in a bad mood it can be terrible. You don't want an elephant as a pet. You want a cat or a dog or a bird...

Williams Syndrome

What about the reverse pattern? Would it be possible to have severe impairments of nonlinguistic functions and nevertheless have good language abilities? Psychologists have long assumed, with much data to support them, that all mentally retarded people have severe language deficits. They saw this rule as almost a logical necessity; anyone who lacked the intelligence to learn simple motor skills would presumably also lack the intelligence to learn and use language.

And then, beginning in the 1960s, psychologists discovered a rare, probably genetic, condition called **Williams syndrome,** in which people are retarded in many other ways but remarkably skilled in their use of language. Such people are unable to learn the simple skills needed to take care of themselves; even as adults, they need the constant supervision of a parent or attendant. They cannot hold even an unskilled job or copy even the simplest drawings. Nevertheless, they can tell stories with great emotional expression, devise their own stories, even compose song lyrics. If someone tells them a sentence and shows them several pictures, they can choose the picture that matches the sentence, even if the sentence is somewhat complicated (Bellugi, Wang, & Jernigan, 1994). Figure 14.16 shows the result when one young woman with Williams syndrome, IQ 49, was asked to draw an elephant and to describe an elephant. Note that the drawing would be uninterpretable if the investigator had not labeled what the woman said she was trying to draw.

The speech of people with Williams syndrome includes more than the ordinary number of unusual words. For example, if asked to "name as many animals as possible," most people list common animals such as dog, horse, and rabbit. People with Williams syndrome include a disproportionate number of uncommon choices such as weasel, newt, ibex, unicorn, and triceratops (Bellugi, Wang, & Jernigan, 1994).

Given that their language skills are so superior to their nonlanguage skills, we might expect to find evidence of right-hemisphere damage. In fact, however, MRI images indicate a reduction in the overall mass of the cerebral cortex and thalamus, with normal size of the limbic system, and no trend toward any imbalance between the left and right hemispheres (Jernigan & Bellugi, 1994). We cannot explain Williams syndrome in terms of the loss or absence of a particular brain area; rather, the problem seems to be an unusual organization of brain connections, in ways that future research will have to explore. In any case, observations on Williams syndrome support the idea that language is a specialized ability that can be kept or lost independently of other functions; it is not simply a by-product of overall intelligence.

Dyslexia

Dyslexia is a specific reading difficulty in a person with adequate vision and at least average skills in academic areas other than reading. Like the terms backache or headache, the term *dyslexia* refers to symptoms, not causes. The causes are varied and certainly not yet well understood; most investigators attribute dyslexia to minor brain abnormalities, but others attribute it to learned habits of visual perception.

According to one extensive review of the literature, dyslexic people are more likely than other people to have a bilaterally symmetrical cerebral cortex, instead of having their planum temporale and certain other areas larger in the left hemisphere than in the right (Hynd & Semrud-Clikeman, 1989). In some dyslexic people, certain language-related areas are actually larger in the right hemisphere than they are in the left (Duara et al., 1991). Also, many dyslexic people have small anatomical abnormalities in their brains, especially on the left side and especially in the frontal and temporal cortex (Hynd & Semrud-Clikeman, 1989). All these results support Geschwind and Galaburda's theory (p. 501) linking anomalous lateralization of function with a predisposition to dyslexia and other problems.

Going beyond the general issue of lateralization, what can we say about impairments of specific neuronal or behavioral processes? Recall from Chapter 6 the distinction between the parvocellular and magnocellular pathways in the visual system. The parvocellular system deals with details, especially of stationary objects. The magnocellular system deals with overall patterns and moving objects. Many people with dyslexia show indications of a relatively unresponsive magnocellular system (Livingstone, Rosen, Drislane, & Galaburda, 1991). Consequently, they are impaired on detecting overall patterns (such as words) and have trouble with rapidly changing stimuli (such as happens when one moves one's eyes across a page). People with dyslexia generally show impairments on reading words and sentences, although they are as quick and accurate as anyone else in reading a single isolated letter.

Here is a demonstration of another process that is relevant to dyslexia. Focus your eyes on the central dot in each display below and, without moving your eyes back and forth, try to read the letters to the left and right of the dot:

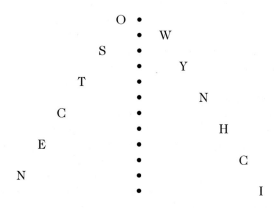

If you are like most people, you found that you had no trouble reading the letters in the first lines, which were close to the fixation point (•). As the spacing increased on successive lines, you found it harder to identify each letter. Depending on many details of procedure, people sometimes show a slightly greater accuracy for letters to the right of the fixation point than for those to the left. The tendency to read better to the right is a function of our long experience in reading from left to right; it is absent in first through third graders (Carmon, Nachson, & Starinsky, 1976) and reversed in people who read Hebrew, which is printed right to left (Pollatsek, Bolozky, Well, & Rayner, 1981).

Now try the following display. The instructions are the same as for the previous display, except that, instead of trying to read one letter, you will try to read the *middle* letter of each three-letter combination:

<pre>
                          NOE •
                                • TWC
                      WSH •
                                •   EYO
                  CTN •
                                •   ONT
              HCW •
                                •   OHW
          IEY •
                                •   WCI
      HNO •
                                •   SIY
</pre>

The task became more difficult because of **lateral masking,** the interference generated by adjacent letters. One can also demonstrate lateral masking by briefly flashing a central fixation point and a letter to its left or right. If the fixation point is literally just a dot, it does not interfere with reading the letter. But if the fixation point is another letter, it does interfere.

For most people, a letter at the fixation point generates little interference with nearby letters but major interference with remotely placed letters. For example, the H does not mask the W in this display:

HW

but it does mask the N in this display:

H   N

(Remember, we are talking about letters flashed briefly on a screen. This interference is less impressive when you have a chance to stare at letters on a page.)

Now, it turns out that the results I just described apply to most people, but not to all. For a certain minority of people, a letter at the fixation point produces noticeable interference for an immediately adjacent letter (like the W in the HW display), but produces less than the normal amount of interference for a remote letter (like the N in the H   N display). People showing this pattern of results suffer from dyslexia! That is, when people with certain kinds of dyslexia focus on one letter, that letter produces lateral masking of the immediately adjacent letters, but not much masking of letters farther to the right (Geiger, Lettvin, & Zegarra-Moran, 1992). So when such a person focuses on a word, he or she is worse than average at reading that word, but better than average at reading the next word over.

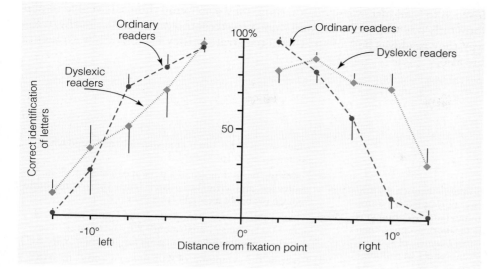

Figure 14.17

Identification of a single letter at various locations left or right of a letter at the fixation point, by normal and dyslexic readers

Normal readers identify a letter most accurately when it is close to the fixation point, and their accuracy drops steadily for letters more remote from that point. People with dyslexia show a small but significant impairment (via lateral masking) for letters just to the right of the fixation point, yet they are substantially more accurate than normal readers are in identifying letters 5–10° to the right of fixation. (Based on Geiger, Lettvin, & Zegarra-Moran, 1992.)

Figure 14.17 shows the mean results for normal readers and for people with dyslexia. Note that normal readers identify letters close to the fixation point with almost 100 percent accuracy. Their accuracy drops for letters farther to the left or right of the fixation point. People with dyslexia are worse than normal at reading letters just to the right of fixation because of strong lateral masking. But for letters 5–10° to the right of fixation, they perform significantly better than normal readers do.

This analysis of dyslexia suggests the possibility of alleviating dyslexia by teaching people to see just one word at a time instead of several. In preliminary studies, a few dyslexic children and adults have been told, as part of their treatment, to place over any page that they are reading a sheet of paper with a window cut out of it, large enough to expose about one word at a time. A reader can either uncover the word at the fixation point, or, if preferred, fixate at one point and uncover a word that is several degrees to the right of that point. In either case, the idea is to focus attention on one word at a time instead of several. In three months, 15 dyslexic children improved their reading skills by 1.22 grade levels (Geiger, Lettvin, & Fahle, 1994). Four dyslexic adults also made spectacular progress; one advanced from a third-grade reading level to a tenth-grade reading level in 4 months (Geiger, Lettvin, & Zegarra-Moran, 1992). After about the first 3 weeks of practice, they no longer needed the special cut-out sheet of paper.

One final twist: Of the four dyslexic adults who went through this process, three decided that they would rather return to being dyslexic! While dyslexic, they could attend to several tasks at once, such as talking to someone, listening to news on the radio, creating a work of art, and so forth. When they learned to read just one word at a time, they also found themselves able to perform only one task at a time, and they missed their old way of life. In short, the way they read was part of an attentional strategy they used in other aspects of life also.

Summary

1. Chimpanzees can learn to communicate through gestures or nonvocal symbols, although their output lacks syntax and does not closely resemble human language. Bonobos (pygmy chimpanzees) have made far more progress than have common chimpanzees, possibly because of species differences and partly because of differences in training methods. (p. 505)

2. People with Broca's aphasia, generally associated with damage to the left frontal cortex, find it difficult to speak or write. They find it especially difficult to use prepositions, conjunctions, and other grammatical connectives. They also fail to understand speech when its meaning depends on grammatical connectives, sentence structure, or word order. (p. 509)

3. People with Wernicke's aphasia, generally associated with damage to the left temporal cortex, have trouble understanding speech and recalling the names of objects. (p. 512)

4. Studies using PET scans indicate that reading without speaking depends on the occipital cortex. Reading tasks that require attention to sound activate the temporal cortex. (p. 514)

5. Certain specialized deficits such as word blindness arise as a result of a disconnection between the language areas and other parts of the brain. (p. 515)

6. The phenomenon of Williams syndrome demonstrates the possibility of developing good language abilities despite a serious deficit in other aspects of intelligence. (p. 518)

7. Dyslexia (severe impairment in reading) may be related to anomalous lateralization or to an unresponsive magnocellular path. It is also linked with a tendency to see more than the normal number of letters to the right of the visual fixation point. (p. 519)

Review Questions

1. How and why do the results of language training with *Pan paniscus* differ from those with common chimpanzees? (p. 506)

2. Describe the differences between Broca's aphasia and Wernicke's aphasia. (p. 509)

3. How can an investigator use a PET scan to determine which areas of the brain are especially activated when a person speaks? (p. 514)

4. Following brain damage, if a person can still speak normally, see, and write, but cannot read, where is the brain damage probably located? (p. 515)

5. What problems were reported for the family with developmental language impairment? Why is it wrong to say that their results indicate a "gene for grammar"? (p. 517)

6. Describe the symptoms of Williams syndrome. (p. 518)

7. What training method has enabled certain people with dyslexia to make rapid progress in learning to read? Why did three of four adults choose to abandon this method? (p. 521)

Thought Questions

1. Most people with Broca's aphasia suffer from partial paralysis on the right side of the body. Most people with Wernicke's aphasia do not. Why?

2. In a syndrome called word deafness, a person cannot understand spoken language, although both language and hearing are normal in other respects. What would be a possible neurological explanation?

Suggestions for Further Reading

Aitchison, J. (1983). *The articulate mammal: An introduction to psycholinguistics* (2nd ed.). New York: Universe Books. Discusses language and the biological specializations that make language possible.

Corballis, M. C. (1991). *The lopsided ape.* New York: Oxford University Press. Thoughtful discussion of lateralization, the physiology of language, and implications concerning the evolution of human behavior.

Damasio, A. R., & Damasio, H. (1992, September). Brain and language. *Scientific American, 267* (3), 87–95. Review of the relationship between language and neural activity in various brain areas.

Krasnegor, N. A., Rumbaugh, D. M., Schiefelbusch, R. L., & Studdert-Kennedy, M. (1991). *Biological and behavioral determinants of language development.* Hillsdale, NJ: Lawrence Erlbaum. Features chapters on language learning by chimpanzees, children, and language-impaired people.

Terms

Broca's area portion of the human left frontal lobe associated with certain aspects of language, especially language production (p. 509)

aphasia lack of language abilities (p. 510)

Broca's aphasia condition marked by loss of fluent speech and impaired use and understanding of prepositions, word endings, and other grammatical devices (p. 510)

Wernicke's area portion of the human left temporal lobe associated with language comprehension (p. 512)

Wernicke's aphasia condition marked by poor language comprehension and great difficulty remembering the names of objects (p. 512)

anomia difficulty recalling the names of objects (p. 512)

alexia physical inability to read despite vision that is otherwise normal (p. 515)

Williams syndrome type of mental retardation in which the person has good use of language in spite of extremely limited abilities in other regards (p. 518)

dyslexia a specific reading difficulty in a person with adequate vision and at least average skills in academic areas other than reading (p. 519)

lateral masking difficulty reading a letter as a result of interference from adjacent letters (p. 520)

RECOVERY FROM BRAIN DAMAGE

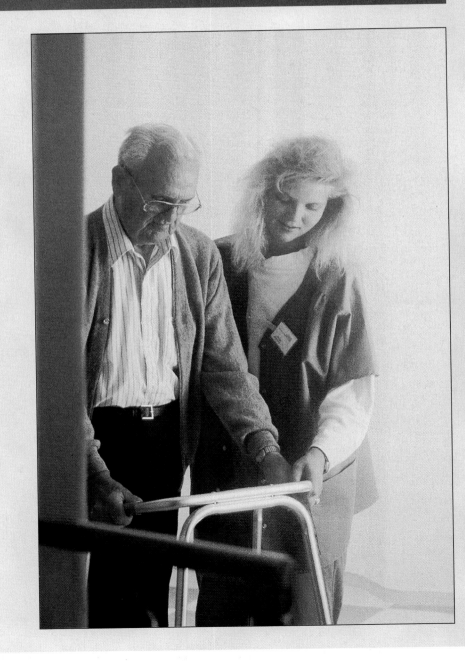

CHAPTER FIFTEEN

1. The human brain can be damaged by a sharp blow, an interruption of blood flow, or several other types of injury. Batteries of tests are available for estimating the location and extent of damage.

2. Although both humans and animals typically recover in part from brain damage, behavior is never as securely established as it would be if the brain had never been damaged. Behavior is likely to deteriorate again as a result of stress or fatigue and in old age.

3. Many mechanisms contribute to recovery from brain damage, including restoration of undamaged neurons to full activity, regrowth of axons, readjustment of surviving synapses, and behavioral adjustments.

4. The degree of recovery from brain damage is sometimes better and sometimes worse if the damage occurs in infancy.

An American soldier who suffered a wound to the left hemisphere of his brain during the Korean War was at first unable to speak at all. Three months later, he was able to speak in short fragments. When he was shown a letterhead, "New York University College of Medicine," and asked to read it, all he could say was, "Doctors—little doctors." Eight years later, when someone asked him again to read the letterhead, he replied, "Is there a catch? It says 'New York University College of Medicine'" (Eidelberg & Stein, 1974).

People with brain damage typically show some behavioral recovery; they are most impaired shortly after the damage and less impaired later on. And yet their recovery is seldom, if ever, complete. For example, people who recover their speech, like the soldier just described, generally show lasting impairments in finding the right words, expressing themselves clearly, or understanding complex speech by others.

Given that the mammalian nervous system cannot replace lost neurons (with the few exceptions mentioned in Chapter 2), we face the theoretical question of how people recover from brain damage at all. From a practical standpoint, we wonder what therapists could do to facilitate recovery. A further reason to study recovery from brain damage is that an understanding of recovery may yield new insights into the functioning of the healthy brain.

Brain Damage and Mechanisms of Recovery

Your body is a partially self-repairing machine. You get a cut, it heals; you lose some skin cells, you grow new ones. When you lose neurons, however, you cannot replace them—with a few exceptions such as olfactory receptors. How, then, does recovery from brain damage take place?

Causes of Human Brain Damage

The human brain can incur damage in many ways. In young adults, the most common cause is a sharp blow to the head from a fall, an automobile or motorcycle accident, a violent assault, or other traumas. About 8 million people receive such closed-head injuries each year in the United States; some 400,000 of them suffer a coma and probable brain damage (Peterson, 1980). Head injuries cause damage partly by subjecting the brain to rotational forces that drive brain tissue against the inside of the skull (see Digression 15.1).

In a **stroke,** also known as a **cerebrovascular accident,** a blood clot or other obstruction closes an artery, or an artery ruptures, interrupting the blood flow—and thus the oxygen supply—to an area of the brain. Deprived of oxygen, the neurons die within a few minutes. **Hypertension** (high blood pressure) greatly increases the probability of a stroke, and it is noteworthy that most strokes occur between 10:00 A.M. and noon when blood pressure is usually highest (J. Marler et al., 1989). Stroke damage may be limited to a fairly sharply defined region; neurons outside that region survive without permanent impairment. Figure 15.1 shows the brain of a person who died immediately after a stroke, the brain of a person who survived for a long time after a stroke, and the brain of a victim of a bullet wound.

Strokes vary in their severity from barely noticeable to immediately fatal. About 30 percent of stroke victims die within the first month after the stroke. Survivors experience various behavioral symptoms, depending on the extent and location of the damage; most experience substantial recovery within the first 2 to 3 months and moderate, gradual improvement that continues long after that (Dombovy & Bach-y-Rita, 1988).

Strokes are rare in young people but become increasingly common beyond age 60 (Kurtzke, 1976). The reported incidence of strokes in the United States declined for a number of years and then rose again, as Figure 15.2 shows. Note that the *reported* incidence is not the same as *actual* incidence, however. The initial decline began with the introduction of treatments to combat hypertension; the later increase probably represents improved reporting of mild strokes after the introduction of CAT scans (Broderick, Phillips, Whisnant, O'Fallon, & Bergstralh, 1989).

Why Don't Woodpeckers Give Themselves Concussions?

When a woodpecker strikes its bill against a tree, it repeatedly bangs its head against an unyielding object at a velocity of 6 to 7 meters per second (about 15 miles per hour). How does it escape brain injury?

P. R. A. May and associates (May, Fuster, Haber, & Hirschman, 1979) used slow-motion photography to observe the behavior of woodpeckers. They found that a woodpecker often makes a pair of quick, preliminary taps against the wood before a hard strike, much like a carpenter lining up a hammer with a nail. When it makes the hard strike, it does so in an almost perfectly straight line, keeping its neck rigid. The result is a near absence of rotational forces and whiplash. The fact that woodpeckers are so careful to avoid rotating their heads during impact supports the claim that rotational forces are a major factor in traumatic brain injuries.

The researchers suggested several implications for football players, race car drivers, and others who wear protective helmets. One implication is that the helmet would give more protection if it extended down to the shoulders, like the metal helmets that medieval knights wore. The advice for non-helmet-wearers: If you see a potential automobile accident or similar trauma about to occur, tuck your chin to your chest and tighten your neck muscles.

A male hairy woodpecker. (Rod Planck)

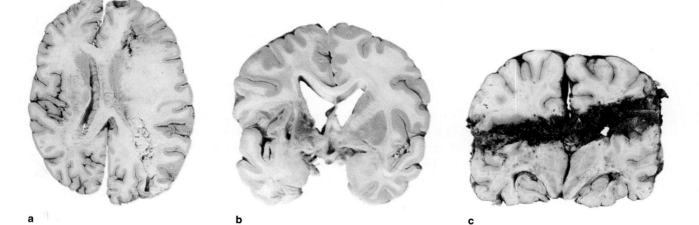

a   b   c

Figure 15.1
Three damaged human brains
(*a*) *Brain of a person who died immediately after a stroke. Note the swelling on the right side.* (*b*) *Brain of a person who survived for a long time after a stroke. Note the cavities on the left side, where many cells were lost.* (*c*) *Brain of a person who suffered a gunshot wound and died immediately. (Photos courtesy of Dana Copeland.)*

Brain Damage and Mechanisms of Recovery

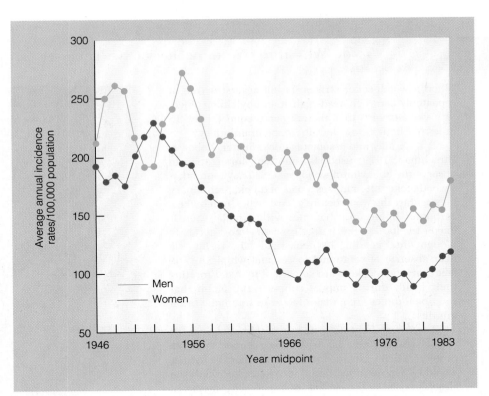

Figure 15.2
Reported incidence of strokes in the United States
Incidence declined for a number of years because of treatments for hypertension; the later rise is probably due to improved accuracy at detecting mild strokes. (From Broderick, Phillips, Whisnant, O'Fallon, & Bergstralh, 1989.)

A stroke kills neurons mostly by overstimulation. A ruptured blood vessel floods nearby neurons with excessive calcium. Recall from Chapter 3 that calcium stimulates the presynaptic terminal to increase its release of neurotransmitters. Recall also from Chapter 13 that calcium enters neurons during certain kinds of excitatory transmission, such as the stimulation of NMDA-type glutamate receptors. The net effect of excess calcium is such a flurry of activity at glutamate synapses that postsynaptic neurons rapidly fill with calcium, sodium, and water, until they actually burst (Rothman, 1992). A high level of calcium can also cause certain neurons to release nitric oxide (NO), which in large quantitites can damage surrounding cells.

Research on rats indicates that stroke damage can be minimized by an injection of magnesium, which blocks calcium from entering neurons (Rothman, 1983); an injection of drugs that block glutamate synapses (Kochhar, Zivin, Lyden, & Mazzarella, 1988; Schurr & Rigor, 1993); or a temporary reduction in body temperature (Strachan, Whittle, & Miller, 1989).

Besides closed-head injuries and strokes, other sources of brain damage include tumors in the brain, certain bacteria and viruses, drugs and toxic substances, bullet wounds, and exposure of the head to radiation. Huntington's disease and Korsakoff's syndrome cause gradual, diffuse damage to many brain areas. In this chapter, we focus mainly on the outcome of strokes and other sudden, localized brain damage.

Diagnosis of Brain Damage

If neuropsychologists know or suspect that a person has suffered brain damage, they administer certain tests to determine the nature of the behavioral deficits and infer the location of the damage. Of greater practical importance, they use the results to plan a program of physical, occupational, or speech therapy to help the person regain control over the activities of daily living. Some behavioral deficits—such as impairments of memory, attention, and abstract thinking—signal brain damage without specifying the type or location of the damage (Goodglass & Kaplan, 1979). Other deficits suggest a particular type of damage.

One battery of tests designed to identify the type and extent of brain damage is the **Halstead-Reitan test.** It consists of a series of measurements ranging from speed of finger tapping to comprehension of language, each of which is especially sensitive to a particular type of brain damage. Other items on the test include placing blocks into the correct holes in a board with one's eyes closed, identifying whether two rhythms are the same or different, and connecting 25 numbered circles in order (Golden, 1981). The Halstead-Reitan test is lengthy, taking about 8 hours to complete.

Another examination used to test for brain damage is the **Luria-Nebraska neuropsychological battery,** pioneered by the Russian psychologist A. R. Luria and revised by researchers at the University of Nebraska (Golden, 1984). The test consists of 269 items divided into 14 scales. Here are a few examples of items:

- Touch your thumb to each of the other four fingers, one at a time.
- Count the number of tones in a musical sequence.
- Localize where you have been touched on the arm.
- Copy drawings of a circle, square, and triangle.
- Memorize a list of seven words.
- Tap a rhythm to copy one that you have heard.

The Luria-Nebraska test can be completed in about 2.5 hours (Golden, 1981). However, many psychologists are not convinced that the information it provides is as reliable or useful as the Halstead-Reitan test.

The reason that both batteries include so many items is that a person may fail a given item for any of several reasons. Interpreting the result on one item requires comparing it with results on other items. For example, someone might fail to copy drawings of circles, squares, and triangles because of poor vision, poor coordination of the hand muscles, or inability to remember the instructions. To evaluate the results of this item, it helps to know whether the person has also failed other visual items, other hand coordination items, or all items in general.

The Precarious Nature of Recovery from Brain Damage

A person or animal that has recovered from brain damage is never fully the same as before the damage. For analogy, someone with a sore foot may be able to walk just about normally under most conditions. The same person carrying a heavy load uphill, however, may slow down greatly, stumble frequently, or even have to quit altogether. Similarly, people and animals that have recovered from brain damage may perform almost normally under most conditions, but their behavior deteriorates under conditions that would only slightly trouble a person without brain damage.

How Stress Impairs Recovered Behavior

Someone who loses some behavior after a stroke and then gradually regains it may lose it again, temporarily, after a couple of beers or a tiring day or toward the end of a long testing session (Fleet & Heilman, 1986). The behavior of

**Figure 15.3
Behavior of a rat after
damage to one side of the
cerebral cortex**

Immediate effect: Sensory
neglect. Rat ignores
sensory stimulus on
opposite side of body.

Later effect: Sensory
extinction. Rat responds
first on the normal side. It
responds to the string on
the opposite side later.

Still later: Rat responds to
both sides equally *unless*
the environment is
changed or the rat is
stressed.

brain-damaged rats also deteriorates under stress or fatigue. For example, in a cool room, both normal rats and rats that have recovered from lateral hypothalamic lesions increase their food intake. (Digesting food generates body heat.) If the room gets colder, a normal rat eats even more, but the animal that has recovered from brain damage may fail to eat altogether, especially if only dry food and water are available (Snyder & Stricker, 1985).

A second example: A normal rat reacts to hypovolemia (decreased blood volume) by drinking and reacts to decreased blood glucose by eating. By contrast, a rat that has recovered from lateral hypothalamic damage temporarily acts the way it did just after the damage: It ignores food and water, does not react to sensory stimuli, and hardly moves (Stricker, Cooper, Marshall, & Zigmond, 1979).

A third example: After damage to one side of the cerebral cortex, especially the parietal cortex, both humans and rats pay less attention to stimuli on the opposite side of the body. At first, they may ignore stimuli on the opposite side altogether. This reaction is known as **sensory neglect** (see Figure 15.3). In milder cases or after partial recovery, they respond to stimuli on the side opposite the brain damage *if* those stimuli are presented alone. If a competing stimulus is present on the normal side of the body, they respond to that stimulus first. If they see similar stimuli on both sides, they report the one on the normal side and not the one on the impaired side (Baylis, Driver, & Rafal, 1993). This tendency for a stimulus on the normal side to overwhelm a stimulus on the impaired side is known as **sensory extinction.**

Eventually, both people and rats respond to stimuli on both sides equally. For example, a rat with strings tied to both forelimbs works equally hard at trying to remove one as the other. However, under mild stress or after a slight change in the environment, the rat loses its recovered behavior. If the experimenter simply turns on the lights or opens the cage door, the rat temporarily goes back to paying more attention to the normal side (Schallert & Whishaw, 1984). Presumably, humans also revert to sensory neglect or sensory extinction under conditions of stress or an altered environment that would scarcely affect a normal individual.

The Loss of Recovered Behavior in Old Age

A recovered rat also deteriorates more in old age than normal rats do. In rats, as in humans, a certain number of neurons die throughout life, and the loss become particularly critical in old age. This natural loss of neurons can

*Chapter 15
Recovery from Brain
Damage*

magnify the effects of a brain lesion long after an individual seems to have recovered from it. By the time a rat that has recovered from lateral hypothalamic damage is 2 years old (old age for a rat), it begins to lose its recovered feeding and drinking behaviors and its responsiveness to sensory stimuli. Eventually, the rat returns to a condition approximating its behavior just after the lesion (Schallert, 1983).

The same principle may hold for humans, Timothy Schallert (1983) speculates. For example, Parkinson's disease may be the result of brain damage suffered early in life, probably not even noticed at the time if it was due to the gradual effects of toxins. When the person reaches old age, losing a small number of additional neurons greatly impairs behavior.

Possible Mechanisms of Recovery from Brain Damage

How can behavior recover after brain damage, given that the brain cannot simply replace the lost neurons? A simple assumption is that some other area of the brain takes over the functions of the damaged area. However, that assumption is valid only in a limited sense. Someone who has injured her left leg may learn to walk on her right leg and crutches. In a sense, we may say that the right leg and the two arms have taken over the function of the damaged leg, but they are simply doing their own functions in a somewhat new way that helps the person compensate for the loss of a leg. In a similar way, a blind person learns to pay more attention to auditory and somatic stimuli; if an animal is blinded throughout infancy, the nonvisual areas of its cortex may grow larger than usual (Burnstine, Greenough, & Tees, 1984). But such changes simply make better use of the nonvisual information available; nonvisual areas of the brain do not take over visual functions.

A brain-damaged individual can recover lost functions by structural changes in the surviving neurons or by learning new ways to solve old problems. Let us consider some of the mechanisms of recovery from brain damage.

Learned Adjustments in Behavior

Much of the recovery that takes place after brain damage is learned; the brain-damaged individual makes better use of abilities unaffected by the damage. For example, someone who has lost vision in all but the center of the visual field may at first fail to see some of the environment. Later, the person moves his or her head back and forth to compensate for the loss in peripheral vision (Marshall, 1985).

A brain-damaged person or animal may also learn to use abilities that at first appeared to be lost but actually were just impaired. For example, it is possible to eliminate most of the sensory information from a leg by cutting the sensory nerves from that leg to the spinal cord (see Figure 15.4). The animal loses sensation from the affected body parts, but it can still control the muscles. Such a limb is referred to as **deafferented.**

Although the animal still *can* control the muscles of the deafferented limb, it ordinarily fails to do so. For example, monkeys with a deafferented limb do not spontaneously use the limb for walking, picking up objects, or any other voluntary behaviors (Taub & Berman, 1968). The investigators initially assumed that the monkey could not use the limb because of the lack of sensory feedback. In a later experiment, however, they cut the afferent nerves of both

Figure 15.4

Figure 15.4
Cross section through the spinal cord
A cut through the dorsal root (as shown) deprives the animal of touch sensations from part of the body, while leaving the motor nerves intact.

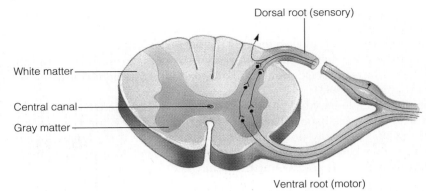

forelimbs; a monkey with this more extensive damage recovered use of both deafferented limbs. The monkey could walk moderately fast, climb upward or sideways on the walls of metal cages, and even pick up a raisin between its thumb and forefinger. Apparently, a monkey fails to use one deafferented forelimb only because walking on three limbs is easier than moving the impaired limb. When both limbs are deafferented, the monkey is forced to use both.

Similarly, many people with brain damage find it easier, especially at first, to struggle along without even trying to use some impaired ability. Many of them are capable of doing more than they are doing and more than they realize they can do. Therapy for brain-damaged people sometimes focuses on showing them how much they are already capable of doing and encouraging them to practice those skills.

Diaschisis and Its Reduction

An individual's behavioral deficit after brain damage reflects more than just the loss of cells. Ordinarily, axons from each neuron provide stimulation that helps to keep other neurons active. When a neuron dies, the other neurons that depended on it for input become less active. For example, after damage to an area in the right hemisphere, the corresponding area in the left hemisphere becomes temporarily less active also (Perani, Vallar, Paulesu, Alberoni, & Fazio, 1993). **Diaschisis** (di-AS-ki-sis, from a Greek term meaning *to shock throughout*) refers to the decreased activity of neurons after they have lost part of their input when other neurons were damaged (Feeney & Baron, 1986).

If diaschisis is an important contributor to behavioral deficits following brain damage, then stimulant drugs should promote recovery from the damage. In a series of experiments, D. M. Feeney and colleagues measured the behavioral effects of cortical damage in rats and cats. Depending on the location of the damage, the animals showed impairments in coordinated movement or depth perception. Injecting amphetamine (which increases dopamine and norepinephrine activity) significantly enhanced the behaviors, and animals that practiced the behaviors under the influence of amphetamine showed long-lasting benefits. Injecting the drug haloperidol (which blocks most of the same synapses) impaired the recovery of behavior (Feeney & Sutton, 1988; Feeney, Sutton, Boyeson, Hovda, & Dail, 1985; Hovda & Feeney, 1989; Sutton, Hovda, & Feeney, 1989).

Similarly, damage to cells in the lateral hypothalamus decreases the activity in certain areas of the cerebral cortex where lateral hypothalamic neurons send their axons (Kolb & Whishaw, 1977). The suppression of cortical activity contributes to the loss of feeding, drinking, and responsiveness to sensory

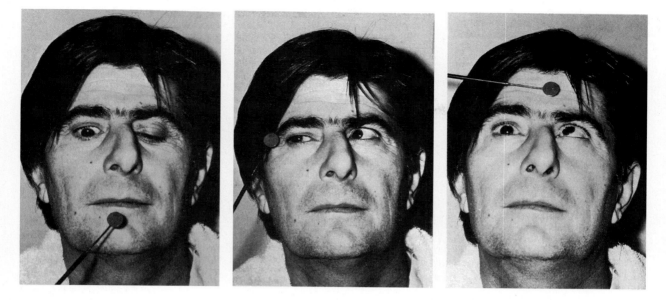

Damaged axons to the muscles of the patient's right eye regenerated but attached incorrectly. When he looks down, his right eyelid opens wide instead of closing, as the other eyelid does. His eye movements are frequently misaimed, and he has trouble moving his right eye upward or to the left. (From P. Thomas, 1988.)

stimuli ordinarily observed after lateral hypothalamic lesions. Behavioral recovery depends partly on a gradual increase in activity by cortical cells.

These results have an important implication for the treatment of stroke patients. People who have just suffered strokes or other brain damage are often given drugs to control blood pressure. Such drugs block norepinephrine synapses and therefore probably interfere with behavioral recovery (Boyeson, Callister, & Cavazos, 1992). The research on diaschisis implies that physicians should use such drugs as sparingly as possible.

Recovery by the Regrowth of Axons

Although a destroyed cell body cannot be replaced, damaged axons do grow back under certain circumstances. A neuron of the peripheral nervous system has its cell body in the spinal cord and an axon that extends into the periphery. When such an axon is crushed, the degenerated portion grows back toward the periphery at a rate of about 1 mm per day. If it is a myelinated axon, the regenerating axon follows the myelin path back to its original target. If the axon was cut instead of crushed, the myelin on the two sides of the cut may not line up correctly, and the regenerating axon may not have a sure path to follow. A sensory nerve finds its way to a sensory receptor, and a motor nerve finds its way to a muscle (Brushart, 1993); still, a motor nerve may not find the correct muscle, as Figure 15.5 illustrates.

Within the mature mammalian brain or spinal cord, a damaged axon regenerates only briefly over an insignificant distance, if at all. That is why the paralysis caused by spinal cord injury is permanent. However, after a cut through the optic nerve or the spinal cord of certain fish species, enough axons regenerate across the cut to restore fairly normal functioning (Bernstein & Gelderd, 1970; Rovainen, 1976; Scherer, 1986; Selzer, 1978).

Why do damaged axons regenerate in the central and peripheral nervous systems of fish and in the peripheral nervous system of mammals, but not in the central nervous system of mammals? Researchers have considered a number of possibilities. One is that a cut through the adult mammalian spinal cord causes too much scar tissue to form. A number of attempts have been made to

Figure 15.6
Collateral sprouting

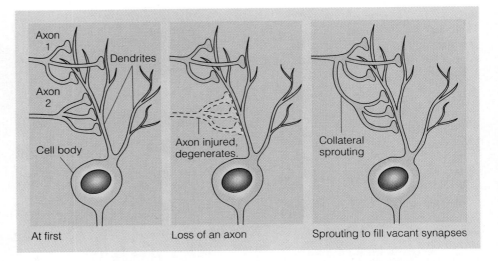

Axon 1

Axon 2

Dendrites

Cell body

Axon injured, degenerates.

Collateral sprouting

At first   Loss of an axon   Sprouting to fill vacant synapses

inhibit the formation of scar tissue, but none of the methods led to any reliable recovery from spinal-cord damage (e.g., McMasters, 1962).

Another possibility is that axons require trophic factors to regenerate, and the adult mammalian nervous system fails to provide those factors. Axons regenerating in the peripheral nervous system follow a path made of myelin. The Schwann cells that form myelin secrete chemicals that promote axon growth. If one implants Schwann cells into a damaged area of the central nervous system, the axons in that area grow into the Schwann cells, growing much more than central nervous system axons ordinarily do (Kromer & Cornbrooks, 1985; Paino & Bunge, 1991). Evidently, Schwann cells produce trophic factors (see p. 161) that promote axon growth; axons in the brain and spinal cord fail to regrow after damage because of the lack of those trophic factors.

Apparently, one reason why axons regenerate in the fish brain and spinal cord is that fish produce trophic factors after damage (Thormodsson, Parker, & Grafstein, 1992). One group of experimenters cut the optic nerves of fish and rabbits. The optic nerve of the fish regenerated; that of the rabbits did not. Then they took a segment of regenerating fish nerve and placed it near an injured rabbit optic nerve. The fish tissues apparently released a chemical that promotes regeneration, because the optic nerve of the rabbit regenerated in part (Schwartz et al., 1985). In the future, injection of such trophic factors into damaged brains may be a means of promoting recovery in humans (Knüsel et al., 1992).

Sprouting

After damage to a set of axons, the cells that had received input from those axons react to their loss of input by secreting chemicals such as nerve growth factor, which we encountered back in Chapter 5 (Van der Zee, Fawcett, & Diamond, 1992). Those chemicals induce nearby uninjured axons to form new branches, or **collateral sprouts,** that attach to the vacant synapses (see Figure 15.6). Gradually, over several months, the sprouts fill in most but not all of the vacated synapses (Matthews, Cotman, & Lynch, 1976). For example, after destruction of about half of the cells in a rat's *locus coeruleus* (a hindbrain area), the brain shows an enormous drop in the number of synapses that the locus coeruleus supplies to the forebrain. Over the next six months, the surviving axons sprout enough to restore almost completely normal input (Fritschy & Grzanna, 1992).

Sprouting is probably a normal condition, not one that occurs only in response to brain damage (Cotman & Nieto-Sampedro, 1982). Periodically, the brain gradually loses old synapses and replaces them via sprouting; in time, the brain loses and replaces some of these new ones.

Sprouting will be most useful in combating the effects of brain damage if the sprouting axon is similar to the damaged one; in that case, it provides a good substitute. However, when an axon sprouts to occupy the synapses previously occupied by an unrelated axon, the usefulness of sprouting is less certain. Perhaps the individual learns to use the new connections appropriately, or perhaps the new connections interfere with normal behavior.

Evidence exists that sprouting is at least sometimes beneficial, although that evidence is largely indirect. For example, **gangliosides** (a class of glycolipids—that is, combined carbohydrate and fat molecules) are believed to enhance collateral sprouting, among other effects. Gangliosides, which are found on the membranes of neurons, reduce the behavioral deficits caused by damage to the caudate nucleus (Sabel, Slavin, & Stein, 1984).

Moreover, the time course of behavioral recovery after brain damage matches the time course of sprouting. In one experiment using rats, connections from one side of the cerebral cortex to one side of the hippocampus were destroyed. Over the next 2 weeks, axons from the opposite side of the cerebral cortex formed collateral sprouts onto the hippocampus on the damaged side. The behaviors that were initially impaired after the lesion recovered over the same two weeks (Scheff & Cotman, 1977). In a follow-up study, researchers measured the degree of behavioral recovery and the amount of electrical activity in the hippocampus. As the electrical activity increased (apparently reflecting collateral sprouting), the behavior recovered proportionately. The animals with the most rapid collateral sprouting had the most rapid behavioral recovery (Reeves & Smith, 1987).

Denervation Supersensitivity

A postsynaptic cell that is deprived of synaptic input for a long time becomes more sensitive to the neurotransmitter. For example, a normal muscle cell responds to the neurotransmitter acetylcholine only at the neuromuscular junction. If the axon is cut, or if it is inactive for days, the muscle cell builds additional receptors, becoming sensitive to acetylcholine over a wider area of its surface (Johns & Thesleff, 1961; Levitt-Gilmour & Salpeter, 1986). The same process occurs in neurons. Heightened sensitivity to the neurotransmitter after the destruction of incoming axons is known as **denervation supersensitivity** (Glick, 1974). Heightened sensitivity as a result of inactivity by incoming axons is called **disuse supersensitivity.** Both kinds of supersensitivity can result from increased numbers of receptors on the surface of the cell or from changes within the cell.

One way to investigate denervation supersensitivity is to remove dopamine synapses selectively by injecting **6-hydroxydopamine (6-OHDA)** into relevant parts of the brain. Because 6-OHDA is chemically similar to dopamine and norepinephrine, the neurons that release these neurotransmitters recognize 6-OHDA and absorb it. After entering the neurons, it is oxidized into toxic chemicals that destroy those neurons. As Figure 15.7 shows, after an injection of 6-OHDA to one side of the brain, postsynaptic cells react to the decreased dopamine input by increasing their number of dopamine receptors on that side (LaHoste & Marshall, 1989).

Brain Damage and Mechanisms of Recovery

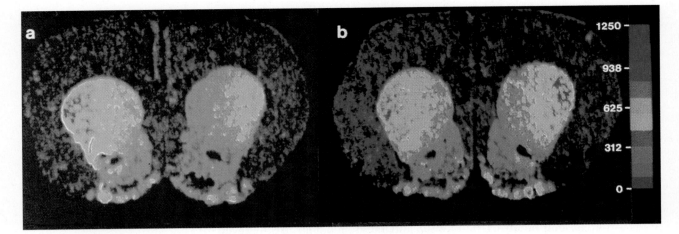

Figure 15.7
Responses of dopamine receptors to decreased input

In these autoradiography slides, red indicates the highest amount of radioactive binding, followed by yellow, green, and blue. (a) An injection of 6-OHDA destroyed dopamine axons in the hemisphere on the left. In response, that hemisphere developed an increased number of D_2 receptors, as indicated by increased binding of a radioactive drug that attaches to those receptors. (b) Rats in another group also received a 6-OHDA lesion to one hemisphere, but they then received daily injections of a drug that blocks D_2 receptors. Here, D_2 receptors increased equally in both hemispheres. (From LaHoste & Marshall, 1989.)

Such changes contribute to recovery by increasing neurons' responses to the limited amount of dopamine that remains. In one study, experimenters injected 6-OHDA on one side of rats' brains, damaging dopamine neurons on that side only (see Figure 15.8). They waited weeks for postsynaptic neurons to become supersensitive to dopamine. Then they injected the rats with either amphetamine or apomorphine. Amphetamine causes dopamine-containing axons to release more neurotransmitter. Because one side of the brain was lacking dopamine axons, the amphetamine stimulated only the intact side of the brain, causing the rats to turn in one direction (toward the brain-injured side). **Apomorphine** is a morphine derivative that directly stimulates dopamine receptors. Because of denervation supersensitivity, apomorphine strongly stimulates the damaged side of the brain, causing the rats to turn in the opposite direction (Marshall, Drew, & Neve, 1983). These results (shown in Figure 15.8) indicate that the denervated side of the brain has become supersensitive to dopamine and to drugs that stimulate dopamine receptors.

Denervation supersensitivity helps to explain why people can lose most of their dopamine-containing axons from the substantia nigra before they begin to show symptoms of Parkinson's disease (Zigmond, Abercrombie, Berger, Grace, & Stricker, 1990). After loss of some of the axons, the remaining axons compensate by increasing their release of dopamine. After still further loss, the receptors on the postsynaptic membrane develop denervation supersensitivity. Such mechanisms can compensate for a loss of up to 75–90 percent of the axons; with still further damage, symptoms of Parkinson's disease start to emerge.

Reorganization of Sensory Representations

As we saw in Chapter 8, during development, many axons form tentative connections with a given postsynaptic neuron. Through a competitive process, the postsynaptic neuron strengthens the synapses with one or more of those axons. The rejected axons may maintain ineffective (inhibited) synapses with the cell, or they may attach to neighboring cells. Now suppose that the originally accepted axon dies or has a prolonged period of inactivity. At that point, one of the previously ineffective synapses may become active, through denervation supersensitivity, or an axon attached to a neighboring cell may produce collateral sprouts.

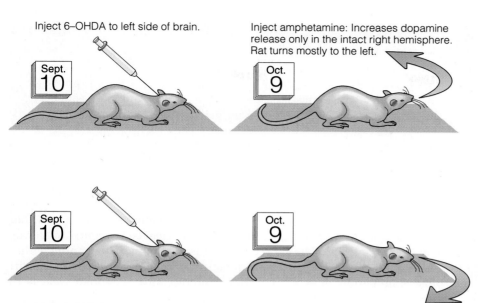

Inject 6–OHDA to left side of brain.

Inject amphetamine: Increases dopamine release only in the intact right hemisphere. Rat turns mostly to the left.

Inject 6–OHDA to left side of brain.

Inject apomorphine: Rat's receptors are stimulated more on the left than on the right. Rat turns mostly to the right.

Figure 15.8
Results of an experiment demonstrating denervation supersensitivity
Injecting 6-OHDA destroys axons releasing dopamine on one side of the brain. Later, amphetamine stimulates only the intact side of the brain because it cannot cause axons to release dopamine on the damaged side. Apomorphine stimulates the damaged side more strongly because it directly stimulates dopamine receptors, which have become supersensitive on that side. (Based on data from Marshall, Drew, & Neve, 1983.)

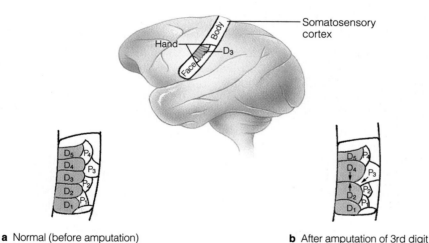

a Normal (before amputation)   **b** After amputation of 3rd digit

Figure 15.9
Changes in the representation of the fingers in the somatosensory cortex of an owl monkey after amputation of the third finger
Note that the cortical area previously responsive to the third finger (D_3) becomes responsive to the second and fourth fingers (D_2 and D_4) and part of the palm (P_3). (Based on Kaas, Merzenich, & Killackey, 1983.)

For example, one section in the primary somatosensory cortex of a monkey is responsive to touch stimuli from the five fingers of one hand, as Figure 15.9a shows. In one study, experimenters amputated finger 3 in an owl monkey. The cortical cells that used to respond to information from that finger now had virtually no input. As time passed, more and more of those neurons became responsive to finger 2, finger 4, or part of the palm, until eventually the cortex had the pattern of responsiveness we see in Figure 15.9b (Kaas, Merzenich, & Killackey, 1983; Merzenich et al., 1984). Evidently, axons representing those adjacent hand parts had established effective synapses through collateral sprouting, denervation supersensitivity, or both. Such reorganization does not cause fingers 2 and 4 to feel like the lost finger. When humans lose a finger, they become more sensitive in the neighboring fingers, better able to localize a sensation on one of them.

Table 15.1	Summary of Mechanisms of Recovery from Brain Damage

1. Learned adjustments in behavior
2. Return of function by undamaged neurons: reduction of diaschisis.
3. Regeneration of damaged axons (occurs in the central and peripheral nervous systems of fish; occurs only in the peripheral nervous system for mature mammals)
4. Changes at synapses: sprouting and denervation supersensitivity

Cortical reorganization after loss of sensation from one finger occurs over short distances. That is, after an area loses its own axons, the new axons that start to excite it are axons that formerly excited cortical cells about 1 mm away (Kahle & Cotman, 1993). The reorganization is fairly quick, beginning within 15 minutes (Gilbert, 1993). Similar reorganization can occur if one body part gets more stimulation than normal. For example, after a monkey learns to respond to a particular stimulation pattern on one finger, or after a blind person spends years reading Braille with one finger, the cortical representation of the stimulated skin grows (Pascual-Leone & Torres, 1993; Recanzone, Merzenich, Jenkins, Kamil, & Dinse, 1992). In other words, reorganization of the cortex is not an unusual phenomenon that happens only after brain damage; it is probably occurring to a small degree almost all the time.

For many years, neuroscientists assumed that cortical reorganization was limited to displacements of an axon's representation over about 1 mm or so—a realistic estimate of how far a cortical axon's branches might extend. Then came a surprise. Investigators recorded from the cerebral cortex of monkeys that had had an entire limb deafferented twelve years previously. (These were the same monkeys discussed under the heading "Learned Adjustments in Behavior," p. 531.) In these monkeys, quite a large stretch of cortex had lost its input representing the fingers, palm, arm, and part of the neck. After this lengthy interval, that whole cortical area had become responsive to the face (Pons et al., 1991). How this occurred is unknown. The cortical cells ordinarily responsive to the face (which were, incidentally, still responsive to the face) were located 10–14 mm away from some of the cells now responding to the face. Researchers found no evidence that axons had grown collateral sprouts over anything close to that distance. The most likely hypothesis is that axons in the spinal cord or the brain stem had sprouted to nearby targets and that the brain stem cells were relaying this altered information to the thalamus and cortex.

Table 15.1 summarizes the mechanisms we have discussed that may contribute to recovery from brain damage.

Summary

1. Strokes are a common cause of brain damage in old age. A sudden blow to the head is a more common cause of brain damage in young people. (p. 526)

2. The Halstead-Reitan and Luria-Nebraska batteries assess brain damage. Because performance on a given item may be impaired for many reasons, these tests compare a person's performance across a variety of items. (p. 529)

3. People and animals that have recovered from brain damage are more likely than normal individuals are to deteriorate under conditions of stress or in old age. (p. 529)

4. Much of the recovery that takes place after brain damage does not require structural changes in the brain; it depends on learned changes in behavior to take advan-

tage of the skills that remain, even if they are impaired. (p. 531)

5. After brain damage, neurons that are remote from the site of damage may become inactive because they receive less input than usual. Behavioral recovery from brain damage depends partly on increased activity by these remote neurons; stimulant drugs promote recovery by facilitating activity in surviving cells. (p. 532)

6. A cut axon may regenerate in the peripheral nervous system of a mammal and in either the central or peripheral nervous system of certain fish. Several explanations have been proposed for why cut axons do not regenerate in the mammalian central nervous system. (p. 533)

7. When one set of axons dies, neighboring axons may, under certain conditions, sprout new branches to innervate the vacant synapses. (p. 534)

8. If many of the axons innervating a given postsynaptic neuron die or become inactive, that neuron may become responsive to other axons. (p. 536)

Review Questions

1. What causes death of neurons after a stroke? (p. 528)
2. Besides closed-head injury and stroke, what are some other causes of human brain damage? (p. 528)
3. Why do the Halstead-Reitan and Luria-Nebraska tests assess many separate behaviors? (p. 529)
4. In what ways is a person or animal that has recovered from brain damage different from one that has never suffered brain damage? (p. 529)
5. What shows that brain-damaged animals are sometimes capable of behaviors that they do not spontaneously engage in? Describe one example. (p. 531)
6. The drug haloperidol is given to many patients suffering from schizophrenia and several other psychological disorders. Why would it be unwise to administer haloperidol to a patient who had recently suffered a stroke? (p. 533)
7. Explain why axons may fail to regenerate across a cut through the mammalian spinal cord. (p. 533)
8. What is the evidence that collateral sprouting sometimes aids in recovery from brain damage? (p. 535)
9. What conditions produce denervation supersensitivity? (p. 535)
10. When the sensory cortex reorganizes its connections following loss of sensation from a finger, what happens to the sensations from neighboring parts of the hand? (p. 537)

Thought Question

1. Ordinarily, patients with Parkinson's disease move very slowly, if at all. However, during an emergency (such as a fire in the building), some such patients move rapidly and vigorously. Suggest a possible explanation.

Suggestions for Further Reading

DeMille, A. (1981). *Reprieve: A memoir.* Garden City, NY: Doubleday. A stroke victim's own account of her stroke and recovery from it, with interpolated commentary by a neurologist, Fred Plum.

Marshall, J. F. (1985). Neural plasticity and recovery of function after brain injury. *International Review of Neurobiology, 26,* 201–247. A general review of mechanisms of recovery.

Zivin, J. A., & Choi, D. W. (July, 1991). Stroke therapy. *Scientific American, 265* (1), 56–63. Description of how a stroke kills neurons and the possible ways of reducing cell death.

Terms

stroke (or **cerebrovascular accident**) brain damage caused when a blood clot or other obstruction interrupts the flow of blood, and therefore oxygen, to a brain area (p. 526)

hypertension high blood pressure (p. 526)

Halstead-Reitan test set of behavioral tests designed to identify the type and extent of brain damage (p. 529)

Luria-Nebraska neuropsychological battery set of behavioral tests designed to identify the type and extent of brain damage (p. 529)

sensory neglect ignoring stimuli on the side of the body opposite an area of brain damage (p. 530)

sensory extinction tendency to respond first and more strongly to stimuli on the same side of the body as brain damage, as opposed to stimuli on the opposite side (p. 530)

deafferent to remove the sensory nerves from a body part (p. 531)

diaschisis decreased activity in neurons that have lost part of their input (p. 532)

collateral sprout newly formed branch from an uninjured axon that forms a synapse vacated when another axon was destroyed (p. 534)

ganglioside molecule composed of combinations of carbohydrates and fats (p. 535)

denervation supersensitivity increased sensitivity by a postsynaptic cell after removal of an axon that formerly innervated it (p. 535)

disuse supersensitivity increased sensitivity by a postsynaptic cell after a period of decreased input by incoming axons (p. 535)

6-hydroxydopamine (6-OHDA) chemical that destroys neurons that release dopamine or norepinephrine (p. 535)

apomorphine morphine derivative that stimulates dopamine receptors (p. 536)

Factors Influencing Recovery from Brain Damage

If two individuals suffer the same brain damage, one of them may show more severe symptoms than the other does. Why? Sometimes it is because they were different ages at the time of the injury. In other cases, it is because one suffered the damage suddenly and the other gradually. Still another possibility is that one received therapy after the damage.

Effects of Age at the Time of the Damage

According to the **Kennard principle,** named after Margaret Kennard, who first stated it (Kennard, 1938), recovery from brain damage early in life will be more complete than will recovery from damage later in life. For example, a child whose left hemisphere is damaged before age 2 eventually develops nearly normal language abilities, in most cases. Similar damage at a later age produces much more severe language deficits, with much less recovery (Satz, Strauss, & Whitaker, 1990). A child with damage to the sensory or motor cortex also shows greater gains than an adult with similar damage (Hécaen, Perenin, & Jeannerod, 1984).

The Kennard principle is no more than partly correct, however. Depending on the location of the damage and the behavioral deficits studied, the effects of early brain damage may be greater than, less than, or the same as the effects of adult brain damage (Kolb & Whishaw, 1989; Stein, Finger, & Hart, 1983). For example, although damage limited to, say, the motor cortex of a young child may only moderately impair motor control, it is likely to produce other, more generalized difficulties not found after adult brain damage, such as slow learning and a low IQ score (Taylor, 1984).

Moreover, the effect of age on recovery from brain damage depends on the cause of damage. Although children may recover better than adults do from the destruction of a limited area of the brain, they recover less from effects on the brain due to infection, poor nutrition, inadequate oxygen, or exposure to alcohol or other drugs (O'Leary & Boll, 1984). Such factors disrupt the organization of developing neurons without killing them, so the neurons may make abnormal connections. The result is a generalized loss of sensory and motor functions and intelligence.

Why might the effects of infant brain damage be different from those of adult brain damage? We can identify several possible reasons.

Altered Connections by Spared Neurons

Infant neurons have greater potential than adult neurons do for collateral sprouting of axons (McWilliams & Lynch, 1983, 1984), axonal regeneration

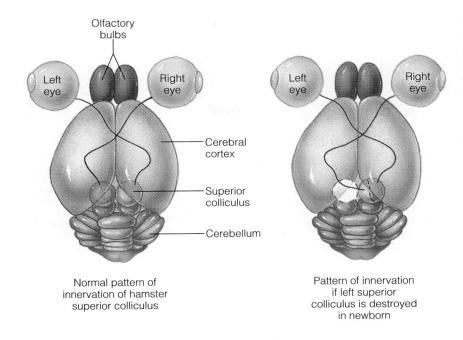

Olfactory bulbs

Left eye

Right eye

Cerebral cortex

Superior colliculus

Cerebellum

Left eye

Right eye

Normal pattern of innervation of hamster superior colliculus

Pattern of innervation if left superior colliculus is destroyed in newborn

Figure 15.10

If the superior colliculus of a newborn hamster is destroyed on one side, the axons that normally inner-vate the damaged side go to the opposite superior colliculus. (Based on results of Schneider & Jhaveri, 1974.)

(Kalil, 1988), dendritic branching (Kolb & Gibb, 1993), and redirection of axons whose normal target is unavailable. For example, suppose that the superior colliculus on the left side of an infant hamster's brain is damaged before the optic nerve reaches it. When axons of the optic nerve do reach the damaged area, they cross to attach to the superior colliculus on the right side instead (see Figure 15.10). The hamsters then show some spatial orientation toward what they see in the right visual field. Unfortunately, they orient in the wrong direction. That is, a hamster that sees something on the right turns to the left. It is as if the right superior colliculus interprets all the input that it receives as coming from the left visual field as usual (Schneider & Jhaveri, 1974). This example shows that early brain damage can lead to a different pattern of connections than adult damage—not necessarily a better one.

Effects on Other, Still Developing Neurons

In normal development, the immature brain produces many more neurons and synapses than will survive to adulthood, as we saw in Chapter 5. As development proceeds, many of the extra neurons and extra connections are lost. During early development, damage to one set of neurons can alter the survival and connections of other immature neurons.

For example, after complete removal of one hemisphere of a rat brain in infancy, the other hemisphere increases in thickness (Kolb, Sutherland, & Whishaw, 1983). Evidently, neurons of each hemisphere compete with neurons of the other hemisphere for the chance to survive; if one hemisphere is damaged, a greater percentage of cells in the opposite hemisphere can survive.

In contrast, after removal of the anterior portion of the cortex in infant rats, the posterior portion of the cortex develops less than normal (Kolb & Holmes, 1983). Apparently, neurons in the posterior cortex require interaction with neurons in the anterior cortex to survive. For that reason, damage to the anterior cortex affects the behavior of infant rats more than it does the behavior of adults.

Here is another example in which early damage can produce either excellent recovery or severe deficits, depending on its location: Patricia Goldman

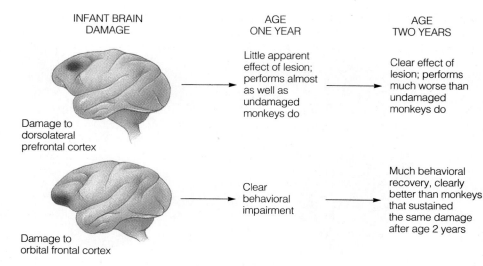

Figure 15.11
Summary of experiments on brain damage in infant monkeys
After damage to the dorsolateral prefrontal cortex, monkeys seem relatively unimpaired at age 1 year but more severely impaired later, when this area ordinarily matures. After damage to the orbital frontal cortex, monkeys show a clear behavioral impairment at first but substantial recovery later. (From P. Goldman, 1976.)

INFANT BRAIN DAMAGE

AGE ONE YEAR

AGE TWO YEARS

Damage to dorsolateral prefrontal cortex

Little apparent effect of lesion; performs almost as well as undamaged monkeys do

Clear effect of lesion; performs much worse than undamaged monkeys do

Damage to orbital frontal cortex

Clear behavioral impairment

Much behavioral recovery, clearly better than monkeys that sustained the same damage after age 2 years

found that damage to the **orbital frontal cortex** (an anterior area of the prefrontal cortex) in infant monkeys produced deficits on the delayed alternation task, in which the monkeys have to alternate between choosing an object on the left and choosing an object on the right. This deficit is quite clear at age 1 year; however, by age 2 years, the behavior improves considerably. Monkeys suffering the same brain damage at a later age show far less recovery (Goldman, 1976; Miller, Goldman, & Rosvold, 1973). Evidently, early damage to the orbital frontal cortex prompts other, later developing areas to change their organization in a way that compensates for the damage.

By contrast, infant damage to the **dorsolateral prefrontal cortex** (also in the prefrontal cortex) produces at first only a moderate deficit on the delayed alternation task. One year after the injury, they performed surprisingly well, almost as well as other 1-year-old monkeys without brain damage. When tested 2 years after the lesion, however, the brain-damaged monkeys showed clear behavioral deficits (Goldman, 1971). That is, the behavioral deficit actually increased over time. The apparent explanation rests on the fact that the dorsolateral prefrontal cortex is slow to mature. The infant lesion produced little effect by age 1 year because the dorsolateral prefrontal cortex, even if healthy, does not do much at that age anyway. But by age 2 years, when that area should start assuming some important functions, its absence begins to make a difference. Figure 15.11 summarizes these results. We shall return to this point in Chapter 16: Some investigators believe that schizophrenia is associated with early damage to the dorsolateral prefrontal cortex, but because of the slow maturation of this area, the effects do not become fully evident until adolescence or early adulthood.

Differences between Slow-Onset and Rapid-Onset Lesions

After sudden damage to the motor cortex on both sides of its brain, a monkey suffers a total and permanent loss of fine movements. However, if the damage occurs in several stages, with a couple of weeks to recover from one small brain injury before the next one occurs, the monkey may continue to walk and to carry on other activities even though the entire motor cortex is ultimately destroyed (Travis & Woolsey, 1956). The **serial-lesion effect** refers to the phenomenon of better recovery after a series of small lesions than after a single lesion of the same total size.

The serial-lesion effect does not occur with all kinds of brain damage; sometimes a series of small lesions produces just as great an effect as one large lesion. When the serial-lesion effect does occur, two explanations are possible: (1) Gradual brain damage may allow for collateral sprouting or other structural changes that cannot occur after sudden, complete damage, or (2) gradual damage may enable the individual to learn new ways of coping and better ways to use the abilities spared by the lesion.

In an experiment that supports the second interpretation, rats with bilateral damage to their somatosensory and motor cortex displayed a variety of sensory and motor impairments from which they recovered only slightly. After unilateral damage to the same areas, rats displayed unilateral impairments from which they made substantial recovery—but only if they were allowed to practice the behaviors. If they then sustained damage on the opposite side of the brain, the behaviors that recovered after the first damage remained intact (deCastro & Zrull, 1988). Evidently, the rats recovered from the first damage largely through some learning process. The learned behaviors survived after damage to the opposite side of the brain.

Therapies for Brain Damage

After someone suffers brain damage, physicians, physical therapists, and others try to help the person recover. Although therapy today consists almost entirely of supervised practice of the impaired behaviors, direct brain interventions may become possible in the future.

Behavioral Interventions

You may fail to find a book that you know the library used to have, either because the library has lost or misplaced the book or because it has lost its record of the book's location. Similarly, brain-damaged people and animals may seem to have forgotten a particular skill either because they completely lost the skill or because they "cannot find" it. Therapists help brain-damaged people find their lost skills or learn to use their remaining abilities more effectively.

For example, some people with frontal lobe damage behave in socially inappropriate ways, such as using obscene language, failing to wash themselves, and making lewd sexual overtures to strangers. Therapists work with such patients, perhaps providing positive reinforcement for polite speech, good grooming, and self-restraint. The brain-damaged people gradually recover the social skills that they appeared to have lost (McGlynn, 1990).

Similarly, a brain-damaged animal that seems to have forgotten a learned skill may still retain it in some hidden manner. After damage to its visual cortex, a rat that had previously learned to approach a white card instead of a black card for food chose randomly between the two cards. Had the rat forgotten the discrimination completely? Evidently not, since it could learn again to approach the white card significantly more easily than it could learn to

Figure 15.12
**Results of an experiment on
brain damage and memory**
*Brain damage impairs
retrieval of a memory but
does not destroy it com-
pletely. (From LeVere and
Morlock, 1973.)*

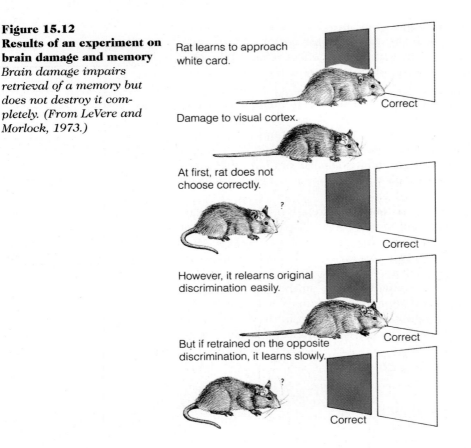

Rat learns to approach
white card.

Correct

Damage to visual cortex.

At first, rat does not
choose correctly.

Correct

However, it relearns original
discrimination easily.

Correct

But if retrained on the opposite
discrimination, it learns slowly.

Correct

approach the black card (LeVere & Morlock, 1973). Apparently, some trace of
the original learning remained after the brain damage. (See Figure 15.12.)

Thomas LeVere (1975) proposed that such a lesion does not destroy the
memory representation but merely impairs the rat's ability to find the memory.
When the rat relearns the task, it is actually relocating or reaccessing the original memory. Moreover, the reaccessing process is not impaired by a drug that
greatly impedes the learning of new tasks (Davis & LeVere, 1979).

Similarly, humans who have suffered brain damage may have trouble
accessing certain skills and memories. Just as a monkey that has no sensation
in one arm may try to get by without using it, a person who has an impaired
sensory system may try to get by without using it (LeVere, 1980). The task of
physical therapists, occupational therapists, and speech therapists is to prod
brain-damaged patients to practice their impaired skills instead of ignoring
them.

In an experiment that supports this approach to therapy, N. D. LeVere and
T. E. LeVere (1982) trained rats with visual cortex lesions on a brightness discrimination task, in which tactile stimuli were also present. For one group of
rats, the tactile stimuli were redundant with the brightness cues; the rats could
solve the problem by responding to either stimulus. This group solved the task
rapidly but paid attention only to the tactile stimuli. If the tactile stimuli were
removed, the rats responded randomly. For a second group of rats, the tactile
stimuli were irrelevant; they could solve the problem only on the basis of
brightness. This group took much longer than normal rats to solve the problem
because their attention to the tactile stimuli distracted them from the relevant

visual cues, but they did eventually solve it. In short, rats with visual cortex lesions can learn about visual stimuli, but they are unlikely to do so if other stimuli are available (Davis & LeVere, 1982). To help humans with similar brain damage, therapists should either simplify the problem by removing distracting stimuli or teach the individual to concentrate on the relevant stimuli.

Drug Therapies

Several drugs have shown signs of aiding recovery from brain damage in animals. So far, no evidence is available concerning their effect on humans.

Nimodipine, a drug that prevents calcium from entering cells, improves memory for visual learning tasks in rats with visual cortex lesions (LeVere, Brugler, Sandin, & Gray-Silva, 1989). It probably acts through two routes: First, recall from Chapter 13 that calcium blockers can improve learning and memory by preventing inappropriate stimulation at NMDA-type glutamate synapses. Second, recall from earlier in this chapter that strokes kill brain cells mainly by flooding them with excess calcium, leading to overstimulation. Calcium blockers administered before or shortly after a stroke can reduce the amount of damage that the stroke causes (LeVere, 1993).

Several studies indicate that gangliosides (which, as we have seen, may enhance collateral sprouting) promote the restoration of damaged brains. Their location on the membranes of neurons suggests that they contribute to the recognition of one neuron by another in early development, guiding axons to the correct locations to form synapses. Daily injections of gangliosides aid the recovery of behavior after several kinds of brain damage (Cahn, Borziex, Aldinio, Toffano, & Cahn, 1989; Ramirez et al., 1987a, 1987b; Sabel, Slavin, & Stein, 1984). Exactly how they do so is unknown.

The Prospects for Therapy by Brain Grafts

At the risk of sounding Frankensteinian, what about the possibility of replacing dead brain cells by transplanting healthy cells from someone else? Surgeons can graft brain tissue from one individual to another with only limited prospect of tissue rejection. Perhaps because the blood-brain barrier protects the brain from foreign substances, the immune system is relatively inactive in the brain (Nicholas & Arnason, 1992). The grafted brain tissue grows, however, only if it comes from a fetus.

In a pioneering study, M. J. Perlow and colleagues (1979) injected the chemical 6-OHDA to make lesions in the substantia nigra on one side of the brain in rats. (The substantia nigra is the part of the brain that degenerates in Parkinson's disease.) Each rat developed movement abnormalities resembling Parkinson's disease just on the side of the body opposite to the brain damage. After the movement abnormalities had stabilized, the experimenters transplanted the substantia nigra from rat fetuses to locations where those cells would normally make synapses in the adult rat brains. The grafts survived in 29 of the 30 rats that received them, making synapses in varying numbers. Four weeks after the grafts were implanted, most recipients had recovered much of their normal movement. Control animals that suffered the same brain damage without receiving the brain grafts showed little or no behavioral recovery.

Inspired by this report, other investigators have tried transplanting fetal tissue to reverse the effects of many types of brain damage, producing successful effects in some cases but not in others (Fisher & Gage, 1993). When it does work, investigators are not altogether sure why it works. In certain cases, the results suggest that the transplanted fetal cells survive, extend their dendrites and axons, and make apparently appropriate synapses (e.g., Hudson, Bickford, Johansson, Hoffer, & Strömberg, 1994). In other cases, the transplant operation leads to behavioral recovery even though the transplanted tissue does not survive or form synapses. Evidently, the transplanted tissue releases trophic factors that stimulate axon and dendrite growth in the surrounding areas of the recipient's own brain (Bohn, Cupit, Marciano, & Gash, 1987; Dunnett, Ryan, Levin, Reynolds, & Bunch, 1987; Ensor, Morley, Redfern, & Miles, 1993).

Although the research on laboratory animals remains inconclusive on some key points, several surgical teams have tried to transplant tissues into damaged brain areas for human Parkinson's patients. The obvious question is: Who will be the donors? Several early studies tried transplanting tissue from the patient's own adrenal gland. Even though that tissue is not composed of neurons, it produces and releases dopamine, the transmitter that is deficient in Parkinson's patients' brains. Unfortunately, the adrenal gland transplants produced little if any benefit in most patients (see, for example, Backlund et al., 1985).

The other possibility is to transplant brain tissue taken from aborted fetuses. Early attempts using this method were complicated by the fact that fetal brain tissue is suitable for transplantation only for a brief period during development. After it is removed, it must be transplanted rapidly into the recipient's brain or the cells will not survive. In many cases, fetal tissues transplanted into the brains of Parkinson's patients either failed to survive at all or produced only minor improvement in the patient's condition (Landau, 1993). Techniques have now been developed for freezing and preserving fetal tissues for use in a later transplant (Redmond et al., 1993). Preliminary studies with a few patients have yielded significant benefits that have lasted months, though they have not accomplished a full cure (Freed et al., 1992; Spencer et al., 1992). Far more research will be needed to determine whether either brain transplants or injections of trophic factors may someday become a useful medical technique.

Summary

1. Recovery from brain damage may be better or worse in infants than in adults, depending on a number of circumstances. (p. 540)

2. Recovery is sometimes better if the damage develops in several stages, instead of all at once, or if the damaged individual had certain experiences before the damage. (p. 542)

3. At present, therapy for brain damage consists mostly of helping the person practice the abilities that have been impaired but not destroyed. (p. 543)

4. Drugs that enhance memory or guide axonal growth promote recovery after certain kinds of brain damage. (p. 545)

5. Animal experiments suggest the possibility of transplanting brain grafts from fetal donors as a therapy for brain damage. However, results with humans have been mostly unencouraging. Benefits may depend on trophic factors rather than new synapses with the transplanted neurons. (p. 545)

Review Questions

1. Why might the effects of infant brain damage differ from those of adult brain damage? Give more than one reason and evidence for each. (p. 540)

2. What are the usual methods and goals of therapy for people with brain damage? (p. 543)

3. What kind of donor must be used in brain graft experiments if the transplanted tissue is to survive and make connections? (p. 545)

Thought Question

1. If brain grafts could be made successfully from fetal monkeys to adult humans, how should we decide whether it is right to conduct such surgery?

Suggestions for Further Reading

Kolb, B., & Whishaw, I. Q. (1989). Plasticity in the neocortex: Mechanisms underlying recovery from early brain damage. *Progress in Neurobiology, 32,* 235–276. Review of research on differences between young and old in recovery from brain damage.

Fisher, L. J., & Gage, F. H. (1993). Grafting in the mammalian central nervous system. *Physiological Reviews, 73,* 583–616. Very thorough review of research on the effects and mechanisms of brain grafting.

Terms

Kennard principle generalization (not always correct) that it is easier to recover from brain damage early in life than later in life (p. 540)

orbital frontal cortex an anterior area of the prefrontal cortex (p. 542)

dorsolateral prefrontal cortex area of the prefrontal cortex (p. 542)

serial-lesion effect tendency for recovery to be more complete after a series of small lesions than after a single, large lesion (p. 543)

BIOLOGY OF MOOD DISORDERS, SCHIZOPHRENIA, AND AUTISM

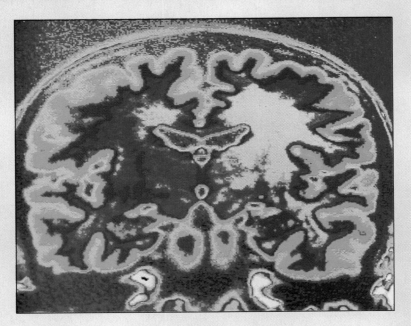

E. F. Torrey & M. F. Casanova/NIMH

CHAPTER SIXTEEN

MAIN IDEAS

1. Mood disorders and schizophrenia are the product of numerous biological and environmental influences.

2. Various drugs used for treating depression and schizophrenia alter transmission at certain types of synapses. The drugs' effectiveness suggests that the underlying causes of the disorders may include some problem affecting particular neurotransmitters.

3. A number of nondrug biological treatments are also effective against certain cases of depression, including electroconvulsive shock, changes in sleep patterns, exposure to bright light, and the use of lithium salts.

4. Autism is a rare childhood disorder that resembles schizophrenia in certain regards, although the underlying causes differ.

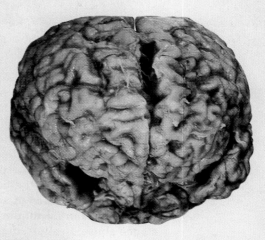

Figure 16.1
The brain of a person with general paresis (the final stage of syphilis)
Many of the gyri in the cerebral cortex are shrunken. (Photo courtesy of Dana Copeland.)

Until the late 1860s, people with aphasia were considered mentally ill. After physicians discovered that aphasia was caused by localized brain damage, those patients were treated by neurologists instead of psychiatrists. Similarly, after physicians discovered that general paresis, a type of intellectual deterioration, was a symptom of the third stage of syphilis infection (see Figure 16.1), people with this problem were classified as neurological rather than psychiatric patients. Apparently, as soon as we find a neurological basis for a psychiatric disorder, people hesitate to call it a mental illness.

If we found neurological bases for all psychological disorders, would psychiatrists and clinical psychologists go out of business? No. Talking with a psychotherapist (psychotherapy) can be helpful for people suffering from aphasia, general paresis, or even a broken leg. Evidence accumulating since about 1950 indicates that anxiety, obsessive-compulsive disorder, sleep disorders, violent behavior, and many other psychological disorders have biological aspects. Psychotherapists have learned to coordinate psychotherapy with biological therapy, but they still find ample demand for psychotherapy. The presence of biological contributors to a disorder does not deny the importance of experiential contributors.

In this chapter, we deal with depression, schizophrenia, and related disorders—disorders that in many cases become so severe that they absolutely dominate a person's life. Researchers disagree, sometimes sharply, about the relative importance of biological and environmental causes for these disorders; they also disagree about the relative advantages and disadvantages of biological therapies, psychotherapies, and combinations of the two. Here we emphasize the biological components of depression, schizophrenia, and autism; *Biological Psychology* is, after all, the title of this book. But this emphasis does not imply that other aspects are unimportant.

Depression

Depression, like all other psychological conditions, can vary enormously in its duration and intensity. Almost everyone has had at least an occasional, brief period of feeling sad and discouraged. When psychologists or psychiatrists talk about depression, they refer to an episode that seriously interferes with a person's life for weeks, months, even years. Even by that more stringent definition, depression is quite widespread. According to one survey of more than 8,000 U.S. adults, about 19 percent of all people suffer some form of psychiatrically significant depression at some time in their lives (Kessler et al., 1994). Moreover, a substantial number of those people also suffer from anxiety or substance abuse. In short, depression is a major human problem.

Types of Depression

A **depressed** person feels fearful and gloomy, helpless and hopeless. Depressed people are generally inactive; when they do anything at all, it is unproductive, such as pacing back and forth, wringing their hands. They say they feel unhappy, and their facial expressions indicate unhappiness.

Depressed people almost invariably have trouble sleeping. On the average, they take longer than most people to fall asleep. After sleeping restlessly, they awaken too early and cannot get back to sleep. During the day, they consequently feel drowsy.

Difficulties in Diagnosing Depression

If you feel sad and gloomy today, are you suffering from a psychological disorder, is your brain chemistry out of balance, and should you arrange to see a therapist? Probably not. You may have good reasons for feeling low today, and you may start feeling better soon. A clinician would consider you depressed only if your distress is persistent and seriously interferes with your everyday life for a long time, generally months.

Even then, depression may not be your main or only problem. One study of patients in the California mental health system found that more than one-third had serious, undiagnosed physical illnesses that could cause or at least aggravate their psychological distress (Koran et al., 1989). Ideally, a therapist should

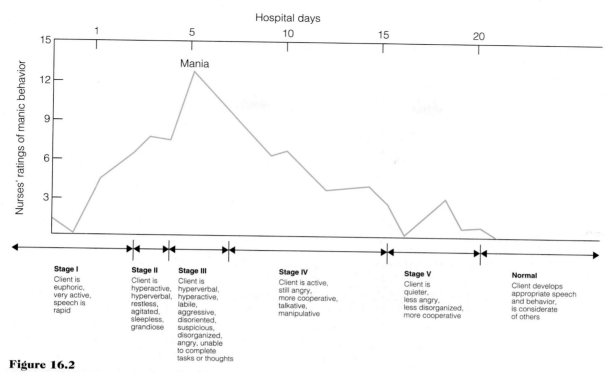

Figure 16.2
Stages of a manic episode of a hospitalized patient over three weeks
(After Janosik and Davies, 1987.)

find out what other problems a person might have before beginning to treat depression.

Unipolar versus Bipolar Disorder

Depression can occur as either a unipolar or a bipolar disorder. **Unipolar disorder** has only one pole, or extreme, of mood. That is, a person varies between normal mood and depression. A person may come out of a period of depression only to have a recurrence at a later time. Depression is diagnosed more frequently in women than in men (Murphy, Sobol, Neff, Olivier, & Leighton, 1984), and the mean age of onset is about 40.

   Bipolar disorder—also known as **manic-depressive disorder**—has two poles, mania and depression. **Mania** is the opposite of depression, characterized by restless activity, excitement, laughter, a mostly happy mood, rambling speech, and loss of inhibitions. In extreme cases, manic people are dangerous to themselves and others. Someone suffering from bipolar disorder alternates between periods of mania and depression, passing through a nearly normal mood on the way. Figure 16.2 represents the rise and fall of a manic episode in one hospitalized patient.

   A cycle from depression to mania and back to depression again may last a year or only a few days (Bunney, Murphy, Goodwin, & Borge, 1972). Some people follow such a regular cycle that one can predict their manic and depressive episodes long in advance (Richter, 1938, 1957b, 1957c), as Figure 16.3 shows. About one person in a thousand is diagnosed with bipolar disorder, but many more have mild, undiagnosed, and untreated cases. The mean age of onset is the late 20s.

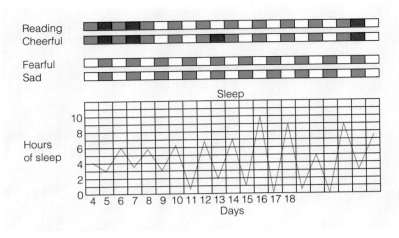

Figure 16.3
One example of bipolar disorder: records for a woman who had 1-day manic periods alternating with 1-day depressed periods
Blue means definitely, red means somewhat, and white means no for each category. Note that days of cheerfulness and reading alternated with days of fearfulness and sadness. Note also that she slept well on her cheerful days and poorly on her sad days. (Based on Richter, 1938.)

Possible Biological Causes of Depression

The causes of depression may differ from one person to another. Further, a given individual may become depressed for more than one reason. We discuss here a few of the possible biological causes. The fact that this discussion focuses on biological factors does not in any way deny the importance of people's experiences; biological predispositions combine with the effects of people's unpleasant or difficult experiences in complex ways to produce depression.

Genetics

Both depression and bipolar disorder run in families. About 10 to 20 percent of the parents, brothers, and sisters of depressed and bipolar patients suffer from these same disorders themselves (Smeraldi, Kidd, Negri, Heimbuch, & Melica, 1979; Weissman et al., 1984). Furthermore, adopted children who become depressed have, on the average, more depressed biological relatives than depressed adoptive relatives (Wender et al., 1986).

While there may exist certain genes that specifically predispose people to become depressed, other genes act in a way that could lead to any of several psychological disorders. For example, having a close relative with depression increases your risk of becoming depressed, as well as your risk of developing alcoholism, other substance abuse, or anxiety disorders (Kendler, Heath, Neale, Kessler, & Eaves, 1993; Kendler, Neale, Kessler, Heath, & Eaves, 1992; Weissman et al., 1987).

Modern methods enable researchers to localize the gene responsible for certain conditions. For example, we now know the exact location of the Huntington's disease gene (Chapter 8). Identifying such a gene enables researchers to investigate what protein that gene produces and how that protein affects the body. Ultimately, investigators may try to reverse the chemical effects of the harmful gene. In pursuit of that goal, many investigators have tried to identify a gene or genes responsible for depression. So far, progress has been elusive. According to one study of the Old Order Amish of Pennsylvania, relatives who resembled one another with regard to bipolar disorder also resembled one another with regard to certain genes known to be on chromosome 11 (Egeland et al., 1987). However, a follow-up study on a larger sample of the Old Order

*Chapter 16
Biology of Mood Disorders, Schizophrenia, and Autism*

552

Amish population and two studies on other populations found no evidence linking bipolar disorder to chromosome 11 (Detera-Wadleigh et al., 1987; Hodgkinson et al., 1987; Kelsoe et al., 1989).

Finding the Huntington's gene was an extremely difficult and time-consuming task, but it was facilitated by the close relationship between the gene and the disease: Researchers knew the disease depended on one gene, that virtually everyone who has the gene gets the disease, and that no one without the gene gets the disease. For depression, the facts appear quite different: There are probably several genes that increase the risk of depression in different ways; many people who have the genes fail to become depressed; and sometimes people with no apparent genetic predisposition become depressed. Under these circumstances, the task of finding the genes that predispose toward depression is extremely challenging, almost overwhelming.

Viruses

Preliminary evidence suggests that some cases of depression may be linked to a little-known viral infection called **Borna disease.** As recently as the 1980s, Borna disease was considered a rare infection that attacks the brains of European farm animals. Gradually, investigators discovered that the virus affects a much greater variety of species over a much greater geographical range. In severe cases, the virus is fatal; in milder cases, it is noted mostly by its behavioral effects, such as an alternation between periods of frantic activity and periods of inactivity.

One group of investigators wondered whether any humans might carry the virus. (Many viruses are passed between humans and other species, even if the effects on humans are quite different from the effects on other species.) In 1985, they reported the results of a blood test given to several hundred humans (Amsterdam et al., 1985). Only 12 people tested positive for Borna disease virus, but *all 12 were suffering from major depression or bipolar disorder.* These 12 were a small percentage of the 265 depressed people tested in the study; still, it is significant that *none* of the 105 undepressed people tested positive for the virus.

A few years passed while virologists improved their methods for measuring the presence of the Borna virus. Studies in the early 1990s examined thousands of people in three continents, finding the Borna virus in about 2 percent of normal people, 30 percent of severely depressed patients, and 13–14 percent of people with certain chronic brain diseases (Bode, Ferszt, & Czech, 1993; Bode, Riegel, Lange, & Ludwig, 1992). Obviously, more research is necessary, but these data suggest some relationship between this virus and depression.

Abnormalities of Hemispheric Dominance

The rate of glucose metabolism, a good indicator of overall brain activity, varies as a function of mania and depression, as Figure 16.4 shows. During mania, activity is higher than normal. During depression, it is lower than normal, especially in the left frontal lobe (Baxter et al., 1985) and parts of the temporal and parietal lobes (Sackeim et al., 1990).

Several other lines of evidence suggest that most depressed people have depressed activity in the left hemisphere, especially the left frontal cortex. The EEG and other measures show more activation in the right hemisphere than in the left hemisphere (Davidson, 1984; Starkstein & Robinson, 1986). In response to an arousing stimulus, depressed people have less than the normal

Figure 16.4
PET scans taken on 3 different days for a patient who went through rapid and enormous changes in mood
Three separate horizontal planes are shown for each day. On May 17 and May 27, when the patient was depressed, brain metabolic rates were low. On May 18, when the patient was in a cheerful, hypomanic mood, the brain metabolic rate was high. Red indicates the highest metabolic rate, followed by yellow, green, and blue. (Courtesy of L. R. Baxter, Jr.)

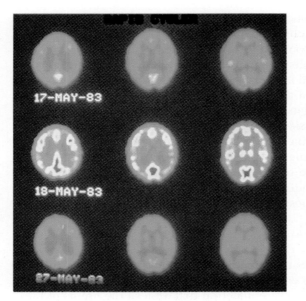

increase in electrical conduction of the skin on the right hand. When dealing with a cognitive problem, their eyes gaze to the left, not to the right as in most people (Lenhart & Katkin, 1986).

Many people with left-hemisphere damage become seriously depressed; fewer people with right-hemisphere damage become depressed (Bolla-Wilson, Robinson, Starkstein, Boston, & Price, 1989). Depending on the exact location of the damage, many people with right-hemisphere damage become emotionally unresponsive; they even have difficulty deciding whether two faces are showing the same or different emotional expressions (Kolb & Taylor, 1981). In rare cases, people with right-hemisphere damage become manic. Nearly all of those who develop mania after a stroke had some predisposition to mania either because of previous subcortical brain damage or a family history of psychiatric disorders (Robinson, Boston, Starkstein, & Price, 1988).

Overall, the evidence suggests that left-hemisphere damage or inactivity is associated with depression. We shall return to this point when we discuss the effects of electroconvulsive shock to the left or right hemisphere.

Events That Trigger Depressed Episodes

For many people, depression occurs in episodes or bouts. A person may feel about normal or perhaps mildly depressed for a few weeks or months and then enter a period of more severe depression. After a time, the depression lifts and the person feels fairly normal again until the next depressed episode.

A variety of events can trigger such a depressed episode. Such events do not necessarily qualify as "causes" of depression; rather, they alter the timing or intensity of depressive episodes. (They are like dust that causes an asthmatic person to sneeze: The dust did not cause the asthma; it just triggered an episode of its expression.)

Hormonal changes are one example of an event that can trigger a depressive episode. Of all women admitted to one psychiatric hospital for depression, 41 percent were admitted on the day before or the first day of menstruation (Abramowitz, Baker, & Fleischer, 1982). Similarly, a certain amount of depression is common just after giving birth. Most women experience "the blues" for a day or two after delivery because of pain, emotional upheaval, the inconvenience of hospital care, and possibly the hormonal changes occurring at this time. About 20 percent experience a moderately serious **postpartum depression**—that is, a depression after giving birth. About one woman in a thousand enters a more serious, long-lasting depression (Hopkins, Marcus, & Campbell, 1984). Generally, however, such a woman was already predisposed to depression and may have suffered several previous depressed episodes unrelated to childbirth (Schöpf, Bryois, Jonquière, & Le, 1984). In short, giving birth may have triggered the onset of a depressive episode, but it was not the underlying cause of the depression.

Allergic reactions can also trigger depressive episodes in certain people (Marshall, 1993). So can a variety of stressful experiences. One study found that the stress of being a mother to a handicapped child did not increase the probability of becoming depressed, but it did increase the intensity of any depression that developed (Breslau & Davis, 1986).

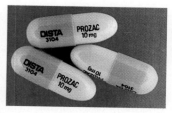

Figure 16.5
Fluoxetine (Prozac) pills
Fluoxetine is an example of a second-generation antidepressant pill, having effects that are limited to a single neurotransmitter. Two other kinds of antidepressant pills are tricyclics and monoamine oxidase inhibitors (Leonard Lessin/ Peter Arnold, Inc.)

Neurotransmitters and Depression

Logically, we might imagine that investigators would first figure out the causes of a psychological disorder and then develop a treatment to address that cause. The sequence in real life has generally been the opposite: First, investigators find a drug or other therapy that appears to be helpful, and then they infer what the underlying cause must have been. Antidepressant drugs, like many other psychiatric drugs, were discovered by accident. (See Digression 16.1.) These therapies led to an understanding of the causes of depression, rather than the other way around.

Antidepressant Drugs and Their Effects

The earliest antidepressant drugs appeared on the scene in the 1950s. Gradually, a pattern emerged: Several investigators independently and almost simultaneously noted that the antidepressant drugs increased the activity at catecholamine synapses in the brain (Garattini & Valzelli, 1960; MacLean, 1962; Stein, 1962). They therefore inferred that depression might be related to deficient stimulation at dopamine and norepinephrine synapses.

Today's antidepressant drugs fall into three major categories: tricyclics, MAOIs, and "second-generation" or "atypical" antidepressants. (See Figure 16.5.) The **tricyclics** (such as imipramine, trade name Tofranil) operate by preventing the presynaptic neuron from reabsorbing catecholamines or serotonin after releasing them; thus, the neurotransmitters remain longer in the synaptic cleft and continue stimulating the postsynaptic cell.

The **monoamine oxidase inhibitors (MAOIs)** (such as phenelzine, trade name Nardil) block the enzyme *monoamine oxidase (MAO)*, which metabolizes catecholamines and serotonin into inactive forms. When MAOIs block this enzyme, released neurotransmitter molecules remain longer than usual at the synapse without being inactivated; they therefore stimulate the postsynaptic cell more than usual. The tricyclics are generally more helpful than the MAOIs for major depressions; most psychiatrists prescribe MAOIs only after tricyclic drugs have proved ineffective for a given patient.

The **second-generation antidepressants** are drugs that exert more specific effects on a single neurotransmitter. For example, fluoxetine (trade name Prozac) blocks the reuptake of serotonin by the presynaptic terminal. The side

Depression

We like to think that basic science comes first and that applied science or technology later applies the discoveries of basic science to solve practical problems. Yet the history of drug therapies, particularly in psychiatry, includes many examples of the reverse, in which useful drugs were stumbled upon by accident and researchers then had to study the effects to explain their success.

Disulfiram, for example, was originally used in the manufacture of rubber. Someone noticed that workers in a certain rubber factory developed a distaste for alcohol and traced the cause to disulfiram, which had altered the workers' metabolism such that they became ill after drinking any alcohol. Disulfiram, now better known by the trade name Antabuse, is often prescribed for people trying to quit drinking alcohol.

Iproniazid was originally marketed as rocket fuel. Eventually, someone discovered that it was useful therapy for tuberculosis. Later, while experimenting on its effects in treating tuberculosis, someone discovered that it was an effective antidepressant (Klerman, 1975).

The use of bromides to control epilepsy was origi-

nally based on a theory, but the theory was all wrong (Friedlander, 1986; Levitt, 1975). People in the 1800s believed that masturbation caused epilepsy and that bromides reduced sexual drive. Therefore, the reasoning went, bromides should reduce epilepsy. It turns out that bromides do relieve epilepsy, but for altogether different reasons.

For decades, the search for new psychiatric drugs was a matter of haphazardly testing as many chemicals as possible, first on laboratory animals and then on humans. For example, investigators looking for new tranquilizers would look for drugs that decreased rats' avoidance of stimuli associated with shock. (A drug that decreased avoidance presumably decreased fear.) Today, because we largely understand how tranquilizers and other drugs affect synapses, drug researchers no longer have to test nearly so many compounds on animals. They start by synthesizing chemicals with properties similar to those of the drugs already in use, evaluating new chemicals in test tubes or tissue samples until they find a drug with stronger or more specific effects on synaptic transmission.

effects of such drugs are more limited and more predictable than those of standard tricyclics and MAOIs, which may affect four or more neurotransmitters (Feighner et al., 1991). Common side effects from tricyclics include dizziness, drowsiness, blurred vision, rapid heartbeat, dry mouth, and excessive sweating. Many people experience such severe side effects that they have to quit taking the drug or reduce the dose to a level where it becomes ineffective. Fluoxetine, however, ordinarily produces only nausea and headache as side effects, and even these two effects are seldom severe. The milder the side effects, the larger amount of drug a person can take, and therefore the greater the benefits are likely to be. The use of fluoxetine has been controversial because of reports that it occasionally provokes suicidal thoughts. That effect is rare, although of course very serious when it does occur. The use of Prozac also provokes some ethical misgivings because the drug sometimes elevates self-esteem, reduces shyness, and in other ways alters people's long-standing ways of relating to other people. Changing people's personalities through psychotherapy is generally a long, slow enterprise with only limited success; a sudden change through drugs is an unsettling prospect (Kramer, 1993).

Implications for the Physiology of Depression

Now that we know what kinds of drugs relieve depression, we can infer what brain abnormalities are responsible for depression, right? Unfortunately, it is not that simple. The results suggest that disorders of serotonin and norepinephrine synapses contribute in some way to depression, but we do not know how these two (and no doubt others as well) combine their effects through some final common path.

One major research problem is to explain the time course of the drugs' effectiveness. For example, a tricyclic drug blocks reuptake of both serotonin and catecholamines quickly after the person takes the drug. A little later, but still within the first few hours, the excess neurotransmitter that accumulates in the synaptic cleft stimulates the **autoreceptors** located on the presynaptic terminal. Stimulation of these receptors decreases further release of the neurotransmitter. In other words, the initial effects of the drug are self-limiting; the drug prolongs the presence of serotonin and catecholamines in the synapse, but that prolonged presence decreases their further release. As still more time passes, the prolonged stimulation of the autoreceptors desensitizes them, restoring something close to the original amount of release (Antelman, Chiodo, & DeGiovanni, 1982; Sulser, Gillespie, Mishra, & Manier, 1984). Meanwhile, the prolonged stimulation of the postsynaptic receptors gradually decreases those receptors' sensitivity. So is the combined result of all these processes an increase or a decrease in the stimulation of the postsynaptic receptors? And why do the drugs' effects on behavior build up so slowly? Some people start getting limited benefits, such as improved sleep, after taking the drugs for a few days, but most people do not experience major antidepressant effects until they have taken the drugs for three weeks or more. What is happening in the brain during all that time?

You may be understandably confused at this point; researchers themselves are confused. What do all these results tell us about the underlying causes of depression? Primarily, they imply that the mechanisms of depression are more complex than simply having "too much" or "too little" of a particular neurotransmitter. We must await new research to clarify how the drugs work and what causes depression in the first place.

Other Therapies for Depression and Bipolar Disorder

Antidepressant drugs have provided safe, effective, relatively inexpensive help for a great many depressed patients, but they do not work for everyone. About two-thirds of depressed patients experience significant benefits, although not all of them get full relief. Cognitive psychotherapy is also successful for about two-thirds of depressed patients, although no one is sure whether those are the *same* two-thirds (Hollon et al., 1992). Cognitive therapy is more likely to produce relief that lasts long after the end of therapy (Evans et al., 1992); many drug-therapy patients have to continue taking the drugs almost indefinitely. However, cognitive therapy has the disadvantage of being more expensive and time-consuming. Let us consider some other possible treatments.

Electroconvulsive Therapy

Electroconvulsive therapy (ECT) has had a stormy history (Fink, 1985). Its use originated with the observation that, among certain people who suffer from both epilepsy and schizophrenia, an increase in the symptoms of one disorder is often associated with a decrease in the symptoms of the other (Trimble & Thompson, 1986). In the 1930s, a Hungarian physician, Ladislas Meduna, intentionally induced a convulsive seizure in schizophrenic patients to see whether it would relieve the symptoms of schizophrenia. Soon other physicians were doing the same, generally inducing the seizures by a large dose of insulin. Insulin shock is a dreadful experience, however, and very difficult to

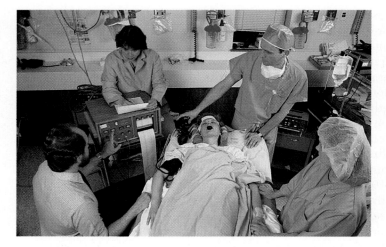

Figure 16.6
Electroconvulsive therapy (ECT)

In contrast to the practices of an earlier era, ECT today is administered with muscle relaxants or anesthetics to minimize discomfort. It can be used only if the patient gives informed consent. (James D. Wilson/Woodfin Camp & Associates.)

control. An Italian physician, Ugo Cerletti, after years of experimentation with animals, developed a method of inducing seizures by an electric shock across the head (Cerletti & Bini, 1938). Electroconvulsive therapy was quicker than insulin; more importantly, most patients awakened from it calmly and did not remember the experience.

Although ECT proved to be only occasionally beneficial in treating schizophrenia, psychiatrists began experimenting with it for other disorders. They discovered that it did seem to help many people suffering from major depression. ECT became a common treatment for depression, even though its use for this disorder was based on no theory at all. Its overuse and misuse, especially during the 1950s, gave it a bad reputation. Certain patients were given ECT a hundred times or more, without their consent, even if it seemed to be doing them no good.

When antidepressant drugs became available in the late 1950s, the use of ECT declined rapidly. All states now have laws that permit the use of ECT only after a patient has given informed consent. Many states have also imposed laws restricting the ages of people who can receive ECT and the disorders for which it can be used (Winslade, Liston, Ross, & Weber, 1984).

Beginning in the 1970s, ECT has made a partial comeback, with many modifications. It is now used almost exclusively for depression, rarely for schizophrenia or other disorders. It is applied on alternate days for usually about two weeks. Patients are given muscle relaxants or anesthetics to minimize discomfort and the possibility of injury (Figure 16.6). To minimize the side effects, the intensity of the shock is much lower than in earlier years. In some cases, physicians administer the shock over just the right hemisphere instead of the whole head. Right-hemisphere ECT can be just as effective as bilateral ECT for relieving depression if the right-side-only ECT is intense enough to induce a seizure (Abrams, Swartz, & Vedak, 1991). Because depression is associated with decreased activity of the left hemisphere, right-hemisphere ECT may promote a better balance of activity between the two hemispheres or it may somehow enhance activity in the left hemisphere.

ECT is used primarily for three kinds of depressed patients (Scovern & Kilmann, 1980; Weiner, 1979). First, it is given to patients who have not responded to any of the antidepressant drugs; ECT produces good results in most such patients (Paul et al., 1981). Second, it is used for patients with suicidal tendencies because it takes effect in about a week, whereas antidepressant drugs usually take 2 to 3 weeks. For a patient likely to attempt suicide, a delay of effect may be fatal. Third, ECT has proved particularly effective for depressed patients who suffer from delusions.

Medical commissions in both the United States and Great Britain have concluded that ECT is both safe and effective (Fink, 1985). According to one extensive review of the literature, 80 percent of all severely depressed patients respond well to ECT, while only 64 percent respond well to tricyclic drugs and even fewer respond to MAOIs (Janicak et al., 1985). The benefits of ECT are not permanent, however; many patients will relapse into depression unless they are given drugs or other therapies to prevent it.

Many people today distrust ECT, partly because it seems barbaric and partly because they believe, rightly or wrongly, that it produces serious side effects. For most patients, the side effects are minor and temporary, including a period of confusion and both retrograde and anterograde amnesia during the first 1 to 6 months after the end of treatment (Squire, Wetzel, & Slater, 1979). However, a few patients experience long-term memory deficits and other health risks (Weiner, 1984). Memory loss is most severe in patients with a long history of psychiatric or neurological problems (Summers, Robins, & Reich, 1979). Applying ECT to only the right hemisphere minimizes memory impairment (Squire & Zouzounis, 1986).

Half a century after the introduction of ECT, no one is yet sure how it relieves depression. It does not act as a punishment, and it need not impair memory to be effective. It must induce a seizure, however. ECT that produces a seizure affects the brain in many ways, such as decreasing the number of norepinephrine receptors at postsynaptic cells (Kellar & Stockmeier, 1986; Lerer & Shapira, 1986). Conflicting results have been reported about whether it increases or decreases receptor sensitivity at autoreceptors (Chiodo & Antelman, 1980; Reches et al., 1984).

Alterations of Sleep Patterns

Most depressed people, especially those who are middle aged or older, experience sleep abnormalities that suggest a disorder of their biological rhythms. Recall from Chapter 9 that a normal undepressed person who goes to bed at the normal time first enters REM sleep about 80 minutes after falling asleep. The normal person has little REM sleep during the first half of the night and an increasing percentage in the second half. That trend is controlled by the time of day, not by how long the person has been asleep. If someone who usually falls asleep at 11 P.M. waits until 3 A.M. to go to sleep, that person is likely to enter REM sleep rapidly and to have a lot of REM sleep per hour. The reason is that REM sleep is related to circadian rhythms, as reflected by changes in body temperature (see Figure 16.7). REM sleep occupies a small percentage of total sleep while body temperature is declining and a larger percentage while body temperature is rising (Czeisler, Weitzman, Moore-Ede, Zimmerman, & Knauer, 1980).

Most depressed people enter REM sleep within 45 minutes after going to bed at their normal time. When the depressed person goes to sleep, body temperature may already be starting to rise, as Figure 16.7 illustrates. For that reason, REM sleep begins early and may occupy a great deal of sleep time throughout the night. Curiously, manic patients also have quick onset of REM sleep (Hudson, Lipinki, Frankenburg, Grochocinski, & Kupfer, 1988).

Several means of adjusting sleep habits can alleviate depression (Gillin, 1983). One promising method is to have the person go to sleep earlier than usual, in phase with his or her temperature cycle. The person goes to sleep at, say, 6 P.M., when the temperature cycle is at about the point it is in undepressed people at 11 P.M.; he or she sleeps 8 hours and awakens at 2 A.M. On

Figure 16.7
Relationship of sleep and REM to the circadian cycle of body temperature
The circadian rhythm is shifted for most depressed people. Depressed people going to bed at their normal time enter REM sleep quickly, as do normal people going to bed several hours later than usual. (Bottom graphs adapted from Hobson, 1989.)

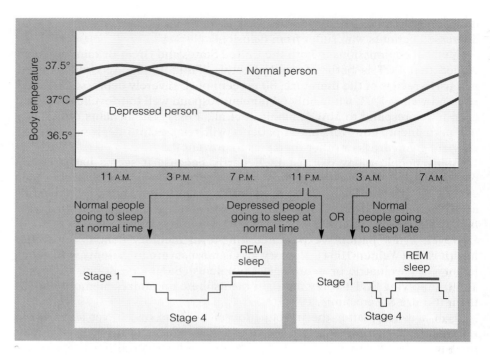

each succeeding night, the person goes to sleep half an hour later, until the bedtime reaches 11 P.M. or some other satisfactory point. In short, therapists treat the depressed patient like someone who is having trouble adjusting to a change in time zones. The result is a relief from depression that lasts for months (Sack, Nurnberger, Rosenthal, Ashburn, & Wehr, 1985).

Another approach is to keep the person awake all night. Doing so produces a rapid relief from depression (Pflug, 1973). Why this procedure is effective is not known; furthermore, its benefits last only a day or two, and depressed patients frankly hate this treatment. It is also possible to relieve depression by depriving the depressed person of REM sleep by awakening him or her whenever signs of REM appear (Vogel, Thompson, Thurmond, & Rivers, 1973). The benefits of REM deprivation develop gradually over days but can last days to weeks. Again, the mechanism of the effect is not known. For nondepressed people, sleep deprivation or REM deprivation makes mood worse, not better (Roy-Byrne, Uhde, & Post, 1986).

Bright Lights

One uncommon form of depression is **seasonal affective disorder,** conveniently abbreviated **SAD.** People who suffer from seasonal affective disorder become depressed, sometimes seriously depressed, every winter. Most of them become at least slightly manic in the summer. The disorder is more common and more severe in regions closer to the poles, where the nights are extra long in winter and very short in summer. Some patients who suffer depression every winter in their far northern homes experience no such depression if they spend the winter in, say, southern California (Pande, 1985; Rosenthal et al., 1984). In many ways, SAD differs from other types of depression; for example, SAD patients have phase-delayed sleep and temperature rhythms, unlike most other depressed patients, who have phase-advanced rhythms (Figure 16.8).

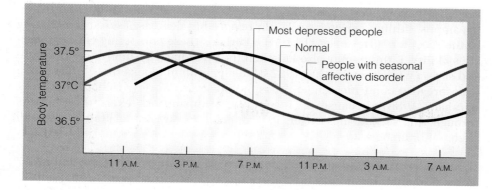

Figure 16.8
Typical sleep and temperature cycles for normal people, depressed patients, and SAD patients
Note that SAD patients are phase delayed, while most other depressed patients are phase advanced.

SAD is not a reaction to the cold of winter but to its darkness. Most people feel more cheerful on a sunny day than on a dark day. According to the results of one survey, more than 90 percent of people experience some seasonal variation in mood, generally feeling happier in summer than in winter (Kasper, Wehr, Bartko, Gaist, & Rosenthal, 1989). For some people, these mood swings are exaggerated, with a small minority reaching levels that qualify as depression and mania (Lewy et al., 1985).

It is possible to relieve SAD by exposing the person to very bright lights (for example, 2,500 lux). The person sits in front of the lights for an hour or more before the sun rises or after it sets, thus artificially creating a longer daylight period. Some research suggests that artificial light has its greatest antidepressant effect early in the morning (Sack et al., 1990); other research indicates that morning and evening light are equally effective (Wirz-Justice et al., 1993). Researchers are not agreed on what causes seasonal affective disorder or on how bright light alleviates it (Blehar & Rosenthal, 1989).

Lithium

The most effective known therapy for bipolar disorder, and for certain cases in which a person alternates regularly between depression and normal mood, is the use of **lithium** salts. The effectiveness of lithium was discovered by accident. An Australian investigator, J. F. Cade, believing that uric acid would be therapeutically useful for treating mania and depression, mixed uric acid with a lithium salt to help it dissolve and then gave the solution to patients. It was indeed helpful, although investigators eventually realized that the lithium was the effective agent.

Lithium levels out the mood of a bipolar patient. With continued use, it prevents a relapse into either mania or depression. The use of lithium must be regulated carefully, however. The therapeutic dose is not much less than the dose that begins to produce toxic effects. Also, lithium sometimes causes serious medical harm if combined with ECT or with the drug haloperidol (Gottfried & Frankel, 1981; Small, Kellams, Milstein, & Small, 1980).

Because lithium is chemically similar to sodium, it may partly take the place of sodium in crossing the membrane and in various other body functions. How it relieves bipolar disorder is not known. Because it alleviates both mania and depression—opposite states—its effects cannot be explained simply in terms of increasing or decreasing the activity at a particular type of synapse. It may act by stabilizing both dopamine and serotonin synapses, preventing alternations between increased and decreased receptor density (Pert,

Depression

Rosenblatt, Sivit, Pert, & Bunney, 1978; Treiser et al., 1981). In the rat hippocampus, lithium elevates serotonin release but decreases serotonin binding to the receptors (Treiser et al., 1981). Perhaps these competing effects generate stability. Lithium may also lengthen the circadian rhythms of temperature and sleep (Wirz-Justice et al., 1982). Finally, lithium blocks the synthesis of a widespread second messenger, phosphoinositide (Worley, Heller, Snyder, & Baraban, 1988). Because so many neurotransmitters exert their effects through this second messenger, it is difficult to determine lithium's overall effect on brain activity.

Summary

1. A person with a unipolar disorder has periods of depression; someone with a bipolar disorder has periods of both depression and mania. (p. 551)

2. Certain genes evidently increase the risk of depression, while also increasing the risk of certain other psychological disorders. Localizing the actual gene or genes will be a very difficult task. (p. 552)

3. Preliminary studies have found the Borna disease virus in a fair number of depressed people and in very few nondepressed people. The relationship between the virus and depression remains for future research to explore. (p. 553)

4. Most depressed people show greater activity in the right than in the left cerebral hemisphere. (p. 553)

5. Certain events such as hormonal changes, allergy attacks, and stressful experiences may trigger an episode of depression, even if they do not cause the underlying problem. (p. 554)

6. Three kinds of antidepressant drugs are in wide use: tricyclics, MAOIs, and second-generation antidepressants. (p. 555)

7. The mechanisms by which drugs relieve depression are as yet only partly understood. (p. 556)

8. Other therapies for depression include cognitive psychotherapy, electroconvulsive therapy, and altered sleep patterns. (p. 557)

9. Bright lights can relieve seasonal affective disorder. Lithium salts are the preferred treatment for bipolar disorder. (p. 560)

Review Questions

1. What are the symptoms of depression and of mania? (p. 551)

2. What is the difference between unipolar disorder and bipolar disorder? (p. 551)

3. Why is it more feasible to find the gene for Huntington's disease than the gene or genes for depression? (p. 552)

4. What are the synaptic effects of tricyclic drugs and MAOIs? (p. 555)

5. Why has fluoxetine become popular as an antidepressant? Why are some people still skeptical about using it? (p. 555)

6. How long after someone starts taking antidepressant drugs is the person likely to experience relief from depression? What happens in the brain during that delay? (p. 557)

7. How are the procedures for delivering ECT different today from what they were in the 1950s? (p. 558)

8. What modification of the procedure for ECT reduces the impairment it causes in memory? (p. 558)

9. What kind of sleep abnormality is most characteristic of depressed people? (p. 559)

10. What change in sleep timing can relieve depression? (p. 559)

Thought Questions

1. Certain people suffer from what they describe as "post-Christmas depression." They claim that they feel depressed as a letdown after all the excitement of the holiday season. What other explanation could you offer?

2. ECT applied over the right hemisphere only can relieve depression with minimum impairment of memory. What result would you expect from ECT applied over just the left hemisphere? Why?

Suggestions for Further Reading

Heston, L. L. (1992). *Mending minds*. New York: W. H. Freeman. A nontechnical description of contemporary, drug-oriented psychiatry. Chapters 1 and 2 deal with mood disorders.

Kramer, P. D. (1993). *Listening to Prozac*. New York: Viking. Describes a psychiatrist's experiences with patients using Prozac and his ethical misgivings about sometimes changing people's personalities as well as their moods.

McNeal, E. T., & Cimbolic, P. (1986). Antidepressants and biochemical theories of depression. *Psychological Bulletin, 99*, 361–374. A good overview of evidence linking depression to abnormalities of transmission at the synapses.

Terms

depression condition in which a person feels fearful, gloomy, helpless, and hopeless, and engages in little productive activity (p. 550)

unipolar disorder mood disorder with only one extreme (or pole), generally depression (p. 551)

bipolar disorder or **manic-depressive disorder** condition in which a person alternates between two poles, mania and depression (p. 551)

mania condition of restless activity, excitement, laughter, mostly happy mood, and few inhibitions (p. 551)

Borna disease viral disease that affects the nervous system of animals, producing results that range from exaggerated activity fluctuations to death (p. 553)

postpartum depression depression after giving birth (p. 555)

tricyclic drug that prevents the presynaptic neuron from reabsorbing catecholamine or serotonin molecules after releasing them (p. 555)

monoamine oxidase inhibitor (MAOI) drug that blocks the enzyme monoamine oxidase (p. 555)

second-generation antidepressant antidepressant drug that is neither a tricyclic nor a monoamine oxidase inhibitor and that has effects largely limited to a single neurotransmitter (p. 555)

autoreceptor presynaptic receptor that responds to the neurotransmitter released by the presynaptic cell itself (p. 557)

electroconvulsive therapy (ECT) attempt to relieve depression or other disorders by an electrically induced convulsion (p. 557)

seasonal affective disorder (SAD) period of depression that reoccurs each winter (p. 560)

lithium an element whose salts are often used as a therapy for bipolar disorder (p. 561)

Schizophrenia and Autism

Here is a conversation between two people diagnosed with schizophrenia (Haley, 1959):

A: Do you work at the air base?
B: You know what I think of work. I'm 33 in June, do you mind?
A: June?
B: 33 years old in June. This stuff goes out the window after I live this, uh—leave this hospital. So I can't get my vocal cords back. So I lay off cigarettes. I'm in a spatial condition, from outer space myself. . . .
A: I'm a real spaceship from across.
B: A lot of people talk that way, like crazy, but Believe it or not, by Ripley, take it or leave it—alone—it's in the *Examiner*, it's in the comic section, Believe it or not, by Ripley, Robert E. Ripley, Believe it or not, but we don't have to believe anything, unless I feel like it. Every little rosette—too much alone.
A: Yeah, it could be possible.
B: I'm a civilian seaman.
A: Could be possible. I take my bath in the ocean.
B: Bathing stinks. You know why? 'Cause you can't quit when you feel like it. You're in the service.

People with schizophrenia say and do things that other people (including most other people with schizophrenia) find difficult to understand. The reasons behind the disorder are still not well understood, but they apparently include a large biological component.

The Characteristics of Schizophrenia

Schizophrenia is a generally severe disorder characterized by deteriorating ability to function in everyday life and some combination of hallucinations, delusions, thought disorder, movement disorder, and inappropriate emotional expressions. The *Diagnostic and Statistical Manual of Mental Disorders, Third Edition Revised (DSM-III-R)*, provides a more formal and complete description (American Psychiatric Association, 1987). One of the difficulties in dealing with schizophrenia is that affected people vary considerably in both their behavioral symptoms and their biological characteristics. For example, some have prominent hallucinations and delusions, others have prominent thought disorders; some have clear signs of brain damage, and others do not. Investigators are still not sure whether they are dealing with one disorder or a family of loosely related disorders (Heinrichs, 1993). If it is a loose family, no wonder the results fluctuate from study to study.

Schizophrenia was originally known as *dementia praecox,* which is Latin for "premature deterioration of the mind." In 1911, Eugen Bleuler introduced the term *schizophrenia,* which has been preferred ever since. Although schizophrenia is Greek for "split mind," it is *not* the same thing as *multiple personality,* a condition in which a person alternates between one personality and another. A person with schizophrenia has only one personality. The split in the schizophrenic mind is between the emotional and intellectual sides of the person. That is, what the person expresses emotionally—or fails to express emotionally—is often at odds with what the person is saying.

Behavioral Symptoms

Most people with schizophrenia have either hallucinations, delusions, or a characteristic thought disorder. **Hallucinations** are sensory experiences that do not correspond to reality, such as hearing voices. Visual hallucinations are rare in schizophrenia and more common among drug abusers. **Delusions** are beliefs that other people regard as unfounded, such as the belief that one is being persecuted severely or the belief that invaders from outer space are trying to control one's behavior.

The most typical **thought disorder** of schizophrenia is a difficulty understanding and using abstract concepts. For example, a schizophrenic person has trouble understanding such proverbs as "When the cat is away, the mice will play," interpreting them literally. Schizophrenic people also show a lack of organizing purpose in their stream of thoughts and have loose associations among ideas, as in a dream.

Hallucinations, delusions, and thought disorder are sometimes known as **positive symptoms** of schizophrenia because they represent the presence of certain behaviors. In contrast, **negative symptoms** represent the absence of certain behaviors: Many schizophrenic people lack emotional expression, fail to interact socially with others, and speak very little.

In some cases, schizophrenia has an **acute** (sudden) onset, a brief duration, and good prospects for a lasting recovery. More frequently, it has a **chronic** (gradual) onset and a long-term course. In childhood and adolescence, the person shows moderately high anxiety levels, difficulty in interpersonal relationships, a lack of ambition, a fear of trying anything new, low levels of pleasure, and mild degrees of thought disorder (Arboleda & Holzman, 1985; Hartmann et al., 1984). These symptoms become worse in the late teens and early 20s, generally leading to a diagnosis of schizophrenia before age 30.

If untreated, the condition continues to deteriorate until the person has great trouble completing the ordinary tasks of everyday life. Before antischizophrenic drugs first became available in the mid-1950s, most schizophrenic people were confined to a mental hospital for life. Today, about one-third of all people with schizophrenia manage to live normally with the aid of drugs and outpatient treatment. The others have either occasional or frequent stays in mental hospitals.

Demographic Data

Because of borderline cases and disagreements about diagnosis, it is difficult to state the exact incidence of schizophrenia. According to one large survey of U.S. adults, about 0.7 percent of all people will suffer from schizophrenia at some point in their lives (Kessler et al., 1994). A number of others, perhaps

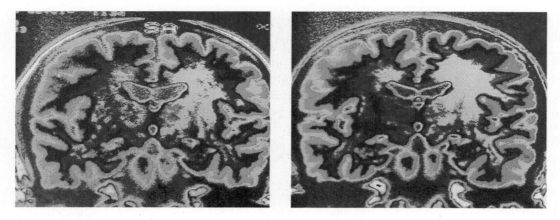

Figure 16.9
Coronal sections through the brains of identical twins
The twin on the left has schizophrenia; the twin on the right does not. Note that the ventricles (near the center of each brain) are larger in the twin with schizophrenia. (Photos courtesy of E. F. Torrey & M. F. Casanova/NIMH.)

another 1 percent, have a milder *schizoid* condition. Schizophrenia occurs in all ethnic groups and in all parts of the world, although it is rare in the tropics. It is reported 10 to 100 times more often in the United States and Europe than in most Third World countries (Torrey, 1986). Within the United States, it is more common in impoverished areas than in wealthy areas. It is about equally common in men and women, although it is generally diagnosed at an earlier age in men (Lewine, 1981).

Brain Atrophy or Dysfunction

Many but not all schizophrenic patients show signs of mild brain damage or atrophy (shrinkage) in parts of the thalamus, cerebral cortex, and hippocampus. Brain damage or atrophy is not typically found in patients suffering from other psychological disorders.

Several lines of evidence point to brain damage in schizophrenia. First, examinations after death reveal that the forebrains of schizophrenic people are about 6 percent lighter than those of other mental patients (R. Brown et al., 1986). Through such techniques as magnetic resonance imaging (MRI) (see Chapter 4), researchers have found that many schizophrenic people have larger-than-normal ventricles (Zipursky, Lim, Sullivan, Brown, & Pfefferbaum, 1992). The ventricles are fluid-filled spaces; enlarged ventricles mean that neurons occupy less space. (See Figure 16.9.) Researchers are not sure why the ventricles are enlarged in some patients and not in others. Scattered reports suggest that enlargement occurs most commonly in males (Andreasen et al., 1990b) or in those with a long history of poor social behavior (Pandurangi, Bilder, Rieder, Mukherjee, & Hamer, 1988). Because enlarged ventricles are about as common in young patients as in old patients (Andreasen et al., 1990b), the cell loss probably occurs early in life rather than accumulating over the life span.

Schizophrenic brains have fewer neurons in the cerebral cortex (Benes, Davidson, & Bird, 1986), the dorsomedial thalamus (Pakkenberg, 1990), the

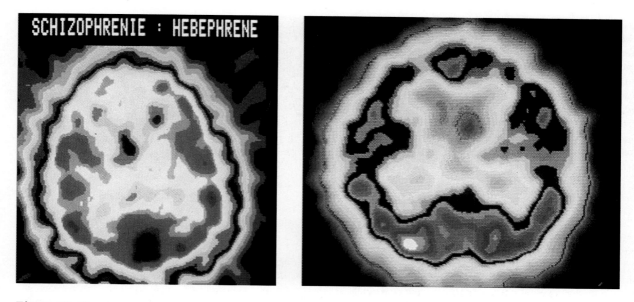

Figure 16.10
PET scans of (left) a person with schizophrenia and (right) a person without schizophrenia
Red indicates the highest level of metabolism, followed by yellow, green, and blue. Several studies have found that people with schizophrenia have lower-than-normal activity in their frontal cortex (toward the top in each figure). (SPL/Photo Researchers, Inc.)

amygdala, and the hippocampus (Altshuler, Casanova, Goldberg, & Kleinman, 1990; Breier et al., 1992; Bogerts, Meertz, & Schönfeldt-Bausch, 1985). Schizophrenic people, including those who have never been medicated, also have lower-than-average levels of brain metabolism, especially in the hippocampus and the temporal and frontal areas of the cortex (Andreasen et al., 1992; Buchsbaum et al., 1992; Tamminga et al., 1992). The general trend of data suggests greater posterior than anterior metabolic rate. (See Figure 16.10.)

Schizophrenic people fail to recruit extra activity in parts of the frontal cortex when necessary. For example, when healthy people sort cards according to complex or changing rules, they recruit metabolic activity in the dorsolateral part of their prefrontal cortex. Generally, the greater the increase in metabolic activity, the better they perform the task. People with schizophrenia fail to show such a rise in metabolic activity when they attempt these tasks (Berman, Torrey, Daniel, & Weinberger, 1992), and they perform the tasks poorly (Goldberg, Weinberger, Berman, Pliskin, & Podd, 1987).

In addition to having fewer and less active neurons than normal, many people with schizophrenia also show signs of disorganization among their neurons. During an early stage of brain maturation, certain developing neurons migrate through layers of white matter to reach their normal destination in the cerebral cortex. In some people with schizophrenia, many of those neurons apparently failed to complete the journey; they remain throughout life somewhere in the midst of the white matter (Akbarian et al., 1993a, 1993b). Even neurons that do approximately reach their normal locations fail to arrange themselves in the neat, orderly manner typical of nonschizophrenic brains (Benes & Bird, 1987). (See Figures 16.11 and 16.12.)

Schizophrenia and Autism

Figure 16.11
The hippocampus of two
normal people (left) and
two people with schizo-
phrenia (right)
*Notice the atrophy of the
brains on the right. (From
Bogerts, Meertz, &
Schönfeldt-Bausch, 1985;
photos courtesy of B.
Bogerts.)*

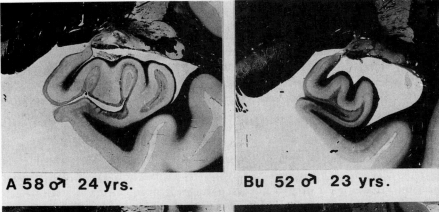
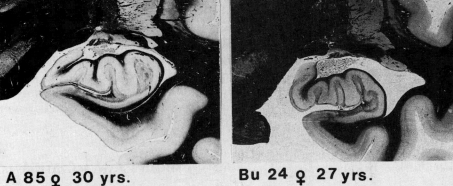

A 58 ♂ 24 yrs.   Bu 52 ♂ 23 yrs.

A 85 ♀ 30 yrs.   Bu 24 ♀ 27 yrs.

People with schizophrenia also show signs of impaired transfer of information across the corpus callosum. For example, an experimenter points at one of the patient's fingers, say the ring finger of the left hand, and asks the patient to raise the same finger on the opposite hand. In general, schizophrenic patients perform poorly on such tasks (Craft, Willerman, & Bigler, 1987). They also show deficits implying a left-hemisphere impairment, such as being slow to shift their attention from an object on their left to an object on their right (Posner, Early, Reiman, Pardo, & Dhawan, 1988). These results suggest that the lateralization of function between the two hemispheres fails to take place properly in the brains of people who eventually become schizophrenic.

Possible Causes of Schizophrenia

The results just discussed indicate that *something* causes brain damage in schizophrenic people. What might that something be?

Over the years, a great many hypotheses have been proposed and considered. A few examples: Schizophrenia may be due to the accumulation of copper or other heavy metal ions in the brain (Bowman & Lewis, 1982). The schizophrenic brain may produce certain chemicals, such as bufotenine, that can induce hallucinations (Kety, 1975; Potkin et al., 1979; Wyatt, Termini, & Davis, 1971). The schizophrenic brain may produce 6-hydroxydopamine, which would destroy norepinephrine synapses, lead to a loss of pleasure and motivated behavior, and sometimes impair movement (Stein & Wise, 1971).

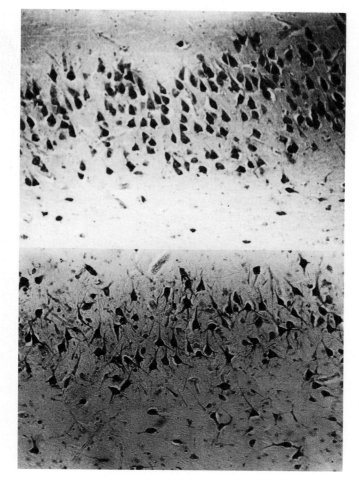

Figure 16.12
Cells of the hippocampus in a normal person (top) and a person with schizophrenia (bottom)
The cells on the bottom are arranged in a more haphazard, disorganized manner. (Photos courtesy of Arnold Scheibel.)

Support for all of those hypotheses, as well as several others, has faded, although we are not in a position to rule them out altogether. Now let us consider some of the possibilities that investigators currently take most seriously.

Genetics

According to most studies, schizophrenia runs in families (Figure 16.13). That is, people with schizophrenia are more likely than others are to have relatives with schizophrenia (Gottesman, 1991). Furthermore, even among the non-schizophrenic relatives of a schizophrenic patient, many show indications of minor brain damage or dysfunction, just as the schizophrenic patients do (Kinney, Woods, & Yurgelun-Todd, 1986; Marcus, Hans, Mednick, Schulsinger, & Michelsen, 1985).

Similarity within a family indicates only that genetics is a possible factor, however. Members of a family may resemble one another because of either genetics or similar environment. We must look further to distinguish between these two possibilities.

Twin Studies   One line of evidence is a comparison of monozygotic (identical) twins and dizygotic (fraternal) twins. (See Appendix A for a review of genetics.) When one monozygotic twin is schizophrenic, the other twin of the pair has about a 50 percent probability of becoming schizophrenic also. Even those who do not become schizophrenic are likely to develop other serious disturbances,

Schizophrenia and Autism

Figure 16.13
**Probability of developing
schizophrenia for people
with various relationships
to a schizophrenic person**
*The probability is highest for
people who are close relatives. (Based on data from
I. I. Gottesman, 1991.)*

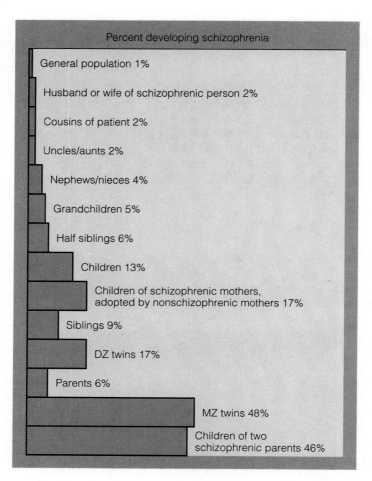

Percent developing schizophrenia

General population 1%

Husband or wife of schizophrenic person 2%

Cousins of patient 2%

Uncles/aunts 2%

Nephews/nieces 4%

Grandchildren 5%

Half siblings 6%

Children 13%

Children of schizophrenic mothers,
adopted by nonschizophrenic mothers 17%

Siblings 9%

DZ twins 17%

Parents 6%

MZ twins 48%

Children of two
schizophrenic parents 46%

including borderline schizophrenia (Kendler & Robinette, 1983). On the other hand, if one dizygotic twin is schizophrenic, the other twin has only about a 15 percent probability of schizophrenia (Kendler, 1983; McGuffin, Farmer, Gottesman, Murray, & Reveley, 1984). That is, monozygotic twins have a 50 percent **concordance** (agreement) for schizophrenia, and dizygotic twins have a 15 percent concordance. Presumably, the monozygotic twins have a greater concordance because they share more genes. Furthermore, those twin pairs who mistakenly thought that they were monozygotic (identical) but who are really dizygotic are less concordant for schizophrenia than those twin pairs who always thought they were dizygotic but who are really monozygotic (Kendler, 1983). That is, *being* monozygotic has a greater effect on a pair of twins than *being treated as* monozygotic.

Curiously, the concordance rate for schizophrenia between monozygotic twins is related to the concordance rate for handedness. Some monozygotic twins are mirror images of one another: One is right handed, the other is left handed, and the two are mirror images in physical appearance (Segal, 1984). Among pairs of monozygotic twins that are both right handed, the schizophrenia concordance rate is 92 percent. That is, if one is schizophrenic, the other has a 92 percent probability of being schizophrenic as well. But among pairs in which one is right handed and the other is left handed, the concordance rate is only 25 percent (Boklage, 1977).

Adopted Children Who Develop Schizophrenia   A second line of evidence supporting a genetic basis for schizophrenia is an examination of adopted children who develop schizophrenia. More of the biological relatives than the adoptive relatives of such children suffer from schizophrenia themselves (Kessler, 1980; Kety, Rosenthal, Wender, Schulsinger, & Jacobsen, 1975; Lowing, Mirsky, & Pereira, 1983). A child of a schizophrenic parent adopted by a normal couple is more likely to develop schizophrenia than is a child of normal parents who has an adopted parent with schizophrenia (Wender, Rosenthal, Kety, Schulsinger, & Welner, 1974). These data point to either genetics or prenatal environment as a determining factor in schizophrenia.

Finally, in rare cases, an adopted child has a **paternal half-sibling** who was also adopted. Paternal half-siblings have the same father but different mothers; they are more closely related than cousins but less closely related than brother and sister. One study in Denmark found sixty-three adopted schizophrenics who had a paternal half-sibling adopted by another family. Eight of the sixty-three half-siblings had schizophrenia also—a concordance well above the approximately 1 percent prevalence of schizophrenia in the population. Note that, because these children had different mothers, they did not share a common environment even before birth.

Children of People with Schizophrenia and Their Twins   Suppose a person with schizophrenia has a twin who does not develop schizophrenia and that both twins eventually become parents. What risk of schizophrenia do their children have?

Researchers have tested this question by going through the medical records of Norway and Denmark. (The Scandinavian countries have kept amazingly thorough records on their citizens throughout the twentieth century.) Those records indicate that the children of the twin without schizophrenia have almost the same risk of schizophrenia as do the children of the twin with schizophrenia (Gottesman & Bertelson, 1989; Kringlen & Cramer, 1989).

What do these data mean? Apparently, both twins inherited genes that predispose a person to schizophrenia. Some unknown influence caused those genes to produce schizophrenia in one twin and not in the other, but both twins were capable of passing the genes to their children. These data indicate that genes are not the whole explanation of schizophrenia; clearly, someone with genes for schizophrenia may avoid developing schizophrenia. They also suggest that people without genes for schizophrenia seldom develop schizophrenia. (If purely environmental factors caused schizophrenia in a twin with no genes for schizophrenia, the other twin would not be likely to have schizophrenic children.)

The Search for Schizophrenia Genes   Data of the types just discussed make a convincing case that genetic predisposition plays an important role in schizophrenia. Most researchers believe that further research of the same type will not tell us much that we do not already know (Holzman & Matthysse, 1990). Future research goals include finding out whether schizophrenia depends on one gene or many, where the gene or genes are located, and how they produce their effects on the brain.

As in the case of the search for depression genes, the search for schizophrenia genes is extremely challenging. Finding a gene that always produces a particular disease, such as Huntington's disease, is a difficult enough needle-in-a-haystack problem. Finding a gene that only sometimes produces a disorder, such as schizophrenia, is almost impossible by present methods.

Figure 16.14
Abnormal pursuit eye movements by two people, one of whom has schizophrenia
(**a**) *Movement of a visual target.* (**b**) *Eye movements of a person without schizophrenia, following the target.* (**c**) *Eye movements of a person with schizophrenia. Note that the person with schizophrenia has clearly apparent but not gross deficits. The eyes stay close to the target but have frequent lags and occasional backward movements. (From Sereno & Holzman, 1993.)*

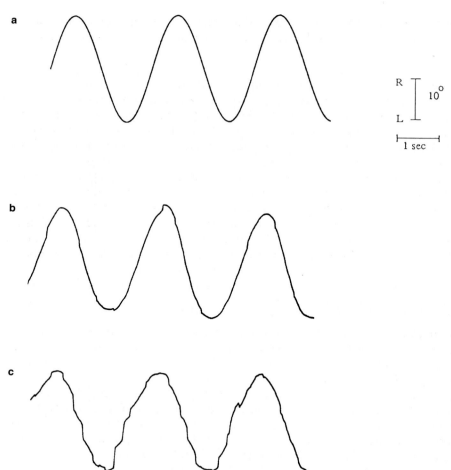

The Search for Schizophrenia Markers   One way to facilitate the search for possible schizophrenia genes is to find some biological marker that will tell us who has the gene and who does not, independently of whether or not those people exhibit the behavioral symptoms of schizophrenia. One such marker is an impairment of smooth pursuit eye movements. People have two kinds of eye movements: saccadic movements and pursuit movements. A **saccadic eye movement** is a sudden shift from one target to another. When you read this page, your eyes jump from one fixation point to another by a saccadic movement. A **pursuit eye movement** is a movement to focus on a moving target, such as watching a person walk by. Most people with schizophrenia have deficits in their pursuit eye movements; either the eyes stop moving while the target continues, or the eyes make a saccadic movement that takes them off the target (Sereno & Holzman, 1993). (See Figure 16.14.) They have such difficulties both before they have started drug treatment (Lieberman et al., 1993) and after drugs have relieved the symptoms. Almost half of their close relatives also have dysfunctions of pursuit eye movements (Holzman, 1985). These results support the hypothesis that impaired pursuit eye movements may indicate vulnerability to schizophrenia.

The pursuit eye movements are not, however, a sufficiently accurate marker by themselves; a number of nonschizophrenic people have impaired pursuit eye movements for other reasons, and some people with schizophrenia show normal pursuit eye movements. Researchers hope that pursuit eye movements in combination with other markers and symptoms may be a more accurate indicator.

Beyond Simple Genetic Determinism   Clearly, heredity is a major contributor to schizophrenia but not the only contributor. Frequently, someone with no known schizophrenic relatives develops schizophrenia. Conversely, the monozygotic twin of a schizophrenic person may develop normally.

Paul Meehl (1989) has proposed that the effect of the gene or genes is to produce a defect of neural activity that he calls "schizotypy," characterized by altered sensory and thought processes. A variety of environmental factors determines whether schizotypy eventually develops into schizophrenia. These environmental factors may include stressful experiences in the family, at school, or in other social settings. But they can also include infections and diseases, dietary insufficiencies, a blow to the head, and other biological influences. At this point, we do not know which environmental factors are most crucial.

Stress as a Possible Trigger for Schizophrenia

Many psychologists once believed that schizophrenia was caused by the parents' behavior. The parents of certain schizophrenics were reported to give confusing "come here, go away" messages, for example. This hypothesis is now considered obsolete. The main reason for its downfall was the results of adoption studies. The probability of schizophrenia relates more to the genes that the biological parents provide than to the environment that the adopting parents provide. Furthermore, the time course of the disorder does not fit the hypothesis; schizophrenia is usually first diagnosed at ages 20 to 30, when parental influence should be lessening.

Other types of experience may have something to do with the onset of schizophrenia, however. Stressful experiences may aggravate the condition, even if they are not the original cause. Curt Richter (1956, 1958a, 1958b) offered an animal model of schizophrenia. He exposed rats to the highly stressful experience of swimming in turbulent water nonstop for 60 hours. The survivors held abnormal positions rigidly for long times and occasionally leaped suddenly, as if they were responding to a hallucinated sight or sound. Promising as this demonstration may have been, however, it was not pursued further.

In humans, extremely stressful experiences can sometimes provoke an acute onset of schizophrenia; more frequently, stress triggers an episode of increased symptoms in a person who had already shown indications of schizophrenia. That is, stress is more likely to exaggerate the symptoms of schizophrenia than to be the cause.

A Virus?

One peculiarity sets schizophrenia apart from other psychological disorders: More schizophrenic people are born during the winter months than during any other season (Bradbury & Miller, 1985). No such tendency is found in the birth dates of people suffering from depression, alcoholism, or other psychological disturbances (Watson, Tilleskjor, Kucala, & Jacobs, 1984). This **season-of-birth effect** for schizophrenia is stronger in the northern United States than in the south; worldwide, the tendency disappears in the tropics. It is particularly pronounced for schizophrenics who have no schizophrenic relatives. That is, a family with several close schizophrenic relatives has a fairly high probability

Figure 16.15

Probability of developing schizophrenia by people who were in various stages of gestation during an influenza epidemic
The probability of schizophrenia is greatest if the epidemic occurred during the second trimester. (Based on data of Mednick, Machon, & Huttunen, 1990.)

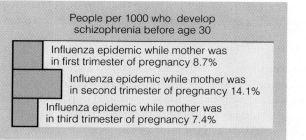

People per 1000 who develop schizophrenia before age 30

Influenza epidemic while mother was in first trimester of pregnancy 8.7%

Influenza epidemic while mother was in second trimester of pregnancy 14.1%

Influenza epidemic while mother was in third trimester of pregnancy 7.4%

that any given child will become schizophrenic, regardless of when that child is born. A family with no history of schizophrenia ordinarily has very little probability of having a child who will develop schizophrenia, but that probability increases if the child is born in the winter (Bradbury & Miller, 1985).

What might account for the season-of-birth effect? One possibility, though not the only one, is viral infection. Viral epidemics are more common in fall than in winter, especially in northern climates. Therefore, the reasoning goes, during a fall epidemic, many pregnant women may become infected with a virus. The second trimester of pregnancy is important for brain development; a woman who is in her second trimester of pregnancy during the fall gives birth in the winter. In short, according to this hypothesis, babies born in the winter have an increased risk of schizophrenia because their mothers may have had a viral infection in the preceding fall.

To test this hypothesis, we can ask several questions. First, is the season-of-birth effect particularly strong in years of a major fall epidemic of some viral disease? The answer is apparently yes. For example, Europe had a major influenza epidemic in the fall of 1957. Women who were in their second trimester of pregnancy that fall gave birth in January to March of 1958. The schizophrenia rate for Finnish children born in January to March of 1958 was almost twice as high as the rate for children born before January or after March (Mednick, Machon, & Huttunen, 1990). (See Figure 16.15.) Data for children born in Edinburgh, Scotland, in 1958 showed a trend in the same direction, although it was not statistically significant (Kendell & Kemp, 1989).

Second, if the incidence of viral disease is greater than usual at some time other than fall, will the incidence of schizophrenia increase for the babies born three months later? Studies in both Denmark and the northeastern United States have supported that hypothesis (Barr, Mednick, & Munk-Jorgensen, 1990; Torrey, Rawlings, & Waldman, 1988). Those studies suggest that almost any viral infection is dangerous; the risk of schizophrenia increased after epidemics of influenza, measles, polio, and chicken pox.

Because all the reported effects are small, we need to examine more data before drawing any firm conclusions. At this point, we can note only a possible relationship between viral epidemics and the season-of-birth effect.

If the relationship is genuine, its explanation is still uncertain. A few viruses can cross the blood-brain barrier, including those for Borna disease, rabies, herpes, and AIDS (Digression 16.2). Most viruses, however, not only fail to cross the blood-brain barrier, but also fail to cross the placenta from the mother to the developing fetus (Coyle, 1991). The likeliest hypothesis is that the virus damages the infant's brain only by some indirect route, such as causing the mother to have a fever at a stage when her fetus's brain cannot tolerate a high temperature.

Acquired immune deficiency syndrome (AIDS) is a fatal condition caused by a retrovirus known as HTLV-III (human T-lymphotropic virus III). Unlike the influenza virus and other viruses that can be transmitted by casual contact between two people, the AIDS virus can be transmitted only if it enters the blood of the recipient. It enters the blood if one receives a blood transfusion from a person with the virus or if one takes an injection with a needle previously used by an infected person. The virus can also be transmitted along with the sperm during sex if the sex partner has a break in the skin where the virus can enter. In heterosexual contact, men can transmit it to women more easily than women can transmit it to men (Kaplan, 1988).

Because the AIDS virus resembles a virus common in African monkeys, humans probably got the virus from those monkeys, perhaps as recently as the 1950s. From its point of origin, it spread slowly at first, then more rapidly. The virus has an incubation period of 5 years or more. That is, a person may have the virus for years before showing any symptoms.

The virus most often infects T4 lymphocytes, which are cells of the immune system (Gallo, 1987). With these cells inactivated, the body becomes more vulnerable to all infections; the person has no defense against any of the viruses and bacteria that it could otherwise fight off without any trouble.

The AIDS virus can cause brain damage in two ways. First, because the virus has weakened the body's immune system, the brain is vulnerable to infections, just as the other organs are. Various patients suffer from encephalitis, meningitis, bacterial infections, brain tumors, and hemorrhage of the brain's blood vessels (Levy, Bredesen, & Rosenblum, 1985). Second, unlike most viruses, the AIDS virus sometimes crosses the blood-brain barrier and invades glia cells and neurons. Behavioral results include apathy, and loss of memory, speech, and muscle control (Johnson, 1992).

One more point about the viral hypothesis: It assumes that the virus damages brain development prior to birth, yet schizophrenia generally develops gradually, with symptoms becoming pronounced by age 20 to 30. Why would the symptoms take so long to emerge?

The time course may not be so puzzling as it seems at first (Weinberger, 1987). One of the primary areas of impairment in schizophrenia is the dorsolateral prefrontal cortex. People with schizophrenia generally perform poorly on tasks known to depend on that area, and they fail to recruit extra metabolic activity in that area when performing such tasks. As we saw in Chapter 15, the dorsolateral prefrontal cortex is one of the last brain areas to reach maturity. Infant monkeys with damage in that area behave normally at first and gradually become *more* impaired at a later age when the dorsolateral prefrontal cortex would ordinarily become mature. Similarly, we can imagine that the same kind of damage in human infants might produce more serious behavioral problems in late adolescence and young adulthood than it did in early childhood. Thus, particular kinds of early brain damage may lead to delayed effects on psychological well-being.

The Biochemistry of Schizophrenia

Whatever the actual cause of schizophrenia may be—genetics, stress, virus—it must act through changes in the brain's structure and chemistry. Since the discovery of antischizophrenic drugs in the 1950s, much research has made it clear that schizophrenia is associated with an abnormality related to the dopamine synapses of the brain. Still, the exact nature of that abnormality remains elusive.

Chemicals That Can Provoke a State Similar to Schizophrenia

Large doses of amphetamine, especially if repeated often within a few days, can induce **amphetamine psychosis,** a condition that includes hallucinations, delusions, and other symptoms similar to schizophrenia. Large doses of methamphetamine, cocaine, LSD, or Antabuse sometimes also induce a state similar to schizophrenia. The main differences between drug-induced psychosis and schizophrenia are that victims of the drug-induced states often report visual hallucinations, while schizophrenic people seldom do, and that a drug-induced psychosis is generally temporary (Ellinwood, 1969; Sato, 1992).

The drugs that can produce psychosis all increase the stimulation of dopamine synapses. For example, amphetamine increases the release of dopamine from the presynaptic endings. The drug L-dopa, which is often given as a treatment for Parkinson's disease, also stimulates dopamine synapses. Among the typical side effects of L-dopa are delusions, such as delusions of persecution, and other behaviors characteristic of schizophrenia (Gershon, Angrist, & Shopsin, 1977). Moreover, L-dopa aggravates the symptoms of people with schizophrenia. In short, overstimulation of dopamine synapses can produce the symptoms of schizophrenia.

Neuroleptics and the Dopamine Hypothesis of Schizophrenia

The strongest link between dopamine synapses and schizophrenia comes from studies of drugs that alleviate schizophrenia. In the 1950s, researchers discovered that the drug **chlorpromazine** (trade name Thorazine) helps to relieve schizophrenia. Before the introduction of chlorpromazine, few schizophrenic patients who entered a mental hospital ever left. Chlorpromazine and related drugs can halt the course of the disease, especially when treatment begins at an early stage. The drugs do not actually cure schizophrenia; rather, they control it, somewhat as insulin controls diabetes. A person with schizophrenia must continue to take the drug—daily or monthly, depending on the drug—or the symptoms are likely to return.

If chlorpromazine were the only drug useful in treating schizophrenia, we would have no easy way to determine how it works because it affects brain chemistry in so many ways. The best way to determine how it works is to find what it has in common with other effective drugs.

Researchers have discovered many antischizophrenic or **neuroleptic drugs.** Most of them belong to two chemical families: the **phenothiazines,** which include chlorpromazine, and the **butyrophenones,** which include **haloperidol** (trade name Haldol). All these drugs block the postsynaptic dopamine receptors (Snyder, Banerjee, Yamamura, & Greenberg, 1974; van Praag, 1977).

Figure 16.16 illustrates the relationship between the antischizophrenic effect of a drug and its ability to block postsynaptic dopamine receptors. For each drug, researchers determined the mean dose prescribed for schizophrenic patients (displayed along the horizontal axis). Presumably, drugs such

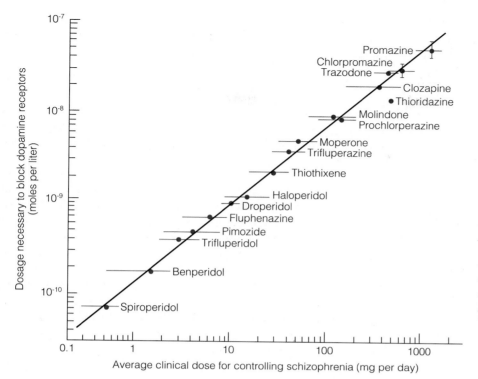

Figure 16.16
Antidopamine effects of neuroleptic drugs
Drugs are arranged along the horizontal axis in terms of the average daily dose prescribed for schizophrenic patients. (Horizontal lines indicate common ranges of dosage.) Along the vertical axis is a measurement of the amount of each drug required to achieve a certain degree of blockage of post-synaptic dopamine receptors. A drug's effectiveness in blocking dopamine synapses is almost perfectly correlated with its ability to control schizophrenia. (From Seeman, Lee, Chau-Wong, & Wong, 1976.)

as spiroperidol (at the lower left in the figure) are prescribed in the lowest doses because they are effective in these low doses; drugs such as chlorpromazine are prescribed in larger doses because such doses are necessary to achieve the desired effect. The investigators also determined what dose of each drug is necessary to block dopamine receptors (displayed along the vertical axis). As the figure shows, the more effective a given drug is for blocking dopamine receptors, the more effectively it relieves schizophrenia (Seeman, Lee, Chau-Wong, & Wong, 1976).

These results give rise to the **dopamine hypothesis of schizophrenia.** According to this hypothesis, schizophrenia results from excess activity at dopamine synapses; neuroleptic drugs relieve schizophrenia by decreasing that activity.

Strengths and Weaknesses of the Dopamine Hypothesis

The fact that dopamine-blocking drugs relieve schizophrenia is certainly strong evidence that the causes of schizophrenia have something to do with dopamine synapses. Furthermore, most patients with schizophrenia blink more frequently than normal, a behavior that probably reflects excessive dopamine stimulation (Kleinman et al., 1984).

Despite the attractiveness of the dopamine hypothesis, it still faces some serious questions (Jaskiw & Weinberger, 1992). First, research has found little evidence that the brains of schizophrenic people have either excess dopamine concentrations or any excess of dopamine receptors. Some studies have found normal concentrations, and others have found slightly elevated concentrations, but few studies have reported concentrations far from the normal range.

One possible resolution to this issue is that people with schizophrenia may have normal dopamine levels at most times but occasional brief periods when the dopamine levels rise sharply (Breier, Davis, Buchanan, Moricle, & Munson, 1993).

A further difficulty for the dopamine hypothesis is the time course for the effects of neuroleptic drugs. Although such drugs block dopamine receptors almost at once, their effects on behavior build up gradually over 2 or 3 weeks (Lipton & Nemeroff, 1978). As with the similar pattern for antidepressant drugs, neuroleptic drugs probably induce gradual changes in both the pattern of release by the presynaptic neuron and the sensitivity of the postsynaptic neuron.

One possibility is that the underlying problem in schizophrenia is not an excess of dopamine activity but a deficit of glutamate activity (Kornhuber, 1983). Glutamate is a neurotransmitter released by axons extending from the cerebral cortex to the limbic system; dopamine synapses are known to inhibit the release of glutamate in that area. One study reported that people with schizophrenia have only about half as much glutamate as normal in their brain (Kim & Kornhuber, 1982). If glutamate levels are low, one way to increase them would be to block the dopamine synapses that inhibit the glutamate synapses. One attraction of the decreased-glutamate hypothesis is that it fits with the evidence of damage to the cerebral cortex.

Side Effects of Neuroleptic Drugs and the Search for Improved Drugs

Most investigators in this field believe that neuroleptic drugs exert their beneficial effects by decreasing the activity of dopamine neurons in the **mesolimbic system,** a set of neurons that project from the midbrain tegmentum to the limbic system. However, the drugs also decrease the activity of other dopamine neurons that are responsible for movement. Consequently, the drugs produce a combination of desired and undesired effects.

Among the unpleasant side effects of neuroleptic drugs, the most serious is **tardive dyskinesia** (TARD-eev dis-kih-NEE-zhee-uh), tremors and other involuntary movements that develop gradually over years of drug use in many but not all people who take neuroleptics. It is most common in older patients and patients who have taken larger doses of neuroleptic drugs (Morgenstern & Glazer, 1993).

A simple, appealing theory is that tardive dyskinesia results from denervation supersensitivity (Chapter 15): Because of prolonged blockage of transmission at dopamine synapses, the postsynaptic neurons develop more receptors and begin to respond vigorously to even small amounts of dopamine. Slight stimulation of these highly responsive synapses leads to bursts of involuntary movements. (As we saw in Chapter 8, dopamine synapses in the basal ganglia stimulate movement.)

However, this simple theory appears to be wrong. In one study, investigators labeled dopamine receptors with a radioactive drug and then examined the brain with a PET scan. They found the same concentration of dopamine receptors in patients with and without tardive dyskinesia (Andersson et al., 1990). Evidently, tardive dyskinesia is not linked to an excess of dopamine receptors, although the actual cause is unknown.

Once tardive dyskinesia emerges, it is apparently permanent, even after the patient stops taking the drug. In fact, without the drug, the dopamine receptors

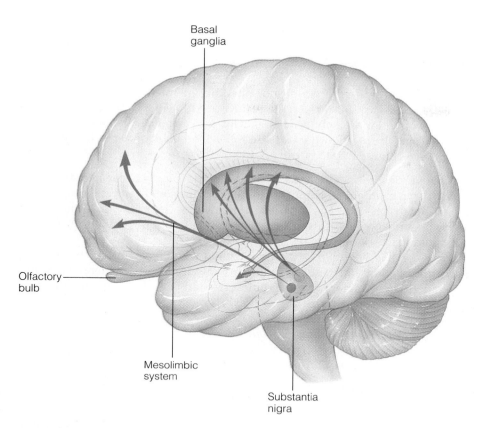

Figure 16.17
Two major dopamine pathways
The mesolimbic system is apparently responsible for the symptoms of schizophrenia; the path to the basal ganglia is responsible for tardive dyskinesia, which sometimes results from use of neuroleptic drugs. (Adapted from Valzelli, 1980.)

are no longer blocked, and the symptoms of tardive dyskinesia grow *worse.* Various drugs are useful in relieving tardive dyskinesia (Thaker et al., 1987).

Given the difficulties of combating tardive dyskinesia after it starts, the best solution is to prevent it from starting. Certain new drugs, called *atypical antipsychotic drugs,* show much promise for alleviating schizophrenia without causing tardive dyskinesia. The brain has several types of dopamine receptors and several dopamine pathways, each with somewhat different drug sensitivities (Albanese, Altavista, & Rossi, 1986). The neuroleptic drugs that produce tardive dyskinesia inhibit both the mesolimbic system and the dopamine path from the substantia nigra to the basal ganglia. Apparently, the mesolimbic system has the most to do with the symptoms of schizophrenia; the path to the basal ganglia is responsible for tardive dyskinesia (see Figure 16.17). The new atypical antipsychotic drugs, such as clozapine and thioridazine, block dopamine activity in the mesolimbic system and thereby alleviate schizophrenia. Because they have less effect on the dopamine receptors in the basal ganglia, they are less likely to produce tardive dyskinesia (White & Wang, 1983). Clozapine, which blocks serotonin receptors as well as certain dopamine receptors, is often helpful even for patients who do not respond well to other neuroleptic drugs.

Schizophrenia and Autism

579

Figure 16.18
An autistic boy with two stereotyped behaviors: pulling on his ears and biting his hand. His right hand is covered with welts and calluses.

Infantile Autism

Infantile autism is a rare condition, affecting about one child in 2,500. It resembles schizophrenia in certain regards, although the underlying causes differ. Like other kinds of abnormal behavior, autism comes in all degrees, from mild to severe. In full-blown cases the following behaviors are characteristic (Creak, 1961; Kanner, 1943; Ornitz & Ritvo, 1976):

1. *Social isolation.* The autistic child largely ignores other people, shows little attachment to parents or other relatives, and retreats into a world of his or her own. Many parents remark that their autistic child was an unresponsive infant from the start, failing to orient to adult faces or to mold to the parent's body when held.
2. *Stereotyped behaviors.* An autistic child rocks back and forth, bites his or her hands, stares at something, rotates an object, or engages in other repetitive behaviors for long, uninterrupted periods. Each autistic child has a special repertoire of preferred stereotyped behaviors. (See Figure 16.18.)
3. *Resistance to any change in routine.* The child establishes strong habits and becomes upset if the routine is changed.
4. *Abnormal responses to sensory stimuli.* The autistic child may ignore visual stimuli and sounds, especially speech, sometimes to such an extent that others assume that the child is deaf. At other times, the child may show an excessive startle reaction to a mild stimulus.
5. *Insensitivity to pain.* At least some of the time, autistic children fail to react to cuts, burns, extreme hot or cold, and other pain.
6. *Inappropriate emotional expressions.* Autistic children have sudden bouts of fear and crying for no obvious reason; at other times, they display utter fearlessness and unprovoked laughter. Their emotions seem to spring from spontaneous internal sources rather than as reactions to any event.
7. *Disturbances of movement.* Certain autistic children may be hyperactive or inactive for prolonged periods.
8. *Poor use of speech.* Some autistic children never speak. A larger number learn the names of many common objects and develop good pronunciation but seldom use language to ask for anything or to enhance social relationships.
9. *Specific, limited intellectual abnormalities.* Many autistic children do well, even unusually well, on certain intellectual tasks but very poorly on others. The exact pattern of impairment varies from child to child. It is difficult to estimate their overall intelligence because they often fail to follow the instructions for a standard IQ test.

Autism has often been compared with schizophrenia because social isolation is a prominent characteristic of both conditions. The two conditions differ in many regards, however. (See Table 16.1.) Childhood autism almost never develops into adult schizophrenia (Petty, Ornitz, Michelman, & Zimmerman, 1984).

One mildly autistic boy who largely recovered from the disorder described his experiences as follows (White & White, 1987, pp. 224–225):

At the age of about two I could say a fair number of words but hardly any full sentences. I was rarely able to hear sentences because my hearing dis-

Table 16.1   Distinctions between Schizophrenia and Autism

Characteristics	Schizophrenia	Autism
Usual age at first diagnosis	15–30 years old	A few months to three years old
Sex ratio	Equal numbers of males and females	Mostly males
Genetics	Clear genetic tendency	Probable but less clear genetic tendency; does not cluster in same families with schizophrenia
Response to neuroleptic drugs	Improvement in most cases	Sedation; no reduction of autistic symptoms

torted them. I was sometimes able to hear a word or two at the start and understand it and then the next lot of words sort of merged into one another and I could not make head or tail of it. . . . I did not get on very well at nursery school. . . . Sometimes when other kids spoke to me I could scarcely hear them and sometimes they sounded like bullets. I thought I was going to go deaf. . . . I was also frightened of the vacuum cleaner, the food mixer and the liquidizer because they sounded about five times as loud as they actually were. . . . Now off to school. . . . Shortly after the start of the [second year] the class went off on a trip to Bristol Zoo. The bus started with a clap of thunder, the engine sounding almost four times as loud as normal and I had my hands in my ears for most of the journey. We finally arrived there. It was a very bright day and very hot. My eyesight blurred several times that day and once I could see no more than a yard in front. I jumped out of my skin when the animals made noises.

Given these sensory distortions, we can begin to understand why an autistic child retreats into his or her own world.

Biological Abnormalities in Autistic Children

Autistic children demonstrate such a wide variety of biological abnormalities that it is difficult to specify which of their many abnormalities is the primary problem. Autistic children give no indication of gross brain atrophy, damage, or malformation (Creasey et al., 1986). However, they do show signs of neurological impairment (Gillberg & Gillberg, 1983), including a very high metabolic rate in some brain regions and a very low rate in others (Rumsey et al., 1985). Many autistic children suffer from various other abnormalities, including deficient response to vestibular sensation (Ornitz, Atwell, Kaplan, & Westlake, 1985), EEG abnormalities, irregular waking-sleeping cycles, presence of potentially hallucinogenic chemicals in their blood, and many minor physical anomalies. One striking and puzzling characteristic, which no theory to date has even attempted to explain, is that most autistic children are unusually good looking. Also surprising is the report that many autistic children huddle around radiators or other heat sources in a room at normal temperature, as if they feel cold (Jeddi, 1970). Moreover, many parents have reported that, whenever their autistic children have a fever, they behave almost normally, with better-than-usual communication with other people and more attention to their surroundings (Sullivan, 1980).

Possible Causes of Autism

Autism, like most other psychological disorders, is probably the product of several causes. At this time, the most likely factors are biological.

Parental Behavior?

The early accounts of autistic children described their parents as well-educated, upper-middle-class, intellectual people who displayed little emotion (Kanner, 1943). Certain theorists suggested that the parents' lack of emotional warmth actually caused the children to become autistic. Virtually all authorities now dismiss this hypothesis for several reasons. One is that later studies have failed to confirm the supposed overrepresentation of autism in intellectual or upper-middle-class families (Koegel, Schreibman, O'Neill, & Burke, 1983; Tsai, Stewart, & August, 1981). Second, nearly all the brothers and sisters of autistic children develop normally. If the parents were bad enough to make one child behave so strangely, we would expect the other children in the family to be a bit odd as well. The normal behavior of the brothers and sisters argues strongly against the bad-parent theory.

Genetics

Given how early the condition develops, it is natural to look for indications of a genetic basis. Twin studies do support a hereditary contribution. It is not easy to find many autistic children who have a twin, because both autism and twinning are rare. One extensive study examined 40 pairs of twins that included at least one autistic child. Of 23 monozygotic pairs, 22 were concordant for autism; of 17 dizygotic pairs, 4 were concordant (Ritvo, Freeman, Mason-Brothers, Mo, & Ritvo, 1985). Autism is unlikely to depend on a single gene, however; among the brothers and sisters of autistic children, the frequency of autism ranges from 2 to 8 percent, according to different studies.

One possible way to reconcile the high concordance in identical twins to the much lower concordance in brothers and sisters is to assume that autism depends on a large number of genes, many of which must be present to produce the condition. The greater frequency of autism in males than in females could mean that females need a greater "dose" of the abnormal genes than males do to become autistic. Indeed, female autistic children have more EEG abnormalities, more movement disturbances, poorer bladder and bowel control, and more evidence of brain dysfunction than equally autistic males have (Tsai, Stewart, & August, 1981). A family with an autistic daughter has a 14.5% risk of autism in any later children—more than double the risk observed if the first autistic child had been a son (Ritvo et al., 1989).

One interesting development in genetic research on autism is the discovery that a large number of autistic children have a fragile X chromosome, a weak spot on an X chromosome that is vulnerable to breakage under certain conditions. The fragile X syndrome has also been noted in many mentally retarded people and in the relatives of autistic and mentally retarded children (August & Lockhart, 1984; Gillberg, Wahlström, & Hagberg, 1984). An explanation in terms of a fragile X chromosome would help to make sense of the disproportionate number of boys with autism: Girls have a second X chromosome that can compete with the effects of a defective one.

Endorphins

Autistic children sometimes fail to react to painful stimuli. One of the most reliable ways to decrease sensitivity to pain is an injection of morphine or other opiate drugs. Consider some other symptoms of morphine intoxication (Desmond & Wilson, 1975; Glass, Evans, & Rajegowda, 1975; Ream, Robinson, Richter, Hegge, & Holloway, 1975): (1) social withdrawal, (2) repetitive and sometimes stereotyped behaviors, (3) ignoring most sensory stimuli but hallucinating others, (4) sedation under most circumstances but sometimes a driven hyperactivity, and (5) happiness and fearlessness. During withdrawal from morphine, the symptoms include restlessness, fear and anxiety, crying, and a jumpy overresponsiveness to stimulation. In short, a person who alternately took morphine injections and then went through withdrawal would show many of the same behaviors associated with autism.

One opiate receptor in the brain, the zeta (ζ) receptor, is known to modify the growth and development of the central nervous system (Zagon, Goodman, & McLaughlin, 1993). Children who are born to narcotic-addicted mothers suffer many defects in brain development and behavior (Householder, Hatcher, Burns, & Chasnoff, 1982). A few of these effects resemble the behavior of autistic children: The children of addicts have delayed learning and language development and decreased responsiveness to their caregivers.

Obviously, autistic children are not morphine addicts, and few of their mothers were narcotics users. But the body does have its own opiates, the endorphins. Perhaps, for some unknown reason, an autistic child's brain sometimes releases excessive amounts of endorphins and at other times releases very low amounts (Kalat, 1978; Panksepp, Herman, & Vilberg, 1978).

Do autistic children have some anomaly in their endorphins? One study measured endorphin levels in the CSF of autistic children and normal children. Of 20 autistic children, 11 had higher endorphin levels than the highest of the 8 normal children (Gillberg, Terenius, & Lönnerholm, 1985). Other studies have found elevated endorphin levels in autistic children with high frequencies of self-injurious behaviors (Sandman et al., 1990).

Therapies for Autism

Autism is generally a lifelong condition, although some individuals become self-sufficient adults. If we take the endorphin hypothesis seriously, we might expect that an opiate-blocking drug, such as naloxone or naltrexone, could help to relieve autism. Several early studies have found that such drugs reduce self-injurious behaviors such as handbiting (Sahley & Panksepp, 1987; Sandman et al., 1990); more data are needed, especially on the effects of such drugs at earlier ages. At present, however, the most successful treatments for autism concentrate on special education rather than on biological interventions (Schopler, 1987).

Summary

1. Schizophrenia is a psychological disorder characterized by deterioration of daily functioning plus some combination of other symptoms that can include hallucinations, delusions, and thought disorder. Psychologists are not certain whether schizophrenia is a single disorder or a family of disorders. (p. 564)

2. Many patients with schizophrenia have a moderate atrophy and disorganization of neurons in the cerebral cortex, thalamus, and hippocampus. Some people also show decreased metabolic activity in the frontal cortex. (p. 566)

3. Studies of twins and adopted children indicate that schizophrenia has a genetic basis, although not everyone with the gene(s) develops schizophrenia. (p. 569)

4. Impairment of pursuit eye movements may be a biological marker indicating vulnerability to schizophrenia. (p. 572)

5. More patients with schizophrenia were born in winter than in other seasons. One possible explanation is that their mothers may have been exposed to a viral infection in the fall before giving birth, when the fetus's brain was at a critical stage of development. (p. 573)

6. Neuroleptics, the drugs that relieve schizophrenia, block dopamine synapses and block the release of dopamine. Consequently, many investigators believe overactivity of dopamine synapses is part of the cause of schizophrenia. (p. 576)

7. Neuroleptic drugs induce tardive dyskinesia as a side effect in certain patients. Certain atypical antipsychotic drugs, such as clozapine, can produce the antischizophrenic effects without tardive dyskinesia. (p. 578)

8. Infantile autism, a rare condition that begins in early childhood, is characterized by social isolation, stereotyped behaviors, and insensitivity to pain. It resembles schizophrenia in certain regards, although the underlying causes are almost certainly different. (p. 580)

9. The biological basis of autism is not yet known; possibilities include genetics and excessive endorphin activity during early brain development. (p. 582)

Review Questions

1. Distinguish between the positive and negative symptoms of schizophrenia. (p. 565)

2. Does the brain damage associated with schizophrenia increase over age? What are the implications of the age pattern in brain damage? (p. 566)

3. If a schizophrenic person has a nonschizophrenic twin, is the nonschizophrenic twin likely to have children who eventually develop schizophrenia? What conclusions follow from this answer? (p. 571)

4. How do saccadic eye movements differ from pursuit eye movements? (p. 572)

5. What is the season-of-birth effect and what is a promising hypothesis to explain it? (p. 573)

6. What is the main behavioral difference between schizophrenia and amphetamine psychosis? (p. 576)

7. What synaptic effects do neuroleptic drugs have? (p. 576)

8. Describe the strengths and weaknesses of the dopamine hypothesis of schizophrenia. (p. 577)

9. What is usually the most troublesome side effect of neuroleptic drugs? (p. 578)

10. Why is it unlikely that autism depends on a single gene? (p. 582)

Thought Questions

1. One problem for any genetic hypothesis of schizophrenia is explaining how the genes responsible for schizophrenia could become as common as they seem to be. Schizophrenic people have a higher-than-normal probability of dying young (Allebeck & Wistedt, 1986) and a lower-than-normal probability of having children. Evolution, it certainly seems, should select strongly against a gene for schizophrenia. How could we account for the apparently high prevalence of this gene in spite of the apparently strong selection against it?

2. People with schizophrenia are reported to have fewer dreams than other people and to have some PGO spikes during wakefulness. Speculate on what this might mean in relation to the causes of schizophrenia.

3. According to available evidence, the concordance rate for autism is higher for dizygotic twins than for brother and sister, even though the genetic similarity is no greater for one relationship than the other. What possible explanation might you offer?

Suggestions for Further Reading

Gottesman, I. I. (1991). *Schizophrenia genesis*. New York: W. H. Freeman. Discussion of the causes of schizophrenia, with emphasis on genetics.

Heston, L. L. (1992). *Mending minds*. New York: W. H. Freeman. A nontechnical description of contemporary, drug-oriented psychiatry. See Chapter 3 on schizophrenia.

Rutter, M., & Schopler, E. (1978). *Autism*. New York: Plenum. Good introduction to research on autistic children.

Terms

schizophrenia disorder characterized by deteriorating ability to function in everyday life and some combination of hallucinations, delusions, thought disorder, movement disorder, and inappropriate emotional expressions (p. 564)

hallucination sensory experience that does not correspond to reality (p. 565)

delusion belief that other people regard as unfounded, such as the belief that one is being severely persecuted (p. 565)

thought disorder impaired thinking, such as difficulty understanding and using abstract concepts (p. 565)

positive symptom presence of a behavior not seen in normal people (p. 565)

negative symptom absence of a behavior ordinarily seen in normal people (p. 565)

acute having a sudden onset (p. 565)

chronic having a gradual onset and long duration (p. 565)

concordance agreement (A pair of twins is concordant for a trait if both of them have it or if neither has it.) (p. 570)

paternal half-siblings people who have the same father but different mothers (p. 571)

saccadic eye movement sudden shift of the eyes from one target to another (p. 572)

pursuit eye movement eye movement that follows a moving target (p. 572)

season-of-birth effect tendency for people born in winter to have a greater probability of developing schizophrenia than do people born in other seasons (p. 573)

amphetamine psychosis condition resembling schizophrenia provoked by a large dose of amphetamine (p. 576)

chlorpromazine first drug found to relieve schizophrenia (p. 576)

neuroleptic drug drug that relieves schizophrenia (p. 576)

phenothiazine a class of neuroleptic drugs, including chlorpromazine (p. 576)

butyrophenone class of neuroleptic drugs, including haloperidol (p. 576)

haloperidol a common neuroleptic drug (p. 576)

dopamine hypothesis of schizophrenia hypothesis that schizophrenia is due to excess activity at dopamine synapses (p. 577)

mesolimbic system set of neurons that project from the midbrain tegmentum to the limbic system (p. 578)

tardive dyskinesia side effect of neuroleptic drugs characterized by tremors and other involuntary movements (p. 578)

infantile autism condition characterized by social isolation, stereotyped behaviors, abnormal responses to sensory stimuli, inappropriate emotional expressions, and abnormal development of speech and intellect (p. 580)

Appendix A
GENETICS AND EVOLUTION

MAIN IDEAS

1. The expression of a given gene depends on the environment and on interactions with other genes.

2. Genes are located on chromosomes, which are composed of the chemical deoxyribonucleic acid (DNA). DNA chains determine the structure of RNA chains, which in turn determine the structure of proteins.

3. It is difficult to measure the contribution of heredity to the variations in human behavior, although several methods are in common use.

4. Although it is often difficult to determine exactly how a species has evolved from its ancestors, the basic process of evolution through natural selection is a logical necessity.

*T*his appendix is not intended to be comprehensive. It presents only those aspects of genetics and evolution that a reader needs to know in order to understand biological psychology. If you already have a strong background in genetics, you may just want to skim over most of this material.

Mendelian Genetics

Prior to the work of Gregor Mendel, a late-nineteenth-century monk, scientists thought that inheritance was a blending process, in which the properties of the sperm and the egg simply mixed, much as one might mix red paint and yellow paint.

Mendel demonstrated that inheritance occurs through **genes,** units of heredity that maintain their structural identity from one generation to another and do not blend with one another. Suppose, as Mendel did in one experiment, we breed a pea plant that has yellow seeds with one that has white seeds. (Most plants reproduce sexually just as animals do.) All the offspring of this cross have yellow seeds. Now we breed two of these offspring with each other. In the next generation, about three-fourths have yellow seeds and one-fourth have white seeds. Thus, although the second generation had only yellow seeds, the genes for white seeds have not been lost.

To account for results like these, Mendel proposed that inheritance depends on structural particles (later called genes) that come in pairs. In the example of the pea plants, one parent has a pair of genes for yellow seeds, which we could represent as *AA.* The other parent has a pair of genes for white seeds, which we could designate *aa.* (Each parent also has millions of other genes that control a wide variety of characteristics.) During reproduction, each parent contributes one gene from each pair. So the first parent contributes an *A* gene (for yellow seeds) and the second parent contributes an *a* gene (for white seeds). The offspring therefore have an *Aa* gene combination. In this case, the gene for yellow seeds, *A,* is **dominant** over the gene for white seeds, *a,* which is **recessive.** If an individual has one of each gene, it exhibits the trait corresponding to the dominant gene.

Although all members of the second generation produce yellow seeds, they carry both an *A* and an *a* gene. Thus, during reproduction, each individual can contribute either gene to offspring. If both parents contribute an *a* gene, they will produce a white-seed offspring, even though both parents have yellow seeds. (On the other hand, if both parents produce only white seeds, none of their offspring can produce yellow seeds. Do you see why?)

Statistically, an *Aa* individual contributes an *A* gene to 50 percent of its offspring and an *a* gene to the other 50 percent. Therefore, an *Aa* and *Aa* mating produces 25 percent *AA* offspring, 50 percent *Aa,* and 25 percent *aa.* (See Figure A.1.)

Many human traits depend on a single gene that follows these simple Mendelian ratios. Examples include eye color (brown dominant, blue recessive), ability to taste the chemical phenylthiocarbamide (ability to taste domi-

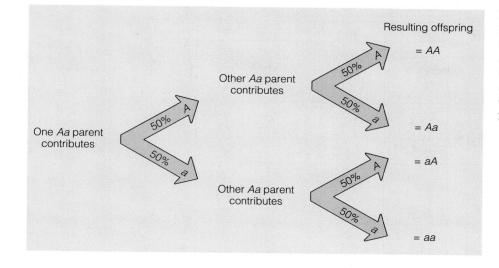

Figure A.1
**Results of an *Aa* by *Aa*
mating**
*Each offspring has a 25 per-
cent chance of receiving the
AA combination, a 25 per-
cent chance of aa, and a 50
percent chance of Aa.*

Resulting offspring

Other *Aa* parent
contributes

= AA

50%

A

50%

a

= Aa

One *Aa* parent
contributes

50%

A

50%

a

Other *Aa* parent
contributes

= aA

50%

A

50%

a

= aa

nant, inability recessive), and ability to curl one's tongue lengthwise (ability
dominant, inability recessive).

An individual who has two identical genes for some trait (either *AA* or *aa*)
is **homozygous** for that gene. One who has different genes (*Aa*) is **heterozygous.**

In many cases, neither gene is dominant; the heterozygous individual is
then intermediate between the two homozygous conditions. In the preceding
example, if neither gene were dominant, the *Aa* individuals might produce light
yellow seeds. A cross between two *Aa* individuals would then yield about 25
percent yellow-seed individuals (*AA*), 50 percent light yellow (*Aa*), and 25 percent white (*aa*).

Many characteristics depend on more than one gene pair. Suppose, for
example, that the length of a worm depends on two gene pairs. Genes *B* and *C*
are dominant genes for long body; genes *b* and *c* are recessive for short body. If
we cross a long worm with *BBCC* **genotype** (gene pattern) and a short worm
with *bbcc* genotype, the first worm contributes a *B* and a *C*; the second contributes a *b* and a *c*. Therefore, all the offspring will have a *BbCc* genotype and
will have long bodies.

Now, let us cross a *BbCc* with another *BbCc*. Assume that the *B* and *C* genes
arrange themselves independently of each other. That is, a parent that contributes a *B* gene can contribute either a *C* or a *c*; it has an equal chance of contributing any of the combinations *BC*, *Bc*, *bC*, and *bc*. The same goes for the
other parent. Thus, the possibilities for offspring are as Figure A.2 shows.

In 9 of the 16 possibilities, the offspring has at least one *B* gene and at least
one *C* gene. Because *B* and *C* are dominant genes, all these offspring are long.
Only one of the possible offspring types has both a *bb* and a *cc* combination;
only the individuals of this type are short. The other six possibilities have at
least one dominant gene at either the *B* or the *C* locus, and two recessive genes
at the other (for example, *Bbcc* or *bbCC*); these worms are intermediate in
length between the two original types.

Things can get more complicated. Perhaps *B* makes more of a difference
than *C,* so that a *Bbcc* worm is longer than a *bbCc*. Or perhaps more than two
gene pairs contribute to body length (or any other characteristic). Furthermore, the effects of a gene may depend on the environment or on what other
genes the individual has.

Figure A.2
Results of a *BbCc* (long) by
***BbCc* (long) cross**
Of the offspring, 9/16 are
long, 6/16 are intermediate,
and 1/16 are short.

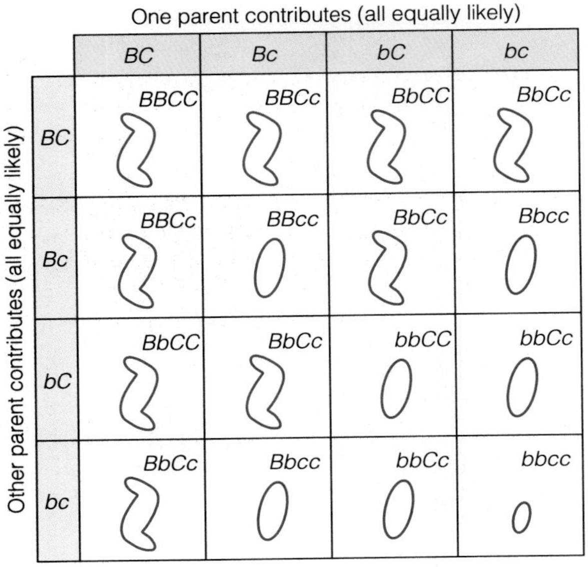

Chromosome Linkage

Up to this point, we have dealt with genes that are inherited independently of one another. Genes can be physically linked so that someone who inherits one gene is likely to inherit a second one, too.

Genes are located on strands of DNA called **chromosomes.** Each chromosome participates in reproduction independently of the others, and each species has a certain number of chromosomes (23 pairs in humans, 4 pairs in fruit flies). Thus, if an individual has a *BbCc* genotype, and if the *B* and *C* genes are on different chromosomes, its contribution of a *B* or *b* gene has nothing to do with whether it contributes a *C* or a *c*. But suppose that they are on the same chromosome. If one chromosome has the *BC* combination and the other has *bc*, then an individual who contributes a *B* gene will probably also contribute a *C*.

The exception to this statement comes about as a result of **crossing over.** During reproduction, a pair of chromosomes may break apart and reconnect such that part of one chromosome attaches to the other part of the second chromosome. If one chromosome has the *BC* combination and the other chromosome has the *bc* combination, crossing over between the *B* locus and the *C* locus leaves new chromosomes with the combinations *Bc* and *bC*. The closer the *B* locus is to the *C* locus, the less often crossing over will occur between them.

Sex-Linked and Sex-Limited Genes

Each individual has a certain number of chromosomes. All but one pair are known as autosomal chromosomes; all genes located on these chromosomes are referred to as **autosomal genes.** The other two chromosomes are the sex chromosomes; genes located on them are known as **sex-linked genes.**

In mammals, the two sex chromosomes are designated X and Y. (Unlike the symbols *A, B,* and *C* that were introduced to illustrate gene pairs, X and Y are standard symbols for sex chromosomes used by all geneticists.) A female mammal has two X chromosomes; a male has an X and a Y. During reproduction, the female necessarily contributes an X chromosome, and the male contributes

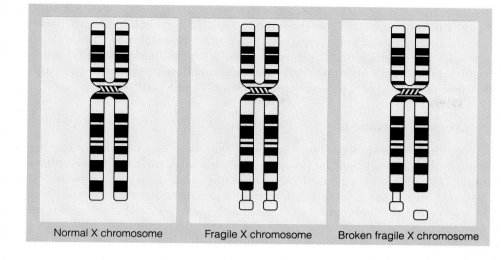

Figure A.3
The fragile X chromosome
Unlike the normal X chromosome, the fragile X chromosome has a portion that can easily break off.

Normal X chromosome   Fragile X chromosome   Broken fragile X chromosome

either an X or a Y. If he contributes an X, the offspring will be female; if he contributes a Y, the offspring will be male. (Birds are different. Male birds have two sex chromosomes alike, designated ZZ; females have two different sex chromosomes, designated ZW.)

The **Y chromosome** is small and carries few, if any, genes other than the gene that causes the individual to develop as a male instead of a female. The **X chromosome,** however, carries many genes. Thus, when biologists speak of sex-linked genes, they ordinarily mean X-linked genes.

Characteristics controlled by sex-linked genes occur more often in one sex than in the other. If a gene is a sex-linked dominant, the characteristic that it controls occurs more often in females than in males because females, with two X chromosomes, have twice the chance that males have of getting the sex-linked gene.

On the other hand, a characteristic that is controlled by a sex-linked recessive gene produces its effects only if the dominant gene is not present. Thus, for a female to show the effects of a sex-linked recessive, she would have to have two such genes. A male, however, has only one X chromosome; if he has an X-linked recessive gene, he cannot have a dominant gene to overrule it. Color blindness is controlled by a sex-linked recessive gene in humans. Most color-blind people are male. For a female to be color blind, she would have to have a color-blind father and a mother with at least one gene for color blindness. Other examples of sex-linked recessive genes are those for hemophilia ("bleeder's disease") and albinism.

Distinct from sex-linked genes are the **sex-limited genes.** A sex-limited gene has an effect in one sex only, or at least it has a much stronger effect in one sex than the other. For instance, genes control the amount of chest hair in men, breast size in women, the amount of crowing in roosters, and the rate of egg production in hens. Such genes need not be on the sex chromosomes; both sexes have the genes, but the genes exert their effects more strongly under the influence of either testosterone or estrogen.

One moderately common genetic cause of mental retardation relates to the sex chromosomes: the **fragile X chromosome** (Brown & Jenkins, 1989). A fragile X chromosome has a segment that can literally snap off (Figure A.3). In people who have a fragile X chromosome, that segment snaps off in some of the body's cells and not in others. In females, a fragile X chromosome generally has no apparent effects, because each cell also has a normal X chromosome. For

Genetics and Evolution

males, if the fragile X chromosome snaps off in many cells, especially brain cells, the individual will be moderately to severely retarded, with poorly formed dendrites and fewer synapses than normal (Rudelli et al., 1985). If the chromosome segment snaps off in fewer cells, the individual may be mildly retarded or normal. About one male in a thousand develops mental retardation because of the fragile X chromosome (Brown & Jenkins, 1989).

Sources of Variation

If reproduction always produced offspring that were exact copies of the parents, evolution would not be possible. One source of variation is **recombination.** The effects of a gene depend on what other genes are present. An offspring, in receiving some genes from one parent and some from the other, may have a new combination of genes that together yield characteristics not found in either parent.

Another source of variation is a **mutation,** or change, in a single gene. For instance, a gene for brown eyes might mutate into a gene for blue eyes. Mutation of a given gene is a rare event, but, because each of us has millions of genes, mutations provide a constant source of variation.

A mutation is a random event; that is, the needs of the organism do not guide it. A mutation is analogous to having an untrained person add, remove, or distort something on the blueprints for your new house. The likely result is to make the house less desirable than it would have been, perhaps even to make it collapse; only rarely would the random change improve the house.

Most mutations produce recessive genes, however. Thus, if you or one of your recent ancestors had a harmful mutation on one of the genes, your children would not show the harmful effects unless you happened to mate with someone who had the same harmful mutant gene. Your mate is unlikely to have the same mutant genes that you have, unless the two of you got that gene from the same ancestor. For this reason, it is unhealthy for people to marry their own relatives.

A third source of variation—almost always disadvantageous—is for one parent to contribute something other than exactly one copy of each chromosome. Occasionally, one parent contributes two or zero copies of a given chromosome. For example, if one human parent contributes two copies of chromosome 21, the child has a total of three copies, counting the one obtained from the other parent. The consequence is **Down syndrome,** a genetic disorder characterized by mental retardation (Figure A.4). The brain anomalies generally include low brain weight, reduced numbers of certain kinds of cells, reduced number and depth of sulci in the cerebral cortex, and shorter-than-normal dendrites (Coyle, Oster-Granite, & Gearhart, 1986). By age 40, people with Down syndrome develop further brain abnormalities of the types also seen in Alzheimer's disease (see Chapter 13).

Down syndrome is rare in children of young mothers but becomes increasingly common in children born to mothers older than 35. The incidence of Down syndrome may or may not be related to the father's age; at this point, the data are inconsistent. At most, the father's age is a minor factor in comparison with the mother's age (Erickson & Bjerkedal, 1981; Regal, Cross, Lamson, & Hook, 1980).

Penetrance   When we refer to, say, "a gene for brown eyes," we mean that the gene makes a difference between having brown eyes and some other color of eyes *under the usual environmental conditions.* Some genes have observable effects only if the individual experiences a certain climate, a particular pattern

a

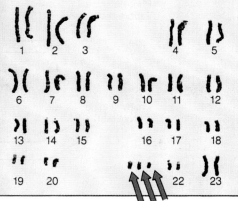

b

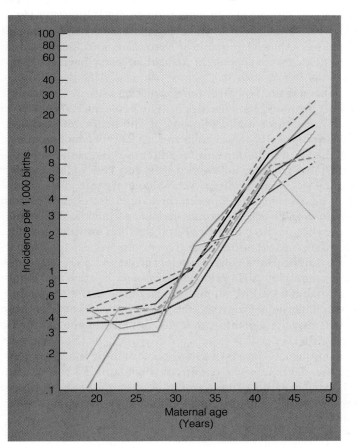

c

Figure A.4
(*a*) *A child with Down syndrome. (A. Sieveking/ PR Inc.)* (*b*) *Chromosomes of a girl with Down syndrome. Arrows indicate the three copies of chromosome 21. Note that this is the smallest of the human chromosomes; an extra copy of one of the larger chromosomes is more likely to be fatal. (Cytogenetics Laboratory, UCSF.)* (*c*) *Increase in frequency of Down syndrome as a function of the mother's age. For mothers over age 35, the probability of giving birth to a Down syndrome child increases. Each line represents the results of a different study. (Based on Lilienfeld, 1969.)*

of light and darkness, a specific diet, a given social setting, or some other environmental condition. A gene may also have effects that emerge only in individuals who have certain other genes. A gene that affects some individuals but not others has partial **penetrance.** That is, its effects "penetrate" into observable characteristics only under certain conditions. The genes for schizophrenia and most other psychological conditions have partial penetrance; a person may have the relevant genes but fail to develop the condition.

Genetics and Evolution

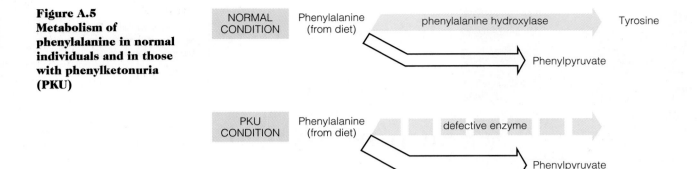

**Figure A.5
Metabolism of
phenylalanine in normal
individuals and in those
with phenylketonuria
(PKU)**

NORMAL CONDITION — Phenylalanine (from diet) — phenylalanine hydroxylase — Tyrosine — Phenylpyruvate

PKU CONDITION — Phenylalanine (from diet) — defective enzyme — Phenylpyruvate

Because of the phenomenon of partial penetrance, it is sometimes possible to reduce the undesirable effects of a gene by changing the environment. One clear example is a condition known as **phenylketonuria** (FEE-nil-KEET-uhn-YOOR-ee-uh), or **PKU**. PKU is one of the most common genetically caused forms of mental retardation. About 1 percent of Europeans and Asians carry the recessive gene for PKU; very few people of African ancestry have the gene (Wang et al., 1989).

The gene for PKU prevents the body from metabolizing *phenylalanine,* an amino acid found in most proteins (see Figure A.5). The consequent buildup of phenylalanine leads to structural malformations of the brain, including a deficit of myelin and a surplus of glia cells. Children with PKU become mentally retarded, restless, irritable, and sometimes prone to temper tantrums.

Physicians can determine whether a newborn baby has PKU by measuring the level of phenylalanine or its metabolites in the blood or urine. This test is routinely performed on nearly all babies born in the United States. If the level is excessively high, indicating PKU, the parents are told to put the child on a strict low-phenylalanine diet. If the parents enforce this diet conscientiously, the child's brain can develop nearly normally and he or she will escape mental retardation. That is, the diet prevents penetrance of the gene.

After a child reaches maturity, it is no longer necessary to stick closely to the diet, except that a woman with PKU should return to the diet during pregnancy and nursing. Even if her baby is normal, the baby's enzymes cannot handle the enormous levels of phenylalanine that accumulate in the mother's bloodstream on a normal diet.

You may have noticed this advisory on beverages containing the sugar substitute NutraSweet: "Phenylketonurics: Contains Phenylalanine." The reason is that NutraSweet is a compound of two amino acids, one of them being phenylalanine. Anyone with PKU must be certain to avoid NutraSweet.

The Biochemistry of Genetics

A chromosome is actually a molecule of the double-stranded chemical deoxyribonucleic acid, or **DNA** (with some proteins attached). Each strand of DNA is composed of four bases in varying orders—guanine, cytosine, adenine, and thymine—attached to a skeleton made of phosphate and a sugar, deoxyribose. The order of these four bases along the chromosome determines all the genetic information. A gene is a small segment of the DNA molecule.

RNA strand G—C—U—A—C—A—G—U—U

DNA strand C—G—A—T—G—T—C—A—A

Figure A.6
A strand of RNA forms by pairing the complementary base to each base in the DNA.

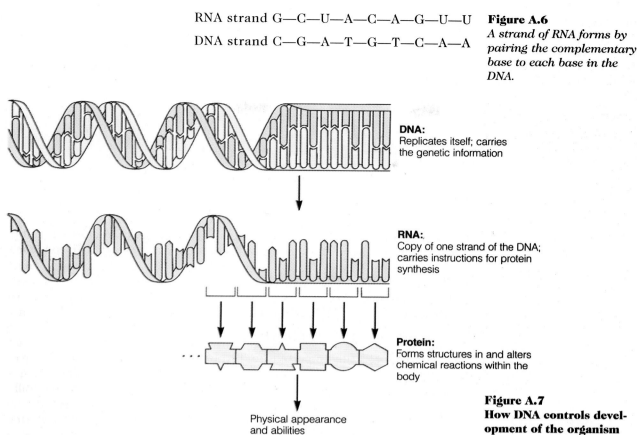

DNA:
Replicates itself; carries the genetic information

RNA:
Copy of one strand of the DNA; carries instructions for protein synthesis

Protein:
Forms structures in and alters chemical reactions within the body

Physical appearance and abilities

Figure A.7
How DNA controls development of the organism
The sequence of bases along a strand of DNA determines the order of bases along a strand of RNA; RNA in turn controls the sequence of amino acids in a protein molecule.

A strand of DNA serves as a **template,** or model, for the synthesis of **RNA** (ribonucleic acid) molecules. RNA is a single strand composed of a sequence of bases—guanine, cytosine, adenine, and uracil—attached to a skeleton made of phosphate and the sugar ribose. The RNA bases are arranged in a manner complementary to those of DNA: Where a DNA chain has guanine, the RNA chain has cytosine; similarly, DNA's cytosine, adenine, and thymine pair up with RNA's guanine, uracil, and adenine, respectively, as Figure A.6 illustrates.

After being synthesized from the DNA template, RNA molecules disperse to various places in the cell. Different kinds of RNA serve different functions. One kind, tRNA (transfer RNA), transports amino acids to the ribosomes of the cell. Another kind, mRNA (messenger RNA), serves as a template for the formation of proteins. An mRNA chain determines the amino-acid structure of a protein by a code: Each sequence of three RNA bases codes for one amino acid. For instance, the RNA sequence guanine-cytosine-guanine codes for the amino acid arginine. The order of RNA bases determines the order of the protein's amino acids. Figure A.7 summarizes the main steps in translating DNA information into proteins.

The proteins then determine the development and properties of the organism. Some proteins form part of the structure of the body; others serve as **enzymes,** or biological catalysts that regulate chemical reactions in the body.

Retroviruses reverse the classical sequence of DNA producing RNA. Viruses are infectious agents composed of RNA. Like any other kind of RNA, they serve as templates for the formation of proteins. One of the proteins produced by a

Genetics and Evolution

Figure A.8
It is pointless to ask whether the area of a rectangle depends more on height or width, but it is meaningful to ask whether the differences in area for a given group of rectangles depend more on differences in height or in width. The same is true for the roles of heredity and environment in determining behavior.

retrovirus, however, causes the formation of a new segment of DNA complementary to the RNA. If that segment of DNA becomes incorporated into one of the chromosomes, it will continue producing more of the retrovirus, in the standard DNA-to-RNA direction. A retrovirus is therefore extremely difficult to attack medically. AIDS and some forms of leukemia are caused by retroviruses.

Measuring the Contributions of Heredity and Environment in Humans

It is often theoretically important to distinguish between the contributions of heredity and environment in the development of behavior. Sometimes people ask, "Which is more important for such-and-so behavior: heredity or environment?" The question is meaningless in that form, although we can rephrase it in a meaningful way. To see what is wrong with the phrasing of the question, consider two analogies:

1. Why does your computer do the things it does? Is it because of the computer's hardware or its software? (You see at once that the question is meaningless. Everything that the computer does depends on both its hardware and its software.)
2. Which is more important for the area of a rectangle, its height or its width? (Again, the question is meaningless; neither height nor width contributes to area independently of the other.)

Now let us rephrase these questions:

1. Why does your computer do some tricks differently from my computer? Is it because the two computers have different hardware or because we are running different software?
2. The rectangles in Figure A.8 differ in area; is that *difference* in area due mostly to differences in height or to differences in width?

Similarly, the proper way to phrase the heredity-environment question is: This group differs from that group in such-and-so behavior; do they *differ* because of differences in their heredity or because of differences in their environment? This question may be difficult to answer in practice, but at least it makes sense in principle. Note that the answer will depend not only on which behavior we examine but also on which groups we compare. For the rectangles in Figure A.8, the differences in area depend mostly on differences in width; for some other set of rectangles, the answer might be different. Similarly, the differences in behavior between red lizards and green lizards might be mostly due to genetic differences, while the differences between green lizards and blue lizards might be due mostly to environmental differences. We have to examine each case separately.

The standard measurement of the contributions of heredity and environment is **heritability.** Heritability is a mathematical construct designed to measure how closely the variations in some characteristic correlate with differences in heredity as opposed to differences in environment. Heritability can vary from zero to 1.0. A heritability of zero means that none of the observed variation is due to differences in heredity; a heritability of 1.0 means that all the observed differences are due to differences in heredity.

It is difficult to get adequate data about heritability in humans. Investigators have no control over who mates with whom or what environment their children grow up in. The time between generations is long, and we are often uncertain about which aspects of the environment are critical.

In many cases, the goal of research is merely to determine whether heredity contributes at all to the differences in behavior. The following types of evidence can be used in studies of the heritability of human behavior, beginning with the *least* convincing and working up from there.

Similarities among Relatives

Does the similarity in behavior between individuals correspond to their degree of genetic relationship? If we designate the genetic relationship between a person and himself or herself as 1.0, then other relationships are as follows:

Relationship	Degree of Relationship
Identical twin	1.0
Fraternal twin	0.5
Brother or sister	0.5
Father, mother, son, daughter	0.5
Grandparent, grandchild	0.25
Uncle, aunt, nephew, niece	0.25
Half-brother, half-sister	0.25
First cousin	0.125
Second cousin	0.0625
Unrelated person	0.0

(These figures assume that people mate randomly rather than choosing genetically similar individuals as mates. Because that assumption is false for humans, the correct numerical coefficients should be somewhat higher.)

If some variation in behavior depends partly on genetics, then the closer the genetic relationship between people, the greater should be the similarity in their behavior. For example, identical twins should resemble each other more than siblings, who should resemble each other more than cousins, and so on.

When this is *not* true—if identical twins resemble each other no more than two unrelated people, for example—we may confidently reject genetics as a significant reason for the variation in behavior. On the other hand, this type of information is never strong evidence *in favor* of a genetic explanation. Identical twins share more of their environment in common than brother and sister, who in turn share more than cousins. Thus, strong similarity between closely related people does not distinguish between genetic and environmental explanations.

Figure A.9

Identical (monozygotic) twins are produced from the same fertilized egg. Fraternal (dizygotic) twins grow from two eggs fertilized by two different sperm.

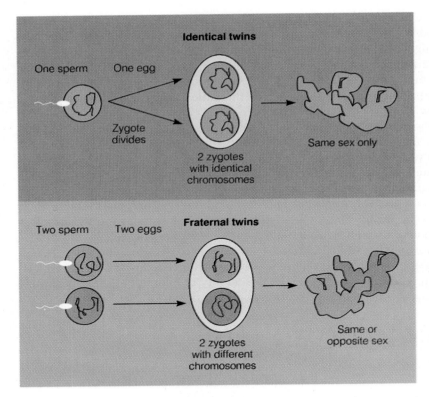

Similarities between Identical Twins and Fraternal Twins

Is the similarity greater between identical twins than between fraternal twins? Fraternal, or nonidentical, twins are also known as **dizygotic** ("two-egg") twins (see Figure A.9). Although they are born at the same time, they are no more closely related genetically than any brother and sister. Identical twins, also known as **monozygotic** ("one-egg") twins, begin as a single egg fertilized by a single sperm; they have identical genetics.

A pair of twins of either kind usually grows up sharing a common environment. Identical twins, however, share more genetics in common. Therefore, if some behavior shows greater similarity between identical twins than between fraternal twins, we can suspect that this added similarity reflects a genetic influence.

However, we should interpret this kind of evidence cautiously. Identical twins are more likely to be treated alike than are fraternal twins by their families and by other people. Thus, identical twins may have greater environmental similarity than fraternal twins as well as greater genetic similarity.

Behavior of Twins Reared in Separate Environments

Do twins reared in separate environments resemble each other? Occasionally, twins are adopted by different families. If we examine a large number of twin pairs who were reared in separate adoptive homes and find that some behavior shows marked similarity within most pairs, one likely interpretation is that genetic similarity is responsible for the behavioral similarity. Two other interpretations are possible: One is that pairs of twins have been adopted by similar families, providing similar environments. (This is a reasonable possibility. Adoption agencies do not place children at random.) The other is that something in the **prenatal** (before-birth) environment strongly influenced development.

Behavior of Adopted Children

Does the behavior of an adopted child more closely resemble that of the genetic relatives or that of the adopted relatives? If a child is adopted at an early age, the people who provide the child's environment are different from those who provided the genes. In some cases, it can be demonstrated that a child's probability of developing some behavior corresponds more closely to the incidence of that behavior among the genetic relatives than to its incidence among the adopted relatives. The most likely interpretation then would be a genetic influence on the behavior or an influence by the prenatal environment.

Although evidence of this type can be fairly strong, it is not without its complications (Kamin, 1974). For example, most adoption agencies try to place a child in an adoptive family that resembles the child's biological family. In some cases, a child may come to resemble his or her biological family because of environmental influences that the adoptive family provides. Still, selective placement in adoptive homes cannot explain cases in which children resemble their biological parents *more* than they resemble their adoptive parents.

Adoption data indicate some role of genetics in IQ scores, activity level, emotionality, sociability versus shyness, schizophrenia, and numerous other behavioral characteristics (Plomin, 1990). In each of these cases, however, the data suggest that the behavioral outcome depends on a large number of genes (not just one) and on the influences of the environment.

Paternal Half-Siblings

How much do adopted paternal half-siblings resemble each other? A sibling is a brother or sister. Half-siblings have one parent in common but not the other. **Paternal half-siblings** have the same father but different mothers.

Occasionally, two paternal half-siblings are adopted at early ages by different families—generally because the same man has fathered illegitimate children by more than one mother. Such children have been reared in different environments and did not even share a common prenatal environment because they had different mothers. Therefore, any strong resemblance between adopted paternal half-siblings is almost certainly due to genetics.

Evidence of this type is potentially about as convincing as any evidence we can get about human heritability. The main problem is that such evidence is scarce. Adopted paternal half-siblings are not easy to locate.

Evolution

Evolution is a change in the gene frequencies for a population over generations. Note that this definition simply specifies *change*; the change is not necessarily an improvement in the long run. For example, many species have evolved specialized adaptations to a specific environment; if that environment changes, those adaptations may become a disadvantage.

It is important to distinguish two questions concerning evolution: How *did* species evolve, and how *do* species evolve? To ask how species did evolve is to ask from *what* they evolved. To answer this question, biologists have to reconstruct a history based on fossils and other kinds of evidence. Their inferences are always subject to revision if new evidence becomes available.

How species *do* evolve is a question of how the process works. We could establish the process of evolution as a logical necessity, even if we had no fossil evidence at all, using the following argument: The study of genetics has demonstrated that offspring generally resemble their parents. We also know, however, that mutations and recombinations lead to a steady supply of new variations within the population and that these new variations are themselves passed on to later generations. If individuals with some genetic variation have an advantage, in the sense that they reproduce more often and more successfully, then their genes will become more common in the population; that is, evolution will occur.

This general principle has long been familiar to animal and plant breeders as **artificial selection.** By selectively breeding only the most productive egg-laying chickens or the dogs that are the best at herding sheep, breeders can develop a new strain of chickens or dogs with a greater degree of the desired characteristic. Darwin's (1859) theory of evolution merely extended this idea, stating that nature acts like a selective breeder. If individuals with a particular new gene combination are more successful than others in finding food, or escaping enemies, or attracting mates, or protecting their offspring, the result will be a gradual increase in the frequency of that gene combination, just as surely as if some breeder had been selecting for that gene.

Note one important point about genetics and natural selection: We *do not* evolve through inheritance of acquired characteristics. Remember: Mutations are random events; what you do in your life does not increase or decrease the chance of a useful mutation. For example, if you exercise your muscles or develop your intellect, you do not thereby increase the chances that your children will be born with excellent muscles or brains. Also, the fact that most people do not make much use of their little toes does *not* mean that later generations will be born with smaller and smaller little toes. A gene that decreased the size of the little toe would spread in the population *only* if that gene (or some other gene tightly linked to it on a chromosome) somehow improved people's chance of surviving long enough to reproduce, or if it helped them to attract a mate—for instance, if having an extremely tiny little toe were considered "sexy." But the mere fact that people use or do not use some part of their body does not change the genes that control the body part.

Summary

1. In a normal environment, every individual with a dominant gene will show its effects. A recessive gene's effects are fully expressed only if no dominant gene is present. (p. 588)

2. If two genes are on the same chromosome, someone who inherits one of those genes is likely to inherit the other as well. (p. 590)

3. Because sex-linked genes are on the X chromosome, sex-linked recessive genes show their effects more in males than in females, whereas sex-linked dominant genes show their effects more frequently in females. Although a sex-limited gene may be on any chromosome, its effects occur only in one sex. (p. 590)

4. A gene is said to have partial penetrance if its effects depend on variations in the environment. (p. 592)

5. Chromosomes are composed of the molecule DNA, which makes RNA copies of itself that, in turn, determine the formation of proteins. (p. 594)

6. It is difficult to estimate the heritability of most significant human behaviors because the available evidence is subject to alternative explanations. (p. 597)

7. Although it is difficult to be certain about which species evolved from which ancestral species and how, the fundamental process of evolution is a logical necessity. (p. 599)

Review Questions

1. Distinguish between dominant and recessive, homozygous and heterozygous. (p. 588)
2. Why do sex-linked dominant genes show their effects more in women than in men? (p. 591)
3. Why do sex-linked recessive genes show their effects mostly in men? (p. 591)
4. What is a sex-limited gene? (p. 591)
5. Why does the fragile X chromosome produce mental retardation in more males than females? (p. 591)
6. What is a mutation? (p. 592)
7. What is the relationship between Down syndrome and the age of the parents at the time of the child's birth ? (p. 592)
8. Describe an example of a gene whose effects can be modified or eliminated by a change in the environment. (p. 594)
9. What are chromosomes composed of? (p. 594)
10. What is the route by which DNA controls the production of proteins? (p. 595)
11. How does a retrovirus reproduce? (p. 595)
12. What is the best way to phrase the heredity-environment question? (p. 596)
13. Describe the strengths and weaknesses of the various lines of evidence used to determine the role of heredity in the development of human behavior. (p. 597)

Suggestion for Further Reading

Plomin, R. (1990). The role of inheritance in behavior. *Science, 248,* 183–188. A brief summary of methods for studying the genetics of behavior in humans and other species.

Terms

gene a physical particle that determines some aspect of inheritance (p. 588)

dominant gene gene that exerts noticeable effects even in an individual who has only one copy of the gene per cell (p. 588)

recessive gene a gene that exerts noticeable effects only in an individual who has two copies of the gene per cell (p. 588)

homozygous having two identical genes for a given characteristic (p. 589)

heterozygous having two unlike genes for a given trait (p. 589)

genotype the total collection of an individual's genes (p. 589)

chromosome strand of DNA bearing the genes (p. 590)

crossing over exchange of parts between two chromosomes during replication (p. 590)

autosomal gene gene on any of the chromosomes other than the sex chromosomes (X and Y) (p. 590)

sex-linked gene gene on either the X or the Y chromosome (p. 590)

Y chromosome a chromosome of which female mammals have none and males have one (p. 591)

X chromosome a chromosome of which female mammals have two and males have one (p. 591)

sex-limited gene gene whose effects are seen only in one sex, although members of both sexes may have the gene (p. 591)

fragile X chromosome condition in which an X chromosome has a segment that can snap off; a common cause of mental retardation in males (p. 591)

recombination a reassortment of genes during reproduction, sometimes leading to a characteristic that is not apparent in either parent (p. 592)

mutation change in a gene during reproduction (p. 592)

Down syndrome condition caused by having three strands of chromosome 21 per cell instead of two, resulting in mental retardation (p. 592)

penetrance the degree of expression of a gene (p. 593)

phenylketonuria (PKU) inherited inability to metabolize phenylalanine, leading to mental retardation unless the afflicted person stays on a strict low-phenylalanine diet throughout childhood (p. 594)

DNA deoxyribonucleic acid, the chemical that composes the chromosomes (p. 594)

template model from which copies are made (p. 595)

RNA ribonucleic acid, a chemical whose structure is determined by DNA and that in turn determines the structure of proteins (p. 595)

enzyme any protein that catalyzes biological reactions (p. 595)

retrovirus virus made of RNA that makes a DNA copy of itself (p. 595)

heritability a correlation coefficient, ranging from zero to 1.0, indicating the degree to which variations in some characteristic depend on variations in heredity for a given population (p. 597)

dizygotic twin fraternal (nonidentical) twin (p. 598)

monozygotic twin identical twin (p. 598)

prenatal before birth (p. 599)

paternal half-siblings individuals with the same father but different mothers (p. 599)

evolution change in the gene pool of a population over generations (p. 599)

artificial selection change in the gene pool of a population by a breeder's selection of desired individuals for mating purposes (p. 600)

Appendix B
BRIEF, BASIC CHEMISTRY

1. All matter is composed of a limited number of elements that combine in endless ways.

2. The component parts of an element—the atoms—consist of protons, neutrons, and electrons. Most atoms can either gain, lose, or share electrons with other atoms.

3. The chemistry of life is predominantly the chemistry of carbon compounds.

*T*o understand certain aspects of biological psychology, particularly the action potential and the molecular mechanisms of synaptic transmission, you need to know a little about chemistry. If you have taken a high school or college course in chemistry and remember the material reasonably well, you should have no trouble with the chemistry in this text. If your knowledge of chemistry is pretty hazy, perhaps this appendix will help. (If you plan to take other courses in biological psychology, you should study as much biology and chemistry as possible.)

Elements and Compounds

If you look around, you will see an enormous variety of materials—dirt, water, wood, plastic, metal, cloth, glass, your own body. All those countless types of objects are composed of a small number of basic building blocks. For example, if a piece of wood catches fire, it breaks down into ashes, gases, and some water vapor. The same is true of your body. In turn, an investigator could take those ashes, gases, and water and break them down by chemical and electrical means into carbon, oxygen, hydrogen, nitrogen, and a few other materials. Eventually, however, the investigator arrives at a set of materials that cannot be broken down further: Pure carbon or pure oxygen, for example, cannot be converted into anything simpler—at least not by ordinary chemical means. (High-power bombardment with subatomic particles is another story.) Evidently, the matter we see is composed of **elements**—materials that cannot be broken down into other materials—and **compounds**—materials made by combining elements.

Chemists have found 92 elements in nature, and they have constructed some more in the laboratory. (Actually, one of the 92—technetium—is so rare as to be virtually unknown in nature.) Figure B.1, the periodic table, lists each of these elements. Of these, only a few are important for life on earth. Table B.1 shows the elements that compose nearly all of the human body.

Note that each element has a one- or two-letter abbreviation, such as O for oxygen, H for hydrogen, and Ca for calcium. These are internationally accepted symbols that facilitate communication among chemists who speak different languages. For example, element number 19 is called potassium in English, potassio in Italian, kālijs in Latvian, and draslík in Czech. But chemists in all countries use the symbol K (from *kalium*, the Latin word for *potassium*). Similarly, the symbol for sodium is Na (from *natrium,* the Latin word for *sodium*), and the symbol for iron is Fe (from the Latin word *ferrum*).

A compound is represented by the symbols for the elements that compose it. For example, NaCl represents sodium chloride (common table salt). H_2O, the symbol for water, indicates that water is formed by combining two parts of hydrogen with one part of oxygen.

Atoms and Molecules

A block of iron can be chopped into finer and finer pieces until a certain point. Eventually, it is divided into tiny pieces that cannot be divided any further. Those pieces are called **atoms**. Every element is composed of atoms.

Periodic Table of the Elements

Period	1 IA	2 IIA	3 IIIB	4 IVB	5 VB	6 VIB	7 VIIB	8 VIIIB	9 VIIIB	10 VIIIB	11 IB	12 IIB	13 IIIA	14 IVA	15 VA	16 VIA	17 VIIA	18 VIIIA
1	1 H hydrogen 1.008																	2 He helium 4.003
2	3 Li lithium 6.941	4 Be beryllium 9.012											5 B boron 10.81	6 C carbon 12.011	7 N nitrogen 14.007	8 O oxygen 16.0	9 F fluorine 18.999	10 Ne neon 20.179
3	11 Na sodium 22.99	12 Mg magnesium 24.305											13 Al aluminum 26.982	14 Si silicon 28.085	15 P phosphorous 30.974	16 S sulfur 32.060	17 Cl chlorine 35.453	18 Ar argon 39.948
4	19 K potassium 39.098	20 Ca calcium 40.08	21 Sc scandium 44.955	22 Ti titanium 47.90	23 V vanadium 50.941	24 Cr chromium 51.996	25 Mn manganese 54.938	26 Fe iron 55.847	27 Co cobalt 58.933	28 Ni nickel 58.70	29 Cu copper 63.546	30 Zn zinc 65.38	31 Ga gallium 69.72	32 Ge germanium 72.59	33 As arsenic 74.922	34 Se selenium 78.96	35 Br bromine 79.904	36 Kr krypton 83.80
5	37 Rb rubidium 85.468	38 Sr strontium 87.62	39 Y yttrium 88.906	40 Zr zirconium 91.22	41 Nb niobium 92.906	42 Mo molybdenum 95.940	43 Tc technetium (97)	44 Ru ruthenium 101.07	45 Rh rhodium 102.905	46 Pd palladium 106.40	47 Ag silver 107.868	48 Cd cadmium 112.41	49 In indium 114.82	50 Sn tin 118.69	51 Sb antimony 121.75	52 Te tellurium 127.60	53 I iodine 126.904	54 Xe xenon 131.30
6	55 Cs cesium 132.905	56 Ba barium 137.33	57 La lanthanum 138.906 †	72 Hf hafnium 178.49	73 Ta tantalum 180.948	74 W tungsten 183.85	75 Re rhenium 186.207	76 Os osmium 190.20	77 Ir iridium 192.22	78 Pt platinum 195.09	79 Au gold 196.967	80 Hg mercury 200.59	81 Tl thallium 204.37	82 Pb lead 207.20	83 Bi bismuth 208.980	84 Po polonium (209)	85 At astatine (210)	86 Rn radon (222)
7	87 Fr francium (223)	88 Ra radium 226.025	89 Ac actinium (227) ‡	104 Rf rutherfordium (261)	105 Ha hahnium (262)	106 Sg seaborgium (263)	107 Ns nielsbohrium (262)	108 Hs hassium (265)	109 Mt meitnerium (266)									

Alkali Metals — 1 IA
Alkaline Earth Metals — 2 IIA
Transition Elements
Noble Gases — 18 VIIIA
Halogens — 17 VIIA

Inner Transition Elements

† Lanthanides 6

58 Ce cerium 140.12	59 Pr praseodymium 140.908	60 Nd neodymium 144.24	61 Pm promethium (145)	62 Sm samarium 150.40	63 Eu europium 151.96	64 Gd gadolinium 157.25	65 Tb terbium 158.925	66 Dy dysprosium 162.50	67 Ho holmium 164.93	68 Er erbium 167.26	69 Tm thulium 168.934	70 Yb ytterbium 173.04	71 Lu lutetium 174.97

‡ Actinides 7

90 Th thorium 232.038	91 Pa protactinium 231.036	92 U uranium 238.029	93 Np neptunium (237)	94 Pu plutonium (244)	95 Am americium (243)	96 Cm curium (247)	97 Bk berkelium (247)	98 Cf californium (251)	99 Es einsteinium (254)	100 Fm fermium (257)	101 Md mendelevium (258)	102 No nobelium (255)	103 Lr lawrencium (260)

Key
atomic number — 1
symbol of element — H
element name — hydrogen
atomic weight — 1.008

Figure B.1
The periodic table of chemistry
It is called "periodic" because certain properties show up at periodic intervals. For example, the column from lithium down consists of metals that readily form salts. The column at the far right consists of gases that do not readily form compounds.

Table B.1 The Elements that Compose Almost All of the Human Body

Element	Symbol	Percent by Weight in Human Body
Oxygen	O	65
Carbon	C	18
Hydrogen	H	10
Nitrogen	N	3
Calcium	Ca	2
Phosphorus	P	1.1
Potassium	K	0.35
Sulfur	S	0.25
Sodium	Na	0.15
Chlorine	Cl	0.15
Magnesium	Mg	0.05
Iron	Fe	Trace
Copper	Cu	Trace
Iodine	I	Trace
Fluorine	F	Trace
Manganese	Mn	Trace
Zinc	Zn	Trace
Selenium	Se	Trace
Molybdenum	Mo	Trace

Similarly, a compound such as water can be divided into tinier and tinier pieces until a certain point. The smallest possible piece of a compound is called a **molecule**. A molecule of water can be decomposed into two atoms of hydrogen and one atom of oxygen, but if that happens it is no longer water. So a molecule is the smallest piece of a compound that retains the properties of the compound.

An atom is composed of subatomic particles. The most important of these are protons, neutrons, and electrons. A proton has a positive electrical charge, a neutron has a neutral charge, and an electron has a negative charge. The center of an atom—its nucleus—contains one or more protons plus some number of neutrons. Electrons are found in the space around the nucleus. An atom has the same number of protons as electrons, so the electrical charges balance out. (Ions, which we shall consider in a moment, have an imbalance of positive and negative charges.)

The difference between one element and another is the number of protons in the nucleus of the atom. Hydrogen has just one proton, for example, and oxygen has eight. The number of protons in the nucleus of an element's atoms is its **atomic number**; this number is recorded on the table at the top of the square for that element. The number at the bottom of each square is the element's **atomic weight**; this indicates the relative weight of the atoms. If a proton has a weight of one unit, a neutron has a weight just trivially greater than one and an electron has a weight just trivially greater than zero. The atomic weight of the element is the number of protons in the atom plus the average number of neutrons. For example, most hydrogen atoms have one proton and no neutrons; a few atoms per thousand have one or two neutrons, giving an average atomic weight of 1.008. Sodium ions have 11 protons; most also have 12 neutrons, and the atomic weight is slightly less than 23. (Can you figure out the number of neutrons in the average potassium atom? Refer to Figure B.1.)

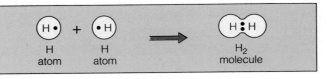

Figure B.3
Structure of a hydrogen molecule
A hydrogen atom has one electron; in the compound, the two atoms share the two electrons equally.

Ions and Chemical Bonds

When an atom gains or loses one or more electrons, it is then called an **ion**. For example, if sodium and chloride come together, the sodium atoms readily lose one electron each and the chloride atoms gain one each. The result is a set of positively charged sodium ions (indicated Na^+) and negatively charged chloride ions (Cl^-). Potassium atoms, like sodium atoms, tend to lose an electron and become positively charged ions (K^+); calcium atoms tend to lose two electrons and gain a double positive charge (Ca^{++}).

Because positive charges attract negative charges, sodium ions attract chloride ions. When dry, sodium and chloride form a crystal structure, as Figure B.2 shows. (In water solution, the two kinds of ion move about haphazardly, occasionally attracting one another but then pulling apart.) The attraction of sodium ions for chloride ions is an **ionic bond**. In contrast, some pairs of atoms may share electrons with each other, instead of transferring an electron from one atom to another. For example, two hydrogen atoms bind as shown in Figure B.3. Two hydrogen atoms bind with an oxygen atom as shown in Figure B.4. In such cases, the atoms are bound by a **covalent bond**—a bond that shares electrons. When a covalent bond forms, an atom is bound to another particular atom. Until that bond is broken, neither atom can move independently of the other.

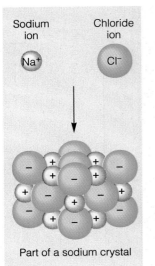

Sodium ion   Chloride ion

Na^+ Cl^-

Part of a sodium crystal

Figure B.2
The crystal structure of sodium chloride
Each sodium ion is surrounded by chloride ions, and each chloride ion is surrounded by sodium ions; no ion is bound to any other single ion in particular.

Reactions of Carbon Compounds

Living organisms depend on the enormously versatile compounds of carbon. Carbon forms covalent bonds with other carbon atoms as well as with hydrogen, oxygen, and a number of other elements. Because of the importance of carbon compounds for life, carbon chemistry is known as organic chemistry.

Carbon forms covalent bonds with other carbon atoms. Two carbon atoms may share one pair of electrons, two pairs, or three pairs. Such bonds can be indicated as shown below:

C – C	Two atoms share one pair of electrons.
C = C	Two atoms share two pairs of electrons.
C $\equiv$ C	Two atoms share three pairs of electrons.

Each carbon atom typically forms a total of four covalent bonds, either with other carbon atoms, with hydrogen atoms, or with other atoms. Many biologically important compounds include long chains of carbon compounds linked to one another, such as:

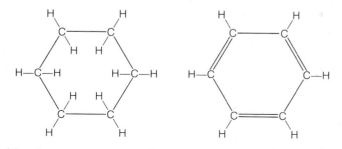

Note that each carbon atom has a total of four bonds, counting each double bond as two. In some molecules, the carbon chain may loop around to form a ring:

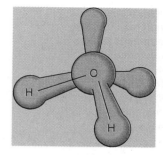

Figure B.4
Structure of a water molecule
The oxygen atom shares a pair of electrons with each hydrogen atom, although it does not share them equally. Oxygen holds the electrons more tightly, making the oxygen part of the molecule more negatively charged than the hydrogen part of the molecule.

Structures like these are common in organic chemistry. To simplify the diagrams, chemists often omit the hydrogen atoms. The reader can simply assume that each carbon atom in the diagram has four covalent bonds and that all the bonds not shown are bonds with hydrogen atoms. To further simplify the diagrams, chemists often omit the carbon atoms themselves, showing only the carbon-to-carbon bonds. For example, the two molecules shown above might be rendered as follows:

If a particular carbon atom has a bond with some atom other than hydrogen, the diagram shows the exception. For example, in each of the two molecules diagrammed below, one carbon has a bond with an oxygen atom, which in turn has a bond with a hydrogen atom. All the bonds that are not shown are carbon-hydrogen bonds.

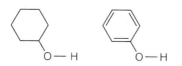

   Figure B.5 illustrates some carbon compounds that are critical for animal life. Purines and pyrimidines form the central structure of DNA and RNA, the chemicals responsible for heredity. Proteins, fats, and carbohydrates are the primary types of fuel that the body uses.
   The body also manufactures its own proteins, fats, and carbohydrates. Proteins form an important part of most body structures. Hemoglobin, the compound in the blood that transports oxygen and carbon dioxide, is a protein. So are actin and myosin, the compounds responsible for the contraction of muscles. Fats and carbohydrates are stored as a source of energy.

Chemical Reactions in the Body

A living organism is an immensely complicated, coordinated set of chemical reactions. Life requires that the rate of each reaction be carefully regulated. In many cases, a reaction produces a chemical that enters into another reaction,

Brief, Basic Chemistry

**Figure B.5
Structure of some
important biological
molecules**
*The R in the protein repre-
sents a point of attachment
for various chains that differ
from one amino acid to
another.*

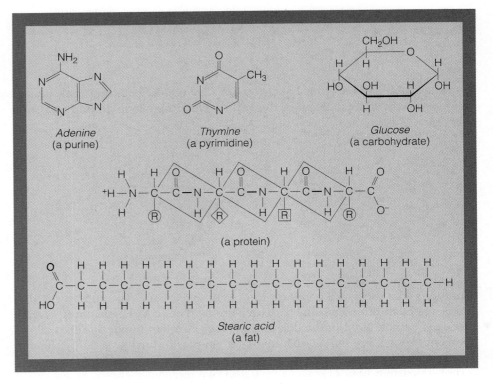

Adenine
(a purine)

Thymine
(a pyrimidine)

Glucose
(a carbohydrate)

(a protein)

Stearic acid
(a fat)

**Figure B.6
ATP (adenosine triphos-
phate), composed of
adenosine, ribose, and
three phosphates**
*ATP can lose one phosphate
group to form ADP (adeno-
sine diphosphate) and then
lose another one to form
AMP (adenosine monophos-
phate). Each time that it
breaks off a phosphate
group, it releases energy.*

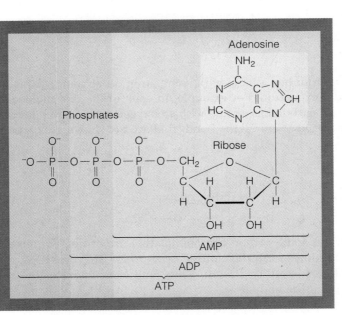

Adenosine

Phosphates

Ribose

AMP

ADP

ATP

which produces another chemical that enters into another reaction, and so
forth. If any one of those reactions proceeds too rapidly, its product will accumulate to levels that might be harmful. If a reaction proceeds too slowly, it will
not produce enough of some needed product at the right time, stalling the reaction that uses that product.

 Enzymes are proteins that control the rate of chemical reactions in the
body. Each reaction is controlled by its own particular enzyme. (Enzymes are

a type of catalyst. A catalyst is any chemical that facilitates a reaction among other chemicals, without being altered itself in the process.)

The Role of ATP

The body relies on one chemical, adenosine triphosphate (**ATP**), as its main way of delivering energy where it is needed (Figure B.6). When food is digested, much of the energy that it releases goes into forming ATP molecules. Those ATP molecules travel to the muscles and other parts of the body that use energy.

ATP consists of the chemical adenosine bound to ribose and three phosphate groups (PO_3). Phosphates form high-energy covalent bonds. That is, a large amount of energy is required to form those bonds and a large amount of energy is released when they break. ATP can break off one or two of its three phosphates to provide energy to the muscles or other body parts.

Summary

1. All naturally occurring matter is composed of 92 elements that combine to form an endless variety of compounds. (p. 603)

2. The smallest piece of an element is an atom. The smallest piece of a compound that maintains the properties of the compound is a molecule. (p. 603)

3. The atoms of some elements can gain or lose an electron, thus becoming ions. Positively charged ions attract negatively charged ions. That attraction is called an ionic bond. (p. 606)

4. In some cases, two or more atoms may share electrons, thus forming a covalent bond. (p. 606)

5. Enzymes are proteins that promote and control certain chemical reactions in the body. (p. 608)

6. The principal carrier of energy in the body is a chemical called ATP. (p. 609)

Review Questions

1. What is the difference between an atom and a molecule? What is the difference between an atom and an ion? (p. 603)

2. What are the most abundant elements in the human body? (p. 605)

3. What does the atomic number of an element represent? What does the atomic weight represent? (p. 605)

4. What kind of bonds do carbon atoms form: ionic or covalent? (p. 606)

Terms

element material that cannot be broken down into other materials (p. 603)

compound material made by combining elements (p. 603)

atom piece of an element that cannot be divided any further (p. 603)

molecule smallest possible piece of a compound (p. 605)

atomic number number of protons in the nucleus of an atom (p. 605)

atomic weight number indicating the weight of an atom relative to a weight of one for a proton (p. 605)

ion atom that has gained or lost one or more electrons (p. 606)

ionic bond chemical attraction between two ions of opposite charge (p. 606)

covalent bond chemical bond between two atoms that share electrons (p. 606)

enzyme protein that controls the rate of chemical reactions in the body (p. 608)

ATP (adenosine triphosphate) a chemical that the body uses as its main way of delivering energy where it is needed (p. 609)

Appendix C

SOCIETY FOR NEURO-SCIENCE GUIDELINES FOR ANIMAL RESEARCH

Introduction

Research in the neurosciences contributes to the quality of life by expanding knowledge about living organisms. This improvement in quality of life stems in part from progress toward ameliorating human disease and disability, in part from advances in animal welfare and veterinary medicine, and in part from the steady increase in knowledge of the abilities and potentialities of human and animal life. Continued progress in many areas of biomedical research requires the use of living animals in order to investigate complex systems and functions because, in such cases, no adequate alternatives exist. Progress in both basic and clinical research in such areas cannot continue without the use of living animals as experimental subjects. The use of living animals in properly designed scientific research is therefore both ethical and appropriate. Nevertheless, our concern for the humane treatment of animals dictates that we weigh carefully the benefits to human knowledge and welfare whenever animal research is undertaken. The investigator using research animals assumes responsibility for proper experimental design, including ethical as well as scientific aspects.

The scientific community shares the concern of society at large that the use of animals in research should conform to standards that are consonant with those applied to other uses of animals by humans. While it is unlikely that any particular set of standards will satisfy everyone, it is appropriate for scientific societies to formulate guidelines that apply to the humane use of laboratory animals in particular areas of research. Ideally, such guidelines should also be acceptable to society at large as reasonable and prudent.

Most of the more specific sections of this document were formulated with respect to research using warm-blooded vertebrates. As a general principle, however, ethical issues involved in the use of any species, whether vertebrate or invertebrate, are best considered in relation to the complexity of that species' nervous system and its apparent awareness of the environment, rather than physical appearance or evolutionary proximity to humans.

Factors That Relate to the Design of Experiments

The primary factor used to evaluate humane treatment in animal research is degree of distress or discomfort assessed by anthropomorphic judgments made by reasonable and prudent human observers. *The fundamental principle of ethical animal research is that experimental animals must not be subjected to avoidable distress or discomfort.* This principle must be observed when designing any experiment that uses living animals.

Although most animal research involves minimal distress or discomfort, certain valid scientific questions may require experimental designs that inevitably produce these effects. Such situations, while uncommon, are extremely diverse and must be evaluated individually. It is critical that distress and discomfort be minimized by careful experimental design. It is also important to recognize that there is no difference between distress and discomfort that may be inherent in a valid experimental design and that which may occur as an unintended side effect. It is therefore incumbent on the investigator to recognize and to eliminate all *avoidable* sources of distress and discomfort in animal subjects. This goal often requires attention to specifics of animal husbandry and to experimental design.

Invasive procedures and paralytic drugs should never be employed without benefit of anesthetic agents unless there is a very strong scientific justification and careful consideration is given to possible alternatives. Advances in experimental techniques, such as the use of devices chronically implanted under anesthesia, can offer alternative approaches. If these are not feasible, it is essential to monitor nociceptive responses (for example, recordings of EEG, blood pressure, and pupillary responses) that may indicate distress in the animal subject, and to use these as signals of the need to alleviate pain, to modify the experimental design, or to terminate the experiment.

When designing research projects, investigators should carefully consider the species and numbers of animals necessary to provide valid information, as well as the question whether living subjects are required to answer the scientific question. As a general rule, experiments should be designed so as to minimize the number of animals used and to avoid the depletion of endangered species. Advances in experimental methods, more efficient use of animals, within-subject designs, and modern statistical techniques all provide possible ways to minimize the numbers of animals used in research. This goal is completely consistent with the critical importance of replication and validation of results to true progress in science.

Factors That Relate to the Conduct of Experiments

Research animals must be acquired and cared for in accordance with the guidelines published in the *NIH Guide for the Care and Use of Laboratory Animals* (National Institutes of Health Publications, No. 85-23, Revised 1985). Investigators must also be aware of the relevant local, state, and federal laws. The quality of research data depends in no small measure on health and general condition of the animals used, as well as on the specifics of experimental design. Thus, proper animal husbandry is integral to the success of any research effort using living animal subjects. General standards for animal husbandry (housing, food quality, ventilation, etc.) are detailed in the *NIH Guide*. The experienced investigator can contribute additional specifics for optimum care for particular experimental situations, or for species not commonly encountered in laboratory settings.

Surgery performed with the intent that the animal will survive (for example, on animals intended for chronic study) should be carried out, or directly supervised, by persons with appropriate levels of experience and training, and with attention to asepsis and prevention of infection. Major surgical procedures should be done using an appropriate method of anesthesia to render the animal insensitive to pain. Muscle relaxants and paralytics have no anesthetic action and should not be used alone for surgical restraint. Postoperative care must include attention to minimize discomfort and the risk of infection.

Many experimental designs call for surgical preparation under anesthetic agents with no intent that the animal should survive. In such cases, the animals ordinarily should be maintained unconscious for the duration of the experiment. At the conclusion of the experiment, the animal should be killed without regaining consciousness and death ensured before final disposition.

Certain experiments may require physical restraint, and/or withholding of food or water, as methodological procedures rather than experimental paradigms. In such cases, careful attention must be paid to minimize discomfort or distress and to ensure that general health is maintained. Immobilization or restraint to which the animals cannot be readily adapted should not be imposed when alternative procedures are practical. Reasonable periods of rest and readjustment should be included in the experimental schedule unless these would be absolutely inconsistent with valid scientific objectives.

When distress and discomfort are unavoidable attributes of a valid experimental design, it is mandatory to conduct such experiments so as to minimize these effects, to minimize the duration of the procedure, and to minimize the numbers of animals used, consistent with the scientific objectives of the study.

References

Numbers or letters in parentheses following citations indicate the chapter or appendix in which a reference is cited.

Abramov, I., Gordon, J., Hendrickson, A., Hainline, L., Dobson, V., & LaBossiere, E. (1982). The retina of the newborn human infant. *Science, 217,* 265-267. (6)

Abramowitz, E.S., Baker, A.H., & Fleischer, S.F. (1982). Onset of depressive psychiatric crises and the menstrual cycle. *American Journal of Psychiatry, 139,* 475-478. (16)

Abrams, R., Swartz, C.M., & Vedak, C. (1991). Antidepressant effect of high-dose right unilateral electroconvulsive therapy. *Archives of General Psychiatry, 48,* 746-748. (16)

Adam, K. (1980). Sleep as a restorative process and a theory to explain why. *Progress in Brain Research, 53,* 289-305. (9)

Adamec, R. (1975). The behavioral basis of prolonged suppression of predatory attack in cats. *Aggressive Behavior, 1,* 297-314. (12)

Adamec, R.E., Stark-Adamec, C., & Livingston, K.E. (1980). The development of predatory aggression and defense in the domestic cat (*Felis catus*): 3. Effects on development of hunger between 180 and 365 days of age. *Behavioral and Neural Biology, 30,* 435-447. (12)

Adams, D.B., Gold, A.R., & Burt, A.D. (1978). Rise in female-initiated sexual activity at ovulation and its suppression by oral contraceptives. *New England Journal of Medicine, 299,* 1145-1150. (11)

Adkins, E.K., & Adler, N.T. (1972). Hormonal control of behavior in the Japanese quail. *Journal of Comparative and Physiological Psychology, 81,* 27-36. (11)

Adkins, E.K., & Pniewski, E.E. (1978). Control of reproductive behavior by sex steroids in male quail. *Journal of Comparative and Physiological Psychology, 92,* 1169-1178. (11)

Adkins-Regan, E. (1988). Sex hormones and sexual orientation in animals. *Psychobiology, 16,* 335-347. (11)

Aggleton, J.P., Blindt, H.S., & Rawlins, J.N.P. (1989). Effects of amygdaloid and amygdaloid-hippocampal lesions on object recognition and spatial working memory in rats. *Behavioral Neuroscience, 103,* 962-974. (13)

Aggleton, J.P., & Passingham, R.E. (1981). Syndrome produced by lesions of the amygdala in monkeys (*Macaca mulatta*). *Journal of Comparative and Physiological Psychology, 95,* 961-977. (12)

Ahlskog, J.E., & Hoebel, B.G. (1973). Overeating and obesity from damage to a noradrenergic system in the brain. *Science, 182,* 166-169. (10)

Ahlskog, J.E., Randall, P.K., & Hoebel, B.G. (1975). Hypothalamic hyperphagia: Dissociation form hyperphagia following destruction of noradrenergic neurons. *Science, 190,* 399-401. (10)

Aird, R.B., Masland, R.L., & Woodbury, D.M. (1984). *The epilepsies: A critical review.* New York: Raven Press. (14)

Akbarian, S., Bunney, W.E., Jr., Potkin, S.G., Wigal, S.B., Hagman, J.O., Sandman, C.A., & Jones, E.G. (1993a). Altered distribution of nicotinamide-adenine dinucleotide phosphate-diaphorase cells in frontal lobe of schizophrenics implies disturbances of cortical development. *Archives of General Psychiatry, 50,* 169-177. (16)

Akbarian, S., Viñuela, A., Kim, J.J., Potkin, S.G., Bunney,W.E., Jr., & Jones, E.G. (1993b). Distorted distribution of nicotinamide-adenine dinucleotide phosphate-diaphorase neurons in temporal lobe of schizophrenics implies anomalous cortical development. *Archives of General Psychiatry, 50,* 178-187. (16)

Albanese, A., Altavista, M.C., & Rossi, P. (1986). Organization of central nervous system dopaminergic pathways. *Journal of Neural Transmission,* Supplementum 22, 3-17. (16)

Alberts, J.R. (1978). Huddling by rat pups: Group behavioral mechanisms of temperature regulation and energy conservation. *Journal of Comparative and Physiological Psychology, 92,* 231-245. (10)

Albright, T.D. (1992). Form-cue invariant motion processing in primate visual cortex. *Science, 255,* 1141-1143. (6)

Aldrich, M.S. (1993). Narcolepsy. *Neurology, 42* (Suppl. 6), 34-43. (9)

Alexander, J.T., Cheung, W.K., Dietz, C.B., & Leibowitz, S.F. (1993). Meal patterns and macronutrient intake after peripheral and PVN injections of the α_2-receptor antagonist idazoxan. *Physiology & Behavior, 53,* 623-630. (10)

Alexander, M.P., Benson, D.F., & Stuss, D.T. (1989). Frontal lobes and language. *Brain and Language, 37,* 656-691. (14)

Allen, L.S., & Gorski, R.A. (1992). Sexual orientation and the size of the anterior commissure in the human brain. *Proceedings of the National Academy of Sciences (U.S.A.), 89,* 7199-7202. (11)

Allison, T., & Cicchetti, D.V. (1976). Sleep in mammals: Ecological and constitutional correlates. *Science, 194,* 732-734. (9)

Allison, T., & Goff, W.R. (1968). Sleep in a primitive mammal, the spiny anteater. *Psychophysiology, 5,* 200-201. (9)

Almli, C.R., Fisher, R.S., & Hill, D.L. (1979). Lateral hypothalamus destruction in infant rats produces consummatory deficits without sensory neglect or attenuated arousal. *Experimental Neurology, 66,* 146-157. (10)

Alper, J. (1993). Echo-planar MRI: Learning to read minds. *Science, 261,* 556. (4)

Al-Rashid, R.A. (1971). Hypothalamic syndrome in acute childhood leukemia. *Clinical Pediatrics, 10,* 53-54. (10)

Altner, H. (1978). Physiology of taste. In R.F. Schmidt (Ed.), *Fundamentals of sensory physiology* (pp. 218-227). New York: Springer-Verlag. (7)

Altshuler, L.L., Casanova, M.F., Goldberg, T.E., & Kleinman, J.E. (1990). The hippocampus and parahippocampus in schizophrenic, suicide, and control brains. *Archives of General Psychiatry, 47,* 1029-1034. (16)

American Medical Association. (1988). *Use of animals in biomedical research.* (1)

American Psychiatric Association. (1987). *Diagnostic and statistical manual of mental disorders* (3rd ed., rev.). Washington, DC : Author. (16)

Amoore, J.E. (1967). Specific anosmia: A clue to the olfactory code. *Nature, 214,* 1095-1098. (7)

Amoore, J.E. (1977). Specific anosmia and the concept of primary odors. *Chemical Senses and Flavor, 2,* 267-281. (7)

Amsterdam, J.D., Winokur, A., Dyson, W., Herzog, S., Gonzalez, F., Rott, R., & Koprowski, H. (1985). Borna disease virus. *Archives of General Psychiatry, 42,* 1093-1096. (16)

Anders, J.J., Dorovini-Zis, K., & Brightman, M.W. (1980). Endothelial and astrocytic cell membranes in relation to the composition of cerebral extracellular fluid. In H.M. Eisenberg & R.L. Suddith (Eds.), *The cerebral microvasculature* (pp. 193-209). New York: Plenum. (2)

Andersen, R.A., Essick, G.K., & Siegel, R.M. (1985). Encoding of spatial location by posterior parietal neurons. *Science, 230,* 456-458. (4)

Anderson, W.J., & Altman, J. (1972). Retardation of cerebellar and motor development in rats by focal x-irradiation beginning at four days. *Physiology & Behavior, 8*, 57-67. (4)

Andersson, U., Eckernäs, S.-Å., Hartvig, P., Ulin, J., Långström, B., & Häggström, J.-E. (1990). Striatal binding of ^{11}C-NMSP studied with positron emission tomography in patients with persistent tardive dyskinesia: No evidence for altered dopamine D_2 receptor binding. *Journal of Neural Transmission, 79*, 215-226. (16)

Andreasen, N.C. (1988). Brain imaging: Applications in psychiatry. *Science, 239*, 1381-1388. (4)

Andreasen, N.C., Rezai, K., Alliger, R., Swayze, V.W. II, Flaum, M., Kirchner, P., Cohen, G., & O'Leary, D.S. (1992). Hypofrontality in neuroleptic-naive patients and in patients with chronic schizophrenia. *Archives of General Psychiatry, 49*, 943-958. (16)

Andreasen, N.C., Swayze, V.W., II, Flaum, M., Yates, W.R., Arndt, S., & McChesney, C. (1990b). Ventricular enlargement in schizophrenia evaluated with computed tomographic scanning. *Archives of General Psychiatry, 47*, 1008-1015. (16)

Anías, J., Holmgren, B., Urbá Holmgren, R., & Eguíbar, J.R. (1984). Circadian rhythm of yawning behavior. *Acta Neurobiologiae Experimentalis, 44*, 179-186. (9)

Antelman, S.M., Chiodo, L.A., & DeGiovanni, L.A. (1982). Antidepressants and dopamine autoreceptors: Implications for both a novel means of treating depression and understanding bipolar illness. *Advances in Biochemical Psychopharmacology, 31*, 121-132. (16)

Antin, J., Gibbs, J., Holt, J., Young, R.C., & Smith, G.P. (1975). Cholecystokinin elicits the complete behavioral sequence of satiety in rats. *Journal of Comparative and Physiological Psychology, 89*, 784-790. (10)

Antin, J., Gibbs, J., & Smith, G.P. (1978). Intestinal satiety requires pregastric food stimulation. *Physiology & Behavior, 20*, 67-70. (10)

Antonini, A., & Stryker, M.P. (1993). Rapid remodeling of axonal arbors in the visual cortex. *Science, 260*, 1819-1821. (6)

Antrobus, J.S. (1986). Dreaming: Cortical activation and perceptual thresholds. *Journal of Mind and Behavior, 7*, 193-211. (9)

Appley, M.H. (1991). Motivation, equilibrium, and stress. In R. Dienstbier (Ed.), *Nebraska symposium on motivation 1990* (pp. 1-67). Lincoln, NE: University of Nebraska Press. (11)

Aram, D.M., & Ekelman, B.L. (1986). Spoken syntax in children with acquired unilateral hemispheric lesions. *Brain and Language, 27*, 75-100. (14)

Arango, V., Ernsberger, P., Marzuk, P.M., Chen, J.-S., Tierney, H., Stanley, M., Reis, D.J., & Mann, J.J. (1990). Autoradiographic demonstration of increased serotonin 5-HT$_2$ and beta-adrenergic receptor binding sites in the brain of suicide victims. *Archives of General Psychiatry, 47*, 1038-1047. (12)

Arboleda, C., & Holzman, P.S. (1985). Thought disorder in children at risk for psychosis. *Archives of General Psychiatry, 42*, 1004-1013. (16)

Arkin, A.M., Toth, M.F., Baker, J., & Hastey, J.M. (1970). The frequency of sleep talking in the laboratory among chronic sleep talkers and good dream recallers. *Journal of Nervous and Mental Disease, 151*, 369-374. (9)

Arnold, A.P. (1980). Sexual differences in the brain. *American Scientist, 68*, 165-173. (1)

Arnold, A.P. (1982). Neural control of passerine song. In D.E. Kroodsma & E.H. Miller (Eds.), *Acoustic communication in birds* (Vol. 1, pp. 75-94). New York: Academic Press. (1)

Arnold, A.P., & Breedlove, S.M. (1985). Organizational and activational effects of sex steroids on brain and behavior: A reanalysis. *Hormones and Behavior, 19*, 469-498. (11)

Arnsten, A.F.T., & Goldman-Rakic, P.S. (1985a). Alpha$_2$-adrenergic mechanisms in prefrontal cortex associated with cognitive decline in aged nonhuman primates. *Science, 230*, 1273-1276. (13)

Arnsten, A.F.T., & Goldman-Rakic, P.S. (1985b). Catecholamines and cognitive decline in aged nonhuman primates. *Annals of the New York Academy of Sciences, 444*, 218-234. (13)

Arvidson, K., & Friberg, U. (1980). Human taste: Response and taste bud number in fungiform papillae. *Science, 209*, 807-808. (7)

Asanuma, H. (1981). The pyramidal tract. In V.B. Brooks (Ed.), *Handbook of physiology: Section 1: The nervous system, Volume 2. Motor control* (Pt. 1, pp. 703-733). Bethesda, MD: American Physiological Society. (8)

Aserinsky, E., & Kleitman, N. (1955). Two types of ocular motility occurring in sleep. *Journal of Applied Physiology, 8*, 1-10. (9)

Astic, L., Sastre, J.-P., & Brandon, A.-M. (1973). Étude polygraphique des états de vigilance chez le foetus de cobaye [Polygraphic study of the states of arousal of the guinea pig fetus]. *Physiology & Behavior, 11*, 647-654. (9)

Attardi, D.G., & Sperry, R.W. (1963). Preferential selection of central pathways by regenerating optic fibers. *Experimental Neurology, 7*, 46-64. (5)

August, G.J., & Lockhart, L.H. (1984). Familial autism and the fragile-X chromosome. *Journal of Autism and Developmental Disorders, 14*, 197-204. (16)

Augustine, G.J., Charlton, M.P., & Smith, S.J. (1987). Calcium action in synaptic transmitter release. *Annual Review of Neuroscience, 10*, 633-693. (3)

Axelrod, J. (1974, June). Neurotransmitters. *Scientific American, 230* (6), 58-71. (10)

Ayala-Guerrero, F., Calderón, A., & Pérez, M.C. (1988). Sleep patterns in a chelonian reptile (*Gopherus flavomarginatus*). *Physiology & Behavior, 44*, 333-337. (9)

Babich, F.R., Jacobson, A.L., Bubash, S., & Jacobson, A. (1965). Transfer of a response to naive rats by injection of ribonucleic acid extracted from trained rats. *Science, 149*, 656-657. (13)

Bachevalier, J., & Mishkin, M. (1984). An early and a late developing system for learning and retention in infant monkeys. *Behavioral Neuroscience, 98*, 770-778. (13)

Backlund, E.-O., Granberg, P.-O., Hamberger, B., Sedvall, G., Seiger, A., & Olson, L. (1985). Transplantation of adrenal medullary tissue to striatum in Parkinsonism. In A. Björklund & U. Stenevi (Eds.), *Neural grafting in the mammalian CNS* (pp. 551-556). Amsterdam: Elsevier. (15)

Bading, H., Ginty, D.D., & Greenberg, M.E. (1993). Regulation of gene expression in hippocampal neurons by distinct calcium signaling pathways. *Science, 260*, 181-186. (13)

Baghdoyan, H.A., Spotts, J.L., & Snyder, S.G. (1993). Simultaneous pontine and basal forebrain microinjections of carbachol suppress REM sleep. *Journal of Neuroscience, 13*, 229-242. (9)

Bahill, A.T., & LaRitz, T. (1984). Why can't batters keep their eyes on the ball? *American Scientist, 72*, 249-253. (8)

Bailey, J.M., & Benishay, D.S. (1993). Familial aggregation of female sexual orientation. *American Journal of Psychiatry, 150*, 272-277. (11)

Bailey, J.M., & Pillard, R.C. (1991). A genetic study of male sexual orientation. *Archives of General Psychiatry, 48*, 1089-1096. (11)

Bailey, J.M., Pillard, R.C., Neale, M.C., & Agyei, Y. (1993). Heritable factors influence sexual orientation in women. *Archives of General Psychiatry, 50*, 217-223. (11)

Bailey, J.M., Willerman, L., & Parks, C. (1991). A test of the maternal stress theory of human male homosexuality. *Archives of Sexual Behavior, 20*, 277-293. (11)

Balasubramaniam, V., & Kanaka, T.S. (1976). Hypothalamotomy in the management of aggressive behavior. In T.P. Morley (Ed.), *Current controversies in neurosurgery* (pp. 768-777). Philadelphia: Saunders. (12)

Ballard, P.A., Tetrud, J.W., & Langston, J.W. (1985). Permanent human parkinsonism due to 1-methyl-4-phenyl-1,2,3,6-tetrahydropyridine (MPTP). *Neurology, 35*, 949-956. (8)

Ballenger, J.C., Burrows, G.D., DuPont, R.L., Jr., Lesser, I.M., Noyes, R., Jr., Pecknold, J.C., Rifkin, A., & Swinson, R.P. (1988). Alprazolam in panic disorder and agoraphobia: Results from a multicenter trial. *Archives of General Psychiatry, 45*, 413-422. (12)

Banks, M.S., Aslin, R.N., & Letson, R.D. (1975). Sensitive period for the development of human binocular vision. *Science, 190*, 675-677. (6)

Baptista, L.F., & Petrinovich, L. (1984). Social interaction, sensitive phases and the song template hypothesis in the white-crowned sparrow. *Animal Behaviour, 32*, 172-181. (1)

Barbaro, N.M. (1988). Studies of PAG/PVG stimulation for pain relief in humans. In H.L. Fields & J.-M. Besson (Eds.), *Progress in brain research* (Vol. 77, pp. 165-173). Amsterdam: Elsevier. (7)

Barbizet, J. (1970). *Human memory and its pathology.* San Francisco: W. H. Freeman. (14)

Bard, P. (1929). The central representation of the sympathetic system. *Archives of*

Neurology and Psychiatry, 22, 230-246. (12)

Bard, P. (1934). On emotional expression after decortication with some remarks on certain theoretical views. *Psychological Review, 41,* 309-329. (12)

Barnes, C.A., & McNaughton, B.L. (1985). An age comparison of the rates of acquisition and forgetting of spatial information in relation to long-term enhancement of hippocampal synapses. *Behavioral Neuroscience, 99,* 1040-1048. (13)

Barr, C.E., Mednick, S.A., & Munk-Jorgensen, P. (1990). Exposure to influenza epidemics during gestation and adult schizophrenia. *Archives of General Psychiatry, 47,* 869-874. (16)

Barre, V., & Petter-Rousseaux, A. (1988). Seasonal variations in sleep-wake cycle in *Microcebus murinus. Primates, 19,* 53-64. (9)

Bartoshuk, L.M. (1991). Taste, smell, and pleasure. In R.C. Bolles (Ed.) *The hedonics of taste* (pp. 15-28). Hillsdale, NJ: Lawrence Erlbaum. (7)

Bartoshuk, L.M., Gentile, R.L., Moskowitz, H.R., & Meiselman, H.L. (1974). Sweet taste induced by miracle fruit (*Synsephalum dulcificum*). *Physiology & Behavior, 12,* 449-456. (7)

Bartus, R.T., Dean, R.L., III, Beer, B., & Lippa, A.S. (1982). The cholinergic hypothesis of geriatric memory dysfunction. *Science, 217,* 408-417. (13)

Bartus, R.T., Dean, R.L., Pontecorvo, M.J., & Flicker, C. (1985). The cholinergic hypothesis: A historical overview, current perspective, and future directions. *Annals of the New York Academy of Sciences, 444,* 332-358. (13)

Bastien, C., & Campbell, K. (1992). The evoked K-complex: All-or-none phenomenon? *Sleep, 15,* 236-245. (9)

Batini, C., Magni, F., Palestini, M., Rossi, G.F., & Zanchetti, A. (1959). Neural mechanisms underlying the enduring EEG and behavioral activation in the midpontine pretrigeminal cat. *Archives Italiennes de Biologie, 97,* 13-25. (9)

Batini, C., Moruzzi, G., Palestini, M., Rossi, G.F., & Zanchetti, A. (1958). Persistent patterns of wakefulness in the pretrigeminal midpontine preparation. *Science, 128,* 30-32. (9)

Batini, C., Moruzzi, G., Palestini, M., Rossi, G.F., & Zanchetti, A. (1959). Effects of complete pontine transections on the sleep-wakefulness rhythm: The midpontine pretrigeminal preparation. *Archives Italiennes de Biologie, 97,* 1-12. (9)

Batini, C., Palestini, M., Rossi, G.F., & Zanchetti, A. (1959). EEG activation patterns in the midpontine pretrigeminal cat following sensory deafferentation. *Archives Italiennes de Biologie, 97,* 26-32. (9)

Baudry, M., & Lynch, G. (1993). Long-term potentiation: Biochemical mechanisms. In M. Baudry, R.F. Thompson, & J.L. Davis (Eds.), *Synaptic plasticity* (pp. 87-115). Cambridge, MA: MIT Press. (13)

Baum, M.J. (1983). Hormonal modulation of sexuality in female primates. *BioScience, 33,* 578-582. (11)

Baum, M.J., & Vreeburg, J.T.M. (1973). Copulation in castrated male rats following combined treatment with estradiol and dihydrotestosterone. *Science, 182,* 283-285. (11)

Baxter, L.R., Phelps, M.E., Mazziotta, J.C., Guze, B.H., Schwartz, J.M., & Selin, C.E. (1987). Local cerebral glucose metabolic rates in obsessive-compulsive disorder. *Archives of General Psychiatry, 44,* 211-218. (12)

Baxter, L.R., Phelps, M.E., Mazziotta, J.C., Schwartz, J.M., Gerner, R.H., Selin, C.E., & Sumida, R.M. (1985). Cerebral metabolic rates for glucose in mood disorders. *Archives of General Psychiatry, 42,* 441-447. (16)

Baxter, L.R., Jr., Schwartz, J.M., Bergman, K.S., Szuba, M.P., Guze, B.H., Mazziotta, J.C., Alazraki, A., Selin, C.E., Ferng, H.-K., Munford, P., & Phelps, M.E. (1992). Caudate glucose metabolic rate changes with both drug and behavior therapy for obsessive-compulsive disorder. *Archives of General Psychiatry, 49,* 681-689. (12)

Bayer, S.A. (1985). Neuron production in the hippocampus and olfactory bulb of the adult rat brain: Addition or replacement? *Annals of the New York Academy of Sciences, 457,* 163-172. (2)

Baylis, G.C., Driver, J., & Rafal, R.D. (1993). Visual extinction and stimulus repetition. *Journal of Cognitive Neuroscience, 5,* 453-466. (15)

Beach, F.A. (1967). Cerebral and hormonal control of reflexive mechanisms involved in copulatory behavior. *Physiological Reviews, 47,* 289-316. (11)

Beach, F.A. (1970). Hormonal effects on socio-sexual behavior in dogs. In M. Gibian & E.J. Plotz (Eds.), *Mammalian reproduction* (pp. 437-466). Berlin: Springer-Verlag. (11)

Beach, F.A. (1976). Sexual attractivity, proceptivity, and receptivity in female animals. *Hormones and Behavior, 7,* 105-138. (11)

Beach, F.A., Buehler, M.G., & Dunbar, I.F. (1982). Competitive behavior in male, female, and pseudohermaphroditic female dogs. *Journal of Comparative and Physiological Psychology, 96,* 855-874. (11)

Beach, F.A., Dunbar, I.F., & Buehler, M.G. (1982). Sexual characteristics of female dogs during successive phases of the ovarian cycle. *Hormones and Behavior, 16,* 414-462. (11)

Bear, D.M., & Fedio, P. (1977). Quantitative analysis of interictal behavior in temporal lobe epilepsy. *Archives of Neurology, 34,* 454-467. (12)

Beatty, W.W., Butters, N., & Janowsky, D.S. (1986). Patterns of memory failure after scopolamine treatment: Implications for cholinergic hypotheses of dementia. *Behavioral and Neural Biology, 45,* 196-211. (13)

Bechara, A., & van der Kooy, D. (1985). Opposite motivational effects of endogenous opioids in brain and periphery. *Nature, 314,* 533-534. (1)

Becker, H.C. (1988). Effects of the imidazobenzodiazepine Ro15-4513 on the stimulant and depressant actions of ethanol on spontaneous locomotor activity. *Life Sciences, 43,* 643-650. (12)

Békésy, G.—See von Békésy, G.

Bellugi, U., Poizner, H., & Klima, E.S. (1983). Brain organization for language: Clues from sign aphasia. *Human Neurobiology, 2,* 155-170. (14)

Bellugi, U., Wang, P.P., & Jernigan, T.L. (1994). Williams syndrome: An unusual neuropsychological profile. In S.H. Broman & J. Grafman (Eds.), *Atypical cognitive deficits in developmental disorders* (pp. 23-56). Hillsdale, NJ: Lawrence Erlbaum. (14)

Benca, R.M., Obermeyer, W.H., Thisted, R.A., & Gillin, J.C. (1992). Sleep and psychiatric disorders. *Archives of General Psychiatry, 49,* 651-668. (9)

Benes, F.M., & Bird, E.D. (1987). An analysis of the arrangement of neurons in the cingulate cortex of schizophrenic patients. *Archives of General Psychiatry, 44,* 608-616. (16)

Benes, F.M., Davidson, J., & Bird, E.D. (1986). Quantitative cytoarchitectural studies of the cerebral cortex of schizophrenics. *Archives of General Psychiatry, 43,* 31-35. (16)

Bennett, E.L., Rosenzweig, M.R., & Flood, J.F. (1979). Role of neurotransmitters and protein synthesis in short- and long-term memory. In J. Obiols, C. Ballús, E. González Monclús, & J. Pujol (Eds.), *Biological psychiatry today* (pp. 211-219). Amsterdam: Elsevier/North Holland Biomedical Press. (13)

Berenbaum, S.A., & Hines, M. (1992). Early androgens are related to childhood sex-typed toy preferences. *Psychological Science, 3,* 203-206. (11)

Berg, J.M. (1986). Etiology update and review. I. Biomedical factors. In J. Wortis (Ed.), *Mental retardation and developmental disabilities* (Vol. 14, pp. 20-35). New York: Elsevier. (A)

Berman, K.F., Torrey, E.F., Daniel, D.G., & Weinberger, D.R. (1992). Regional cerebral blood flow in monozygotic twins discordant and concordant for schizophrenia. *Archives of General Psychiatry, 49,* 927-934. (16)

Berman, K.F., Zec, R.F., & Weinberger, D.R. (1986). Physiologic dysfunction of dorsolateral prefrontal cortex in schizophrenia: II. Role of neuroleptic treatment, attention, and mental effort. *Archives of General Psychiatry, 43,* 126-135. (4, 16)

Bernstein, J.J., & Gelderd, J.B. (1970). Regeneration of the long spinal tracts in the goldfish. *Brain Research, 20,* 33-38. (15)

Berridge, K.C., Venier, I.L., & Robinson, T.E. (1989). Taste reactivity analysis of 6-hydroxydopamine-induced aphagia: Implications for arousal and anhedonia hypotheses of dopamine function. *Behavioral Neuroscience, 103,* 36-45. (10)

Biben, M. (1979). Predation and predatory play behaviour of domestic cats. *Animal Behaviour, 27,* 81-94. (12)

Bickford, R.G., Dodge, H.W., Jr., & Uihlein, A. (1960). Electrographic and behavioral effects related to depth stimulation in human patients. In E.R. Ramey & D.S. O'Doherty (Eds.), *Electrical stimulation in the unanesthetized brain* (pp. 248-261). New York: P.B. Hoeber. (1)

Billington, C.J., & Levine, A.S. (1992). Hypothalamic neuropeptide Y regulation of feeding and energy metabolism. *Current Opinion in Neurobiology, 2,* 847-851. (10)

Bisiach, E., & Luzzatti, C. (1978). Unilateral neglect of representational space. *Cortex, 14,* 129-133. (4)

Björklund, A. (1992). Dopaminergic transplants in experimental parkinsonism: Cellular mechanisms of graft-induced functional recovery. *Current Opinion in Neurobiology, 2,* 683-689. (8)

Blake, R., & Hirsch, H.V.B. (1975). Deficits in binocular depth perception in cats after alternating monocular deprivation. *Science, 190,* 1114-1116. (6)

Blakemore, C., & Sutton, P. (1969). Size adaptation: A new aftereffect. *Science, 166,* 245-247. (6)

Blass, E.M., & Epstein, A.N. (1971). A lateral preoptic osmosensitive zone for thirst in the rat. *Journal of Comparative and Physiological Psychology, 76,* 378-394. (10)

Blass, E.M., & Hall, W.G. (1976). Drinking termination: Interactions among hydrational, orogastric, and behavioral controls in rats. *Psychological Review, 83,* 356-374. (10)

Blass, E.M., & Teicher, H.M. (1980). Suckling. *Science, 210,* 15-22. (10)

Blehar, M.C., & Rosenthal, N.E. (1989). Seasonal affective disorders and phototherapy. *Archives of General Psychiatry, 46,* 469-474. (16)

Bleuler, E. (1950). *Dementia praecox, or the group of schizophrenias.* New York: International Universities Press. (Original work published 1911) (16)

Bliss, T.V.P., & Lømo, T. (1973). Long-lasting potentiation of synaptic transmission in the dentate area of the anaesthetized rabbit following stimulation of the perforant path. *Journal of Physiology* (London), *232,* 331-356. (13)

Block, B.A., Finnerty, J.R., Stewart, A.F.R., & Kidd, J. (1993). Evolution of endothermy in fish: Mapping physiological traits on a molecular phylogeny. *Science, 260,* 210-214. (10)

Bloom, F.E. (1987). Molecular diversity and cellular functions of neuropeptides. In E.R. deKloet, V.M. Wiegant, & D. deWied (Eds.), *Progress in brain research* (Vol. 72, pp. 213-220). Amsterdam: Elsevier. (3)

Blumberg, M.S., & Alberts, J.R. (1990). Ultrasonic vocalizations by rat pups in the cold: An acoustic by-product of laryngeal braking? *Behavioral Neuroscience, 104,* 808-817. (10)

Blumberg, M.S., Efimova, I.V., & Alberts, J.R. (1992). Ultrasonic vocalizations by rat pups: The primary importance of ambient temperature and the thermal significance of contact comfort. *Developmental Psychobiology, 25,* 229-250. (10)

Bode, L., Ferszt, R., & Czech, G. (1993). Borna disease virus infection and affective disorders in man. *Archives of Virology,* Suppl. 7, 159-167. (16)

Bode, L., Riegel, S., Lange, W., & Ludwig, H. (1992). Human infections with Borna disease virus: Seroprevalence in patients with chronic diseases and healthy individuals. *Journal of Medical Virology, 36,* 309-315. (16)

Bodnoff, S.R., Suranyi-Cadotte, B.E., Quirion, R., & Meaney, M.J. (1989). Role of the central benzodiazepine receptor system in behavioral habituation to novelty. *Behavioral Neuroscience, 103,* 209-212. (12)

Bogardus, C., Lillioja, S., Ravussin, E., Abbott, W., Zawadzki, J.K., Young, A., Knowler, W.C., Jacobowitz, R., & Moll, P.P. (1986). Familial dependence of the resting metabolic rate. *New England Journal of Medicine, 315,* 96-100. (10)

Bogerts, B., Meertz, E., & Schönfeldt-Bausch, R. (1985). Basal ganglia and limbic system pathology in schizophrenia. *Archives of General Psychiatry, 42,* 784-791. (16)

Boklage, C.E. (1977). Schizophrenia, brain asymmetry development, and twinning: Cellular relationship with etiological and possibly prognostic implications. *Biological Psychiatry, 12,* 19-35. (16)

Bolla-Wilson, K., Robinson, R.G., Starkstein, S.E., Boston, J., & Price, T.R. (1989). Lateralization of dementia of depression in stroke patients. *American Journal of Psychiatry, 146,* 627-634. (12)

Booth-Kewley, S., & Friedman, H.S. (1987). Psychological predictors of heart disease: A quantitative review. *Psychological Bulletin, 101,* 343-362. (12)

Boring, E.G. (1950). *A history of experimental psychology* (2nd ed.). New York: Appleton-Century-Crofts. (14)

Borod, J.C., Koff, E., Lorch, M., & Nicholas, M. (1986). The expression and perception of facial emotion in brain-damaged patients. *Neuropsychologia, 24,* 169-180. (14)

Bowmaker, J.K., & Dartnall, H.J.A. (1980). Visual pigments of rods and cones in a human retina. *Physiological Science, 298,* 501-511. (6)

Bowman, M.B., & Lewis, M.S. (1982). The copper hypothesis of schizophrenia: A review. *Neuroscience & Biobehavioral Reviews, 6,* 321-328. (16)

Boyeson, M.G., Callister, T.R., & Cavazos, J.E. (1992). Biochemical and behavioral effects of a sensorimotor cortex injury in rats pretreated with the noradrenergic neurotoxin DSP-4. *Behavioral Neuroscience, 106,* 964-973. (15)

Bozarth, M.A., & Wise, R.A. (1984). Anatomically distinct opiate receptor fields mediate reward and physical dependence. *Science, 224,* 516-517. (12)

Bracke-Tolkmitt, R., Linden, A., Canavan, A.G.M., Rockstroh, B., Scholz, E., Wessel, K., & Diener, H.-C. (1989). The cerebellum contributes to mental skills. *Behavioral Neuroscience, 103,* 442-446. (13)

Bradbury, M. (1979). Why a blood-brain barrier? *Trends in Neurosciences, 2,* 36-38. (2)

Bradbury, T.N., & Miller, G.A. (1985). Season of birth in schizophrenia: A review of evidence, methodology, and etiology. *Psychological Bulletin, 98,* 569-594. (16)

Bradford, J.M.W. (1988). Organic treatment for the male sexual offender. *Annals of the New York Academy of Sciences, 528,* 193-202. (11)

Bradshaw, J.L., & Nettleton, N.C. (1981). The nature of hemispheric specialization in man. *Behavioral and Brain Sciences, 4,* 51-91. (14)

Brady, J.V., Porter, R.W., Conrad, D.G., & Mason, J.W. (1958). Avoidance behavior and the development of gastroduodenal ulcers. *Journal of the Experimental Analysis of Behavior, 1,* 69-72. (12)

Brain, P.F. (1979). Steroidal influences on aggressiveness. In J. Obiols, C. Ballús, E. González Monclús, & J. Pujol (Eds.), *Biological psychiatry today* (pp. 1204-1208). Amsterdam: Elsevier/North Holland Biomedical Press. (11)

Braus, H. (1960). *Anatomie des Menschen, 3. Band: Periphere Leistungsbahnen II. Centrales Nervensystem, Sinnesorgane. 2. Auflage* [Human anatomy: Vol. 3. Peripheral pathways II. Central nervous system, sensory organs (2nd ed.)]. Berlin: Springer-Verlag. (4, 7)

Breedlove, S.M. (1992). Sexual dimorphism in the vertebrate nervous system. *Journal of Neuroscience, 12,* 4133-4142. (11)

Breer, H., & Boekhoff, I. (1992). Second messenger signalling in olfaction. *Current Opinion in Neurobiology, 2,* 439-443. (7)

Breier, A., Buchanan, R.W., Elkashef, A., Munson, R.C., Kirkpatrick, B., & Gellad, F. (1992). Brain morphology and schizophrenia: A magnetic resonance imaging study of limbic prefrontal cortex, and caudate structures. *Archives of General Psychiatry, 49,* 921-926. (16)

Breier, A., Davis, O.R., Buchanan, R.W., Moricle, L.A., & Munson, R.C. (1993). Effects of metabolic perturbation on plasma homovanillic acid in schizophrenia. *Archives of General Psychiatry, 50,* 541-550. (16)

Brenner, E., Cornelissen, F., & Nuboer, W. (1990). Striking absence of long-lasting effects of early color deprivation on monkey vision. *Developmental Psychobiology, 23,* 441-448. (6)

Brenowitz, E.A. (1991). Altered perception of species-specific song by female birds after lesions of a forebrain nucleus. *Science, 251,* 303-305. (1)

Breslau, N., & Davis, G.C. (1986). Chronic stress and major depression. *Archives of General Psychiatry, 43,* 309-314. (16)

Bridgeman, B., & Staggs, D. (1982). Plasticity in human blindsight. *Vision Research, 22,* 1199-1203. (6)

Bridges, R.S., DiBiase, R., Loundes, D.D., & Doherty, P.C. (1985). Prolactin stimulation of maternal behavior in female rats. *Science, 227,* 782-784. (11)

Broderick, J.P., Phillips, S.J., Whisnant, J.P., O'Fallon, W.M., & Bergstralh, E.J. (1989). Incidence rates of stroke in the eighties: The end of the decline in stroke? *Stroke, 20,* 577-582. (15)

Bronson, F.H. (1974). Pheromonal influences on reproductive activities in rodents. In M.C. Birch (Ed.), *Pheromones* (pp. 344-365). Amsterdam: North Holland. (7)

Brooks, D.C., & Bizzi, E. (1963). Brain stem electrical activity during deep sleep. *Archives Italiennes de Biologie, 101,* 648-665. (9)

Brown, G.L., Ebert, M.H., Goyer, P.F., Jimerson, D.C., Klein, W.J., Bunney, W.E., & Goodwin, F.K. (1982). Aggression, suicide, and serotonin: Relationships of CSF amine metabolites. *American Journal of Psychiatry, 139,* 741-746. (12)

Brown, R., Colter, N., Corsellis, N., Crow, T.J., Frith, C., Jagoe, R., Johnstone, E.C., & Marsh, L. (1986). Postmortem evidence of structural brain changes in schizophrenia. *Archives of General Psychiatry, 43,* 36-42. (16)

Brown, R.E. (1986). Paternal behavior in the male Long-Evans rat (*Rattus norvegicus*). *Journal of Comparative Psychology, 100,* 162-172. (11)

Brown, W.T., & Jenkins, E.C. (1989). Mental retardation, fragile X syndrome. In G. Adelman (Ed.), *Neuroscience year* (pp. 102-104). Boston: Birkhäuser. (A)

Brownell, K.D., Greenwood, M.R.C., Stellar, E., & Shrager, E.E. (1986). The effects of repeated cycles of weight loss and regain in rats. *Physiology & Behavior, 38*, 459-464. (10)

Brunelli, S.A., Shindledecker, R.D., & Hofer, M.A. (1987). Behavioral responses of juvenile rats (*Rattus norvegicus*) to neonates after infusion of maternal blood plasma. *Journal of Comparative Psychology, 101*, 47-59. (11)

Brushart, T.M.E. (1993). Motor axons preferentially reinnervate motor pathways. *Journal of Neuroscience, 13*, 2730-2738. (15)

Bruyer, R., Dupuis, M., Ophoven, E., Rectem, D., & Reynaert, C. (1985). Anatomical and behavioral study of a case of asymptomatic callosal agenesis. *Cortex, 21*, 417-430. (14)

Buchsbaum, M.S., Haier, R.J., Potkin, S.G., Nuechterlein, K., Bracha, H.S., Katz, M., Lohr, J., Wu, J., Lottenberg, S., Jerabek, P.A., Trenary, M., Tafalla, R., Reynolds, C., & Bunney, W.E., Jr. (1992). Frontostriatal disorder of cerebral metabolism in never-medicated schizophrenics. *Archives of General Psychiatry, 49*, 935-942. (16)

Buck, L., & Axel, R. (1991). A novel multigene family may encode odorant receptors: A molecular basis for odor recognition. *Cell, 65*, 175-187. (7)

Buell, S.J., & Coleman, P.D. (1981). Quantitative evidence for selective dendritic growth in normal human aging but not in senile dementia. *Brain Research, 214*, 23-41. (2)

Buggy, J., Fisher, A.E., Hoffman, W.E., Johnson, A.K., & Phillips, M.I. (1975). Ventricular obstruction: Effect on drinking induced by intracranial injection of angiotensin. *Science, 190*, 72-74. (10)

Buisseret, P., & Imbert, M. (1976). Visual cortical cells: Their developmental properties in normal and dark reared kittens. *Journal of Physiology, 255*, 511-525. (6)

Bundgaard, M. (1986). Pathways across the vertebrate blood-brain barrier: Morphological viewpoints. *Annals of the New York Academy of Sciences, 481*, 7-19. (2)

Bunney, W.E., Jr., Murphy, D.L., Goodwin, F.K., & Borge, G.F. (1972). The "switch process" in manic-depressive illness. *Archives of General Psychiatry, 27*, 295-302. (16)

Bunsey, M., Kramer, D., Kesler, M., & Strupp, B.J. (1990). A vasopressin metabolite increases attentional selectivity. *Behavioral Neuroscience, 104*, 277-287. (13)

Burn, D.J., Mark, M.H., Playford, E.D., Maraganore, D.M., Zimmerman, T.R., Jr., Duvoisin, R.C., Harding, A.E., Marsden, C.D., & Brooks, D.J. (1992). Parkinson's disease in twins studied with ^{18}F-dopa and positron emission tomography. *Neurology, 42*, 1894-1900. (8)

Burnstine, T.H., Greenough, W.T., & Tees, R.C. (1984). Intermodal compensation following damage or deprivation: A review of behavioral and neural evidence. In C.R. Almli & S. Finger (Eds.), *Early brain damage* (Vol. 1, pp. 3-34).

Orlando, FL: Academic Press. (15)

Butterfield, P.G., Valanis, B.G., Spencer, P.S., Lindeman, C.A., & Nutt, J.G. (1993). Environmental antecedents of young-onset Parkinson's disease. *Neurology, 43*, 1150-1158. (8)

Cahn, R., Borziex, M.-G., Aldinio, C., Tofano, G., & Cahn, J. (1989). Influence of monosialoganglioside inner ester on neurologic recovery after global cerebral ischemia in monkeys. *Stroke, 20*, 652-656. (15)

Cain, D.P., & Vanderwolf, C.H. (1990). A critique of Rushton on race, brain size, and intelligence. *Personality and Individual Differences, 11*, 777-784. (5)

Caine, S.B., & Koob, G.F. (1993). Modulation of cocaine self-administration in the rat through D-3 dopamine receptors. *Science, 260*, 1814-1816. (3)

Calford, M.B., Graydon, M.L., Huerta, M.F., Kaas, J.H., & Pettigrew, J.D. (1985). A variant of the mammalian somatotopic map in a bat. *Nature, 313*, 477-479. (4)

Calne, D.B., Langston, J.W., Martin, W.R.W., Stoessl, A.J., Ruth, T.J., Adam, M.J., Pate, B.D., & Schulzer, M. (1985). Positron emission tomography after MPTP: Observations relating to the cause of Parkinson's disease. *Nature, 317*, 246-248. (8)

Camel, J.E., Withers, G.S., & Greenough, W.T. (1986). Persistence of visual cortex dendritic alterations induced by post-weaning exposure to a "superenriched" environment in rats. *Behavioral Neuroscience, 100*, 810-813. (2)

Campbell, C.B.G., & Hodos, W. (1991). The *scala naturae* revisited: Evolutionary scales and anagenesis in comparative psychology. *Journal of Comparative Psychology, 105*, 211-221. (5)

Campbell, J.C., & Seiden, L.S. (1973). Performance influence on the development of tolerance to amphetamine. *Pharmacology, Biochemistry, and Behavior, 1*, 703-708. (10)

Campbell, S.S., & Tobler, I. (1984). Animal sleep: A review of sleep duration across phylogeny. *Neuroscience & Biobehavioral Reviews, 8*, 269-300. (9)

Cannon, W.B. (1929). Organization for physiological homeostasis. *Physiological Reviews, 9*, 399-431. (10)

Cannon, W.B. (1942). "Voodoo" death. *American Anthropologist, 44*, 169-181. (12)

Cappannari, S.C., Rau, B., Abram, W.S., & Buchanan, D.C. (1975). Voodoo in the general hospital. *Journal of the American Medical Association, 232*, 938-940. (12)

Capranica, R.R., & Frishkopf, L.S. (1966). Responses of auditory units in the medulla of the cricket frog. *Journal of the Acoustical Society of America, 40*, 1263. (7)

Capranica, R.R., Frishkopf, L.S., & Nevo, E. (1973). Encoding of geographic dialects in the auditory system of the cricket frog. *Science, 182*, 1272-1275. (7)

Caramazza, A. (1988). Some aspects of language processing revealed through the analysis of acquired aphasia: The lexical system. *Annual Review of Neuroscience, 11*, 395-421. (14)

Carani, C., Zini, D., Baldini, A., Della Casa, L., Ghizzani, A., & Marrama, P. (1990).

Effects of androgen treatment in impotent men with normal and low levels of free testosterone. *Archives of Sexual Behavior, 19*, 223-234. (11)

Carlsson, A. (1987). Perspectives on the discovery of central monoaminergic neurotransmission. *Annual Review of Neuroscience, 10*, 19-40. (3)

Carlton, P.L., & Wolgin, D.L. (1971). Contingent tolerance to the anorexigenic effects of amphetamine. *Physiology & Behavior, 7*, 221-223. (10)

Carmignoto, G., & Vicini, S. (1993). Activity-dependent decrease in NMDA receptor responses during development of the visual cortex. *Science, 258*, 1007-1011. (13)

Carmon, A., Nachson, I., & Starinsky, R. (1976). Developmental aspects of visual hemifield differences in perception of verbal material. *Brain and Language, 3*, 463-469. (14)

Carpenter, G.A., & Grossberg, S. (1984). A neural theory of circadian rhythms: Aschoff's rule in diurnal and nocturnal mammals. *American Journal of Physiology, 247*, R1067-R1082. (9)

Carson, C.C., Huelskamp, R.M., & Woodall, T.D. (1993). Perspectives on education in America. *Journal of Educational Research, 86*, 259-310. (5)

Carter, C.S. (1992). Hormonal influences on human sexual behavior. In J. B. Becker, S.M. Breedlove, & D. Crews (Eds.), *Behavioral endocrinology* (pp. 131-142). Cambridge, MA: MIT Press. (11)

Castellucci, V.F., & Kandel, E.R. (1974). A quantal analysis of the synaptic depression underlying habituation of the gill-withdrawal reflex in *Aplysia*. *Proceedings of the National Academy of Sciences, U.S.A., 71*, 5004-5008. (13)

Castellucci, V.F., Pinsker, H., Kupfermann, I., & Kandel, E. (1970). Neuronal mechanisms of habituation and dishabituation of the gill-withdrawal reflex in *Aplysia*. *Science, 167*, 1745-1748. (13)

Catterall, W.A. (1984). The molecular basis of neuronal excitability. *Science, 223*, 653-661. (2)

Caul, W.F., Jones, J.R., & Barrett, R.J. (1988). Amphetamine's effects on food consumption and body weight: The role of adaptive processes. *Behavioral Neuroscience, 102*, 441-450. (10)

Cerletti, U. & Bini, L. (1938). L'Elettroshock [Electroshock]. *Archivio Generale di Neurologia e Psichiatria e Psicoanalisi, 19*, 266-268. (16)

Cespuglio, R., Laurent, J.P., & Jouvet, M. (1975). Étude des relations entre l'activité ponto-géniculo-occipitale (PGO) et la motricité oculaire chez le chat sous reserpine [Study of the relations between ponto-geniculo-occipital activity (PGO) and ocular motility in the cat under reserpine]. *Brain Research, 83*, 319-335. (9)

Chandra, V., Bharucha, N.E., & Schoenberg, B.S. (1984). Mortality data for the U.S. for deaths due to and related to twenty neurologic diseases. *Neuroepidemiology, 3*, 149-168. (8)

Changeux, J.-P., Devillers-Thiéry, A., & Chemouilli, P. (1984). Acetylcholine receptor: An allosteric protein. *Science, 225*, 1335-1345. (3)

Chase, C. (1993, July/August). Intersexual rights. *The Sciences, 33* (4), 3. (11)

Chase, M.H., Soja, P.J., & Morales, F.R. (1989). Evidence that glycine mediates the postsynaptic potentials that inhibit lumbar motoneurons during the atonia of active sleep. *Journal of Neuroscience, 9,* 743-751. (9)

Chase, T.N., Baronti, F., Fabbrini, G., Heuser, I.J., Juncos, J.L., & Mouradian, M.M. (1989). Rationale for continuous dopaminomimetic therapy of Parkinson's disease. *Neurology, 39*(Suppl. 2), 7-10. (8)

Chase, T.N., Wexler, N.S., & Barbeau, A. (1979). *Advances in neurology: Vol. 23. Huntington's disease.* New York: Raven. (8)

Chiarello, C. (1980). A house divided? Cognitive functioning with callosal agenesis. *Brain and Language, 11,* 128-158. (14)

Chiodo, L.A., & Antelman, S.M. (1980). Electroconvulsive shock: Progressive dopamine autoreceptor subsensitivity independent of repeated treatment. *Science, 210,* 799-801. (16)

Chiueh, C.C. (1988). Dopamine in the extrapyramidal motor function: A study based upon the MPTP-induced primate model of Parkinsonism. *Annals of the New York Academy of Sciences, 515,* 226-248. (8)

Chugani, H.T., & Phelps, M.E. (1986). Maturational changes in cerebral function in infants determined by ^{18}FDG positron emission tomography. *Science, 231,* 840-843. (4, 5)

Cicone, N., Wapner, W., Foldi, N.S., Zurif, E., & Gardner, H. (1979). The relation between gesture and language in aphasic communication. *Brain and Language, 8,* 324-349. (14)

Cirignotta, F., Todesco, C.V., & Lugaresi, E. (1980). Temporal lobe epilepsy with ecstatic seizures (so-called Dostoevsky epilepsy). *Epilepsia, 21,* 705-710. (12)

Clark, R.E., & Lavond, D.G. (1993). Reversible lesions of the red nucleus during acquisition and retention of a classically conditioned behavior in rabbits. *Behavioral Neuroscience, 107,* 264-270. (13)

Clarke, S., Assal, G., & deTribolet, N. (1993). Left hemisphere strategies in visual recognition, topographical orientation and time planning. *Neuropsychologia, 31,* 99-113. (14)

Cleary, L.J., Hammer, M., & Byrne, J.H. (1989). Insights into the cellular mechanisms of short-term sensitization in *Aplysia.* In T.J. Carew & D.B. Kelley (Eds.), *Perspectives in neural systems and behavior* (pp. 105-119). New York: Alan R. Liss. (13)

Clohessy, A.B., Posner, M.I., Rothbart, M.K., & Vecera, S.P. (1991). The development of inhibition of return in early infancy. *Journal of Cognitive Neuroscience, 3,* 345-350. (6)

Cloninger, C.R., Bohman, M., & Sigvardsson, S. (1981). Inheritance of alcohol abuse: Cross-fostering analysis of adopted men. *Archives of General Psychiatry, 38,* 861-868. (3)

Cohen, N.J., Eichenbaum, H., Deacedo, B.S., & Corkin, S. (1985). Different memory systems underlying acquisition of procedural and declarative knowledge.

Annals of the New York Academy of Sciences, 444, 54-71. (13)

Cohen, S., Kaplan, J.R., Cunnick, J.E., Manuck, S.B., & Rabin, B.S. (1992). Chronic social stress, affiliation, and cellular immune response in nonhuman primates. *Psychological Science, 3,* 301-304. (12)

Cohen, S., & Williamson, G.M. (1991). Stress and infectious disease in humans. *Psychological Bulletin, 109,* 5-24. (12)

Coile, D.C., & Miller, N.E. (1984). How radical animal activists try to mislead humane people. *American Psychologist, 39,* 700-701. (1)

Comings, D.E., & Amromin, G.D. (1974). Autosomal dominant insensitivity to pain with hyperplastic myelinopathy and autosomal dominant indifference to pain. *Neurology, 24,* 838-848. (7)

Coons, E.E., Levak, M., & Miller, N.E. (1965). Lateral hypothalamus: Learning of food-seeking response motivated by electrical stimulation. *Science, 150,* 1320-1321. (1)

Cooper, S.J., Dourish, C.T., & Barber, D.J. (1990). Reversal of the anorectic effect of (+)-fenfluramine in the rat by the selective cholecystokinin receptor antagonist MK-329. *British Journal of Pharmacology, 99,* 65-70. (10)

Corda, M.G., Blaker, W.D., Mendelson, W.B., Guidotti, A., & Costa, E. (1983). Beta-carbolines enhance shock-induced suppression of drinking in rats. *Proceedings of the National Academy of Sciences, U.S.A., 80,* 2072-2076. (12)

Corder, E.H., Saunders, A.M., Strittmatter, W.J., Schmechel, D.E., Gaskell, P.C., Small, G.W., Roses, A.D., Haines, J.L., & Pericak-Vance, M.A. (1993). Gene dose of apolipoprotein E type 4 allele and the risk of Alzheimer's disease in late onset families. *Science, 261,* 921-923. (13)

Coren, S., & Porac, C. (1977). Fifty centuries of right-handedness: The historical record. *Science, 198,* 631-632. (14)

Corkin, S. (1984). Lasting consequences of bilateral medial temporal lobectomy: Clinical course and experimental findings in H.M. *Seminars in Neurology, 4,* 249-259. (13)

Corso, J.F. (1973). Hearing. In B.B. Wolman (Ed.), *Handbook of general psychology* (pp. 348-381). Englewood Cliffs, NJ: Prentice-Hall. (7)

Corso, J.F. (1985). Communication, presbycusis, and technological aids. In H.K. Ulatowska (Ed.), *The aging brain: Communication in the elderly* (pp. 33-51). San Diego, CA: College Hill. (7)

Coss, R.G., Brandon, J.G., & Globus, A. (1980). Changes in morphology of dendritic spines on honeybee calycal interneurons associated with cumulative nursing and foraging experiences. *Brain Research, 192,* 49-59. (2)

Coss, R.G., & Globus, A. (1979). Social experience affects the development of dendritic spines and branches on tectal interneurons in the Jewel fish. *Developmental Psychobiology, 12,* 347-358. (2)

Cotman, C.W., Monaghan, D.T., & Ganong, A.H. (1988). Excitatory amino acid neurotransmission: NMDA receptors and Hebb-type synaptic transmission. *Annual Review of Neuroscience, 11,* 61-80. (13)

Cotman, C.W., & Nieto-Sampedro, M.

(1982). Brain function, synapse renewal, and plasticity. *Annual Review of Psychology, 33,* 371-401. (15)

Cowan, J.D. (1983). Testing the escape hypotheses: Alcohol helps users to forget their feelings. *Journal of Nervous and Mental Disease, 171,* 40-48. (3)

Coyle, J.T., Oster-Granite, M.L., & Gearhart, J.D. (1986). The neurobiologic consequences of Down syndrome. *Brain Research Bulletin, 16,* 773-787. (A)

Coyle, P.K. (1991). Viral infections of the developing nervous system. *Seminars in the Neurosciences, 3,* 157-163. (16)

Craft, S., Willerman, L., & Bigler, E.D. (1987). Callosal dysfunction in schizophrenia and schizo-affective disorder. *Journal of Abnormal Psychology, 96,* 205-213. (16)

Craner, S.L., Hoffman, G.E., Lund, J.S., Humphrey, A.L., & Lund, R.D. (1992). cFos labeling in rat superior colliculus: Activation by normal retinal pathways and pathways from intracranial retinal transplants. *Experimental Neurology, 117,* 219-229. (5)

Crawley, J.N. (1990). Coexistence of neuropeptides and "classical" neurotransmitters. *Annals of the New York Academy of Sciences, 579,* 233-245. (3)

Crawshaw, L.I., Moffitt, B.P., Lemons, D.E., & Downey, J.A. (1981). The evolutionary development of vertebrate thermoregulation. *American Scientist, 69,* 543-550. (10)

Creak, M. (1961). Schizophrenic syndrome in childhood. *British Medical Journal, 2,* 889-890. (16)

Creasey, H., Rumsey, J.M., Schwartz, M., Duara, R., Rapoport, J.L., & Rapoport, S.I. (1986). Brain morphometry in autistic men as measured by volumetric computed tomography. *Archives of Neurology, 43,* 669-672. (16)

Cremers, C.W.R.J., & van Rijn, P.M. (1991). Acquired causes of deafness in childhood. *Annals of the New York Academy of Sciences, 630,* 197-202. (7)

Crenshaw, A.G., Fridén, J., Thornell, L.-E., & Hargens, A.R. (1991). Extreme endurance training: Evidence of capillary and mitochondria compartmentalization in human skeletal muscle. *European Journal of Applied Physiology, 63,* 173-178. (8)

Cruikshank, S.J., Edeline, J.-M., & Weinberger, N.M. (1992). Stimulation at a site of auditory-somatosensory convergence in the medial geniculate nucleus is an effective unconditioned stimulus for fear conditioning. *Behavioral Neuroscience, 106,* 471-483. (12)

Cserr, H.F., & Bundgaard, M. (1986). The neuronal microenvironment: A comparative view. *Annals of the New York Academy of Sciences, 481,* 1-6. (2)

Culebras, A. (1992). Neuroanatomic and neurologic correlates of sleep disturbances. *Neurology, 42* (Suppl. 6), 19-27. (9)

Culebras, A., & Moore, J.T. (1989). Magnetic resonance findings in REM sleep behavior disorder. *Neurology, 39,* 1519-1523. (9)

Cummings, J.L., & Victoroff, J.I. (1990). Noncognitive neuropsychiatric syndromes in Alzheimer's disease. *Neuropsychiatry, Neuropsychology, & Behavioral Neurology, 3,* 140-158. (13)

Cusick, C.G., Wall, J.T., & Kaas, J.H. (1986). Representations of the face, teeth and oral cavity in areas 3b and 1 of somatosensory cortex in squirrel monkeys. *Brain Research, 370,* 359-364. (4)

Cutler, W.B., Preti, G., Krieger, A., Huggins, G.R., Garcia, C.R., & Lawley, H.J. (1986). Human axillary secretions influence women's menstrual cycles: The role of donor extract from men. *Hormones and Behavior, 20,* 463-473. (7)

Cynader, M., & Chernenko, G. (1976). Abolition of direction selectivity in the visual cortex of the cat. *Science, 193,* 504-505. (6)

Czeisler, C.A., Johnson, M.P., Duffy, J.F., Brown, E.N., Ronda, J.M., & Kronauer, R.E. (1990). Exposure to bright light and darkness to treat physiologic maladaptation to night work. *New England Journal of Medicine, 322,* 1253-1259. (9)

Czeisler, C.A., Weitzman, E.D., Moore-Ede, M.C., Zimmerman, J.C., & Knauer, R.S. (1980). Human sleep: Its duration and organization depend on its circadian phase. *Science, 210,* 1264-1267. (9, 16)

Dabbs, J.M., & Morris, R. (1990). Testosterone, social class, and antisocial behavior in a sample of 4,462 men. *Psychological Science, 1,* 209-211. (11)

Dakof, G.A., & Mendelsohn, G.A. (1986). Parkinson's disease: The psychological aspects of a chronic illness. *Psychological Bulletin, 99,* 375-387. (8)

Dalby, J.T., Arboleda-Florez, J., & Seland, T.P. (1989). Somatic delusions following left parietal lobe injury. *Neuropsychiatry, Neuropsychology, and Behavioral Neurology, 2,* 306-311. (4)

Dale, N., Schacher, S., & Kandel, E.R. (1988). Long-term facilitation in *Aplysia* involves increase in transmitter release. *Science, 239,* 282-285. (13)

Dalton, K. (1968). Ante-natal progesterone and intelligence. *British Journal of Psychiatry, 114,* 1377-1382. (11)

Daly, M., Wilson, M., & Weghorst, S.J. (1982). Male sexual jealousy. *Ethology & Sociobiology, 3,* 11-27. (12)

Damasio, A. (1979). The frontal lobes. In K.M. Heilman & E. Valenstein (Eds.), *Clinical neuropsychology* (pp. 360-412). New York: Oxford University Press. (4)

Damasio, A.R. (1983). Language and the basal ganglia. *Trends in Neurosciences, 6,* 442-444. (4)

Damasio, A.R., & Geschwind, N. (1984). The neural basis of language. *Annual Review of Neuroscience, 7,* 127-147. (14)

Damasio, H., & Damasio, A.R. (1980). The anatomical basis of conduction aphasia. *Brain, 103,* 337-350. (14)

Damsma, G., Pfaus, J.G., Wenkstern, D., Phillips, A.G., & Fibiger, H.C. (1992). Sexual behavior increases dopamine transmission in the nucleus accumbens and striatum of male rats: Comparison with novelty and locomotion. *Behavioral Neuroscience, 106,* 181-191. (11)

Darley, S.A., & Katz, I. (1973). Heart rate changes in children as a function of test versus game instructions and test anxiety. *Child Development, 44,* 784-789. (12)

Darwin, C. (1859). *On the origin of species.* Reprinted by various publishers. (A)

Dascombe, M.J. (1986). The pharmacology of fever. *Progress in Neurobiology, 25,* 327-373. (10)

Daum, I., Ackermann, H., Schugens, M.M., Reimold, C., Dichgans, J., & Birbaumer, N. (1993). The cerebellum and cognitive functions in humans. *Behavioral Neuroscience, 107,* 411-419. (8)

Daum, I., Schugens, M.M., Ackermann, H., Lutzenberger, W., Dichgans, J., & Birbaumer, N. (1993). Classical conditioning after cerebellar lesions in humans. *Behavioral Neuroscience, 107,* 748-756. (13)

Davidson, J.M. (1966). Activation of male rat's sexual behavior by intracerebral implantation of androgen. *Endocrinology, 79,* 783-794. (11)

Davidson, R.J. (1984). Affect, cognition, and hemispheric specialization. In C.E. Izard, J. Kagan, & R.B. Zajonc (Eds.), *Emotions, cognition, & behavior* (pp. 320-365). Cambridge, England: Cambridge University Press. (16)

Davidson, T.L., McKernan, M.G., & Jarrard, L.E. (1993). Hippocampal lesions do not impair negative patterning: A challenge to configural association theory. *Behavioral Neuroscience, 107,* 227-234. (13)

Davies, P. (1985). A critical review of the role of the cholinergic system in human memory and cognition. *Annals of the New York Academy of Sciences, 444,* 212-217. (13)

Davis, H.P., & Squire, L.R. (1984). Protein synthesis and memory: A review. *Psychological Bulletin, 96,* 518-559. (13)

Davis, J.D., Wirtshafter, D., Asin, K.E., & Brief, D. (1981). Sustained intracerebroventricular infusion of brain fuels reduces body weight and food intake in rats. *Science, 212,* 81-83. (10)

Davis, K.L., Mohs, R.C., Tinklenberg, J.R., Pfefferbaum, A., Hollister, L.E., & Kopell, B.S. (1978). Physostigmine: Improvement of long-term memory processes in normal humans. *Science, 201,* 272-274. (13)

Davis, M. (1992). The role of the amygdala in fear and anxiety. *Annual Review of Neuroscience, 15,* 353-375. (12)

Davis, N., & LeVere, T.E. (1979). Recovery of function after brain damage: Different processes and the facilitation of one. *Physiological Psychology, 7,* 233-240. (15)

Davis, N., & LeVere, T.E. (1982). Recovery of function after brain damage: The question of individual behaviors or functionality. *Experimental Neurology, 75,* 68-78. (15)

Deacon, T.W. (1990a). Problems of ontogeny and phylogeny in brain-size evolution. *International Journal of Primatology, 11,* 237-282. (5)

Deacon, T.W. (1990b). Rethinking mammalian brain evolution. *American Zoologist, 30,* 629-705. (5)

Deacon, T.W. (1992). Brain-language coevolution. In J.A. Hawkins & M. Gell-Mann (Eds.), *The evolution of human languages* (pp. 49-83). Reading, MA: Addison-Wesley. (5, 14)

Deacon, T.W. (1994). *Symbolic origins.* New York: W. W. Norton (5)

DeArmond, S.J., Fusco, M.M., & Dewey, M.M. (1974). *Structure of the human brain.* New York: Oxford University Press. (10)

deCastro, J.M., & Zrull, M.C. (1988). Recovery of sensorimotor function after frontal cortex damage in rats: Evidence that the serial lesion effect is due to serial recovery. *Behavioral Neuroscience, 102,* 843-851. (15)

DeCoursey, P. (1960). Phase control of activity in a rodent. *Cold Spring Harbor symposia on quantitative biology, 25,* 49-55. (9)

Delgado, J.M.R. (1969). *Physical control of the mind.* New York: Harper & Row. (1, 11)

Delgado, J.M.R. (1981). Neuronal constellations in aggressive behavior. In L. Valzelli & L. Morgese (Eds.), *Aggression and violence: A psycho/biological and clinical approach* (pp. 82-98). Milan, Italy: Edizioni Saint Vincent. (12)

Delgado, J.M.R., & Hamlin, H. (1960). Spontaneous and evoked electrical seizures in animals and in humans. In E.R. Ramey & D.S. O'Doherty (Eds.), *Electrical studies on the unanesthetized brain* (pp. 133-158). New York: P.B. Hoeber. (12)

Deliagina, T.G., Orlovsky, G.N., & Pavlova, G.A. (1983). The capacity for generation of rhythmic oscillations is distributed in the lumbosacral spinal cord of the cat. *Experimental Brain Research, 53,* 81-90. (8)

DeLong, M.R. (1974). Motor functions of the basal ganglia: Single-unit activity during movement. In F.O. Schmitt & F.G. Worden (Eds.), *The neurosciences, third study program* (pp. 319-325). Cambridge, MA: MIT Press. (8)

DeLong, M.R., Alexander, G.E., Georgopoulos, A.P., Crutcher, M.D., Mitchell, S.J., & Richardson, R.T. (1984). Role of basal ganglia in limb movements. *Human Neurobiology, 2,* 235-244. (8)

Delwaide, P.J., Devoitille, J.M., & Ylieff, M. (1980). Acute effect of drugs upon memory of patients with senile dementia. *Acta Psychiatrica Belgica, 80,* 748-754. (13)

Dement, W. (1960). The effect of dream deprivation. *Science, 131,* 1705-1707. (9)

Dement, W. (1972). *Some must watch while some must sleep.* San Francisco: W.H. Freeman. (9)

Dement, W.C. (1990). A personal history of sleep disorders medicine. *Journal of Clinical Neurophysiology, 7,* 17-47. (9)

Dement, W., Ferguson, J., Cohen, H., & Barchas, J. (1969). Non-chemical methods and data using a biochemical model: The REM quanta. In A.J. Mandell & M.P. Mandell (Eds.), *Psychochemical research in man* (pp. 275-325). New York: Academic Press. (9)

Dement, W., & Kleitman, N. (1957a). Cyclic variations in EEG during sleep and their relation to eye movements, body motility, and dreaming. *Electroencephalography and Clinical Neurophysiology, 9,* 673-690. (9)

Dement, W., & Kleitman, N. (1957b). The relation of eye movements during sleep to dream activity: An objective method for the study of dreaming. *Journal of Experimental Psychology, 53,* 339-346. (9)

Dement, W., & Wolpert, E.A. (1958). The relation of eye movements, body motility, and external stimuli to dream content. *Journal of Experimental Psychology, 55,* 543-553. (9)

Dennett, D.C. (1991). *Consciousness explained.* Boston, MA: Little, Brown, and Co. (6)

Dennett, D.C., & Kinsbourne, M. (1992). Time and the observer: The where and when of consciousness in the brain. *The Behavioral and Brain Sciences, 15,* 183-247. (6)

Déprés, J.-P., Pouliot, M.-C., Moorjani, S., Nadeau, A., Tremblay, A., Lupien, P.J., Thériault, G., & Bouchard, C. (1991). Loss of abdominal fat and metabolic response to exercise training in obese women. *American Journal of Physiology, 261,* E159-E167. (10)

Desiderato, O., MacKinnon, J.R., & Hissom, H. (1974). Development of gastric ulcers in rats following stress termination. *Journal of Comparative and Physiological Psychology, 87,* 208-214. (12)

DeSimone, J.A., Heck, G.L., & Bartoshuk, L.M. (1980). Surface active taste modifiers: A comparison of the physical and psychophysical properties of gymnemic acid and sodium lauryl sulfate. *Chemical Senses, 5,* 317-330. (7)

Desimone, J.A., Heck, G.L., Mierson, S., & Desimone, S.K. (1984). The active ion transport properties of canine lingual epithelia in vitro. *Journal of General Physiology, 83,* 633-656. (7)

Desimone, R. (1991). Face-selective cells in the temporal cortex of monkeys. *Journal of Cognitive Neuroscience, 3,* 1-8. (6)

Desimone, R., Albright, T.D., Gross, C.G., & Bruce, C. (1984). Stimulus-selective properties of inferior temporal neurons in the macaque. *Journal of Neuroscience, 4,* 2051-2062. (6)

Desimone, R., & Gross, C.G. (1979). Visual areas in the temporal cortex of the macaque. *Brain Research, 178,* 363-380. (6)

Désir, D., van Cauter, E., Fang, V.S., Martino, E., Jadot, C., Spire, J.-P., Noël, P., Refetoff, S., Copinschi, G., & Golstein, J. (1981). Effects of "jet lag" on hormonal patterns. I. Procedure variations in total plasma proteins, and disruption of adrenocorticotropin-cortisol periodicity. *Journal of Clinical Endocrinology and Metabolism, 52,* 628-641. (9)

Desmond, M.M., & Wilson, G.S. (1975). Neonatal abstinence syndrome: Recognition and diagnosis. *Addictive Diseases, 2,* 113-121. (16)

Desor, J.A., & Beauchamp, G.K. (1974). The human capacity to transmit olfactory information. *Perception & Psychophysics, 16,* 551-556. (7)

Detera-Wadleigh, S.D., Berrettini, W.H., Goldin, L.R., Boorman, D., Anderson, S., & Gershon, E.S. (1987). Close linkage of c-Harvey- *ras*-1 and the insulin gene to affective disorder is ruled out in three North American pedigrees. *Nature, 325,* 806-808. (16)

Deutsch, J.A., & Ahn, S.J. (1986). The splanchnic nerve and food intake regulation. *Behavioral and Neural Biology, 45,* 43-47. (10)

Deutsch, J.A., & Gonzalez, M.F. (1980). Gastric nutrient content signals satiety. *Behavioral and Neural Biology, 30,* 113-116. (10)

Deutsch, J.A., Young, W.G., & Kalogeris, T.J. (1978). The stomach signals satiety. *Science, 201,* 165-167. (10)

DeValois, R.L., & Jacobs, G.H. (1968). Primate color vision. *Science, 162,* 533-540. (6)

Devane, W.A., Dysarz, F.A., III, Johnson, M.R., Melvin, L.S., & Howlett, A.C. (1988). Determination and characterization of a cannabinoid receptor in rat brain. *Molecular Pharmacology, 34,* 605-613. (3)

Devane, W.A., Hanuš, L., Breuer, A., Pertwee, R.G., Stevenson, L.A., Griffin, G., Gibson, D., Mandelbaum, A., Etinger, A., & Mechoulam, R. (1992). Isolation and structure of a brain constituent that binds to the cannabinoid receptor. *Science, 258,* 1946-1949. (3)

Diamond, I.T. (1979). The subdivisions of neocortex: A proposal to revise the traditional view of sensory, motor, and association areas. *Progress in Psychobiology and Physiological Psychology, 8,* 1-43. (4)

Diamond, I.T. (1983). Parallel pathways in the auditory, visual, and somatic systems. In G. Macchi, A. Rustioni, & R. Spreafico (Eds.), *Somatosensory integration in the thalamus* (pp. 251-272). Amsterdam: Elsevier. (4)

Diamond, M. (1982). Sexual identity, monozygotic twins reared in discordant sex roles and a BBC follow-up. *Archives of Sexual Behavior, 11,* 181-186. (11)

Diamond, M., Llacuna, A., & Wong, C.L. (1973). Sex behavior after neonatal progesterone, testosterone, estrogen, or antiandrogens. *Hormones and Behavior, 4,* 73-88. (11)

Dichgans, J. (1984). Clinical symptoms of cerebellar dysfunction and their topodiagnostic significance. *Human Neurobiology, 2,* 269-279. (8)

DiLorenzo, P.M., & Hecht, G.S. (1993). Perceptual consequences of electrical stimulation in the gustatory system. *Behavioral Neuroscience, 107,* 130-138. (6)

Dimond, S.J. (1979). Symmetry and asymmetry in the vertebrate brain. In D.A. Oakley & H.C. Plotkin (Eds.), *Brain, behaviour, and evolution* (pp. 189-218). London: Methuen. (14)

Dinarello, C.A., & Wolff, S.M. (1982). Molecular basis of fever in humans. *American Journal of Medicine, 72,* 799-819. (10)

DiPelligrino, G., & Wise, S.P. (1991). A neurophysiological comparison of three distinct regions of the primate frontal lobe. *Brain, 114,* 951-978. (8)

Dixson, A.F. (1987). Effects of adrenalectomy upon proceptivity, receptivity, and sexual attractiveness in ovariectomized marmosets (*Callithrix jacchus*). *Physiology & Behavior, 39,* 495-499. (11)

Dombovy, M.L., & Bach-y-Rita, P. (1988). Clinical observations on recovery from stroke. In S.G. Waxman (Ed.), *Advances in neurology* (Vol. 47, pp. 265-276). New York: Raven Press. (15)

Domenici, L., Parisi, V., & Maffei, L. (1992). Exogenous supply of nerve growth factor prevents the effects of strabismus in the rat. *Neuroscience, 51,* 19-24. (6)

Dörner, G. (1974). Sex-hormone-dependent brain differentiation and sexual functions. In G. Dörner (Ed.), *Endocrinology of sex* (pp. 30-37). Leipzig: J.A. Barth. (11)

Dowling, J.E. (1987). *The retina.* Cambridge, MA: Harvard University Press. (6)

Dowling, J.E., & Boycott, B.B. (1966). Organization of the primate retina. *Proceedings of the Royal Society of London,* B, *166,* 80-111. (6)

Drachman, D.A., & Leavitt, J. (1974). Human memory and the cholinergic system. *Archives of Neurology, 30,* 113-121. (13)

Drachman, D.B. (1978). Myasthenia gravis. *New England Journal of Medicine, 298,* 136-142, 186-193. (8)

Dreyfus-Brisac, C. (1970). Ontogenesis of sleep in human prematures after 32 weeks of conceptional age. *Developmental Psychobiology, 3,* 91-121. (9)

Duara, R., Kushch, A., Gross-Glenn, K., Barker, W.W., Jallad, B., Pascal, S., Loewenstein, D.A., Sheldon, J., Rabin, M., Levin, B., & Lubs, H. (1991). Neuroanatomic differences between dyslexic and normal readers on magnetic resonance imaging scans. *Archives of Neurology, 48,* 410-416. (14)

Dubocovich, M.L. (1984). Presynaptic alpha-adrenoceptors in the central nervous system. *Annals of the New York Academy of Sciences, 430,* 7-25. (3)

Duggan, J.P., & Booth, D.A. (1986). Obesity, overeating, and rapid gastric emptying in rats with ventromedial hypothalamic lesions. *Science, 231,* 609-611. (10)

Dunlap, J.L., Zadina, J.E., & Gougis, G. (1978). Prenatal stress interacts with prepubertal social isolation to reduce male copulatory behavior. *Physiology and Behavior, 21,* 873-875. (11)

Duvoisin, R.C., Eldridge, R., Williams, A., Nutt, J., & Calne, D. (1981). Twin study of Parkinson disease. *Neurology, 31,* 77-80. (8)

Dyal, J.A. (1971). Transfer of behavioral bias: Reality and specificity. In E.J. Fjerdingstad (Ed.), *Chemical transfer of learned information* (pp. 219-263). New York: American Elsevier. (13)

Dykes, R.W., Sur, M., Merzenich, M.M., Kaas, J.H., & Nelson, R.J. (1981). Regional segregation of neurons responding to quickly adapting, slowly adapting, deep and Pacinian receptors within thalamic ventroposterior lateral and ventroposterior inferior nuclei in the squirrel monkey (*Saimiri sciureus*). *Neuroscience, 6,* 1687-1692. (7)

Easter, S.S. Jr., Purves, D., Rakic, P., & Spitzer, N.C. (1985). The changing view of neural specificity. *Science, 230,* 507-511. (5)

Eccles, J.C. (1964). *The physiology of synapses.* Berlin: Springer-Verlag. (3)

Eccles, J.C. (1986). Chemical transmission and Dale's principle. In T. Hökfelt, K. Fuxe, & B. Pernow (Eds.), *Progress in brain research* (Vol. 68, pp. 3-13). Amsterdam: Elsevier. (3)

Edeline, J.-M., Pham, P., & Weinberger, N.M. (1993). Rapid development of learning-induced receptive field plasticity in the auditory cortex. *Behavioral Neuroscience, 107,* 539-551. (13)

Edeline, J.-M., & Weinberger, N.M. (1992). Associative retuning in the thalamic source of input to the amygdala and auditory cortex: Receptive field plasticity in the medial division of the medial geniculate body. *Behavioral Neuroscience, 106*, 81-105. (13)

Edelman, G.M. (1987). *Neural Darwinism*. New York: Basic Books. (5)

Edelstein, E.L. (1981). Vasopressins and other neuropeptides as CNS mental modulators: A review. *Israel Journal of Psychiatry & Related Sciences, 18*, 229-236. (13)

Edman, G., Åsberg, M., Levander, S., & Schalling, D. (1986). Skin conductance habituation and cerebrospinal fluid 5-hydroxyindoleacetic acid in suicidal patients. *Archives of General Psychiatry, 43*, 586-592. (12)

Egeland, J.A., Gerhard, D.S., Pauls, D.L., Sussex, J.N., Kidd, K.K., Allen, C.R., Hostetter, A.M., & Housman, D.E. (1987). Bipolar affective disorders linked to DNA markers on chromosome 11. *Nature, 325*, 783-787. (16)

Ehman, G.K., Albert, D.J., & Jamieson, J.L. (1971). Injections into the duodenum and the induction of satiety in the rat. *Canadian Journal of Psychology, 25*, 147-166. (10)

Ehret, C.F., Potter, V.R., & Dobra, K.W. (1975). Chronotypic action of theophylline and of pentobarbital as circadian Zeitgebers in the rat. *Science, 188*, 1212-1215. (9)

Ehrhardt, A.A., Meyer-Bahlburg, H.F.L., Rosen, L.R., Feldman, J.F., Veridiano, N.P., Zimmerman, I., & McEwen, B.S. (1985). Sexual orientation after prenatal exposure to exogenous estrogen. *Archives of Sexual Behavior, 14*, 57-77. (11)

Ehrhardt, A.A., & Money, J. (1967). Progestin-induced hermaphroditism: IQ and psychosexual identity in a study of ten girls. *Journal of Sex Research, 3*, 83-100. (11)

Eichenbaum, H. (1992). The hippocampal system and declarative memory in animals. *Journal of Cognitive Neuroscience, 4*, 217-231. (13)

Eidelberg, E., & Stein, D.G. (1974). Functional recovery after lesions of the nervous system. *Neurosciences Research Program Bulletin, 12*, 191-303. (15)

Eisenstein, E.M., & Cohen, M.J. (1965). Learning in an isolated prothoracic insect ganglion. *Animal Behaviour, 13*, 104-108. (13)

Ellinwood, E.H., Jr. (1969). Amphetamine psychosis: A multi-dimensional process. *Seminars in Psychiatry, 1*, 208-226. (16)

Elliott, T.R. (1905). The action of adrenalin. *Journal of Physiology* (London), *32*, 401-467. (3)

Ellis, L. (1986). Evidence of neuroandrogenic etiology of sex roles from a combined analysis of human, nonhuman primate and nonprimate mammalian studies. *Personality and Individual Differences, 7*, 519-552. (11)

Ellis, L., & Ames, M.A. (1987). Neurohormonal functioning and sexual orientation: A theory of homosexuality-heterosexuality. *Psychological Bulletin, 101*, 233-258. (11)

Ellis, L., Ames, M.A., Peckham, W., & Burke, D. (1988). Sexual orientation of human offspring may be altered by severe maternal stress during pregnancy. *Journal of Sex Research, 25*, 152-157. (11)

Engel, A.K., König, P., Kreiter, A.K., & Singer, W. (1991). Interhemispheric synchronization of oscillatory neuronal responses in cat visual cortex. *Science, 252*, 1177-1179. (6)

Engel, B.T. (1985). Stress is a noun! No, a verb! No, an adjective! In T.M. Field, P.M. McCabe, & N. Schneiderman (Eds.), *Stress and coping* (pp. 3-12). Hillsdale, NJ: Lawrence Erlbaum. (12)

Ensor, D.M., Morley, J.S., Redfern, R.M., & Miles, J.B. (1993). The activity of an analogue of MPF (β-endorphin 28-31) in a rat model of Parkinson's disease. *Brain Research, 610*, 166-168. (13)

Epstein, A.N. (1983). The neuropsychology of drinking behavior. In E. Satinoff & P. Teitelbaum (Eds.), *Handbook of behavioral neurobiology: Vol. 6. Motivation* (pp. 367-423). New York: Plenum. (10)

Epstein, A.N. (1990). Prospectus: Thirst and salt appetite. In E.M. Stricker (Ed.), *Handbook of behavioral neurobiology, Vol. 10: Neurobiology of food and fluid intake* (pp. 489-512). New York: Plenum. (10)

Erbas, E.A., Meinertzhagen, I.A., & Shaw, S.R. (1991). Evolution in nervous systems. *Annual Review of Neuroscience, 14*, 9-38. (6)

Erickson, C., & Lehrman, D. (1964). Effect of castration of male ring doves upon ovarian activity of females. *Journal of Comparative and Physiological Psychology, 58*, 164-166. (11)

Erickson, C.J., & Zenone, P.G. (1976). Courtship differences in male ring doves: Avoidance of cuckoldry? *Science, 192*, 1353-13 54. (11)

Erickson, J.D., & Bjerkedal, T.O. (1981). Down syndome associated with father's age in Norway. *Journal of Medical Genetics, 18*, 22-28. (A)

Ernhart, C.B., Sokol, R.J., Martier, S., Moron, P., Nadler, D., Ager, J.W., & Wolf, A. (1987). Alcohol teratogenicity in the human: A detailed assessment of specificity, critical period, and threshold. *American Journal of Obstetrics and Gynecology, 156*, 33-3 9. (5)

Eslinger, P.J., & Damasio, A.R. (1986). Preserved motor learning in Alzheimer's disease: Implications for anatomy and behavior. *Journal of Neuroscience, 6*, 3006-3009. (13)

Etcoff, N.L., Freeman, R., & Cave, K.R. (1991). Can we lose memories of faces? content specificity and awareness in a prosopagnosic. *Journal of Cognitive Neuroscience, 3*, 25-41. (6)

Evans, D.A., Funkenstein, H.H., Albert, M.S., Scherr, P.A., Cook, N.R., Chown, M.J., Hebert, L.E., Hennekens, C.H., & Taylor, J.O. (1989). Prevalence of Alzheimer's disease in a community population of older persons. *Journal of the American Medical Association, 262*, 2551-2556. (13)

Evans, M.D., Hollon, S.D., DeRubeis, R.J., Piasecki, J.M., Grove, W.M., Garvey, M.J., & Tuason, V.B. (1992). Differential relapse following cognitive therapy and pharmacotherapy for depression. *Archives of General Psychiatry, 49*, 802-808. (16)

Evarts, E.V. (1979). Brain mechanisms of movement. *Scientific American, 241* (3), 164-179. (8)

Factor, E.M., Mayer, A.D., & Rosenblatt, J.S. (1993). Peripenduncular nucleus lesions in the rat: I. Effects on maternal aggression, lactation, and maternal behavior during pre- and postpartum periods. *Behavioral Neuroscience, 107*, 166-185. (11)

Fanselow, M.S. (1993). Associations and memories: The role of NMDA receptors and long-term potentiation. *Current Directions in Psychological Science, 2*, 152-156. (13)

Fantz, R.L. (1963). Pattern vision in newborn infants. *Science, 140*, 296-279. (6)

Farah, M.J. (1990). *Visual agnosia*. Cambridge, MA: MIT Press. (6)

Farah, M.J. (1992). Is an object an object an object? Cognitive and neuropsychological investigations of domain specificity in visual object recognition. *Current Directions in Psychological Science, 1*, 164-169. (6)

Farwell, L.A., & Donchin, E. (1988). Talking off the top of your head: Toward a mental prosthesis utilizing event-related brain potentials. *Electroencephalography and Clinical Neurophysiology, 70*, 510-523. (4)

Feder, H.H. (1981). Estrous cyclicity in mammals. In N.T. Adler (Ed.), *Neuroendocrinology of reproduction* (pp. 279-348). New York: Plenum. (11)

Federman, D.D. (1967). *Abnormal sexual development*. Philadelphia, PA: W.B. Saunders. (11)

Feeney, D.M. (1987). Human rights and animal welfare. *American Psychologist, 42*, 593-599. (1)

Feeney, D.M., & Baron, J.-C. (1986). Diaschisis. *Stroke, 17*, 817-830. (15)

Feeney, D.M., & Sutton, R.L. (1988). Catecholamines and recovery of function after brain damage. In D.G. Stein & B.A. Sabel (Eds.), *Pharmacological approaches to the treatment of brain and spinal cord injury* (pp. 121-142). New York: Plenum. (15)

Feeney, D.M., Sutton, R.L., Boyeson, M.G., Hovda, D.A., & Dail, W.G. (1985). The locus coeruleus and cerebral metabolism: Recovery of function after cerebral injury. *Physiological Psychology, 13*, 197-203. (15)

Feighner, J.P., Gardner, E.A., Johnston, J.A., Batey, S.R., Khayrallah, M.A., Ascher, J.A., & Lineberry, C.G. (1991). Double-blind comparison of bupropion and fluoxetine in depressed outpatients. *Journal of Clinical Psychiatry, 52*, 329-335. (16)

Fendrich, R., Wessinger, C.M., & Gazzaniga, M.S. (1992). Residual vision in a scotoma: Implications for blindsight. *Science, 258*, 1489-1491. (6)

Fentress, J.C. (1973). Development of grooming in mice with amputated forelimbs. *Science, 179*, 704-705. (8)

Ferguson, N.B.L., & Keesey, R.E. (1975). Effect of a quinine-adulterated diet upon body weight maintenance in male rats with ventromedial hypothalamic lesions. *Journal of Comparative and Physiological Psychology, 89*, 478-488. (10)

Fernald, R.D. (1989). Seeing through a growing eye. In T.J. Carew & D.B. Kelley (Eds.), *Perspectives in Neural Systems and Behavior* (pp. 151-174). New York: Alan R. Liss. (6)

Fettiplace, R. (1990). Transduction and tuning in auditory hair cells. *Seminars in the Neurosciences, 2,* 33-40. (7)

File, S.E., Pellow, S., & Braestrup, C. (1985). Effects of the beta-carboline, FG7142, in the social interaction test of anxiety and the holeboard: Correlations between behaviour and plasma concentrations. *Pharmacology Biochemistry & Behavior, 22,* 941-944. (12)

Fink, M. (1985). Convulsive therapy: Fifty years of progress. *Convulsive Therapy, 1,* 204-216. (16)

Finlay, B.L., & Pallas, S.L. (1989). Control of cell number in the developing mammalian visual system. *Progress in Neurobiology, 32,* 207-234. (5)

Fisher, L.J., & Gage, F.H. (1993). Grafting in the mammalian central nervous system. *Physiological Reviews, 73,* 583-616. (15)

Fitzsimons, J.T. (1961). Drinking by nephrectomized rats injected with various substances. *Journal of Physiology, 155,* 563-579. (10)

Fitzsimons, J.T. (1973). Some historical perspectives in the physiology of thirst. In A.N. Epstein, H.R. Kissileff, & E. Stellar (Eds.), *The neurophysiology of thirst* (pp. 3-33). Washington, DC: Winston. (10)

Fjerdingstad, E.J. (1973). Transfer of learning in rodents and fish. In W.B. Essman & S. Nakajima (Eds.), *Current biochemical approaches to learning and memory* (pp. 73-98). Flushing, NY: Spectrum. (13)

Flatz, G. (1987). Genetics of lactose digestion in humans. *Advances in Human Genetics, 16,* 1-77. (10)

Fleet, W.S., & Heilman, K.M. (1986). The fatigue effect in hemispatial neglect. *Neurology, 36* (Suppl. 1), 258. (15)

Fletcher, P. (1990). Speech and language defects. *Nature, 346,* 226. (14)

Fletcher, R., & Voke, J. (1985). *Defective colour vision.* Bristol, England: Adam Hilger. (6)

Flood, J.F., Smith, G.E., & Morley, J.E. (1987). Modulation of memory processing by cholecystokinin: Dependence on the vagus nerve. *Science, 236,* 832-834. (13)

Flynn, J.P. (1973). Patterning mechanisms, patterned reflexes, and attack behavior in cats. *Nebraska Symposium on Motivation 1972,* 125-153. (12)

Flynn, J.P., Edwards, S.B., & Bandler, R.J., Jr. (1971). Changes in sensory and motor systems during centrally elicited attack. *Behavioral Science, 16,* 1-19. (12)

Folkard, S., Hume, K.I., Minors, D.S., Waterhouse, J.M., & Watson, F.L. (1985). Independence of the circadian rhythm in alertness from the sleep/wake cycle. *Nature, 313,* 678-679. (9)

Foltz, E.L., & Millett, F.E. (1964). Experimental psychosomatic disease states in monkeys. I. Peptic ulcer—"executive monkeys." *Journal of Surgical Research, 4,* 445-453. (12)

Foote, S.L., & Morrison, J.H. (1987). Extrathalamic modulation of cortical function. *Annual Review of Neuroscience, 10,* 67-95. (4)

Forger, N.G., & Breedlove, S.M. (1987). Motoneuronal death during human fetal development. *Journal of Comparative Neurology, 264,* 118-122. (5)

Forman, R.F., & McCauley, C. (1986). Validity of the positive control polygraph test using the field practice model. *Journal of Applied Psychology, 71,* 691-698. (13)

Foster, R.G. (1993). Photoreceptors and circadian systems. *Current Directions in Psychological Science, 2,* 34-39. (9)

Foulkes, D. (1967). Nonrapid eye movement mentation. *Experimental Neurology* (Suppl. 4), 28-38. (9)

Frank, P.W. (1981). A condition for a sessile strategy. *American Naturalist, 118,* 288-290. (8)

Frank, R.A., Mize, S.J.S., Kennedy, L.M., de los Santos, H.C., & Green, J. (1992). The effect of *Gymnema sylvestre* extracts on the sweetness of eight sweeteners. *Chemical Senses, 17,* 461-479. (7)

Freed, C.R., Breeze, R.E., Rosenberg, N.L., Schneck, S.A., Kriek, E., Qi, J.-X., Lone, T., Zhang, Y.-B., Snyder, J.A., Wells, T.H., Ramig, L.O., Thompson, L., Mazziotta, J.C., Huang, S.C., Grafton, S.T., Brooks, D., Sawle, G., Schroter, G., & Ansari, A.A. (1992). Survival of implanted fetal dopamine cells and neurologic improvement 12 to 46 months after transplantation for Parkinson's disease. *New England Journal of Medicine, 327,* 1549-1555. (15)

Freed, D.M., & Corkin, S. (1988). Rate of forgetting in H.M.: 6-month recognition. *Behavioral Neuroscience, 102,* 823-827. (13)

Freedman, R.D., & Thibos, L.N. (1975). Contrast sensitivity in humans with abnormal visual experience. *Journal of Physiology, 247,* 687-710. (6)

Fregly, M.J., & Rowland, N.E. (1991). Effect of a nonpeptide angiotensin II receptor antagonist, DuP 753, on angiotensin-related water intake in rats. *Brain Research Bulletin, 27,* 97-100. (10)

French, A.R. (1988). The patterns of mammalian hibernation. *American Scientist, 76,* 568-575. (9)

Frese, M., & Harwich, C. (1984). Shiftwork and the length and quality of sleep. *Journal of Occupational Medicine, 26,* 561-566. (9)

Friedlander, W.J. (1986). Who was "the father of bromide treatment of epilepsy"? *Archives of Neurology, 43,* 505-507. (3)

Friedman, M.I., & Stricker, E.M. (1976). The physiological psychology of hunger: A physiological perspective. *Psychological Review, 83,* 409-431. (10)

Frisch, R.E. (1972). Weight at menarche: Similarity for well nourished and undernourished girls at differing ages, and evidence for historical constancy. *Pediatrics, 50,* 445-450. (11)

Frisch, R.E. (1983). Fatness, puberty, and fertility: The effects of nutrition and physical training on menarche and ovulation. In J. Brooks-Gunn & A.C. Petersen (Eds.), *Girls at puberty* (pp. 29-49). New York: Plenum. (11)

Frisch, R.E. (1984). Body fat, puberty and fertility. *Biological Reviews, 59,* 161-188. (11)

Fritsch, G., & Hitzig, E. (1870). Über die elektrische Erregbarkeit des Grosshirns [Concerning the electrical stimulability of the cerebrum]. *Archiv für Anatomie Physiologie und Wissenschaftliche Medicin,* 300-332. (1, 8)

Fritschy, J.-M., & Grzanna, R. (1992). Degeneration of rat locus coeruleus neurons is not accompanied by an irreversible loss of ascending projections. *Annals of the New York Academy of Sciences, 648,* 275-278. (15)

Frutiger, S.A. (1986). Changes in self-stimulation at stimulation-bound eating and drinking sites in the lateral hypothalamus during food or water deprivation, glucoprivation, and intracellular or extracellular dehydration. *Behavioral Neuroscience, 100,* 221- 229. (12)

Fukuda, Y., Hsiao, C.-F., & Watanabe, M. (1985). Morphological correlates of Y, X, and W type ganglion cells in the cat's retina. *Vision Research, 25,* 319-327. (6)

Fuller, R.K., & Roth, H.P. (1979). Disulfiram for the treatment of alcoholism: An evaluation in 128 men. *Annals of Internal Medicine, 90,* 901-904. (3)

Fuster, J.M. (1989). *The prefrontal cortex* (2nd ed.). New York: Raven Press. (4)

Gabrielli, W.F., Jr., & Plomin, R. (1985). Drinking behavior in the Colorado adoptee and twin sample. *Journal of Studies on Alcohol, 46,* 24-31. (3)

Gaito, J. (1976). Molecular psychobiology of memory: Its appearance, contributions, and decline. *Physiological Psychology, 4,* 476-484. (13)

Galef, B.G., Jr. (1992). Weaning from mother's milk to solid foods: The developmental psychobiology of self-selection of foods by rats. *Annals of the New York Academy of Sciences, 662,* 37-52. (10)

Galin, D., Johnstone, J., Nakell, L., & Herron, J. (1979). Development of the capacity for tactile information transfer between hemispheres in normal children. *Science, 204,* 1330-1332. (14)

Gallistel, C.R. (1980). *The organization of action: A new synthesis.* Hillsdale, NJ: Erlbaum. (8)

Gallistel, C.R. (1981). Bell, Magendie, and the proposals to restrict the use of animals in neurobehavioral research. *American Psychologist, 36,* 357-360. (1)

Gallistel, C.R., Gomita, Y., Yadin, E., & Campbell, K.A. (1985). Forebrain origins and terminations of the medial forebrain bundle metabolically activated by rewarding stimulation or by reward-blocking doses of pimozide. *Journal of Neuroscience, 5,* 1246-1261. (12)

Gallo, R.C. (1987, January). The AIDS virus. *Scientific American, 256* (1), 46-56. (16)

Gallup, G.G., Jr., & Suarez, S.D. (1980). On the use of animals in psychological research. *Psychological Record, 30,* 211-218. (1)

Gallup, G.G., Jr., & Suarez, S.D. (1985). Alternatives to the use of animals in psychological research. *American Psychologist, 40,* 1104-1111. (1)

Gamse, R., Leeman, S.E., Holzer, P., & Lembeck, F. (1981). Differential effects of capsaicin on the content of somatostatin, substance P, and neurotensin in the nervous system of the rat. *Naunyn-Schmiedeberg's Archives of Pharmacology, 317,* 140-148. (7)

Garattini, S., & Valzelli, L. (1960). Sulla valutazione farmacologica delle sostanze antidepressive [On the pharmacological validation of antidepressive substances].

In *Le sindromi depressive* (pp. 7-30.) (16)

Garcia, J. (1981). Tilting at the paper mills of academe. *American Psychologist, 36*, 149-158. (inside cover)

Gardner, B.T., & Gardner, R.A. (1975). Evidence for sentence constituents in the early utterances of child and chimpanzee. *Journal of Experimental Psychology: General, 104*, 244-267. (14)

Gardner, H., & Zurif, E.B. (1975). *Bee but not be*: Oral reading of single words in aphasia and alexia. *Neuropsychologia, 13*, 181-190. (14)

Garrick, T. (1990). The role of gastric contractility and brain thyrotropin-releasing hormone in cold restraint-induced gastric mucosal injury. *Annals of the New York Academy of Sciences, 597*, 51-70. (12)

Garrick, T., Minor, T.R., Bauck, S., Weiner, H., & Guth, P. (1989). Predictable and unpredictable shock stimulates gastric contractility and causes mucosal injury in rats. *Behavioral Neuroscience, 103*, 124-130. (12)

Gawin, F.H. (1991). Cocaine addiction: Psychology and neurophysiology. *Science, 251*, 1580-1586. (3)

Gaze, R.M., & Sharma, S.C. (1970). Axial differences in the reinnervation of the goldfish optic tectum by regenerating optic fibers. *Experimental Brain Research, 10*, 171-181. (5)

Gazzaniga, M.S., LeDoux, J.E., & Wilson, D.H. (1977). Language, praxis, and the right hemisphere: Clues to some mechanisms of consciousness. *Neurology, 27*, 1144-1147. (14)

Geiger, G., Lettvin, J.Y., & Fahle, M. (1994). Dyslexic children learn a new visual strategy for reading: A controlled experiment. *Vision Research, 34*, 1223-1233. (14)

Geiger, G., Lettvin, J.Y., & Zegarra-Moran, O. (1992). Task-determined strategies of visual process. *Cognitive Brain Research, 1*, 39-52. (14)

Geliebter, A., Westreich, S., Hashim, S.A., & Gage, D. (1987). Gastric balloon reduces food intake and body weight in obese rats. *Physiology & Behavior, 39*, 399-402. (10)

Gent, J.F., & Bartoshuk, L.M. (1983). Sweetness of sucrose, neohesperidin dihydrochalcone, and saccharin is related to genetic ability to taste the bitter substance 6-n-propylthiouracil. *Chemical Senses, 7*, 265-272. (7)

George, D.T., Nutt, D.J., Walker, W.V., Porges, S.W., Adinoff, B., & Linnoila, M. (1989). Lactate and hyperventilation substantially attenuate vagal tone in normal volunteers. *Archives of General Psychiatry, 46*, 153-156. (12)

Gershon, S., Angrist, B., & Shopsin, B. (1977). Pharmacological agents as tools in psychiatric research. In E.S. Gershon, R.H. Belmaker, S.S. Kety, & M. Rosenbaum (Eds.), *The impact of biology on modern psychiatry* (pp. 65-93). New York: Spectrum. (16)

Geschwind, N. (1970). The organization of language and the brain. *Science, 170*, 940-944. (14)

Geschwind, N. (1972). Language and the brain. *Scientific American, 226*(4), 76-83. (14)

Geschwind, N. (1975). The apraxias: Neural mechanisms of disorders of learned movements. *American Scientist, 63*, 188-195. (5, 8)

Geschwind, N., & Galaburda, A.M. (1985). Cerebral lateralization: Biological mechanisms, associations, and pathology: I. A hypothesis and a program for research. *Archives of Neurology, 42*, 428-459. (14)

Geschwind, N., & Levitsky, W. (1968). Human brain: left-right asymmetries in temporal speech region. *Science, 161*, 186-187. (14)

Getchell, T.V., & Getchell, M.L. (1987). Peripheral mechanisms of olfaction: Biochemistry and neurophysiology. In T.E. Finger & W.L. Silver (Eds.), *Neurobiology of taste and smell* (pp. 91-123). New York: John Wiley. (7)

Gibbs, F.P. (1983). Temperature dependence of the hamster circadian pacemaker. *American Journal of Physiology, 244*, R607-R610. (9)

Gibbs, J., Young, R.C., & Smith, G.P. (1973). Cholecystokinin decreases food intake in rats. *Journal of Comparative and Physiological Psychology, 84*, 488-495. (10)

Gilbert, C.D. (1993). Rapid dynamic changes in adult cerebral cortex. *Current Opinion in Neurobiology, 3*, 100-103. (15)

Gillberg, C., & Gillberg, I.C. (1983). Infantile autism: A total population study of reduced optimality in the pre-, peri-, and neonatal period. *Journal of Autism and Developmental Disorders, 13*, 153-166. (16)

Gillberg, C., Terenius, L., & Lönnerholm, G. (1985). Endorphin activity in childhood psychosis. *Archives of General Psychiatry, 42*, 780-783. (16)

Gillberg, C., Wahlström, J., & Hagberg, B. (1984). Infantile autism and Rett's syndrome: Common chromosomal denominator? *Lancet, ii* (8411), 1094-1095. (16)

Gillin, J.C. (1983). The sleep therapies of depression. *Progress in Neuro-Psychopharmacology & Biological Psychiatry, 7*, 351-364. (16)

Giraudat, J., & Changeux, J.-P. (1981). The acetylcholine receptor. In J.W. Lamble (Ed.), *Towards understanding receptors* (pp. 34-43). Amsterdam: Elsevier/North Holland Biomedical Press. (3)

Gjedde, A. (1984). Blood-brain transfer of galactose in experimental galactosemia, with special reference to the competitive interaction between galactose and glucose. *Journal of Neurochemistry, 43*, 1654-1662. (2)

Glaser, D., van der Wel, H., Brouwer, J.N., Dubois, G.E., & Hellekant, G. (1992). Gustatory responses in primates to the sweetener aspartame and their phylogenetic implications. *Chemical Senses, 17*, 325-335. (7)

Glaser, J.H., Etgen, A.M., & Barfield, R.J. (1987). Temporal aspects of ventromedial hypothalamic progesterone action in the facilitation of estrous behavior in the female rat. *Behavioral Neuroscience, 101*, 534-545. (11)

Glaser, R., Rice, J., Speicher, C.E., Stout, J.C., & Kiecolt-Glaser, J.K. (1986). Stress depresses interferon production by leukocytes concomitant with a decrease in natural killer cell activity. *Behavioral Neuroscience, 100*, 675-678. (12)

Glass, A.V., Gazzaniga, M.S., & Premack, D. (1973). Artificial language training in global aphasics. *Neuropsychologia, 11*, 95-103. (14)

Glass, L., Evans, H.E., & Rajegowda, B.K. (1975). Neonatal narcotic withdrawal. In R.W. Richter (Ed.), *Medical aspects of drug abuse* (pp. 124-133). Hagerstown, MD: Harper & Row. (16)

Glick, S.D. (1974). Changes in drug sensitivity and mechanisms of functional recovery following brain damage. In D.G. Stein, J.J. Rosen, & N. Butters (Eds.), *Plasticity and recovery of function in the central nervous system* (pp. 339-372). New York: Academic Press. (15)

Glickman, S.E., Frank, L.G., Licht, P., Yalcinkaya, T., Siiteri, P.K., & Davidson, J. (1992). Sexual differentiation of the female spotted hyena: One of nature's experiments. *Annals of the New York Academy of Sciences, 662*, 135-159. (11)

Glickstein, M. (1992). The cerebellum and motor learning. *Current Opinion in Neurobiology, 2*, 802-806. (13)

Gloning, I., Gloning, K., Weingarten, K., & Berner, P. (1954). Über einen Fall mit Alexie der BRAILLEschrift [On a case with alexia for Braille writing]. *Wiener Zeitschrift für Nervenheilkunde, 10*, 260-273. (14)

Goate, A., Chartier-Harlin, M.C., Mullan, M., Brown, J., Crawford, F., Fidani, L., Giuffra, L., Haynes, A., Irving, N., James, L., Mant, R., Newton, P., Rooke, K., Roques, P., Talbot, C., Pericak-Vance, M., Roses, A., Williamson, R., Rossor, M., Owen, M., & Hardy, J. (1991). Segregation of a missense mutation in the amyloid precursor protein gene with familial Alzheimer's disease. *Nature, 349*, 704-706. (13)

Gold, P.E. (1987). Sweet memories. *American Scientist, 75*, 151-155. (13)

Gold, R.M. (1973). Hypothalamic obesity: The myth of the ventromedial hypothalamus. *Science, 182*, 488-490. (10)

Goldberg, T.E., Weinberger, D.R., Berman, K.F., Pliskin, N.H., & Podd, M.H. (1987). Further evidence for dementia of the prefrontal type in schizophrenia? *Archives of General Psychiatry, 44*, 1008-1014. (16)

Golden, C.J. (1981). *Diagnosis and rehabilitation in clinical neuropsychology* (2nd ed.). Springfield, IL: Charles C. Thomas. (15)

Golden, C.J. (1984). Rehabilitation and the Luria-Nebraska neuropsychological battery. In B.A. Edelstein & E.T. Couture (Eds.), *Behavioral assessment and rehabilitation of the traumatically brain-damaged* (pp. 83-120). New York: Plenum. (15)

Goldman, B.D. (1981). Puberty. In N.T. Adler (Ed.), *Neuroendocrinology of reproduction* (pp. 229-239). New York: Plenum. (11)

Goldman, M.S. (1983). Cognitive impairment in chronic alcoholics: Some cause for optimism. *American Psychologist, 38*, 1045-1054. (3)

Goldman, P.S. (1971). Functional development of the prefrontal cortex in early life and the problem of neuronal plasticity. *Experimental Neurology, 32*, 366-387. (15)

Goldman, P.S. (1976). The role of experience in recovery of function following orbital prefrontal lesions in infant monkeys. *Neuropsychologia, 14*, 401-412. (15)

Goldman-Rakic, P.S. (1987). Development of cortical circuitry and cognitive function. *Child Development, 58*, 601-622. (4)

Goldman-Rakic, P.S. (1988). Topography of cognition: Parallel distributed networks in primate association cortex. *Annual Review of Neuroscience, 11*, 137-156. (inside cover, 4)

Goldman-Rakic, P.S. (1994). Specification of higher cortical functions. In S.H. Broman & J. Grafman (Eds.), *Atypical cognitive deficits in developmental disorders* (pp. 3-17). Hillsdale, NJ: Lawrence Erlbaum. (13)

Goldman-Rakic, P.S., Bates, J.F., & Chafee, M.V. (1992). The prefrontal cortex and internally generated motor acts. *Current Opinion in Neurobiology, 2*, 830-835. (8)

Goldstein, L.A., & Sengelaub, D.R. (1992). Timing and duration of dihydrotestosterone treatment affect the development of motoneuron number and morphology in a sexually dimorphic rat spinal nucleus. *Journal of Comparative Neurology, 326*, 147-157. (11)

Goldstein, M. (1974). Brain research and violent behavior. *Archives of Neurology, 30*, 1-35. (11, 12)

Gonzalez, M.F., & Deutsch, J.A. (1981). Vagotomy abolishes cues of satiety produced by gastric distension. *Science, 212*, 1283-1284. (10)

Goodglass, H., & Kaplan, E. (1979). Assessment of cognitive deficit in the brain-injured patient. In M.S. Gazzaniga (Ed.), *Handbook of behavioral neurology* (Vol. 2, pp. 3-22). New York: Plenum. (15)

Goodman, W.K., Price, L.H., Delgado, P.L., Palumbo, J., Krystal, J.H., Nagy, L.M., Rasmussen, S.A., Heninger, G.R., & Charney, D.S. (1990). Specificity of serotonin reuptake inhibitors in the treatment of obsessive-compulsive disorder. *Archives of General Psychiatry, 47*, 577-585. (12)

Gopnik, M., & Crago, M.B. (1991). Familial aggregation of a developmental language disorder. *Cognition, 39*, 1-50. (14)

Gorman, J.M., Battista, D., Goetz, R.R., Dillon, D.J., Liebowitz, M.R., Fyer, A.J., Kahn, J.P., Sandberg, D., & Klein, D.F. (1989). A comparison of sodium bicarbonate and sodium lactate infusion in the induction of panic attacks. *Archives of General Psychiatry, 46*, 145-150. (12)

Gorman, J.M., Cohen, B.S., Liebowitz, M.R., Fyer, A.J., Ross, D., Davies, S.O., & Klein, D.F. (1986). Blood gas changes and hypophosphatemia in lactate-induced panic. *Archives of General Psychiatry, 43*, 1067-1071. (12)

Gorski, R.A. (1980). Sexual differentiation of the brain. In D.T. Krieger & J.C. Hughes (Eds.), *Neuroendocrinology* (pp. 215-222). Sunderland, MA: Sinauer. (11)

Gorski, R.A. (1985). The 13th J.A.F. Stevenson memorial lecture. Sexual differentiation of the brain: Possible mechanisms and implications. *Canadian Journal of Physiology and Pharmacology, 63*, 577-594. (11)

Gottesman, I.I. (1991). *Schizophrenia genesis*. New York: W.H. Freeman. (16)

Gottesman, I.I., & Bertelson, A. (1989). Confirming unexpressed genotypes for schizophrenia. *Archives of General Psychiatry, 46*, 867-872. (16)

Gottfried, S., & Frankel, M. (1981). New data on lithium and haloperidol incompatibility. *American Journal of Psychiatry, 138*, 818-821. (16)

Götz, M., Novak, N., Bastmeyer, M., & Bolz, J. (1992). Membrane-bound molecules in rat cerebral cortex regulate thalamic innervation. *Development, 116,* 507-519. (5)

Graziadei, P.P.C., & deHan, R.S. (1973). Neuronal regeneration in frog olfactory system. *Journal of Cell Biology, 59*, 525-530. (2)

Graziadei, P.P.C., & Monti Graziadei, G.A. (1985). Neurogenesis and plasticity of the olfactory sensory neurons. *Annals of the New York Academy of Sciences, 457*, 127-142. (2)

Green, D.J., & Gillette, R. (1982). Circadian rhythm of firing rate recorded from single cells in the rat suprachiasmatic brain slice. *Brain Research, 245*, 198-200. (9)

Greenblatt, S.H. (1973). Alexia without agraphia or hemianopsia: Anatomical analysis of an autopsied case. *Brain, 96*, 307-316. (14)

Greene, E., & Naranjo, J.N. (1987). Degeneration of hippocampal fibers and spatial memory deficit in the aged rat. *Neurobiology of Aging, 8*, 35-43. (13)

Greenough, W.T. (1975). Experiential modification of the developing brain. *American Scientist, 63*, 37-46. (2)

Gresty, M.A., Bronstein, A.M., Brandt, T., & Dieterich, M. (1992). Neurology of otolith function. *Brain, 115,* 647-673. (7)

Griffin, D.R., Webster, F.A., & Michael, C.R. (1960). The echolocation of flying insects by bats. *Animal Behaviour, 8*, 141-154. (7)

Grisham, W., Castro, J.M., Kashon, M.L., Ward, I.L., & Ward, O.B. (1992). Prenatal flutamide alters sexually dimorphic nuclei in the spinal cord of male rats. *Brain Research, 578*, 69-74. (11)

Gross, C.G., & Sergent, J. (1992). Face recognition. *Current Opinion in Neurobiology, 2*, 156-161. (6)

Grossman, S.P., Dacey, D., Halaris, A.E., Collier, T., & Routtenberg, A. (1978). Aphagia and adipsia after preferential destruction of nerve cell bodies in hypothalamus. *Science, 202*, 537-539. (10)

Gubernick, D.J., & Alberts, J.R. (1983). Maternal licking of young: Resource exchange and proximate controls. *Physiology & Behavior, 31*, 593-601. (11)

Guidotti, A., Ferrero, P., Fujimoto, M., Santi, R.M., & Costa, E. (1986). Studies on endogenous ligands (endocoids) for the benzodiazepine/beta carboline binding sites. *Advances in Biochemical Pharmacology, 41*, 137-148. (12)

Guidotti, A., Forchetti, C.M., Corda, M.G., Konkel, D., Bennett, C.D., & Costa, E. (1983). Isolation, characterization, and purification to homogeneity of an endogenous polypeptide with agonistic action on benzodiazepine receptors. *Proceedings of the National Academy of Sciences, U.S.A., 80*, 3531-3535. (12)

Guile, M.N. (1987). Differential gastric ulceration in rats receiving shocks on either fixed-time or variable-time sched-

ules. *Behavioral Neuroscience, 101*, 139-140. (12)

Gulick, W.L. (1971). *Hearing: physiology and psychophysics*. New York: Oxford University Press. (7)

Gusella, J.F., Tanzi, R.E., Anderson, M.A., Hobbs, W., Gibbons, K., Raschtchian, R., Gilliam, T.C., Wallace, M.R., Wexler, N.S., & Conneally, P.M. (1984). DNA markers for nervous system diseases. *Science, 225*, 1320-1326. (A)

Gustafsson, B., & Wigström, H. (1990). Basic features of long-term potentiation in the hippocampus. *Seminars in the Neurosciences, 2*, 321-333. (13)

Guyton, A.C. (1974). *Function of the human body* (4th ed.). Philadelphia: Saunders. (2)

Gwinner, E. (1986). Circannual rhythms in the control of avian rhythms. *Advances in the Study of Behavior, 16*, 191-228. (9)

Habib, M., Gayraud, D., Oliva, A., Regis, J., Salamon, G., & Khalil, R. (1991). Effects of handedness and sex on the morphology of the corpus callosum: A study with brain magnetic resonance imaging. *Brain and Cognition, 16*, 41-61. (14)

Haley, J. (1959). An interactional description of schizophrenia. *Psychiatry, 22*, 321-332. (16)

Hall, J.L., & Gold, P.E. (1990). Adrenalectomy-induced memory deficits: Role of plasma glucose levels. *Physiology & Behavior, 47*, 27-33. (13)

Hall, M.J., Bartoshuk, L.M., Cain, W.S., & Stevens, J.C. (1975). PTC taste blindness and the taste of caffeine. *Nature, 253*, 442-443. (7)

Hamer, D.H., Hu, S., Magnuson, V.L., Hu, N., & Pattatucci, A.M.L. (1993). A linkage between DNA markers on the X chromosome and male sexual orientation. *Science, 261*, 321-327. (11)

Hampson, R.E., Heyser, C.J., & Deadwyler, S.A. (1993). Hippocampal cell firing correlates of delayed-match-to-sample performance in the rat. *Behavioral Neuroscience, 107*, 715-739. (13)

Hansen, S., Harthon, C., Wallin, E., Löfberg, L., & Svensson, K. (1991). Mesotelencephalic dopamine system and reproductive behavior in the female rat: Effects of ventral tegmental 6-hydroxydopamine lesions on maternal and sexual responsiveness. *Behavioral Neuroscience, 105*, 588-598. (11)

Harada, S., Agarwal, D.P., Goedde, H.W., Tagaki, S., & Ishikawa, B. (1982). Possible protective role against alcoholism for aldehyde dehydrogenase isozyme deficiency in Japan. *Lancet, ii* (8302), 827. (3)

Harris, K.M., & Stevens, J.K. (1989). Dendritic spines of CA1 pyramidal cells in the rat hippocampus: Serial electron microscopy with reference to their biophysical characteristics. *Journal of Neuroscience, 9*, 2982-2997. (2)

Harris, R.A., Brodie, M.S., & Dunwiddie, T.V. (1992). Possible substrates of ethanol reinforcement: GABA and dopamine. *Annals of the New York Academy of Sciences, 654*, 61-69. (3)

Harrison, J.M., & Irving, R. (1966). Visual and nonvisual auditory systems in mammals. *Science, 154*, 738-743. (5)

Hart, B.L. (Ed.) (1976). *Experimental psychobiology*. San Francisco: W.H. Freeman. (10)

Hartline, H.K. (1949). Inhibition of activity of visual receptors by illuminating nearby retinal areas in the Limulus eye. *Federation Proceedings, 8*, 69. (6)

Hartmann, E., Milofsky, E., Vaillant, G., Oldfield, M., Falke, R., & Ducey, C. (1984). Vulnerability to schizophrenia. *Archives of General Psychiatry, 41*, 1050-1056. (16)

Harvey, P.H., & Krebs, J.R. (1990). Comparing brains. *Science, 249*, 140-146. (5)

Hauri, P. (1979). What can insomniacs teach us about the functions of sleep? In R. Drucker-Colín, M. Shkurovich, & M.B. Sterman (Eds.), *The functions of sleep* (pp. 251-271). New York: Academic Press. (9)

Hawkins, R.A., & Biebuyck, J.F. (1979). Ketone bodies are selectively used by individual brain regions. *Science, 205*, 325-327. (2)

Hayaishi, O. (1988). Sleep-wake regulation by prostaglandins D_2 and E_2. *Journal of Biological Chemistry, 263*, 14593-14596. (9)

Hayman, C.A.G., & Macdonald, C.A. (1993). The role of repetition and associative interference in new semantic learning in amnesia: A case experiment. *Journal of Cognitive Neuroscience, 5*, 375-389. (13)

Heath, R.G. (1963). Electrical self-stimulation of the brain in man. *American Journal of Psychiatry, 120*, 571-577. (12)

Heath, R.G. (1964). Pleasure response of human subjects to direct stimulation of the brain: Physiologic and psychodynamic considerations. In R.G. Heath (Ed.), *Role of pleasure in behavior* (pp. 219-243). New York: Harper. (1)

Hebb, D.O. (1949). *Organization of behavior*. New York: Wiley. (inside cover, 14)

Hécaen, H., & Kremin, H. (1976). Neurolinguistic research on reading disorders resulting from left hemisphere lesions: Aphasic and "pure" alexias. In H. Whitaker & H.A. Whitaker (Eds.), *Studies in neurolinguistics* (Vol. 2, pp. 269-329). New York: Academic Press. (14)

Hécaen, H., Perenin, M.T., & Jeannerod, M. (1984). The effects of cortical lesions in children: Language and visual functions. In C.R. Almli & S. Finger (Eds.), *Early brain damage* (pp. 277-298). Orlando, FL: Academic Press. (15)

Heffner, R.S., & Heffner, H.E. (1982). Hearing in the elephant (*Elephas maximus*): Absolute sensitivity, frequency discrimination, and sound localization. *Journal of Comparative and Physiological Psychology, 96*, 926-944. (7)

Heinrichs, R.W. (1993). Schizophrenia and the brain. *American Psychologist, 48*, 221-233. (16)

Heller, W., & Levy, J. (1981). Perception and expression of emotion in right-handers and left-handers. *Neuropsychologia, 19*, 263-272. (14)

Helzer, J.E., Canino, G.J., Yeh, E.-K., Bland, R.C., Lee, C.K., Hwu, H.-G., & Newman, S. (1990). Alcoholism—North America and Asia. *Archives of General Psychiatry, 47*, 313-319. (3)

Henley, K., & Morrison, A.R. (1974). A re-evaluation of the effects of lesions of the pontine tegmentum and locus coeruleus on phenomena of paradoxical sleep in the cat. *Acta Neurobiologiae Experimentalis, 34*, 215-232. (9)

Hennig, R., & Lømo, T. (1985). Firing patterns of motor units in normal rats. *Nature, 314*, 164-166. (8)

Herkenham, M. (1992). Cannabinoid receptor localization in brain: Relationship to motor and reward systems. *Annals of the New York Academy of Sciences, 654*, 19-32. (3)

Herkenham, M., Lynn, A.B., de Costa, B.R., & Richfield, E.K. (1991). Neuronal localization of cannabinoid receptors in the basal ganglia of the rat. *Brain Research, 547*, 267-274. (3)

Herkenham, M., Lynn, A.B., Little, M.D., Johnson, M.R., Melvin, L.S., deCosta, B.R., & Rice, K.C. (1990). Cannabinoid receptor localization in brain. *Proceedings of the National Academy of Sciences, U.S.A., 87*, 1932-1936. (4)

Herman, L.M., Pack, A.A., & Morrel-Samuels, P. (1993). Representational and conceptual skills of dolphins. In H.L. Roitblat, L.M. Herman, & P.E. Nachtigall (Eds.), *Language and communication: Comparative perspectives* (pp. 403-442). Hillsdale, NJ: Lawrence Erlbaum. (14)

Hernandez, L., & Hoebel, B.G. (1988). Feeding and hypothalamic stimulation increase dopamine turnover in the accumbens. *Physiology & Behavior, 44*, 599-606. (10)

Hernandez, L., Murzi, E., Schwartz, D.H., & Hoebel, B.G. (1992). Electrophysiological and neurochemical approach to a hierarchical feeding organization. In P. Bjorntorp & B.N. Brodoff (Eds.), *Obesity* (pp. 171-183). Philadelphia, PA: J.B. Lippincott. (10)

Herrero, S. (1985). *Bear attacks: Their causes and avoidance*. Piscataway, NJ: Winchester. (7, 10)

Hess, W.R. (1944). Das Schlafsyndrom als Folge dienzephaler Reizung [Sleep syndrome as a consequence of diencephalic stimulation]. *Helvetica Physiologica Acta, 2*, 305-344. (1)

Hettinger, T.P., & Frank, M.E. (1992). Information processing in mammalian gustatory systems. *Current Opinion in Neurobiology, 2*, 469-478. (7)

Hibbard, L.S., McGlone, J.S., Davis, D.W., & Hawkins, R.A. (1987). Three-dimensional representation and analysis of brain energy metabolism. *Science, 236*, 1641-1646. (4)

Higgins, J.W., Mahl, G.F., Delgado, J.M.R., & Hamlin, H. (1956). Behavioral changes during intracerebral electrical stimulation. *Archives of neurology and psychiatry, 76*, 399-419. (12)

Hines, M., Davis, F.C., Coquelin, A., Goy, R.W., & Gorski, R.A. (1985). Sexually dimorphic regions in the medial preoptic area and the bed nucleus of the stria terminalis of the guinea pig brain: A description and an investigation of their relationship to gonadal steroids in adulthood. *Journal of Neuroscience, 5*, 40-47. (11)

Hitchcock, J.M., & Davis, M. (1991). Efferent pathway of the amygdala involved in conditioned fear as measured with the fear-potentiated startle paradigm. *Behavioral Neuroscience, 105*, 826-842. (12)

Hobson, J.A. (1989). *Sleep*. New York: Scientific American Library. (16)

Hobson, J.A. (1992). Sleep and dreaming: Induction and mediation of REM sleep by cholinergic mechanisms. *Current Opinion in Neurobiology, 2*, 759-763. (9)

Hobson, J.A., & McCarley, R.W. (1977). The brain as a dream state generator: An activation-synthesis hypothesis of the dream process. *American Journal of Psychiatry, 134*, 1335-1348. (9)

Hockfield, S., & Kalb, R.G. (1993). Activity-dependent structural changes during neuronal development. *Current Opinion in Neurobiology, 3*, 87-92. (6)

Hodgkinson, S., Sherrington, R., Gurling, H. Marchbanks, R., Reeders, S., Mallet, J., McInnis, M., Petursson, H., & Brynjolfsson, J. (1987). Molecular genetic evidence for heterogeneity in manic depression. *Nature, 325*, 805-806. (16)

Hoebel, B.G. (1988). Neuroscience and motivation: Pathways and peptides that define motivational systems. In R.C. Atkinson, R.J. Herrnstein, G. Lindzey, & R.D. Luce (Eds.), *Stevens' handbook of experimental psychology* (2nd ed.) (pp. 547-625). New York: John Wiley. (10)

Hoebel, B.G., & Hernandez, L. (1993). Basic neural mechanisms of feeding and weight regulation. In A.J. Stunkard & T.A. Wadden (Eds.), *Obesity: Theory and therapy*, 2nd ed. (pp. 43-62). New York: Raven Press. (10)

Hoffman, P.L., Tabakoff, B., Szabó, G., Suzdak, P.D., & Paul, S.M. (1987). Effect of an imidazobenzodiazepine, Ro15-4513, on the incoordination and hypothermia produced by ethanol and pentobarbital. *Life Sciences, 41*, 611-619. (12)

Hökfelt, T., Holets, V.R., Staines, W., Meister, B., Melander, T., Schalling, M., Schultzberg, M., Freedman, J. Björklund, H., Olson, L., Lindh, B., Elfvin, L.-G., Lundberg, J.M., Lindgren, J.A., Samuelsson, B., Pernow, B., Terenius, L., Post, C., Everitt, B., & Goldstein, M. (1986). Coexistence of neuronal messengers—an overview. *Progress in brain research* (Vol. 68, pp. 33-70). Amsterdam: Elsevier. (3)

Hökfelt, T., Johansson, O., & Goldstein, M. (1984). Chemical anatomy of the brain. *Science, 225*, 1326-1334. (3)

Hollander, E., DeCaria, C.M., Nitescu, A., Gully, R., Suckow, R.F., Cooper, T.B., Gorman, J.M., Klein, D.F., & Liebowitz, M.R. (1992). Serotonergic function in obsessive-compulsive disorder. *Archives of General Psychiatry, 49*, 21-28. (12)

Hollon, S.D., DeRubeis, R.J., Evans, M.D., Wiemer, M.J., Garvey, M.J., Grove, W.M., & Tuason, V.B. (1992). Cognitive therapy and pharmacotherapy for depression. *Archives of General Psychiatry, 49*, 774-781. (16)

Holst—see von Holst

Holzman, P.S. (1985). Eye movement dysfunctions and psychosis. *International Review of Neurobiology, 27*, 179-205. (16)

Holzman, P.S., & Matthysse, S. (1990). The genetics of schizophrenia: A review. *Psychological Science, 1*, 279-286. (16)

Hoover, J.E., & Strick, P.L. (1993). Multiple output channels in the basal ganglia. *Science, 259*, 819-821. (8)

Hopkins, J., Marcus, M., & Campbell, S.B. (1984). Postpartum depression: A critical review. *Psychological Bulletin, 95,* 498-515. (16)

Hoptman, M.J., & Levy, J. (1988). Perceptual asymmetries in left- and right-handers for cartoon and real faces. *Brain & Cognition, 8,* 178-188. (14)

Horne, J.A. (1988). *Why we sleep.* Oxford, England: Oxford University Press. (9)

Horne, J.A., & Minard, A. (1985). Sleep and sleepiness following a behaviourally "active" day. *Ergonomics, 28,* 567-575. (9)

Horridge, G.A. (1962). Learning of leg position by the ventral nerve cord in headless insects. *Proceedings of the Royal Society of London, B, 157,* 33-52. (13)

Householder, J., Hatcher, R., Burns, W., & Chasnoff, I. (1982). Infants born to narcotic-addicted mothers. *Psychological Bulletin, 92,* 453-468. (16)

Hovda, D.A., & Feeney, D.M. (1989). Amphetamine-induced recovery of visual cliff performance after bilateral visual cortex ablation in cats: Measurements of depth perception thresholds. *Behavioral Neuroscience, 103,* 574-584. (15)

Howland, H.C., & Sayles, N. (1984). Photorefractive measurements of astigmatism in infants and young children. *Investigative Ophthalmology and Visual Science, 25,* 93-102. (6)

Hubel, D.H. (1963, November). The visual cortex of the brain. *Scientific American, 209* (5), 54-62. (6)

Hubel, D.H., & Wiesel, T.N. (1959). Receptive fields of single neurons in the cat's striate cortex. *Journal of Physiology, 148,* 574-591. (6)

Hubel, D.H., & Wiesel, T.N. (1963). Receptive fields of cells in striate cortex of very young, visually inexperienced kittens. *Journal of Neurophysiology, 26,* 944-1002. (6)

Hubel, D.H., & Wiesel, T.N. (1965). Binocular interaction in striate cortex of kittens reared with artificial squint. *Journal of Neurophysiology, 28,* 1041-1059. (6)

Hubel, D.H., & Wiesel, T.N. (1977). Functional architecture of macaque monkey visual cortex. *Proceedings of the Royal Society of London, B, 198,* 1-59. (6)

Hudson, J.I., Lipinski, J.F., Frankenburg, F.R., Grochocinski, V.J., & Kupfer, D.J. (1988). Electroencephalographic sleep in mania. *Archives of General Psychiatry, 45,* 267-273. (16)

Hudson, J.L., Bickford, P., Johansson, M., Hoffer, B.J., & Strömberg, I. (1994). Target and neurotransmitter specificity of fetal central nervous system transplants: Importance for functional reinnervation. *Journal of Neuroscience, 14,* 283-290. (15)

Hudspeth, A.J. (1985). The cellular basis of hearing: The biophysics of hair cells. *Science, 230,* 745-752. (7)

Hughes, J., Smith, T.W., Kosterlitz, H.W., Fothergill, L.A., Morgan, B.A., & Morris, H.R. (1975). Identification of two related pentapeptides from the brain with potent opiate agonist activity. *Nature, 258,* 577-579. (7)

Hull, E.M., Eaton, R.C., Markowski, V.P., Moses, J., Lumley, L.A., & Loucks, J.A. (1992). Opposite influence of medial preoptic D1 and D2 receptors on genital reflexes: Implications for copulation. *Life Sciences, 51,* 1705-1713. (11)

Hull, E.M., Eaton, R.C., Moses, J., & Lor-

rain, D. (1993). Copulation increases dopamine activity in the medial preoptic area of male rats. *Life Sciences, 52,* 935-940. (11)

Humphrey, P.P.A., Hartig, P., & Hoyer, D. (1993). A proposed new nomenclature for 5-HT receptors. *Trends in Pharmacological Sciences, 14,* 233-236. (3)

Hunter, W.S. (1923). *General Psychology* (revised edition). Chicago: University of Chicago Press. (4)

Huntington's Disease Collaborative Research Group (1993). A novel gene containing a trinucleotide repeat that is expanded and unstable on Huntington's disease chromosomes. *Cell, 72,* 971-983. (8)

Hurvich, L.M., & Jameson, D. (1957). An opponent-process theory of color vision. *Psychological Review, 64,* 384-404. (6)

Hyman, B.T., van Hoesen, G.W., Damasio, A.R., & Barnes, C.L. (1984). Alzheimer's disease: Cell-specific pathology isolates the hippocampal formation. *Science, 225,* 1168-1170. (13)

Hynd, G.W., & Semrud-Clikeman, M. (1989). Dyslexia and brain morphology. *Psychological Bulletin, 106,* 447-482. (14)

Iadecola, C. (1993). Regulation of the cerebral microcirculation during neural activity: Is nitric oxide the missing link? *Trends in Neurosciences, 16,* 206-214. (4)

Iggo, A., & Andres, K.H. (1982). Morphology of cutaneous receptors. *Annual Review of Neuroscience, 5,* 1-31. (7)

Imamura, K., Mataga, N., & Mori, K. (1992). Coding of odor molecules by mitral/tufted cells in rabbit olfactory bulb. I. Aliphatic compounds. *Journal of Neurophysiology, 68,* 1986-2002. (7)

Imperato-McGinley, J., Guerrero, L., Gautier, T., & Peterson, R.E. (1974). Steroid 5 alpha-reductase deficiency in man: An inherited form of male pseudohermaphroditism. *Science, 186,* 1213-1215. (11)

Innocenti, G.M. (1980). The primary visual pathway through the corpus callosum: Morphological and functional aspects in the cat. *Archives Italiennes de Biologie, 118,* 124-188. (14)

Innocenti, G.M., & Caminiti, R. (1980). Postnatal shaping of callosal connections from sensory areas. *Experimental Brain Research, 38,* 381-394. (14)

Innocenti, G.M., Frost, D.O., & Illes, J. (1985). Maturation of visual callosal connections in visually deprived kittens: A challenging critical period. *Journal of Neuroscience, 5,* 255-267. (14)

Inoué, S., Uchizono, K., & Nagasaki, H. (1982). Endogenous sleep-promoting factors. *Trends in Neurosciences, 5,* 218-220. (9)

Inouye, S.T., & Kawamura, H. (1979). Persistence of circadian rhythmicity in a mammalian hypothalamic "island" containing the suprachiasmatic nucleus. *Proceedings of the National Academy of Sciences, U.S.A., 76,* 5962-5966. (9)

Irwin, M., Daniels, M., Risch, S.C., Bloom, E., & Weiner, H. (1988). Plasma cortisol and natural killer cell activity during bereavement. *Biological Psychiatry, 24,* 173-178. (12)

Isaacson, R.L. (1972). Hippocampal destruction in man and other animals.

Neuropsychologia, 10, 47-64. (13)

Ivy, G.O., & Killackey, H.P. (1981). The ontogeny of the distribution of callosal projection neurons in the rat parietal cortex. *Journal of Comparative Neurology, 195,* 367-389. (14)

Izard, C. (1977). *Human emotions.* New York: Plenum. (12)

Jacobs, B.L. (1987). How hallucinogenic drugs work. *American Scientist, 75,* 386-392. (3)

Jancsó, G., Kiraly, E., & Jancsó-Gábor, A. (1977). Pharmacologically induced selective degeneration of chemosensitive primary sensory neurones. *Nature, 270,* 741-743. (7)

Janicak, P.G., Davis, J.M., Gibbons, R.D., Ericksen, S., Chang, S., & Gallagher, P. (1985). Efficacy of ECT: A meta-analysis. *American Journal of Psychiatry, 142,* 297-302. (15)

Janosik, E.H., & Davies, J.L. (1986). *Psychiatric mental health nursing.* Boston: Jones & Bartlett. (16)

Janowsky, J.S., Shimamura, A.P., Kritchevsky, M., & Squire, L.R. (1989). Cognitive impairment following frontal lobe damage and its relevance to human amnesia. *Behavioral Neuroscience, 103,* 548-560. (13)

Jarrard, L.E., Okaichi, H., Steward, O., & Goldschmidt, R.B. (1984). On the role of hippocampal connections in the performance of place and cue tasks: Comparisons with damage to hippocampus. *Behavioral Neuroscience, 98,* 946-954. (13)

Jaskiw, G.E., & Weinberger, D.R. (1992). Dopamine and schizophrenia—a cortically corrective perspective. *Seminars in the Neurosciences, 4,* 179-188. (16)

Jeddi, E. (1970). Confort du contact et thermoregulation comportementale [Contact comfort and behavioral thermoregulation]. *Physiology & Behavior, 5,* 1487-1493. (16)

Jeeves, M.A., & Temple, C.M. (1987). A further study of language function in callosal agenesis. *Brain and Language, 32,* 325-335. (14)

Jenner, P. (1990). Parkinson's disease: Clues to the cause of cell death in the substantia nigra. *Seminars in the Neurosciences, 2,* 117-126. (8)

Jenner, P., Schapira, A.H.V., & Marsden, C.D. (1992). New insights into the cause of Parkinson's disease. *Neurology, 42,* 2241-2250. (8)

Jerison, H.J. (1985). Animal intelligence as encephalization. *Philosophical Transactions of the Royal Society of London, B, 308,* 21-35. (5)

Jernigan, T.L., & Bellugi, U. (1994). Neuroanatomical distinctions between Williams and Down syndromes. In S.H. Broman & J. Grafman (Eds.), *Atypical cognitive deficits in developmental disorders* (pp. 57-66). Hillsdale, NJ: Lawrence Erlbaum. (14)

Jiao, S., Gurevich, V., & Wolff, J.A. (1993). Long-term correction of rat model of Parkinson's disease by gene therapy. *Nature, 362,* 450-453. (8)

Johns, T.R., & Thesleff, S. (1961). Effects of motor inactivation on the chemical sensitivity of skeletal muscle. *Acta Physiologica Scandinavica, 51,* 136-141. (15)

Johnson, D. (1990). Animal rights and

human lives: Time for scientists to right the balance. *Psychological Science, 1,* 213-214 . (1)

Johnson, L.C. (1969). Physiological and psychological changes following total sleep deprivation. In A. Kales (Ed.), *Sleep: Physiology & pathology* (pp. 206-220). Philadelphia: Lippincott. (9)

Johnson, M.H., Posner, M.I., & Rothbart, M.K. (1991). Components of visual orienting in early infancy: Contingency learning, anticipatory looking, and disengaging. *Journal of Cognitive Neuroscience, 3,* 335-344. (6)

Johnson, R.T. (1992). Retroviruses and nervous system disease. *Current Opinion in Neurobiology, 2,* 663-670. (16)

Johnson, W.G., & Wildman, H.E. (1983). Influence of external and covert food stimuli on insulin secretion in obese and normal subjects. *Behavioral Neuroscience, 97,* 1025-1028. (10)

Joly, E., Mucke, L., & Oldstone, M.B.A. (1991). Viral persistence in neurons explained by lack of major histocompatibility class I expression. *Science, 253,* 1283-1285. (2)

Jones, D.G. (1988). Influence of ethanol on neuronal and synaptic maturation in the central nervous system—morphological investigations. *Progress in Neurobiology, 31,* 171-197. (5)

Jones, E.G. (1985). *The thalamus.* New York: Plenum. (4)

Jones, H.S., & Oswald, I. (1968). Two cases of healthy insomnia. *Electroencephalography and Clinical Neurophysiology, 24,* 378-380. (9)

Jones, R.A. (1987). Cigarettes, respiratory rate, and the relaxation paradox. *International Journal of the Addictions, 22,* 803-809. (1)

Jordan, H.A. (1969). Voluntary intragastric feeding. *Journal of Comparative and Physiological Psychology, 68,* 498-506. (10)

Jouvet, M. (1960). Telencephalic and rhombencephalic sleep in the cat. In G.E.W. Wolstenholme & M. O'Connor (Eds.), *CIBA foundation symposium on the nature of sleep* (pp. 188-208). Boston: Little, Brown. (9)

Jouvet, M., & Delorme, F. (1965). Locus coeruleus et sommeil paradoxal [Locus coeruleus and paradoxical sleep]. *Comptes Rendus des Séances de la Société de Biologie, 159,* 895-899. (9)

Jouvet, M., & Renault, J. (1966). Insomnie persistante après lésions des noyaux du raphe chez le chat [Persistent insomnia after lesions of the raphe nuclei in the cat]. *Comptes Rendus des Séances de la Société de Biologie, 160,* 1461-1465. (9)

Kaas, J.H. (1983). What, if anything, is SI? Organization of first somatosensory area of cortex. *Physiological Reviews, 63,* 206-231. (7)

Kaas, J.H. (1989). Why does the brain have so many visual areas? *Journal of Cognitive Neuroscience, 1,* 121-135. (5, 6)

Kaas, J.H., & Krubitzer, L.A. (1991). The organization of extrastriate visual cortex. In B. Dreher & S.R. Robinson (Eds.), *Neuroanatomy of the visual pathways and their development* (Vision and visual dysfunction, Vol. 3). (pp. 302-323). Boca Raton, FL: CRC Press. (6)

Kaas, J.H., Merzenich, M.M., & Killackey, H.P. (1983). The reorganization of somatosensory cortex following peripheral nerve damage in adult and developing mammals. *Annual Review of Neuroscience, 6,* 325-356. (15)

Kaas, J.H., Nelson, R.J., Sur, M., Lin, C.-S., & Merzenich, M.M. (1979). Multiple representations of the body within the primary somatosensory cortex of primates. *Science, 204,* 521-523. (4)

Kahle, J.S., & Cotman, C.W. (1993). Synaptic reorganization in the hippocampus: An electrophysiological analysis. *Annals of the New York Academy of Sciences, 702,* 61-74. (15)

Kalat, J.W. (1978). Letter to the editor: Speculations on similarities between autism and opiate addiction. *Journal of Autism and Childhood Schizophrenia, 8,* 477-479. (16)

Kales, A., & Kales, J.D. (1984). *Evaluation and treatment of insomnia.* New York: Oxford. (9)

Kales, A., Scharf, M.B., & Kales, J.D. (1978). Rebound insomnia: A new clinical syndrome. *Science, 201,* 1039-1041. (9)

Kales, A., Soldatos, C.R., Bixler, E.O., & Kales, J.D. (1983). Early morning insomnia with rapidly eliminated benzodiazepines. *Science, 220,* 95-97. (9)

Kalil, K. (1990). Regeneration of pyramidal tract axons. In S.G. Waxman (Ed.), *Advances in neurology* (Vol. 47, pp. 67-85). New York: Raven Press. (15)

Kalsner, S. (1990). Heteroreceptors, autoreceptors, and other terminal sites. *Annals of the New York Academy of Sciences, 604,* 1-6. (3)

Kamarck, T., & Jennings, J.R. (1991). Biobehavioral factors in sudden cardiac death. *Psychological Bulletin, 109,* 42-75. (12)

Kamin, L.J. (1974). *The science and politics of IQ.* New York: Wiley. (A)

Kandel, E.R., & Schwartz, J.H. (1982). Molecular biology of learning: Modulation of transmitter release. *Science, 218,* 433-443. (13)

Kanner, L. (1943). Autistic disturbances of affective contact. *Nervous Child, 2,* 217-250. (16)

Kaplan, M.S. (1985). Formation and turnover of neurons in young and senescent animals: An electromicroscopic and morphometric analysis. *Annals of the New York Academy of Sciences, 457,* 173-192. (2)

Karmanova, I.G. (1982). *Evolution of sleep.* Basel: Karger. (9)

Karno, M., Golding, J.M., Sorenson, S.B., & Burnam, A. (1988). The epidemiology of obsessive-compulsive disorder in five US communities. *Archives of General Psychiatry, 45,* 1094-1099. (12)

Karrer, T., & Bartoshuk, L. (1991). Capsaicin desensitization and recovery on the human tongue. *Physiology & Behavior, 49,* 757-764. (7)

Kasper, S., Wehr, T.A., Bartko, J.J., Gaist, P.A., & Rosenthal, N.E. (1989). Epidemiological findings of seasonal changes in mood and behavior. *Archives of General Psychiatry, 46,* 823-833. (16)

Kawai, N. (1991). Neuroactive toxins of spider venoms. *Journal of Toxicology—Toxin Reviews, 10,* 131-167. (3)

Kaye, W.H., Berrettini, W., Gwirtsman, H., & George, D.T. (1990). Altered cerebrospinal fluid neuropeptide Y and peptide YY immunoreactivity in anorexia and bulimia nervosa. *Archives of General Psychiatry, 47,* 548-556. (10)

Kellar, K.J., & Stockmeier, C.A. (1986). Effects of electroconvulsive shock and serotonin axon lesions on beta-adrenergic and serotonin-2 receptors in rat brain. *Annals of the New York Academy of Sciences, 462,* 76-90. (16)

Kelso, S.R., Ganong, A.H., & Brown, T.H. (1986). Hebbian synapses in hippocampus. *Proceedings of the National Academy of Sciences, U.S.A., 83,* 5326-5330. (13)

Kelsoe, J.R., Ginns, E.I., Egeland, J.A., Gerhard, D.S., Goldstein, A.M., Bale, S.J., Pauls, D.L., Long, R.T., Kidd, K.K., Conte, G., Housman, D.E., & Paul, S.M. (1989). Re-evaluation of the linkage relationship between chromosome 11p loci and the gene for bipolar affective disorder in the Old Order Amish. *Nature, 342,* 238-243. (16)

Kendell, R.W., & Kemp, I.W. (1989). Maternal influenza in the etiology of schizophrenia. *Archives of General Psychiatry, 46,* 8 78-882. (16)

Kendler, K.S. (1983). Overview: A current perspective on twin studies of schizophrenia. *American Journal of Psychiatry, 140,* 1413-1425. (16)

Kendler, K.S., Heath, A.C., Neale, M.C., Kessler, R.C., & Eaves, L.J. (1993). Alcoholism and major depression in women. *Archives of General Psychiatry, 50,* 690-698. (16)

Kendler, K.S., Neale, M.C., Kessler, R.C., Heath, A.C., & Eaves, L.J. (1992). Major depression and generalized anxiety disorder. *Archives of General Psychiatry, 49,* 716-722. (16)

Kendler, K.S., & Robinette, C.D. (1983). Schizophrenia in the National Academy of Sciences-National Research Council twin registry—A 16-year update. *American Journal of Psychiatry, 140,* 1551-1563. (16)

Kennard, M.A. (1938). Reorganization of motor function in the cerebral cortex of monkeys deprived of motor and premotor areas in infancy. *Journal of Neurophysiology, 1,* 477-496. (15)

Kesner, R.P. (1990). Learning and memory in rats with an emphasis on the role of the hippocampal formation. In R.P. Kesner & D.S. Olton (Eds.), *Neurobiology of comparative cognition* (pp. 179-204). Hillsdale, NJ: Lawrence Erlbaum. (13)

Kessler, R.C., McGonagle, K.A., Zhao, S., Nelson, C.B., Hughes, M., Eshleman, S., Wittchen, H.-U., & Kendler, K.S. (1994). Lifetime and 12-month prevalence of *DSM-III-R* psychiatric disorders in the United States. *Archives of General Psychiatry, 51,* 8-19. (16)

Kessler, S. (1980). The genetics of schizophrenia: A review. *Schizophrenia Bulletin, 6,* 404-416. (16)

Kety, S.S. (1975). Progress toward an understanding of the biological substrates of schizophrenia. In R.R. Fieve, D. Rosenthal, & H. Brill (Eds.), *Genetic research in psychiatry* (pp. 15-26). Baltimore, MD: Johns Hopkins University Press. (16)

Kety, S.S., Rosenthal, D., Wender, P.H., Schulsinger, F., & Jacobsen, B. (1975).

Mental illness in the biological and adoptive families of adopted individuals who have become schizophrenic. In R.R. Fieve, D. Rosenthal, & H. Brill (Eds.), *Genetic research in psychiatry* (pp. 147-165). Baltimore, MD: Johns Hopkins University Press. (16)

Kiecolt-Glaser, J.K., & Glaser, R. (1993). Mind and immunity. In D. Goleman & J. Gurin (Eds.), *Mind body medicine* (pp. 39-61). Yonkers, NY: Consumer Reports Books. (12)

Killackey, H.P. (1990). Neocortical expansion: An attempt toward relating phylogeny and ontogeny. *Journal of Cognitive Neuroscience, 2*, 1-17. (4, 5)

Killackey, H.P., & Chalupa, L.M. (1986). Ontogenetic change in the distribution of callosal projection neurons in the postcentral gyrus of the fetal rhesus monkey. *Journal of Comparative Neurology, 244*, 331-348. (14)

Killeffer, F.A., & Stern, W.E. (1970). Chronic effects of hypothalamic injury. *Archives of Neurology, 22*, 419-429. (10)

Kim, J.J., Fanselow, M.S., DeCola, J.P., & Landeira-Fernandez, J. (1992). Selective impairment of long-term but not short-term conditional fear by the N-methyl-D-aspartate antagonist APV. *Behavioral Neuroscience, 106*, 591-596. (13)

Kim, J.S., & Kornhuber, H.H. (1982). The glutamate theory in schizophrenia: Clinical and experimental evidence. In N. Namba & H. Kaiya (Eds.), *Psychobiology of schizophrenia* (pp. 221-234). Oxford, England: Pergamon. (16)

Kim, M., & Davis, M. (1993). Electrolytic lesions of the amygdala block acquisition and expression of fear-potentiated startle even with extensive training but do not prevent reacquisition. *Behavioral Neuroscience, 107*, 580-595. (12)

Kimelberg, H.K., & Norenberg, M.D. (1989, April). Astrocytes. *Scientific American, 260*(4), 66-76. (2)

King, B.M., Smith, R.L., & Frohman, L.A. (1984). Hyperinsulinemia in rats with ventromedial hypothalamic lesions: Role of hyperphagia. *Behavioral Neuroscience, 98*, 152-155. (10)

Kinnamon, J.C. (1987). Organization and innervation of taste buds. In T.E. Finger and W.L. Silver (Eds.) *Neurobiology of taste and smell* (pp. 277-297). New York: John Wiley. (7)

Kinney, D.K., Woods, B.T., & Yurgelun-Todd, D. (1986). Neurologic abnormalities in schizophrenic patients and their families. *Archives of General Psychiatry, 43*, 665-668. (16)

Kinsbourne, M., & McMurray, J. (1975). The effect of cerebral dominance on time sharing between speaking and tapping by preschool children. *Child Development, 46*, 240-242. (14)

Klein, D.F. (1993). False suffocation alarms, spontaneous panics, and related conditions. *Archives of General Psychiatry, 50*, 306-317. (12)

Klein, T., Martens, H., Dijk, D.-J., Kronauer, R.E., Seely, E.W., & Czeisler, C.A. (1993). Circadian sleep regulation in the absence of light perception: Chronic non-24-hour circadian rhythm sleep disorder in a blind man with a regular 24-hour sleep-wake schedule. *Sleep, 16*, 333-343. (9)

Kleinman, J.E., Karson, C.N., Weinberger,

D.R., Freed, W.J., Berman, K.F., & Wyatt, R.J. (1984). Eye-blinking and cerebral ventricular size in chronic schizophrenic patients. *American Journal of Psychiatry, 141*, 1430-1432. (16)

Kleinschmidt, A., Bear, M.F., & Singer, W. (1987). Blockade of "NMDA" receptors disrupts experience-dependent plasticity of kitten striate cortex. *Science, 238*, 355-358. (13)

Kleitman, N. (1963). *Sleep and wakefulness* (rev. ed.). Chicago: University of Chicago Press. (9)

Klerman, G.L. (1975). Relationships between preclinical testing and therapeutic evaluation of antidepressive drugs: The importance of new animal models for theory and practice. In A. Sudilovsky, S. Gershon, & B. Beer (Eds.), *Predictability in psychopharmacology* (pp. 159-178). New York: Raven. (16)

Kluger, M.J. (1978). The evolution and adaptive value of fever. *American Scientist, 66*, 38-43. (10)

Kluger, M.J., & Rothenburg, B.A. (1979). Fever and reduced iron: Their interaction as a host defense response to bacterial infection. *Science, 203*, 374-376. (10)

Kluger, M.J., & Vaughn, L.K. (1978). Fever and survival in rabbits infected with *Pasteurella multocida*. *Journal of Physiology, 282*, 243-251. (10)

Klüver, H., & Bucy, P.C. (1939). Preliminary analysis of functions of the temporal lobes in monkeys. *Archives of Neurology and Psychiatry, 42*, 979-1000. (4)

Knierim, J.J., & Van Essen, D.C. (1992). Visual cortex: Cartography, connectivity, and concurrent processing. *Current Opinion in Neurobiology, 2*, 150-155. (6)

Knudsen, E.I., & Konishi, M. (1978). Space and frequency are represented separately in the auditory midbrain of the owl. *Journal of Neurophysiology, 41*, 870-884. (7)

Knüsel, B., Beck, K.D., Winslow, J.W., Rosenthal, A., Burton, L.E., Widmer, H.R., Nicolics, K., & Hefti, F. (1992). Brain-derived neurotrophic factor administration protects basal forebrain cholinergic but not nigral dopaminergic neurons from degenerative changes after axotomy in the adult rat brain. *Journal of Neuroscience, 12*, 4391-4402. (15)

Koch, C., & Zador, A. (1993). The function of dendritic spines: Devices subserving biochemical rather than electrical compartmentalization. *Journal of Neuroscience, 13*, 413-422. (2)

Kochhar, A., Zivin, J.A., Lyden, P.D., & Mazzarella, V. (1988). Glutamate antagonist therapy reduces neurologic deficits produced by focal central nervous system ischemia. *Archives of Neurology, 45*, 148-153. (15)

Kodama, J., Fukushima, M., & Sakata, T. (1978). Impaired taste discrimination against quinine following chronic administration of theophylline in rats. *Physiology & Behavior, 20*, 151-155. (7)

Koegel, R.L., Schreibman, L., O'Neill, R.E., & Burke, J.C. (1983). The personality and family-interaction characteristics of parents of autistic children. *Journal of Consulting & Clinical Psychology, 51*, 683-692. (16)

Kolb, B., & Gibb, R. (1993). Possible

anatomical basis of recovery of function after neonatal frontal lesions in rats. *Behavioral Neuroscience, 107*, 799-811. (15)

Kolb, B., & Holmes, C. (1983). Neonatal motor cortex lesions in the rat: Absence of sparing of motor behaviors and impaired spatial learning concurrent with abnormal cerebral morphogenesis. *Behavioral Neuroscience, 97*, 697-709. (15)

Kolb, B., Sutherland, R.J., & Whishaw, I.Q. (1983). Abnormalities in cortical and subcortical morphology after neonatal neocortical lesions in rats. *Experimental Neurology, 79*, 223-244. (15)

Kolb, B., & Taylor, L. (1981). Affective behavior in patients with localized cortical excisions: Role of lesion site and side. *Science, 214*, 89-90. (13, 16)

Kolb, B., & Whishaw, I.Q. (1977). Effects of brain lesions and atropine on hippocampal and neocortical electroencephalograms in the rat. *Experimental Neurology, 56*, 1-22. (15)

Kolb, B., & Whishaw, I.Q. (1989). Plasticity in the neocortex: Mechanisms underlying recovery from early brain damage. *Progress in Neurobiology, 32*, 235-276. (15)

Koller, W.C. (1992). How accurately can Parkinson's disease be diagnosed? *Neurology, 42* (Suppl. 1), 6-16. (8)

Komisaruk, B.R., Adler, N.T., & Hutchison, J. (1972). Genital sensory field: Enlargement by estrogen treatment in female rats. *Science, 178*, 1295-1298. (11)

Konishi, M. (1969). Hearing, single-unit analysis, and vocalizations in songbirds. *Science, 166*, 1178-1181. (1)

Koran, L.M., Sox, H.C., Jr., Marton, K.I., Moltzen, S., Sox, C.H., Kraemer, H.C., Imai, K., Kelsey, T.G., Rose, T.G., Jr., Levin, L.C., & Chandra, S. (1989). Medical evaluation of psychiatric patients. *Archives of General Psychiatry, 46*, 733-740. (16)

Kornhuber, H.H. (1974). Cerebral cortex, cerebellum, and basal ganglia: An introduction to their motor functions. In F.O. Schmitt & F.G. Worden (Eds.), *The neurosciences: Third study program* (pp. 267-280). Cambridge, MA: MIT Press. (8)

Kornhuber, H.H. (1983). Chemistry, physiology and neuropsychology of schizophrenia: Towards an earlier diagnosis of schizophrenia I. *Archiv für Psychiatrie und Nervenkrankheiten, 233*, 415-422. (16)

Kowall, N.W., Beal, M.F., Busciglio, J., Duffy, L.K., & Yankner, B.A. (1991). An *in vivo* model for the neurodegenerative effects of β amyloid and protection by substance P. *Proceedings of the National Academy of Sciences (U.S.A.), 88*, 7247-7251. (13)

Kraly, F.S. (1990). Drinking elicited by eating. *Progress in Psychobiology and Physiological Psychology, 14*, 67-133. (10)

Kramer, P.D. (1993). *Listening to Prozac*. New York: Viking. (16)

Kringlen, E., & Cramer, G. (1989). Offspring of monozygotic twins discordant for schizophrenia. *Archives of General Psychiatry, 46*, 873-877. (16)

Krnjević, K., & Reinhardt, W. (1979). Choline excites cortical neurons. *Science, 206*, 1321-1323. (3)

Kromer, L.F., & Cornbrooks, C.J. (1985). Transplants of Schwann cell cultures promote axonal regeneration in the adult mammalian brain. *Proceedings of the National Academy of Sciences (U.S.A.), 82*, 6330-6334. (15)

Kroodsma, D.E. (1976). Reproductive development in a female songbird: Differential stimulation by quality of male song. *Science, 192*, 574-575. (1)

Kroodsma, D.E., & Miller, E.H. (1982). Introduction. In D.E. Kroodsma & E.H. Miller (Eds.), *Acoustic communication in birds* (Vol. 1, pp. xxi-xxxvi). New York: Academic Press. (1)

Krueger, J.M., Pappenheimer, J.R., & Karnovsky, M.L. (1982). The composition of sleep-promoting factor isolated from human urine. *Journal of Biological Chemistry, 257*, 1664-1669. (9)

Kruesi, M.J.P., Hibbs, E.D., Zahn, T.P., Keysor, C.S., Hamburger, S.D., Bartko, J.J., & Rapoport, J.L. (1992). A 2-year prospective follow-up of children and adolescents with disruptive behavior disorders. *Archives of General Psychiatry, 49*, 429-435. (12)

Krupa, D.J., Thompson, J.K., & Thompson, R.F. (1993). Localization of a memory trace in the mammalian brain. *Science, 260*, 989-991. (13)

Kryger, M. (Ed.), with perspectives by C. Guilleminault, J.D. Parkes, M. Dahlitz, M. Mitler, M. Erman, & R. Hajdukovic. (1993). Amphetamines and narcolepsy. *Sleep, 16*, 199-206. (9)

Kupfermann, I., Castellucci, V., Pinsker, H., & Kandel, E. (1970). Neuronal correlates of habituation and dishabituation of the gill withdrawal reflex in *Aplysia. Science, 167*, 1743-1745. (13)

Kurtzke, J.R. (1976). An introduction to the epidemiology of cerebrovascular disease. In F. Scheinberg (Ed.), *Cerebrovascular diseases* (pp. 239-253). New York: Raven. (15)

Kuypers, H.G.J.M. (1989). Motor system organization. In G. Adelman (Ed.), *Neuroscience year* (pp. 107-110). Boston: Birkhäuser. (8)

Lagarde, D., Laurent, J., Milhaud, C., Andre, E., Aubin, H.J., & Anton, G. (1990). Behavioral effects induced by beta CCE in free or restrained rhesus monkeys (*Macaca mulatta*). *Pharmacology Biochemistry & Behavior, 35*, 713-719. (12)

Lague, L., Raiguel, S., & Orban, G.A. (1993). Speed and direction selectivity of macaque middle temporal neurons. *Journal of Neurophysiology, 69*, 19-39. (6)

LaHoste, G.J., & Marshall, J.F. (1989). Non-additivity of D2 receptor proliferation induced by dopamine denervation and chronic selective antagonist administration: Evidence from quantitative autoradiography indicates a single mechanism of action. *Brain Research, 502*, 223-232. (15)

Lai, Y.Y., & Siegel, J.M. (1991). Pontomedullary glutamate receptors mediating locomotion and muscle tone suppression. *Journal of Neuroscience, 11*, 2931-2937. (9)

LaMantia, A.-S., & Purves, D. (1989). Development of glomerular pattern visualized in the olfactory bulbs of living mice. *Nature, 341*, 646-649. (5)

Lamb, M.E. (1975). Physiological mechanisms in the control of maternal behavior in rats: A review. *Psychological Review, 82*, 104-119. (11)

Lamb, T.D., & Pugh, E.N., Jr. (1990). Physiology of transduction and adaptation in rod and cone photoreceptors. *Seminars in the Neurosciences, 2*, 3-13. (6)

Land, E.H., Hubel, D.H., Livingstone, M.S., Perry, S.H., & Burns, M.M. (1983). Colour-generating interactions across the corpus callosum. *Nature, 303*, 616-618. (6)

Land, E.H., & McCann, J.J. (1971). Lightness and retinex theory. *Journal of the Optical Society of America, 61*, 1-11. (6)

Land, M.F., & Fernald, R.D. (1992). The evolution of eyes. *Annual Review of Neuroscience, 15*, 1-29. (6)

Landau, W.M. (1993). Clinical neuromythology X. Faithful fashion: Survival status of the brain transplant cure for parkinsonism. *Neurology, 43*, 644-649. (15)

Landis, D.M.D. (1987). Initial junctions between developing parallel fibers and Purkinje cells are different from mature synaptic junctions. *Journal of Comparative Neurology, 260*, 513-525. (3)

Lang, R.A., Flor-Henry, P., & Frenzel, R.R. (1990). Sex hormone profiles in pedophilic and incestuous men. *Annals of Sex Research, 3*, 59-74. (11)

Langworthy, R.A., & Jennings, J.W. (1972). Oddball, abstract olfactory learning in laboratory rats. *Psychological Record, 22*, 487-490. (5)

Lashley, K.S. (1929). *Brain mechanisms and intelligence.* Chicago: University of Chicago Press. (4, 13)

Lashley, K.S. (1930). Basic neural mechanisms in behavior. *Psychological Review, 37*, 1-24. (inside cover)

Lashley, K.S. (1950). In search of the engram. *Symposia of the Society for Experimental Biology, 4*, 454-482. (13)

Lassonde, M., Bryden, M.P., & Demers, P. (1990). The corpus callosum and cerebral speech lateralization. *Brain and Language, 38*, 195-206. (14)

Laudenslager, M.L. (1976). Proportional hypothalamic control of behavioral thermoregulation in the squirrel monkey. *Physiology & Behavior, 17*, 383-390. (10)

Laurent, J.-P., Cespuglio, R., & Jouvet, M. (1974). Dèlimitation des voies ascendantes de l'activité ponto-géniculo-occipitale chez le chat [Demarcation of the ascending paths of ponto-geniculo-occipital activity in the cat]. *Brain Research, 65*, 29-52. (9)

LeDoux, J.E., Iwata, J., Cicchetti, P., & Reis, D.J. (1988). Different projections of the central amygdaloid nucleus mediate autonomic and behavioral correlates of conditioned fear. *Journal of Neuroscience, 8*, 2517-2529. (12)

Lee, M.K., Graham, S.N., & Gold, P.E. (1988). Memory enhancement with post-training intraventricular glucose injections in rats. *Behavioral Neuroscience, 102*, 591-595. (13)

Lees, G.J. (1993). The possible contribution of microglia and macrophages to delayed neuronal death after ischemia. *Journal of the Neurological Sciences, 114*, 119-122. (2)

Lehrman, D.S. (1964). The reproductive behavior of ring doves. *Scientific American, 211*(5), 48-54. (11)

Leibowitz, S.F., & Alexander, J.T. (1991). Analysis of neuropeptide Y-induced feeding: Dissociation of Y1 and Y2 receptor effects on natural meal patterns. *Peptides, 12*, 1251-1260. (10)

Leibowitz, S.F., Alexander, J.T., Cheung, W.K., & Weiss, G.F. (1993). Effects of serotonin and the serotonin blocker metergoline on meal patterns and macronutrient selection. *Pharmacology Biochemistry & Behavior, 45*, 185-194. (10)

Leibowitz, S.F., Hammer, N.J., & Chang, K. (1981). Hypothalamic paraventricular nucleus lesions produce overeating and obesity in the rat. *Physiology & Behavior, 27*, 1031-1040. (10)

Leibowitz, S.F., Weiss, G.F., & Suh, J.S. (1990). Medial hypothalamic nuclei mediate serotonin's inhibitory effect on feeding behavior. *Pharmacology Biochemistry & Behavior, 37*, 735-742. (10)

Leiner, H.C., Leiner, A.L., & Dow, R.S. (1989). Reappraising the cerebellum: What does the hindbrain contribute to the forebrain? *Behavioral Neuroscience, 103*, 998-1008. (4)

LeMagnen, J. (1981). The metabolic basis of dual periodicity of feeding in rats. *Behavioral and Brain Sciences, 4*, 561-607. (10)

Lenhart, R.E., & Katkin, E.S. (1986). Psychophysiological evidence for cerebral laterality effects in a high-risk sample of students with subsyndromal bipolar depressive disorder. *American Journal of Psychiatry, 143*, 602-607. (16)

Lennartz, R.C., & Weinberger, N.M. (1992). Frequency-specific receptive field plasticity in the medial geniculate body induced by Pavlovian fear conditioning is expressed in the anesthetized brain. *Behavioral Neuroscience, 106*, 484-497. (13)

Lentz, T.L., Burrage, T.G., Smith, A.L., Crick, J., & Tignor, G.H. (1982). Is the acetylcholine receptor a rabies virus receptor? *Science, 215*, 182-184. (12)

Leonard, H.L., Swedo, S.E., Rapoport, J.L., Koby, E.V., Lenane, M.C., Cheslow, D.L., & Hamburger, S.D. (1989). Treatment of obsessive-compulsive disorder with clomipramine and desipramine in children and adolescents. *Archives of General Psychiatry, 46*, 1088-1092. (12)

Lerer, B., & Shapira, B. (1986). Neurochemical mechanisms of mood stabilization. *Annals of the New York Academy of Sciences, 462*, 367-375. (15)

Lesse, S. (1984). Psychosurgery. *American Journal of Psychotherapy, 38*, 224-228. (4)

Lester, L.S., & Fanselow, M.S. (1985). Exposure to a cat produces opioid analgesia in rats. *Behavioral Neuroscience, 99*, 756-759. (7)

Lettvin, J.Y., Maturana, H.R., McCulloch, W.S., & Pitts, W.H. (1959). What the frog's eye tells the frog's brain. *Proceedings of the Institute of Radio Engineers, 47*, 1940-1951. (7)

LeVay, S. (1991). A difference in hypothalamic structure between heterosexual and homosexual men. *Science, 253*, 1034-1037. (11)

LeVay, S. (1993). *The sexual brain*. Cambridge, MA: MIT Press. (11)

LeVere, N.D., & LeVere, T.E. (1982). Recovery of function after brain damage: Support for the compensation theory of the behavioral deficit. *Physiological Psychology, 10*, 165-174. (15)

LeVere, T.E. (1975). Neural stability, sparing and behavioral recovery following brain damage. *Psychological Review, 82*, 344-358. (15)

LeVere, T.E. (1980). Recovery of function after brain damage: A theory of the behavioral deficit. *Physiological Psychology, 8*, 297-308. (15)

LeVere, T.E. (1993). Recovery of function after brain damage: The effects of nimodipine on the chronic behavioral deficit. *Psychobiology, 21*, 125-129. (15)

LeVere, T.E., Brugler, T., Sandin, M., & Gray-Silva, S. (1989). Recovery of function after brain damage: Facilitation by the calcium entry blocker nimodipine. *Behavioral Neuroscience, 103*, 561-565. (15)

LeVere, T.E., & Morlock, G.W. (1973). Nature of visual recovery following posterior neodecortication in the hooded rat. *Journal of Comparative and Physiological Psychology, 83*, 62-67. (15)

Levi-Montalcini, R. (1987). The nerve growth factor 35 years later. *Science, 237*, 1154-1162. (5)

Levine, B., Hardwick, J.M., Trapp, B.D., Crawford, T.O., Bollinger, R.C., & Griffin, D.E. (1991). Antibody-mediated clearance of alphavirus infection from neurons. *Science, 254*, 856-860. (2)

Levine, D.N., Warach, J.D., Benowitz, L., & Calvanio, R. (1986). Left spatial neglect: Effects of lesion size and premorbid brain atrophy on severity and recovery following right cerebral infarction. *Neurology, 36*, 362-366. (4)

Levine, J.D., Fields, H.L., & Basbaum, A.I. (1993). Peptides and the primary afferent nociceptor. *Journal of Neuroscience, 13*, 2273-2286. (7)

Levitt, R.A. (1975). *Psychopharmacology*. Washington, DC: Hemisphere. (16)

Levitt-Gilmour, T.A., & Salpeter, M.M. (1986). Gradient of extrajunctional acetylcholine receptors early after denervation of mammalian muscle. *Journal of Neuroscience, 6*, 1606-1612. (15)

Levitzki, A. (1988). From epinephrine to cyclic AMP. *Science, 241*, 800-806. (3)

Levy, J. (1983). Language, cognition, and the right hemisphere: A response to Gazzaniga. *American Psychologist, 38*, 538-541. (14)

Levy, J., Heller, W., Banich, M.T., & Burton, L.A. (1983). Asymmetry of perception in free viewing of chimeric faces. *Brain and Cognition, 2*, 404-419. (14)

Levy, J., Nebes, R.D., & Sperry, R.W. (1971). Expressive language in the surgically separated minor hemisphere. *Cortex, 7*, 49-58. (14)

Lewine, R.R.J. (1981). Sex differences in schizophrenia: Timing or subtypes? *Psychological Bulletin, 90*, 432-444. (16)

Lewis, E.R., Everhart, T.E., & Zeevi, Y.Y. (1969). Studying neural organization in *Aplysia* with the scanning electron microscope. *Science, 165*, 1140-1143. (3)

Lewis, V.G., Money, J., & Epstein, R. (1968). Concordance of verbal and nonverbal ability in the adrenogenital syndrome. *Johns Hopkins Medical Journal, 122*, 192-195. (11)

Lewy, A.J., Nurnberger, J.I., Jr., Wehr, T.A., Pack, D., Becker, L.E., Powell, R.-L., Newsome, D.A. (1985). Supersensitivity to light: Possible trait marker for manic-depressive illness. *American Journal of Psychiatry, 142*, 725-727. (16)

Lieberman, J.A., Jody, D., Alvir, J.M.J., Ashtari, M., Levy, D.L., Bogerts, B., Degreef, G., Mayerhoff, D.I., & Cooper, T. (1993). Brain morphology, dopamine, and eye-tracking abnormalities in first-episode schizophrenia. *Archives of General Psychiatry, 50*, 357-368. (16)

Liebeskind, J.C., & Paul, L.A. (1977). Psychological and physiological mechanisms of pain. *Annual Review of Psychology, 28*, 41-60. (7)

Lilienfeld, A. (1969). *Epidemiology of mongolism*. Baltimore, MD: Johns Hopkins University Press. (A)

Lin, L.-F., Doherty, D.H., Lile, J.D., Bektesh, S., & Collins, F. (1993). GDNF: A glial cell line-derived neurotrophic factor for midbrain dopaminergic neruons. *Science, 260*, 1130-1132. (5)

Lindberg, N.O., Coburn, C., & Stricker, E.M. (1984). Increased feeding by rats after subdiabetogenic streptozotocin treatment: A role for insulin in satiety. *Behavioral Neuroscience, 98*, 138-145. (10)

Lindsay, P.H., & Norman, D.A. (1972). *Human information processing*. New York: Academic Press. (7)

Lindstrom, J. (1979). Autoimmune response to acetylcholine receptors in myasthenia gravis and its animal model. *Advances in Immunology, 27*, 1-50. (3, 8)

Lipton, M.A., & Nemeroff, C.B. (1978). An overview of the biogenic amine hypothesis of schizophrenia. In W.E. Fann, I. Karacan, A. Pokorny, & R.L. Williams (Eds.), *Phenomenology and treatment of schizophrenia* (pp. 431-453). New York: Spectrum. (16)

Livingstone, M.S. (1988, January). Art, illusion and the visual system. *Scientific American, 258*(1), 78-85. (6)

Livingstone, M.S., & Hubel, D. (1988). Segregation of form, color, movement, and depth: Anatomy, physiology, and perception. *Science, 240*, 740-749. (6)

Livingstone, M.S., Rosen, G.D., Drislane, F.W., & Galaburda, A.M. (1991). Physiological and anatomical evidence for a magnocellular defect in developmental dyslexia. *Proceedings of the National Academy of Sciences (U.S.A.), 88*, 7943-7947. (14)

Llinás, R.R. (1975, January). The cortex of the cerebellum. *Scientific American, 232*(1), 56-71. (8)

Loewenstein, W.R. (1960, August). Biological transducers. *Scientific American, 203*(2), 98-108. (7)

Loewi, O. (1960). An autobiographic sketch. *Perspectives in Biology, 4*, 3-25. (3)

Logothetis, N.K. (1991). Is movement perception color blind? *Current Biology, 1*, 298-300. (6)

London, E.D., Cascella, N.G., Wong, D.F., Phillips, R.L., Dannals, R.F., Links, J.M., Herning, R., Grayson, R., Jaffe, J.H., & Wagner, H.N. (1990). Cocaine-induced reduction of glucose utilization in human brain. *Archives of General Psychiatry, 47*, 567-574. (3)

Loring, D.W., Meador, K.J., Lee, G.P., Murro, A.M., Smith, J.R., Flanigin, H.F., Gallagher, B.B., & King, D.W. (1990). Cerebral language lateralization: Evidence from intracarotid amobarbital testing. *Neuropsychologia, 28*, 831-838. (14)

Lott, I.T. (1982). Down's syndrome, aging, and Alzheimer's disease: A clinical review. *Annals of the New York Academy of Sciences, 396*, 15-27. (13)

Lowing, P.A., Mirsky, A.F., & Pereira, R. (1983). The inheritance of schizophrenia spectrum disorders: A reanalysis of the Danish adoptee study plan. *American Journal of Psychiatry, 140*, 1167-1171. (16)

Luciana, M., Depue, R.A., Arbisi, P., & Leon, A. (1992). Facilitation of working memory in humans by a D_2 dopamine receptor agonist. *Journal of Cognitive Neuroscience, 4*, 58-68. (13)

Lund, R.D., Lund, J.S., & Wise, R.P. (1974). The organization of the retinal projection to the dorsal lateral geniculate nucleus in pigmented and albino rats. *Journal of Comparative Neurology, 158*, 383-404. (6)

Lurito, J.T., Georgakopoulos, T., & Georgopoulos, A.P. (1991). Cognitive spatial-motor processes. 7. The making of movements at an angle from a stimulus direction: Studies of motor cortical activity at the single cell and population levels. *Experimental Brain Research, 87*, 562-580. (8)

Lyman, C.P., O'Brien, R.C., Greene, G.C., & Papafrangos, E.D. (1981). Hibernation and longevity in the Turkish hamster *Mesocricetus brandti*. *Science, 212*, 668-670. (9)

Lynch, G., & Baudry, M. (1991). Reevaluating the constraints on hypotheses regarding LTP expression. *Hippocampus, 1*, 9-14. (13)

Lynch, J.A., & Aserinsky, E. (1986). Developmental changes of oculomotor characteristics in infants when awake and in the "active state of sleep." *Behavioural Brain Research, 20*, 175-183. (9)

Lynch, J.C. (1980). The functional organization of posterior parietal association cortex. *The Behavioral and Brain Sciences, 3*, 485-534. (4)

Lytle, L.D., Messing, R.B., Fisher, L., & Phebus, L. (1975). Effects of long-term corn consumption on brain serotonin and the response to electric shock. *Science, 190*, 692-694. (12)

Maccoby, E.E., & Jacklin, C.N. (1974). *The psychology of sex differences*. Stanford, CA: Stanford University Press. (11)

Macdonald, R.L., Weddle, M.G., & Gross, R.A. (1986). Benzodiazepine, β-carboline, and barbiturate actions on GABA responses. *Advances in Biochemical Psychopharmacology, 41*, 67-78. (12)

MacFarlane, J.G., Cleghorn, J.M., & Brown, G.M. (1985a). Melatonin and core temperature rhythms in chronic insomnia. In G.M. Brown & S.D. Wainwright (Eds.), *The pineal gland: Endocrine aspects* (pp. 301-306). New York: Pergamon. (9)

MacFarlane, J.G., Cleghorn, J.M., & Brown, G.M. (1985b, September). *Circadian rhythms in chronic insomnia*. Paper presented at the 4th World Congress of *Biological Psychiatry*, Philadelphia. (9)

MacLean, P.D. (1949). Psychosomatic disease and the "visceral brain": Recent developments bearing on the Papez theory of emotion. *Psychosomatic Medicine, 11*, 338-353. (12)

MacLean, P.D. (1954). Studies on limbic system ("visceral brain") and their bearing on psychosomatic problems. In E.D. Wittkower & R.A. Cleghorn (Eds.), *Recent developments in psychosomatic medicine* (pp. 101-125). Philadelphia: Lippincott. (12)

MacLean, P.D. (1958). Contrasting functions of limbic and neocortical systems of the brain and their relevance to psychophysiological aspects of medicine. *American Journal of Medicine, 25*, 611-626. (12)

MacLean, P.D. (1962). Neurophysiologie. In *Monoamines et système nerveux central* (pp. 269-276). Geneva: Georg a Cie, 1962. (16)

MacLean, P.D. (1970). The limbic brain in relation to the psychoses. In P. Black (Ed.), *Physiological correlates of emotion* (pp. 129-146). New York: Academic Press. (12)

MacLusky, N.J., & Naftolin, F. (1981). Sexual differentiation of the central nervous system. *Science, 211*, 1294-1303. (11)

Macphail, E.M. (1985). Vertebrate intelligence: The null hypothesis. *Philosophical Transactions of the Royal Society of London, B, 308*, 37-51. (4)

Mahowald, M.W., & Schenck, C.H. (1992). Dissociated states of wakefulness and sleep. *Neurology, 42* (Suppl. 6), 44-52. (9)

Majewska, M.D., Harrison, N.L., Schwartz, R.D., Barker, J.L., & Paul, S.M. (1986). Steroid hormone metabolites are barbiturate-like modulators of the GABA receptors. *Science, 232*, 1004-1007. (12)

Malcuit, G. (1973). Cardiac responses in aversive situation with and without avoidance possibility. *Psychophysiology, 10*, 295-306. (12)

Mangiapane, M.L., & Simpson, J.B. (1980). Subfornical organ: Forebrain site of pressor and dipsogenic action of angiotensin II. *American Journal of Physiology, 239*, R382-R389. (10)

Mangiapane, M.L., Thrasher, T.N., Keil, L.C., Simpson, J.B., & Ganong, W.F. (1983). Deficits in drinking and vasopressin secretion after lesions of the nucleus medianus. *Neuroendocrinology, 37*, 73-77. (10)

Mann, J.J., Arango, V., & Underwood, M.D. (1990). Serotonin and suicidal behavior. *Annals of the New York Academy of Sciences, 600*, 476-485. (12)

Mann, J.J., Stanley, M., McBride, A., & McEwen, B.S. (1986). Increased serotonin$_2$ and β-adrenergic receptor binding in the frontal cortices of suicide victims. *Archives of General Psychiatry, 43*, 954-959. (12)

Marcus, J., Hans, S.L., Mednick, S.A., Schulsinger, F., & Michelsen, N. (1985). Neurological dysfunctioning in offspring of schizophrenics in Israel and Denmark. *Archives of General Psychiatry, 42*, 753-761. (16)

Margolskee, R.F. (1993). The biochemistry and molecular biology of taste transduction. *Current Opinion in Neurobiology, 3*, 526-531. (7)

Mark, V.H., & Ervin, F.R. (1970). *Violence and the brain*. New York: Harper & Row. (12)

Markham, C.H., & Diamond, S.G. (1981). Evidence to support early levodopa therapy in Parkinson disease. *Neurology, 31*, 124-131. (8)

Marler, J.R., Price, T.R., Clark, G.L., Muller, J.E., Robertson, T., Mohr, J.P., Hier, D.B., Wolf, P.A., Caplan, L.R., & Foulkes, M.A. (1989). Morning increase in onset of ischemic stroke. *Stroke, 20*, 473-476. (15)

Marler, P. (1970). A comparative approach to vocal learning: Song development in white-crowned sparrows. *Journal of Comparative and Physiological Psychology, 71* (No. 2, Pt. 2), 1-25. (1)

Marler, P., & Nelson, D. (1992). Neuroselection and song learning in birds: Species universals in a culturally transmitted behavior. *Seminars in the Neurosciences, 4*, 415-423. (5)

Marler, P., & Peters, S. (1977). Selective vocal learning in a sparrow. *Science, 198*, 519-521. (1)

Marler, P., & Peters, S. (1981). Sparrows learn adult song and more from memory. *Science, 213*, 780-782. (1)

Marler, P., & Peters, S. (1982). Long-term storage of learned birdsongs prior to production. *Animal Behaviour, 30*, 479-482. (1)

Marler, P., & Peters, S. (1987). A sensitive period for song acquisition in the song sparrow, *Melospiza melodia*: A case of age-limited learning. *Ethology, 76*, 89-100. (1)

Marler, P., & Peters, S. (1988). Sensitive periods for song acquisition from tape recordings and live tutors in the swamp sparrow, *Melospiza georgiana*. *Ethology, 77*, 76-84. (1)

Marques, P.R., Spencer, R.L., Burks, T.F., & McDougal, J.N. (1984). Behavioral thermoregulation, core temperature, and motor activity: Simultaneous quantitative assessment in rats after dopamine and prostaglandin E1. *Behavioral Neuroscience, 98*, 858-867. (10)

Marrocco, R.T. (1986). The neurobiology of perception. In J.E. LeDoux & W. Hirst (Eds.), *Mind and brain* (pp. 33-88). Cambridge, England: Cambridge University Press. (6)

Marsden, C.D. (1984). Motor disorders in basal ganglia disease. *Human Neurobiology, 2*, 245-250. (8)

Marsden, C.D. (1992). Dopamine and basal ganglia disorders in humans. *Seminars in the Neurosciences, 4*, 171-178. (8)

Marshall, J.C., & Halligan, P.W. (1990). Line bisection in a case of visual neglect: Psychophysical studies with implications for theory. *Cognitive Neuropsychology, 7*, 107-130. (4)

Marshall, J.F. (1985). Neural plasticity and recovery of function after brain injury. *International Review of Neurobiology, 26*, 201-247. (15)

Marshall, J.F., Drew, M.C., & Neve, K.A. (1983). Recovery of function after mesotelencephalic dopaminergic injury in senescence. *Brain Research, 259*, 249-260. (15)

Marshall, P.S. (1993). Allergy and depression: A neurochemical threshold model of the relation between the illnesses. *Psychological Bulletin, 113*, 23-43. (16)

Martin, A.R. (1977). Junctional transmission. II. Presynaptic mechanisms. In E.R. Kandel (Ed.), *Handbook of physiology* (Sect. 1, Vol. 1, Pt. 1, pp. 329-355). Bethesda, MD: American Physiological Society. (3)

Martin, J.V., Cook, J.M., Hagen, T.J., & Mendelson, W.B. (1989). Inhibition of sleep and benzodiazepine receptor binding by a beta-carboline derivative. *Pharmacology Biochemistry & Behavior, 34*, 37-42. (12)

Martin, R.C., & Blossom-Stach, C. (1986). Evidence of syntactic deficits in a fluent aphasic. *Brain and Language, 28*, 196-234. (14)

Martinez, J.L., Jr., Jensen, R.A., & McGaugh, J.L. (1981). Attenuation of experimentally induced amnesia. *Progress in Neurobiology, 16*, 155-186. (13)

Martinez-Vargas, M.C., & Erickson, C.J. (1973). Some social and hormonal determinants of nest-building behaviour in the ring dove (*Streptopelia risoria*). *Behaviour, 45*, 12-37. (11)

Mash, D.C., Flynn, D.D., & Potter, L.T. (1985). Loss of M2 muscarine receptors in the cerebral cortex in Alzheimer's disease and experimental cholinergic denervation. *Science, 228*, 1115-1117. (13)

Masterton, R.B. (1974). Adaptation for sound localization in the ear and brainstem of mammals. *Federation Proceedings, 33*, 1904-1910. (7)

Matthews, D.A., Cotman, C., & Lynch, G. (1976). An electron microscopic study of lesion-induced synaptogenesis in the dentate gyrus of the adult rat. II. Reappearance of morphologically normal synaptic contacts. *Brain Research, 115*, 23-41. (15)

Mawson, A.R., & Jacobs, K.W. (1978). Corn, tryptophan, and homicide. *Journal of Orthomolecular Psychiatry, 7*, 227-230. (12)

May, P.R.A., Fuster, J.M., Haber, J., & Hirschman, A. (1979). Woodpecker drilling behavior: An endorsement of the rotational theory of impact brain injury. *Archives of Neurology, 36*, 370-373. (15)

Mayer, A.D., & Rosenblatt, J.S. (1979). Hormonal influences during the ontogeny of maternal behavior in female rats. *Journal of Comparative and Physiological Psychology, 93*, 879-898. (11)

Mayer, A.D., & Rosenblatt, J.S. (1984). Postpartum changes in maternal responsiveness and nest defense in *Rattus norvegicus*. *Journal of Comparative Psychology, 98*, 177-188. (11)

Mayer, J. (1953). Glucostatic mechanism of regulation of food intake. *New England Journal of Medicine, 249*, 13-16. (10)

Mayer, W., & Scherer, I. (1975). Phase shifting effect of caffeine in the circadian rhythm of *Phaseolus coccineus* L. *Zeitschrift für Naturforschung, C, 30*, 855-856. (9)

McBurney, D.H., & Bartoshuk, L.M. (1973). Interactions between stimuli with different taste qualities. *Physiology & Behavior, 10*, 1101-1106. (7)

McCarley, R.W., & Hobson, J.A. (1977). The neurobiological origins of psychoanalytic dream theory. *American Journal of Psychiatry, 134,* 1211-1221. (9)

McCarley, R.W., & Hoffman, E. (1981). REM sleep, dreams, and the activation-synthesis hypothesis. *American Journal of Psychiatry, 138,* 904-912. (9)

McClintock, M.K. (1971). Menstrual synchrony and suppression. *Nature, 229,* 244-245. (7)

McConnell, J.V. (1962). Memory transfer through cannibalism in planarians. *Journal of Neuropsychiatry, 3* (Suppl. 1), 42-48. (13)

McConnell, S.K. (1992). The genesis of neuronal diversity during development of cerebral cortex. *Seminars in the Neurosciences, 4,* 347-356. (5)

McConnell, S.K., Ghosh, A., & Shatz, C.J. (1989). Subplate neurons pioneer the first axon pathway from the cerebral cortex. *Science, 245,* 978-982. (5)

McCormick, D.A. (1989). Acetylcholine: Distribution, receptors, and actions. *Seminars in the Neurosciences, 1,* 91-101. (3)

McCormick, D.A., & Thompson, R.F. (1984). Cerebellum: Essential involvement in the classically conditioned eyelid response. *Science, 223,* 296-299. (13)

McEwen, B.S., & Pfaff, D.W. (1985). Hormone effects on hypothalamic neurons: Analysing gene expression and neuromodulator action. *Trends in Neurosciences, 8,* 105-110. (11)

McGaugh, J.L. (1990). Significance and remembrance: The role of neuromodulatory systems. *Psychological Science, 1,* 15-25. (13)

McGlynn, S.M. (1990). Behavioral approaches to neuropsychological rehabilitation. *Psychological Bulletin, 108,* 420-441. (15)

McGuffin, P., Farmer, A.E., Gottesman, I.I., Murray, R.M., & Reveley, A.M. (1984). Twin concordance for operationally defined schizophrenia. *Archives of General Psychiatry, 41,* 541-545. (16)

McHugh, P.R. (1989). The neuropsychology of basal ganglia disorders. *Neuropsychiatry, Neuropsychology, and Behavioral Neurology, 2,* 239-247. (8)

McHugh, P.R., & Moran, T.H. (1985). The stomach: A conception of its dynamic role in satiety. *Progress in Psychobiology and Physiological Psychology, 11,* 197-232. (10)

McKinnon, W., Weisse, C.S., Reynolds, C.P., Bowles, C.A., & Baum, A. (1989). Chronic stress, leukocyte-subpopulations, and humoral response to latent viruses. *Health Psychology, 8,* 389-402. (12)

McLean, S., Skirboll, L.R., & Pert, C.B. (1985). Comparison of substance P and enkephalin distribution in rat brain: An overview using radioimmunocytochemistry. *Neuroscience, 14,* 837-852. (7)

McLeod, P.J., & Brown, R.E. (1988). The effects of prenatal stress and postweaning housing conditions on parental and sexual behavior of male Long-Evans rats. *Psychobiology, 16,* 372-380. (11)

McMahon, C.E. (1975). The wind of the cannon ball: An informative anecdote from medical history. *Psychotherapy & Psychosomatics, 26,* 125-131. (12)

McMahon, S.B., & Koltzenburg, M. (1992). Itching for an explanation. *Trends in Neurosciences, 15,* 497-501. (7)

McManus, I.C., & Bryden, M.P. (1991). Geschwind's theory of cerebral lateralization: Developing a formal, causal model. *Psychological Bulletin, 110,* 237-253. (14)

McMasters, R.E. (1962). Regeneration of the spinal cord in the rat: Effects of Piromen and ACTH upon the regenerative capacity. *Journal of Comparative Neurology, 119,* 113-121. (15)

McMinn, M.R. (1984). Mechanisms of energy balance in obesity. *Behavioral Neuroscience, 98,* 375-393. (10)

McWilliams, J.R., & Lynch, G. (1983). Rate of synaptic replacement in denervated rat hippocampus declines precipitously from the juvenile period to adulthood. *Science, 221,* 572-574. (15)

McWilliams, J.R., & Lynch, G. (1984). Synaptic density and axonal sprouting in rat hippocampus: Stability in adulthood and decline in late adulthood. *Brain Research, 294,* 152-156. (15)

Meddis, R. (1979). The evolution and function of sleep. In D.A. Oakley & H.C. Plotkin (Eds.), *Brain, behaviour and evolution* (pp. 99-125). London: Methuen. (9)

Meddis, R., Pearson, A.J.D., & Langford, G. (1973). An extreme case of healthy insomnia. *EEG and Clinical Neurophysiology, 35,* 213-214. (9)

Mednick, S.A., Machon, R.A., & Huttunen, M.O. (1990). An update on the Helsinki influenza project. *Archives of General Psychiatry, 47,* 292. (16)

Meehl, P.E. (1989). Schizotaxia revisited. *Archives of General Psychiatry, 46,* 935-944. (16)

Mehiel, R. (1991). Hedonic-shift conditioning with calories. In R.C. Bolles (Ed.), *The hedonics of taste* (pp. 107-126). Hillsdale, NJ: Lawrence Erlbaum. (10)

Meisel, R.L., Dohanich, G.P., & Ward, I.L. (1979). Effects of prenatal stress on avoidance acquisition, open-field performance and lordotic behavior in male rats. *Physiology & Behavior, 22,* 527-530. (11)

Meister, M., Wong, R.O.L., Baylor, D.A., & Shatz, C.J. (1991). Synchronous bursts of action potentials in ganglion cells of the developing mammalian retina. *Science, 252,* 939-943. (5)

Meldrum, B.S. (1990). Excitotoxicity in neuronal degenerative disorders. *Seminars in the Neurosciences, 2,* 127-132. (8)

Melzack, R. (1990). Phantom limbs and the concept of a neuromatrix. *Trends in Neurosciences, 13,* 88-92. (7)

Melzack, R., & Wall, P.D. (1965). Pain mechanisms: A new theory. *Science, 150,* 971-979. (7)

Menco, B. (1992). Ultrastructural studies on membrane, cytoskeletal, mucous, and protective compartments in olfaction. *Microscopy Research and Technique, 22,* 215-224. (7)

Merton, P.A. (1972). How we control the contraction of our muscles. *Scientific American, 226*(5), 30-37. (8)

Merzenich, M.M., Nelson, R.J., Stryker, M.P., Cynader, M.S., Schoppman, A., & Zook, J.M. (1984). Somatosensory cortical map changes following digit amputation in adult monkeys. *Journal of Comparative Neurology, 224,* 591-605. (15)

Messing, R.B., & Sparber, S.B. (1985). Greater task difficulty amplifies the facilitatory effect of des-glycinamide arginine vasopressin on appetitively motivated learning. *Behavioral Neuroscience, 99,* 1114-1119. (13)

Michael, R.P., Zumpe, D., & Bonsall, R.W. (1990). Estradiol administration and the sexual activity of castrated male rhesus monkeys (*Macaca mulatta*). *Hormones and Behavior, 24,* 71-88. (11)

Mignard, M., & Malpeli, J.G. (1991). Paths of information flow through visual cortex. *Science, 251,* 1249-1251. (6)

Miles, F.A., & Evarts, E.V. (1979). Concepts of motor organization. *Annual Review of Psychology, 30,* 327-362. (8)

Miller, E.A., Goldman, P.S., & Rosvold, H.E. (1973). Delayed recovery of function following orbital prefrontal lesions in infant monkeys. *Science, 182,* 304-306. (15)

Miller, E.H. (1982). Character and variance shift in acoustic signals of birds. In D.E. Kroodsma & E.H. Miller (Eds.), *Acoustic communication in birds*, (Vol. 1, pp. 253-295). New York: Academic Press. (1)

Miller, K.W. (1985). The nature of the site of general anesthesia. *International Review of Neurobiology, 27,* 1-61. (2)

Miller, N.E. (1985). The value of behavioral research on animals. *American Psychologist, 40,* 423-440. (1)

Miller, W.C., & DeLong, M.R. (1988). Parkinsonian symptomatology: An anatomical and physiological analysis. *Annals of the New York Academy of Sciences, 515,* 287-302. (8)

Millhorn, D.E., Bayliss, D.A., Erickson, J.T., Gallman, E.A., Szymeczek, C.L., Czyzyk-Krzeska, M., & Dean, J.B. (1989). Cellular and molecular mechanisms of chemical synaptic transmission. *American Journal of Physiology, 257* (6 Part 1), L289-L310. (3)

Milner, B. (1959). The memory defect in bilateral hippocampal lesions. *Psychiatric Research Reports, 11,* 43-58. (13)

Milner, B., Corkin, S., & Teuber, H.-L. (1968). Further analysis of the hippocampal amnesic syndrome: 14-year follow-up study of H.M. *Neuropsychologia, 6,* 215-234. (13)

Miselis, R.R., Shapiro, R.E., & Hand, P.J. (1979). Subfornical organ efferents to neural systems for control of body water. *Science, 205,* 1022-1025. (10)

Mishkin, M., & Manning, F.J. (1978). Nonspatial memory after selective prefrontal lesions in monkeys. *Brain Research, 143,* 313-323. (13)

Mistlberger, R.E. (1992). Nonphotic entrainment of circadian activity rhythms in suprachiasmatic nuclei-ablated hamsters. *Behavioral Neuroscience, 106,* 192-202. (9)

Mitchell, D.E. (1980). The influence of early visual experience on visual perception. In C.S. Harris (Ed.), *Visual coding and adaptability* (pp. 1-50). Hillsdale, NJ: Erlbaum. (6)

Mogil, J.S., Sternberg, W.F., & Liebeskind, J.C. (1993). Studies of pain, stress and immunity. In C.R. Chapman & K.M. Foley (Eds.), *Current & emerging issues in cancer pain: Research & practice* (pp. 31-47). New York: Raven Press. (7, 12)

Moltz, H., Lubin, M., Leon, M., & Numan, M. (1970). Hormonal induction of maternal behavior in the ovariectomized nulliparous rat. *Physiology & Behavior, 5,* 1373-1377. (11)

Money, J. (1970). Matched pairs of hermaphrodites: Behavioral biology of sexual differentiation from chromosomes to gender identity. *Engineering and Science (Cal. Tech.), 33,* 34-39. (11)

Money, J., & Ehrhardt, A.A. (1968). Prenatal hormonal exposure: Possible effects on behaviour in man. In R.P. Michael (Ed.), *Endocrinology and human behaviour* (pp. 32-48). London: Oxford University Press. (11)

Money, J., & Ehrhardt, A.A. (1972). *Man & woman, boy & girl.* Baltimore, MD: Johns Hopkins University Press. (11)

Money, J., & Lewis, V. (1966). IQ, genetics and accelerated growth: Adrenogenital syndrome. *Bulletin of the Johns Hopkins Hospital, 118,* 365-373. (11)

Money, J., & Schwartz, M. (1978). Biosocial determinants of gender identity differentiation and development. In J.B. Hutchison (Ed.), *Biological determinants of sexual behaviour* (pp. 765-784). Chichester, England: John Wiley. (11)

Mook, D.G. (1990). Satiety, specifications, and stop rules: Feeding as voluntary action. *Progress in Psychobiology and Physiological Psychology, 14,* 1-65. (10)

Moonen, C.T.W., van Zijl, P.C.M., Frank, J.A., LeBihan, D., & Becker, E.D. (1990). Functional magnetic resonance imaging in medicine and physiology. *Science, 250,* 53-61. (4)

Moorcroft, W.J. (1989). *Sleep, dreaming, & sleep disorders.* Lanham, MD: University Press of America. (9)

Moore, F.L., & Orchinik, M. (1991). Multiple molecular actions for steroids in the regulation of reproductive behaviors. *Seminars in the Neurosciences, 3,* 489-496. (11)

Moore-Ede, M.C., Czeisler, C.A., & Richardson, G.S. (1983a). Circadian timekeeping in health and disease. *New England Journal of Medicine, 309,* 469-476. (9)

Moore-Ede, M.C., Czeisler, C.A., & Richardson, G.S. (1983b). Circadian timekeeping in health and disease. Part 2. Clinical implications of circadian rhythmicity. *New England Journal of Medicine, 309,* 530-536. (9)

Morgan, D.G., & Finch, C.E. (1988). Dopaminergic changes in the basal ganglia: A generalized phenomenon of aging in mammals. *Annals of the New York Academy of Sciences, 515,* 145-159. (8)

Morgenstern, H., & Glazer, W.M. (1993). Identifying risk factors for tardive dyskinesia among long-term outpatients maintained with neuroleptic medications. *Archives of General Psychiatry, 50,* 723-733. (16)

Mori, K., Mataga, N., & Imamura, K. (1992). Differential specificities of single mitral cells in rabbit olfactory bulb for a homologous series of fatty acid odor molecules. *Journal of Neurophysiology, 67,* 786-789. (7)

Morley, J.E., Bartness, T.J., Gosnell, B.A., & Levine, A.S. (1985). Peptidergic regulation of feeding. *International Review of Neurobiology, 27,* 207-298. (10)

Morley, J.E., Levine, A.S., Grace, M., & Kneip, J. (1985). Peptide YY (PYY), a potent orexigenic agent. *Brain Research, 341,* 200-203. (10)

Morris, J.F., & Pow, D.V. (1993). New anatomical insights into the inputs and outputs from hypothalamic magnocellular neurons. *Annals of the New York Academy of Sciences, 689,* 16-33. (11)

Morris, M., Lack, L., & Dawson, D. (1990). Sleep-onset insomniacs have delayed temperature rhythms. *Sleep, 13,* 1-14. (9)

Morrow, L., Ratcliff, G., & Johnston, C.S. (1986). Externalising spatial knowledge in patients with right hemispheric lesions. *Cognitive Neuropsychology, 2,* 265-273. (14)

Moruzzi, G., & Magoun, H.W. (1949). Brain stem reticular formation and activation of the EEG. *Electroencephalography and Clinical Neurophysiology, 1,* 455-473. (9)

Moscovitch, M. (1985). Memory from infancy to old age: Implications for theories of normal and pathological memory. *Annals of the New York Academy of Sciences, 444,* 78-96. (13)

Moscovitch, M. (1989). Confabulation and the frontal systems: Strategic versus associative retrieval in neuropsychological theories of memory. In H.L. Roediger, III, & F.I.M. Craik (Eds.), *Varieties of memory and consciousness: Essays in honour of Endel Tulving* (pp. 133-160). Hillsdale, NJ: Lawrence Erlbaum. (13)

Moscovitch, M. (1992). Memory and working-with-memory: A component process model based on modules and central systems. *Journal of Cognitive Neuroscience, 4,* 257-267. (13)

Mountcastle, V.B. (1957). Modality and topographic properties of single neurons of cat's somatic sensory cortex. *Journal of Neurophysiology, 20,* 408-434. (4)

Moyer, K.E. (1974). Sex differences in aggression. In R.C. Friedman, R.M. Richart, & R.L. VandeWiele (Eds.), *Sex differences in behavior* (pp. 335-372). New York: Wiley. (11)

Mrosovsky, N. (1990). *Rheostasis: The physiology of change.* New York: Oxford University Press. (10)

Murison, R., & Overmier, J.B. (1990). Proactive actions of psychological stress on gastric ulceration in rats—Real psychobiology. *Annals of the New York Academy of Sciences, 597,* 191-200. (12)

Murphy, J.M., Sobol, A.M., Neff, R.K., Olivier, D.C., & Leighton, A.H. (1984). Stability of prevalence. *Archives of General Psychiatry, 41,* 990-997. (16)

Murphy, M.G., & O'Leary, J.L. (1973). Hanging and climbing functions in raccoon and sloth after total cerebellectomy. *Archives of Neurology, 28,* 111-117. (8)

Murphy, M.R., Checkley, S.A., Seckl, J.R., & Lightman, S.L. (1990). Naloxone inhibits oxytocin release at orgasm in man. *Journal of Clinical Endocrinology and Metabolism, 71,* 1056-1058. (11)

Murrell, J., Farlow, M., Ghetti, B., & Benson, M.D. (1991). A mutation in the amyloid precursor protein associated with hereditary Alzheimer's disease. *Science, 254,* 97-99. (13)

Myers, J.J., & Sperry, R.W. (1985). Interhemispheric communication after section of the forebrain commissures. *Cortex, 21,* 249-260. (14)

Nachman, M. (1962). Taste preferences for sodium salts by adrenalectomized rats. *Journal of Comparative and Physiological Psychology, 55,* 1124-1129. (10)

Nadel, L. (1992). Multiple memory systems: What and why. *Journal of Cognitive Neuroscience, 4,* 179-188. (13)

Nakanishi, S. (1992). Molecular diversity of glutamate receptors and implications for brain function. *Science, 258,* 597-603. (13)

Nantwi, K.D., & Schoener, E.P. (1993). Cocaine and dopaminergic actions in rat neostriatum. *Neuropharmacology, 32,* 807-817. (3)

Nathans, J., Davenport, C.M., Maumenee, I.H., Lewis, R.A., Hejtmancik, J.F., Litt, M., Lovrien, E., Weleber, R., Bachynski, B., Zwas, F., Klingaman, R., & Fishman, G. (1989). Molecular genetics of human blue cone monochromacy. *Science, 245,* 831-838. (6)

Nathans, J., Piantanida, T.P., Eddy, R.L., Shows, T.B., & Hogness, D.S. (1986). Molecular genetics of inherited variations in human color vision. *Science, 232,* 203-210. (6)

Nathans, J., Thomas, D., & Hogness, D.S. (1986). Molecular genetics of human color vision: The genes encoding blue, green, and red pigments. *Science, 232,* 193-202. (6)

Nebes, R.D. (1974). Hemispheric specialization in commissurotomized man. *Psychological Bulletin, 81,* 1-14. (14)

Nee, L.E., Eldridge, R., Sunderland, T., Thomas, C.B., Katz, D., Thompson, K.E., Weingartner, H., Weiss, H., Julian, C., & Cohen, N. (1987). Dementia of the Alzheimer type: Clinical and family study of 22 twin pairs. *Neurology, 37,* 359-363. (13)

Neitz, J., & Jacobs, G.H. (1986). Reexamination of spectral mechanisms in the rat (*Rattus norvegicus*). *Journal of Comparative Psychology, 100,* 21-29. (6)

Nelson, D.O., & Prosser, C.L. (1981). Intracellular recordings from thermosensitive preoptic neurons. *Science, 213,* 787-789. (10)

Nelson, T.O., McSpadden, M., Fromme, K., & Marlatt, G.A. (1986). Effects of alcohol intoxication on metamemory and on retrieval from long-term memory. *Journal of Experimental Psychology: General, 115,* 247-254. (3)

Netter, F.H. (1983). *CIBA collection of medical illustrations: Vol. 1. Nervous system.* New York: CIBA. (11)

Nicholas, M.K., & Arnason, B.G.W. (1992). Immunologic responses in central nervous system transplantation. *Seminars in the Neurosciences, 4,* 273-283. (15)

Nicklas, W.J., Saporito, M., Basma, A., Geller, H.M., & Heikkila, R.E. (1992). Mitochondrial mechanisms of neurotoxicity. *Annals of the New York Academy of Sciences, 648,* 28-36. (8)

Nicoll, R.A., & Madison, D.V. (1982). General anesthetics hyperpolarize neurons in the vertebrate central nervous system. *Science, 217,* 1055-1057. (2)

Nieuwenhuys, R. (1988). *The human central nervous system: A synopsis and atlas.* New York: Springer Verlag. (4, 10)

North, R.A. (1989). Neurotransmitters and their receptors: From the clone to the clinic. *Seminars in the Neurosciences, 1,* 81-90. (3)

633

North, R.A. (1992). Cellular actions of opiates and cocaine. *Annals of the New York Academy of Sciences, 654,* 1-6. (3)

Nottebohm, F. (1980a). Testosterone triggers growth of brain vocal control nuclei in adult female canaries. *Brain Research, 189,* 429-436. (1)

Nottebohm, F. (1980b). Brain pathways for vocal learning in birds: A review of the first 10 years. *Progress in Psychobiology and Physiological Psychology, 9,* 85-124. (1)

Nutt, D.J. (1989). Altered central α_2-adrenoceptor sensitivity in panic disorder. *Archives of General Psychiatry, 46,* 165-169. (12)

Obeso, J.A., Grandas, F., Vaamonde, J., Luquin, M.R., Artieda, J., Lera, G., Rodríguez, M.E., & Martínez-Lage, J.M. (1989). Motor complications associated with chronic levodopa therapy in Parkinson's disease. *Neurology, 39* (Suppl. 2), 11-19. (8)

O'Dowd, B.F., Lefkowitz, R.J., & Caron, M.G. (1989). Structure of the adrenergic and related receptors. *Annual Review of Neuroscience, 12,* 67-83. (3)

Ojemann, G., & Mateer, C. (1979). Human language cortex: Localization of memory, syntax, and sequential motor-phoneme identification systems. *Science, 205,* 1401-1403. (14)

Ojemann, G.A., & Whitaker, H.A. (1978). Language localization and variability. *Brain and Language, 6,* 239-260. (14)

Ojemann, J.G., Ojemann, G.A., & Lettich, E. (1992). Neuronal activity related to faces and matching in human right nondominant temporal cortex. *Brain, 115,* 1-13. (6)

O'Keefe, J. (1983). Spatial memory within and without the hippocampal system. In W. Seifert (Ed.), *Neurobiology of the hippocampus* (pp. 375-403). London: Academic Press. (13)

Olds, J. (1958). Satiation effects in self-stimulation of the brain. *Journal of Comparative and Physiological Psychology, 51,* 675-678. (12)

Olds, J. (1962). Hypothalamic substrates of reward. *Physiological Reviews, 42,* 554-604. (12)

Olds, J., & Milner, P. (1954). Positive reinforcement produced by electrical stimulation of the septal area and other regions of the rat brain. *Journal of Comparative and Physiological Psychology, 47,* 419-428. (12)

O'Leary, A. (1990). Stress, emotion, and human immune function. *Psychological Bulletin, 108,* 363-382. (12)

O'Leary, D.S., & Boll, T.J. (1984). Neuropsychological correlates of early generalized brain dysfunction in children. In C.R. Almli & S. Finger (Eds.), *Early brain damage* (pp. 215-229). Orlando, FL: Academic Press. (15)

Olsen, T.S., Bruhn, P., & Öberg, R.G.E. (1986). Cortical hypoperfusion as a possible cause of "subcortical aphasia." *Brain, 109,* 393-410. (14)

Olton, D.S., & Papas, B.C. (1979). Spatial memory and hippocampal function. *Neuropsychologia, 17,* 669-682. (13)

Olton, D.S., Walker, J.A., & Gage, F.H. (1978). Hippocampal connections and spatial discrimination. *Brain Research, 139,* 295-308. (13)

Ornitz, E.M., Atwell, C.W., Kaplan, A.R., & Westlake, J.R. (1985). Brain-stem dysfunction in autism. *Archives of General Psychiatry, 42,* 1018-1025. (16)

Ornitz, E.M., & Ritvo, E.R. (1976). Medical assessment. In E.R. Ritvo (Ed.), *Autism* (pp. 7-23). New York: Spectrum. (16)

Overman, W., Bachevalier, J., Turner, M., & Peuster, A. (1992). Object recognition versus object discrimination: Comparison between human infants and infant monkeys. *Behavioral Neuroscience, 106,* 15-29. (13)

Overmier, J.B., Murison, R., Ursin, H., & Skoglund, E.J. (1987). Quality of post-stressor rest influences the ulcerative process. *Behavioral Neuroscience, 101,* 246-253. (12)

Owren, M.J., Hopp, S.L., Sinnott, J.M., & Petersen, M.R. (1988). Absolute auditory thresholds in three old world monkey species (*Cercopithecus aethiops, C. neglectus, Macaca fuscata*) and humans (*Homo sapiens*). *Journal of Comparative Psychology, 102,* 99-107. (7)

Paez, X., Stanley, B.G., & Leibowitz, S.F. (1993). Microdialysis analysis of norepinephrine levels in the paraventricular nucleus in association with food intake at dark onset. *Brain Research, 606,* 167-170. (10)

Page, G.G., Ben-Eliyahu, S., Yirmiya, R., & Liebeskind, J.C. (1993). Morphine attenuates surgery-induced enhancement of metastatic colonization in rats. *Pain, 54,* 21-28. (7)

Pagel, M.D., & Harvey, P.H. (1989). Taxonomic differences in the scaling of brain on body weight among mammals. *Science, 244,* 1589-1593. (5)

Paino, C.L., & Bunge, M.B. (1991). Induction of axon growth into Schwann cell implants grafted into lesioned adult rat spinal cord. *Experimental Neurology, 114,* 254-257. (15)

Pakkenberg, B. (1990). Pronounced reduction of total neuron number in mediodorsal thalamic nucleus and nucleus accumbens in schizophrenics. *Archives of General Psychiatry, 47,* 1023-1028. (16)

Palay, S.L., & Chan-Palay, V. (1977). General morphology of neurons and neuroglia. In J.M. Brookhart & V.M. Mountcastle (Eds.), *Handbook of physiology: Section 1. The nervous system* (Vol. 1, Pt. 1, pp. 5-37). Bethesda, MD: American Physiological Society. (2)

Pande, A.C. (1985). Light-induced hypomania. *American Journal of Psychiatry, 142,* 1126. (16)

Pandurangi, A.K., Bilder, R.M., Rieder, R.O., Mukherjee, S., & Hamer, R.M. (1988). Schizophrenic symptoms and deterioration. *Journal of Nervous and Mental Disease, 176,* 200-206. (16)

Panksepp, J., Herman, B., & Vilberg, T. (1978). An opiate excess model of childhood autism. *Neuroscience Abstracts, 4* (Abstract 1601), 500. (16)

Papanicolaou, A.C., Moore, B.D., Deutsch, G., Levin, H.S., & Eisenberg, H.M. (1988). Evidence for right-hemisphere involvement in recovery from aphasia. *Archives of Neurology, 45,* 1025-1029. (14)

Papez, J.W. (1937). A proposed mechanism of emotion. *Archives of Neurology and Psychiatry, 38,* 725-743. (12)

Pappone, P.A., & Cahalan, M.D. (1987). *Pandinus imperator* scorpion venom blocks voltage-gated potassium channels in nerve fibers. *Journal of Neuroscience, 7,* 3300-3305. (2)

Parker, G.H. (1922). *Smell, taste, and allied senses in the vertebrates.* Philadelphia: Lippincott. (7)

Pascual-Leone, A., & Torres, F. (1993). Plasticity of the sensorimotor cortex representation of the reading finger in Braille readers. *Brain, 116,* 39-52. (15)

Passingham, R.E. (1979). Brain size and intelligence in man. *Brain, Behavior, and Evolution, 16,* 253-270. (5)

Patrick, C.J., & Iacono, W.G. (1989). Psychopathy, threat, and polygraph test accuracy. *Journal of Applied Psychology, 74,* 347-355. (13)

Paul, S.M., Extein, I., Calil, H.M., Potter, W.Z., Chodoff, P., & Goodwin, F.K. (1981). Use of ECT with treatment-resistant depressed patients at the National Institute of Mental Health. *American Journal of Psychiatry, 138,* 486-489. (16)

Paulson, O.B., & Newman, E.A. (1987). Does the release of potassium from astrocyte endfeet regulate cerebral blood flow? *Science, 237,* 896-898. (4)

Peachey, J.E., & Naranjo, C.A. (1983). The use of disulfiram and other alcohol-sensitizing drugs in the treatment of alcoholism. *Research Advances in Alcohol and Drug Problems, 7,* 397-431. (3)

Peck, J.W., & Novin, D. (1971). Evidence that osmoreceptors mediating drinking in rabbits are in the lateral preoptic area. *Journal of Comparative and Physiological Psychology, 74,* 134-147. (10)

Pedersen, C.A., Ascher, J.A., Monroe, Y.L., & Prange, A.J., Jr. (1982). Oxytocin induces maternal behavior in virgin female rats. *Science, 216,* 648-650. (11)

Pellegrino, L.J., & Cushman, A.J. (1967). *A stereotaxic atlas of the rat brain.* New York: Appleton-Century-Crofts. (4)

Pellis, S.M., O'Brien, D.P., Pellis, V.C., Teitelbaum, P., Wolgin, D.L., & Kennedy, S. (1988). Escalation of feline predation along a gradient from avoidance through "play" to killing. *Behavioral Neuroscience, 102,* 760-777. (4)

Penfield, W. (1955). The permanent record of the stream of consciousness. *Acta Psychologica, 11,* 47-69. (13)

Penfield, W., & Milner, B. (1958). Memory deficit produced by bilateral lesions in the hippocampal zone. *Archives of Neurology and Psychiatry, 79,* 475-497. (13)

Penfield, W., & Perot, P. (1963). The brain's record of auditory and visual experience. *Brain, 86,* 595-696. (13)

Penfield, W., & Rasmussen, T. (1950). *The cerebral cortex of man.* New York: Macmillan. (4)

Penfield, W., & Roberts, L. (1959). *Speech and brain mechanisms.* Princeton, NJ: Princeton University Press. (1)

Pepperberg, I.M. (1981). Functional vocalizations by an African grey parrot. *Zeitschrift für Tierpsychologie, 55,* 139-160. (14)

Pepperberg, I.M. (1993). Cognition and communication in an African grey parrot (*Psittacus erithacus*): Studies on a non-human, nonprimate, nonmammalian subject. In H.L. Roitblat, L.M. Herman, & P.E. Nachtigall (Eds.), *Language and communication: comparative perspectives* (pp. 221-248). Hillsdale, NJ: Lawrence Erlbaum. (14)

Perani, D., Vallar, G., Paulesu, E., Alberoni, M., & Fazio, F. (1993). Left and right hemisphere contributions to recovery from neglect after right hemisphere damage—An [^{18}F]FDG PET study of two cases. *Neuropsychologia, 31*, 115-125. (15)

Pericak-Vance, M.A., Bebout, J.L., Gaskell, P.C. Jr., Yamaoka, L.H., Hung, W.-Y., Alberts, M.J., Walker, A.P., Bartlett, R.J., Haynes, C.A., Welsh, K.A., Earl, N.L., Heyman, A., Clark, C.M., & Roses, A.D. (1991). Linkage studies in familial Alzheimer disease: Evidence for chromosome 19 linkage. *American Journal of Human Genetics, 48*, 1034-1050. (13)

Perlow, M.J., Freed, W.J., Hoffer, B.J., Seiger, A., Olson, L., & Wyatt, R.J. (1979). Brain grafts reduce motor abnormalities produced by destruction of nigrostriatal dopamine system. *Science, 204*, 643-647. (15)

Pert, A., Rosenblatt, J.E., Sivit, C., Pert, C.B., & Bunney, W.E., Jr. (1978). Long-term treatment with lithium prevents the development of dopamine receptor supersensitivity. *Science, 201*, 171-173. (16)

Pert, C.B., & Snyder, S.H. (1973). The opiate receptor: Demonstration in nervous tissue. *Science, 179*, 1011-1014. (7)

Petersen, S.E., Fox, P.T., Posner, M.I., Mintun, M., & Raichle, M.E. (1988). Positron emission tomographic studies of the cortical anatomy of single-word processing. *Nature, 331*, 585-589. (14)

Peterson, G.C. (1980). Organic mental disorders associated with brain trauma. In H.I. Kaplan, A.M. Freedman, & B.J. Sadlock (Eds.), *Comprehensive textbook of psychiatry* (3rd ed.), (Vol. 2, pp. 1422-1437). Baltimore, MD: Williams & Wilkins. (15)

Petty, L.K., Ornitz, E.M., Michelman, J.D., & Zimmerman, E.G. (1984). Autistic children who become schizophrenic. *Archives of General Psychiatry, 41*, 129-135. (16)

Pfaffmann, C., Frank, M., & Norgren, R. (1979). Neural mechanisms and behavioral aspects of taste. *Annual Review of Psychology, 30*, 283-325. (7)

Pfaus, J.G., & Phillips, A.G. (1991). Role of dopamine in anticipatory and consummatory aspects of sexual behavior in the male rat. *Behavioral Neuroscience, 105*, 727-743. (11)

Pflug, B. (1973). Therapeutic aspects of sleep deprivation. In W.P. Koella & P. Levin (Eds.), *Sleep: Physiology, biochemistry, psychology, pharmacology, clinical implications* (pp. 185-191). Basel: Karger. (16)

Phelps, M.E., & Mazziotta, J.C. (1985). Positron emission tomography: Human brain function and biochemistry. *Science, 228*, 799-809. (4)

Phillips, R.G., & LeDoux, J.E. (1992). Differential contribution of amygdala and hippocampus to cued and contextual fear conditioning. *Behavioral Neuroscience, 106*, 274-285. (12)

Phoenix, C.H., Slob, A.K., & Goy, R.W. (1973). Effects of castration and replacement therapy on sexual behavior of adult male rhesuses. *Journal of Comparative and Physiological Psychology, 84*, 472-481. (11)

Pincus, J.H. (1980). Can violence be a manifestation of epilepsy? *Neurology, 30*, 304-307. (12)

Pincus, J.H., & Tucker, G.J. (1985). *Behavioral neurology* (3rd ed.). New York: Oxford University Press. (14)

Pinel, J.P.J., Treit, D., & Rovner, L.I. (1977). Temporal lobe aggression in rats. *Science, 197*, 1088-1089. (12)

Pini, A. (1993). Chemorepulsion of axons in the developing mammalian central nervous system. *Science, 261*, 95-98. (5)

Pi-Sunyer, X., Kissileff, H.R., Thornton, J., & Smith, G.P. (1982). C-terminal octapeptide of cholecystokinin decreases food intake in obese men. *Physiology & Behavior, 29*, 627-630. (10)

Plomin, R. (1990). The role of inheritance in behavior. *Science, 248*, 183-188. (A)

Plomin, R., Corley, R., DeFries, J.C., & Fulker, D. (1990). Individual differences in television viewing in early childhood: Nature as well as nurture. *Psychological Science, 1*, 371-377. (11)

Poling, A., Schlinger, H., & Blakely, E. (1988). Failure of the partial inverse benzodiazepine agonist Ro15-4513 to block the lethal effects of ethanol in rats. *Pharmacology Biochemistry & Behavior, 31*, 945-947. (12)

Pollak, J.M. (1979). Obsessive-compulsive personality: A review. *Psychological Bulletin, 86*, 225-241. (12)

Pollatsek, A., Bolozky, S., Well, A.D., & Rayner, K. (1981). Asymmetries in the perceptual span for Israeli readers. *Brain and Language, 14*, 174-180. (14)

Pollitt, E. (1988). Developmental impact of nutrition on pregnancy, infancy, and childhood: Public health issues in the United States. In N.W. Bray (Ed.), *International review of research in mental retardation* (Vol. 15, pp. 33-80). San Diego: Academic Press. (5)

Pomerantz, S.M., & Goy, R.W. (1983). Proceptive behavior of female rhesus monkeys during tests with tethered males. *Hormones and Behavior, 17*, 237-248. (11)

Pomeranz, B., & Chung, S.H. (1970). Dendritic-tree anatomy codes form-vision physiology in tadpole retina. *Science, 170*, 983-984. (4)

Pomeranz, B.H. (1989). Transcutaneous electrical nerve stimulation (TENS). In G. Adelman (Ed.), *Neuroscience year* (pp. 161-164). Boston: Birkhäuser. (7)

Pons, T.P., Garraghty, P.E., Ommaya, A.K., Kaas, J.H., Taub, E., & Mishkin, M. (1991). Massive cortical reorganization after sensory deafferentation in adult macaques. *Science, 252*, 1857-1860. (15)

Porter, R.H., Balogh, R.D., Cernoch, J.M., & Franchi, C. (1986). Recognition of kin through characteristic body odors. *Chemical Senses, 11*, 389-395. (7)

Posner, M.I., Early, T.S., Reiman, E., Pardo, P.J., & Dhawan, M. (1988). Asymmetries in hemispheric control of attention in schizophrenia. *Archives of General Psychiatry, 45*, 814-821. (16)

Posner, M.I., Petersen, S.E., Fox, P.T., & Raichle, M.E. (1988). Localization of cognitive operations in the human brain. *Science, 240*, 1627-1631. (14)

Pothos, E., Rada, P., Mark, G.P., & Hoebel, B.G. (1991). Dopamine microdialysis in the nucleus accumbens during acute and chronic morphine, naloxone-precipitated withdrawal and clonidine treatment. *Brain Research, 566*, 348-350. (3)

Potkin, S.G., Karoum, F., Chuang, L.-W., Cannon-Spoor, H.E., Phillips, I., & Wyatt, R.J. (1979). Phenylethylamine in paranoid chronic schizophrenia. *Science, 206*, 470-471. (16)

Preilowski, B. (1975). Bilateral motor interaction: Perceptual-motor performance of partial and complete split-brain patients. In K.J. Zülch, O. Creutzfeldt, & G.C. Galbraith (Eds.), *Cerebral localization* (pp. 115-132). New York: Springer Verlag. (14)

Premack, A.J. (1976). *Why chimps can read*. New York: Harper & Row. (14)

Premack, A.J., & Premack, D. (1972). Teaching language to an ape. *Scientific American, 227* (4), 92-99. (14)

Preti, G., Cutler, W.B., Garcia, C.R., Huggins, G.R., & Lawley, H.J. (1986). Human axillary secretions influence women's menstrual cycles: The role of donor extract of females. *Hormones and Behavior, 20*, 474-482. (7)

Pritchard, T.C., Hamilton, R.B., Morse, J.R., & Norgren, R. (1986). Projections of thalamic gustatory and lingual areas in the monkey, *Macaca fascicularis*. *Journal of Comparative Neurology, 244*, 213-228. (7)

Provine, R.R. (1979). "Wing-flapping" develops in wingless chicks. *Behavioral and Neural Biology, 27*, 233-237. (8)

Provine, R.R. (1981). Wing-flapping develops in chickens made flightless by feather mutations. *Developmental Psychobiology, 14*, 481-486. (8)

Provine, R.R. (1984). Wing-flapping during development and evolution. *American Scientist, 72*, 448-455. (8)

Provine, R.R. (1986). Yawning as a stereotyped action pattern and releasing stimulus. *Ethology, 72*, 109-122. (8)

Provine, R.R., & Westerman, J.A. (1979). Crossing the midline: Limits of early eye-hand behavior. *Child Development, 50*, 437-441. (14)

Purves, D., & Hadley, R.D. (1985). Changes in the dendritic branching of adult mammalian neurones revealed by repeated imaging *in situ*. *Nature, 315*, 404-406. (2)

Purves, D., & Lichtman, J.W. (1980). Elimination of synapses in the developing nervous system. *Science, 210*, 153-157. (5)

Quadagno, D.M., Briscoe, R., & Quadagno, J.S. (1977). Effect of perinatal gonadal hormones on selected nonsexual behavior patterns: A critical assessment of the non-human and human literature. *Psychological Bulletin, 84*, 62-80. (11)

Raczkowski, D., Hamos, J.E., & Sherman, S.M. (1988). Synaptic circuitry of physiologically identified W-cells in the cat's dorsal lateral geniculate nucleus. *Journal of Neuroscience, 8*, 31-48. (6)

Rada, P., Pothos, E., Mark, G.P. & Hoebel, B.G. (1991). Microdialysis evidence that acetylcholine in the nucleus accumbens is involved in morphine withdrawal and in its treatment with clonidine. *Brain Research, 561*, 354-356. (3)

Rafal, R., Smith, J., Krantz, J., Cohen, A., & Brennan, C. (1990). Extrageniculate vision in hemianopic humans: Saccade inhibition by signals in the blind field. *Science, 250*, 118-121. (6)

Raisman, G. (1991). Glia, neurons, and plasticity. *Annals of the New York Academy of Sciences, 633*, 209-213. (2)

Rakic, P. (1978). Neuronal migration and contact guidance in the primate telencephalon. *Postgraduate Medical Journal, 54* (Suppl. 1), 25-37. (5)

Rakic, P. (1985). DNA synthesis and cell division in the adult primate brain. *Annals of the New York Academy of Sciences, 457*, 193-211. (2)

Rakic, P. (1988). Specification of cerebral cortical areas. *Science, 241*, 170-176. (5)

Ralph, M.R., Foster, R.G., Davis, F.C., & Menaker, M. (1990). Transplanted suprachiasmatic nucleus determines circadian period. *Science, 247*, 975-978. (9)

Ralph, M.R., & Menaker, M. (1988). A mutation of the circadian system in golden hamsters. *Science, 241*, 1225-1227. (9)

Raming, K., Krieger, J., Strotman, J., Boekhoff, I., Kubick, S., Baumstark, C., & Breer, H. (1993). Cloning and expression of odorant molecules. *Nature, 361*, 353-356. (7)

Ramirez, J.J., Fass, B., Karpiak, S.E., & Steward, O. (1987a). Ganglioside treatments reduce locomotor hyperactivity after bilateral lesions of the entorhinal cortex. *Neuroscience Letters, 75*, 283-287. (15)

Ramirez, J.J., Fass, B., Kilfoil, T., Henschel, B., Grones, W., & Karpiak, S.E. (1987b). Ganglioside-induced enhancement of behavioral recovery after bilateral lesions of the entorhinal cortex. *Brain Research, 414*, 85-90. (15)

Ramsay, D.J., & Thrasher, T.N. (1990). Thirst and water balance. In E.M. Stricker (Ed.), *Handbook of behavioral neurobiology, Vol. 10: Neurobiology of food and fluid intake* (pp. 353-386). New York: Plenum Press. (10)

Ranson, S.W., & Clark, S.L. (1959). *The anatomy of the nervous system: Its development and function* (10th ed.). Philadelphia: W.B. Saunders Co. (4)

Rapoport, S.I., & Robinson, P.J. (1986). Tight-junctional modification as the basis of osmotic opening of the blood-brain barrier. *Annals of the New York Academy of Sciences, 481*, 250-267. (2)

Rasmussen, S.A. (1985). Obsessive compulsive disorder in dermatologic practice. *Journal of the American Academy of Dermatology, 13*, 965-967. (12)

Rasmussen, T., & Milner, B. (1977). The role of early left-brain injury in determining lateralization of cerebral speech functions. *Annals of the New York Academy of Sciences, 299*, 355-369. (14)

Rausch, G., & Scheich, H. (1982). Dendritic spine loss and enlargement during maturation of the speech control system in the Mynah bird (*Gracula religiosa*). *Neuroscience Letters, 29*, 129-133. (5)

Rawlins, J.N.P., Lyford, G.L., Seferiades, A., Deacon, R.M.J., & Cassaday, H.J. (1993). Critical determinants of nonspatial working memory deficits in rats with

conventional lesions of the hippocampus or fornix. *Behavioral Neuroscience, 107*, 420-433. (13)

Ream, N.W., Robinson, M.G., Richter, R.W., Hegge, F.W., & Holloway, H.C. (1975). Opiate dependence and acute abstinence. In R.W. Richter (Ed.), *Medical aspects of drug abuse* (pp. 81-123). Hagerstown, MD: Harper & Row. (14)

Recanzone, G.H., Merzenich, M.M., Jenkins, W.M., Kamil, A.G., & Dinse, H.R. (1992). Topographic reorganization of the hand representation in cortical area 3b of owl monkeys trained in a frequency-discrimination task. *Journal of Neurophysiology, 67*, 1031-1056. (15)

Reches, A., Wagner, H.R., Barkai, A.I., Jackson, V., Yablonskaya-Alter, E., & Fahn, S. (1984). Electroconvulsive treatment and haloperidol: Effects on pre- and postsynaptic dopamine receptors in rat brain. *Psychopharmacology, 83*, 155-158. (16)

Rechtschaffen, A., Gilliland, M.A., Bergmann, B.M., & Winter, J.B. (1983). Physiological correlates of prolonged sleep deprivation in rats. *Science, 221*, 182-184. (9)

Redmond, D.E., Jr., Roth, R.H., Spencer, D.D., Naftolin, F., Leranth, C., Robbins, R.J., Marek, K.L., Elsworth, J.D., Taylor, J.R., Sass, K.J., & Sladek, J.R., Jr. (1993). Neural transplantation for neurodegenerative diseases: Past, present, and future. *Annals of the New York Academy of Sciences, 695*, 258-266. (15)

Reed, T.E. (1985). Ethnic differences in alcohol use, abuse, and sensitivity: A review with genetic interpretation. *Social Biology, 32*, 195-209. (3)

Reeves, A.G., & Plum, F. (1969). Hyperphagia, rage, and dementia accompanying a ventromedial hypothalamic neoplasm. *Archives of Neurology, 20*, 616-624. (10)

Reeves, T.M., & Smith, D.C. (1987). Reinnervation of the dentate gyrus and recovery of alternation behavior following entorhinal cortex lesions. *Behavioral Neuroscience, 101*, 179-186. (15)

Refinetti, R., & Carlisle, H.J. (1986a). Complementary nature of heat production and heat intake during behavioral thermoregulation in the rat. *Behavioral and Neural Biology, 46*, 64-70. (10)

Refinetti, R., & Carlisle, H.J. (1986b). Effects of anterior and posterior hypothalamic temperature changes on thermoregulation in the rat. *Physiology & Behavior, 36*, 1099-1103. (10)

Refinetti, R., & Menaker, M. (1992). The circadian rhythm of body temperature. *Physiology & Behavior, 51*, 613-637. (9)

Regal, R.R., Cross, P.K., Lamson, S.H., & Hook, E.B.U. (1980). A search for evidence for a paternal age effect independent of a maternal age in birth certificate reports of Down's syndome in New York state. *American Journal of Epidemiology, 112*, 650-655. (A)

Regan, T. (1986). The rights of humans and other animals. *Acta Physiologica Scandinavica, 128* (Suppl. 554), 33-40. (1)

Reichling, D.B., Kwiat, G.C., & Basbaum, A.I. (1988). Anatomy, physiology, and pharmacology of the periaqueductal gray contribution to antinociceptive controls. In H.L. Fields & J.-M. Besson (Eds.), *Progress in brain research* (Vol. 77, pp. 31-46). Amsterdam: Elsevier. (7)

Rémillard, G.M., Andermann, F., Testa, G.F., Gloor, P., Aube, M., Martin, J.B. Feindel, W., Guberman, A., & Simpson, C. (1983). Sexual ictal manifestations predominate in women with temporal lobe epilepsy: A finding suggesting sexual dimorphism in the human brain. *Neurology, 33*, 323-330. (12)

Rensch, B. (1964). Memory and concepts of higher animals. *Proceedings of the Zoological Society of Calcutta, 17*, 207-221. (5)

Rensch, B. (1971). Probleme des Gedächtnisspuren. [Problems of the memory trace]. *Rheinisch-Westfälische Akademie der Wissenschaften, 221*, 7-67. (5)

Rensch, B. (1973). *Gedächtnis Begriffsbildung und Planhandlungen bei Tieren.* [Memory, concept formation, and planned behavior in animals]. Berlin: Verlag Paul Parey. (5)

Rensch, B., & Dücker, G. (1963). Haptisches Lern- und Unterscheidungs- Vermögen bei einem Waschbären [Haptic learning and discrimination abilities of a raccoon]. *Zeitschrift für Tierpsychologie, 20*, 608-615. (5)

Rettig, R., Ganten, D., & Johnson, A.K. (1981). Isoproterenol-induced thirst: Renal and extrarenal mechanisms. *American Journal of Physiology, 241*, R152-R157. (10)

Richter, C.P. (1922). A behavioristic study of the activity of the rat. *Comparative Psychology Monographs, 1*, 1-55. (9)

Richter, C.P. (1936). Increased salt appetite in adrenalectomized rats. *American Journal of Physiology, 115*, 155-161. (10)

Richter, C.P. (1938). Two-day cycles of alternating good and bad behavior in psychotic patients. *Archives of Neurology and Psychiatry, 39*, 587-598. (16)

Richter, C.P. (1950). Taste and solubility of toxic compounds in poisoning of rats and humans. *Journal of Comparative and Physiological Psychology, 43*, 358-374. (7, 10)

Richter, C.P. (1956). Ovulation cycles and stress. In C.A. Villee (Ed.), *Gestation—Transactions of the third conference* (pp. 53-70). New York: Josiah Macy, Jr. Foundation. (16)

Richter, C.P. (1957a). On the phenomenon of sudden death in animals and man. *Psychosomatic Medicine, 19*, 191-198. (12)

Richter, C.P. (1957b). Behavior and metabolic cycles in animals and man. In P.H. Hoch & J. Zubin (Eds.), *Experimental psychopathology* (pp. 34-54). New York: Grune & Stratton. (16)

Richter, C.P. (1957c). Hormones and rhythms in man and animals. In G. Pincus (Ed.), *Recent progress in hormone research* (Vol. 13, pp. 105-159). New York: Academic Press. (16)

Richter, C.P. (1958a). Neurological basis of responses to stress. In G.E.W. Wolstenholme & C.M. O'Connor (Eds.), *CIBA foundation symposium on the neurological basis of behaviour* (pp. 204-217). Boston: Little, Brown. (16)

Richter, C.P. (1958b). Abnormal but regular cycles in behavior and metabolism in rats and catatonic-schizophrenics. In M. Reiss (Ed.), *Psychoendocrinology* (pp. 168-181). New York: Grune & Stratton. (16)

Richter, C.P. (1967). Psychopathology of periodic behavior in animals and man. In J. Zubin & H.F. Hunt (Eds.), *Comparative psychopathology* (pp. 205-227). New York: Grune & Stratton. (9)

Richter, C.P. (1975). Deep hypothermia and its effect on the 24-hour clock of rats and hamsters. *Johns Hopkins Medical Journal, 136,* 1-10. (9)

Richter, C.P., & Langworthy, O.R. (1933). The quill mechanism of the porcupine. *Journal für Psychologie und Neurologie, 45,* 143-153. (4)

Riley, J.N., & Walker, D.W. (1978). Morphological alterations in hippocampus after long-term alcohol consumption in mice. *Science, 201,* 646-648. (2)

Rinn, W.E. (1984). The neuropsychology of facial expression: A review of the neurological and psychological mechanisms for producing facial expressions. *Psychological Bulletin, 95,* 52-77. (8, 14)

Riska, B., & Atchley, W.R. (1985). Genetics of growth predict patterns of brain-size evolution. *Science, 229,* 668-671. (5)

Ritvo, E.R., Freeman, B.J., Mason-Brothers, A., Mo, A., & Ritvo, A.M. (1985). Concordance for the syndrome of autism in 40 pairs of afflicted twins. *American Journal of Psychiatry, 142,* 74-77. (16)

Ritvo, E.R., Jorde, L.B., Mason-Brothers, A., Freeman, B.J., Pingree, C., Jones, M.B., McMahon, W.M., Petersen, P.B., Jenson, W.R., & Mo, A. (1989). The UCLA-University of Utah epidemiological survey of autism: Recurrence risk estimates and genetic counseling. *American Journal of Psychiatry, 146,* 1032-1036. (16)

Robbins, T.W., & Everitt, B.J. (1992). Functions of dopamine in the dorsal and ventral striatum. *Seminars in the Neurosciences, 4,* 119-127. (8)

Robillard, T.A.J., & Gersdorff, M.C.H. (1986). Prevention of pre- and perinatal acquired hearing defects, Part I: Study of causes. *Journal of Auditory Research, 26,* 207-237. (7)

Robins, L.N., Helzer, J.E., Weissman, M.M., Orvaschel, H., Gruenberg, E., Burke, J.D., Jr., & Regier, D.A. (1984). Lifetime prevalence of specific psychiatric disorders in three sites. *Archives of General Psychiatry, 41,* 949-958. (12, 6)

Robinson, R.G., Boston, J.D., Starkstein, S.E., & Price, T.R. (1988). Comparison of mania and depression after brain injury: Causal factors. *American Journal of Psychiatry, 145,* 172-178. (12)

Rogers, J., & Morrison, J.H. (1985). Quantitative morphology and regional and laminar distributions of senile plaques in Alzheimer's disease. *Journal of Neuroscience, 5,* 2801-2808. (13)

Roland, P.E., Larsen, B., Lassen, N.A., & Skinhøj, R. (1980). Supplementary motor area and other cortical areas in organization of voluntary movements in man. *Journal of Neurophysiology, 43,* 118-136. (8)

Romanski, L.M., Clugnet, M.-C., & LeDoux, J.E. (1993). Somatosensory and auditory convergence in the lateral nucleus of the amygdala. *Behavioral Neuroscience, 107,* 444-450. (12)

Rome, L.C., Loughna, P.T., & Goldspink, G. (1984). Muscle fiber activity in carp as a function of swimming speed and muscle temperature. *American Journal of Psy-*

chiatry, 247, R272-R279. (8)

Romer, A.S. (1962). *The vertebrate body.* Philadelphia, PA: Saunders. (5)

Rose, J.E., Brugge, J.F., Anderson, D.J., & Hind, J.E. (1967). Phase-locked response to low-frequency tones in single auditory nerve fibers of the squirrel monkey. *Journal of Neurophysiology, 30,* 769-793. (7)

Rosen, J.B., Hitchcock, J.M., Sananes, C.B., Miserendino, M.J.D., & Davis, M. (1991). A direct projection from the central nucleus of the amygdala to the acoustic startle pathway: Anterograde and retrograde tracing studies. *Behavioral Neuroscience, 105,* 817-825. (12)

Rosenberg, R.N. (1993). A causal role for amyloid in Alzheimer's disease: The end of the beginning. *Neurology, 43,* 851-856. (13)

Rosenblatt, J.S. (1967). Nonhormonal basis of maternal behavior in the rat. *Science, 156,* 1512-1514. (11)

Rosenblatt, J.S. (1970). Views on the onset and maintenance of maternal behavior in the rat. In L.R. Aronson, E. Tobach, D.S. Lehrman, & J.S. Rosenblatt (Eds.), *Development and evolution of behavior* (pp. 489-515). San Francisco: W.H. Freeman. (11)

Rosenthal, N.E., Sack, D.A., Gillin, C.J., Lewy, A.J., Goodwin, F.K., Davenport, Y., Mueller, P.S., Newsome, D.A., & Wehr, T.A. (1984). Seasonal affective disorder. *Archives of General Psychiatry, 41,* 72-80. (16)

Ross, R.M., Losey, G.S., & Diamond, M. (1983). Sex change in a coral-reef fish: Dependence of stimulation and inhibition on relative size. *Science, 217,* 574-576. (11)

Rosvold, H.E., Mirsky, A.F., & Pribram, K.H. (1954). Influence of amygdalectomy on social behavior in monkeys. *Journal of Comparative and Physiological Psychology, 47,* 173-178. (12)

Roth, R.H. (1984). CNS dopamine autoreceptors: Distribution, pharmacology, and function. *Annals of the New York Academy of Sciences, 430,* 27-53. (3)

Rothman, S.M. (1983). Synaptic activity mediates death of hypoxic neurons. *Science, 220,* 536-537. (15)

Rothman, S.M. (1992). Excitotoxins: Possible mechanism of action. *Annals of the New York Academy of Sciences, 648,* 132-139. (15)

Rouet-Smih, F., Tonon, M.-C., Pelletier, G., & Vaudry, H. (1992). Characterization of endozepine-related peptides in the central nervous system and in peripheral tissues of the rat. *Peptides, 13,* 1219-1225. (12)

Rovainen, C.M. (1976). Regeneration of Müller and Mauthner axons after spinal transection in larval lampreys. *Journal of Comparative Neurology, 168,* 545-554. (15)

Rovee-Collier, C., Kupersmidt, J., O'Brien, L., Collier, G., & Tepper, V. (1991). Behavioral thermoregulation and immobilization: Conflicting demands for survival. *Journal of Comparative Psychology, 105,* 232-242. (11)

Rowland, N. (1980). Drinking behavior: Physiological, neurological, and environmental factors. In T.M. Toates & T.R. Halliday (Eds.), *Analysis of motivational*

processes (pp. 39-59). London: Academic Press. (10)

Rowland, N., & Flamm, C. (1977). Quinine drinking: More regulatory puzzles. *Physiology & Behavior, 18,* 1165-1170. (10)

Roy, A., DeJong, J., & Linnoila, M. (1989). Cerebrospinal fluid monoamine metabolites and suicidal behavior in depressed patients. *Archives of General Psychiatry, 46,* 609-612. (12)

Roy-Byrne, P.P., Uhde, T.W., & Post, R.M. (1986). Effects of one night's sleep deprivation on mood and behavior in panic disorder. *Archives of General Psychiatry, 43,* 895-899. (16)

Rozin, P. (1984). The acquisition of food habits and preferences. In J.D. Matarazzo, S.M. Weiss, J.A. Herd, N.E. Miller, & S.M. Weiss (Eds.), *Behavioral health: A handbook of health enhancement and disease prevention* (pp. 590-607). New York: John Wiley. (10)

Rozin, P. (1990). Getting to like the burn of chili pepper. In B.G. Green, J.R. Mason, & M.R. Kare (Eds.), *Chemical senses,* (Vol. 2, pp. 231-269). New York: Marcel Dekker. (10)

Rozin, P., & Fallon, A.E. (1987). A perspective on disgust. *Psychological Review, 94,* 23-41. (10)

Rozin, P., & Jonides, J. (1977). Mass reaction time measurement of the speed of the nerve impulse and the duration of mental processes in class. *Teaching of Psychology, 4,* 91-94. (2)

Rozin, P., & Kalat, J.W. (1971). Specific hungers and poison avoidance as adaptive specializations of learning. *Psychological Review, 78,* 459-486. (10, 13)

Rozin, P., & Pelchat, M.L. (1988). Memories of mammaries: Adaptations to weaning from milk. *Progress in Psychobiology and Physiological Psychology, 13,* 1-29. (10)

Rozin, P., & Schull, J. (1988). The adaptive-evolutionary point of view in experimental psychology. In R.C. Atkinson, R.J. Herrnstein, G. Lindzey, & R.D. Luce (Eds.), *Stevens' handbook of experimental psychology (2nd ed.), Vol. 1: Perception and motivation* (pp. 503-546). (13)

Rozin, P., & Vollmecke, T.A. (1986). Food likes and dislikes. *Annual Review of Nutrition, 6,* 433-456. (10)

Rozin, P., & Zellner, D. (1985). The role of Pavlovian conditioning in the acquisition of food likes and dislikes. *Annals of the New York Academy of Sciences, 443,* 189-202. (10)

Rubens, A.B., & Benson, D.F. (1971). Associative visual agnosia. *Archives of Neurology, 24,* 305-316. (6)

Rudelli, R.D., Brown, W.T., Wisniewski, K., Jenkins, E.C., Laure-Kamionowska, M., Connell, F., & Wisniewski, H.M. (1985). Adult fragile X syndrome. Clinico-neuropathologic findings. *Acta Neuropathologica, 67,* 289-295. (A)

Rumbaugh, D.M. (1990). Comparative psychology and the great apes: Their competency in learning, language, and numbers. *Psychological Record, 40,* 15-39. (14)

Rumsey, J.M., Duara, R., Grady, C., Rapoport, J.L., Margolin, R.A., Rapoport, S.I., & Cutler, N.R. (1985). Brain metabolism in autism. *Archives of General Psychiatry, 42,* 448-455. (16)

Rusak, B. (1977). The role of the suprachiasmatic nuclei in the generation of circadian rhythms in the golden hamster, *Mesocricetus auratus. Journal of Comparative Physiology* A, *118*, 145-164. (9)

Rusak, B., & Zucker, I. (1979). Neural regulation of circadian rhythms. *Physiological Reviews, 59*, 449-526. (9)

Rushton, J.P. (1988). Race differences in behaviour: A review and evolutionary analysis. *Personality and Individual Differences, 9*, 1009-1024. (5)

Russell, M.J., Switz, G.M., & Thompson, K. (1980). Olfactory influences on the human menstrual cycle. *Pharmacology, Biochemistry, and Behavior, 13*, 737-738. (7)

Sabel, B.A., Slavin, M.D., & Stein, D.G. (1984). GM₁ ganglioside treatment facilitates behavioral recovery from bilateral brain damage. *Science, 225*, 340-342. (15)

Sack, D.A., Nurnberger, J., Rosenthal, N.E., Ashburn, E., & Wehr, T.A. (1985). Potentiation of antidepressant medications by phase advance of the sleep-wake cycle. *American Journal of Psychiatry, 142*, 606-608. (16)

Sack, R.L., Lewy, A.J., White, D.M., Singer, C.M., Fireman, M.J., & Vandiver, R. (1990). Morning vs. evening light treatment for winter depression. *Archives of General Psychiatry, 47*, 343-351. (16)

Sackeim, H.A., Prohovnik, I., Moeller, J.R., Brown, R.P., Apter, S., Prudic, J., Devanand, D.P., & Mukherjee, S. (1990). Regional cerebral blood flow in mood disorders. I. Comparison of major depressives and normal controls at rest. *Archives of General Psychiatry, 47*, 60-70. (16)

Sackeim, H.A., Putz, E., Vingiano, W., Coleman, E., & McElhiney, M. (1988). Lateralization in the processing of emotionally laden information, I. Normal functioning. *Neuropsychiatry, Neuropsychology, and Behavioral Neurology, 1*, 97-110. (14)

Sahley, T.L., & Panksepp, J. (1987). Brain opioids and autism: An updated analysis of possible linkages. *Journal of Autism and Developmental Disorders, 17*, 201-216. (16)

Sakai, R.R., & Epstein, A.N. (1990). Dependence of adrenalectomy-induced sodium appetite on the action of angiotensin II in the brain of the rat. *Behavioral Neuroscience, 104*, 167-176. (10)

Sakai, R.R., Frankmann, S.P., Fine, W.B., & Epstein, A.N. (1989). Prior episodes of sodium depletion increase the need-free sodium intake of the rat. *Behavioral Neuroscience, 103*, 186-192. (10)

Sakurai, Y. (1990). Cells in the rat auditory system have sensory-delay correlates during the performance of an auditory working memory task. *Behavioral Neuroscience, 104*, 856-868. (13)

Salthouse, T.A. (1984, February). The skill of typing. *Scientific American, 250*(2), 128-135. (8)

Sananes, C.B., & Davis, M. (1992). N-methyl-D-aspartate lesions of the lateral and basolateral nuclei of the amygdala block fear-potentiated startle and shock sensitization of shock. *Behavioral Neuroscience, 106*, 72-80. (12)

Sanberg, P.R., & Coyle, J.T. (1984). Scientific approaches to Huntington's disease. *CRC Critical Reviews in Clinical Neurobiology, 1*, 1-44. (8)

Sanberg, P.R., Pevsner, J., Autuono, P.G., & Coyle, J.T. (1985). Fetal methylazoxymethanol acetate-induced lesions cause reductions in dopamine receptor-mediated catalepsy and stereotypy. *Neuropharmacology, 24*, 1057-1062. (4)

Sanders, R.J. (1989). Sentence comprehension following agenesis of the corpus callosum. *Brain and Language, 37*, 59-72. (14)

Sanderson, W.C., Rapee, R.M., & Barlow, D.H. (1989). The influence of an illusion of control on panic attacks induced via inhalation of 5.5% carbon dioxide-enriched air. *Archives of General Psychiatry, 46*, 157-162. (12)

Sandman, C.A., Barron, J.L., Demet, E.M., Chicz-Demet, A., Rothenberg, S.J., & Zea, F.J. (1990). Opioid peptides and perinatal development: Is beta-endorphin a natural teratogen? *Annals of the New York Academy of Sciences, 579*, 91-108. (16)

Sanes, J.R. (1993). Topographic maps and molecular gradients. *Current Opinion in Neurobiology, 3*, 67-74. (5)

Saron, C.D., & Davidson, R.J. (1989). Visual evoked potential measures of interhemispheric transfer time in humans. *Behavioral Neuroscience, 103*, 1115-1138. (14)

Sáry, G., Vogels, R., & Orban, G.A. (1993). Cue-invariant shape selectivity of macaque inferior temporal neurons. *Science, 260*, 995-997. (6)

Sassoon, D.A., Gray, G.E., & Kelley, D.B. (1987). Androgen regulation of muscle fiber type in the sexually dimorphic larynx of *Xenopus laevis. Journal of Neuroscience, 7*, 3198-3206. (8)

Satinoff, E. (1964). Behavioral thermoregulation in response to local cooling of the rat brain. *American Journal of Physiology, 206*, 1389-1394. (10)

Satinoff, E. (1988). Thermal influences on REM sleep. In R. Lydic & J.F. Biebuyck (Eds.), *Clinical physiology of sleep* (pp. 135-144). Bethesda, MD: American Physiological Society. (9)

Satinoff, E. (1991). Developmental aspects of behavioral and reflexive thermoregulation. In H.N. Shanir, G.A. Barr, & M.A. Hofer (Eds.), *Developmental psychobiology: New methods and changing concepts* (pp. 169-188). New York: Oxford University Press. (10)

Satinoff, E., Liran, J., & Clapman, R. (1982). Aberrations of circadian body temperature rhythms in rats with medial preoptic lesions. *American Journal of Physiology, 242*, R352-R357. (10)

Satinoff, E., McEwen, G.N., Jr., & Williams, B.A. (1976). Behavioral fever in newborn rabbits. *Science, 193*, 1139-1140. (10)

Satinoff, E., & Rutstein, J. (1970). Behavioral thermoregulation in rats with anterior hypothalamic lesions. *Journal of Comparative and Physiological Psychology, 71*, 77-82. (10)

Satinoff, E., Valentino, D., & Teitelbaum, P. (1976). Thermoregulatory cold-defense deficits in rats with preoptic/anterior hypothalamic lesions. *Brain Research Bulletin, 1*, 553-565. (10)

Sato, M. (1992). A lasting vulnerability to psychosis in patients with previous methamphetamine psychosis. *Annals of the New York Academy of Sciences, 654*, 160-170. (16)

Satz, P., Strauss, E., & Whitaker, H. (1990). The ontogeny of hemispheric specialization: Some old hypotheses revisited. *Brain and Language, 38*, 596-614. (15)

Sauerwein, H.C., Lassonde, M.C., Cardu, B., & Geoffroy, G. (1981). Interhemispheric integration of sensory and motor functions in agenesis of the corpus callosum. *Neuropsychologia, 19*, 445-454. (14)

Savage-Rumbaugh, E. (1991). Language learning in the bonobo: How and why they learn. In N.A. Kresnegor, D.M. Rumbaugh, R.L. Schiefelbusch, & M. Studdert-Kennedy (Eds.), *Biological and behavioral determinants of language development* (pp. 209-233). Hillsdale, NJ: Lawrence Erlbaum. (14)

Savage-Rumbaugh, E.S. (1990). Language acquisition in a nonhuman species: Implications for the innateness debate. *Developmental Psychobiology, 23*, 599-620. (14)

Savage-Rumbaugh, E.S. (1993). Language learnability in man, ape, and dolphin. In H. L. Roitblat, L.M. Herman, & P.E. Nachtigall (Eds.), *Language and communication: Comparative perspectives* (pp. 457-473). Hillsdale, NJ: Lawrence Erlbaum. (14)

Savage-Rumbaugh, E.S., Murphy, J., Sevcik, R.A., Brakke, K.E., Williams, S.L., & Rumbaugh, D.M. (1993). Language comprehension in ape and child. *Monographs of the Society for Research in child development, 58*, serial no. 233. (14)

Savage-Rumbaugh, E.S., Sevcik, R.A., Brakke, K.E., & Rumbaugh, D.M. (1992). Symbols: Their communicative use, communication, and combination by bonobos (*Pan paniscus*). In L.P. Lipsitt & C. Rovee-Collier (Eds.), *Advances in infancy research* (Vol. 7, pp. 221-278). Norwood, NJ: Ablex. (14)

Scalia, F., & Winans, S.S. (1976). New perspectives on the morphology of the olfactory system: Olfactory and vomeronasal pathways in mammals. In R.L. Doty (Ed.), *Mammalian olfaction, reproductive processes and behavior* (pp. 7-28). New York: Academic Press. (7)

Schacher, S., Castellucci, V.F., & Kandel, E.R. (1988). cAMP evokes long-term facilitation in *Aplysia* sensory neurons that requires new protein synthesis. *Science, 240*, 1667-1669. (13)

Schacter, D.L. (1983). Amnesia observed: Remembering and forgetting in a natural environment. *Journal of Abnormal Psychology, 92*, 236-242. (13)

Schacter, D.L. (1985). Priming of old and new knowledge in amnesic patients and normal subjects. *Annals of the New York Academy of Sciences, 444*, 41-53. (13)

Schallert, T. (1983). Sensorimotor impairment and recovery of function in brain-damaged rats: Reappearance of symptoms during old age. *Behavioral Neuroscience, 97*, 159-164. (15)

Schallert, T., & Whishaw, I.Q. (1984). Bilateral cutaneous stimulation of the somatosensory system in hemidecorticate rats. *Behavioral Neuroscience, 98*, 518-540. (15)

Scheff, S.W., & Cotman, C.W. (1977). Recovery of spontaneous alternation following lesions of the entorhinal cortex in adult rats: Possible correlation to axon sprouting. *Behavioral Biology, 21*, 286-293. (15)

Scheibel, A.B. (1983). Dendritic changes. In B. Reisberg (Ed.), *Alzheimer's disease* (pp. 69-73). New York: Free Press. (13)

Scheibel, A.B. (1984). A dendritic correlate of human speech. In N. Geschwind & A.M. Galaburda (Eds.), *Cerebral dominance* (pp. 43-52). Cambridge, MA: Harvard University Press. (4)

Scheibel, M.E., & Scheibel, A.R. (1963). Some structure-functional correlates of development in young cats. *Electroencephalography and Clinical Neurophysiology, 15* (Suppl. 24), 235-246. (4)

Schellenberg, G.D., Bird, T.D., Wijsman, E.M., Orr, H.T., Anderson, L., Nemens, E., White, J.A., Bonnycastle, L., Weber, J.L., Alonso, M.E., Potter, H., Heston, L.L., & Martin, G.M. (1992). Genetic linkage evidence for a familial Alzheimer's disease locus on chromosome 14. *Science, 258*, 668-671. (13)

Schelling, T.C. (1992). Addictive drugs: The cigarette experience. *Science, 255*, 430-433. (3)

Schenk, L., & Bear, D. (1981). Multiple personality and related dissociative phenomena in patients with temporal lobe epilepsy. *American Journal of Psychiatry, 138*, 1311-1316. (12)

Scherer, S.S. (1986). Reinnervation of the extraocular muscles in goldfish is nonselective. *Journal of Neuroscience, 6*, 764-77 3. (15)

Schieber, M.H., & Hibbard, L.S. (1993). How somatotopic is the motor cortex hand area? *Science, 261*, 489-492. (8)

Schiffman, S.S. (1983). Taste and smell in disease. *New England Journal of Medicine, 308*, 1275-1279, 1337-1343. (7)

Schiffman, S.S., & Erickson, R.P. (1971). A psychophysical model for gustatory quality. *Physiology & Behavior, 7*, 617-633. (7)

Schiffman, S.S., & Erickson, R.P. (1980). The issue of primary tastes versus a taste continuum. *Neuroscience & Biobehavioral Reviews, 4*, 109-117. (7)

Schiffman, S.S., Lockhead, E., & Maes, F.W. (1983). Amiloride reduces the taste intensity of Na$^+$ and Li$^+$ salts and sweeteners. *Proceedings of the National Academy of Sciences, U.S.A., 80*, 6136-6140. (7)

Schiffman, S.S., McElroy, A.E., & Erickson, R.P. (1980). The range of taste quality of sodium salts. *Physiology & Behavior, 24*, 217-224. (7)

Schiffman, S.S., Simon, S.A., Gill, J.M., & Beeker, T.G. (1986). Bretylium tosylate enhances salt taste. *Physiology & Behavior, 36*, 1129-1137. (7)

Schiller, F. (1979). *Paul Broca*. Berkeley: University of California Press. (14)

Schiller, P.H., & Lee, K. (1991). The role of the primate extrastriate area V4 in vision. *Science, 251*, 1251-1253. (6)

Schmidt, J.T., Cicerone, C.M., & Easter, S.S. (1977). Expansion of the half retinal projection to the tectum in goldfish: An electrophysiological and anatomical study. *Journal of Comparative Neurology, 177*, 257-278. (5)

Schneider, B.A., Trehub, S.E., Morrongiello, B.A., & Thorpe, L.A. (1986). Auditory sensitivity in preschool children. *Journal of the Acoustical Society of America, 79*, 447-452. (7)

Schneider, G.E., & Jhaveri, S.R. (1974). Neuroanatomical correlates of spared or altered function after brain lesions in the newborn hamster. In D.G. Stein, J.J. Rosen, & N. Butters (Eds.), *Plasticity and recovery of function in the central nervous system* (pp. 65-109). New York: Academic Press. (15)

Schöpf, J., Bryois, C., Jonquière, M., & Le, P.K. (1984). On the nosology of severe psychiatric post-partum disorders. *European Archives of Psychiatry and Neurological Sciences, 234*, 54-63. (16)

Schopler, E. (1987). Specific and nonspecific factors in the effectiveness of a treatment system. *American Psychologist, 42*, 376-383. (16)

Schulkin, J. (1991). *Sodium hunger: The search for a salty taste.* Cambridge, England: Cambridge University Press. (10)

Schuman, E.M., & Madison, D.V. (1991). A requirement for the intercellular messenger nitric oxide in long-term potentiation. *Science, 254*, 1503-1506. (13)

Schurr, A., & Rigor, B.M. (1993). Kainate toxicity in energy-compromised rat hippocampal slices: Differences between oxygen and glucose deprivation. *Brain Research, 614*, 10-14. (15)

Schwartz, D.H., McClane, S., Hernandez, L., & Hoebel, B. (1989). Feeding increases extracellular serotonin in the lateral hypothalamus of the rat as measured by microdialysis. *Brain Research, 479*, 349-354. (10)

Schwartz, J.C., Giros, B., Martres, M.-P., & Sokoloff, P. (1992). The dopamine receptor family: Molecular biology and pharmacology. *Seminars in the Neurosciences, 4*, 99-108. (3)

Schwartz, M., Belkin, M., Harel, A., Solomon, A., Lavie, V., Hadani, M., Rachailovich, I., & Stein-Izsak, C. (1985). Regenerating fish optic nerves and a regeneration-like response in injured optic nerves of adult rabbits. *Science, 228*, 600-603. (15)

Scott, T.R. (1987). Coding in the gustatory system. In T.E. Finger & W.L. Silver (Eds.), *Neurobiology of taste and smell* (pp. 355-378). New York: John Wiley. (7)

Scott, T.R. (1992). Taste: The neural basis of body wisdom. In A.P. Simopoulos (Ed.), *Nutritional triggers for health and in disease* (pp. 1-39). Basel: Karger. (7)

Scott, T.R., & Chang, F.-C.T. (1984). The state of gustatory neural coding. *Chemical Senses, 8*, 297-314. (7)

Scott, T.R., & Perrotto, R.S. (1980). Intensity coding in pontine taste area: Gustatory information is processed similarly throughout rat's brain stem. *Journal of Neurophysiology, 44*, 739-750. (7)

Scott, T.R., & Plata-Salaman, C.R. (1991). Coding of taste quality. In T.V. Getchell et al. (Eds.), *Smell and taste in health and disease* (pp. 345-368). New York: Raven Press. (7)

Scovern, A.W., & Kilmann, P.R. (1980). Status of electroconvulsive therapy: Review of the outcome literature. *Psychological Bulletin, 87*, 260-303. (16)

Scoville, W.B., & Milner, B. (1957). Loss of recent memory after bilateral hippocampal lesions. *Journal of Neurology, Neurosurgery, and Psychiatry, 20*, 11-21. (13)

Seeman, P., Lee, T., Chau-Wong, M., & Wong, K. (1976). Antipsychotic drug doses and neuroleptic/dopamine receptors. *Nature, 261*, 717-719. (16)

Segal, N. (1984). Asymmetries in monozygotic twins. *American Journal of Psychiatry, 141*, 1638. (16)

Sejnowski, T.J., Chattarji, S., & Stanton, P.K. (1990). Homosynaptic long-term depression in hippocampus and neocortex. *Seminars in the Neurosciences, 2*, 355-363. (13)

Selzer, M.E. (1978). Mechanisms of functional recovery and regeneration after spinal cord transection in larval sea lamprey. *Journal of Physiology, 277*, 395-408. (15)

Sereno, A.B., & Holzman, P.S. (1993). Express saccades and smooth pursuit eye movement function in schizophrenic, affective disorder, and normal subjects. *Journal of Cognitive Neuroscience, 5*, 303-316. (16)

Shah, A., & Lisak, R.P. (1993). Immunopharmacologic therapy in myasthenia gravis. *Clinical Neuropharmacology, 16*, 97-103. (8)

Shalev, A.Y., Orr, S.P., Peri, T., Schreiber, S., & Pitman, R.K. (1992). Physiologic responses to loud tones in Israeli patients with posttraumatic stress disorder. *Archives of General Psychiatry, 49*, 870-875. (12)

Shanon, B. (1980). Lateralization effects in musical decision tasks. *Neuropsychologia, 18*, 21-31. (14)

Shapiro, B.E., & Danly, M. (1985). The role of the right hemisphere in the control of speech prosody in propositional and affective contexts. *Brain and Language, 25*, 19-36. (14)

Shapiro, C.M., Bortz, R., Mitchell, D., Bartel, P., & Jooste, P. (1981). Slow-wave sleep: A recovery period after exercise. *Science, 214*, 1253-1254. (9)

Shapiro, D.J., Barton, M.C., McKearin, D.M., Chang, T.-C., Lew, D., Blume, J., Nielsen, D.A., & Gould, L. (1989). Estrogen regulation of gene transcription and mRNA stability. *Recent Advances in Hormone Research, 45*, 29-64. (11)

Shatz, C.J. (1992, September). The developing brain. *Scientific American, 267* (9), 60-67. (5)

Shepherd, G.M. (1988). *Neurobiology* (2nd ed.). New York: Oxford University Press. (3)

Sherman, S.M., & Spear, P.D. (1982). Organization of visual pathways in normal and visually deprived cats. *Physiological Reviews, 62*, 738-855. (6)

Sherrington, C.S. (1906). *The integrative action of the nervous system.* New York: Scribner's. (2nd ed.). New Haven, CT: Yale University Press. (3)

Sherwin, B.B. (1988). A comparative analysis of the role of androgen in human male and female sexual behavior: Behavioral specificity, critical thresholds, and sensitivity. *Psychobiology, 16*, 416-425. (11)

Shields, S.A. (1983). Development of autonomic nervous system responsivity in children: A review of the literature. *International Journal of Behavioral Development, 6*, 291-319. (12)

Shik, M.L., & Orlovsky, G.N. (1976). Neurophysiology of locomotor automatism. *Physiological Reviews, 56,* 465-501. (8)

Shimamura, A.P., Janowsky, J.S., & Squire, L.R. (1990). Memory for the temporal order of events in patients with frontal lobe lesions and amnesic patients. *Neuropsychologia, 28,* 803-813. (13)

Shirley, S.G., & Persaud, K.C. (1990). The biochemistry of vertebrate olfaction and taste. *Seminars in the Neurosciences, 2,* 59-68. (7)

Shoulson, I. (1990). Huntington's disease: Cognitive and psychiatric features. *Neuropsychiatry, Neuropsychology, and Behavioral Neurology, 3,* 15-22. (8)

Shozu, M., Akasofu, K., Harada, T., & Kubota, Y. (1991). A new cause of female pseudohermaphroditism: Placental aromatase deficiency. *Journal of Clinical Endocrinology and Metabolism, 72,* 560-566. (11)

Shutts, D. (1982). *Lobotomy: Resort to the knife.* New York: Van Nostrand Reinhold. (4)

Sidman, R.L., Green, M.C., & Appel, S.H. (1965). *Catalog of the neurological mutants of the mouse.* Cambridge, MA: Harvard University Press. (4)

Sidtis, J.J., Volpe, B.T., Holtzman, J.D., Wilson, D.H., & Gazzaniga, M.S. (1981). Cognitive interaction after staged callosal section: Evidence for transfer of semantic activation. *Science, 212,* 344-346. (14)

Siegel, A., & Brutus, M. (1990). Neural substrates of aggression and rage in the cat. *Progress in Psychobiology and Physiological Psychology, 14,* 135-233. (12)

Siegel, A., & Pott, C.B. (1988). Neural substrates of aggression and flight in the cat. *Progress in Neurobiology, 31,* 261-283. (12)

Siegel, J.M., Nienhuis, R., Fahringer, H.M., Paul, R., Shiromani, P., Dement, W.C., Mignot, E., & Chiu, C. (1991). Neuronal activity in narcolepsy: Identification of cataplexy-related cells in the medial medulla. *Science, 252,* 1315-1318. (9)

Silinsky, E.M. (1989). Adenosine derivatives and neuronal function. *Seminars in the Neurosciences, 1,* 155-165. (3)

Simmons, J.A., Wever, E.G., & Pylka, J.M. (1971). Periodical cicada: Sound production and hearing. *Science, 171,* 212-213. (7)

Simpson, J.L. (1976). *Disorders of sexual differentiation.* New York: Academic Press. (11)

Singer, W. (1986). Neuronal activity as a shaping factor in postnatal development of visual cortex. In W.T. Greenough & J.M. Jusaska (Eds.), *Developmental neuropsychobiology* (pp. 271-293). Orlando, FL: Academic Press. (6)

Sirigu, A., Grafman, J., Bressler, K., & Sunderland, T. (1991). Multiple representations contribute to body knowledge processing. Evidence from a case of autopagnosia. *Brain, 114,* 629-642. (7)

Sitaram, N., Weingartner, H., & Gillin, J.C. (1978). Human serial learning: Enhancement with arecholine and choline and impairment with scopolamine. *Science, 201,* 274-276. (13)

Sjöström, M., Friden, J., & Ekblom, B. (1987). Endurance, what is it? Muscle morphology after an extremely long distance run. *Acta Physiologica Scandinavica, 130,* 513-520. (8)

Sjöström, M., Johansson, C., & Lorentzon, R. (1988). Muscle pathomorphology in m. quadriceps of marathon runners. Early signs of strain disease or functional adaptation? *Acta Physiologica Scandinavica, 132,* 537-542. (8)

Sklar, L.S., & Anisman, H. (1981). Stress and cancer. *Psychological Bulletin, 89,* 369-406. (12)

Small, J.G., Kellams, J.J., Milstein, V., & Small, I.F. (1980). Complications with electroconvulsive treatment combined with lithium. *Biological Psychiatry, 15,* 103-112. (16)

Smeraldi, E., Kidd, K.K., Negri, F., Heimbuch, R., & Melica, A.M. (1979). Genetic studies of affective disorders. In J. Obiols, C. Ballús, E. González Monclús, & J. Pujol (Eds.), *Biological psychiatry today* (pp. 60-65). Amsterdam: Elsevier/North Holland Biomedical Press. (16)

Smith, C., & Wong, P.T.P. (1991). Paradoxical sleep increases predict successful learning in a complex operant task. *Behavioral Neuroscience, 105,* 282-288. (9)

Smith, C.A.D., Gough, A.C., Leigh, P.N., Summers, B.A., Harding, A.E., Maranganore, D.M., Sturman, S.G., Schapira, A.H.V., Williams, A.C., Spurr, N.K., & Wolf, C.R. (1992). Debrisoquine hydroxylase gene polymorphism and susceptibility to Parkinson's disease. *Lancet, 339,* 1375-1377. (8)

Smith, D.C. (1981). Functional restoration of vision in the cat after long-term monocular deprivation. *Science, 213,* 1137-1139. (6)

Smith, D.V., VanBuskirk, R.L., Travers, J.B., & Bieber, S.L. (1983). Coding of taste stimuli by hamster brain stem neurons. *Journal of Neurophysiology, 50,* 541-558. (7)

Smith, L.T. (1975). The interanimal transfer phenomenon: A review. *Psychological Bulletin, 81,* 1078-1095. (13)

Smith, S.S., O'Hara, B.F., Persico, A.M., Gorelick, D.A., Newlin, D.B., Vlahav, D., Solomon, L., Pickens, R., & Uhl, G.R. (1992). Genetic vulnerability to drug abuse: The D_2 dopamine receptor Taq1B1 restriction fragment length polymorphism appears more frequently in polysubstance abusers. *Archives of General Psychiatry, 49,* 723-727. (3)

Snyder, G.L., & Stricker, E.M. (1985). Effects of lateral hypothalamic lesions on food intake of rats during exposure to cold. *Behavioral Neuroscience, 99,* 310-322. (15)

Snyder, S.H. (1984). Drug and neurotransmitter receptors in the brain. *Science, 224,* 22-31. (3)

Snyder, S.H. (1992). Nitric oxide and neurons. *Current Opinion in Neurobiology, 2,* 323-327. (3)

Snyder, S.H., Banerjee, S.P., Yamamura, H.I., & Greenberg, D. (1974). Drugs, neurotransmitters, and schizophrenia. *Science, 184,* 1243-1253. (16)

Somjen, G.G. (1988). Nervenkitt: Notes on the history of the concept of neuroglia. *Glia, 1,* 2-9. (2)

Sonderegger, T.B. (1970). Intracranial stimulation and maternal behavior. *APA Convention Proceedings, 78th meeting,* 245-246. (12)

Spencer, D.D., Robbins, R.J., Naftolin, F., Marek, K.L., Vollmer, T., Leranth, C., Roth, R.H., Price, L.H., Gjedde, A., Bunnery, B.S., Sass, K.J., Elsworth, J.D., Kier, E.L., Makuch, R., Hoffer, P.B., & Redmond, D.E., Jr. (1992). Unilateral transplantation of human fetal mesencephalic tissue into the caudate nucleus of patients with Parkinson's disease. *New England Journal of Medicine, 327,* 1541-1548. (15)

Spencer, P.S., Ludolph, A.C., & Kisby, G.E. (1992). Are human neurodegenerative disorders linked to environmental chemicals with excitotoxic properties? *Annals of the New York Academy of Sciences, 648,* 154-160. (8)

Sperry, R.W. (1943). Visuomotor coordination in the newt (*Triturus viridescens*) after regeneration of the optic nerve. *Journal of Comparative Neurology, 79,* 33-55. (5)

Sperry, R.W. (1961). Cerebral organization and behavior. *Science, 133,* 1749-1757. (14)

Sperry, R.W. (1993). The impact and promise of the cognitive revolution. *American Psychologist, 48,* 878-885. (1)

Spiegel, T.A. (1973). Caloric regulation of food intake in man. *Journal of Comparative and Physiological Psychology, 84,* 24-37. (10)

Spies, G. (1965). Food versus intra-cranial self-stimulation reinforcement in food-deprived rats. *Journal of Comparative and Physiological Psychology, 60,* 153-157. (12)

Spoont, M.R. (1992). Modulatory role of serotonin in neural information processing: Implications for human psychopathology. *Psychological Bulletin, 112,* 330-350. (12)

Spurzheim, J.G. (1908). *Phrenology* (rev. ed.). Philadelphia: Lippincott. (4)

Squire, L.R. (1992). Memory and the hippocampus: A synthesis from findings with rats, monkeys, and humans. *Psychological Review, 99,* 195-231. (13)

Squire, L.R., Amaral, D.G., & Press, G.A. (1990). Magnetic resonance imaging of the hippocampal formation and mammillary nuclei distinguish medial temporal lobe and diencephalic amnesia. *Journal of Neuroscience, 10,* 3106-3117. (13)

Squire, L.R., & Spanis, C.W. (1984). Long gradient of retrograde amnesia in mice: Continuity with the findings in humans. *Behavioral Neuroscience, 98,* 345-348. (13)

Squire, L.R., Wetzel, C.D., & Slater, P.C. (1979). Memory complaint after electroconvulsive therapy: Assessment with a new self-rating instrument. *Biological Psychiatry, 14,* 791-801. (16)

Squire, L.R., & Zouzounis, J.A. (1986). ECT and memory: Brief pulse versus sine wave. *American Journal of Psychiatry, 143,* 596-601. (16)

Staller, J., Buchanan, D., Singer, M., Lappin, J., & Webb, W. (1978). Alexia without agraphia: An experimental case study. *Brain and Language, 5,* 378-387. (14)

Stanford, L.R. (1987). Conduction velocity variations minimize conduction time differences among retinal ganglion cell axons. *Science, 238,* 358-360. (6)

Stanley, B.G., Schwartz, D.H., Hernandez, L., Leibowitz, S.F., & Hoebel, B.G. (1989). Patterns of extracellular

5-hydroxyindoleacetic acid (5-HIAA) in the paraventricular hypothalamus (PVN): Relation to circadian rhythm and deprivation-induced eating behavior. *Pharmacology, Biochemistry, & Behavior, 33,* 257-260. (10)

Starke, K. (1981). Presynaptic receptors. *Annual Review of Pharmacology and Toxicology, 21,* 7-30. (3, 16)

Starkstein, S.E., & Robinson, R.G. (1986). Cerebral lateralization in depression. *American Journal of Psychiatry, 143,* 1631. (16)

Starr, C., & Taggart, R. (1989). *Biology: The unity and diversity of life.* Belmont, CA: Wadsworth. (7, 8, 11)

Stein, D.G., Finger, S., & Hart, T. (1983). Brain damage and recovery: Problems and perspectives. *Behavioral and Neural Biology, 37,* 185-222. (15)

Stein, L. (1962). Effects and interactions of imipramine, chlorpromazine, reserpine, and amphetamine on self-stimulation: Possible neurophysiological basis of depression. In J. Wortis (Ed.), *Recent advances in biological psychiatry* (Vol. 4, pp. 288-308). New York: Plenum. (16)

Stein, L., & Wise, C.D. (1971). Possible etiology of schizophrenia: Progressive damage to the noradrenergic reward system by 6-hydroxydopamine. *Science, 171,* 1032-1036. (16)

Stein, M., Miller, A.H., & Trestman, R.L. (1991). Depression, the immune system, and health and illness. *Archives of General Psychiatry, 48,* 171-177. (12)

Stephan, F.K. (1992). Resetting of a feeding-entrainable circadian clock in the rat. *Physiology & Behavior, 52,* 985-995. (9)

Stephenson, F.A., & Dolphin, A.C. (1989). GABA and glycine neurotransmission. *Seminars in the Neurosciences, 1,* 115-123. (3)

Steriade, M. (1992). Basic mechanisms of sleep generation. *Neurology, 42* (Suppl. 6), 9-18. (9)

Stockman, E.R., Callaghan, R.S., Gallagher, C.A., & Baum, M.J. (1986). Sexual differentiation of play behavior in the ferret. *Behavioral Neuroscience, 100,* 563-568. (11)

Stolerman, I.P. (1991). Behavioural pharmacology of nicotine: Multiple mechanisms. *British Journal of Addiction, 86,* 533-536. (3)

Stoner, G.R., & Albright, T.D. (1993). Image segmentation cues in motion processing: Implications for modularity in vision. *Journal of Cognitive Neuroscience, 5,* 129-149. (6)

Strachan, R.D., Whittle, I.R., & Miller, J.D. (1989). Hypothermia and severe head injury. *Brain Injury, 3,* 51-55. (15)

Streissguth, A.P., Barr, H.M., & Martin, D.C. (1983). Maternal alcohol use and neonatal habituation assessed with the Brazelton scale. *Child Development, 54,* 1109-1118. (5)

Strichartz, G., Rando, T., & Wang, G.K. (1987). An integrated view of the molecular toxinology of sodium channel gating in excitable cells. *Annual Review of Neuroscience, 10,* 237-267. (2)

Stricker, E.M. (1969). Osmoregulation and volume regulation in rats: Inhibition of hypovolemic thirst by water. *American Journal of Physiology, 217,* 98-105. (10)

Stricker, E.M. (1976). Drinking by rats after lateral hypothalamic lesions: A new look

at the lateral hypothalamic syndrome. *Journal of Comparative and Physiological Psychology, 90,* 127-143. (10)

Stricker, E.M. (1983). Thirst and sodium appetite after colloid treatment in rats: Role of the renin-angiotensinaldosterone system. *Behavioral Neuroscience, 97,* 725-737. (10)

Stricker, E.M., & Coburn, P.C. (1978). Osmoregulatory thirst in rats after lateral preoptic lesions. *Journal of Comparative and Physiological Psychology, 92,* 350-361. (10)

Stricker, E.M., Cooper, P.H., Marshall, J.F., & Zigmond, M.J. (1979). Acute homeostatic imbalances reinstate sensorimotor dysfunctions in rats with lateral hypothalamic lesions. *Journal of Comparative and Physiological Psychology, 93,* 512-521. (15)

Stricker, E.M., & Macarthur, J.P. (1974). Physiological bases for different effects of extravascular colloid treatments on water and NaCl solution drinking by rats. *Physiology & Behavior, 13,* 389-394. (10)

Stricker, E.M., Rowland, N., Saller, C.F., & Friedman, M.I. (1977). Homeostasis during hypoglycemia: Central control of adrenal secretion and peripheral control of feeding. *Science, 196,* 79-81. (10)

Stricker, E.M., Swerdloff, A.F., & Zigmond, M.J. (1978). Intrahypothalamic injections of kainic acid produce feeding and drinking deficits in rats. *Brain Research, 158,* 470-473. (10)

Stryker, M.P., & Sherk, H. (1975). Modification of cortical orientation selectivity in the cat by restricted visual experience: A reexamination. *Science, 190,* 904-906. (6)

Stryker, M.P., Sherk, H., Leventhal, A.G., & Hirsch, H.V.B. (1978). Physiological consequences for the cat's visual cortex of effectively restricting early visual experience with oriented contours. *Journal of Neurophysiology, 41,* 896-909. (6)

Stunkard, A.J., Sorensen, T.I.A., Hanis, C., Teasdale, T.W., Chakraborty, R., Schull, W.J., & Schulsinger, F. (1986). An adoption study of human obesity. *New England Journal of Medicine, 314,* 193-198. (10)

Stuss, D.T., & Benson, D.F. (1984). Neuropsychological studies of the frontal lobes. *Psychological Bulletin, 95,* 3-28. (4)

Sullivan, R.C. (1980). Why do autistic children...? *Journal of Autism and Developmental Disorders, 10,* 231-241. (16)

Sulser, F., Gillespie, D.D., Mishra, R., & Manier, D.H. (1984). Desensitization by antidepressants of central norepinephrine receptor systems coupled to adenylate cyclase. *Annals of the New York Academy of Sciences, 430,* 91-101. (16)

Summers, W.K., Robins, E., & Reich, T. (1979). The natural history of acute organic mental syndrome after bilateral electroconvulsive therapy. *Biological Psychiatry, 14,* 905-912. (16)

Surprenant, A. (1989). The neurotransmitter noradrenaline and its receptors. *Seminars in the Neurosciences, 1,* 125-136. (3)

Sutton, R.L., Hovda, D.A., & Feeney, D.M. (1989). Amphetamine accelerates recovery of locomotor function following bilateral frontal cortex ablation in rats.

Behavioral Neuroscience, 103, 837-841. (15)

Suzdak, P.D., Glowa, J.R., Crawley, J.N., Schwartz, R.D., Skolnick, P., & Paul, S.M. (1986). A selective imidazobenzodiazepine antagonist of ethanol in the rat. *Science, 234,* 1243-1247. (12)

Swaab, D.F., & Fliers, E. (1985). A sexually dimorphic nucleus in the human brain. *Science, 228,* 1112-1115. (11)

Swaab, D.F., & Hofman, M.A. (1990). An enlarged suprachiasmatic nucleus in homosexual men. *Brain Research, 537,* 141-148. (11)

Swan, H., & Schatte, C. (1977). Antimetabolic extract from the brain of the hibernating ground squirrel *Citellus tridecemlineatus. Science, 195,* 84-85. (9)

Swash, M. (1972). Released involuntary laughter after temporal lobe infarction. *Journal of Neurology, Neurosurgery, and Psychiatry, 35,* 108-113. (12)

Swedo, S.E., Leonard, H.L., Rapoport, J.L., Lenane, M.C., Goldberger, E.L., & Cheslow, D.L. (1989). A double-blind comparison of clomipramine and desipramine in the treatment of trichotillomania (hairpulling). *New England Journal of Medicine, 321,* 497-501. (12)

Szechtman, H., Ornstein, K., Teitelbaum, P., & Golani, I. (1985). The morphogenesis of stereotyped behavior induced by the dopamine receptor agonist apomorphine in the laboratory rat. *Neuroscience, 14,* 783-798. (8)

Szél, Á., Röhlich, P., Caffé, A.R., Juliusson, B., Aguirre, G., & van Veen, T. (1992). Unique topographic separation of two spectral classes of cones in the mouse retina. *Journal of Comparative Neurology, 325,* 327-342. (6)

Szymusiak, R., DeMory, A., Kittrell, M.W., & Satinoff, E. (1985). Diurnal changes in thermoregulatory behavior in rats with medial preoptic lesions. *American Journal of Physiology, 249,* R219-R227. (10)

Takeuchi, A. (1977). Junctional transmission: I. Postsynaptic mechanisms. In E.R. Kandel (Ed.), *Handbook of physiology Section 1: Neurophysiology, Vol. 1. Cellular biology of neurons* (Pt. 1, pp. 295-327). Bethesda, MD: American Physiological Society. (3)

Talbot, J.D., Marrett, S., Evans, A.C., Meyer, E., Bushnell, M.C., & Duncan, G.H. (1991). Multiple representations of pain in human cerebral cortex. *Science, 251,* 1355-1358. (7)

Tamminga, C.A., Thaker, G.K., Buchanan, R., Kirkpatrick, B., Alphs, L.D., Chase, T.N., & Carpenter, W.T. (1992). Limbic system abnormalities identified in schizophrenia using positron emission tomography with fluorodeoxyglucose and neocortical alterations with deficit syndrome. *Archives of General Psychiatry, 49,* 522-530. (16)

Tanaka, K., Sugita, Y., Moriya, M., & Saito, H.-A. (1993). Analysis of object motion in the ventral part of the medial superior temporal area of the macaque visual cortex. *Journal of Neurophysiology, 69,* 128-142. (6)

Taub, E., & Berman, A.J. (1968). Movement and learning in the absence of sensory feedback. In S.J. Freedman (Ed.), *The neuropsychology of spatially oriented behavior* (pp. 173-192). Homewood, IL: Dorsey. (15)

Tauc, L., & Poulain, B. (1991). Vesigate hypothesis of neurotransmitter release explains the formation of quanta by a non-vesicular mechanism. *Physiological Research, 40,* 279-291. (3)

Taylor, H.G. (1984). Early brain injury and cognitive development. In C.R. Almli & S. Finger (Eds.), *Early brain damage* (pp. 325-345). Orlando, FL: Academic Press. (15)

Teitelbaum, P. (1955). Sensory control of hypothalamic hyperphagia. *Journal of Comparative and Physiological Psychology, 48,* 156-163. (10)

Teitelbaum, P. (1961). Disturbances in feeding and drinking behavior after hypothalamic lesions. In M.R. Jones (Ed.), *Nebraska symposia on motivation 1961* (pp. 39-69). Lincoln, NE: University of Nebraska Press. (10)

Teitelbaum, P. & Epstein, A.N. (1962). The lateral hypothalamic syndrome. *Psychological Review, 69,* 74-90. (10)

Teitelbaum, P., & Pellis, S.M. (1992). Toward a synthetic physiological psychology. *Psychological Science, 3,* 4-20. (1)

Teitelbaum, P., Pellis, V.C., & Pellis, S.M. (1991). Can allied reflexes promote the integration of a robot's behavior? In J.A. Meyer & S.W. Wilson (Eds.), *From animals to animats: Simulation of animal behavior* (pp. 97-104). Cambridge, MA: MIT Press/Bradford Books. (8)

Tempel, D.L., Kim, T., & Leibowitz, S.F. (1993). The paraventricular nucleus is uniquely responsive to the feeding stimulatory effects of steroid hormones. *Brain Research, 614,* 197-204. (10)

Tempel, D.L., Leibowitz, K.J., & Leibowitz, S.F. (1988). Effects of PVN galanin on macronutrient selection. *Peptides, 9,* 309-314. (10)

Temple, C.M., Jeeves, M.A., & Vilarroya, O. (1989). Ten pen men: Rhyming skills in two children with callosal agenesis. *Brain and Language, 37,* 548-564. (14)

Terman, G.W., & Liebeskind, J.C. (1986). Relation of stress-induced analgesia to stimulation-produced analgesia. *Annals of the New York Academy of Sciences, 467,* 300-308. (7)

Terman, G.W., Shavitt, Y., Lewis, J.W., Cannon, J.T., & Liebeskind, J.C. (1984). Intrinsic mechanisms of pain inhibition: Activation by stress. *Science, 226,* 1270-1277. (7)

Terrace, H.S., Petitto, L.A., Sanders, R.J., & Bever, T.G. (1979). Can an ape create a sentence? *Science, 206,* 891-902. (14)

Tetrud, J.W., & Langston, J.W. (1989). The effect of deprenyl (Selegiline) on the natural history of Parkinson's disease. *Science, 245,* 519-522. (8)

Tetrud, J.W., Langston, J.W., Garbe, P.L., & Ruttenber, A.J. (1989). Mild parkinsonism in persons exposed to 1-methyl-4-phenyl-1,2,3,6-tetrahydropyridine (MPTP). *Neurology, 39,* 1483-1487. (8)

Teyler, T., & Grover, L. (1993). Forms of long-term potentiation induced by NMDA and non-NMDA receptor activation. In M. Baudry, R.F. Thompson, & J.L. Davis (Eds.), *Synaptic plasticity* (pp. 73-86). Cambridge, MA: MIT Press. (13)

Teyler, T.J., & DiScenna, P. (1986). The hippocampal memory indexing theory. *Behavioral Neuroscience, 100,* 147-154. (13)

Thaker, G.K., Tamminga, C.A., Alphs, L.D., Lafferman, J., Ferraro, T.N., & Hare, T.A. (1987). Brain gamma-aminobutyric acid abnormality in tardive dyskinesia. *Archives of General Psychiatry, 44,* 522-529. (16)

Thomas, P.K. (1988). Clinical aspects of PNS regeneration. In S.G. Waxman (Ed.), *Advances in neurology* (Vol. 47, pp. 9-29). New York: Raven Press. (15)

Thomas, R.K. (1980). Evolution of intelligence: An approach to its assessment. *Brain Behavior and Evolution, 17,* 454-472. (5)

Thompson, D.A., & Campbell, R.G. (1977). Hunger in humans induced by 2-deoxy-D-glucose: Glucoprivic control of taste preference and food intake. *Science, 198,* 1065-1068. (10)

Thompson, J.K., Jarvie, G.J., Lahey, B.B., & Cureton, K.J. (1982). Exercise and obesity: Etiology, physiology, and intervention. *Psychological Bulletin, 91,* 55-79. (10)

Thompson, R.F. (1986). The neurobiology of learning and memory. *Science, 233,* 941-947. (13)

Thormodsson, F.R., Parker, T.S., & Grafstein, B. (1992). Immunochemical studies of extracellular glycoproteins (X-GPs) of goldfish brain. *Experimental Neurology, 118,* 275-283. (15)

Ticku, M.K., & Kulkarni, S.K. (1988). Molecular interactions of ethanol with GABAergic system and potential of Ro15-4513 as an ethanol antagonist. *Pharmacology Biochemistry & Behavior, 30,* 501-510. (12)

Tinbergen, N. (1951). *The study of instinct.* Oxford, England: Oxford University Press. (1)

Tinbergen, N. (1973). The search for animal roots of human behavior. In N. Tinbergen, *The animal in its world* (Vol. 2, pp. 161-174). Cambridge, MA: Harvard University Press. (1)

Tippin, J., & Henn, F.A. (1982). Modified leukotomy in the treatment of intractable obsessional neurosis. *American Journal of Psychiatry, 139,* 1601-1603. (4)

Tolstoy, L. (1978). *Tolstoy's letters: Vol. 1. 1828-1879.* New York: Scribner's. (12)

Tomkins, S. (1980). Affect as amplification: Some modifications in theory. In R. Plutchik & H. Kellerman (Eds.), *Emotion: Theory, research, and experience* (Vol. 1, pp. 141-164). New York: Academic Press. (12)

Tordoff, M.G., Novin, D., & Russek, M. (1982). Effects of hepatic denervation on the anorexic response to epinephrine, amphetamine, and lithium chloride: A behavioral identification of glucostatic afferents. *Journal of Comparative and Physiological Psychology, 96,* 361-375. (10)

Torrey, E.F. (1986). Geographic variations in schizophrenia. In C. Shagass, R.C. Josiassen, W.H. Bridger, K.J. Weiss, D. Stoff, & G. M. Simpson (Ed.), *Biological psychiatry 1985* (pp. 1080-1082). New York: Elsevier. (16)

Torrey, E.F., Rawlings, R., & Waldman, I.N. (1988). Schizophrenic births and viral diseases in two states. *Schizophrenia Research, 1,* 73-77. (16)

Travers, S.P., Pfaffmann, C., & Norgren, R. (1986). Convergence of lingual and palatal gustatory neural activity in the nucleus of the solitary tract. *Brain Research, 365,* 305-320. (7)

Travis, A.M., & Woolsey, C.N. (1956). Motor performance of monkeys after bilateral partial and total cerebral decortications. *American Journal of Physical Medicine, 35,* 273-310. (15)

Treiser, S.L., Cascio, C.S., O'Donohue, T.L., Thoa, N.B., Jacobowitz, D.M., & Kellar, K.J. (1981). Lithium increases serotonin release and decreases serotonin receptors in the hippocampus. *Science, 213,* 1529-1532. (16)

Trevarthen, C. (1974). Cerebral embryology and the split brain. In M. Kinsbourne & W.L. Smith (Eds.), *Hemispheric disconnection and cerebral function* (pp. 208-236). Springfield, IL: Charles C. Thomas. (14)

Trimble, M.R., & Thompson, P.J. (1986). Neuropsychological and behavioral sequelae of spontaneous seizures. *Annals of the New York Academy of Sciences, 462,* 284-292. (16)

Tsai, L., Stewart, M.A., & August, G. (1981). Implication of sex differences in the familial transmission of infantile autism. *Journal of Autism and Developmental Disorders, 11,* 165-173. (16)

Ts'o, D.Y., & Gilbert, C.D. (1988). The organization of chromatic and spatial interactions in the primate striate cortex. *Journal of Neuroscience, 8,* 1712-1727. (6)

Tucker, D.M. (1981). Lateral brain function, emotion, and conceptualization. *Psychological Bulletin, 89,* 19-46. (14)

Turek, F.W., & Losee-Olson, S. (1986). A benzodiazepine used in the treatment of insomnia phase-shifts the mammalian circadian clock. *Nature, 321,* 167-168. (9)

Turner, S.M., Beidel, D.C., & Nathan, R.S. (1985). Biological factors in obsessive-compulsive disorders. *Psychological Disorders, 97,* 430-450. (12)

Udin, S.B., & Scherer, W.J. (1990). Restoration of the plasticity of binocular maps by NMDA after the critical period in *Xenopus. Science, 249,* 669-672. (13)

Udry, J.R., & Morris, N.M. (1968). Distribution of coitus in the menstrual cycle. *Nature, 220,* 593-596. (11)

Uhl, G., Blum, K., Noble, E., & Smith, S. (1993). Substance abuse vulnerability and D₂ receptor genes. *Trends in Neurosciences, 16,* 83-88. (3)

Uphouse, L. (1980). Reevaluation of mechanisms that mediate brain differences between enriched and impoverished animals. *Psychological Bulletin, 88,* 215-232. (5)

Vaillant, G.E., & Milofsky, E.S. (1982). The etiology of alcoholism. *American Psychologist, 37,* 494-503. (3)

Valenstein, E.S., & Beer, B. (1962). Reinforcing brain stimulation in competition with water reward and shock avoidance. *Science, 137,* 1052-1054. (12)

Valenstein, E.S., Cox, V.C., & Kakolewski, J.W. (1970). Reexamination of the role of the hypothalamus in motivation. *Psychological Review, 77,* 16-31. (1)

Vallacher, R.R., & Wegner, D.M. (1987). What do people think they're doing? Action identification and human behavior. *Psychological Review, 94,* 3-15. (8)

Valvo, A. (1971). *Sight restoration after long-term blindness.* New York: American Foundation for the Blind. (6)

Valzelli, L. (1973). The "isolation syndrome" in mice. *Psychopharmacologia, 31,* 305-320. (12)

Valzelli, L. (1980). *An approach to neuroanatomical and neurochemical psychophysiology.* Torino, Italy: C.G. Edizioni Medico Scientifiche. (10, 16)

Valzelli, L., & Bernasconi, S. (1979). Aggressiveness by isolation and brain serotonin turnover changes in different strains of mice. *Neuropsychobiology, 5,* 129-135. (12)

Valzelli, L., & Garattini, S. (1972). Biochemical and behavioural changes induced by isolation in rats. *Neuropharmacology, 11,* 17-22. (12)

Vandenbergh, J.G. (1987). Regulation of puberty and its consequences on population dynamics of mice. *American Zoologist, 27,* 891-898. (11)

Vanderweele, D.A., Novin, D., Rezek, M., & Sanderson, J.D. (1974). Duodenal or hepatic-portal glucose perfusion: Evidence for duodenally based satiety. *Physiology & Behavior, 12,* 467-473. (10)

Van der Zee, C.E.E.M., Fawcett, J., & Diamond, J. (1992). Antibody to NGF inhibits collateral sprouting of septohippocampal fibers following entorhinal cortex lesion in adult rats. *Journal of Comparative Neurology, 326,* 91-100. (15)

Van Hoesen, G.W. (1993). The modern concept of association cortex. *Current Opinion in Neurobiology, 3,* 150-154. (4)

Van Hoesen, G.W., Hyman, B.T., & Damasio, A.R. (1991). Entorhinal cortex pathology in Alzheimer's disease. *Hippocampus, 1,* 1-8. (13)

van Praag, H.M. (1977). The significance of the cerebral dopamine metabolism in the pathogenesis and treatment of psychotic disorders. In E.S. Gershon, R.H. Belmaker, S.S. Kety, & M. Rosenbaum (Eds.), *The impact of biology on modern psychiatry* (pp. 1-26). New York: Plenum. (16)

VanTwyver, H., & Allison, T. (1970). Sleep in the opossum *Didelphis marsupialis. Electroencephalography and Clinical Neurophysiology, 29,* 181-189. (9)

Van Zoeren, J.G., & Stricker, E.M. (1977). Effects of preoptic, lateral hypothalamic, or dopamine-depleting lesions on behavioral thermoregulation in rats exposed to the cold. *Journal of Comparative and Physiological Psychology, 91,* 989-999. (10)

Vargha-Khadem, F., & Passingham, R.E. (1990). Speech and language deficits. *Nature, 346,* 226. (14)

Varon, S.S., & Somjen, G.G. (1979). Neuron-glia interactions. *Neurosciences Research Program Bulletin, 17,* 1-239. (2)

Victor, M., Adams, R.D., & Collins, G.H. (1971). *The Wernicke-Korsakoff syndrome.* Philadelphia: F.A. Davis. (13)

Viney, W., King, D.B., & Berndt, J. (1990). Animal research in psychology: Declining or thriving? *Journal of Comparative Psychology, 104,* 322-325. (1)

Virkkunen, M., DeJong, J., Bartko, J., Goodwin, F.K., & Linnoila, M. (1989). Relationship of psychobiological variables to recidivism in violent offenders and impulsive fire setters. *Archives of General Psychiatry, 46,* 600-603. (12)

Virkkunen, M., Nuutila, A., Goodwin, F.K., & Linnoila, M. (1987). Cerebrospinal fluid monoamine metabolite levels in male arsonists. *Archives of General Psychiatry, 44,* 241-247. (12)

Vizi, E.S. (1984). *Non-synaptic interactions between neurons: Modulation of neurochemical transmission.* Chichester, England: John Wiley. (3)

Vogel, G.W., Thompson, F.C., Jr., Thurmond, A., & Rivers, B. (1973). The effect of REM deprivation on depression. In W.P. Koella & P. Levin (Eds.), *Sleep: Physiology, biochemistry, psychology, pharmacology, clinical implications* (pp. 191-195). Basel: Karger. (16)

Volavka, J. (1990). Aggression, electroencephalography, and evoked potentials: A critical review. *Neuropsychiatry, Neuropsychology, and Behavioral Neurology, 3,* 249-259. (12)

Vollhardt, L.T. (1991). Psychoneuroimmunology: A literature review. *American Journal of Orthopsychiatry, 61,* 35-47. (12)

von Békésy, G. (1956). Current status of theories of hearing. *Science, 123,* 779-783. (7)

von Békésy, G. (1957). The ear. *Scientific American, 197(2),* 66-78. (7)

Voneida, T.J., & Fish, S.E. (1984). Central nervous system changes related to the reduction of visual input in a naturally blind fish (*Astyanax hubbsi*). *American Zoologist, 24,* 775-784. (5)

von Holst, E., & von St. Paul, U. (1960). Vom Wirkungsgefüge der Triebe [Concerning the stratification of drives]. *Naturwissenschaften, 47,* 409-422. (1)

Wald, G. (1968). Molecular basis of visual excitation. *Science, 162,* 230-239. (6)

Waldvogel, J.A. (1990). The bird's eye view. *American Scientist, 78,* 342-353. (6)

Wallace, M.A., & Farah, M.J. (1992). Savings in relearning face-name associations as evidence for "covert recognition" in prosopagnosia. *Journal of Cognitive Neuroscience, 4,* 150-154. (6)

Wallen, K., Winston, L.A., Gaventa, S., Davis-DaSilva, M., & Collins, D.C. (1984). Periovulatory changes in female sexual behavior and patterns of ovarian steroid secretion in group-living rhesus monkeys. *Hormones and Behavior, 18,* 431-450. (11)

Wallesch, C.-W., Henriksen, L., Kornhuber, H.-H., & Paulson, O.B. (1985). Observations on regional cerebral blood flow in cortical and subcortical structures during language production in normal man. *Brain and Language, 25,* 224-233. (14)

Wang, H.-W., Wysocki, C.J., & Gold, G.H. (1993). Induction of olfactory receptor sensitivity in mice. *Science, 260,* 998-1000. (7)

Wang, T., Okano, Y., Eisensmith, R., Huang, S.Z., Zeng, Y.T., Wilson, H.Y.L., & Woo, S.L. (1989). Molecular genetics of phenylketonuria in Orientals: Linkage disequilibrium between a termination mutation and haplotype 4 of the phenylalanine hydroxylase gene. *American Journal of Human Genetics, 45,* 675-680. (A)

Ward, I.L. (1972). Prenatal stress feminizes and demasculinizes the behavior of males. *Science, 175,* 82-84. (11)

Ward, I.L. (1977). Exogenous androgen activates female behavior in noncopulating, prenatally stressed male rats. *Journal of Comparative and Physiological Psychology, 91,* 465-471. (11)

Ward, I.L., & Reed, J. (1985). Prenatal stress and prepubertal social rearing conditions interact to determine sexual behavior in male rats. *Behavioral Neuroscience, 99,* 301-309. (11)

Ward, I.L., & Ward, O.B. (1985). Sexual behavior differentiation: Effects of prenatal manipulations in rats. In N. Adler, D. Pfaff, & R.W. Goy (Eds.), *Handbook of behavioral neurobiology,* Vol. 7 (pp. 77-98). New York: Plenum Press. (11)

Ward, O.B., Monaghan, E.P., & Ward, I.L. (1986). Naltrexone blocks the effects of prenatal stress on sexual behavior differentiation in male rats. *Pharmacology Biochemistry & Behavior, 25,* 573-576. (11)

Watson, C.G., Tilleskjor, C., Kucala, T., & Jacobs, L. (1984). The birth seasonality effect in nonschizophrenic psychiatric patients. *Journal of Clinical Psychology, 40,* 884-888. (16)

Waxman, S.G., & Ritchie, J.M. (1985). Organization of ion channels in the myelinated nerve fiber. *Science, 228,* 1502-1507. (2)

Webb, W.B. (1974). Sleep as an adaptive response. *Perceptual and Motor Skills, 38,* 1023-1027. (9)

Weinberger, D.R. (1987). Implications of normal brain development for the pathogenesis of schizophrenia. *Archives of General Psychiatry, 44,* 660-669. (16)

Weindl, A. (1973). Neuroendocrine aspects of circumventricular organs. In W. F. Ganong & L. Martini (Eds.), *Frontiers in neuroendocrinology 1973* (pp. 3-32). New York: Oxford University Press. (10)

Weiner, R.D. (1979). The psychiatric use of electrically induced seizures. *American Journal of Psychiatry, 136,* 1507-1517. (16)

Weiner, R.D. (1984). Does electroconvulsive therapy cause brain damage? *Behavioral and Brain Sciences, 7,* 1-53. (16)

Weiskrantz, L., Warrington, E.K., Sanders, M.D., & Marshall, J. (1974). Visual capacity in the hemianopic field following a restricted occipital ablation. *Brain, 97,* 709-728. (6)

Weiss, J.M. (1968). Effects of coping responses on stress. *Journal of Comparative and Physiological Psychology, 65,* 251-260. (12)

Weiss, J.M. (1971a). Effects of coping behavior in different warning signal conditions on stress pathology in rats. *Journal of Comparative and Physiological Psychology, 77,* 1-13. (12)

Weiss, J.M. (1971b). Effects of punishing the coping response (conflict) on stress pathology in rats. *Journal of Comparative and Physiological Psychology, 77,* 14-21. (12)

Weiss, P. (1924). Die funktion transplantierter amphibienextremitäten. Aufstellung einer resonanztheorie der motorischen nerventätigkeit auf grund abstimmter endorgane [The function of transplanted amphibian limbs. Presentation of a resonance theory of motor nerve action upon tuned end organs]. *Archiv für Mikroskopische Anatomie und Entwicklungsmechanik, 102,* 635-672. (5)

Weisse, C.S. (1992). Depression and immunocompetence: A review of the literature. *Psychological Bulletin, 111,* 475-489. (12)

Weissman, M.M., Gammon, G.D., John, K., Merikangas, K.R., Warner, V., Prusoff, B.A., Sholomskas, D. (1987). Children of depressed parents: Increased psychopathology and early onset of major depression. *Archives of General Psychiatry, 44,* 847-853. (16)

Weissman, M.M., Gershon, E.S., Kidd, K.K., Prusoff, B.A., Leckman, J.F., Dibble, E., Hamovit, J., Thompson, D., Pauls, D.L., & Guroff, J.J. (1984). Psychiatric disorders in the relatives of probands with affective disorders. *Archives of General Psychiatry, 41,* 13-21. (16)

Weitzman, E.D. (1981). Sleep and its disorders. *Annual Review of Neurosciences, 4,* 381-417. (9)

Wender, P.H., Kety, S.S., Rosenthal, D., Schulsinger, F., Ortmann, J., & Lunde, I. (1986). Psychiatric disorders in the biological and adoptive families of adopted individuals with affective disorders. *Archives of General Psychiatry, 43,* 923-929. (16)

Wender, P.H., Rosenthal, D., Kety, S.S., Schulsinger, F., & Welner, J. (1974). Crossfostering: A research strategy for clarifying the role of genetic and experiential factors in the etiology of schizophrenia. *Archives of General Psychiatry, 30,* 121-128. (16)

Wenger, J.R., Berlin, V., & Woods, S.C. (1980). Learned tolerance to the behaviorally disruptive effects of ethanol. *Behavioral and Neural Biology, 28,* 418-430. (10)

Wenger, J.R., Tiffany, T.M., Bombardier, C., Nicholls, K., & Woods, S.C. (1981). Ethanol tolerance in the rat is learned. *Science, 213,* 575-577. (10)

West, J.R., Hodges, C.A., & Black, A.C., Jr. (1981). Prenatal exposure to ethanol alters the organization of hippocampal mossy fibers in rats. *Science, 211,* 957-959. (2)

Westbrook, G.L., & Jahr, C.E. (1989). Glutamate receptors in excitatory neurotransmission. *Seminars in the Neurosciences, 1,* 103-114. (3)

Whishaw, I.Q., & Tomie, J.-A. (1991). Acquisition and retention by hippocampal rats of simple, conditional, and configural tasks using tactile and olfactory cues: Implications for hippocampal function. *Behavioral Neuroscience, 105,* 787-797. (13)

Whitam, F.L., Diamond, M., & Martin, J. (1993). Homosexual orientation in twins: A report on 61 pairs and three triplet sets. *Archives of Sexual Behavior, 22,* 187-206. (11)

White, B.B., & White, M.S. (1987). Autism from the inside. *Medical Hypotheses, 24,* 223-229. (16)

White, F.J., & Wang, R.Y. (1983). Differential effects of classical and atypical antipsychotic drugs on A9 and A10 dopamine neurons. *Science, 221,* 1054-1057. (16)

Whitman, B.W., & Packer, R.J. (1993). The photic sneeze reflex: Literature review and discussion. *Neurology, 43,* 868-871. (8)

Wiesel, T.N. (1982). Postnatal development of the visual cortex and the influence of environment. *Nature, 299,* 583-591. (6)

Wiesel, T.N., & Hubel, D.H. (1963). Single-cell responses in striate cortex of kittens deprived of vision in one eye. *Journal of Neurophysiology, 26,* 1003-1017. (6)

Wiggins, S., Whyte, P., Huggins, M., Adam, S., Theilman, J., Bloch, M., Sheps, S.B., Schechter, M.T., & Hayden, M.R., for the Canadian collaborative study of predictive testing. (1992). The psychological consequences of predictive testing for Huntington's disease. *New England Journal of Medicine, 327,* 1401-1405. (8)

Wild, H.M., Butler, S.R., Carden, D., & Kulikowski, J.J. (1985). Primate cortical area V4 important for colour constancy but not wavelength discrimination. *Nature, 313,* 133-135. (6)

Willerman, L. (1991). Commentary on Rushton's Mongoloid-Caucasoid differences in brain size. *Intelligence, 15,* 361-364. (5)

Willerman, L., Schultz, R., Rutledge, J.N., & Bigler, E.D. (1991). *In vivo* brain size and intelligence. *Intelligence, 15,* 223-228. (5)

Williams, C.L. (1986). A reevaluation of the concept of separable periods of organizational and activational actions of estrogens in development of brain and behavior. *Annals of the New York Academy of Sciences, 474,* 282-292. (11)

Williams, R.W., & Herrup, K. (1988). The control of neuron number. *Annual Review of Neuroscience, 11,* 423-453. (2)

Willner, J., Gallagher, M., Graham, P.W., & Crooks, G.B., Jr. (1992). N-methyl-D-aspartate antagonist D-APV selectively disrupts taste-potentiated odor aversion learning. *Behavioral Neuroscience, 106,* 315-323. (13)

Wilson, F.A.W., Ó Scalaidhe, S.P., & Goldman-Rakic, P.S. (1993). Dissociation of object and spatial processing domains in primate prefrontal cortex. *Science, 260,* 1955-1958. (6)

Wilson, J.D., George, F.W., & Griffin, J.E. (1981). The hormonal control of sexual development. *Science, 211,* 1278-1284. (11)

Winfree, A.T. (1983). Impact of a circadian clock on the timing of human sleep. *American Journal of Physiology, 245,* R497-R504. (9)

Winocur, G., & Moscovitch, M. (1990). Hippocampal and prefrontal cortex contributions to learning and memory: Analysis of lesion and aging effects on maze learning in rats. *Behavioral Neuroscience, 104,* 544-551. (13)

Winslade, W.J., Liston, E.H., Ross, J.W., & Weber, K.D. (1984). Medical, judicial, and statutory regulation of ECT in the United States. *American Journal of Psychiatry, 141,* 1349-1355. (16)

Winson, J. (1993). The biology and function of rapid eye movement sleep. *Current Opinion in Neurobiology, 3,* 243-248. (9)

Wintrob, R.M. (1973). The influence of others: Witchcraft and rootwork as explanations of behavior disturbances. *Journal of Nervous and Mental Disease, 156,* 318-326. (12)

Wirz-Justice, A., Graw, P., Kräuchi, K., Gisin, B., Jochum, A., Arendt, J., Fisch, H.-U., Buddeberg, C., & Pöldinger, W. (1993). Light therapy in seasonal affective disorder is independent of time of day or circadian phase. *Archives of General Psychiatry, 50,* 929-937. (16)

Wirz-Justice, A., Groos, G.A., & Wehr, T.A. (1982). The neuropharmacology of circadian timekeeping in mammals. In J. Aschoff, S. Daan, & G.A. Groos (Eds.), *Vertebrate circadian rhythms* (pp. 183-193). Berlin: Springer-Verlag. (16)

Wise, R.A., & Bozarth, M.A. (1984). Brain reward circuitry: Four circuit elements "wired" in apparent series. *Brain Research Bulletin, 12,* 203-208. (12)

Wise, R.A., & Bozarth, M.A. (1987). A psychomotor stimulant theory of addiction. *Psychological Review, 94,* 469-492. (12)

Wise, R.A., & Rompre, P.-P. (1989). Brain dopamine and reward. *Annual Review of Psychology, 40,* 191-225. (12)

Witelson, S.F. (1985). The brain connection: The corpus callosum is larger in left-handers. *Science, 229,* 665-668. (14)

Witelson, S.F., & Pallie, W. (1973). Left hemisphere specialization for language in the newborn: Neuroanatomical evidence of asymmetry. *Brain, 96,* 641-646. (14)

Wolgin, D.L., Cytawa, J., & Teitelbaum, P. (1976). The role of activation in the regulation of food intake. In D. Novin, W. Wyrwicka, & G. Bray (Eds.), *Hunger: Basic mechanisms and clinical implications* (pp. 179-191). New York: Raven. (10)

Wong, D.F., Wagner, H.N., Jr., Dannals, R.F., Links, J.M., Frost, J.J., Ravert, H.T., Wilson, A.A., Rosenbaum, A.E., Gjedde, A., Douglass, K.H., Petronis, J.D., Folstein, M.F., Toung, J.K.T., Burns, H.D., & Kuhar, M.J. (1984). Effects of age on dopamine and serotonin receptors measured by positron tomography in the living human brain. *Science, 226,* 1393-1396. (13)

Wong-Riley, M.T.T. (1989). Cytochrome oxidase: An endogenous metabolic marker for neuronal activity. *Trends in Neurosciences, 12,* 94-101. (3)

Woodruf-Pak, D.S., Lavond, D.G., & Thompson, R.F. (1985). Trace conditioning: Abolished by cerebellar nuclear lesions but not lateral cerebellar cortex aspirations. *Brain Research, 348,* 249-260. (13)

Woods, S.W., Charney, D.S., Loke, J., Goodman, W.K., Redmond, D.E., Jr., & Heninger, G.R. (1986). Carbon dioxide sensitivity in panic anxiety. *Archives of General Psychiatry, 43,* 900-909. (12)

Woodworth, R.S. (1934). *Psychology,* 3rd ed. New York: Henry Holt and Company. (2)

Woolverton, W.L., Kandel, D., & Schuster, C.R. (1978). Tolerance and cross-tolerance to cocaine and d-amphetamine. *Journal of Pharmacology and Experimental Therapeutics, 205,* 525-535. (10)

Worley, P.F., Heller, W.A., Snyder, S.H., & Baraban, J.M. (1988). Lithium blocks a phosphoinositide-mediated cholinergic response in hippocampal slices. *Science, 239,* 1428-1429. (16)

Wulfeck, B., & Bates, E. (1991). Differential sensitivity to errors of agreement and word order in Broca's aphasia. *Journal of Cognitive Neuroscience, 3,* 258-272. (14)

Wurtman, J.J. (1985). Neurotransmitter control of carbohydrate consumption. *Annals of the New York Academy of Sciences, 443,* 145-151. (3)

Wurtman, R.J. (1982). Nutrients that modify brain function. *Scientific American, 246*(4), 50-59. (3)

Wurtman, R.J. (1983). Behavioural effects of nutrients. *Lancet, i* (8334), 1145-1147. (3)

Wurtman, R.J., Hefti, F., & Melamed, E. (1981). Precursor control of neurotransmitter synthesis. *Pharmacological Reviews, 32,* 315-335. (3)

Wyatt, R.J., Termini, B.A., & Davis, J. (1971). Biochemical and sleep studies of schizophrenia: A review of the literature 1960-1970: Part I. Biochemical studies. *Schizophrenia Bulletin, 4,* 10-66. (16)

Yalcinkaya, T.M., Siiteri, P.K., Vigne, J.-L., Licht, P., Pavgi, S., Frank, L.G., & Glickman, S.E. (1993). A mechanism for virilization of female spotted hyenas in utero. *Science, 260,* 1929-1931. (11)

Yamamoto, T. (1984). Taste responses of cortical neurons. *Progress in Neurobiology, 23,* 273-315. (7)

Yarsh, T.L., Farb, D.H., Leeman, S.E., & Jessell, T.M. (1979). Intrathecal capsaicin depletes substance P in the rat spinal cord and produces prolonged thermal analgesia. *Science, 206,* 481-483. (7)

Yaryura-Tobias, J.A. (1977). Obsessive-compulsive disorders: A serotoninergic hypothesis. *Journal of Orthomolecular Psychiatry, 6,* 317-326. (12)

Yau, K.-W., Matthews, G., & Baylor, D.A. (1979). Thermal activation of the visual transduction mechanism in retinal rods. *Nature, 279,* 806-807. (6)

Yaxley, S., Rolls, E.T., & Sienkiewicz, Z.J. (1990). Gustatory responses of single neurons in the insula of the macaque monkey. *Journal of Neurophysiology, 63,* 689-700. (7)

Yeni-Komshian, G.H., & Benson, D.A. (1976). Anatomical study of cerebral asymmetry in the temporal lobe of humans, chimpanzees, and rhesus monkeys. *Science, 192,* 387-389. (14)

Yeomans, J.S., & Pollard, B.A. (1993). Amygdala efferents mediating electrically evoked startle-like responses and fear potentiation of acoustic startle. *Behavioral Neuroscience, 107,* 596-610. (12)

Yoon, M. (1971). Reorganization of retinotectal projection following surgical operations on the optic tectum in goldfish. *Experimental Neurology, 33,* 395-411. (5)

Yost, W.A., & Nielsen, D.W. (1977). *Fundamentals of hearing.* New York: Holt, Rinehart, & Winston. (7)

Young, A.B., Greenamyre, J.T., Hollingsworth, Z., Albin, R., D'Amato, C., Shoulson, I., & Penney, J.B. (1988). NMDA receptor losses in putamen from patients with Huntington's disease. *Science, 241,* 981-983. (8)

Young, M.P., & Yamane, S. (1992). Sparse population coding of faces in the inferotemporal cortex. *Science, 256,* 1327-1331. (6)

Young, W.C., Goy, R.W., & Phoenix, C.H. (1964). Hormones and sexual behavior. *Science, 143,* 212-218. (11)

Zagon, I.S., Goodman, S.R., & McLaughlin, P.J. (1993). Zeta (ζ), the opioid growth factor receptor: Identification and characterization of binding subunits. *Brain Research, 605,* 50-56. (16)

Zagrodzka, J., & Fonberg, E. (1979). Alimentary instrumental responses and neurological reflexes in amygdalar cats. *Acta Neurobiologiae Experimentalis, 39,* 143-156. (12)

Zaidel, D., & Sperry, R.W. (1977). Some long-term motor effects of cerebral commissurotomy in man. *Neuropsychologia, 15,* 193-204. (14)

Zaidel, E. (1983). Advances and retreats in laterality research. *Behavioral and Brain Sciences, 6,* 523-528. (14)

Zeigler, H.P., Jacquin, M.F., & Miller, M.G. (1985). Trigeminal orosensation and ingestive behavior in the rat. *Progress in Psychobiology and Physiological Psychology, 11,* 63-196. (10)

Zeki, S. (1980). The representation of colours in the cerebral cortex. *Nature, 284,* 412-418. (6)

Zeki, S. (1983). Colour coding in the cerebral cortex: The responses of wavelength-selective and colour-coded cells in monkey visual cortex to changes in wavelength composition. *Neuroscience, 9,* 767-781. (6)

Zeki, S. (1990). A century of cerebral achromatopsia. *Brain, 113,* 1721-1777. (6)

Zeki, S. (1993). The visual association cortex. *Current Opinion in Neurobiology, 3,* 155-159. (4)

Zeki, S., & Shipp, S. (1988). The functional logic of cortical connections. *Nature, 335,* 311-317. (6)

Žernicki, B., Gandolfo, G., Glin, L., & Gottesmann, C. (1984). Cerveau isolé and pretrigeminal rats. *Acta Neurobiologiae Experimentalis, 44,* 159-177. (9)

Zigmond, M.J., Abercrombie, E.D., Berger, T.W., Grace, A.A., & Stricker, E.M. (1990). Compensations after lesions of central dopaminergic neurons: Some clinical and basic implications. *Trends in Neurosciences, 13,* 290-296. (8, 15)

Zihl, J., von Cramon, D., & Mai, N. (1983). Selective disturbance of movement vision after bilateral brain damage. *Brain, 106,* 313-340. (6)

Zilles, K., Armstrong, E., Moser, K.H., Schleicher, A., & Stephan, H. (1989). Gyrification in the cerebral cortex of primates. *Brain, Behavior, and Evolution, 34,* 143-150. (5)

Zimmerman, M.B., Blaine, E.H., & Stricker, E.M. (1981). Water intake in hypovolemic sheep: Effects of crushing the left atrial appendage. *Science, 211,* 489-491. (10)

Zipursky, R.B., Lim, K.O., Sullivan, E.V., Brown, B.W., & Pfefferbaum, A. (1992). Widespread cerebral gray matter volume deficits in schizophrenia. *Archives of General Psychiatry, 49,* 195-205. (16)

Zuckerman, M., & Brody, N. (1988). Oysters, rabbits and people: A critique of "race differences in behaviour" by J.P. Rushton. *Personality and Individual Differences, 9,* 1025-1033. (5)

Zurif, E.B. (1980). Language mechanisms: A neuropsychological perspective. *American Scientist, 68,* 305-311. (14)

Zwislocki, J.J. (1981). Sound analysis in the ear: A history of discoveries. *American Scientist, 69,* 184-192. (7)

Acknowledgments

Page 1: Photo courtesy of the Cincinnati Zoo.
Page 6: Figure 1.1 from "Sexual differences in the brain" by A. P. Arnold, *American Scientist*, 1980, 68:165–173. Top Photos courtesy of A. P. Arnold. Bottom photo © Ed Reschke.
Page 7: Top photo © Russell Fieber/FPG International Corp. Bottom photo: © Rod Planck.
Page 11: Historical illustration René Descartes.
Page 14: Figure 1.3 redrawn from "Vom Wirkungsgefüge der Triebe" by E. von Holst and U. von St. Paul in *Naturwissenschaften*, 1960, 47:409–422. Used by permission of Springer-Verlag.
Page 19: Figure 1.6 courtesy of the Foundation for Biomedical Research.

Page 24: Photo © Ed Reschke.
Page 27: Figure 2.2 micrograph courtesy of Dennis M. D. Landis.
Page 28: Figure 2.3 photo © Dan McCoy/Scheibel/Rainbow.
Page 30: Figure 2.5 redrawn from *Journal of Neuroscience,* Harris & Stevens, 1989.
Page 33: Figure 2.8 from R. G. Coss, *Brain Research,* 1982. Used by permission of R. G. Coss.
Page 35: Figure 2.10 from "Changes in the dendritic branching of adult mammalian neurons revealed by repeated imaging in situ" by D. Purves and R. D. Hadley, *Nature,* 315:404–406. Copyright © 1985 Macmillan Magazines. Reprinted by permission. Photos provided by D. Purves.
Page 42: Figure 2.13(b) photo by Fritz Goro.

Page 56: Photo © Custom Medical Stock Photo.
Page 72: Figure 3.10(b) micrograph courtesy of Dennis M. D. Landis (c) From "Studying neural organization in *Aplysia* with the scanning electron microscope" by E. R. Lewis et al., *Science,* 1969, 165:1142. Copyright 1969 by the AAAS. Reprinted by permission of AAAS and E. R. Lewis.
Page 75: Figure 3.12 redrawn from "Autoimmune response to acetylcholine receptors in myasthenia gravis and its animal model" by J. Lindstrom, in H. G. Kunkel and F. J. Dixon (eds.), *Advances in Immunology,* 1979, 27:1–50. Used by permission of Academic Press, Inc. and J. Lindstrom.
Page 85: Figure 3:16 from "Cocaine-induced reduction of glucose utilization in human brain" by E. D. London et al.,

Archives of General Psychiatry, 1990, 47:567–574. Copyright 1990, American Medical Association. Used by permission of AMA and E. D. London.
Page 87: Photo © Scott Camazine/Photo Researchers, Inc.

Page 94: Photo © FPG International Corp.
Page 100: Figure 4.4 photo © Manfred Kage/Peter Arnold, Inc.
Page 101: Figure 4.5 photo © Manfred Kage/Peter Arnold, Inc.
Page 102: Figure 4.6 from *Biology: The Unity and Diversity of Life,* 5th Edition, by Cecie Starr and Ralph Taggart, 1989, Wadsworth Publishing Company.
Page 109: Figure 4.11 photos courtesy of Dr. Dana Copeland.
Page 110, 111, 112: Figures 4.12, 4.13, 4.14 modified after *The Human Central Nervous System,* by R. Nieuwenhuys et al., 1988, Springer-Verlag, Berlin.
Page 113: Figure 4.15 photo courtesy of Dr. Dana Copeland.
Page 117: Figure 4.16 photos courtesy of Dr. Dana Copeland.
Page 118: Figure 4.17 from *The Anatomy of the Nervous System* by S. W. Ranson and S. L. Clark, 1959. Reprinted by permission of W. B. Saunders Co.
Page 122: Figure 4.21 after *The Cerebral Cortex of Man* by W. Penfield and R. Rasmussen, 1950. Used by permission of Macmillan Publishing Co.
Page 124: Figure 4.23 after *The Prefrontal Cortex* by J. M. Fuster, 1989, Raven Press. Used by permission of Raven Press and J. M. Fuster.
Page 125: Photo courtesy of Dr. Dana Copeland.
Page 126: Figure 4.24 photos by Doug Goodman/Monkmeyer Press.
Page 130: Figure 4.26 photo provided by James W. Kalat.
Page 131: Figure 4.28 from *A Stereotaxic Atlas of the Rat Brain,* 2nd Edition, by L. J. Pellegrino, A. S. Pellegrino, and A. J. Cushman, 1979. Reprinted by permission of Plenum Publishing Corp. and Louis Pellegrino.
Page 132: Photo © Ed Reschke/Peter Arnold, Inc.
Page 135: Figure 4.29 from "Dendritic-tree anatomy codes form vision physiology in tadpole retina" by B. Pomeranz and S. H. Chung, *Science,* 1970, 170:983–984. Copyright 1970 by AAAS. Reprinted by permission of AAAS and B. Pomeranz. Photos provided courtesy of B. Pomeranz.

Page 136: Figure 4.30 (b) photo © Dan McCoy/Rainbow.
Page 137: Figure 4.31 photo © Dan McCoy/Rainbow.
Page 139: Figure 4.32 (above) from "Brain electrical correlates of pattern recognition" by E. Donchin in G. F. Inbar (ed.), *Signal Analysis and Pattern Recognition in Biomedical Engineering* © 1975 Keter Publishing House Ltd., Jerusalem. Used by permission. (Below) from L. A. Farwell and E. Donchin, *Electroencephalography and Clinical Neurophysiology,* 1988, 70:510–533. Used by permission of L. A. Farwell.
Page 140: Figure 4.33 photos courtesy of Michael E. Phelps and John C. Mazziotta, University of California, Los Angeles, School of Medicine.
Page 140: Figure 4.34 photo © Burt Glinn/Magnum.
Page 141: Figure 4.35 photo courtesy of Karen Berman and Daniel Weinberger, National Institute of Mental Health.

Page 144: Illustration © Tim Grajek/Stockworks.
Page 148: Figure 5.2 photo courtesy of Dr. Dana Copeland.
Page 149: Figure 5.3 from "Development of glomerulare pattern visualized in the olfactory bulbs of living mice" by A.S. LaMantia and D. Purves. Reprinted by permission from *Nature,* 1989, 341:646–649. Copyright © 1989 Macmillan Magazines Ltd. Photo courtesy of Dale Purves.
Page 150: Figure 5.4 photo © George Steinmetz.
Page 151: Figure 5.5 from "Spine stems on tectal interneurons are shortened by social stimulation" by R. G. Coss and A. Globus, *Science,* 1978, 200:787–790. Copyright 1978 by the AAAS. Reprinted by permission of AAAS and Richard G. Coss.
Page 152: Figure 5.6 photo "Dendritic spine loss and enlargement during maturation of the speech control system in the mynah bird (*Gracula religiosa*)" *Neuroscience Letters* (1982) 129–133, Elsevier/North-Holland Scientific Publishers Ltd. Used by permission of G. Rausch & H. Scheich.
Page 154: Figure 5.7 modified after *The Vertebrate Body* by A. S. Romer, 1962, W. B. Saunders, Philadelphia.
Page 155: Figure 5.9 from "Preferential selection of central pathways by regenerating optic fibers" by D. G. Attardi and R. W. Sperry, *Experimental Neurology,* 1963,

7:46–64. Used by permission of Academic Press and R. W. Sperry.

Page 159: Figure 5.13 after "Elimination of synapses in the developing nervous system" by D. Purves and J. W. Lichtman, *Science*, 1980, 210:153–157. Copyright 1980 by the AAAS. Used by permission of AAAS and Dale Purves.

Page 160: Figure 5.14 from "Motoneuronal death in the human fetus" by N.G. Forger and S. M. Breedlove, *Journal of Comparative Neurology*, 1987, 264:118–122. Copyright 1987 Alan R. Liss, Inc. Used by permission of Nancy G. Forger.

Page 166: Figure 5.16 modified after *The Vertebrate Body* by A. S. Romer, 1962, W. B. Saunders, Philadelphia.

Page 167: Figure 5.17 photo David Hinds, courtesy of Sharon L. Cummings, Ph.D., University of California, Davis.

Page 168: Figure 5.18 (a and b) from *Zeitschrift für Tierpsychologie*, 1963, 608–615, Von B. Rensch and G. Dücker.

Pages 169, 170: Figures 5.19, 5.20 courtesy of T. W. Deacon.

Page 171: Figure 5.21 photo Dan McCoy/Rainbow.

Page 172: Figure 5.22 adapted from "Animal intelligence as encephalization" by H. J. Jerison, *Philosophical Transactions of the Royal Society of London,* 1985, B 308: 21–35. Used by permission of The Royal Society and H. J. Jerison.

Page 174: Top photo, Historical Pictures Services, Chicago/FPG International Corp.; Bottom photo, Dr. Thomas Harvey.

Page 178: Photo, Tom McHugh/The National Audubon Collection/Photo Researchers, Inc.

Page 184: Figure 6.3, Photo © Chase Swift.

Pages 185, 200: Figure 6.4(a), 6.17: After "Organization of the primate retina" by J. E. Dowling and B. B. Boycott, *Proceedings of the Royal Society of London*, B, 1966, 166:80–111. Used by permission of the Royal Society of London and John Dowling.

Page 185: Figure 6.4b photo © Ed Reschke.

Page 188: Figure 6.7b micrograph courtesy of E. R. Lewis, F. S. Werblin, and Y. Y. Zeevi.

Page 191: Figure 6.9 used by permission of J. K. Bowmaker and H. J. A. Dartnall.

Page 197: Figure 6.12 from *The Retina* by John E. Dowling, 1987, Belknap Press of Harvard University Press. Micrograph by M. Tachibana and A. Kaneko. Reprinted by permission of John E. Dowling.

Page 198: Figure 6.13 photo © Don Wong/Science Source/Photo Researchers, Inc.

Page 204: Figure 6.20 photo © 1995 Artists Rights Society (ARS), New York/ADAGP, Paris.

Page 204: Figure 6.21 from "Segregation of form, color, movement, and depth: Anatomy, physiology, and perception" by M. Livingstone and D. Hubel, *Science*, 1988, 240:740–749. Copyright 1988 by the AAAS. Reprinted by permission of AAAS and Margaret Livingstone.

Pages 207, 208: Figure 6.24 and 6.25: Based on "Receptive fields of single neurons in the cat's striate cortex" by D. H. Hubel and T. N. Wiesel, in *Journal of Physiology*, 1959, 148:574–591. Used by permission of the *Journal of Physiology* and David Hubel.

Page 211: Figure 6.28 adapted from "The visual cortex of the brain" by David Hubel,

Scientific American, November 1963, Vol. 209, No. 5, pp. 54–63. Copyright © 1963 by Scientific American, Inc. All rights reserved. Reprinted by permission.

Page 222: Figure 6.33 photos courtesy of Russell D. Fernald, University of Oregon.

Page 228: Figure 6.38 photo courtesy of Helmut V. Hirsch.

Page 232: Photo © Michael Tamborrino/FPG International, Inc.

Page 237: by permission of A. J. Hudspeth. Photos courtesy of A. J. Hudspeth, R. Jacobs, P. Leake and M. Miller.

Page 240: Photo courtesy of Gallaudet University.

Page 242: Figure 7.7 after *Human Information Processing* by P. H. Lindsay and D. A. Norman, 1972. Used by permission of Academic Press and P. H. Lindsay.

Page 243: Photo © Telegraph Colour Library/FPG International.

Page 248: Photo © Ed Reschke.

Page 249: Figure 7.13 from *Biology: The Unity and Diversity of Life*, 5th Edition, by Cecie Starr and Ralph Taggart, 1989, Wadsworth Publishing Company.

Page 253: Figure 7.16 from "Multiple representations of pain in human cerebral cortex," *Science*, 251,1355–1358. Used by permission of Dr. Jeanne D. Talbot, Université de Montreal.

Page 256: Photo © Tim Malyon and Paul Biddle/Science Photo Library/FPG International.

Page 261: Figure 7.19(b) photo © SIU/Peter Arnold, Inc.

Page 269: Figure 7.22 from *Cell,* 65, 175–187. Used by permission of L. Buck and R. Axel, 1991.

Page 272: Photo © Al Tielemans/Duomo.

Page 275: Figure 8.1 art after Cecie Starr and Ralph Taggart, *Biology: The Unity and Diversity of Life*, 5th Edition, 1989, Wadsworth Publishing Company.

Page 275: Figures 8.1 and 8.2 photos © Ed Reschke.

Page 276: Figures 8.3 and 8.4 after Cecie Starr and Ralph Taggart, *Biology: The Unity and Diversity of Life*, 5th Edition, 1989, Wadsworth Publishing Company.

Page 278: Figure 8.5 © Bill Curtsinger Photography.

Page 281: Photo © Johnny Johnson/Natural Selection.

Page 283: Photo © L. West/The National Audubon Society/Photo Researchers, Inc.

Page 293: Figure 8.14 from *Experimental Brain Research*, 87, 562–580, J. T. Lurito, T. Georgakopoulos and A. P. Georgopoulos. Used by permission of A. Georgopoulos.

Page 299: Figure 8.16 from "Mortality data for the U.S. for deaths due to and related to twenty neurologic diseases" by V. Chandra, N. E. Bharucha, and B. S. Shoenberg, *Neuroepidemiology*, 1984, 3:149–168. Used by permission of S. Karger AG, Basel and V. Chandra.

Page 302: Figure 8.18 from "Dopamine in the extrapyramidal motor function: A study based upon the MPTP-induced primate model of Parkinsonism" by C. C. Chiueh, 1988, *Annals of the New York Academy of Sciences*, 515:226–248. Reprinted by permission of the New York Academy of Sciences and C. C. Chiueh.

Page 308: Photo courtesy of NASA.

Page 311: Figure 9.1 from "Phase control of activity in a rodent" by P. J. DeCoursey, *Cold Spring Harbor Symposia on Quantitative Biology,* 1960, 25:49–55. Used by permission of Cold Spring Harbor Laboratory and P. J. DeCoursey.

Page 312: Figure 9.2 from "Sleep-onset insomniacs have delayed temperature rhythms" by M. Morris, L. Lack, and D. Dawson, *Sleep*, 1990, 13:1–14. Reprinted by permission of Raven Press and Leon Lack.

Page 313: Figure 9.3 from *Sleep and Wakefulness* by N. Kleitman. Used by permission of The University of Chicago Press and N. Kleitman. Copyright 1963 by the University of Chicago. All rights reserved.

Page 317: Figure 9.5 from "Suprachiasmatic nucleus: Use of 14-C-labeled deoxyglucose uptake as a funtional marker" by W. J. Schwartz and H. Gainer, *Science*, 1977, 197:1089–1091. Copyright by the AAAS. Used by permission of AAAS and W. J. Schwartz.

Page 323: Figure 9.7 photo by Richard Nowitz.

Page 324: Records provided by T. E. LeVere.

Page 326: Figure 9.9 photo from Dr. J. Allan Hobson.

Page 327: Figure 9.10 from "Cyclic variations in EEG during sleep and their relation to eye movements, body motility, and dreaming" by W. Dement and N. Kleitman, *Electroencephalography and Clinical Neuropsychology*, 1957, 9:673–690. Reproduced by permission of Elsevier/North-Holland Biomedical Press and W. C. Dement.

Page 328: Photo © Tom McHugh/Photo Researchers, Inc.

Page 328: Figure 9.11 from "Ontogenetic Development of Human Sleep-Dream Cycle" by H. P. Roffwarg, J. N. Muzio and W. C. Dement, *Science*, 1966, 152:604–609. Copyright 1966 by the AAAS. Used by permission of AAAS and W. C. Dement.

Page 342: Photo © Kent and Donna Dannen/Photo Researchers, Inc.

Page 347: Figure 10.1 modified after *The Human Central Nervous System* by R. Nieuwenhuys et al., 1988, Springer-Verlag.

Page 348: Figure 10.2 © Stephen Dalton/Photo Researchers, Inc.

Page 349: Figure 10.3 © A. Cosmos Blank/NAS/Photo Researchers, Inc.

Page 350: Figure 10.4 based on data from Blumber, Efimova and Alberts, 1992.

Page 371: Figure 10.17 from "The role of activation in the regulation of food intake" by D. L. Wolgin, J. Cytawa, and P. Teitelbaum in D. Novin, W. Wyrwicka and G. Bray (eds.), *Hunger: Basic Mechanisms and Clinical Implications*, 1976. Copyright 1976 by Raven Press. Reprinted by permission of Raven Press. Photo courtesy of P. Teitelbaum.

Page 373: Figure 10.19 (a) photo © Yoav Levy/Phototake; (b) from "Disturbances in feeding and drinking behavior after hypothalamic lesions" by P. Teitelbaum in M. R. Jones (ed.), *1961 Nebraska Symposium on Motivation*, pp.39–69. Copyright 1961 by University of Nebraska Press. Used by permission.

Page 375: Figure 10.21 from "Peptide YY (PYY), a potent orexigenic agent" *Brain Research*, 341, 200-203. By J. E. Morley, A. S. Levine, M. Grace and J. Kneip (1985).

Page 378: Photo © Ron Chapple/FPG International.

Pages 381, 383, 384, 387, 388: Figures 11.1, 11.2, 11.4, 11.5, 11.6, 11.7, 11.8 from Cecie Starr and Ralph Taggart, *Biology: The Unity and Diversity of Life*, 5th Edition, 1989. Wadsworth Publishing Company.

Page 391: Figure 11.11 courtesy of Kay E. Holekamp.

Page 397: Figure 11.13 from "Rise in female-initiated sexual activity at ovulation and its suppression by oral contraceptives" by D. B. Adams, A. R. Gold and A. D. Burt, in *New England Journal of Medicine*, 1978, 299:1145–1150. Reprinted by permission from *The New England Journal of Medicine*.

Page 398: Figure 11.14 adapted from "Weight at menarche: Similarity for well-nourished girls at differing ages, and evidence for historical constancy" by R. E. Frisch, *Pediatrics*, 1972, 50:445–450. Copyright by Pediatrics. Reprinted by permission.

Page 405: Figure 11.16 from *Abnormal Sexual Development* by D. D. Federman, 1967. Used by permission of W. B. Saunders Company.

Page 409: Figure 11.19 from "Sex-hormone-dependent brain differentiation and sexual functions" by G. Dorner, in G. Dorner (ed.), *Endocrinology of Sex*. Copyright 1975 by Johann Ambrosius Barth. Reprinted by permission of Johann Ambrosius Barth.

Page 411: Figures 11.20, 11.21 from "A Difference in Hypothalamic Structure Between Heterosexual and Homosexual Men" by S. LeVay, *Science*, 253:1034–1037, 1991. Copyright 1991 by the AAAS. Reprinted by permission of AAAS and S. LeVay.

Page 414: Johann W. Elzenga/Tony Stone Worldwide.

Page 417: Figure 12.1 © Alon Reininger/Contact Press Images/Woodfin Camp.

Page 419: Figure 12.2 from "Avoidance behavior and the development of gastroduodenal ulcers" by J. V. Brady, R. W. Porter, D. G. Conrad, and J. W. Mason, *Journal of the Experimental Analysis of Behavior*, 1958, 1:69–72. Copyright 1958 by the Society for the Experimental Analysis of Behavior, Inc. Reprinted by permission of the Society for the Experimental Analysis of Behavior and J. V. Brady.

Page 428: Figure 12.5 based on "Psychosomatic disease and the 'visceral brain': Recent developments bearing on the Papez theory of emotion" by P. D. MacLean, *Psychosomatic Medicine*, 1949, 11:338–353. Used by permission of the American Psychosomatic Society.

Page 429: Figure 12.6 redrawn from "Studies on limbic systems ('visceral brain') and their bearing on psychosomatic problems" by P. D. MacLean in E. D. Wittkower and R. A. Cleghorn (eds.) *Recent Developments in Psychosomatic Medicine*, 1954. Copyright Sir Isaac Pitman & Sons, Ltd. Used by permission of J. B. Lippincott Co. and Sir Isaac Pitman & Sons, Ltd.

Page 469: Figure 12.10 based on "Studies on endogenous ligands (endacoids) for the benzodiazepine/beta-carboline binding sites" by A. Guidotti, P. Ferrero, M. Fujimoto, R. M. Santi and E. Costa, 1986, *Advances in Biochemical Psychopharmacology*, 41:137–148. Used by permission from Raven Press, New York.

Page 436: Photo courtesy of Jules Asher. From "New Drug Counters Alcohol Intoxication" by G. Kolata, 1986, *Science*, 234:1199. Copyright 1986 by the AAAS. Used by permission of AAAS.

Page 439: Figure 12.12 from "Neural substrates of aggression and rage in the cat" by A. Siegel and M. Brutus, *Progress in Psychobiology and Physiological Psychology*, 1990, 14:135–233. Reprinted by permission of Academic Press and A. Siegel.

Page 440: Figure 12.13 from "Neuronal constellations in aggressive behavior" by Jose Delgado, in L. Valzelli and L. Morgese (eds.) *Aggression and Violence: A Psycho/biological and Clinical Approach*, Edizioni Saint Vincent, 1981. Used by permission of Jose Delgado.

Page 441: Figure 12.14 photo courtesy of Dr. Dana Copeland.

Page 448: Photo © Dan McCoy/Rainbow.

Page 459: Figure 13.5 (b) photo courtesy of Dr. Dana Copeland.

Page 462: Figure 13.7 photo courtesy of Dr. Robert D. Terry, Department of Neurosciences, School of Medicine, University of California at San Diego.

Page 463: Figure 13.8 after "Dendritic Changes" by A. B. Scheibel, Figure 8-1, p. 70, in B. Reisberg (ed.) *Alzheimer's Disease*, 1983, Free Press.

Page 463: Figure 13.9 from "Quantitative morphology and regional and laminar distributions of senile plaques in Alzheimer's disease" by J. Rogers and J. H. Morrison, *Journal of Neuroscience*, 1985, 5:2801–2808. Copyright 1985 by the Society for Neuroscience. Photo courtesy of Dr. Joseph Rogers. Reprinted by permission of Dr. Joseph Rogers.

Page 465: Figure 13:10 photo © Hank Morgan/Rainbow.

Page 474: Figure 13.13 based on "Learning of leg position by the ventral nerve cord in headless insects" by G. A. Horridge, in *Proceedings of the Royal Society of London*, B, 1962, 157: 33–52. Used by permission of the Royal Society of London and G. A. Horridge.

Page 475: Figure 13.14 photo from H. Chaumeton/Nature.

Page 477: Figure 13:16 redrawn from "Neuronal mechanisms of habituation and dishabituation of the gill-withdrawal reflex in *Aplysia*" by V. Castellucci, H. Pinsker, I. Kupfermann and E. R. Kandel, *Science*, 1970, 167:1745–1748. Copyright 1970 by the AAAS. Used by permission of AAAS and V. Castellucci.

Page 486: Photo FPG International.

Page 491: Figure 14.3 (b) photo courtesy of Dr. Dana Copeland.

Page 496: Figure 14.5 from "Asymmetry of perception in free viewing of chimeric faces" by J. Levy, W. Heller, M. T. Banich and L. A. Burton, *Brain and Cognition*, 1983, 2:404–419. Used by permission of Academic Press.

Page 498: Figure 14.6 from "Human brain: Left-right asymmetries in temporal speech region" by N. Geschwind and W. Levitsky, *Science*, 1968, 161:186–187. Copyright 1968 by the AAAS. Reprinted by permission of AAAS and N. Geschwind.

Page 505: Figure 14.9 photo courtesy of Ann Premack.

Page 506: Figure 14.10 photo courtesy of Duane Rumbaugh from Georgia State University's Language Research Center, operated with Yerkes Primate Center of Emory.

Page 508: Figure 14.11 photo © David Carter.

Page 511: Figure 14.13 from "Observations on regional cerebral blood flow in cortical and subcortical structures during language production in normal man" by C. W. Wallesch, L. Henriksen, H. H. Kornhuber and O. B. Paulson, 1985, *Brain and Language*, 25: 224–233. Used by permission of Academic Press and O. B. Paulson.

Page 515: Figure 14.14 from "Localization of cognitive operations in the human brain" by M. Posner, S. E. Petersen, P. T. Fox and M. E. Raichle, *Science*, 1988, 240:1627–1631. Copyright 1988 by the AAAS. Reprinted by permission of AAAS and M. I. Posner.

Page 516: Figure 14.15 from "Positron emission tomographic studies of the cortical anatomy of single-word processing" by S. E. Petersen, P. T. Fox, M. I. Posner, M. Mintun and M. E. Raichle. Reprinted by permission from *Nature*, 1988, 331:585–589. Copyright © 1988 Macmillan Magazines Ltd. Photos provided by S. E. Petersen.

Page 518: Figure 14.16 from "Williams Syndrome: An unusual neuropsychological profile" by U. Bellugi, P. P. Wang, and T. L. Jernigan, in S. H. Broman & J. Grafman (eds.) *Atypical Cognitive Deficits in Developmental Disorders*, 1987, Hillsdale, NJ: Lawrence Erlbaum. Printed by permission.

Page 521: Figure 14.17 from "Task-determined strategies of visual process" by G. Geiger, J. Y. Lettvin and O. Zegarra-Moran, *Cognitive Brain Research*, 1:39–52 (1992). Reprinted by permission G. Geiger, J. Y. Lettvin and O. Zegarra-Moran and Elsevier Publishers, Academic Publishing Division.

Page 524: Photo © Jeff Zaruba/Tony Stone Worldwide.

Page 527: Photo © Rod Planck Photography.

Page 527: Figure 15.1 photos courtesy of Dr. Dana Copeland.

Page 528: Figure 15.2 from "Incidence rates of stroke in the eighties: The end of the decline in stroke?" by J. P. Broderick, S. J. Phillips, J. P. Whisnant, W. M. O'Fallon and E. J. Bergstrahl, *Stroke*, 1989, 20:577–582. Used by permission of the American Heart Association and J. P. Whisnant.

Page 533: Figure 15.5 from "Clinical aspects of PNS regeneration" by P. K. Thomas in S. G. Waxman (ed.), *Advances in Neurology, Vol 47: Functional Recovery in Neurological Disease*, 1988, Raven Press. Reprinted by permission of Raven Press and P. K. Thomas. Photo by Michael D. Sanders.

Page 536: Figure 15.7 from "Non-additivity of D2 receptor proliferation induced by dopamine denervation and chronic selective antagonist administration" by G. J.

LaHoste and J. F. Marshall, *Brain Research*, 1989, 502:223–232. Reprinted by permission of Elsevier Science Publishers. Photos courtesy of G. J. LaHoste.
Page 537: Figure 15.9 redrawn by permission from *The Annual Review of Neuroscience*, Volume 6, copyright 1983 by Annual Reviews, Inc. Used by permission of Annual Reviews, Inc. and Jon H. Kaas.

Page 548: Photo courtesy E. F. Torrey and M. F. Casanova/NIMH.
Page 549: Photo courtesy of Dr. Dana Copeland.
Page 551: Figure 16.2 redrawn from E. Janosik and J. Davies, *Psychiatric Mental Health Nursing*, p. 173. © 1986 Jones and Bartlett Publishers: Boston. Used by permission.
Page 552: Figure 16.3 from "Two-day cycles of alternating good and bad behavior in psychotic patients" by C. P. Richter, *Archives of Neurology and Psychiatry*, 1938, 39:587–598. Copyright 1938, American Medical Association. Used by permission.
Page 554: Figure 16.4 reprinted by permission of L. R. Baxter Jr. Photo courtesy of L. R. Baxter Jr.
Page 555: Figure 16.5 © Leonard Lessin, Peter Arnold, Inc.
Page 558: Figure 16.6 © James D. Wilson/Woodfin Camp & Assoc.
Page 560: Figure 16.7 adapted from *Sleep* by J. Allan Hobson, Scientific American Library, 1989. Reprinted by permission of W. H. Freeman and Company.
Page 566: Figure 16.9 photos courtesy of E. F. Torrey and M. F. Casanova/NIMH.
Page 567: Figure 16.10 photos © CEA-Orsay/CNRI/SPL/Photo Researchers, Inc.
Page 568: Figure 16.11 photos courtesy of B. Bogerts.
Page 569: Figure 16.12 photos courtesy of Arnold Scheibel.
Page 572: Figure 16.14 from Sereno and Holzman, "Express saccades and smooth pursuit eye movement function in schizophrenic, affective disorder and normal subjects," *Journal of Cognitive Neuroscience*, Vol. 5, pp. 303–316 (1993). Reprinted by permission.
Page 577: Figure 16:16 from "Antipsychotic drug doses and neuroleptic/dopamine receptors" by P. Seeman, T. Lee, M. Chau-Wong, and K. Wong, *Nature*, 261, (1976), 717–719. Copyright 1976 Macmillan Magazines Limited. Reprinted by permission of *Nature* and Phillip Seeman.

Page 593: Figure A4 (a) photo © A. Sieveking/Photo Researchers, Inc.

Sources for Endsheet Quotations

Ramon y Cajal, S. (1937). Recollections of my life. *Memoirs of the American Philosophical Society*, 8, parts 1 and 2. (Photo from Bettman Archive.)
Sherrington, C.S. (1941). *Man on his nature*. New York: Macmillan, p. 104.
Goldman-Rakic, P.S. (1988). Topography of cognition: Parallel distributed networks in primate association cortex. *Annual Review of Neuroscience*, 11, 137–156. (p. 152.)
Sperry, R.W. (1975). In search of psyche. In F.G. Worden, J.P. Swazey, & G. Adelman (Eds.) *The neurosciences: Paths of Discovery* (pp. 424–434). Cambridge, MA: MIT Press.
Jerre Levy: personal communication.
Geschwind, N. (1965). Disconnexion syndromes in animals and man. *Brain*, 88, 237–294, 585–644.
Susan S. Schiffman: personal communication.
Candace Pert: personal communication.
David Hubel: personal communication.
Wiesel, T. N. (1982). Postnatal development of the visual cortex and the influence of environment. *Nature*, 299, 583–591.
Levi-Montalcini, R. (1988). *In praise of imperfection*. New York: Basic Books, p. 94.
Dement, W. (1972). *Some must watch while some must sleep*. San Francisco: W. H. Freeman.
Cannon, W. B. (1945). *The way of an investigator*. New York: Norton.
Edward Stricker: personal communication.
Beach, Frank A. "In memoriam: Frank A. Beach" (1988). *Hormones and Behavior*, 22, 419–443; and personal communication.
Curt P. Richter: personal communication.
Paul MacLean: personal communication.
Luigi Valzelli: personal communication.
Lashley, K. S. (1930). Basic neural mechanisms in behavior. *Psychology Review*, 37, 1–24.
Hebb, D. O. (1949). *Organization of behavior*. New York: John Wiley & Sons. (p.xiii.)
Garcia, J. (1981). Tilting at the paper mills of Academe. *American Psychologist*, 36, 149–158. (p. 151.)
Eric R. Kandel: personal communication.
Duane Rumbaugh and Sue Savage-Rumbaugh: personal communication.
Carla J. Schatz: personal communication.

Subject Index

To The Owner Of This Book

I hope that you have enjoyed *Biological Psychology, Fifth Edition* as much as I enjoyed writing it. I would like to know as much about your experience as you would care to offer. Only through your comments and those of others can I learn how to make this a better text for future readers.

School _____ Your instructor's name _____

1. What did you like the most about *Biological Psychology, Fifth Edition*? _____

_____

_____

_____

2. Do you have any recommendations for ways to improve the next edition of this text? _____

_____

_____

_____

3. In the space below or in a separate letter, please write any other comments you have about the book. (For example, were any chapters or concepts particularly difficult?) I'd be delighted to hear from you!

_____

_____

_____

_____

_____

_____

_____

_____

_____

_____

Optional:

Your name: _____ Date: _____

May Brooks/Cole quote you, either in promotion for *Biological Psychology, Fifth Edition*
or in future publishing ventures?

Yes: _____ No: _____

Sincerely,

James W. Kalat

FOLD HERE

- -

NO POSTAGE
NECESSARY
IF MAILED
IN THE
UNITED STATES

BUSINESS REPLY MAIL

FIRST CLASS   PERMIT NO. 358   PACIFIC GROVE, CA

POSTAGE WILL BE PAID BY ADDRESSEE

ATT: *James W. Kalat* _____

Brooks/Cole Publishing Company
511 Forest Lodge Road
Pacific Grove, California 93950-9968

FOLD HERE